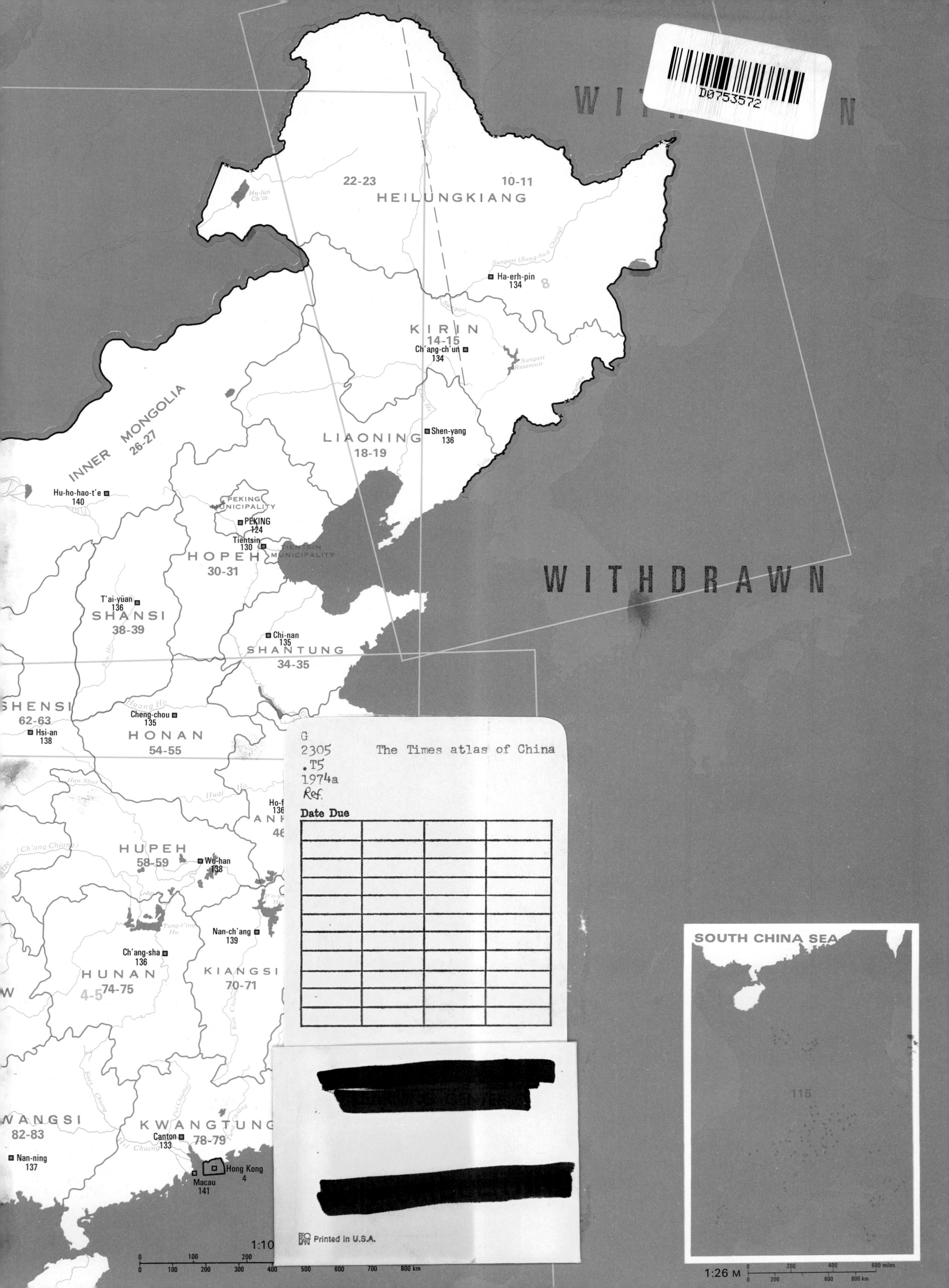
HEILUNGKIANG
22-23
10-11
Hu-lun Ch'ih
Sungari (Sung-hua Chiang)
Ha-erh-pin
134
8
KIRIN
14-15
Ch'ang-ch'un
134
Sungari Reservoir
LIAONING
18-19
Shen-yang
136
INNER MONGOLIA
26-27
Hu-ho-hao-t'e
140
PEKING MUNICIPALITY
PEKING
124
Tientsin
130
TIENTSIN MUNICIPALITY
HOPEH
30-31
T'ai-yüan
136
SHANSI
38-39
Chi-nan
135
SHANTUNG
34-35
SHENSI
62-63
Hsi-an
138
Huang Ho
Cheng-chou
135
HONAN
54-55
Han Shui
Huai Ho
HUPEH
58-59
Wu-han
138
(Ch'ang Chiang)
Tung-t'ing Hu
Nan-ch'ang
139
Ch'ang-sha
136
HUNAN
74-75
4-5
KIANGSI
70-71
KWANGSI
82-83
Nan-ning
137
KWANGTUNG
Canton
133
78-79
Hsi Chiang
Hong Kong
4
Macau
141
SOUTH CHINA SEA
115
1:26 M
0 200 400 600 miles
0 200 600 800 km
0 100 200 400 500 600 700 800 km

THE TIMES ATLAS OF CHINA

THE TIMES ATLAS OF CHINA

[redacted]

[redacted]

NYT

QUADRANGLE/THE NEW YORK TIMES BOOK CO.

Editors and chief contributors **P. J. M. Geelan**
D. C. Twitchett
Professor of Chinese, University of Cambridge

Cartographic consultant **John C. Bartholomew**

Contributors **Maurice Corina**
Industrial Editor, The Times

W. W. Easey
School of Oriental and African Studies,
University of London

K. C. Jordan FRGS

Richard King
Faculty of Oriental Studies, University of Cambridge

H. A. G. Lewis OBE

The publishers would like to thank
James L. Payne, U.S. Government Printing Office,
Washington, D.C. for permission to use maps from the
Atlas of China, published by the
Central Intelligence Agency, 1971
Theodore Shabad of the New York Times
C. Kumei and M. Kikuchi of Kyobunkaku Limited
and M. Nitta of Tokyo for their kind co-operation and
assistance.

Publishing Manager: Barry Winkleman
Publishing assistant: Elizabeth Bland
Design and art direction: Ivan and Robin Dodd

Cartography by Kyobunkaku Limited, Tokyo
John Bartholomew & Son Limited, Edinburgh
and Hunting Surveys Limited, Boreham Wood

Text set by Yendall and Company, London

Chinese and English lists set by
Regal Company, Hong Kong

Printed by John Bartholomew & Son Limited

Data processing of the index by
Computer Data Processing Limited, London

Index computer set by Computaprint Limited, London

Index printed and books bound by
Hazell Watson and Viney, Aylesbury

First published (in part) by
Kyobunkaku Limited, Tokyo, 1973
First published in Great Britain in 1974 by
Times Books, the book publishing division of
Times Newspapers Limited
New Printing House Square, Gray's Inn Road,
London WC1X 8EZ

ISBN 0 7230 0118 9

CONTENTS

INTRODUCTION

It is with some diffidence that *The Times* presents this atlas to a world increasingly interested in China. Modern Chinese cartography has as yet provided nothing comparable to the maps and atlases available for most other countries. Despite the ancient origins of map-making in China, the People's Republic was initially poorly endowed with maps. Even if a great part of the archival material which did exist had not been removed to Taiwan, the quality and extent of coverage fell far short of what would be required by a modern, industrialised nation. By the tenth anniversary of the People's Republic, however, the more densely settled areas had been newly surveyed and mapped. Mapping the rest, including the outlying regions of Sinkiang, Tibet and Inner Mongolia, which were virtually unmapped, will occupy cartographic staffs for decades to come. These remarkable achievements have, unfortunately, not resulted in the publication of general maps to satisfy the external demand for information about the immense and rapidly-changing country. Detailed geographical and particularly statistical information at the time of writing is, by Western standards, hard to come by, but in spite of these difficulties this book will, it is hoped, fulfil an essential function: to submit to the discipline of an atlas the wide variety of information available from disparate sources about the land and people of China.

The first section of the atlas comprises maps and text concerned with a variety of historical, economic and physical topics. Maps illustrate the settlement and frontiers of China as they evolved through the great dynasties to the era of Communism; the ethnic minorities, climate, agriculture, communications, minerals and energy resources, industry and administration of modern China. The second section is a series of maps showing the physical structure of the country. The third and principal section of the atlas consists of maps of the provinces of China. These were originally compiled by a Japanese publisher, Kyōbunkaku, and have been transcribed, extensively updated and have been supplemented by hill shading to indicate the relief of the terrain. The maps are accompanied by text and a list of regions, districts, counties and municipalities for each province, in English and Chinese. The Chinese characters used in the administrative summaries for all provinces with the exception of Taiwan are the modern simplified characters which are used in the People's Republic.

During the preparation of this atlas three major problems emerged. The first concerned the choice of transcription system for the place-names in the atlas. Place-names present enormous difficulties. Transcription of Chinese, complex enough in itself, offers unlimited scope to sinologists and others to create widely varying spelling systems. 'Hsüan Te' and 'Seuen Tih', for example, although apparently unrelated, are different transcriptions of the reign-name of a Ming emperor. Of the two principal transcription systems, Wade-Giles and Pinyin, the former was selected on the grounds that, although Pinyin is now used for certain purposes in the People's Republic itself, Wade-Giles has been used in almost all technical literature about China, and by British and American cartographers, for many years. A more detailed discussion of the arguments which influenced this decision will be found on page 142.

The second problem was that posed by the existence of conventional names for many Chinese provinces and cities. In the case of the provinces, conventional forms of the names have been used throughout this atlas, except in the administrative summaries which follow each province plate, where the full names in Chinese and in Wade-Giles have been given. Cities whose conventional names have become widely used seemed to demand similar treatment, but this led to many inconsistencies and the decision was taken to use Wade-Giles spellings throughout the atlas, with only four exceptions: Peking, Tientsin, Canton and Shanghai. In the index conventional names, Post Offices spellings and the variant spellings of Tibetan and other minority-language names are all cross-referenced to the Chinese names given on the maps.

A third problem was raised by a characteristic of local administration in China, particularly in the western part of the country; this is the constant shifting of *hsien* (county) centres. These are as often known by the names of the *hsien* as by their own names. Furthermore, when a town increases its status to become a *shih* (municipality), it may acquire a new name as well as additional territory. Ambiguities of nomenclature may result. In the atlas an attempt has been made to indicate visually such names which may for these reasons be difficult to identify. All *hsien* and *shih* are symbolised according to the location of their centres in December 1972; but where the *hsien* or *shih* name differs from that of the place in which it was then situated, it is shown in square brackets. Thus Chung-shu [Jen-huai] indicates that the place called Chung-shu currently serves as the centre of Jen-huai Hsien and will on that account often be called Jen-huai. The square brackets serve also as a warning that this is not a permanent situation: a map based on 1966 information will have applied the name of Jen-huai to a place some 20 kilometres north-west whose actual name is Mao-t'ai but which *at that time* was the centre of Jen-huai Hsien.

Names of minority administrative areas are often descriptive in character and unwieldy when transcribed from their full Chinese forms. They have been given in whole or partial translation on the province maps. Thus, in Sinkiang, the K'o-tzu-le-su K'o-erh-k'o-tzu Tzu-chih-chou is referred to as the Kizil Su Kirghiz Autonomous District; the Su-pei Meng-ku-tsu Tzu-chih-hsien appears as North Kansu Mongol A.H. The full Chinese forms of all such names will be found in the administrative summaries following each province plate. These lists also include the names of those few *hsien* whose centres lie in *shih* which carry their own symbol. No distinction is made in the lists between sub-province level and lower level municipalities, since precise information is not available. Municipalities of the first category are probably those whose known boundaries are shown on the province plates and on the map on pages xxxvi and xxxvii which also contains a general account of the administrative divisions of the People's Republic.

In recent years much political significance has been read into the work of map and atlas publishers as far as boundary depiction and the spelling of place-names are concerned. The position of *The Times* as publisher of this and other atlases is quite clear. Its role is not one of international arbitration, nor does it seek in the depiction of boundaries to apportion lands to one state or another. An atlas publisher strays beyond his proper sphere if he tries to adjudicate between the rights and wrongs of a dispute, rather than to set out facts as he can best determine them. It follows that *The Times* in its atlases aims to show the territorial situation obtaining at the time of going to press, without regard to the *de jure* position in contentious areas or the rival claims of the contending parties. The portrayal of boundaries and the spelling of place-names in such areas must not be taken to indicate approval by *The Times* of the political status of the territories. Still less must it be inferred that *The Times* propagates the views of the government of the United Kingdom, the United States of America or any other nation.

CHINA'S HISTORY

Pre-history and the Shang period The main developments in prehistoric times were concentrated in Northern China, particularly in the area of loess soils in the provinces of Shensi, Shansi, and Honan, where conditions favoured primitive agriculture. The Shang was the first highly organised state from which we have records. It was also the first culture using metal (bronze). Scattered Shang sites are found over a much wider area than that shown, which includes all the major sites indicating a high level of culture.

The Warring States period The Shang was replaced in the 11th century BC by the Chou, who controlled most of northern and north-eastern China, which was administered through a system of fiefs. Its first capital was near modern Hsi-an. After 771 BC its centre was moved to the vicinity of modern Lo-yang, and the central authority of the Chou declined. Gradually the larger feudal states absorbed the smaller, until by the 3rd century BC only a handful of powerful states remained. The Chou kings had by this time lost all political power.

The Han Empire The larger states had already become powerful and highly centralised by the 3rd century BC. The Ch'in state, centred in the Wei river valley in the north-west, was the most powerful. In 221 BC Ch'in overcame the last of its rivals and unified all of China under a single centralised imperial regime, and expanded its frontiers southwards into Kwangtung. The authoritarian Ch'in empire collapsed in 207–6 BC, however, and was replaced from 202 BC by the Han, who controlled China, with a brief inter-regnum (AD 9–25) until AD 220. The map shows China at the time of the first recorded census (AD 2), when the population was 57,671,000, the great majority of whom lived in the north.

The Three Kingdoms At the final collapse of the Han in AD 220 China was divided into three regional regimes. Although briefly reunited under the Western Chin in 265 China passed through a period of political disunion which lasted until 589.

The Northern and Southern Dynasties During the period of disunion the south remained under a series of comparatively stable regimes, which gradually extended Chinese settlement and administration over the south and south-east. The north was invaded by a series of foreign peoples, and politically fragmented during the 4th century AD. The north was eventually reunified under the Toba Turkish Wei dynasty during the 5th century.

T'ang China The empire was again reunited under the Sui in 589. The new dynasty overtaxed its resources in a series of foreign wars, and fell in 617 to be replaced by the T'ang (618–907). During the T'ang, Chinese power extended far into Central Asia, while Chinese culture and institutions were widely adopted in Japan, Korea and Vietnam. The map shows T'ang China (though not its Central Asian territories) at the height of its power in 742. From the 8th century major changes began – the rapid growth of central and southern China as the main economic region; widespread development of cities and urban growth. The highly centralised state was challenged by powerful regional regimes.

The Five Dynasties In 881 the T'ang capital fell, and although the dynasty lasted in name until 907, China was split up into a number of independent states. From 907–960 a series of five short-lived dynasties in the north claimed to be the legitimate rulers of the empire, but in fact China remained fragmented and the last of the states surrendered to the new dynasty of Sung only in 979. These independent regimes are known as the Ten Kingdoms (Shih-kuo).

The Southern Sung and Chin The Sung had never been able to reconquer the area around Peking taken during the early 10th century by the Khitans, who established a powerful semi-Chinese state (Liao) in modern Manchuria. In the north-west another highly organised state, Hsi-hsia, was set up by the Tanguts. In the early 12th century the Jurchen, a Tungusic people from Manchuria, vassals of the Liao, replaced their overlords and set up a new state of Chin, which in 1127 forced the Sung to abandon their capital, and conquered most of northern China. Large parts of northern China were thus under successive foreign dynasties from 936 until 1368. During this period Sung China co-existed with several other Chinese-style bureaucratic states under alien rulers.

Sung China The Sung arose as a purely northern dynasty in 960, and gradually incorporated the independent states into a single empire by 979, although it could not recover some northern territories occupied by foreign powers. Under the Sung China enjoyed great internal prosperity. The population doubled between 742 and 1080, and by the end of the 11th century was about 100,000,000. This growth was concentrated in south and central China, while northern China declined.

The Mongol World Empire The rise of the Mongols in the early 13th century led to the conquest of Chin in 1234, and later to the conquest of the Southern Sung in 1278. China now became a part of the Mongol Empire, which stretched across Eurasia. This empire, however, was divided into a number of very different Khanates.

The Mongol Yüan period In China, Mongol rule was imposed very harshly after the conquest of the Chin in 1234, and the northern territories which then became Mongol suffered great destruction. However, the Mongols gradually adopted many Chinese institutions, and by the time the south was conquered in 1278, the Mongols applied policies which were far less harsh. Under the Mongols south-western China, hitherto under a series of independent kingdoms, was finally incorporated into the empire.

Ming China In 1368, with the establishment of the Ming, China was reunited under a Chinese dynasty for the first time for more than four centuries. The Ming was an inward looking period after the mid-15th century, but internally China underwent steady growth. Trade flourished, agriculture and industry grew steadily more productive, and the population rose rapidly to 150,000,000 by 1600.

The Ming Voyages Under the Sung and the Mongols China had become a major sea power, with Chinese ships trading with Indonesia, south-east Asia, India and the Persian Gulf. In the early 15th century the Emperor Yung-lo sent a series of massive maritime expeditions to south-east Asia and into the Indian Ocean, where they ranged as far as the Red Sea and the East African coast. The voyages soon came to an end, however, and the Chinese abandoned the use of sea power, just as the first western penetration of the Indian Ocean was about to begin.

The Ch'ing Empire In 1644 the Ming empire came to an end, conquered by the Manchus, descendents of the Jurchen who had formed the Chin state from 1127–1234. The Manchus not only established a powerful internal regime under which China prospered as never before, with a population reaching 315,000,000 in 1800 and 430,000,000 by 1850; they also extended China's external frontiers to incorporate Mongolia, Manchuria, Sinkiang and Tibet within China's frontiers for the first time. China exercised, too, some influence over a further series of tributary states, including Korea, Vietnam and Nepal. At the height of its power in about 1800, Ch'ing China faced serious internal economic problems, widespread social unrest and rebellions. From 1840 the western powers also began to force trading concessions from the Chinese and to exert pressure on the Chinese government.

Foreign influence in China The Opium War (1839–42) exposed China's weakness in the face of modern western military technology. As a result Hong Kong was ceded to Britain, and a number of ports opened to foreign trade. In the 1850s China faced a series of internal rebellions during which the western powers extracted further concessions, and Russia secured extensive territories east of the rivers Amur and Ussuri. In 1894–5 Japan's easy victory over China led to a period when the great powers attempted to define spheres of influence in China, and to compete for economic concessions, particularly for the right to build railways. With the collapse of the Ch'ing empire Mongolia became an independent state, Chinese influence in Tibet lapsed, Sinkiang came increasingly under Soviet influence, and Manchuria under the dominance of Japan which had already annexed Taiwan in 1895. In 1932 Manchuria became the Japanese puppet state of Manchukuo. In 1937 Japan invaded China itself, and occupied large areas until 1945.

The growth of the Communist regime The Chinese Communist Party had controlled large parts of Kiangsi and some neighbouring areas in the early 1930s. They were driven out by the Nationalists and established their base at Yen-an in Shensi from which they conducted their war of resistance against the Japanese. During the war many liberated areas within Japanese territory were communist dominated. With the coming of peace in 1945 the Russian occupation of Manchuria and Inner Mongolia ensured Communist dominance of these areas. After the outbreak of Civil War with the Nationalists in 1946 the Communist armies rapidly over-ran the north, and in 1949 the People's Republic was established in Peking, while the remaining members of the Nationalist government fled to Taiwan.

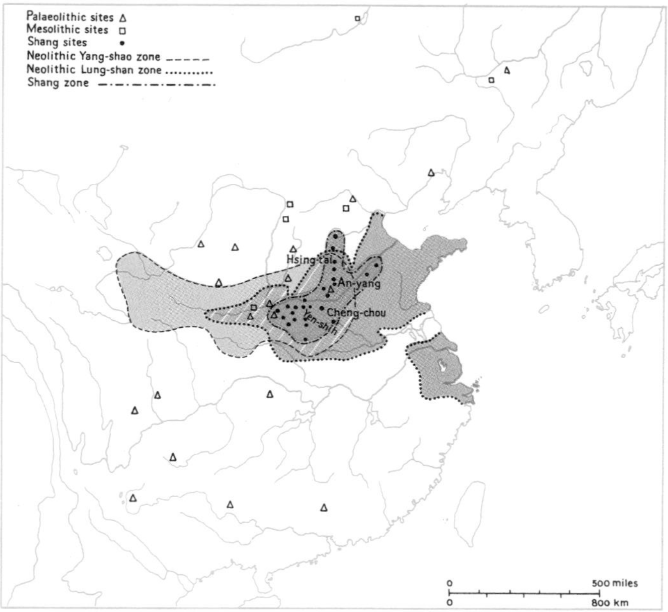

PRE-HISTORY AND THE SHANG PERIOD

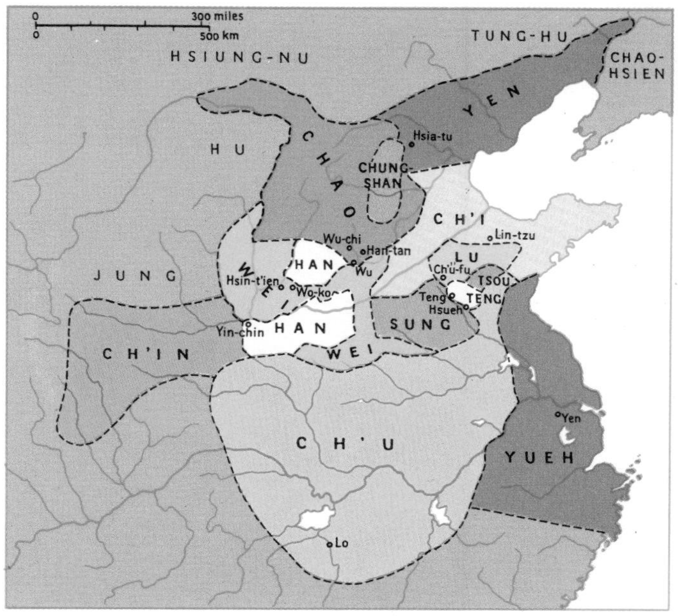

THE WARRING STATES PERIOD

THE HAN EMPIRE 2 AD

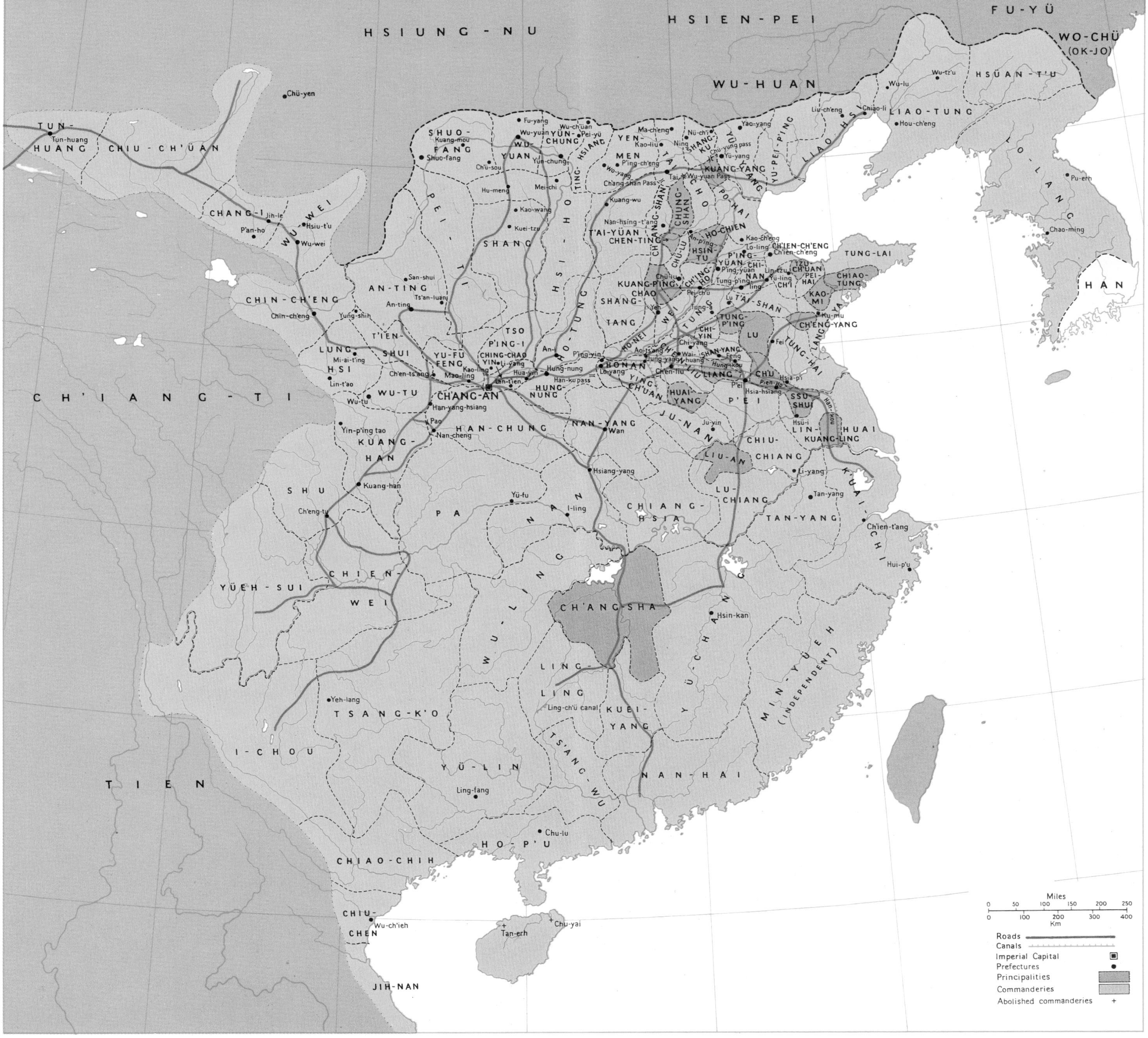

THE THREE KINGDOMS 220–265 AD

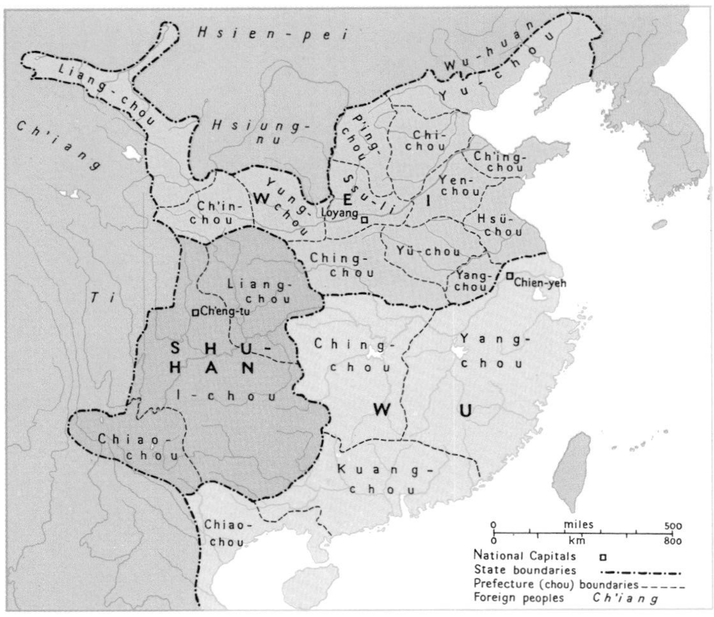

THE NORTHERN AND SOUTHERN DYNASTIES

T'ANG CHINA 742 AD

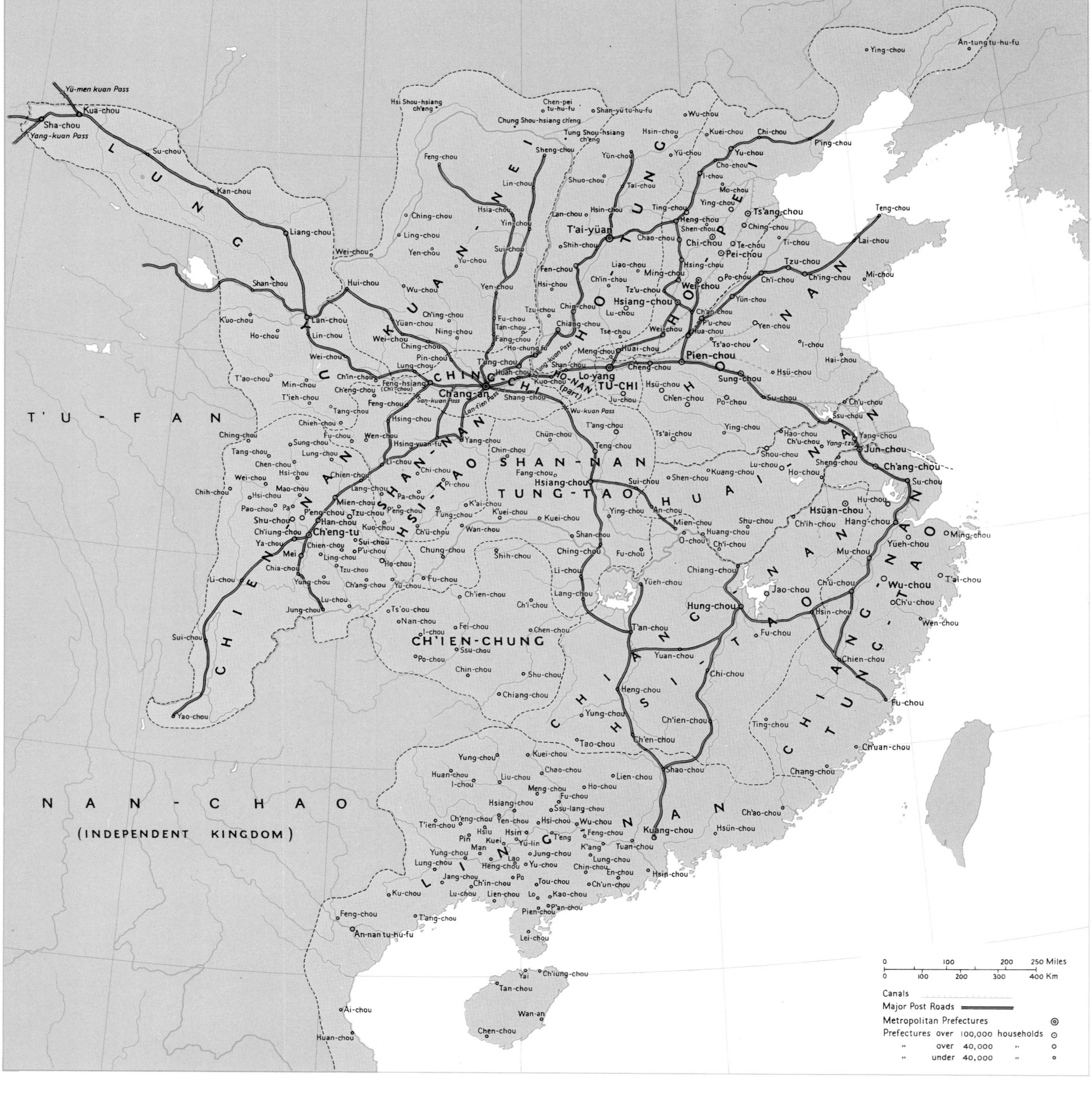

THE FIVE DYNASTIES

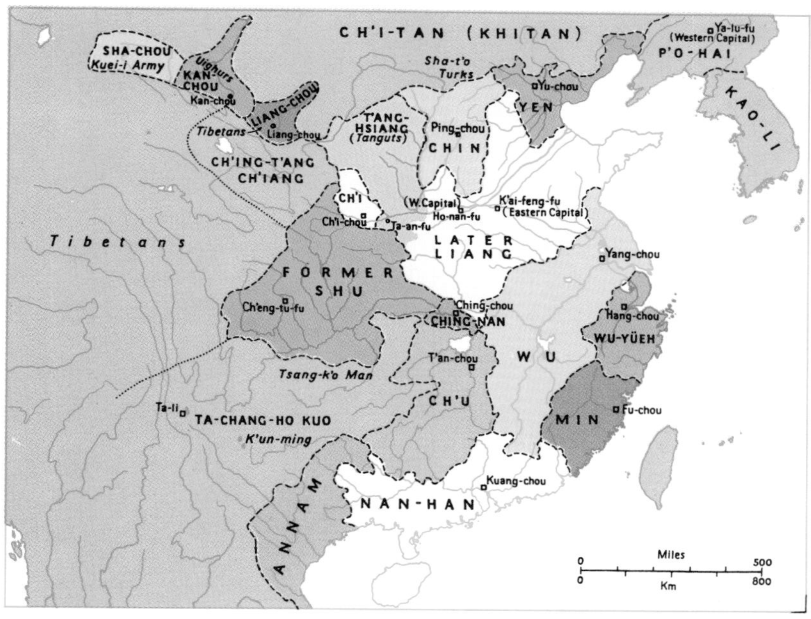

THE SOUTHERN SUNG AND CHIN

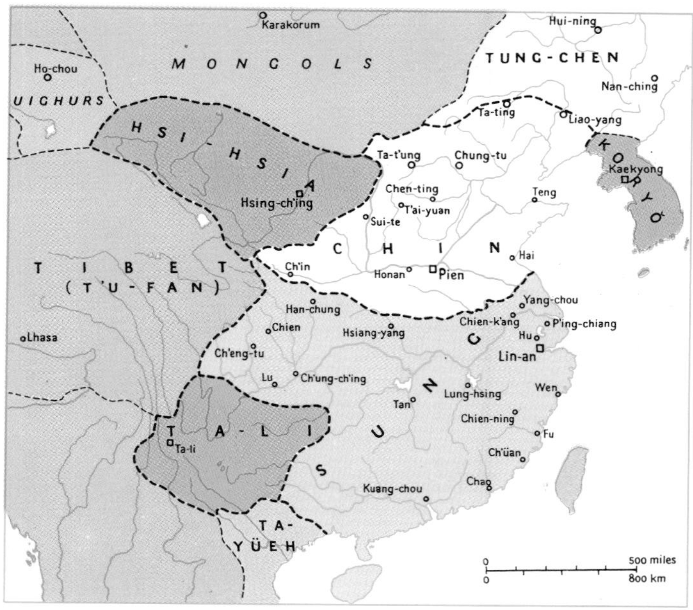

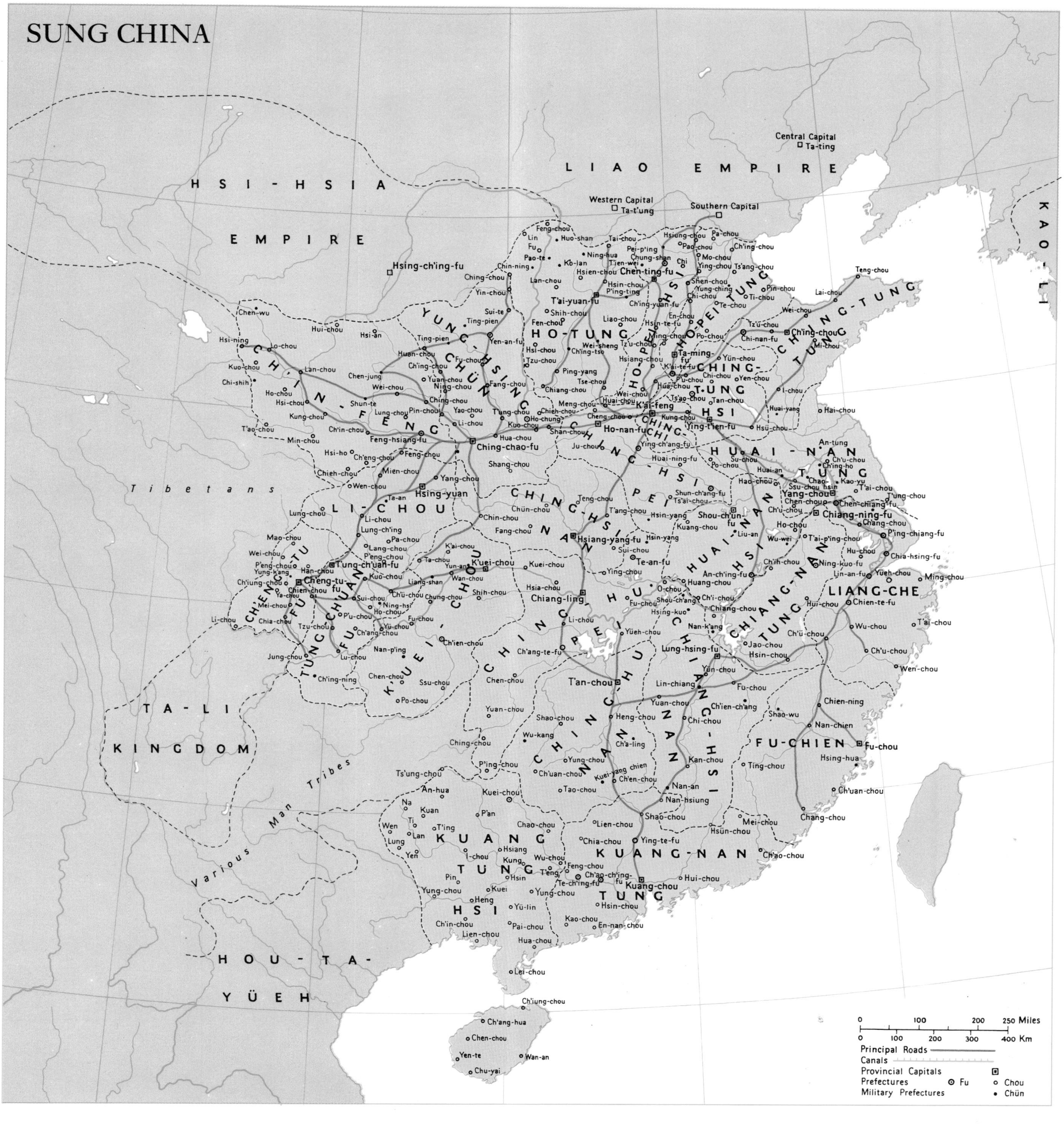

THE MONGOL WORLD EMPIRE

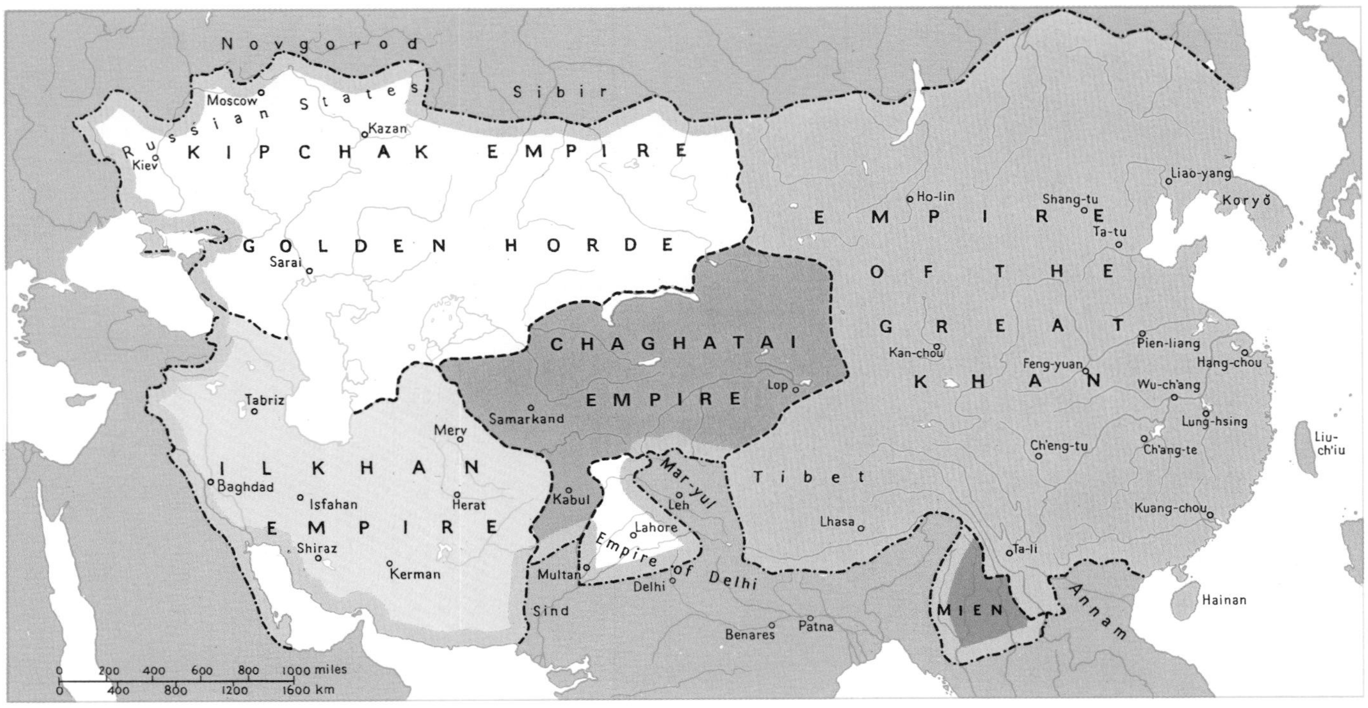

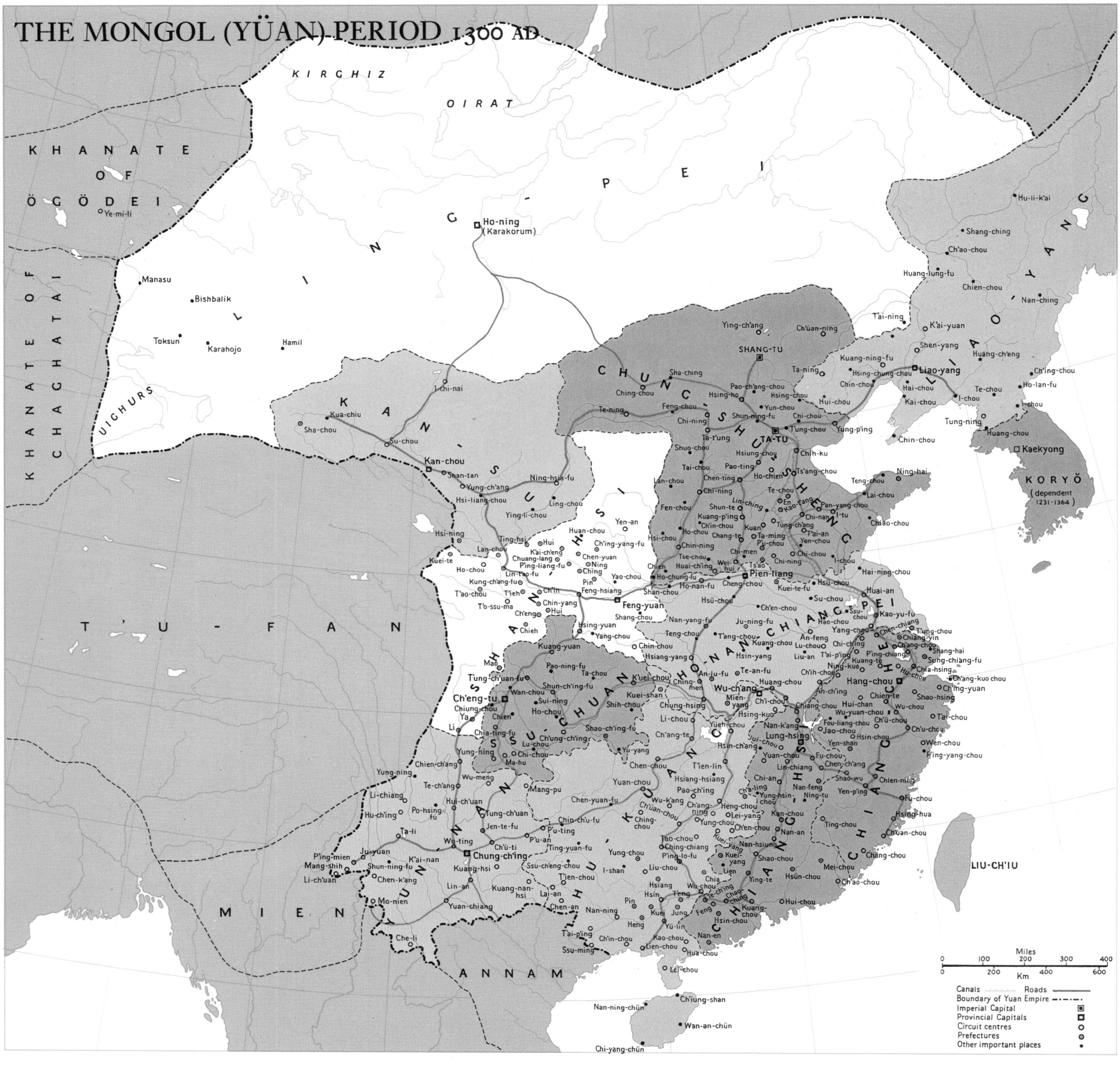

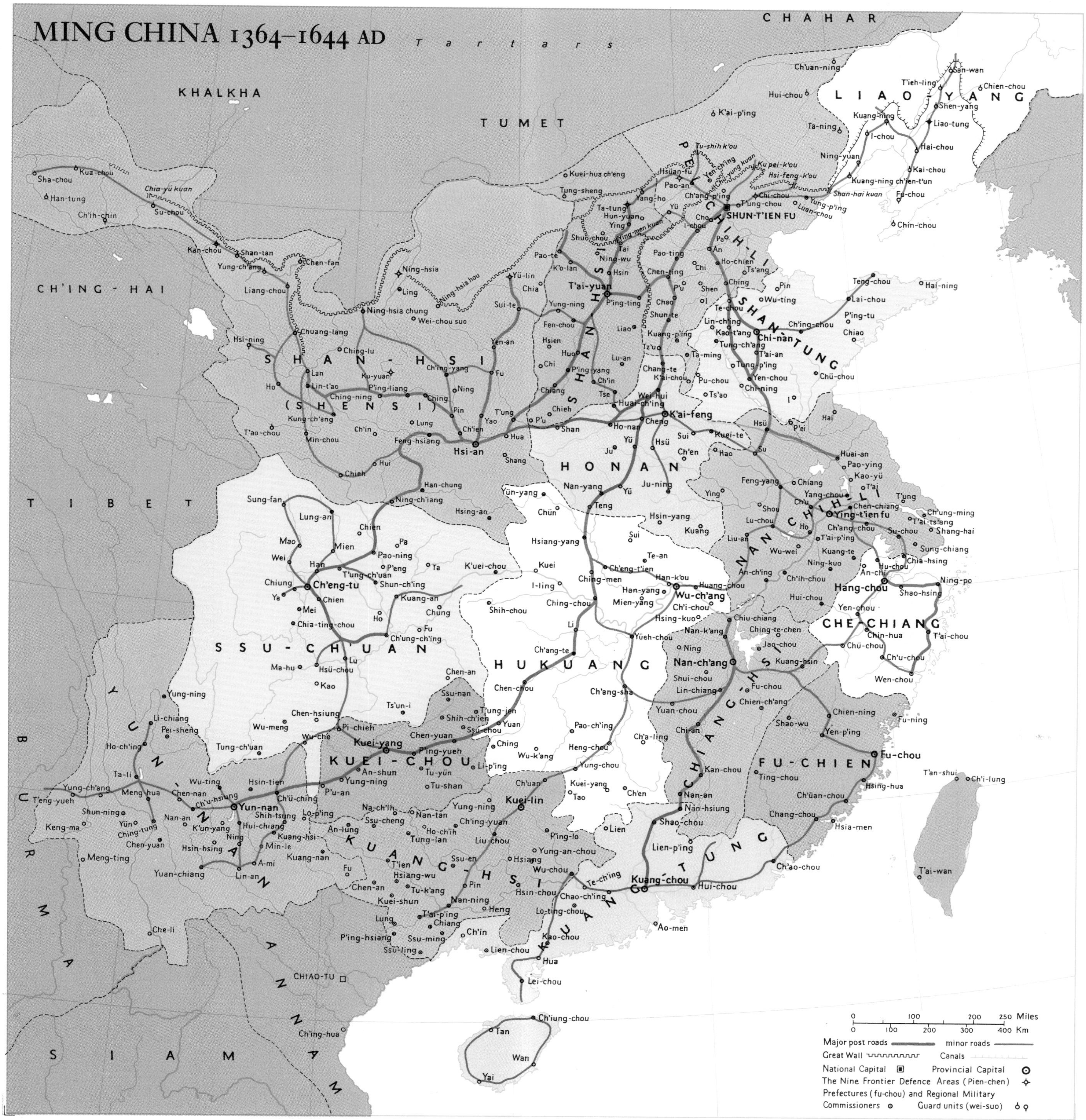

THE MING VOYAGES

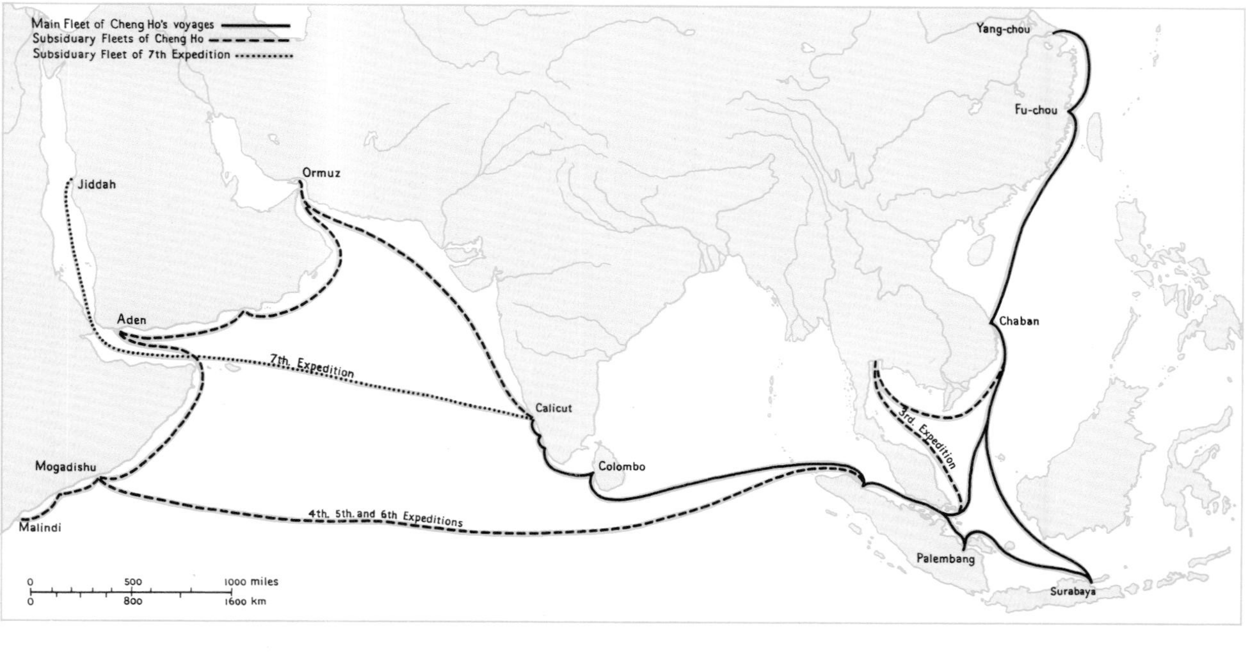

THE CH'ING EMPIRE

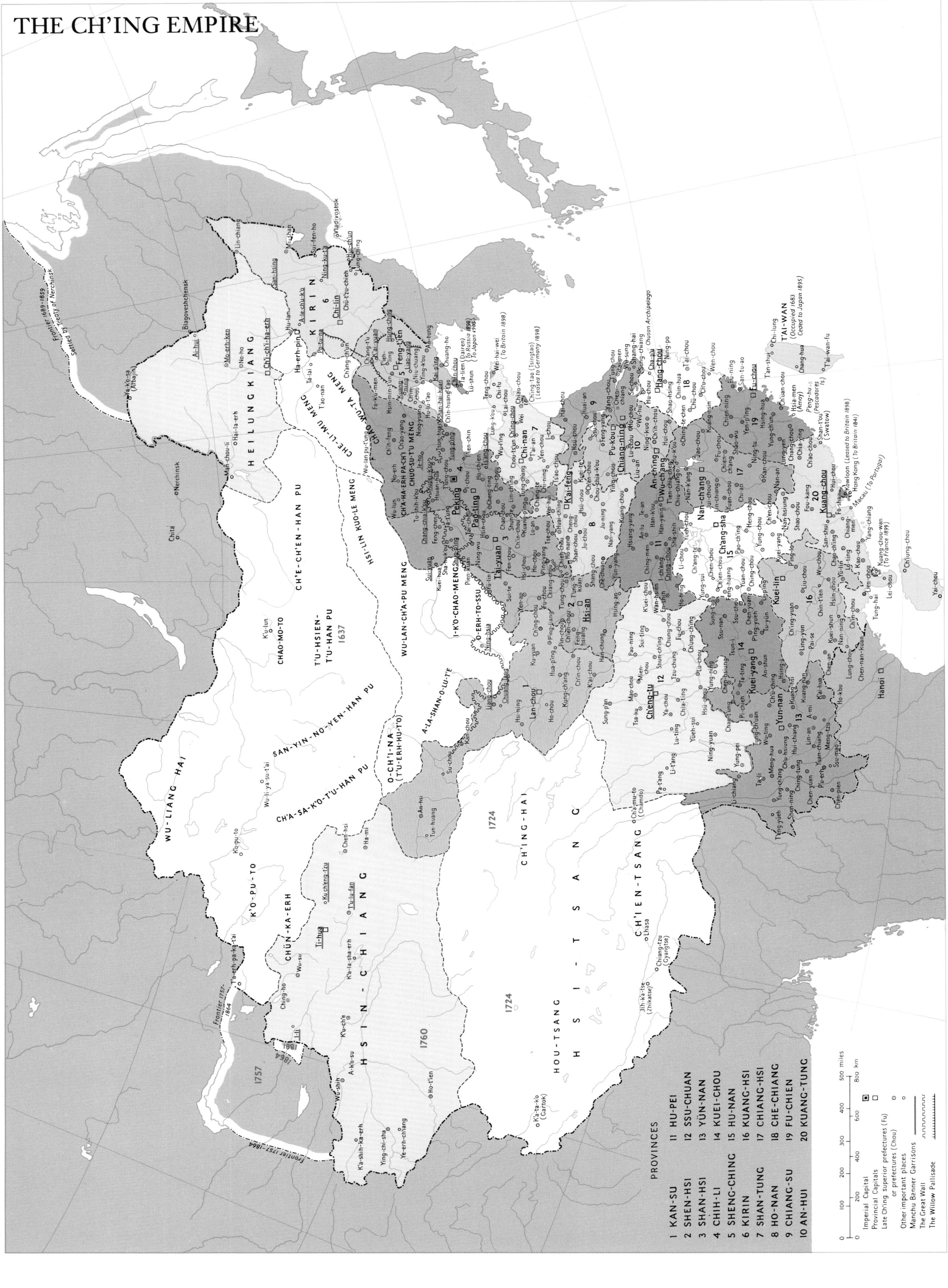

FOREIGN INFLUENCE IN CHINA

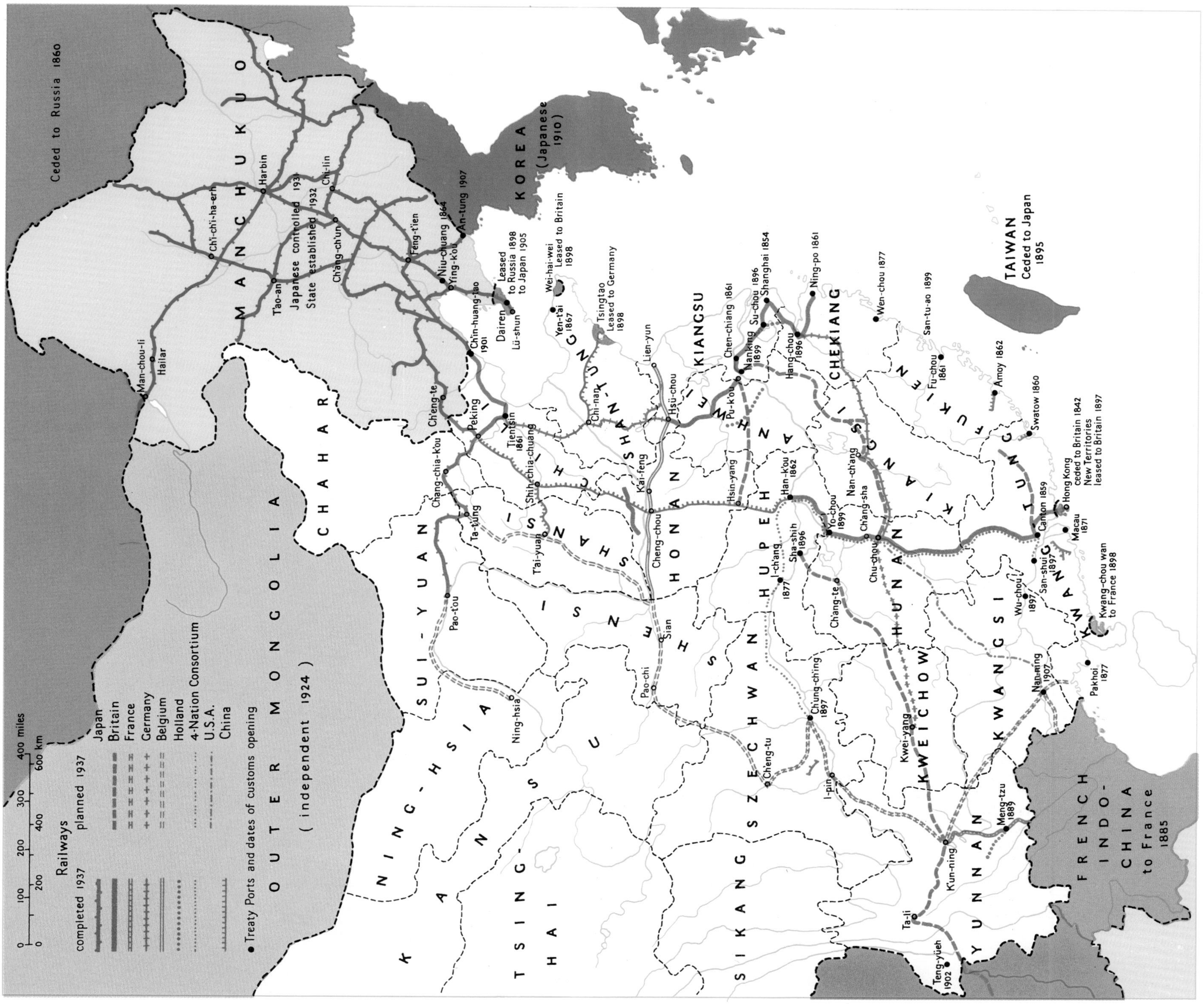
Railways
completed 1937
planned 1937
Japan
Britain
France
Germany
Belgium
Holland
4-Nation Consortium
U.S.A.
China
• Treaty Ports and dates of customs opening
0 100 200 300 400 miles
0 200 400 600 km
OUTER MONGOLIA
(independent 1924)
Ceded to Russia 1860
MANCHUKUO
Japanese controlled 1931
State established 1932
KOREA
(Japanese 1910)
TAIWAN
Ceded to Japan
1895
FRENCH INDO-CHINA
to France
1885
CHAHAR
SUI-YUAN
NING-HSIA
KANSU
TSING-HAI
SIKANG
SZECHWAN
SHENSI
SHANSI
HOPEI
SHANTUNG
HONAN
HUPEH
HUNAN
KIANGSU
ANHWEI
CHEKIANG
KIANGSI
FUKIEN
KWANGTUNG
KWANGSI
KWEICHOW
YUNNAN

THE GROWTH OF THE COMMUNIST REGIME 1945–1949

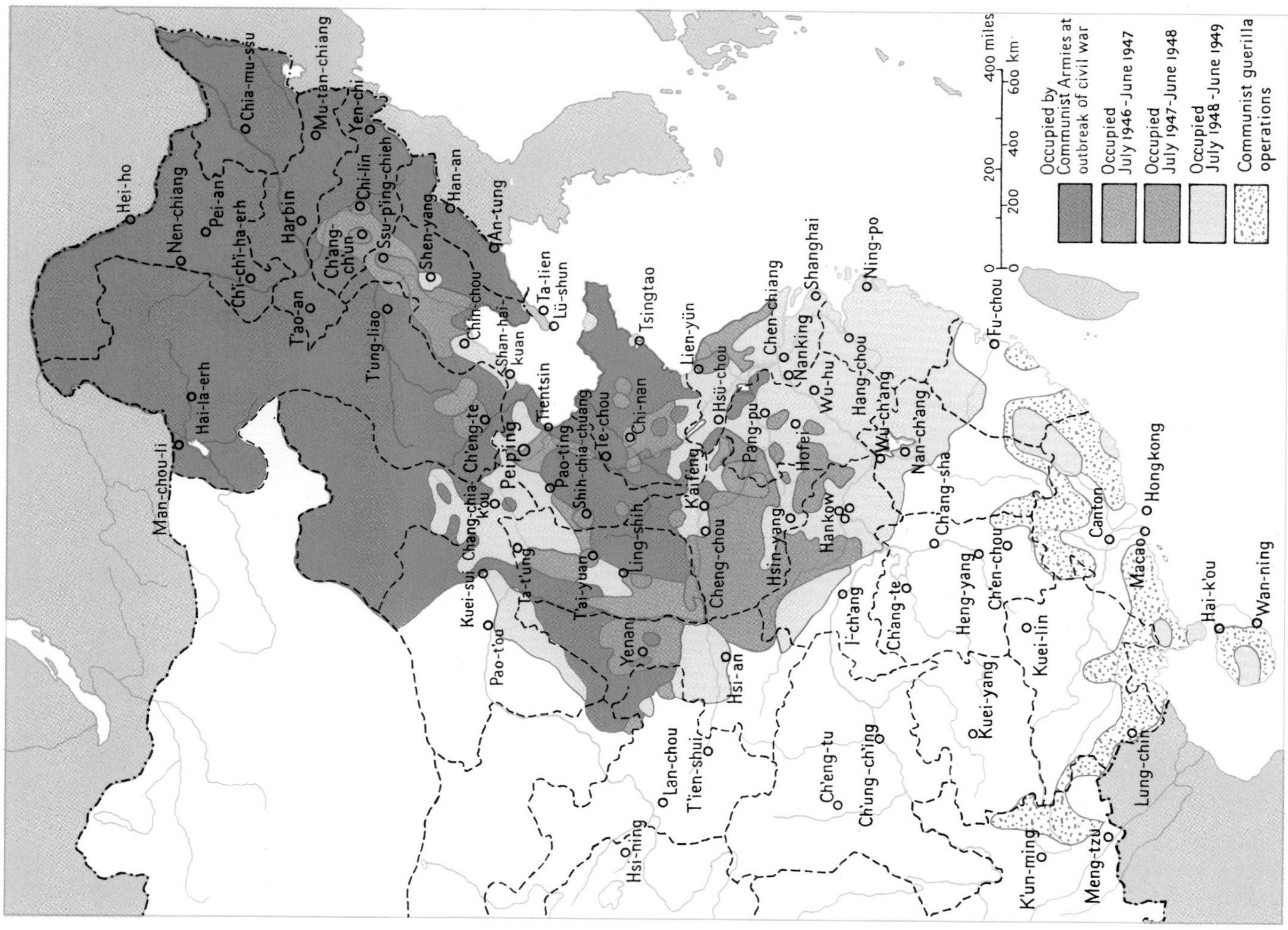
Occupied by Communist Armies at outbreak of civil war
Occupied July 1946-June 1947
Occupied July 1947-June 1948
Occupied July 1948-June 1949
Communist guerilla operations
0 200 400 miles
0 200 400 600 km

ROUGHLY a quarter of the world's people live in China. The 1953 Census gave a total of 583,000,000. The exact figure at the present time is unknown, and estimates range from 750,000,000 to more than 900,000,000. The majority of observers place the total at more than 800,000,000.

The total Chinese population has always been very large by comparison with European countries, but has grown very rapidly in recent centuries. Until about AD 800 it remained stable at around 50,000,000. Between that date and AD 1200 it rose rapidly to more than 100,000,000 persons. Following the Mongol conquest it fell to about 65,000,000 in the late 14th century, and then rose steadily to about 150,000,000 in 1600. During the rebellions at the end of the Ming dynasty (1367–1644) and during the conquest of the Manchus, there was great loss of life, and the population only recovered to this level in the first decade of the 18th century. The peaceful and prosperous 18th century saw a tremendous population 'explosion'. From 150,000,000 in 1710 the total leapt to more than double (313,000,000) by 1800, and by 1850 had nearly trebled at 430,000,000.

The outbreak of the T'ai-p'ing rebellion and the series of risings and civil wars which followed, such as the Nien rebellion and the Moslem risings in Turkestan and Yunnan caused the loss of countless millions of lives, and in the 1870s and 1880s a series of terrible famines caused at least 20,000,000 deaths in northern China. These disasters led not only to a drop in the total population, but also prompted considerable internal migration and a marked fall in the rate of population increase. Under the Republic (1912–49) social and political instability, natural disasters and famines, and the massive loss of life during the war of resistance against the Japanese and the ensuing civil war, again kept population increase in check.

Nevertheless in 1953 the population had increased to nearly 600,000,000. Since 1949 internal peace and political stability, more adequate distribution of food supplies and rapidly improving standards of medical care and public hygiene have caused a further rapid population increase. A radical decrease in infant mortality has also led to a population whose average age is very young, when compared with the rapidly ageing populations of western countries. 86 per cent of the Chinese population is below 50, and 40 per cent under 18 years of age. At present the population is probably increasing at a rate of 15,000,000 per year.

Over-population was already becoming a problem at the end of the 18th century, when the necessity of feeding a rapidly increasing population began to strain the available food supply. In the mid-1950s this problem again became a subject of public debate, and a number of prominent economists began to advocate the limitation of runaway population growth by contraception, abortion and the encouragement of later marriages. This line was adopted by Chou En-lai in a speech in 1955, and became official policy. A widespread educational campaign began. However, at the time of the Great Leap Forward in 1958 there was a reversal of official policy, which promoted the theory that a large population and the largest possible labour force was an economic asset rather than a liability.

However, in the years of severe food shortages (1959–61) following the Great Leap Forward, official policy changed once again, and since 1962 the government has continued to encourage planned childbirth and late marriages. The 'normal' age of marriage is accepted as 25–29 for men, and 23–27 for women. These policy changes have had far greater impact upon the urban workers than among the rural population.

The Chinese population is almost entirely concentrated in the eastern half of the country. The western regions, Sinkiang, Tsinghai and Tibet, which only came under Chinese domination under the Manchu Ch'ing dynasty in the 18th century, and which are unsuited for permanent settlement, remain very sparsely peopled. Except for small oases they are largely inhabited by nomadic or semi-nomadic pastoral peoples. These three provinces, which comprise 37.5 per cent of the total land area of China, contain only 1.4 per cent of the population. Similarly the Inner Mongolian and Ningsia border areas, arid grasslands and semi-desert unsuited to permanent agriculture, which account for another 13 per cent of the total area, contain only 1.7 per cent of the population. Thus the arid western and north-western half of China contains barely 3 per cent of its people, and large areas are completely uninhabited.

In contrast to these areas, the eastern half of China is very densely peopled and the entire cultivable area has been settled for many centuries. Only the plains of the three provinces of the north-east, formerly the homeland of the Manchus, have been settled in the last century and a half. The only areas with low population densities are the mountainous regions, and marginal and uncultivated uplands. Something like 30 per cent of the total land area is under cultivation, and in these areas the population is extremely dense. Most of eastern China has population densities of more than 100 per square mile. In the fertile farmlands of the great eastern plain, the Yangtze valley, Szechwan and Kwangtung, densities are commonly over 500 per square mile, and in the great plain sometimes over 1,000 per square mile. Most densely peopled of all is the province of Szechwan. In the fertile plain around Ch'eng-tu the population density reaches 1,500 per square mile.

The great majority of the Chinese population remains rural and agricultural. At the time of the 1953 census only 13 per cent of the Chinese were urban dwellers. Even of this total, a third lived in small rural market towns and minor local administrative centres with less than 20,000 persons.

In the 1950s urban population was rapidly expanded as a result of the drive towards industrialisation, under the First Five Year Plan and the Great Leap Forward. Between 1957 and 1960 the total urban population shot up from 92,000,000 (14.3 per cent of the total) to 130,000,000 (18.5 per cent). Most of this increase resulted from the migration of workers from the countryside, but it was also affected by the abnormally high birth-rate in the cities, which was twice the national average. This enormous rate of increase among the urban population led to a shortage of urban housing, and consequent pressure on the construction industry which was unable to meet the demand for housing.

The collapse of the Great Leap Forward led to a considerable decrease in urban population. By 1962 some 20,000,000 urban workers had been returned to the countryside as the result of the closing down of many new and uneconomic industrial plants.

A third of the urban population live in the 17 great cities with populations of more than one million. These cities, which also accounted for more than 60 per cent of China's total industrial capacity in 1960, are concentrated in the coastal provinces and in Manchuria, with the exception of the great regional economic centres, T'ai-yüan, Hsi-an (Sian), Ch'eng-tu and Ch'ung-ch'ing, which were developed by deliberate policy in the 1950s. Besides these great metropolitan centres there are about a hundred regional urban centres with more than 100,000 people, and another hundred with more than 50,000. Well over 90 per cent of these urban centres are in eastern China, and a large proportion are in the north and north-east. The sparsely peopled western half of the country has very few urban centres of any size, and there are comparatively few large cities in southern China.

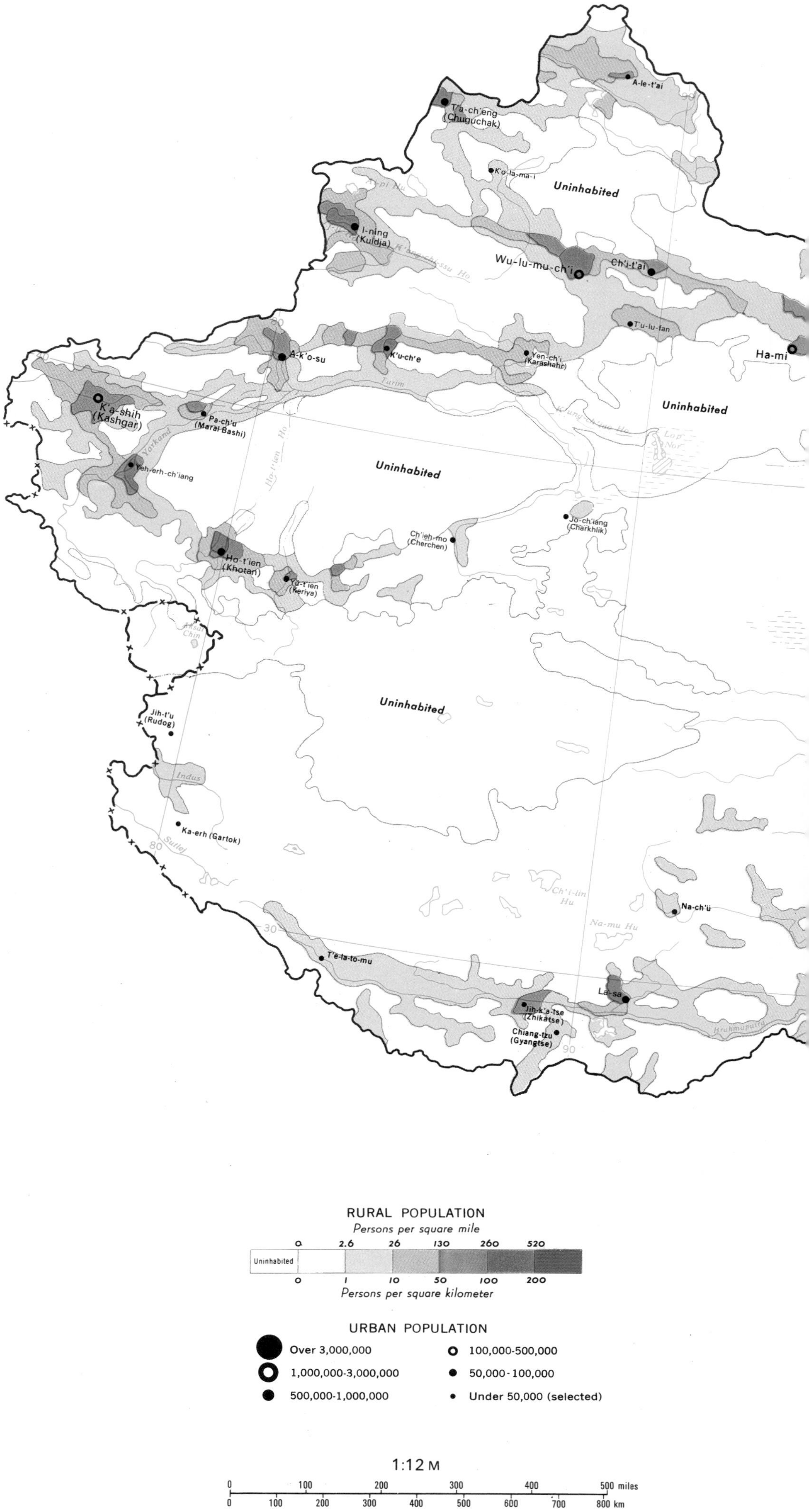

POPULATION

Population

	Population (1972) (1,000)	Density per sq. km.
PRC	**750,000**	**79**
Europe	469,000	95
Africa	364,000	12
S. America	300,000	15
USSR	248,000	11
N. America	233,000	11
Japan	106,000	287
World	3,782,000	28

Literacy

(% of Population over 15 years old)

N. America	99
Europe & USSR	96
Oceania	90
L. America	76
PRC	**60**
Asia (general)	53
Africa	26

Structure of agricultural employment

(% of economically active population)

	1960	1970
Africa	80.5	75.5
PRC	**75.2**	**66.7**
L. America	47.9	41.5
USSR/E. Europe	42.6	32.4
Japan	33.0	21.0
W. Europe	23.5	17.2
Oceania	12.0	8.9
N. America	7.2	4.4
World	57.8	51.4

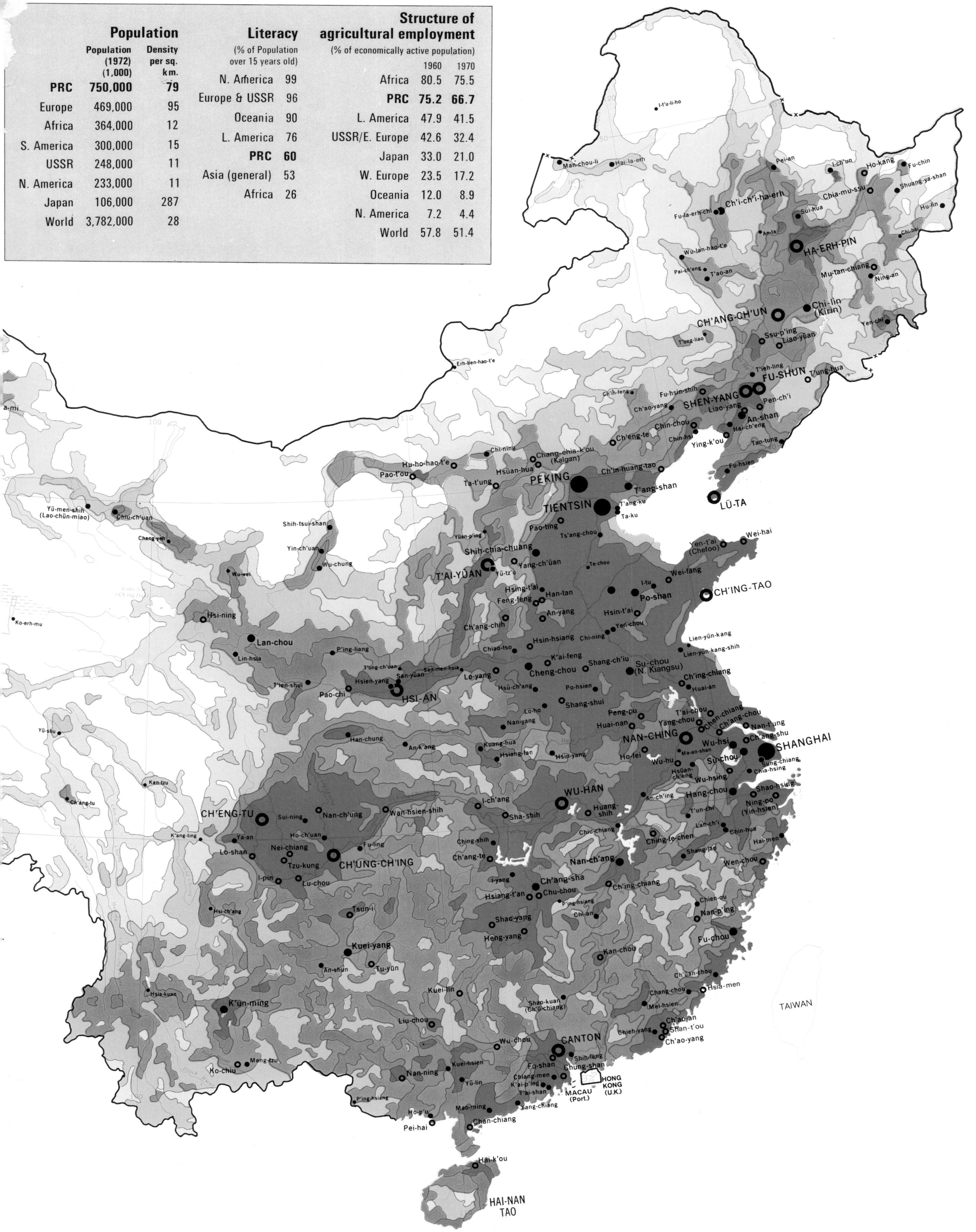

ABOUT 95 per cent of the total Chinese population is composed of Han Chinese peoples, speaking one or other of the dialects of Chinese. The other 5 per cent is made up of the members of a great number of national minorities, ethnically and linguistically different from the Chinese. Despite their relatively small numbers, the minorities are politically significant for they occupy between them almost half of the area of China, including the vitally important strategic border areas with the Soviet Union, the Mongolian People's Republic, India, Burma, Vietnam and Korea.

The Tibetans There are about three million Tibetans, who occupy most of the Tibetan Autonomous Region, Tsinghai province, western Szechwan and north-western Yunnan. They were until recent times an independent people whose culture and social institutions have developed along quite different lines from the Chinese, and they remained to a large degree semi-autonomous, bound together by the complete political and social dominance of the Lamaistic church. Tibet was finally brought under firm Chinese central control after the rebellion of 1959, and in 1965 the Tibet Autonomous Region was set up to administer the area.

The Turkic peoples The various Turkic peoples, all of them Moslem, total about 4,300,000 and inhabit most of Sinkiang and the north-western parts of Tsinghai and Kansu. The most important of these peoples are the Uighurs, who inhabit the oases and towns of Sinkiang, and who were the dominant group in Central Asia until the Manchu conquest in the 18th century. The Uzbeks are also mostly settled in the oasis towns. The other main groups are the Kazakhs and the Kirghiz, pastoral nomads who live along the western border of Sinkiang and the Soviet Union, and whose peoples also live across the frontier. During their long and complex history, these Turkic peoples have enjoyed long periods of independence, but since 1949 many Chinese have been settled in the area, and although Sinkiang is an Autonomous Region, its Turkic peoples are no longer so dominant.

The Mongols The Mongols, totalling about one and a half million, inhabit the entire border region abutting on the Mongolian People's Republic, from Kansu in the west to Heilungkiang. The Mongols of this frontier zone comprise a great number of tribes speaking different dialects. They are organised into tribal Leagues and Banners each of which has its own territory. In the past the nomadic existence of the Mongols, in grasslands too dry for permanent agriculture, distinguished them from their Chinese neighbours, but since the late 19th century Chinese settlers have encroached on their pasturelands and attempted to open the frontier area for agriculture, and now many of the Mongols live in permanent settlements.

In addition to this main frontier zone of Mongol settlement there are scattered tribes and settlements of Mongols in the Dzungarian region of Sinkiang. In Tsinghai live the Monguor (Tu) people, who have been separated from the main Mongol peoples for many centuries and preserve an archaic form of the language and many ancient customs. Kansu is the home of the Pao-an and Tung-hsiang, Mongol peoples who live among the Chinese Moslems of the area and have been converted to Islam, although most of the Mongols were strongly influenced by Lamaistic Buddhism until recent times.

The Mongols, once rulers of all China and much of northern Asia, have always been very independent, even under the Manchu dynasty. In the early years of this century a powerful nationalist movement grew up, which led to the foundation of the independent Mongolian Republic. In 1947 an Inner Mongolian Autonomous District was established, which in 1954 was enlarged to form the Inner Mongolian Autonomous Region stretching from the borders of Heilungkiang to Sinkiang, with an area of 450,000 square miles. The Region was reduced, in 1969, to about a third of that area.

The Tungusic peoples The most important Tungusic people, the Manchus, who number perhaps two and a half millions, have been almost completely assimilated into the Han Chinese population, no longer speak their own language, and do not form separate ethnic communities. Most of them live in the provinces of Liaoning, Kirin and Heilungkiang.

The Koreans There is a considerable Korean minority numbering more than a million living in the north-east. The main community lives in the area around Yen-chi in eastern Kirin, where they settled as refugees in the 1870s.

The Chinese Moslems (Hui) The Chinese Moslems are not strictly an ethnic minority, since they are of Han Chinese descent and speak dialects of Mandarin. But they form a powerful religious minority which tends to live in separate communities concentrated in the north-west (Ningsia, for instance, forms a Hui Autonomous Region), in Peking and Tientsin, and among the city populations of Hopeh, Honan, Anhwei and Hunan.

The south-western minorities Most of the south-west, Kwangsi, Kweichow and Yunnan, has been colonised by Han Chinese only in comparatively recent times. Even today in these areas Chinese settlement is largely confined to the more fertile mountain basins and valleys, leaving the uplands and more remote districts in the hands of a great number of minority peoples. These peoples, whose insulation from Chinese influence until quite recently has made them China's most numerous, backward and fragmented minorities, divide into three main groups. The first includes half a million Thai tribesmen who live in the areas of Yunnan bordering on Burma, Laos and North Vietnam; the seven million Chuang who since 1958 have had their own province, Kwangsi Chuang Autonomous Region, and the Pu-yi. The second group comprises the three million Miao-Yao with settlements in southern Kweichow, in Yunnan, Kwangsi, Hunan and Kwangtung, and the She people who live in the mountains of Fukien and Chekiang. The third group includes the Sino-Tibetan peoples in western Yunnan and south-western Szechwan; the Min-chia living around Ta-li and the Tu-chia of western Hunan; the Hani on the Vietnamese border, and the Lisu and the Lahu in western Yunnan.

THE MINORITY PEOPLES

CLIMATIC features, above all else, dictate the uses to which much of China's landscape can be put. The country is sharply divided into two parts, the north-western and western half, an arid or semi-arid region with less than 20 inches of annual precipitation, where temperature variations are extreme, and where permanent agriculture is possible only in sheltered or well-irrigated pockets; and, in contrast to this, the more humid regions of the south and south-east where the climate is much less variable.

The Chinese climatic pattern is dictated by the winter and summer monsoons. The monsoon pattern of climate is subject to wide local variation, and the continental high pressure and low pressure systems are far more extreme and more persistent in some years than in others. The annual variations have made the climate very unpredictable, and China has suffered seriously in the past from the effects of flood and, more particularly, of drought. In winter, the bitterly cold continental areas of Siberia and Central Asia become the centre of a massive and persistent high pressure system. Strong northerly or north-westerly winds (the winter monsoons) flow out from this system to the Pacific. Blowing into China from the Gobi desert, these winds generate frequent dust storms in northern China, but bring very little precipitation. Throughout China only a small proportion of the annual precipitation falls during the winter months and during the spring. From May onwards the air masses are reversed. Siberia and Central Asia heat up and become the centre of a low pressure system, and China's climate is dominated by southerly and south-easterly winds (the summer monsoons) flowing in from the Pacific. These are heavily moisture-laden and bring the summer rains (the 'plum rains'). Everywhere in China summer and autumn are the wettest seasons. This is especially the case in northern and north-eastern China where almost three-quarters of the annual rainfall comes between mid-June and mid-September.

In northern China spring droughts are frequent, and these are commonly followed by floods in early summer. Moreover, the summer rains fall during the period when losses through evaporation are highest, and their effects are thus significantly reduced. Although the concentration of rainfall in summer and autumn is almost universal, except in the western areas with minimum rainfall, it does not present such a serious problem in southern and south-eastern China. Here the annual rainfall rises to 50 or 80 inches, and even the drier winter months have adequate rainfall. Moreover, unlike northern China, the south is not subject to great variations in rainfall from one year to the next.

Average temperatures vary greatly throughout the country. The average January temperatures are below freezing throughout the west and north of the Chin-ling mountain range and the Huai river. In the north of Manchuria they fall well below −18°C (0°F) and there are areas where the subsoil is permanently frozen. In the north-east the winters are so severe that the rivers are icebound for upwards of 180 days each year. The average winter temperatures in central and southern China rise steadily towards the coastal zone of Fukien and Kwangtung, where they are about 15.5°C (60°F).

Whereas winter temperatures vary according to latitude, in summer the average temperatures are very much more uniform throughout the country. The average July temperatures are above 21°C (70°F) everywhere, and in general decrease from the coast westward. The average July temperatures in the south-east coastal zone, and in the Szechwan basin in the interior, are above 29.5°C (85°F).

The annual temperature range thus varies greatly. The most extreme variations of climate are to be found in northern Manchuria, where the average temperatures range from −25°C (−13°F) in January to 21°C (70°F) in July, and in the inland deserts of Sinkiang. The least variation is to be found in the southern coastal areas, where the seasons are far less sharply differentiated, and where the growing season lasts the whole year round.

These are broad generalisations. Local conditions and topography greatly influence climate, especially in the mountainous western half of the country. In the high plateaux of western China and Tibet sheer altitude also has a great effect. There are very great variations in the micro-climates of these areas, and for most of western China no adequate climatic data are available to permit of detailed description.

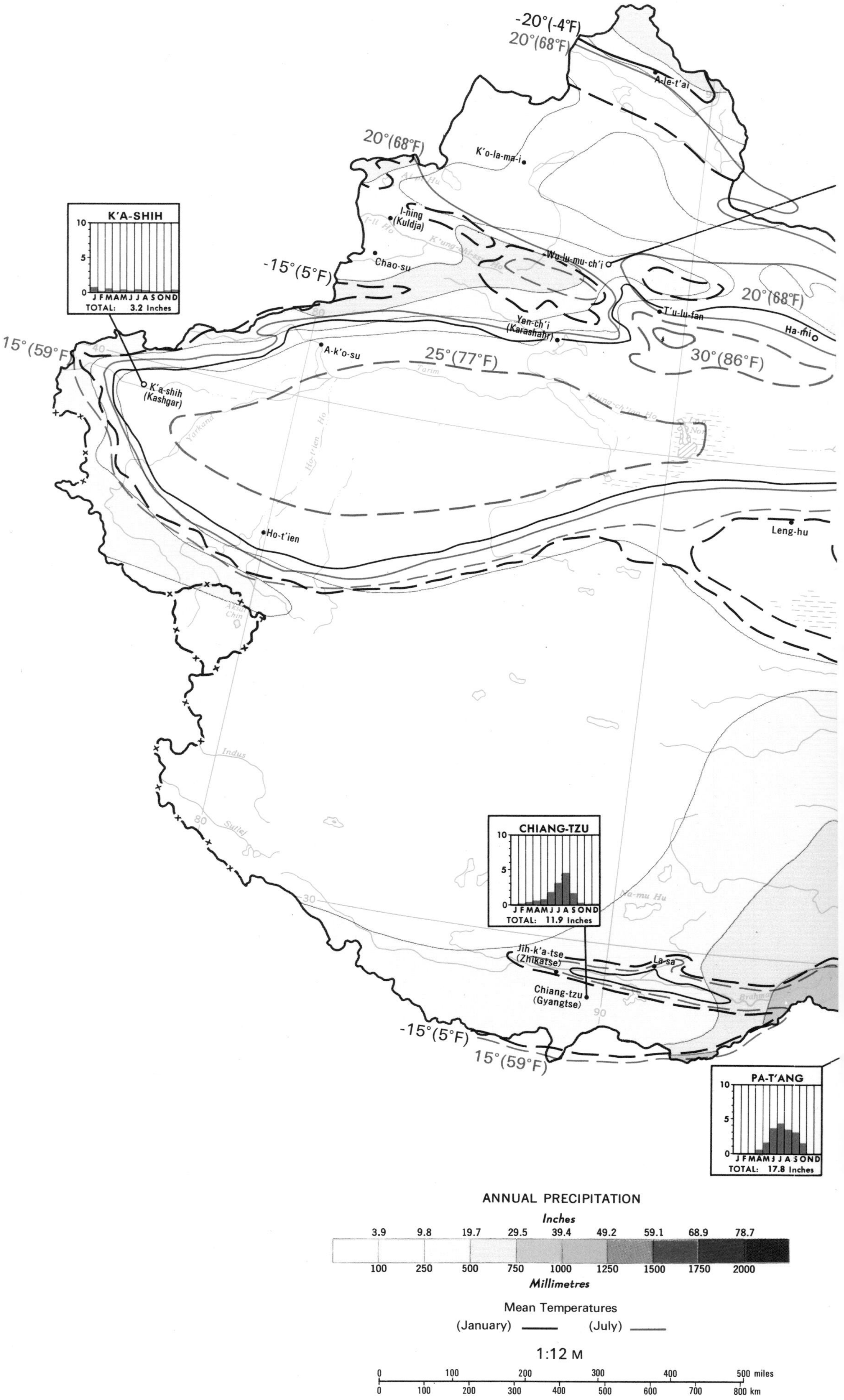

CLIMATE

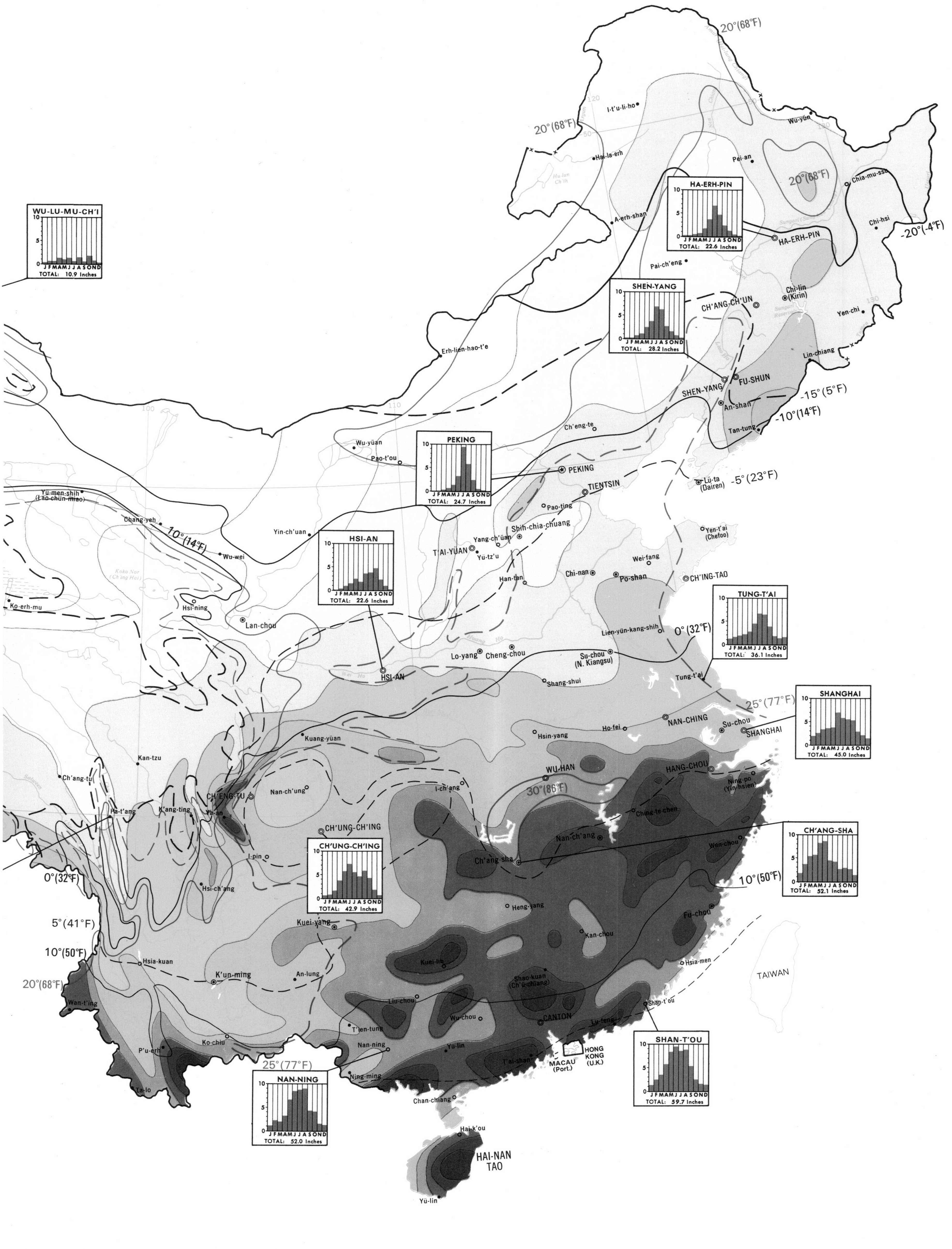

WU-LU-MU-CH'I
TOTAL: 10.9 Inches
HA-ERH-PIN
TOTAL: 22.6 Inches
SHEN-YANG
TOTAL: 28.2 Inches
PEKING
TOTAL: 24.7 Inches
HSI-AN
TOTAL: 22.6 Inches
TUNG-T'AI
TOTAL: 36.1 Inches
SHANGHAI
TOTAL: 45.0 Inches
CH'UNG-CH'ING
TOTAL: 42.9 Inches
CH'ANG-SHA
TOTAL: 52.1 Inches
SHAN-T'OU
TOTAL: 59.7 Inches
NAN-NING
TOTAL: 52.0 Inches
J F M A M J J A S O N D
20°(68°F)
-20°(-4°F)
-15°(5°F)
-10°(14°F)
-5°(23°F)
10°(14°F)
0°(32°F)
25°(77°F)
30°(86°F)
10°(50°F)
5°(41°F)
I-t'u-li-ho
Wu-yün
Hai-la-erh
Pei-an
Chia-mu-ssu
A-erh-shan
HA-ERH-PIN
Chi-hsi
Pai-ch'eng
CH'ANG-CH'UN
Chi-lin (Kirin)
Yen-chi
Erh-lien-hao-t'e
Lin-chiang
FU-SHUN
SHEN-YANG
An-shan
Tan-tung
Ch'eng-te
Wu-yüan
Pao-t'ou
PEKING
TIENTSIN
Lü-ta (Dairen)
Yü-men-shih (Lao-chün-miao)
Pao-ting
Chang-yeh
Yin-ch'uan
Shih-chia-chuang
Yang-ch'üan
Yen-t'ai (Chefoo)
T'AI-YÜAN
Yü-tz'u
Wu-wei
Wei-fang
Chi-nan
Po-shan
CH'ING-TAO
Han-tan
Ko-erh-mu
Hsi-ning
Lan-chou
Lien-yün-kang-shih
Lo-yang
Cheng-chou
Su-chou (N. Kiangsu)
HSI-AN
Shang-shui
Tung-t'ai
NAN-CHING
Su-chou
SHANGHAI
Ho-fei
Hsin-yang
Kuang-yüan
Kan-tzu
Ch'ang-tu
WU-HAN
HANG-CHOU
Ning-po (Yin-hsien)
Nan-ch'ung
I-ch'ang
CH'ENG-TU
Ba-t'ang
K'ang-ting
Ya-an
Ching-te-chen
CH'UNG-CH'ING
Nan-ch'ang
Wen-chou
Ch'ang-sha
I-pin
Hsi-ch'ang
Heng-yang
Fu-chou
Kuei-yang
Kan-chou
Hsia-kuan
Kuei-lin
Hsia-men
TAIWAN
K'un-ming
An-lung
Shao-kuan (Ch'ü-chiang)
Wan-t'ing
Liu-chou
Shan-t'ou
Wu-chou
CANTON
T'ien-tung
Ko-chiu
Yü-lin
HONG KONG (U.K.)
MACAU (Port.)
P'u-erh
Nan-ning
T'ai-shan
Ning-ming
Ta-lo
Chan-chiang
Hai-k'ou
HAI-NAN TAO
Yü-lin

CHINA has always been an agrarian society, and agricultural techniques were already advanced by the 14th century when most of the crops, techniques and implements characteristic of Chinese agriculture were already in use. From that time onwards Chinese agriculture has had to support an ever-increasing population. By the end of the 16th century most of the good farmland in China itself was already under cultivation. Although new foreign crops, such as maize, sweet potatoes and ground nuts enabled farmers to utilise poor upland soils, much good land was devoted to the cultivation of another import – tobacco – and later of opium. Careless cultivation of hill lands also led to widespread soil erosion. In ordinary farming, few technical innovations were made. Farming became more and more labour-intensive and the average size of farms decreased. Although some frontier areas were brought under cultivation, climatic and physical conditions severely limited expansion of the cultivated area, and the same area which had fed 100,000,000 people in the 14th century had to feed more than 400,000,000 by the 19th century. By about 1800 China faced an economic crisis.

By the present century this crisis was acute. Although after 1850 Chinese settlers began to move into Manchuria and to open up some of the frontier zone in Inner Mongolia which had been traditional pasturelands of the Mongol tribes, there was little further room for expansion. Early in this century the population had reached 450,000,000 and famine was frequent, particularly in the poor northern provinces. Although about half of the farmers cultivated their own land, tenancy was widespread, particularly in the Yangtze provinces, in the south and in Szechwan. In the 1930s most people, of all political parties, believed that the inequalities of land-ownership were the source of China's agrarian problems, and landlordism, tenancy, indebtedness and the exploitation of the peasantry were blamed for agriculture's inefficiency. They believed that a more equitable redistribution of land would automatically increase the efficiency of agriculture. After 1949 planners continued to stress the primary need for such social and institutional changes. Although land reform was rapidly carried out throughout China, many inequalities persisted, and the average size of farms remained very small and uneconomic.

The next stage of planning was the organisation of individual farmers into larger productive units, first into mutual aid teams, whose members retained ownership of their lands, then into producer co-operatives and higher collectives in which all land was owned by the members. By 1956, 96 per cent were incorporated into producer co-operatives and 88 per cent were fully collectivised. These higher collectives averaged some 170 households – the equivalent of a large village – and were subdivided into production brigades of about 20 households. A further step towards full collectivisation came with the organisation of the People's Communes (Jen-min kung-she) in 1958. These combined the existing higher collectives into much larger units, which also took over the functions of the lowest level of local government, the *hsiang*. The communes, unlike the collectives, thus combined economic management with ordinary administrative functions. They were not only a step towards full communal control of all the means of production, but were also an essential part of the policy of administrative de-centralisation begun in 1957. By September 1958 the collectives had been merged into 26,400 communes, with an average size of 4,600 households or 25,000 persons. The largest were in the independent municipalities of Peking and Shanghai and in the most modernised areas with good communications – Hopeh, Honan, Kiangsu, Chekiang, the middle Yangtze plain around Wu-han and Kwangtung. The original communes proved to be too large, and after 1961 their number was greatly increased and their size reduced. By 1963 there were about 74,000 communes controlling the natural economic and social areas served by traditional local markets.

Internally the communes are divided into production brigades and smaller production teams which manage and perform agricultural work and production. The commune as a whole manages repair and construction work, handicrafts and small scale local industries, and has tended to become an organ of low-level local administration, with responsibility for law and order, rural education, health services, irrigation and water-control, and local transport. These changes in the nature of the communes occurred in the period of economic crisis and widespread shortages which followed the failure of the Great Leap Forward. The abandonment of very large productive units coincided with the end of attempts to impose a pattern of strictly communal living, and farmers regained control of their own private plots of land. At the same time the basic policy of the government towards agriculture changed. The social and institutional changes in favour of collective or communal use of land had now been pressed to completion, and the government now began to encourage technical improvement in agricultural production. Capital investment, which had been almost exclusively devoted to heavy industry in the 1950s was now diverted to the support of agriculture. Fertiliser production had been very backward but after 1962 many large plants and also a great number of small local factories were constructed. Although the use of chemical fertilisers still falls far below that of more highly developed countries, their wide-spread availability has led to great increases in crop yields. A further significant technical development was the mechanisation of agriculture. At the time of the Great Leap Forward local light engineering industries were established, mostly designed for the manufacture and repair of farm implements. The production of tractors began in the 1950s in large centralised plants built on Soviet models, producing machines designed for large scale farming. Since the early 1960s, however, many small local plants have been producing a wide range of tractors designed for Chinese conditions, while other local industries have developed seed-drills, earth-moving machinery and chemical sprays. Large scale rural electrification has also made possible the use of electrical pumping equipment for irrigation schemes and much of this equipment, too, is manufactured in local plants.

Great attention has also been given to the improvement of crop varieties. New strains of wheat have been cultivated in areas of the west and north with extremely harsh climates. New types of rice have pushed the limits both of rice cultivation and of double cropping of rice much farther north than in earlier times. The use of insecticides and pest control have also improved production. New techniques of cultivation have been tried and the terracing of fields, contour ploughing to check soil erosion, irrigation and afforestation schemes have considerably increased the area under cultivation.

In the early years, from 1949–61, agrarian production in China rose only very slowly, in spite of collectivisation, and the years 1959–61 were years of disastrous food shortages, crop failures and widespread hardship. Since 1962, however, grain production has risen steadily, and successfully provided for the increase in the population. Agriculture remains by far the most important sector of the Chinese economy, employing a very large proportion of the work-force, and providing both raw material for industry and roughly one-third of China's total exports.

Oases—Agricultural potential limited by availability of irrigation water. Wide variety of food grains, industrial crops (cotton), and fruit and vegetable specialties—grapes and melons.

Tibetan Highlands—High elevations limit cultivation mainly to fast-maturing barley. Some tubers and hardy vegetables grown; wheat and other grains planted at lower elevations.

Szechwan Rice—Single crop rice followed by wheat, rape, or peas is common cropping system. Corn and sweet potatoes extensively cultivated in non-irrigated fields.

AGRICULTURE

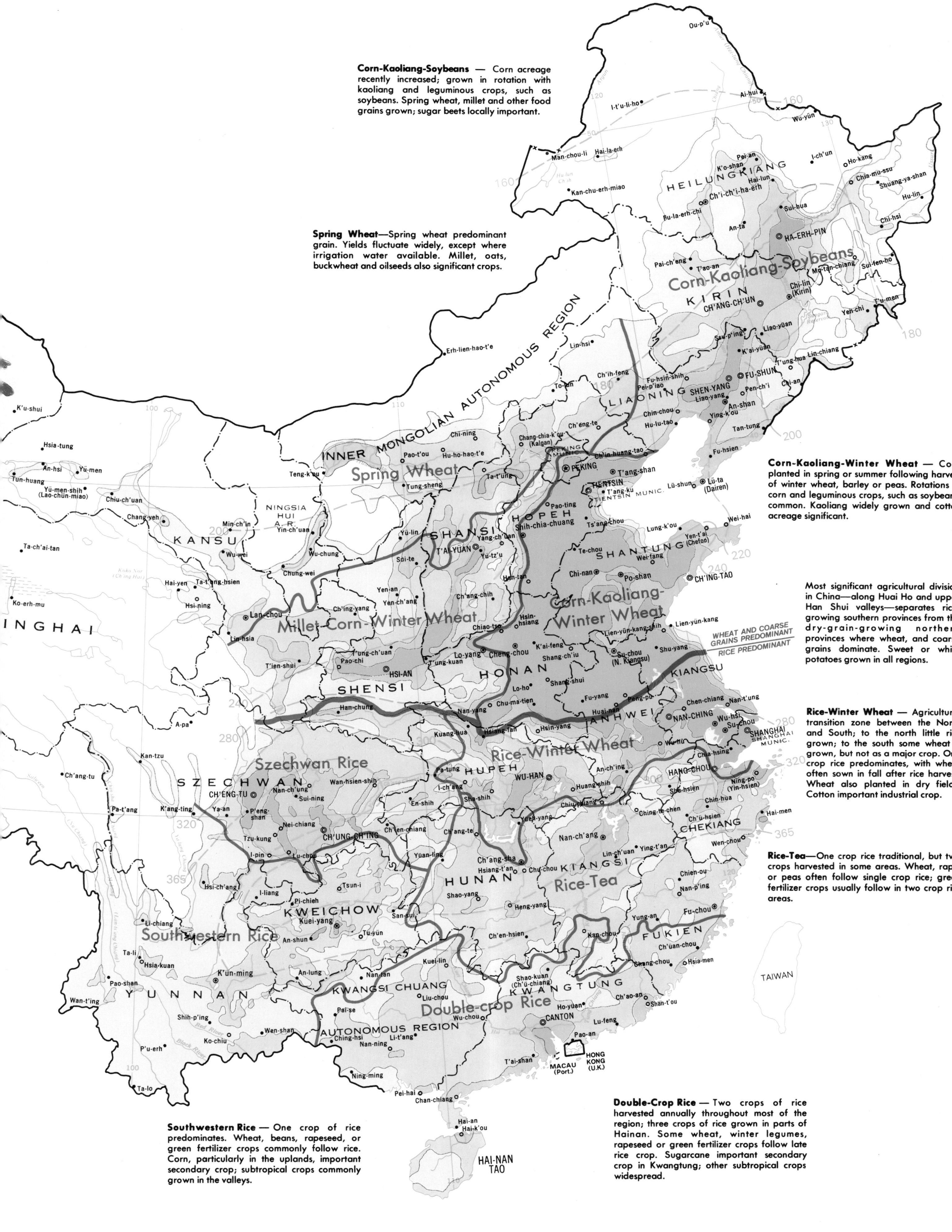

Corn-Kaoliang-Soybeans — Corn acreage recently increased; grown in rotation with kaoliang and leguminous crops, such as soybeans. Spring wheat, millet and other food grains grown; sugar beets locally important.

Spring Wheat—Spring wheat predominant grain. Yields fluctuate widely, except where irrigation water available. Millet, oats, buckwheat and oilseeds also significant crops.

Corn-Kaoliang-Winter Wheat — Corn planted in spring or summer following harvest of winter wheat, barley or peas. Rotations of corn and leguminous crops, such as soybeans, common. Kaoliang widely grown and cotton acreage significant.

Most significant agricultural division in China—along Huai Ho and upper Han Shui valleys—separates rice-growing southern provinces from the dry-grain-growing northern provinces where wheat, and coarse grains dominate. Sweet or white potatoes grown in all regions.

Rice-Winter Wheat — Agricultural transition zone between the North and South; to the north little rice grown; to the south some wheat is grown, but not as a major crop. One crop rice predominates, with wheat often sown in fall after rice harvest. Wheat also planted in dry fields. Cotton important industrial crop.

Rice-Tea—One crop rice traditional, but two crops harvested in some areas. Wheat, rape, or peas often follow single crop rice; green fertilizer crops usually follow in two crop rice areas.

Southwestern Rice — One crop of rice predominates. Wheat, beans, rapeseed, or green fertilizer crops commonly follow rice. Corn, particularly in the uplands, important secondary crop; subtropical crops commonly grown in the valleys.

Double-Crop Rice — Two crops of rice harvested annually throughout most of the region; three crops of rice grown in parts of Hainan. Some wheat, winter legumes, rapeseed or green fertilizer crops follow late rice crop. Sugarcane important secondary crop in Kwangtung; other subtropical crops widespread.

Production of selected crops (1971) 1,000 metric tons

	Europe	USSR	USA	PRC	Japan	World
Wheat	79,634	92,000	44,620	**32,000**	444	343.1
Rye	15,757	12,000	1,294	—	1	30.9
Barley	51,484	36,000	10,070	**18,500**	503	152.4
Oats	18,711	15,000	12,712	**1,690**	60	57.7
Maize	41,160	11,500	140,733	**28,500**	30	307.8
Millet & Sorghum	451	3,000	22,739	**22,000**	16	101.1
Rice paddy	1,841	1,420	3,820	**104,000**	14,139	307.4
includes mixed/misc. **All cereals**	231,212	172,640	236,146	**210,500**	15,207	1309.0
Sugar cane	462	—	21,769	**30,500**	815	585,482
Sugar beets	105,463	78,324	23,766	**5,200**	2,332	228,151
Centrifugal sugar	15,843	8,150	5,134	**3,300**	466	72,268
Non-centrifugal sugar	—	—	—	**726**	3	11,339
Potatoes	134,704	92,300	14,451	1965 **27,000**	3,156	306,445
Sweet potatoes & Yams	81	—	626	1965 **81,000**	2,564	147,713
Dry beans	913	68	744	**1,400**	167	11,686
Apples	12,533	—	2,791	**400**	1,050	19,954
Pears	4,509	—	665	**900**	470	7,399
Grapes	35,223	1,087	2,830	1970 **135**	234	54,838
Oranges/Tangerines	4,414	95	7,841	**700**	3,000	—
Soy beans	193	610	31,823	**11,500**	122	48,291
Groundnuts in shell	72	1	1,357	**2,700**	111	18,480
Cotton-seed	326	4,646	3,978	**3,036**	—	21,976
Rape-seed	2,076	3	1	**1,000**	25	7,880
Cotton (Lint)	183	2,394	2,299	**1,518**	—	11,799
Sesame-seed	78	1	4	**3,700**	30	20,981
Sunflower-seed	2,137	5,700	110	**70**	—	9,694
Castor beans	17	70	15	**90**	—	797
Jute	—	50	—	**500**	15	3,474
100 metric tons **Tung oil**	—	7	20	**900**	—	1,201
100 metric tons **Tea**	1	678	—	**1,730**	930	13,048
100 metric tons **Tobacco**	5,918	2,880	8,101	**7,850**	1,497	46,592

Meat, milk and egg production

	(1,000 metric tons) ***meat	**milk	(100 metric tons) poultry	eggs
Europe	22,017	150,431	—	60,393
USSR	8,750	83,100	11,000	23,000
USA	16,939	53,796	63,321	42,185
PRC	***13,310**	**400,932**	**26,350**	**33,100**
Japan	941	5,004	3,810	18,500

—beyond estimate
*of which 3,460 pork
**cow, buffalo, goat, sheep
***beef-veal, mutton-lamb, pork

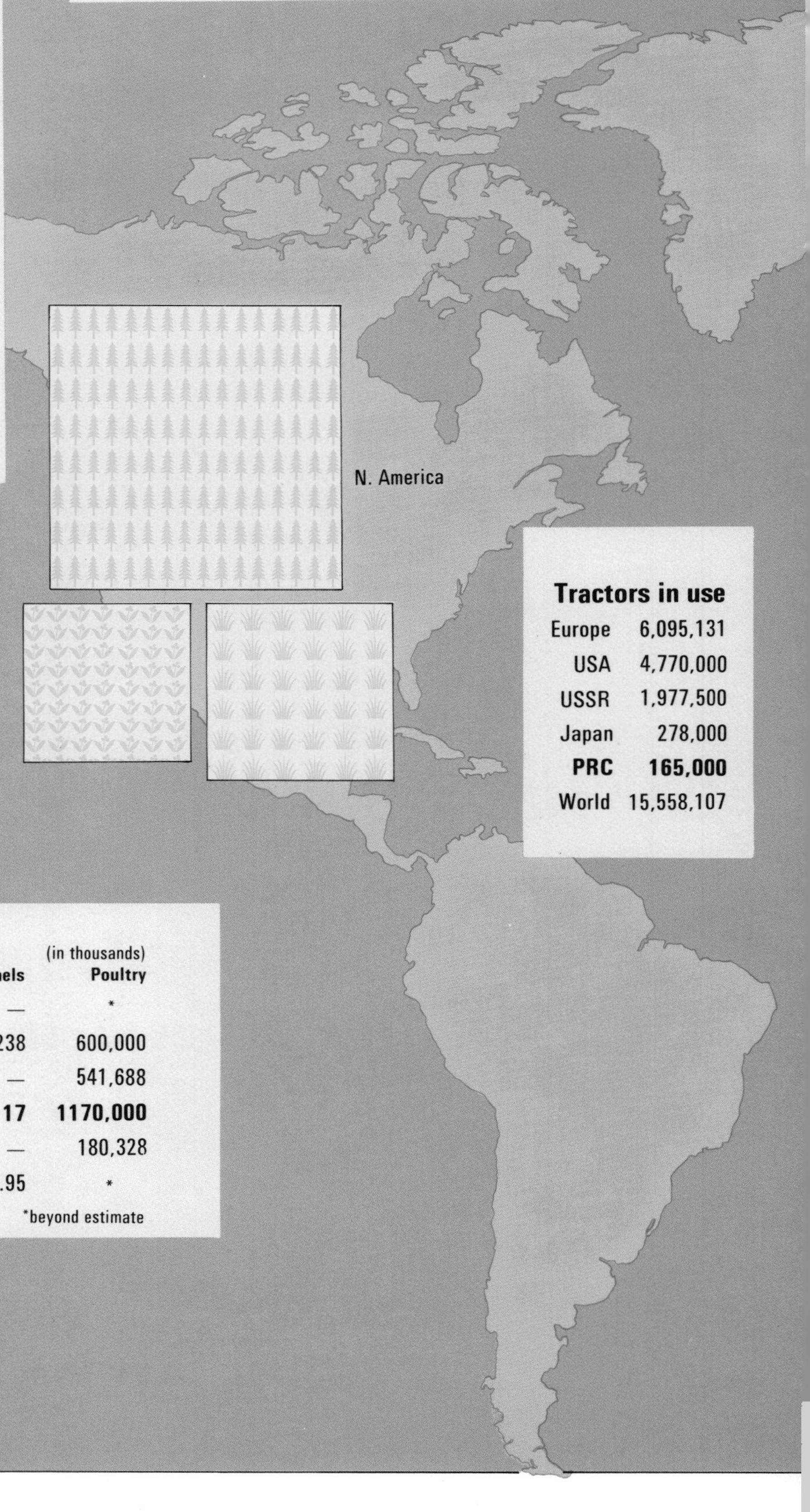

Raw silk
(not cocoons)
metric tons

Japan	20,515
PRC	**10,200**
USSR	3,020
Europe	801
USA	—
World	40,268

Wool Production
100 metric tons

	Greasy	Clean
USSR	4,240	2,544
Europe	2,620	1,421
USA	871	385
PRC	**600**	**360**
Japan	2	1
World	27,368	15,865

Tractors in use

Europe	6,095,131
USA	4,770,000
USSR	1,977,500
Japan	278,000
PRC	**165,000**
World	15,558,107

Livestock and poultry numbers

	(in millions) Horses	Mules	Asses	Cattle	Pigs	Sheep	Goats	Buffaloes	Camels	(in thousands) Poultry
Europe	7.7	1.1	1.7	122.6	139.4	127.4	12.6	0.3	—	*
USSR	7.4	—	0.6	99.1	67.4	137.9	5.4	0.5	238	600,000
USA/Canada	8.1	—	—	126.8	75.2	20.3	2.1	—	—	541,688
PRC	**7.2**	**1.6**	**11.7**	**63.2**	**223.0**	**71.0**	**57.5**	**29.4**	**17**	**1170,000**
Japan	0.1	—	—	3.6	6.9	0.2	0.2	—	—	180,328
World	66.3	14.7	41.9	1141.2	667.7	1074.7	383.0	125.3	145.95	*

—Figures not available *beyond estimate

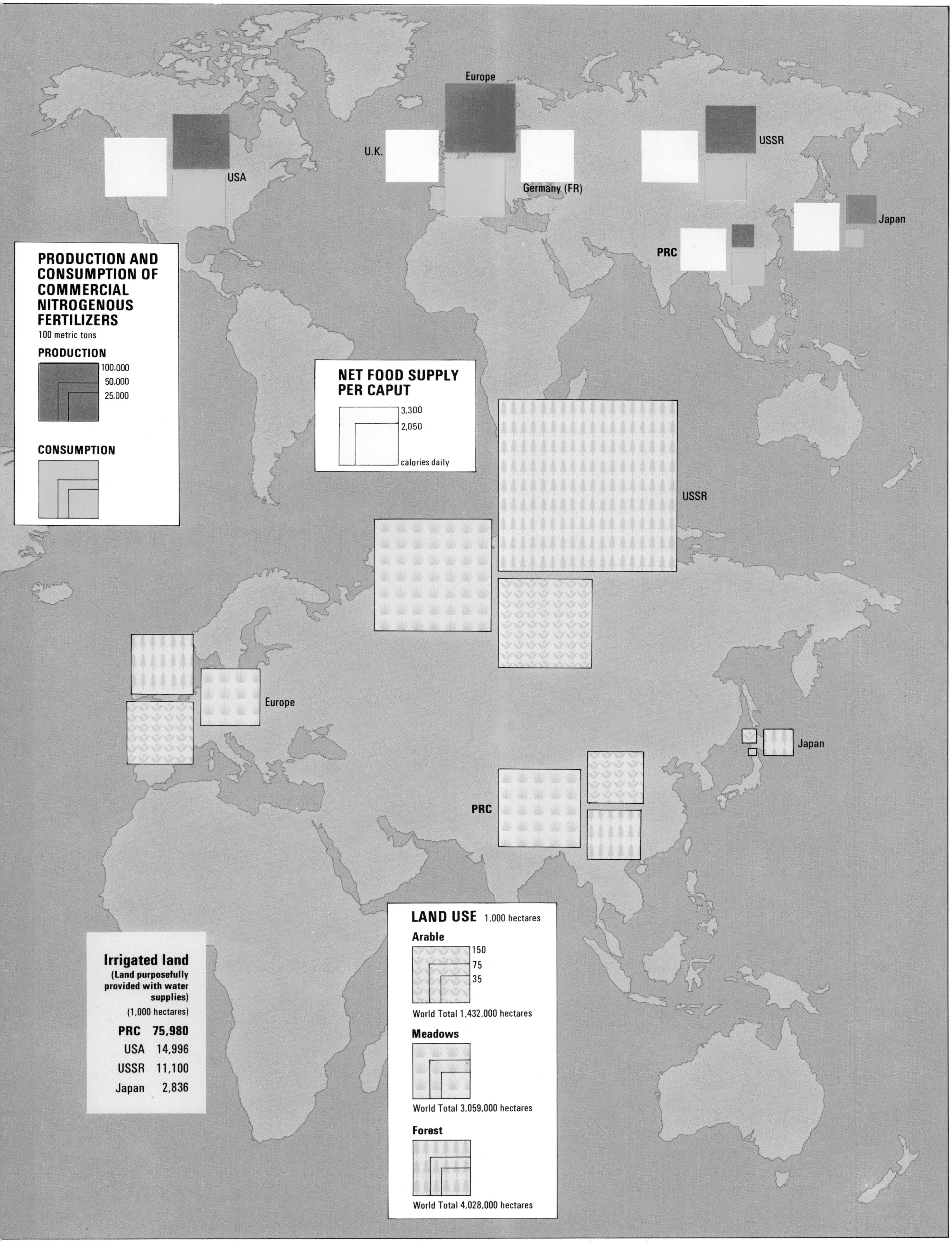
PRODUCTION AND CONSUMPTION OF COMMERCIAL NITROGENOUS FERTILIZERS
100 metric tons
PRODUCTION
100,000
50,000
25,000
CONSUMPTION
Europe
U.K.
Germany (FR)
USA
USSR
Japan
PRC
NET FOOD SUPPLY PER CAPUT
3,300
2,050
calories daily
USSR
Europe
Japan
PRC
Irrigated land
(Land purposefully provided with water supplies)
(1,000 hectares)
PRC 75,980
USA 14,996
USSR 11,100
Japan 2,836
LAND USE 1,000 hectares
Arable
150
75
35
World Total 1,432,000 hectares
Meadows
World Total 3,059,000 hectares
Forest
World Total 4,028,000 hectares

UNTIL the construction of railways, China depended upon its traditional transport network. The country was divided into roughly 60,000 primary market areas, which formed the basic social and economic divisions of the country, and which were the centres of perhaps three-quarters of all commerce. Within these areas the peasant producers carried their own goods to market, delivered their own rents to landlords, paid their taxes to the authorities and carried home their own purchases. Transfer of goods between these markets, and from the local markets to larger commercial centres was undertaken partly by professional carriers, partly by peasants working for hire as a subsidiary means of livelihood. Such local transport depended in northern China largely upon the roads, goods being carried by carts drawn by oxen, mules or horses, by pack animals, by wheelbarrows and human porters. In southern China, the natural river systems and a dense network of canals provided a means of transport. In general, the waterways, which also served the needs of drainage, flood control and irrigation, were much better maintained than the primitive roads of the north, and though water transport was still expensive, it was much cheaper than transport by road, which gave central and southern China a marked economic advantage over the north.

The long-distance transport system which was superimposed on the dense network of local communication was supported and maintained by the central government. Although the Ch'in and Han built a system of trunk highways in the 3rd and 2nd centuries BC, these were allowed to fall into disrepair and the road system remained poor and ill-maintained. However a nationwide network of post stations and courier services for official communications was maintained and these trunk routes became important routes for ordinary trade and travel. Besides maintaining communications throughout their empire, the government also had to collect vast revenues, and to transfer huge quantities of grain to provision their armies. Water transport was the only practicable means of handling such traffic. The main grain surplus areas were in central China, and the capitals and the bulk of the military establishment were in the north. Since the main river systems of the great eastern plain (the Yangtze, Huai Ho and Huang Ho) ran west to east, canals were built to join these river systems and carry the south to north traffic. The first canal between the Yangtze and Huai was built during the Warring States period. Under the Sui, in AD 607–9, a canal was built linking the Huang Ho to the Huai river and thence to the Yangtze and beyond to Hang-chou. Another canal joined the Huang Ho to a place near modern Tientsin. In the 14th century this canal system was replaced by the Grand Canal which linked Peking to the Yangtze by a different route. Until the 18th century this provided a very efficient transport system, with its own administrative and maintenance staff and large fleets of barges. In the middle of the 19th century, however, the system was seriously damaged. In 1851–5 the Huang Ho, which had flowed into the sea south of the Shantung peninsula, changed its course, blocking the northern section of the Grand Canal. Subsequently the southern sections of the canal were seriously damaged during the T'ai-p'ing and Nien rebellions. The Chinese government began to ship grain and other goods from Shanghai to Tientsin by sea, using both foreign steamers and ships of its own Chinese Merchants' Steam Navigation Company. Chinese owned steamboats became numerous and by 1913 over 1,000 steamers were in use on inland waterways. Although steamships were much faster, the costs of transport were about the same as for native junks, and these continued to carry the bulk of the goods.

As the steamship gradually changed the long-distance transport of bulk cargoes, the government communications system was also completely revolutionised in the late 19th century. A telegraph system was begun in 1881, a modern postal service was founded in 1896 and a telephone service in 1903, and the Chinese statesmen, who were convinced of the necessity of an effective system of transport as a means of strengthening the country, put all their efforts into railway construction. The beginnings of a modern highway system came much later than railways – in 1912 there were no roads fit for motor traffic at all – but rapid progress was made, and under the Nationalist government, from 1928–37, there was a serious attempt to build a planned highway network in the provinces of Chekiang, Kiangsu, Anhwei, Honan, Kiangsi, Hunan and Hopeh. By 1937 there were 114,000 kilometres of highway, more than two-thirds of which had been built since 1928, and almost all of which was in the coastal provinces. The outbreak of war, and the flight of the Chinese government to the south-west led to extensive highway construction in western China and the interior. A highway carried heavy truck traffic through the north-west and Sinkiang to the Soviet Union, and in the south-west a road was built through Yunnan to Burma. However, road transport remained severely hampered by the lack of automotive industry, a chronic shortage of fuels and a lack of technical skills and maintenance facilities. In 1949 the traditional forms of transport, slow, inefficient and extremely costly, continued to carry most goods.

Since 1949 the highway system has been extended and improved, and existing highways renovated. A network of strategic highways has been built to open up the sparsely peopled and remote areas of the south-west and west and have played a major role in the firm integration into the Chinese state of the ethnic minorities of these outlying areas. They have also made possible the exploitation of economic resources such as the oil fields of K'o-la-ma-i (Karamai) and the Tsaidam Basin. The road network of China is now estimated to total some 500,000 kilometres but well over half of this total is merely unsurfaced earth tracks, and there are still only a few thousand kilometres of modern concrete or bituminous-surfaced roads. Traffic is very light, however, as vehicles are few and petrol scarce. The Chinese automotive industry, concentrated in Ch'ang-ch'un, with smaller plants in Tientsin, Shanghai, Wu-han, Nan-ch'ang and Canton, is still very small. The first trucks were produced in 1957, but production virtually came to a halt in 1961, and only began to recover in about 1966. In 1971 output of trucks was about 75,000.

Waterways remain an important part of the transport system, although water transport in the north is badly limited by severe winters. In the 1950s, after a long period of neglect, considerable investment was made in the waterways. A major scheme, begun under the First Five Year Plan, to repair and re-open the Grand Canal as a trunk route has apparently been completed as far as the borders of Shantung, and the water-control and conservancy schemes on the Hai Ho, Huang Ho and Huai Ho systems, and improvements to the upper course of the Yangtze, have all added to the mileage of waterway navigable by small craft. As on the roads, however, traditional forms of transport prevail, and most water traffic is still carried by shallow-draught junks.

ROADS AND WATERWAYS

THE development of railways in China began only late in the 19th century. Although some modernising statesmen had advocated building a rail system in the 1860s, as a means of unifying the country, attempts to build railways met strong opposition, and the first experimental line built in 1876 from Shanghai to Wu-sung had to be dismantled. The government later built a short line from the T'ang-shan coal mines to Tientsin in 1881, but as late as 1895 there were only 288 kilometres of railway in the whole country.

After China's defeat by Japan in the war of 1894, the inevitability of modernisation was accepted, and opposition to railways ceased. From 1898 to 1911 there was a great wave of railway construction, almost all of it undertaken by foreign companies and financed by foreign loans. Resentment against the foreign influence represented by the railways and concessions led to powerful popular protest, and a campaign for the nationalisation of the rail network played a large part in the fall of the empire in 1911. But by this time 9,600 kilometres of track had been laid. These first lines were designed primarily for strategic rather than economic purposes, and for long-distance traffic. Peking and Tientsin were linked to Manchuria, a line was built by Chinese engineers to Chang-chia-k'ou (Kalgan) on the Mongolian border, and two great trunk lines were built from the north to the Yangtze, one from Peking to Han-k'ou (modern Wu-han), the other from Tientsin to P'u-k'ou on the Yangtze opposite Nan-ching. The Russians built the Chinese Eastern Railway, linking the Trans-Siberian line with Vladivostok across Manchuria, and a branch linking this line to the new port they developed at Lü-ta (Dairen), and in Shantung the Germans built a line from their new port Ch'ing-tao (Tsingtao).

After 1912 railway development came to a virtual halt. Internal instability and civil war prevented long-term planning and disrupted what services there were, and foreign investment ceased with the outbreak of the First World War. Between 1912 and 1927 only 3,400 kilometres of new lines were constructed, more than half of this in Manchuria where the Japanese had established a sphere of influence after the Russo-Japanese War. The railway, however, was extended further along the Mongolian border, and a beginning was made to two important trunk routes, from Han-k'ou to Canton, and the Lung-hai railway from the coast at Lien-yün-kang to the west. The restoration of some degree of political stability in 1927 improved the situation, and between 1928 and 1937 the Lung-hai and Canton-Han-k'ou lines were completed and a major line was built from Chekiang into Kiangsi and Hunan provinces. But the greatest progress continued to be in Manchuria, where some 4,500 kilometres were built by the Japanese after 1931 – 50 per cent more than in all the rest of China. After the outbreak of the Sino-Japanese War in 1937 there was some limited construction for strategic purposes, but immense damage was done to the existing railway system. Even greater damage was done during the civil war before 1949.

Throughout this early period only a narrow belt of territory along the railways found its economy much affected by the new form of transport. No network of feeder lines was built, and the traditional transport system – carriers and animal-drawn carts – operating on extremely primitive roads was both slow and expensive. All the railways were heavily in debt to foreign creditors, and their revenues were used in the repayment of loans and interest. Capital equipment was neglected, and maintenance kept to the barest minimum. By 1949 almost all of China's railways were obsolescent, with the exception of the Manchurian rail network which was better planned and dense enough to affect the economy of the whole region. After a programme of repair and reconstruction was completed, however, much of the old system was re-equipped and a major expansion of the rail system was undertaken between 1952 and 1960. A great new trunk line joined the new industrial centres of Pao-t'ou and Lan-chou in the north-west with the existing system, and a line was constructed into Szechwan. Another major trunk line was built into Sinkiang in the far west, designed to link up with the Soviet system and to serve the new oil fields at Yü-men and K'o-la-ma-i (Karamai). This line was completed only as far as Wu-lu-mu-ch'i (Urumchi) when the Sino-Soviet dispute broke out, though another line, connecting with the Soviet system via Mongolia, had been opened in 1956. In the south-west, Kwangsi and Kweichow provinces were given rail access to a new port developed at Chan-chiang, and in the south-western province of Fulkien a railway was built to Hsia-men (Amoy) and Fu-chou.

In 1960 the collapse of the Great Leap Forward brought an end to new railway construction. Development started again only in 1964, and further growth was planned under the Third Five Year Plan for 1966–70, but this again suffered a setback with the disruption resulting from the Cultural Revolution during 1967–68. Since 1968, however, some new construction has been completed, particularly in the south-west, and much track has been doubled, modern marshalling yards constructed, major bridges built across the Yangtze at Nan-ching, Wu-han and Ch'ung-ch'ing, and new industrial plant built.

Even after half a century of carefully planned growth, the Chinese rail system is inadequate. It is still concentrated in the north-east and the coastal regions; it is still very sparse compared with the rail network of Europe or North America; it still remains a network of strategic trunk lines, dependent on the traditional forms of transport for the distribution and collection of goods. Most of the network remains single tracked and steam traction is almost universal. However, as internal air traffic is very meagre, the highway system remains poor and motor transport comparatively rare, the railway retains the sort of monopoly for long-distance passenger traffic and freight which it enjoyed in western countries at the turn of the century.

Rail traffic (Passenger miles)		Railway track (km)	
Japan	179,037,000,000	USSR	135,200
USSR	164,915,000,000	USA	127,408
PRC	**13,644,000,000**	India	59,500
USA	10,770,000,000	**PRC**	**35,000**
		Japan	27,855

THE RAILWAY SYSTEM

CHINA'S very considerable mineral resources are more than adequate to support her industry. Modern large-scale mining was situated originally in the coastal provinces and in Manchuria, and most mines were financed by foreign capital. The exploitation, though, of mineral resources was hampered by lack of detailed geological surveys until the 1920s and 1930s, lack of capital and poor transport facilities. Since 1949 extensive surveying has discovered many new mineral resources and the extension of the rail network has made the exploitation of new mines possible. The government has invested heavily in mining, and in spite of a sharp decrease in mineral and metal production after 1960, by 1970 production was again increasing steadily while notable advances had been made in the techniques both of mining and ore processing.

Iron and steel China has very large iron reserves, although a large part of these consist of very low grade ores. The first modern ironworks in China was Han-yeh-ping, established at Wu-han at the end of the 19th century. In 1937 the iron and steel industry was almost entirely confined to southern Manchuria, at Pen-ch'i and at An-shan. Smaller ironworks were set up at Shih-ching-shan outside Peking, at T'ai-yüan and, during the war at Ch'ung-ch'ing. After 1945 the Soviet occupying forces dismantled most of the An-shan plant, and in 1949 iron and steel production had virtually ceased. Under the Communist regime iron and steel production was given the highest priority, both during the years of reconstruction (1949–52) and under the First Five Year Plan. During this period An-shan was developed into a large integrated iron and steel complex, which was supplemented by other new plants developed under the programme for the relocation of industry in the interior. During the Great Leap Forward a large number of iron and steel works were established, though many of these new developments proved uneconomical and inefficient and were shut down or abandoned in the years following the collapse of the Great Leap Forward in 1960. Overall production revived by 1966 and is now running well above the peak level of 1960. In recent years small scale local mining and smelting has been encouraged. There are eight major centres for the iron and steel industry. An-shan is still the largest integrated plant in China, and Pen-ch'i produces a wide range of special steels and steel products. Lung-yen, in northern Hopeh, is a major source of iron ore used by iron and steel complexes at Shih-ching-shan outside Peking, and at T'ai-yüan. Pao-t'ou has a new complex, started in the 1950s, using ore from the rich mines at Pai-yün-o-po to the north, and Wu-han has a large iron and steel plant supplied from Ta-yeh in Hupeh. Ma-an-shan on the Yangtze, is a major centre of iron mining, which was first exploited by the Japanese during the Second World War and has been a steel-making centre since 1964. Ch'ung-ch'ing has a large complex and Chiu-ch'üan, in the Kansu corridor, began production in the late 1960s. Hai-nan Island is also a major source of iron ore.

Ferrous alloys Although China is deficient in chrome, nickel and cobalt, there is however a large surplus over current needs of tungsten, of which China is a major world producer (15.4 per cent of the world supply). Tungsten is mined in many areas of the Nan-ling mountains in Kwangtung, Fukien and particularly in southern Kiangsi and Hunan. China also has more than adequate supplies of molybdenum, mostly from Chin-hsi in Liaoning, and manganese from Liaoning and Hunan.

Light metals Aluminium was first produced by the Japanese at Fu-shun and this plant was rehabilitated in 1957. Production is also reported from small plants in Shantung, Hopeh, Inner Mongolia, Kansu, Honan, Szechwan, Hunan and Chekiang. Magnesium metal is refined at Ying-k'ou in Liaoning.

Non-ferrous metals Copper deposits are widely scattered but small and production remains deficient. The most important producers are T'ung-ch'uan in Yunnan, Hwang-shih in Hupeh, Pai-yin and Wu-wei in Kansu and Hung-tao-shan in Liaoning. Two important centres have recently been brought into large scale production: T'ung-ling on the south bank of the Yangtze and Shou-wang-fen in Hopeh. Lead and zinc are produced in Hunan, Anhwei and Kiangsi, and a large amount of lead in southern Yunnan. Tin, of which China provides 4.6 per cent of the world's supply, is produced in Yunnan, Kwangsi and Kiangsi. China produces 18.3 per cent of the world's antimony, mainly from central Hunan, from Kwangsi and from Kwangtung. Most of the production of mercury, for export as well as for domestic use, is in Kweichow and Hunan.

By western standards China's consumption of fuels and energy is very low and in many fields human and animal power still provide a major resource. Coal is estimated to account for almost 90 per cent of China's energy resources, though the generation of hydro-electric power has increased steadily since 1960.

Coal China's coal reserves are perhaps between 70 and 80 billion tons, a total exceeded only by the USA and the USSR. Large scale coal mining was one of the first modern industries to be developed in the late 19th century. By the 1930s more than thirty million tons were produced annually, and nearly 66 million tons during the Japanese war effort in occupied China, though by 1949, as a result of the destruction and deliberate closure of mines in the intervening war years, production had fallen to about 32 million tons. By 1957 total production had reached 131 million tons, 123 million of which came from large modernised mines. Production was still further increased during the Great Leap Forward and a target of 425 million tons was set for 1960 (actual production in 1960 was perhaps 300 million tons), but the collapse of the Great Leap Forward led to a sharp cut-back to 160 million tons in 1961. Production slowly recovered to about 200 million tons in 1966 and has risen steadily to about 300 million tons in 1970. Some two-thirds of the total production comes from the established coal fields of the north-east and is used to feed the industrial base in Manchuria and northern China. Since the 1950s important new coal fields have been developed in Honan and Anhwei and on the borders of Ningsia and Inner Mongolia, but the south and west remain deficient in coal.

Petroleum Before 1949 oil production in China was minimal. After 1949 extensive prospecting was carried out and important new reserves were discovered. The small Yü-men field in western Kansu was greatly developed and linked by rail to a new refinery at Lan-chou and in the 1950s a much more important field was discovered at K'o-la-ma-i (Karamai) in Sinkiang, which was also linked by rail to Lan-chou and central China, and fields were brought into production in the remote Tsaidam region of Tsinghai and at Nan-ch'ung in Szechwan. By 1960 total production had reached about 3 million tons. Up to this point, however, China continued to rely heavily on supplies from the Soviet Union, and the major refinery centre at Lan-chou was constructed with Soviet aid in 1958. The country was self-sufficient by 1966, though, when domestic output reached 8 million tons, following the discovery of major oil fields at Ta-ch'ing and Sheng-li which were developed entirely by Chinese technicians. By 1970 total output was about 20 million tons. Oil refining plant is concentrated in the coastal consuming areas at Shanghai, Lü-ta (Dairen) and Chin-hsi, and major modern refineries have been built at Nan-ching and Peking. There are smaller refineries at Nan-ch'ung, Yü-men, K'o-la-ma-i and Leng-hu. Shale-oil extraction, established by the Japanese in Manchuria, continues at the old plant at Fu-shun in Liaoning and at a new plant at Mao-ming in Kwangsi. Total production is over 2 million tons.

Natural gas Natural gas, has been used as a fuel for the evaporation of brine from salt wells in parts of Szechwan since the middle ages. This field, centred at Tzu-kung, is still exploited and a large gas field was brought into production in the 1960s near Ch'ung-ch'ing.

Electric power Coal-fired thermal plants, concentrated in the north and north-eastern regions, provide most of China's installed generating capacity, 90 per cent of which is used by industry. Rural electrification is largely supplied by small local generating plants. The development of hydro-electric schemes was comparatively late – the only major schemes brought into operation before 1949 were the large Feng-man and Sup'ung schemes built by the Japanese in Manchuria – but during the 1950s great stress was laid on electrification, and Soviet and East European engineers installed many new plants. Two huge projects on the Huang Ho, at Liu-chia and San-men were begun. There are three areas with a co-ordinated power system connected to a regional grid. The most advanced of these remains the Manchurian system which in 1957 produced almost half of China's electric power. It has now been linked with the Peking-Tientsin-T'ang-shan industrial area, which also has considerable generating capacity. A second power grid, fed by the very large hydro-electric station at Hsin-an-chiang in Chekiang, links Shanghai, Hang-chou and Nan-ching. The third power system was designed to take power from the San-men scheme on the Huang Ho (which was left unfinished by the withdrawal of Soviet aid) and joins the newly-developed industrial centres of Hsi-an (Sian), Lo-yang, Cheng-chou and T'ai-yüan. The electricity generating industry has expanded steadily and in 1970 installed capacity had reached 18 million kilowatts, compared with 11 million in 1960 and 1.8 million in 1949. However, in spite of China's immense potential hydro-electric resources and although the Chinese can now themselves manufacture most necessary equipment, hydro-electricity remains relatively undeveloped by western standards.

MINERALS AND ENERGY

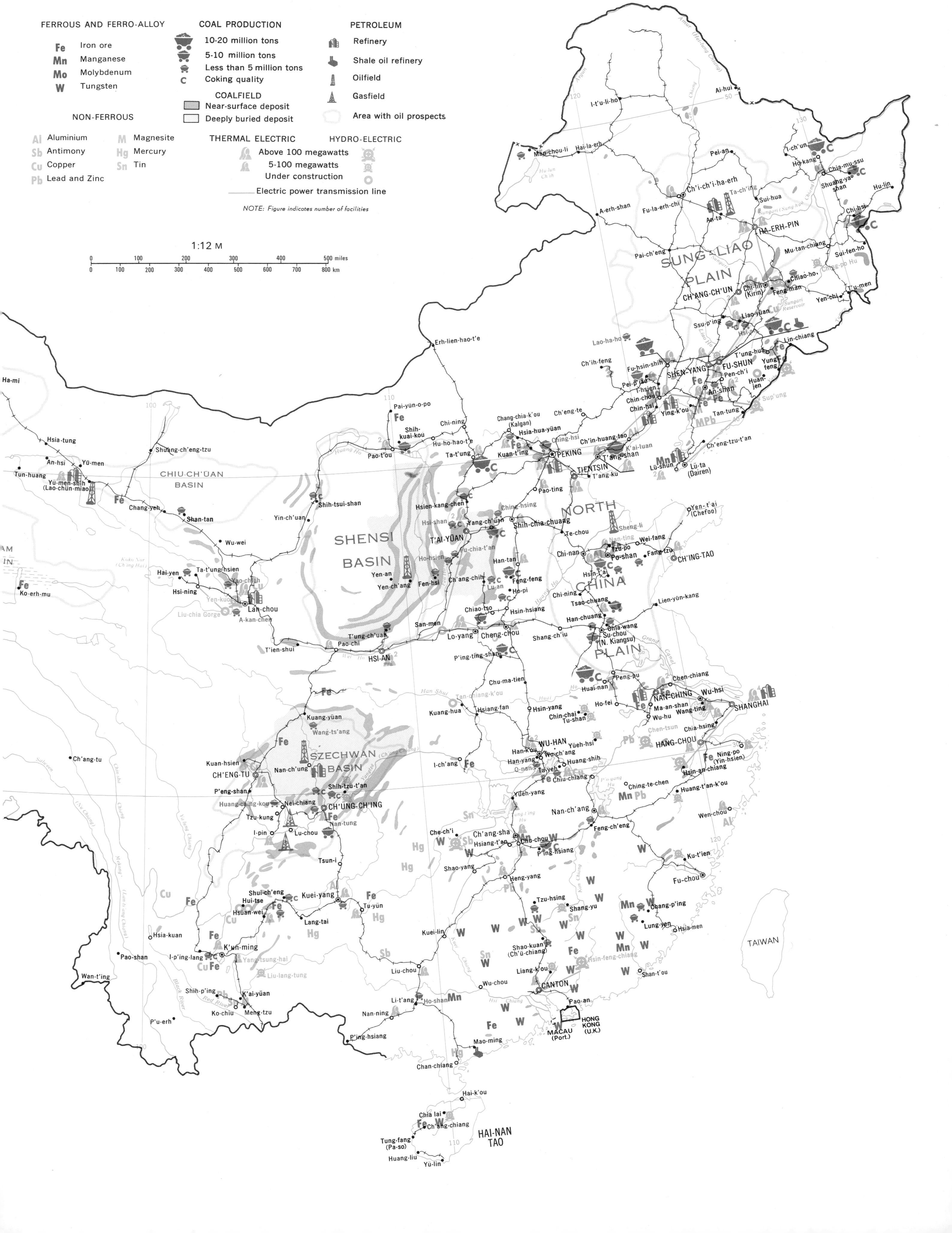
FERROUS AND FERRO-ALLOY
Fe Iron ore
Mn Manganese
Mo Molybdenum
W Tungsten
NON-FERROUS
Al Aluminium
Sb Antimony
Cu Copper
Pb Lead and Zinc
M Magnesite
Hg Mercury
Sn Tin
COAL PRODUCTION
10-20 million tons
5-10 million tons
Less than 5 million tons
C Coking quality
COALFIELD
Near-surface deposit
Deeply buried deposit
PETROLEUM
Refinery
Shale oil refinery
Oilfield
Gasfield
Area with oil prospects
THERMAL ELECTRIC
Above 100 megawatts
5-100 megawatts
HYDRO-ELECTRIC
Under construction
Electric power transmission line
NOTE: Figure indicates number of facilities
1:12 M
0 100 200 300 400 500 miles
0 100 200 300 400 500 600 700 800 km
SUNG-LIAO PLAIN
SHENSI BASIN
SZECHWAN BASIN
NORTH CHINA PLAIN
CHIU-CH'ÜAN BASIN
HAI-NAN TAO
TAIWAN
PEKING
TIENTSIN
SHANGHAI
HA-ERH-PIN
CH'ANG-CH'UN
SHEN-YANG
FU-SHUN
T'AI-YÜAN
HSI-AN
CH'ENG-TU
CH'UNG-CH'ING
WU-HAN
NAN-CHING
HANG-CHOU
CANTON
K'un-ming
Kuei-yang
Lan-chou
Ch'ang-sha
Nan-ch'ang
Cheng-chou
Lo-yang
Chi-nan
Ch'ing-tao
An-shan
Pen-ch'i
Lü-ta (Dairen)
T'ang-shan
Ta-t'ung
Pao-t'ou
Yü-men
Yü-men-shih (Lao-chün-miao)
Ta-ch'ing
Ch'i-ch'i-ha-erh
Chi-lin (Kirin)
Fu-hsin-shih
Ying-k'ou
Chin-chou
Chin-hsi
Kai-luan
Ch'in-huang-tao
Hsia-hua-yüan
Chang-chia-k'ou (Kalgan)
Shih-chia-chuang
Yang-ch'üan
Han-tan
Feng-feng
Chiao-tso
P'ing-ting-shan
Huai-nan
Ma-an-shan
Wu-hsi
Ning-po (Yin-hsien)
Fu-chou
Hsia-men
Shan-t'ou
Hong Kong (U.K.)
Macau (Port.)
Hai-k'ou
Hai-la-erh
Man-chou-li
Ai-hui
Chia-mu-ssu
Mu-tan-chiang
Ha-mi
Hsi-ning
Tzu-kung
Nan-ch'ung
Lu-chou
Kuan-hsien
Liu-chia Gorge
San-men
Tan-chiang-k'ou
Hsin-an-chiang
Amur (Hei-lung Chiang)
Huang Ho
Yangtze
Hsi Chiang

MINERALS AND ENERGY COMPARISONS

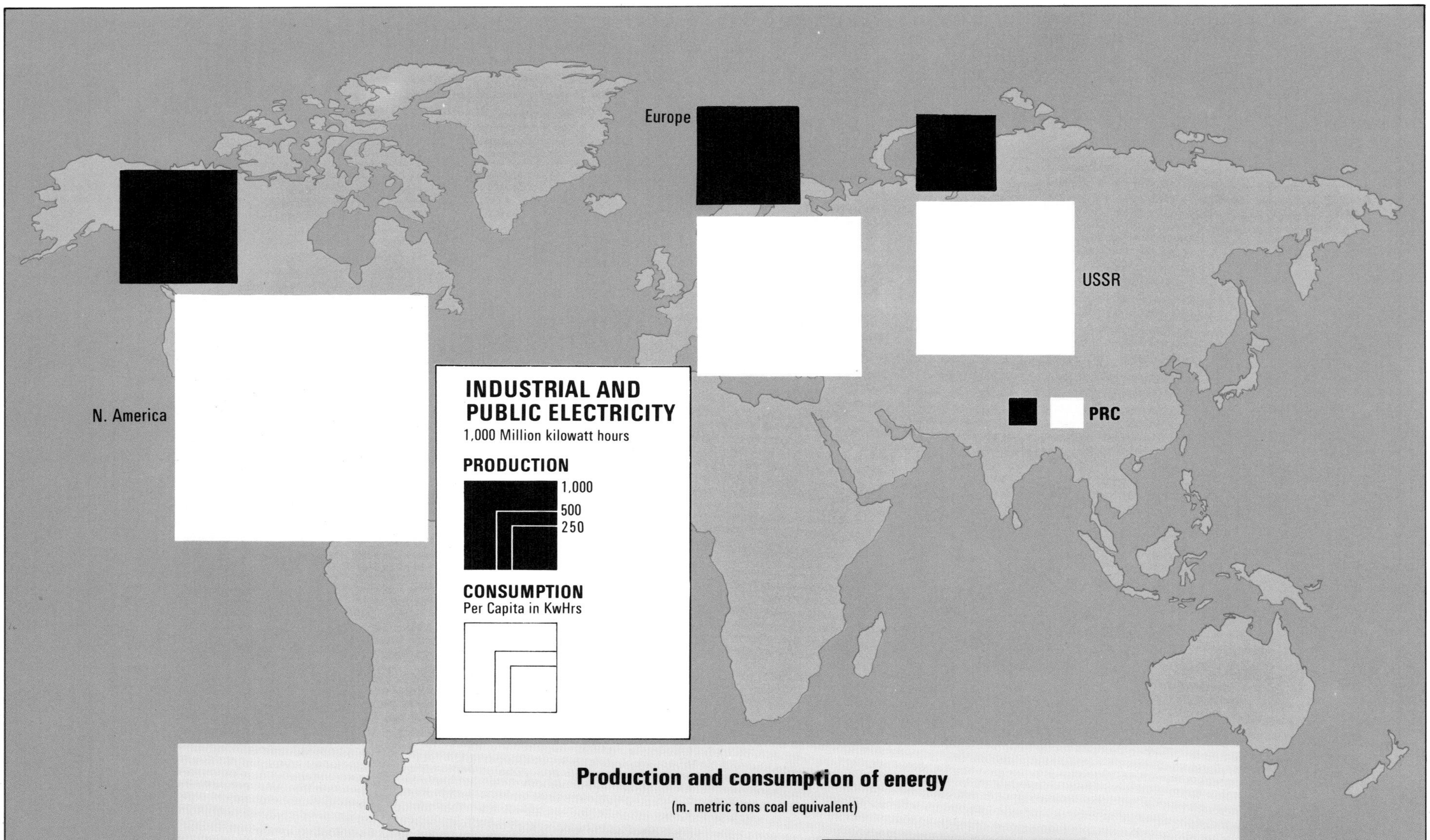

Production and consumption of energy

(m. metric tons coal equivalent)

	PRODUCTION					CONSUMPTION				
	Total Energy	Coal & Lignite	Crude Petroleum	Natural Gas	Elec. Hydro Nuclear	Aggregate	Solid Fuels	Liquid Fuels	Gas	Hydro Nuclear Elec.
PRC	**395.919**	**364.473**	**26.117**	—	**4.106**	**404.160**	**363.838**	**34.994**	—	**4.106**
W. Europe	556.857	378.755	25.415	105.052	47.634	1350.964	441.434	753.488	108.216	47.826
USSR	1210.593	472.600	458.346	263.663	15.985	1076.861	452.065	345.470	264.004	15.322
USA	2053.775	543.347	649.503	826.808	34.117	2278.966	470.712	933.740	840.115	35.399
Japan	54.822	39.759	1.006	3.499	10.558	332.370	89.394	227.250	5.168	10.558

Aluminium

Production (1,000 metric tons)

USA	3,739.8
W. Europe	2,500.3
USSR	1,750.0
PRC	**155.0**
World	11,505.6

Tin

Mine Production (1,000 metric tons)

PRC	**23.0**
USSR	12.0
W. Europe	4.5
USA	—
World	235.6

Asbestos fibre

(1,000 short tons)

N. America	1,827
USSR	1,350
PRC	**190**
World	4,160

Antimony

Mine Production (metric tons)

Africa	15,543
PRC	**14,000**
Bolivia	13,105
Asia	7,580
USSR	7,500
W. Europe*	4,132
USA	411
World	69,029

*includes Yugoslavia: 2,100

Tungsten ores and Concentrates output

(metric tons)

PRC	**8,000**
USSR	6,500
USA	4,266
World	32,700

Copper

Mine Production (1,000 metric tons)

USA	1,490.3
USSR	1,050.0
W. Europe	272.1
PRC	**135.0**
World	7,022.0

Zinc

(million metric tons)

W. Europe	740.6
USSR	620·0
USA	476.8
PRC	**150.0**
World	5,661.5

Phosphate rock

(1,000 metric tons)

USA	38,500
USSR	21,000
PRC	**2,600**
World	91,616

Lead

Mine Production (1,000 metric tons)

USA	584.9
USSR	495.0
W. Europe	466.9
PRC	**125.0**
World	3,523.5

Iron ore

(million metric tons)

USSR	196.00
W. Europe	117.00
USA	89.00
PRC	**40.00**
World	750.00

Crude oil production

(million tons)

M. East	895
USA	532
USSR	394
PRC	**30**
W. Europe	22

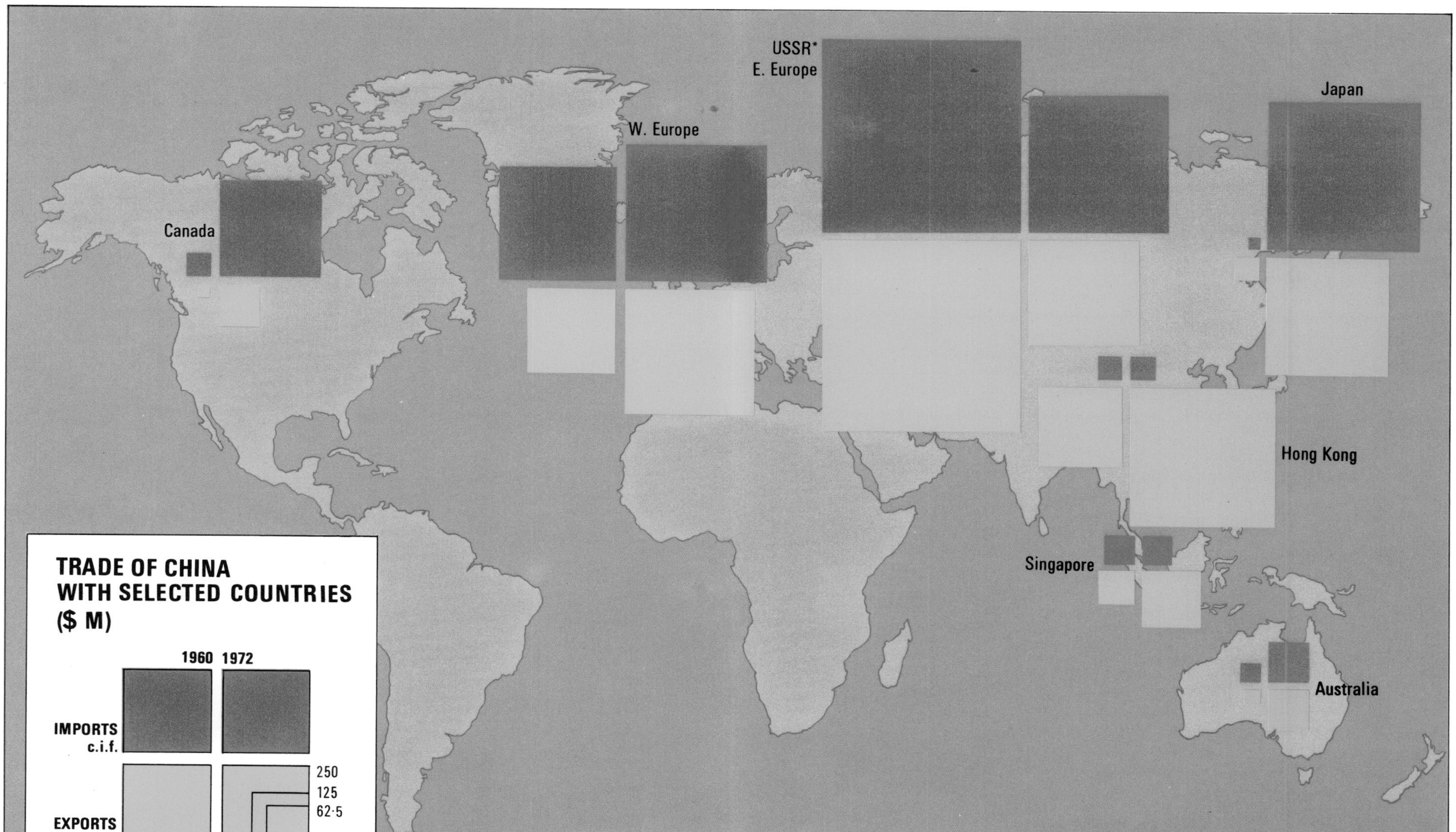

GNP at market prices (million US $)

	GNP	GNP per capita	GNP growth 1960–70
USA	975,240	4,760	3.2%
USSR	434,870*	1,790	5.8%
Japan	198,840	1,920	9.6%
F. R. Germany	180,260	2,930	3.5%
PRC	**121,870***	**160**	**2.1%**
India	57,290	110	1.2%

*Net material product, converted

	Cement (1,000 short tons)	Cotton yarn (1,000 short tons)
USSR	104,992	1,582
USA	74,684	1,670
Japan	63,039	559
PRC	**11,016**	**1,602**

Steel (1,000 metric tons)

	Crude steel output	Finished steel products
EEC	139	101
USSR	126	**90
USA	121	*80
Japan	97	82
PRC	**23**	****14**

*deliveries **estimate

	Cars in use	Motor vehicles
USA	92,082,000	10,671,654
Europe	71,057,000	12,727,000
Japan	10,572,000	5,810,774
USSR	1,600,000	1,130,000
PRC (1970)	**133,000**	**160,000**
World	199,000,000	*32,944,068

Production (inc. cars)
*Main Producing countries only.

	Radio sets (1,000)	TV sets (1,000)
USA	290,000	84,600
USSR	94,600	34,800
Japan	25,742	22,658
PRC	**11,500**	**300**

Merchant shipping fleet (1,000 gross tons)

Japan	30,509
USA	16,266
USSR	16,194
PRC	**1,022**

Non-cellulosic man made fibre

USA	3,893
Japan	1,520
USSR	330
PRC	**26**
World	9,975

Paper and Board (1,000 metric tons)

	Consumption	Production
USA	49.2	45.2
Japan	12.6	12.9
USSR	6.8	6.5
PRC	**3.4**	**1.7**

THE development of modern industry in China began in the period following the T'ai-p'ing rebellion in the 1860s, when although manufacturing by foreign firms was illegal, some small factories were established in the Treaty Ports, first at Shanghai and later also at Tientsin. After 1895 the Treaty of Shimonoseki legalised foreign industry in the Treaty Ports, and a large number of foreign companies began operations not only in Shanghai and Tientsin, but also in Wu-han, Shantung and in Manchuria. Chinese-controlled modern industry had meanwhile followed a different course. It had begun as an off-shoot of the 'self-strengthening' movement of the 1860s and 1870s and was predominantly military. The first enterprises were shipyards and arsenals, in Shanghai (1865), Nan-ching (1865), Fu-chou (1867) and Wu-han (1890). These arsenals not only manufactured modern weapons and built modern ships, but also conducted training programmes for engineers, technicians and translators, who were familiar with western technology and ideas and who were far more important in China's modernisation than the weapons produced by the arsenals. From 1872–95, however, a number of Chinese owned and managed modern industrial enterprises were founded with commercial objectives. Some of the larger ones were official or semi-official enterprises, but many were private concerns, engaged in mining, metal-working, textiles, paper-making and flour-milling. Most were poorly managed and under-capitalised and eventually many came under the control of foreign interests.

After 1895 Chinese industry expanded rapidly and a large number of companies, concerned mostly with mining, public utilities, food-processing and tobacco manufacture were founded in the early years of this century. By the end of the Ch'ing empire in 1911, however, industry was still of only very minor importance in the economy, and foreign investment was concentrated in mining, communications and finance. The outbreak of the First World War altered the Chinese economy in two ways. First, the Japanese came to control more and more of the foreign industry and eventually established economic control over Manchuria, where they had been predominant since their defeat of the Russians in the Russo-Japanese War. Until about 1931 they treated Manchuria simply as a market for their goods and as a source of raw material for Japanese industry. After this, when their control of Manchuria was complete, they formulated a long-term plan to transform Manchuria into a base of heavy industry, with large scale modern iron and steel, engineering and chemical industries, and highly productive mining, forestry and agriculture. The other major consequence of the War was that the involvement of the western powers in war production reduced the availability of imported goods in China, and Chinese industry expanded to meet the demand. It was not until the war ended, however, that this expansion was fully realised and 1918–22 was the period of most rapid growth in Chinese industry, with new investment in the traditional fields of textiles, food processing and mining. By 1922, political unrest had seriously disrupted the production of raw materials for industry and the distribution of manufactured goods, and the Chinese again began to invest their capital in the Treaty Ports under foreign protection. At the outbreak of war with Japan in 1937, industry was limited to Manchuria, then under Japanese control, to the coastal provinces, and to the Treaty Ports. The war prompted the Chinese to move many strategic plants from Shanghai and Wu-han into Szechwan and Yunnan, and at the same time the Japanese began to plan the relocation of industry in occupied China, expanding industry in Shansi and founding iron and steel works at Pao-t'ou in Inner Mongolia and at Ma-an-shan on the Yangtze.

In 1945 Chinese industry lay in ruins and before any real progress could be made to restore order, civil war, the inefficiency of the Kuomintang government and ever-spiralling inflation had effectively ruined the economy. The first years of the Communist regime were devoted to the restoration of basic industries and of the transport network. In 1952 this stage was completed and most industries were roughly back to where they had been in 1936. Between 1953 and 1957 the First Five Year Plan was put into operation. Rapid increase in industrial production was the first aim, using the existing base of heavy industry in Manchuria. This plan involved the relocation of industry and its development in the interior provinces, partly for strategic reasons, and some two-thirds of the new industrial installations and of the plants installed with Soviet aid were situated inland. Major concentrations of industry grew up in T'ai-yüan and Ta-t'ung; in Pao-t'ou; in Hsi-an (Sian) and Lan-chou; in Lo-yang and Cheng-chou; in Ch'eng-tu and Ch'ung-ch'ing. After 1957, however, growth once again tended to be concentrated in the established industrial complexes of Manchuria, Shanghai, Peking-Tientsin and the old Treaty Ports.

The Great Leap Forward, set in motion in 1958, attempted to accelerate industrial growth at an impossible pace. During 1958–60 every type of industrial enterprise was set enormously inflated targets, and great numbers of small plants were built in the provinces, many of them hopelessly inefficient and uneconomic. Over-extension of industrial effort was accompanied by a major agricultural crisis in 1959–61, and as a final blow, in 1960 the Soviet Union suddenly ceased all economic assistance to China and many crucial Soviet-planned projects were abandoned. Government investment in industry fell back to the level of 1953 and 20,000,000 urban workers were sent back to the countryside.

After 1963 a gradual recovery began. The earlier exclusive concentration on heavy industry was replaced by a diversified and more local spread of industry, and a great deal of production was now devoted to the support of agriculture. Investment was concentrated in chemical and fertiliser plants and in the production of tractors and agricultural implements. Another setback in industrial production followed the outbreak of the Cultural Revolution and only in mid-1969 did it recover to 1966 levels, but since then there has been a steady improvement. The lack of skilled technicians and managers has been made good, although China continues to rely heavily on foreign technology and design, and great attention is now paid to the development of local technical skills. The most marked feature of recent growth has been the development in parallel of modern, highly mechanised industry concentrated in large central plants and of small scale, often technically primitive, local industries designed to serve the needs of rural agriculture. Today, for example, there are more than one thousand small chemical fertiliser plants, which account for 60 per cent of the country's total output. The decentralisation of plants is partly due to the continuing shortcomings of the transport system, but is also designed as a deliberate policy to spread simple technology to the countryside, and as a means of absorbing local labour surpluses. Some of the local industries – electrical plants, cement and iron works, engineering shops – are run by the counties, others by the communes. Similar local organisations manage other industries processing agricultural goods, oil extraction, flour milling, cotton ginning, sugar refining, small scale canning and preservation of foods, and also textile manufacture and a wide variety of local handicrafts.

Metallurgy	Machine Building		Light Industry	Chemicals-Other
Aluminium	Agricultural machinery	Locomotives	Ceramics	Cement
Copper	Bearings	Machine tools	Silk	Chemicals
Iron	Cutting tools	Railroad cars	Sugar	Fertiliser
Lead	Electrical equipment	Shipbuilding	Textiles	Glass
Steel	Electronics	Tractors		Paper
Tin	Heavy machinery	Trucks		Pharmaceuticals
Zinc	Instruments			Rubber
				Tyres

Economic region boundary

Major industrial area

1:12 M

0 100 200 300 400 500

0 100 200 300 400 500 600 700 800

INDUSTRY

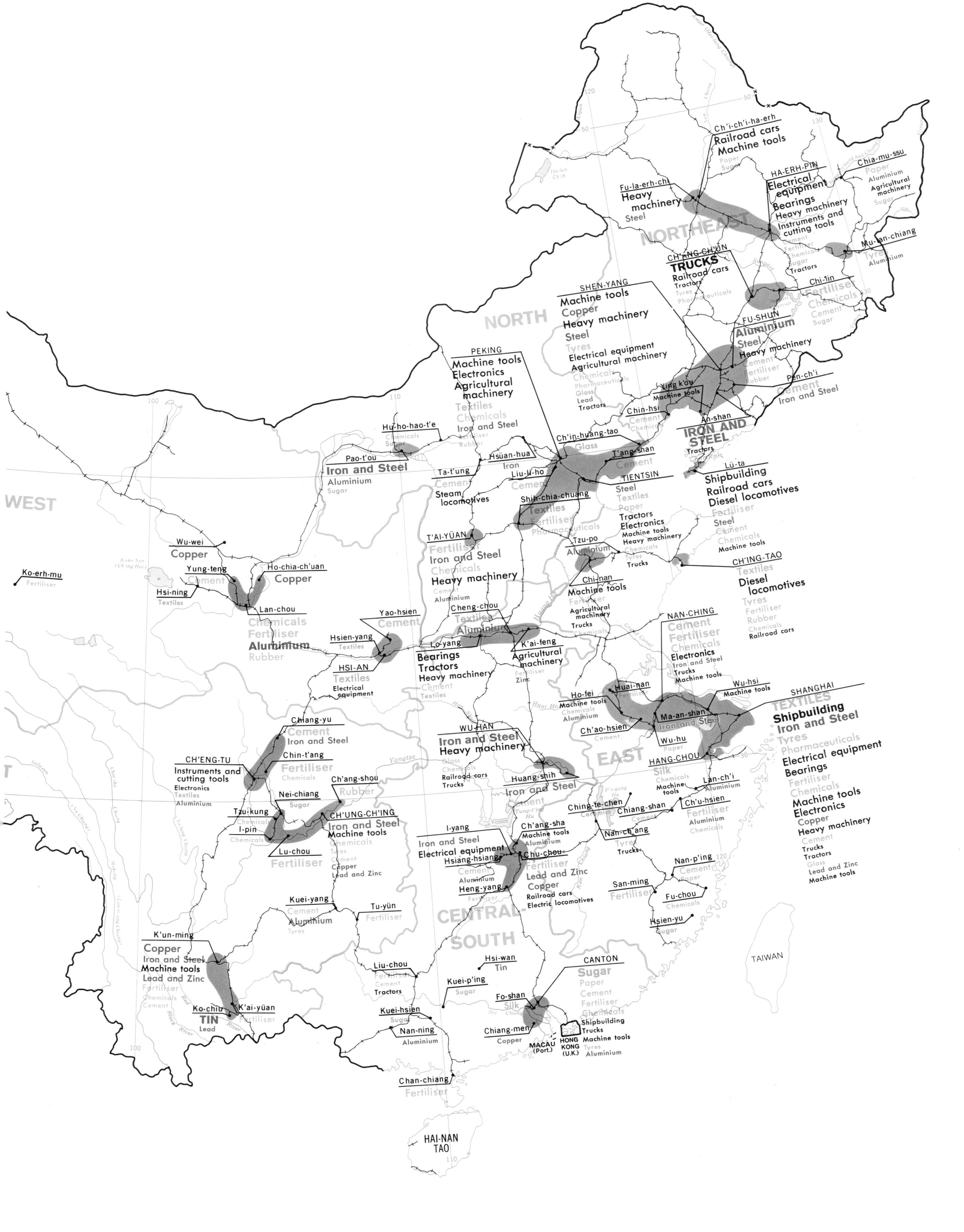

NORTHEAST
NORTH
WEST
EAST
CENTRAL-SOUTH
Ch'i-ch'i-ha-erh
Railroad cars
Machine tools
Paper
Sugar
HA-ERH-PIN
Electrical equipment
Bearings
Heavy machinery
Instruments and cutting tools
Cement
Fertiliser
Chemicals
Sugar
Tractors
Chia-mu-ssu
Paper
Aluminium
Agricultural machinery
Sugar
Mu-tan-chiang
Tyres
Aluminium
Fu-la-erh-chi
Heavy machinery
Steel
CH'ANG-CH'UN
TRUCKS
Railroad cars
Tractors
Tyres
Pharmaceuticals
Chi-lin
Fertiliser
Chemicals
Cement
Sugar
SHEN-YANG
Machine tools
Copper
Heavy machinery
Steel
Tyres
Electrical equipment
Agricultural machinery
Chemicals
Pharmaceuticals
Glass
Lead
Tractors
FU-SHUN
Aluminium
Steel
Heavy machinery
Cement
Fertiliser
Rubber
Pen-ch'i
Cement
Iron and Steel
Ying-k'ou
Machine tools
Chin-hsi
Cement
Chemicals
An-shan
IRON AND STEEL
Tractors
Chemicals
Lü-ta
Shipbuilding
Railroad cars
Diesel locomotives
PEKING
Machine tools
Electronics
Agricultural machinery
Textiles
Chemicals
Iron and Steel
Fertiliser
Rubber
Ch'in-huang-tao
Glass
T'ang-shan
Cement
TIENTSIN
Steel
Textiles
Paper
Tractors
Electronics
Machine tools
Heavy machinery
Fertiliser
Steel
Cement
Chemicals
Machine tools
Hu-ho-hao-t'e
Chemicals
Sugar
Pao-t'ou
Iron and Steel
Aluminium
Sugar
Hsüan-hua
Iron
Ta-t'ung
Cement
Steam locomotives
Liu-li-ho
Cement
Shih-chia-chuang
Textiles
Fertiliser
Pharmaceuticals
T'AI-YÜAN
Fertiliser
Iron and Steel
Chemicals
Heavy machinery
Cement
Aluminium
Tzu-po
Aluminium
Tyres
Trucks
Chemicals
Chi-nan
Machine tools
Fertiliser
Agricultural machinery
Trucks
Chemicals
CH'ING-TAO
Textiles
Diesel locomotives
Tyres
Fertiliser
Rubber
Chemicals
Railroad cars
Wu-wei
Copper
Ko-erh-mu
Fertiliser
Yung-teng
Cement
Hsi-ning
Textiles
Ho-chia-ch'uan
Copper
Lan-chou
Chemicals
Fertiliser
Aluminium
Rubber
Yao-hsien
Cement
Hsien-yang
Textiles
HSI-AN
Textiles
Electrical equipment
Cheng-chou
Textiles
Aluminium
Lo-yang
Bearings
Tractors
Heavy machinery
Cement
Textiles
K'ai-feng
Agricultural machinery
Fertiliser
Zinc
NAN-CHING
Cement
Fertiliser
Chemicals
Electronics
Iron and Steel
Trucks
Machine tools
Huai-nan
Fertiliser
Ho-fei
Machine tools
Chemicals
Aluminium
Wu-hsi
Machine tools
Ma-an-shan
Iron and Steel
Ch'ao-hsien
Cement
Wu-hu
Paper
SHANGHAI
TEXTILES
Shipbuilding
Iron and Steel
Tyres
Pharmaceuticals
Electrical equipment
Bearings
Fertiliser
Chemicals
Machine tools
Electronics
Copper
Heavy machinery
Cement
Trucks
Tractors
Glass
Lead and Zinc
Machine tools
HANG-CHOU
Silk
Chemicals
Machine tools
Lan-ch'i
Aluminium
Chiang-yu
Cement
Iron and Steel
CH'ENG-TU
Instruments and cutting tools
Electronics
Textiles
Aluminium
Chin-t'ang
Fertiliser
Chemicals
Ch'ang-shou
Rubber
Nei-chiang
Sugar
Tzu-kung
Chemicals
I-pin
Chemicals
CH'UNG-CH'ING
Iron and Steel
Machine tools
Chemicals
Tyres
Cement
Copper
Lead and Zinc
Lu-chou
Fertiliser
WU-HAN
Iron and Steel
Heavy machinery
Glass
Chemicals
Railroad cars
Trucks
Huang-shih
Iron and Steel
Cement
Ching-te-chen
Ceramics
Chiang-shan
Ch'u-hsien
Fertiliser
Aluminium
Chemicals
Nan-ch'ang
Tyres
Trucks
I-yang
Iron and Steel
Electrical equipment
Ch'ang-sha
Machine tools
Aluminium
Hsiang-hsiang
Cement
Aluminium
Chu-chou
Fertiliser
Lead and Zinc
Copper
Railroad cars
Electric locomotives
Heng-yang
Fertiliser
Nan-p'ing
Cement
Paper
San-ming
Fertiliser
Fu-chou
Chemicals
Hsien-yu
Sugar
TAIWAN
Kuei-yang
Cement
Aluminium
Tyres
Tu-yün
Fertiliser
K'un-ming
Copper
Iron and Steel
Machine tools
Lead and Zinc
Fertiliser
Chemicals
Cement
Ko-chiu
TIN
Lead
K'ai-yüan
Fertiliser
Liu-chou
Fertiliser
Cement
Tractors
Hsi-wan
Tin
Kuei-p'ing
Sugar
Kuei-hsien
Sugar
Nan-ning
Aluminium
CANTON
Sugar
Paper
Cement
Fertiliser
Chemicals
Shipbuilding
Trucks
Machine tools
Tyres
Aluminium
Fo-shan
Silk
Chiang-men
Copper
MACAU (Port.)
HONG KONG (U.K.)
Chan-chiang
Fertiliser
HAI-NAN TAO
Yangtze
Black River
Red River

SINCE the foundation of the People's Republic of China in 1949, there have been many changes in its internal administration. By that year the country had passed through several decades of unrest, civil war, foreign invasion and a general decline of civil order. In many areas central control had been totally lacking for many years. The country was divided into 35 provinces, within which there was great variation of local government. From 1949 to 1958 there were constant changes and rationalisation of the local administrative structure, leading to amalgamation of some of the smaller provinces in Manchuria and the north-eastern border areas, and to many changes at lower levels. Since 1958 the administrative structure at the provincial level has remained comparatively unchanged, with the exception of the redistribution of a large part of the territory of the Inner Mongolian Autonomous Region to other provinces in 1969.

Provincial Level At the highest level of local administration the country is divided into units of three distinct types. In most of China the highest unit is the province (*sheng*). In the areas inhabited largely by national minorities, however, the province is replaced by the Autonomous Region (*tzu-chih-ch'ü*). These were established in Inner Mongolia (1947, but boundary changes were frequent until 1966 and further changes occurred in 1969); Sinkiang (1955); Ningsia (1958); Kwangsi (1958) and Tibet (1965). Finally Peking, Shanghai and Tientsin and their surrounding areas form provincial level municipalities (*chih-hsia-shih*) directly subordinate to central government.

Sub-provincial Level The level of administrative unit directly under the province subsumes several different types of administrative unit. The normal unit is the 'region' (*ti-ch'ü*) which was usually called 'special district' (*chuan-ch'u*) until 1971. Areas with substantial minority populations, however, are administered as 'autonomous districts' (*tzu-chih-chou*). In Inner Mongolia the equivalent administrative division is the 'league' (*meng*) or tribal federation. Important cities are given status as sub-provincial municipalities (*sheng-hsia-shih*), which have equivalent standing with the 'region' or local municipalities (*ti-hsia-shih*). 178 cities currently have such semi-autonomous status. The island of Hai-nan, under Kwangtung province, has a unique sub-provincial status as an 'administrative district' (*hsing-cheng-ch'ü*).

County Level The basic level of local administration is the 'county' (*hsien*). In minority areas some non-Chinese peoples are organised in 'autonomous hsien' (*tzu-chih-hsien*), and in Inner Mongolia the equivalent level of local administration is the 'banner' (*ch'i*) a tribal unit dating from Manchu times. The Mongol minority in Western Heilungkiang province is also organised in 'autonomous banners' (*tzu-chih-ch'i*). In Tibet, although the official term used is the *hsien*, the common local name for this level of administration is the *dzong*, rendered in Chinese as *tsung*.

Local Level Beneath the county level administrations, the traditional level of rural organisation until the mid-1950s was the 'locality' (*hsiang*). During the successive stages of collectivisation, however, the *hsiang* was gradually replaced in its administrative functions by the collectives and then by the people's communes (*jen-min kung-she*). These number some 75,000 at the present time, whereas there were formerly some 200,000 *hsiang*. Each commune is normally subdivided into production brigades (*sheng-chang ta-tui*) usually co-extensive with a village unit, and production teams (*sheng-chan tui*). Urban administrations beneath the county level are called 'towns' (*chen*). These are normally local market centres, the status of which is purely administrative.

Administrative changes at the lower levels have been frequent and continuous. The county seems to have been the level at which change was least frequent, but even here the administrative seat of counties has been frequently changed from one local town to another.

Parallel with the civil administration outlined above are two higher level regional organisations. For planning purposes China is organised in six economic co-ordination regions:

1 North-east: Heilungkiang, Kirin and Liaoning provinces.
2 East: Shantung, Kiangsu, Anhwei, Chekiang, Kiangsi and Fukien provinces, with Shanghai municipality.
3 North: Hopeh and Shansi provinces, Peking and Tientsin municipalities, with Inner Mongolia.
4 Central-south: Honan, Hupeh, Hunan, Kwangtung provinces and Kwangsi Autonomous Region.
5 South-west: Szechwan, Kweichow and Yunnan provinces and Tibet.
6 North-west: Kansu, Tsinghai, and Shensi provinces, Ningsia and Sinkiang Autonomous Regions.

These correspond roughly to the six 'greater administrative regions' (*ta hsing-cheng-ch'ü*) established in 1950 to oversee the work of reconstruction. These were reduced to a supervisory role in 1952 and abolished as administrative entities in 1954, although the Communist Party continued to maintain regional bureaux which had supra-provincial powers.

The second large-scale organisation is the military command system. China is divided into twelve major military commands:

1 Shen-yang: Heilungkiang, Kirin and Liaoning provinces.
2 Peking: Hopeh, Shansi, Peking, Tientsin and Inner Mongolia.
3 Chi-nan: Shantung.
4 Nan-ching: Kiangsu, Anhwei, Chekiang, Shanghai.
5 Fu-chou: Fukien and Kiangsi.
6 Wu-han: Hupeh and Honan.
7 Canton: Kwangtung, Kwangsi and Hunan.
8 Lan-chou: Kansu, Shensi, Ningsia and Tsinghai.
9 Sinkiang (Wu-lu-mu-ch'i): Sinkiang Autonomous Region.
10 Ch'eng-tu: Szechwan.
11 K'un-ming: Yunnan and Kweichow.
12 Tibet (La-sa): the Tibet Autonomous Region.

These military command areas played an important role in the period following the Cultural Revolution in 1966, when the Party regional bureaux ceased to function, and the military began to play a major role in civilian administration. Each province also functions as a military district.

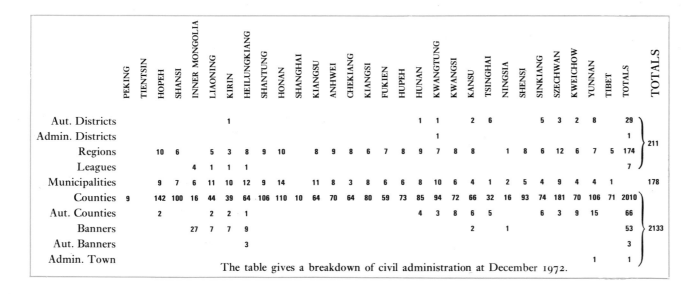

	PEKING	TIENTSIN	HOPEH	SHANSI	INNER MONGOLIA	LIAONING	KIRIN	HEILUNGKIANG	SHANTUNG	HONAN	SHANGHAI	KIANGSU	ANHWEI	CHEKIANG	KIANGSI	FUKIEN	HUPEH	HUNAN	KWANGTUNG	KWANGSI	KANSU	TSINGHAI	NINGSIA	SHENSI	SINKIANG	SZECHWAN	KWEICHOW	YUNNAN	TIBET	TOTALS	TOTALS
Aut. Districts							1											1	1		2	6			5	3	2	8		29	
Admin. Districts																			1											1	
Regions			10	6		5	3	8	9	10		8	9	8	6	7	8	9	7	8	8		1	8	6	12	6	7	5	174	211
Leagues					4	1	1	1																						7	
Municipalities			9	7	6	11	10	12	9	14		11	8	3	8	6	6	8	10	6	4	1	2	5	4	9	4	4	1		178
Counties	9		142	100	16	44	39	64	106	110	10	64	70	64	80	59	73	85	94	72	66	32	16	93	74	181	70	106	71	2010	
Aut. Counties			2			2	2	1										4	3	8	6	5			6	3	9	15		66	
Banners					27	7	7	9													2		1							53	2133
Aut. Banners								3																						3	
Admin. Town																												1		1	

The table gives a breakdown of civil administration at December 1972.

ADMINISTRATIVE DIVISIONS

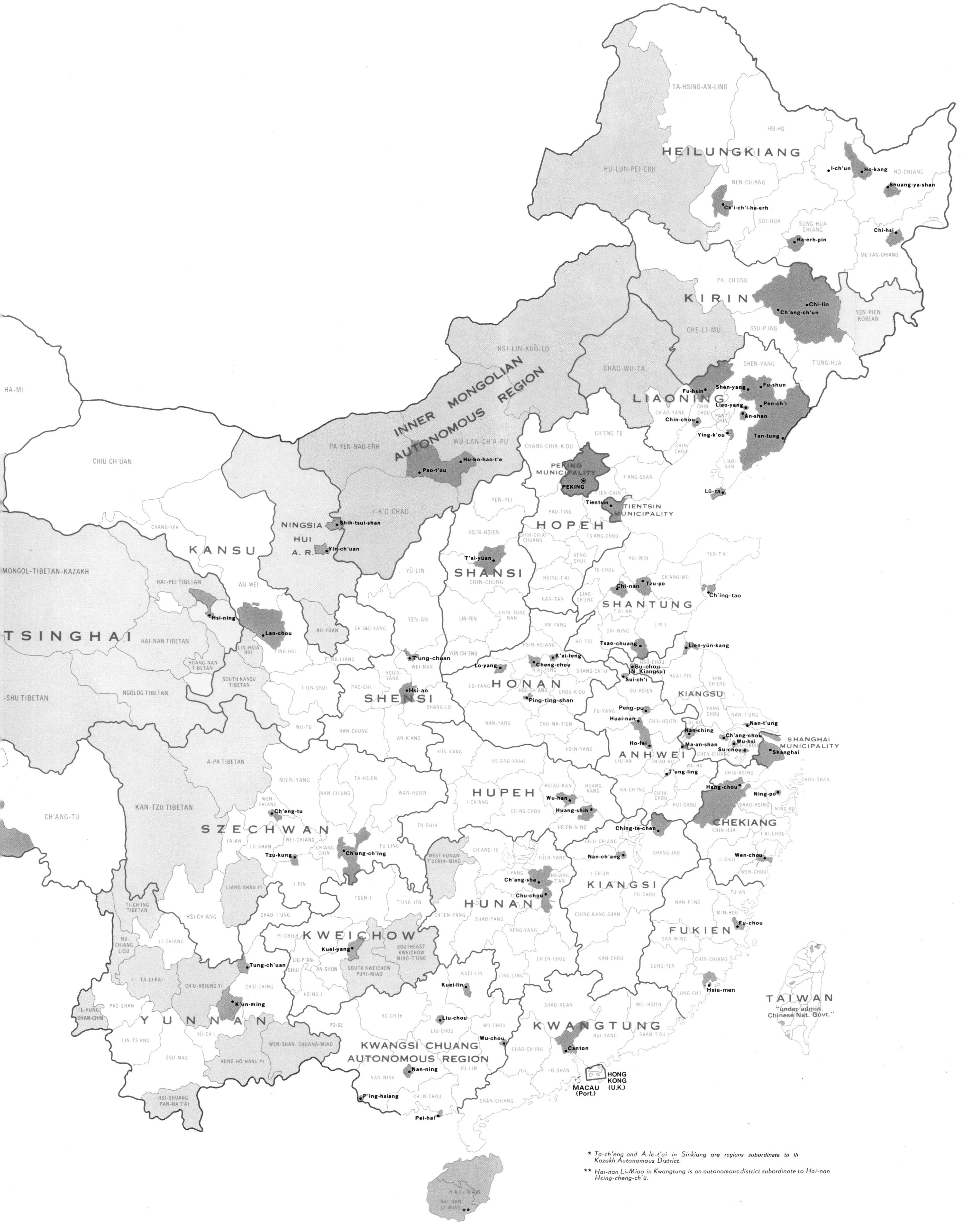

HEILUNGKIANG
TA-HSING-AN-LING
HEI-HO
HU-LUN-PEI-ERH
NEN-CHIANG
I-ch'un
Ho-kang
HO-CHIANG
Shuang-ya-shan
Ch'i-ch'i-ha-erh
SUI-HUA
SUNG-HUA-CHIANG
Ha-erh-pin
Chi-hsi
MU-TAN-CHIANG
PAI-CH'ENG
KIRIN
Chi-lin
Ch'ang-ch'un
YEN-PIEN KOREAN
CHE-LI-MU
SSU-P'ING
T'UNG-HUA
HSI-LIN-KUO-LO
CHAO-WU-TA
INNER MONGOLIAN AUTONOMOUS REGION
SHEN-YANG
LIAONING
Fu-hsin
Shen-yang
Fu-shun
Liao-yang
Pen-ch'i
An-shan
Chin-chou
Ying-k'ou
Tan-tung
LIAO-NAN
Lü-ta
CH'ENG-TE
PA-YEN-NAO-ERH
WU-LAN-CH'A-PU
CHANG-CHIA-K'OU
Hu-ho-hao-t'e
Pao-t'ou
PEKING MUNICIPALITY
PEKING
T'ANG-SHAN
Tientsin
TIENTSIN MUNICIPALITY
HA-MI
CHIU-CH'UAN
CHANG-YEH
NINGSIA HUI A.R.
Shih-tsui-shan
Yin-ch'uan
I-K'O-CHAO
KANSU
YEN-PEI
PAO-TING
HOPEH
HSIN-HSIEN
SHIH-CHIA-CHUANG
TS'ANG-CHOU
HENG-SHUI
T'ai-yüan
SHANSI
CHIN-CHUNG
YÜ-LIN
HSING-T'AI
HAN-TAN
MONGOL-TIBETAN-KAZAKH
HAI-PEI TIBETAN
WU-WEI
Hsi-ning
Lan-chou
TSINGHAI
HAI-NAN TIBETAN
LIN-HSIA HUI
HUANG-NAN TIBETAN
SOUTH KANSU TIBETAN
NGOLOG TIBETAN
KU-YÜAN
TING-HSI
CH'ING-YANG
YEN-AN
LIN-FEN
CHIN-TUNG-NAN
YÜN-CH'ENG
T'ung-chuan
WEI-NAN
P'ING-LIANG
T'IEN-SHUI
PAO-CHI
HSIEN-YANG
Hsi-an
SHENSI
SHANG-LO
HAN-CHUNG
AN-K'ANG
WU-TU
Lo-yang
LO-YANG
HONAN
HSIN-HSIANG
AN-YANG
K'ai-feng
Cheng-chou
HSU-CH'ANG
Ping-ting-shan
NAN-YANG
CHU-MA-TIEN
CHOU-K'OU
SHANG-CH'IU
Chi-nan
Tzu-po
CH'ANG-WEI
YEN-T'AI
Ch'ing-tao
SHANTUNG
T'AI-AN
CHI-NING
LIN-I
HO-TSE
Tsao-chuang
Lien-yün-kang
Su-chou (N. Kiangsu)
Sui-ch'i
SU-HSIEN
HUAI-YIN
KIANGSU
FU-YANG
Peng-pu
Huai-nan
CH'U-HSIEN
Nan-ching
Ma-an-shan
Ho-fei
ANHWEI
LIU-AN
CH'AO-HU
Nan-t'ung
Ch'ang-chou
Wu-hsi
Su-chou
SHANGHAI MUNICIPALITY
Shanghai
T'ung-ling
AN-CH'ING
WU-HU
HUI-CHOU
CHIA-HSING
Hang-chou
Ning-po
SHAO-HSING
CHOU-SHAN
CHEKIANG
CHIN-HUA
T'AI-CHOU
LI-SHUI
Wen-chou
WEN-CHOU
HSIN-YANG
YÜN-YANG
HSIANG-YANG
HUPEH
HSIAO-KAN
HUANG-KANG
I-CH'ANG
CHING-CHOU
Wu-han
Huang-shih
HSIEN-NING
EN-SHIH
A-PA TIBETAN
KAN-TZU TIBETAN
CH'ANG-TU
MIEN-YANG
TA-HSIEN
NAN-CH'UNG
WAN-HSIEN
WEN-CHIANG
Ch'eng-tu
SZECHWAN
YA-AN
LO-SHAN
NEI-CHIANG
Tzu-kung
Ch'ung-ch'ing
FU-LING
I-PIN
LIANG-SHAN YI
WEST HUNAN T'UCHIA-MIAO
CH'ANG-TE
YÜEH-YANG
I-YANG
Ch'ang-sha
HSIANG-T'AN
Chu-chou
HUNAN
SHAO-YANG
HENG-YANG
CH'IEN-YANG
CH'EN-CHOU
LING-LING
Ching-te-chen
CHIU-CHIANG
Nan-ch'ang
SHANG-JAO
I-CH'UN
KIANGSI
FU-CHOU
CHING-KANG-SHAN
KAN-CHOU
NAN-P'ING
FU-AN
MIN-HOU
Fu-chou
FUKIEN
SAN-MING
LUNG-YEN
CHIN-CHIANG
Hsia-men
LUNG-CH'I
TAIWAN
"under admin. Chinese Nat. Govt."
TI-CH'ING TIBETAN
HSI-CH'ANG
CHAO-T'UNG
TSUN-I
T'UNG-JEN
PI-CHIEH
KWEICHOW
Kuei-yang
SOUTHEAST KWEICHOW MIAO-T'UNG
SOUTH KWEICHOW PUYI-MIAO
AN-SHUN
LIU-P'AN-SHUI
NU-CHIANG LISU
LI-CHIANG
TA-LI PAI
CH'U-HSIUNG YI
Tung-ch'uan
CH'Ü-CHING
K'un-ming
HSING-I
TE-HUNG SHAN-CHIN
PAO-SHAN
YUNNAN
YÜ-CH'I
LIN-TS'ANG
SSU-MAO
HUNG-HO HANI-YI
WEN-SHAN CHUANG-MIAO
HSI-SHUANG-PAN-NA T'AI
PO-SE
HO-CH'IH
KUEI-LIN
Kuei-lin
LIU-CHOU
Liu-chou
WU-CHOU
Wu-chou
KWANGSI CHUANG AUTONOMOUS REGION
Nan-ning
NAN-NING
YÜ-LIN
P'ing-hsiang
CH'IN-CHOU
Pei-hai
SHAO-KUAN
MEI-HSIEN
KWANGTUNG
HUI-YANG
SHAN-T'OU
CHAO-CH'ING
Canton
FO-SHAN
HONG KONG (U.K.)
MACAU (Port.)
CHAN-CHIANG
HAI-NAN
HAI-NAN LI-MIAO

* *Ta-ch'eng and A-le-t'ai in Sinkiang are regions subordinate to Ili Kazakh Autonomous District.*

** *Hai-nan Li-Miao in Kwangtung is an autonomous district subordinate to Hai-nan Hsing-cheng-ch'ü.*

TOPOGRAPHIC surveys and maps, for use in the planning of the country's reconstruction, were pressing needs of the People's Republic of China in its first years. Although the bulk of the professionally qualified had departed for Taiwan, taking with them much archival material, Russian advisers assisted during the first decade and progress was swift. For public use only a few small scale maps and atlases were issued, but these did intimate China's standpoint on her national frontiers. Since that time, China has on several occasions declared her resolve to settle international boundary questions by discussion but has expressed equal determination to oppose unilateral action by others. In pursuance of this policy, agreement has been reached with Afghanistan (1963), Burma (1960), Mongolia (1962), Nepal (1961) and Pakistan (1963). Boundary agreements have also been made with Korea and Vietnam. Borders with the USSR and India and sovereignty of the islands in the South China Sea (see page 116) have yet to be finally resolved.

The Sino-Russian Frontier Towards the end of the 16th century Russian expansion into Siberia began in earnest. New towns were established from the Urals to the Pacific in a little over sixty years. The first expeditions were small, often numbered in tens, rarely in hundreds, but they were followed by the settlers who were to make their homes in Siberia. At this time China had no real frontiers in the sense of definable lines: the limits of Chinese territory were the most distant lands tributary to China.

From about 1573 the Ming Empire began its decline. In 1644 Manchu tribes overran China and founded the Ch'ing or Manchu Dynasty.

A party of 130 Russians reached the Amur river just when the Ming Dynasty was in its death throes. They travelled down it to the Sea of Okhotsk and founded the port of Okhotsk. When Khabarovsk arrived six years later he met stiff Manchu resistance which he successfully quelled but found himself and his country engaged in conflict with Manchu China. Forty years of hostilities ended in the Treaty of Nerchinsk, the first treaty ever signed by the Chinese Empire. The Russians gave up the Amur and agreed on a boundary which followed the Argun river to its confluence with the Amur and then along the Shilka river to the Stanovoy and Yablonovyy mountains. In 1850, however, a military detachment, seeking an alternative to the difficult overland route to Okhotsk, hoisted the Russian flag on the north bank of the river and in 1854 they were joined by a force which sailed in from the Pacific. China had no power to resist, after the crushing defeat of the Opium Wars (1838–42). The Treaties of Aigun (1858) and Peking (1860) made the Amur river the boundary and gave Russia the land between the Ussuri river and the Pacific. The USSR regards the boundary in this area as following Pritok (channel) Kazakevicheva thus making the island of Hei-hsia-tzu Soviet. China claims a 'thalweg' boundary – the line followed by the main navigational channels of the rivers. This would place the confluence at Khabarovsk and would make Hei-hsia-tzu Chinese (see section A).

Sixty-four villages on the north bank of the Amur lying between the rivers Zeya (Zela) and Bureya were to remain Manchu. The inhabitants were ejected during the Boxer Rebellion (1900). China has yet to agree the resulting river boundary (see section B).

A subsequent treaty (Tsitsihar, 1911) moved the Russian boundary a few miles further into China in two areas each about 50 miles in extent. China did not ratify this treaty although it was signed (see section C).

By 1850 Russian occupation of Siberia extended to Lake Balkhash, the Ili river and Lake Issyk-Kul'. Appeals for help from various Kirgiz tribes brought the Russians deeper into Kirgizia. In 1871 disorder reigned further up the Ili river in the region of Kul'dzha. The Russians moved in to restore order. Ten years later the Ili valley and Kul'dzha were returned to China. Treaties of 1864, 1870 and 1881 were signed with China to define the boundaries in this area (see section D).

Russian expansion towards India alarmed the British. A treaty was signed in 1895 in which the Wakhan corridor, a salient of Afghan territory, barred further Russian progress southwards. China was not a party to the Treaty but since the Russians had achieved a common frontier with Afghanistan in the Pamirs, the Khrebet Sarykol'skiy watershed became the Russo-Chinese boundary south of Kizil-Jik-Dawan (see section E).

The Sino-Indian Frontier Tibet was nominally under Chinese suzerainty at the fall of the Manchu Empire in 1911. At Simla in 1914 Britain and China discussed the division of Tibet into a western, autonomous region and an eastern, Chinese-administered region. At the same time a line, the McMahon Line – named after the British representative – was added to the final map to define the boundary between Tibet and India, including a part of what is now Burma. All three representatives signed the map and documents relating to the proposed boundaries. The Chinese Government, however, rejected their plenipotentiary's agreement, on the grounds of the portrayal of the boundary between Tibet and China (see section G). Chinese agreement with Burma (1960) includes acceptance of part of the McMahon Line, but China has yet to reach agreement with India and claims the correct boundary is in the foothills, thus excluding the North East Frontier Agency which India claims has long been under Indian administration.

Equally serious are the rival claims in Aksai Chin. China occupies this area, which India claims is her territory. A road built by China to link Sinkiang with Tibet now runs through it (see section F).

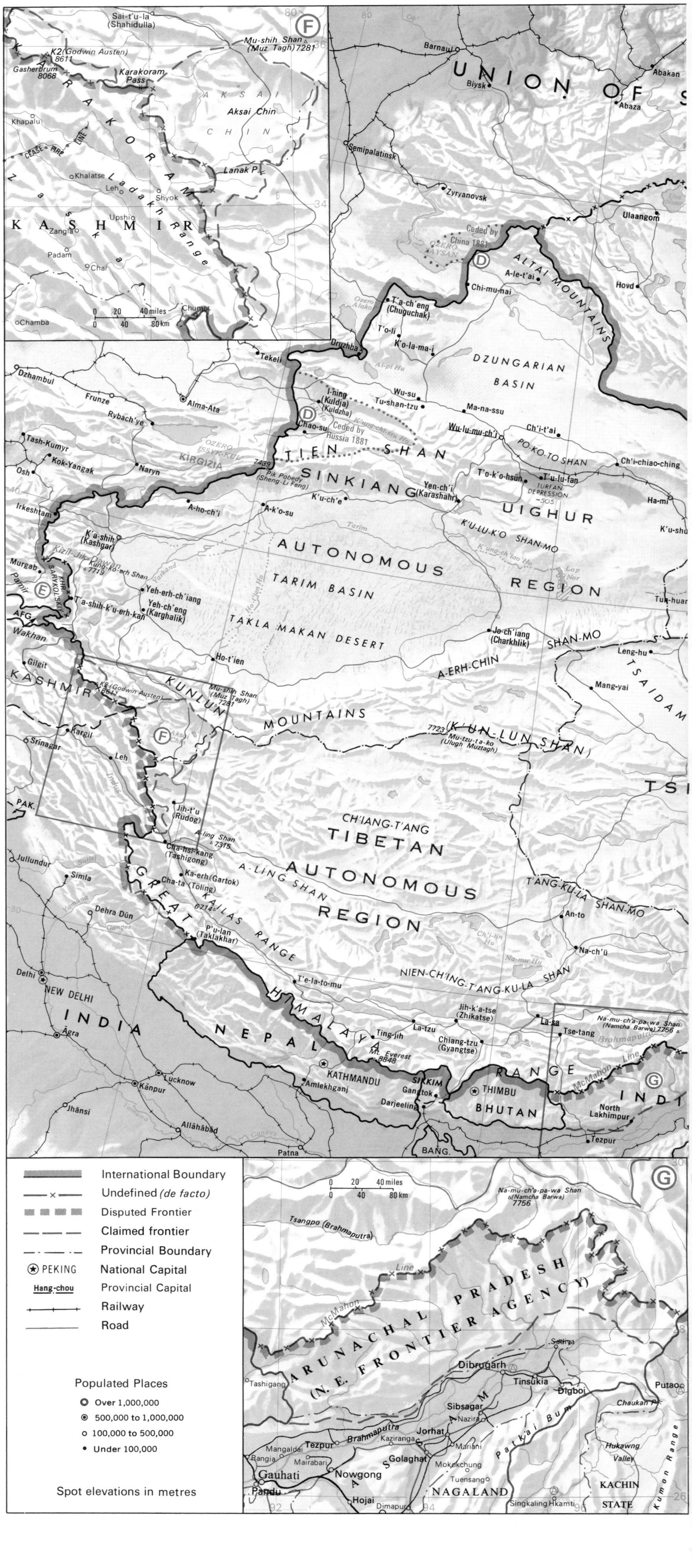

CHINA'S FRONTIERS

SYMBOLS

PHYSICAL MAPS (2-8)

Boundaries

- International
- Undelimited
- Administrative

Communications

- Railways
- Roads
- Tracks
- Navigable Canals
- Airports

Other Features

- River, Stream
- Seasonal Watercourses
- Seasonal Flood-Plain
- Pass ; Gorges
- Dam, Barrage
- Waterhole, Well
- Summit, Peak
- Ancient Walls

Lake Types

- Fresh-water
- Perennial Salt Lake
- Seasonal Salt Lake
- Saline Mud Flat
- Salt Flat

Landscape Features

- Ice-field and Glaciers
- Sand Desert, Dunes
- Saline Marsh, Salt Desert
- Marsh, Swamp
- Tidal Area

PROVINCIAL MAPS (10-119)

Administrative Centres

- Provincial Capital
- Shih (Municipality)
- Hsien (County) or Ch'i (Banner) centre
- Other populated place
- [Ta-pu] Name of Shih, Hsien or Ch'i where different from name of centre
- Wu-hu Centre of Autonomous District, League or Region

N.B. Regional name is shown only where different from name of centre

Boundaries

- International
- Undelimited
- Provincial
- Autonomous District (A.D.); Meng (League) Hsien (Taiwan only)
- Shih (Municipality) Ti - ch'ü (Region)

Abbreviations

A.D. - Autonomous District
A.H. - Autonomous Hsien
Aut. Bann. - Autonomous Banner
E. Bann. - Eastern Banner
W. Bann. - Western Banner

Communications

- Railway
- Road, Track
- Waterway
- Shipping Route
- Port ; Airport

Other Features

- River, Stream
- Seasonal Watercourse
- Subterranean Stream
- Undefined River Course
- Canal, Ditches
- Dam, Reservoir

- Seasonal Lake
- Marsh, Flood area
- Salt Marsh
- Desert
- Reef, Shoal
- Ancient Wall
- Historic Site
- Summit, Peak
- Pass
- Gorge
- Hot Spring

CITY PLANS (124-141)

- Built-up area
- Station Railway
- Trolley-bus/bus route; stop
- Ferry
- Airport
- Bridge
- Park, Recreation Area
- City Wall
- Named buildings
- Tomb
- Memorial
- Stadium

THE ORIENT

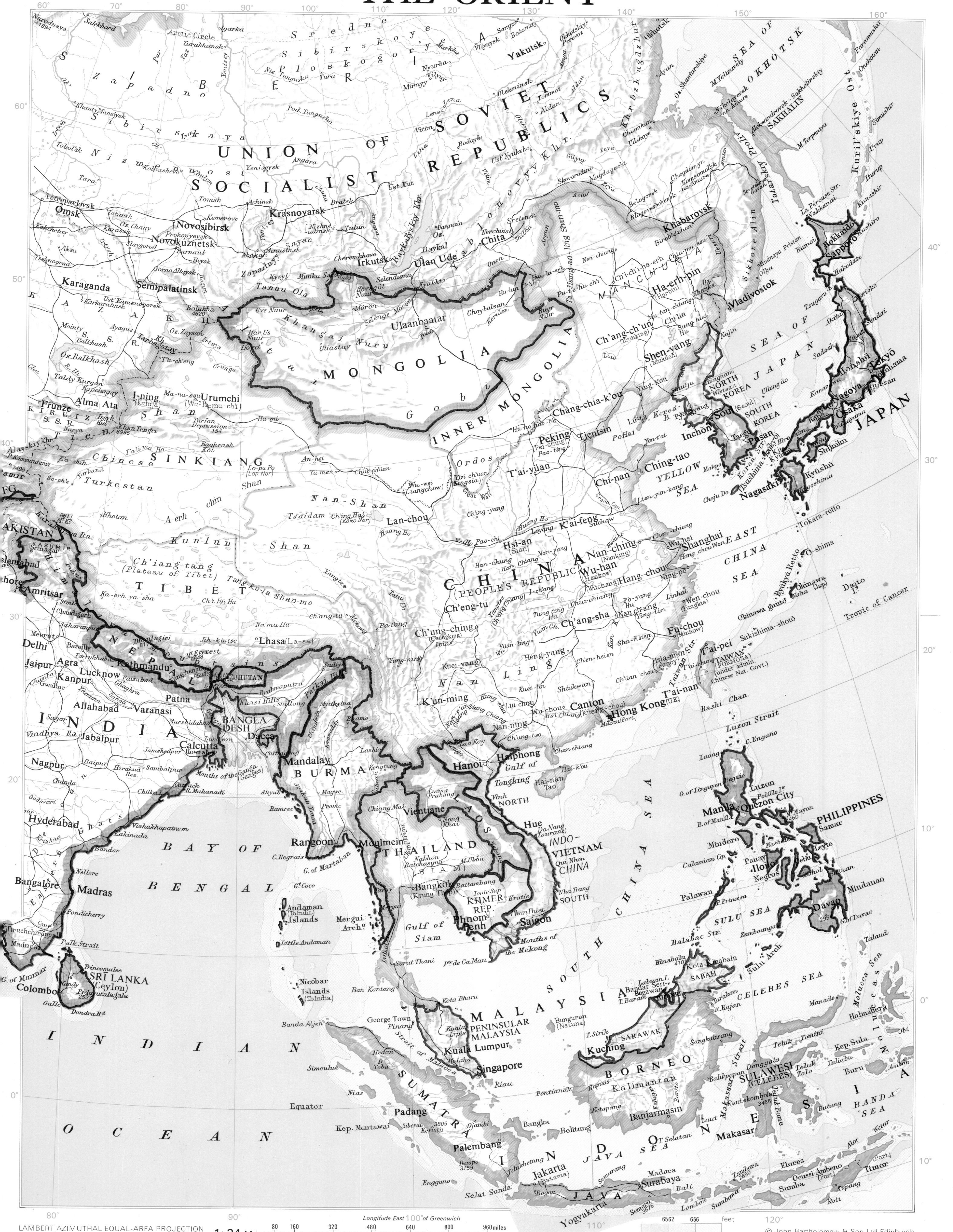

LAMBERT AZIMUTHAL EQUAL-AREA PROJECTION

1:24 M

Longitude East 100° of Greenwich

© John Bartholomew & Son Ltd Edinburgh

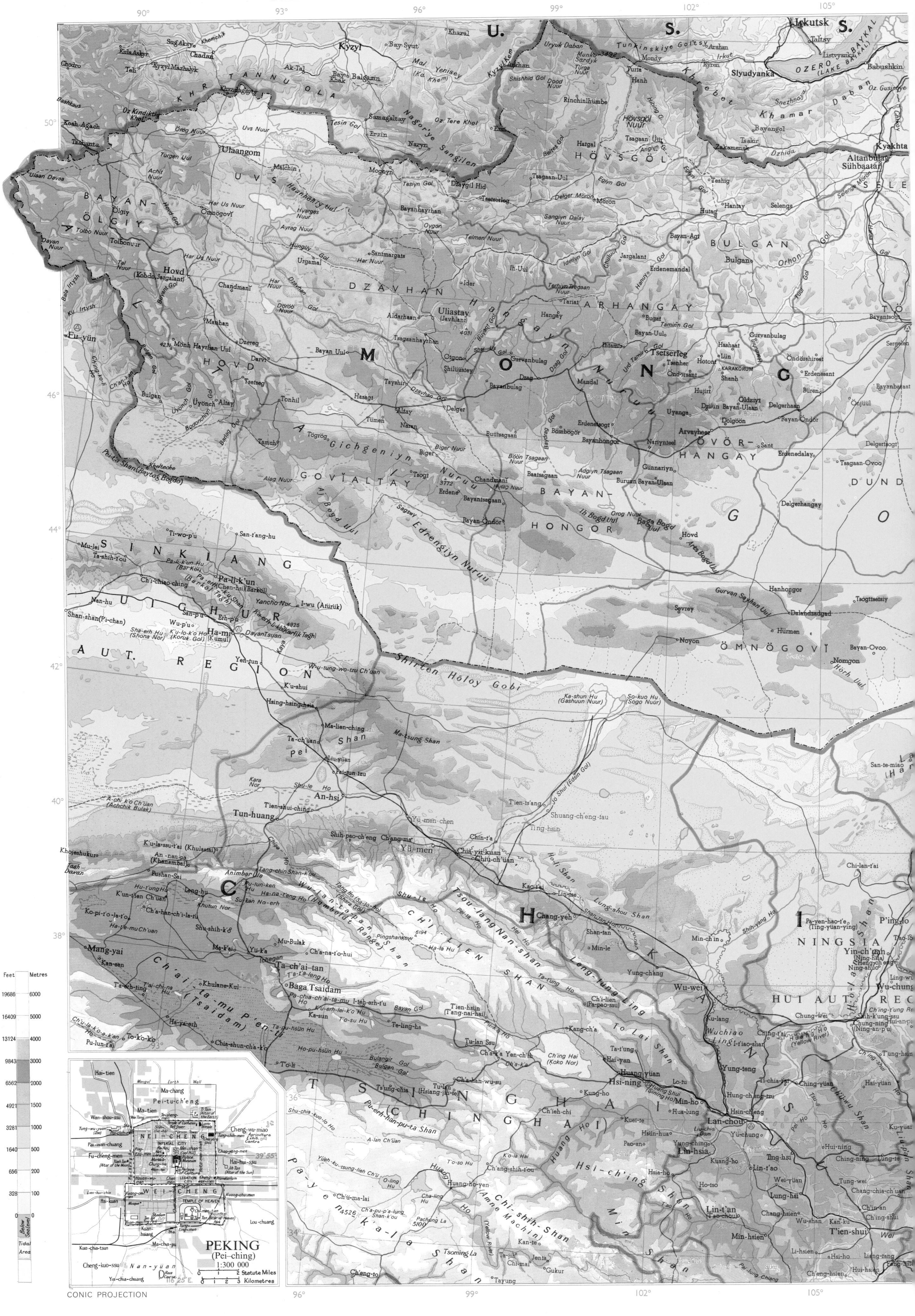
U. S. S.
M O N G O
SINKIANG UIGHUR AUT. REGION
TSINGHAI (CHINGHAI)
KANSU
NINGSIA HUI AUT. REGION
BAYAN-ÖLGIY
HOVD
UVS
DZAVHAN
ARHANGAY
HÖVSGÖL
BULGAN
GOVI ALTAY
BAYAN-HONGOR
ÖVÖR-HANGAY
ÖMNÖGOVI
DUND GOVI
SELENGE
Kyzyl
Irkutsk
Slyudyanka
Ozero Baykal (Lake Baikal)
Ulaangom
Uvs Nuur
Hovd (Kobdo, Jargalant)
Ölgiy
Uliastay (Javhlant)
Tsetserleg
Altay
Bayanhongor
Dalandzadgad
Altanbulag Sühbaatar
Kyakhta
Hami (Kumul)
Pa-li-k'un
Tun-huang
An-hsi
Yü-men
Chiu-ch'üan
Chang-yeh
Wu-wei
Lan-chou
Hsi-ning
Ch'ing Hai (Koko Nor)
Lin-hsia
T'ien-shui
Yin-ch'uan
Ch'ai-ta-mu P'en-ti (Tsaidam)
Ch'i-lien Shan
Nan-shan
A-nyê-ma-ch'in Shan
Pei Shan
Shiliin Höloy Gobi
Gobi Altay
Hangay Nuruu
Khrebet Tannu Ola
PEKING (Pei-ching) 1:300 000
NEI-CH'ENG
WAI-CH'ENG
IMPERIAL CITY
TEMPLE OF HEAVEN
Statute Miles
Kilometres
Feet
Metres
19686 6000
16409 5000
13124 4000
9843 3000
6562 2000
4921 1500
3281 1000
1640 500
656 200
328 100
0 0
Below Sea level
Tidal Area
90°
93°
96°
99°
102°
105°
50°
46°
44°
42°
40°
38°
36°
34°

NORTH CHINA AND MONGOLIA

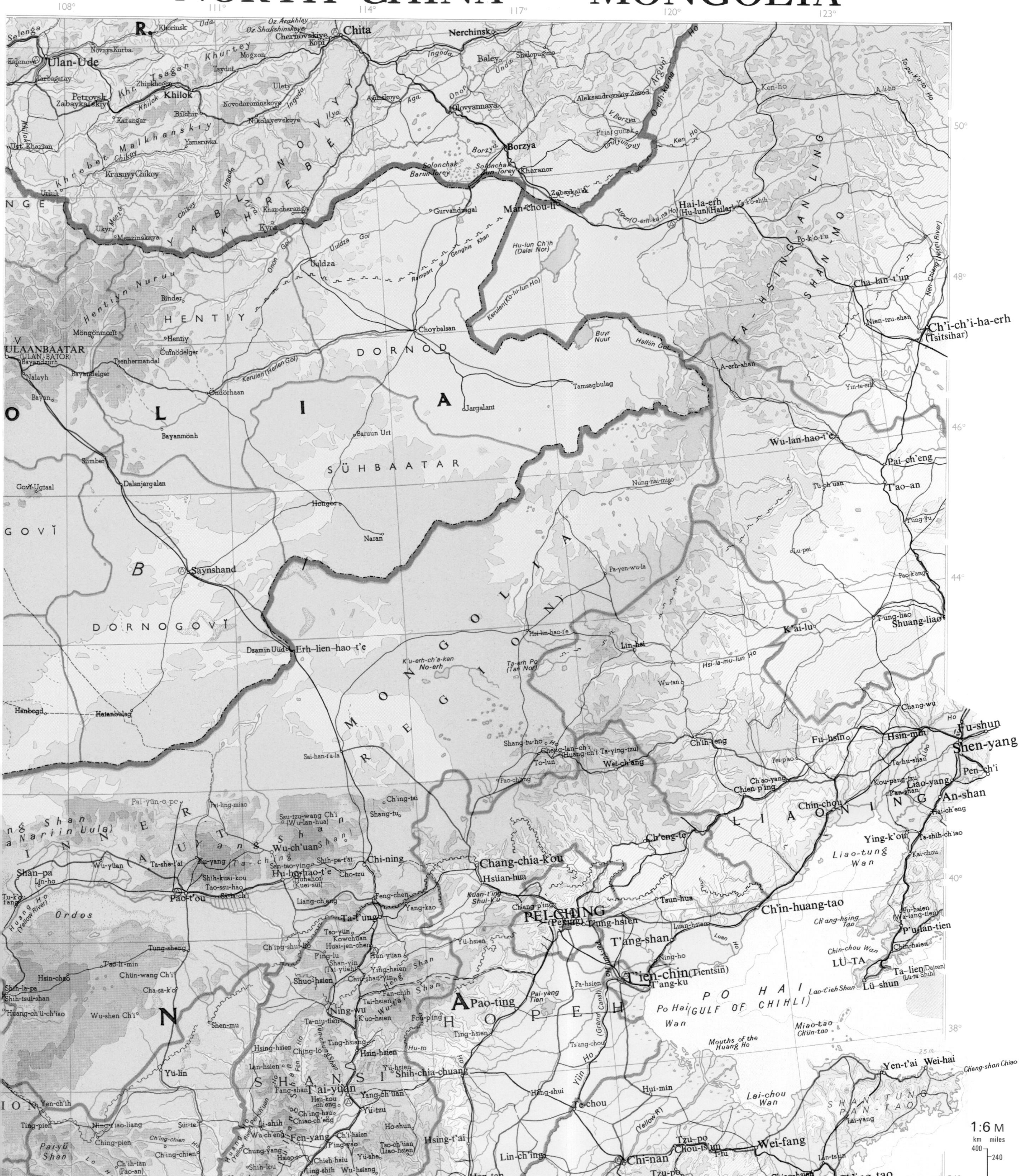

TSINGHAI
KANSU
SHENSI
SZECHWAN
KWEICHOW
YUNNAN
KWANGSI CHUANG AUT. REGION
CHAMDO
INDIA
BURMA
LAOS
NORTH VIETNAM
GULF OF TONGKING
LEI-CHOU PAN-TAO (Luichow Peninsula)
Ch'eng-tu
Ch'ung-ch'ing
Kun-ming
Kuei-yang
Nan-ning
Lan-chou
Hsi-an (Sian)
Han-chung
Ya-an
Kang-ting (Tatsienlu)
Liu-chou
Kuei-lin
Hai-k'ou
Tsun-i
Lu-chou
Nei-chiang
Nan-ch'ung
Chan-chiang
Pei-hai
Myitkyina
Lashio
Putao
HANOI
Haiphong
Lao Cai
Ch'in ling Shan
Ta-pa Shan
Hsi-ch'ing Shan
Min Shan
Kung-ka Shan (Minya Konka) 7590
Wu-chih Shan 1879
THE TRIANGLE
Ssu-ch'uan P'en-ti (Red Basin)
HONG KONG
1:300 000
Kowloon
Victoria
Aberdeen
Tsuen Wan
Sha Tin
Lantau
Lamma I.
Stanley
Port Shelter
Tolo Harbour
Feet
Metres
19686 6000
16409 5000
13124 4000
9843 3000
6562 2000
4921 1500
3281 1000
1640 500
656 200
328 100
0 0
Tidal Area
164 50
328 100
656 200
6562 2000
96°
99°
102°
105°
108°
34°
32°
30°
28°
26°
24°
22°
114°5'
114°10'
114°20'
CONIC PROJECTION

YELLOW SEA
(HUANG HAI)
SHANTUNG
SHANSI
HONAN
KIANGSU
ANHWEI
HUPEH
HUNAN
KIANGSI
CHEKIANG
FUKIEN
KWANGTUNG
Cheng-chou
K'ai-feng
Lo-yang
Hsü-chou
Lien-yün-kang
Nan-ching
Shanghai
Su-chou
Wu-hsi
Hang-chou
Ning-po
Wu-han
Ho-fei
Nan-ch'ang
Ch'ang-sha
Heng-yang
Fu-chou
Wen-chou
Hsia-men
Chin-men (Quemoy)
Shan-t'ou (Swatow)
Canton
Kowloon
Victoria
HONG KONG (To U.K.)
Macau (To Port.)
FORMOSA STRAIT
(T'AI-WAN HAI-HSIA)
TAIWAN
(FORMOSA)
(under admin. Chinese Nat. Govt.)
T'ai-pei
Chi-lung
Kao-hsiung
P'eng-hu Lieh-tao
(Pescadores)
Sakishima-shotō
SOUTH CHINA SEA
(NAN HAI)
HAI-NAN TAO
Chou-shan Ch'ün-tao
Ch'ang Chiang-k'ou (Mouth of the Yangtze)
SHANGHAI
1:300 000
Statute Miles
Kilometres
1:6 M
km miles
Longitude East of Greenwich
Heights in metres

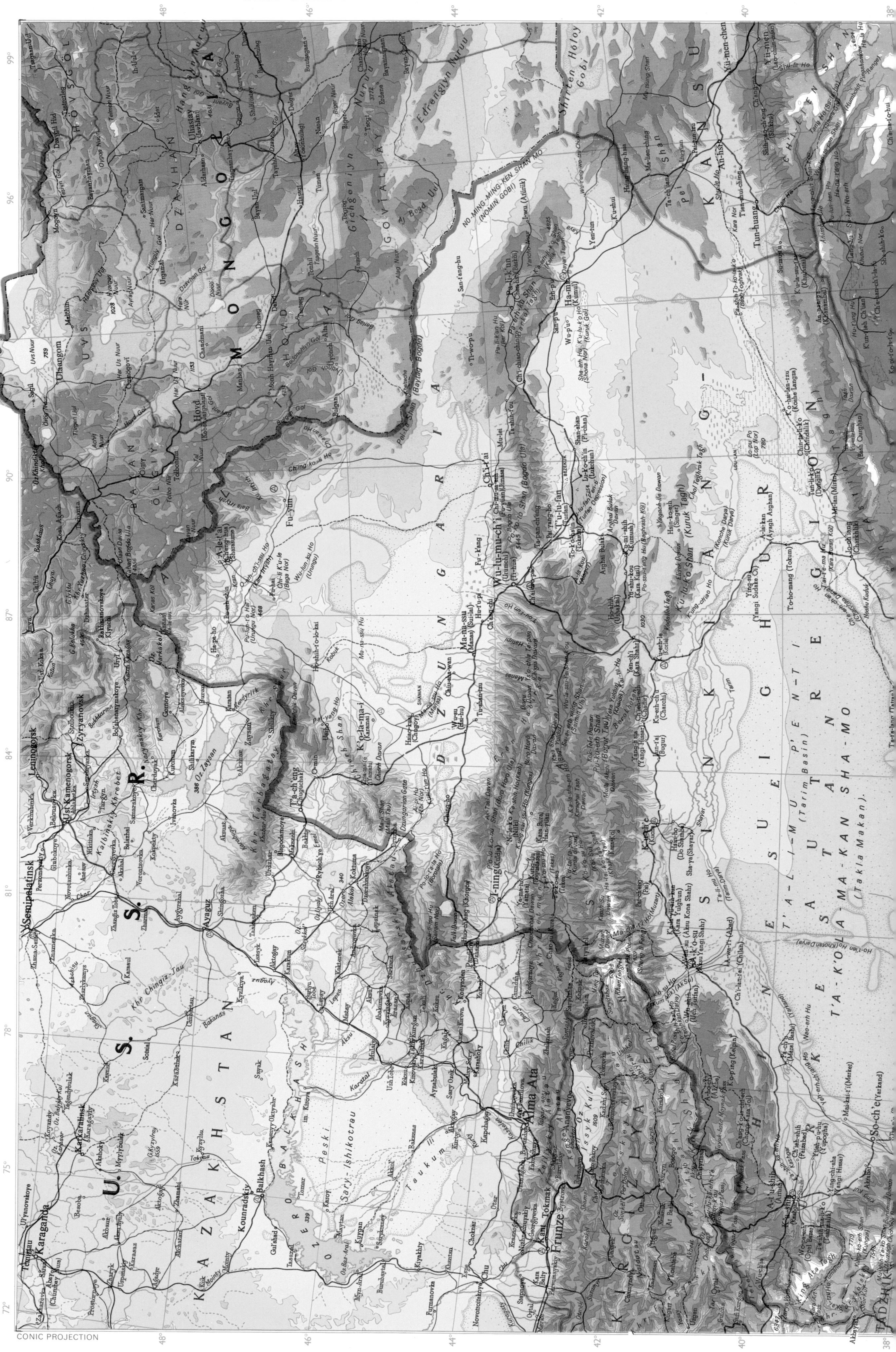

1:6M

0 20 40 80 120 160 200 240 miles

0 40 80 160 240 320 400 km

CONIC PROJECTION

BURMA
BHUTAN
SIKKIM
NEPAL
KATHMANDU
DELHI
Lucknow
Kanpur
Agra
Gwalior
Amritsar
Srinagar
Lhasa
Darjeeling
Longitude East 87° of Greenwich
Heights in metres
Feet 0 328 656 1640 3281 4921 6562 9843 13124 16409 19686
Metres 0 100 200 500 1000 1500 2000 3000 4000 5000 6000

© John Bartholomew & Son Ltd, Edinburgh

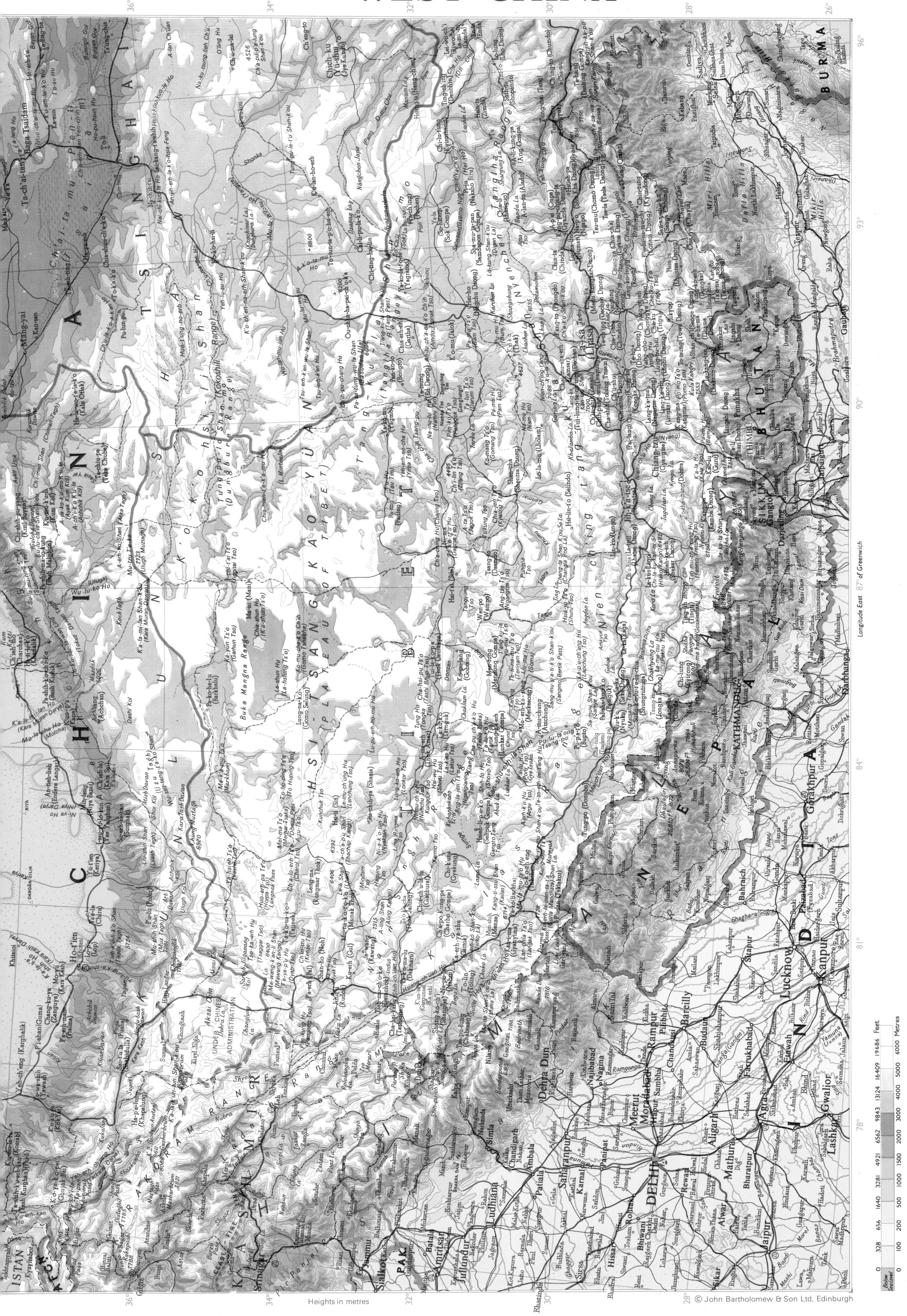

NORTH-EAST CHINA

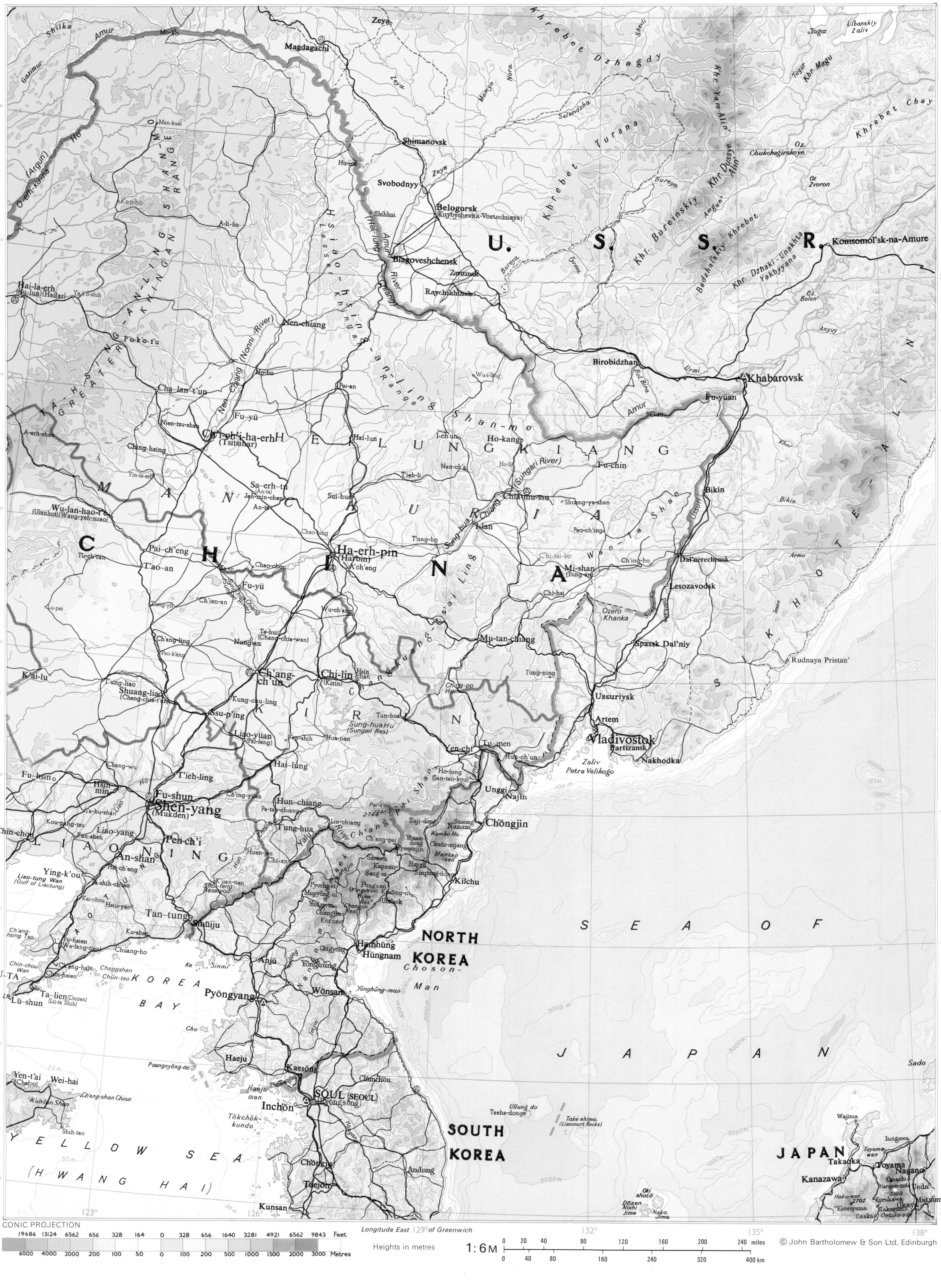

HEILUNGKIANG
PROVINCE

HEILUNGKIANG is the most northerly of all the Chinese provinces, and one of the largest since the boundary changes of 1969. It is an area which was until recent times on the fringe of the Chinese empire. First incorporated in a Chinese-style state under the Liao (937–1125) Khitan dynasty and then under the larger and more sinified Chin (1125–1234) Jurchen dynasty, this area remained under a degree of central control during the period of the Mongol dynasty (1234–1368). In the late 14th century and the early 15th the Chinese Ming dynasty (1368–1644) attempted to exercise a form of indirect rule over the tribal population, but this gradually became ineffective. During the Manchu Ch'ing dynasty, which had its origins in the north-east, Russian expansion across Siberia reached the Amur river region in the mid-17th century. This was checked, and the Treaty of Nerchinsk (1689) recognised Chinese sovereignty over the whole Amur region to the north of the present boundary. This northern area was placed under a Manchu military governor. In 1858–60 Russia annexed the whole area north of the Amur river, and the coastal area south to Vladivostok.

Until this time the province remained very thinly peopled, with few Chinese farmers. Settlement in the plains of the Sungari (Sung-hua) and Nonni (Nen Chiang) rivers began only in the late 19th century. Heilungkiang, even more than Kirin and Liaoning, remained largely peopled by various Tungusic peoples. At the end of the 19th century, when the foreign powers began to divide China into spheres of influence, Heilungkiang came under Russian domination. The Russians constructed the Chinese Eastern Railway across the province to Vladivostok, and after the Boxer rebellion occupied the railway zone for some years. Russian influence remained here, even after the Russo–Japanese War of 1904–5, and a large number of White Russians settled in the cities after the Revolution of 1917. In 1931 the province, with the rest of Manchuria, came under Japanese control. By this time there had already been considerable Chinese immigration into Heilungkiang, and this continued. The Japanese also built a railway network, and began the exploitation of the province's resources. Under the Communist regime this growth has continued. The population rose from about 12,000,000 in 1953 to 21,000,000 by 1964. The increase is partly the result of extensive immigration from other parts of China.

In the post-war years the western section of the province, with a large Mongol population, became a part of the Inner Mongolian Autonomous Region, forming the Hu-lun-pei-erh (Hulunbuir) League. Late in 1969 this area was transferred to Heilungkiang.

Heilungkiang has a very harsh climate. Even the southern plain has average winter temperatures of −20.1°C (−4°F). In the Amur valley in the north temperatures drop to −27.6°C (−18°F). The winters are very long and there are many areas of permafrost. The summers are short and hot ranging from 20°C to 24°C (68°F to 75°F). The growing season is about 165 days in the Sung-hua plain, and less than 160 days in the north. Rainfall is adequate, about 500 mm to 600 mm in the plain, decreasing towards the west. Most of this falls in the summer months.

The natural vegetation of the central plains was steppe grassland, while the mountains are covered in dense mixed forest. There are still very large areas of natural forest, and Heilungkiang produces about 40 per cent of China's timber.

The Sung-hua river plain This is an area of natural grassland with extremely rich black soils, which was first brought into cultivation on a large scale in the early part of this century, when the coming of the railway gave it good communications with the outside. This is the most important agricultural area of Heilungkiang, where grain (corn, spring wheat, millet, kaoliang) soy beans, flax and sugarbeet are grown. There is also a dairy industry, and animal husbandry is important.

Ha-erh-pin (Harbin), the provincial capital, is the main city of this region. At the beginning of this century it was a small river port on the Sung-hua, but the railways transformed it into the natural communication centre for the province. Already a city of 380,000 in 1932, it doubled in the next decade under the Japanese, when it developed extensive food processing industries. Since 1949 Ha-erh-pin has developed more varied industry. It has become a major producer of heavy machinery (especially turbines and boilers) for power generating, for electrical equipment, for precision tools and bearings and for tractors. It also produces cement, fertilisers and chemicals, and refines sugar. Its population has continued to grow and is currently estimated at about 2,000,000.

Shao-tung and *Hu-lan* are important industrial satellite towns.

The Nen-chiang river plain lies to the west and north-west. It is slightly less fertile, and has a somewhat lower rainfall and a shorter growing season. It is mainly a grain-growing area, with winter wheat, corn, kaoliang and rice taking up most of the land. Soy beans and sugarbeet are also important economic crops. This area has well developed animal husbandry and a dairy industry concentrated around Ch'i-ch'i-ha-erh and An-ta.

Ch'i-ch'i-ha-erh is the main city of the area. An old post town under the Manchus, this was the first area settled by Chinese in the 18th century. It began to develop rapidly after 1903 when the Chinese Eastern Railway was completed, and by the 1930s already had a wide range of industries. Further industrial development followed under the Japanese and this has continued under the Communist regime. Ch'i-ch'i-ha-erh has a major engineering industry, producing railway locomotives and rolling stock, machine tools and mine machinery. It also has a large sugar-refining industry and paper mills, as well as extensive food-processing plants.

Fu-la-erh-chi is a satellite industrial city, with a steel plant, and heavy machinery factories.

Ta-ch'ing oilfield This oilfield, the precise location of which has never been specified, but which is south-west of An-ta, was discovered in 1959, and began production in 1962. By 1965 the field produced half of China's total oil production, 3,500,000 tons. Production has increased considerably since. Part of this oil is refined locally, the rest shipped by rail to refineries at Ta-lien and Chin-chou in Liaoning. The field remains China's largest source of oil, and has made a considerable contribution to China's self-sufficiency.

The Ho Chiang plain This is the plain where the Amur, Sungari and Ussuri rivers converge. It is a low-lying ill-drained area, with many swamps and a tendency to flood. There has been considerable work on water-conservancy schemes in the area since 1949, and there are many large state farms. The main crops are spring wheat, corn, kaoliang and rice, and sugarbeet, soy beans and flax are also grown.

Chia-mu-ssu is the principal route centre and market of this area. Its growth was comparatively late, dating from the completion of the railways in 1939 and the beginning of coal-mining in the nearby region. Growth has continued since 1949. It has a large power plant, and much diversified industry, including paper making, using wood from the forests of the Hsiao-hsing-an range to the north, sugar refining, the manufacture of farm equipment and aluminium smelting. It is also important for the lumber trade and for transport of coal.

Ho-kang is a major coal field, which first came into operation in 1936. It was producing 2,500,000 tons by 1943. Production has been greatly increased since 1949. It was nearly 5,000,000 tons in 1957, and is now probably about 10,000,000 tons.

Shuang-ya-shan, south-east of Chia-mu-ssu, is another important coal town, which was developed in the 1940s and has continued to grow. It produced 2,300,000 tons in 1957 and now probably produces about 5,000,000 tons.

The Hsiao-hsing-an mountains This heavily-forested mountain belt lies between the Amur and the Sungari plain. It is sparsely peopled, has little cultivated land, and is important mainly as a lumbering region.

I-ch'un is the main town of the area and the centre of the lumber industry.

The Hei-ho area This includes the lower and middle plain of the Amur and the northern slopes of the Hsiao-hsing-an range. It is extremely cold, and apart from the narrow alluvial plain along the Amur, has difficult and complex terrain, heavily covered with forest. It developed very late. Settlement began around Hei-ho early in this century, after a minor gold-rush in the 1880s. Extensive settlement took place in the 1950s, and there is now a small population producing spring wheat, corn and soy beans, with some hardy rice. Agriculture, however, is still confined to a very small area. The timber industry is very important, but communications are very poor.

South-eastern Heilungkiang uplands This area was virtually unpopulated virgin forest until the construction of the Chinese Eastern railway in the early years of this century, when lumbering became a major industry and Chinese settlers moved into the area. The main crops grown here are soy beans, corn, spring wheat and some rice.

Mu-tan-chiang is the region's major city. Formerly a small settlement, as the traditional regional centre had been Ning-an, it grew to importance as a lumbering centre, where the Mu-tan Chiang river crossed the new railway route. It retains its importance as a lumbering centre, but has also developed other industries in recent times, including aluminium smelting, a tyre manufacturing plant and, more recently, a small iron and steel plant.

Chi-hsi to the north-east is a very important coal mining centre. First developed by the Japanese in the 1930s, it has continued to grow steadily. It produced 5,800,000 tons in 1957, and now probably produces over 10,000,000 tons annually.

See also notes on page 21.

AREA
710,000 square kilometres

POPULATION
21,390,000 (other estimates up to 25,000,000)

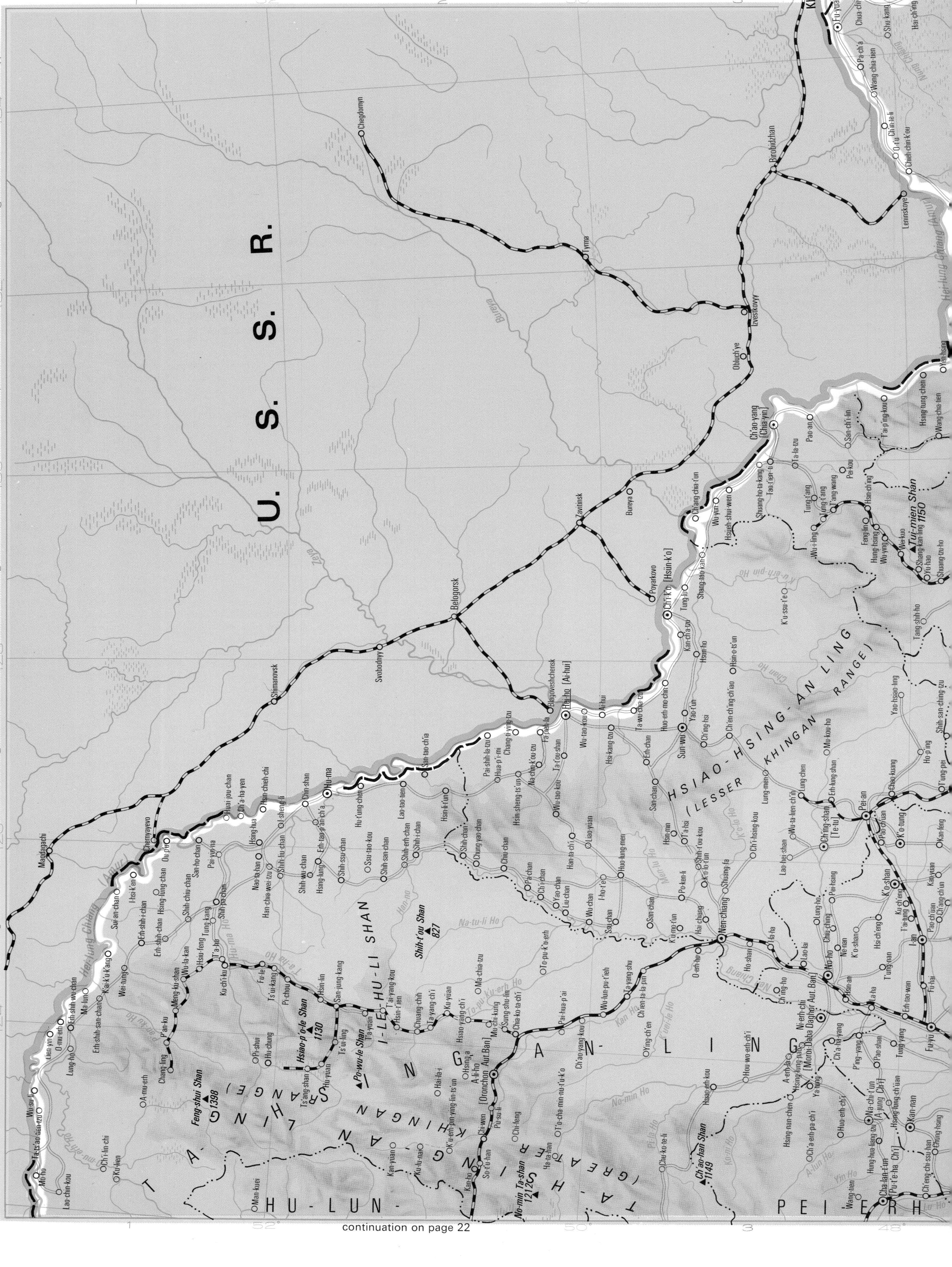

continuation on page 22

HEILUNGKIANG

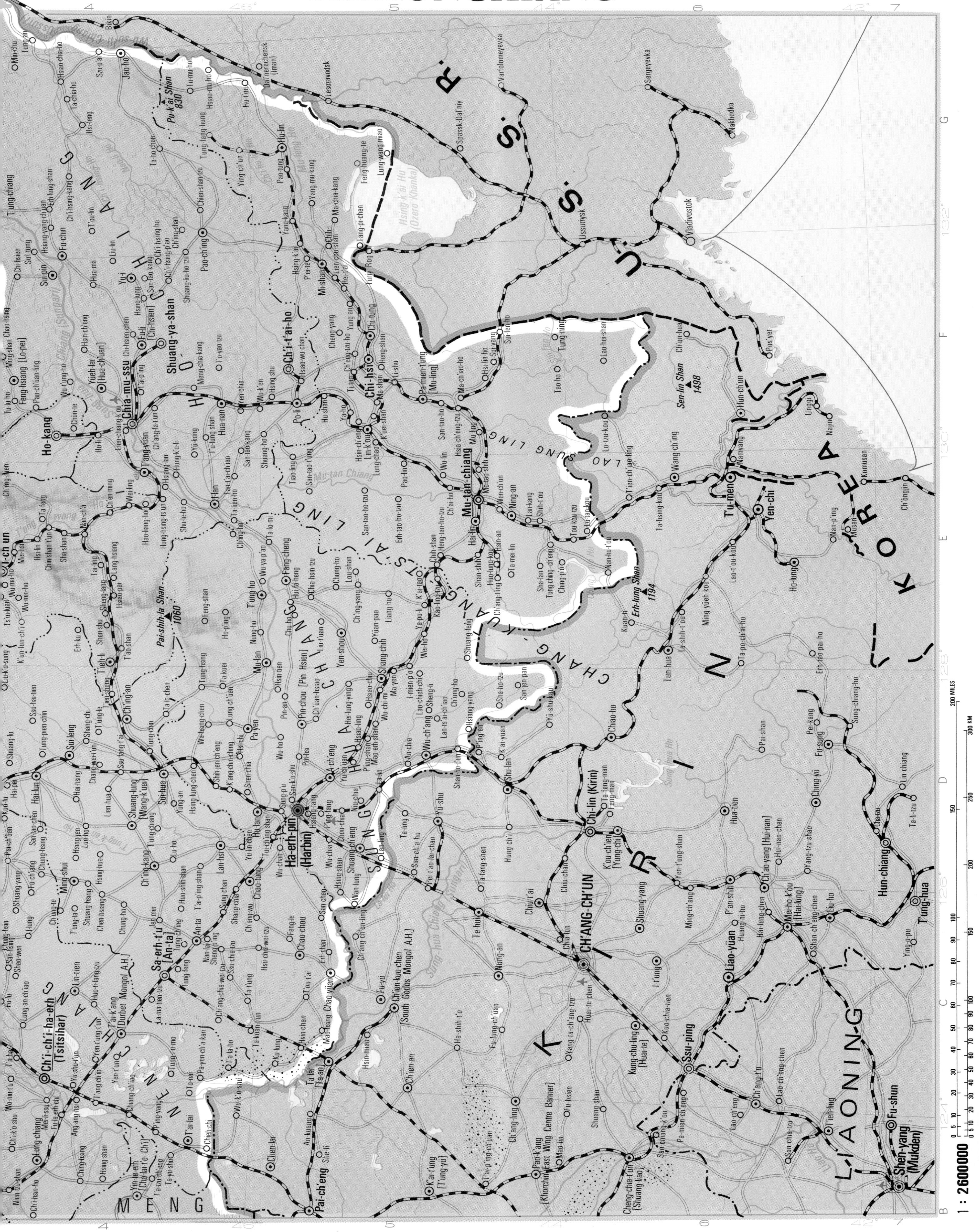

HEILUNGKIANG PROVINCE 黑龙江省
HEI-LUNG-CHIANG SHENG

12 shih	*municipalities*
1 meng	*league*
8 ti-ch'ü	*regions*
64 hsien	*counties*
1 tzu-chih-hsien	*autonomous county*
9 ch'i	*banners*
3 tzu-chih-ch'i	*autonomous banners*

capital **Ha-erh-pin Shih**	D5	哈尔滨市
An-ta Shih	C4	安达市
Chia-mu-ssu Shih	G4	佳木斯市
Ch'i-ch'i-ha-erh Shih	B4	齐齐哈尔市
Chi-hsi Shih	F5	鸡西市
Ch'i-t'ai-ho Shih	F5	七台河市
Hai-la-erh Shih	A3	海拉尔市
Ho-kang Shih	F4	鹤岗市
I-ch'un Shih	E4	伊春市
Man-chou-li Shih	B3	满州里市
Mu-tan-chiang Shih	E5	牡丹江市
Shuang-ya-shan Shih	F4	双鸭山市

Hei-ho Ti-ch'ü		黑河地区
Ai-hui Hsien		爱辉县
centre: Hei-ho	D2	黑河
Hsün-k'o Hsien		逊克县
centre: Ch'i-k'o	E3	奇克
Nen-chiang Hsien	C3	嫩江县
Pei-an Hsien	D3	北安县
Sun-wu Hsien	D3	孙吴县
Te-tu Hsien		德都县
centre: Ch'ing-shan	D3	青山

Ho-chiang Ti-ch'ü		合江地区
centre: Chia-mu-ssu	G4	佳木斯
Chi-hsien Hsien		集贤县
centre: Fu-li	F4	福利
Fu-chin Hsien	G4	富锦县
Fu-yüan Hsien	H3	抚远县
Hua-ch'uan Hsien		桦川县
centre: Yüeh-lai	F4	悦来
Hua-nan Hsien	F4	桦南县
I-lan Hsien	E4	依兰县
Jao-ho Hsien	G4	饶河县
Lo-pei Hsien		萝北县
centre: Feng-hsiang	F4	风翔
Pao-ch'ing Hsien	G4	宝清县
Po-li Hsien	F5	勃利县
Sui-pin Hsien	F4	绥滨县
T'ang-yüan Hsien	E4	汤原县
T'ung-chiang Hsien	G4	同江县
Yu-i Hsien	F4	友谊县

Hu-lun-pei-erh Meng		呼伦贝尔盟
centre: Hai-la-erh	A3	海拉尔
A-jung Ch'i		阿荣旗
centre: Na-chi-t'un	B3	那吉屯
Cha-lai-t'e Ch'i		扎赉特旗
centre: Yin-te-erh	B4	音德尔
Ch'en-pa-erh-hu Ch'i Old Barga Banner	C3	陈巴尔虎旗
centre: Pa-yen-k'u-jen		巴彦库仁
Hsi-kuei-t'u Ch'i	D3	喜桂图旗
centre: Ya-k'o-shih		牙克石
Hsin-pa-erh-hu Tso-ch'i New Barga East Banner	C3	新巴尔虎左旗
centre: A-mu-ku-lang		阿穆古郎
Hsin-pa-erh-hu Yu-ch'i New Barga West Banner	B3	新巴尔虎右旗
centre: A-erh-t'ai-mien-chen		阿尔太面镇
O-erh-ku-na Tso-ch'i Argun East Banner	D2	额尔古纳左旗
centre: Ken-ho		根河
O-erh-ku-na Yu-ch'i Argun West Banner	D2	额尔古纳右旗
centre: La-pu-ta-lin		拉布达林
O-wen-k'o Tzu-chih-ch'i Evenki Autonomous Banner	C3	鄂温克自治旗
centre: Nan-t'un		南屯
Pu-t'e-ha Ch'i		布特哈旗
centre: Cha-lan-t'un	B3	札兰屯

I-ch'un Ti-ch'ü		伊春地区
Chia-yin Hsien		嘉荫县
centre: Ch'ao-yang	F3	朝阳
T'ien-li Hsien	E4	铁力县

Mu-tan-chiang Ti-ch'ü		牡丹江地区
Chi-tung Hsien	F5	鸡东县
Hai-lin Hsien	E5	海林县
Hu-lin Hsien	G5	虎林县
Lin-k'ou Hsien	F5	林口县
Mi-shan Hsien	F5	密山县
Mu-ling Hsien		穆棱县
centre: Pa-mien-t'ung	F5	八面通
Ning-an Hsien	E5	宁安县
Tung-ning Hsien	F5	东宁县

Nen-chiang Ti-ch'ü		嫩江地区
centre: Ch'i-ch'i-ha-erh	B4	齐齐哈尔
Fu-yü Hsien	C4	富裕县
I-an Hsien	C4	依安县
Kan-nan Hsien	B4	甘南县
K'o-shan Hsien	C3	克山县
K'o-tung Hsien	D3	克东县
Lin-tien Hsien	C4	林甸县
Lung-chiang Hsien	B4	龙江县
No-ho Hsien	C3	讷河县
Pai-ch'üan Hsien	D4	拜泉县
T'ai-lai Hsien	B4	泰来县
Tu-erh-po-t'e Meng-ku-tsu Tzu-chih-hsien Durbet Mongol Autonomous Hsien		杜尔伯持蒙古族 自治县
centre: T'ai-k'ang	F4	泰康

Sui-hua Ti-ch'ü		绥化地区
An-ta Hsien	C4	安达县
Chao-chou Hsien	C5	肇州县
Chao-tung Hsien	C4	肇东县
Chao-yüan Hsien	C5	肇源县
Ch'ing-an Hsien	D4	青安县
Ch'ing-kang Hsien	D4	青冈县
Hai-lun Hsien	D4	海伦县
Lan-hsi Hsien	D4	兰西县
Ming-shui Hsien	C4	明水县
Sui-hua Hsien	D4	绥化县
Sui-leng Hsien	D4	绥棱县
Wang-k'uei Hsien		望奎县
centre: Shuang-lung	D4	双龙

Sung-hua-chiang Ti-ch'ü		松花江地区
centre: Ha-erh-pin	D5	哈尔滨
A-ch'eng Hsien	D5	阿城县
Fang-cheng Hsien	E5	方正县
Hu-lan Hsien	D4	呼兰县
Mu-lan Hsien	E5	木兰县
Pa-yen Hsien	D4	巴彦县
Pin Hsien		宾县
centre: Pin-chou	D5	宾州
Shang-chih Hsien	D5	尚志县
Shuang-ch'eng Hsien	D5	双城县
T'ung-ho Hsien	E4	通河县
Wu-ch'ang Hsien	D5	五常县
Yen-shou Hsien	E5	延寿县

Ta-hsing-an-ling Ti-ch'ü		大兴安岭地区
centre: Chia-ko-ta-ch'i	C2	加格达奇
Hu-ma Hsien	C1	呼玛县
Mo-li-ta-wa Ta-wo-erh-tsu Tzu-chih-ch'i Moroi-Daba Daghor Autonomous Banner		莫力达瓦达斡尔族 自治旗
centre: Ni-erh-chi	C3	尼尔基
O-lun-ch'un-tsu Tzu-chih-ch'i Oronchon Autonomous Banner		鄂伦春族自治旗
centre: A-li-ho	B2	阿里河

KIRIN
PROVINCE

KIRIN (Chi-lin) was first created as a province in 1907, when the restrictions on Chinese settlement in Manchuria were finally lifted. Its present boundaries were established in 1954, with the exception of the sections of the Hu-lun pei-erh and Che-li-mu Leagues which were detached from Inner Mongolia in 1969. Its administrative capital was moved from Chi-lin (Kirin city) to Ch'ang-ch'un in 1954. This region was always on the border of the Chinese cultural sphere. From the 8th century it formed a part of the powerful Po-hai state, which was destroyed in 927 by the Khitan, who in turn established a powerful Chinese-style dynasty, the Liao, which controlled Manchuria and parts of north-eastern China. In the 12th century the Jurchen, one of the Liao's subject peoples of Tungusic stock, who inhabited central Kirin and Heilungkiang, established their own independent state, which in 1125 destroyed the Liao and went on to conquer all northern China. They were destroyed in 1234 by the Mongols, whose control extended over this region. After the restoration of Chinese rule under the Ming in 1368, Manchuria remained a tributary region. In the late 16th century the Jurchen again grew powerful, and in 1616 set up an independent state in Manchuria, which included parts of Liaoning as well as Kirin and Heilungkiang. In 1633 this state took the name of Manchu, and in 1644 conquered China, establishing the Ch'ing empire which was to last until 1911. The Manchus, in an attempt to preserve their racial and cultural identity, forbade Chinese settlement in their homelands. But some Chinese peasants had begun to settle in Kirin in the 18th century, and after 1860, with the Russian occupation of the region beyond the Amur, this ban was not strictly enforced. It lingered until 1907, however, and it was not until the very end of the 19th century and early in the present century that large-scale settlement began.

In 1931 Kirin was occupied by the Japanese, and in 1932 became part of the puppet state of Manchukuo. It was during this period that the province developed a rail and power network, and large-scale industrial development began. Since 1949 the population has continued to grow, as industry and agriculture have become more and more productive.

Kirin is a transitional area between the bleak northern climate of Heilungkiang and the comparatively mild Liaoning. Winters are extremely cold. Ch'ang-ch'un's average January temperature is −16.9°C (1°F). The rivers are frozen for at least five months per year, and the growing season is between 160–170 days. Summers are very hot, with July average of 23.6°C (75°F). The rainfall, most of which falls in the summer months, decreases westwards from 1,000 mm in the Ch'ang-pai Shan mountains to only 400 mm in the western plateau. The natural vegetation was dense mixed forest in the eastern mountain areas, and good natural grassland in the plains.

The Ch'ang-ch'un plain This is a flat fertile plain, with rich, black earth soils. It is densely cultivated, the most important crops being corn, kaoliang, soy beans, sugar beet and millet.

Ch'ang-ch'un is the dominant city in the area, and has been, since 1954, the provincial capital. Ch'ang-ch'un is a modern city, which grew up as a major railway junction after 1905 and became a major market for the agriculture of the region. In 1932 it was selected by the Japanese as the capital of the Manchukuo state, and grew into a fine modern city. Its population rose by 1945 to 862,000 people, many of whom were Japanese, and it became a major cultural centre as well as an administrative capital. After the war it declined somewhat, but by 1957 its population had reached 975,000. It is currently estimated at over one million. After 1949, however, Ch'ang-ch'un's character changed. Previously its dominant industry had been food-processing. In the 1950s it was developed into a major heavy industrial city. It has the largest automotive industry in China, which began producing lorries in 1956, diesel engine and tractor works, tyre manufacturing, and a major plant producing railway locomotives, rolling stock and equipment. It also has a pharmaceutical chemicals industry. It has many institutions of higher education, and is a major centre of the film industry.

The Ssu-p'ing plain This is the southern part of the central plain, separated from the Ch'ang-ch'un area by the low watershed between the Sung-hua (Sungari) river system and the drainage basin of the Liao river system. This, too, is a fertile plain, the main grain producing area of the province, growing corn, kaoliang, millet, soy beans and sugar beet.

Ssu-p'ing, like Ch'ang-ch'un, developed early in this century as a railway junction and as a market and collecting centre for local agricultural produce. The city was almost destroyed during the civil war. After 1949 it developed into a minor industrial city, with farm-machinery and chemical plants, and oil-extraction, flour milling and lumber working industries. Although the city was designated for further development in the late 1950s, this does not seem to have taken place.

Liao-yüan, to the south-east, is the centre of a major coalfield, producing some three million tons per annum of good quality steam coal. It has a large thermal generating plant, and some industry, including fertiliser and paper manufacturing.

The Chi-lin area This is a region of hills, quite high in the east, more rounded and rolling in the west, with only a small area of plain. The mountains are deeply dissected by the headwaters of the Sung-hua river. Above Chi-lin these were dammed at Feng-man to form a very large hydro-electric scheme. This was completed by the Japanese before 1942. Other schemes were planned in the same area in the 1950s.

The lowlands of this area grow soy beans and rice, with less concentration on corn and kaoliang than elsewhere in Kirin. Flax and tobacco are also cultivated. The hills are mostly forested, although much of the forest has been cut over.

Chi-lin, unlike Ch'ang-ch'un, is an old Chinese city, first established in the 17th century. Early in this century it was predominantly a centre of lumbering, and a regional market centre. As the Japanese began to develop Manchuria as a base for war industry in the 1930s, industries with a stress on chemicals concerned with the production of petroleum from coal, cement, and paper-making were established. In the 1950s the Feng-man hydro-electric plant, which had been partly dismantled during the Russian occupation, was restored, and industrial growth resumed. A number of very large chemical and fertiliser plants, and a major ferro-alloy industry were set up. Chi-lin is also a centre for sugar refining.

The Yen-pien mountain region This is the most mountainous and rugged area of Kirin, with a series of ranges, the Ch'ang-pai Shan, Nan-kang Shan, Wei-hu Ling, and Lao-sung Ling, whose peaks rise from 1,000 m to 1,600 m. It is still heavily forested, and was settled later than the plain areas to the east. It is the centre of a large Korean minority, who emigrated into the Yen-chi–T'u-men area in the 1870s and 1880s. They now number about 600,000 in this area alone. This area is essentially a lumbering district, with timber exported by rail to Chi-lin or to the Mu-tan-chiang area of Heilungkiang. There is also some copper mining at T'ien-pao-shan. The agriculture of the area concentrates on rice, soy beans and millet.

Yen-chi is the administrative centre of this Korean Autonomous District and the main market for the agriculture of the surrounding area.

T'u-men, on the North Korean border, is a major rail junction, and also a centre of the paper-making industry.

The T'ung-hua area This comprises the south-eastern corner of Kirin. It is a mountainous area drained by the headwaters of the Sung-hua and of the Ya-lu rivers. More than two-thirds of the area remains under dense forest, and forestry is a major industry. It also has rich reserves of iron ore and coal. Agriculture is confined to limited areas, and corn, soy beans, millet and kaoliang are grown.

T'ung-hua is the main city of this area. A centre of the lumber industry from the late 19th century, it was reached by a railway in 1937, and later became important as a transportation centre for the local coalfield at Hun-chiang and the iron mines at Ta-li-tzu, to which branch lines were built. In the late 1950s the construction of a major iron and steel plant was planned here, but it was never built. Local coal and iron-ore is transported by rail to An-shan.

Hun-chiang, to the north-east of T'ung-hua, is a major coal mining city, producing some two to three million tons of good coking coal annually.

See also notes on page 21.

AREA
290,000 square kilometres

POPULATION
17,890,000 (other estimates up to 21,000,000)

A
B
C
D
E
F
121°
122°
123°
124°
125°
126°
42°
41°
continuation on page 23
INNER MONGOLIA
CHE LI MU MENG
L I A O N I N G
H E
K I R I N
HA TA LING
CH'ANG-CH'UN SHIH
TA HEI SHAN
LUNG KANG
LAO LING
Lao-t'ou Shan
1394
LIAO-TUNG WAN
Liao Ho
Hun Ho
Sung-hua Chiang (Sungari)
Pai-ch'eng
T'ao-nan
[T'ao-an]
Wu-lan-hao-t'e
[Khorchin West Wing South Banner]
Pai-yin-hu-shih
[Khorchin West Wing Centre Banner]
K'ai-t'ung
[T'ung-yü]
T'u-ch'üan
Chen-lai
Ta-lai
[Ta-an]
Lu-pei
[Cha-lu-t'e Ch'i]
Pao-k'ang
[Khorchin East Wing Centre Banner]
T'ung-liao
K'ai-lu
Kan-ch'i-k'a
[Khorchin East Wing North Banner]
Ta-ch'in-t'a-la
[Nai-man Ch'i]
K'u-lun-chen
[K'u-lun Ch'i]
Ch'ien-kuo-chen
[South Gorlos Mongol A.H.]
Ch'ang-ch'un
Ssu-p'ing
Liao-yüan
[Tung-liao]
Cheng-chia-t'un
[Shuang-liao]
Kung-chu-ling
[Huai-te]
Ch'ang-ling
Fu-yü
Nung-an
Shuang-yang
Mei-ho-k'ou
[Hai-lung]
Ch'ao-yang
[Hui-nan]
Tung-feng
Liu-ho
P'an-shih
Hui-nan
Fu-hsin-chen
[Fu-hsin Mongol A.H.]
Fu-hsin
Chang-wu
Fa-k'u
K'ai-yüan
T'ieh-ling
Ch'ang-t'u
Hsi-feng
K'ang-p'ing
Hsin-min
SHEN-YANG
(MUKDEN)
Fu-shun
Ch'ing-yüan
Hsin-pin
T'ung-hua
K'uai-ta-mao
[T'ung-hua]
Hun-chiang
Chi-an
Huan-jen
Pen-ch'i
Liao-yang
An-shan
Hai-ch'eng
Liao-chung
T'ai-an
Chin-chou
I-hsien
Pei-chen
P'an-shan
Chao-tung
Chao-chou
Chao-yüan
Shuang-ch'eng
Lan-hsi
Yüeh-liang P'ao
Ta-pu-su P'ao

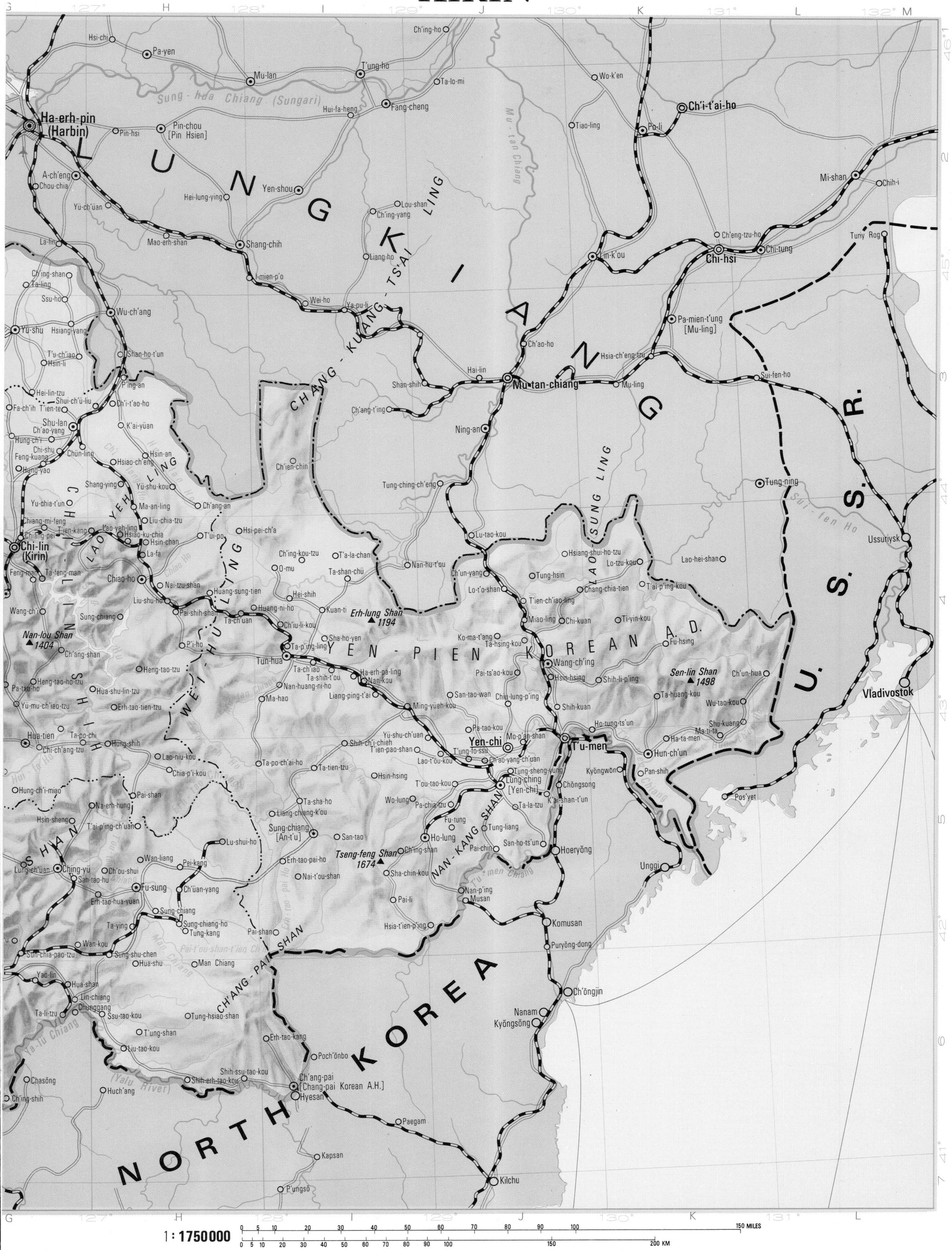

1 : 1750000

0 5 10 20 30 40 50 60 70 80 90 100 150 MILES

0 5 10 20 30 40 50 60 70 80 90 100 150 200 KM

KIRIN PROVINCE 吉林省
CHI-LIN SHENG

10 shih	*municipalities*
1 tzu-chih-chou	*autonomous district*
1 meng	*league*
3 ti-ch'ü	*regions*
39 hsien	*counties*
2 tzu-chih-hsien	*autonomous counties*
7 ch'i	*banners*

capital **Ch'ang-ch'un Shih**	**F4**	长春市
Chiu-t'ai Hsien	**F3**	九台县
Nung-an Hsien	**F3**	农安县
Shuang-yang Hsien	**F4**	双阳县
Te-hui Hsien	**F3**	德惠县
Yü-shu Hsien	**G3**	榆树县
Chi-lin Shih	**G4**	吉林市
Chiao-ho Hsien	**H4**	蛟河县
Hua-tien Hsien	**G5**	桦甸县
P'an-shih Hsien	**G5**	磐石县
Shu-lan Hsien	**G3**	舒兰县
Yung-chi Hsien		永吉县
centre: K'ou-ch'ien	**G4**	口前
Hun-chiang Shih	**G6**	浑江市
Liao-yüan Shih	**F5**	辽源市
Pai-ch'eng Shih	**C2**	白城市
Ssu-p'ing Shih	**E4**	四平市
T'u-men Shih	**J5**	图们市
T'ung-hua Shih	**F6**	通化市
T'ung-liao Shih	**C4**	通辽市
Yen-chi Shih	**J5**	延吉市
Che-li-mu Meng		哲里木盟
centre: T'ung-liao	**C4**	通辽
Cha-lu-t'e Ch'i		扎鲁特旗
centre: Lu-pei	**A3**	鲁北
K'ai-lu Hsien	**B4**	开鲁县
K'o-erh-ch'in Tso-i Chung-ch'i Khorchin East Wing Centre Banner		科尔泌左翼中旗
centre: Pao-k'ang	**D3**	保康
K'o-erh-ch'in Tso-i Hou-ch'i Khorchin East Wing North Banner		科尔泌左翼后旗
centre: Kan-ch'i-k'a	**C5**	甘旗卡
K'o-erh-ch'in Yu-i Chung-ch'i Khorchin West Wing Centre Banner		科尔泌右翼中旗
centre: Pai-yin-hu-shih	**B2**	白音胡硕
K'u-lun Ch'i		库伦旗
centre: K'u-lun-chen	**B5**	库伦镇
Nai-man Ch'i		奈曼旗
centre: Ta-ch'in-t'a-la	**A5**	大泌他拉
T'ung-liao Hsien	**C4**	通辽县
Pai-ch'eng Ti-ch'ü		白城地区
Ch'ang-ling Hsien	**D3**	长岭县
Chen-lai Hsien	**D2**	镇赉县
Ch'ien-an Hsien	**E2**	乾安县
Ch'ien-kuo-erh-lo-ssu Meng-ku-tsu Tzu-chih-hsien South Gorlos Mongol Autonomous Hsien		前郭尔罗斯蒙古族 自治县
centre: Ch'ien-kuo-chen	**E2**	前郭镇
Fu-yü Hsien	**E2**	扶余县
K'o-erh-ch'in Yu-i Ch'ien-ch'i Khorchin West Wing South Banner		科尔泌右翼前旗
centre: Wu-lan-hao-t'e	**C1**	乌兰浩特
Ta-an Hsien		大安县
centre: Ta-lai	**E2**	大赉
T'ao-an Hsien		洮安县
centre: T'ao-nan	**C2**	洮南
T'u-ch'üan Hsien	**B2**	突泉县
T'ung-yü Hsien		通榆县
centre: K'ai-t'ung	**D3**	开通
Ssu-p'ing Ti-ch'ü		四平地区
Huai-te Hsien		怀德县
centre: Kung-chu-ling	**E4**	公主岭
I-t'ung Hsien	**F4**	伊通县
Li-shu Hsien	**E4**	梨树县
Shuang-liao Hsien		双辽县
centre: Cheng-chia-t'un	**D4**	郑家屯
Tung-feng Hsien	**F5**	东丰县
Tung-liao Hsien		东辽县
centre: Liao-yüan	**F5**	辽源
T'ung-hua Ti-ch'ü		通化地区
Ch'ang-pai Ch'ao-hsien-tsu Tzu-chih-hsien Ch'ang-pai Korean Autonomous Hsien	**I6**	长白朝鲜族 自治县
Chi-an Hsien	**G6**	集安县
Ching-yü Hsien	**G5**	靖宇县
Fu-sung Hsien	**H5**	抚松县
Hai-lung Hsien		海龙县
centre: Mei-ho-k'ou	**F5**	梅河口
Hui-nan Hsien		辉南县
centre: Ch'ao-yang	**G5**	朝阳
Liu-ho Hsien	**D2**	柳河县
T'ung-hua Hsien		通化县
centre: K'uai-to-mao	**F6**	快大茂
Yen-pien Ch'ao-hsien-tsu Tzu-chih-chou Yen-pien Korean Autonomous District		延边朝鲜族 自治州
centre: Yen-chi	**J5**	延吉
An-t'u Hsien		安图县
centre: Sung-chiang	**I5**	松江
Ho-lung Hsien	**F3**	和龙县
Hun-ch'un Hsien	**K5**	珲春县
Tun-hua Hsien	**I4**	敦化县
Wang-ch'ing Hsien	**J4**	汪清县
Yen-chi Hsien		延吉县
centre: Lung-ching	**J5**	龙井

LIAONING
PROVINCE

LIAONING consists of two very different sections. The eastern half, which contains almost all the population, comprises the southern section of Manchuria (the Liaotung peninsula and the eastern mountains), the Liao Ho plain, and the corridor of land leading from Hopeh. This area constituted Liaoning until 1969 when, with the dismemberment of the Inner Mongolian Autonomous Region, the Chao-wu-ta (Jo-uda) League was incorporated into Liaoning. Liaoning is the oldest area of Chinese settlement in Manchuria. It formed a part of the Han empire, and was partially incorporated in the T'ang empire during the 7th century. But little settlement took place. It was an important base for the Liao and Chin, two Chinese-style dynasties under non-Chinese (Khitan and Jurchen) peoples which controlled much of northern China between the 10th and 13th centuries, and in the early 17th century the Manchus built up a powerful state in the area before their conquest of all China in 1644. By that time there was a considerable Chinese population in Liaoning. The Manchus attempted to restrict Chinese immigration into Manchuria, however, and although this policy was less rigid in Liaoning than in the northern areas of Manchuria, it was only in the late 19th and early 20th century that large-scale immigration took place. At first much of this migration was of seasonal labourers from Hopeh and Shantung, but permanent settlement soon followed.

Modern development came with the railways. Shen-yang (Mukden) was linked to Peking early in the century, and between 1896 and 1903 the Russians built a railway linking Ta-lien, where they had acquired the lease of territory and built a modern port after 1898, with Ha-erh-pin and the Chinese Eastern Railway across northern Manchuria. After the Russo-Japanese War of 1904–5 the railway and Ta-lien port were transferred to Japan, and the area came increasingly under Japanese influence. In 1932 Liaoning became a part of the Japanese puppet state of Manchukuo, and serious development of the area began. At first Manchuria was seen as a source of raw materials for Japanese industry, but during the 1930s it was decided to industrialise the area as a base for the Japanese military. Before 1945 Liaoning acquired the best rail system in China, a huge hydro-electric scheme at Shui-feng, major coal and iron mines, and a great concentration of heavy industry. Although much of its equipment was looted during the Soviet occupation in 1945, southern Manchuria was the only systematically industrialised area of China outside the coastal ports. Under the Communist regime the restoration of this area was a first priority, and during the 1950s its heavy industry produced much of the plant for industrial growth elsewhere in China. It remains the most heavily industrialised, and also the most urbanised province in China.

The Liaotung peninsula This is a rugged area, with mountains generally about 300 m to 400 m but rising to peaks of over 1,000 m. It is a continuation of the Shantung peninsula in structure. It has a comparatively mild climate. At Lü-ta January temperatures average −5°C (23°F) but the growing season is from 200–210 days and rainfall is between 500 m to 700 m, falling mostly in summer. Much of the forest cover of this area was cut over long ago, and the hills are badly eroded. Agriculture is very diversified. The main grain crop is corn but the production of peanuts and soy beans for oil, and cotton (on the west coast) are important crops, and vegetables are grown near the cities. Fruit growing is extremely important and most of China's apple production comes from this area.

Ta-lien (Dairen) is the area's main city. It is a modern city, built by the Russians as an ice-free port and naval base at the end of the 19th century, and later developed by the Japanese into the main port for Manchuria and into a major industrial city. It has continued to grow, and the municipality (which includes the neighbouring port and naval base of Lü-shun) had a population of one and a half million in 1958. It has a steel plant and extensive engineering industries – ship-building, locomotives and railway rolling-stock, diesel and electric motors and machine tools. There is a large chemical industry with both fertiliser and industrial chemical plants, and a major oil refinery, processing crude oil from the Ta-ch'ing field in Heilungkiang. Ta-lien has a large canning industry, and textile mills.

The South-eastern highlands lie east of Shen-yang and north of the Liao-tung peninsula. This is a highland area gradually rising to the complex mountains of the southern Chang-pai-shan range. The mountainous areas close to the Korean and Kirin borders are still little settled and have large areas of natural forest. The area has a good rainfall (up to 1,000 mm), but a rather short growing season of about 180 days. Agriculture concentrates on the production of corn, millet and kaoliang. Soy beans and tobacco are also widely grown, especially around Feng-ch'eng.

Pen-ch'i at the western edge of this district is a major industrial city with a steel industry now some 50 years old. It has local supplies of coal and phospherous-free iron ore from Miao-erh-kou and Wai-t'ou-shan. It produces large quantities of pig-iron and high grade steels. Pen-ch'i also has a large cement industry.

Tan-tung, situated on the estuary of the Ya-lu river on the Korean border, began to develop after 1907, when a railway was built from Shenyang to P'yong-yang. It is the natural commercial centre for the eastern part of this area. Its main industries are textiles, mainly tussah silk weaving and rayon, and paper-making.

Shui-feng further up the Ya-lu river, has a very large hydro-electric plant built under the Japanese in 1941, which supplies both Korea and the Manchurian power system. Construction of another major scheme at Huan-jen, begun in the late 1950s, appears never to have been completed.

The An-shan–Ying-k'ou plain This area comprises the lower reaches of the Hun Ho and Liao Ho rivers. It is a very productive agricultural area growing corn, kaoliang, rice, soy beans, vegetables and cotton.

Liao-yang is the ancient centre of this area, a historic administrative city which plays an important commercial role as the market centre for local agriculture, and large textile and food-processing industries.

An-shan, nearby, is a creation of modern industrialisation. It is China's main iron and steel producer. The steel industry was established by the Japanese in 1917, and by 1945 had been developed into a major iron and steel complex. It now produces some six million tons of steel ingot annually. The installations were dismantled by the Soviet occupying forces in 1945, but An-shan's steel industry was reconstructed and re-equipped from 1949 onwards, to the point where it could play a major role in industrial growth under the First Five Year Plan (1953–8). During this period the smelting and steel-making plants were greatly expanded, and a wide variety of finished products were produced. Additional iron mines were built. Since the late 1950s An-shan's total dominance of the Chinese iron and steel industry has been reduced, but it is still by far the greatest centre of the industry.

Ying-k'ou at the mouth of the Liao Ho was the chief port for Manchurian trade until the rise of Ta-lien. It remains a minor port and industrial city with a machine-tool industry, food-processing and canning, textile and paper manufactures. It is also the commercial centre for the lower Liao valley, where much reclamation has been carried out in recent years.

The Shen-yang–Fu-shun plain This central plain is a low undulating area, with many poorly drained sections. It is intensively cultivated, although it has a short growing season of 170–180 days. Corn, millet, rice, kaoliang and soy beans are the main crops. Peanuts, cotton, tobacco and sugarbeet are also important. The land is naturally fertile and the degree of mechanisation of agriculture higher than in most parts of China. But cultivation is not intensive by the standards of other provinces. Liaoning is a grain-deficit area, importing grain from northern Manchuria to feed its cities.

Shen-yang (Mukden) is the provincial capital and Liaoning's largest city, with an estimated population of 3,000,000. An ancient city, it was the capital of the Manchus before their conquest of China, and remained an important administrative and commercial centre. Under the Japanese, Shen-yang became the political and economic centre of southern Manchuria. Its population rose from 420,000 in 1931 to 1,890,000 by 1945, and it had already become a major industrial city. Industrial growth has continued since the beginning of the Communist regime. Shen-yang has become a major centre of the engineering industry, supplied with steel from An-shan and Pen-ch'i. It produces heavy machinery and industrial equipment, machine tools, electrical equipment, tractors and aircraft. There are major smelteries for copper, zinc and lead. It also produces agricultural machinery, vehicle tyres, textiles and glass. There is a very large chemical industry, producing pharmaceuticals and industrial chemicals. It remains a major administrative and cultural centre, with a variety of institutions for higher education and research.

Fu-shun, to the north-east, is a major coal producing city, where mines were first opened in 1902. There are enormous reserves of coal, and production was already 10,000,000 tons per annum under the Japanese in 1944. Since 1949 it has increased still further, and is now estimated at between 15,000,000 and 20,000,000 tons annually. Fu-shun has an oil-shale industry, also developed under the Japanese after 1929, and a petro-chemical complex. It has copper mines, and is a major producer of aluminium, another industry dating from the Japanese occupation. It produces cement, rubber (synthetic) and fertiliser. There is an engineering industry which specialises in heavy plant and machinery, and a very large power plant. The population of the city is now estimated at over a million.

The western plain and coastal area This area is a plain similar to that of the An-shan region, rising to the broken, hilly country behind the coastal strip from Shan-hai-kuan to Chin-chou and thence to the Mongolian plateau. Much of this area has scattered woodland. The main crops are corn, kaoliang, millet and rice, with a good deal of cotton. There is also some fruit growing, especially of pears and apples.

Chin-chou is the main centre of this region, an important rail junction and an ancient administrative centre. It was built into an industrial area by the Japanese, closely connected with Chin-hsi and the port of Hu-lu-tao to the south. Under the Japanese a variety of industries were established, using coal from the rich field nearby in Fu-hsin. Under the Communist regime Chin-chou has developed a diversified electronic industry.

Chin-hsi on the coast to the south has a large oil refinery. A synthetic petroleum plant, using Fu-hsin coal, was built here by the Japanese, and Chin-hsi has since been developed into a major chemical producing area. It also has a cement industry.

Fu-hsin was developed as a coalfield later than Fu-shun – large-scale mining began in 1937. Under the Communist regime very large strip mines have been opened, and Fu-hsin is estimated to be producing from 15,000,000 to 20,000,000 tons annually. Most of this is used in power-generating plants.

The western plateau This area of rolling grasslands is really a part of the Inner Mongolian Plateau, and still has a considerable Mongol ethnic minority totalling some 350,000 people, in the west. An area of rather low rainfall, it is on the border between the agrarian and pastoral zones.

Ch'ih-feng is the main centre, situated in a large basin of culivated land. At the end of a railway line, it acts as the collecting and market centre for the area.

See also notes on page 21.

AREA
230,000 square kilometres

POPULATION
29,500,000

continuation on page 23

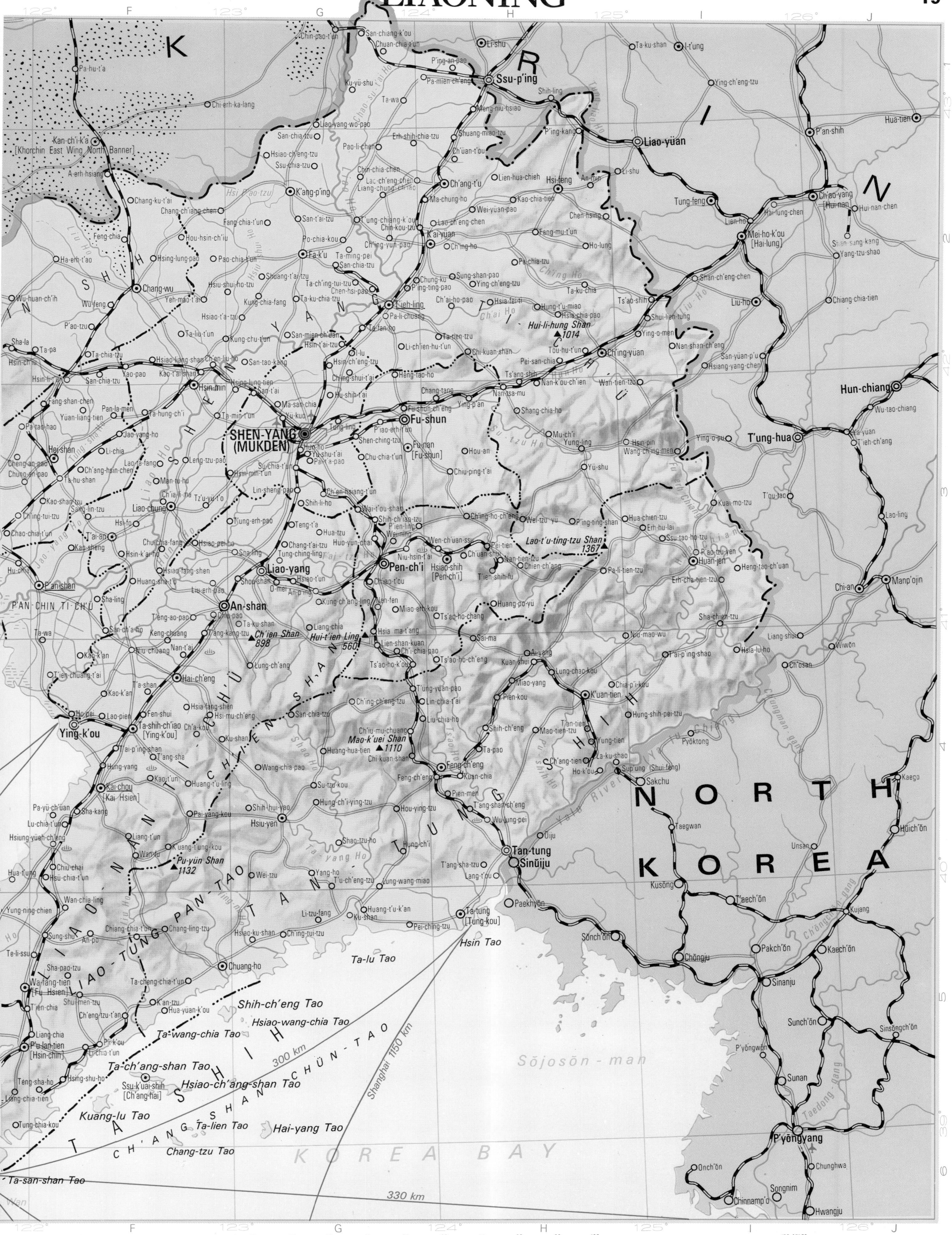

1:1540000

0 5 10 20 30 40 50 60 70 80 90 100 150 MILES

0 5 10 20 30 40 50 60 70 80 90 100 150 200 KM

LIAONING PROVINCE 辽宁省
LIAO-NING SHENG

11 shih	*municipalities*
1 meng	*league*
5 ti-ch'ü	*regions*
44 hsien	*counties*
2 tzu-chih-hsien	*autonomous counties*
7 ch'i	*banners*

capital **Shen-yang Shih**	G3	沈阳市
An-shan Shih	F3	鞍山市
Ch'ih-feng Shih	B2	赤峰市

Fu-hsin Shih	E2	阜新市
Chang-wu Hsien	F2	彰武县
Fu-hsin Meng-ku-tsu Tzu-chih-hsien		阜新蒙古族自治县
Fu-hsin Mongol Autonomous Hsien		
centre: Fu-hsin-chen	E2	阜新镇

Fu-shun Shih	G3	抚顺市
Fu-shun Hsien		抚顺县
centre: Fu-nan	G3	抚南
Liao-yang Shih	G3	辽阳市

Lü-ta Shih	E6	旅大市
Ch'ang-hai Hsien		长海县
centre: Ssu-k'uai-shih	F5	四块石

Pen-ch'i Shih	G3	本溪市
Pen-ch'i Hsien		本溪县
centre: Hsiao-shih	H3	小市

Tan-tung Shih	H4	丹东市
Chuang-ho Hsien	F5	庄河县
Feng-ch'eng Hsien	H4	凤城县
Hsiu-yen Hsien	G4	岫岩县
Huan-jen Hsien	I3	桓仁县
K'uan-tien Hsien	H4	宽甸县
Tung-kou Hsien		东沟县
centre: Ta-tung	H5	大东
Ying-k'ou Shih	F4	营口市

Chao-wu-ta Meng		昭乌达盟
centre: Ch'ih-feng	B2	赤峰
A-lu-k'o-erh-ch'in Ch'i		阿鲁科尔沁旗
Aru-Khorchin Banner		
centre: T'ien-shan	D6	天山
Ao-han Ch'i		敖汉旗
centre: Hsin-hui	C2	新惠
Ch'ih-feng Hsien	B2	赤峰县
K'a-la-ch'in Ch'i		喀喇沁旗
Kharachin Banner		
centre: Chin-shan-chen	B3	锦山镇
K'o-shih-k'o-t'eng Ch'i		克什克腾旗
centre: Ching-feng	A1	景峰
Lin-hsi Hsien	A1	林西县
Ning-ch'eng Hsien		宁城县
centre: T'ien-i	C3	天义
Pa-lin Tso-ch'i		巴林左旗
Bairin East Banner		
centre: Lin-tung	C6	林东
Pa-lin Yu-ch'i		巴林右旗
Bairin West Banner		
centre: Ta-pan	B1	大板
Weng-niu-t'e Ch'i		翁牛特旗
centre: Wu-tan	B2	乌丹

Ch'ao-yang Ti-ch'ü		朝阳地区
Ch'ao-yang Hsien	D3	朝阳县
Chien-ch'ang Hsien	C4	建昌县
Chien-p'ing Hsien		建平县
centre: Yeh-pai-shou	C3	叶柏寿
K'a-la-ch'in Tso-i Meng-ku-tsu Tzu-chih-hsien		喀喇沁左翼蒙古族自治县
Kharachin East Wing Mongol Autonomous Hsien		
centre: Ta-ch'eng-tzu	C3	大城子
Ling-yüan Hsien	C3	凌源县
Pei-p'iao Hsien	D3	北票县

Chin-chou Ti-ch'ü		锦州地区
Chin-hsi Hsien	D4	锦西县
Chin Hsien		锦县
centre: Ta-ling-ho	E3	大凌河
Hei-shan Hsien	F3	黑山县
Hsing-ch'eng Hsien	D4	兴城县
I Hsien		义县
centre: I-hsien	E3	
Pei-chen Hsien	E3	北镇县
Sui-chung Hsien	D4	绥中县

Liao-nan Ti-ch'ü		辽南地区
centre: Kai-chou	F4	盖州
Chin Hsien		金县
centre: Chin-hsien	E5	
Fu Hsien		复县
centre: Wa-fang-tien	E5	瓦房店
Hai-ch'eng Hsien	F4	海城县
Hsin-chin Hsien		新金县
centre: P'u-lan-tien	E5	普兰店
Kai Hsien		盖县
centre: Kai-chou	F4	盖州
Liao-yang Hsien	G3	辽阳县
Ying-k'ou Hsien		营口县
centre: Ta-shih-ch'iao	F4	大石桥

P'an-chin Ti-ch'ü		盘锦地区
centre: P'an-shan	F3	盘山
P'an-shan Hsien	F3	盘山县

Shen-yang Ti-ch'ü		沈阳地区
centre: T'ieh-ling		
Ch'ang-t'u Hsien	H2	昌图县
Ch'ing-yüan Hsien	H2	清原县
Fa-k'u Hsien	G2	法库县
Hsi-feng Hsien	H2	西丰县
Hsin-min Hsien	F3	新民县
Hsin-pin Hsien	I3	新宾县
K'ai-yüan Hsien	H2	开原县
K'ang-p'ing Hsien	G2	康平县
Liao-chung Hsien	F3	辽中县
T'ai-an Hsien	F3	台安县
T'ieh-ling Hsien	G2	铁岭县

WEST
HEILUNGKIANG, KIRIN, LIAONING
PROVINCES

THESE areas no longer constitute an administrative unity. Until 1969 the whole region formed a part of the Inner Mongolia Autonomous Region. The western part of Heilungkiang and the north-west of Kirin formed the Mongolian Hu-lun-pei-erh League, south-western Kirin the Che-li-mu (Jerim) League, and western Liaoning the Chao-wu-ta (Jo-uda) League, all of which were areas with a predominantly Mongol population. These areas seem to have been detached from Inner Mongolia largely because of the difficulties of administering the former provincial territories, which had no developed system of lateral communications.

The region comprises the north-south range of mountains known as the Great Khingan Range (Ta Hsing-an Shan-mo), which forms the western border of the Manchurian Central Plain, and the Mongolian plateau beyond. The northern part of this area drains either into the Argun, and thence into the Amur river, or into the interior drainage basins of Bayr Nur (on the Mongolian border) or Hu-lun Ch'ih (Hulunbuir) lake. The latter sometimes discharges into the Argun. The Khingan range is broadest and most complex in the north, where most of the peaks are between 1,000 m and 1,300 m. Towards the south in Kirin and Liaoning they are narrower and occasional higher peaks reach 1,700 m to 2,000 m. In general the ranges have comparatively sharp eastern escarpments, with more gentle slopes westwards into the Mongolian plateau. The land forms are mostly rounded. The mountains in Heilungkiang are still densely forested, particularly on the wetter eastern face, where rainfall is above 500 mm per annum. To the west the climate becomes progressively drier, and forest is replaced by steppe grassland. The forest cover on the southern mountains, which have a lower rainfall, is sparser and has been extensively cut.

The climatic regime of the whole area is harsh. Average winter temperatures are as low as −22°C to −30°C (−7°F to −22°F), and for some six months of the year average temperatures are below freezing. The growing season lasts only about 160 days, and some areas have permafrost in the subsoil. Summers are hot, averaging above 20°C (68°F), except in the north of the Hsing-an mountains.

This whole area has so far been little settled by Chinese farmers. Only in the east of the region has there been any considerable development of agriculture, and even here in most cases Chinese agriculture, cultivation of mainly corn, kaoliang, soy beans, spring wheat, millet and sugar beet, exists side by side with pastoral industry. In the west, where the rainfall is mostly below 300 mm, agriculture gives way entirely to pasture, the only areas of cultivated farmland being along the railway line near Man-chou-li and Hai-la-erh. In the pasturelands surrounding this region dairy-farming is also well-developed.

Chinese settlement has largely been confined to the railway zone in Heilungkiang, and the eastern foothills. The western pasturelands of the plateau are largely inhabited by Mongols. The remote forests of the northern Hsing-an mountains are inhabited predominantly by Tungusic forest tribes, the Evenki and the Oronchon, who subsist on forestry and hunting.

There is no major industry in the area. *Man-chou-li*, the border town on the old Chinese Eastern Railway, has a variety of minor industries, and nearby coal mines produce soft coal. *Hai-la-erh* is the market centre for the agricultural and dairy region west of the Hsing-an range, and has food processing, chemical and wood-working industries. *Pai-ch'eng*, in the Kirin plain, acts as the main collecting centre for the central area, as it is the terminus of a railway to Hu-lan-hao-t'e, and beyond the Hsing-an range to I-erh-shih near the Mongolian border.

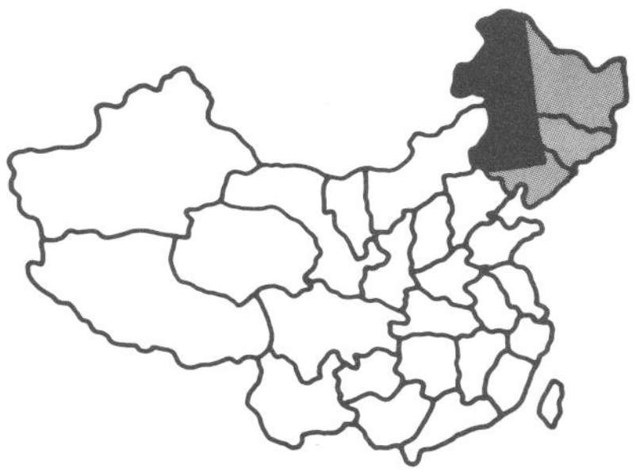

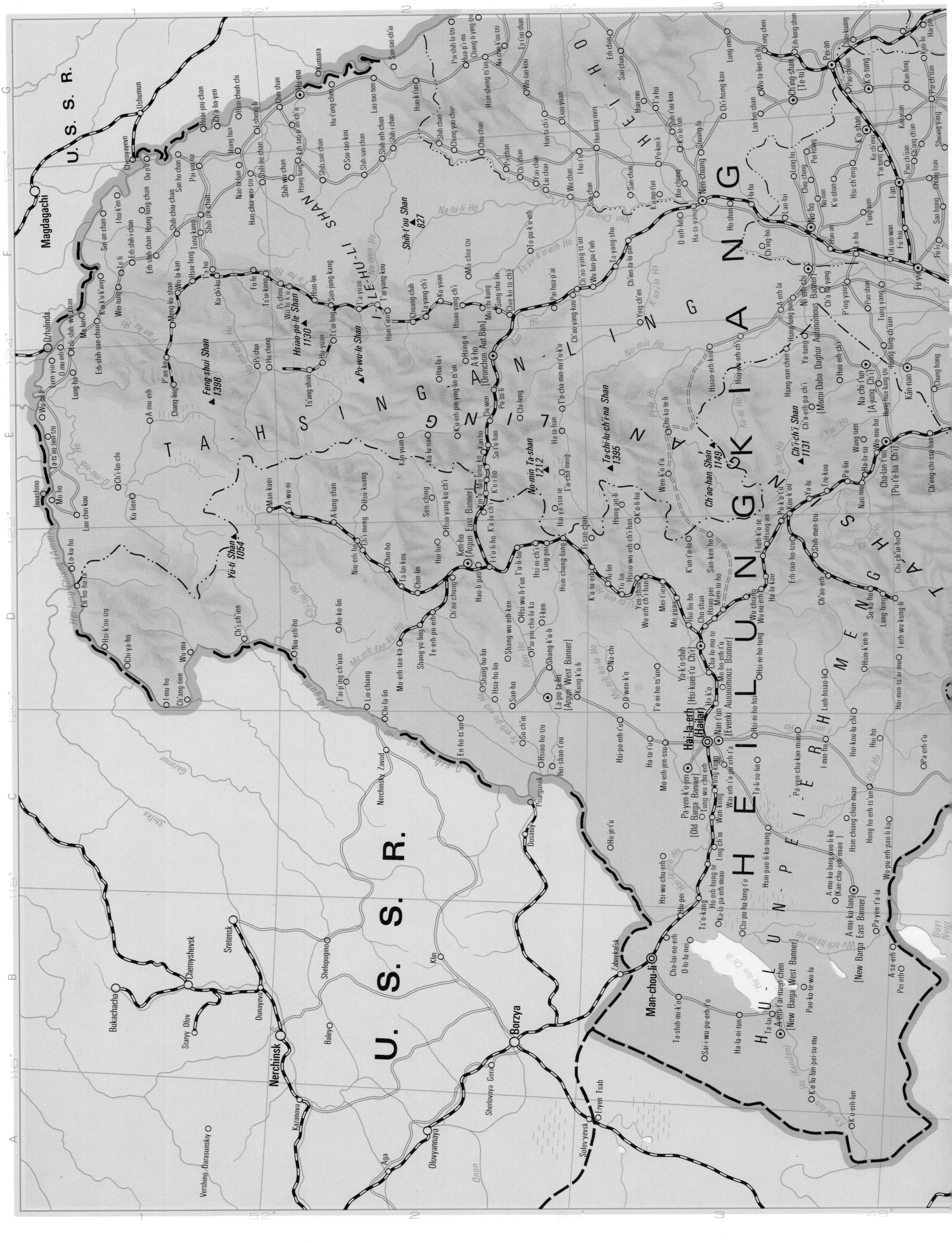
U. S. S. R.
U. S. S. R.
Magdagachi
Ushumun
Chernyayevo
Dzhalinda
Kumara
Hu-ma
Amur
TA HSING AN LING
I LE HU LI SHAN
HEILUNGKIANG
HU-LUN-PEI-ERH MENG
Feng-shui Shan 1398
Yi-ti Shan 1054
Hsiao-po-le Shan 1130
Po-wu-le Shan
Shih-t'ou Shan 827
No-min Ta-shan 1212
Ta-chi-lu-ch'i-na Shan 1395
Ch'ao-han Shan 1149
Ch'i-ch'i Shan 1131
Ken-ho [Argun East Banner]
La-pu-ta-lin [Argun West Banner]
A-li-ho [Oronchon Aut. Banner]
Na-chi-t'un [A-jung Ch'i]
Chan-lan-t'un [Pu-t'e-ha Ch'i]
[Morin-Daba Daghor Autonomous Banner]
Ya-k'o-shih [Hsi-kuei-t'u Ch'i]
[Evenki Autonomous Banner]
Hai-la-erh (Hailar)
Pa-yen-k'u-jen [Old Barga Banner]
A-mu-ku-lang [New Barga East Banner]
[New Barga West Banner]
Man-chou-li
Zabaykalsk
Priargunsk
Nen-chiang
Pei-an
Nerchinsk
Sretensk
Chernyshevsk
Bukachacha
Borzya
Olovyannaya
Solov'yevsk
Nerchinskiy Zavod
Kazanova
Aga
Onon
Shilka
Gazimur

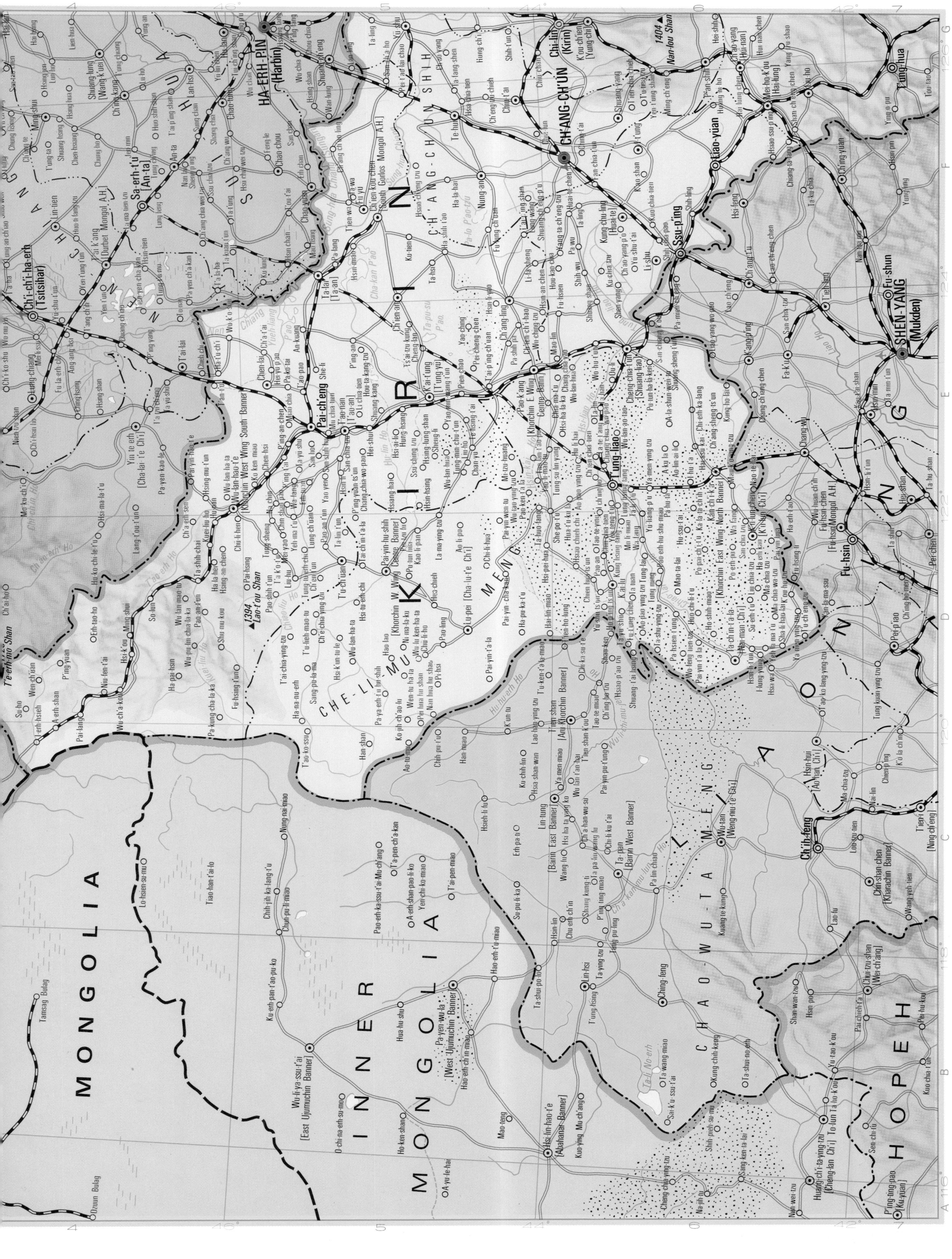
MONGOLIA
INNER MONGOLIA
KIRIN
LIAONING
HOPEH
HA-ERH-PIN (Harbin)
CH'ANG-CH'UN
SHEN-YANG (Mukden)
Ch'i-ch'i-ha-erh (Tsitsihar)
Chi-lin (Kirin)
Ssu-p'ing
T'ung-liao
Pai-ch'eng
Fu-hsin
Fu-shun
Ch'ih-feng
CHE-LI-MU MENG
CHAO-WU-TA MENG
1 : 2600000

Administrative summaries for
the provinces of Heilungkiang, Kirin
and Liaoning can be found on
the following pages:

HEILUNGKIANG
12

KIRIN
16

LIAONING
20

INNER MONGOLIA
AUTONOMOUS REGION

THIS area, though not politically separate, was traditionally beyond the frontiers of China. Its southern frontier is a major natural frontier, beyond which the climate is too harsh and too arid to support Chinese agriculture. It was therefore left in the hands of nomadic Mongolian herdsmen, and until this century Chinese settlement was confined to border trading towns, and a few irrigated areas in the valley of the Huang Ho and the plain between Pao-t'ou and Hu-ho-hao-t'e. Later the pressure of Chinese over-population, and the building of a railway from Peking to Chang-chia-k'ou (Kalgan), Ta-t'ung and Pao-t'ou between 1905 and 1923, brought an influx of Chinese settlers, who attempted to convert the border pasturelands into farmland. The efforts were often disastrous, destroying the natural grass cover, and leading to erosion and soil depletion.

Mongol independence movements began in the early years of this century. The claims of the Mongol population for some measure of autonomy were first recognised by the Japanese puppet state of Manchukuo in 1932, and later, when the Japanese occupied northern China, a Japanese-sponsored Mongol Autonomous Government was set up in what is now the Inner Mongolian Autonomous Region under the Mongol prince Te-wang. In 1945 the Communists, who had already liberated some of the area, were placed in control of Inner Mongolia by the Soviet and Mongolian armies which had occupied it. In 1947 the Communist regime set up the Inner Mongolian Autonomous Region, with its capital at Wang-ye-miao (Ulan-hoto). From 1949 to 1956 its borders were successively extended, until in 1956 it comprised the entire Mongol-peopled frontier area from the Amur river in Heilungkiang to the borders of Sinkiang. At the same time its capital was moved first to Chang-chia-k'ou in 1950, and then in 1952 to Kuei-sui, renamed Hu-ho-hao-t'e in 1954.

This region, established in accord with current views on the autonomy of national minority peoples, was never unified by any system of transport, and its constituent areas developed independently. In 1969, possibly for defence as well as for administrative reasons, the Autonomous Region was divided: the north-eastern areas were placed under the three Manchurian provinces, while the western areas were placed under Ningsia and Kansu. In the whole of this area, the Mongol population remains a small minority, although they occupy the vast bulk of its territory. In the Autonomous Region, at its fullest extent before 1969, there were slightly less than a million Mongols, out of a total population estimated at 13 million. In the reduced area of today there are estimated to be some 600,000 Mongols out of a total of 9 million.

Inner Mongolia comprises a number of different environmental regions, all of which share an extremely harsh continental climate. The winters are long and extremely cold. Average January temperatures range from −6°C (21°F) in the Ordos to −22°C (−8°F) in the north, and the winter is made even more harsh by continuous, violent north-westerly winds, bringing dust-storms from the Gobi. Rainfall is very low, ranging from 300 mm in the south-east to 100 mm and below in the north, and comes almost entirely in summer, when temperatures are high (20°C–22°C; 68°F–72°F). Drought is common.

The Inner Mongolian Plateau Bounded on the south by the uplands of the Yin-shan ranges, the northern plateau is about 1,000 m above sea level, and is an area of interior drainage, the few rivers flowing north into the borders of the Gobi, or into small saline lakes such as the K'u-lo-ch'a-kan No-erh and Ta-erh Po. This rolling plain is covered with natural grassland, rich in the east of the province and becoming poorer and more arid towards the north and the west. This is the most important area in China for the production of animal products. The pastoral industry is almost entirely in the hands of the Mongols, whose herds include horses, sheep, cattle and camels. In the main pasturelands the flocks and herds are kept in open grazing areas assigned to one or other of the tribal 'banner' groups. In the areas nearer the Chinese border the Mongol population has become semi-sedentary, and engages in some farming. In the 1950s there were estimated to be over 20,000,000 head of livestock in the area.

Trade from this region traditionally passed through border market cities such as To-lun, Chang-chia-k'ou, Chi-ning, and Hu-ho-hao-t'e, in the Chinese border area. Much of the transport of the area still uses animals, but some motor roads have been constructed. After 1955, too, the plateau was crossed by a railway, extending to Ulan Bator and the Soviet Union. This line joins the Peking-Pao-t'ou railway at Chi-ning and crosses the border at Erh-lien Hao-t'e, which has become a minor local centre of trade and minor industry. The discovery of oil in this area was reported recently.

The Yin-shan mountains The southern border of the plateau is marked by the long ridge of mountains, some 1,500 m high with occasional peaks up to 2,100 m, which extends eastwards from the Lang Shan range to the north of the great bend of the Huang Ho. In the east a second range, the Ta-ch'ing Shan, runs parallel to the south of the Yin-shan itself. The most important resources of this area are minerals.

Pai-yün-o-po some 120 km north of Pao-t'ou, to which it was linked by rail in 1959, is one of China's main sources of high grade iron ore. This is used in the huge iron and steel complex at Pao-t'ou.

Shui-mo-tan (Shih-kuai-kou), 30 km north-east of Pao-t'ou in the Ta-ch'ing range, is the centre of an important coalfield, producing 1,500,000 tons annually. The first mines went into production in 1957.

Mica and asbestos are also produced in this area.

The Ho-tao plain and Pao-t'ou – Hu-ho-hao-t'e plains These two plains form the main centre of agricultural production, and contain a large proportion of the total population. The Ho-tao plain is an extensive alluvial plain north of the Huang Ho, 160 km long and 60 km wide. A dense irrigation system was established here about a century ago. In the western plain, stretching from Pao-t'ou to the valley of the Ta-hei-ho around Hu-ho-hao-t'e, the irrigation system, based on the Min-sheng canal, is more recent, dating from 1918, and much extended under the Communist regime. These areas of irrigated agriculture fall within the spring wheat area. Some hardy rice is grown around Pao-t'ou and Wu-yuan, but wheat and kaoliang are the main foodcrops. Oats and millet are grown on marginal lands. The main cash crops are soy beans, hemp, rape-seed, tobacco, and various medicinal plants such as licorice. In the western area, livestock are also important. Sugar beet is a major crop. These plains are an old east-west route, where a railway was constructed which reached Pao-t'ou in 1923, and extended westward to Ningsia and Kansu in 1958. On this route lie all the province's main cities.

Chi-ning is an important rail junction and commercial centre for the east of the frontier area.

Hu-ho-hao-t'e, the provincial capital and a city of 320,000 in 1957, is an old-established Chinese trading and frontier administrative centre, formerly known as Kuei-sui. During the 1950s it also began to develop industrially. It has chemical and fertiliser plants, a diesel engine factory dating from 1966, and a large sugar-refining industry, using local sugar beet.

Pao-t'ou was also an old frontier trading city. During the Japanese occupation plans were made to build an iron works here, using local coal and iron ore, and in the 1950s it was rapidly built into a major industrial city, according to the general policy of relocating heavy industry in the interior. Using coal from nearby Shui-mo-tan, from Shih-tsui-shan in Ningsia, and from the mines of Wu-ta and Hai-po-wan on the Huang Ho in the extreme south-west of the region, and iron from Pai-yün-o-po, a large generating plant and the first blast furnaces began operation in 1958–9. Development was held up after the failure of the Great Leap Forward, but resumed in the late 1960s, when new blast furnaces and rail and girder rolling mills were installed. Pao-t'ou ranks after An-shan, Wu-han and Shanghai as one of China's largest steel producers. Annual production is estimated at 1,700,000 tons of pig iron, 2,000,000 tons of steel ingot, and 1,100,000 tons of finished steel. Pao-t'ou has also become an important producer of aluminium, chemicals, fertiliser, and cement. There is some engineering, food-processing – especially sugar refining – and textiles. The population of Pao-t'ou increased almost five times in the years between 1953 and 1958, from 150,000 to 700,000.

Teng-k'ou is the commercial centre of the western Ho-tao plain.

Wu-ta and *Hai-po-wan* are twin coal-mining centres, producing more than a million tons annually.

The O-erh-to-ssu (Ordos) Region The region south of the Huang Ho is occupied by the Ordos plateau, an area forming the northern section of the Shensi plateau. The area is bounded to the south and south-east by the old Great Wall, which is roughly the boundary beyond which permanent agriculture is impracticable. The Ordos is an area of very poor grassland merging into large tracts of stony desert and sand dunes. It is sparsely people by Mongol herdsmen. The desert has tended to spread south-eastwards, and in the early 1960s a belt of hardy trees was planted along the line of the wall and other measures taken to prevent the southward shifting of sand dunes.

AREA
450,000 square kilometres

POPULATION
9,000,000

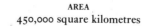

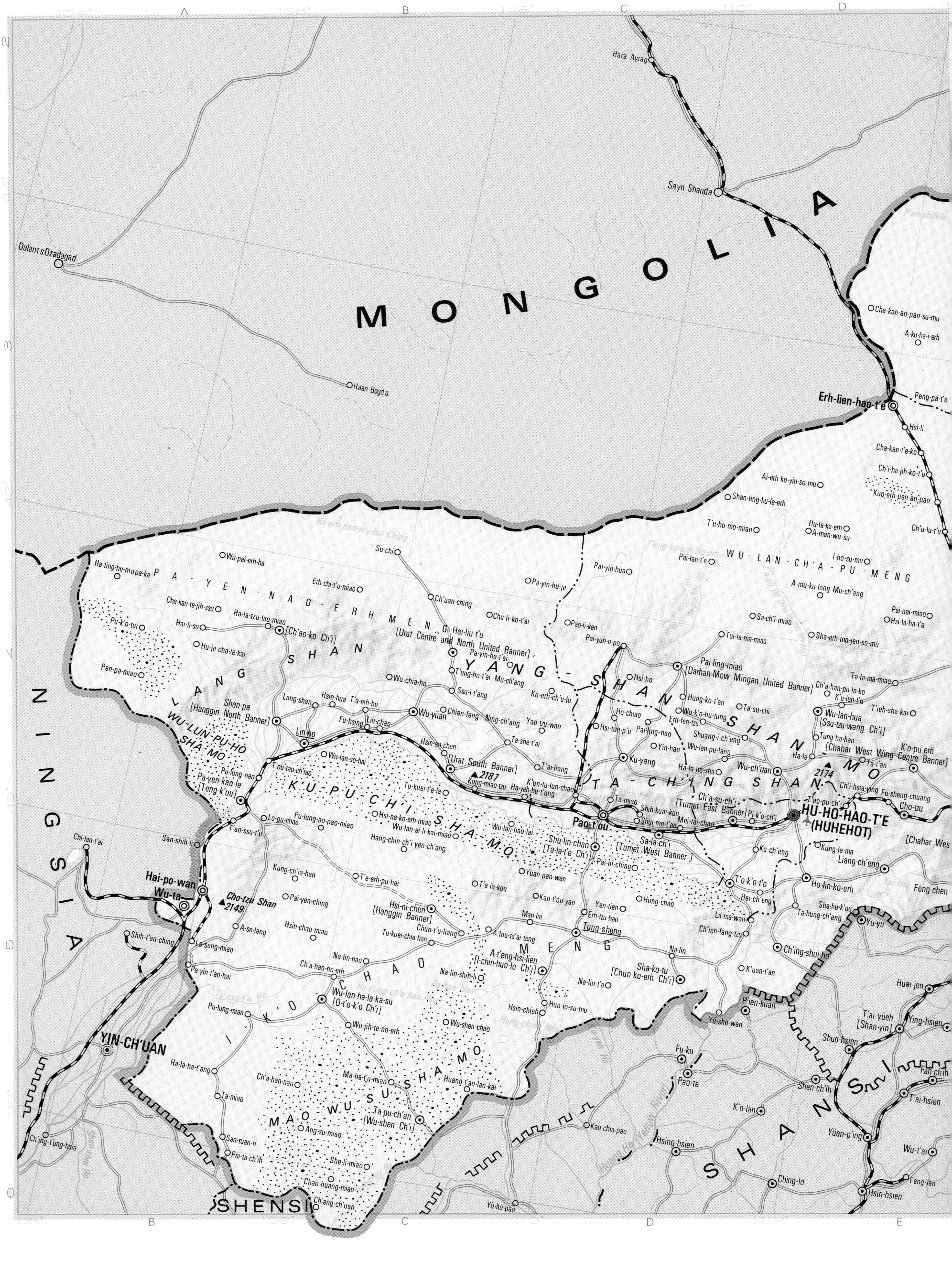
MONGOLIA
Hara Ayrag
Sayn Shanda
Dalant s Dzadagad
Haan Bogd o
Erh-lien-hao-t'e
Cha-kan-ao-pao-su-mu
A-ku-ha-i-erh
Peng-pa-t'e
Hsi-li
Cha-kan-t'e-ko
Ch'i-ha-jih-ko-t'u
Ai-erh-ko-yin-so-mu
Shan-ting-hu-la-erh
Kuo-erh-pen-ao-pao
T'u-ho-mo-miao
Hu-la-ka-erh
A-man-wu-su
Ch'u-lu-t'u
Ku-erh-pan-wu-lan Ching
Su-chi
T'eng-ko-erh No-erh
Pai-lan-t'e
WU-LAN-CH'A-PU MENG
I-ho-su-mu
Pai-yin-hua
A-mu-ku-lang Mu-ch'ang
Ha-ting-hu-mo-pa-ka
Wu-pai-erh-ha
PA-YEN-NAO-ERH MENG
Erh-chi-t'u-miao
Pa-yin-hu-je
Cha-kan-te-jih-ssu
Ch'uan-ching
Ha-la-tzu-lao-miao
Hai-li-su
Chu-li-ko-t'ai
Pao-li-ken
Sa-ch'i-miao
Pai-nai-miao
Hsi-la-ha-t'a
Pu-k'o-tui
Ch'ao-ko Ch'i
Hai-liu-t'u
[Urat Centre and North United Banner]
Pai-yün-o-po
Tui-la-ma-miao
Sha-erh-mo-jen-so-mu
Hu-je-cha-te-kai
SHAN
Pa-yin-ha-t'ai
T'ung-ho-t'ai Mu-ch'ang
YANG-SHAN
Pai-ling-miao
[Darhan-Mow Mingan United Banner]
Ta-la-ma-miao
Pen-pa-miao
LANG SHAN
Hsi-ho
Wu-chia-ho
Ssu-i-t'ang
Ko-erh-ch'u-lu
Hung-ko-t'an
Ch'a-han-pu-le-ko
K'u-lun-t'u
Shan-pa
[Hanggin North Banner]
Lang-shan
Hsin-hua
T'a-erh-hu
Wu-yüan
Chien-feng
Ning-ch'ang
Ho-chiao
Wu-k'o-hu-tung
Ta-su-chi
Wu-lan-hua
[Ssu-tzu-wang Ch'i]
T'ieh-sha-kai
WU-LUN-PU-HO SHA-MO
Fu-hsing
Liu-chao
Yao-tzu-wan
Hsi-tou-p'u
Pai-ling-nao
Erh-fen-tzu
Shuang-i-ch'eng
Tung-ha-hao
[Chahar West Wing Centre Banner]
K'o-pu-erh
Lin-ho
Hsin-an-chen
Ta-she-t'ai
Yin-hao
Wu-lan-pu-lang
Ha-le
T'a-t'an
Wu-lan-so-hai
[Urat South Banner]
Ku-yang
Ha-la-ho-sha
Wu-ch'uan
2174
Pu-lung-nao
T'ou-tao-ch'iao
2187
T'ai-liang
TA-CH'ING SHAN
MO
Ch'i-hsia-ying
Fu-sheng-chuang
Pa-yen-kao-le
[Teng-k'ou]
KU-PU-CHI SHA-MO
Tu-kuei-t'e-la
Kung-miao-tzu
Ha-yeh-hu-t'ung
K'un-tu-lun-chao
Ta-miao
Shih-kuai-kou
Ch'a-su-ch'i
[Tumet East Banner]
T'ao-pu-ch'i
Cho-tzu
Lo-pu-chao
Pu-lung-ao-pao-miao
Hsi-na-ko-erh-miao
Wu-lan-ai-li-kai-miao
Wu-lan-hao-lai
Pao-t'ou
Shui-mo-t'an
Mei-tai-chao
Pi-k'o-ch'i
HU-HO-HAO-T'E
(HUHEHOT)
T'ao-ssu-t'u
Chi-lan-t'ai
San-shih-li
Hang-chin-ch'i-yen-ch'ang
Shu-lin-chao
[Ta-la-t'e Ch'i]
Sa-la-ch'i
[Tumet West Banner]
Ku-ch'eng
Kung-la-ma
[Chahar Wes
Liang-ch'eng
Huang Ho (Yellow River)
Kung-ch'ia-han
Pai-ni-ching
Yuan-pao-wan
T'o-k'o-t'o
Ho-lin-ko-erh
Tai Hai
Feng-chen
Hai-po-wan
Wu-ta
Cho-tzu Shan
2149
T'e-erh-pu-hai
T'a-la-kou
Pai-yen-ching
Kao-t'ou-yao
Hung-chao
Hei-ch'eng
Sha-hu-k'ou
Ta-hung-ch'eng
Yu-yu
Hsi-ni-chen
[Hanggin Banner]
Yen-tien
Erh-tzu-hao
La-ma-wan
Shih-t'an-ching
A-se-lang
Hsin-chao-miao
Ch'ün-t'u-liang
Man-lai
A-lou-ts'ai-teng
Tung-sheng
Ch'ien-fang-tzu
La-seng-miao
Tu-kuei-chia-han
Na-lin
Ch'ing-shui-ho
Na-lin-nao
A-t'eng-hsi-lien
[I-chin-huo-lo Ch'i]
Sha-ko-tu
[Chun-ko-erh Ch'i]
K'uan-t'an
Pa-yin-t'ao-hai
Ch'a-han-no-erh
Na-lin-shih-li
Na-lin-t'a
I-K'O-CHAO MENG
Huai-jen
Tu-ssu-t'u Ho
Ho-t'ung-ch'a-han Nao
Pa-han Nao
Wu-lan-ha-la-ka-su
[O-t'o-k'o Ch'i]
Hsin-chieh
Huo-lo-su-mu
P'ien-kuan
T'ai-yüeh
[Shan-yin]
Ying-hsien
Pu-lung-miao
Wu-shen-chao
Hung-chien Nao
Yu-shu-wan
Shuo-hsien
YIN-CH'UAN
Wu-jih-te-no-erh
Fu-ku
Ha-la-ha-t'eng
Ma-ha-t'u-miao
Huang-t'ao-lao-kai
MAO-WU-SU SHA-MO
Pao-te
Shen-ch'ih
Fan-chih
Ch'a-han-nao
T'ai-hsien
Ta-miao
Ta-pu-ch'an
[Wu-shen Ch'i]
K'o-lan
Ang-su-miao
Kao-chia-pao
SHANSI
Ch'ing-t'ung-hsia
Shan-shui Ho
San-tuan-ti
Huang Ho (Yellow River)
Hsing-hsien
Yüan-p'ing
Wu-t'ai
Pei-ta-ch'ih
She-li-miao
Chao-huang-miao
Ching-lo
Fang-lan
Hsin-hsien
SHENSI
Ch'eng-ch'uan
Yü-ho-pao
NINGSIA

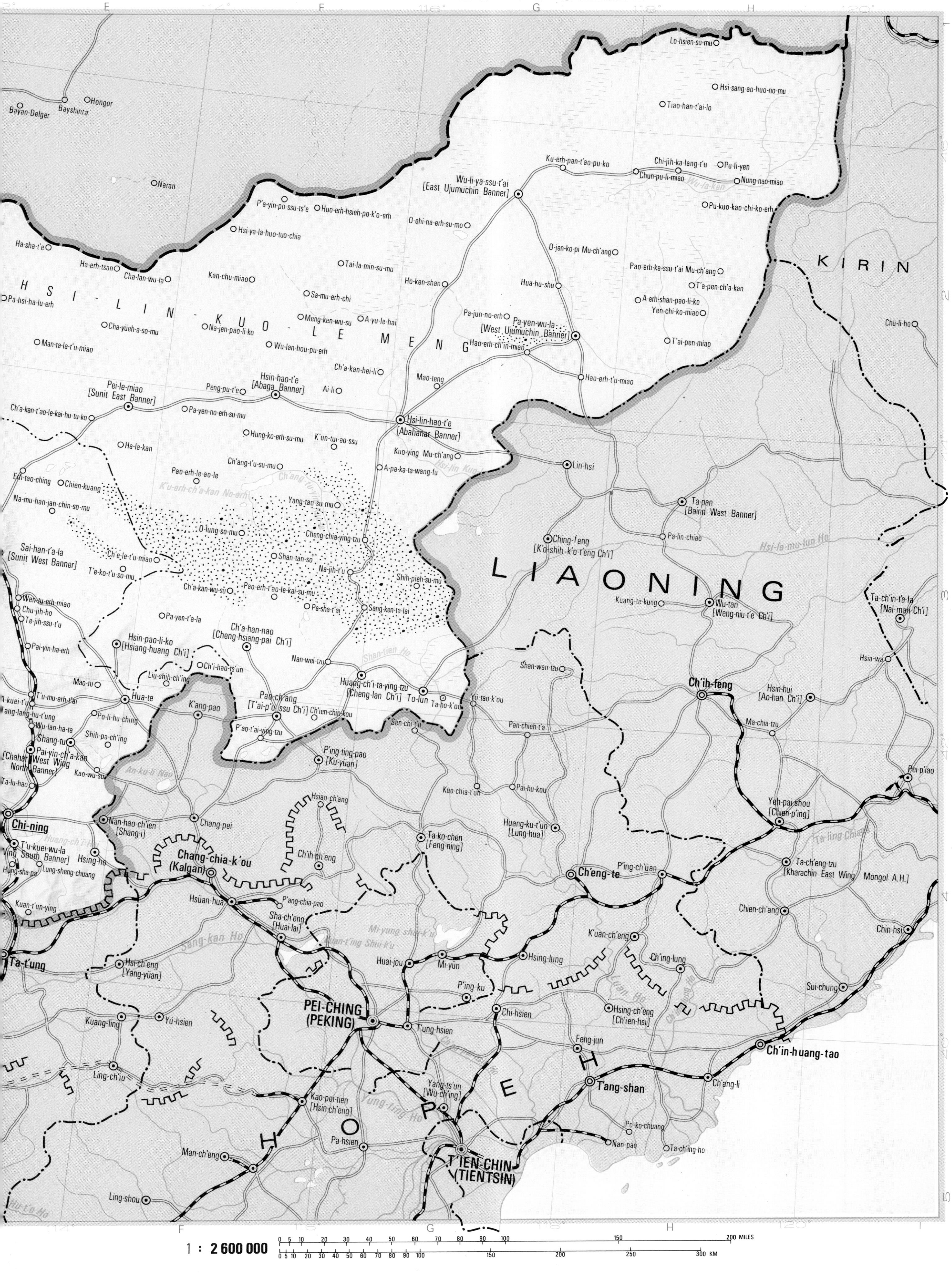
HSI-LIN-KUO-LE MENG
KIRIN
LIAONING
HOPEH
Lo-hsien-su-mu
Hsi-sang-ao-huo-no-mu
Tiao-han-t'ai-lo
Bayan-Delger
Bayshinta
Hongor
Naran
Ku-erh-pan-t'ao-pu-ko
Chi-jih-ka-lang-t'u
Pu-li-yen
Chun-pu-li-miao
Wu-la-ken
Nung-nao-miao
Pu-kuo-kao-chi-ko-erh
Wu-li-ya-ssu-t'ai
[East Ujumuchin Banner]
P'a-yin-po-ssu-ts'e
Huo-erh-hsieh-po-k'o-erh
O-ehi-na-erh-su-mo
Hsi-ya-la-huo-tuo-chia
Ha-sha-t'e
O-jen-ko-pi Mu-ch'ang
Ha-erh-tsan
Cha-lan-wu-la
Kan-chu-miao
Tai-la-min-su-mo
Pao-erh-ka-ssu-t'ai Mu-ch'ang
T'a-pen-ch'a-kan
Ho-ken-shan
Hua-hu-shu
A-erh-shan-pao-li-ko
Yen-chi-ko-miao
Pa-hsi-ha-lu-erh
Sa-mu-erh-chi
Meng-ken-wu-su
A-yu-le-hai
Pa-jun-no-erh
Pa-yen-wu-la
[West Ujumuchin Banner]
Cha-yüeh-a-so-mu
Na-jen-pao-li-ko
Hao-erh-ch'in-miao
T'ai-pen-miao
Chü-li-ho
Man-ta-la-t'u-miao
Wu-lan-hou-pu-erh
Ch'a-kan-hei-li
Mao-teng
Hao-erh-t'u-miao
Pei-le-miao
[Sunit East Banner]
Hsin-hao-t'e
[Abaga Banner]
Peng-pu-t'e
Ai-li
Ch'a-kan-t'ao-le-kai-hu-tu-ko
Pa-yen-no-erh-su-mu
Hsi-lin-hao-t'e
[Abahanar Banner]
Hung-ko-erh-su-mu
K'un-tui-ao-ssu
Ha-la-kan
Kuo-ying Mu-ch'ang
Hsi-lin Kuo-le
Lin-hsi
Ch'ang-t'u-su-mu
A-pa-ka-ta-wang-fu
Pao-erh-le-ao-le
Erh-tao-ching
Chien-kuang
K'u-erh-ch'a-kan No-erh
Ch'ang-tu-ying
Yang-tao-su-mu
Ta-pan
[Bairin West Banner]
Na-mu-han-jan-chin-so-mu
O-lung-so-mu
Cheng-chia-ying-tzu
Ching-feng
[K'o-shih-k'o-t'eng Ch'i]
Pa-lin-chiao
Hsi-la-mu-lun Ho
Sai-han-t'a-la
[Sunit West Banner]
Ch'e-le-t'u-miao
Shan-tan-so
T'e-ko-t'u-so-mu
Na-jih-t'u
Shih-pieh-su-mu
Ch'a-kan-wu-su
Pao-erh-t'ao-le-kai-su-mu
Kuang-te-kung
Wu-tan
[Weng-niu-t'e Ch'i]
Ta-ch'in-t'a-la
[Nai-man Ch'i]
Wen-tu-erh-miao
Chu-jih-ho
Te-jih-ssu-t'u
Pa-sha-t'ai
Sang-ken-ta-lai
Pa-yen-t'a-la
Ch'a-han-nao
[Cheng-hsiang-pai Ch'i]
Hsin-pao-li-ko
[Hsiang-huang Ch'i]
Pai-yin-ha-erh
Shan-tien Ho
Nan-wei-tzu
Ch'i-hao-ts'un
Liu-shih-ch'ing
Shan-wan-tzu
Hsia-wa
Mao-tu
Huang-ch'i-ta-ying-tzu
[Cheng-lan Ch'i]
To-lun
Ta-ho-k'ou
Ch'ih-feng
Hsin-hui
[Ao-han Ch'i]
A-kuei-t'u
T'u-mu-erh-t'ai
Hua-te
Pao-ch'ang
[T'ai-p'u-ssu Ch'i]
Ch'ien-chin-kou
Yu-tao-k'ou
Wang-lang-hu-t'ung
Wu-lan-ha-ta
Po-li-hu-ching
K'ang-pao
P'ao-t'ai-ying-tzu
Sen-chi-t'u
Pan-chieh-t'a
Ma-chia-tzu
Shang-tu
Shih-pa-ch'ing
Pai-yin-ch'a-kan
[Chahar West Wing North Banner]
P'ing-ting-pao
[Ku-yüan]
Kao-wu-su
Ta-lu-hao
An-ku-li Nao
Kuo-chia-t'un
Pai-hu-kou
Pei-p'iao
Hsiao-ch'ang
Yeh-pai-shou
[Chien-p'ing]
Chi-ning
Nan-hao-ch'ien
[Shang-i]
Chang-pei
Huang-ku-t'un
[Lung-hua]
Ta-ling Chiang
Huang-ch'i Hai
T'u-kuei-wu-la
[West Wing South Banner]
Hsing-ho
Ta-ko-chen
[Feng-ning]
Ch'ih-ch'eng
Hung-sha-pa
Lung-sheng-chuang
Chang-chia-k'ou
(Kalgan)
Ch'eng-te
P'ing-ch'üan
Ta-ch'eng-tzu
[Kharachin East Wing Mongol A.H.]
Hsüan-hua
P'ang-chia-pao
Kuan-t'un-ying
Sha-ch'eng
[Huai-lai]
Chien-ch'ang
Mi-yung shui-k'u
Kuan-t'ing Shui-k'u
K'uan-ch'eng
Chin-hsi
Sang-kan Ho
Ta-t'ung
Hsi-ch'eng
[Yang-yüan]
Huai-jou
Mi-yün
Hsing-lung
Ch'ing-lung
Luan Ho
Ch'ing-lung Ho
P'ing-ku
Sui-chung
PEI-CHING
(PEKING)
Chi-hsien
Hsing-ch'eng
[Ch'ien-hsi]
Kuang-ling
Yü-hsien
T'ung-hsien
Ch'ao-pai Ho
Feng-jun
Ch'in-huang-tao
Ling-ch'iu
Yang-ts'un
[Wu-ch'ing]
T'ang-shan
Ch'ang-li
Kao-pei-tien
[Hsin-ch'eng]
Yung-ting Ho
Po-ko-chuang
Pa-hsien
Nan-pao
Ta-ch'ing-ho
Man-ch'eng
T'IEN-CHIN
(TIENTSIN)
Ling-shou
Hu-t'o Ho
114°
116°
118°
120°
46°
44°
42°
40°
E
F
G
H
I
1
2
3
4
5
1 : 2 600 000
0 5 10 20 30 40 50 60 70 80 90 100 150 200 MILES
0 5 10 20 30 40 50 60 70 80 90 100 150 200 250 300 KM

INNER MONGOLIA AUTONOMOUS REGION 內蒙古自治区
NEI-MENG-KU TZU-CHIH-CH'Ü

6 shih	*cities*
4 meng	*leagues*
16 hsien	*counties*
27 ch'i	*banners*

capital **Hu-ho-hao-t'e Shih**	D4	呼和浩特市
T'o-k'o-t'o Hsien	D4	托克托县
T'u-mo-t'e Tso-ch'i		土默特左旗
Tumet East Banner		
centre: Ch'a-su-ch'i	D4	察素齐
Pao-t'ou Shih	D4	包头市
Ku-yang Hsien	D4	固阳县
T'u-mo-t'e Yu-ch'i		土默特右旗
Tumet West Banner		
centre: Sa-la-ch'i	D4	萨拉齐
Chi-ning Shih	E4	集宁市
Erh-lien-hao-t'e Shih	D3	二连浩特市
Hai-po-wan Shih	B5	海勃湾市
Wu-ta Shih	B5	乌达市
Hsi-lin-kuo-le Meng		锡林郭勒盟
centre: Hsi-lin-hao-t'e	G3	锡林浩特
A-pa-ha-na-erh Ch'i		阿巴哈纳尔旗
Abahanar Banner		
centre: Hsi-lin-hao-t'e	G3	锡林浩特
A-pa-ka Ch'i		阿巴嘎旗
Abaga Banner		
centre: Hsin-hao-t'e	F2	新浩特
Cheng-hsiang-pai Ch'i		正镶白旗
centre: Ch'a-han-nao	F3	察汗淖
Cheng-lan Ch'i		正蓝旗
centre: Huang-ch'i-ta-ying-tzu	G3	黄旗大营子
Hsiang-huang Ch'i		镶黄旗
centre: Hsin-pao-li-ko	E3	新宝力格
Hsi-wu-chu-mu-ch'in Ch'i		西乌珠穆沁旗
West Ujumuchin Banner		
centre: Pa-yen-wu-la	G2	巴彦乌拉
Su-ni-t'e Tso-ch'i		苏尼特左旗
Sunit East Banner		
centre: Pei-le-miao	E3	贝勒庙
To-lun Hsien	G3	多伦县
Tung-wu-chu-mu-ch'in Ch'i		东乌珠穆沁旗
East Ujumuchin Banner		
centre: Wu-li-ya-ssu-t'ai	G2	乌利亚斯太
I-k'o-chao Meng		伊克昭盟
centre: Tung-sheng	C5	东胜
Chun-ko-erh Ch'i		准格尔旗
centre: Sha-ko-tu	D5	沙圪堵
Hang-chin Ch'i		杭锦旗
Hanggin Banner		
centre: Hsi-ni-chen	C5	锡尼镇
I-chin-huo-lo Ch'i		伊金霍洛旗
centre: A-t'eng-hsi-lien	C5	阿腾席连
O-t'o-k'o Ch'i		鄂托克旗
centre: Wu-lan-ha-la-ka-su	B5	乌兰哈拉嘎苏
Ta-la-t'e Ch'i		达拉特旗
centre: Shu-lin-chao	D4	树林召
Tung-sheng Hsien	C5	东胜县
Wu-shen Ch'i		乌审旗
centre: Ta-pu-ch'an	C5	达卜缠
Pa-yen-nao-erh Meng		巴彦淖尔盟
centre: Lin-ho	B4	临河
Ch'ao-ko Ch'i		潮格旗
centre: not known	B4	
Hang-chin Hou-ch'i		杭锦后旗
Hanggin North Banner		
centre: Shan-pa	B4	陕坝
Lin-ho Hsien	B4	临河县
Teng-k'ou Hsien		磴口县
centre: Pa-yen-kao-le	B4	巴彦高勒
Wu-la-t'e Ch'ien-ch'i		乌拉特前旗
Urat South Banner		
centre: not known	C4	
Wu-la-t'e Chung-hou-lien-ho-ch'i		乌拉特中后联合旗
Urat Centre and North United Banner		
centre: Hai-liu-t'u	C4	海流图
Wu-yüan Hsien	C4	五原县
Wu-lan-ch'a-pu Meng		乌兰察布盟
centre: Chi-ning	E4	集宁
Ch'a-ha-erh Yu-i Ch'ien-ch'i		察哈尔右翼前旗
Chahar West Wing South Banner		
centre: T'u-kuei-wu-la	E4	土贵乌拉
Ch'a-ha-erh Yu-i Chung-ch'i		察哈尔右翼中旗
Chahar West Wing Centre Banner		
centre: K'o-pu-erh	E4	科布尔
Ch'a-ha-erh Yu-i Hou-ch'i		察哈尔右翼后旗
Chahar West Wing North Banner		
centre: Pai-yin-ch'a-kan	E4	白音察干
Ch'ing-shui-ho Hsien	D5	清水河县
Cho-tzu Hsien	D4	卓资县
Feng-chen Hsien	E4	丰镇县
Ho-lin-ko-erh Hsien	D4	和林格尔县
Hsing-ho Hsien	F4	兴和县
Hua-te Hsien	E4	化德县
Liang-ch'eng Hsien	E4	凉城县
Shang-tu Hsien	E4	商都县
Ssu-tzu-wang Ch'i		四子王旗
centre: Wu-lan-hua	D4	乌兰花
Su-ni-t'e Yu-ch'i		苏尼特右旗
Sunit West Banner		
centre: Sai-han-t'a-la	D4	赛汉塔拉
Ta-erh-han-mao Ming-an Lien-ho-ch'i		达尔罕茂明安联合旗
Darhan-Mow Mingan United Banner		
centre: Pai-ling-miao	D4	百灵庙
Wu-ch'uan Hsien	D4	武川县

HOPEH PROVINCE

PEKING AND TIENTSIN MUNICIPALITIES

THIS region comprises the province of Hopeh and the province-level municipalities of Peking and Tientsin. It includes not only the traditional province of Hopeh (known under the Manchus as Chih-li) but also the northern plateau and hill areas which once formed parts of the provinces of Chahar and Jehol. These areas have very different environments and histories. The Great Plain of southern Hopeh was already incorporated in the Chinese cultural area by the end of the second millenium BC. Although it was many centuries before the poorly drained marshy plain itself was brought under cultivation, the foothill zone along the T'ai-hang range in the west already had a number of notable cities. Under the unified empire of the Han (206 BC–AD 220) the plain itself was drained and brought under cultivation, and maintained a very dense population. It continued to be the most densely peopled and productive area in China until about the 8th century, when the economic centre of the empire shifted to the Yangtze valley. In the early 10th century the northern half of Hopeh came under the dominance of the Khitan state of Liao in 936, and remained under foreign rulers – first the Jurchen and then the Mongols until 1368. During this period Peking first became a national capital, and after the restoration of Chinese rule under the Ming in 1368, Peking again became the capital in 1421. Hopeh province suffered badly from floods and drought during the late 19th century. There was considerable emigration to Manchuria, to the borderlands of Inner Mongolia, and into the north-west.

The northern section of the province, beyond the Great Wall, has a very different environment, dry uplands unsuited to traditional Chinese farming. This has always remained a frontier zone comparatively sparsely peopled, and administratively distinct from Hopeh province. Apart from minor adjustments, the province took its present shape in 1956.

The Southern Hopeh plain This area forms a vast alluvial plain, almost entirely below 50 m, watered by a series of rivers. From south to north the Wei Ho, Chang Ho, Fu-yang Ho, Hu-t'o Ho, Ta-ch'ing Ho and Yung-ting Ho flow together in the vicinity of Tientsin to form the Hai Ho. The whole region is one of very poor drainage, with many large areas of marsh, such as the Wen-an marsh and the Pai-yang lake, and large tracts of saline land. Formerly an area perennially devastated by widespread flooding, since 1949 very extensive water control works have been carried out. Additional outlets to the sea have been constructed to reduce the build up of spring flood waters around Tientsin; dams constructed on the upper streams of the various rivers to control their flow and reduce their silt-load; extensive dykes and retention basins constructed, and some attempt made to reduce the salinity of the soil.

The area has a very hard climate. Average temperatures in January are about –4°C (25°F), and the rivers are icebound for about three months in winter. Summers are very hot, with average July temperatures of 25°C (77°F) in the north. Rainfall is low: below 750 mm everywhere, and below 500 mm in the central part of the plain. It is subject to great annual variations, spring droughts being very common, and almost three quarters of the rain falls in June, July and August. The growing season is about 260 days in the south, falling to 220 days in the Peking area.

Agriculture is extremely intensive. Apart from the saline soils of the coastal belt, and the marshlands west and south-west of Tientsin, a very large proportion of the total area is farmed. The commonest crops are winter wheat, barley or peas followed by corn. Kaoliang and soy beans are widely grown, and cotton is a very important crop, especially in the south and west.

The main cities lie at the foot of the T'ai-hang mountains, which rise from the plain to the west and form the border with Shansi province. This higher ground has been a major communications route since pre-historic times, and since the early years of this century has been followed by the main Peking to Han-k'ou railway. The area has also some important coal deposits.

Han-tan is an ancient city, which was a minor commercial and administrative centre until recent times. In the 1950s it became an important cotton textile town. Later, important coal mines were opened at Feng-feng, and iron mines at Tz'u-shan provided raw materials for an iron and steel plant, built in 1958–60. Another mining centre is nearby at K'uang-shan-ts'un. Large cement and thermal power plants have also been built.

Shih-chia-chuang, the provincial capital, is an entirely modern city. A small satellite village of the old administrative city of Cheng-ting until the beginning of the century, Shih-chia-chuang became a rail junction for the railway to T'ai-yüan, growing into an important commercial centre and a centre of light industry in the 1920s and 1930s. In 1939 another rail line linked it with Te-chou and Chi-nan in Shantung, increasing its commercial area. After 1949 it was built up into a major centre of the cotton textile industry, and has since developed a woollen industry and chemical and fertiliser plants. Its population rose from 373,000 in 1953 to 598,000 in 1958, when it became the provincial capital.

Pao-t'ing is another very ancient city and a former capital of Hopeh. It is the chief commercial and market centre for central Hopeh, and also an important cultural centre, with various museums and institutions of higher education. It has a variety of agriculture-based industries, flour milling, oil extraction, leather and woollen manufacture, and it produces rayon.

Ts'ang-chou, on the old Grand Canal near the coast, and on the Tientsin–P'u-k'ou railway, is the main administrative and commercial centre of the coastal plain. It has a variety of minor industries. Salt is produced in the nearby coastal area.

The Peking area Peking (Pei-ching), situated at the north of the great plain, and at the mouth of various routes into the Mongolian borderlands, has been an important city throughout historical times, and the national capital, with brief intervals, since the 13th century, when the Mongols set their capital here. It became the terminus of the Grand Canal, which brought in supplies from southern China, and the focus of the national system of post-roads. In this century the rail system has converged upon Peking. Until the end of the Manchu regime in 1911, Peking remained essentially an administrative and cultural capital, with a flourishing commercial life, but little industry. Later some industry grew up to the west, with the exploitation of coal mines at Men-t'ou-kou and the construction of an iron and steel plant at Shih-ching-shan. During the 1950s there was rapid industrial growth in the east towards T'ung-hsien. Peking's iron and steel industry was also greatly developed, and fully integrated in 1969. The Shih-ching-shan plant now produces more than 1,000,000 tons of iron annually. Heavy engineering plant producing bridge girders, locomotives, machine tools, motor vehicles, ball-bearings and agricultural equipment was developed, and electronic, chemical and textile industries. Peking has a large thermal generating plant, and is joined by a power grid to a hydro-electric plant at Kuan-t'ing, to Tientsin, T'ang-shan, and to the Manchurian power grid.

Peking is not only the nation's political capital, but also its cultural centre, with many museums, universities and institutions of higher education and research.

The municipality includes a large area of hills to the north of the city, and includes the mining and industrial centres in the vicinity. Its population was 2,768,000 in 1953, and had grown to 4,010,000 in 1958. It is currently estimated at about 7,000,000.

Tientsin (T'ien-ching), like Peking, has the status of a provincial-level municipality, which it was granted in 1967. Although it is China's third largest city, Tientsin is not an ancient city like Peking, but a product of modern economic development. A minor port until the 19th century, it was opened to foreign trade in 1860, and in the various foreign concessions which were set up thereafter, western trade and industry began on a large scale, and Tientsin became a centre of modern and western ideas second only to Shanghai. Tientsin also became China's second port, although the Hai Ho was impassable for large ships, and an outport at Ta-ku had to tranship most goods. During the War the Japanese began to construct a modern port, and this was completed in 1952 at T'ang-ku. Tientsin was always an important centre for canal and river traffic, and had rail communications from the early years of this century. Before 1949 most of Tientsin's industry was textiles (both cotton and woollens) and food-processing. Textiles remain very important, but the city has more recently developed a steelworks, a diversified engineering industry producing heavy machinery, tractors, lorries, diesel engines and industrial equipment of various kinds, an electronic industry, chemical and paper plants, and a plant manufacturing automobile tyres.

Tientsin is also a very important centre for education, with several universities and institutes of higher education, museums and libraries. Its growth since 1949 has not been as rapid as Peking's. It had 2,694,000 people in 1953, 3,200,000 in 1957 and is estimated to have over 4,000,000 today.

Eastern Hopeh This area includes the coastal plain east of Tientsin, which gradually narrows until the hills of the interior meet the coast at Shan-hai-kuan. This is an area with an agriculture similar to that of the plain, although cotton is not so commonly grown. It is mainly remarkable for its coalfield.

T'ang-shan is the main centre of the mining area. Its growth began in the 1880s with the exploitation by British capital of the K'ai-luan coal mines, which exported their output, by China's first railway, to Lu-t'ai and thence by boat to Tientsin and Shanghai. These mines have since been greatly expanded, and the complex of mines now produces between 10,000,000 and 15,000,000 tons annually. T'ang-shan developed a large scale cement industry in the early years of this century, and a large thermal generating plant which provides power for Tientsin and Peking as well as for T'ang-shan industrial complex. It has recently developed a large iron and steel industry, engineering works and a variety of other industries including textiles, paper making and food processing.

The Jehol uplands lie to the north of the Great Wall and east of Peking. It is an area of complex hills of 500 m to 1,000 m, with individual peaks up to 1,500 m, and ranges striking roughly south-west to north-east. These ranges, known collectively as the Yen Shan, are rugged and sparsely peopled, but they enclose some small basins which are carefully cultivated. The climate is very severe here, with January temperatures down to –14°C (7°F), and the climate is drier towards the north-west. The growing season is much shorter than elsewhere in the province – about 190–200 days.

Ch'eng-te, formerly the capital of Jehol, is the main city. It is the commercial and market centre for the densely peopled basin, and the main administrative centre for north-eastern Hopeh.

The North-western plateau This area stretches from north-west of Peking municipality to the border of Inner Mongolia. An area of high plateau, rising to between 1,000 m and 1,500 m, it is crossed by the Hsiung-erh Shan and Ta-ma-chün Shan ranges, striking from south-west to north-east, and rising to the north-west of the province. This area was formerly part of the province of Chahar, and still retains a small Mongol minority. It is marginal land for permanent agriculture. In the latter part of the 19th century and during the present century, Chinese farmers attempted to expand the area under cultivation into what were traditional pasturelands, often with disastrous results, as they destroyed the natural grassland.

Chang-chia-k'ou (Kalgan) was the traditional centre of this region, a border trading city and garrison town, where there was a major market for trade from the steppes, the collection of wool and hides, and the export of Chinese goods to the Mongols. Chang-chia-k'ou's importance was greatly increased in 1909 when a railway was built from Peking, which was subsequently extended further west. It was already a large city with extensive food processing and similar industries, but since the 1950s it has grown further and developed woollen and cotton textile mills, a rayon plant, and a large industry building mining machinery.

Hsüan-hua is a satellite city of Chang-chia-k'ou, with important iron mines at Lung-yen, and coal mines. It has a major power plant, and an iron and steel plant. But most of the iron ore from Lung-yen is sent to the steel works in T'ai-yüan, Shih-ching-shan or An-shan.

HOPEH AREA
190,000 square kilometres

POPULATION
41,410,000 (other estimates up to 46,000,000)

PEKING AREA
8,400 square kilometres

POPULATION
7,570,000

TIENTSIN AREA
3,900 square kilometres

POPULATION
4,280,000

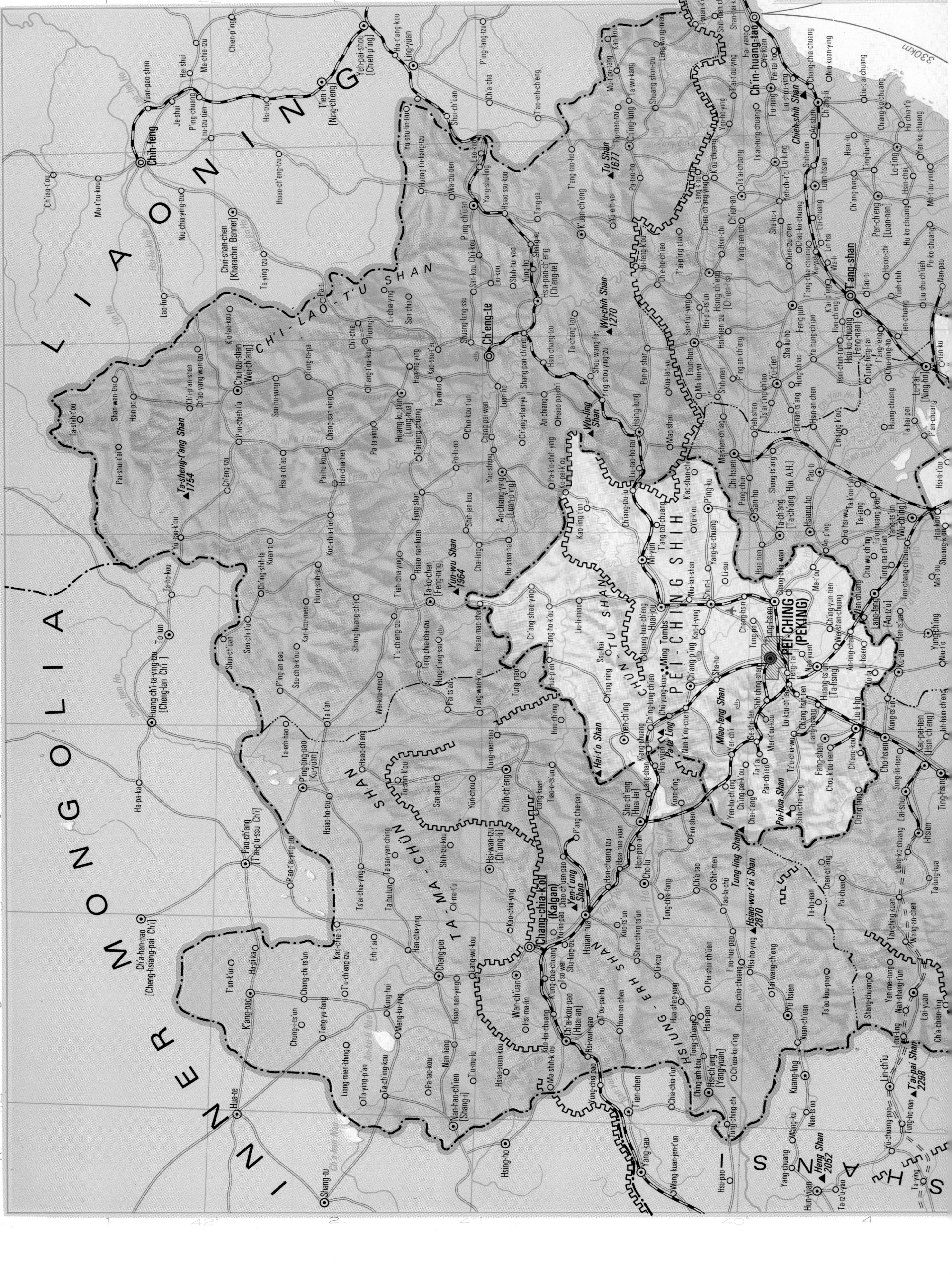
INNER MONGOLIA
LIAONING
PEI-CHING SHIH
PEI-CHING (PEKING)
CH'I-LAO-T'U SHAN
TA-MA-CH'ÜN SHAN
HSIUNG-ERH SHAN
CHÜN-TU SHAN
Chih-feng
Ch'eng-te
Chang-chia-k'ou (Kalgan)
T'ang-shan
Ch'in-huang-tao
Ta-sheng-t'ang Shan 1754
Yün-wu Shan 1964
Wu-ling Shan
Tu Shan 1677
Wu-chih Shan 1270
Hsiao-wu-t'ai Shan 2870
T'ai-pai Shan 2298
Heng Shan 2052
Ming Tombs
330km

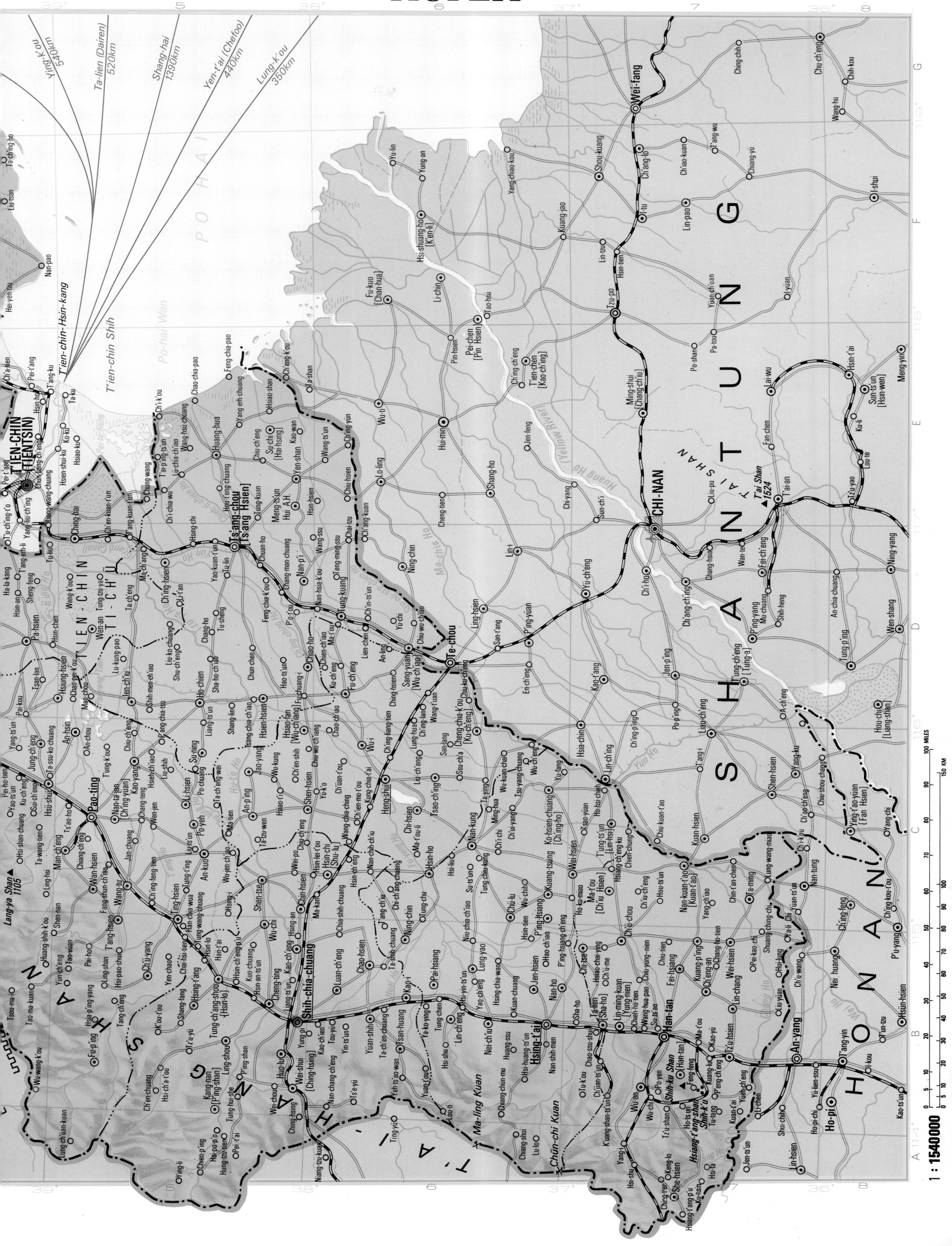
Ying-k'ou 540km
Ta-lien (Dairen) 520km
Shang-hai 1390km
Yen-t'ai (Chefoo) 440km
Lung-k'ou 350km
T'ien-chin-Hsin-kang
T'ien-chin Shih
PO HAI
Po-hai Wan
T'IEN-CHIN (TIENTSIN)
TIEN-CHIN TI-CH'Ü
Ts'ang-chou (Ts'ang Hsien)
Te-chou
Pao-ting
Shih-chia-chuang
Hsing-t'ai
Han-tan
An-yang
CHI-NAN
Wei-fang
Tzu-po
T'ai Shan 1524
T'AI SHAN
Lang-ya Shan 1105
Huang Ho (Yellow River)
SHANTUNG
HONAN
SHANSI
T'AI-HANG SHAN
Ma-ling Kuan
Ch'ün-chi Kuan
1 : 1540000

HOPEH PROVINCE 河北省
HO-PEI SHENG

9 shih	*municipalities*
10 ti-ch'ü	*regions*
142 hsien	*counties*
2 tzu-chih-hsien	*autonomous counties*

capital Shih-chia-chuang Shih	B5	石家庄市
Chang-chia-k'ou Shih	B3	张家口市
Ch'eng-te Shih	E3	承德市
Ch'in-huang-tao Shih	G4	秦皇岛市
Han-tan Shih	B7	邯郸市
Hsing-t'ai Shih	B6	邢台市
Pao-ting Shih	C5	保定市
T'ang-shan Shih	F4	唐山市
Ts'ang-chou Shih	D5	沧州市

Chang-chia-k'ou Ti-ch'ü		张家口地区
Chang-pei Hsien	B2	张北县
Ch'ih-ch'eng Hsien	C3	赤城县
Cho-lu Hsien	C3	涿鹿县
Ch'ung-li Hsien		崇礼县
centre: Hsi-wan-tzu	C3	西湾子
Hsüan-hua Hsien	C3	宣化县
Huai-an Hsien		怀安县
centre: Ch'ai-kou-pao	B3	柴沟堡
Huai-lai Hsien		怀来县
centre: Sha-ch'eng	C3	沙城
K'ang-pao Hsien	B2	康保县
Ku-yüan Hsien		古源县
centre: P'ing-ting-pao	C2	平定堡
Shang-i Hsien		尚义县
centre: Nan-haò-ch'ien	A2	南壕堑
Wan-ch'üan Hsien	B3	万全县
Yang-yüan Hsien		阳原县
centre: Hsi-ch'eng	B3	西城
Yü Hsien		蔚县
centre: Yü-hsien	B4	

Ch'eng-te Ti-ch'ü		承德地区
Ch'eng-te Hsien		承德县
centre: Hsia-pan-ch'eng	F3	下板城
Ch'ing-lung Hsien	F3	青龙县
Feng-ning Hsien		丰宁县
centre: Ta-ko-chen	D2	大阁镇
Hsing-lung Hsien	E3	兴隆县
K'uan-ch'eng Hsien	F3	宽城县
Luan-p'ing Hsien		滦平县
centre: An-chiang-ying	E3	鞍匠营
Lung-hua Hsien		隆化县
centre: Huang-ku-t'un	E2	皇姑屯
P'ing-ch'üan Hsien	F2	平泉县
Wei-ch'ang Hsien		围场县
centre: Chui-tzu-shan	E2	锥子山

Han-tan Ti-ch'ü		邯郸地区
Ch'eng-an Hsien	B7	成安县
Chi-tse Hsien	B7	鸡泽县
Ch'iu Hsien		丘县
centre: Ma-t'ou	C7	马头
Ch'ü-chou Hsien	B7	曲周县
Fei-hsiang Hsien	B7	肥乡县
Han-tan Hsien		邯郸县
centre: not known	B7	
Kuang-p'ing Hsien	B7	广平县
Kuan-t'ao Hsien		馆陶县
centre: Nan-kuan-t'ao	C7	南馆陶
Lin-chang Hsien	B7	临漳县
She Hsien		涉县
centre: She-hsien	A7	
Ta-ming Hsien	C7	大名县
Tz'u Hsien		磁县
centre: Tz'u-hsien	B7	
Wei Hsien		魏县
centre: Wei-hsien	B7	
Wu-an Hsien	B7	武安县
Yung-nien Hsien		永年县
centre: Lin-ming-kuan	B7	临洺关

Heng-shui Ti-ch'ü		衡水地区
An-p'ing Hsien	C5	安平县
Chi Hsien		冀县
centre: Chi-hsien	C6	
Ching Hsien		景县
centre: Ching-hsien	D5	
Fu-ch'eng Hsien	D6	阜城县
Heng-shui Hsien	C6	衡水县
Jao-yang Hsien	C5	饶阳县
Ku-ch'eng Hsien		古城县
centre: Cheng-chia-k'ou	C6	郑家口
Shen Hsien		深县
centre: Shen-hsien	C5	
Tsao-ch'iang Hsien	C6	枣强县
Wu-ch'iang Hsien		武强县
centre: Hsiao-fan	C5	小范
Wu-i Hsien	C6	武邑县

Hsing-t'ai Ti-ch'ü		邢台地区
Ch'ing-ho Hsien		清河县
centre: Ko-hsien-chuang	C6	葛仙庄
Chu-lu Hsien	C6	巨鹿县
Hsing-t'ai Hsien	B6	邢台县
Hsin-ho Hsien	C6	新河县
Jen Hsien		任县
centre: Jen-hsien	B6	
Kuang-tsung Hsien	C6	广宗县
Lin-ch'eng Hsien	B6	临城县
Lin-hsi Hsien		临西县
centre: T'ung-ts'un	C7	童村
Lung-yao Hsien	B6	隆尧县
Nan-ho Hsien	B6	南河县
Nan-kung Hsien	C6	南宫县
Nei-ch'iu Hsien	B6	内丘县
Ning-chin Hsien	B6	宁晋县
Pai-hsiang Hsien	B6	柏乡县
P'ing-hsiang Hsien	C6	平乡县
Sha-ho Hsien		沙河县
centre: Ta-lien	B7	褡裢
Wei Hsien		威县
centre: Wei-hsien	C7	

Pao-ting Ti-ch'ü		保定地区
An-hsin Hsien	C5	安新县
An-kuo Hsien	C5	安国县
Ch'ing-yüan Hsien		清苑县
centre: Nan-ta-jan	C5	南大冉
Cho Hsien		涿县
centre: Cho-hsien	C4	
Ch'ü-yang Hsien	B5	曲阳县
Fu-p'ing Hsien	B5	阜平县
Hsin-ch'eng Hsien		新城县
centre: Kao-pei-tien	C4	高碑店
Hsiung Hsien		雄县
centre: Hsiung-hsien	D4	
Hsü-shui Hsien	C4	徐水县
I Hsien		易县
centre: I-hsien	C4	
Jung-ch'eng Hsien	C4	容城县
Kao-yang Hsien	C5	高阳县
Lai-shui Hsien	C4	涞水县
Lai-yüan Hsien	B4	涞源县
Li Hsien		蠡县
centre: Li-hsien	C5	
Man-ch'eng Hsien	C5	满城县
Po-yeh Hsien	C5	博野县
T'ang Hsien		唐县
centre: T'ang-hsien	B5	
Ting Hsien		定县
centre: Ting-hsien	B5	
Ting-hsing Hsien	C4	定兴县
Wang-tu Hsien	C5	望都县
Wan Hsien		完县
centre: Wan-hsien	C5	

Shih-chia-chuang Ti-ch'ü		石家庄地区
Chao Hsien		赵县
centre: Chao-hsien	B6	
Cheng-ting Hsien	B5	正定县
Ching-hsing Hsien		井陉县
centre: Wei-shui	B5	微水
Chin Hsien		晋县
centre: Chin-hsien	C5	
Hsing-t'ang Hsien	B5	行唐县
Hsin-lo Hsien		新乐县
centre: Tung-ch'ang-shou	B5	东长寿
Huo-lu Hsien	B5	获鹿县
Kao-ch'eng Hsien	B5	藁城县
Kao-i Hsien	B6	高邑县
Ling-shou Hsien	B5	灵寿县
Luan-ch'eng Hsien	B6	栾城县
P'ing-shan Hsien		平山县
centre: Kang-nan	B5	岗南
Shen-tse Hsien	C5	深泽县
Shu-lu Hsien		束鹿县
centre: Hsin-chi	C6	辛集
Tsan-huang Hsien	B6	赞皇县
Wu-chi Hsien	B5	无极县
Yüan-shih Hsien	B6	元氏县

T'ang-shan Ti-ch'ü		唐山地区
Ch'ang-li Hsien	G4	昌黎县
Ch'ien-an Hsien	F3	迁安县
Ch'ien-hsi Hsien		迁西县
centre: Hsing-ch'eng	F3	兴城
Feng-jun Hsien	F4	丰润县
Feng-nan Hsien		丰南县
centre: Hsü-ko-chuang	F4	胥各庄
Fu-ning Hsien	G4	抚宁县
Lo-t'ing Hsien	F4	乐亭县
Luan Hsien		滦县
centre: Luan-hsien	F4	
Luan-nan Hsien		滦南县
centre: Pen-ch'eng	F4	倴城
Lu-lung Hsien	F4	卢龙县
Tsun-hua Hsien	E3	遵化县
Yü-t'ien Hsien	E4	玉田县

T'ien-chin Ti-ch'ü		天津地区
centre: Lang-fang	D4	
An-tz'u Hsien		安次县
centre: Lang-fang	D4	廊坊
Chi Hsien		蓟县
centre: Chi-hsien	E3	
Ching-hai Hsien	D5	静海县
Hsiang-ho Hsien	E4	香河县
Ku-an Hsien	D4	固安县
Ning-ho Hsien		宁河县
centre: Lu-t'ai	E4	芦台
Pa Hsien		霸县
centre: Pa-hsien	D4	
Pao-ti Hsien	E4	宝坻县
San-ho Hsien	E4	三河县
Ta-ch'ang Hui-tsu Tzu-chih-hsien Ta-ch'ang Hui Autonomous Hsien	D4	大厂回族自治县
Ta-ch'eng Hsien	D5	大城县
Wen-an Hsien	D5	文安县
Wu-ch'ing Hsien		武清县
centre: Yang-ts'un	E4	杨村
Yung-ch'ing Hsien	D4	永清县

Ts'ang-chou Ti-ch'ü		沧州地区
Chiao-ho Hsien	D5	交河县
Ch'ing Hsien		青县
centre: Ch'ing-hsien	D5	
Hai-hsing Hsien		海兴县
centre: Su-chi	E5	苏基
Ho-chien Hsien	D5	河间县
Hsien Hsien		献县
centre: Hsien-hsien	D5	
Huang-hua Hsien	E5	黄骅县
Jen-ch'iu Hsien	D5	任丘县
Meng-ts'un Hui-tsu Tzu-chih-hsien Meng-ts'un Hui Autonomous Hsien	E5	孟村回族自治县
Nan-p'i Hsien	D5	南皮县
Su-ning Hsien	C5	肃宁县
Ts'ang Hsien		沧县
centre: Ts'ang-chou	D5	沧州
Tung-kuang Hsien	D6	东光县
Wu-ch'iao Hsien		吴桥县
centre: Sang-yüan	D6	桑园
Yen-shan Hsien	E5	盐山县

PEKING MUNICIPALITY 北京市
PEI-CHING SHIH D4

9 hsien *counties*

Ch'ang-p'ing Hsien	D3	昌平县
Fang-shan Hsien	C4	房山县
Huai-jou Hsien	D3	怀柔县
Mi-yün Hsien	D3	密云县
P'ing-ku Hsien	E3	平谷县
Shun-i Hsien	D3	顺义县
Ta-hsing Hsien		大兴县
centre: Huang-ts'un	D4	黄村
T'ung Hsien		通县
centre: T'ung-hsien	D4	
Yen-ch'ing Hsien	C3	延庆县

TIENTSIN MUNICIPALITY 天津市
T'IEN-CHIN SHIH E5

SHANTUNG
PROVINCE

SHANTUNG is China's second most populous province (after Szechwan), with 8.3 per cent of the total population living on 1.6 per cent of the total area. Its density of population is exceeded only by Kiangsu.

It is a region which has been settled since Neolithic times, and in early Chinese history was one of the most important centres of Chinese culture. In the first millenium BC its principal state, Ch'i, was already famous for its teeming population, for its advanced economy, and for its political institutions. It continued to be important throughout the Chinese medieval period, when its ports became the chief outlets for the North China plain and for the trade with Korea and Japan. Under the Mongols its role as a communications link were strengthened by the construction of the new imperial canal route through western Shantung in 1293, and by a canal across the neck of the peninsula. These reduced the importance of its coastal trade. Although the first settlements in Shantung were in the uplands, the western and northern plains were already densely peopled by the 1st century BC. These areas, in spite of costly flood control works, were constantly threatened by floods as the Huang Ho changed its course. Particularly serious floods occurred at the end of the 12th century, when the Huang Ho left its northern course to discharge into the sea south of the Shantung peninsula, and in 1853–5 when it took its present course, which destroyed the northern section of the Grand Canal, flooded vast areas of rich farmland, and caused enormous loss of life. At the end of the 19th century, a series of droughts and famines, coupled with ever-increasing population pressure, led to large-scale emigration from Shantung to the newly-opened lands in Manchuria and along the Inner Mongolian border. This emigration, which began in the 1890s, reached a peak in the late 1920s, when more than four million people emigrated from the province between 1923 and 1930. Under the Communist regime, too, emigration has continued, both to Manchuria and to developing areas such as Sinkiang.

At the end of the 19th century Shantung came under strong foreign influence. In 1898 the Germans were granted a lease of the Chiao-chou bay, where they built a modern port, Ch'ing-tao (Tsingtao), while Britain leased Wei-hai-wei as a naval base. The Germans built a railway inland to Chi-nan (Tsinan) in 1905, and began to establish coal mines and other industries. During the First World War, in 1915, the Japanese took over German interests, and continued to occupy parts of Shantung until 1923.

Shantung divides into a number of very different regions.

The Shantung Peninsula The mountains of central Shantung and the Peninsula form part of the ancient mountain range which continues across the Gulf of Po-hai into the Liao-tung peninsula and the Chang-pai Shan range of eastern Manchuria. The average height of the hills of the peninsula is about 250 m. Individual peaks reach 900 m, but the landscape is one of rounded hills and small inter-montane basins. The coast is mostly sheer, and there are a series of good harbours. The climate is more temperate than the western areas of Shantung, and the growing season somewhat shorter. The agriculture of the area concentrates upon winter wheat and kaoliang, with foxtail millet and peanuts as important secondary crops. The hills were deforested in very early times, and the area has suffered badly from soil erosion. The area is also famous for wild silk, and for the production of fruit, particularly pears grown around Lai-yang, and grapes from Chi-mo.

Yen-t'ai (once known as Chefoo) was formerly a minor local port, which became the major centre of this area following the construction of a railway to Ch'ing-tao in 1955. It has recently seen the growth of some minor industry, including a small steel plant, and a major canning and processing industry. Yen-t'ai is a major fishing port. Its population was 116,000 in 1953.

The Chiao-lai plain This wide lowland plain separates the hills of the peninsula from the massif of central Shantung. A fertile and densely peopled agricultural area, it produces winter wheat, kaoliang, soy beans and sweet potatoes as staple crops, but is also an important producing area for cotton and tobacco, for which the Wei-fang area is famous. The area is traversed by the railway from Ch'ing-tao to Chi-nan.

Wei-fang is the major centre of this agricultural region, with processing plants for tobacco, peanut-oil extraction and flour milling. It is also close to a minor coalfield at Fang-tzu. Its population in 1953 was 149,000.

Ch'ing-tao, the largest city and industrial centre of Shantung, was the creation of western colonialisation. Although formerly a small fishing village, after the lease of the area to Germany in 1898, Ch'ing-tao was built up as a naval base and as the outlet for trade carried by the railway to Chi-nan. Ch'ing-tao remains a major port, exporting soy beans, peanuts and coal from the interior, and is also a fishing port even more important than Yen-t'ai. Ch'ing-tao's industrial growth began under the Germans, and was continued under the Japanese, who occupied the former German territory in 1915. Beside food manufacturing, oil extraction, and textiles, based on local produce, Ch'ing-tao is also a major centre of heavy industry, manufacturing diesel locomotives and railway rolling stock, rubber, especially automobile tyres, cement, chemicals and fertiliser. Its population was 1,121,000 in 1957.

The central Shantung massif This is a higher and more complex hill area than the peninsula. The northern section comprises three parallel ranges (from west to east, T'ai Shan, Lu Shan, I Shan) with a roughly south-west to north-east axis. They average 300–500 m, with peaks over 1,000 m, the highest being the most famous of China's traditional holy mountains, T'ai Shan (1,524 m). These ranges present a steep escarpment to the north. The southern and south-eastern sections of the massif are less rugged and lower, with broad cultivated river valleys draining south into the Huai. Once forested, these hills have long since been denuded of trees, with resultant soil erosion, although some attempt at reforestation has been made since 1949.

The agriculture of this area is mainly winter wheat, kaoliang, soy beans and millet, with areas specialising in production of wild silk and fruits, and peanuts as a widespread cash crop. Some sheep are also reared in the upland districts.

The area is important as a major coal producer, and centre of metal working. From very early times central Shantung was a major centre of the copper and iron industry. Modern development, however, began during the period of German influence before the First World War. The first major coal mines were those of Po-shan (in *Tzu-po* municipality) which produces some 10,000,000 tons annually. This mining centre has developed, since 1950, into an industrial district, with an important ceramic, refractory and glass industry, and an aluminium industry. To the north at Chin-ling-chen is a very rich source of high-grade iron ore. In recent years, following the discovery of the Sheng-li oilfield, Tzu-po has also become the centre of a petro-chemical industry. The municipality of Tzu-po, which includes the mining towns of Po-shan, Tzu-ch'uan, and Chin-ling-chen as well as the administrative centre Chang-tien, had a population in 1957 of 806,000.

Tsao-chuang in the south-west of the highlands was also developed as a coal mining centre before the First World War, when the Tientsin–Pu-k'ou railway first made it accessible. The mines were destroyed during the Second World War, but were rebuilt and modernised in the mid-1950s. The Tsao-chuang mines produce good coking coal, and output is estimated at over 6,000,000 tons. Another coalfield in this area is at Hsin-wen, which produces about 1,500,000 tons annually.

Chi-nan, the provincial capital and Shantung's second largest city, lies at the foot of the north-western corner of the massif. Chi-nan is an ancient city, a traditional administrative and transportation centre. Its modern growth began with the construction of the railway to Ch'ing-tao in 1905 and the Tientsin–Chi-nan–Pu-k'ou railway, which made it a major railway junction. It remains an important administrative and cultural centre. Industrial growth was at first concentrated in textiles, flour milling, oil extraction and similar processing industries, but in the late 1950s a small iron and steel complex was built, and Chi-nan has developed a large power plant, and a machine-building industry, specialising in machine tools, agricultural machinery, trucks, precision instruments and electrical equipment. It also manufactures fertilisers, industrial chemicals and paper.

The northern Shantung plain To the north of the central mountains is the flat, alluvial plain of the mouth of the Huang Ho. This is a rich area of farmland, whose only drawbacks are the highly saline soils of the delta area. In recent decades this plain has been extensively drained and irrigated. Its agriculture produces winter wheat, kaoliang, corn, soy beans and sweet potatoes. In the saline soils near the Huang Ho delta, cotton is a very important crop.

The area is also the site of a new oilfield, Sheng-li, the precise location of which is not clear. It is still a minor producer, with an output of 500,000 tons per year, but the field is thought to extend under the sea in the Po Hai gulf.

The coastal area is also a major source of salt, produced by evaporation.

Te-chou, at the point where the railway from Chi-nan to Tientsin crosses the Grand Canal and joins the railway to Shih-chia-chuang, is the main commercial and transportation centre of this area.

The western Shantung plain The plain lies to the west of the central massif. This is a part of the Great North China Plain of Hopeh and Honan, a rich alluvial area with a very dense agricultural population.

The area is traversed by the Grand Canal, which is supplied with water from a series of lakes in the south-west of the province. The agriculture of this region concentrates upon winter wheat, soy beans, kaoliang and cotton.

Chi-ning, the chief commercial and marketing centre of the region was formerly an important canal port, from which grain was shipped to Peking. The change of course of the Huang Ho in 1853–5, however, blocked the canal to the north, and ambitious plans to modernise and reopen the canal in the 1950s seem not to have been completed north of Chi-ning. Chi-ning is however linked to the Chi-nan–Pu-k'ou railway, and remains the chief city of this area. It had a population of 86,000 in 1953.

AREA
153,300 square kilometres

POPULATION
55,520,000 (estimate for 1970: 62,500,000)

A
B
C
D
116°
117°
118°
1
2
3
4
5
38°
37°
36°
HOPEH
HUI-MIN
HONAN
HO-TSE
LU SHAN
CHI-NAN SHIH
T'AI SHAN
MENG SHAN
ANHWEI
KIANGSU
LIN-I
Ts'ang-chou
Chun-chen
Tung-kuan
Chuan-ho
Chiu-ch'eng
Hsiao-shan
An-p'ing
Jao-yang
Shen-tse
Hsien-hsien
Meng-ts'un
[Meng-ts'un Hui A.H.]
Yen-shan
Hsiao-fan
[Wu-ch'iang]
Fu-chuang-i
Chiao-ho
Po-t'ou
Nan-p'i
Hsin-chi
[Shu-lu]
Shen-hsien
Hsin-chi
Ch'eng-k'ou
Pai-t'ou
Ta-shan
Fu-chia-t'ai-tzu
Hsin-ch'ien-hu
T'ai-ping-chen
Tiao-k'ou-chen
I-hui Ho
Tung-kuang
Ch'ien-mo-t'ou
Wu-i
Fu-ch'eng
Chai-tzu
Chiu-hsien
Ch'ing-yün
Ch'ang-chia-chuang
Ch'e-chen
I-ho-chuang
Po-hai
Nan-chih-ch'iu
Lien-chen
Ch'ang-kuan
Huang-chia
Hsieh-chia-chi
[Ch'ing-yün]
Shui-wan
Yü-hsiang
Li-chia
Lo-chen
Fu-yang Ho
Heng-shui
Ching-hsien
Yün Ho (Grand Canal)
Tu-chi
Lo-ling
Wu-ti
Chan-ch'eng
Fu-kuo
[Chan-hua]
Li-kuo
Ch'en-chia-kuang
Sang-yüan
[Wu-ch'iao]
Ning-chin
Ma-chia Ho
Yang-hsin
Chi-hsien
Pao-tien
Ch'ai-hu-tien
K'ung-chen
Yang-an
Wen-chia-tien
Pai-t'ou-chen
Hsi-shuang-ho
[K'en-li]
Min-feng
Hsin-ho
Tsao-ch'iang
Yung-an
Te-chou
Te-p'ing
Cheng-tien
Shih-miao
Hui-min
Sang-lo-shu
Pin-hsien
Li-chin
Hsin-tien
Pien-li-chen
Mi-chen
Huai-jen
Pei-chen
[Pin-hsien]
Hsin-chen
Tung-chiu-kung
Nan-kung
Chiu-ku-ch'eng
Ku-ch'eng
T'u-ch'iao
Huang-ho-ya
Ling-hsien
Shen-t'ou
Yin-hsiang
Tsao-hu-li
Hsin-tien
Shang-tien
Li-tse-chen
Shih-k'ou
Liu-hu
Ta-ying
T'eng-chuang
Ssu-nu-ssu
Wang-ts'un-tien
Lin-tzu-chieh
Cheng-chia-chai
Shang-ho
Cheng-chia
Tzu-chiao
Ch'ing-ho-chen
Yellow River
Huang Ho
Niu-chuang
Ch'i-chi
Wu-kuan-chai
San-t'ang
Tao-hsü
Ch'un-hua-chen
Chao-chia-chü
Chü-lu
Chia-ma-ying
P'ing-yüan
Ta-li-chia
Lin-i
Meng-ssu
Wang-p'an-chen
Hsiao-ying
Pei-ssu
Chiu-ch'eng
Wu-ch'eng
En-ch'eng
Jen-feng
Ch'ing-ch'eng
Hsin-sheng-tien
Su-liu-chuang
Lin-chuang
Hsin-tien
Sha Ho
T'ien-chen
[Kao-ch'ing]
Po-hsing
Kuang-tsung
Ko-hsien-chuang
[Ch'ing-ho]
Hsing-lung
Ch'ü-t'i
Kao-yüan
Liu-ch'iao
Kuang-jao
Cheng-pao-t'un
Chang-chuang
Hsia-k'ou
Wei-chia-ch'iao
Sun-chen
Ch'ing-chia-chuang
Tao-chuang
Ho-ku-miao
Wei-hsien
Hsia-chin
Liang-ts'un
Yin-chi
Fang-ssu
Chang-pao-t'un
Chi-yang
Lü-chia-chai
Chiu-hu
Huan-t'ai-ch'eng
So-chen
[Huan-t'ai]
Hsing-fu
T'ien-liu
Ma-t'ou
[Ch'iu Hsien]
Tsao-yüan
Yü-ch'eng
Hui-ho
Hsin-chai
Ch'ang-shan
Chu-t'ai
Ta-wang
Feng-ch'eng
Ho-hsi-chieh
Lin-ch'ing
Sung-lin
Kao-t'ang
An-jen
Wang-tzu-chuang
Sun-keng
Shui-chai
Chiu-chang-ch'iu
Tsou-p'ing
Chang-tien
[Tzu-po]
Ma-shang
Chin-ling-chen
Lin-tzu
Shou-kuang
K'ou-pu
Hsiang-ch'eng-ku
K'ang-chuang
Sung-chuang
Lun-chen
Sang-tzu-tien
Ya-wang-k'ou
Kuo-tien
Ming-shui
[Chang-ch'iu]
Chou-ts'un
Nan-ting
Feng-shui
Hsin-tien
Tzu-ho-tien
Mi Ho
Wei-wan
Ch'ing-p'ing
Liu-li-ssu
Yen-ch'eng
Ch'i-ho
Tsao-yüan
P'ing-ling-ch'eng
P'u-chi
Ta-lin-ch'ih
Lo-chia-chuang
T'an-chia-fang
Yao-kou
Liu-lin
Tou-hu-t'un
Lo-k'ou
Hung-chia-lou
[Li-ch'eng]
Tzu-chuan
Chiu-kuan-t'ao
Ch'ing-shui
Ch'ih-p'ing
P'an-tien
Chiao-miao
CHI-NAN
(TSINAN)
Pu-ts'un
Wang-ts'un
Hung-shan
Lung-k'ou
Chu-ya
I-tu
Nan-kuan-t'ao
[Kuan-t'ao]
Liang-shui-chen
Po-p'ing
P'ing-an-tien
Tang-chia-chuang
Wen-tsu
Ta-k'un-lun
Lung-kang
Chia-chen
Ch'ang-ch'ing
Jen-li-chi
Hsi-ying
Hsi-ho
T'ai-ho
Lin-ch'ü
T'ang-i
Chao-kuan-chen
Ku-shan
Kuei-te
Chung-kung
Liu-pu
Po-shan
Kuan-hsien
Liao-ch'eng
Chiang-kuan-t'un
Kao-chi
Chang-hsia
Shih-t'an-wu
Pa-tou
Wu-ching
Liu-shan-chai
Hsin-chai
Sang-a-chen
Niu-chiao-tien
Hsüeh-yeh-chuang
Yüan-ch'üan
Chih-yüan
Kao-ya
Chang Ho
Chin-t'an-chen
Wang-feng
T'ung-ch'eng
[Tung-a]
Hsiao-li-p'u
Ling-yen-ssu
Ta-ming
Sha-chen
Yü-chi
Yen-tien
Ku-kuan-t'un
Wan-te
K'ou-chen
Miao-shan
Ch'ang-chuang
Chai-li
Lung-wang-miao
Chang-lu
Kuo-tien-t'un
P'ing-yin
Shou-chieh
Chu-vang
1108
San-ch'a-tien
Chiang-yü
Hsin-hsien
Hsiao-kou
T'ai Shan
1524
Fang-hsia
Lu Shan
I Shan
1032
Fei-ch'eng
Mu-chuang
T'ai-an
Fan-chen
Lai-wu
Hsin-chuang
Lu-ts'un
Yüeh-chuang
Ku-liu-shu
A-ch'eng
Tung-a-chen
Shih-heng
Tao-fang
Nan-ma
[I-yüan]
Chiu-shan
Nan-lo
Yang-ku
Chang-ch'iu
Hsia-chih
T'un-t'ou
I-yang
Chu-tien
Chiu-hsien
Shih-ch'iao
Mu-ling Kuan
Ch'ien-k'ou
Chao-ch'eng
Ta-yang
An-lin-chan
Hsia-chang
Hung-kou
Nan-shang-chuang
Yen-chuang
Huang-chuang
Ya-chuang
Ma-chan
Chiu-shou-chang
Tung-a-ping Hu
Tung-pei-chi-p'o
Kuan-ch'eng
Ku-ch'eng
Hua-lan-tien
Man-chuang
Ts'u-lai Shan
1027
Chang-chuang
Tung-li-tien
Chu-ko
Ch'ing-feng
An-chia-chuang
Ta-wen Ho
Ta-wen-k'ou
Yang-liu-tien
Han-wang
Kao-ch'iao
Hsü-ch'eng
Ta-ching
Tung-liang-chuang
Kung-li
Kuo-tu
Pei-shih-tien
Yang-chia-chai
Ying-t'ao-yüan
[Fan Hsien]
An-shan
Tung-p'ing
Tz'u-yao
Lou-te
Hsin-t'ai
Lung-yen
Pu-li
Tao-to
Hei-hu-miao
Hou-chi
[Liang-shan]
Sha-ho-chen
Yang-liu-tien
Kang-ch'eng
Nan-i
Hua-feng
Ku-li
Sun-ts'un
[Hsin-wen]
Tung-tu
Ch'ing-ho-t'ou
Chin-ch'eng
Hsiao-p'i-k'ou
Liang Shan
Hsia-wei
Ts'ui-chia-yü
Yang-chi
Ning-yang
Hsieh-ma-t'ing
Shih-lai
Ch'ang-lu
T'an-pu
I-shui
P'u-ch'eng
Lo-lou
P'an-ch'i-tu
Ch'ang-chuang
Che-kou
Meng-yin
Yao-chia-tien-tzu
Ssu-shih-li-p'u
Chiu-ch'eng
Yang-chuang-chi
Wen-shang
Wu-ts'un
Hsing-ts'un
Chung-ts'e
Wu-t'ai
Hsieh-wu
Chi-shan
K'ai-ho
Ch'eng-chia-chuang
Yao-ts'un
Ssu-shui
Hsia-ch'iao
Chung-ts'un
Su-ts'un
Tung-ching
Chüan-ch'eng
Ch'en-p'o
Yün-ch'eng
Huang-ho
Nan-wang
Tz'u-ch'iu
K'ang-chuang-i
Ch'ü-fu
1155
Kuei-meng Ting
Chieh-p'ai
Meng-liang-ku
Tung-k'ou
Yin-ma
Liang-pao-ssu
Yen-chou
Ch'eng-chia-chuang
Nan-hsin
Chang-chuang
T'ien-huang
P'ing-i
To-chuang
Chieh-hu
[I-nan]
Lin-p'u-chi
Huang-an
Wu-an-chi
Shen-li-p'u
Sun-shih-tien
P'u-wang
Shen-chi
Chao-wang Ho
Shuang-hou
Liu-chuang
Hsiao-liu-chi
Chia-yang
Chi-ning
Wang-yu
Tsou-hsien
Ta-shu
T'ang-ts'un
Tung-yang
T'ung-shih
Hsia-ch'iao
Shang-chih
Ching-t'o-ssu
Ho-yang
Hsia-chuang
Tung-ming
Chü-yeh
Hsia-kuan-t'un
An-chü
Chung-hsin-tien
Chang-chuang
Ch'eng-ch'ien
Ti-fang
Ko-kou
Ch'i-wang-chi
Hsin-chi
Sha-t'u-chi
Lung-ku-chi
Ta-i
T'ai-p'ing-ch'iao
Liang-hsia-tien
I Shan
Chu-shui Ho
Hsieh-chuang
Wang-kou
Shih-ch'iao
T'ang-t'ou
Yu-t'an-chai
Ho-tse
Tu-shan-chi
Ma-p'o
Cheng-ch'eng
Chu-t'ien
Fei-hsien
Tung-ming-chi
Chang-feng-chi
Kuo-li-chi
Chieh-ho
Tung-kuo
Liu-lin-chi
Lu-ch'iao
Liu-chia-chuang
Hsin-chuang
Liang-ch'iu
T'an-i
I-t'ang
O-chuang
Wang-huo-t'un
Yang-shan
Ta-i-chi
Liang-ch'eng
Wan-fu Ho
Ta-wu
Sang-ts'un
Tu-shu-t'ou
Pan-ch'üan
Chiao-yüan
Ma-t'ou-chi
Ting-t'ao
Nan-lu-chi
Nan-yang
T'eng-hsien
Shan-t'ing
Hsin-chuang
Ma-chuang
Hsiang-kung-chuang
T'ao-yüan
Han-chi
Ma-chi
Jan-ku
Ma-miao
Lo-t'un
Chin-hsiang
Tu-shan Hu
Nan-sha-ho
Hsü-chuang
Lin-i
Chiu-ch'ü
Chung-kou
Ku-t'ing
[Yü-t'ai]
Chung-ts'un
Ta-wang-chi
Ch'eng-wu
Chi-shu-chi
Yü-ch'eng
Man-k'ou
Hsi-kang
Yang-chuang
Pao-tu Ku
Lo-chuang
Hsia-chuang
[Lin-shu]
Wei-wan
T'ien-kuan-miao
Lung-ku
Kuan-ch'iao
Hsi-chi
Fu-chuang
Ch'i-ts'un
Tsao-chuang
Huang-ssu
Ts'ao-ma-chi
Hsia-chen
[Wei-shan]
T'ao-chuang
Tsou-wu
Shui-kuo
Hsiang-ch'eng
T'ang-chuang
Li-chia-chuang
Nan-ku-chuang
Ts'ao-hsien
Shan-hsien
Chung-hsing
Hsüeh-ch'eng
I-ch'eng
Pien-chuang
[Ts'ang-shan]
Mo-shan
Ts'ao-chuang
Ta-hsing-chen
Ta-i-chi
Ch'ing-ku-chi
Lung-wang-miao
Sha-kou
Lan-ling
Ts'eng-shan
Ta-p'u
Shih-men
Min-ch'üan
Huang-kang-chi
Feng-hsien
P'ei-hsien
Weishan Hu
Chou-ying
Lan-ch'eng
Ch'ang-ch'eng
Liang-t'i-t'ou
Yang-lou
Han-chuang
Ma-t'ou-chen
Liu-ho
Ma-liang-chi
T'ai-erh-chuang
Chung-fang
Kang-shang
T'an-ch'eng
Li-kou-i
Chien-t'ou-chi
Niu-shan
[Tung-hai]
Ning-ling
Chu-chi
[Shang-ch'iu]
Ching-an-chi
Yang-chi
Hung-hua-pu
Tang-shan
Fei-huang Ho
Liu-ch'üan
Shang-ch'iu
Liu-ti-ch'üan
Huang-k'ou
Chia-wang
Kuan-hu
Hsin-an
[Hsin-i]
Yang-lou

1 : 1350000

0 5 10 20 30 40 50 60 70 80 90 100 MILES

0 5 10 20 30 40 50 60 70 80 90 100 150 KM

SHANTUNG PROVINCE 山东省

SHAN-TUNG SHENG

9 shih	*municipalities*
9 ti-ch'ü	*regions*
106 hsien	*counties*

capital **Chi-nan Shih**	**C3**	济南市
Li-ch'eng Hsien		历城县
centre: Hung-chia-lou	**C3**	洪家楼
Ch'ing-tao Shih	**F3**	青岛市
Lao-shan Hsien		崂山县
centre: Li-ts'un	**F3**	李村
Chi-ning Shih	**B4**	济宁市
Te-chou Shih	**B2**	德州市
Tsao-chuang Shih	**C5**	枣庄市
Tzu-po Shih	**D3**	淄博市
centre: Chang-tien		张店
Wei-fang Shih	**E3**	潍坊市
Wei-hai Shih	**H2**	威海市
Yen-t'ai Shih	**G2**	烟台市

Ch'ang-wei Ti-ch'ü 昌潍地区

centre: Wei-fang	**E3**	潍坊
An-ch'iu Hsien	**E3**	安丘县
Ch'ang-i Hsien	**E3**	昌邑县
Ch'ang-lo Hsien	**D3**	昌乐县
Chiao Hsien		胶县
centre: Chiao-hsien	**F3**	
Chiao-nan Hsien		胶南县
centre: Wang-ko-chuang	**E4**	王哥庄
Chu-ch'eng Hsien	**E4**	诸城县
I-tu Hsien	**D3**	益都县
Kao-mi Hsien	**E3**	高密县
Lin-ch'ü Hsien	**D3**	临朐县
P'ing-tu Hsien	**E3**	平度县
Shou-kuang Hsien	**D3**	寿光县
Wei Hsien		潍县
centre: Han-t'ing	**E3**	寒亭
Wu-lien Hsien		五莲县
centre: Hung-ning	**E4**	洪凝

Chi-ning Ti-ch'ü 济宁地区

Chia-hsiang Hsien	**B4**	嘉祥县
Chin-hsiang Hsien	**B4**	金乡县
Chi-ning Hsien	**B4**	济宁县
Ch'ü-fu Hsien	**B4**	曲阜县
Ssu-shui Hsien	**C4**	泗水县
T'eng Hsien		滕县
centre: T'eng-hsien	**C4**	
Tsou Hsien		邹县
centre: Tsou-hsien	**B4**	
Wei-shan Hsien		微山县
centre: Hsia-chen	**C5**	夏镇
Wen-shang Hsien	**B4**	汶上县
Yen-chou Hsien	**B4**	兖州县
Yü-t'ai Hsien		鱼台县
centre: Ku-t'ing	**B4**	谷亭

Ho-tse Ti-ch'ü 菏泽地区

Ch'eng-wu Hsien	**A5**	成武县
Chüan-ch'eng Hsien	**A4**	鄄城县
Chü-yeh Hsien	**B4**	巨野县
Ho-tse Hsien	**A4**	菏泽县
Liang-shan Hsien		梁山县
centre: Hou-chi	**B4**	后集
Shan Hsien		单县
centre: Shan-hsien	**B5**	
Ting-t'ao Hsien	**A4**	定陶县
Ts'ao Hsien		曹县
centre: Ts'ao-hsien	**A5**	
Tung-ming Hsien	**A4**	东明县
Yün-ch'eng Hsien	**A4**	郓城县

Hui-min Ti-ch'ü 惠民地区

centre: Pei-chen	**D2**	北镇
Chan-hua Hsien		沾化县
centre: Fu-kuo	**D2**	富国
Huan-t'ai Hsien		桓台县
centre: So-chen	**D3**	索镇
Hui-min Hsien	**C2**	惠民县
Kao-ch'ing Hsien		高青县
centre: T'ien-chen	**C2**	田镇
K'en-li Hsien		垦利县
centre: Hsi-shuang-ho	**D2**	西双河
Kuang-jao Hsien	**D2**	广饶县
Li-chin Hsien	**D2**	利津县
Pin Hsien		滨县
centre: Pei-chen	**D2**	北镇
Po-hsing Hsien	**D2**	博兴县
Tsou-p'ing Hsien	**C3**	邹平县
Wu-ti Hsien	**C2**	无棣县
Yang-hsin Hsien	**C2**	阳信县

Liao-ch'eng Ti-ch'ü 聊城地区

Ch'ih-p'ing Hsien	**B3**	茌平县
Hsin Hsien		莘县
centre: Hsin-hsien	**A3**	
Kao-t'ang Hsien	**B3**	高唐县
Kuan Hsien		冠县
centre: Kuan-hsien	**A3**	
Liao-ch'eng Hsien	**A3**	聊城县
Lin-ch'ing Hsien	**A3**	临清县
Tung-a Hsien		东阿县
centre: T'ung-ch'eng	**B3**	铜城
Yang-ku Hsien	**A3**	阳谷县

Lin-i Ti-ch'ü 临沂地区

Chü Hsien		莒县
centre: Chü-hsien	**D4**	
Chü-nan Hsien		莒南县
centre: Shih-tzu-lu	**D4**	十字路
Fei Hsien		费县
centre: Fei-hsien	**C4**	
I-nan Hsien		沂南县
centre: Chieh-hu	**D4**	界湖
I-shui Hsien	**D4**	沂水县
I-yüan Hsien		沂源县
centre: Nan-ma	**D3**	南麻
Jih-chao Hsien	**E4**	日照县
Lin-i Hsien	**D4**	临沂县
Lin-shu Hsien		临沭县
centre: Hsia-chuang	**D5**	夏庄
Meng-yin Hsien	**C4**	蒙阴县
P'ing-i Hsien	**C4**	平邑县
T'an-ch'eng Hsien	**D5**	郯城县
Ts'ang-shan Hsien		苍山县
centre: Pien-chuang	**D5**	卞庄

T'ai-an Ti-ch'ü 泰安地区

Ch'ang-ch'ing Hsien	**B3**	长清县
Chang-ch'iu Hsien		章丘县
centre: Ming-shui	**C3**	明水
Fei-ch'eng Hsien	**B3**	肥城县
Hsin-t'ai Hsien	**C4**	新泰县
Hsin-wen Hsien		新文县
centre: Sun-ts'un	**C4**	孙村
Lai-wu Hsien	**C3**	莱芜县
Ning-yang Hsien	**B4**	宁阳县
P'ing-yin Hsien	**B3**	平阴县
T'ai-an Hsien	**C3**	泰安县
Tung-p'ing Hsien	**B4**	东平县

Te-chou Ti-ch'ü 德州地区

Ch'i-ho Hsien	**B3**	齐河县
Ch'ing-yün Hsien		庆云县
centre: Hsieh-chia-chi	**C2**	解家集
Chi-yang Hsien	**C3**	济阳县
Hsia-chin Hsien	**A3**	夏津县
Ling Hsien		陵县
centre: Ling-hsien	**B2**	
Lin-i Hsien	**B2**	临邑县
Lo-ling Hsien	**C2**	乐陵县
Ning-chin Hsien	**B2**	宁津县
P'ing-yüan Hsien	**B2**	平原县
Shang-ho Hsien	**C2**	商河县
Wu-ch'eng Hsien	**A2**	武城县
Yü-ch'eng Hsien	**B3**	禹城县

Yen-t'ai Ti-ch'ü 烟台地区

Ch'ang-tao Hsien		长岛县
centre: Ssu-hou	**F2**	寺后
Chao-yüan Hsien	**F2**	招远县
Chi-mo Hsien	**F3**	即墨县
Fu-shan Hsien	**G2**	福山县
Hai-yang Hsien		海阳县
centre: Tung-ts'un	**G3**	东村
Hsi-hsia Hsien	**F2**	栖霞县
Huang Hsien		黄县
centre: Huang-hsien	**F2**	
Jung-ch'eng Hsien		荣成县
centre: Ya-t'ou	**H2**	崖头
Ju-shan Hsien		乳山县
centre: Hsia-ts'un	**G3**	夏村
Lai-hsi Hsien		莱西县
centre: Shui-chi	**F3**	水集
Lai-yang Hsien	**F3**	莱阳县
Mou-p'ing Hsien	**G2**	牟平县
P'eng-lai Hsien	**F2**	蓬莱县
Wen-teng Hsien	**H2**	文登县
Yeh Hsien		掖县
centre: Yeh-hsien	**E2**	

SHANSI
PROVINCE

SHANSI province, especially the southern half, was one of the earliest areas of Chinese civilisation, the territory of the state of Chin. Later, after the unification of the empire in 221 BC the northern part of the province became one of the key defensive areas between China and her semi-nomadic northern neighbours. From the 3rd to the 6th century Shansi came under the control of a succession of alien dynasties. In AD 386–532 it was the base from which the Toba established the Northern Wei state (its first capital was at Ta-t'ung) which reunified northern China. In the early 7th century it was the power base for the establishment of the T'ang, and a crucial strategic area in their subsequent struggles with the Turks. In later times, when the political centre of China moved from the north-west, and the Shensi area went into an economic decline, Shansi remained relatively isolated and poor, bearing a heavy defensive establishment. During the late Ming and Ch'ing periods, the inhabitants of central Shansi became prominent in trade, and began to set up a widespread banking system, used for government transfers of funds, which had branches throughout China, but especially in the north and central provinces. These local banks ceased to be important after the end of the empire (1911). During the Republican period Shansi was controlled by Yen Hsi-shan, a powerful warlord whose autonomous regime attempted to institute some measure of industrial growth and modernisation. The first railway, joining T'ai-yüan to Shih-chia-chuang in Hopeh was built from 1904–7 by a Sino-French company, and Ta-t'ung was linked with Chang-chia-k'ou (Kalgan) and Peking shortly afterwards. Yen Hsi-shan built a further railway from Ta-t'ung to T'ai-yüan and later extended this to P'u-chou in the south-west of the province in 1937. Shansi was the scene of fierce resistance to the Japanese invasion and during the Second World War the Japanese carried out further development of industry and coal mining around T'ai-yüan, although the mountainous areas in both eastern and western Shansi were in the hands of Communist guerilla forces.

Under the Communists, after 1949, the serious exploitation of Shansi's mineral wealth and the development of T'ai-yüan into a major industrial city have continued.

Shansi consists of a great upraised plateau, with an average height of from 500–1,000 m, broken by a series of fault trenches and basins down the middle of the province. It falls into a number of distinct regions.

Western Shansi The western edge of the plateau, north of the Fen river valley, is dominated by the folded range of the Lü-liang mountains, which average 1,500 m, with individual peaks of more than 2,500 m. To the west of this range, rivers drain into the Huang Ho, which runs through a series of gorges culminating at Lung-men, and is unnavigable. The climate is very dry, with 300–400 mm of rain, and the area, which is heavily loess covered, sustains rather poor agriculture, although spring wheat, millet and kaoliang are grown. The area has very poor communications, and is rather impoverished. In the 1950s various plans for improvements were made in connection with the reclamation plan for the Huang Ho basin, but few of these were implemented.

The An-i basin The extreme south-western corner of the province is occupied by the An-i basin, lying between the Chi-wang Shan range to the north and the higher Chung-t'iao Shan range which forms the province's southern border. This is a heavily cultivated area, with a longer growing season (240 days or more) than other parts of Shansi. It grows winter wheat, corn, kaoliang and some cotton. This area, the main centre of which is Yün-ch'eng, is also a very important producer of salt, from the Chieh-i salt lake. This yields some 600,000 tons of household salt annually, and also sustains a small local chemical industry.

The Yang-ch'eng and Ch'ang-chih basins Drained by northern tributaries of the Huang Ho, the Ch'in Ho and Ta Ho respectively, these basins, which occupy the south-east of the province, are closely connected with Honan province. Intensively cultivated, this is the area of the province with the most rainfall (500 mm or more). Agriculture concentrates on winter wheat, corn, kaoliang, cotton and hemp. In addition to agriculture, the Ch'ang-chih area is an old-established centre of the iron industry. There is a coal field at Lu-an, north of Ch'ang-chih, which has been linked by rail to Honan since 1961. Ch'ang-chih itself has a small iron and steel works, cement manufacturing, and rubber works. Much of the coal from this area is shipped by rail to the industrial cities of Honan.

The Fen- Ho valley and T'ai-yüan basin The Fen Ho drains central Shansi, running from north-east to south-west through a series of fault basins. The valley has been irrigated from early times, but the irrigation system suffered neglect and was extensively repaired and broadened from the 1930s onwards. The agriculture is based on winter wheat, kaoliang and millet, while cotton and hemp are also widely grown. The largest and most productive area of cultivation is the basin around T'ai-yüan. These central basins have important coal mines, and the province as a whole has enormous reserves of coal. The Fen-hsi coal field on the west of the Fen Ho valley has mines at Ho-hsien, Fu-chia-t'un and Fen-hsi producing coking coal for the steel industry at T'ai-yüan. Further north is the newer I-t'ang field, developed in the 1960s. These fields are served by spur railways. A more important field is the Hsi-shan field west of T'ai-yüan itself which produces annually nearly 5 million tons of coking and steam coals.

T'ai-yüan is the provincial capital, the administrative centre and largest city of Shansi since very early historical times. Modern industry, together with western-style education, was established there in the first years of this century, and further developed under the 'planned economy' instituted by warlord Yen Hsi-shan in the 1930s. It was not only an important food processing and textile centre, using locally grown cotton in modern mills, but it also had a wide range of engineering industries. After 1949 T'ai-yüan was one of the first inland centres to be developed into a major industrial complex under the industrial dispersion policy of the First Five Year Plan. The major industry first developed was iron and steel, using local coal and iron ore, and also ore from Lung-yen in Hopeh. In the late 1950s T'ai-yüan ranked after An-shan as China's second centre of steel production, although it has since been overtaken by Wu-han, Shanghai and possibly Pao-t'ou. Heavy machinery manufacture was also developed, and industrial chemical, fertiliser and plastics plants were set up after 1958. It has also become a major producer of aluminium. Yü-tz'u, a satellite city in the south-east, is a major producer of textile machinery. T'ai-yüan's population exceeded a million in 1957, and is estimated at about 1,100,000.

The Yang-ch'üan basin A small inter-montane basin situated west of the T'ai-hang mountains, east of T'ai-yüan. A minor agricultural district, Yang-ch'üan became an important producer of coal early in the century with the completion of the Shih-chia-chuang to Tai-yüan railway. Producing anthracite and low-sulphur coals, Yang-ch'üan yields between 5 and 10 million tons annually, much of which is exported to Hopeh as well as shipped to T'ai-yüan. There is also a local steel industry. The city has about 200,000 people.

The T'ai-hang mountains This is the general name given to the formidable mountain barrier which constitutes Shansi's eastern border with Hopeh. Presenting a steep 1,500–2,000 m escarpment to the east, broken only by a handful of passes cut by river valleys, these mountains have been a major cultural barrier throughout Chinese history. On the west the profile is much more gentle, and they slope down into the plateau. The northern end of the T'ai-hang proper is the valley of the Hu-t'o river. To the north are the complex series of north-east to south-west ranges making up the Wu-t'ai Shan and Heng Shan system, with peaks over 2,000 m. A largely barren area with only pockets of agriculture, this area was historically important as one of the great centres of Chinese Buddhism.

The Sang-kan basin The northernmost and largest of the basin plains in Shansi is that of the San-kan river, south of the great wall. This has always been a semi-frontier area for agriculture, because of its short growing season (less than 200 days) and low rainfall (below 500 mm). These, combined with bitterly cold winters, make it impossible to raise winter wheat, so agriculture largely depends on spring wheat, millet and kaoliang. Sesame and other oil seeds are important cash crops, and grazing of animals is important in the marginal lands.

Ta-t'ung is the chief city of the area. Traditionally an important political centre and a trading centre for the Inner Mongolian frontier, Ta-t'ung has been a major rail junction since the 1930s. Since the 1920s it has also been one of China's major coalfields, producing some ten million tons in the early 1960s. This field is of excellent bituminous coal. It is used for the generation of power, for the railways, and for the steel industries at Pao-t'ou and T'ai-yüan. Ta-t'ung also has a large cement industry, and engineering works specialising in railway plant and steam locomotives. It also remains a very important centre for local agricultural produce and for hides and wool from the Inner Mongolian frontier. It has a population of about 250,000.

Minority peoples Almost the entire population are Han Chinese, although on the northern border are a few Mongols and settlements of Chinese Moslems, who are also to be found in the T'ai-yüan and Ch'ang-chih areas.

AREA
157,000 square kilometres

POPULATION
Estimates range from 18,000,000 to 20,000,000

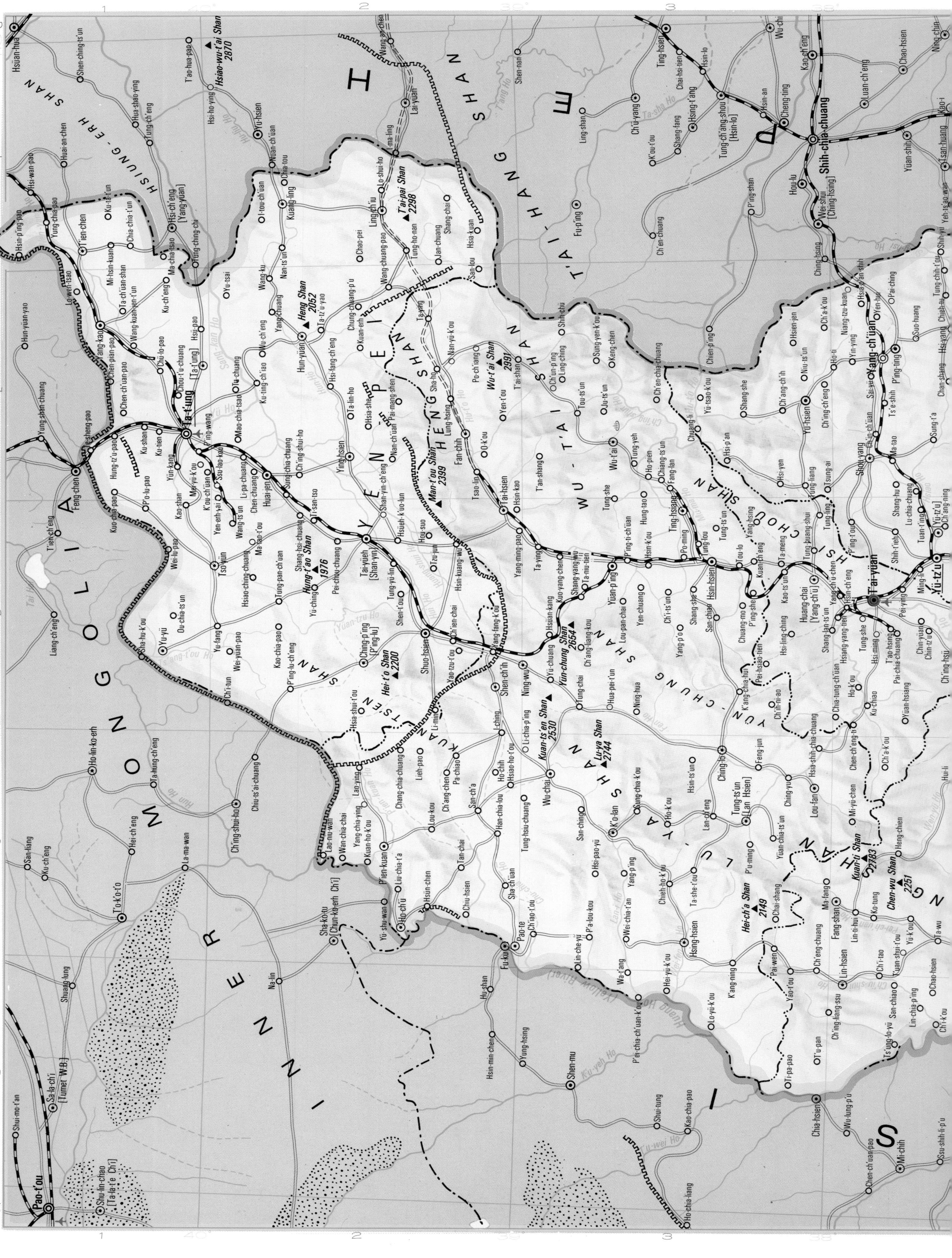
H
SHAN
HSIUNG-ERH SHAN
T'AI-HANG SHAN
WU-T'AI SHAN
HENG SHAN
YEN PEI
KUAN-TS'EN SHAN
YÜN-CHUNG SHAN
HSI SHAN
LÜ-LIANG SHAN
CHOU
INNER MONGOLIA
Hsiao-wu-t'ai Shan 2870
T'ai-pai Shan 2298
Heng Shan 2052
Wu-t'ai Shan 2991
Man-t'ou Shan 2399
Hung-t'ao Shan 1976
Hei-t'o Shan 2200
Yün-chung Shan 2654
Kuan-ts'en Shan 2530
Lu-ya Shan 2744
Hei-ch'a Shan 2149
Kuan-t'u Shan 2183
Chen-wu Shan 2251
Hsüan-hua
Ta-t'ung
Feng-chen
T'ai-yüan
Shih-chia-chuang
Yang-ch'üan
Hsin-hsien
Tai-hsien
Shuo-hsien
Ning-wu
Wu-chai
Ching-lo
Hsing-hsien
Lin-hsien
Pao-te
Fu-ku
Ho-ch'ü
Pao-t'ou
Sa-la-ch'i [Tumet W.B.]
Shu-lin-chao [Ta-la-t'e Ch'i]
Sha-ko-tu [Chun-ko-erh Ch'i]
Ho-lin-ko-erh
T'o-k'o-t'o
Ch'ing-shui-ho
Shen-mu
Chia-hsien
Mi-chih
Huang Ho (Yellow River)

SHANSI

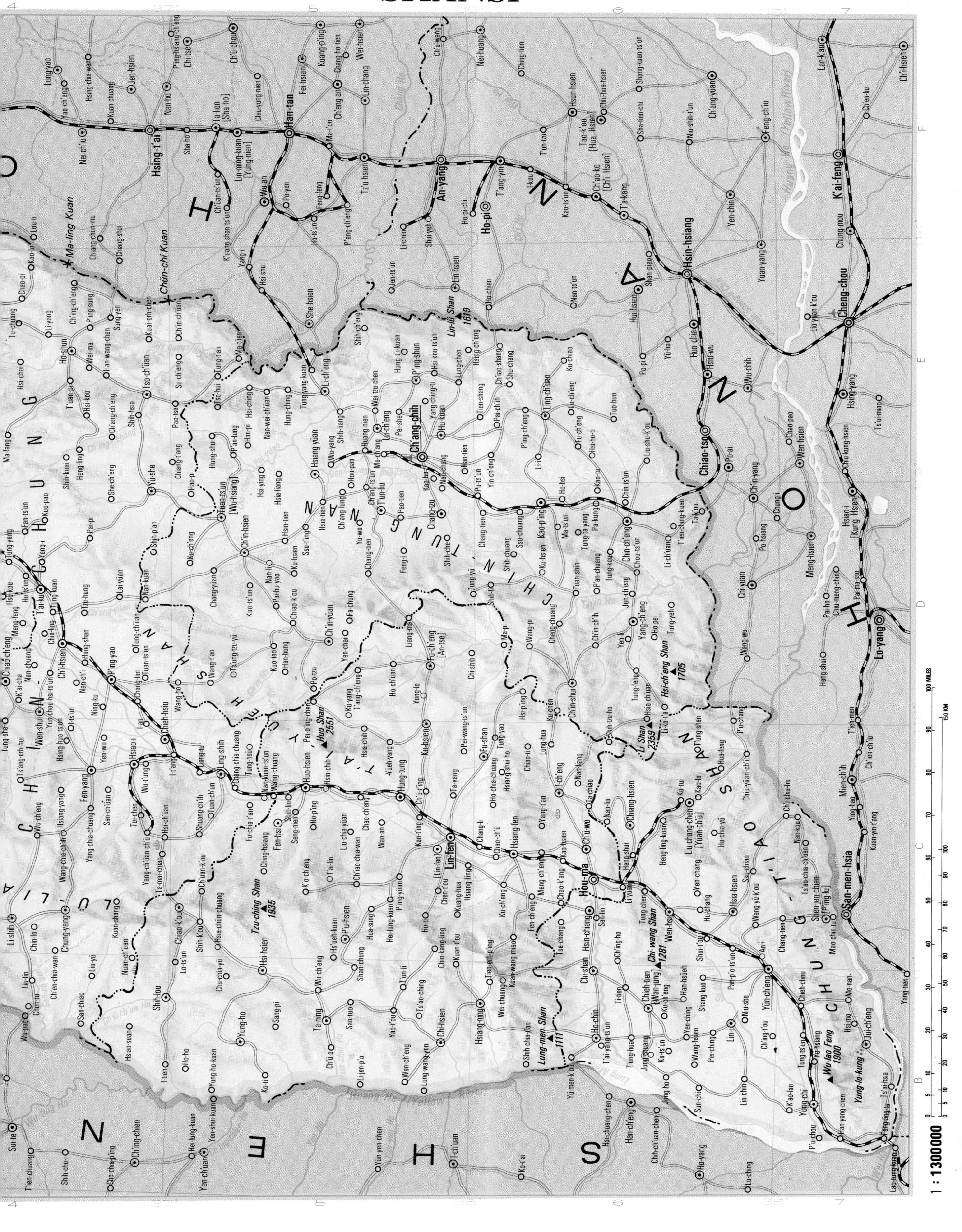
Han-tan
Hsing-t'ai
An-yang
Ho-pi
Hsin-hsiang
K'ai-feng
Cheng-chou
Chiao-tso
Lo-yang
San-men-hsia
Ch'ang-chih
Lin-fen
Hou-ma
Huo Shan 2551
Lin-lü Shan 1619
Chi-wang Shan 1281
Tzu-ching Shan 1935
Lung-men Shan 1111
Wu-lao Feng 1900
Huang Ho (Yellow River)
1 : 1300000
100 MILES
150 KM

SHANSI PROVINCE 山西省

SHAN-HSI SHENG

7 shih	*municipalities*
6 ti-ch'ü	*regions*
100 hsien	*counties*

capital T'ai-yüan Shih	D4	太原市
Ch'ing-hsü Hsien	D4	清徐县
Yang-ch'ü Hsien		阳曲县
centre: Huang-chai	D3	
Ch'ang-chih Shih	E5	长治市
Hou-ma Shih	C6	侯马市
Lin-fen Shih	C5	临汾市
Ta-t'ung Shih	E1	大同市
Yang-ch'üan Shih	E4	阳泉市
Yü-tz'u Shih	D4	榆次市

Chin-chung Ti-ch'ü		晋中地区
centre: Yü-tz'u	D4	榆次
Chiao-ch'eng Hsien	D4	交城县
Chieh-hsiu Hsien	C4	介休县
Ch'i Hsien		祁县
centre: Ch'i-hsien	D4	
Chung-yang Hsien	C4	中阳县
Fang-shan Hsien	C4	方山县
Fen-yang Hsien	C4	汾阳县
Ho-shun Hsien	E4	和顺县
Hsiao-i Hsien	C4	孝义县
Hsi-yang Hsien	E4	昔阳县
Ling-shih Hsien	C5	灵石县
Lin Hsien		临县
centre: Lin-hsien	B4	
Li-shih Hsien	C4	离石县
P'ing-ting Hsien	E4	平定县
P'ing-yao Hsien	D4	平遥县
Shou-yang Hsien	E4	寿阳县
T'ai-ku Hsien	D4	太谷县
Tso-ch'üan Hsien	E4	左权县
Wen-shui Hsien	D4	文水县
Yü Hsien		盂县
centre: Yü-hsien	E3	
Yü-she Hsien	D4	榆社县
Yü-tz'u Hsien		榆次县
centre: not known	D4	

Chin-tung-nan Ti-ch'ü		晋东南地区
centre: Ch'ang-chih	E5	长治
Ch'ang-chih Hsien	E5	长治县
Chang-tzu Hsien	D5	长子县
Chin-ch'eng Hsien	D6	晋城县
Ch'in Hsien		沁县
centre: Ch'in-hsien	D5	
Ch'in-shui Hsien	D6	沁水县
Ch'in-yüan Hsien	D5	沁源县
Hsiang-yüan Hsien	E5	襄垣县
Hu-kuan Hsien	E5	壶关县
Kao-p'ing Hsien	D6	高平县
Li-ch'eng Hsien	E5	黎城县
Ling-ch'uan Hsien	E6	陵川县
Lu-ch'eng Hsien	E5	潞城县
P'ing-shun Hsien	E5	平顺县
T'un-liu Hsien	D5	屯留县
Wu-hsiang Hsien		武乡县
centre: Tuan-ts'un	D5	段村
Yang-ch'eng Hsien	D6	阳城县

Hsin-hsien Ti-ch'ü		忻县地区
Ching-lo Hsien	C3	静乐县
Fan-chih Hsien	E2	繁峙县
Ho-ch'ü Hsien	C2	河曲县
Hsing Hsien		兴县
centre: Hsing-hsien	C3	
Hsin Hsien		忻县
centre: Hsin-hsien	D3	
K'o-lan Hsien	C3	岢岚县
Lan Hsien		岚县
centre: Tung-ts'un	C3	东村
Lou-fan Hsien	C3	娄烦县
Ning-wu Hsien	D2	宁武县
Pao-te Hsien	C2	保德县
P'ien-kuan Hsien	C2	偏关县
Shen-ch'ih Hsien	D2	神池县
Tai Hsien		代县
centre: Tai-hsien	D2	
Ting-hsiang Hsien	D3	定襄县
Wu-chai Hsien	C3	五寨县
Wu-t'ai Hsien	E3	五台县
Yüan-p'ing Hsien	D3	原平县

Lin-fen Ti-ch'ü		临汾地区
An-tse Hsien		安泽县
centre: Fu-ch'eng	D5	府城
Chiao-k'ou Hsien	C5	交口县
Chi Hsien		吉县
centre: Chi-hsien	B5	
Ch'ü-wo Hsien	C6	曲沃县
Fen-hsi Hsien	C5	汾西县
Fu-shan Hsien	C6	浮山县
Hsiang-fen Hsien	C6	襄汾县
Hsiang-ning Hsien	B6	乡宁县
Hsi Hsien		隰县
centre: Hsi-hsien	B5	
Hung-tung Hsien	C5	洪洞县
Huo Hsien		霍县
centre: Huo-hsien	C5	
I-ch'eng Hsien	C6	翼城县
Ku Hsien		古县
centre: Ku-hsien	C5	
Lin-fen Hsien		临汾县
centre: not known	C5	
P'u Hsien		蒲县
centre: P'u-hsien	C5	
Shih-lou Hsien	B4	石楼县
Ta-ning Hsien	B5	大宁县
Yung-ho Hsien	B5	永和县

Yen-pei Ti-ch'ü		雁北地区
centre: Ta-t'ung	E1	大同
Huai-jen Hsien	E2	怀仁县
Hun-yüan Hsien	E2	浑源县
Kuang-ling Hsien	F2	广灵县
Ling-ch'iu Hsien	F2	灵丘县
P'ing-lu Hsien		平鲁县
centre: Ching-p'ing	D2	井坪
Shan-yin Hsien		山阴县
centre: Tai-yüeh	D2	岱岳
Shuo Hsien		朔县
centre: Shuo-hsien	D2	
Ta-t'ung Hsien		大同县
centre: not known	E1	
T'ien-chen Hsien	F1	天镇县
Tso-yün Hsien	D2	左云县
Yang-kao Hsien	E1	阳高县
Ying Hsien		应县
centre: Ying-hsien	E2	
Yu-yü Hsien	D1	右玉县

Yün-ch'eng Ti-ch'ü		运城地区
Chiang Hsien		绛县
centre: Chiang-hsien	C6	
Chi-shan Hsien	B6	稷山县
Ho-chin Hsien	B6	河津县
Hsia Hsien		夏县
centre: Hsia-hsien	C6	
Hsin-chiang Hsien	C6	新绛县
Jui-ch'eng Hsien	B7	芮城县
Lin-i Hsien	B6	临猗县
P'ing-lu Hsien		平陆县
centre: Sheng-jen-chien	C7	圣人涧
Wan-jung Hsien		万荣县
centre: Chieh-tien	B6	解店
Wen-hsi Hsien	C6	闻喜县
Yüan-ch'ü Hsien		垣曲县
centre: Liu-chang-chen	C6	刘张镇
Yün-ch'eng Hsien	B6	运城县
Yung-chi Hsien	B7	永济县

KIANGSU PROVINCE

SHANGHAI MUNICIPALITY

THE Kiangsu–Shanghai region is the most populous and densely peopled area in China. Settled from very early times, this area, apart from its north-western extremity, formed part of the state of Wu from at least the 6th century BC. Wu was conquered by the Yüeh state in 473 BC, and then by the great Yangtze valley state of Ch'u in 334 BC. During this period the area developed a highly individual culture. Annexed by the Ch'in in 223 BC, the area became a part of the Chinese empire. But with the division of the empire in 220, the area became the main centre of a series of southern regimes, which were only reincorporated into the empire under the Sui in 589. After this the importance of Kiangsu grew rapidly. By the 8th century its population had grown and it had become a major grain-surplus area, exporting rice in huge quantities to the north via the canal system built by the Sui in the early 7th century. By the 12th century, this area had become the economic centre of the empire, with vastly productive agriculture, many great cities, and flourishing trade. With the conquest of northern China by the Chin in 1126, Hang-chou (Lin-an) became the capital of the Southern Sung empire, and grew into a huge and flourishing metropolis. The political capital of the empire remained in the south, at Nan-ching, when the Ming finally restored Chinese control over all of China in 1368. But even after 1421, when the seat of government moved, the region continued to prosper, and developed a highly productive economy, with a dense network of irrigation works and waterways, a complex textile industry, and a wealthy gentry which played a very important role in China's political and cultural life. Nan-ching once again became the political centre of China under the Nationalist government from 1928. But from the mid-19th century, with the growth of Shanghai as China's chief port and main centre of modern industry, the region became a centre for modernising influences. The present boundaries of the Shanghai Municipality and of Kiangsu date from 1958.

Virtually the entire region is a flat alluvial plain lying less than 50 m above sea-level. The hills are in the extreme north-west and the south-western corner of the province. A large proportion of the coastal areas have been reclaimed from the sea in historical times, and the coastline is constantly moving eastward. The plain is covered with a dense network of canals, irrigation ditches and canalised rivers, which form a very largely man-made landscape, intensively farmed.

Northern Kiangsu The area to the north of the Huai river was traditionally the poorest and most backward part of the province. It is drier than the rest of the province (less than 750 mm in the Hsü-chou area) and has a shorter growing season (250–260 days). As almost half of the annual rainfall comes in July and August, the area has a history of repeated droughts and disastrous floods. The main crops are winter wheat, followed by kaoliang or millet, with some corn. Sweet potatoes, peanuts and soy beans are also grown. Cotton cultivation has spread in this area since the mid-1950s, especially around Hsü-chou and the Huai valley. This area also has important coal deposits around Hsü-chou, an extension of the Tsao-chuang field in Shantung.

Hsü-chou, an important traditional route centre on the Grand Canal, became a major rail centre early in this century, at the point where the Tientsin–P'u-k'ou railway crossed the east–west Lung-hai route from the coast to the interior. Since the early 1950s, the Grand Canal south of Hsü-chou has been reconstructed, and has again become a major waterway. Hsü-chou's coalfield is at Chia-wang to the north-east, producing some 2,600,000 tons annually. Another coalfield to the south at Sui-ch'i produces some 5,000,000 tons. Hsü-chou is also a secondary industrial city, with textile and machine-making industries.

Lien-yün-kang is the port for the region. It is a modern city, built in the 1930s as the terminus of the Lung-hai railway, to replace the old port of Hai-chou which had silted up. It is the only port on the north Kiangsu coast, which is extremely shallow.

The Chiang-pei area The plain between the Huai and Yangtze rivers is divided into three zones. The coastal area, recently reclaimed from the sea, is an area of salt-pans which have been a major source of salt for many centuries. Further inland is an area of cultivated, but still very saline soils. This area is a major cotton-growing district. The western section is broken up by a series of lakes and marshes, and is largely a rice-producing area. The Chiang-pei area is served by a dense network of waterways, based on four main canals; the ancient Grand Canal between the Huai river at Huai-yin and the Yangtze near Yang-chou; the T'ung-yang canal running eastwards from Yang-chou to the coastal area of Huai-an; the Northern Kiangsu Canal, built to provide an adequate outlet from the Hung-tse lake to the sea; and the Ch'uan-ch'ang canal which runs parallel to the coast and was formerly much used by the salt industry. The most densely peopled and intensively farmed area lies in the south along the northern shore of the Yangtze mouth. In this area little rice is grown, the staple grains being wheat, barley and corn. Much of the land is planted to cotton, oilseeds, jute, soy beans, indigo and other specialised economic crops.

Yang-chou was, during the period from the 7th to the 11th centuries, one of China's richest trading cities, and the trans-shipment point for Yangtze trade on to the Grand Canal. Later it gradually declined, although it remained the home of the great salt merchants of Kiangsu. It is now mainly a commercial centre and market for northern Kiangsu salt and rice production.

Nan-t'ung began to rival Yang-chou as the chief city of the area at the end of the 19th century, when a local official, Chang Chien, provided it with modern schools, among the first in China, and various western-style industries. It now has cotton textiles, food processing, oil pressing and light engineering industries.

Ch'ing-chiang is the main town of the north, situated at the junction of the Grand Canal with the Huai. Once a major transport centre, much of its trade is now diverted to the railway further west in Anhwei. Like Yang-chou, it is now largely a commercial town and a major market for salt and rice.

Yen-ch'eng is the main centre of the coastal area, particularly for the salt industry.

The Nan-ching area comprises the part of Kiangsu south of the Yangtze and west of the T'ai Hu lake. This is the only hilly area in Kiangsu, but the hills, which have a south-west to north-east axis, do not exceed more than 200 m for the most part. The climate here is much more favourable than in the north of Kiangsu; rainfall is over 1,000 m and the growing season lasts for some 280 days. The lowland areas are intensively cultivated, largely double cropped with winter wheat followed by rice. Hill land occupies about a third of the region, and tea production is important, especially around I-hsing.

Nan-ching (Nanking) dominates this area. A major regional centre from at least the 2nd century BC, and from time to time the capital of various southern regimes, Nan-ching was the national capital from 1368–1421 and again from 1928–49. Until 1949 it was essentially a great administrative and commercial centre, with little industry. Since the early 1950s it has become a major industrial city. In addition to its traditional textile industry, it has become an important centre of the chemical industry; of fertiliser and cement manufacture; has a small iron and steel plant, engineering works producing lorries, machine tools and agricultural implements; electronics and plastics industries. Its communications were greatly improved in 1969 with the completion of a massive rail and road bridge across the Yangtze. Its population is estimated to be 1,700,000.

Chen-chiang is an old-established city at the northern end of the section of the Grand Canal south of the Yangtze. It became an important river port and centre of foreign trade in the late 19th century, but was gradually overshadowed by the growth of Shanghai. It remains a trading city, and its importance has been increased by the repairs to the Grand Canal, which leave it a major transfer point for goods from the area south of the Yangtze, like Yang-chou in the north. It has some minor industries – flour milling, oil-extraction and paper making. It is also an important centre of the lumber trade, where log rafts from the upper Yangtze are broken up for trans-shipment.

The T'ai Hu plain comprises the part of southern Kiangsu east of Chen-chiang. It is a huge, continuous expanse of alluvial plain, with only a few hills surrounding the T'ai Hu lake. The area has been heavily settled and intensively cultivated since at least the 6th century, and irrigation and reclamation work has been continuous for well over a thousand years. The soil is naturally fertile, the climate is warmer and wetter than other parts of Kiangsu, and the level of agricultural technique is extremely high. The basis of agriculture is doubled-cropped wheat and rice, but in some areas two crops of rice are grown. Grain is rotated with green fertiliser crops or rape-seed. Cotton is grown on the sandy lands in the north along the Yangtze. But the area is famous as one of China's chief districts for silk. The hills around T'ai Hu produce many fruits and also tea. Fresh-water fishing is also very important in this area.

Su-chou is a very ancient city, the capital of Wu in the 5th century BC, and a great administrative centre, famous for its cultured élite, its high level of education, its handicrafts and its wealth. It remains a tourist centre, with many beauty-spots and ancient monuments. Since 1949 it has become partially industrialised, although it has been rivalled by the growth of Shanghai and Wu-hsi. The old-established silk-industry has been greatly expanded; the city has developed a chemical industry, paper making, and has begun to produce cotton textiles.

Wu-hsi lies at the north-eastern corner of the T'ai Hu lake, also on the Grand Canal. It, too, is an ancient city, though of lesser importance than Su-chou until recent times. With the construction of the railway from Shanghai to Nan-ching in 1908, it grew into a very important market for the shipment of food to Shanghai, and grew rapidly into one of China's chief rice markets. Modern industry also began here rather early – the first modern textile mill was founded in 1894. Wu-hsi merchants played an important role in the industrial growth of Shanghai, and the city grew wealthy. After 1949 Wu-hsi's commercial role as a rice market diminished, and considerable industrial growth followed. Silk and cotton textiles are the main industry, but food processing, oil-extraction and machinery-making (diesel engines and machine tools) are of great importance.

Ch'ang-chou lies north-west of Wu-hsi, also on the canal and the railway. A local commercial city in former times, Ch'ang-chou developed a large-scale cotton textile industry after 1937. It is still the largest textile producer in the area, and also an important producer of textile machinery. It also has large engineering works, producing locomotives and railway rolling stock, diesel engines and electrical equipment.

The Shanghai Delta area Since 1958 this area, with Ch'ung-ming island in the mouth of the Yangtze, has formed the provincial-level municipality of Shanghai. The whole area is a flat plain broken by innumerable watercourses. Its agriculture is extremely intensive, and is largely concentrated on the production of foodstuffs for the Shanghai market, which dominates the whole area. Cotton and rice, wheat and rape-seed are the main crops, but vegetables and dairy produce are important commodities. Ch'ung-ming island is an important producer of cotton.

Shanghai is China's largest city, and one of its main industrial centres. Until 1842 Shanghai was a minor trading port, but once it had been opened up to foreign trade and foreign settlement, it grew at a phenomenal rate, outstripping the traditional ports of the Yangtze area, and the great cities like Su-chou in its hinterland. It became not only China's chief port, but also the major centre for modern western-owned industry, from which western ideas and modern technology were disseminated throughout the country.

Before 1937 Shanghai had a large share of Chinese industrial plant, industrial capital and modern industrial labour force, for the unsettled conditions in the inland provinces during the 1920s and 1930s encouraged industrial investment in Shanghai which was under western protection. Textiles and other light industries made up most of Shanghai's industry, and heavy industry was comparatively unimportant. After 1949, although the textile industry continued to grow – Shanghai is still by far the largest producer of textiles in China, manufacturing cotton, wool, silk and synthetic fibres – heavy industry was also developed. In the 1950s a major steel industry, using pig iron from Ma-an-shan and An-shan, was founded. This was converted in 1959–60 into a fully integrated iron and steel plant, producing 2 million tons of steel a year. Shanghai is also a major producer of copper, lead and zinc. There is a large and diversified engineering industry, and ship-building is a major industry. The chemical industry grew rapidly in the 1960s, producing industrial and pharmaceutical chemicals, plastics, synthetic fibres, and fertilisers. There is a large petro-chemical industry and refineries using crude oil from Ta-ch'ing in Manchuria.

Shanghai has three very large thermal power generating plants, and is the focus of a power grid, which connects it with Su-chou, Wu-hsi and Nan-ching, and with Hang-chou and the very large Hsin-an-chiang hydro-electric plant in Chekiang.

Shanghai's population is currently estimated at approximately twelve million.

KIANGSU AREA
102,200 square kilometres

POPULATION
45,230,000 (1957) (current estimates 47,000,000 to 51,000,000)

SHANGHAI AREA
5,600 square kilometres

POPULATION
12,000,000

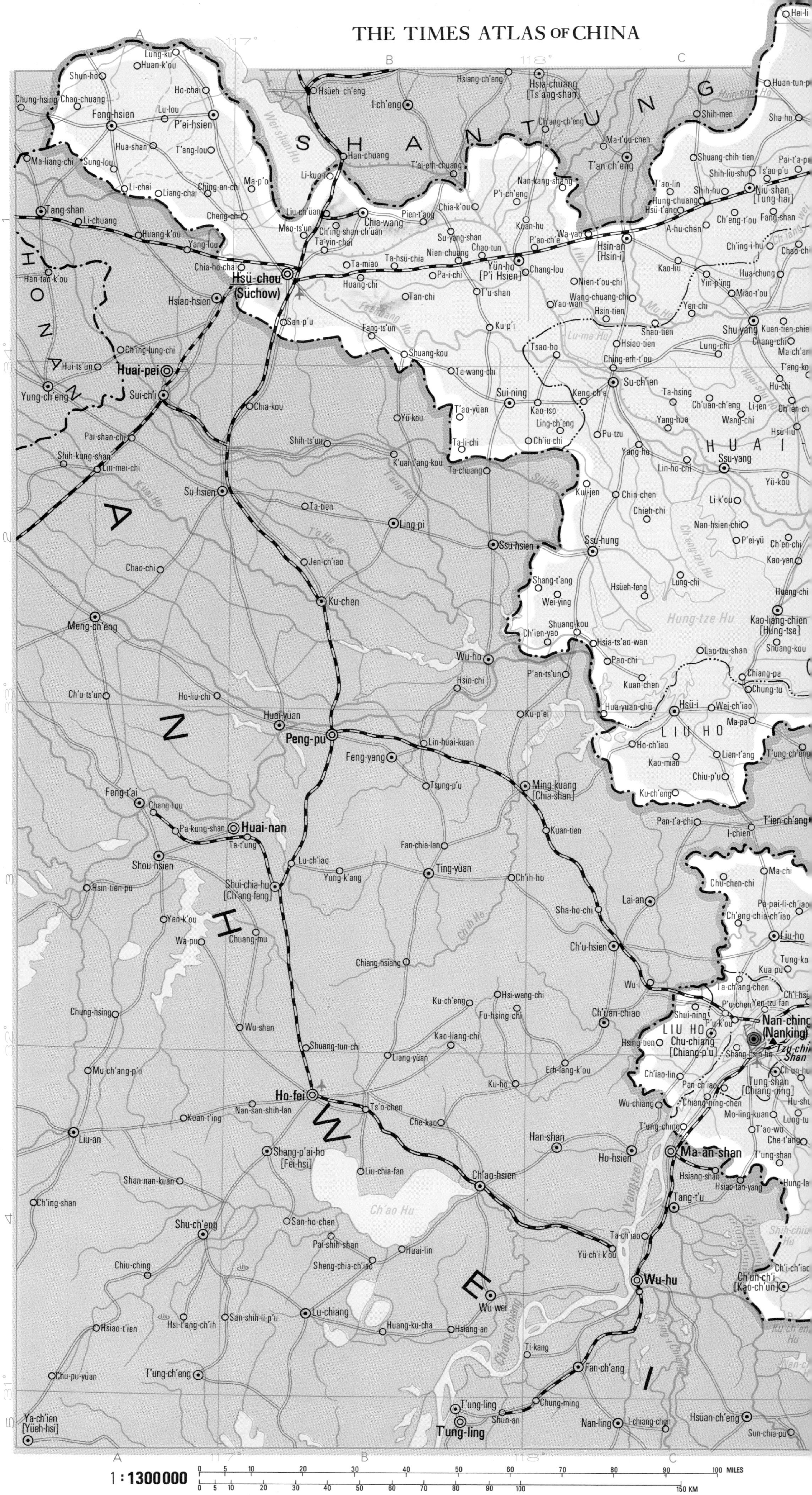

1 : 1300000

0 5 10 20 30 40 50 60 70 80 90 100 MILES

0 5 10 20 30 40 50 60 70 80 90 100 150 KM

Che-wang
Hai-chou Wan
Hai-t'ou
Yü-ch'eng
Ch'in-shan Tao
Ch'ing-k'ou [Kan-yü]
Tung-hsi-yün Tao
Hsü-kou
T'ai-pei
Lien-yün-kang
Tun-shang
Yün-t'ai Shan
Lien-yün-kang
Hai-chou
Nan-ch'eng
Hsü-yü
Pan-p'u
Yen-wei-kang
Hsin-pa
Tung-chi
T'ung-hsing-chieh
Lung-chü
Yang-chi
Ch'en-chia-kang
Ta-i-shan [Kuan-yün]
T'ien-lou
Hsin-shih-ts'un
Ta-yu
Ta-yu-chien
Wu-chi
Pai-tsao
Ch'en-chi
Hsin-i Ho
Hsiang-shui
Liu-t'ao
Pa-t'an
Li-chi
Hsin-an-chen [Kuan-nan]
Kuo-chi
Liu-t
Yün-ho-chi
Tung-k'an [Pin-hai]
(North Kiangsu Canal)
Kao-kou
Hui-tun
Wu-fan
Pa-ta-chia
Wu-kang
T'ang-chi
Ch'ien-ch'iu
Ch'eng-chi
Huang-ying
Ssu-ming
T'ung-yang-kang
T'ung-hsing
Ch'en-shih-an
Yang-chai
Fu-ning
Ch'en-chi
Lien-shui
Ho-te [She-yang]
Ch'en-yang
YIN
Pan-hu
Kou-tun
Wang-ying
Ch'in-kung
Ch'ing-chiang
Su-chia-chü
Tung-kou
Yung-hsing
Ts'ao-yen
Chung-hsing-ch'iao
Hsi-ch'iao
I-lin
Pan-cha
Kao-tso
Shang-kang
Huang-chia-chien
Huai-an
Chu-ch'iao
Ching-k'ou
Chien-yang
Hu-to [Chien-hu]
Hsin-hsing
Hsin-yang Kang
Tung-ch'iao
Nan-yang
San-lung
P'ing-ch'iao
An-feng
Yen-ch'eng
Ching-ho
She-yang
Lung-kang
Ts'ao-tien
Wu-yu
Ssu-ch'a-ho
Lou-wang
Ch'in-nan
Hsin-feng-chen
Ch'a-ho
Pao-ying
Ta-kang
Yü-hua
Lu-to
Ta-chung-chi [Ta-feng]
Ta-tsung Hu
Liu-pao
Sha-kou
Liu-chuang
Lü-liang-ch'iao
Liu-pao
Ta-chou
Nan-yang
Fan-shui
An-feng
Pai-chü
Li-ch'eng [Chin-hu]
Lin-tse
Hsiao-hai
Chieh-shou
Ch'en-tsao
Ta-ch'iao
Tai-chia-yao
Ts'ao-nien
Hsin-hsing [Hsing-hua]
Ta-to
P'an-te-hsing
Min-ch'iao
Ti-to
Tung-t'ai
Ssu-tsao
Ts'ao-p'ieh
Ch'ing-shui-t'an
Ho-k'ou
Ch'en-lun
Kao-yu Hu
San-to
Chiang-miao
Liang-to
San-ts'ang
Kao-yu
Chou-chuang
Tai-nan
An-feng
Liu-li-she
Shih-yen
Ch'iang-kang
Tung-lo
Pa-ch'iao-chen
Fu-an
Lu-chin
Fan-ch'uan
Ts'ou-t'ung
T'ang-yang
Sung-chia-ch'iao
Hsiao-chi
Kang-k'ou
Hsin-t'ung-yang-yün Ho
Hai-an
Li-pao
Chiao-hsieh
Huang-chüeh-ch'iao
Ting-kou
Pai-mu
Hu-chi
T'ai-chou
Shao-po
Chiang-yen [T'ai Hsien]
Pen-ch'a
Ta-i-chi
Ch'ü-t'ang
Ting-chia-so
Ch'en-chi
I-ling
Ssu-kang-k'ou
Feng-li
Hsieh-chia-chi
Hsien-nü-miao [Chiang-tu]
Ya-chou
Tung-ch'en
Chü-chen
Pei-k'an
Chang-t'ien
Chiang-to
Ju-kao
Ting-yen
Ch'a-ho
LIU-HO
Yang-chou
Ta-ch'iao
Tao-p'u
Shuang-tien
Ma-t'ang
Chüeh-kang [Ju-tung]
Hsin-ch'eng
San-chiang-ying
Shih-chia-ch'iao
K'ou-an
Pan-ching
I-cheng
Hsüan-chia-p'u
Mo-t'ou
Kua-chou
Liu-wei
Shih-kang
Ta-t'ung-chen
Ch'uan-yao Kang
Pai-p'u
Chen-chiang
Tan-tou-chen
Yang-chung
Ma-tien
Huang-ch'iao
Ch'i-an-chen
Ta-kang
T'ai-hsing
Chi-chia-shih
Shih-chuang
Kuo-chia-yüan
Lung-t'an
Hsia-shu
Kao-tzu
Chien-pi
K'uai-ch'eng
Yu-fang
Kuang-ling
P'ing-ch'ao
Hsi-t'ing
San-yü-chen
Pa-ch'iao-chen
Hsieh-ch'iao
Erh-an
T'ang-cha
Chin-sha [Nan-t'ung]
Lü-ssu
Hsin-feng
Ta-ch'eng-ch'iao
Hsin-shih
T'ien-sheng-kang
Yü-hsi
T'ang-shan
Tung-ch'ang-chieh
Meng-ho
Ching-chiang
Nan-t'ung-kang
Nan-t'ung
Yü-tung
Hai-fu-chen
Sheng-tz'u-chen
Hsiao-hai-chen
Erh-chia-chen
Ssu-chia-pa
Tan-yang
Hsi-hsia-shu
Pa-yü-kang
Shih-i-yü
Lang Shan
Ch'i-lin-chen
San-yang-chen
Pai-mien
Wei-ts'un
Hou-ch'eng
Ch'uan-kang
Chü-jung
Yen-k'ou
Hsia-kang
Chiang-yin
Mao-chia-chen [Hai-men]
San-ch'ang
Ling-tien-chen
Chiu-lung-chen
T'u-ch'iao
Yen-ling
Lü-ch'eng
An-chia-she
Shen-kang
Lu-yüan
Pao-nien
Erh-ling
Hsi-shih-ch'iao
Hua-shih
Yang-she [Sha-chou]
Tung-an-chen
Ch'ien-pai-shu
Pen-niu
Chiao-ch'i
Ch'iao-ch'i
Pei-hsin-chen
Hui-lung-chen [Ch'i-tung]
Kuo-chuang-miao
Chih-ch'i-ch'iao
Huang-t'ang
Ch'ang-chou
Tse-yang-chen
San-hsing
Ch'ung-ming Tao
T'ien-wang-ssu
Chin-t'an
Pu-i-ch'iao
Ch'i-shu-yen
Fu-shan
Hsü-p'u
Miao-chen
T'ai-an-kang
Yin-yang
Hsüeh-pu
Chu-lin
Hu-t'ang-ch'iao
Yü-ch'i
Chu-t'ang
Mei-li
Hsü-shih
Ch'ang-tang Hu
Shui-pei
Wu-huang
Chang-ching-ch'iao
Yü Shan
Ch'ung-ming
Hsin-k'ai-ho
Ch'ang Chiang-k'ou
MAO SHAN
Huang-li
Li-chia-ch'iao
Ch'ang-shu
Huang-ching
Li-shui
Wo Hu
Hui Shan
Lien-t'ang
Sha-ch'i
Fu-lu
Pao-chen
Shang-hsing-chen
P'i-ch'iao
Chai-ch'iao
Hu-tai
An-chen
Pai-mao
Ch'en-chia-chen
Chu-tse-ch'iao
Shang-huang
Wu-hsi
T'ang-k'ou
T'ang-shih
(Mouth of the Yangtze)
K'ung-chen
Kuan-lin
Ts'ao-ch'iao
Hsin-chuang
Shuang-feng
Liu-ho
(Yangtze)
Yang-hsiang
Hsin-an
Wang-t'ing
Pa-ch'eng
T'ai-ts'ang
Nan-tu
Hsüeh-yen-ch'iao
Wei-ching-t'ang
Lou-t'ang
Lo-tien
Pao-shan
Li-yang
Ho-ch'iao
Nan-fang-ch'üan
Ch'ang-hsing Tao
Chou-t'ieh-ch'iao
Huang-tai-chen
K'un-shan
Chia-ting
Wu-sung
Huang Sha
Ya-ch'i
Ch'a-t'ing
Hsü-she
I-hsing
Hu-kuan-chen
Lu-mu
Nan-hsiang
Ta-ch'ang
Kao-ch'iao
She-chu
Sui-t'ing
Cheng-i
Lu-chia
An-t'ing
SHANG-HAI SHIH
Tai-pu
Kuang-fu
Lu-chih-chen
Tung-pa
Ting-shu-chen
Su-chou (Soochow)
Chang-pu
Mei-chu
Chang-chu
Ling-yen Shan
Tung-fang
Soochow Creek
SHANG-HAI
Pen-tu
T'ai Hu
Ch'en-mu
Ch'uan-sha
Yang-tien
Heng-ching
Ch'ing-pu
Ch'i-pao
Chou-p'u
Hsi-tung-t'ing Shan
Tung-ho-chen
T'ung-li
Chu-ch'iao
Lang-ch'i
Tung-tung-t'ing Shan
Wu-chiang
Ssu-ching
Hsin-chuang [Shang-hai]
Nagasaki
CHE
Mei-shan
Tung-shan
Chou-chuang
Tien-shan Hu
Nan-hui
Hawaii
Shan-pei
Sung-chiang
Hsin-ch'ang
Ch'ang-hsing
Li-li
Lu-hsü
Lien-t'ang
Min-hsing
Ta-t'uan
Shi-tzu-p'u
KIANG
P'ing-wang
CHEKIANG
Whangpoo R.
Canton
Li-chia-kang
Nan-ch'iao [Feng-hsien]
Feng-ch'eng
Ssu-an
Sheng-tse
Kang-ching
T'ing-lin
Ni-ch'eng
Kuang-te
Chieh-p'ai
Hu-chou [Wu-hsing]
Chen-tse
Huang-p'u Chiang
Chin-shan
Che-lin
Nan-hsün
Chia-shan
Lü-kang
Chang-yen
Ning-po
Chin-shan-wei
700km
Ta Sha
YELLOW SEA
(HUANG HAI)
Tsingtao—Shanghai 740km
Tan-tung 1150km
Ch'ang Sha
Pei Sha
Ch'in-huang-tao 1280km
Yao Sha
P'u-tzu Sha
An Sha
Huang-tzu Sha
Chin-chia Sha
Chuang-chia Sha
Lang-chia Sha
Ta-lien 1040km
Wu-nan Sha
Yen-t'ai 960km
D
E
F
G
119°
120°
121°
122°
31°
32°
33°
34°
1
2
3
4
5

KIANGSU PROVINCE 江苏省
CHIANG-SU SHENG

11 shih	*municipalities*
8 ti-ch'ü	*regions*
64 hsien	*counties*

capital **Nan-ching Shih**	C3	南京市
Ch'ang-chou Shih	D4	常州市
Chen-chiang Shih	D3	镇江市
Ch'ing-chiang Shih	D2	清江市
Hsü-chou Shih	B1	徐州市
Lien-yün-kang Shih	D1	连云港市
Nan-t'ung Shih	E3	南通市
Su-chou Shih	E4	苏州市
T'ai-chou Shih	D3	泰州市
Wu-hsi Shih	E4	无锡市
Yang-chou Shih	D3	扬州市

Chen-chiang Ti-ch'ü		镇江地区
Chiang-ning Hsien		江宁县
centre: Tung-shan	C4	东山
Chin-t'an Hsien	D4	金坛县
Chü-jung Hsien	D4	句容县
I-hsing Hsien	D4	宜兴县
Kao-ch'un Hsien		高淳县
centre: Ch'un-ch'i	C4	淳溪
Li-shui Hsien	D4	溧水县
Li-yang Hsien	D4	溧阳县
Tan-t'u Hsien		丹徒县
centre: Chen-chiang	D3	镇江
Tan-yang Hsien	D4	丹阳县
Wu-chin Hsien		武进县
centre: Ch'ang-chou	D4	常州
Yang-chung Hsien	D3	扬中县

Hsü-chou Ti-ch'ü		徐州地区
Feng Hsien		丰县
centre: Feng-hsien	A1	
Hsin-i Hsien		新沂县
centre: Hsin-an	C1	新安
Kan-yü Hsien		赣榆县
centre: Ch'ing-k'ou	D1	青口
P'ei Hsien		沛县
centre: P'ei-hsien	A1	
P'i Hsien		邳县
centre: Yün-ho	B1	运河
Sui-ning Hsien	B2	睢宁县
Tung-hai Hsien		东海县
centre: Niu-shan	C1	牛山
T'ung-shan Hsien		铜山县
centre: Hsü-chou	B1	徐州

Huai-yin Ti-ch'ü		淮阴地区
centre: Ch'ing-chiang	D2	清江
Huai-an Hsien	D2	淮安县
Huai-yin Hsien		淮阴县
centre: Ch'ing-chiang	D2	清江
Hung-tse Hsien		洪泽县
centre: Kao-liang-chien	C2	高良涧
Kuan-nan Hsien		灌南县
centre: Hsin-an-chen	D1	新安镇
Kuan-yün Hsien		灌云县
centre: Ta-i-shan	D1	大伊山
Lien-shui Hsien	D2	涟水县
Shu-yang Hsien	C1	沭阳县
Ssu-hung Hsien	C2	泗洪县
Ssu-yang Hsien	C2	泗阳县
Su-ch'ien Hsien	C2	宿迁县

Liu-ho Ti-ch'ü		六合地区
Chiang-p'u Hsien		江浦县
centre: Chu-chiang	C3	珠江
Chin-hu Hsien		金湖县
centre: Li-ch'eng	D2	黎城
Hsü-i Hsien	C2	盱眙县
I-cheng Hsien	D3	仪征县
Liu-ho Hsien	C3	六合县

Nan-t'ung Ti-ch'ü		南通地区
Ch'i-tung Hsien		启东县
centre: Hui-lung-chen	F4	汇龙镇
Hai-an Hsien	E3	海安县
Hai-men Hsien		海门县
centre: Mao-chia-chen	F4	茅家镇
Ju-kao Hsien	E3	如皋县
Ju-tung Hsien		如东县
centre: Chüeh-kang	F3	掘港
Nan-t'ung Hsien		南通县
centre: Chin-sha	F3	金沙

Su-chou Ti-ch'ü		苏州地区
Ch'ang-shu Hsien	E4	常熟县
Chiang-yin Hsien	E4	江阴县
K'un-shan Hsien	E4	昆山县
Sha-chou Hsien		沙州县
centre: Yang-she	E4	杨舍
T'ai-ts'ang Hsien	F4	太仓县
Wu-chiang Hsien	E4	吴江县
Wu-hsi Hsien	E4	无锡县
Wu Hsien		吴县
centre: Su-chou	E4	苏州

Yang-chou Ti-ch'ü		扬州地区
Chiang-tu Hsien		江都县
centre: Hsien-nü-miao	D3	仙女庙
Ching-chiang Hsien	E3	靖江县
Han-chiang Hsien		邗江县
centre: Yang-chou	D3	扬州
Hsing-hua Hsien		兴化县
centre: Hsin-hsing	D3	新兴
Kao-yu Hsien	D3	高邮县
Pao-ying Hsien	D2	宝应县
T'ai Hsien		泰县
centre: Chiang-yen	E3	姜堰
T'ai-hsing Hsien	E3	泰兴县

Yen-ch'eng Ti-ch'ü		盐城地区
Chien-hu Hsien		建湖县
centre: Hu-tuo	D2	湖垛
Fu-ning Hsien	D2	阜宁县
Hsiang-shui Hsien	D1	响水县
Pin-hai Hsien		滨海县
centre: Tung-k'an	D1	东坎
She-yang Hsien		射阳县
centre: Ho-te	E2	合德
Ta-feng Hsien		大丰县
centre: Ta-chung-chi	E2	大中集
Tung-t'ai Hsien	E3	东台县
Yen-ch'eng Hsien	E2	盐城县

SHANGHAI MUNICIPALITY

SHANG-HAI SHIH	F4	上海市
Chia-ting Hsien	F4	嘉定县
Ch'ing-p'u Hsien	F4	青浦县
Chin-shan Hsien	F5	金山县
Ch'uan-sha Hsien	F4	川沙县
Ch'ung-ming Hsien	F4	崇明县
Feng-hsien Hsien		奉贤县
centre: Nan-ch'iao	F5	南桥
Nan-hui Hsien	F4	南汇县
Pao-shan Hsien	F4	宝山县
Shang-hai Hsien		上海县
centre: Hsin-chuang	F4	莘庄
Sung-chiang Hsien	F4	松江县

ANHWEI
PROVINCE

ANHWEI province took its present form for the first time under the Ch'ing dynasty (1644–1911), and has remained the same since then, apart from minor changes to the boundary with Kiangsu. It falls into two quite distinct areas. The north of the province forms a part of the great plain of eastern China; this was settled heavily in Han times. The southern area between the Yangtze and the Huai river was first heavily settled in the 7th and 8th centuries. The section of Anhwei south of the Yangtze was settled somewhat later, but developed a distinct character of its own, as it was the home of a remarkably successful group of merchants (the Hui-chou or Hsin-an merchants), who played a most important role in China's internal trade during the Ming and early Ch'ing period, and became immensely wealthy.

The North Anhwei plain This is a great area of level plain lying to the north of the Huai Ho river, and drained by a series of tributaries running into the Huai. The plain is broken only by some low hills in the area where Shantung, Kiangsu and Anhwei meet. There is no natural watershed between the Huai and the Huang Ho, and on many occasions there has been disastrous flooding in this area caused by the diversion of waters from the Huang Ho into the Huai river system. The last of these was deliberately caused in 1938 by the Nationalist army as a means of halting the Japanese armies. This caused immense destruction, and gravely damaged the drainage system of northern Anhwei, which suffered badly from flooding throughout the 1940s. Since 1951 a great deal of work has been done to control the Huai. It has been dyked, its headwaters dammed to provide irrigation waters and hydro-electricity, and more recently a canal (the New Pien canal) was constructed across the north of the area to relieve its tributary rivers. These works have increased the amount of irrigated land, reduced the danger of floods, and improved river transport. In the past northern Anhwei was largely an area of dry farming, with winter wheat or barley followed by a summer crop of corn. Soy beans and kaoliang were also commonly grown. Recently rice has begun to rival wheat as the staple grain crop in some southern areas. Cotton and various oilseeds such as rape are widely cultivated.

In the northern tip of the province there is an important coalfield known as the Huai-pei field. This is centred on Sui-ch'i, which was designated a municipality in 1961. The field is estimated to produce five million tons per annum.

Pang-pu is the chief city of northern Anhwei, at the point where the Tientsin–Pu-k'ou railway crosses the Huai river. A traditional river port and market centre, it grew rapidly in the early part of this century. Since the 1950s, while retaining its role as the centre of this rich agricultural area, and as a major market for wheat and other farm produce, it also developed considerable industry. Beside food processing and cotton textiles, and glass and paper manufacture, it has an engineering industry.

The Huai-nan hills Between the Huai river and the Yangtze valley lies a belt of hilly land, the eastward extension of the Ta-pieh Shan range on the border between Honan and Hupeh. In the west, on the Hupeh border, the hills are high and mountainous, with considerable areas over 1,500 m, and a peak, T'ien-chu Shan, of 1,751 m. The axis of these hills is mainly south-west to north-east. In the east the hills are low, rarely over 300 m, and rounded. In the middle is the basin of a large lake, the Chao Hu. The richest and most closely cultivated area is the central zone around the Chao Hu, which is carefully irrigated and is primarily a rice producing district. The southern basin of the upper Huai around Liu-an was formerly badly affected by flooding. It has greatly benefited from the works completed to control the Huai headwaters. Flooding is now less common, and irrigation has been greatly extended. Although wheat used to be the major crop, rice has become more widespread in the last decades. The high hills and mountains of the Ta-pieh Shan in the west still have much forest cover. The area produces wheat, corn, sweet potatoes and hemp. But it has suffered seriously from erosion in the past. Tea is also an important crop. The hilly area north and east of the Chao Hu lake is also a rice producing area, although it is not as intensively cultivated. The area suffers from drought in spring, and has a rather low rainfall (750 mm or below). Irrigation is common, but the schemes are very small and often inefficient. Rice, with winter wheat, is grown in low irrigated land. On the hilly uplands wheat, barley, sweet potatoes and corn are the main crops. Tobacco and peanuts are also grown.

Ho-fei (formerly Lu-chou) is the main city and the provincial capital. Situated on the Huai-nan railway, near the Chao Hu lake, it also has water communication with the Yangtze. Until 1950 Ho-fei was a small administrative city with only 40,000 people and no industry. Since then it has grown greatly. In the early years of the Communist period many light industries were relocated here from Shanghai. In the late 1950s a small steel plant was built, and an engineering industry grew up, manufacturing machine tools and mining equipment. There is also an aluminium plant. The population rose from 183,000 in 1953 to 360,000 in 1957, and is now estimated at about 500,000.

Huai-nan on the south bank of the Huai is the centre of a rich coalfield which began operations in 1929, and grew rapidly after the construction of a rail link to Yü-ch'i-k'ou on the Yangtze in 1936. Production was greatly increased after 1950, and the field is one of the biggest in China, with an annual output of more than 10,000,000 tons. Huai-nan also has a large thermal power plant, which is linked by a grid with various small hydro-electric schemes on the upper Huai tributaries, and with Pang-pu and Wu-hu south of the Yangtze.

The Yangtze valley This broad alluvial plain broken by low hills has a much warmer, wetter climate than the northern areas of Anhwei, with about 1,000 mm of rain, and a growing season of 230–250 days. Almost all of the cultivated land is irrigated paddy field. It is a great rice producing region, with very high yields. In the western part of the valley double-cropped rice is very common. In the east rice is usually grown following winter wheat. Cotton and rape-seed are widely grown, and some ramie and sugar cane. Tea is produced in the hills on the southern bank of the Yangtze.

Wu-hu was the traditional centre of the rice trade in southern Anhwei, and the building of the railway to Nan-ching increased its importance. Wu-hu remains an extremely important commercial and transport centre, but it has little industry except for paper and board manufacturing, cotton spinning, and food processing.

An-ch'ing, formerly the provincial capital, had a similar role on the northern bank of the Yangtze. It has no rail communications, however, and since losing its administrative status it has remained comparatively unimportant and little industry has been developed in the city.

Ma-an-shan on the southern bank of the Yangtze is a very important source of iron ore, first exploited by the Japanese during the Second World War, when blast furnaces were installed. In the early 1950s these were restored, and Ma-an-shan began to produce pig-iron in bulk for the Shanghai steel industry. It was greatly expanded in the late 1950s and early 1960s, and converted into an integrated iron and steel complex. Most of its pig-iron is still shipped to Shanghai, however.

T'ung-ling, also on the southern bank of the Yangtze, is an important mining centre for copper. There is also an iron mine at T'ao-chung to the east.

The Southern Anhwei hills The south of the province is an area of rugged hills and mountains, with rather narrow valleys and little cultivated land. Most of the uplands are between 600 m and 100 m, but individual peaks rise to 1,323 m (Chiu-hua Shan) and 1,841 m (Huang Shan). The climate is sub-tropical, with a growing season of 300 days or more, and abundant rainfall (1,750 mm to 2,000 mm). The area is thickly forested, and timber is an important product. Farming is concentrated in the valleys, where rice, wheat, barley, sweet potatoes, corn and rape-seed are the main crops. Tea production is a very important local industry – the area produces about a tenth of China's total tea crop.

T'un-ch'i is the chief route centre and communication node for this area. The city has replaced, in this respect, the older cities of She-hsien and Chi-men, although the latter remains an important centre of tea production.

Hsuan-ch'eng plays a similar role in the eastern mountains, with routes reaching into Chekiang, with which the area is closely linked.

AREA
130,000 square kilometres

POPULATION
31,240,000 (other estimates up to 39,000,000)

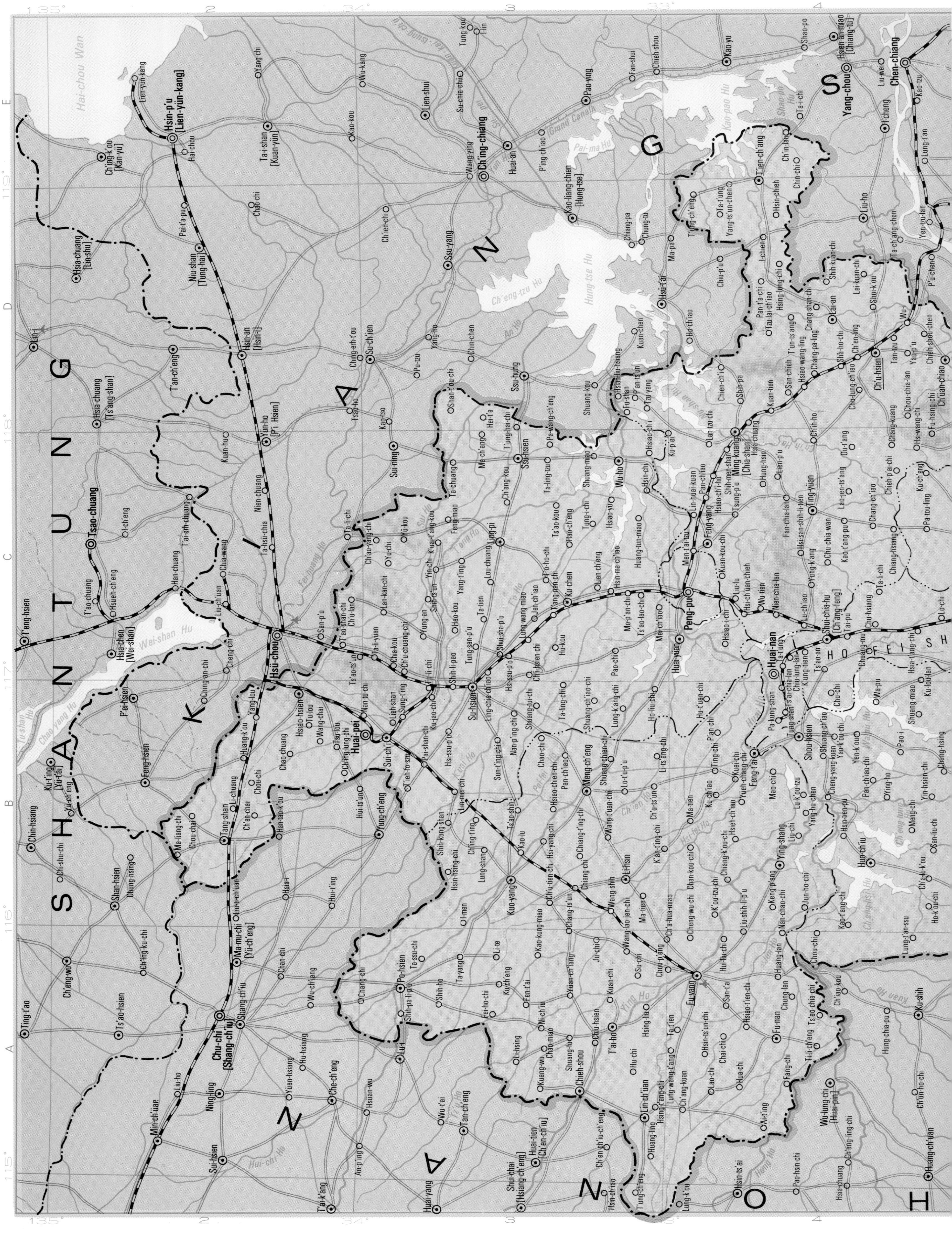
Hai-chou Wan
Hsin-p'u [Lien-yün-kang]
Ch'ing-chiang
Huai-an
Grand Canal
Hung-tse Hu
Ch'eng-tzu Hu
Kao-yu
Yang-chou
Chen-chiang
Pao-ying
Su-ch'ien
Hsin-an [Hsin-i]
Tsao-chuang
Wei-shan Hu
Hsü-chou
Su-hsien
Huai-pei
Peng-pu
Huai-nan
Huai-yüan
Ming-kuang [Chia-shan]
Ch'u-hsien
Ting-yüan
Shou-hsien
Feng-t'ai
Meng-ch'eng
Kuo-yang
Po-hsien
Fu-yang
Chu-chi [Shang-ch'iu]
Lin-ch'üan
Chieh-shou
Huai-yang
Ying Ho
Huai Ho
Ku-shih
Wu-lung-chi [Huai-pin]
Huang-ch'uan
S H A N T U N G
K I A N G S U
A N H W E I
H O N A N
H O F E I

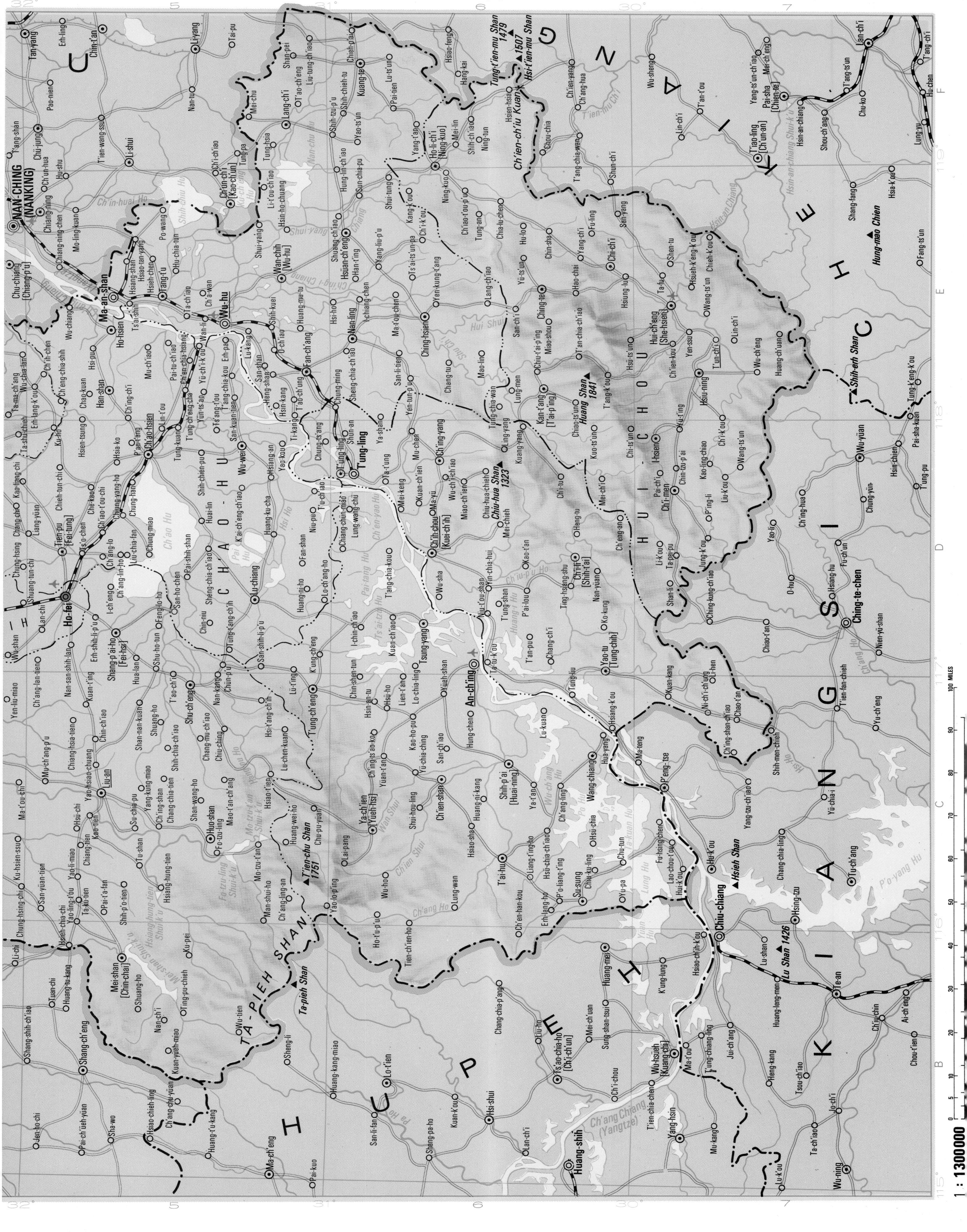

NAN-CHING (NANKING)
Ma-an-shan
Wu-hu
Ho-fei
An-ch'ing
Tung-ling
Chiu-chiang
Ching-te-chen
Huang-shih
Hui-ch'eng [She-hsien]
Huang Shan 1841
Chiu-hua Shan 1323
T'ien-chu Shan 1751
Lu Shan 1426
Hsieh Shan
Ta-pieh Shan
TA-PIEH SHAN
Shih-erh Shan
Hung-mao Chien
Tung-t'ien-mu Shan 1479
Hsi-t'ien-mu Shan 1507
Ch'ien-ch'iu Kuan
CHAO-HU
HUI-CHOU
Ch'ao Hu
P'o-yang Hu
Ch'ang Chiang (Yangtze)
KIANGSU
CHEKIANG
KIANGSI
HUPEH
1 : 1300000
MILES

ANHWEI PROVINCE 安徽省
AN-HUI SHENG

8 shih *municipalities*
9 ti-ch'ü *regions*
70 hsien *counties*

capital **Ho-fei Shih**	D5	合肥市
Ch'ang-feng Hsien		长丰县
centre: Shui-chia-hu	D4	水家湖
An-ch'ing Shih	D6	安庆市
Huai-nan Shih	D4	淮南市
Huai-pei Shih	C3	淮北市
Ma-an-shan Shih	E5	马鞍山市
Peng-pu Shih	D4	蚌埠市
T'ung-ling Shih	D6	铜陵市
Wu-hu Shih	E5	芜湖市

An-ch'ing Ti-ch'ü		安庆地区
Ch'ien-shan Hsien	C6	潜山县
Huai-ning Hsien		怀宁县
centre: Shih-p'ai	C6	石牌
Su-sung Hsien	C6	宿松县
T'ai-hu Hsien	C6	太湖县
Tsung-yang Hsien	D6	枞阳县
T'ung-ch'eng Hsien	C5	桐城县
Wang-chiang Hsien	C6	望江县
Yüeh-hsi Hsien		岳西县
centre: Ya-ch'ien	C6	衙前

Ch'ao-hu Ti-ch'ü		巢湖地区
centre: Ch'ao-hsien	D5	巢县
Ch'ao Hsien		巢县
centre: Ch'ao-hsien	D5	
Fei-tung Hsien		肥东县
centre: Tien-pu	D5	店埠
Han-shan Hsien	E5	含山县
Ho Hsien		和县
centre: Ho-hsien	E5	
Lu-chiang Hsien	D5	庐江县
Wu-wei Hsien	D5	无为县

Ch'ih-chou Ti-ch'ü		池州地区
Ch'ing-yang Hsien	D6	青阳县
Kuei-ch'ih Hsien		贵池县
centre: Ch'ih-chou	C6	池州
Shih-t'ai Hsien		石台县
centre: Ch'i-li	D6	七里
Tung-chih Hsien		东至县
centre: Yao-tu	D6	尧度
T'ung-ling Hsien	D6	铜陵县

Ch'u-hsien Ti-ch'ü		滁县地区
Chia-shan Hsien		嘉山县
centre: Ming-kuang	D4	明光
Ch'üan-chiao Hsien	E4	全椒县
Ch'u Hsien		滁县
centre: Ch'u-hsien	E4	
Feng-yang Hsien	D4	凤阳县
Lai-an Hsien	E4	来安县
T'ien-ch'ang Hsien	E4	天长县
Ting-yüan Hsien	D4	定远县

Fu-yang Ti-ch'ü		阜阳地区
Chieh-shou Hsien	B3	界首县
Feng-t'ai Hsien	C4	凤台县
Fu-nan Hsien	B4	阜南县
Fu-yang Hsien	B4	阜阳县
Kuo-yang Hsien	C3	涡阳县
Li-hsin Hsien	C3	利辛县
Lin-ch'üan Hsien	B3	临泉县
Meng-ch'eng Hsien	C3	蒙城县
Po Hsien		亳县
centre: Po-hsien	B3	
T'ai-ho Hsien	B3	太和县
Ying-shang Hsien	C4	颍上县

Hui-chou Ti-ch'ü		徽州地区
centre: T'un-ch'i	E7	屯溪
Chi-ch'i Hsien	E6	绩溪县
Ch'i-men Hsien	D7	祁门县
Ching-te Hsien	E6	旌德县
Hsiu-ning Hsien	E7	休宁县
I Hsien		黟县
centre: I-hsien	D7	
Ning-kuo Hsien		宁国县
centre: Ho-li-ch'i	E6	河历溪
She Hsien		歙县
centre: Hui-ch'eng	E7	徽城
T'ai-p'ing Hsien		太平县
centre: Kan-t'ang	E6	甘棠

Liu-an Ti-ch'ü		六安地区
Chin-chai Hsien		金寨县
centre: Mei-shan	B5	梅山
Fei-hsi Hsien		肥西县
centre: Shang-p'ai-ho	D5	上派河
Huo-ch'iu Hsien	C4	霍丘县
Huo-shan Hsien	C5	霍山县
Liu-an Hsien	C5	六安县
Shou Hsien		寿县
centre: Shou-hsien	C4	
Shu-ch'eng Hsien	C5	舒城县

Su-hsien Ti-ch'ü		宿县地区
Hsiao Hsien		萧县
centre: Hsiao-hsien	C2	
Huai-yüan Hsien	D4	怀远县
Ku-chen Hsien	D3	固镇县
Ling-pi Hsien	D3	灵壁县
Ssu Hsien		泗县
centre: Ssu-hsien	D3	
Su Hsien		宿县
centre: Su-hsien	C3	
Sui-ch'i Hsien	C3	濉溪县
Tang-shan Hsien	C2	砀山县
Wu-ho Hsien	D3	五河县

Wu-hu Ti-ch'ü		芜湖地区
Ching Hsien		泾县
centre: Ching-hsien	E6	
Fan-ch'ang Hsien	E5	繁昌县
Hsüan-ch'eng Hsien	E6	宣城县
Kuang-te Hsien	F6	广德县
Lang-ch'i Hsien	F5	郎溪县
Nan-ling Hsien	E6	南陵县
Tang-t'u Hsien	E5	当涂县
Wu-hu Hsien		芜湖县
centre: Wan-chih	E5	湾址

CHEKIANG
PROVINCE

THE smallest of the mainland provinces of China, Chekiang has a dense population, and an importance out of proportion with its size. The province falls into two quite different parts, the area north of Hang-chou, which forms a part of the Yangtze delta region, very similar to southern Kiangsu, and the southern part of the province, which is mountainous, and is really a continuation of the mountains of northern Fukien. The first of these areas originally formed part of the Wu state, and was incorporated into the Ch'in and Han empires after 223 BC. The southern and eastern sections formed part of the territory occupied by the Yüeh peoples. Although the Han gradually claimed control of it, it was only slowly incorporated into the empire and settled. Its final period of growth began in the 6th and 7th centuries. After this it became increasingly important, particularly after the capital of the southern Sung was established at Hang-chou (1127–1280). The area became famous for its tradition of education and culture.

The whole province has a warm, damp, sub-tropical climate. In winter, January temperatures average about 4°C (39°F) in the north, 7.5°C (45.5°F) in the southern coastal area. In summer the whole province has average July temperatures of around 28–29°C (82–84°F). All of Chekiang has more than 1,000 mm of rainfall, with considerably more on the mountains of the south. The north, which has been intensively cultivated for well over a thousand years, long ago lost its natural vegetation cover. The mountains of the south are still richly covered with mixed forest.

The northern Chekiang plain This comprises the southern half of the Yangtze delta plain, to the south of the T'ai Hu lake. It is a continuation of the plain of Kiangsu and Shanghai, and the provincial boundary is purely arbitrary. It is a flat, featureless plain with a dense network of waterways, canals and irrigation channels, the most important of which is the Grand Canal, leading from Chia-hsing to Hang-chou. The chief crop is rice, grown after a spring crop of rape-seed, wheat or beans. Jute and cotton are widely grown, and fine tobacco around Tung-hsiang. The area raises many sheep, and in the Hu-chou and Wu-hsing areas silk culture is very important. In the hills to the south-west of the T'ai Hu lake, which occupy the west of this region, tea, bamboo and timber are important products.

Chia-hsing is a transport centre on the Grand Canal, and the main market and commercial centre for the north-east of the plain. It had 78,000 people in 1953. It is a silk manufacturing centre, with some modern engineering and chemicals.

Hu-chou plays a similar role in the area along the southern shore of the T'ai Hu lake. It has an old-established silk industry, and is a very important rice market.

Hang-chou is the provincial capital, and by far the largest city in Chekiang. An ancient city, which rose to prominence in the 7th and 8th centuries, and which later became the immensely wealthy capital of the Southern Sung empire. Hang-chou became important as the southern terminus of the Grand Canal. Although it was once a seaport, its harbour has for many centuries been fit only for the smallest coastal shipping, and for river shipping on the Ch'ien-t'ang river leading into the interior of the province. Traditionally the centre of a wide variety of handicrafts, producing silks, cottons and paper, Hang-chou has been considerably industrialised since 1949. The silk industry has been greatly expanded, and some plants installed for the manufacture of cotton textiles and burlap from local jute. There is a small steel plant, some engineering works and a diversified chemical industry. It also remains a major transport centre, both for canal traffic, and for rail traffic from Kiangsi and Hunan. Hang-chou is a great beauty spot, with many famous historical sites, and remains a major cultural centre, with a number of institutions of higher education.

The Shao-hsing–Ning-po plain Along the southern shore of Hang-chou bay are a series of low alluvial plains, backed by the hilly uplands of the Kuiai-chi Shan, Ssu-ming Shan and T'ien-t'ai Shan ranges, which rise to 1,000 m or so. Here the valleys are cultivated in paddy fields, while much of the hill land remains wooded. The coastal plain has a dense irrigation system and canals linking Ning-po with the estuary of the Ch'ien-t'ang river. Flood control works have made life in this plain more secure in recent years. The main crop is rice. Double-cropped rice was first cultivated in this area, and is sometimes grown with a third spring-ripening crop. In the uplands, rice is usually grown with wheat or barley. Cotton, mostly exported to Shanghai is widely grown, and jute, ramie and rape-seed are important economic crops. The uplands are one of the great tea-producing areas of China. Timber is an important local resource, although most of the primary forest was cut long ago, and silk is produced widely. Along the coast fisheries are important, particularly in the Chou-shan archipelago off the coast. Salt is also produced in large quantities in the coastal districts.

Shao-hsing is situated in the middle of the waterway system of the plain and has been a major administrative town since early times. Famous in the past for its handicrafts, and above all for its rice wines, it remains largely an agricultural market centre, although some modern industry, including a small steel plant, was developed in the late 1950s.

Ning-po rose to importance later than Shao-hsing, during the 7th and 8th centuries, when it became a major port. It was a port for both the coastal trade, and also for the trade with the Ryukyu Islands and Japan. It later flourished as a trading city for exports from Chekiang, and its merchants were very important as bankers in the 18th and early 19th centuries. As Shanghai rose, however, Ning-po's importance dwindled, although it remained an important second rank port. There was some industrial development before the Second World War, and the city's importance grew after 1955 when it first received a rail link. Traditionally its industries were textiles and food-processing. These were greatly expanded in the 1950s, and an engineering industry was founded, making diesel engines, agricultural implements, and building small ships for the fishing industry. It is a very important fishing port.

The south-western uplands These comprise the upper basin of the Ch'ien-t'ang river and its tributaries. It is the most sparsely peopled and backward port of Chekiang, a region of wooded hills, mostly under 1,000 m, separated by valleys and river basins. In these plains paddy fields make up most of the acreage, growing double-cropped rice often with corn, wheat or barley. Sugar-cane is grown in the Chin-hua and I-niao areas. Since 1949 the silk industry has been considerably developed and tea is produced around Ch'un-an and Chien-te. The Chin-hua basin is famous for its citrus fruits and there is a great deal of excellent timber. Although Chekiang has little coal, there is considerable development of hydro-electric power. There are two major schemes on the Ch'ien-t'ang river, one at Huang-t'an-k'ou near Chü-hsien, the other, a very large project on the Hsin-an Chiang near the Anhwei border. This plant is linked by a power grid to Hang-chou and Shanghai.

Chin-hua on the railway from Hang-chou to Kiangsi, is the main market centre of this region. It has developed some food-processing industry.

Lan-ch'i has developed an aluminium industry, using electric power from the Hsin-an Chiang scheme.

The south-eastern uplands This area of coastal highlands is drained by the Ou Chiang and Ling Chiang. It is the highest and most rugged land in Chekiang, with steep slopes and narrow valleys with little cultivable land. What land there is is intensively farmed using double-cropped rice, with green fertiliser crops of wheat, barley, rape-seed, sweet potatoes. Sugar cane is widely grown on the coast, and jute, ramie and cotton are important economic crops. Citrus fruits are a speciality of the area, and there is a good deal of tea production. Forestry is also important, and the area produces timber and wood oils, which are collected for shipment at Wen-chou.

Wen-chou is the region's main city and commercial centre. Although the city is hampered by poor communications with its hinterland, it is an important local port, exporting tea, timber and fruits. It has a paper industry, and various food-processing industries. Most of its exports go to Shanghai.

AREA
101,800 square kilometres

POPULATION
31,000,000

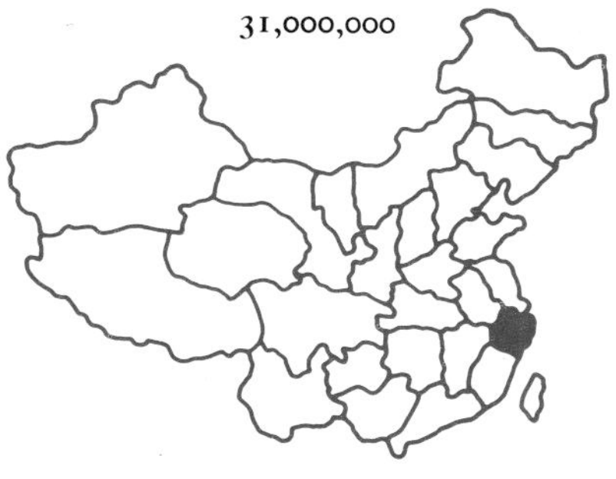

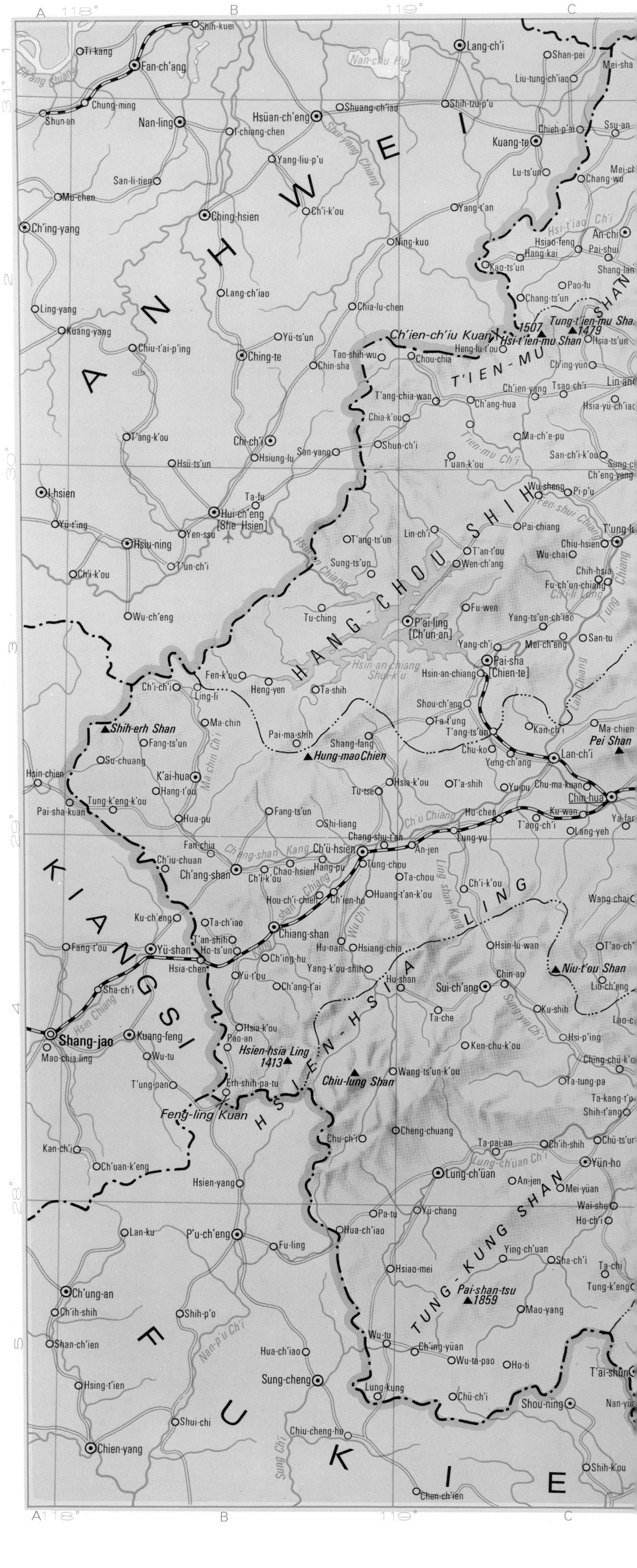
A 118° B 119° C
1
2
3
4
5
31°
30°
29°
28°
ANHWEI
KIANGSI
FUKIEN
CHEKIANG
T'IEN-MU SHAN
HANG-CHOU SHIH
HSIEN-HSIA LING
TUNG-KUNG SHAN
Shih-kuei
Ti-kang
Fan-ch'ang
Ch'ang Chiang
Chung-ming
Shun-an
Nan-ling
Hsüan-ch'eng
I-chiang-chen
Shuang-ch'iao
Shui-yang Chiang
Nan-chu Hu
Lang-ch'i
Shih-tzu-p'u
Shan-pei
Liu-tung-ch'iao
Mei-sha
Chieh-p'ai
Ssu-an
Kuang-te
Lu-ts'un
Chang-wu
Yang-liu-p'u
San-li-tien
Mu-chen
Ching-hsien
Ch'i-k'ou
Yang-t'an
Ch'ing-yang
Ning-kuo
Hsi-t'iao Ch'i
An-chi
Hsiao-feng
Hang-kai
Pai-shui
Kao-ts'un
Shang-lan
Pao-fu
Chang-ts'un
Lang-ch'iao
Ling-yang
Chia-lu-chen
Kuang-yang
Yü-ts'un
Ch'ien-ch'iu Kuan
1507
Hsi-t'ien-mu Shan
Tung-t'ien-mu Shan
1479
Hsia-ts'un
Chiu-t'ai-p'ing
Ching-te
Tao-shih-wu
Heng-lu-t'ou
Chou-chia
Chin-sha
Ch'ing-yun
Lin-an
T'ang-chia-wan
Ch'ien-yang
Tsao-ch'i
Ch'ang-hua
Hsia-yu-ch'iao
Chia-k'ou
T'ien-mu Ch'i
Ma-ch'e-pu
T'ang-k'ou
Chi-ch'i
Shun-ch'i
San-ch'i-k'ou
San-yang
Hsiung-lu
Hsü-ts'un
T'uan-k'ou
Ch'eng-yang
I-hsien
Wu-sheng
Pi-p'u
Ta-fu
Hui-ch'eng
[She Hsien]
Fen-shui Chiang
Yü-t'ing
Yen-ssu
Pai-chiang
T'ung-lu
Hsiu-ning
Lin-ch'i
T'ang-ts'un
T'an-t'ou
Chiu-hsien
Wu-chai
T'un-ch'i
Hsin-an Chiang
Sung-ts'un
Wen-ch'ang
Ch'i-k'ou
Chih-hsia
Fu-ch'un-chiang
Ch'i-li Lung
Wu-ch'eng
Tu-ching
Fu-wen
P'ai-ling
[Ch'un-an]
Yang-ts'un-ch'iao
Mei-ch'eng
San-tu
Yang-ch'i
Hsin-an-chiang Shui-k'u
Pai-sha
[Chien-te]
Hsin-an-chiang
Fen-k'ou
Heng-yen
Ta-shih
Ch'i-ch'i
Ling-li
Shou-ch'ang
Ma-chin
Ta-t'ung
Kan-ch'i
Ma-chien
Shih-erh Shan
T'ang-ts'un
Pei Shan
Pai-ma-shih
Shang-fang
Fang-ts'un
Chu-ko
Lan-ch'i
Hung-mao Chien
Yung-ch'ang
Su-chuang
Ma-chin Ch'i
K'ai-hua
Hsin-chien
Hang-t'ou
Hsia-k'ou
T'a-shih
Yu-pu
Chu-ma-kuan
Tu-tse
Chin-hua
Tung-k'eng-k'ou
Pai-sha-kuan
Fang-ts'un
Hu-chen
Ku-wan
Hua-pu
Shih-liang
Ch'ü Chiang
T'ang-ch'i
Lang-yeh
Fan-chia
Ch'ang-shan Kang
Shang-shu-t'an
Lung-yu
Ch'ü-hsien
An-jen
Ch'iu-chuan
Hang-pu
Ch'ang-shan
Chao-hsien
Tung-chou
Ta-chou
Ch'i-k'ou
Ling-shan Kang
Hou-ch'i-chieh
Ch'ien-ho
Huang-t'an-k'ou
Wang-chai
Ku-ch'eng
Ta-ch'iao
Chiang-shan
T'an-shih
Fang-t'ou
Yü-shan
Ho-ts'un
Hu-nan
Hsiang-chia
Hsin-lu-wan
T'ao-ch'i
Hsia-chen
Ch'ing-hu
Yang-k'ou-shih
Niu-t'ou Shan
Yü-t'ou
Ch'ang-t'ai
Hu-shan
Chin-ap
Sui-ch'ang
Lo-ch'eng
Sha-ch'i
Hsin Chiang
Ta-che
Ku-shih
Sung-yin Ch'i
Hsia-k'ou
Shang-jao
Kuang-feng
Pao-an
Hsi-p'ing
Mao-chia-ling
Wu-tu
Hsien-hsia Ling
1413
Ken-chu-k'ou
Ching-chü-k'ou
T'ung-pan
Chiu-lung Shan
Wang-ts'un-k'ou
Ta-tung-pa
Erh-shih-pa-tu
Ta-kang-t'o
Feng-ling Kuan
Shih-t'ang
Chu-ch'i
Cheng-chuang
Ta-pai-an
Ch'ih-shih
Chü-ts'un
Kan-ch'i
Lung-ch'üan Ch'i
Ch'uan-k'eng
Yün-ho
Lung-ch'üan
An-jen
Mei-yüan
Hsien-yang
Wai-she
Pa-tu
Yu-chang
Ho-ch'i
Lan-ku
P'u-ch'eng
Hua-ch'iao
Fu-ling
Ying-ch'uan
Sha-ch'i
Ta-chi
Hsiao-mei
Tung-k'eng
Ch'ung-an
Pai-shan-tsu
1859
Ch'ih-shih
Shih-p'o
Mao-yang
Nan-p'u Ch'i
Shan-ch'ien
Wu-tu
Ch'ing-yüan
Hua-ch'iao
Wu-ta-pao
Ho-ti
T'ai-shun
Hsing-t'ien
Sung-cheng
Lung-kung
Chü-ch'i
Shou-ning
Nan-yang
Shui-chi
Chiu-cheng-ho
Sung Ch'i
Chien-yang
Shih-k'ou
Chen-ch'ien

CHEKIANG

KIANGSU
SHANG-HAI
SHANGHAI
CHIA HSING
Nagasaki 850km
Hawaii 17610km
Ta-lien
Wu-chiang
Ch'uan-sha
Chou-p'u
Nan-hui
Sung-chiang
Hsi-tung-t'ing Shan
Tung-tung-t'ing Shan
Tung-ho-chen
Tung-shan
T'ai Hu
Ch'ang-hsing
Chin-ts'un
Yang-p'u
Ho-ch'i
Lu-hsü
P'ing-wang
Hsin-ch'ang
Lin-ch'eng
Li-chia-kang
Hung-hsing-ch'iao
Chen-tse
Sheng-tse
Hsi-t'ang
T'ien-ning
Nan-ch'iao [Feng-hsien]
Hu-chou [Wu-hsing]
Ho-p'ing
Chih-li
Nan-hsün
Chin-shan
Chia-shan
Che-lin
Shih-chia-ch'iao
Hsin-ch'eng
Hsin-tai
Hsiao-shu
Shuang-lin
Chia-hsing
Chin-ssu-niang-ch'iao
Chin-shan-wei
Ch'ing-shan
Ling-hu
Wu-chen
Lien-shih
Hsin-feng
P'ing-hu
Mo-kan Shan
724
T'ai-ch'i
Shan-lien
Pu-yüan
Chung-kuan
Shih-men
Wang-tien
Ch'üan-kung-t'ing
Sou-ts'un
San-ch'iao
Hsin-shih
T'ung-hsiang
Cha-p'u
T'an-hu Shan
Wang-p'an Shan
Wang-p'an Yang
P'ai-t'ou
Wu-k'ang
Te-ch'ing
Shen-tang
Ch'ung-te
Wu-yüan-chen [Hai-yen]
Huang-hu
T'ang-hsi
Hsia-shih [Hai-ning]
Hsieh-ch'iao
Ch'ang-an-chen
T'ung-yüan
Lin-p'ing [Yü-hang]
P'eng-kung
P'ing-yao
Hsu-ts'un
Yen-kuan
Hsin-ts'ang
Kan-p'u
Liang-chu
Huang-wan
Heng-fang
Ch'ien-t'ang Chiang
Ch'iao-ssu
Chien-ch'iao
T'ou-p'eng
Hang-chou Wan
Hui-pieh Yang
Hang-chou
Chiu-yü-hang
Ch'ing-shan
Liu-hsia
Hsi-hsing
Hsiao-shan
Chuan-t'ang
Ch'ang-ho
Ch'ien-ch'ing
An-ch'ang
Kua-li
Ma-an
Hsia-fang-ch'iao
An-tung
Ch'ang-ho-shih
Chou-hsiang
Ssu-men
Hsiao-lin
Hu-shan [Tz'u-ch'i]
Ti-t'ang
Lin-shan
Hsin-p'u-yen
Kuan-ch'eng
Shen-shih-ch'iao
Ming-ho-ch'ang
Fan-shih
Fu-yang
I-ch'iao
Ling-ch'iao
Pai-lu-t'ang
Li-hai
Sung-hsia
Yü-yao
Ma-chu
Chang-t'ing
Ta-yüan
Lin-p'u
K'o-ch'iao
Tung-p'u
T'ao-yen
Shao-hsing
Tung-kuan-chen
Pai-kuan [Shang-yü]
Ts'ao-o
Lu-chia-pu
Ta-yin
Hsia-p'u
Tz'u-ch'eng
Chen-hai
Yung Chiang
Li-kang
Ch'en-kang
Chin-t'ang Shan
Ting-hai
Pai-ch'üan
Ta-chan
P'u-t'o
Huang-ta Yang
CHOU-SHAN TAO
Chou-shan Ch'ün-tao
CHOU-SHAN
Tai Shan
Tung-sha-chiao
Ta-ch'ang-t'u Shan
Kao-t'ing-chen [Tai-shan]
Liang-hsiung-ti Tao
Ssu-tzu-mei Tao
Tao-tou-ao
Ta-ch'ü Shan
Lang-kang-shan Lieh-tao
HUANG-TSE YANG
Ta-yang Shan
Hsiao-yang Shan
Ta-huang-lung Shan
Ts'ai-yüan-chen [Sheng-ssu]
Ssu-chiao Shan
Ch'en-ch'ien Shan
SHENG-SSU LIEH-TAO
Hua-niao Shan
260km
Fu-ch'un
P'u-yang
Ho-shang-chen
Mei-ch'ih
Ch'ang-k'ou
Chai-ch'i
Chang-ts'un
Li-chu
P'ing-shui
Shang-p'u
Feng-hui
Liang-nung
Hung-t'ang
Chuang-ch'iao
Chuang-shih
Ta-hsieh-t'ou
Ning-po
Ch'uan-shan
Chung-tse
Ch'ai-ch'iao
Wu-hsiang-ch'i
Ch'iu-chieh
Chiang-shan
Kuo-chü
Chu-chia Chen
T'ao-hua Tao
Chiao-t'ou
Hsia-ch'i Tao
T'ang-p'u
Hsia-kuan
Ting-chia-fan
Chih-pu
Hung-men
Feng-ch'iao
Wang-t'ang
Shang-yen-t'an
Chang-chen
San-chieh
Hsüeh-tou Shan
Hsiao-wang-miao
Ch'i-k'ou
Chiang-k'ou
Heng-ch'i
Ta-kung
Hsi-wu
Feng-hua
T'ing-hsia
Ma-chien
San-tou
Chu-chi
Ts'ao-t'a
Wai-ch'en
P'ai-t'ou
Chung-yu
An-hua
Hsien-yen
Ku-lai
Ssu-ming Shan
SSU-MING SHAN
HUI-CHI SHAN
Ch'en-ts'ai
Huang-shan
Ch'ung-jen
Sheng-hsien
Huang-tse
Pei-chuang-shih
Sha-ch'i
Sung-ao
Ch'iu-ts'un
Ling-chao
Ts'ui-chia-ao
Liu-heng Tao
Hsiang-shan Kang
Ta-hsü
Hang-k'ou-p'ing
Cheng-chia-wu
Kan-lin
Hsin-ch'ang
Pa-mao
Ta-yen
Hsi-tien
Hsi-chou
Tan-ch'eng [Hsiang-shan]
Chüeh-ch'i
P'u-chiang
Huang-chai
Ta-ch'en
Su-ch'i
Ch'ang-lo
Ch'eng-t'an
Ta-shih-chin
Shen-ch'üan
Mei-lin
Ch'iao-t'ou-hu
Ssu-chou-t'ou
Chiu-shan Lieh-tao
Hou-chai
Kuei-men
EAST CHINA SEA
(TUNG HAI)
Heng-ch'i
Hua-ch'i
Ju-ao
Shang-hu
Shang-ch'i
Chin-hua Chiang
I-hsiao
Wei-shan
Lu-shih-k'ou
Ko-shan-ts'un
Huang-t'an
Ning-hai
Ch'a-yüan
Li-yang
Tung-yang
Hua-ting Shan
Ch'ang-chieh
Ting-t'ang
Shih-p'u
I-t'ing
Hsieh-t'ang
Fo-t'ang
Ling-k'ou
Chien-shan
Pai-hou
Sang-chou
Sha-liu
San-men Wan
Hsiao-shun
Hou-ling-shan
Hu-ch'i
P'ing-chen
T'ien-t'ai
T'IEN-T'AI SHAN
Ho-p'u
Niu-t'ou Shan
Nan-tien
T'ang-ya
Ch'ih-an
Nan-ma
Shang-hu
Chieh-t'ou
Shih-feng Ch'i
F'an-t'ou
Hai-yu [San-men]
Feng-p'u
Kao-chien
Chien-t'iao
Ta-fo Shan
T'ang-hsien
Ssu-lu-k'ou
An-wen
Hua-yang
Ling-hsia-chin
T'ing-p'ang
Shanghai 440km
Shang-chiao-tao
Ku-shan
Tien-ch'ien
Li-p'u
Nichai
Chih-ying
Hsin-wo
Hou-ko
Pai-shui-yang
Ta-t'ien
Tung-cheng
Hua-ch'iao
San-chiao-t'ang
Wu-i
Yung-k'ang
Ch'e-k'ou
Yü-shan Lieh-tao
Wu-i Chiang
Shih-chu
Kuan-lu
Hsien-chü
Chang-chia-tu
T'ai-chou [Lin-hai]
T'ao-chu
Chiang-erh Ao
1375
Kua-ts'ang Shan
Fan-ch'iao
Hu-chen
Pu-lu
Tu-hsia-ch'iao
Ling Chiang
Hsin-chien
Heng-ch'i
Pai-t'a
Chu-ch'i
Yu-ch'i
Yung-ch'üan
Shang-p'an
Hao Ch'i
P'an-t'an
Ch'ien-so
Kao Tao
Chin-yün
Hai-men
T'ai-chou Wan
Ko-fan
Shu-hung
Yung-an Ch'i
Huang-yen
Chiang-shan Tao
Shuang-ch'i
Ta-yüan
Ch'ang-t'an
Ning-ch'i
Yüan-ch'iao
Lu-ch'iao
Lang-chi Shan
Huang-ts'un
KUA-TS'ANG SHAN
Tse-kuo
Chin-ch'ing
Ch'ien-ts'un
Hsin-ho
Ta-ch'i
T'ai-chou Lieh-tao
Li-shui
Yen-t'an
Chiu-lung
Pei-yen-tang Shan
Ta-ching
Jo-heng
1001
Pai-ch'i
Wen-ling
Sung-men
Pi-hu
Fu-i
Hai-k'ou
Yen-t'ou
Ho-sheng
Pi-lien
Feng-lin
Fu-jung
Shih-t'ang
Shanghai 590km
Chih-ch'i-t'ou
Ch'üan-liao
Ch'ing-chiang
Tu-kang
Ling-men
Hung-ch'iao
Ch'u-men
Ai-wan Wan
Wen-ch'i
Ch'iao-hsia-chieh
P'u-ch'i
Huan-shan [Yü-huan]
Yung-chia
Hsiao Ch'i
Ch'ing-t'ien
Ou Chiang
Huang-t'ien
Pai-shih
Lo-ch'ing
K'an-men
Ta-shun
Pai-yen
Shan-k'ou
Kang-t'ou
Liu-shih
Lung-wan
Yü-huan Tao
Wen-chou
Weng-yang
Fu-chou—Shanghai 870km
Chi-lung—Shanghai 780km
Ch'ü-ch'i
Wu-yen
Tung-t'ou Shan
Nan-t'ien
Hu-ling
Yung-chung
Wen-chou Wan
Ta-men Tao
Yü-hu
T'ao-shan
Ta-hsüeh [Wen-ch'eng]
Kao-lou
T'ang-hsia
Hsien-chiang
Tung-t'ou
Huang-yang
Hsüeh-k'ou
Jui-an
Hsin-cheng
Fei-yün Chiang
Ma-yü
P'ing-yang-k'eng
Pa-shih-mou
Nan-yen-t'ang Shan
1121
Hsia-men—Shanghai 1040km
Pai-chang-k'ou
P'ing-yang
Pei-lung Shan
Pei-chi Shan
Shan-ch'i
Shui-t'ou
Ch'ien-ts'ang
Ao-chiang
Ma-pu
Hsiao-chiang
Canton—Shanghai 1690km
WEYEN TANG SHAN
Ao Chiang
Ling-ch'i
I-shan
P'ing-yang Tsui
Ta-an
Ch'iao-tun
Nan-chi Shan
P'eng-ch'i
Fen-shui-kuan
Chin-hsiang
Fu-chou 350km
Fan-shan
Kuan-shan Tao
Fu-ting
Ma-chan
Che-jung
Kuan-yang
Ting-ts'ao Yü
Pei-kuan Tao
120°
121°
122°
123°
D
E
F
1
2
30°
3
29°
4
28°
5
1:1 320 000
0 5 10 20 30 40 50 60 70 80 90 100 MILES
0 5 10 20 30 40 50 60 70 80 90 100 150 KM

CHEKIANG PROVINCE 浙江省

CHE-CHIANG SHENG

3 shih	*municipalities*
8 ti-ch'ü	*regions*
64 hsien	*counties*

capital **Hang-chou Shih**	D2	杭州市
Chien-te Hsien		建德县
centre: Pai-sha	C3	白沙
Ch'un-an Hsien		淳安县
centre: P'ai-ling	C3	排岭
Fu-yang Hsien	C2	富阳县
Hsiao-shan Hsien	D2	萧山县
Lin-an Hsien	C2	临安县
T'ung-lu Hsien	C3	桐庐县
Yü-hang Hsien		余杭县
centre: Lin-p'ing	D2	临平县

Ning-po Shih	E3	宁波市
Wen-chou Shih	D5	温州市

Chia-hsing Ti-ch'ü		嘉兴地区
centre: Hu-chou	D2	湖州
An-chi Hsien	C2	安吉县
Ch'ang-hsing Hsien	C1	长兴县
Chia-hsing Hsien	D2	嘉兴县
Chia-shan Hsien	D2	嘉善县
Hai-ning Hsien		海宁县
centre: Hsia-shih	D2	硖石
Hai-yen Hsien		海盐县
centre: Wu-yüan-chen	D2	武原镇
P'ing-hu Hsien	E2	平湖县
Te-ch'ing Hsien	D2	德清县
T'ung-hsiang Hsien	D2	桐乡县
Wu-hsing Hsien		吴兴县
centre: Hu-chou	D2	湖州

Chin-hua Ti-ch'ü		金华地区
Ch'ang-shan Hsien	B4	常山县
Chiang-shan Hsien	B4	江山县
Chin-hua Hsien	C3	金华县
Ch'ü Hsien		衢县
centre: Ch'ü-hsien	B4	
I-wu Hsien	D3	义乌县
K'ai-hua Hsien	B3	开化县
Lan-ch'i Hsien	C3	兰溪县
P'u-chiang Hsien	C3	浦江县
Tung-yang Hsien	D3	东阳县
Wu-i Hsien	C4	武义县
Yung-k'ang Hsien	D4	永康县

Chou-shan Ti-ch'ü		舟山地区
centre: Ting-hai	F2	定海
P'u-t'o Hsien	F3	普陀县
Sheng-ssu Hsien		嵊泗县
centre: Ts'ai-yüan-chen	F2	菜园镇
Tai-shan Hsien		岱山县
centre: Kao-t'ing-chen	F2	高亭镇
Ting-hai Hsien	F2	定海县

Li-shui Ti-ch'ü		丽水地区
Ch'ing-t'ien Hsien	D4	青田县
Chin-yün Hsien	D4	缙云县
Li-shui Hsien	C4	丽水县
Lung-ch'üan Hsien	C4	龙泉县
Sui-ch'ang Hsien	C4	遂昌县
Yün-ho Hsien	C4	云和县

Ning-po Ti-ch'ü		宁波地区
Chen-hai Hsien	E3	镇海县
Feng-hua Hsien	E3	奉化县
Hsiang-shan Hsien		象山县
centre: Tan-ch'eng	E3	丹城
Ning-hai Hsien	E3	宁海县
Tz'u-ch'i Hsien		慈溪县
centre: Hu-shan	E2	浒山
Yin Hsien		鄞县
centre: Ning-po	E3	宁波
Yü-yao Hsien	E2	余姚县

Shao-hsing Ti-ch'ü		绍兴地区
Sheng Hsien		
centre: Sheng-hsien	D3	嵊县
Chu-chi Hsien	D3	诸暨县
Hsin-ch'ang Hsien	D3	新昌县
Shang-yü Hsien		上虞县
centre: Pai-kuan	D2	百官
Shao-hsing Hsien	D2	绍兴县

T'ai-chou Ti-ch'ü		台州地区
Hsien-chü Hsien	D4	仙居县
Huang-yen Hsien	E4	黄岩县
Lin-hai Hsien		临海县
centre: T'ai-chou	E4	台州
San-men Hsien		三门县
centre: Hai-yu	E3	海游
T'ien-t'ai Hsien	E3	天台县
Wen-ling Hsien	E4	温岭县
Yü-huan Hsien		玉环县
centre: Huan-shan	E4	环山

Wen-chou Ti-ch'ü		温州地区
Jui-an Hsien	D5	瑞安县
Lo-ch'ing Hsien	D4	乐清县
P'ing-yang Hsien	D5	平阳县
T'ai-shun Hsien	C5	泰顺县
Tung-t'ou Hsien	E5	洞头县
Wen-ch'eng Hsien		文城县
centre: Ta-hsüeh	D5	大峃
Yung-chia Hsien	D4	永嘉县

HONAN
PROVINCE

HONAN is one of the smallest Chinese provinces, and one of the most densely peopled. Only Kiangsu and Shantung have denser populations. It is also one of the oldest settled areas of China. The north of the province was the site of various neolithic cultures, the homeland of the Shang state in the 2nd century BC, and the first Chinese bronze culture. The area of Lo-yang became the second capital of the Chou dynasty, and the capital of the Later Han and of many other dynasties during the first millenium. During this period the plain of eastern Honan was the most populous and heavily peopled area of China. In the 10th century K'ai-feng, already one of China's richest commercial cities, became the capital of the Sung dynasty (from 960–1127). Although the area never regained its former political eminence, it has remained an important economic region, in spite of the fact that it has suffered a succession of natural disasters: flooding of the Huang Ho, which has changed its course several times, causing great destruction, droughts, and plagues of locusts. Since 1949 water-control schemes have been constructed both on the Huang Ho and on the Huai river in the south of the province, which have reduced the danger of floods and made irrigation possible over far more of the plain. In addition, the region including Cheng-chou, Lo-yang and K'ai-feng was built up during the 1950s as a centre of modern industry.

Northern Honan This area, which lies to the north of the Huang Ho at the foot of the towering T'ai-hang range on the Shansi border, forms a part of the great plain of Hopeh and western Shantung. Apart from some saline areas in the north-east, it is a fertile alluvial plain. Its climate is harsher than that of the rest of the province, with a rainfall of 500 mm to 650 mm and a growing season of 240 frost-free days. January temperatures average only −2°C (28°F). The rainfall is very largely confined to the summer; spring droughts are common. The summers are hot, with average temperatures around 27°C (81°F). Much of the land has traditionally been farmed in dry fields, the main crops being winter wheat followed by kaoliang or corn. New varieties of wheat introduced in the 1950s greatly increased production. The main economic crop is cotton, which is widely cultivated between Hsin-hsiang and An-yang. On the poor lands along the Huang Ho peanuts are an important crop. Elsewhere rape-seed and sesame are grown. Tobacco is grown to some extent.

River control on the Huang Ho has strengthened the dykes, and also involved the construction of a canal from the Huang Ho to the Wei river. This has provided a water route from Hsin-hsiang to Tientsin, and also made possible a system of irrigation in the plain north of the Huang Ho between Cheng-chou and Hsin-hsiang. This was completed in 1953.

Along the foot of the T'ai-hang mountains are a number of important coal-mining centres. The oldest of these is at *Chiao-tso*, which produces over five million tons of anthracite per annum. Further north, near An-yang, are a series of mines at *Ho-pi*, which produce a further three million tons per year.

The main cities of the area all lie on the ancient road along the foot of the T'ai-hang range, followed since early in this century by the Peking–Han-k'ou railway.

An-yang, the last capital of the Shang, and an ancient administrative city is the northernmost. An-yang's modern industrial growth began in 1957 with the development of the nearby Ho-pi coalfield. A small iron and steel plant was built in 1958–60 using local iron ore.

Hsin-hsiang further south is a major transport centre, where the Peking–Han-k'ou railway crosses the Wei, which provides a water route to Tientsin. It also has a railway to the coal mines at Chiao-tso, which has been extended to Ch'ang-chih and the coalfield at Lu-an in south-eastern Shansi. It remains an important regional centre and an industrial town with textile and food-processing plants. It also has cement and rayon factories.

The Lo-yang – Cheng-chou – K'ai-feng region This belt of the middle Huang Ho valley has characteristics similar to those of the northern plain, but it is notable as the main industrial region of the province. It was an ancient east-west route, unified in this century by the Lung-hai railway. The main industrial centres are linked by a power grid which was to have been fed by the ambitious San-men hydro-electric scheme, left uncompleted in the early 1960s when Soviet aid ceased. The grid is fed by thermal generating plants at Lo-yang and Cheng-chou.

Lo-yang, one of China's most ancient cities and several times a dynastic capital, declined after the 10th century AD into a provincial administrative centre. Under the First Five Year Plan, it was chosen as a new industrial city under the scheme to relocate industry. It rapidly became a very important centre of the engineering industry, producing heavy machinery, mining plant, ball bearings and tractors. It also produces cotton textiles and cement on a large scale.

Cheng-chou became the provincial capital in 1954. It too had been an ancient city, the seat of one of the capitals of the Shang in the second millenium BC, but had later declined into a small provincial city. Its modern growth began with the construction of the Peking–Han-k'ou railway, and then the Lung-hai railway, which made it a vital rail junction. It rapidly rivalled and surpassed K'ai-feng as the chief market and communication centre for the rich Honan plain. In the 1950s it was selected for industrial development, particularly as a centre of the cotton textile industry. It also builds textile machinery on a large scale, and has large flour mills and oil-extraction plants. In recent times it has also become a major centre of aluminium production.

K'ai-feng was formerly the provincial capital. It first became important as a major commercial centre in the 7th and 8th centuries, as a port at the head of the Pien Canal, joining the Huang Ho to the Huai and the Yangtze. From 907 until 1127 it was the national capital. Later, the new Grand Canal built under the Mongols passed further east, and K'ai-feng gradually declined. With the coming of railways K'ai-feng was again left on one side, until the construction of the Lung-hai line, and its function as a regional market centre was assumed by Cheng-chou. In the 1950s, however, it too began a period of industrial growth, as a centre of production for agricultural machinery. In the 1960s it acquired a large fertiliser plant, and began smelting zinc. It has not, however, undergone rapid expansion on the scale of Lo-yang or Cheng-chou.

The western Honan mountains The western third of Honan is taken up by a complex of mountain ranges and basins, which represent the eastern extremity of the great Chin-ling range. The main ranges are the south-west to north-east Hsiung-erh Shan range in the north, mainly between 1,000 and 1,500 m, the hills south of the Lo valley culminating in the ancient holy mountain of Sung Shan (1,359 m), and the Fu-niu range with peaks up to 2,343 m, which strikes north-west to south-east. This region is comparatively sparsely peopled, and much of it still has forest cover. In the valleys and basins, the agriculture is mainly based on winter wheat grown in combination with millet, corn or kaoliang. Oats and buckwheat are grown in the upland areas. Goats and sheep are raised in considerable numbers. The area has poor communications and few towns of any size. In the north the Huang Ho flows in a narrow valley between the mountains of Honan and those of south-western Shansi. At one point it flows through a series of narrow gorges at San-men. This was the site of the hydro-electric scheme begun in the late 1950s.

The Nan-yang basin In the south-west of the province, between the Fu-niu Shan and T'ung-pai Shan ranges is the fertile basin around Nan-yang, part of the drainage basin of the Han Shui and its tributaries. This area, sheltered by the mountains, has a much warmer climate, with winter temperatures about 3°C (37°F), about 1,000 mm of rainfall and a growing season of more than 280 days. This area grows rice and winter wheat. Cotton, sesame, rape-seed are also important. It is also a major silk producing area.

Nan-yang is its commercial centre, and the centre of an extensive highway network. It was joined by rail to Lo-ho in 1969. However, its natural connections have always been with Hsiang-fan in northern Hupeh, rather than with Honan.

The east Honan plain This flat, featureless alluvial plain forms part of the drainage basin of the Huai river. In the 1950s much work was done on flood control in this area and a series of dams were built on various headwaters of the Huai Ho, in the foothills of the western mountains. In the mid-1960s the new Pien-ho canal was built to relieve the overloaded northern tributaries of the Huai, diverting some of their waters through northern Anhwei. The climate of this area becomes both warmer and wetter towards the south. In the north annual rainfall is about 750 mm, in the south 1,000 mm, with a growing season of more than 280 days. Most of this plain is devoted to the cultivation of winter wheat with corn, kaoliang and sweet potatoes. Cotton is also an important crop, and tobacco is grown widely in the region around Hsü-ch'ang. Along the foothills of the western mountains are a series of important coal mining centres. In the north are two new and comparatively small mines at Mi-hsien and Yi-yang near Lo-yang. The most important mining centre, producing somewhat less than 10,000,000 tons annually, and with vast reserves, is *P'ing-ting-shan*. These mines began production in the late 1950s, and produce coking coal, much of which is sent to the iron and steel complex at Wu-han.

The main regional market centres of the plain are *Hsü-ch'ang*, which is the chief outlet for the south-western district around Nan-yang, and the centre of the tobacco trade; *Shang-ch'iu*, which is the main market and collecting centre for the eastern plain and for the adjoining areas in Shantung and Anhwei; and *Hsin-yang* in the upper Huai Ho valley in the extreme south. Hsin-yang is the centre of an area where extensive irrigation works have been built since the 1950s, and where rice and winter wheat are the main crops. It is a market for rice and wheat, and for sesame, which is an important local crop.

AREA
167,000 square kilometres

POPULATION
50,320,000 (other estimates up to 55,000,000)

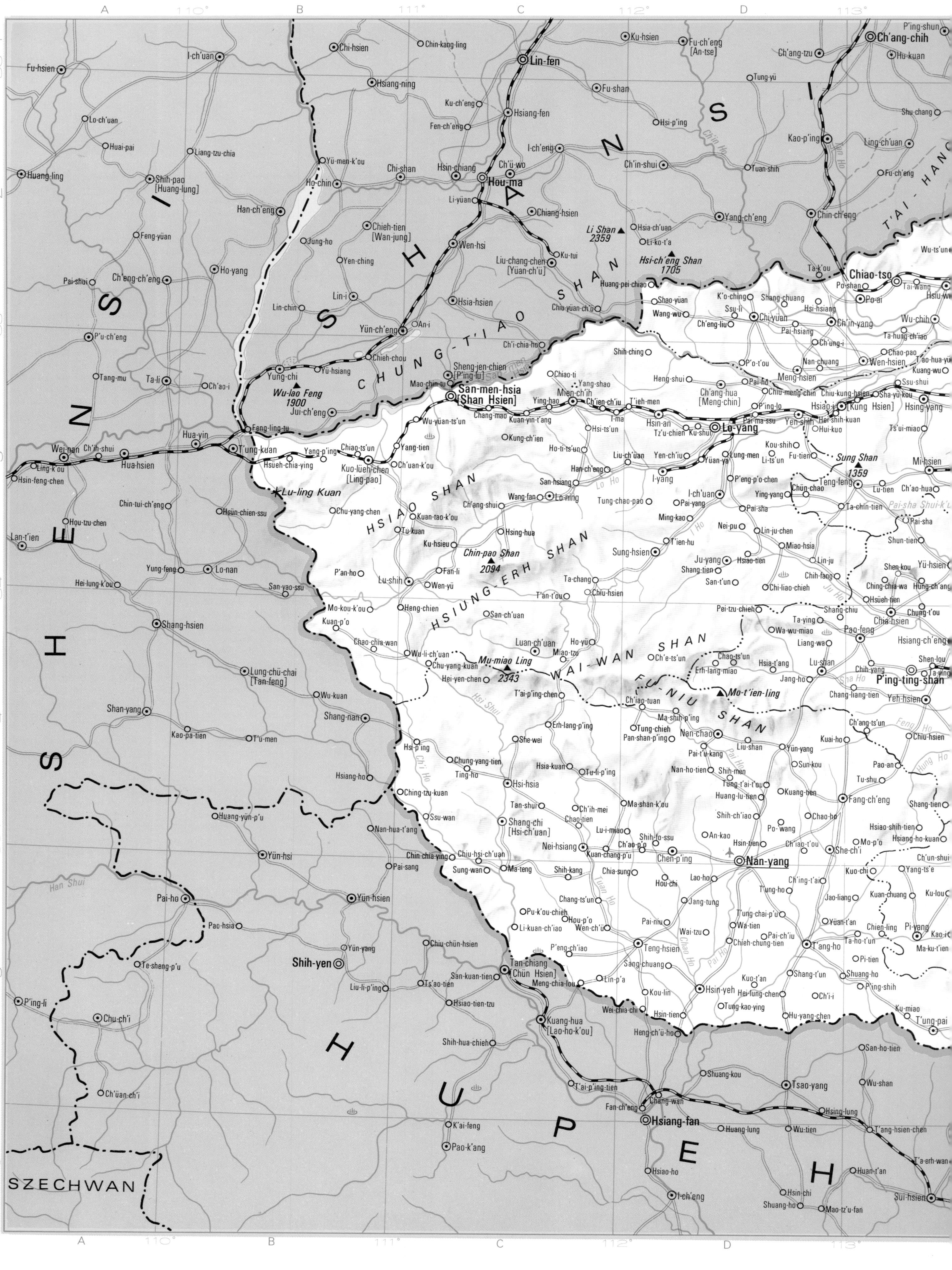

A
110°
B
111°
C
112°
D
113°
SHANSI
SHENSI
HUPEH
HONAN
SZECHWAN
T'AI-HANG
CHUNG-T'IAO SHAN
HSIAO SHAN
HSIUNG-ERH SHAN
WAI-WAN SHAN
FU-NIU SHAN
Li Shan 2359
Hsi-ch'eng Shan 1705
Wu-lao Feng 1900
Chin-pao Shan 2094
Mu-miao Ling 2343
Mo-t'ien-ling
Sung Shan 1359
Lu-ling Kuan
Lin-fen
Ch'ang-chih
Hou-ma
Chiao-tso
San-men-hsia [Shan Hsien]
Lo-yang
P'ing-ting-shan
Nan-yang
Hsiang-fan
Shih-yen
Fu-hsien
I-ch'uan
Chi-hsien
Chin-kang-ling
Ku-hsien
Fu-ch'eng [An-tse]
Ch'ang-tzu
Hu-kuan
Tung-yü
Hsiang-ning
Fu-shan
Ku-ch'eng
Hsiang-fen
Fen-ch'eng
Hsi-p'ing
Lo-ch'uan
Huai-pai
Liang-tzu-chia
Yü-men-k'ou
Huang-ling
Shih-pao [Huang-lung]
Ho-chin
Chi-shan
Hsin-chiang
Ch'ü-wo
I-ch'eng
Ch'in-shui
Kao-p'ing
Ling-ch'uan
Tuan-shih
Fu-ch'eng
Li-yüan
Han-ch'eng
Chiang-hsien
Yang-ch'eng
Chin-ch'eng
Feng-yüan
Chieh-tien [Wan-jung]
Hsia-ch'uan
Jung-ho
Wen-hsi
Li-ko-t'a
Ku-tui
Ho-yang
Yen-ching
Liu-chang-chen [Yüan-ch'ü]
Pai-shui
Ch'eng-ch'eng
Huang-pei-chiao
Ta-k'ou
Lin-i
Hsia-hsien
Shao-yüan
Lin-chin
Chiu-yüan-ch'ü
Yün-ch'eng
An-i
Wang-wu
Ch'i-yüan
Ch'in-yang
Wu-chih
P'u-ch'eng
Ch'i-chia-ho
Chieh-chou
Sheng-jen-chien
Yung-chi
Yü-hsiang
Tang-mu
Ta-li
Ch'ao-i
Mao-chin-tu
Wen-hsien
Meng-hsien
Ying-hao
Mien-ch'ih
Ch'ien-ch'iu
T'ieh-men
Ch'ang-hua [Meng-chin]
Hsing-yang
Jui-ch'eng
Feng-ling-tu
Hua-yin
T'ung-kuan
Wei-nan
Ch'ih-shui
Hua-hsien
Ling-k'ou
Hsin-feng-chen
Yang-p'ing
Chiao-ts'un
Yang-tien
Ch'uan-k'ou
Hsüeh-chia-ying
Kuo-lüeh-chen [Ling-pao]
Ch'ang-mao
Kuan-yin-t'ang
Hsin-an
Kung-ch'ien
Ho-ti-ts'un
Liu-ch'üan
Yen-ch'iu
Yüan-ya
Lung-men
I-yang
Han-ch'eng
San-hsiang
Wang-fan
Lo-ning
Teng-feng
I-ch'uan
Ch'ang-shui
Chu-yang-chen
Kuan-tao-k'ou
Tu-kuan
Hsing-hua
Ku-hsieu
Sung-hsien
Ju-yang
Lu-shih
Fan-li
Wen-yü
Ta-chang
T'an-t'ou
Chiu-hsien
Pao-feng
Lan-t'ien
Hou-tzu-chen
Chin-tui-ch'eng
Hsün-chien-ssu
Yung-feng
Lo-nan
Hei-lung-k'ou
San-yao-ssu
Shang-hsien
Mo-kou-k'ou
Heng-chien
San-ch'uan
Kuan-p'o
Chao-chia-wan
Luan-ch'uan
Wu-li-ch'uan
Chu-yang-kuan
Hei-yen-chen
Lung-chü-chai [Tan-feng]
Wu-kuan
Shan-yang
Shang-nan
Kao-pa-tien
T'u-men
T'ai-p'ing-chen
Ch'iao-tuan
Nan-chao
Yeh-hsien
Erh-lang-p'ing
She-wei
Hsi-p'ing
Chung-yang-tien
Ting-ho
Hsiang-ho
Ching-tzu-kuan
Hsi-hsia
Ssu-wan
Shang-chi [Hsi-ch'uan]
Huang-yün-p'u
Nan-hua-t'ang
Fang-ch'eng
Yün-hsi
Chin-chia-ying
Chiu-hsi-ch'uan
Nei-hsiang
Kuan-chang-p'u
Chen-p'ing
Pai-sang
Ma-teng
Sung-wan
Pai-ho
Han Shui
Yün-hsien
Pao-hsia
Te-sheng-p'u
Yün-yang
Chiu-chün-hsien
Tan-chiang [Chün Hsien]
Teng-hsien
Hsin-yeh
Pi-yang
T'ang-ho
P'ing-li
Chu-ch'i
Liu-li-p'ing
Ts'ao-tien
San-kuan-tien
Hsiao-tien-tzu
Kuang-hua [Lao-ho-k'ou]
Shih-hua-chieh
Ch'üan-ch'i
T'ai-p'ing-tien
Shuang-kou
Tsao-yang
Wu-shan
Fan-ch'eng
Chang-wan
Hsing-lung
Huang-lung
Wu-tien
T'ang-hsien-chen
K'ai-feng
Pao-k'ang
Hsiao-ho
I-ch'eng
Hsin-chi
Shuang-ho
Mao-tz'u-fan
Sui-hsien
Huan-t'an
T'a-erh-wan
Lo Ho
Hsi Shui
Tuan Ho
Pai Ho
Chao Ho
Ju Ho
Sha Ho
Ch'in Ho
Tan Ho

HONAN

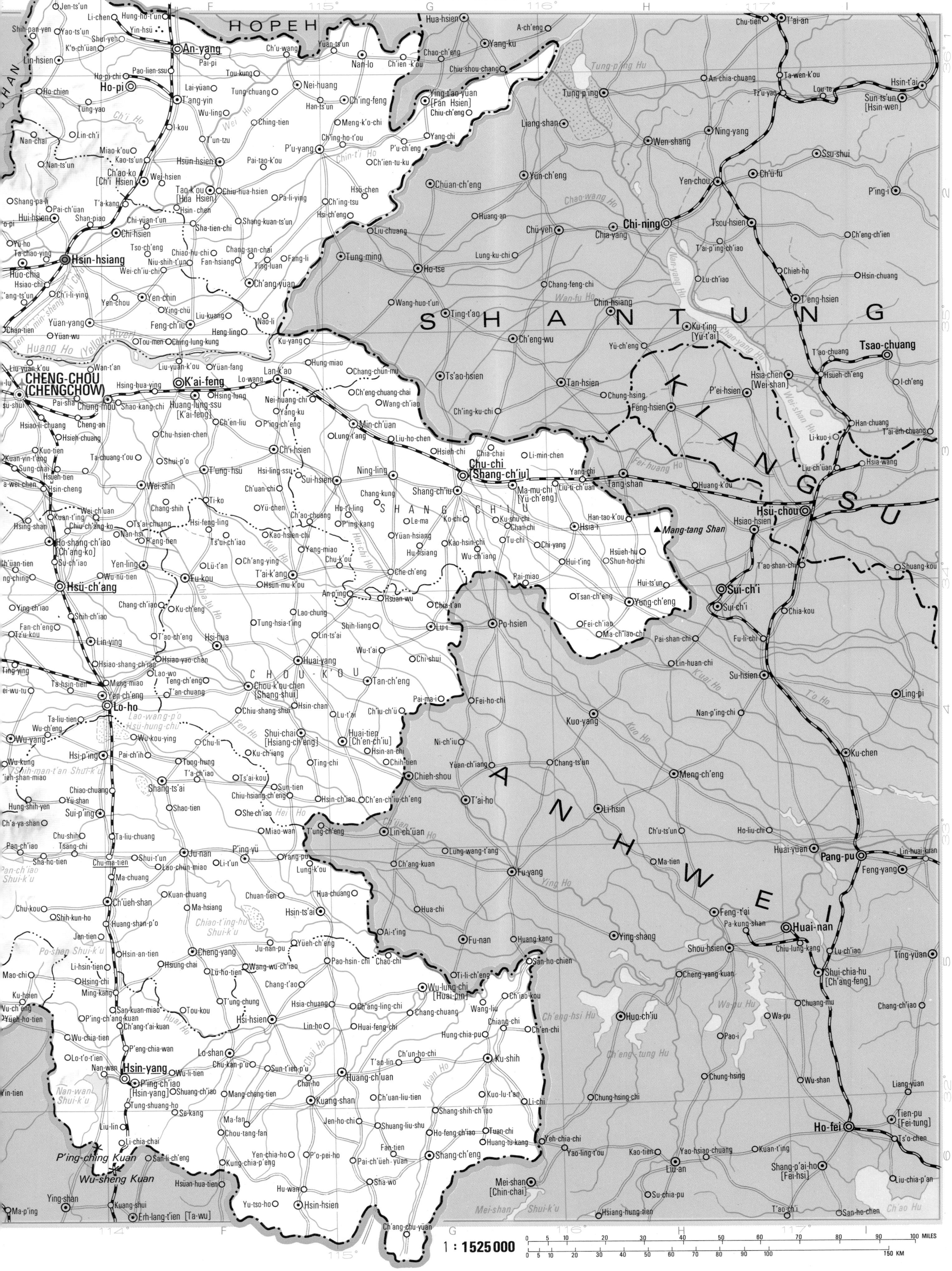
HOPEH
SHANTUNG
KIANGSU
ANHWEI
CHENG-CHOU
(CHENGCHOW)
K'ai-feng
An-yang
Hsin-hsiang
Ho-pi
Hsü-ch'ang
Lo-ho
Chu-chi
[Shang-ch'iu]
Hsin-yang
Chi-ning
Hsü-chou
Tsao-chuang
Pang-pu
Huai-nan
Ho-fei
SHANG-CH'IU
CHOU-K'OU
Huang Ho (Yellow River)
Mang-tang Shan
P'ing-ching Kuan
Wu-sheng Kuan
1 : 1525000
MILES
KM

HONAN PROVINCE 河南省
HO-NAN SHENG

14 shih	*municipalities*
10 ti-ch'ü	*regions*
110 hsien	*counties*

capital **Cheng-chou Shih**	E3	郑州市
An-yang Shih	F1	安阳市
Chiao-tso Shih	E2	焦作市
Ho-pi Shih	F2	鹤壁市
Hsin-hsiang Shih	E2	新乡市
Hsin-yang Shih	F5	信阳市
Hsü-ch'ang Shih	E3	许昌市
K'ai-feng Shih	F3	开封市
Lo-ho Shih	F4	漯河市
Lo-yang Shih	D3	洛阳市
Nan-yang Shih	D4	南阳市
P'ing-ting-shan Shih	E4	平顶山市
San-men-hsia Shih	C3	三门峡市
Shang-ch'iu Shih		商丘市
centre: Chu-chi	G3	朱集

An-yang Ti-ch'ü		安阳地区
An-yang Hsien	F1	安阳县
Ch'ang-yüan Hsien	F2	长垣县
Ch'i Hsien		淇县
centre: Ch'ao-ko	F2	朝歌
Ch'ing-feng Hsien	G2	清丰县
Fan Hsien		范县
centre: Ying-t'ao-yüan	G2	樱桃园
Hsün Hsien		浚县
centre: Hsün-hsien	F2	
Hua Hsien		滑县
centre: Tao-k'ou	F2	道口
Lin Hsien		林县
centre: Lin-hsien	E1	
Nan-lo Hsien	G1	南乐县
Nei-huang Hsien	F2	内黄县
P'u-yang Hsien	G2	濮阳县
T'ang-yin Hsien	F2	汤阴县

Chou-k'ou Ti-ch'ü		周口地区
centre: Chou-k'ou-chen	F4	周口镇
Ch'en-ch'iu Hsien		沈丘县
centre: Huai-tien	G4	槐店
Fu-kou Hsien	F3	扶沟县
Hsiang-ch'eng Hsien		项城县
centre: Shui-chai	F4	水寨
Hsi-hua Hsien	F4	西华县
Huai-yang Hsien	F4	淮阳县
Lu-i Hsien	G4	鹿邑县
Shang-shui Hsien		商水县
centre: Chou-k'ou-chen	F4	周口镇
T'ai-k'ang Hsien	F3	太康县
Tan-ch'eng Hsien	G4	郸城县

Chu-ma-tien Ti-ch'ü		驻马店地区
Cheng-yang Hsien	F5	正阳县
Ch'üeh-shan Hsien	F5	确山县
Hsin-ts'ai Hsien	F5	新蔡县
Hsi-p'ing Hsien	E4	西平县
Ju-nan Hsien	F5	汝南县
P'ing-yü Hsien	F5	平舆县
Pi-yang Hsien	E5	泌阳县
Shang-ts'ai Hsien	F4	上蔡县
Sui-p'ing Hsien	E4	遂平县

Hsin-hsiang Ti-ch'ü		新乡地区
Chi Hsien		汲县
centre: Chi-hsien	F2	
Ch'in-yang Hsien	D2	沁阳县
Chi-yüan Hsien	D2	济源县
Feng-ch'iu Hsien	F2	封丘县
Hsin-hsiang Hsien	E2	新乡县
Hsiu-wu Hsien	E2	修武县
Hui Hsien		辉县
centre: Hui-hsien	E2	
Huo-chia Hsien	E2	获嘉县
Meng Hsien		孟县
centre: Meng-hsien	D3	
Po-ai Hsien	E2	博爱县
Wen Hsien		温县
centre: Wen-hsien	E3	
Wu-chih Hsien	E2	武陟县
Yen-chin Hsien	F2	延津县
Yüan-yang Hsien	E2	原阳县

Hsin-yang Ti-ch'ü		信阳地区
Hsi Hsien		息县
centre: Hsi-hsien	F5	
Hsin Hsien		新县
centre: Hsin-hsien	F6	
Hsin-yang Hsien		信阳县
centre: P'ing-ch'iao	F5	平桥
Huai-pin Hsien		淮滨县
centre: Wu-lung-chi	G5	乌龙集
Huang-ch'uan Hsien	G5	潢川县
Kuang-shan Hsien	F5	光山县
Ku-shih Hsien	G5	固始县
Lo-shan Hsien	F5	罗山县
Shang-ch'eng Hsien	G6	商城县

Hsü-ch'ang Ti-ch'ü		许昌地区
Ch'ang-ko Hsien		长葛县
centre: Ho-shang-ch'iao	E3	和尚桥
Chia Hsien		郏县
centre: Chia-hsien	E4	
Hsiang-ch'eng Hsien	E4	襄城县
Hsü-ch'ang Hsien	E3	许昌县
Lin-ying Hsien	E4	临颍县
Lu-shan Hsien	D4	鲁山县
Pao-feng Hsien	E4	宝丰县
Wu-yang Hsien	E4	舞阳县
Yeh Hsien		叶县
centre: Yeh-hsien	E4	
Yen-ch'eng Hsien	E4	郾城县
Yen-ling Hsien	F3	鄢陵县
Yü Hsien		禹县
centre: Yü-hsien	E3	

K'ai-feng Ti-ch'ü		开封地区
Ch'i Hsien		杞县
centre: Ch'i-hsien	F3	
Chung-mou Hsien	F3	中牟县
Hsin-cheng Hsien	E3	新郑县
Hsing-yang Hsien	E3	荥阳县
K'ai-feng Hsien		开封县
centre: Huang-lung-ssu	F3	黄龙寺
Kung Hsien		巩县
centre: Hsiao-i	D3	孝义
Lan-k'ao Hsien	F3	兰考县
Mi Hsien		密县
centre: Mi-hsien	E3	
Teng-feng Hsien	E3	登封县
T'ung-hsü Hsien	F3	通许县
Wei-shih Hsien	F3	尉氏县

Lo-yang Ti-ch'ü		洛阳地区
Hsin-an Hsien	D3	新安县
I-ch'uan Hsien	D3	伊川县
I-yang Hsien	D3	宜阳县
Ju-yang Hsien	D3	汝阳县
Ling-pao Hsien		灵宝县
centre: Kuo-lüeh-chen	B3	虢略镇
Lin-ju Hsien	D3	临汝县
Lo-ning Hsien	C3	洛宁县
Luan-ch'uan Hsien	C4	栾川县
Lu-shih Hsien	C3	卢氏县
Meng-chin Hsien		孟津县
centre: Ch'ang-hua	D3	长华
Mien-ch'ih Hsien	C3	渑池县
Shan Hsien		陕县
centre: San-men-hsia	C3	三门峡
Sung Hsien		嵩县
centre: Sung-hsien	D3	
Yen-shih Hsien	D3	偃师县

Nan-yang Ti-ch'ü		南阳地区
Chen-p'ing Hsien	D4	镇平县
Fang-ch'eng Hsien	D4	方城县
Hsi-ch'uan Hsien		淅川县
centre: Shang-chi	C4	上集
Hsi-hsia Hsien	C4	西峡县
Hsin-yeh Hsien	D5	新野县
Nan-chao Hsien	D4	南召县
Nan-yang Hsien	D4	南阳县
Nei-hsiang Hsien	C4	内乡县
She-ch'i Hsien	D4	社旗县
T'ang-ho Hsien	D5	唐河县
Teng Hsien		邓县
centre: Teng-hsien	D5	
T'ung-pai Hsien	E5	桐柏县

Shang-ch'iu Ti-ch'ü		商丘地区
centre: Chu-chi	G3	朱集
Che-ch'eng Hsien	G3	柘城县
Hsia-i Hsien	H3	夏邑县
Min-ch'üan Hsien	G3	民权县
Ning-ling Hsien	G3	宁陵县
Shang-ch'iu Hsien	G3	商丘县
Sui Hsien		睢县
centre: Sui-hsien	G3	
Yü-ch'eng Hsien		虞城
centre: Ma-mu-chi	G3	马牧集
Yung-ch'eng Hsien	H4	永城县

HUPEH
PROVINCE

HUPEH province comprises two quite different regions. The eastern two-thirds of the province is an area of low-lying plain forming the northern half of the central Yangtze basin, bounded on the north by the Huai-yang ranges and on the south-east by the Mu-fu Shan range. This plain is drained by the Yangtze and its main northern tributary, the Han Shui. The western third of the province is a very different area, of rugged highlands with small cultivated basins and valleys, which divide Hupeh from Szechwan. The plain area has been settled by the Chinese since the first millenium BC. From the 7th century onwards it was intensively settled, and in the 11th century was already a rice-surplus producing area. In the late 19th century it was the first area in the Chinese interior to undergo considerable modern industrial growth. The mountainous west was very sparsely peopled until comparatively recent times.

The whole province is sheltered from northerly air masses by the northern mountains. It has winter temperatures of about 5°C (41°F), and very hot humid summers with average temperatures of 29°C (84°F) and more. The annual rainfall is over 1,000 mm except in the extreme north of the Han Shui valley, and very much more (1,500 mm and more) in the south-western mountains. The growing season is about 280 days in the north and 300 days in the south. Most of the rain falls in summer, but there is more winter rainfall than in northern China. The whole area was naturally forested, but the lowlands have long ago been cleared. The western mountains, however, are still heavily forested.

South-eastern Hupeh Apart from an area of forested hills and mountains on the south-east border with Kiangsi, along the Mu-fu Shan range, this region consists of a great alluvial plain drained by the Yangtze and the lower course of the Han Shui. The area was originally very swampy. There are still vast areas of lakes, and the Yangtze and other rivers meander through a landscape covered with a dense network of waterways. In the past this area was frequently flooded, and since 1954 two large retention basins have been built, one south of the Yangtze near Sha-shih, the other between the Han Shui and Yangtze west of Han-yang, to accommodate flood water in times of critical flooding. The plain is very intensively cultivated. The main crops are rice, winter wheat, barley and corn, with large areas devoted to the cultivation of cotton and of ramie. The hills of the south are an important tea-producing district.

The main importance of this area, however, is as the industrial region of Hupeh. The south-eastern hills have extremely important iron mines at Ta-yeh and some small anthracite mines. This area was the site of the first modern iron and steel plant in China. The Ta-yeh mines were first opened up in the 1890s to feed an iron and steel works at Han-yang (Wu-han). Coal was brought from P'ing-hsiang in Kiangsi. Later the ironworks passed into the possession of the Japanese, who shut down local production of steel, but exported ore from Ta-yeh to Japan. During the Second World War, the plant of the Han-yang iron works was moved to Ch'ung-ch'ing.

Wu-han is by far the region's largest city, and one of the most important industrial complexes in China. It consists of three separate cities, at the confluence of the Han Shui and Yangtze; Han-k'ou, the largest, which developed into a major commercial centre for foreign trade in the Yangtze area during the late 19th century; Han-yang, site of the old iron and steel complex and a major industrial area; and Wu-ch'ang, the administrative centre of the province, with universities and other public buildings. This is the oldest of the three cities, which replaced Chiang-ling as the main administrative and commercial centre of Hupeh during the Ming period. The three cities were joined by two rail and road bridges over the Han (1954) and the Yangtze (1957). Although the old iron and steel plant was dismantled during the war, Wu-han was designated a major centre for industrial growth in the 1950s, and a huge integrated iron and steel complex was constructed between 1956 and 1959, and later extended. Wu-han produces steel rails and constructional steel, and supplies a varied engineering industry, which manufactures heavy machinery, boilers, diesel engines, lorries, railway rolling stock, ball bearings etc. An aluminium plant was also installed in 1971, and there are various chemical industries and glass-making plants and cement works. Han-k'ou and Han-yang have also large cotton textile mills, and paper mills.

Wu-han's combined population rose from 1,400,000 in 1953 to 2,100,000 in 1957 and is currently estimated to be about 2,700,000.

Huang-shih, about 80 km downstream from Wu-han, is a new industrial centre established in 1950, to include the iron-mining centre of Ta-yeh, Shih-hui-yao the port from which the ore was shipped, and Huang-shih-kang, a major cement manufacturing centre. Huang-shih has an old-established iron and steel plant rebuilt in the late 1950s. But most of the local ore is sent by rail to Wu-han.

O-ch'eng, between Huang-shih and Wu-han on the railway, also has a small iron and steel complex, built between 1958–60.

Sha-shih is the principal city of the western section of the Hupeh plain. It is not only an important port on the Yangtze, but also has a more direct water-route to Wu-han through the maze of waterways north of the river. Sha-shih's growth began in the last century, when it was opened to foreign trade. It rapidly displaced nearby Chiang-ling, the traditional administrative centre of the area. After 1949 there was a good deal of industrial growth here, and Sha-shih has become an important manufacturing city for cotton textiles and cotton yarn, and has many other small food-processing and other industries. It also remains a very important local commercial and marketing centre.

The middle Han Shui basin is an area of flat alluvial plains and low hills, rising to little more than 150 m to 400 m. Intensively cultivated and heavily peopled, though not to the extent of the southern plain, it too is a productive area where agriculture concentrates upon rice, winter wheat, barley, corn, rape-seed and cotton. Wheat is far more important than in the south-eastern plain, since the climate is noticeably cooler, with a shorter growing season, and rice is mostly confined to the area around Hsiang-fan.

Hsiang-fan is the main city of the area, formed in 1950 by the amalgamation of the ancient administrative city of Hsiang-yang and the newer city of Fan-ch'eng. Traditionally a transport centre at the junction of the Han Shui with its northern tributaries the Pei Ho and T'ang Ho, which provide an easy route into Ho-nan, Hsiang-yang lost some of its importance when the Peking–Han-k'ou railway was constructed on a route further east, although it remained the commercial and market centre of the region and an important river port. In 1965 it was connected with Wu-han by rail, as the first stage of a line designed to follow the Han valley westwards. It supports a variety of minor textile and food-processing industries.

Kuang-hua (also known as Lao-ho-k'ou), further up the Han valley, is at the western extremity of the plain, and also plays an important role in trade from the mountainous district of the north-west, and from the Nan-yang basin in southern Honan. A very important trading city before the Second World War, its role has largely been assumed by Hsiang-fan.

North-western Hupeh is a rugged mountainous area drained by the Han Shui and its tributaries. The mountains are not very high – mostly below 1,000 m – but the small basins around Yün-hsien, Chün-hsien, Fang-hsien and Chu-shan are the only areas with any considerable agricultural population. The area is colder than other areas of Hupeh, and has a rainfall below 750 mm, with frequent winter droughts. Wheat, corn, sweet potatoes, some rice, cotton and sesame are the main crops. The productivity of the area, however, is low. Forest products are cultivated; pears, persimmons, walnuts and tung-oil are important. The area has no sizeable towns, and little industry of any sort. At the eastern edge of this region, the Han Shui flows through steep gorges. In 1958 a hydro-electric scheme was inaugurated at Tan-chiang, but has not, apparently, been completed.

North-eastern Hupeh This area consists of the hilly land rising to the ranges known collectively as the Huai-yang ranges – the T'ung-pai Shan and Ta-pieh Shan forming the border with Honan and Anhwei, and the Ta-hung Shan forming the area's western border. The hills are mostly very low (200 m to 300 m), and there are extensive plains. The mountain ranges themselves are formed of much weathered granite and gneiss, and the highest peaks are only about 1,000 m. With the exception of the mountain ranges, this is a densely peopled and highly cultivated area. Rice is the main crop, grown with wheat, cotton, soy beans, ramie, sesame and rape-seed. There is little industry.

The south-western Hupeh mountains This is the most mountainous region of the province, an area of rugged topography with many mountains above 1,000 m, comprising the Wu Shan ranges, which form the boundary between Hupeh and Szechwan, and through which the Yangtze runs in a series of spectacular gorges, and the mountainous basin of the Ch'ing Chiang on the Hunan border. It is an area with large areas of natural forest cover, and with a climate which varies widely. In general it has warmer winters than the Wu-han area, because of the protection given by the mountains against cold winter winds. It also has a very abundant rainfall. Only the area of the Yangtze valley around I-ch'ang, and the basins around En-shih and Hsüan-en, are heavily cultivated. The main crops are rice, corn, wheat, sweet potatoes, yams and soy beans. Corn is the main staple crop in the uplands. Rape-seed, ramie and cotton are also grown. Livestock are extensively raised, and tea production is widespread. Citrus fruits and forest products like tung-oil, varnish and tallow are important. The population is very sparse, however, and the area is the most backward in Hupeh.

I-ch'ang, a river port at the western end of the Yangtze gorges, is the area's only sizeable city. Always an important commercial centre, since the 1950s it has developed chemical and food-processing industries.

I-tu, further downstream, is the main commercial outlet for the Ch'ing Chiang valley, exporting timber, tea and other forest products.

AREA
180,000 square kilometres

POPULATION
33,710,000 (other estimates up to 35,000,000)

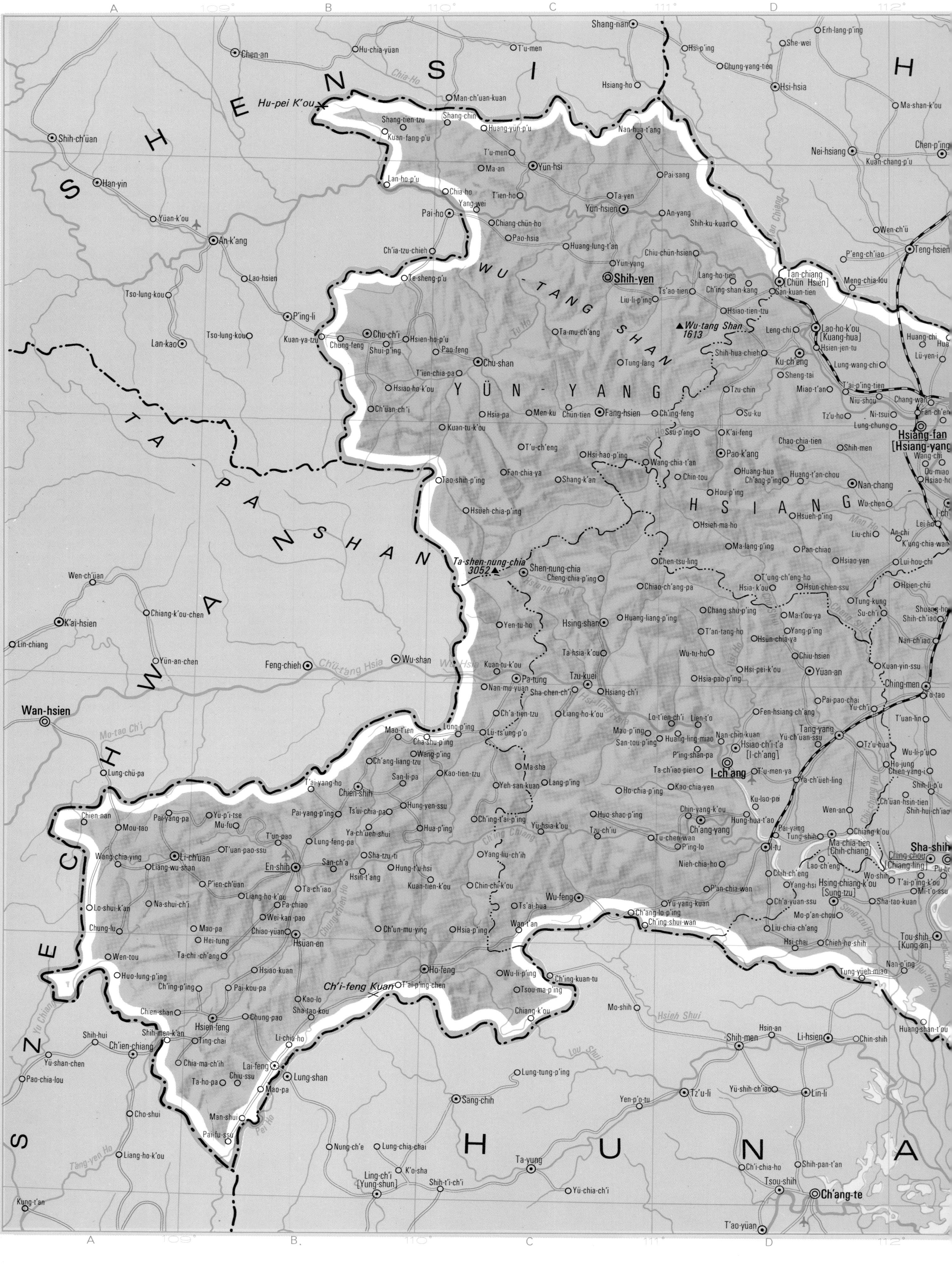

A
B
C
D
109°
110°
111°
112°
1
2
3
4
5
6
33°
32°
31°
30°
29°
S H E N S I
H
Shang-nan
Chen-an
Hu-chia-yüan
T'u-men
Chia Ho
Hsi-p'ing
Erh-lang-p'ing
She-wei
Chung-yang-tien
Hsiang-ho
Hsi-hsia
Man-ch'uan-kuan
Hu-pei K'ou
Shang-tien-tzu
Shang-chin
Huang-yün-p'u
Nan-hua-t'ang
Ma-shan-k'ou
Shih-ch'üan
Kuan-fang-p'u
T'u-men
Ma-an
Yün-hsi
Pai-sang
Nei-hsiang
Kuan-chang-p'u
Chen-p'ing
Han-yin
Lan-ho-p'u
Chia-ho
T'ien-ho
Ta-yen
Yang-wei
Yün-hsien
An-yang
Pai-ho
Chiang-chün-ho
Shih-ku-kuan
Han Chiang
Yüan-k'ou
Pao-hsia
Wen-ch'ü
An-k'ang
Huang-lung-t'an
Ch'ia-tzu-chieh
Yün-yang
Chiu-chün-hsien
P'eng-ch'iao
Teng-hsien
WU-TANG SHAN
Shih-yen
Lang-ho-tien
Tan-chiang [Chün Hsien]
Meng-chia-lou
Lao-hsien
Te-sheng-p'u
Ts'ao-tien
Ch'ing-shan-kang
San-kuan-tien
Tso-lung-kou
Liu-li-p'ing
Hsiao-tien-tzu
P'ing-li
Wu-tang Shan 1613
Leng-chi
Lao-ho-k'ou [Kuang-hua]
Lan-kao
Tso-lung-kou
Kuan-ya-tzu
Chu-ch'i
Hsien-ho-p'u
Ta-mu-ch'ang
Hsien-jen-tu
Huang-chi
Chung-feng
Shui-p'ing
Tu Ho
Shih-hua-chieh
Ku-ch'eng
Lü-yen-i
Pao-feng
Chu-shan
Tung-lang
Lung-wang-chi
Sheng-tai
T'ien-chia-pa
Hsiao-ho-k'ou
YÜN-YANG
Tzu-chin
Miao-t'an
T'ai-p'ing-tien
TA-PA SHAN
Niu-shou
Chang-wan
Ch'üan-ch'i
Hsia-pa
Men-ku
Chün-tien
Fang-hsien
Ch'ing-feng
Su-ku
Tz'u-ho
Ni-tsui
Fan-ch'eng
Lung-chung
Kuan-tu-k'ou
Nan Ho
Ssu-p'ing
K'ai-feng
Hsiang-fan [Hsiang-yang]
T'u-ch'eng
Chao-chia-tien
Shih-men
Wang-chi
Hsi-hao-p'ing
Wang-chia-t'an
Pao-k'ang
Ou-miao
Fan-chia-ya
Huang-hua
Hsiao-ho
Shang-k'an
Chin-tou
Ch'ang-p'ing
Huang-t'an-chou
Tao-shih-p'ing
Nan-chang
Hou-p'ing
HSIANG
Wu-chen
Hsüeh-chia-p'ing
Hsüeh-p'ing
Hsieh-ma-ho
Lei-ho
Man Ho
Liu-chi
An-chi
K'ung-chia-wan
Ma-lang-p'ing
Pan-chiao
Chen-tsu-ling
Hsiao-yen
Lui-hou-chi
Ta-shen-nung-chia 3052
Shen-nung-chia
Cheng-chia-p'ing
T'ung-ch'eng-ho
Wen-ch'üan
Chiao-ch'ang-pa
Hsia-k'ou
Hsün-chien-ssu
Hsien-chü
Hsiang Ch'i
Tung-kung
Chiang-k'ou-chen
Chang-shu-p'ing
Ma-t'ou-ya
Su-ch'i
Shuang-ho
K'ai-hsien
Hsing-shan
Huang-liang-p'ing
Shih-ch'iao
Yen-tu-ho
Yang-p'ing
Lin-chiang
T'an-tang-ho
Hsün-chia-ya
Nan-ch'iao
Ta-hsia-k'ou
Chiu-hsien
Wu-tu-ho
Hei Ho
Yün-an-chen
Feng-chieh
Ch'ü-t'ang Hsia
Wu-shan
Wu Hsia
Kuan-tu-k'ou
Tzu-kuei
Hsi-pei-k'ou
Kuan-yin-ssu
Yüan-an
Pa-tung
Hsia-pao-p'ing
Ching-men
Nan-mu-yüan
Sha-chen-ch'i
Hsiang-ch'i
Hsi-ling Hsia
Pai-pao-chai
Ching-tao
Wan-hsien
Ch'a-tien-tzu
Liang-ho-k'ou
Lo-t'ien-ch'i
Lien-t'o
Fen-hsiang-ch'ang
Yü-ch'i
T'uan-lin
Mo-tao Ch'i
Mao-t'ien
Lung-p'ing
Lü-ts'ung-p'o
Mao-p'ing
Huang-ling-miao
Nan-chin-kuan
Yü-ch'üan-ssu
Tang-yang
Ch'a-shu-p'ing
San-tou-p'ing
Hsiao-ch'i-t'a [I-ch'ang]
Tz'u-hua
Wu-li-p'u
Ch'ang-liang-tzu
Wang-p'ing
P'ing-shan-pa
Lung-chü-pa
Ma-sha
Ta-ch'iao-pien
I-ch'ang
T'u-men-ya
Ho-jung
Chien-yang-i
San-li-pa
Kao-tien-tzu
Shih-li-p'u
T'ai-yang-ho
Chien-shih
Yeh-san-kuan
Lang-p'ing
Ho-chia-p'ing
Kao-chia-yen
Ya-ch'üeh-ling
Hung-yen-ssu
Ku-lao-pei
Ch'üan-hsin-tien
Chien-nan
Pai-yang-pa
Yü-p'i-tse
Pai-yang-p'ing
Ts'ui-chia-pa
Shih-hui-ch'ien
Mou-tao
Mu-fu
Hua-p'ing
Ch'ing-t'ai-p'ing
Huo-shao-p'ing
Chin-yang-k'ou
Hung-hua-t'ao
Wen-an
Ya-ch'üeh-shui
Yü-hsia-k'ou
Tzu-ch'iu
Ch'ang-yang
Pai-yang
Chiang-k'ou
T'un-pao
Ch'ing Chiang
Tu-chen-wan
Tung-shih
Ma-chia-tien [Chih-chiang]
Sha-shih
Wang-chia-ying
Li-ch'uan
T'uan-pao-ssu
Lung-feng-pa
P'ing-lo
I-tu
Ching-chou [Chiang-ling]
Liang-wu-shan
En-shih
San-ch'a
Sha-tzu-ti
Hung-t'u-hsi
Yang-liu-ch'ih
Nieh-chia-ho
Lao-ch'eng
Pu-hu
Hsin-t'ang
Chih-ch'eng
Wo-shih
T'ai-p'ing-k'ou
P'ien-ch'üan
Ta-ch'iao
Kuan-tien-k'ou
Chin-chi-k'ou
Yang-hsi
Hsing-chiang-k'ou [Sung-tzu]
Mi-t'o-ssu
Liang-ho-k'ou
P'an-chia-wan
Na-shui-ch'i
Pa-chiao
Ts'ai-hua
Wu-feng
Yü-yang-kuan
Ch'a-yuan-ssu
Sha-tao-kuan
Lo-shui-k'an
Wei-kan-pao
Ch'ang-lo-p'ing
Mo-p'an-chou
Chiao-yüan
Wan-t'an
Ch'ing-shui-wan
Liu-chia-ch'ang
Chung-lu
Mao-pa
Hsüan-en
Ch'un-mu-ying
Hsia-p'ing
Hsi-chai
Chieh-ho-shih
Tou-shih [Kung-an]
Hei-tung
Chung-chien Ho
Sung-tzu Ho
Wen-tou
Ta-chi-ch'ang
Hu-tu Ho
Huo-lung-p'ing
Hsiao-kuan
Ho-feng
Wu-li-p'ing
Tung-yüeh-miao
Nan-p'ing
Ch'ing-p'ing
Pai-kou-pa
Ch'i-feng Kuan
T'ai-p'ing-chen
Ch'ing-kuan-tu
Tsou-ma-p'ing
Kao-lo
Mo-shih
Yü Chiang
Chien-shan
Chung-pao
Sha-tao-kou
Chiang-k'ou
Hsieh Shui
Huang-shan-t'ou
Hsien-feng
Shih-hui
Shih-men-k'an
Ting-chai
Li-chia-ho
Hsin-an
Shih-men
Li-hsien
Chin-shih
Ch'ien-chiang
Lou Shui
Chia-ma-ch'ih
Lai-feng
Lung-shan
Yü-shan-chen
Chiu-ssu
Lung-tung-p'ing
Pao-chia-lou
Ta-ho-pa
Mao-pa
Yü-shih-ch'iao
Tz'u-li
Lin-li
Sang-chih
Yen-p'o-tu
Cho-shui
Man-shui
Pai-fu-ssu
Pei Ho
Nung-ch'e
Lung-chia-chai
Liang-ho-k'ou
S Z E C H W A N
H U N A
T'ang-yen Ho
K'o-sha
Ta-yung
Ch'i-chia-ho
Shih-pan-t'an
Ling-ch'i [Yung-shun]
Shih-t'i-ch'i
Yü-chia-ch'i
Tsou-shih
Ch'ang-te
Kung-t'an
T'ao-yüan

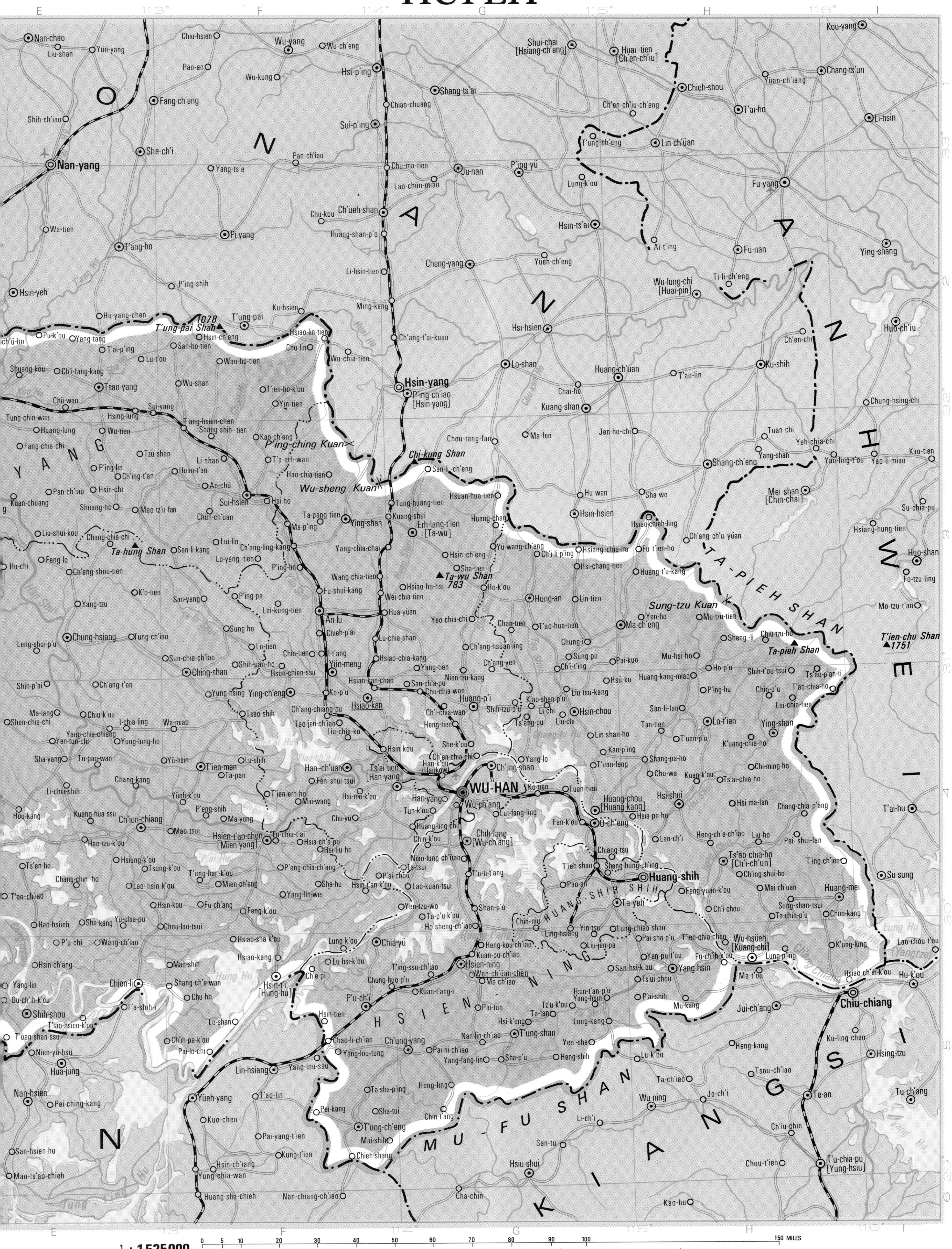

1 : 1525000

0 5 10 20 30 40 50 60 70 80 90 100 150 MILES

0 5 10 20 30 40 50 60 70 80 90 100 150 200 KM

HUPEH PROVINCE 湖北省

HU-PEI SHENG

6 shih	*municipalities*
8 ti-ch'ü	*regions*
73 hsien	*counties*

capital **Wu-han Shih**	G4	武汉市
Hsiang-fan Shih	E2	襄樊市
Huang-shih Shih	H4	黄石市
Ta-yeh Hsien	G4	大冶县
I-ch'ang Shih	D4	宜昌市
Sha-shih Shih	E4	沙市市
Shih-yen Shih	C2	十堰市

Ching-chou Ti-ch'ü		**荆州地区**
Chiang-ling Hsien		江陵县
centre: Ching-chou	E4	荆州
Ch'ien-chiang Hsien	E4	潜江县
Chien-li Hsien	E5	监利县
Ching-men Hsien	E3	荆门县
Ching-shan Hsien	F3	京山县
Chung-hsiang Hsien	E3	钟祥县
Hung-hu Hsien		洪湖县
centre: Hsin-t'i	F5	新堤
Kung-an Hsien		公安县
centre: Tou-shih	E4	斗市
Mien-yang Hsien		沔阳县
centre: Hsien-t'ao-chen	F4	仙桃镇
Shih-shou Hsien	E5	石首县
Sung-tzu Hsien		松滋县
centre: Hsin-chiang-k'ou	D4	新江口
T'ien-men Hsien	F4	天门县

En-shih Ti-ch'ü		**恩施地区**
Chien-shih Hsien	B4	建始县
En-shih Hsien	B4	恩施县
Ho-feng Hsien	C5	鹤峰县
Hsien-feng Hsien	B5	咸丰县
Hsüan-en Hsien	B4	宣恩县
Lai-feng Hsien	B5	来凤县
Li-ch'uan Hsien	A4	利川县
Pa-tung Hsien	C3	巴东县

Hsiang-yang Ti-ch'ü		**襄阳地区**
centre: Hsiang-fan	E2	襄樊
Hsiang-yang Hsien		襄阳县
centre: Hsiang-fan	E2	襄樊
I-ch'eng Hsien	E3	宜城县
Kuang-hua Hsien		光化县
centre: Lao-ho-k'ou	D2	老河口
Ku-ch'eng Hsien	D2	谷城县
Nan-chang Hsien	D3	南漳县
Pao-k'ang Hsien	D3	保康县
Sui Hsien		随县
centre: Sui-hsien	F3	
Tsao-yang Hsien	E2	枣阳县

Hsiao-kan Ti-ch'ü		**孝感地区**
An-lu Hsien	F3	安陆县
Han-ch'uan Hsien	F4	汉川县
Han-yang Hsien		汉阳县
centre: Ts'ai-tien	G4	蔡甸
Hsiao-kan Hsien	F4	孝感县
Huang-p'i Hsien	G4	黄陂县
Ta-wu Hsien		大悟县
centre: Erh-lang-tien	G3	二郎店
Ying-ch'eng Hsien	F4	应城县
Ying-shan Hsien	F3	应山县
Yün-meng Hsien	F3	云梦县

Hsien-ning Ti-ch'ü		**咸宁地区**
centre: Wen-ch'üan-chen	G5	温泉镇
Chia-yü Hsien	F5	嘉鱼县
Ch'ung-yang Hsien	G5	崇阳县
Hsien-ning Hsien	G5	咸宁县
O-ch'eng Hsien	G4	鄂城县
P'u-ch'i Hsien	F5	蒲圻县
T'ung-ch'eng Hsien	F5	通城县
T'ung-shan Hsien	G5	通山县
Wu-ch'ang Hsien		武昌县
centre: Chih-fang	G4	纸坊
Yang-hsin Hsien	H5	阳新县

Huang-kang Ti-ch'ü		**黄冈地区**
Ch'i-ch'un Hsien		蕲春县
centre: Ts'ao-chia-ho	H4	漕家河
Hsin-chou Hsien	G4	新洲县
Hsi-shui Hsien	H4	浠水县
Huang-kang Hsien		黄冈县
centre: Huang-chou	G4	黄州
Huang-mei Hsien	H4	黄梅县
Hung-an Hsien	G3	红安县
Kuang-chi Hsien		广济县
centre: Wu-hsüeh	H5	武穴
Lo-t'ien Hsien	H4	罗田县
Ma-ch'eng Hsien	H3	麻城县
Ying-shan Hsien	H4	英山县

I-ch'ang Ti-ch'ü		**宜昌地区**
Ch'ang-yang Hsien	D4	长阳县
Chih-chiang Hsien		枝江县
centre: Ma-chia-tien	D4	马家店
Hsing-shan Hsien	C3	兴山县
I-ch'ang Hsien		宜昌县
centre: Hsiao-ch'i-t'a	D4	小溪塔
I-tu Hsien	D4	宜都县
Shen-nung-chia Hsien	C3	神农架县
Tang-yang Hsien	D4	当阳县
Tzu-kuei Hsien	C3	秭归县
Wu-feng Hsien	C4	五峰县
Yüan-an Hsien	D3	远安县

Yün-yang Ti-ch'ü		**郧阳地区**
centre: Shih-yen	C2	十堰
Chu-ch'i Hsien	B2	竹溪县
Chün Hsien		均县
centre: Tan-chiang	D2	丹江
Chu-shan Hsien	C2	竹山县
Fang Hsien		房县
centre: Fang-hsien	C2	
Yün-hsi Hsien	C2	郧西县
Yün Hsien		郧县
centre: Yün-hsien	C2	

SHENSI
PROVINCE

THE northern part of Shensi, especially the Wei Ho valley, is one of the longest settled areas of China. The seat of early Mesolithic and Neolithic cultures, the area constituted an important route between China and Central Asia. At the end of the 2nd millenium BC it was the homeland of the Chou people, who established some degree of political authority over much of north China from their capital Hao near Hsi-an (Sian). Later, the Ch'in, who first established a unified Chinese empire in 221 BC had their origins in the Wei valley, and this area remained a powerful centre of political authority until the end of the 9th century. After the fall of the T'ang in 907, the province gradually declined in importance, as the political centre of the empire moved to the east, and became a poor and backward region.

The province took roughly its present form, including the area of mountains south of the Chin-ling, in 1235. It suffered from serious rebellions and disorders from 1340–68, again from 1620–44, and in 1867–78 when the great Moslem rising led to the death of more than 600,000 Shensi Moslems. The province was also visited by terrible famines in 1876–8, when five millions died and in 1915, 1921 and 1928, when there were three million victims.

During the early republican period (1912–28) Shensi also suffered civil war and virtual anarchy for long periods. In 1936 the Communist armies, driven out of their bases in Kiangsi on the 'Long March' eventually passed through western Shensi and established themselves in Yen-an which from 1937 became the base first for their war of resistance against the Japanese, and then, after 1945, for their conquest of all China.

The Shensi Plateau The northern part of Shensi is a great upland plateau roughly 1,000 m above sea level. The western rim of this plateau is formed by the Liu-pan mountains, and the plateau is divided by the low Liang Shan and Huang-lung Shan ranges into a north-western area which drains directly into the Huang Ho, and a south-eastern area drained by the Lo Ho and Ching Ho and other northern tributaries of the Wei Ho. The plateau is covered with a thick layer of wind-blown loess soil, which masks the original land forms, and has in its turn been deeply eroded, forming a characteristic landscape of deep ravines and almost vertical cliff faces. This erosion has been intensified by the effects of long human occupation, which has completely destroyed the natural vegetation cover.

This plateau area has a hard climate, with a growing period of from 220 days in the south to 190 days in the north. Rainfall is about 500 mm in the south-east, and decreases towards the north and west to about 300 mm. Almost all this rain falls in summer when evaporation is high. Agriculture depends heavily on techniques for conserving moisture, and the north-western border with Inner Mongolian Autonomous Region, roughly coinciding with the old Great Wall, remains a major cultural frontier, beyond which the conditions for agriculture are extremely precarious. The plateau is too cold in winter for winter wheat to survive. Spring wheat and millet are the main grain crops. Less than a quarter of the land is cultivated, however, and grazing for horses and sheep becomes more important towards the northern and western borders.

The plateau is structurally a basin of sedimentary rocks, which include immense reserves of coal. The only mines so far exploited, owing to the lack of modern transport facilities, are those at T'ung-ch'uan on the southern edge of the plateau. There are good prospects for oil production, but to date the only production is at a minor field at Yen-ch'ang and Yen-ch'uan, near Yen-an. Further exploitation of the area's resources is inhibited by the poor communications – limited to roads – on the plateau. There are no cities of any size, though Yen-an enjoys great prestige as a national shrine.

The Wei Ho Valley The Wei Ho, a tributary of the Huang Ho, flows eastwards across the province at the foot of the towering Ch'in-ling Shan range. Its valley is a major tectonic trough, bounded by a complex zone of faults and fractures along the foot of the mountains, which forms an area of seismic instability, very vulnerable to earthquakes. The northern border of the Wei valley trench is much less abrupt, and the Ching Ho and Lo Ho, northern tributaries of the Wei, have formed large alluvial plains which merge into the Wei valley. The whole valley, and the northern face of the Ch'in-ling range are deeply mantled with loess, and the plain is largely formed of redeposited loess washed off the plateau. All the rivers are heavily silted.

The climate is much less harsh than that of the plateau. The growing season is longer (about 240 days) and winter temperatures higher. The rainfall is also heavier, between 500–650 mm. Most of the rain comes between May and October, and spring and early summer are usually dry. The climate is not seriously deficient in rainfall, but the area is periodically subject to long and severe droughts.

The Wei valley is naturally fertile, and has been intensively cultivated since early times. It was the site of the first major irrigation network in China, built in the 3rd century BC. Although the irrigation system was neglected after the 9th century, it was rehabilitated in the 1930s, and has been further repaired and extended since 1949. Well over half of the land is under cultivation, and the area supports a dense agricultural population. The valley grows rice in irrigated areas, winter wheat, tobacco and cotton. Millet, corn, barley and kaoliang, are also increasingly important crops. On the higher ground millet, oats and buckwheat are the main crops. In the upper Wei and Ching Ho valleys, hemp and sesame are widely grown, and oats are raised as fodder for the important animal husbandry of the marginal areas.

The Wei valley has been an important communication route since prehistoric times, where the great east-west route from Kansu to the north China plain is joined by various routes across the Ch'in-ling range into Szechwan, and by roads across the plateau to the north. The first railway reached Hsi-an in 1934, and was extended west to Pao-chi in 1937. Since the 1950s this route has been extended into the far west, and a link built from Pao-chi into Szechwan. This led to some limited industrial growth in the area.

Hsi-an is one of China's most ancient towns. The Chou, Ch'in, Han and T'ang had their capitals here, and from the late 6th to the 9th centuries Ch'ang-an, as it was then called, was the world's largest metropolis, with a population of more than a million. It declined, however, and was until recently a large regional administrative city, with some minor industries. Since 1949 it has been rapidly and systematically developed into a major regional industrial metropolis. The coal mines at T'ung-ch'uan to the north provide fuel for two large thermal generating plants, and the city was linked with the power grid joining the unfinished San-men project on the Huang Ho to the industrial cities of Honan. The new industrial growth has involved large textile mills, producing both cotton and woollen goods, and a large and diversified electrical industry. An iron and steel plant was built during the Great Leap Forward, but it may have been abandoned after 1962. An engineering industry produces agricultural and mining equipment, and there are some chemical plants. Hsi-an is also a very important administrative and cultural centre with an important university and other institutes, libraries and museums. Its population in 1958 was estimated at 1,368,000, and is now perhaps 1,500,000. *San-yüan* and *Hsien-yang* are both more or less satellite cities of Hsi-an, important route centres which have also undergone some development of modern industry, particularly in cotton textiles.

Pao-chi, the chief centre of the western Wei valley, is Shensi's second city, with about 180,000 people in 1958. It has its own large power plant and has a large cotton textile industry. It is a very important rail junction, with a line branching southwards into Szechwan, and has railway workshops and other light engineering industries.

Southern Shensi The south of the province is quite different from the north in every way. It is a rugged and highly mountainous area. In the north are the wide ranges of the Ch'in-ling, a complex mountain belt rising to 2,500 m, and individual peaks rising to 3,500 m. These mountains have always been a major environmental and cultural divide, crossed by only four passes. They are separated from the Ta-pa Shan range which forms the border with Szechwan by the valley of the Han Shui, which broadens out in the region of Han-chung to form a fertile basin about 144 kilometres long by 48 kilometres broad.

This mountainous southern area also has a totally different climate. Sheltered from the north by the Ch'in-ling ranges, it has a sub-tropical climate similar to that of Szechwan or the Central Yangtze. Although it is slightly less hot than the Yangtze valley, winter temperatures are well above freezing, and the growing season is between 260–280 days. Rainfall is from 750 mm to 1,000 mm, mostly falling in late summer and early autumn. The spring and early summer are dry. Climate varies greatly owing to the very varied topography. The natural vegetation was mixed forest, and there are still great areas of natural timber, which has not been cut owing to the difficulty of access.

This area remained very sparsely peopled until the late 17th century, apart from the Han-chung basin, where paddy rice followed by winter wheat have long been grown intensively. In the late 17th century, the introduction of corn and sweet potatoes made the cultivation of uplands possible, and there was extensive immigration from the 1770s from Szechwan, Hupeh and other parts of central China. Upland farming often led to serious erosion problems, however. Most of the cultivated land in the province is below the 1,000 m line. Rice is still the main crop in the Han-chung plain; corn and winter wheat are grown elsewhere in the mountainous districts. Sub-tropical crops such as tea, tung-oil and citrus fruits are grown, while apples, pears, apricots and grapes are also widely produced. The southern region has very poor communications. An east-west highway follows the Han Shui valley, and a railway was planned to follow the same route, but only a short section in the west has been completed.

Han-chung is the communication centre and administrative centre for this southern area, and serves as the market and commercial centre of the surrounding plain. It has some minor light industry, mainly food processing and cotton textiles.

AREA
195,800 square kilometres

POPULATION
Estimated 22,000,000

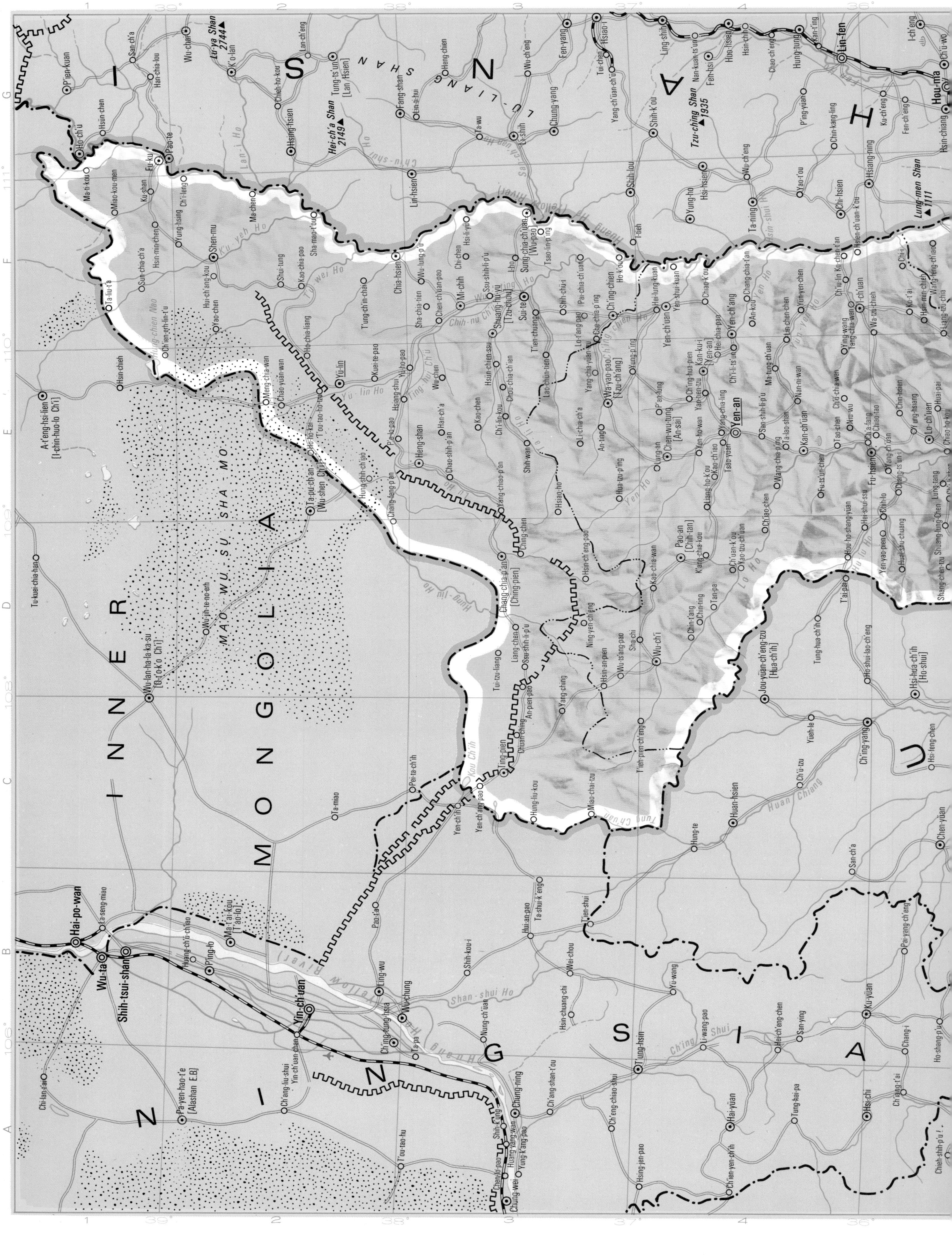
INNER MONGOLIA
NINGSIA
SHENSI
SHANSI
MAO-WU-SU SHA MO
LU-LIANG SHAN
Lu-ya Shan 2744
Hei-ch'a Shan 2149
Tzu-ching Shan 1935
Lung-men Shan 1111
Huang Ho (Yellow River)
Wu-ting Ho
Yen Ho
Lo Ho
Ch'ing Shui
Hai-po-wan
Wu-ta
Shih-tsui-shan
Yin-ch'uan
Wu-chung
Chung-ning
Chung-wei
Ku-yüan
Hsi-chi
Hai-yüan
T'ung-hsin
Yen-ch'ih
Ting-pien
Ching-pien
Yü-lin
Heng-shan
Shen-mu
Fu-ku
Pao-te
Sui-te
Mi-chih
Wu-pao
Ch'ing-chien
Yen-ch'uan
Yen-ch'ang
Yen-an
Pao-an
Wu-ch'i
Chih-tan
An-sai
Tzu-ch'ang
Kan-ch'üan
Fu-hsien
Lo-ch'uan
Huan-hsien
Ch'ing-yang
Ho-shui
Hua-ch'ih
Chen-yüan
Lin-fen
Hou-ma
Hsin-chiang
Chi-hsien
Hsiang-ning
Ta-ning
Hsi-hsien
Shih-lou
Lin-hsien
Li-shih
Fang-shan
Hsing-hsien
Lan-hsien
Chia-hsien
Wu-lan-ha-la-ka-su
A-t'eng-hsi-lien
Pa-yen-hao-t'e

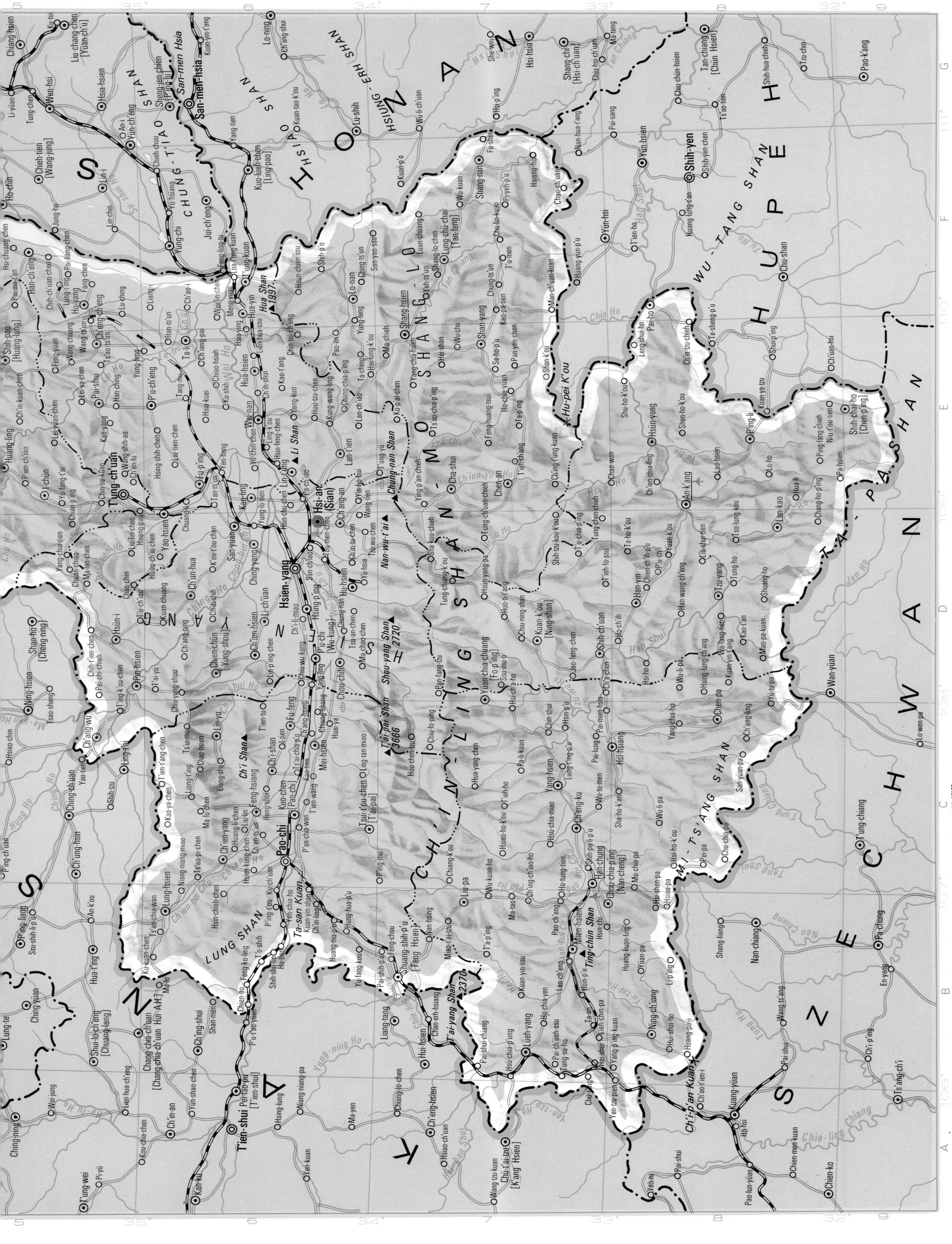

Hsi-an (Sian)
Hsien-yang
Pao-chi
Han-chung
An-k'ang
Shang-hsien
Yen-an
Tung-ch'uan
Wei-nan
San-men-Hsia
Shih-yen
Yün-hsien
Tien-shui
Kuang-yüan
CH'IN-LING SHAN
TA-PA SHAN
MI-TS'ANG SHAN
WU-TANG SHAN
SHANG-LO
CHUNG-T'IAO SHAN
HSIAO-SHAN
LUNG SHAN
T'ai-pai Shan 3666
Hua Shan 1997
Li Shan
Chung-nan Shan
Nan-wu-t'ai
Shou-yang Shan 2720
Ch'i Shan
T'ai-yang Shan 2370
Ting-chün Shan
Ta-san Kuan
Ch'i-p'an Kuan
Hu-pei K'ou
Han Shui
Wei Ho
Chia-ling Chiang
HO-NAN
HU-PEI
SZECHWAN
KANSU
SHANSI
1 : 1750000

SHENSI PROVINCE 陕西省

SHAN-HSI SHENG

5 shih	*municipalities*
8 ti-ch'ü	*regions*
93 hsien	*counties*

capital **Hsi-an Shih**	**D6**	西安市
Hsien-yang Shih	**D6**	咸阳市
Ch'ang-an Hsien	**D6**	长安县
Pao-chi Shih	**C6**	宝鸡市
T'ung-ch'uan Shih	**E5**	铜川市
Yen-an Shih	**E4**	延安市

An-k'ang Ti-ch'ü		安康地区
An-k'ang Hsien	**D8**	安康县
Chen-p'ing Hsien		镇坪县
centre: Shih-chai-ho	**E9**	石寨河
Han-yin Hsien	**D8**	汉阴县
Hsün-yang Hsien	**E8**	旬阳县
Lan-kao Hsien	**D8**	岚皋县
Ning-shan Hsien		宁陕县
centre: Kuan-k'ou	**D7**	关口
Pai-ho Hsien	**F8**	白河县
P'ing-li Hsien	**E8**	平利县
Shih-ch'üan Hsien	**D7**	石泉县
Tzu-yang Hsien	**D8**	紫阳县

Han-chung Ti-ch'ü		汉中地区
Ch'eng-ku Hsien	**C7**	城固县
Chen-pa Hsien	**C8**	镇巴县
Fo-p'ing Hsien		佛坪县
centre: Yüan-chia-chuang	**D7**	袁家庄
Han-chung Hsien	**C7**	汉中县
Hsi-hsiang Hsien	**C8**	西乡县
Liu-pa Hsien	**B7**	留坝县
Lüeh-yang Hsien	**B7**	略阳县
Mien Hsien		勉县
centre: Mien-hsien	**B7**	
Nan-cheng Hsien		南郑县
centre: Chou-chia-p'ing	**B7**	周家坪
Ning-ch'iang Hsien	**B8**	宁强县
Yang Hsien		洋县
centre: Yang-hsien	**C7**	

Hsien-yang Ti-ch'ü		咸阳地区
Ch'ang-wu Hsien	**C5**	长武县
Ch'ien Hsien		乾县
centre: Ch'ien-hsien	**D6**	
Ching-yang Hsien	**D6**	泾阳县
Chou-chih Hsien	**D6**	周至县
Ch'un-hua Hsien	**D6**	淳化县
Hsing-p'ing Hsien	**D6**	兴平县
Hsün-i Hsien	**D5**	旬邑县
Hu Hsien		户县
centre: Hu-hsien	**D6**	
Kao-ling Hsien	**E6**	高陵县
Li-ch'üan Hsien	**D6**	礼泉县
Pin Hsien		彬县
centre: Pin-hsien	**D5**	
San-yüan Hsien	**D6**	三原县
Yung-shou Hsien		永寿县
centre: Chien-chün	**D6**	监军

Pao-chi Ti-ch'ü		宝鸡地区
Ch'ien-yang Hsien	**C6**	千阳县
Ch'i-shan Hsien	**C6**	岐山县
Feng-hsiang Hsien	**C6**	凤翔县
Feng Hsien		凤县
centre: Shuang-shih-p'u	**B7**	双石铺
Fu-feng Hsien	**C6**	扶风县
Lin-yu Hsien	**C6**	麟游县
Lung Hsien		陇县
centre: Lung-hsien	**B6**	
Mei Hsien		眉县
centre: Mei-hsien	**C6**	
Pao-chi Hsien		宝鸡县
centre: Kuo-chen	**C6**	虢镇
T'ai-pai Hsien		太白县
centre: Tsui-t'ou-chen	**C6**	咀头镇
Wu-kung Hsien		武功县
centre: P'u-chi	**D6**	普集

Shang-lo Ti-ch'ü		商洛地区
centre: Shang-hsien		商县
Cha-shui Hsien	**E7**	柞水县
Chen-an Hsien	**E7**	镇安县
Lo-nan Hsien	**F6**	洛南县
Shang Hsien		商县
centre: Shang-hsien	**E7**	
Shang-nan Hsien	**F7**	商南县
Shan-yang Hsien	**E7**	山阳县
Tan-feng Hsien		丹凤县
centre: Lung-chü-chai	**F7**	龙驹寨

Wei-nan Ti-ch'ü		渭南地区
Ch'eng-ch'eng Hsien	**E5**	澄城县
Fu-p'ing Hsien	**E6**	富平县
Han-ch'eng Hsien	**F5**	韩城县
Ho-yang Hsien	**F5**	合阳县
Hua Hsien		华县
centre: Hua-hsien	**E6**	
Hua-yin Hsien	**F6**	华阴县
Lan-t'ien Hsien	**E6**	蓝田县
Lin-t'ung Hsien	**E6**	临潼县
Pai-shui Hsien	**E5**	白水县
P'u-ch'eng Hsien	**E6**	蒲城县
Ta-li Hsien	**E6**	大荔县
T'ung-kuan Hsien	**F6**	潼关县
Wei-nan Hsien	**E6**	渭南县
Yao Hsien		耀县
centre: Yao-hsien	**D6**	

Yen-an Ti-ch'ü		延安地区
An-sai Hsien		安塞县
centre: Chen-wu-tung	**E4**	眞武洞
Chih-tan Hsien		志丹县
centre: Pao-an	**D4**	保安
Fu Hsien		富县
centre: Fu-hsien	**E5**	
Huang-ling Hsien	**E5**	黄陵县
Huang-lung Hsien		黄龙县
centre: Shih-pao	**E5**	石堡
I-ch'uan Hsien	**F4**	宜川县
I-chün Hsien	**E5**	宜君县
Kan-ch'üan Hsien	**E4**	甘泉县
Lo-ch'uan Hsien	**E5**	洛川县
Tzu-ch'ang Hsien		子长县
centre: Wa-yao-pao	**E3**	瓦窑堡
Wu-ch'i Hsien	**D4**	吴旗县
Yen-an Hsien		延安县
centre: ?Kan-ku-i	**E4**	甘谷驿
Yen-ch'ang Hsien	**F4**	延长县
Yen-ch'uan Hsien	**F4**	延川县

Yü-lin Ti-ch'ü		榆林地区
Chia Hsien		佳县
centre: Chia-hsien	**F2**	
Ch'ing-chien Hsien	**F3**	清涧县
Ching-pien Hsien		靖边县
centre: Chang-chia-p'an	**D3**	张家畔
Fu-ku Hsien	**G1**	府谷县
Heng-shan Hsien	**E3**	横山县
Mi-chih Hsien	**F3**	米脂县
Shen-mu Hsien	**F2**	神木县
Sui-te Hsien	**F3**	绥德县
Ting-pien Hsien	**C3**	定边县
Tzu-chou Hsien		子州县
centre: Shuang-hu-yü	**F3**	双湖峪
Wu-pao Hsien		吴堡县
centre: Sung-chia-ch'uan	**F3**	宋家川
Yü-lin Hsien	**E2**	榆林县

FUKIEN
PROVINCE

FUKIEN, one of the most individual of the Chinese provinces, was brought under Chinese domination at a comparatively late date. Under the Former Han (206 BC–AD 7) it remained outside the political boundaries of China, under the aboriginal Min-yüeh people. The first Chinese penetration of the area came under the Chin (AD 265–420), who established a loose network of administration. However, real settlement began only in T'ang times. In the late 8th century a movement of Chinese settlers into Fukien transformed the province from a frontier area into a densely populated and wealthy region. The population increased many times. The province's new prosperity was largely associated with trade. Fu-chou and Ch'üan-chou were important ports, both for internal trade and for international commerce. Tea from the north and sugar from the south were exported to northern China, and local industries such as lacquer and porcelain, paper and silk manufacture rapidly grew. By the 12th century Fukien was a rich province, which was famous for the high level of its education and literary culture, whose gentry had great influence in the empire.

Under the Ming, Fukien bore the brunt of attacks by the Japanese pirates (Wo-k'ou), and both the Ming and Ch'ing governments pursued policies inimical to foreign trade, even at times withdrawing the population from the coastal zone. Fukien lost its prosperous trade, and when this revived in the late 17th and 18th centuries, it was concentrated at Canton. Although Fukien had a very high standard of agricultural technique, population density led to emigration. In the late 17th century, the settlement of Taiwan – which had become a part of the province – began, and great numbers of Fukienese emigrated to south-east Asia.

Both Fu-chou and Hsia-men (Amoy) were opened to trade as treaty ports in 1842, and in the 1860s Fu-chou developed one of the first modern shipyards and arsenals in China, the activities of which did much to spread western technology. However, towards the end of the century the traditional tea trade went into a decline as a result of competition from India and Ceylon, while after the Japanese occupation of Taiwan in 1895, the rapid development of the Taiwan sugar industry took away much of the province's market for sugar. In the pre-war period Fukien had a serious adverse trade balance, and small scale attempts at industrial growth mostly ended in failure. The war with Japan, from 1937–45, led to much destruction, the occupation of Fu-chou and a complete disruption of the trade upon which the province depended. Even after 1949, the vital coastal trade was continually hampered by the blockade of coastal ports by Nationalist forces in Taiwan, and by their continued occupation of key offshore islands.

Economic growth in the province recovered slowly, especially after the completion of railways linking both Hsia-men and Fu-chou with the interior in 1955. There is still very little industry, although agricultural production has increased rapidly, and the province is self-sufficient in food-stuffs. Nevertheless, the province has little arable land, and population pressure is very high.

Fukien has a semi-tropical or tropical climate. Winter temperatures at Fu-chou average 10·6°C (52°F), and 28·6°C (83°F) is the July average. On the coast, the growing season lasts throughout the year. The mountainous inland areas, particularly in the north, have a more moderate climate, and the winters can be cold. The climate is wet, most of the province having from 1,500 mm to 2,000 mm rainfall per year, most of which falls in summer between May and September. The area is frequently subject to typhoons.

The whole province is extremely hilly and complex in its relief. An ancient massif of mountains, with a general north-east to south-west axis, the province has a very high and rugged range forming the boundary with Kiangsi, the Wu-i Shan. It is divided by a series of valleys, drained by the upper tributaries of the Min Chiang and Han Chiang, from a complicated series of coastal ranges, the Po-p'ing Shan and Tai-yün Shan. The coast, much indented and with many islands, has a series of small alluvial plains, on which the major cities are located.

North-eastern Fukien This area, north of Lo-yüan, is a region of rolling hills, mostly under 700 m. It is drier and considerably cooler than the coastal area further south. Forestry is important, producing pine, fir, oak, tung-oil and tea-oil. Agriculture is mainly single cropped rice grown with soy beans, wheat and rape-seed. Tea of very high quality, which was the main source for the Fu-chou tea trade, is the most important product of this area.

The Fu-chou region This area comprises the lower valley of the Min Chiang, and the alluvial plain (about 500 square kilometres) around Fu-chou. This area has been longer settled than the north-east, has a warmer climate, more level land, and better conditions for agriculture. Rice is the main crop, mostly double cropped. Sweet potatoes, corn and wheat are also grown, together with sugar cane, jute, rape-seed and peanuts. On the hillsides fruit growing is a major industry. Oranges are a notable local product, though bananas, peaches and olives are also grown. The fishing industry is particularly important along the whole northern coast.

Fu-chou is the provincial capital, and the traditional administrative centre of the province. As a port it was the natural outlet for the valley of the Min Chiang, and most of the interior of the province. The navigation of the Min Chiang was much improved in the 1950s, and in 1958 Fu-chou was linked by rail with the Hsia-men–Kiangsi railway, but Fu-chou now has to rely on its outport Ma-wei, which has shipbuilding and a navy yard. Fu-chou is famous for its many handicrafts, and exports lacquer, porcelain and silk textiles, as well as tea and lumber. In 1958 a small steel plant was built, and in 1959 a chemical complex, which produces fertiliser, plastics and rayon. Paper making is another well established industry. Fu-chou depends for electric power upon the Ku-t'ien Ch'i hydro-electric plant, to the north-west. Population (553,000 in 1953) is now estimated at about 700,000.

Northern Fukien comprises the interior basin of the Min Chiang's main tributaries, the Chien Ch'i, Fu-t'un Ch'i, Chin Ch'i and the lower valley of the Sha Ch'i. It is a very hilly region, rising to steep mountains in the west and north. The area is heavily forested, and lumbering, for pine and fir, is an important local industry. Lumber is floated by raft to Nan-p'ing, and thence to Fu-chou. Camphor and bamboo are also important products.

For agriculture, the terrain has little level land, and the climate is considerably more temperate than in coastal areas. Single-crop rice, soy beans, corn, wheat and rape-seed are the main crops. There is some considerable tea production, but not on the same scale as in north-east Fukien.

Nan-p'ing is the chief centre of this region, at the junction of the Chien Ch'i with the Min Chiang. It was a traditional transhipment point, whose importance has grown with the coming of the railway to Kiangsi, Fu-chou and Hsia-men. It has important lumber and paper mills, and a large cement plant. It had about 65,000 people in 1958.

Shao-wu in the north-west has also grown into a major market centre since the coming of the railway. The surrounding area has deposits of tungsten.

Southern Fukien This comprises the coastal ranges of the Po-p'ing Shan and Tai-yün Shan, together with the rather extensive alluvial plains of the Chiu-lung Chiang, Chin Chiang and Han Chiang around Hsia-men, Ch'üan-chou and Chang-chou. These plains are farmed more intensively than any other part of Fukien, with very complex irrigation and drainage systems, and support a very dense population. The main crops are double-cropped rice, often grown with wheat or peas to produce three crops annually. On dry fields wheat, corn and sweet potatoes are grown. Sugar cane, jute, and peanuts are important economic crops, and sisal, soy beans, ramie, sesame, rape-seed, and tobacco are also grown.

On the hills fruits are very widely cultivated – bananas, oranges, grapefruit, longan, lichee, and pineapples. In the area around An-ch'i there is an important tea district.

Fishing is an important industry all along the coast.

Hsia-men (Amoy) is Fukien's second city. It had 224,000 people in 1953, and is currently estimated to have a population of 350,000. It has a very good port, which supplanted Chang-chou in the 18th and 19th centuries, and handles the trade in local sugar, fruits and tea. Industrially it is less important than Fu-chou, concentrating largely on food processing. Hsia-men has very strong connections with the overseas Chinese.

Chang-chou was formerly a very important seaport, with a flourishing trade with the Philippines and south-east Asia. However, the river silted up, and the port was replaced by Hsia-men. A centre of silk textile and sugar production, it had 80,000 people in 1953.

Ch'üan-chou was China's leading port for trade with south-east Asia and the Near East from the 11th to the 14th centuries. It declined after the 15th century, partly because of the decline of Chinese long range shipping, partly because the port gradually silted up. It is the main commercial centre and market for the Chin Chiang basin, and a port for the coastal trade. It has some sugar-refining, oil-pressing, jute-weaving and fertiliser industry. The population in 1953 was 108,000.

Western Fukien The south-western area is one of complex terrain, extremely hilly, drained by the upper waters of the Han Chiang and the Sha Ch'i. It was relatively inaccessible, until the construction of the Hsia-men railway in 1955–7, and the natural outlet for the southern section was Shan-t'ou (Swatow). It was the last area of Fukien to be settled, and is rather backward. There are few irrigation and drainage schemes, and agriculture is comparatively primitive. Rice, soy beans, corn, tobacco and rape-seed are the main crops.

The area has some small coal mines at Lung-yen and Chang-p'ing, and San-ming, further north has a medium sized fertiliser plant.

Yung-an is the traditional commercial and market centre of the region.

AREA
123,100 square kilometres

POPULATION
16,760,000 (other estimates up to 18,000,000)

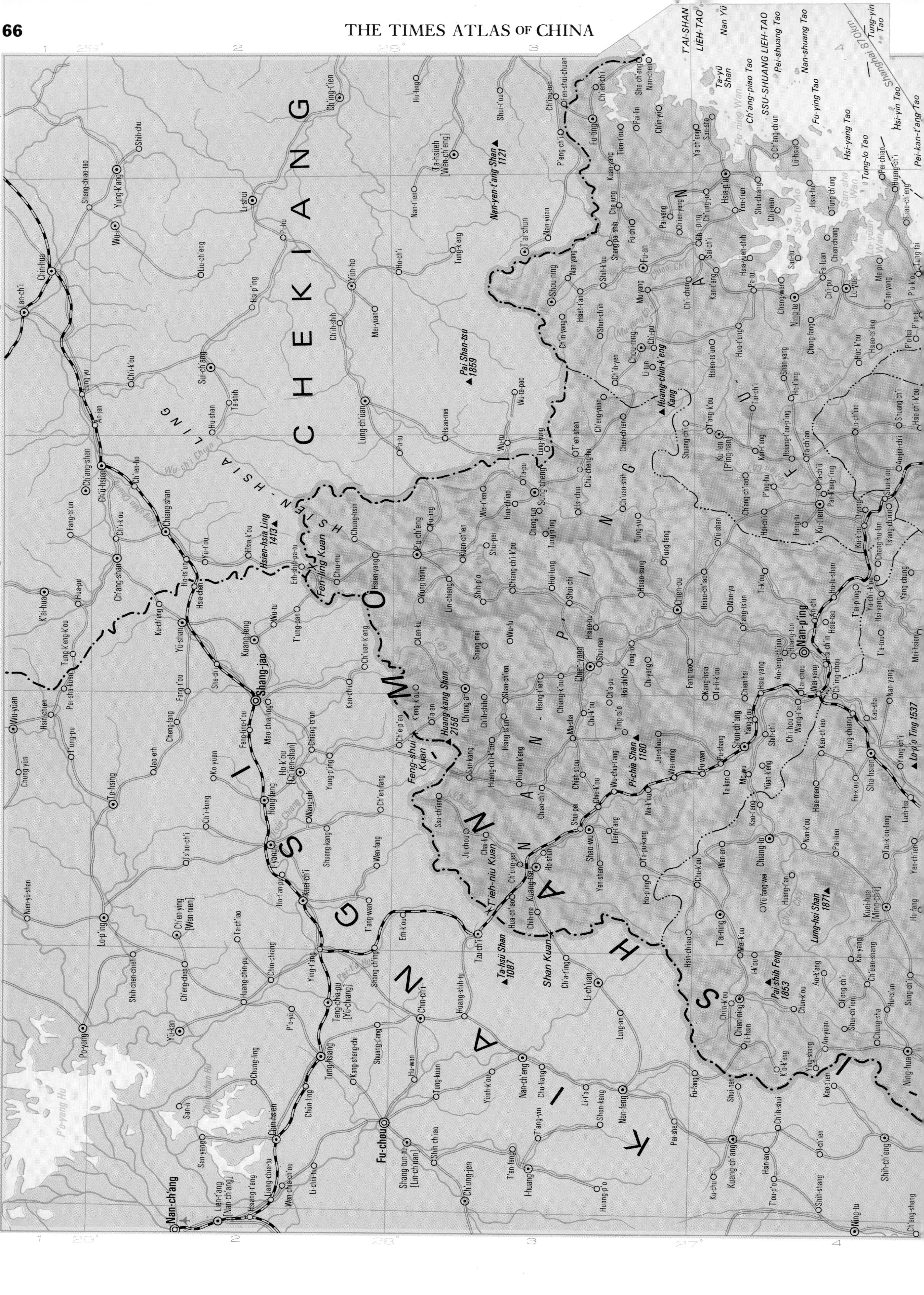

CHEKIANG
KIANGSI
FUKIEN
HSIEN-HSIA LING
WU-I SHAN
NAN-P'ING
Hsien-hsia Ling 1413
Pai Shan-tsu 1859
Nan-yen-t'ang Shan 1121
Huang-kang Shan 2158
Pi-chia Shan 1180
Lung-hsi Shan 1871
Pai-shih Feng 1853
Ta-hsü Shan 1087
Lo-p'o Ting 1537
Fen-ling Kuan
Feng-shui Kuan
T'ieh-niu Kuan
Shan Kuan
Huang-chin-k'eng Kang
Shang-jao
Nan-ch'ang
Fu-chou
Nan-p'ing
Chien-ou
Shao-wu
Chien-yang
Ning-te
Fu-an
Kuan-yang
Chin-hua
Lan-ch'i
Li-shui
P'o-yang Hu
T'AI-SHAN LIEH-TAO
SSU-SHUANG LIEH-TAO
Shanghai 870 km

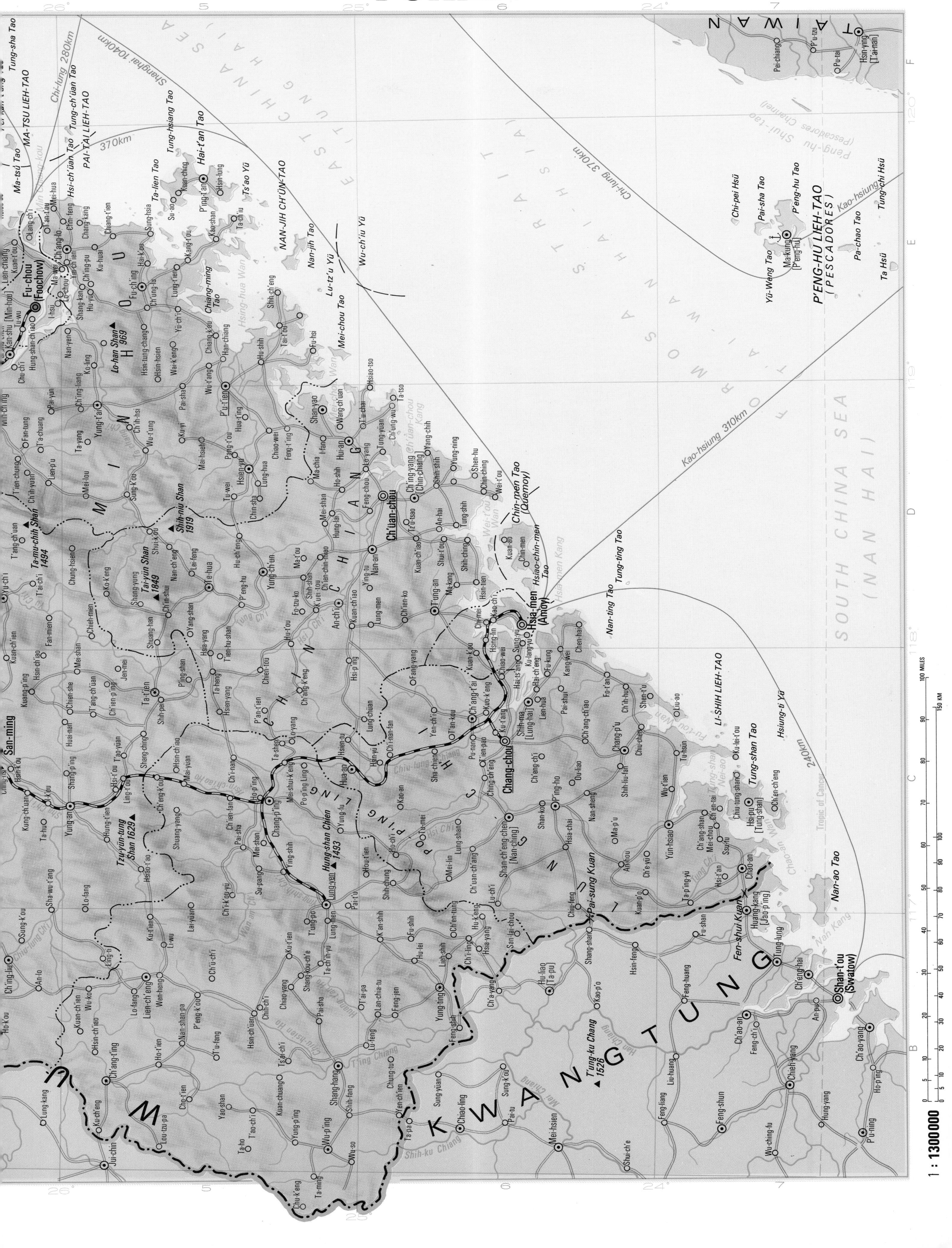

TAIWAN
FORMOSA STRAIT (T'AI-WAN HAI-HSIA)
EAST CHINA SEA (TUNG HAI)
SOUTH CHINA SEA (NAN HAI)
MIN
CHIANG
KWANGTUNG
Fu-chou (Foochow)
Ch'üan-chou
Hsia-men (Amoy)
Chang-chou
Shan-t'ou (Swatow)
San-ming
Lung-yen
P'ENG-HU LIEH-TAO (PESCADORES)
Ma-kung [P'eng-hu]
Chin-men Tao (Quemoy)
MA-TSU LIEH-TAO
PAI-TAI LIEH-TAO
NAN-JIH CH'ÜN-TAO
LI-SHIH LIEH-TAO
Nan-ao Tao
Tung-shan Tao
Hai-t'an Tao
Nan-jih Tao
Mei-chou Tao
P'eng-hu Shui-tao (Pescadores Channel)
Shanghai 1040km
Chi-lung 370km
Kao-hsiung 310km
Tropic of Cancer
Shih-niu Shan 1919
Ta-mu-chin Shan 1494
T'ai-yün Shan 1849
Lo-han Shan 969
Hung-shan Chien 1493
Tzu-yün-tung Shan 1629
T'ung-ku Chang 1526
Pai-sung Kuan
Fen-shui Kuan
Chiu-lung Chiang
Han Chiang
Mei Chiang
T'ing Chiang
1 : 1300000
100 MILES
150 KM

FUKIEN PROVINCE 福建省

FU-CHIEN SHENG

6 shih	*municipalities*
7 ti-ch'ü	*regions*
59 hsien	*counties*

capital **Fu-chou Shih**	E4	福州市
Chang-chou Shih	C6	漳州市
Ch'üan-chou Shih	D6	泉州市
Hsia-men Shih	D6	厦门市
Nan-p'ing Shih	D4	南平市
San-ming Shih	C4	三明市

Chin-chiang Ti-ch'ü		晋江地区
centre: Ch'üan-chou	D6	泉州
An-ch'i Hsien	D5	安溪县
Chin-chiang Hsien		晋江县
centre: Ch'ing-yang	D6	青阳
Hui-an Hsien	D5	惠安县
Nan-an Hsien	D6	南安县
Te-hua Hsien	D5	德化县
T'ung-an Hsien	D6	同安县
Yung-ch'un Hsien	D5	永春县

Fu-an Ti-ch'ü		福安地区
centre: Ning-te	E4	宁德
Chou-ning Hsien	E3	周宁县
Fu-an Hsien	E3	福安县
Fu-ting Hsien	F3	福鼎县
Hsia-p'u Hsien	E4	霞浦县
Ku-t'ien Hsien	D4	古田县
Lien-chiang Hsien	E4	连江县
Lo-yüan Hsien	E4	罗源县
Ning-te Hsien	E4	宁德县
P'ing-nan Hsien		屏南县
centre: Ku-fen	D4	古坋
Shou-ning Hsien	E3	寿宁县

Lung-ch'i Ti-ch'ü		龙溪地区
centre: Chang-chou	C6	漳州
Chang-p'u Hsien	C6	漳浦县
Ch'ang-t'ai Hsien	C6	长泰县
Chao-an Hsien	C7	诏安县
Hua-an Hsien	C5	华安县
Lung-hai Hsien		龙海县
centre: Shih-ma	C6	石码
Nan-ching Hsien		南靖县
centre: Shan-ch'eng-chen	C6	山城镇
P'ing-ho Hsien	C6	平和县
Tung-shan Hsien		东山县
centre: Hsi-pu	C7	西埔
Yün-hsiao Hsien	C7	云霄县

Lung-yen Ti-ch'ü		龙岩地区
Chang-p'ing Hsien	C5	漳平县
Ch'ang-t'ing Hsien	B5	长汀县
Lien-ch'eng Hsien	B5	连城县
Lung-yen Hsien	C5	龙岩县
Shang-hang Hsien	B5	上杭县
Wu-p'ing Hsien	B5	武平县
Yung-ting Hsien	B6	永定县

Min-hou Ti-ch'ü		闽侯地区
centre: P'u-t'ien	D5	莆田
Ch'ang-lo Hsien	E5	长乐县
Fu-ch'ing Hsien	E5	福清县
Hsien-yu Hsien	D5	仙游县
Min-ch'ing Hsien	D4	闽清县
Min-hou Hsien		闽侯县
centre: Kan-shu	E4	甘蔗
P'ing-t'an Hsien	E5	平潭县
P'u-t'ien Hsien	D5	莆田县
Yung-t'ai Hsien	D5	永泰县

Nan-p'ing Ti-ch'ü		南平地区
centre: Chien-yang	D3	建阳
Chien-ou Hsien	D3	建瓯县
Chien-yang Hsien	D3	建阳县
Ch'ung-an Hsien	D3	崇安县
Kuang-tse Hsien	C3	光泽县
P'u-ch'eng Hsien	D3	浦城县
Shao-wu Hsien	C3	邵武县
Shun-ch'ang Hsien	C4	顺昌县
Sung-cheng Hsien	D3	松政县

San-ming Ti-ch'ü		三明地区
Chiang-lo Hsien	C4	将乐县
Chien-ning Hsien	B4	建宁县
Ch'ing-liu Hsien	B4	清流县
Ming-ch'i Hsien		明溪县
centre: Kuei-hua	C4	归化
Ning-hua Hsien	B4	宁化县
Sha Hsien		沙县
centre: Sha-hsien	C4	
T'ai-ning Hsien	C4	泰宁县
Ta-t'ien Hsien	C5	大田县
Yu-ch'i Hsien	D4	尤溪县
Yung-an Hsien	C5	永安县

KIANGSI
PROVINCE

KIANGSI province was first incorporated into the Chinese empire at an early stage but remained sparsely peopled until the 8th century AD. Before this the main expansion of the Chinese settlement south of the Yangtze had been in Hunan, through which ran the main route to Kwangtung. Later the route through Kiangsi became the more important, after the construction of the canal system in the early 7th century diverted traffic to southern China through Yang-chou and the lower Yangtze. The prosperity of Kiangsi developed with the growth of tea planting and silver mining in the province in the late 8th century, when Kiangsi merchants became famous for their wealth. In the late T'ang and Sung (8th to 13th centuries) the area was rapidly settled by Chinese farmers, and became renowned for its academies, and for its scholars and statesmen. In the 19th century Kiangsi's role as a major transport route from Canton to the north was much reduced by the opening of coastal ports to foreign shipping. In the early part of this century Kiangsi first suffered from war-lordism, and later, after 1927, became one of the main bases of the Communist movement. After years of fighting and destruction, the Nationalist government drove the Communists from Kiangsi, on the Long March to the north (1934–5). Almost immediately afterwards came the war with Japan, and Kiangsi was under Japanese occupation from 1938–45.

Kiangsi is more or less co-extensive with the drainage basin of the Kan Chiang, the great tributary of the Yangtze which flows into the Po-yang lake. It is surrounded by mountains, but these have many gaps and easy passes into the neighbouring provinces. Apart from the alluvial plains around the Po-yang lake and the major river in the north, most of the province is hilly country lying between 200 m and 1,000 m.

The climate is sub-tropical, with a growing season lasting about 320 days in the north, and all year round in the far south. The rainfall is abundant – most of the province has more than 1,500 mm per year, apart from the Kan-chou area in the south, which has about 1,250 mm. The north and north-east have considerably more, in some places more than 2,000 mm. There is a marked maximum in the summer months, but even in the winter there is adequate rain. Temperatures average 4° to 5°C (39° to 41°F) in January, slightly lower in the north. The summers are very hot (average 29°C; 84°F) and extremely humid. The province was originally an area of sub-tropical forest. Most of the central areas have long ago been cleared, but the mountainous areas still have very extensive areas of forest.

The central Kiangsi plain The area around the southern side of the Po-yang lake, the lower valleys of the Kan Chiang and Fu Ho rivers, form a broad, low-lying, featureless, alluvial plain with some higher hills to the south and west. The Po-yang lake, which varies greatly in size and shape from season to season, has been surrounded by a complex network of flood-prevention works, and the whole plain has a dense network of waterways, used for drainage, irrigation and local transport. This area is economically the longest settled, most intensively cultivated and most developed part of Kiangsi, forming not only an important route south from the Yangtze, but also a major east-west route from Chekiang and Shanghai to Hunan. Agriculture concentrates mainly on very intensive cultivation of double-cropped rice with winter wheat. Cotton, sesame and soy beans are important crops.

Nan-ch'ang is the traditional provincial capital, the main trade and administrative centre of the province. The city was formerly a very important staging post on the main trunk route from Peking and Nan-ching to Canton, but suffered something of an eclipse after the 1860s. However, it remained the major regional centre for a rich and productive area, and its importance revived with the building of a rail link to the coast in 1936–7. Since 1949 it has been steadily industrialised and has grown considerably. Its industry largely concentrates on agriculture-based industries (food-processing, cotton textiles, oil extraction), on lumbering and paper-making. But there is also an important engineering industry producing tractors, diesel engines, lorries and aircraft. It also makes automobile tyres. It has a large thermal generating plant using coal from the Shang-t'ang coalfield, near Feng-ch'eng to the south-west. This field, developed since 1959, produces some 2,000,000 tons per year.

Fu-chou is the main regional market centre for the south-eastern plain. It has some rice-milling and fertiliser manufacture.

North-east Kiangsi comprises a hilly and mountainous area to the south of the Yangtze. The only extensive flat areas lie along the valley of the Hsin Chiang and on the eastern shores of the Po-yang lake. These lowlands are intensively farmed and densely populated. Rice predominates. Double cropped rice is common, or rice grown together with winter wheat, rape-seed or soy beans. Cotton, jute, and sesame are also grown. In the uplands single-crop rice is grown in the valleys; wheat, soy beans, corn and sesame on dry upland fields. The uplands are one of China's most important tea-planting areas, particularly in the north and east of the region.

Shang-jao is the traditional economic centre for north-eastern Kiangsi, situated on the railway between Nan-ch'ang and Chekiang. It has some minor industry engaged in tea-processing and waxed paper making.

Ying-t'an, the junction between the Nan-ch'ang–Chekiang railway and the newer railway to Hsia-men and Fu-chou in Fukien was a minor market town until the 1950s but has to some extent replaced Shang-jao as an outlet for goods from Fukien.

Ching-te-chen, in the uplands to the north, is the centre of China's largest and most famous ceramic industry. Although the production of porcelain fell off during the early years of this century, the industry has been revived and extensively modernised since 1949, and the population of Ching-te-chen, most of whom are engaged in the industry in some way, has grown from 50,000 in 1949 to 270,000 today.

North-western Kiangsi This, too, is an area of rugged uplands, the only lowlands being the Yangtze valley and the valley of the Hsiu Shui. The Yangtze lowland, an area of dyked reclaimed land, is largely cultivated with cotton, ramie and rape-seed. In the hilly districts, wheat is more important than rice as a grain crop. Cotton is also grown, tea is cultivated, and potatoes and sweet potatoes are common crops.

Chiu-chiang is the main city. Situated near the Po-yang lake where it drains into the Yangtze, it was the natural outlet for Kiangsi's trade, and a major river port. It was opened to foreign trade in 1858 and became the port not only for Kiangsi, but also for eastern Hupeh and Anhwei. It remained very important until the 1930s, when first the civil disturbances in Kiangsi, and then the construction of the railway to Shanghai, giving Nan-ch'ang a direct outlet to the sea, diverted a good deal of its trade. It remains the economic centre for northern Kiangsi, a major market for grain, tea, tobacco and ramie, and has an important cotton textile and food-processing industry.

Western Kiangsi This area comprises the hilly middle basin of the Kan Chiang, rising to the series of ranges which form the border with Hunan. Apart from the narrow river plains, much of this area remains forest covered. It is comparatively sparsely peopled, and agriculture is much less intensive and productive than in the northern plains. Rice, sweet potatoes, soy beans and rape-seed are the main crops. The area around Chi-an produces cotton, jute, sesame and sugar cane.

Chi-an is the main economic centre of the middle Kan Chiang valley. A river port, above which the Kan Chiang flows through a series of rapids, it has some industry, including rice mills and a camphor factory.

P'ing-hsiang in the extreme west, on the railway to Ch'ang-sha, is the centre of the most densely peopled area. It is also important as the centre of a very productive coalfield. This was first extensively developed in the 1890s as a fuel source for the Han-yeh-p'ing iron works at Han-yang (Wu-han). After the iron industry closed down in the late 1920s, coal production fell off drastically. However, since the 1950s it has again been developed, and is now the biggest coalfield in southern China, producing somewhat less than 10,000,000 tons per year, much of which is shipped to the industrial cities of Hunan and to the steel complex at Wu-han. It also has an important ceramic industry.

South-eastern Kiangsi This is a very hilly and mountainous area, above 500 m except a few valleys and basins. It has a very warm, wet climate with a very long growing period. The cultivated valleys produce rice, which is mainly double-cropped, soy beans, rape-seed and sweet potatoes. The uplands produce peanuts. In the valleys, jute and sugar cane are important crops. The mountains still have extensive forests, and lumbering is a major winter occupation. Rafts of pine and cedar are floated down to Kan-chou. The forests also produce pitch, resin and turpentine.

The region has considerable mineral reserves. Tungsten is mined in several districts and tin and copper near Ta-yü.

Kan-chou is the main regional centre, a market for grain, sugar, timber and tungsten ore. It has some miscellaneous manufacturing, producing paper, and farming and mining equipment. Its industry is supplied with power from a hydro-electric scheme at Shang-yu, completed between 1954–7.

AREA
160,000 square kilometres

POPULATION
21,070,000 (other estimates up to 25,000,000)

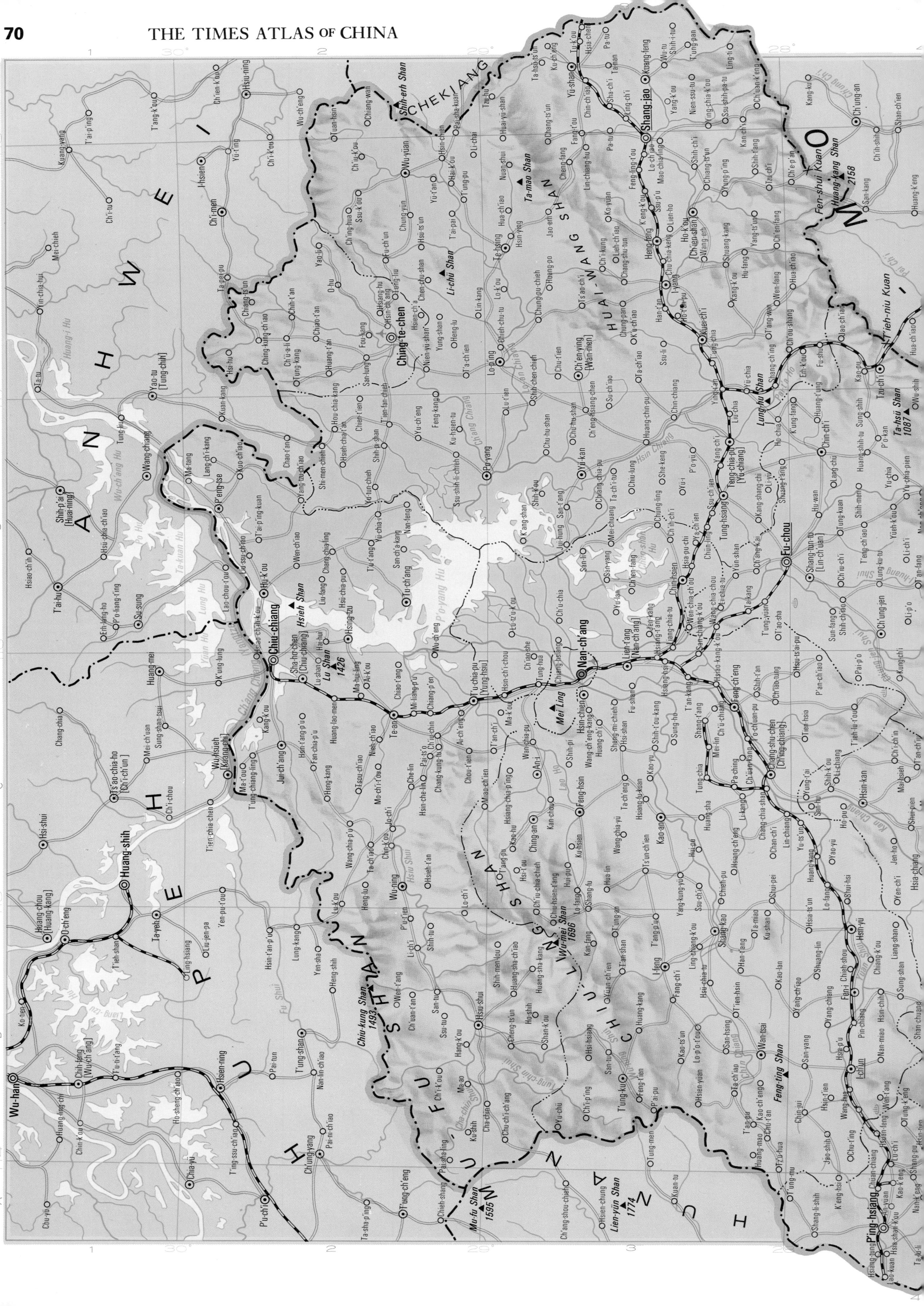
ANHWEI
HUPEH
KIANGSI
CHEKIANG
FUKIEN
HUNAN
HUAI-YÜ SHAN
MU-FU SHAN
CHIU-LING SHAN
Wu-han
Huang-shih
Chiu-chiang
Nan-ch'ang
Ching-te-chen
Shang-jao
Fu-chou
P'o-yang Hu
Lu Shan 1426
Chiu-kung Shan 1493
Mu-fu Shan 1595
Lien-yün Shan 1774
Huang-kang Shan 2158
Ta-hsü Shan 1087
Wu-mei Shan 1696
Ying-t'an
Ping-hsiang
Ch'ung-jen
Kao-an
Nan-ch'ang
Feng-ch'eng
Hsin-yü
I-ch'un
Wu-ning
Hsiu-shui
T'ung-ku
Kuei-ch'i
Te-hsing
Po-yang
Yü-kan
Wu-yüan
Kan Chiang
Hsin Chiang
Fu Shui
Hsiu Shui
Chin Chiang
Yüan Shui

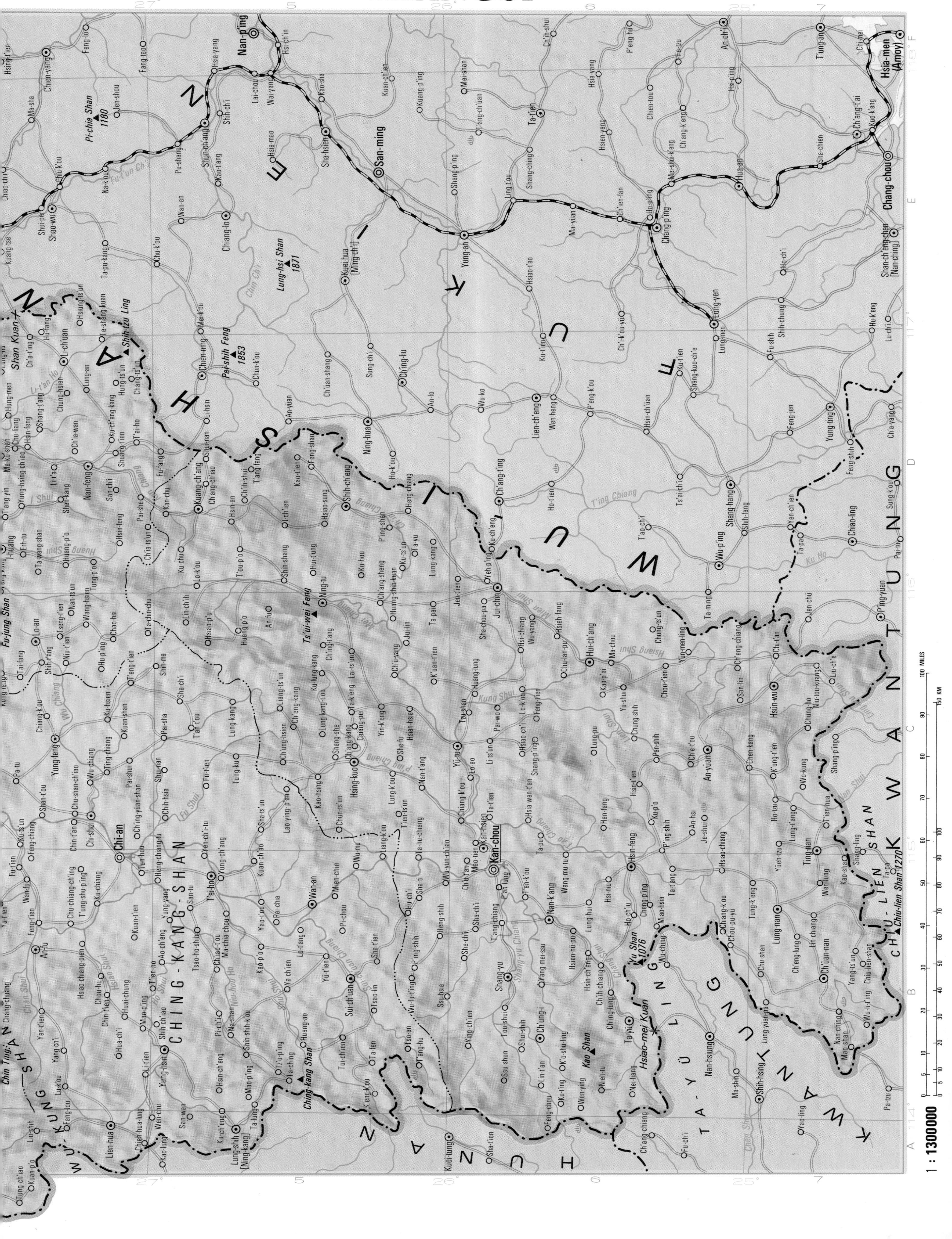

Nan-p'ing
San-ming
Sha-hsien
Yung-an
Chang-p'ing
Lung-yen
Chang-chou
Hsia-men (Amoy)
Shan-ch'eng-chen [Nan-ching]
Hua-an
T'ung-an
An-ch'i
Shao-wu
Shun-ch'ang
Chiang-lo
Pi-chia Shan 1180
Lung-hsi Shan 1871
Pai-shih Feng 1853
Shih-tzu Ling
Shan Kuan
Li-ch'uan
Chien-ning
Ning-hua
Ch'ing-liu
Kuei-hua [Ming-ch'i]
Lien-ch'eng
Ch'ang-t'ing
Shang-hang
Wu-p'ing
Yung-ting
Chiao-ling
Shih-ch'eng
Kuang-ch'ang
Nan-feng
Ning-tu
Ts'ui-wei Feng
Jui-chin
Hui-ch'ang
Hsün-wu
An-yüan
Lung-nan
Ting-nan
Ch'üan-nan
Chiu-lien Shan 1270
Yü-tu
Kan-chou
Hsing-kuo
Wan-an
T'ai-ho
Chi-an
Yung-feng
Chi-shui
An-fu
Lien-hua
Yung-hsin
Ning-kang
Lung-shih
Ching-kang Shan
Sui-ch'uan
Shang-yu
Nan-k'ang
Hsin-feng
Ch'ung-i
Ta-yü
Hsiao-mei Kuan
Yu Shan 1076
Kao Shan
Nan-hsiung
Shih-hsing
Kuei-tung
Fu-jung Shan
Chin Ting
FUKIEN
WU-I SHAN
CHING-KANG-SHAN
KWANGTUNG
CHIU-LIEN SHAN
TA-YÜ LING
HUNAN
WU-KUNG SHAN
1 : 1300000

KIANGSI PROVINCE 江西省

CHIANG-HSI SHENG

8 shih	*municipalities*
6 ti-ch'ü	*regions*
80 hsien	*counties*

capital **Nan-ch'ang Shih**	**C3**	南昌市
Chi-an Shih	**B4**	吉安市
Ching-te-chen Shih	**E2**	景德镇市
Chiu-chiang Shih	**C2**	九江市
Fu-chou Shih	**D3**	抚州市
Kan-chou Shih	**B6**	赣州市
P'ing-hsiang Shih	**A4**	萍乡市
Shang-jao Shih	**E3**	上饶市

Ching-kang-shan Ti-ch'ü		井冈山地区
centre: Chi-an	**B4**	吉安
An-fu Hsien	**B4**	安福县
Chi-an Hsien	**B4**	吉安县
Chi-shui Hsien	**C4**	吉水县
Hsia-chiang Hsien	**C4**	峡江县
Hsin-kan Hsien	**C4**	新干县
Lien-hua	**A4**	莲花县
Ning-kang Hsien		宁冈县
centre: Lung-shih	**A5**	砻市
Sui-ch'uan Hsien	**B5**	遂川县
T'ai-ho Hsien	**B5**	泰和县
Wan-an Hsien	**B5**	万安县
Yung-feng Hsien	**C4**	永丰县
Yung-hsin Hsien	**B5**	永新县

Chiu-chiang Ti-ch'ü		九江地区
Chiu-chiang Hsien		九江县
centre: Sha-ho-chen	**C2**	沙河镇
Hsing-tsu Hsien	**D2**	星子县
Hsiu-shui Hsien	**B2**	修水县
Hu-k'ou Hsien	**D2**	湖口县
Jui-ch'ang Hsien	**C2**	瑞昌县
P'eng-tse Hsien	**D2**	彭泽县
Te-an Hsien	**C2**	德安县
Tu-ch'ang Hsien	**D2**	都昌县
Wu-ning Hsien	**C2**	武宁县
Yung-hsiu Hsien		永修县
centre: T'u-chia-pu	**C2**	涂家埠

Fu-chou Ti-ch'ü		抚州地区
Chin-ch'i Hsien	**D4**	金溪县
Ch'ung-jen Hsien	**D4**	崇仁县
I-huang Hsien	**D4**	宜黄县
Li-ch'uan Hsien	**D4**	黎川县
Lin-ch'uan Hsien		临川县
centre: Shang-tun-tu	**D4**	上顿渡
Lo-an Hsien	**C4**	乐安县
Nan-ch'eng Hsien	**D4**	南城县
Nan-feng Hsien	**D4**	南丰县
Tzu-ch'i Hsien	**E3**	资溪县

I-ch'un Ti-ch'ü		宜春地区
An-i Hsien	**C3**	安义县
Ching-an Hsien	**C3**	靖安县
Ch'ing-chiang Hsien		清江县
centre: Chang-shu-chen	**C3**	樟树镇
Chin Hsien		进县
centre: Chin-hsien	**D3**	
Feng-ch'eng Hsien	**C3**	丰城县
Feng-hsin Hsien	**C3**	奉新县
Fen-i Hsien	**B4**	分宜县
Hsin-chien Hsien	**C3**	新建县
Hsin-yü Hsien	**B4**	新余县
I-ch'un Hsien	**B4**	宜春县
I-feng Hsien	**B3**	宜丰县
Kao-an Hsien	**C3**	高安县
Nan-ch'ang Hsien		南昌县
centre: Lien-t'ang	**C3**	莲塘
Shang-kao Hsien	**B3**	上高县
T'ung-ku Hsien	**B3**	铜鼓县
Wan-tsai Hsien	**B3**	万载县

Kan-chou Ti-ch'ü		赣州地区
An-yüan Hsien	**C6**	安远县
Ch'üan-nan Hsien	**B7**	全南县
Ch'ung-i Hsien	**B6**	崇义县
Hsin-feng Hsien	**B6**	信丰县
Hsing-kuo Hsien	**C5**	兴国县
Hsün-wu Hsien	**C7**	灵乌县
Hui-ch'ang Hsien	**C6**	会昌县
Jui-chin Hsien	**D6**	瑞金县
Kan Hsien		赣县
centre: Kan-hsien	**C6**	
Kuang-ch'ang Hsien	**D5**	广昌县
Lung-nan Hsien	**B7**	龙南县
Nan-k'ang Hsien	**B6**	南康县
Ning-tu Hsien	**C5**	宁都县
Shang-yu Hsien	**B6**	上犹县
Shih-ch'eng Hsien	**D5**	石城县
Ta-yü Hsien	**B6**	大余县
Ting-nan Hsien	**C7**	定南县
Yü-tu Hsien	**C6**	于都县

Shang-jao Ti-ch'ü		上饶地区
Ch'ien-shan Hsien		铅山县
centre: Ho-k'ou	**E3**	河口
Heng-feng Hsien	**E3**	横峰县
I-yang Hsien	**E3**	弋阳县
Kuang-feng Hsien	**F3**	广丰县
Kuei-ch'i Hsien	**E3**	贵溪县
Lo-p'ing Hsien	**E3**	乐平县
Po-yang Hsien	**D2**	波阳县
Shang-jao Hsien	**E3**	上饶县
Te-hsing Hsien	**E3**	德兴县
Tung-hsiang Hsien	**D3**	东乡县
Wan-nien Hsien		万年县
centre: Ch'en-ying	**E3**	陈营
Wu-yüan Hsien	**E2**	婺源县
Yü-chiang Hsien		余江县
centre: Teng-chia-pu	**D3**	邓家埠
Yü-kan Hsien	**D3**	余干县
Yü-shan Hsien	**F3**	玉山县

HUNAN
PROVINCE

HUNAN, particularly the northern area around Ch'ang-sha, was the seat of one of the most important and powerful Chinese states, Ch'u, from the 7th to the 3rd centuries BC. Ch'u was a rich and influential state with an artistic and literary culture very different from that of northern China. Under the Ch'in and Han dynasties (221 BC to AD 220) its former territories became a part of the newly unified Chinese empire, and many settlers from the north occupied the Ch'ang-sha area and the Hsiang Chiang valley, which formed the main route to Canton and the south. The hill areas remained in the hands of various aboriginal peoples. The main period of growth came between the 8th and 11th centuries, when its population increased five-fold. Under the Ming (1368–1644) and Ch'ing (1644–1911) Hunan became a great grain producing area, shipping vast quantities of rice to the cities of the lower Yangtze region. It also developed a strong sense of regional identity. By the 19th century it began to suffer from population pressure, land shortage, and landlordism, and from the mid-19th century there was a great deal of peasant unrest, among both the Chinese farmers and the minority peoples of the border areas. In the 1920s and 1930s the border area with Kiangsi became a principal stronghold of the Chinese Communists, and Mao Tse-tung and many other prominent leaders came from the province.

Hunan comprises the drainage basin of the Tung-ting lake, into which four major tributaries of the Yangtze flow. These are the Hsiang Chiang, the Tzu Shui, the Yüan Chiang and Li Shui. Apart from the northern plain, most of the province is hilly, and large areas are still forest-covered. The climate is wet, with 1,500 mm of rain in the north and east, and 1,200 mm in the west. The mountainous areas have as much as 1,900 mm. Seventy per cent of the rain falls in summer. Winters are short, dry and cold, with January averages of 3°C to 5°C (37°F to 41°F), and occasional waves of severe cold. Summer temperatures average about 28°C (82°F), and 30°C (86°F) and more in the humid low-lying northern plain. The frost-free growing period is about 260 days in the north and 300 days in the south of the province.

The Tung-ting Lake plain The north of the province is occupied with the flat lacustrine basin around the southern shores of the Tung-ting Lake. This lake has been silting up, and its area has been much reduced since the beginning of this century. The shorelands are gradually being reclaimed, and flood control works extended to bring the polders under cultivation. Most of the land in this region is irrigated paddy field, and it has traditionally been a very important rice surplus area. Much of the land is double cropped. The dry, unirrigated fields are largely used for the cultivation of cotton, which is grown in rotation either with wheat or soy beans, or with rape-seed. Ramie is another important fibre crop, grown in the Yüan Chiang valley and around Han-shou. Jute is grown widely on poor, dry fields unsuitable for cotton.

Ch'ang-te is a major port and trans-shipment point not only for agricultural produce of the Tung-ting plain, but also for the upper valley of the Yüan Chiang. It has a large trade in timber and tung oil as well as in rice and cotton.

Yueh-yang is another port and commercial centre at the outlet from the lake into the Yangtze. It too is an important centre of the timber trade, lumber being shipped downstream in rafts to Wu-han, or exported by rail.

The lower Hsiang Chiang basin This area of alluvial plain is surrounded by low, gently rolling hills, rising to the series of south-west to north-east ranges forming the Kiangsi border in the east. It is the oldest, most intensively cultivated, most densely peopled and most highly developed area in the province. As in the northern plain, most of the cultivated area is irrigated paddy field, devoted largely to the production of rice. Multiple cropping has been practised at least since the 18th century. Corn, sweet potatoes, wheat and buckwheat are also grown, but the tendency has been to concentrate more and more on intensive rice culture. Rape-seed, grown for oil, is the only major economic crop. This area, the main industrial district of Hunan, uses power generated in thermal power stations at Ch'ang-sha and Chu-chou, and also hydro-electricity from the Che-ch'i scheme on the Tzu Shui river further west. There are some coal deposits, but coal is brought by rail from the P'ing-hsiang mines in Kiangsi.

Ch'ang-sha is the traditional centre of Hunan, the provincial capital and its main cultural centre. It is a major port, long prosperous as a major rice market, and as a centre of trade in tea, lumber, cotton, ramie and livestock. Since the beginning of the century it has had a diversity of industry, cotton textiles, foodstuffs, rice milling, tea processing, oil extraction, tobacco making. Its growth was accelerated by the extension of a railway from Wu-han in 1918. More recently it has become a centre of precision engineering and machine tool manufacture, agricultural equipment and agricultural chemicals. In the early 1970s an aluminium industry was developed. The population of Ch'ang-sha was 703,000 in 1957.

Chu-chou, unlike Ch'ang-sha, is an entirely modern town. Formerly a small market town, it became the river port for the P'ing-hsiang coal mines at the beginning of the century, when it was connected with P'ing-hsiang by rail. It later became a very important railway junction with the Canton–Wu-han line, and grew into a centre for the manufacture of railway equipment, locomotives and rolling stock. It has also become an important centre of the copper and lead and zinc industries, processing ore from Shui-k'ou-shan, and has established a major chemical fertiliser industry. Its population is estimated at 500,000.

Hsiang-tan was a river port and market centre, which stagnated early in this century when the railway took away much of its trade. Its industrial growth began in 1937. In 1947 its major modern industry, the production of electrical equipment, electric cables and wire was founded. A steel industry was founded in 1959–60 and expanded in the late 1960s. Hsiang-tan also has a large cement works, and cotton textile mills. A recent development has been aluminium smelting. Its population is estimated at about 400,000.

The central Hunan hills This region comprises the middle and upper valleys of the Tzu Shui, Lien Shui and Wu Shui rivers. To the west of the Tzu Shui are quite rugged hills, 500 m and more high. The western part of the region has lower hills, and a larger proportion of the land under cultivation.

The valleys of this area are intensively farmed, but there is a much higher proportion of dry farming than in the north, and there is little grain surplus. Rice is important, but wheat, corn and sweet potatoes are also staples. Rape-seed, peanuts and tobacco are grown as cash crops. This area is the main tea-producing district of Hunan. Tea production began here in the 10th century, and reached a peak in the 19th century. By 1949 the industry had fallen into a decline, but it has since been revived. Timber is also a very important resource of the area, and there is considerable mineral wealth as Hsi-k'uang-shan, near Hsin-hua, is a very important source of antimony. There are considerable coal and iron reserves, and tungsten is also mined.

Shao-yang is the chief communication and market centre of the area, joined by rail to Ch'ang-sha in 1960. It is an important centre of handicrafts, especially wood and bamboo working, and has a large paper industry. Its population had risen to 118,000 in 1953.

Southern Hunan The south of the province is an area of hills rising to the complex ranges of the Nan-ling, which reach 500–1,000 m. Much of the area is still thickly forested. The main settlements are in the broad upper valleys of the Hsiang Chiang and its tributaries. These valleys are intensively farmed and well irrigated. Paddy rice is the major crop, but double cropping is rare. Dry fields are cultivated with sweet potatoes and wheat. Some peanuts and rape-seed are grown. Timber and forest products, particularly tea-oil are very important. Leng-shui-t'an is the major centre of the lumber industry. The area also has great mineral wealth. There are major lead and zinc mines at Shui-k'ou-shan, south of Heng-yang, and at Ch'en-hsien; reserves of tungsten at I-chang, Ju-ch'eng and elsewhere; tin mines, sulphur, and copper deposits near Ch'en-hsien.

Heng-yang is the major city of southern Hunan, with a population estimated at 300,000. An old-fashioned strategic and route centre, it grew rapidly after the construction of the Canton-Wu-han railway in 1937, and became an important Nationalist base until 1944, when there was considerable industrial growth. Badly damaged in the latter stages of the Second World War, its industry was restored after 1949, but has been overshadowed by the growth of Chu-chou and Ch'ang-sha. It manufactures mining equipment and machinery, diesel and electric motors, tractors, agricultural chemicals and agricultural implements. It has a large thermal generating station. Heng-yang remains a very important rail junction and regional transportation and market centre for the area.

Western Hunan Uplands In the upper valleys of the Yüan Chiang and Li Shui, the country is rugged highlands rising to the Kweichow plateau. The mountains rise to 500–1,000 m and have steep slopes and narrow valleys, with little land suitable for cultivation. The rivers are of little use for navigation and transport is difficult. Much of the area is still settled by minority peoples who cultivate scattered areas in the hills. The uplands produce corn, sweet potatoes and wheat. The valleys are cultivated with rice, wheat and corn, and some cotton, ramie and rape-seed are grown. Timber, tea-oil, tung-oil and tea are important products. But communications are poor, the population sparse, and towns few and small.

Minority Peoples About 97 per cent of Hunan's population are Han Chinese. There are four important minorities. In the western uplands live the Miao (370,000) and T'u-chia (390,000). They have their own autonomous districts. In the extreme south-west are some 125,000 T'ung, a Tai people who have assimilated Chinese culture. They too have their own autonomous *hsien*. Lastly, along the southern border of the province are numerous scattered communities of Yao peoples (70,000) engaged in hill farming and forestry.

AREA
210,500 square kilometres

POPULATION
41,000,000

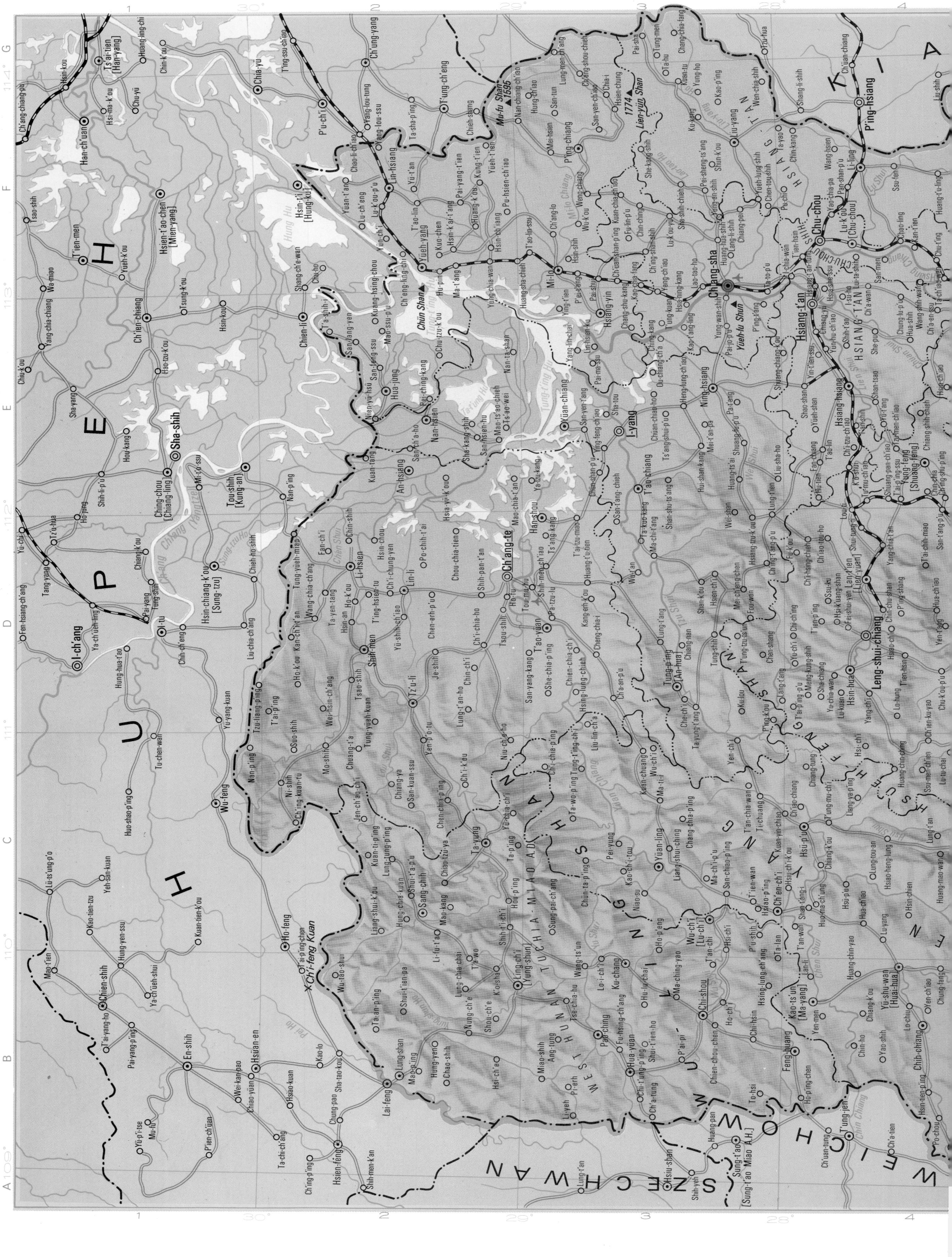
Ch'ang-sha
Hsiang-t'an
Chu-chou
Ch'ang-te
Sha-shih
I-ch'ang
Yüeh-yang
Shih-men
Hsin-hua
Leng-shui-chiang
P'ing-hsiang
En-shih
Chi-shou
Lai-feng
Wu-feng
Ning-hsiang
I-yang
Yüan-ling
Ta-yung
Han-shou
Chien-li
Chien-shih
Hsüan-en
Hsien-feng
Tung-jen

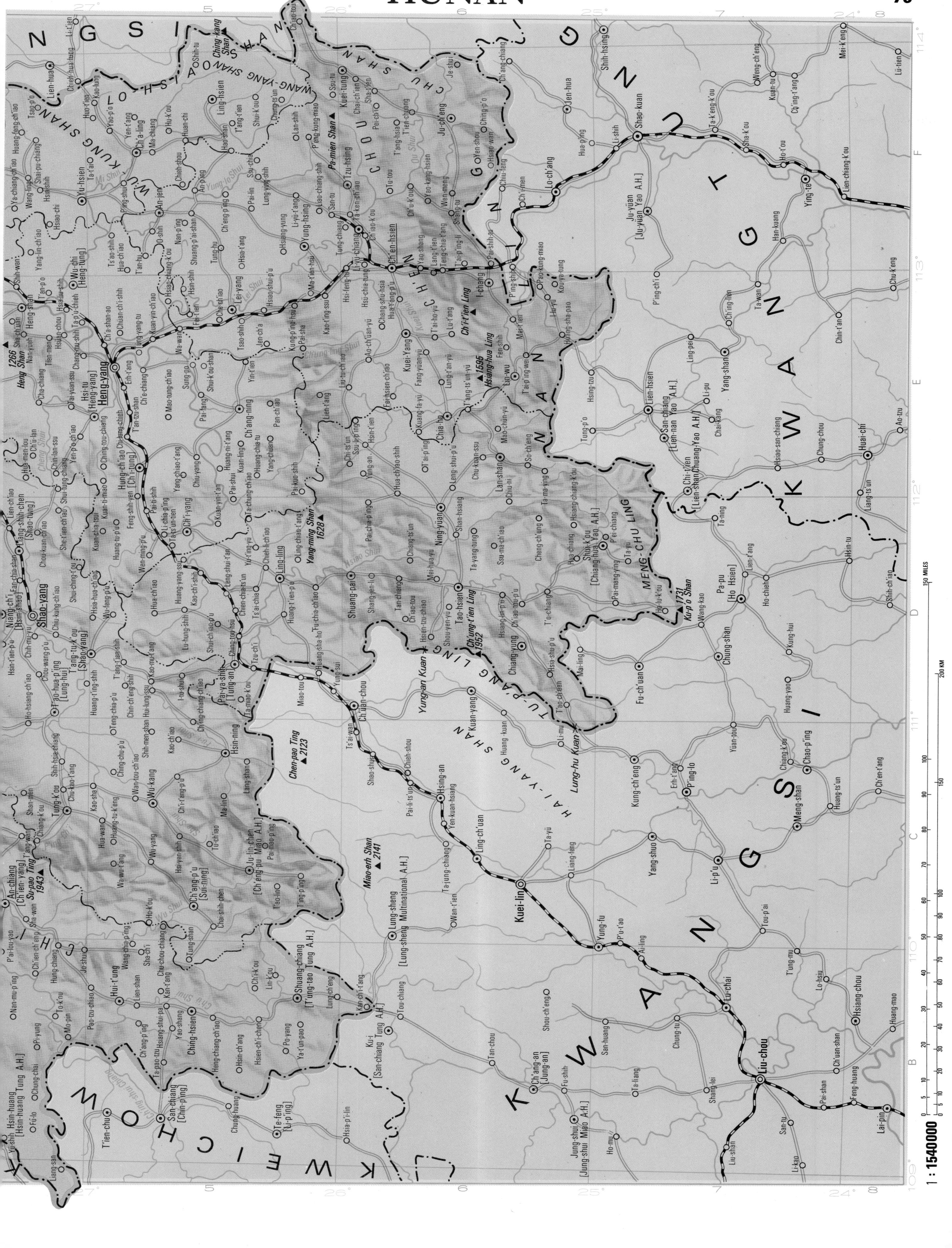

KWANGSI
KWANGTUNG
KWEICHOW
WU-KUNG SHAN
LO-HSIAO SHAN
WANG-YANG SHAN
CHU SHAN
CHOU
NAN LING
MENG-CHU LING
TU-P'ANG LING
HAI-YANG SHAN
Ching-kang Shan
Pa-mien Shan
Ch'i-t'ien Ling
1595 Hsiang-hua Ling
Yang-ming Shan 1628
Ch'ung-t'ien Ling 1952
1731 Ku-p'o Shan
Chen-pao Ting 2123
Miao-erh Shan 2141
Su-pao Ting 1943
1266 Heng Shan
Yung-an Kuan
Lung-hu Kuan
Lien-hua
Ling-hsien
Ch'a-ling
Yu-hsien
An-jen
Kuei-tung
Tzu-hsing
Ju-ch'eng
Yung-hsing
Ch'en-hsien
I-chang
Lei-yang
Shao-kuan
Lo-ch'ang
Ju-yüan [Ju-yüan Yao A.H.]
Ying-te
Wu-chi [Heng-tung]
Heng-shan
Heng-yang
Hsi-tu [Heng-yang]
Ch'ang-ning
Kuei-yang
Lin-wu
Chia-ho
Lan-shan
Ning-yüan
Tao-hsien
Chiang-yung
Shuang-p'ai
Ling-ling
Ch'i-yang
Hung-ch'iao [Ch'i-tung]
Shao-yang
T'ang-tu-k'ou [Shao-yang]
Tung-an
Hsin-ning
Ch'üan-chou
Hsing-an
Ling-ch'uan
Kuei-lin
Yang-shuo
Li-p'u
P'ing-lo
Chao-p'ing
Meng-shan
Fu-ch'uan
Chung-shan
Pa-pu [Ho Hsien]
Huai-chi
Lien-hsien
Yang-shan
Wu-kang
Tung-k'ou
Ch'eng-pu [Ch'eng-pu Miao A.H.]
Sui-ning
Ching-hsien
Shuang-chiang [T'ung-tao Tung A.H.]
Hui-t'ung
Lung-sheng [Lung-sheng Multinational A.H.]
San-chiang [Chin-p'ing]
Yung-fu
Liu-chai
Liu-chou
Hsiang-chou
Lai-pin
Ch'ang-an [Jung-an]
Jung-shui [Jung-shui Miao A.H.]
Te-feng [Li-p'ing]
An-chiang [Ch'ien-yang]
Hsin-huang [Hsin-huang Tung A.H.]
Chih-chiang
1 : 1540000

HUNAN PROVINCE 湖南省
HU-NAN SHENG

8 shih	*municipalities*
1 tzu-chih-chou	*autonomous district*
9 ti-ch'ü	*regions*
85 hsien	*counties*
4 tzu-chih-hsien	*autonomous counties*

capital **Ch'ang-sha Shih**	E3	长沙市
Ch'ang-sha Hsien	E3	长沙县
Ch'ang-te Shih	D2	常德市

Chu-chou Shih	F4	株州市
Chu-chou Hsien		株州县
centre: Lu-k'ou	F4,	渌口
Heng-yang Shih	E5	衡阳市
Hsiang-t'an Shih	E4	湘潭市
I-yang Shih	E3	益阳市
Leng-shui-chiang Shih	D4	冷水江市
Shao-yang Shih	D4	邵阳市

Ch'ang-te Ti-ch'ü		常德地区
An-hsiang Hsien	E2	安乡县
Ch'ang-te Hsien	D2	常德县
Han-shou Hsien	D3	汉寿县
Li Hsien		沣县
centre: Li-hsien	D2	
Lin-li Hsien	D2	临澧县
Shih-men Hsien	D2	石门县
T'ao-yüan Hsien	D3	桃源县
Tz'u-li Hsien	D2	慈利县

Ch'en-chou Ti-ch'ü		郴州地区
centre: Ch'en-hsien	F6	郴县
An-jen Hsien	F5	安仁县
Ch'en Hsien		郴县
centre: Ch'en-hsien	F6	
Chia-ho Hsien	E6	嘉禾县
I-chang Hsien	E6	宜章县
Ju-ch'eng Hsien	F6	汝城县
Kuei-tung Hsien	F6	桂东县
Kuei-yang Hsien	E6	桂阳县
Lei-yang Hsien	E5	耒阳县
Lin-wu Hsien	E6	临武县
Tzu-hsing Hsien	F6	资兴县
Yung-hsing Hsien	F5	永兴县

Ch'ien-yang Ti-ch'ü		黔阳地区
Ch'en-ch'i Hsien	C3	辰溪县
Ch'ien-yang Hsien		黔阳县
centre: An-chiang	C4	安江
Chih-chiang Hsien	B4	芷江县
Ching Hsien		靖县
centre: Ching-hsien	B5	
Hsin-huang T'ung-tsu Tzu-chih-hsien Hsin-huang Tung Autonomous Hsien		新晃侗族自治县
centre: Hsin-huang	B4	
Hsü-p'u Hsien	C4	溆浦县
Huai-hua Hsien		怀化县
centre: Yü-shu-wan	B4	榆树湾
Hui-t'ung Hsien	B5	会同县
Ma-yang Hsien		麻阳县
centre: Kao-ts'un	B4	高村
T'ung-tao T'ung-tsu Tzu-chih-hsien T'ung-tao Tung Autonomous Hsien		通道侗族自治县
centre: Shuang-chiang	B5	双江
Yüan-ling Hsien	C3	沅陵县

Heng-yang Ti-ch'ü		衡阳地区
Ch'ang-ning Hsien	E5	常宁县
Ch'i-tung Hsien		祁东县
centre: Hung-ch'iao	E5	洪桥
Ch'i-yang Hsien	D5	祁阳县
Heng-nan Hsien		衡南县
centre: Heng-yang	E5	衡阳
Heng-shan Hsien	E4	衡山县
Heng-tung Hsien		衡东县
centre: Wu-chi	E4	吴集
Heng-yang Hsien		衡阳县
centre: Hsi-tu	E5	西渡

Hsiang-hsi T'u-chia-tsu Miao-tsu Tzu-chih-chou West Hunan Tuchia-Miao Autonomous District		湘西土家族苗族自治州
centre: Chi-shou	B3	吉首
Chi-shou Hsien	B3	吉首县
Feng-huang Hsien	B4	凤凰县
Hua-yüan Hsien	B3	花垣县
Ku-chang Hsien	B3	古丈县
Lu-ch'i Hsien		泸溪县
centre: Wu-ch'i	C3	武溪
Lung-shan Hsien	B2	龙山县
Pao-ching Hsien	B3	保靖县
Sang-chih Hsien	C2	桑植县
Ta-yung Hsien	C2	大庸县
Yung-shun Hsien		永顺县
centre: Ling-ch'i	B2	灵溪

Hsiang-t'an Ti-ch'ü		湘潭地区
Ch'a-ling Hsien	F5	茶陵县
Hsiang-hsiang Hsien	E4	湘乡县
Hsiang-t'an Hsien	E4	湘潭县
Li-ling Hsien	F4	醴陵县
Ling Hsien		酃县
centre: Ling-hsien	F5	
Liu-yang Hsien	F3	浏阳县
Yu Hsien		攸县
centre: Yu-hsien	F4	

I-yang Ti-ch'ü		益阳地区
An-hua Hsien		安化县
centre: Tung-p'ing	D3	东坪
I-yang Hsien	E3	益阳县
Nan-Hsien		南县
centre: Nan-hsien	E2	
Ning-hsiang Hsien	E3	宁乡县
T'ao-chiang Hsien	E3	桃江县
Yüan-chiang Hsien	E3	沅江县

Ling-ling Ti-ch'ü		零陵地区
Chiang-hua Yao-tsu Tzu-chih-hsien Chiang-hua Yao Autonomous Hsien		江华瑶族自治县
centre: Shui-k'ou	D7	水口
Chiang-yung Hsien	D6	江永县
Hsin-t'ien Hsien	E6	新田县
Lan-shan Hsien	E6	蓝山县
Ling-ling Hsien	D5	零陵县
Ning-yüan Hsien	D6	宁远县
Shuang-pai Hsien	D6	双牌县
Tao Hsien		道县
centre: Tao-hsien	D6	
Tung-an Hsien		东安县
centre: Pai-ya-shih	D5	白牙市

Shao-yang Ti-ch'ü		邵阳地区
Ch'eng-pu Miao-tsu Tzu-chih-hsien Ch'eng-pu Miao Autonomous Hsien		城步苗族自治县
centre: Ju-lin-chen	C5	儒林镇
Hsin-hua Hsien	D4	新化县
Hsin-ning Hsien	C5	新宁县
Hsin-shao Hsien		新邵县
centre: Niang-ch'i	D4	酿溪
Lien-yüan Hsien		涟源县
centre: Lan-t'ien	D4	蓝田
Lung-hui Hsien		隆回县
centre: T'ao-hua-p'ing	D4	桃花坪
Shao-tung Hsien		邵东县
centre: Liang-shih-chen	D4	两市镇
Shao-yang Hsien		邵阳县
centre: T'ang-tu-k'ou	D5	塘渡口
Shuang-feng Hsien		双峰县
centre: Yung-feng	E4	永丰
Sui-ning Hsien		绥宁县
centre: Ch'ang-p'u	C5	长铺
Tung-k'ou Hsien	C4	洞口县
Wu-kang Hsien	C5	武冈县

Yüeh-yang Ti-ch'ü		岳阳地区
Hsiang-yin Hsien	E3	湘阴县
Hua-jung Hsien	E2	华容县
Lin-hsiang Hsien	F2	临湘县
Mi-lo Hsien	F3	汨罗县
P'ing-chiang Hsien	F3	平江县
Yüeh-yang Hsien	F2	岳阳县

KWANGTUNG
PROVINCE

THE Kwangtung area was first included in China by the Ch'in in 214 BC, when the Chinese general, Chao T'o, subdued the area. After the fall of Ch'in he set up an independent state, which resisted the Chinese until the end of the 2nd century BC, when the Chinese finally conquered all Kwangtung, and incorporated it into the empire. Thereafter the Chinese maintained a strong control over Canton and the surrounding delta area, and a general control over other parts of the province. It was, however, many centuries before the province was settled by Chinese. As late as the T'ang period (AD 618–907), although Canton was a major seaport for trade with South-east Asia, India and the Persian Gulf, with a large foreign trading community the rest of the province had only small, scattered Chinese settlements among a predominantly aboriginal population. The region was considered a place of banishment. At the fall of the T'ang, Kwangtung was for a while an independent kingdom, Nan-Han, but after re-unification with the empire under the Sung, Chinese settlement began again in earnest, accelerating after the 12th century. Chinese settlers continued to pour into the region, some of whom formed the distinct K'o-chia (Hakka) group, who, as late-comers, were largely forced to occupy the less fertile and productive lands.

The growth of Kwangtung was particularly rapid under the Ming (1368–1644) and by the 17th century the pressure of population led to extensive emigration. Cantonese moved into the adjoining province of Kwangsi, into the ravaged and depopulated areas of Szechwan after the mid-17th century rebellions there, and into Taiwan and south-east Asia. In the mid-19th century emigration spread to America and even to South Africa.

From the 17th century onwards the area around Canton was a focus for foreign influence: Canton increasingly became China's major port for foreign trade, which was channelled through its immensely rich, licensed merchants (*cohong*); Macau had been a Portuguese enclave since the 16th century; Hong Kong became a British colony in 1842, following the Opium War. As a result, when relations between China and the western powers became strained, the tension was concentrated in the Canton area.

The entire province has a wet, tropical or sub-tropical climate. The average temperatures in January range from 13°C to 16°C (55°F to 61°F), and those in July from 28°C to 30°C (82°F to 86°F). There is virtually no winter and frost is extremely rare except on high land in the north. Rainfall is heavy – over 2,000 mm along the coast, but gradually decreasing towards the north-west. Only western Hainan, the Lei-chou peninsula and the Mei-hsien area in the north-east have less than 1,500 mm. The rainfall comes very largely in summer, from mid-April until October. The growing season lasts throughout the year.

The Pearl River Delta The centre of the province is the alluvial delta plain of the Chu Chiang (Pearl River), into which flow the Hsi Chiang from Kwangsi, the Pei Chiang from the northern mountains of the Nan-ling, and the Tung Chiang draining north-eastern Kwangtung. The plain, some 11,000 square kilometres in extent, is crossed by a dense network of distributary streams and canalised rivers, broken by some outlying hills. Much of the land is reclaimed, and reclamation continues. The area supports an extraordinary density of population. The main crop is rice, which produces two crops a year, but sweet potatoes, wheat and rape-seed are also important. The area is a major producer of silk, and there are a large number of other subsidiary crops – tobacco in the western delta, jute in the east, tropical fruits of many types, sugar cane. The area also produces large quantities of livestock, particularly hogs for the urban markets of Canton and Hong Kong. Fish rearing, in ponds, is also a very important local industry.

To the west, in the valley of the Hsi Chiang, the plain merges into an area of hills with some remnants of forest cover. On these uplands the main crops are wheat, sweet potatoes, taro, kaoliang, rape-seed and peanuts.

Canton (Kuang-chou) is the largest city in Kwangtung. The provincial capital since Han times, Canton has always been a port and a centre of foreign trade, although it can only take ships of medium tonnage. It has become a major industrial city in recent times and a very important centre of sugar refining, the waste from which is used in a large newsprint mill, one of the largest in China. There is a large cement industry, and chemical and fertiliser plants. There is a small iron and steel works and a varied engineering industry, producing machine tools, trucks, and small ships. Other plants produce aluminium and automobile tyres. There is also much light industry, food-processing and textile manufacture. Canton is also a very important cultural and educational centre. Its population was 1,800,000 in 1957, and is currently estimated at about 3,000,000, including the suburbs within its municipal area.

Fo-shan (Fatshan, Namhoi) lies south-west of Canton. It is the centre of the silk industry of the delta, it produces ceramics, and has recently acquired a large chemical plant.

Chiang-men (Kongmoon), with 85,000 people in 1953, is the major centre of the western delta. Primarily a major trading and market centre it has a copper industry, and is a producer of paper and board.

Eastern Kwangtung This area, forming the drainage basins of the Tung Chiang and the Han Chiang is a region of low hills, long ago denuded of natural cover, which have suffered seriously from erosion. The northern part of the region rises to the high watershed of the Nan-ling ranges, which still have more extensive areas of forest cover. In general the north-eastern area around Mei-hsien is comparatively unproductive. The chief areas of intensive agriculture are in the lower valley of the Tung Chiang, where rice and sugar cane are important crops, and above all the alluvial plain around Shan-t'ou, the delta of the Han Chiang. This area is intensively farmed for rice, sugar and sweet potatoes, with some jute production. It is a very important producer of citrus fruits.

Shan-t'ou (Swatow) is the major city of this area. An old-established port, with 280,000 people in 1953, Shan-t'ou is the natural outlet and market centre not only for the surrounding plain, but also for the Han Chiang valley and the Mei-hsien region. It has little industry.

Northern Kwangtung This area is largely the drainage basin of the Pei Chiang, to the north of the Canton delta. Rising to the Nan-ling ranges of the Hunan–Kiangsi borders, the northern areas still have rich forest reserves, and important mineral resources, especially tungsten, antimony and iron. Agriculture in the area is mainly confined to the valleys. Rice is the main crop, double-cropped in the southern districts. Tobacco, sugar cane and ramie are grown extensively, and the area is an important tea producing centre.

Shao-kuan is the focus of this region, historically important as a route centre controlling the access to Kwangtung from both Hunan and Kiangsi. There is a small coalfield nearby (the only major source of coal in Kwangtung), which provides fuel for a thermal generating plant and a small iron and steel works. There are important smelters for non-ferrous metals produced in the area, and some machine building.

South-western Kwangtung This is an area of low hills, with few rivers and much poor barren land. It has a very hot tropical climate, with more than 1,500 mm of rain, mostly falling in summer. The only comparatively dry area is the Lei-chou peninsula. It is an area where three crops per year are possible. Paddy rice is the main crop, where conditions are suitable, but tubers – sweet potato, cassava, taro – are important. It is an area which produces various tropical crops – jute, sisal, sea island cotton, sugar cane. Tropical fruits (bananas, pineapples, mangoes) are widely grown. Rubber has also been extensively planted in the north and south of the Lei-chou peninsula since the 1950s.

Chan-chiang (Tsamkong) on the eastern side of the Lei-chou peninsula, is the area's most important city. Formerly the centre of the French leased territory of Kwangchowwan, it was returned to China in 1945. In 1955 it was linked by rail to Kwangsi, since when it has grown into a major port. It has two large fertiliser plants, and an important coastal salt industry.

Mao-ming, which is linked to Chan-chiang by rail, is important as a producer of oil from oil-shale. This industry has been developed since 1958, and the town has its own refineries producing a variety of fuel oils and gasoline.

Hainan Island Hainan has a tropical climate with an annual average temperature of 25°C (77°F), with a year-round growing season. The mountainous centre of the island is still densely forested, and the south still has a large non-Chinese minority of Li peoples (360,000 in all). The coastal areas produce rice (three crops a year in some places), and large quantities of sugar cane. There have been attempts to plant rubber, coconuts, coffee, sisal and other tropical crops.

Iron ore of very high quality is produced in the west near Ch'ang-chiang, which is linked by rail to the port of Tung-fang, from where it is exported to Chan-chiang on the mainland. There is a small local iron smelting industry.

Hai-k'ou on the north coast is the chief city of Hainan, and the port for the fertile agricultural plain of the north of the island. It has some minor food processing industry.

Kwangtung province also administers the various islands in the South China Sea, belonging to China.

Minority Peoples The vast majority of the population of mainland Kwangtung are Han Chinese, speaking the Cantonese dialects. Among these live the Hakka, speaking a different language, with different customs. They immigrated into Kwangtung some time after the Cantonese population, perhaps from Sung times onwards, from northern and central China, by way of Fukien and Kiangsi. There was much friction between these two groups, which lead to extensive warfare in the mid-19th century. The only minority people on the mainland are the small settlements of Yao living along the Hunan border, in the far north. The Chinese population of Hainan is largely composed of speakers of Min (i.e. Fukien) dialects. The Li peoples, who inhabit the mountains and most of southern Hainan, are of Thai race. There are also a small number of Miao people in Hainan.

AREA
220,000 square kilometres

POPULATION
42,800,000 (other estimates up to 48,000,000)

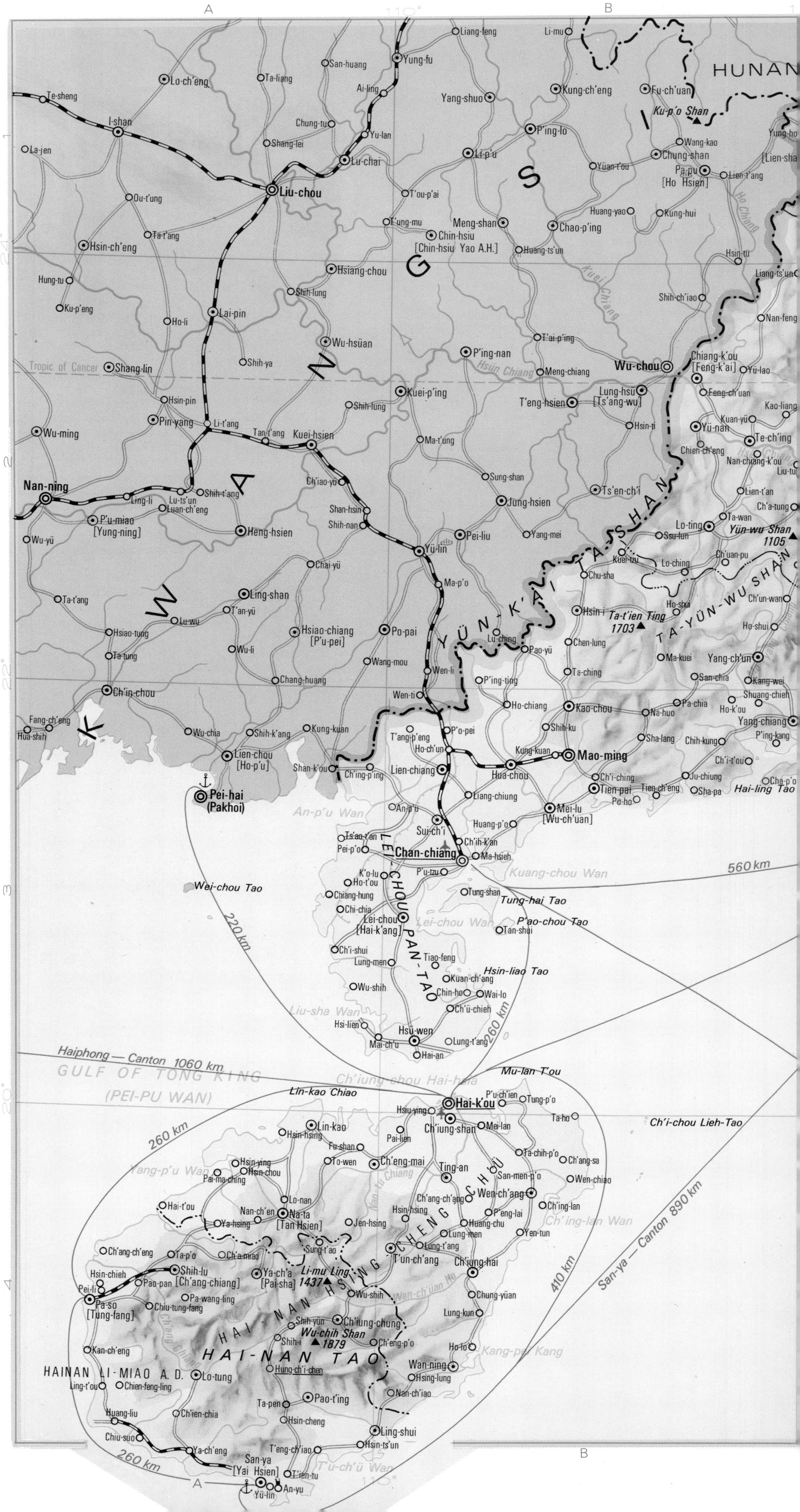
HUNAN
KWANGSI
Ku-p'o Shan
Liang-feng
Li-mu
Yung-fu
San-huang
Lo-ch'eng
Ta-liang
Ai-ling
Yang-shuo
Kung-ch'eng
Fu-ch'uan
Te-sheng
I-shan
Chung-tu
Yu-lan
P'ing-lo
Wang-kao
Chung-shan
La-jen
Shang-lei
Lu-chai
Li-p'u
Yüan-t'ou
Pa-pu [Ho Hsien]
Lien-t'ang
Liu-chou
T'ou-p'ai
Ou-t'ung
Huang-yao
Kung-hui
T'ung-mu
Meng-shan
Chao-p'ing
Ta-t'ang
Chin-hsiu [Chin-hsiu Yao A.H.]
Huang-ts'un
Hsin-ch'eng
Hsiang-chou
Kuei Chiang
Hung-tu
Shih-lung
Shih-ch'iao
Ku-p'eng
Lai-pin
Ho-li
Nan-feng
Wu-hsüan
T'ai-p'ing
P'ing-nan
Tropic of Cancer
Shang-lin
Shih-ya
Hsün Chiang
Meng-chiang
Wu-chou
Chiang-k'ou [Feng-k'ai]
Yü-lao
Kuei-p'ing
Lung-hsü [Ts'ang-wu]
Feng-ch'uan
Hsin-pin
Shih-lung
T'eng-hsien
Pin-yang
Li-t'ang
Kuan-yü
Kao-liang
Hsin-ti
Yü-nan
Te-ch'ing
Wu-ming
Tan-t'ang
Kuei-hsien
Ma-t'ung
Chien-ch'eng
Nan-chiang-k'ou
Nan-ning
Shih-t'ang
Ch'iao-yü
Sung-shan
Ts'en-ch'i
Lien-t'an
Ling-li
Lu-ts'un
Jung-hsien
Ch'a-tung
P'u-miao [Yung-ning]
Luan-ch'eng
Shan-hsin
Shih-nan
Ta-wan
Lo-ting
Yün-wu Shan 1105
Wu-yü
Heng-hsien
Pei-liu
Yang-mei
Ssu-lun
Yü-lin
Ch'uan-pu
Kuei-tzu
Lo-ching
Chai-yü
Chu-sha
Ma-p'o
YÜN-K'AI TA-SHAN
TA-YÜN-WUSHAN
Ling-shan
Ch'un-wan
Ta-t'ang
T'an-yü
Hsin-i
Ta-t'ien Ting 1703
Lu-wu
Ho-shui
Hsiao-tung
Hsiao-chiang [P'u-pei]
Po-pai
Lu-ching
Pao-yü
Chen-lung
Wu-li
Ma-kuei
Yang-ch'un
Ta-tung
Wang-mou
Wen-li
Te-ching
San-chia
Kang-wei
Chang-huang
P'ing-ting
Shuang-chieh
Ch'in-chou
Wen-ti
Ho-chiang
Kao-chou
Na-huo
Pa-chia
Ho-k'ou
Fang-ch'eng
Hua-shih
Shih-ku
Yang-chiang
Wu-chia
Shih-k'ang
Kung-kuan
T'ang-p'eng
P'o-pei
Sha-lang
Chih-kung
P'ing-kang
Lien-chou [Ho-p'u]
Ho-ch'un
Kung-kuan
Mao-ming
Ch'i-t'ou
Shan-k'ou
Ch'ing-p'ing
Lien-chiang
Hua-chou
Ch'i-ching
Ju-chiung
Cha-p'o
Pei-hai (Pakhoi)
Tien-pai
Tien-ch'eng
Sha-pa
Hai-ling Tao
Liang-chiung
Po-ho
An-p'u Wan
An-p'u
Mei-lu [Wu-ch'uan]
Huang-p'o
Sui-ch'i
Ts'ao-t'an
Ch'ih-k'an
Pei-p'o
Chan-chiang
Ma-hsieh
LEI-CHOU PAN-TAO
K'o-lu
P'u-tzu
Kuang-chou Wan
560 km
Wei-chou Tao
Ho-t'ou
Tung-shan
Tung-hai Tao
Chiang-hung
P'ao-chou Tao
Chi-chia
Lei-chou [Hai-k'ang]
Lei-chou Wan
Tan-shui
220 km
Ch'i-shui
Tiao-feng
Hsin-liao Tao
Lung-men
Kuan-ch'ang
Wu-shih
Chin-ho
Wai-lo
Ch'ü-chieh
Liu-sha Wan
Hsi-lien
Hsü-wen
Lung-t'ang
260 km
Mai-ch'u
Hai-an
Haiphong — Canton 1060 km
GULF OF TONG KING
(PEI-PU WAN)
Ch'iung-chou Hai-hsia
Mu-lan T'ou
Lin-kao Chiao
P'u-ch'ien
Tung-p'o
Hsiu-ying
Hai-k'ou
Ch'iung-shan
Mei-lan
Ta-ho
Ch'i-chou Lieh-Tao
260 km
Lin-kao
Hsin-hsing
Pai-lien
Fu-shan
Ta-chih-p'o
Ch'ang-sa
To-wen
Ch'eng-mai
Hsin-ying
Hsin-chou
Yang-p'u Wan
Ting-an
San-men-p'o
Pai-ma-ching
Wen-chiao
Nan-tu Chiang
Ch'ang-ch'ang
Wen-ch'ang
Lo-nan
Hsin-hsing
Ch'ing-lan
Hai-t'ou
Nan-ch'en
Na-ta [Tan Hsien]
P'eng-lai
Ch'ing-lan Wan
Ya-hsing
Jen-hsing
Huang-chu
San-ya — Canton 890 km
Lung-men
Yen-tun
Ch'ang-ch'eng
Sung-t'ao
Lung-t'ang
Ta-p'o
Ch'a-miao
T'un-ch'ang
Ch'iung-hai
Shih-lu
Ya-ch'a [Pai-sha]
Li-mu Ling 1437
Hsin-chieh
Pao-pan
[Ch'ang-chiang]
410 km
Pei-li
Chung-yüan
Pa-so [Tung-fang]
Pa-wang-ling
Wu-shih
Wan-ch'üan Ho
Chiu-tung-fang
Lung-kun
HAI-NAN HSING CHENG CH'Ü
Shih-yün
Ch'iung-chung
Ch'ang Chiang
Wu-chih Shan 1879
Shih-i
Ch'eng-p'o
Kan-ch'eng
HAI-NAN TAO
Ho-lo
Kang-pei Kang
HAINAN LI-MIAO A. D.
Lo-tung
Wan-ning
Hung-ch'i-chen
Hsing-lung
Ling-t'ou
Chien-feng-ling
Nan-ch'iao
Pao-t'ing
Ta-pen
Huang-liu
Ch'ien-chia
Hsin-cheng
Ling-shui
Chiu-suo
Ya-ch'eng
T'eng-ch'iao
Hsin-ts'un
T'u-ch'ü Wan
260 km
San-ya [Yai Hsien]
T'ien-tu
Yü-lin
An-yu

KIANGSI
FUKIEN
CHIU-LIEN SHAN
Chiu-lien Shan 1270
YAO SHAN
Shih-k'eng K'ung 1929
Hsiao-mei Kuan
Pai-sung Kuan
T'ung-ku Chang 1526
Ta-lo Shan 1024
Lo-fu Shan 1296
Lien-hua Shan 1028
Ku-tou Shan 890
KUAN-YIN SHAN
HUI-YANG
Shao-kuan
Lo-ch'ang
Nan-hsiung
Jen-hua
Ying-te
Ch'ing-yüan
CANTON (KUANG-CHOU)
Fo-shan [Nan-hai]
Huang-p'u (Whampoa)
Shih-ch'iao [P'an-yü]
Ta-liang [Shun-te]
Chiang-men (Kongmoon)
Hsin-hui
Shih-ch'i [Chung-shan]
Chao-ch'ing [Kao-yao]
Tseng-ch'eng
Tung-kuan
Hui-chou
Shen-chen [Pao-an]
Kowloon
HONG KONG (To U.K.)
Macau (To Port.)
Ho-yüan
Hsing-ning
Mei-hsien
Wu-hua
Lung-ch'uan
Ho-p'o [Chieh-hsi]
Chieh-yang
Ch'ao-an
Shan-t'ou (Swatow)
Ch'ao-yang
P'u-ning
Hui-lai
Lu-feng
Hai-feng
P'ing-hai
Tung-shan Tao
Nan-ao Tao
NAN-P'ENG LIEH-TAO
Shen-ch'üan Kang
Chia-tzu Kang
Chieh-shih Wan
Hung-hai Wan
Ta-ya Wan
San-men Tao
TAN-KAN LIEH-TAO
WAN-SHAN CH'ÜN-TAO
CHIA-P'ENG LIEH-TAO
Kao-lan Tao
Shang-ch'uan Tao
Hsia-ch'uan Tao
Nan-p'eng Tao
Pei-chin Wan
Canton—Shanghai 1690 km
Hong Kong—Yokohama 2930 km
Canton—Swatow 540 km
Hong Kong—Kao-hsiung 630 km
Singapore—Hong Kong 2670 km
Hong Kong—Manila 1170 km
Conakry—Canton 19220 km
Jakarta—Canton 3340 km
Chan-chiang — Singapore 2480 km
SOUTH CHINA SEA
(NAN HAI)
1 : 2180000
MILES
KM

KWANGTUNG PROVINCE 广东省
KUANG-TUNG SHENG

10 shih	*municipalities*
1 hsing-cheng-ch'ü	*administrative district*
1 tzu-chih-chou	*autonomous district*
7 ti-ch'ü	*regions*
94 hsien	*counties*
3 tzu-chih-hsien	*autonomous counties*

capital **Kuang-chou Shih**	C2	广州市
Hua Hsien		花县
centre: Hua-hsien	C2	
Ts'ung-hua Hsien	C2	从化县
Chan-chiang Shih	B3	湛江市
Chao-ch'ing Shih	C2	肇庆市
Chiang-men Shih	C2	江门市
Fo-shan Shih	C2	佛山市
Hai-k'ou Shih	B3	海口市
Hui-chou Shih	D2	惠州市
Mao-ming Shih	B3	茂名市
Shan-t'ou Shih	E2	汕头市
Shao-kuan Shih	C1	韶关市

Chan-chiang Ti-ch'ü		湛江地区
Hai-k'ang Hsien		海康县
centre: Lei-chou	B3	雷州
Hsin-i Hsien	B2	信宜县
Hsü-wen Hsien	B3	徐闻县
Hua-chou Hsien	B3	化州县
Kao-chou Hsien	B3	高州县
Lien-chiang Hsien	B3	廉江县
Sui-ch'i Hsien	B3	遂溪县
Tien-pai Hsien	B3	电白县
Wu-ch'uan Hsien		吴川县
centre: Mei-lu	B3	梅绿
Yang-chiang Hsien	B3	阳江县
Yang-ch'un Hsien	B2	阳春县

Chao-ch'ing Ti-ch'ü		肇庆地区
Feng-k'ai Hsien		封开县
centre: Chiang-k'ou	B2	江口
Hsin-hsing Hsien	C2	新兴县
Huai-chi Hsien	C2	怀集县
Kao-yao Hsien		高要县
centre: Chao-ch'ing	C2	肇庆
Kuang-ning Hsien		广宁县
centre: Nan-chieh	C2	南街
Lo-ting Hsien	B2	罗定县
Ssu-hui Hsien	C2	四会县
Te-ch'ing Hsien	B2	德庆县
Yü-nan Hsien	B2	郁南县
Yün-fu Hsien	C2	云浮县

Fo-shan Ti-ch'ü		佛山地区
Chu-hai Hsien		珠海县
centre: Hsiang-chou	C2	香州
Chung-shan Hsien		中山县
centre: Shih-ch'i	C2	石岐
En-p'ing Hsien	C2	恩平县
Hsin-hui Hsien	C2	新会县
K'ai-p'ing Hsien		开平县
centre: San-pu	C2	三埠
Kao-ho Hsien		高鹤县
centre: Sha-p'ing	C2	沙坪
Nan-hai Hsien		南海县
centre: Fo-shan	C2	佛山
P'an-yü Hsien		番禺县
centre: Shih-ch'iao	C2	市桥
San-shui Hsien		三水县
centre: Hsi-nan	C2	西南
Shun-te Hsien		顺德县
centre: Ta-liang	C2	大艮
T'ai-shan Hsien	C2	台山县
Tou-men Hsien		斗门县
centre: Ching-an	C2	井岸

Hai-nan Hsing-cheng-ch'ü		海南行政区
centre: Hai-k'ou	B3	海口
Ch'eng-mai Hsien	A4	澄迈县
Ch'iung-hai Hsien	B4	琼海县
Ch'iung-shan Hsien	B4	琼山县
Lin-kao Hsien	A4	临高县
Tan Hsien		儋县
centre: Na-ta	A4	那大
Ting-an Hsien	B4	定安县
T'un-ch'ang Hsien	B4	屯昌县
Wan-ning Hsien	B4	万宁县
Wen-ch'ang Hsien	B4	文昌县

Hai-nan Li-tsu Miao-tsu Tzu-chih-chou Hainan Li-Miao Autonomous District		海南黎族苗族自治州
centre: Hung-ch'i-chen	A4	红旗镇
Ch'ang-chiang Hsien		昌江县
centre: Shih-lu	A4	石碌
Ch'iung-chung Hsien	A4	琼中县
Ling-shui Hsien	B4	陵水县
Lo-tung Hsien	A4	乐东县
Pao-t'ing Hsien	A4	保亭县
Pai-sha Hsien		白沙县
centre: Ya-ch'a	A4	牙叉
Tung-fang Hsien		东方县
centre: Pa-so	A4	八所
Yai Hsien		崖县
centre: San-ya	A4	三亚

Hui-yang Ti-ch'ü		惠阳地区
centre: Hui-chou	D2	惠州
Ho-p'ing Hsien		和平县
centre: Yang-ming	D1	阳明
Ho-yüan Hsien	D2	河源县
Hui-tung Hsien		惠东县
centre: P'ing-shan	D2	平山
Hui-yang Hsien		惠阳县
centre: Hui-chou	D2	惠州
Lien-p'ing Hsien	D1	连平县
Lung-ch'uan Hsien		龙川县
centre: Lao-lung	D1	老隆
Lung-men Hsien	D2	龙门县
Pao-an Hsien		宝安县
centre: Shen-chen	D2	深圳
Po-lo Hsien	D2	博罗县
Tseng-ch'eng Hsien	C2	增城县
Tung-kuan Hsien	C2	东莞县
Tzu-chin Hsien	D2	紫金县

Mei-hsien Ti-ch'ü		梅县地区
Chiao-ling Hsien	E1	蕉岭县
Feng-shun Hsien	E2	丰顺县
Hsing-ning Hsien	D1	兴宁县
Mei Hsien		梅县
centre: Mei-hsien	E1	
P'ing-yüan Hsien	D1	平远县
Ta-pu Hsien		大埔县
centre: Hu-liao	E1	湖寮
Wu-hua Hsien	D2	五华县

Shan-t'ou Ti-ch'ü		汕头地区
Ch'ao-an Hsien	E2	潮安县
Ch'ao-yang Hsien	E2	潮阳县
Ch'eng-hai Hsien	E2	澄海县
Chieh-hsi Hsien		揭西县
centre: Ho-p'o	D2	河婆
Chieh-yang Hsien	E2	揭阳县
Hai-feng Hsien	D2	海丰县
Hui-lai Hsien	E2	惠来县
Jao-p'ing Hsien		饶平县
centre: Huang-kang	E2	黄岗
Lu-feng Hsien	D2	陆丰县
Nan-ao Hsien	E2	南澳县
P'u-ning Hsien	E2	普宁县

Shao-kuan Ti-ch'ü		韶关地区
Ch'ing-yüan Hsien	C2	清远县
Ch'ü-chiang Hsien		曲江县
centre: Ma-pa	C1	马坝
Fo-kang Hsien		佛冈县
centre: Shih-chiao	C2	石角
Hsin-feng Hsien	D1	新丰县
Jen-hua Hsien	C1	仁化县
Ju-yüan Yao-tsu Tzu-chih-hsien Ju-yüan Yao Autonomous Hsien		乳源瑶族自治县
centre: Ju-yüan	C1	
Lien Hsien		连县
centre: Lien-hsien	C1	
Lien-nan Yao-tsu Tzu-chih-hsien Lien-nan Yao Autonomous Hsien		连南瑶族自治县
centre: San-chiang	C1	三江
Lien-shan Chuang-tsu Yao-tsu Tzu-chih-hsien Lien-shan Chuang-Yao Autonomous Hsien		连山壮族瑶族自治县
centre: Chi-t'ien	C1	吉田
Lo-ch'ang Hsien	C1	乐昌县
Nan-hsiung Hsien	D1	南雄县
Shih-hsing Hsien	D1	始兴县
Weng-yüan Hsien		翁源县
centre: Lung-hsien	D1	龙仙
Yang-shan Hsien	C1	阳山县
Ying-te Hsien	C1	英德县

KWANGSI CHUANG
AUTONOMOUS REGION

KWANGSI first came into the political orbit of the Chinese under the Ch'in, when in 214 BC a large army was sent to conquer Kwangtung, and also the eastern sections of Kwangsi. At this time Chinese authority was not securely established, and for the next centuries the area lay on the periphery of the Chinese empire, with Chinese occupation of the eastern and south-eastern parts of the province, and a system of indirect rule through chieftains of the aboriginal Chuang peoples in the more westerly districts. This situation was complicated by the settlement in the northern parts of the province of Yao and Miao tribesmen, driven from their homes in southern Hunan and Kiangsi by the advance of Chinese settlement. Unlike the Chuang, who easily assimilated Chinese customs, the Miao and Yao remained in the hills districts, often harshly oppressed by Chinese settlers. There was continuous trouble, with major risings in the 1830s, and the initial outbreak of the T'ai-p'ing rebellion occurred in Kwangsi, involving many Hakka, as well as some Chuang. The province remained a comparatively poor area until the present century. In the Republican period its military leaders formed the Kwangsi Clique, the principal opposition to Chiang Kai-shek within the Kuomintang, and controlled much of Kwangtung, Hunan and Hupeh for long periods between 1926–37. During this time some effort was made to modernise Kwangsi itself. After the outbreak of the war with Japan, the province was the scene of much fighting and destruction. Since 1949, the province has been enlarged by the addition of the coastal area, giving Kwangsi an outlet to the port of Pei-hai (Pakhoi).

The province is almost coextensive with the basin of the Hsi Chiang river system, which provides good water communications throughout the region. The topography is mostly hilly, with rather poor, infertile soils. The land gradually rises to the north, where it merges into the Kweichow plateau in the west, and the steep ranges of the Nan Shan on the Hunan and Kwangtung borders. The climate is tropical in the south and sub-tropical in the northern half of the province, where the mountains are comparatively cool. Temperatures have a rather small seasonal range. At Kuei-lin January averages 9–10°C (48–50°F); July about 26°C (79°F). The rainfall is heavy – above 1,000 mm everywhere except in the west and north-west, and up to 2,000 mm on the coast and in mountainous districts in the east. Most rain falls from May to October, and the summers are extremely hot and humid. The growing seasons lasts throughout the year.

South-west Kwangsi This is a very hilly area, drained by the Yu Chiang and Tso Chiang rivers, with comparatively narrow river plains, and rather a low proportion of cultivated land. Rice is the main crop. Double-cropping is normal in the east around Nan-ning. In the west single-cropped rice grown together with corn is more common. Sugar cane is an important crop in the east and south. It is mostly refined at Nan-ning. Peanuts are widely grown, and tobacco is grown in the eastern valleys, to be processed in Liu-chou.

Nan-ning, the provincial capital, is the centre of this region. It is an old-established route centre, and became the provincial capital in 1912. It is the main cultural and educational city in Kwangsi. Traditionally a river port, its importance has grown greatly since the construction of the railway in the early 1950s. It has a thermal generating station using coal from the Ho-shan mines at Lai-pin to the north-east. Its industry concentrates on processing local agricultural produce such as sugar. But some modern industry has also grown up – engineering and machine building, a wide range of chemicals and fertilisers, and aluminium are local industries. Its population is now estimated at about 400,000.

The Coastal Area Acquired finally by Kwangsi in 1965, the coastal area mostly consists of rather barren hills. Agriculture concentrates on rice, with much cultivation of tubers such as taro, sweet potatoes and cassava. Jute, sugar and ramie are important economic crops.

Pei-hai (Pakhoi) is an old-established port, but too shallow for modern shipping and it has lost much of its trade to Chan-chiang in Kwangtung, the terminus of the railway to Kwangsi. Pei-hai, however, remains a very important fishing port.

South-eastern Kwangsi This area, which is the part of the province that has been settled the longest, has a well developed agriculture. Double-cropped rice is normal, often with a third winter crop such as wheat, tobacco, vegetables or sweet potatoes. Ground nuts are widely grown on sandy soils. Sugar cane and jute are important industrial crops, and there are sugar refineries at Wu-chou and Kuei-hsien. The area to the west of Wu-chou has some manganese mines.

Wu-chou is the chief centre of this district. Before the railways were constructed, most of Kwangsi's trade went via Wu-chou to Canton, and it remains a very important river port and market centre, although the railway has taken away some of its trade. It has recently become a centre of sugar refining, and the largest manufacturer of pitch in China.

North-eastern Kwangsi The basin of the Kuei Chiang river is a very hilly area, much of it composed of limestone with spectacular karst landscapes. Although it was one of the first settled areas of Kwangsi, it has a very low proportion of cultivated land. Rice is the main crop, but double cropping is only slowly spreading from the south. Ramie fibre is an important crop, grown on hill slopes and terraced fields. Peanuts are also important. Some tea of good quality is grown.

Kuei-lin is the regional centre. It is an ancient city, and was the provincial capital until 1912. It supports a very wide range of local handicraft industries, and various food-processing industries based on local agriculture.

North-western Kwangsi This area, too, is very hilly with a very low proportion of cultivated land. Much of the area is composed of limestone, and lack of water is a major problem. Agriculture is mainly rice growing, with double cropping in the south, and corn grown extensively on upland fields. Cotton, ramie, hemp, peanuts and some sugar cane are also grown in the south.

The area still has a good deal of natural forest, and lumbering is an important industry in the valleys of the Hung Shui and Liu Chiang. The main trees are pine, fir, oak, maple and camphor. Lumber is floated down the rivers to lumber-mills at Liu-chou.

This region also has some minerals. Coal is mined at Ho-shan, south of Liu-chou, and antimony is produced near Nan-tan.

Liu-chou is the main route centre of this area, and its importance has grown greatly since the railways were constructed. It is the junction of main lines to Kuei-yang, and to Kuei-lin and Hunan. It has become the major industrial city of the province. It has a large thermal generating plant, using coal from Ho-shan, and a small steel works at Lu-sai, a few miles to the north-east. Liu-chou has developed an engineering industry, making tractors, farm-machinery and railway equipment. It has large fertiliser and cement works, an electronic industry, and a major lumber-milling industry.

National Minorities The main minority people in Kwangsi are the Chuang, a Thai people, of whom there are 6,500,000 living in the province. They are China's largest national minority. Kwangsi was constituted a Chuang Autonomous Region in 1958. The Chuang have assimilated Chinese culture and generally speak Chinese. They form the bulk of the population in the more sparsely peopled western half of the province. Other minorities are the Tung living on the Hunan border; the Yao and the Miao, who live in scattered communities in the north, in the coastal zone, and along the Vietnamese border. There are estimated to be about 470,000 Yao, 200,000 Miao and 150,000 Tung in the province.

AREA
230,000 square kilometres

POPULATION
20,840,000 (other estimates up to 25,000,000)

104°
A
105°
B
106°
C
107°
D
108°
26°
25°
24°
23°
22°
21°
YUNNAN
KWEICHOW
NORTH VIETNAM
Pan-ch'iao
Yang-ch'ang
Yen-fang
P'an-hsien
P'an-shui [P'u-an]
Lien-ch'eng [Ch'ing-lung]
Kuan-so [Kuan-ling]
Chen-ning [Chen-ning Puyi-Miao A.H.]
Ta-yung
Ta-shan-shao
Lang-tai
Huang-kuo-shu
Ch'ang-shun
Hui-shui
San-tu
Kou-ch'ang
Tuan-shan
Tzu-yün [Tzu-yün Miao-Puyi A.H.]
Hua-chiang
Lao-ch'ang
Niu-ch'ang
Hou-ch'ang
P'ing-fa
Mo-ch'ung
Lung-ch'üan [Tan-chai]
San-tu [San-tu Shui A.H.]
Wu-lo
Keng-ting Shan 1663
P'ing-hu [P'ing-t'ang]
Ya-chou
Tu-shan
T'ung-chou
Pien-yang
Shang-ssu
Chia-liang
Chou-t'an
Chiu-ch'ien
Feng-tung
Ling-yang
Lung-p'ing [Lo-tien]
Li-po
Ma-wei
Liu-chai
Ma-ch'uan-lo
Shang-ch'ao
Hsing-jen
Pa-ling
Pao-t'ien
Fu-lo
T'un-chiao
Chen-feng [Chen-feng Puyi-Miao A.H.]
Ta-i
Ting-hsiao
Hsing-i
Fu-hsing [Wang-mo Puyi-Miao A.H.]
An-lung [An-lung Puyi-Miao A.H.]
Ts'e-yang
Che-lou [Ts'e-heng Puyi A.H.]
Tan-feng [Shih-tsung]
Lo-p'ing
Pan-ch'iao
Ta-t'ung
Pang-cha
Pa-chieh
Ko-pu
Che-pao
Lung-lin [Lung-lin Multi-national A.H.]
Pien-ya
Sha-li
Pa-tu
Chiu-chou
San-chiang-k'ou
Pa-ta-ho
Ma-feng
Ku-chiang
Ni-tung
Pa-ta [Hsi-lin]
Lung-huo
Wei-lo
Pan-t'ao
Pai-lo
Na-lao
Hsi-p'ing
Ting-an
Fu-ta
Pa-tu
Che-ta
Na-tso
Jih-che
Ch'iu-pei
Kuang-nan
Chu-lin
Hsi-yang-chieh
Pa-pao
Che-sang
Fu-ning
Po-ai
Ch'ang-ling-chieh
A-meng
Yen-shan
Ma-t'ang
Wen-shan
Hsi-ch'ou
Hsi-ch'ou-hsin-chieh
Ma-li-p'o
Ma-kuan
Tu-lung-hsin-chieh
Ha Giang
Lao Cai
Cao Bang
Ngan Son
Bac Kan
Thai Nguyen
Phu Tho
Bac Ninh
Phulang Thuong
Hanoi
Hai Duong
Haiphong
Hon Gay
Dinh Lap
Lang Son
Mong Cai
Red River (Song Hong)
Tu-k'ou
Hsiang-yang
Ma-chuang
Yu-p'ing
Ya-ch'ang
Lo-yeh
Kao-lou Ling 1424
Keng-hsin
Hsin-hua
Kan-t'ien
Wang-hung
Chia-yu
Hang-tung
Chin-ya
Ch'iao-yin
Lang-p'ing
T'ai-wang Lao-shan 2062
Lu-ch'eng
Ling-yün
Lo-li [T'ien-lin]
Lo-lou
P'ing-lo
Feng-shan
Hsia-chia
Pa-kuei
Wang-tien
Lung-ch'uan
T'ung-kang
Yung-lo
Po-se
Yang-yü
Ssu-t'ang
T'ien-yang
Yen-li
Ta-leng
Fu-lu
Na-p'o
Na-man
P'o-hung
Ku-mei
Hsiang-chou
P'ing-ma [T'ien-tung]
Lin-p'eng
Tung-ling
Wu-ts'un
Pa-t'ou
Tso-teng
Na-p'o
Lung-ho
K'uei-yü
P'o-ho
An-te
Te-lung
Te-pao
Tu-an
Tsu-jung
Jung-hua
Lung-lin
Hsin-yü
Nan-p'o
Ching-hsi
Ti-chou
Lung-kuang
Yen-t'ung
Hsiang-tu
Pa-la
P'o-chieh
Liu-p'ai [T'ien-o]
Pan-mo
Lo-fu
Wu-ai
Nan-tan
Hsiao-ch'ang
Yao-chai
Pa-yü
Tse-ling
Ch'e-ho
Ch'ang-lao
Ch'ang-chiang
San-wang
Ai-tung
Tung-lan
Chiu-yü
Ch'ang-lo
P'o-hsin
Chung-ho
San-shih
P'o-yüeh
Chia-chuan
Feng-huang
Pa-ma [Pa-ma Yao A.H.]
Shan-chiao
Yen-tung
Yü-feng
Tu-yang
Chiu-huai
Li-ming
Pang-yü
Shuo-liang
Feng-wu
Hai-ch'eng
Hsing-ning
T'ai-p'ing
P'o-tsao
Ssu-lin
Yin-ch'a
Kuo-hua
P'ing-kuo
Yü Chiang
Chin-chieh
Tu-chieh
Yen-chiang
Lung-an
Pa-ho
T'ien-teng
Shang-ying
Nan-yü
Ch'iao-chien
Na-t'ung
Lung-ming
Ch'üan-ming
P'ing-shan
Lung-men
Shih-lung
Na-ling
Ta-hsin
Na-lung
Chung-tung
Lan-yü
T'o-lu
Chin-chou
Pao-yü
T'ai-p'ing
Tso-chou
Hsin-ho
Wu-te
Shui-k'ou-kuan
Hsia-tung
Hsiang-shui
Ku-p'o
Ch'ung-tso
Tso Chiang
Lung-chou
Shang-chin
Ch'ü-chiu
Lai-t'uan
Tung-lo
T'ien-hsi
P'ing-erh-kuan
Na-k'an
Ning-ming
T'ing-liang
Hsia-shih
P'ing-hsiang
Ming-chiang
Yu-i-kuan
Pan-kun
Chih-lang
Na-nan
Kung-an
Pei-lun Ai
SHIH-WAN TA-SHAN
Ta-lü
Hua-shih
Kuei-wei
Chiang-p'ing
Ta-ts'un
Tung-hsing [Tung-hsing Multinational A.H.]
Hai-yüan
Na-k'an
P'ing-fu
Ming Chiang
Na-tang
Ch'i-men-t'un
Tsai-miao
Shang-ssu
Pai-pao
Kung-cheng
Kuei-t'ai
Na-ch'in
Pan-li
Hsi-ch'ang
Tung-men
Lo-pai
Shan-yü
Na-pai
Na-ch'en
Su-yü
Ta-ling
Ch'ü-li
Fu-sui
Wu-yü
Chin-chi-ts'un
T'ing-tzu
Lung-t'ou
Wei-lo
Lao-k'ou
Nan-ning
Kan-yü
Na-lung
T'an-lo
Fu-shu
Shuang-ch'iao
Ting-tang
Wu-ming
Wu-ming Ho
Li-chen
Lo-yü
Ling-ma
Fu-ch'eng
Chou-lu
Yang-yü
Kung-ch'uan
Ch'iao-li
Ma-shan
Ta-hua
Mien-yü
Tu-an [Tu-an Yao A.H.]
Kao-ling
Pao-an
Ta-hsing
La-lieh
Pan-ling
Hsia-yao
La-jen
Pao-p'ing
Lung-t'ou
Pai-t'u
La-lang
Chin-ch'eng-chiang [Ho-ch'ih]
Ho-ch'ih
Tung-chiang
Tu-chieh
Huan-chiang
Pa-kung
Shui-yüan
Hsia-nan
Lo-yang
Ch'üan-shan
Yung-an
Li-hu
GULF (PEI

KWANGSI

1 : 1750000

0 5 10 20 30 40 50 60 70 80 90 100 150 MILES

0 5 10 20 30 40 50 60 70 80 90 100 150 200 KM

KWANGSI CHUANG AUTONOMOUS REGION
KUANG-HSI CHUANG-TSU TZU-CHIH-CH'Ü
广西壮族自治州

6 shih	*municipalities*
8 ti-ch'ü	*regions*
72 hsien	*counties*
8 tzu-chih-hsien	*autonomous counties*

capital **Nan-ning Shih**	E5	南宁市
Kuei-lin Shih	G2	桂林市
Liu-chou Shih	F3	柳州市
Pei-hai Shih	F6	北海市
P'ing-hsiang Shih	C5	凭祥市
Wu-chou Shih	H4	梧州市

Ch'in-chou Ti-ch'ü		钦州地区
Ch'in-chou Hsien	E6	钦州县
Ho-p'u Hsien		合浦县
centre: Lien-chou	F6	廉州
Ling-shan Hsien	F5	灵山县
P'u-pei Hsien		浦北县
centre: Hsiao-chiang	F5	小江
Shang-ssu Hsien	D5	上思县
Tung-hsing Ko-tsu Tzu-chih-hsien Tung-hsing Multi-national Autonomous Hsien		东兴各族自治县
centre: Tung-hsing	E6	

Ho-ch'ih Ti-ch'ü		河池地区
Feng-shan Hsien	D3	凤山县
Ho-ch'ih Hsien		河池县
centre: Chin-ch'eng-chiang	E3	金城江
Huan-chiang Hsien	E3	环江县
I-shan Hsien	E3	宜山县
Lo-ch'eng Hsien	E3	罗城县
Nan-tan Hsien	D3	南丹县
Pa-ma Yao-tsu Tzu-chih-hsien Pa-ma Yao Autonomous Hsien		巴马瑶族自治县
centre: Pa-ma	D3	
T'ien-o Hsien		天峨县
centre: Liu-p'ai	D2	六排
Tu-an Yao-tsu Tzu-chih-hsien Tu-an Yao Autonomous Hsien		都安瑶族自治县
centre: Tu-an	E4	
Tung-lan Hsien	D3	东兰县

Kuei-lin Ti-ch'ü		桂林地区
Ch'üan-chou Hsien	H2	全州县
Hsing-an Hsien	G2	兴安县
Kuan-yang Hsien	H2	灌阳县
Kung-ch'eng Hsien	G3	恭城县
Ling-ch'uan Hsien	G2	灵川县
Lin-kuei Hsien		临桂县
centre: Kuei-lin	G2	桂林
Li-p'u Hsien	G3	荔浦县
Lung-sheng Ko-tsu Tzu-chih-hsien Lung-sheng Multi-national Autonomous Hsien		龙胜各族自治县
centre: Lung-sheng	G2	
P'ing-lo Hsien	G3	平乐县
Tzu-yüan Hsien	G1	资源县
Yang-shuo Hsien	G3	阳朔县
Yung-fu Hsien	G2	永福县

Liu-chou Ti-ch'ü		柳州地区
Chin-hsiu Yao-tsu Tzu-chih-hsien Chin-hsiu Yao Autonomous Hsien		金秀瑶族自治县
centre: Chin-hsiu	G3	
Hsiang-chou Hsien	F4	象州县
Hsin-ch'eng Hsien	E3	忻城县
Jung-an Hsien		融安县
centre: Ch'ang-an	F2	长安
Jung-shui Miao-tsu Tzu-chih-hsien Jung-shui Miao Autonomous Hsien		融水苗族自治县
centre: Jung-shui	F2	
Lai-pin Hsien	F4	来宾县
Liu-ch'eng Hsien		柳城县
centre: Ta-p'u	F3	大埔
Liu-chiang Hsien	F3	柳江县
Lu-chai Hsien	F3	鹿寨县
San-chiang T'ung-tsu Tzu-chih-hsien San-chiang Tung Autonomous Hsien		三江洞族自治县
centre: Ku-i	F2	古宜
Wu-hsüan Hsien	F4	武宣县

Nan-ning Ti-ch'ü		南宁地区
Ch'ung-tso Hsien	D5	崇左县
Fu-sui Hsien	D5	扶绥县
Heng Hsien		横县
centre: Heng-hsien	F5	
Lung-an Hsien	D4	隆安县
Lung-chou Hsien	C5	龙州县
Ma-shan Hsien	E4	马山县
Ning-ming Hsien	D5	宁明县
Pin-yang Hsien	E4	宾阳县
Shang-lin Hsien	E4	上林县
Ta-hsin Hsien	D5	大新县
T'ien-teng Hsien	D4	天等县
Wu-ming Hsien	E4	武鸣县
Yung-ning Hsien		邕宁县
centre: P'u-miao	E5	蒲庙

Po-se Ti-ch'ü		百色地区
Ching-hsi Hsien	C4	靖西县
Hsi-lin Hsien		西林县
centre: Pa-ta	B3	八达
Ling-yün Hsien	C3	凌云县
Lo-yeh Hsien	C3	乐业县
Lung-lin Ko-tsu Tzu-chih-hsien Lung-lin Multi-national Autonomous Hsien		隆林各族自治县
centre: Lung-lin	B3	
Na-p'o Hsien	B4	那坡县
Po-se Hsien	C4	百色县
P'ing-kuo Hsien	D4	平果县
Te-pao Hsien	C4	德保县
T'ien-lin Hsien		田林县
centre: Lo-li	C3	乐里
T'ien-tung Hsien		田东县
centre: P'ing-ma	D4	平马
T'ien-yang Hsien	C4	田阳县

Wu-chou Ti-ch'ü		梧州地区
Chao-p'ing Hsien	G3	昭平县
Chung-shan Hsien	H3	钟山县
Fu-ch'uan Hsien	H3	富川县
Ho Hsien		贺县
centre: Pa-pu	H3	八步
Meng-shan Hsien	G3	蒙山县
T'eng Hsien		藤县
centre: T'eng-hsien	G4	
Ts'ang-wu Hsien		苍梧县
centre: Lung-hsü	H4	龙圩
Ts'en-ch'i Hsien	H5	岑溪县

Yü-lin Ti-ch'ü		玉林地区
Jung Hsien		容县
centre: Jung-hsien	G5	
Kuei Hsien		贵县
centre: Kuei-hsien	F4	
Kuei-p'ing Hsien	G4	桂平县
Lu-ch'uan Hsien	G5	陆川县
Pei-liu Hsien	G5	北流县
P'ing-nan Hsien	G4	平南县
Po-pai Hsien	F5	博白县
Yü-lin Hsien	G5	玉林县

SZECHWAN
PROVINCE

SZECHWAN, one of the largest provinces in China, and the most populous, contains over 11 per cent of the total population. The present province was formed in 1955 by the fusion of the old province of Szechwan with Sikang in the western highlands. Although the new territory is almost half of the area, it is sparsely peopled, with probably about 4,000,000 people.

The two areas have had a very different history. Szechwan, although it had been peopled from much earlier times, first became a part of the Chinese political system in the late 4th century BC, when it was invaded by the state of Ch'in. In the 3rd century BC, the Ch'in government first built the irrigation system in the plain around Ch'eng-tu, which was to remain the economic centre of the province. Szechwan grew steadily until the 13th century, when it had already a dense population engaged in intensive farming. It was much damaged by the Mongol invasion, and again seriously depopulated and ravaged in the wars at the end of the Ming period (1368–44). After this, the province was largely resettled by people from Central and Southern China. In the early Republican period it was very unstable, the scene of constant fighting between rival war-lords. Its modern development dates from the Second World War, when the Nationalist government, in the face of the Japanese advance, withdrew to the south-west, bringing with it many industries dismantled in the coastal cities, and many institutions of higher learning.

Since the beginning of the Communist regime Szechwan has been more firmly integrated into the Chinese state by the construction of railways. The first line reached Ch'eng-tu from Pao-chi in 1956, and the province now also has rail links with Yunnan and Kweichow. The Yangtze, formerly the chief artery for Szechwan's trade, has also had its channels through the gorges in the east of the province cleared and improved for shipping. The western and north-western sections of the province have also been given a much improved highway system.

The Szechwan Basin The eastern half of the province is a basin, drained by the Yangtze and its tributaries, and surrounded by high mountains. It lies at an altitude of about 1,000 m. The south-eastern part of this basin is quite high, with a series of steep ranges with a south-west to north-east axis. To the south of the Yangtze valley these rise to the Kweichow plateau. In the extreme east of the province the ranges join the Ta-pa Shan, a very high and rugged range which forms the border with Shansi. This eastern knot of mountains is traversed by the Yangtze in a series of spectacular gorges. The western part of the basin is also hilly. The only area of flat land is the Ch'eng-tu plain in the north-west. The whole basin has a moist humid and temperate climate, protected from north and north-westerly winds by the great mountain ranges. Rainfall is between 750 and 1,250 mm, with even heavier falls in the south-western mountains. Most rain falls in summer. Winter temperatures average 10°C (50°F); summers average 29°C (84°F) and are very humid. The growing season lasts eleven months throughout the basin, and virtually the whole year in the southern section.

The Ch'eng-tu plain The major agricultural region of Szechwan, this is a large alluvial fan formed by the Min Chiang river which has been irrigated since the 3rd century BC and now supports one of the densest rural populations in the world. Most of the land is rice-paddy, the rice crop being followed by wheat, rape-seed or peas as a winter crop. On the higher ground corn, sweet potatoes, cotton and hemp are grown, and on the hill-lands citrus fruits, especially tangerines, are widely cultivated.

Ch'eng-tu is the traditional centre of this area, and the provincial capital. Founded in the 4th century BC it was always an important regional metropolis and trading city, the centre of a very important silk industry. During the Second World War modern industry begun to grow, and this was accelerated after the completion of a railway to Ch'ung-ch'ing in 1952, and a railway linking Ch'eng-tu with Pao-chi in Shensi in 1956, connecting with the main Chinese rail network. Industry has continued to grow, but not on the scale of Ch'ung-ch'ing. Ch'eng-tu has a large textile industry, and precision engineering, instrument making, electronics and radio plants. A large thermal power plant is fed by coal from nearby Kuan-hsien.

Chin-t'ang to the north-east is a centre of the chemical and fertiliser industries, with a large plant built by the Czechs and completed in 1959–60.

Chiang-yu, even further to the north-east, is a major producer of cement, and has a small iron and steel industry.

The South-western basin This area is bounded by the lower courses of the Min Chiang and To Chiang and the valley of the Yangtze. An area of alluvial plain separated by areas of low hills, it is hotter and wetter than the Ch'eng-tu area. The northern part is very intensively farmed. Rice is the main crop, and in the river valleys sugar cane is widely grown, usually in rotation with corn, sweet potatoes or peanuts. On higher land corn and cotton are widely grown. The upland western area around Lo-shan is a major silk producing area.

Nei-chiang is a major market and route centre, and an important rail junction. It is the main centre of the sugar refining industry, also has light engineering and textile (cottons) plants, and produces paper.

Tzu-kung is the main city of the region. The centre of an ancient salt industry, using brine from deep wells, Tzu-kung has developed into a centre of the chemical industry, and also manufactures machine tools and electrical equipment.

I-pin, the traditional market on the Yangtze, has also developed a chemical industry.

The Ch'ung-ch'ing area occupies the south-east of the Szechwan basin. This, too, is a very warm and wet area, with intensive irrigation and a 320-day growing period. It is a major rice-producing region, where double cropping of rice is common. Wheat, corn, sweet potatoes and kaoliang are important subsidiary crops. Oranges, tangerines, lichees and longan fruits are widely grown, and the area is an important producer of silk.

Ch'ung-ch'ing (Chungking) is the chief centre of the area. A traditional regional centre and river port, with routes across Szechwan and into Kweichow by river and rail, Ch'ung-ch'ing's modern growth began during the Second World War, when it became the capital of the Nationalist government. This period was also the beginning of its transformation into a major centre of heavy industry. A steel industry was founded here in 1940, using plant dismantled in Han-yang. Building on this base, the Communist regime developed Ch'ung-ch'ing into a major heavy industrial base for south-western China. In 1960 it became a fully integrated iron and steel complex, producing over 1 million tons of steel annually. It has also developed other industry, producing machine tools, electrical equipment, small ships, railway rolling stock, cement, copper, lead and zinc, plastics and chemicals. Its population (1,770,000 in 1953), is now estimated at over 4,400,000.

Ch'ang-shou, a small industrial town downstream on the Yangtze, is a major centre of the synthetic rubber industry.

Lu-chou, the main market centre for the western part of the area, has also developed a large fertiliser and chemical industry.

The Eastern Basin This area, the lower basins of the Chia-ling and Ch'ü rivers, is comparatively hilly, with little flat land. The valleys grow rice, wheat and sweet potatoes, and cotton and silk are also produced. The higher north-eastern sections have still much forested land, and grow tea, tree oils and citrus fruits, and draft animals are bred in large numbers.

Nan-chung is a major route and market centre for this area, and the traditional centre of the silk industry. In recent times its importance has grown, owing to the discovery in 1956 of a major oil-field, which began production in 1958, and produces between 500,000 and 1,000,000 tons annually. Some of this is refined locally, but most is sent down the Yangtze by tanker.

The Northern Basin lies east of the Ch'eng-tu plain and south of the Lung-men Shan range and occupies the upper basins of the Fu Chiang and Chia-ling rivers. It is mostly a hilly district, with little level land except in the valleys in the south-west. Much of the area is under dry farming, producing corn, soy beans, cotton and tea. It also has a very old-established silk industry.

Mien-yang is the traditional market for this region, and also an important centre of the silk industry.

Kuang-yuan, on the railway to Pao-chi, is the centre of the north-eastern part of this area. It produces iron ore on a small scale and has coal mines at Wang-tsang and Pai-shui.

The Yangtze Gorge region This eastern extremity of Szechwan is mountainous with a complex, difficult terrain, and poor communications. There is little cultivation, except in the valleys, where rice, wheat and rape-seed are the main crops. The forested mountains produce quantities of tung- and tea-oil.

Wan-hsien, a minor port city on the Yangtze, is the main outlet for the area north of the river and the adjoining parts of Hupeh.

Fu-ling plays the same role for the areas of the Chien Chiang valley, which provides a route into northern Kweichow.

The Apa region This region occupies the mountains and plateaux of north-western Szechwan, beyond the basin itself, and is a high area of rugged ranges and high plateaux, with very varied climatic regimes. The area is only sparsely peopled. Chinese (Han) settlement is confined to the southern and north-eastern valleys, where rice, corn, buckwheat and potatoes with some rape-seed and tobacco are grown. Most of the area is inhabited by Tibetans, who make up 70 per cent of the population. Pastoral industry is very important. Much of the land remains forested, and there is some lumbering.

The Kan-tzu–Ya-an region Formerly a part of Sikang province, this area comprises the towering Ta-hsüeh Shan range, the eastern border of the Szechwan basin, and the high plateau broken by another high north-south range, the Sha-lu-li Shan, to the west. Much of this region lies above 3,000 m. It has a short growing season of between 100 and 200 days. Agriculture is confined to the lower valleys in the south-east around Ya-an, where wheat, barley and peas are the main crops. Tea is also grown extensively in the Ya-an and Jung-ching areas. The northern and western parts of this area are sparsely peopled, largely by Tibetans, and are mainly pastoral areas, where sheep, horses and yaks are bred. Grain is imported into this area from Ya-an. Along the valleys of the Ta-tu and Ya-lung rivers are extensive forests.

Ya-an is the traditional market town of the southern area, and an important trading town on the highway to Tibet. It was capital of Sikang from 1950–55.

K'ang-ting, the main centre of the Tibetan population of the western plateau, and a traditional trading centre between Chinese and Tibetans, with a woollen manufacturing industry, was capital of Sikang until 1950. It is an important route centre with highways leading into both Tibet and Tsinghai.

The South-western plateau The plateau of the south-west is slightly lower (2,000–2,500 m), warmer and wetter than the Kan-tzu area. Most parts have a 200–300-day growing period, and agriculture is important. Where possible, corn, paddy rice, wheat or buckwheat are grown, according to the altitude. Rape-seed and peanuts are important crops, and livestock, especially cattle, are raised by farmers.

AREA
560,000 square kilometres

POPULATION
67,960,000 (other estimates up to 75,000,000)

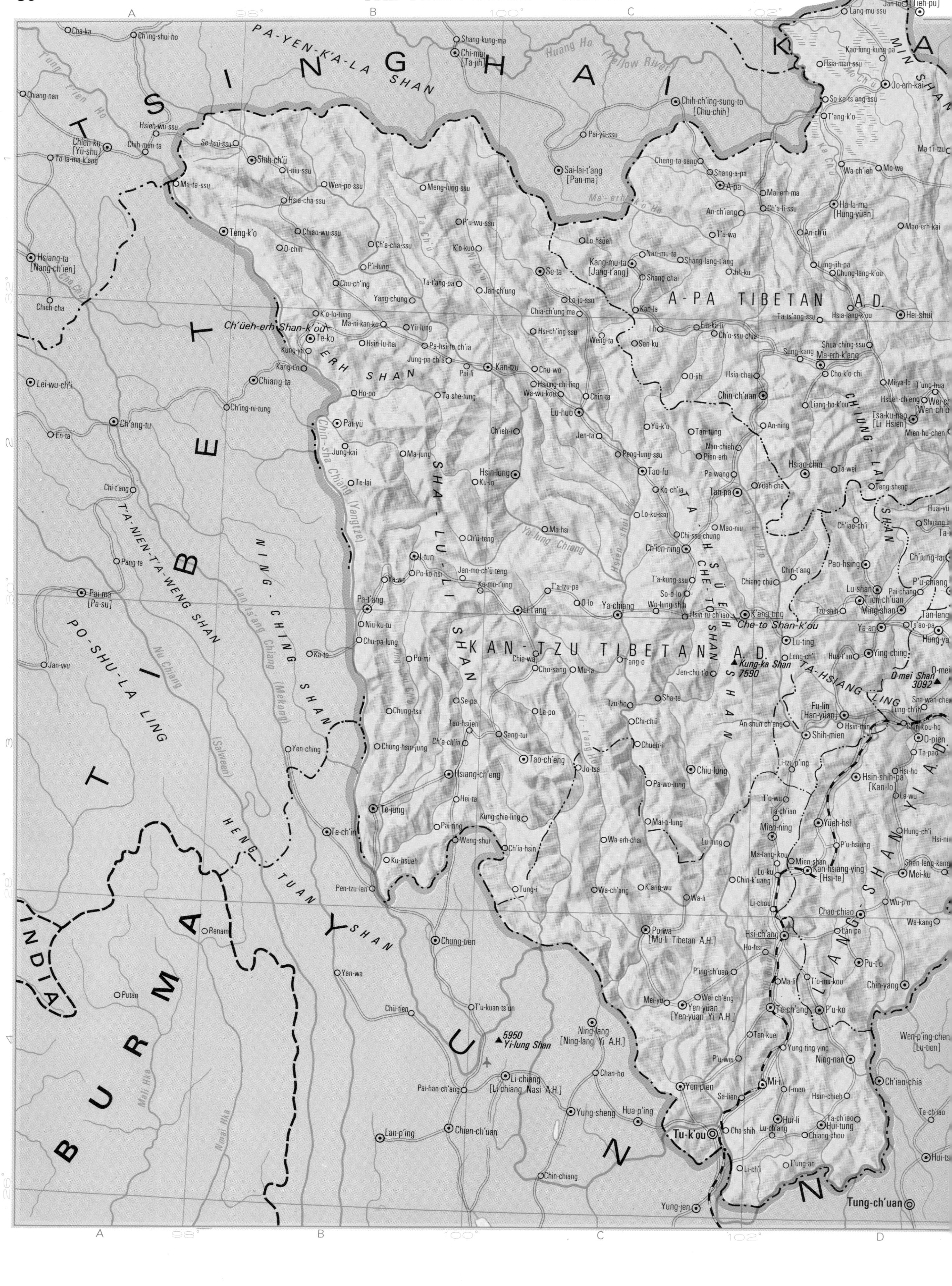

A
B
C
D
98°
100°
102°
1
2
3
4
32°
30°
28°
26°
T S I N G H A I
PA-YEN-K'A-LA SHAN
Huang Ho (Yellow River)
T'ung t'ien Ho
Cha-ka
Ch'ing-shui-ho
Chiang-nan
Hsieh-wu-ssu
Chieh-ku [Yü-shu]
Chih-men-ta
To-la-ma-k'ang
Se-hsü-ssu
Shih-ch'ü
I-niu-ssu
Ma-ta-ssu
Wen-po-ssu
Hsia-cha-ssu
Meng-lung-ssu
Teng-k'o
Chiao-wu-ssu
O-chih
Ch'a-cha-ssu
P'u-wu-ssu
K'o-kuo
Hsiang-ta [Nang-ch'ien]
Cha Ch'ü
Chieh-cha
P'i-lung
Chu-ch'ing
Ta-t'ang-pa
Jan-ch'ung
Yang-chung
Shang-kung-ma
Chi-mai [Ta-jih]
Chih-ch'ing-sung-to [Chiu-chih]
Pai-yü-ssu
Sai-lai-t'ang [Pan-ma]
Ma-erh-k'o Ho
Cheng-ta-sang
Shang-a-pa
A-pa
Mai-erh-ma
Ch'a-li-ssu
An-ch'iang
T'a-wa
Lo-hsüeh
Kang-mu-ta [Jang-t'ang]
Nan-mu-ta
Shang-lang-t'ang
Shang-chai
Jih-ku
Se-ta
Lo-jo-ssu
Chia-ch'ung-ma
Kan-la
A-PA TIBETAN A.D.
Tien-ka-ssu
Jan-to [Tieh-pu]
Lang-mu-ssu
Kao-lung-kung-pa
Hsia-man-ssu
Mo Ch'ü
Jo-erh-kai
So-ko-ts'ang-ssu
T'ang-k'o
Ka Ch'ü
MIN SHAN
Ma-t'i-tzu
Wa-ch'ieh
Mo-wa
Ha-la-ma [Hung-yüan]
An-ch'ü
Mao-erh-kai
Lung-jih-pa
Chung-lang-k'ou
Ta-ts'ang-ssu
Hsia-lang-k'ou
Hei-shui
Ch'üeh-erh Shan-k'ou
K'o-lo-tung
Ma-ni-kan-ko
Yü-lung
Te-ko
Kung-ya
Kang-t'o
Hsin-lu-hai
Pa-hsi-to-ch'ia
Jung-pa-ch'a
Pai-li
Kan-tzu
Hsi-ch'ing-ssu
Weng-ta
Chu-wo
I-li
Erh-ka-li
Ch'o-ssu-chia
San-ku
Sung-kang
Ma-erh-k'ang
Shua-ching-ssu
ERH SHAN
Chiang-ta
Lei-wu-ch'i
Ch'ing-ni-tung
Ho-po
Ta-she-tung
Hsiung-chi-ling
Wa-wu-kou
Chin-ta
O-jih
Hsia-chai
Cho-k'o-chi
Mi-ya-lo
T'ung-hua
Hsüeh-ch'eng
Wei-ch'
[Wen-ch'u]
Ch'ang-tu
En-ta
Pai-yü
Jung-kai
Lu-huo
Chin-ch'uan
Liang-ho-k'ou
Tsa-ku-nao [Li Hsien]
Mien-hu-chen
CH'IUNG-LAI SHAN
Ch'ieh-i
Jen-ta
Yü-k'o
Tan-tung
An-ning
Ma-jung
Nan-chieh
Pien-erh
Peng-lung-ssu
Chin-sha Chiang (Yangtze)
Te-lai
SHA-LU-LI SHAN
Hsin-lung
Ku-lo
Tao-fu
Pa-wang
Hsiao-chin
Ta-wei
Yüeh-cha
Teng-sheng
Chi-t'ang
T'A-NIEN-T'A-WENG SHAN
NING-CHING SHAN
Lan-ts'ang Chiang (Mekong)
Nu Chiang (Salween)
Ko-ch'ia
Tan-pa
Ta-tu Ho
TA HSÜEH SHAN
Lo-ku-ssu
Ma-hsi
Mao-niu
Chi-ssu-chung
Ch'iao-ch'i
Huai-yü
Shuang
Ch'ü-teng
Ya-lung Chiang
Hsien-shui Ho
Ch'ien-ning
Pang-ta
I-tun
Ya-wa
Po-ko-hsi
Jan-mo-ch'ü-teng
Ko-mo-t'ung
Chin-t'ang
Pao-hsing
Ch'iung-lai
P'u-chiang
Chiang-chü
T'a-kung-ssu
So-o-lo
Wo-lung-shih
Hsin-tu-ch'iao
K'ang-ting
Che-to Shan-k'ou
CHE-TO SHAN
Lu-shan
T'ien-ch'uan
Ming-shan
Pai-chang
Tzu-shih
Tan-leng
Ya-an
Ts'ao-pa
Hung-ya
Pai-ma [Pa-su]
PO-SHU-LA LING
Pa-t'ang
T'a-tzu-pa
O-lo
Ya-chiang
Li-t'ang
Niu-ku-tu
Chu-pa-lung
KAN-TZU TIBETAN A.D.
Ka-to
Po-mi
Chia-wa
Cho-sang
Mu-la
T'ang-o
Lu-ting
Leng-ch'i
Hua-t'an
Ying-ching
Kung-ka Shan 7590
Jen-chu-t'o
O-mei Shan 3092
O-mei
Jan-wu
Sha-te
TA-HSIANG LING
Sha-wan-chen
Se-pa
Tzu-ho
Chi-chü
Fu-lin [Han-yüan]
Lung-ch'ih
Chung-tsa
La-po
An-shun-ch'ang
Hsin-min
Chin-kou-ho
Tao-hsüeh
Sang-tui
Shih-mien
O-pien
Ch'a-ch'ia
Li-t'ang Ho
Ch'üeh-i
Ta-pao
Yen-ching
Chung-hsin-jung
Tao-ch'eng
Jo-tsa
Chiu-lung
Li-tzu-p'ing
Hsi-ho
Hsiang-ch'eng
Pa-wo-lung
Hsin-shih-pa [Kan-lo]
Hei-ta
Le-wu
T'o-wu
Te-jung
Kung-chia-ling
Mai-ti-lung
Ta-ch'iao
Mien-ning
Yüeh-hsi
Te-ch'in
Pai-ting
HENG-TUAN SHAN
Weng-shui
Ch'ia-hsin
Wa-erh-chai
Lu-ning
Hung-ch'i
Hsi-ni
P'u-hsiung
Ma-fang-kou
Mien-shan
Kan-hsiang-ying [Hsi-te]
Shan-leng-kang
Ku-hsüeh
Lu-ku
Chin-k'uang
Mei-ku
Pen-tzu-lan
Tung-i
Wa-ch'ang
K'ang-wu
Wa-li
LIANG SHAN YI A.D.
Li-chou
Wu-p'o
Chao-chiao
Wa-kang
Po-wa [Mu-li Tibetan A.H.]
Hsi-ch'ang
Lan-pa
Ho-hsi
Renam
INDIA
BURMA
Y U N N A N
Chung-tien
Yan-wa
P'ing-ch'uan
Ma-li
T'o-mu-kou
Pu-t'o
Chin-yang
Putao
Wai-ch'eng
Mei-yü
Yen-yüan [Yen-yuan Yi A.H.]
Te-ch'ang
P'u-ko
Chü-tien
T'u-kuan-ts'un
5950 Yi-lung Shan
Ning-lang [Ning-lang Yi A.H.]
Tan-kuei
Yung-ting-ying
Wen-p'ing-chen [Lu-tien]
Mali Hka
Nmai Hka
P'u-wei
Ning-nan
Li-chiang [Li-chiang Nasi A.H.]
Pai-han-ch'ang
Chan-ho
Yen-pien
Mi-i
I-men
Ch'iao-chia
Sa-lien
Hsin-chieh
Yung-sheng
Hua-p'ing
Hui-li
Ta-ch'iao
Hui-tung
Ta-ch'iao
Lan-p'ing
Chien-ch'uan
Tu-k'ou
Cha-shih
Lu-ch'ang
Chiang-chou
Hui-ts
Chin-chiang
Li-ch'i
T'ung-an
Yung-jen
Tung-ch'uan

SZECHWAN

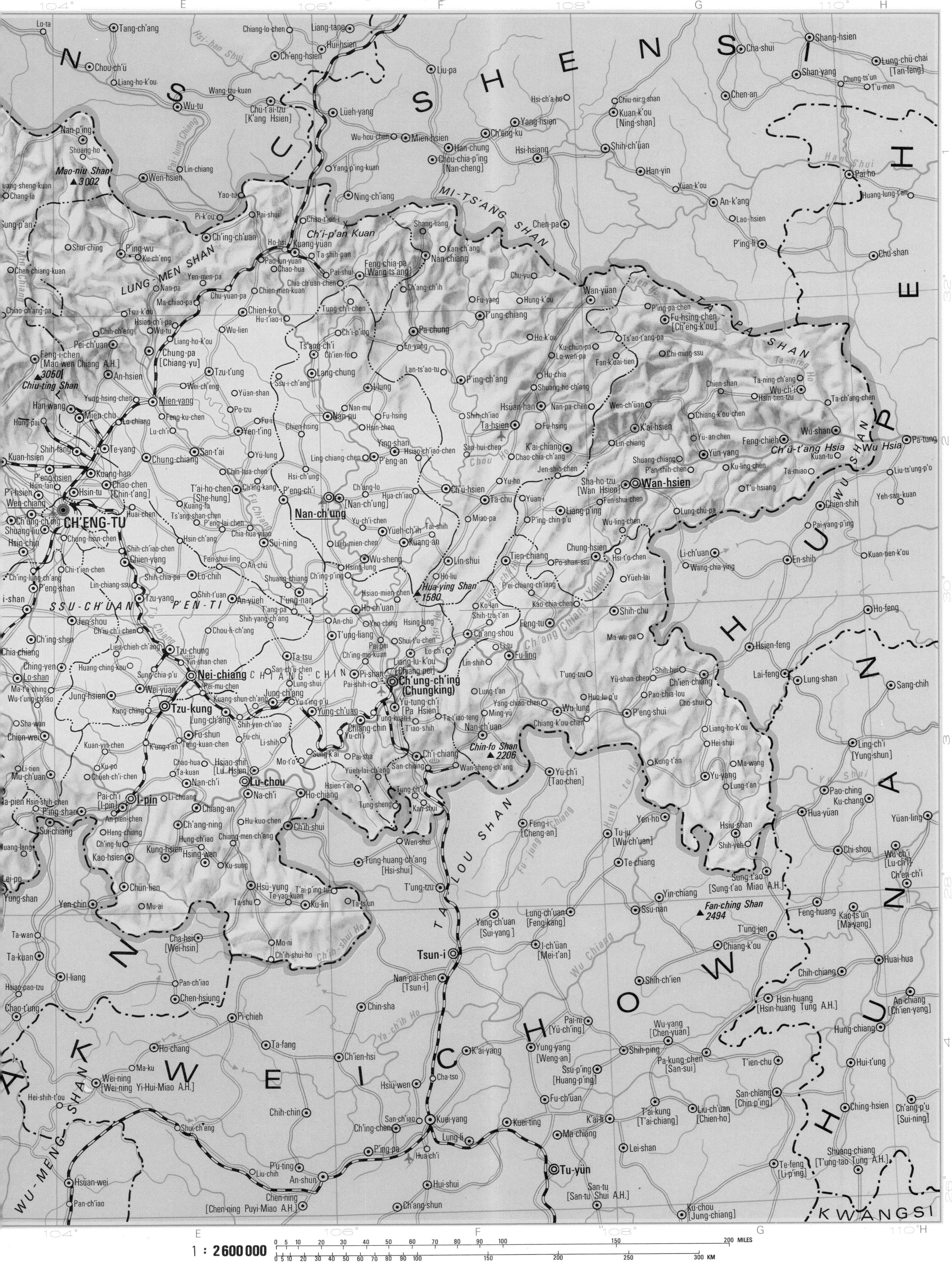

1 : 2600000

0 5 10 20 30 40 50 60 70 80 90 100 150 200 MILES

0 5 10 20 30 40 50 60 70 80 90 100 150 200 250 300 KM

SZECHWAN PROVINCE 四川省
SSU-CH'UAN SHENG

9 shih	*municipalities*
3 tzu-chih-chou	*autonomous districts*
12 ti-ch'ü	*regions*
181 hsien	*counties*
3 tzu-chih-hsien	*autonomous counties*

capital **Ch'eng-tu Shih**	E2	成都市
Ch'ung-ch'ing Shih	F3	重庆市
Ch'ang-shou Hsien	F3	长寿县
Ch'i-chiang Hsien	F3	綦江县
Pa Hsien		巴县
centre: Yü-tung-ch'i	F3	鱼洞溪
I-pin Shih	E3	宜宾市
Lu-chou Shih	E3	泸州市
Nan-ch'ung Shih	F2	南充市
Nei-chiang Shih	E3	内江市
Tu-k'ou Shih	C4	渡口市
Tzu-kung Shih	E3	自贡市
Wan-hsien Shih	G2	万县市

A-pa Tsang-tsu Tzu-chih-chou 阿坝藏族自治州
A-pa Tibetan Autonomous District

centre: Ma-erh-k'ang	D2	马尔康
A-pa Hsien	C1	阿坝县
Chin-ch'uan Hsien	D2	金川县
Hei-shui Hsien	D1	黑水县
Hsiao-chin Hsien	D2	小金县
Hung-yüan Hsien		红原县
centre: Ha-la-ma	D1	哈拉玛
Jang-t'ang Hsien		壤塘县
centre: Kang-mu-ta	C1	刚木达
Jo-erh-kai Hsien	D1	若尔盖县
Li Hsien		理县
centre: Tsa-ku-nao	D2	杂谷脑
Ma-erh-k'ang Hsien	D2	马尔康县
Mao-wen Ch'iang-tsu Tzu-chih-hsien Mao-wen Chiang Autonomous Hsien		茂汶羌族自治县
centre: Feng-i-chen	D2	凤仪镇
Nan-p'ing Hsien	E1	南坪县
Sung-p'an Hsien	D1	松潘县
Wen-ch'uan Hsien		汶川县
centre: Wei-chou	D2	威州

Chiang-chin Ti-ch'ü 江津地区

centre: Yung-ch'uan	E3	永川
Chiang-chin Hsien	F3	江津县
Chiang-pei Hsien		江北县
centre: Liang-lu-k'ou	F3	两路口
Ho-ch'uan Hsien	F2	合川县
Jung-ch'ang Hsien	E3	荣昌县
Pi-shan Hsien	F3	璧山县
Ta-tsu Hsien	E3	大足县
T'ung-liang Hsien	F3	铜梁县
Yung-ch'uan Hsien	E3	永川县

Fu-ling Ti-ch'ü 涪陵地区

Ch'ien-chiang Hsien	G3	黔江县
Feng-tu Hsien	F3	丰都县
Fu-ling Hsien	F3	涪陵县
Hsiu-shan Hsien	G3	秀山县
Nan-ch'uan Hsien	F3	南川县
P'eng-shui Hsien	G3	彭水县
Shih-chu Hsien	G3	石柱县
Tien-chiang Hsien	F2	垫江县
Wu-lung Hsien	F3	武隆县
Yu-yang Hsien	G3	酉阳县

Hsi-ch'ang Ti-ch'ü 西昌地区

Hsi-ch'ang Hsien	D4	西昌县
Hui-li Hsien	D4	会理县
Hui-tung Hsien	D4	会东县
Mien-ning Hsien	D3	冕宁县
Mi-i Hsien	D4	米易县
Mu-li Tsang-tsu Tzu-chih-hsien Mu-li Tibetan Autonomous Hsien		木里藏族自治县
centre: Po-wa	C4	博瓦
Ning-nan Hsien	D4	宁南县
Te-ch'ang Hsien	D4	德昌县
Yen-pien Hsien	C4	盐边县
Yen-yüan I-tsu Tzu-chih-hsien Yen-yüan Yi Autonomous Hsien		盐源彝族自治县
centre: Yen-yüan	C4	

I-pin Ti-ch'ü 宜宾地区

Ch'ang-ning Hsien	E3	长宁县
Chiang-an Hsien	E3	江安县
Chün-lien Hsien	E3	筠连县
Fu-shun Hsien	E3	富顺县
Ho-chiang Hsien	E3	合江县
Hsing-wen Hsien	E3	兴文县
Hsü-yung Hsien	E3	叙永县
I-pin Hsien		宜宾县
centre: Pai-ch'i	E3	柏溪
Kao Hsien		高县
centre: Kao-hsien	E3	
Ku-lin Hsien		古蔺县
Kung Hsien		珙县
centre: Kung-hsien	E3	
Lu-Hsien		泸县
centre: Hsiao-shih	E3	小市
Lung-ch'ang Hsien	E3	隆昌县
Na-ch'i Hsien	E3	纳溪县
Nan-ch'i Hsien	E3	南溪县
P'ing-shan Hsien	E3	屏山县

Kan-tzu Tsang-tsu Tzu-chih-chou 甘孜藏族自治州
Kan-tzu Tibetan Autonomous District

centre: K'ang-ting	C2	康定
Ch'ien-ning Hsien	C2	乾宁县
Chiu-lung Hsien	C3	九龙县
Hsiang-ch'eng Hsien	B3	乡城县
Hsin-lung Hsien	C2	新龙县
I-tun Hsien	B2	义敦县
K'ang-ting Hsien	C2	康定县
Kan-tzu Hsien	B2	甘孜县
Li-t'ang Hsien	C2	理塘县
Lu-huo Hsien	C2	炉霍县
Lu-ting Hsien	D3	泸定县
Pai-yü Hsien	B2	白玉县
Pa-t'ang Hsien	B2	巴塘县
Se-ta Hsien	C1	色达县
Shih-ch'ü Hsien	B1	石渠县
Tan-pa Hsien	C2	丹巴县
Tao-ch'eng Hsien	C3	稻城县
Tao-fu Hsien	C2	道孚县
Te-jung Hsien	B3	得荣县
Te-ko Hsien	B2	德格县
Teng-k'o Hsien	A1	邓柯县
Ya-chiang Hsien	C2	雅江县

Liang-shan I-tsu Tzu-chih-chou 凉山彝族自治州
Liang-shan Yi Autonomous District

centre: Chao-chiao	D3	昭觉
Chao-chiao Hsien	D3	昭觉县
Chin-yang Hsien	D4	金阳县
Hsi-te Hsien		喜德县
centre: Kan-hsiang-ying	D3	甘相营
Kan-lo Hsien		甘洛县
centre: Hsin-shih-pa	D3	新市坝
Lei-po Hsien	D3	雷波县
Ma-pien Hsien	D3	马边县
Mei-ku Hsien	D3	美姑县
O-pien Hsien	D3	峨边县
P'u-ko Hsien	D4	普格县
Pu-t'o Hsien	D4	布拖县
Yüeh-hsi Hsien	D3	越西县

Lo-shan Ti-ch'ü 乐山地区

Chia-chiang Hsien	D3	夹江县
Chien-wei Hsien	D3	犍为县
Ch'ing-shen Hsien	D3	青神县
Ching-yen Hsien	E3	井研县
Hung-ya Hsien	D3	洪雅县
Jen-shou Hsien	E3	仁寿县
Lo-shan Hsien	D3	乐山县
Mei-shan Hsien	D2	眉山县
Mu-ch'uan Hsien	D3	沐川县
O-mei Hsien	D3	峨眉县
P'eng-shan Hsien	D2	彭山县
Tan-leng Hsien	D2	丹棱县

Mien-yang Ti-ch'ü 绵阳地区

An Hsien		安县
centre: An-hsien	E2	
Chiang-yu Hsien		江油县
centre: Chung-pa	E2	中坝
Chien-ko Hsien	E1	剑阁县
Ch'ing-ch'uan Hsien	E1	青川县
Chung-chiang Hsien	E2	中江县
Kuang-yüan Hsien	E1	广元县
Mien-chu Hsien	E2	绵竹县
Mien-yang Hsien	E2	绵阳县
Pei-ch'uan Hsien	E2	北川县
P'eng-ch'i Hsien	E2	蓬溪县
P'ing-wu Hsien	E1	平武县
San-t'ai Hsien	E2	三台县
She-hung Hsien		射洪县
centre: T'ai-ho-chen	E2	太和镇
Sui-ning Hsien	E2	遂宁县
Te-yang Hsien	E2	德阳县
T'ung-nan Hsien	E2	潼南县
Tzu-t'ung Hsien	E2	梓潼县
Wang-ts'ang Hsien		旺苍县
centre: Feng-chia-pa	F1	冯家坝
Yen-t'ing Hsien	E2	盐亭县

Nan-ch'ung Ti-ch'ü 南充地区

Hsi-ch'ung Hsien	E2	西充县
I-lung Hsien	F2	仪陇县
Kuang-an Hsien	F2	广安县
Lang-chung Hsien	E2	阆中县
Nan-ch'ung Hsien		南充县
centre: not known	F2	
Nan-pu Hsien	F2	南部县
P'eng-an Hsien	F2	蓬安县
Ts'ang-ch'i Hsien	E2	苍溪县
Wu-sheng Hsien	F2	武胜县
Ying-shan Hsien	F2	营山县
Yüeh-ch'ih Hsien	F2	岳池县

Nei-chiang Ti-ch'ü 内江地区

An-yüeh Hsien	E2	安岳县
Chien-yang Hsien	E2	简阳县
Jung Hsien		荣县
centre: Jung-hsien	E3	
Lo-chih Hsien	E2	乐至县
Nei-chiang Hsien	E3	内江县
Tzu-chung Hsien	E3	资中县
Tzu-yang Hsien	E2	资阳县
Wei-yüan Hsien	E3	威远县

Ta-hsien Ti-ch'ü 达县地区

Ch'ü Hsien		渠县
centre: Ch'ü-hsien	F2	
Hsüan-han Hsien	F2	宣汉县
K'ai-chiang Hsien	F2	开江县
Lin-shui Hsien	F2	邻水县
Nan-chiang Hsien	F1	南江县
Pa-chung Hsien	F2	巴中县
P'ing-ch'ang Hsien	F2	平昌县
Ta-chu Hsien	F2	大竹县
Ta Hsien		达县
centre: Ta-hsien	F2	
T'ung-chiang Hsien	F2	通江县
Wan-yüan Hsien	G1	万源县

Wan-hsien Ti-ch'ü 万县地区

Ch'eng-k'ou Hsien		城口县
centre: Fu-hsing-chen	G2	复兴镇
Chung Hsien		忠县
centre: Chung-hsien	G2	
Feng-chieh Hsien	G2	奉节县
K'ai Hsien		开县
centre: K'ai-hsien	G2	
Liang-p'ing Hsien	F2	梁平县
Wan Hsien		万县
centre: Sha-ho-tzu	G2	沙河子
Wu-ch'i Hsien	G2	巫溪县
Wu-shan Hsien	G2	巫山县
Yün-yang Hsien	G2	云阳县

Wen-chiang Ti-ch'ü 温江地区

Chin-t'ang Hsien		金堂县
centre: Chao-chen	E2	赵镇
Ch'iung-lai Hsien	D2	邛崃县
Ch'ung-ch'ing Hsien	D2	崇庆县
Hsin-chin Hsien	D2	新津县
Hsin-tu Hsien	E2	新都县
Kuang-han Hsien	E2	广汉县
Kuan Hsien		灌县
centre: Kuan-hsien	D2	
P'eng Hsien		彭县
centre: P'eng-hsien	D2	
P'i Hsien		郫县
centre: P'i-hsien	D1	
P'u-chiang Hsien	D2	蒲江县
Shih-fang Hsien	E2	什邡县
Shuang-liu Hsien	D2	双流县
Ta-i Hsien	D2	大邑县
Wen-chiang Hsien	D2	温江县

Ya-an Ti-ch'ü 雅安地区

Han-yüan Hsien		汉源县
centre: Fu-lin	D3	富林
Lu-shan Hsien	D2	芦山县
Ming-shan Hsien	D2	名山县
Pao-hsing Hsien	D2	宝兴县
Shih-mien Hsien	D3	石棉县
T'ien-ch'üan Hsien	D2	天全县
Ya-an Hsien	D3	雅安县
Ying-ching Hsien	D3	荥经县

KWEICHOW
PROVINCE

KWEICHOW province was until recent times one of the most backward and sparsely peopled areas in China. Although a Chinese administration was set up in the area under the Han (206 BC–AD 220), the Chinese officials merely attempted to maintain some measure of control over the non-Chinese tribes which occupied the area, and Chinese penetration was confined to the north and east of the modern province. The area was provided with a provincial government and took the name Kuei-chou under the Ming (1368–1644). From the 16th century onward Chinese began to settle and farm the valleys of the eastern part of Kweichow, many of them impoverished Hakka, gradually forcing the native minority peoples out of the most fertile areas. Another wave of migration in the late 19th century brought many settlers from Hunan and Szechwan into the province in search of land. But Kweichow remained poor and backward, the communications of the province very poor, and transport costs prohibitive. When the Japanese invasion forced the Nationalist government to retreat to the south-west, the modernisation of the province was begun. Highways to the neighbouring provinces were constructed, a rail link built to Kwangsi, and some industries set up in Kuei-yang and Tsun-i. Much of this activity ceased with the end of the Second World War, and modern growth was revived only with the construction of railways in the late 1950s. Kuei-yang was connected with the Kwangsi province in 1958, with Szechwan in 1966, and with Yunnan in about 1969. Modern transport has made possible some industrial development, and the exploitation of mineral resources. Highways have also made accessible the southern and western districts.

The Kuei-yang Basin This area is centred on the valleys of the Wu Chiang and its tributaries, which have provided the main east-west route through the province. Its role as the communication centre of Kweichow has been further strengthened since the construction of railways. It has grown into the main industrial area of Kweichow, producing over two thirds of its total industrial output. The area is also well developed agriculturally. The main crops are rice and wheat in the valleys, with corn and rape-seed on upland fields. Tobacco is grown on fertile, sandy soils where irrigation is possible. The tobacco curing industry is centred at Kuei-ting.

The area has scattered coal deposits, considerable reserves of iron and, in the area north of Kuei-yang, reserves of bauxite.

Kuei-yang is the main city. The provincial capital since Ming times, it is an old-established administrative and communications centre, the nodal point of the highway system, and since the 1960s a major rail junction. Apart from temporary industrial growth through the Second World War, it had little industry apart from food processing and handicrafts before 1949. Under the first Five Year Plan it was industrialised to some degree, and its population grew from 271,000 to 504,000 between 1953–7. A large thermal generating station using local coal was built, and since then there has been much diversified industrial growth. A small iron and steel complex was established during the Great Leap Forward. A machine building industry was set up to produce electrical equipment, diesel engines, railway rolling stock and mine machinery. There is a large cement works, and a chemical industry making fertilisers. More recently a rubber tyre industry has gained importance, and Kuei-yang has become a producer of aluminium. In addition, there are still important textile, food processing, leather and paper-making industries. Kuei-yang produces 75 per cent of the province's industrial output. Its population has been recently estimated at approximately 800,000.

An-shun is the chief commercial centre of the western part of this central basin, and its importance has grown since the construction of the Kweichow–Yunnan rail link in 1969. It has some small scale oil-extraction, flour-milling and iron-working industries.

Northern Kweichow This area comprises the lower valley of the Wu Chiang, and the valleys of the Ch'ih Shui and other rivers flowing north into the Yangtze in Szechwan. It is a high plateau area, climbing northwards to the series of ranges such as the Ta-lou Shan, rising to 1,500 m and more, which form the border with Szechwan. This is the main agricultural region of Kweichow, with better developed irrigation systems than elsewhere. In the east (the Wu Chiang area) rice and wheat are the main crops, with cotton which was formerly exported to Shanghai and Canton, an important cash crop. In the northern area (the Fu-yung Chiang and Ch'ih Shui valleys) rice and sweet potatoes are the main crops, and ramie is widely grown.

Tsun-i is the main centre of this area. The area is an important producer of manganese, which is exported to the steel complex at Ch'ung-ch'ing. There is a small local iron industry, machinery making, and a large phosphate fertiliser plant. It also has a textile industry, using local cotton and ramie, and rice and flour mills.

Eastern Kweichow This is the area drained by the headwaters of the Yuan Chiang on the border of Hunan. Comparatively sparsely peopled, much of this area is occupied by Miao and Tung minority peoples. In the valleys paddy rice, wheat, rape-seed and cotton are the main crops. In the more westerly areas tobacco is widely grown and sent to be processed in Kuei-ting. There has been considerable reafforestation in this region as forestry is very important among the Miao and Tung peoples and fir, tung-oil and camellia oil are produced. Mining is also significant – the area has one of China's main sources of mercury at Wan-shan.

K'ai-li is the main town, the chief commercial centre, and has some industry: engineering, soft wood working, and newsprint production.

T'ung-jen is the chief market centre for the north of this region, with oil extraction, small fertiliser plants and agricultural implement manufacture.

Southern Kweichow This area is the drainage basin of the Hung-shui Ho which forms the border with Kwangsi. It is lower than most of Kweichow, has extensive areas of karst landscape similar to Kwangsi, and has a much warmer sub-tropical climate than the centre and north of the province.

Over half of the population are Pu-i and Miao minority peoples, who lived formerly by shifting 'slash and burn' farming, but are now mostly settled. In the valleys paddy rice is grown intensively, particularly around Tu-yün, Tu-shan and An-lung. A very important product in the extreme south-west of the province is sugar cane, which is refined at a plant in Hsing-i. The area around Tu-yün is an important producer of ramie fibre. Much of the area is densely forested, and lumbering is an important industry. Lumber is floated down the Hung-shui Ho to Kwangsi. The area is also an important producer of mercury, which is mined at Hsing-i.

Tu-yün was a minor town of about 10,000 people in the 1930s. Temporarily important as the railhead into the province after 1940, it revived after the railway was rebuilt in 1958. It has some local coalmines and a thermal power station. There is some minor industry – engineering, textiles (ramie linen), iron working and paper making.

Tu-shan is an important local market and commercial centre in the east of the region.

Western Kweichow The west of the province is a high, cold, mountainous plateau area rising to above 2,000 m, with peaks of almost 3,000 m. A remote, sparsely peopled area, it has recently been linked by rail both to Kuei-yang and to Yunnan province. It was traditionally an area where pastoral industry was important, as it has a cool climate and a short growing season, and the production of sheep, goats and horses represents about one third of all agricultural production. Agriculture in this area is comparatively recent. The main crops in the lower valleys are corn and rice, with some wheat, barley, rape-seed and beans. In the uplands the principal crops are potatoes, buckwheat and oats.

Hua-chieh is the main market and communication centre for the north-eastern part of this region, with communications with south-east Szechwan.

Shui-ch'eng is the main centre of the more southerly area bordering on Yunan. It has been connected with Kuei-yang by rail since 1969. There are important coal mines and iron mines in the vicinity. Since the coming of the railway it has largely displaced Wei-ning, further west, as the main commercial centre of this region.

National Minority Peoples Kweichow has a very complex ethnic population, which is reflected in the various autonomous administrative units. The Pu-i (Chung-chia) who inhabit much of southern Kweichow are a Thai people related to the Chuang of Kwangsi. They live interspersed with communities of Miao. They total 1,200,000 people. In the far west live the Yi (about 275,000). East of the Pu-i live the Tung and Shui, also of Thai stock. They number 700,000 and 134,000 respectively. The north-eastern border region is largely peopled by Miao, whose settlements are also found scattered all over the south of the province. They total 1,400,000. In general, the minority peoples are concentrated in the southern, eastern and western border areas of the province. Han Chinese settlement has been mainly in the centre and north, in the lowlands, leaving much of the higher land to the minority peoples.

AREA
174,000 square kilometres

POPULATION
17,000,000 (some estimates as high as 20,000,000)

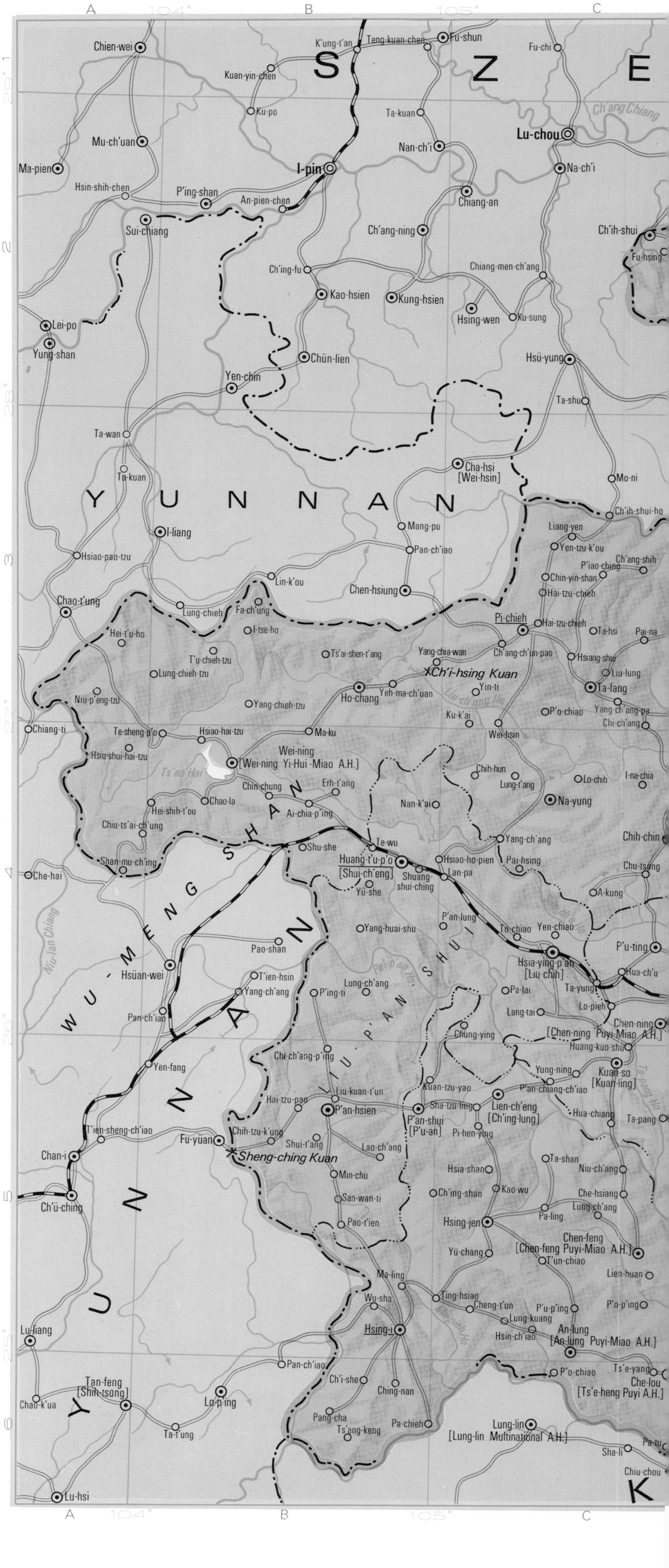
A
104°
B
105°
C
S Z E
K'ung-t'an
Teng-kuan-chen
Fu-shun
Fu-chi
Chien-wei
Kuan-yin-chen
Ch'ang Chiang
Ku-po
Ta-kuan
Lu-chou
Mu-ch'uan
Nan-ch'i
Ma-pien
I-pin
Na-ch'i
Hsin-shih-chen
P'ing-shan
An-pien-chen
Chiang-an
Sui-chiang
Ch'ang-ning
Ch'ih-shui
Fu-hsing
Chiang-men-ch'ang
Ch'ing-fu
Kao-hsien
Kung-hsien
Hsing-wen
Ku-sung
Lei-po
Yung-shan
Chün-lien
Hsü-yung
Yen-chin
Ta-shu
Ta-wan
Cha-hsi
[Wei-hsin]
Ta-kuan
Mo-ni
Y U N N A N
Ch'ih-shui-ho
Mang-pu
Liang-yen
I-liang
Yen-tzu-k'ou
Pan-ch'iao
P'iao-ching
Ch'ang-shih
Hsiao-pao-tzu
Chin-yin-shan
Lin-k'ou
Hai-tzu-chieh
Chen-hsiung
Chao-t'ung
Lung-chieh
Fa-ch'ung
Pi-chieh
Hai-tzu-chieh
I-tse-ho
Ta-hsi
Pai-na
Hei-t'u-ho
T'u-chieh-tzu
Ts'ai-shen-t'ang
Yang-chia-wan
Ch'ang-ch'un-pao
Hsiang-shui
Ch'i-hsing Kuan
Liu-lung
Lung-chieh-tzu
Yin-ti
Ta-fang
Niu-p'eng-tzu
Ho-chang
Yeh-ma-ch'uan
Liu-ch'ung Ho
Yang-chieh-tzu
P'o-chiao
Yang-ch'ang-pa
Ku-k'ai
Chi-ch'ang
Chiang-ti
Te-sheng-p'o
Hsiao-hai-tzu
Ma-ku
Wei-hsin
Hsiu-shui-hai-tzu
Wei-ning
[Wei-ning Yi-Hui-Miao A.H.]
Ts'ao Hai
Chih-hun
Lo-chih
I-na-chia
Lung-t'ang
Chin-chung
Erh-t'ang
Chao-la
Nan-k'ai
Na-yung
Hei-shih-t'ou
Ai-chia-p'ing
Chiu-ts'ai-ch'ung
Te-wu
Yang-ch'ang
Chih-chin
Shu-she
Huang-t'u-p'o
[Shui-ch'eng]
Hsiao-ho-pien
Pai-hsing
Shan-mu-ch'ing
Shuang-shui-ching
Lan-pa
Chu-tsang
Che-hai
Yu-she
A-kung
Niu-lan Chiang
P'an-lung
WU-MENG SHAN
Yang-huai-shu
To-chiao
Yen-chiao
P'u-ting
Pao-shan
Hsia-ying-p'an
[Lu-chih]
Hua-ch'u
Hsüan-wei
T'ien-hsin
Yang-ch'ang
Lung-ch'ang
P'ing-ti
Pa-lai
Ta-yung
Pei-p'an Ho
Pan-ch'iao
Lang-tai
Lo-pieh
Chen-ning
[Chen-ning Puyi-Miao A.H.]
LIU-P'AN SHUI
Chung-ying
Huang-kuo-shu
Chi-ch'ang-p'ing
Yen-fang
Yung-ning
Kuan-so
[Kuan-ling]
Kuan-tzu-yao
P'an-chiang-ch'iao
Liu-kuan-t'un
Hai-tzu-pao
Sha-tzu-ling
Lien-ch'eng
[Ch'ing-lung]
P'an-hsien
P'an-shui
[P'u-an]
Hua-chiang
Ta-pang
Pi-hen-ying
Chih-tzu-k'ung
T'ien-sheng-ch'iao
Shui-t'ang
Fu-yüan
Lao-ch'ang
Chan-i
Sheng-ching Kuan
Ta-shan
Hsia-shan
Niu-ch'ang
Min-chu
Kao-wu
San-wan-ti
Ch'ing-shan
Che-hsiang
Ch'ü-ching
Pa-ling
Lung-ch'ang
Pao-t'ien
Hsing-jen
YUN NAN
Chen-feng
[Chen-feng Puyi-Miao A.H.]
Yü-chang
T'un-chiao
Lien-huan
Ma-ling
Ting-hsiao
Wu-sha
Cheng-t'un
P'u-p'ing
P'o-p'ing
Lung-kuang
Lu-liang
Hsing-i
An-lung
Hsin-ch'iao
[An-lung Puyi-Miao A.H.]
Pan-ch'iao
Ts'e-yang
P'o-chiao
Che-lou
[Ts'e-heng Puyi A.H.]
Tan-feng
[Shih-tsung]
Ch'i-she
Ching-nan
Chao-k'ua
Lo-p'ing
Pang-cha
Lung-lin
[Lung-lin Multinational A.H.]
Pa-chieh
Ts'ang-keng
Ta-t'ung
Pa-tu
Sha-li
Chiu-chou
Lu-hsi
K

1 : 1540000

0 5 10 20 30 40 50 60 70 80 90 100 MILES

0 5 10 20 30 40 50 60 70 80 90 100 150 KM

KWEICHOW PROVINCE 贵州省
KUEI-CHOU SHENG

4 shih	*municipalities*
2 tzu-chih-chou	*autonomous districts*
6 ti-ch'ü	*regions*
70 hsien	*counties*
9 tzu-chih-hsien	*autonomous counties*

capital **Kuei-yang Shih**	D4	贵阳市
An-shun Shih	C4	安顺市
Tsun-i Shih	D3	遵义市
Tu-yün Shih	E4	都匀市

An-shun Ti-ch'ü		安顺地区
An-shun Hsien	C4	安顺县
Chen-ning Pu-i-tsu Miao-tsu Tzu-chih-hsien Chen-ning Puyi-Miao Autonomous Hsien		镇宁布依族苗族 自治县
centre: Chen-ning	C4	
Ch'ing-chen Hsien	D4	清镇县
Hsi-feng Hsien	D3	息烽县
Hsiu-wen Hsien	D4	修文县
K'ai-yang Hsien	D3	开阳县
Kuan-ling Hsien		关岭县
centre: Kuan-so	C5	关索
P'ing-pa Hsien	D4	平坝县
P'u-ting Hsien	C4	普定县
Tzu-yün Miao-tsu Pu-i-tsu Tzu-chih-hsien Tzu-yün Miao-Puyi Autonomous Hsien		紫云苗族布依族 自治县
centre: Tzu-yün	D5	

Ch'ien-nan Pu-i-tsu Miao-tsu Tzu-chih-chou South Kweichow Puyi-Miao Autonomous District		黔南布依族苗族 自治州
centre: Tu-yün	E4	都匀
Ch'ang-shun Hsien	D4	长顺县
Fu-ch'üan Hsien	E4	福泉县
Hui-shui Hsien	D4	惠水县
Kuei-ting Hsien	E4	贵定县
Li-po Hsien	E5	荔波县
Lo-tien Hsien		罗甸县
centre: Lung-p'ing	D5	龙坪
Lung-li Hsien	D4	龙里县
P'ing-t'ang Hsien		平塘县
centre: P'ing-hu	E5	平湖
San-tu Shui-tsu Tzu-chih-hsien San-tu Shui Autonomous Hsien		三都水族自治县
centre: San-tu	E4	
Tu-shan Hsien	E5	独山县
Tu-yün Hsien	E4	都匀县
Weng-an Hsien		瓮安县
centre: Yung-yang	E3	雍阳

Ch'ien-tung-nan Miao-tsu T'ung-tsu Tzu-chih-chou Southeast Kweichow Miao-Tung Autonomous District		黔东南苗族侗族 自治州
centre: K'ai-li	E4	凯里
Chen-yüan Hsien		镇远县
centre: Wu-yang	F3	㵲阳
Chien-ho Hsien		剑河县
centre: Liu-ch'uan	F4	柳川
Chin-p'ing Hsien		锦屏县
centre: San-chiang	G4	三江
Huang-p'ing Hsien		黄平县
centre: Ssu-p'ing	E4	四屏
Jung-chiang Hsien		榕江县
centre: Ku-chou	F5	古州
K'ai-li Hsien	E4	凯里县
Lei-shan Hsien	F4	雷山县
Li-p'ing Hsien		黎平县
centre: Te-feng	G4	德凤
Ma-chiang Hsien	E4	麻江县
San-sui Hsien		三穗县
centre: Pa-kung-chen	F4	八弓镇
Shih-ping Hsien	F3	施秉县
T'ai-chiang Hsien		台江县
centre: T'ai-kung	E4	台拱
Tan-chai Hsien		丹寨县
centre: Lung-ch'üan	E4	龙泉
T'ien-chu Hsien	G4	天柱县
Ts'en-kung Hsien		岑巩县
centre: Ssu-yang	F3	思旸
Ts'ung-chiang Hsien		从江县
centre: Ping-mei	F5	丙妹

Hsing-i Ti-ch'ü		兴义地区
An-lung Pu-i-tsu Miao-tsu Tzu-chih-hsien An-lung Puyi-Miao Autonomous Hsien		安龙布依族苗族 自治县
centre: An-lung	C5	
Cheng-feng Pu-i-tsu Miao-tsu Tzu-chih-hsien Chen-feng Puyi-Miao Autonomous Hsien		贞丰布依族苗族 自治县
centre: Chen-feng	C5	
Ch'ing-lung Hsien		晴隆县
centre: Lien-ch'eng	C5	莲城
Hsing-i Hsien	B5	兴义县
Hsing-jen Hsien	C5	兴仁县
P'u-an Hsien		普安县
centre: P'an-shui	B5	盘水
Ts'e-heng Pu-i-tsu Tzu-chih-hsien Ts'e-heng Puyi Autonomous Hsien		册亨布依族自治县
centre: Che-lou	C6	者楼
Wang-mo Pu-i-tsu Miao-tsu Tzu-chih-hsien Wang-mo Puyi-Miao Autonomous Hsien		望谟布依族苗族 自治县
centre: Fu-hsing	D5	复兴

Liu-p'an-shui Ti'ch'ü		六盘水地区
centre: Huang-t'u-p'o	B4	黄土坡
Liu-chih Hsien		六枝县
centre: Hsia-ying-p'an	C4	下营盘
P'an Hsien		盘县
centre: P'an-hsien	B5	
Shui-ch'eng Hsien		水城县
centre: Huang-t'u-p'o	B4	黄土坡

Pi-chieh Ti-ch'ü		毕节地区
Ch'ien-hsi Hsien	D3	黔西县
Chih-chin Hsien	C4	织金县
Chin-sha Hsien	D3	金沙县
Ho-chang Hsien	B3	赫章县
Na-yung Hsien	C4	纳雍县
Pi-chieh Hsien	C3	毕节县
Ta-fang Hsien	C3	大方县
Wei-ning I-tsu Hui-tsu Miao-tsu Tzu-chih-hsien Wei-ning Yi-Hui-Miao Autonomous Hsien		威宁彝族回族苗族 自治县
centre: Wei-ning	B4	

Tsun-i Ti-ch'ü		遵义地区
Cheng-an Hsien		正安县
centre: Feng-i	E2	凤仪
Ch'ih-shui Hsien	C2	赤水县
Feng-kang Hsien		凤冈县
centre: Lung-ch'üan	E3	龙泉
Hsi-shui Hsien		习水县
centre: Tung-huang-ch'ang	D2	东皇场
Jen-huai Hsien		仁怀县
centre: Chung-shu	D3	中枢
Mei-t'an Hsien		湄潭县
centre: I-ch'üan	E3	义泉
Sui-yang Hsien		绥阳县
centre: Yang-ch'uan	E3	洋川
Tao-chen Hsien		道镇县
centre: Yü-ch'i	E2	玉溪
Tsun-i Hsien		遵义县
centre: Nan-pai-chen	D3	南白镇
T'ung-tzu Hsien	D2	桐梓县
Wu-ch'uan Hsien		务川县
centre: Tu-ju	F2	都濡
Yü-ch'ing Hsien		余庆县
centre: Pai-ni	E3	白泥

T'ung-jen Ti-ch'ü		铜仁地区
Chiang-k'ou Hsien	F3	江口县
Shih-ch'ien Hsien	F3	石阡县
Ssu-nan Hsien	F3	思南县
Sung-t'ao Miao-tsu Tzu-chih-hsien Sung-t'ao Miao Autonomous Hsien		松桃苗族自治县
centre: Sung-t'ao	G2	
Te-chiang Hsien	F2	德江县
T'ung-jen Hsien	G3	铜仁县
Wan-shan Hsien	G3	万山县
Yen-ho Hsien	F2	沿河县
Yin-chiang Hsien	F2	印江县
Yü-p'ing Hsien	F3	玉屏县

YUNNAN
PROVINCE

YUNNAN, the large province occupying the south-west of China proper, became an integrated part of China at a comparatively late stage. Under the Han (206BC–AD220) the kingdom of Tien, in the area of modern K'un-ming, came under Chinese suzerainty, but Chinese control, never very strong, soon lapsed. The area was populated by a large number of non-Chinese aboriginal peoples, without any strong political organisation. In the 8th century the area was dominated by the powerful Nan-chao state, centred on Ta-li. This kingdom became very powerful, and for a while exerted great influence in parts of northern Burma and Thailand and north-western Vietnam. After it fell at the beginning of the 10th century, its place was taken by another independent state, the Ta-li kingdom. The area was finally incorporated into China under the Mongol Yüan dynasty in the 13th century. It remained a frontier area, however, with scattered Chinese garrisons and settlements in the valleys and intermontane basins living beside a very mixed aboriginal population which occupied the uplands. In the 17th and 18th centuries Yunnan became an important source of copper, but this trade died out in the mid-19th century. At this time the province was much disrupted by rebellions of the Chinese Moslem (Hui) population (1855–73), and by tribal risings. The province provided a great deal of opium in the 19th century, a trade which was encouraged as a source of revenue by the war-lords who controlled the province in the early republican period. Its modern development eventually began with the retreat of the government into the south-west during the war with Japan (1937–45). A highway system was built giving the province access to Kweichow and Szechwan, and to northern Burma, and many Chinese refugees moved into the province. After 1949 the Communist government further developed the highway system, and began to develop the railways. The French, who claimed Yunnan as part of their 'sphere of influence', built a first railway from Haiphong to K'un-ming early in the century. This was rebuilt after being destroyed during the war, and in 1969 K'un-ming was connected by rail with Kuei-yang, and with the main Chinese railway network. A direct rail link with Szechwan is also planned.

The whole province is situated on the high south-western plateau, at altitudes of 1,300 m and above, rising towards the west and the north. The plateau is deeply divided by river valleys, and by occasional low-lying basins, the most notable of which are those of the T'ien-ch'ih lake south of K'un-ming, and the Ta-li basin in the west. The western part of Yunnan is occupied by extremely high north-south mountain ranges separated by the deep and inaccessible valleys of the upper Salween, Mekong and Yangtze. Here peaks reach over 5,000 m. The climate is wet, with 750 mm of rain almost everywhere in the province, and as much as 1,750 mm in the extreme south-west. The winters are dry, almost all the rain falling between May and October. Temperatures are much modified by the great altitudes. Winter averages in the K'un-ming area are about 11°C (52°F), and the summers are cool at about 23°C (73°F).

The plateau is mostly covered with rich forest, zoned by altitude. Conifers predominate. Only about 5 per cent of the area is actually under cultivation.

North-eastern Yunnan This is the longest settled, most populous part of Yunnan, with a large proportion of the province's cultivated land, concentrated in the north-eastern plains along the Chin-sha (upper Yangtze) river, and in the lake basins around K'un-ming, where there are considerable areas of flat, cultivable land. The main crops are rice, wheat, corn (especially in the north-east) and rape-seed. Some cotton is grown around K'un-ming, tobacco is a very important cash crop everywhere, and some sugar cane is planted. Since 1949 great efforts have been made to increase productivity by irrigation works, by introducing new types of rice and by terracing hill-slopes. Pigs and sheep are reared in the mountainous areas.

Tung-ch'uan is the centre of Yunnan's copper industry. Very important in the 17th and 18th centuries, the mines in northern Yunnan were revived during the Second World War, and extended after 1954. Ore is smelted in K'un-ming.

The area also has important reserves of iron ore, which are mined at Wu-ting north-west of K'un-ming; and of coal, which is mined at I-p'ing-lang, west of K'un-ming.

K'un-ming is the provincial capital, and by far its largest city and cultural and industrial centre. Traditionally a provincial administrative centre, with about 85,000 people in 1910, its modern growth began with the construction by the French of a narrow-gauge railway to Haiphong in 1910. It then became a prosperous commercial city. Industrial growth came between 1939–45, when the government was removed to western China, and many industrial plants, banks, and businesses moved to K'un-ming from the coastal provinces. After 1940 it flourished as the terminus of the Burma Road, and of the air route to India. It rapidly grew into a large city. Its population, 147,000 in 1936, doubled by 1945 to 300,000. A temporary setback followed the end of the war, and the return of many enterprises to the east. But under the Communist regime a deliberate effort was made to build it up as an industrial base for the south-west. It has become a major producer of copper, lead and zinc. An iron and steel works has been built in nearby An-ning. K'un-ming produces machine-tools, electrical equipment, and since 1969, trucks. There are large chemical, fertiliser and cement plants. It has both hydro-electric and thermal power plants. The population of K'un-ming was estimated to be 900,000 in 1958.

The Ko-chiu region This occupies the south-east of the province. It is comparatively low-lying, at about 1,000–1,500 m, an area of limestone mountains and karst landscape similar to neighbouring parts of Kweichow and Kwangsi. The climate is temperate all year round and there is heavy rainfall, ranging from 1,200 mm in the north to 1,800 mm in the south-west. The valleys have a frost-free sub-tropical climate. Agriculture is rather ill-developed and there is little irrigated land. The main crops are rice and corn, with sugar cane grown on wet lowlands, and peanuts on dry upland fields. There is considerable timber, tea-oil and tung-oil production.

Ko-chiu is China's most important tin-mining centre producing over 90 per cent of the country's tin. Tin has been mined here since the late 18th century, but modern production began with the building of the railway to Haiphong. Before the Second World war the tin was exported to refineries in Hong Kong. During the 1950s the mines were expanded and refineries built on the spot. Lead is also produced locally, and some chemicals.

K'ai-yüan is the main transportation and commercial centre of the area. It also has important coal mines nearby at Hsiao-lung-tan, which feed a thermal generating station producing power for Ko-chiu.

North-west Yunnan This is the highest and most rugged part of the province, much of it above 3,000 m, an area of high mountain ranges divided by deep inaccessible valleys. There is much natural grassland on the higher slopes above the tree-line. The population is sparse. Cultivation is concentrated on the flat lands around lake Erh Hai and in the river valleys of the north and south-east. Rice and winter wheat are widely grown. Cotton is an important cash crop, and great efforts have been made to improve the crop strains. Sugar cane is grown in low, irrigated land. The area is also an important producer of tea, which was first introduced to the Ta-li area in the late 19th century. In the north-western uplands ranching is important and large flocks of cattle, sheep and yaks are reared by the Tibetan, Pai, Li-su, and I minority peoples. The area around Erh Hai is a famous dairy-farming district, producing large quantities of dried milk products. Forestry is also important.

Hsia-kuan is the area's major city, which has replaced nearby Ta-li, the traditional centre of the region, since the construction of the Burma Road. It is a major market for tea, cotton and sugar, and has various industries processing agricultural products.

South-west Yunnan This region is much lower-lying. Apart from mountain ranges such as the Ai-lao and Wu-liang, much of it is below 1,500 m. It is also much hotter. Areas below 1,000 m are virtually frost-free all the year. Rainfall is heavy, from 1,250–1,750 mm, 90 per cent of it falling between May and October. Agriculture is confined to the river valleys, and is rather primitive. The most important crops are rice, glutinous rice, corn, sweet potatoes, with some barley and soy beans. Tea is quite an important product, and its cultivation has a very long history. Most of it is grown by minority peoples.

Yün-ching-hung (Ching-hung) is the chief town of the south-west and the main political centre for the Tai peoples. The town has been linked to K'un-ming by a highway since 1953, and has some minor industry, but is mainly a market and commercial centre for the area.

Ssu-mao was opened up to foreign trade in the last years of the 19th century, and was a base for French enterprise in Yunnan. It fell into decay however, and was a ghost-town by 1949, although it has now recovered, and is again a regional town of some importance.

P'u-erh was the traditional centre of the tea trade.

Minority Peoples Yunnan has the most varied ethnic population in China. In the north-east the chief group are the I (Lolo, No-su). In the north-west there are a variety of Tibeto-Burman peoples, the Pai, I, Li-su, Na-si etc. In the north-east are communities of I, and of Chinese Moslems. The south-west is particularly complex, with Tibeto-Burman Hani, Lahu, and Tuchia; Tai peoples such as the T'ung and Pu-yi, and Mon-khmer peoples like the Puman and Kawa. The Ko-chiu area has many Hani, I, Chinese Moslems, Tai, and Miao and Yao tribes. There are altogether 28 different nationalities in Yunnan, totalling some 7 million persons.

AREA
380,000 square kilometres

POPULATION
20,510,000 (other estimates up to 24,000,000)

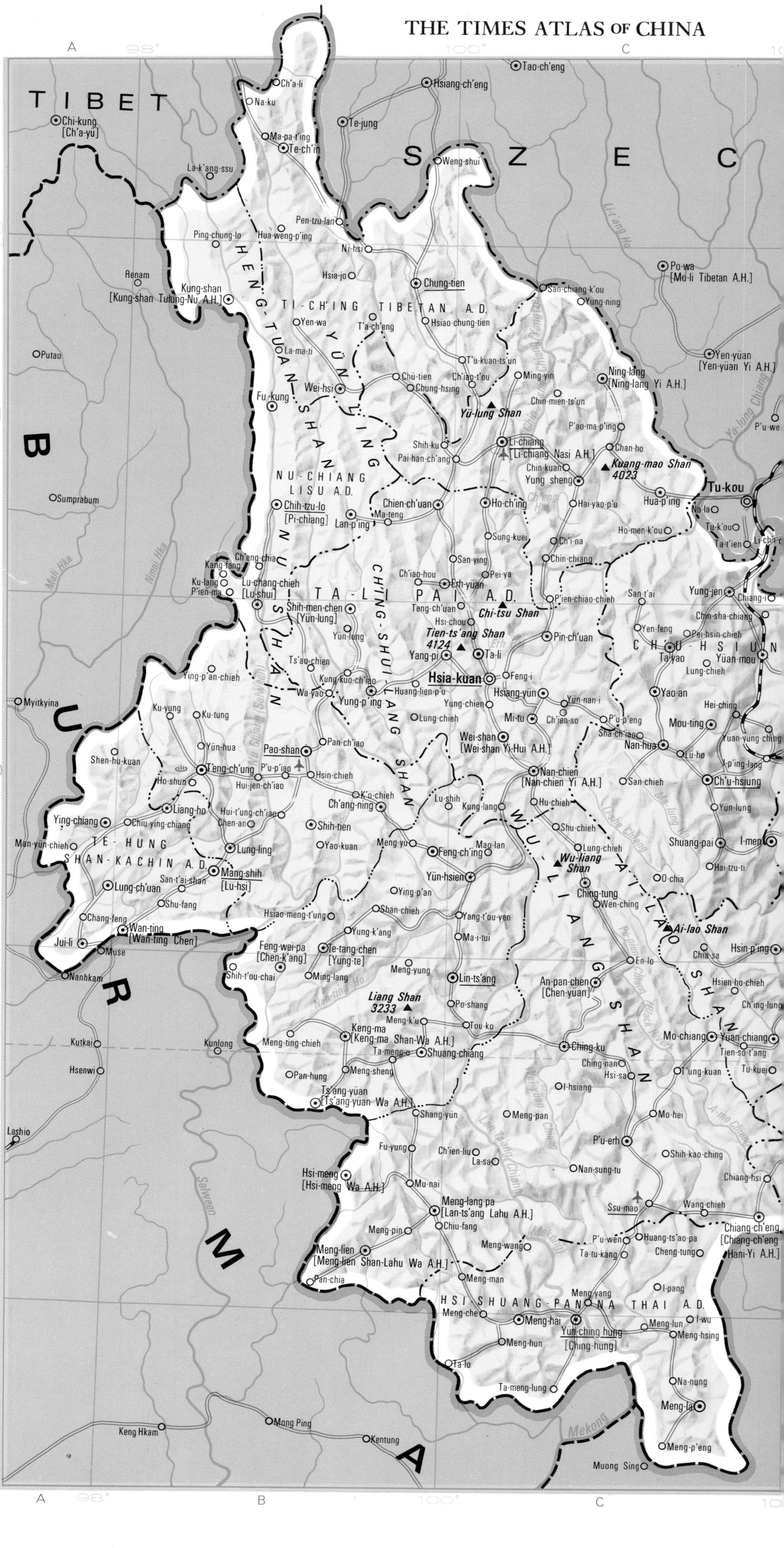
TIBET
SZECH
BURMA
Chi-kung
[Ch'a-yü]
Ch'a-li
Na-ku
Hsiang-ch'eng
Tao-ch'eng
Te-jung
Ma-pa-t'ing
Te-ch'in
La-k'ang-ssu
Weng-shui
Pen-tzu-lan
Ping-chung-lo
Hua-weng-p'ing
Ni-hsi
Renam
Hsia-jo
Chung-tien
San-chiang-k'ou
Yung-ning
Po-wa
[Mu-li Tibetan A.H.]
Kung-shan
[Kung-shan Tulung-Nu A.H.]
TI-CH'ING TIBETAN A.D.
HENG-TUAN-SHAN
YÜN-LING
Hsiao-chung-tien
Yen-wa
T'a-ch'eng
La-ma-ti
Putao
T'u-kuan-ts'un
Yen-yüan
[Yen-yüan Yi A.H.]
Chü-tien
Ch'iao-t'ou
Ming-yin
Ning-lang
[Ning-lang Yi A.H.]
Wei-hsi
Chung-hsing
Chin-mien-ts'un
Fu-kung
Yü-lung Shan
P'ao-ma-p'ing
P'u-wei
Shih-ku
Li-chiang
[Li-chiang Nasi A.H.]
Chan-ho
Pai-han-ch'ang
Chin-kuan
Kuang-mao Shan
4023
NU-CHIANG
LISU A.D.
Yung sheng
Tu-kou
Sumprabum
Chih-tzu-lo
[Pi-chiang]
Chien-ch'uan
Ho-ch'ing
Hai-yao-p'u
Hua-p'ing
Na-la
Lan-p'ing
Ma-teng
Tu-k'ou
Sung-kuei
Ho-men-k'ou
Ch'i-na
Ta-t'ien
Ch'eng-chia
San-ying
Chin-chiang
Kang-fang
Mali Hka
Nmai Hka
Ku-lang
Lu-chang-chieh
Ch'iao-hou
Pei-ya
P'ien-ma
[Lu-shui]
Erh-yüan
TA-LI PAI A.D.
Yung-jen
San-t'ai
Shih-men-chen
[Yün-lung]
Teng-ch'uan
P'ien-chiao-chieh
Chiang-i
Hsi-chou
Chi-tsu Shan
Chin-sha-chiang
Yün-lung
Tien-ts'ang Shan
4124
Pin-ch'uan
Yen-feng
Pei-hsin-chieh
Ts'ao-chien
Yang-pi
Ta-li
CH'U-HSIUNG
Ta-yao
Yüan-mou
Ying-p'an-chieh
Kung-kuo-ch'iao
Hsia-kuan
Feng-i
Lung-chieh
Huang-lien-p'u
Myitkyina
Wa-yao
Yung-p'ing
Hsiang-yün
Yao-an
Yung-chien
Yün-nan-i
Hei-ching
Ku-yung
Ku-tung
Lung-chieh
Mi-tu
Ch'ien-so
P'u-p'eng
Mou-ting
Sha-ch'iao
Yüan-yung-ching
Yün-hua
Pan-ch'iao
Wei-shan
[Wei-shan Yi-Hui A.H.]
Nan-hua
Lü-ho
Shen-hu-kuan
Pao-shan
I-p'ing-lang
T'eng-ch'ung
P'u-p'iao
Hsin-chieh
Nan-chien
[Nan-chien Yi A.H.]
Ch'u-hsiung
Ho-shun
Hui-jen-ch'iao
San-chieh
K'o-chieh
Lu-shih
Hu-chieh
Liang-ho
Hui-t'ung-ch'iao
Ch'ang-ning
Kung-lang
Yün-lung
Chen-an
Ying-chiang
Chiu-ying-chiang
Shih-tien
Shu-chieh
TE-HUNG
Meng-yu
Mao-lan
Shuang-pai
I-men
SHAN-KACHIN A.D.
Man-yün-chieh
Yao-kuan
Lung-chieh
Lung-ling
Feng-ch'ing
Wu-liang Shan
Hai-tzu-ti
San-t'ai-shan
Mang-shih
[Lu-hsi]
Yün-hsien
Lung-ch'uan
Ch'ing-tung
O-chia
Ying-p'an
Wen-ching
Shu-fang
Shan-chieh
Chang-feng
Hsiao-meng-t'ung
Yang-t'ou-yen
Wan-ting
[Wan-ting Chen]
Ai-lao Shan
Yung-k'ang
Ma-i-tui
Jui-li
Muse
Feng-wei-pa
[Chen-k'ang]
Te-tang-chen
[Yung-te]
Chia-sa
Hsin-p'ing
En-lo
Nanhkam
Shih-t'ou-chai
Ming-lang
Meng-yung
Lin-ts'ang
An-pan-chen
[Chen-yüan]
Hsien-ho-chieh
Liang Shan
3233
Po-shang
Ch'ing-lung
Meng-k'u
Tou-ko
Keng-ma
[Keng-ma Shan-Wa A.H.]
Meng-ting-chieh
Mo-chiang
Yüan-chiang
Kutkai
Kunlong
Ta-meng-o
Shuang-chiang
Ching-ku
Tien-so-t'ang
Ching-nan
Hsi-sa
Hsenwi
Meng-sheng
T'ung-kuan
Tu-kuei
Pan-hung
I-hsiang
Ts'ang-yüan
[Ts'ang-yüan Wa A.H.]
Shang-yün
Meng-pan
Mo-hei
Lashio
Fu-yung
Ch'ien-liu
P'u-erh
La-sa
Shih-kao-ching
Hsi-meng
[Hsi-meng Wa A.H.]
Nan-sung-tu
Chiang-hsi
Salween
Mu-nai
Meng-lang-pa
[Lan-ts'ang Lahu A.H.]
Ssu-mao
Wang-chieh
Meng-pin
Chiu-fang
Chiang-ch'eng
[Chiang-ch'eng
Hani-Yi A.H.]
P'u-wen
Huang-ts'ao-pa
Meng-wang
Cheng-tung
Meng-lien
[Meng-lien Shan-Lahu Wa A.H.]
Ta-tu-kang
Pan-chia
Meng-man
I-pang
Meng-yang
HSI-SHUANG-PAN-NA THAI A.D.
Meng-che
Meng-hai
Yün-ching hung
[Ching-hung]
Meng-lun
I-wu
Meng-hsing
Meng-hun
Ta-lo
Na-nung
Ta-meng-lung
Meng-la
Keng Hkam
Mong Ping
Kentung
Mekong
Meng-p'eng
Muong Sing
A
B
C
98°
100°
1
2
3
4
5
28°
26°
24°
22°

1 : 2600000

0 5 10 20 30 40 50 60 70 80 90 100 150 200 MILES

0 5 10 20 30 40 50 60 70 80 90 100 150 200 250 300 KM

YUNNAN PROVINCE 云南省
YÜN-NAN SHENG

4 shih — *municipalities*
8 tzu-chih-chou — *autonomous districts*
7 ti-ch'ü — *regions*
106 hsien — *counties*
15 tzu-chih-hsien — *autonomous counties*
1 chen — *administrative town*

capital **K'un-ming Shih** D3 昆明市
An-ning Hsien D3 安宁县
Ch'eng-kung Hsien D3 呈贡县
Chin-ning Hsien D3 晋宁县
Fu-min Hsien D3 富民县
Hsia-kuan Shih C3 下关市
Ko-chiu Shih D4 个旧市
Tung-ch'uan Shih D2 东川市

Chao-t'ung Ti-ch'ü 昭通地区
Chao-t'ung Hsien D2 昭通县
Chen-hsiung Hsien E2 镇雄县
Ch'iao-chia Hsien D2 巧家县
I-liang Hsien E2 彝良县
Lu-tien Hsien 鲁甸县
centre: Wen-p'ing-chen D2 文屏镇
Sui-chiang Hsien D1 绥江县
Ta-kuan Hsien D2 大关县
Wei-hsin Hsien 威信县
centre: Cha-hsi E2 扎西
Yen-chin Hsien E1 盐津县
Yung-shan Hsien D1 永善县

Ch'ü-ching Ti-ch'ü 曲靖地区
Chan-i Hsien D3 沾益县
Ch'ü-ching Hsien D3 曲靖县
Fu-yüan Hsien E3 富源县
Hsüan-wei Hsien E2 宣威县
Hsün-tien Hsien D3 寻甸县
Hui-tse Hsien D2 会泽县
I-liang Hsien D3 宜良县
Lo-p'ing Hsien E3 罗平县
Lu-liang Hsien D3 陆良县
Lu-nan I-tsu Tzu-chih-hsien 路南彝族自治县
Lu-nan Yi Autonomous Hsien
centre: Lu-nan D3
Ma-lung Hsien 马龙县
centre: T'ung-ch'üan-chen D3 通泉镇
Shih-tsung Hsien 师宗县
centre: Tan-feng D3 丹凤
Sung-ming Hsien D3 嵩明县

Ch'u-hsiung I-tsu Tzu-chih-chou 楚雄彝族自治州
Ch'u-hsiung Yi Autonomous District
Ch'u-hsiung Hsien C3 楚雄县
Lu-ch'üan Hsien D3 禄劝县
Lu-feng Hsien D3 禄丰县
Mou-ting Hsien C3 牟定县
Nan-hua Hsien C3 南华县
Shuang-pai Hsien C3 双柏县
Ta-yao Hsien C3 大姚县
Wu-ting Hsien D3 武定县
Yao-an Hsien C3 姚安县
Yüan-mou Hsien C3 元谋县
Yung-jen Hsien C2 永仁县

Hsi-shuang-pan-na T'ai-tsu Tzu-chih-chou 西双版纳傣族自治州
Hsi-shuang-pan-na Thai Autonomous District
centre: Yün-ching-hung C5 允景洪
Ching-hung Hsien 景洪县
centre: Yün-ching-hung C5 允景洪
Meng-hai Hsien C5 勐海县
Meng-la Hsien C5 勐腊县

Hung-ho Ha-ni-tsu I-tsu Tzu-chih-chou 红河哈尼族彝族自治州
Hung-ho Hani-Yi Autonomous District
centre: Ko-chiu D4 个旧
Chien-shui Hsien D4 建水县
Chin-p'ing Hsien D4 金平县
Ho-k'ou Yao-tsu Tzu-chih-hsien 河口瑶族自治县
Ho-k'ou Yao Autonomous Hsien
centre: Ho-k'ou D4
Hung-ho Hsien D4 红河县
K'ai-yüan Hsien D4 开远县
Lü-ch'un Hsien D4 绿春县
Lu-hsi Hsien D3 沪西县
Meng-tzu Hsien D4 蒙自县
Mi-le Hsien D3 弥勒县
P'ing-pien Miao-tsu Tzu-chih-hsien 屏边苗族自治县
P'ing-pien Miao Autonomous Hsien
centre: P'ing-pien D4
Shih-p'ing Hsien D4 石屏县
Yüan-yang Hsien D4 元阳县

Li-chiang Ti-ch'ü 丽江地区
Hua-p'ing Hsien C2 华坪县
Li-chiang Na-hsi-tsu Tzu-chih-hsien 丽江纳西族自治县
Li-chiang Nasi Autonomous Hsien
centre: Li-chiang C2
Ning-lang I-tsu Tzu-chih-hsien 宁蒗彝族自治县
Ning-lang Yi Autonomous Hsien
centre: Ning-lang C2
Yung-sheng Hsien C2 永胜县

Lin-ts'ang Ti-ch'ü 临沧地区
Chen-k'ang Hsien 镇康县
centre: Feng-wei-pa B4 凤尾坝
Feng-ch'ing Hsien B3 凤庆县
Keng-ma T'ai-tsu Wa-tsu Tzu-chih-hsien 耿马傣族佤族自治县
Keng-ma Shan-Wa Autonomous Hsien
centre: Keng-ma B4
Lin-ts'ang Hsien C4 临沧县
Shuang-chiang Hsien B4 双江县
Ts'ang-yüan Wa-tsu Tzu-chih-hsien 沧源佤族自治县
Ts'ang-yüan Wa Autonomous Hsien
centre: Ts'ang-yüan B4
Yung-te Hsien 永德县
centre: Te-tang-chen B3 德党镇
Yün Hsien 云县
centre: Yün-hsien C3

Nu-chiang Li-su-tsu Tzu-chih-chou 怒江傈僳族自治州
Nu-chiang Lisu Autonomous District
centre: Chih-tzu-lo B2 知子罗
Fu-kung Hsien B2 福贡县
Kung-shan Tu-lung-tsu Nu-tsu Tzu-chih-hsien 贡山独龙族怒族自治县
Kung-shan Tulung-Nu Autonomous Hsien
centre: Kung-shan B2
Lan-p'ing Hsien B2 兰坪县
Lu-shui Hsien 泸水县
centre: Lu-chang-chieh B3 鲁掌街
Pi-chiang Hsien 碧江县
centre: Chih-tzu-lo B2 知子罗

Pao-shan Ti-ch'ü 保山地区
Ch'ang-ning Hsien B3 昌宁县
Lung-ling Hsien B3 龙陵县
Pao-shan Hsien B3 保山县
Shih-tien Hsien B3 施甸县
T'eng-ch'ung Hsien B3 腾冲县

Ssu-mao Ti-ch'ü 思茅地区
Chen-yüan Hsien 镇源县
centre: An-pan-chen C4 按板镇
Chiang-ch'eng Ha-ni-tsu I-tsu Tzu-chih-hsien 江城哈尼族彝族自治县
Chiang-ch'eng Hani-Yi Autonomous Hsien
centre: Chiang-ch'eng C4
Ching-ku Hsien C4 景谷县
Ching-tung Hsien C3 景东县
Hsi-meng Wa-tsu Tzu-chih-hsien 西盟佤族自治县
Hsi-meng Wa Autonomous Hsien
centre: Hsi-meng B4
Lan-ts'ang La-hu-tsu Tzu-chih-hsien 澜沧拉祜族自治县
Lan-ts'ang Lahu Autonomous Hsien
centre: Meng-lang-pa B4 孟朗坝
Meng-lien T'ai-tsu La-hu-tsu Wa-tsu Tzu-chih-hsien 孟连傣族拉祜族佤族自治县
Meng-lien Shan-Lahu-Wa Autonomous Hsien
centre: Meng-lien B4
Mo-chiang Hsien C4 墨江县
P'u-erh Hsien C4 普洱县

Ta-li Pai-tsu Tzu-chih-chou 大理白族自治州
Ta-li Pai Autonomous District
centre: Hsia-kuan B2 下关
Chien-ch'uan Hsien B2 剑川县
Erh-yüan Hsien B2 洱源县
Ho-ch'ing Hsien C2 鹤庆县
Hsiang-yün Hsien C3 祥云县
Mi-tu Hsien C3 弥渡县
Nan-chien I-tsu Tzu-chih-hsien 南涧彝族自治县
Nan-chien Yi Autonomous Hsien
centre: Nan-chien C3
Pin-ch'uan Hsien C3 宾川县
Ta-li Hsien C3 大理县
Wei-shan I-tsu Hui-tsu Tzu-chih-hsien 巍山彝族回族自治县
Wei-shan Yi-Hui Autonomous Hsien
centre: Wei-shan C3
Yang-p'i Hsien B3 漾濞县
Yung-p'ing Hsien B3 永平县
Yün-lung Hsien 云龙县
centre: Shih-men-chen B3 石门镇

Te-hung T'ai-tsu Ching-p'o-tsu Tzu-chih-chou 德宏傣族景颇族自治州
Te-hung Shan-Kachin Autonomous District
centre: Mang-shih B3 芒市
Jui-li Hsien A3 瑞丽县
Liang-ho Hsien B3 梁河县
Lu-hsi Hsien 潞西县
centre: Mang-shih B3 芒市
Lung-ch'uan Hsien A3 陇川县
Wan-ting Chen 畹町镇
centre: Wan-ting B3
Ying-chiang Hsien A3 盈江县

Ti-ch'ing Tsang-tsu Tzu-chih-chou 迪庆藏族自治州
Ti-ch'ing Tibetan Autonomous District
centre: Chung-tien B2 中甸
Chung-tien Hsien B2 中甸县
Te-ch'in Hsien B1 德钦县
Wei-hsi Hsien B2 维西县

Wen-shan Chuang-tsu Miao-tsu Tzu-chih-chou 文山壮族苗族自治州
Wen-shan Chuang-Miao Autonomous District E4
Ch'iu-pei Hsien E3 丘北县
Fu-ning Hsien E4 富宁县
Hsi-ch'ou Hsien E4 西畴县
Kuang-nan Hsien E3 广南县
Ma-kuan Hsien E4 马关县
Ma-li-p'o Hsien E4 麻栗坡县
Wen-shan Hsien E4 文山县
Yen-shan Hsien E4 砚山县

Yü-ch'i Ti-ch'ü 玉溪地区
Ch'eng-chiang Hsien D3 澄江县
Chiang-ch'uan Hsien D3 江川县
Hsin-p'ing Hsien C3 新平县
Hua-ning Hsien D3 华宁县
I-men Hsien C3 易门县
O-shan I-tsu Tzu-chih-hsien 峨山彝族自治县
O-shan Yi Autonomous Hsien
centre: O-shan D3
T'ung-hai Hsien D3 通海县
Yüan-chiang Hsien C4 元江县
Yü-ch'i Hsien D3 玉溪县

KANSU
PROVINCE

KANSU is a large and diverse province, which has formed a part of the Chinese state since very early times, playing an extremely important role as the major route for Chinese commercial, political and cultural contacts with Central Asia and the West. It was, however, always on the edge of the empire, a semi-frontier area with a semi-arid climate, liable to frequent droughts and famines. It was an impoverished province, whose natives played little part in national politics. In the late 19th century it suffered terrible destruction and massive bloodshed in the Moslem rebellion which lasted from 1862–78, and in the brutal suppression which brought it to an end. Millions of lives were lost, and untold destruction of cities and property brought ruin to the province. In the late 19th century famine on a massive scale also brought death to millions of Kansu's people.

Kansu's boundaries have undergone many changes in recent times. From 1954 to 1958 the province included the Ningsia Hui Autonomous Region. From 1956 to 1969 the Alashan desert area was incorporated in the Inner Mongolian Autonomous Region, being returned to Kansu's jurisdiction after the dismemberment of Inner Mongolia in 1969.

Eastern Kansu This region, east of the Liu-pan range, forms an integral part of the Shensi plateau and peneplain some 800–1,000 m above sea level, covered in a thick but deeply dissected mantle of wind-blown loess soil. This area is drained by the Ching Ho and other tributaries of the Wei Ho. It is the only part of Kansu where winter temperatures (here only slightly below freezing) are warm enough to permit the growth of winter wheat. Its rainfall – around 500 mm annually, mostly in summer – is also higher than in the west, and the area grows grain crops such as kaoliang, millets and oats, with soy beans, cotton, hemp and tobacco as cash crops. The chief marketing and distribution centres are Ping-liang and Ching-yang.

The Liu-pan mountains These are formed by the upturned western edge of the Shensi plateau. The forest which once covered parts of the mountains was long ago destroyed and the area is badly eroded.

The Lung-hsi basin West of the Liu-pan range is the fertile basin around T'ien-shui and Lan-chou, traditionally known as the Lung-hsi basin. It is drained by the Huang Ho, which flows in through a series of gorges above Lan-chou, and by its southern tributary the T'ao Ho. On the south-west it is bounded by the extensions of the ranges of eastern Tsinghai, and in the north by the Wu-chiao range, an outlier of the Ch'i-lien Shan range. The basin is heavily covered with loess, and is the most fertile section of the province. The climate however is harsh. Winter temperatures between 6°C (43°F) and 10°C (50°F) and a low rainfall (below 500 mm, almost entirely in the summer when evaporation losses are high) make the climate precarious. The agriculture of the basin is founded on spring wheat, millet and kaoliang. Around Lan-chou, tobacco and melons are important crops. Fruit culture is also important, peaches being a speciality of T'ien-shui, and citrus fruits of Hsi-ku. In the uplands of the south-west, cattle and sheep rearing is important.

Lan-chou, the chief city of the area and provincial capital has been an important garrison town and transport centre since ancient times. Situated on major routes north-west along the Kansu corridor into Central Asia, westward into Tsinghai and Tibet, southward into Szechwan and north-west along the Huang Ho to Ningsia, Pao-t'ou and northern Shansi, Lan-chou was a major centre for caravan traffic into the border regions until the Second World War. During the war it became the terminus of a motor road across Sinkiang to the Soviet Union, which became a crucial source of wartime supplies. The first railway reached Kansu only in 1945, when the Lung-hai railway was extended from Pao-chi to T'ien-shui. This line reached Lan-chou in 1952, and in the 1950s was extended west to Wu-lu-mu-ch'i (Urumchi), with the intention of joining up with the Soviet system. In 1958 another line linked Lan-chou to Pao-t'ou, and in 1959 a line was begun westward into Tsinghai.

Following these developments, Lan-chou, which had previously had only minor processing industries based on local agriculture, was developed into a major industrial city destined to become the principal industrial base for the North-western Economic Region (Kansu, Shensi, and Sinkiang). A large thermal power plant, built with Soviet aid in 1957, employs coal from two large coalfields near Lan-chou, A-kan-chen and Yao-chieh, each producing between one and two million tons annually. In 1958–60 two very large hydro-electric schemes were also begun on the Huang Ho gorges west of Lan-chou, at Yen-kuo and Liu-chia. Neither, however, appears to have been completed. North of Lan-chou is one of China's largest sources of copper, Pai-yin Chang, which began production in 1958. This area has been incoporated into Lan-chou municipality. Lan-chou also produces aluminium on a large scale. It is the seat of various machine-making industries – producing oil-field equipment, railway equipment, machine tools and ball bearings. But the major industry is chemicals. The city has a large oil refinery, linked by a pipe line to Yü-men, which also processes crude oil from K'o-la-ma-i (Karamai) and the Ch'ai-ta-mu P'en-ti (Tsaidam Basin). There are plants for fertiliser, and for synthetic rubber. Since the early 1960s Lan-chou has been the centre of the Chinese atomic industry, with a uranium enrichment plant which began operations in 1963.

With this massive and rapid industrial growth, Lan-chou grew from a city of 200,000 in 1949 to 900,000 a decade later. It is also an important cultural centre, with several university and technical institutes.

T'ien-shui, until the early 1950s a major transport centre and railhead, has since been replaced in this function by Lan-chou, and is now merely the distribution and market centre of the eastern Lung-hsi basin.

The Kansu Corridor To the north-west of Lan-chou extends the Kansu corridor, a narrow belt of land extending along the northern piedmont of the towering Ch'i-lien ranges which form the border with Tsinghai. This is an area of inland drainage. A series of streams, fed by the snows on the Ch'i-lien ranges, flows out into the desert plateau to the north. Only two flows any considerable distance: the Jo Shui (Edsin Gol), which flows into two saline lakes near the Mongolian border, and the Shu-le, which flows into the far north-west near An-hsi. The whole area has very little rainfall – less than 300 mm annually – and agriculture is confined to the ten or so oases ranging in size from 200 to 1,500 square kilometres watered by these mountain streams, where irrigation can be practised. In the most easterly oases, Wu-wei and Chang-ye, special hardy varieties of rice have long been cultivated. Elsewhere, millet, kaoliang and spring wheat are the important crops. In the foothills of the mountains there is a well developed pastoral economy, raising horses, cattle, sheep and camels.

The towns of the Kansu corridor were traditionally a series of oases on a major caravan route. However, the coming of modern transport has led to some industrial developments.

Yü-men was the first major oil-field developed in China. Production began on a small scale in 1939, and throughout the war about 100,000 tons were produced annually and shipped out by lorry. In 1956 a rail link was built to Lan-chou, and a pipe-line constructed in the next year. The refinery at Yü-men itself was enlarged and modernised. In the late 1960s annual production was about two million tons.

Chiu-ch'üan was designated as the site of a major iron and steel complex to serve the north-west in the late 1950s. Very large iron reserves were discovered in the Ch'i-lien range south of the town, while an important coal field was opened up at Shan-tan to the east, producing a million tons annually. The plans for an integrated iron and steel plant seem to have been abandoned when the Great Leap Forward collapsed, but it seems possible that work has gone ahead with this plan since 1965.

Shuang-ch'eng-tzu about 140 miles north-east of Chiu-ch'uan in the valley of the Jo Shui, is China's space and missile launching centre.

The Alashan Desert To the north of the Kansu corridor lies the forbidding Alashan Desert, a virtually uninhabited plateau broken by low ranges of hills, which stretches to the Mongolian border. With an annual rainfall of 100 mm or less, much of this area is true desert, the rest very sparse grassland. It is inhabited entirely by nomadic Mongol herdsmen.

Minority Peoples Kansu has considerable variety of minority peoples. Most numerous are the Chinese Moslems (Hui), who were even more numerous until the great Moslem rebellions of the 19th century, during which millions perished. Their most important settlement is around Lin-hsia in the plain south-east of Lan-chou. Another large community lives on the Shensi border north of Tien-shui. Associated with the Hui settlement around Lin-hsia is a community of Tung-hsiang, a Moslem Mongol minority.

Tibetan minorities occupy much of the mountainous border district in the south-west, and live scattered along the Ch'i-lien range, and in the Wu-chiao range north of Lan-chou.

All of northern Kansu is peopled by Mongols, and a separate Mongol community is to be found in the Ch'i-lien mountains on the Tsinghai border. In the extreme north-western tip of Kansu is a Kazakh minority.

AREA
530,000 square kilometres

POPULATION
12,650,000
Other estimates 13,000,000

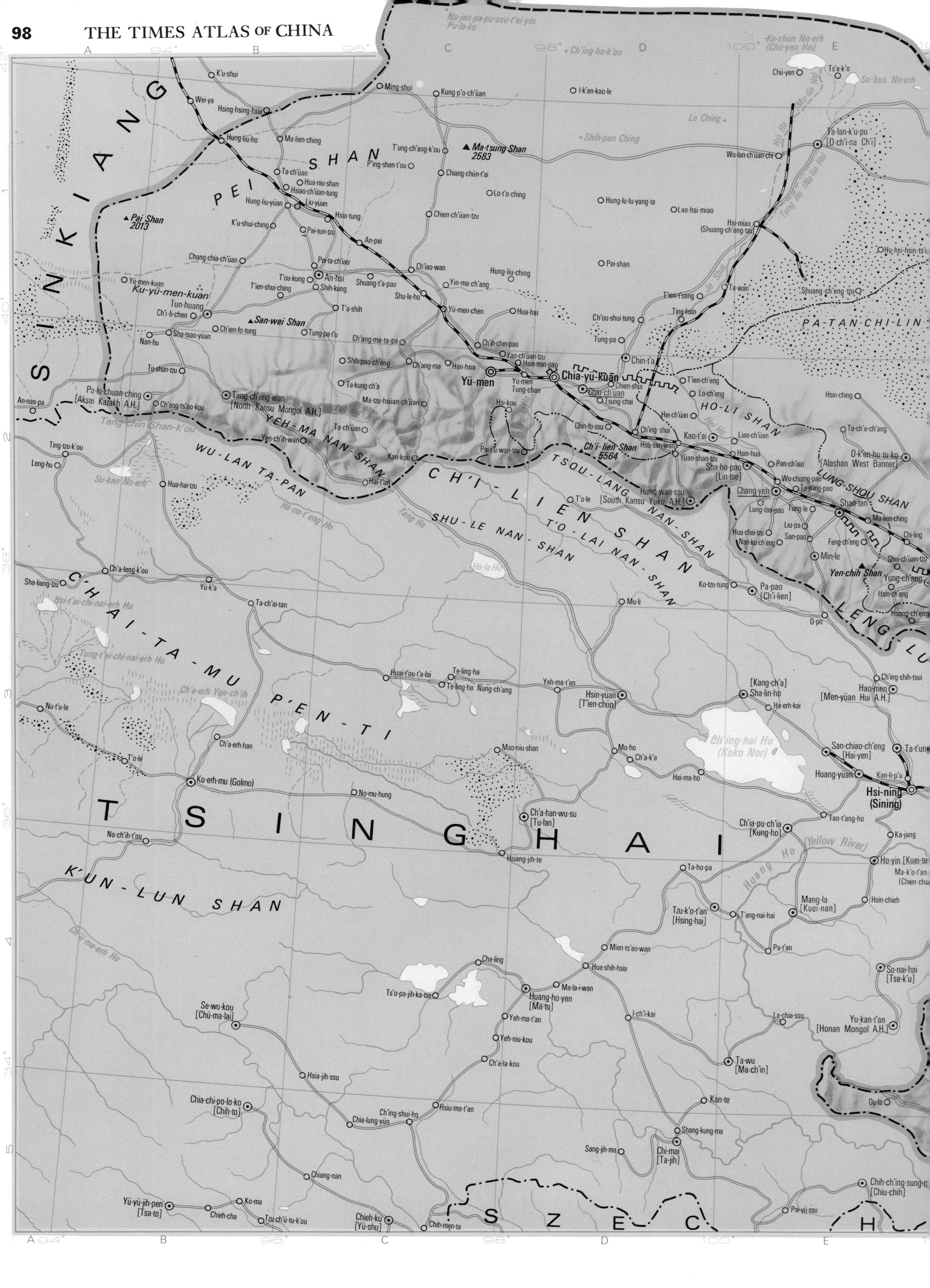
A
B
C
D
E
94°
96°
98°
100°
42°
40°
38°
36°
34°
1
2
3
4
5
Na-jan-pa-pu-ssu-t'ai-yin
Pu-la-ko
Ch'ing-ho-k'ou
Ka-shun No-erh
(Chü-yen Hai)
Chü-yen
Ts'e-k'o
So-kuo No-erh
K'u-shui
Wei-ya
Hsing-hsing-hsia
Ming-shui
Kung-p'o-ch'üan
I-k'en-kao-le
Lo Ching
Shih-pan Ching
Hsi Ho
Mu-lin Ho
Ta-lan-k'u-pu
[O-ch'i-na Ch'i]
Wu-lan-ch'üan-chi
Tung Ho (Na-lin Ho)
Hung-liu-ho
Ma-lien-ching
T'ung-ch'ang-k'ou
Ma-tsung Shan
2583
P'ing-shan-t'ou
SINKIANG
PEI SHAN
Ta-ch'üan
Hua-niu-shan
Hsiao-ch'üan-tung
Chiang-chün-t'ai
Lo-t'o-ching
Hung-liu-yüan
Liu-yüan
Hung-lu-lu-yang-ta
Lao-hsi-miao
Hsi-miao
(Shuang-ch'eng-tzu)
Pai Shan
2013
K'u-shui-ching
Hsia-tung
Chien-ch'üan-tzu
Pai-tun-tzu
An-pei
Hu-hsi-hsin-ts'un
Chang-chia-ch'üan
Pei-ta-ch'iao
Ch'iao-wan
Pei-shan
Yü-men-kuan
Ku-yü-men-kuan
T'ou-kung
An-hsi
Shuang-t'a-pao
Hung-liu-ching
Yin-ma-ch'ang
T'ien-shui-ching
Shih-kung
Jo Shui
Ta-wan
Shuang-ch'eng-tzu
Tun-huang
Ch'i-li-chen
Shu-le-ho
T'ien-ts'ang
T'a-shih
Yü-men-chen
Hua-hai
Ting-hsin
San-wei Shan
Ch'ien-fo-tung
Ch'ou-shui-tung
PA-TAN-CHI-LIN
Nan-hu
Sha-tsao-yüan
Tung-pa-t'u
Ch'ang-ma-ta-pa
Tung-pa
Ch'ih-chin-pao
Chin-t'a
Yao-ch'üan-tzu
Shih-pao-ch'eng
Ch'ang-ma
Han-hsia
Hsin-min-pao
Chia-yü-kuan
Tu-shan-tzu
Yü-men
Yü-men
Tung-chen
Chiu-ch'üan
Chien-shui
T'ien-ch'eng
Ta-kung-ch'a
Lo-ch'eng
Po-lo-chuan-ching
[Aksai Kazakh A.H.]
Tang-ch'eng-wan
[North Kansu Mongol A.H.]
Ma-tzu-hsüan-ch'üan
Tsung-chai
HO-LI SHAN
Hsin-ching
An-nan-pa
Ch'ang-ts'ao-kou
Hsi-kou
Hei-ch'üan
Tang-chin Shan-k'ou
YEH-MA NAN-SHAN
Ta-ch'üan
Chin-fo-ssu
Ch'ing-shui
Hei Ho
Liao-ch'üan
Ta-ch'e-ch'ang
Yen-ch'ih-wan
Kao-t'ai
Ting-tzu-k'ou
WU-LAN TA-PAN
Kan-kou
Pai-t'u-wan-tzu
Ch'i-lien Shan
5564
Hsü-san-wan
Hsin-hua
O-k'en-hu-tu-ko
[Alashan West Banner]
Leng-hu
Yüan-shan-tzu
Pan-ch'iao
Sha-ho-pao
[Lin-tse]
Su-kan No-erh
Hua-hai-tzu
Hai-t'un
CH'I-LIEN SHAN
TSOU-LANG NAN-SHAN
Wu-chiang-pao
LUNG-SHOU SHAN
Hung-wan-ssu
[South Kansu Yuku A.H.]
Chang-yeh
Ta-p'ing-pao
T'o-le
Lung-tao-pao
Shan-tan
Ha-na-t'eng Ho
Tang Ho
SHU-LE NAN-SHAN
T'O-LAI NAN-SHAN
Tung-le
Ma-lien-ching
Liu-pa
Hua-chai-tzu
San-pao
Chi-ling
Nan-ku-ch'eng
Feng-ch'eng
Min-le
Ha-la Hu
Shui-ch'üan-tzu
Yen-chih Shan
Yung-ch'ang
Ch'a-leng-k'ou
Sha-liang-tzu
Yü-k'a
Ko-tzu-tung
Pa-pao
[Ch'i-lien]
Hsin-ch'eng
Hsi-t'ai-chi-nai-erh Hu
Ta-ch'ai-tan
Mu-li
O-po
Huang-ch'eng
LENG-LU
CH'AI-TA-MU P'EN-TI
Tung-t'ai-chi-nai-erh Hu
Te-ling-ha
Huai-t'ou-t'a-lai
Te-ling-ha Nung-ch'ang
Ch'ing-shih-tsui
Hao-men
[Men-yüan Hui A.H.]
Yeh-ma-t'an
Hsin-yüan
[T'ien-chün]
[Kang-ch'a]
Sha-lin-ho
Ch'a-erh Yen-ch'ih
Ha-erh-kai
Nu-t'u-le
Ch'a-erh-han
Mao-niu-shan
Mo-ho
Ch'ing-hai Hu
(Koko Nor)
San-chiao-ch'eng
[Hai-yen]
Ta-t'ung
Ch'a-k'a
Huang-yüan
Kan-li-p'u
T'o-le
Ko-erh-mu (Golmo)
Hei-ma-ho
Hsi-ning
(Sining)
No-mu-hung
Ch'a-han-wu-su
[Tu-lan]
Tao-t'ang-ho
TSINGHAI
Ch'ia-pu-ch'ia
[Kung-ho]
Na-ch'ih-t'ou
Ka-jang
(Yellow River)
Huang Ho
Hsiang-jih-te
Ho-yin [Kuei-te]
Ta-ho-pa
Ma-k'o-t'an
(Chien-cha)
K'UN-LUN SHAN
Mang-la
[Kuei-nan]
Hsin-chieh
Tzu-k'o-t'an
[Hsing-hai]
T'ang-nai-hai
Ch'ü-ma-erh Ho
Pa-t'an
Mien-ts'ao-wan
Cha-ling
Hua-shih-hsia
So-nai-hai
[Tse-k'u]
Ma-la-i-wan
Ts'o-p'a-jih-ka-tse
Huang-ho-yen
[Ma-to]
Se-wu-kou
[Chü-ma-lai]
I-ch'i-kai
La-chia-ssu
Yeh-ma-t'an
Yu-kan-t'an
[Honan Mongol A.H.]
Yeh-niu-kou
Ch'a-la-kou
Ta-wu
[Ma-ch'in]
Hsia-jih-ssu
Chia-chi-po-lo-ko
[Chih-to]
Hsiu-ma-t'an
Ou-la
Kan-te
Ch'ing-shui-ho
Chia-lung-yün
Shang-kung-ma
Sang-jih-ma
Chi-mai
[Ta-jih]
Chiang-nan
Chih-ch'ing-sung-to
[Chiu-chih]
Yü-yü-jih-pen
[Tsa-to]
Ko-ma
Pai-yü-ssu
Chieh-cha
Tzu-ch'ü-t'u-k'ou
Chieh-ku
[Yü-shu]
Chih-men-ta
SZECH

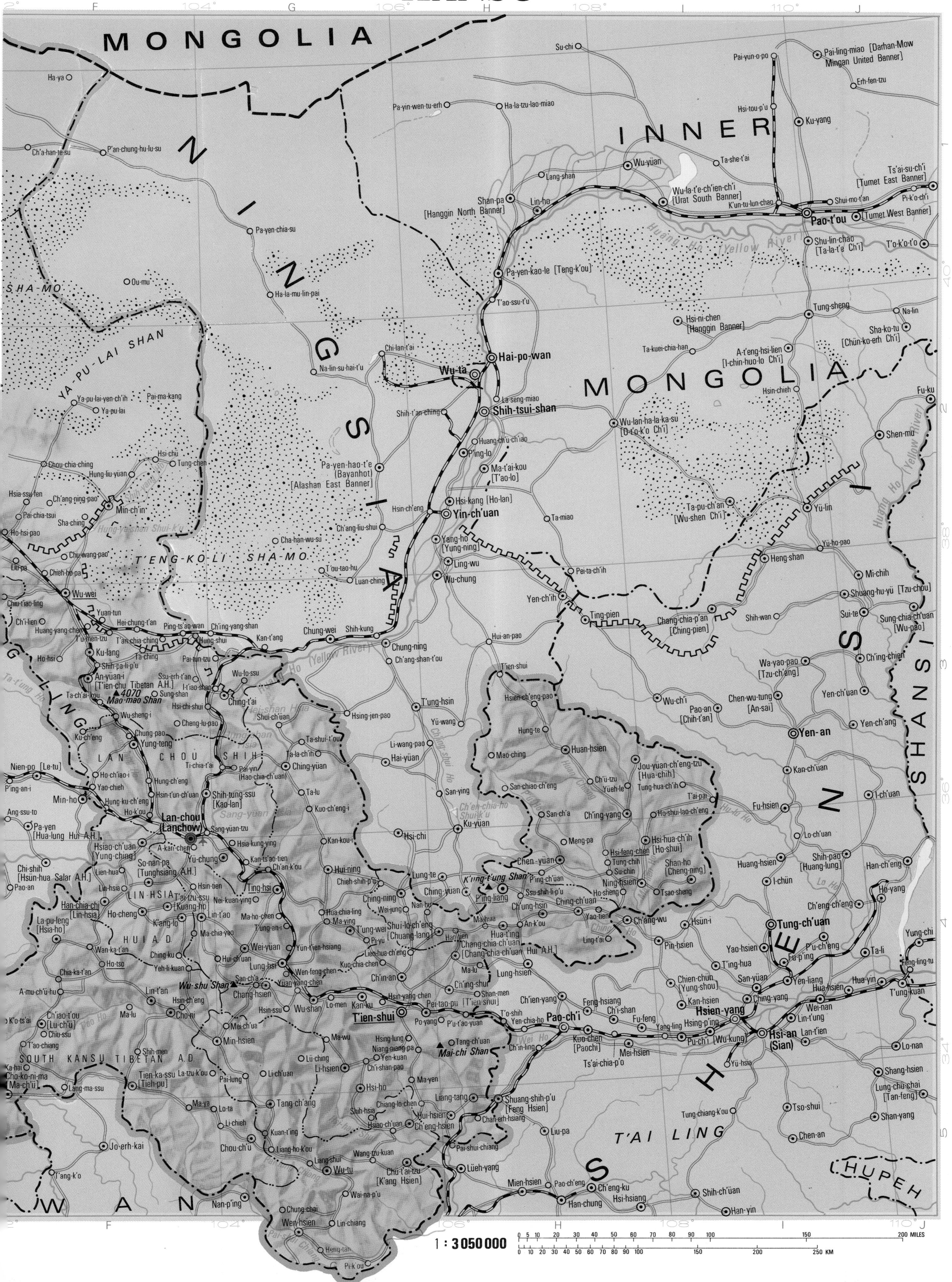
MONGOLIA
NINGSIA
INNER MONGOLIA
SHENSI
SHANSI
SZECHWAN
HUPEH
T'ENG-KO-LI SHA-MO
YA-PU-LAI SHAN
T'AI LING
LAN CHOU SHIH
LIN-HSIA HUI A.D.
SOUTH KANSU TIBETAN A.D.
Huang Ho (Yellow River)
Wei Ho
Ching Ho
Lan-chou (Lanchow)
Yin-ch'uan
Hai-po-wan
Wu-ta
Shih-tsui-shan
Pao-t'ou
Yen-an
Hsi-an (Sian)
Hsien-yang
Pao-chi
T'ien-shui
Tung-ch'uan
Wu-wei
Yü-lin
Han-chung
Mao-mao Shan
4070
Wu-shu Shan
Mai-chi Shan
K'ung-t'ung Shan
Pa-yen-hao-t'e (Bayanhot) [Alashan East Banner]
Pai-ling-miao [Darhan-Mow Mingan United Banner]
Wu-la-t'e-ch'ien-ch'i [Urat South Banner]
Shan-pa [Hanggin North Banner]
Pa-yen-kao-le [Teng-k'ou]
Hsi-ni-chen [Hanggin Banner]
Ta-pu-ch'an [Wu-shen Ch'i]
Wu-lan-ha-la-ka-su [O-t'o-k'o Ch'i]
Ts'ai-su-ch'i [Tumet East Banner]
Tumet West Banner
Chung-wei
Wu-chung
Ku-yüan
P'ing-liang
Hsi-ning
Lin-hsia
Wu-tu
Min-hsien
1 : 3 050 000
0 5 10 20 30 40 50 60 70 80 90 100 150 200 MILES
0 10 20 30 40 50 60 70 80 90 100 150 200 250 KM

KANSU PROVINCE 甘肃省
KAN-SU SHENG

4 shih	*municipalities*
2 tzu-chih-chou	*autonomous districts*
8 ti-ch'ü	*regions*
66 hsien	*counties*
6 tzu-chih-hsien	*autonomous counties*
2 ch'i	*banners*

capital **Lan-chou Shih**	F4	兰州市
Kao-lan Hsien		皋兰县
centre: Shih-tung-ssu	F3	石洞寺
Yü-chung Hsien	G4	榆中县
Yung-teng Hsien	F3	永登县
Chia-yü-kuan Shih	D2	嘉峪关市
T'ien-shui Shih	H3	天水市
Yü-men Shih	C2	玉门市

Kan-nan Tsang-tsu Tzu-chih-chou South Kansu Tibetan Autonomous District		甘南藏族自治州
centre: Ho-tso	F4	合作
Cho-ni Hsien	F4	卓尼县
Chou-ch'ü Hsien	G5	舟曲县
Hsia-ho Hsien		夏河县
centre: La-pu-leng	F4	拉卜楞
Lin-t'an Hsien	F4	临潭县
Lu-ch'ü Hsien		碌曲县
centre: Ch'iao-t'ou	F4	桥头
Ma-ch'ü Hsien		玛曲县
centre: Cho-ko-ni-ma	F4	卓格尼玛
Tieh-pu Hsien		迭部县
centre: Tien-ka-ssu	F4	电尕寺

Lin-hsia Hui-tsu Tzu-chih-chou Lin-hsia Hui Autonomous District		临夏回族自治州
centre: Han-chia-chi	F4	韩家集
Ho-cheng Hsien	F4	和政县
K'ang-lo Hsien	F4	康乐县
Kuang-ho Hsien		广河县
centre: T'ai-tzu-ssu	F4	太子寺
Lin-hsia Hsien		临夏县
centre: Han-chia-chi	F4	韩家集
Tung-hsiang-tsu Tzu-chih-hsien Tunghsiang Autonomous Hsien		东乡族自治县
centre: So-nan-pa	F4	锁南坝
Yung-ching Hsien		永靖县
centre: Hsiao-ch'uan	F4	小川

Chang-yeh Ti-ch'ü		张掖地区
Chang-yeh Hsien	E2	张掖县
Kao-t'ai Hsien	D2	高台县
Lin-tse Hsien		临泽县
centre: Sha-ho-pao	E2	沙河堡
Min-le Hsien	E2	民乐县
Shan-tan Hsien	E2	山丹县
Su-nan Yü-ku-tsu Tzu-chih-hsien South Kansu Yüku Autonomous Hsien		肃南裕固族自治县
centre: Hung-wan-ssu	D2	红湾寺

Ch'ing-yang Ti-ch'ü		庆阳地区
centre: Hsi-feng-chen	H4	
Cheng-ning Hsien		正宁县
centre: Shan-ho	I4	山河
Chen-yüan Hsien	H4	镇原县
Ch'ing-yang Hsien	H4	庆阳县
Ho-shui Hsien		合水县
centre: Hsi-hua-ch'ih	I4	西华池
Hua-ch'ih Hsien		华池县
centre: Jou-yüan-ch'eng-tzu	H3	柔远城子
Huan Hsien		环县
centre: Huan-hsien	H3	
Ning Hsien		宁县
centre: Ning-hsien	H4	

Chiu-ch'üan Ti-ch'ü		酒泉地区
A-k'o-sai Ha-sa-k'o-tsu Tzu-chih-hsien Aksai Kazakh Autonomous Hsien		阿克塞哈萨克族自治县
centre: Po-lo-chuan-ching	B2	博罗转井
An-hsi Hsien	B1	安西县
Chin-t'a Hsien	D2	金塔县
Chiu-ch'üan Hsien	D2	酒泉县
O-chi-na Ch'i Edsin Banner		额济纳旗县
centre: Ta-lan-k'u-pu	E1	达兰库布
Su-pei Meng-ku-tsu Tzu-chih-hsien North Kansu Mongol Autonomous Hsien		肃北蒙古族自治县
centre: Tang-ch'eng-wan	B2	党城湾
Tun-huang Hsien	B1	敦煌县

P'ing-liang Ti-ch'ü		平凉地区
Ching-ch'uan Hsien	H4	泾川县
Ching-ning Hsien	G4	静宁县
Chuang-lang Hsien		庄浪县
centre: Shui-lo-ch'eng	H4	水洛城
Ch'ung-hsin Hsien	H4	崇信县
Hua-t'ing Hsien	H4	华亭县
Ling-t'ai Hsien	H4	灵台县
P'ing-liang Hsien	H4	平凉县

T'ien-shui Ti-ch'ü		天水地区
Chang-chia-ch'uan Hui-tsu Tzu-chih-hsien Chang-chia-ch'uan Hui Autonomous Hsien	H4	张家川回族自治县
Chang Hsien		漳县
centre: Chang-hsien	G4	
Ch'in-an Hsien	G4	秦安县
Ch'ing-shui Hsien	H4	清水县
Hsi-ho Hsien	G4	西河县
Hui Hsien		
centre: Hui-hsien	H5	徽县
Kan-ku Hsien	G4	甘谷县
Liang-tang Hsien	H5	两当县
Li Hsien		礼县
centre: Li-hsien	G4	
T'ien-shui Hsien		天水县
centre: Pei-tao-pu	G4	北道埠
Wu-shan Hsien	G4	武山县

Ting-hsi Ti-ch'ü		定西地区
Ching-yüan Hsien	G3	靖远县
Hui-ning Hsien	G4	会宁县
Lin-t'ao Hsien	F4	临洮县
Lung-hsi Hsien	G4	陇西县
Ting-hsi Hsien	G4	定西县
T'ung-wei Hsien	G4	通渭县
Wei-yüan Hsien	G4	渭源县

Wu-tu Ti-ch'ü		武都地区
Ch'eng Hsien		成县
centre: Ch'eng-hsien	G5	
K'ang Hsien		康县
centre: Chü-t'ai-tzu	G5	咀台子
Min Hsien		岷县
centre: Min-hsien	F4	
Tang-ch'ang Hsien	G5	宕昌县
Wen Hsien		文县
centre: Wen-hsien	G5	
Wu-tu Hsien	G5	武都县

Wu-wei Ti-ch'ü		武威地区
A-la-shan Yu-ch'i Alashan West Banner		阿拉善右旗
centre: O-k'en-hu-tu-ko	E2	额肯呼都格
Ching-t'ai Hsien	G3	景泰县
Ku-lang Hsien	F3	古浪县
Min-ch'in Hsien	F2	民勤县
T'ien-chu Tsang-tsu Tzu-chih-hsien T'ien-chu Tibetan Autonomous Hsien		天祝藏族自治县
centre: An-yüan-i	F3	安远驿
Wu-wei Hsien	F3	武威县
Yung-ch'ang Hsien	E2	永昌县

SINKIANG
UIGHUR AUTONOMOUS REGION

THE Sinkiang region became a part of China only following the Manchu wars of conquest in Central Asia during the 18th century. Before this, the Chinese had occupied the major oases of the Tarim basin under the Han, at the end of the 2nd century BC, and again during the early T'ang period in the 7th and early 8th centuries, when Chinese influence reached to Lake Balkhash, and Chinese garrisons held the area around the Issyk Qul. After the 9th century the area was divided into a number of independent non-Chinese kingdoms, most powerful of which were the Uighurs. The 18th century occupation led to uneasy Chinese domination, broken in the 19th century by a long and destructive rising of the Moslem population, which was suppressed only after great loss of life in 1877. During the Republican period Sinkiang became to all intents independent under warlord Sheng Shih-ts'ai, and in the 1930s came under strong Soviet influence. This lasted to some extent even after the Communist victory in China, when the exploitation of mineral resources until the end of 1954 was carried out by joint Chinese-Soviet enterprises. The province of Sinkiang was changed to a Uighur Autonomous Region in 1955. At that time more than 90 per cent of the population were non-Chinese minority peoples. As the industrial development of the province proceeded during the 1950s and 1960s there was a large influx of Chinese, who now form the majority in the northern area, while the Uighurs continue to predominate in the southern Tarim area.

The Tarim Basin Sinkiang is divided into two major regions by the east-west ranges of the T'ien-shan. To the south of the T'ien-shan, and north of the K'un-lun range, which forms the border with Tsinghai, lies the great basin of the Tarim. Surrounded by mountains reaching 6,000 m and more, this is a flat depression lying about 1,000 m above sea level. It is an area of interior drainage, with many streams flowing off the surrounding mountains to lose themselves in the sands of the desert which occupies the centre of the basin, the Taklamakan. The streams on the northern side flow into the Tarim river, which flows eastward into the vast salt marsh and lake of Lop-nor. The Basin is an extremely arid region, with under 100 mm of rain per annum.

K'a-shih (Kashgar) has only 60 mm. The climate is extreme, with January temperatures about −7°C (19°F) and July temperatures as high as 27°C (81°F). The foothills of the mountains have more rainfall, and are covered with grassland, which is richer on the moister northern rim of the basin. The Taklamakan is true desert. Cultivation is only possible in the oases of irrigated land centred on the larger streams flowing into the basin. These oases, which maintained lively cultures of their own from early in the Christian era, were also important stops on the traditional 'silk road', China's main link with Central Asia and the west until recent times. These oases, which are largely peopled by Uighurs, support a flourishing irrigated agriculture, based on a variety of food grains, spring wheat, corn, rice and millet, cotton, and the extensive culture of fruits such as grapes, apples and pears. The grasslands of the foothills also support an extensive pastoral industry rearing sheep and horses. The communications are entirely by road. From Kashgar in the far west, roads lead over the high passes of the Pamir into Afghanistan and Pakistan, and south over the K'un-lun range into western Tibet.

In the Pamir region live a minority of Tadzikhs, while in the western section of the T'ien-shan there is a population of nomadic Kirghiz. *K'a-shih* is the largest of the oasis cities. It is an ancient trading city and administrative centre, famous for its textiles and rugs. Since the 1950s some minor industry has been established – small engineering and chemical works, cement manufacture, and a cotton weaving and dyeing plant. Its population is about 140,000. *K'u-ch'e (Kucha)* further east, and *Ho-t'ien (Khotan)* further south are also important centres. Ho-t'ien also has a cotton industry.

Lop-nor The eastern end of the Tarim basin drains into an area of marshes and salt lakes, whose outlines and position vary greatly as a result of climatic variation from year to year. An almost uninhabited area of very poor grassland and semi-desert, Lop-nor has been the chief test-site for China's atomic programme since 1964.

The T'u-lu-fan (Turfan) and Ha-mi depressions East of Wu-lu-mu-ch'i (Urumchi), the T'ien-shan ranges split into a southern range, the Ku-lu-k'o Shan, and a higher northern range, the Po-ko-ta Shan. Between these ranges are two very deep depressions, Ha-mi and T'u-lu-fan. They are fault depressions, that of Ha-mi falling to about 200 m, and T'u-lu-fan to 160 m *below* sea level. Practically rainless, and with intensely hot summers (July average at T'u-lu-fan is 33.7°C; 93°F) agriculture depends entirely on irrigation. T'u-lu-fan is famous for grapes, melons, apricots and peaches; Ha-mi for its melons. Ha-mi is also important as a coal mining centre, where a large modern strip mine began work in 1970. The coal is shipped by rail to the industries of Wu-lu-mu-ch'i, and feed a local generating plant. In the late 1950s an iron and steel industry was planned here, using local ore, but this does not seem to have materialised. Both T'u-lu-fan and Ha-mi are served by the Sinkiang railway, which reached Ha-mi in 1960.

The Ili valley West of Wu-lu-mi-ch'i the T'ien-shan range divides, the northern Po-lo-k'o-nu range being separated from the southerly Ha-erh-k'o-t'a-ma Shan range by the Ili valley, which drains westwards into the Soviet Union, discharging into Lake Balkhash. The only part of Sinkiang with an adequate rainfall (300–500 mm, and up to 700 mm in the T'ien-shan) this is a prosperous agricultural and pastoral area. It is famous for apples and pears, and for its horses and sheep.

Its population is very mixed, with Kirghiz, Kazakhs, Chinese, and a colony of Sibo, Manchu descendants of the Ch'ing garrison of the area. *I-ning* is its commercial and administrative centre.

The Wu-lu-mu-ch'i (Urumchi) area Along the northern face of the T'ien-shan ranges facing the Dzungarian basin, is an area which has been the centre of extensive colonisation since the 1950s, and one of the areas where large scale state farms have been developed, utilising the streams flowing off the mountains for irrigation. Unlike the oases in the Tarim, which had always been well-cultivated, much of this new land had never been cultivated. The climate is colder than in the Tarim. Wheat, corn, rice, soy beans, cotton and sugar beet are the main crops.

The chief centres of this agricultural zone are *Ma-na-ssu* and *Shih-ho-tzu*, which has textile and sugar-refining plants.

The mountain ranges are also important sources of minerals. Coal and iron are mined on a considerable scale near Wu-lu-mu-ch'i, while Ch'i-t'ai is a source of uranium.

Wu-lu-mu-ch'i formerly called Ti-hua, is the provincial capital, and the largest city in Sinkiang. It is an ancient strategic and trading centre situated in a break in the T'ien-shan ranges north-west of the T'u-lu-fan depression. Under the Communist regime its importance has grown with the completion of a railway to Lan-chou in 1963, and with the rapid growth of the population and production of oil in the Dzungarian region.

The major centre of industry in the province, Wu-lu-mu-ch'i has thermal power plants fired by local coal, a medium-sized iron and steel plant founded in 1951, small scale engineering, cement manufacture, chemical plants and cotton textile mills. It has a population of about 400,000.

The Dzungarian Basin North of the T'ien-shan piedmont, the Dzungarian Basin extends northward to the high Altai mountains on the border of Mongolia, bounded on the west by the Tarbagatai and Ala-tau ranges on the Soviet border. The Dzungarian plain is less arid than the Tarim, and has only limited areas of true desert, most of it being grassland, supporting a pastoral population. The chief rivers are the Ma-na-ssu and the U-lun-ku which drain into a number of marshes and lakes. Most of the population are nomadic herders of sheep, with some horses, cattle and camels. They are largely either Kazakhs or, in the east, Torgut Mongols.

The principal resource of this region, is the rich oilfield in the western part of the plain, known as the K'o-la-ma-i (Karamai) field. Oil was discovered in the late 1930s at Tu-shan-tzu near Wu-su, where production began in 1940 and a small refinery was built. In 1955 fields were discovered to the north at K'o-la-ma-i and U-erh-ho further to the north-east. Production began in 1958, the old refinery at Tu-shan-tzu was joined by pipeline to the new field, and a refinery built at K'o-la-ma-i. Production by the mid-1960s had reached 2,000,000 tons and is limited mainly by the costs of transporting refined petroleum and crude oil to the railway at Wu-lu-mu-ch'i, some 150 km away.

K'o-la-ma-i, with a population of 40,000 in 1958, is almost entirely dependent on the oil industry, and its municipal boundaries are large, including all the Dzungarian oilfields.

The Altai Mountains The northern and north-western borders of Dzungaria are formed by the Altai, a great range reaching 3,000 m, with occasional peaks above 4,000 m. The area has a substantial rainfall, and the mountains are either tree-covered or form rich pasture. The population comprises largely nomadic Kazakh or Oirat Mongol herdsmen.

AREA
1,646,800 square kilometres

POPULATION
8,000,000

WU-LU-MU-CH'I AREA
K'O-ERH-PAN-T'UNG-KU-T'E SHA-MO
K'o-la-ma-i (Karamai)
Pai-k'ou-ch'üan
A-k'o-pa-ssu-t'ao
Pai-chien-t'an
Yueh-chih-hsin-ts'un
Ma-na-ssu Hu
San-ko-chuang
Ta-pu-hsün
Ma-na-nu-i-k'u-tu-k'o
Che-k'o-sen-ching
San-pa-ssu-ti-wu
Ti-shui Ch'üan
Chu-k'e-ta-hu
Hung-shan-chu
O-lun-pu-la-k'o
Ta-kuai
Chung-kuai
T'a-ch'a-k'ou
Ha-sa-fen
Hsiao-kuai
Ch'ien-shan-lao-pa
Hsin-kuang
Lung-k'ou
Ch'e-p'ai-tzu-ssu-ch'ang
Hsin-ch'e-p'ai-u-tzu
Kung-ch'ing-t'uan Hung-ch'ang
Liu-k'o-shu-ching
Sha-men-tzu
Ma-na-ssu Ho
Sha-ch'iu-ho
Mo-so-wan-erh-ch'ang
Ch'e-p'ai-tzu
Hsia-pa-hu
Erh-i-ch'ang
Mo-so-wan
Ma-ch'iao
Shuang-ching-tzu
T'ou-t'ai
Kung-ch'ing-t'uan Nung-ch'ang
Pa-ni-tzu-ti
Shuang-ho
Huang-kung
Lao-sha-wan
Ta-tung-kou
Ta-ching
Chiang-chün-miao
Mei-yao
Lao-hsi-hu
Pei-wu-ch'a
Pai-chia Hai
Ssu-k'o-shu
Wu-su
Hung-ch'i-ch'ang
Mo-ku-hu Shui-k'u
Yueh-chin Shui-k'u
Hsin-hu
Kan-ho-tzu
K'uei-t'un
Fang-ts'ao-hu
Ch'a-chia-hu
An-chi-hai
Ch'e-ma-tien
Huang-ts'ao-hu
Chi-chi-hu
Hsi-ta-kou
Sung-sheng-kung
Ma-na-ssu (Manas)
Tu-shan-tzu
San-tao-ho-tzu [Sha-wan]
Shih-ho-tzu
Pao-chia-tien
Ts'ao-yüan
Chang-chia-chuang
Pa-i Nung-ch'ang
Tung-hu
Ch'ing-ko-ta
Wu-mu-k'o
Pa-yin-k'ou
Liang-sa-hu
Hsia-san-chiang
Hu-t'u-pi
Chiu-yün-chieh
Tzu-ni-ch'üan
Hsi-ti
Ssu-ch'ang-pa
Pei-tao-ch'iao
Wu-ch'ia-ch'ü
Wu-k'o-shu
Le-t'u-yi
Ta-t'u-ku-li
Erh-shih-li-tien-tzu
Po-erh-t'ung-ku
Tung-wan
Shih-hui-yao-tzu
Yü-shu-kou
Fu-k'ang
Kan-ho-tzu
Shuang-ch'a-ho-tzu
San-t'ai
Ch'i-t'ai
K'o-p'u-k'u-t'u-k'o
Hsi-ko-pi
Erh-kung
Ch'ang-shan-tzu
Huang-shan-chieh
Chi-mu-sa-erh
Mu-lei
Po-lu-k'o-ch'ieh
Hung-kou
Ch'ing-shui-ho-tzu
Ch'ang-chi
Ku-mu-ti [Mi-ch'üan]
T'ien Ch'ih
P'an-chia-t'ai
T'ou-kung
Ta-ch'üan
[Mu-lei Kazakh A.H.]
Lao-ch'i t'ai
Shih-t'i-tzu
An-ning-ch'ü
Wu-lu-mu-ch'i (Urumchi)
Po-ko-ta Feng 5445
Ta-yu
T'an-ch'ang
Tung-kou
T'ou-t'un-ho
Ch'üan-tzu-chieh
Chi-pu-k'u
Pan-chieh-kou
Tung-ch'eng
K'a-shih Ho
Po-lo-k'o-nu Ta-pan
Yung-feng-ch'ü
Miao-erh-kou
Chi-chi-tsao-tzu
Kou-sha-ch'ü
Shui-mo-kou
Pai-yang-kou
Shih-yao-tzu
Mu-tzu Ta-pan
A-shih-li
Huang-ts'ao-liang
Chai-wo-pao
Yen-hu
Hua-shu-lin
Tung-kou
P'an-chia-ti
Nan-chuang
Yang-chuan-kou
Ta-pan-ch'eng
Ta-ho-yen
K'a-lan-ku-kuo-le
Ch'a-erh-t'o-k'ai
Kung-nai-ssu Ho
Kung-nai-ssu-lin-ch'ang
Hou-hsia
Hsiao-erh-pu-la-k'o
T'a-erh-lan
Sha-men-tzu
Shen-chia
Pa-ko
A-erh-hsien
Sheng-li Ta-pan
Pai-yang-ho
T'u-lu-fan
Ch'i-ch'üan-hu
Huo-yen-shan
K'o-k'o-ya
Pa-yin-pu-lu-k'o
Pa-yin-ho-shuo
Ch'a-han-no-erh
Pa-yin-kou
I-k'o-shu
Hsiao-ts'ao-hu
T'ou-tao-ho
Hung-liu-ho
Ta-pu-erh-ku-ssu-t'ai
Yao-tien-tzu
Sheng-chin-t'ai
Su-pa-shih
Shan-shan
Wu-erh-kou
Pu-erh-chien
Mo-t'o-sha-la
Wu-la-ssu-t'ai
T'u-lu-fan (Turfan)
San-p'u
Lien-mu-ch'in
Pa-yin-su-mu-k'u-je
1 : 2 500 000
0 5 10 20 30 40 50 MILES
0 5 10 20 30 40 50 KM
Wu-i-kung-she
A-la Kou
I-la-hu
Ha-tung
Shu-ko
Lu-k'o-ch'in
Ta-lang-k'an
Wu-la-leng-ko
Huo-hei-erh Shan 4332
Pa-lun-t'ai
Wu-wa-men
T'o-k'o-hsün (Toksun)
Ai-ting Hu
Su-pa-shih
Ti-k'an-erh
Ayaguz
Aktogay
Urdzhar
Ozero Sasykkol'
Ozero Alakol'
R.
Druzh
A-k'o-su-man
Wen-ch'üan
Po-lo
BORO TALA
Wu-t'ai
Sai-li-mu Hu
San-t'ai
MO
Panfilov
Huo-ch'eng
Shui-ting [Huo-ch'eng]
Chi-lin-yü-tzu [I-ning]
I-ning (Kuldja)
Su-pu-t'ai
S.
Ch'a-pu-ch'a-erh [Chapchal Sibo A.H.]
Ya-ma-tu
Kung-liu
T'e-k'o-ssu (Tekes)
Chao-su
T'e-k'o-ssu Ho
Sa-erh-huo-pu
Han-ya-ni-k'o
Han-t'eng-ko-li Feng 6995
T' I E N S H A N
Naryn
Kok-Yangak
Osh
T'u-lu-ka-erh-t'e Shan-K'ou
U.
Pai-ch'eng
Hei-tzu-erh
Ta-wan-ch'i
Ch'a-erh-ch'i
Mu-cha-t'i Ho
Yang-t'a-k'o-k'u-tu-k'o
T'u-mu-hsiu-k'o
T'o-shih-kan Ho
Wen-su
Wu-shih
A-k'o-su (Aksu)
A-ho-ya
K'a-la-yü-erh-kun
A-ho-ch'i
Ha-la-ch'i
K'IZIL SU KIRGHIZ A.D.
Sha-ching-tzu
Ma-t'an
K'o-ping
Ha-la-t'a
Ch'i-lan-t'ai
A-ch'ia
A-wa-t'i (Abad)
Ai-man-k'u-le
A-la-erh
Sheng-li-shih chiu-ch'ang
Ha-erh-chün
Sary-Tash
Wu-lu-k'o-ch'ia-t'i
Pa-yin-k'u-lu-t'i
K'ang-ssu
Wu-ch'ia
A-t'u-shih
Pa-p'an-shui-mo
K'an-pieh-ti
Shang-yu-i-ch'ang
Shang-yu Shui-k'u
P'i-se-le-k'o
K'o-tzu-le Ho (Kizil Su)
K'a-shih-ka-erh Ho
(Kashgar Darya)
San-ch'a-k'ou
A-k'o-t'a-mu
K'a-la-k'o-ch'in
Hsia-hu
K'a-shih (Kashgar)
Pe-ch'u
Hsia-ma-le
Hsiao-hsi-hai-tzu Shui-k'u
Nao-erh Hu
Shu-fu
Shu-le
Ch'ieh-shih
Kai-tzu Ho
A-k'o-t'ao
Yüeh-p'u-hu
Se-li-pu-ya
T A - L I
(T A R I
Wu-tzu-pieh-li Shan-K'ou
Ying-chi-sha
A-wa-t'ai
Pu-lun-k'ou
Kung-ko-erh Shan
I-ko-tzu-ya
Mai-kai-t'i (Merket)
Pa-shih-k'u-le-ya
T'A-K'O-LA-M
Pu-k'o-sha-ma-la-le
(T A K L A
So-ch'e (Sha-ch'e) (Yarkand)
Ch'ia-je-k'o
Ma-cha-t'a-ko
T'ang-ku-tzu-pa-ssu-t'e
K'u-ssu-la-fu
Tse-p'u (Posgam)
K'a-ch'ün
Hai-san-le-pa-ko
Yeh-ch'eng (Karghalik)
K'uo-shih-la-shih
T'a-shih-k'u-erh-kan [Tash Kurghan Tajik A.H.]
P'i-shan (Guma)
Mi-sha-lieh-i
AFGHANISTAN
Ming-t'ieh-kai
K'u-k'o-ya
Mu-chi
Tu-hsien-pai-pa-cha
T'u-le-k'o-ch'i-k'u-le
Ming-t'ieh-kai Ta-pan (Mintaka Pass)
PAK.
Hung-chi-la-fu Ta-pan (Khunjerab Pass)
K'o-shih-t'a-ko
A-k'o-mi-ch'i-t'e
Tsang-kui
Mo-yü (Kara Kash)
Ma-cha
Sang-chu
Cha-wa
Ho-t'ien (Khotan)
Lo-p'u
Lang-ju
Baltit
A-la-sa-le
P'u-chi-ya
Su-la-k'o
K'a-la-k'a-shih Ho
Ts'e-le (Chira Bazar)
Ha-lang-kou
Ta-shih-man
Min-feng (Niya)
Ma-cha
Yeh-erh-ch'iang Ho (Yarkand Darya)
Hsi-ti-la
Su-kai-t'i
P'u-sa
T'ieh-k'o-li-k'o Shan 5466
Ch'ia-ha
Yü-t'ien (Keriya)
Ao-i-t'o-ko-la-k'o
Gilgit
K'UN LUN SHAN
K'ang-hsi-wa
P'i-hsia
Hei-shan
Wu-k'u
Nu-jih
A-t'e-ch'iang
Lü-shih
Ch'iao-ko-li Feng (Mt. Godwin Austen) 8611
Yin-ti-la-k'o-li Shan-k'ou
T'a-ko-ma-po
Ta-hung-liu-t'an
Mu-shih Shan
P'u-lu
Ho-ho-le-k'o
Chi-shih-wa-chan
Hsieh-li-k'o-k'o-shih
K A S H M I R
K'a-la-k'un-lun Shan-k'ou (Karakoram Pass)
AKSAI CHIN
K'o-shih-erh-ts'un
T'ien-shui-hai
Ch'üan-shui-kou
Aksai Chin
A-ma-p'a-hsia
T'ieh-lung-t'an
Chi-li-ya Shan-k'ou
T
A
B
C

1 : 4360000

0 5 10 20 30 40 50 60 70 80 90 100 150 200 250 300 350 400 MILES

0 10 20 30 40 50 60 70 80 90 100 150 200 250 300 350 400 450 500 550 600 KM

SINKIANG UIGHUR AUTONOMOUS REGION 新疆维吾尔自治区

HSIN-CHIANG WEI-WU-ERH TZU-CHIH-CH'Ü

4 shih	*municipalities*
5 tzu-chih-chou	*autonomous districts*
6 ti-ch'ü	*regions*
74 hsien	*counties*
6 tzu-chih-hsien	*autonomous counties*

capital **Wu-lu-mu-ch'i Shih**	D2	乌鲁木齐市
Wu-lu-mu-ch'i Hsien	D2	乌鲁木齐县
K'o-la-ma-i Shih	D1	克拉玛依市
K'a-shih Shih	A3	喀什市
I-ning Shih	C2	伊宁市
Hsien under direct provincial administration:—		
Shan-shan Hsien	E2	鄯善县
T'o-k'o-hsün Hsien	E2	托克逊县
T'u-lu-fan Hsien	E2	吐鲁番县

Ch'ang-chi Hui-tsu Tzu-chih-chou		昌吉回族自治州
Ch'ang-chi Hui Autonomous District		
centre: Ch'ang-chi	D1	
Ch'ang-chi Hsien	D1	昌吉县
Chi-mu-sa-erh Hsien	E1	吉木萨尔县
Ch'i-t'ai Hsien	E1	奇台县
Fu-k'ang Hsien	D1	阜康县
Hu-t'u-pi Hsien	D1	呼图壁县
Ma-na-ssu Hsien	D1	玛纳斯县
Mi-ch'üan Hsien		米泉县
centre: Ku-mu-ti	D2	古牧地
Mu-lei Ha-sa-k'o Tzu-chih-hsien		木垒哈萨克自治县
Mu-lei Kazakh Autonomous Hsien		
centre: Mu-lei	E2	

I-li Ha-sa-k'o Tzu-chih-chou		伊犁哈萨克自治州
Ili Kazakh Autonomous District		
centre: I-ning	C2	伊宁
Chao-su Hsien	C2	昭苏县
Ch'a-pu-ch'a-erh Hsi-po Tzu-chih-hsien		察布查尔锡伯自治县
Chapchal Sibo Autonomous Hsien		
centre: Ch'a-pu-ch'a-erh	C2	
Hsin-yüan Hsien	C2	新源县
Huo-ch'eng Hsien		霍城县
centre: Shui-ting	C1	水定
I-ning Hsien		伊宁县
centre: Chi-lin-yü-tzu	C2	吉林圩子
Kung-liu Hsien	C2	巩留县
Ni-le-k'o Hsien	C2	尼勒克县
T'e-k'o-ssu Hsien	C2	特克斯县

A-le-t'ai Ti-ch'ü		阿勒泰地区
Altai Region		
centre: A-le-t'ai	E1	
A-le-t'ai Hsien	E1	阿勒泰县
Chi-mu-nai Hsien		吉木乃县
centre unknown	D1	
Ch'ing-ho Hsien	E1	青河县
Fu-hai Hsien	D1	福海县
Fu-yün Hsien	E1	富蕴县
Ha-pa-ho Hsien	D1	哈巴河县
Pu-erh-chin Hsien	D1	布尔津县

T'a-ch'eng Ti-ch'ü		塔城地区
centre: T'a-ch'eng	C1	
Ho-pu-k'o-sai-erh Meng-ku Tzu-chih-hsien		和布克赛尔蒙古自治县
Kobuk Saur Mongol Autonomous Hsien		
centre: Ho-pu-k'o-sai-erh	D1	
O-min Hsien	C1	额敏县
Sha-wan Hsien		沙湾县
centre: San-tao-ho-tzu	D1	三道河子
T'a-ch'eng Hsien	C1	塔城县
T'o-li Hsien	C1	托里县
Wu-su Hsien	D1	乌苏县
Yü-min Hsien		裕民县
centre: Ha-la-pu-la	C1	哈拉布拉

K'o-tzu-le-su K'o-erh-k'o-tzu Tzu-chih-chou		克孜勒苏柯尔克孜自治州
Kizil Su Kirghiz Autonomous District		
centre: A-t'u-shih	B3	阿图什
A-ho-ch'i Hsien	B2	阿合奇县
A-k'o-t'ao Hsien	A3	阿克陶县
A-t'u-shih Hsien	B3	阿图什县
Wu-ch'ia Hsien	A3	乌恰县

Pa-yin-kuo-leng Meng-ku Tzu-chih-chou		巴音郭楞蒙古自治州
Bayan Gol Mongol Autonomous District		
centre: K'u-erh-le	D2	库尔勒
Ch'ieh-mo Hsien	D3	且末县
Ho-ching Hsien	D2	和静县
Ho-shuo Hsien	D2	和硕县
Jo-ch'iang Hsien	E3	若羌县
K'u-erh-le Hsien	D2	库尔勒县
Lun-t'ai Hsien	D2	轮台县
Po-hu Hsien	D2	博湖县
Yen-ch'i Hui-tsu Tzu-chih-hsien		焉耆回族自治县
Yen-ch'i Hui Autonomous Hsien	D2	
Yü-li Hsien	D2	尉犁县

Po-erh-t'a-la Meng-ku Tzu-chih-chou		博尔塔拉蒙古自治州
Boro Tala Mongol Autonomous District		
centre: Po-lo	C1	博乐
Ching-ho Hsien	C1	精河县
Po-lo Hsien	C1	博乐县
Wen-ch'üan Hsien	C1	温泉县

A-k'o-su Ti-ch'ü		阿克苏地区
Aksu Region		
A-k'o-su Hsien	C2	阿克苏县
A-wa-t'i Hsien	C2	阿瓦提县
Hsin-ho Hsien	C2	新和县
K'o-p'ing Hsien	B2	柯坪县
K'u-ch'e Hsien	C2	库车县
Pai-ch'eng Hsien	C2	拜城县
Sha-ya Hsien	C2	沙雅县
Wen-su Hsien	C2	温宿县
Wu-shih Hsien	B2	乌什县

Ha-mi Ti-ch'ü		哈密地区
Ha-mi Hsien	F2	哈密县
I-wu Hsien	F2	伊吾县
Pa-li-k'un Ha-sa-k'o Tzu-chih-hsien		巴里坤哈萨克自治县
Bar Kol Kazakh Autonomous Hsien		
centre: Pa-li-k'un	F2	

Ho-t'ien Ti-ch'ü		和田地区
Ho-t'ien Hsien	B3	和田县
Lo-p'u Hsien	C3	洛浦县
Min-feng Hsien	C3	民丰县
Mo-yü Hsien	B3	墨玉县
P'i-shan Hsien	B3	皮山县
Ts'e-le Hsien	C3	策勒县
Yü-t'ien Hsien	C3	于田县

K'a-shih Ti-ch'ü		喀什地区
Kashgar Region		
Ch'ieh-shih Hsien	B3	伽师县
Mai-kai-t'i Hsien	B3	麦盖提县
Pa-ch'u Hsien	B3	巴楚县
Shu-fu Hsien	A3	疏附县
Shu-le Hsien	B3	疏勒县
So-ch'e Hsien	B3	莎车县
T'a-shih-k'u-erh-kan T'a-chi-k'o Tzu-chih-hsien		塔什库尔干塔吉克自治县
Tash Kurghan Tajik Autonomous Hsien		
centre: T'a-shih-k'u-erh-kan	A3	
Tse-p'u Hsien	B3	泽普县
Yeh-ch'eng Hsien	B3	叶城县
Ying-chi-sha Hsien	B3	英吉沙县
Yüeh-p'u-hu Hsien	B3	岳普湖县

TSINGHAI
PROVINCE

WITH the exception of the eastern area around Hsi-ning, the province of Tsinghai was incorporated into China in comparatively recent times, following the Manchu conquest of Tibet in the early 18th century. Before that time it had been occupied by a succession of semi-nomadic peoples; the Ch'iang, the T'u-yü-hun and the Tibetans, intermingled with Mongol and Turkic groups. Most of Tsinghai is still occupied by national minorities.

The province falls into three major regions.

Eastern Tsinghai The eastern part of Tsinghai is a high plateau between the complex Ch'i-lien and Nan-shan ranges on the north and the Pa-yen-ku-la range in the south. The plateau is between 2,500 and 3,000 metres above sea level, and is broken by a series of ranges with their axes north-west to south-east, which range up to 4,000 and 5,000 metres. These ranges enclose the basin of the large Ch'ing-hai (Kokonor) lake, from which the province takes its name, and the area is drained by the headwaters of the Huang Ho and its tributaries. The climate is extreme, with long, bitterly cold winters (average January temperature at Hsi-ning is −6.5°C; 20°F), short warm summers (July 18°C; 64°F) and low precipitation, from 150 mm in the east, decreasing to about 100 mm in the west, most of which falls in summer. A few small areas of the mountains in the east have forest cover, but most of the area is rich natural grassland.

The area around Hsi-ning in the east contains most of the population, most of the settled agriculture, and almost all the industry of the province. Sedentary agriculture is concentrated in the valleys of the Huang Ho and of its tributaries the Huang Shui and Ta-t'ung Ho, to the east of the Ch'ing-hai lake. The growing season is very short. Agriculture is mainly based on the cultivation of barley and spring wheat, and has been greatly aided by the development of new quick-ripening varieties of hardy wheats. Other grains, millets, oats and buckwheat, and hemp are also grown, with some hardy fruits. In this agricultural belt there has been considerable colonisation by Han Chinese settlers since the 1950s.

The surrounding uplands, and the region west of the Ch'ing-hai lake have good pasturelands, famous since early times for their fine horses, for cattle, and above all for sheep. Hsi-ning is famous for its wool, which is mostly used in rug and carpet manufacture.

The southern slopes of the Ch'i-lien and Nan-shan ranges have a number of coal deposits, most important of which is at Ta-t'ung. There are also copper deposits and reserves of iron ore in this area.

Hsi-ning The provincial capital is a long-established Chinese city, a military garrison and trading centre since the 16th century. It has always been an important communication centre with routes joining it to Lan-chou in the east, and to the Tsaidam (Ch'ai-ta-mu) region and La-sa in the west and south-west. Until 1959 it was largely an administrative centre, and a trading city with minor industries processing the agricultural products of the surrounding area. However, in 1959 it was linked by rail to Lan-chou and to the main Chinese rail network. Shortly afterwards a branch line was built to the local coalfield at Ta-t'ung in 1960, while the main line was extended to the west as far as Hai-yen, north-east of the Ch'ing-hai lake. This railway was planned to be extended still further into the Tsaidam region, but construction was halted in 1961. In the 1950s Hsi-ning also was linked by highways to both the Tsaidam region, and to La-sa. At the same time industry began to develop: a thermal power station using Ta-t'ung coal was followed by a small local hydro-electric plant in 1966. In 1959–60 a medium-sized iron and steel plant was built, and a small metal finishing industry arose making ball bearings, farm implements and electrical equipment. In the mid 1960s a chemical industry was also begun, with a plastic plant (1965) and fertiliser plant (1966), using mineral products from the west of the province. Hsi-ning grew from 94,000 people in 1953 to an estimated 300,000 in 1970, and remains the only large city in Tsinghai.

Kuei-te to the south of Hsi-ning in the valley of the Huang Ho, is a market and collecting centre for the agricultural areas of the Huang Ho and its tributaries, and for the pastoral industry of south-eastern Tsinghai.

The Tsaidam Basin The north-western part of the province is occupied by the Tsaidam depression, a great basin formed between the A-erh-chin range on the north, and the Ch'i-man and K'un-lun ranges to the south, and a south-easterly outlying range of the Nan-shan on the east. The depression is the lowest-lying region of the province, averaging between 2,600 and 3,000 metres above sea level. It is an area of interior drainage, the many streams from the surrounding ranges flowing into a series of salt marshes and saline lakes. The climate is extremely dry, with annual rainfall ranging from 150 mm down to virtually nil. The climate is harsh, with extremely cold winters. The western and north-western parts of the Tsaidam are true desert. The marginal areas are arid pasture and scrub. Another area of true desert is in the subsidiary northern basin around Lake Su-kan-no-erh.

Until the 1950s the Tsaidam remained virtually uninhabited, except by some nomadic Mongol and Kazakh herdsmen. It was difficult of access, except from the Ch'ing-hai area. In the north, only one pass (T'ang-chin) led into western Kansu. Development began in the 1950s when surveys revealed rich mineral reserves, especially of oil. In the mid 1950s highways were built into the region, state farms established on its borders, and a rail link was projected in anticipation of industrial growth.

The mineral deposits proved to be rich. Oil fields were developed, one around Leng-hu, in the northern Tsaidam, and the other at Yu-ch'üan-tzu, Yu-sha-shan and Yu-t'un-tzu near Mang-yai. Small refineries were built at both fields, and the oil transported to Lan-chou by truck.

Rich coal deposits were also found in the area of Ta-chai-tan and nearby Yu-k'a. Iron deposits were discovered near Ko-erh-mu, and vast resources of soda, borax, potash and bromine were found around the salt lakes near Ta-chai-tan.

Great plans were made to develop the region industrially, and for a while Ko-erh-mu, Ta-ch'ai-tan and Leng-hu were made municipalities. But large scale development was abandoned in 1962–3, and has only been renewed on a limited scale since 1969.

Southern Tsinghai The third major region, southern Tsinghai, is a very high plateau region crossed by many ranges between the Pa-yen-ku-la range, which divides the drainage basins of the upper Huang Ho from those of the Yangtze, and the T'ang-ku-la range which forms the province's southern boundary with Tibet. Both of these ranges are very high, with peaks up to 6,500 metres and more. The area is drained by the headwaters of the Yangtze and of the Mekong, and the various mountain ranges mostly have axes running north-west to south-east. The entire region lies at about 3,500 metres above sea level, with the ranges much higher. The climate here is extreme: the winters are very long and extremely cold, and, because of the altitude, summer temperatures are not high. There is more rain than in the Tsaidam (250–500 mm), mostly falling in summer. But apart from areas in the extreme east, which have some forest cover, the area is predominantly upland pasture or semi-tundra.

The population is almost entirely composed of semi-nomadic Tibetan herdsmen, rearing sheep, goats and yaks. There is very little agriculture and few settlements.

Yü-shu (formerly known as Chieh-ku) is the chief centre. A market and collection point for sheep-skins and wool, it has road connections with western Szechwan, Hsi-ning and Tibet.

Minorities Ethnic composition of the population is very varied. Han Chinese settlement is largely confined to the Hsi-ning area and to the new settlements in the Tsaidam. Apart from the Hsi-ning area the whole province is comprised of autonomous districts of various minorities. By far the most widespread are the Tibetans who are found throughout the province. There are Mongol communities in the Tsaidam and in the extreme south-eastern corner of the province, and large communities of Monguors (Tu) in the area north of Hsi-ning and Ta-t'ung. There is a Kazakh community in the west of the Tsaidam. South-east of Hsi-ning are settlements of Chinese Moslems (Hui) and the Turkic Salar people.

AREA

721,000 square kilometres

POPULATION

1953 census 1,675,000

1970 estimate 2,140,000

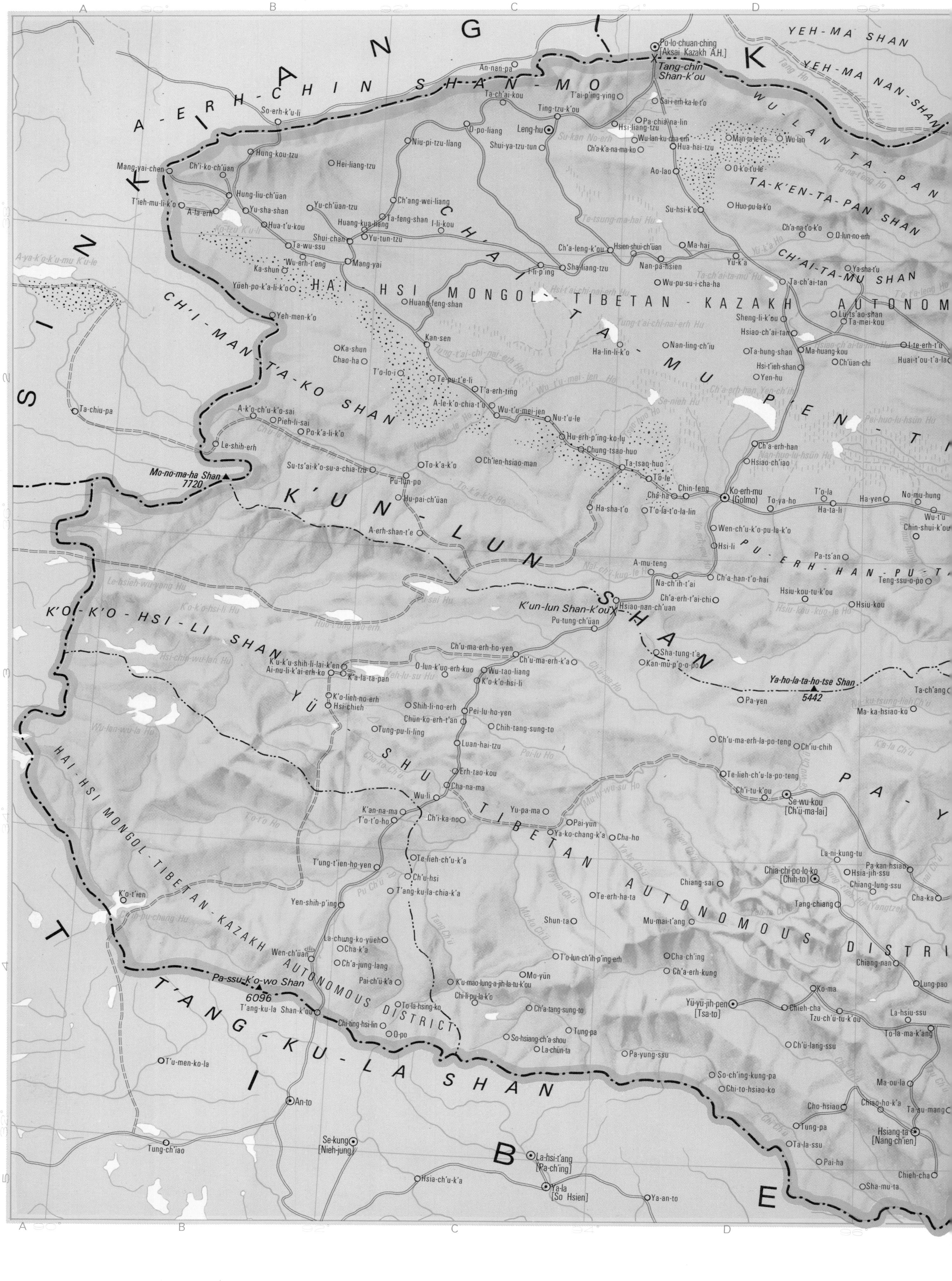

SINKIANG
A-ERH-CHIN SHAN-MO
YEH-MA SHAN
YEH-MA NAN-SHAN
WU-LAN TA-PAN
TA-K'EN-TA-PAN SHAN
CH'AI-TA-MU SHAN
HAI HSI MONGOL-TIBETAN-KAZAKH AUTONOM
CH'AI-TA-MU P'EN-TI
CH'I-MAN-T'A-KO SHAN
K'UN-LUN SHAN
PU-ERH-HAN-PU-TA
K'O-K'O-HSI-LI SHAN
YÜ-SHU TIBETAN AUTONOMOUS DISTRICT
HAI-HSI MONGOL-TIBETAN-KAZAKH AUTONOMOUS DISTRICT
T'ANG-KU-LA SHAN
TIBET
PA-Y
Po-lo-chuan-ching
[Aksai Kazakh A.H.]
Tang-chin Shan-k'ou
An-nan-pa
Ta-ch'ai-kou
T'ai-p'ing-ying
Sai-i-erh-ka-le-t'o
Ting-tzu-k'ou
Leng-hu
O-po-liang
So-erh-k'u-li
Pa-chia-na-lin
Hsi-liang-tzu
Wu-lan-ku-cha-erh
Ch'a-k'a-na-ma-ko
Hua-hai-tzu
Man-ta-le-t'a
Wu-lan
Niu-pi-tzu-liang
Shui-ya-tzu-tun
Mang-yai-chen
Ch'i-ko-ch'üan
Hung-kou-tzu
Hei-liang-tzu
Ao-lao
O-k'o-t'u-le
Hung-liu-ch'üan
T'ieh-mu-li-k'o
A-la-erh
Yu-sha-shan
Yu-ch'üan-tzu
Ch'ang-wei-liang
Hua-t'u-kou
Ta-feng-shan
Huang-kua-liang
I-li-kou
Su-hsi-k'o
Huo-pu-la-k'o
Ch'a-na-t'o-k'o
O-lun-no-erh
Shui-chan
Yu-tun-tzu
Ta-wu-ssu
Wu-erh-t'eng
Mang-yai
Ka-shun
Ch'a-leng-k'ou
Hsien-shui-ch'üan
Ma-hai
Yü-k'a
Nan-pa-hsien
Sha-liang-tzu
I-li-p'ing
Wu-pu-su-i-cha-ha
Ta-ch'ai-tan
Ya-sha-t'u
Yüeh-po-k'a-li-k'o
Huang-feng-shan
Yeh-men-k'o
Sheng-li-k'ou
Lu-ts'ao-shan
Ta-mei-kou
Hsiao-ch'ai-tan
Ka-shun
Chao-ha
Kan-sen
Ha-lin-li-k'o
Nan-ling-ch'iu
Ta-hung-shan
Ma-huang-kou
I-te-erh-t'u
Huai-t'ou-t'a-la
Ch'üan-chi
Hsi-t'ieh-shan
Yen-hu
T'o-lo-i
Te-pu-t'e-li
T'a-erh-ting
A-le-k'o-chia-t'u
Wu-t'u-mei-jen
Ta-chiu-pa
A-k'o-ch'u-k'o-sai
Pieh-li-sai
Nu-t'u-le
Po-k'a-li-k'o
Hu-erh-p'ing-ko-lu
Chung-tsao-huo
Le-shih-erh
Ch'a-erh-han
Hsiao-ch'iao
To-k'a-k'o
Ch'ien-hsiao-man
Ta-tsao-huo
Su-ts'ai-k'o-su-a-chia-tzu
Mo-no-ma-ha Shan
7720
Pu-lun-po
T'o-le
Chin-feng
Cha-ha
Ko-erh-mu
(Golmo)
To-ya-ho
T'o-la
Ha-ta-li
Ha-yen
No-mu-hung
Wu-t'u
Chin-shui-k'ou
Hu-pai-ch'üan
Ha-sha-t'o
T'o-la-t'o-la-lin
Wen-ch'u-k'o-pu-la-k'o
A-erh-shan-t'e
Hsi-li
Pa-ts'an
A-mu-teng
Na-ch'ih-t'ai
Ch'a-han-t'o-hai
Teng-ssu-o-po
Ch'a-erh-t'ai-chi
Hsiu-kou-tu-k'ou
Hsiu-kou
K'un-lun Shan-k'ou
Hsiao-nan-ch'uan
Pu-tung-ch'üan
Ch'u-ma-erh-ho-yen
Sha-tung-t'a
Ch'u-ma-erh-k'a
Kan-mu-p'o-o-po
K'u-k'u-shih-li-lai-k'en
Ai-nu-li-k'ai-erh-ko
O-lun-k'uo-erh-kuo
Wu-tao-liang
K'a-la-ta-pan
K'o-k'o-hsi-li
Ya-ho-la-ta-ho-tse Shan
5442
Ta-ch'ang
Pa-yen
Ma-ka-hsiao-ko
K'o-lieh-no-erh
Hsi-chieh
Shih-li-no-erh
Pei-lu-ho-yen
Chün-ko-erh-t'an
Tung-pu-li-ling
Chih-tang-sung-to
Luan-hai-tzu
Ch'u-ma-erh-la-po-teng
Ch'iu-chih
Erh-tao-kou
Te-lieh-ch'u-la-po-teng
Cha-na-ma
Ch'i-tu-k'ou
Wu-li
Se-wu-kou
[Ch'ü-ma-lai]
K'an-na-ma
Yu-pa-ma
T'o-t'o-ho
Ch'i-ka-no
Pai-yün
Ya-ko-chang-k'a
Cha-ho
T'ung-t'ien-ho-yen
Te-lieh-ch'u-k'a
La-ni-kung-tu
Pa-kan-hsiao
Chia-chi-po-lo-ko
[Chih-to]
Hsia-jih-ssu
Chiang-lung-ssu
Ch'u-hsi
T'ang-ku-la-chia-k'a
Chiang-sai
Cha-ka
K'o-t'ien
Yen-shih-p'ing
Te-erh-ha-ta
Tang-chiang
Shun-ta
Mu-mai-t'ang
La-chung-ko-yüeh
Cha-k'a
Wen-ch'üan
Ch'a-jung-lang
T'o-lun-ch'ih-p'ing-erh
Cha-ch'ing
Ch'a-erh-kung
Chiang-nan
Pai-ch'ü-k'a
Mo-yün
K'u-mao-lung-a-jih-la-tu-k'ou
Lung-pao
Pa-ssu-k'o-wo Shan
6096
Ch'i-li-pu-la-k'o
Ko-ma
T'ang-ku-la Shan-k'ou
To-la-hsing-ko
Ch'a-tang-sung-to
Yü-yü-jih-pen
[Tsa-to]
Chieh-cha
Tzu-ch'ü-tu-k'ou
La-hsiu-ssu
Chi-ting-hsi-lin
O-po
Tung-pa
To-la-ma-k'ang
So-hsiang-ch'a-shou
La-chün-ta
Ch'ü-lang-ssu
Pa-yung-ssu
T'u-men-ko-la
So-ch'ing-kung-pa
Chi-to-hsiao-ko
Ma-ou-la
Chiao-ho-k'a
Ta-su-mang
An-to
Cho-hsiao
Hsiang-ta
[Nang-ch'ien]
Tung-pa
Ta-la-ssu
Tung-ch'iao
Se-kung
[Nieh-jung]
La-hsi-t'ang
[Pa-ch'ing]
Pai-ha
Chieh-cha
Hsia-ch'u-k'a
Ya-la
[So Hsien]
Sha-mu-ta
Ya-an-to
A
B
C
D

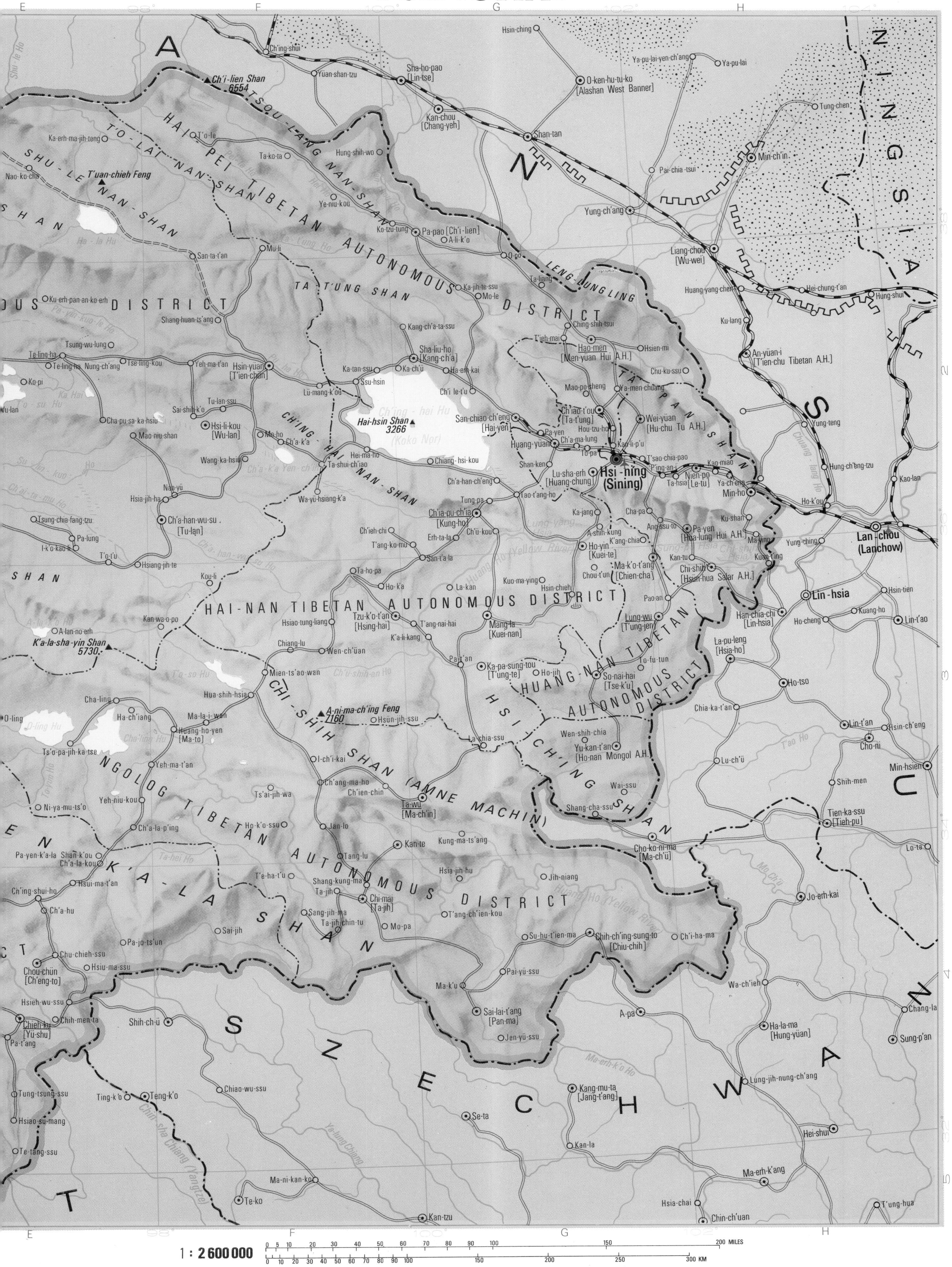

1 : 2 600 000

0 5 10 20 30 40 50 60 70 80 90 100 150 200 MILES

0 10 20 30 40 50 60 70 80 90 100 150 200 250 300 KM

TSINGHAI PROVINCE 青海省
CH'ING-HAI SHENG

1 shih	*municipality*
6 tzu-chih-chou	*autonomous districts*
32 hsien	*counties*
5 tzu-chih-hsien	*autonomous counties*

capital **Hsi-ning Shih**		西宁市
Ta-t'ung Hsien		大通县
centre: Ch'iao-t'ou	**G2**	桥头
Hsien under direct provincial administration:		
Huang-chung Hsien		湟中县
centre: Lu-sha-erh	**G2**	鲁沙尔
Huang-yüan Hsien	**G2**	湟源县
Le-tu Hsien		乐都县
centre: Nien-po	**H2**	碾伯
Min-ho Hsien	**H2**	民和县
Ho-nan Meng-ku-tsu Tzu-chih-hsien Ho-nan Mongol Autonomous Hsien		河南蒙古族自治县
centre: Yu-kan-t'an	**G3**	有干滩
Hsün-hua Sa-la-tsu Tzu-chih-hsien Hsün-hua Salar Autonomous Hsien		循化撒拉族自治县
centre: Chi-shih	**H3**	积石
Hua-lung Hui-tsu Tzu-chih-hsien Hua-lung Hui Autonomous Hsien		化隆回族自治县
centre: Pa-yen	**H2**	巴燕
Hu-chu T'u-tsu Tzu-chih-hsien Hu-chu Tu Autonomous Hsien		互助土族自治县
centre: Wei-yüan	**G2**	威运

Hai-hsi Meng-ku-tsu Tsang-tsu Ha-sa-k'o-tsu Tzu-chih-chou Hai-hsi Mongol-Tibetan-Kazakh Autonomous District		**海西蒙古族藏族哈萨克族自治州**
centre: Te-ling-ha	**E2**	德令哈
Ko-erh-mu Hsien	**D2**	格尔木
T'ien-chün Hsien		天竣县
centre: Hsin-yüan	**F2**	新源
Tu-lan Hsien		都兰县
centre: Ch'a-han-wu-su	**F2**	察汗乌苏
Wu-lan Hsien		乌兰县
centre: Hsi-li-kou	**F2**	希里沟

Hai-nan Tsang-tsu Tzu-chih-chou Hai-nan Tibetan Autonomous District		**海南藏族自治州**
centre: Ch'ia-pu-ch'ia	**G2**	恰卜恰
Hsing-hai Hsien		兴海县
centre: Tzu-k'o-t'an	**F3**	子科滩
Kuei-nan Hsien		贵南县
centre: Mang-la	**G3**	茫拉
Kuei-te Hsien		贵德县
centre: Ho-yin	**G2**	河阴
Kung-ho Hsien		共和县
centre: Ch'ia-pu-ch'ia	**G2**	恰卜恰
T'ung-te Hsien		同德县
centre: Ka-pa-sung-tou	**G3**	尕巴松都

Hai-pei Tsang-tsu Tzu-chih-chou Hai-pei Tibetan Autonomous District		**海北藏族自治州**
centre: Hao-men	**G2**	治门
Ch'i-lien Hsien		祁连县
centre: Pa-pao	**G1**	八宝
Hai-yen Hsien		海晏县
centre: San-chiao-ch'eng	**G2**	三角城
Kang-ch'a Hsien		刚察县
centre: Sha-liu-ho	**G2**	沙柳河
Men-yüan Hui-tsu Tzu-chih-hsien Men-yüan Hui Autonomous Hsien		门源回族自治县
centre: Hao-men	**G2**	治门

Huang-nan Tsang-tsu Tzu-chih-chou Huang-nan Tibetan Autonomous District		**黄南藏族自治州**
centre: Lung-wu	**H3**	隆务
Chien-cha Hsien		尖扎县
centre: Ma-k'o-t'ang	**G3**	马克唐
Tse-k'u Hsien		泽库县
centre: So-nai-hai	**G3**	贤乃亥
T'ung-jen Hsien		同仁县
centre: Lung-wu	**H3**	隆务

Kuo-lo Tsang-tsu Tzu-chih-chou Ngolog Tibetan Autonomous District		**果洛藏族自治州**
centre: Ta-wu	**G3**	大武
Chiu-chih Hsien		久治县
centre: Chih-ch'ing-sung-to	**F4**	智清松多
Kan-te Hsien	**F3**	甘德县
Ma-ch'in Hsien		玛沁县
centre: Ta-wu	**G3**	大武
Ma-to Hsien		玛多县
centre: Huang-ho-yen	**F3**	黄河沿
Pan-ma Hsien		班玛县
centre: Sai-lai-t'ang	**F4**	赛来堂
Ta-jih Hsien		达日县
centre: Chi-mai	**G4**	吉迹

Yü-shu Tsang-tsu Tzu-chih-chou Yü-shu Tibetan Autonomous District		**玉树藏族自治州**
centre: Chieh-ku	**G4**	结古
Ch'eng-to Hsien		称多县
centre: Chou-chün	**G4**	周均
Chih-to Hsien		治多县
centre: Chia-chi-po-lo-ko	**D4**	加吉博洛格
Ch'ü-ma-lai Hsien		曲麻莱县
centre: Se-wu-kou	**D3**	包吾沟
Nang-ch'ien Hsien		囊谦县
centre: Hsiang-ta	**E4**	香达
Tsa-to Hsien		杂多县
centre: Yü-yü-jih-pen	**D4**	于玉日本
Yü-shu Hsien		玉树县
centre: Chieh-ku	**G4**	结古

TIBET
AUTONOMOUS REGION

TIBET has historically been an area culturally quite separate from China. Since the first emergence of an organised Tibetan state around the end of the 6th century, the Tibetan people have continuously dominated the area of the present Autonomous Region, developing their own form of society, culture, and a way of life adapted to the bleak conditions of the Tibetan plateau. At times Tibetan power encroached into Chinese Turkestan (Sinkiang) and into the western borders of Szechwan. The Mongols briefly brought Tibet under the control of the Yüan dynasty in the 13th century. The area was again conquered by the Manchus in the 18th century, and remained a protectorate of the Ch'ing empire, with a governor (Amban) at La-sa (Lhasa). However, the country remained virtually independent under its religious leader the Dalai Lama and the Lamaistic Buddhist hierarchy, which completely dominated Tibetan society, and whose influence was also widespread among the Mongols. In the early years of this century Tibet formed links with British India, and became completely independent of Chinese control. The Communist government finally established control of Tibet late in 1951, when their troops entered La-sa, the Dalai Lama's capital. In the 1950s conflict arose between the Chinese and the religious hierarchy, who violently opposed reforms proposed by the Chinese. A rebellion arose among the Khamba tribes of eastern Tibet, and in 1959 a rebellion broke out in La-sa, leading to the flight of the Dalai Lama. The rebellion was suppressed, and in the following years the powers of the Lamaistic church and the temporal power of the great monasteries was completely broken. In 1965 Tibet was finally organised as an Autonomous Region.

The Chang-tang plateau This immense plateau lies at an altitude of between 4,000 and 5,000 m, a region of barren, desolate rolling uplands broken by a series of west-east ranges, the most important of which is the eastern extension of the Karakoram range and the T'ang-ku-la (Tanglha) range in the east. The plateau is bounded on the north by the K'un-lun and K'o-k'o-hsi-li ranges and on the south by the Kang-ti-ssu (Kailas, Trans-Himalaya) range with peaks rising above 7,000 m. It is an area with meagre rainfall (below 200 mm) and extreme temperatures. Although temperatures vary greatly according to altitude, many areas have only two months per year with average temperatures above freezing. The whole plateau is barren, alpine desert, with some poor mountain grassland towards the south-east. An area of interior drainage, its rivers flow into a great number of salt lakes and saline marshes. Agriculture is impossible. Since the 1950s the area has been traversed by a motor road from Na-ch'ü to the southern border of Sinkiang province, but the whole area is very sparsely inhabited.

The Ch'ang-tu (Chamdo) area The Ch'ang-tu area of eastern Tibet, lying south of the T'ang-ku-la (Tanglha) and north of the Nien-ch'ing T'ang-ku-la (Nyenchen Tanglha) ranges is a somewhat lower section of plateau, drained by the headwaters of the Salween and Mekong and Upper Yangtze. In the east are a series of steep ranges (from west to east the Po-shu-la; Heng-tuan; T'a-nien-t'a-weng; Ta-ma-la and Ning-ching ranges), separated by steep forested gorges. This is an area with considerably more rainfall than other parts of Tibet, and a much more favourable climate. The main town and route centres are Hei-ho (Na-ch'ü) in the west and Ch'ang-tu in the east.

The Southern Tibetan valleys Between the Himalaya ranges of the India-Nepal border and the Kang-ti-ssu and Nien-ch'ing T'ang-ku-la ranges of the southern plateau lies a series of high valley basins, drained by the upper waters of the Sutlej in the west and by the Brahmaputra in the east. The altitudes here are less extreme than on the northern plateau, and temperatures are more tolerable. The January temperature of La-sa which lies just below 4,000 m, averages just below freezing, and July temperature 17°C (63°F). Rainfall is also higher, averaging between 250 mm and 700 mm in the La-sa region. Most of this falls during the summer monsoon season from June to September, but rainfall varies greatly from year to year.

In these valleys live most of the Tibetan population. There has always been some cultivation in this area, based on hardy upland barley. Since 1951 there has been a systematic effort to increase production of barley and hardy varieties of wheat, rye, buckwheat and peas. In the southern valleys tea has been cultivated successfully since 1952. The cultivated area extends from the Jih-k'a-tse (Shigatse) area in the west to La-to in the east. On the uplands surrounding these cultivated areas pastoral industry is important, with sheep, yaks and horses the most common animals.

There has been considerable population increase and extension of the cultivated area since the 1950s. Many new settlements have been established, and the area has been linked by a network of highways.

La-sa, the traditional Tibetan capital, remains the political centre and by far the most important city. It has been provided with electric power from local hydro-electric sources, and has developed small textile, chemical and engineering industries. Its population is estimated at between 70,000 and 80,000.

Chiang-tzu (Gyangtse) is the chief centre of the southern part of this area and an important route centre on the main road to India via Gangtok in Sikkim. It has a small hydro-electric plant.

Jih-k'a-tse (Shigatse) was formerly the seat of the Panchen Lama, the second figure in the Tibetan religious hierarchy, and is the main centre for the western part of the region, dominating the highway to the western valleys, and the new highway across the Nepalese border to Katmandu. It has many handicraft industries, and a population of about 30,000.

Ka-erh (Gartok) was the traditional trade centre of the western valley of the Sutlej, but has been replaced as administrative centre by K'un-sa (Gargunsa) and a new Chinese settlement Shih-ch'üan-ho at the junction of the new highways across western Tibet and into Sinkiang.

Minority Peoples The population of Tibet is almost entirely Tibetan, apart from the small numbers of Chinese who have settled in the larger administrative centres, and some Chinese colonists in the south.

AREA
1,220,000 square kilometres

POPULATION
1,250,000

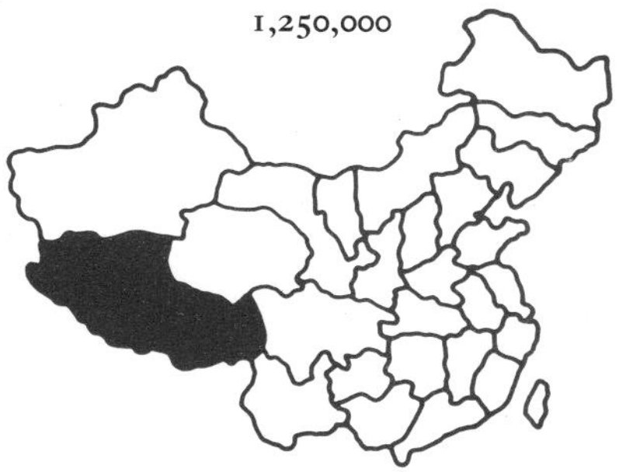

S I N K I A N G
K'U N L U N S H A N
WU-SSU-TENG-T'A-KO SHAN
K'O-K'O-HSI
AKSAI CHIN
KASHMIR
HSI-TSANG KAO-YÜAN
(PLATEAU OF TIBET)
A L I
N A
T'ANG-KU
(TANG
KANG-TI-SSU SHAN
(KAILAS RANGE)
HI-MA-LA-YA SHAN
[HSI-MA-LA-YA SHAN]
NIEN
NEPAL
INDIA
SIKKIM
BH
BANGL
Ch'ieh-mo
Ha-ti-le-k'o
An-ti-erh-lan-kan
Ya-t'ung-ku-tzu-lan-kan
Mo-yü
Ho-t'ien
Lo-p'u
Ts'e-le
Yü-t'ien
Min-feng
Yeh-i-k'o
Hsi-ti-la
Wu-k'u
Nu-jih
P'u-lu
Ta-chiu-pa
A-ch'i-k'o K'u-le
Mu-tzu T'a-ko 7723
K'a-la-mi-lan Shan-k'ou
K'o-su-k'o
A-liu-sha
Ta-hung-liu-t'an
Ch'uan-shui-kou
T'ieh-lung-t'an
Ch'i-li-ya Shan-k'ou
La-chu-lung
K'o-erh-lu-kai Shan-k'ou
Pa-k'o-ha-lu
Su-ko-t'e
Ma-ni
Ch'iao-li-ma
K'a-mu-li
T'o-ma-erh
P'a-ko-lieh-t'o-k'o
Ku-lo-kung-pa
To-mu-la
P'i-pu-k'o
Ting-to
Lun-to
Lei-p'ai-k'o Shan 6356
Ao-wa-ch'in
Shan-ho
Ta-ya-erh
Jih-t'u (Rudok)
Ko-mu
Le-li Shan 6407
Mi-to
Hsi-ti
Ni-shan
P'eng-wa-ming-t'e Shan 6549
Cha-pu
Ch'a-ch'u
Po-wei-erh Shan-k'ou
K'a-p'a-ch'ung-ku
Sha-li
Je-wang
Hsü-hei-no
Sha-chih-ya
Pa-li-chia-ssu (Demchok)
A-ling Shan 7315
Pu-lan-cha-k'a
Shih-ch'üan-ho
Na-p'o [Ko-chi]
Ch'a-k'a
Tsu-hsia-kung-pu
T'o-k'o-ting-ling
Shih-chia-sha-lung
P'a-ting
Ya-ko-mu
Cha-hsi-kang
Lang-chü-ts'a-ch'ü
Ts'o-k'o-cha
Lu-lo
Yu-lang-lo-p'u-chiang-ssu
Po-t'o-cho
K'un-sa (Gargunsa) [Ka-erh]
Man-ko
Kai-tse
Chi-chin
Sha-k'o-ti
Mu-chia-li-pu
Sang-to-lang
La-ka-la-pu Shan-k'ou
Ta-erh-cho
Ma-sao
T'a-ku-k'o
La-chung
Tu-chia-li
Ka-erh-ya-sha (Gartok)
Lu-ma-hsia
Hsi-t'ai
Ni-ma
Yüeh-chu
T'o-lin [Cha-ta]
Chin-lo
K'un-mi-teng-li
Sang-ch'in La
Kung-hsieh-ya
K'o-yang-k'o-erh Shan 6371
Wen-po
P'u-pao [Pan-ko]
Men-shih
Kang-ti-ssu Shan 6714
Men-tung [Ts'o-ch'in]
Lung-ka-erh
Chia-to
Tsang-to
Teng-lung
Pa-ko
Mo-erh-k'o-sung
Shen-cha
T'o-ya
Ma-yu-mu Shan-k'ou
K'ang-ma-erh
Lang-ma
P'u-lan (Purang)
Sang-mu-sang
A-mu-chung
Sa-hsi-k'o-kung-pa
P'a-yang
La-p'a
K'o-shang-ta-mu
Na-mu-cha Shan-k'ou
Chung-pa
Pu-p'a-t'o
Hsi-lin-t'o
Lin-ka-kuo-k'o
Cha-tung (Tradom) [Chung-pa]
Nan-mu-lin (Namling)
Silgarhi
Jumla
P'ing-tu Shan-k'ou
Li-la-ssu
Sa-ka
La-ka
Mei-k'ang-sha
Hsieh-t'ung-men
Wu-yü
Chia-chia [Sa-ka]
T'ang-chia La
Sang-sang
Ang-jen
P'eng-ts'o-lin
Jih-k'a-tse (Shigatse)
Ta-chu-ch'a
Chiao-lo [Pai-lang]
Moradabad
Tsung-ka (Jongkha) [Chi-lung]
Lei-lung
La-kuo
Ch'ü-hsia [La-tzu]
Wang-tan
8172 Dhaulagiri
Manaslu
Chia-la Shan-k'ou
Man-k'a-pa
Hsieh-ko-erh (Shekar) [Ting-jih]
Sa-chia (Sakya)
Jen-tzu
Chiang-tzu (Gyangtse)
Bareilly
8078 Annapurna
Chi-lung (Kyerong)
8012 Hsi-hsia-pang-ma Feng
Ting-jih (Tingri)
To-cha-chung
K'ang-ma
Chiang-ka [Ting-chieh]
Ting-chieh
Kang-pa (Kampa)
Shahjahanpur
Ch'ung-tui [Nieh-la-mu]
Jung-hsia
Ch'ia-la
8848 Mt. Everest (Chu-mu-lang-ma Feng)
Je-ka-la Shan-k'ou
Kangchenjunga 8598
Pa-li
Ya-tung
Punakha
KATHMANDU
Bhadgaon
Patan
Gangtok
Darjeeling
Kalimpong
Lucknow
Gorakhpur
Dhankuta
Kanpur
Siliguri
Muzaffarpur
Ganges (Ganga)
Allahabad
Varanasi
Patna
Bhagalpur
A
B
C
D
80°
84°
88°
1
2
3
4
36°
32°
28°

1 : 4360000

0 10 20 30 40 50 60 70 80 90 100 150 200 250 300 350 400 MILES

0 10 20 30 40 50 60 70 80 90 100 150 200 250 300 350 400 450 500 550 600 KM

TIBET AUTONOMOUS REGION 西藏自治区

HSI-TSANG TZU-CHIH-CH'Ü

1 shih *municipality*
5 ti-ch'ü *regions*
71 hsien *counties*

capital **La-sa Shih**	**D3**	拉萨市
Ch'ü-shui Hsien	**D3**	曲水县
Kung-pu-chiang-ta Hsien		工布江达县
centre: Hsia-lung-hsiang	**E3**	峡龙乡
Lin-chih Hsien	**E3**	林芝县
Lin-chou Hsien		林周县
centre: Sung-p'an	**D3**	松盘
Mi-lin Hsien		米林县
centre: Tung-to	**E3**	东多
Mo-chu-kung-k'a Hsien		墨竹工卡县
centre: Kung-k'a	**E3**	工卡
Mo-t'o Hsien	**E3**	墨脱县
Ni-mu Hsien		尼木县
centre: T'a-jung	**D3**	塔荣
Tang-hsiung Hsien	**D3**	当雄县
Ta-tzu Hsien		达孜县
centre: Te-ch'ing	**D3**	德庆
Tui-lung-te-ch'ing Hsien		堆龙德庆县
centre: Lang-ka	**D3**	朗嘎

A-li Ti-ch'ü 阿里地区
Ari Region

centre: Shih-ch'üan-ho	**A2**	狮泉河
Cha-ta Hsien		札达县
centre: T'o-lin	**A3**	托林
Jih-t'u Hsien	**A2**	日土县
Ka-erh Hsien		噶尔县
centre: K'un-sa	**A2**	昆萨
Kai-tse Hsien	**C2**	改则县
Ko-chi Hsien		革吉县
centre: Na-p'o	**B2**	那坡
P'u-lan Hsien	**B3**	普兰县
Ts'o-ch'in Hsien		措勤县
centre: Men-tung	**C3**	门董

Ch'ang-tu Ti-ch'ü 昌都地区
Chamdo Region

centre: Ch'ang-tu	**F3**	
Ch'ang-tu Hsien	**F3**	昌都县
Ch'a-ya Hsien		察雅县
centre: Yen-to	**F3**	烟多
Ch'a-yü Hsien		察隅县
centre: Chi-kung	**F3**	吉公
Chiang-ta Hsien	**F3**	江达县
Kung-chiao Hsien		贡觉县
centre: Mo-lo	**F3**	莫洛
Lei-wu-ch'i Hsien	**F3**	类乌齐县
Lo-lung Hsien		洛隆县
centre: Tzu-t'o	**E3**	孜托
Mang-k'ang Hsien		芒康县
centre: Chu-k'a	**F3**	竹卡
Pa-su Hsien		八宿县
centre: Pai-ma	**F3**	白马
Pien-pa Hsien	**E3**	边坝县
Po-mi Hsien		波密县
centre: Cha-mu	**E3**	扎木
Ting-ch'ing Hsien	**E3**	丁青县
Tso-kung Hsien		左贡县
centre: Ya-chung	**F3**	亚中

Jih-k'a-tse Ti-ch'ü 日喀则地区
Shigatse Region

centre: Jih-k'a-tse	**D3**	
Ang-jen Hsien	**C3**	昂仁县
Chiang-tzu Hsien	**D3**	江孜县
Chi-lung Hsien		吉隆县
centre: Tsung-ka	**C3**	宗嘎
Chung-pa Hsien		仲巴县
centre: Cha-tung	**C3**	扎东
Hsieh-t'ung-men Hsien	**D3**	谢通门县
Jen-pu Hsien		仁布县
centre: Ch'iang-ch'in-hsüeh	**D3**	强钦雪
Jih-k'a-tse Hsien	**D3**	日喀则县
K'ang-ma Hsien	**D3**	康马县
Kang-pa Hsien	**D3**	岗巴县
La-tzu Hsien		拉孜县
centre: Ch'ü-hsia	**C3**	曲下
Nan-mu-lin Hsien	**D3**	南木林县
Nieh-la-mu Hsien		聂拉木县
centre: Ch'ung-tui	**C3**	冲堆
Pai-lang Hsien		白朗县
centre: Chiao-lo	**D3**	觉洛
Sa-chia Hsien	**D3**	萨加县
Sa-ka Hsien		萨噶县
centre: Chia-chia	**C3**	加加
Ting-chieh Hsien		定结县
centre: Chiang-ka	**C3**	江嘎
Ting-jih Hsien		定日县
centre: Hsieh-ko-erh	**C3**	协格尔
Ya-tung Hsien	**D4**	亚东县

Na-ch'ü Ti-ch'ü 那曲地区
Nagchu Region

centre: Hei-ho	**E3**	黑河
An-to Hsien	**D2**	安多县
Chia-li Hsien	**E3**	嘉黎县
Na-ch'ü Hsien		那曲县
centre: Hei-ho	**E3**	黑河
Nieh-jung Hsien		聂荣县
centre: Se-kung	**E2**	色贡
Pa-ch'ing Hsien		巴青县
centre: La-hsi-t'ang	**E2**	拉西堂
Pan-ko Hsien		班戈县
centre: P'u-pao	**D3**	普保
Pi-ju Hsien	**E3**	比如县
Shen-cha Hsien	**D3**	申扎县
So Hsien Hsien		索县
centre: Ya-la	**E3**	亚拉

Shan-nan Ti-ch'ü 山南地区
Loka Region

centre: Tse-tang	**D3**	泽当
Cha-nang Hsien		札囊县
centre: Cha-t'ang	**D3**	扎唐
Chia-ch'a Hsien		加查县
centre: Chung-pa	**E3**	仲巴
Ch'iung-chieh Hsien	**D3**	穷结县
Ch'ü-sung Hsien		曲松县
centre: La-chia-li	**E3**	拉叻里
Kung-ka Hsien		贡噶县
centre: Chi-hsiung	**D3**	吉雄
Lang-k'a-tzu Hsien	**D3**	浪卡子县
Lang Hsien		郎县
centre: La-to	**E3**	拉多
Lo-cha Hsien		洛扎县
centre: Ka-po	**D3**	嘎波
Lung-tzu Hsien		隆子县
centre: Hsin-pa	**E3**	新巴
Nai-tung Hsien	**D3**	乃东县
Sang-jih Hsien	**E3**	桑日县
Ts'o-mei Hsien		措美县
centre: Tang-hsü	**D3**	当许
Ts'o-na Hsien		错那县
centre: Hsüeh-hsia	**D4**	雪下

NINGSIA

HUI AUTONOMOUS REGION

NINGSIA, which had traditionally been a part of Kansu, became an independent province (though with different boundaries from the present ones) in 1928, and remained a province until 1954, when it was again absorbed by Kansu. In 1958 the areas of the Ningsia plain and the area around Ku-yuan, which had a largely Moslem (Hui) population, and were already organised in Hui autonomous districts, were constituted into the Hui Autonomous Region of Ningsia with provincial status. In 1969, following the dismemberment of Inner Mongolia, a large area of the Alashan Desert was added to Ningsia, which now extended north to the Mongolian frontier.

The Ningsia plain The central area of the province is formed by the broad alluvial plain of the Huang Ho, bounded on the east by the edge of the Shensi plateau, and on the west by the Ho-lan-shan (Alashan) mountain range. The plain is covered by a network of braided channels of the Huang Ho, further complicated by an extensive irrigation system, the beginnings of which go back to the Han period in the 1st century BC, when the area was first settled by the Chinese. Irrigation is essential for agriculture since the area is very arid, with only about 250 mm of rainfall, almost all of which falls in summer, and which is highly variable. It is an area of hard, cold winters, with temperatures too low for winter wheat. In the best irrigated areas non-glutinous rice of hardy varieties is grown; elsewhere spring wheat, with millets and kaoliang are the main grain crop. Soy beans, cotton, tobacco and hemp are important cash crops. Until the 1950s, transport in this area was very poor, and the region was almost exclusively agricultural. The coming of the railway between Pao-t'ou and Lan-chou in 1958, which traversed the Ningsia plain led to the development of some mining and industry.

Shih-tsui-shan at the northern extremity of the plain developed into an important coal-mining centre, specialising in the production of coking coal which is used in the Pao-t'ou iron and steel complex. Shih-tsui-shan is a part of an extensive coalfield, with mines at P'ing-lo, further south, and a northern extension into Inner Mongolia, where Wu-ta and Hai-po-wan are situated on the same seams. Shih-tsui-shan had a population of approximately 60,000 in 1959.

Yin-ch'uan is the old traditional centre of the Ningsia plain, and the provincial capital. It is an important highway centre, with routes leading westward into the desert, and situated at a bridgehead over the Huang Ho to the east. It was traditionally both an administrative and commercial centre, with processing industries using local grain, oil-seeds, wool and hides. Since the arrival of the railway in 1958 some modern industry, including textile mills, has been introduced.

Wu-chung is the main market and commercial centre of the southern section of the plain.

Southern Ningsia The southern extension of the province comprises the valley of the Ch'ing-shui Ho lying to the east of the Liu-pan mountain range. This area is the western extension of the Shensi plateau. Slightly less arid than the Ningsia plain, the area is devoted to spring-wheat agriculture, with a good deal of pastureland. Pastoral industry, particularly the rearing of horses and sheep, is very important.

Ku-yüan is the chief town, market and distribution centre.

The desert of north-western Ningsia The Ningsia plain is sharply bounded by the Ho-lan-shan (Alashan) range on the west. Beyond this range lies the Inner Mongolian plateau, an area of very arid grassland merging westward and north-westward into the true deserts of Sheng-ko-li and Pa-yin Chi-lin respectively. These desert areas are crossed by a low range of hills, the Ya-pu-lai range, which is a westerly extension of the Lang-shan and Yin-shan ranges in Inner Mongolia. The area is virtually uninhabited except for a small population of nomadic Mongol herdsmen. One important resource of the area is salt, which is produced at Lake Chi-lin-t'ai, terminus of a spur railway from Shih-tsui-shan.

Pa-yin-hao-t'e is the traditional centre of the Mongol banners of the Alashan region, and was joined to Yin-ch'uan by a highway in the 1950s.

Minority Peoples The whole of Ningsia has a very high proportion of Chinese Moslems, mostly settled in the Ningsia plain and around Ku-yüan in the south. Altogether they make up about one-third of the total population. The west and north-west of the province are almost exclusively peopled by Mongols.

NINGSIA HUI AUTONOMOUS REGION 宁夏回族自治区

NING-HSIA HUI-TSU TZU-CHIH-CH'Ü

2 shih	*municipalities*	
1 ti-ch'ü	*region*	
16 hsien	*counties*	
1 ch'i	*banner*	
capital **Yin-ch'uan Shih**	C2	银川市
Shih-tsui-shan Shih	C2	石咀山市
11 counties and one banner under direct regional administration:		
Ch'ing-t'ung-hsia Hsien	C2	青铜峡县
Chung-ning Hsien	C3	中宁县
Chung-wei Hsien	C3	中卫县
Ho-lan Hsien		贺兰县
centre: Hsi-kang	C2	习岗
Ling-wu Hsien	C2	灵武县
P'ing-lo Hsien	C2	平罗县
T'ao-lo Hsien		陶乐县
centre: Ma-t'ai-kou	C2	马太沟
T'ung-hsin Hsien	C3	同心县
Wu-chung Hsien	C2	吴忠县
Yen-ch'ih Hsien	D3	盐池县
Yung-ning Hsien		永宁县
centre: Yang-ho	C2	养和
A-la-shan Tso-ch'i Alashan East Banner		阿拉善左旗
centre: Pa-yen-hao-t'e	C2	巴彦浩特
Ku-yüan Ti-ch'ü	C3	固原地区
Ching-yüan Hsien	C4	泾源县
Hai-yüan Hsien	C3	海原县
Hsi-chi Hsien	C4	西吉县
Ku-yüan Hsien	C3	固原县
Lung-te Hsien	C4	隆德县

AREA
77,000 square kilometres

POPULATION
2,500,000

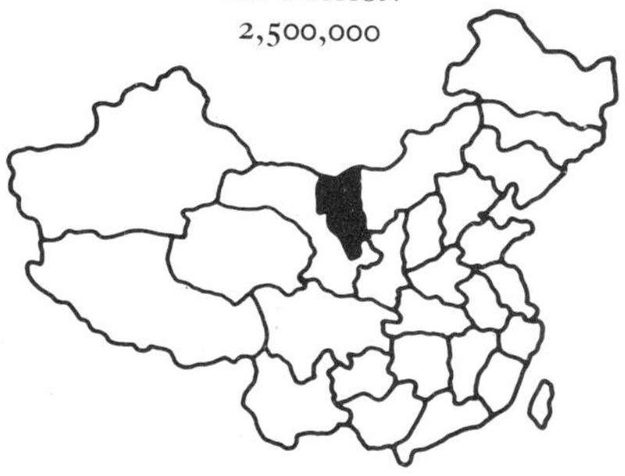

NINGSIA

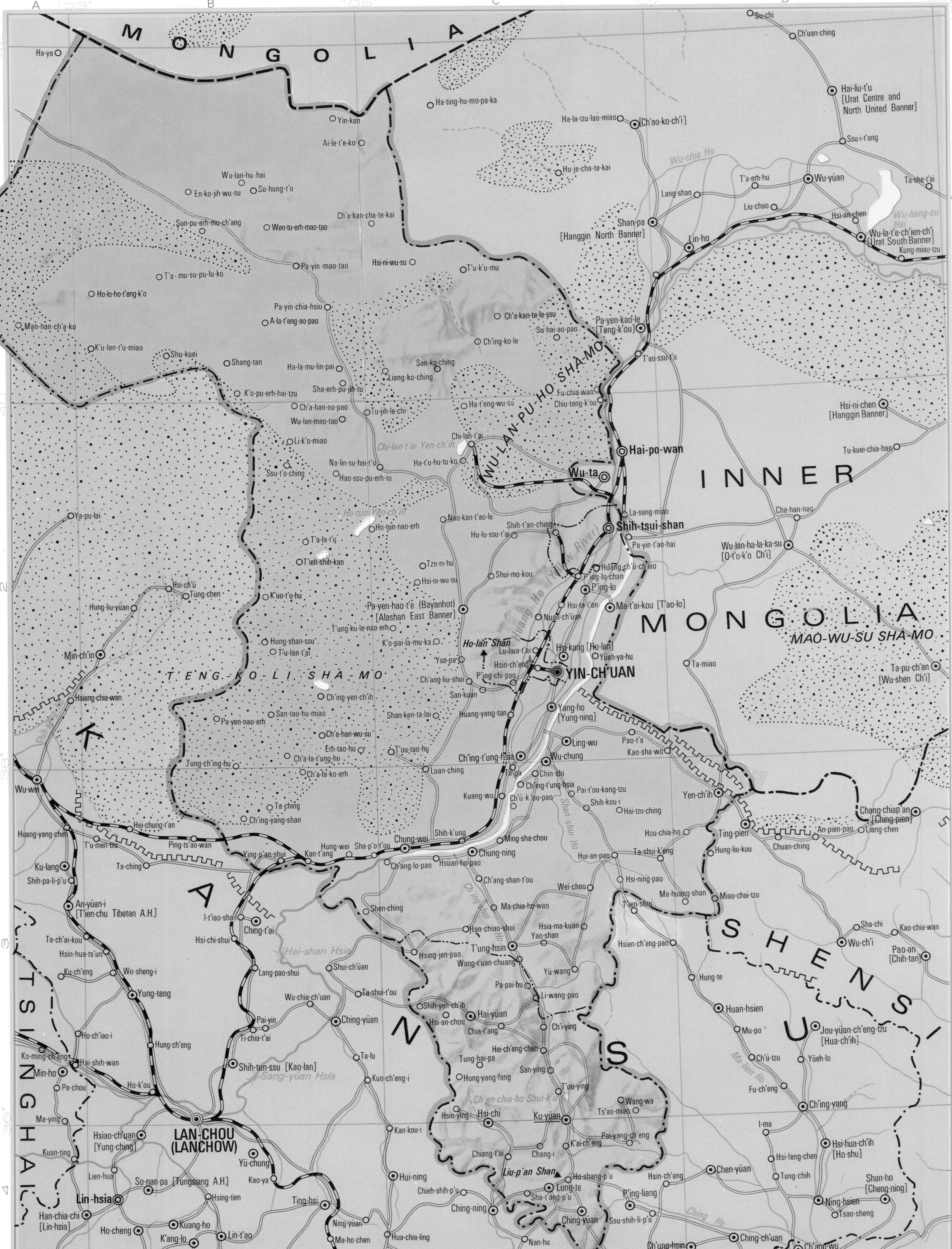

1 : 2 240 000

0 5 10 20 30 40 50 60 70 80 90 100 150 MILES

0 5 10 20 30 40 50 60 70 80 90 100 150 200 KM

SOUTH CHINA SEA ISLANDS

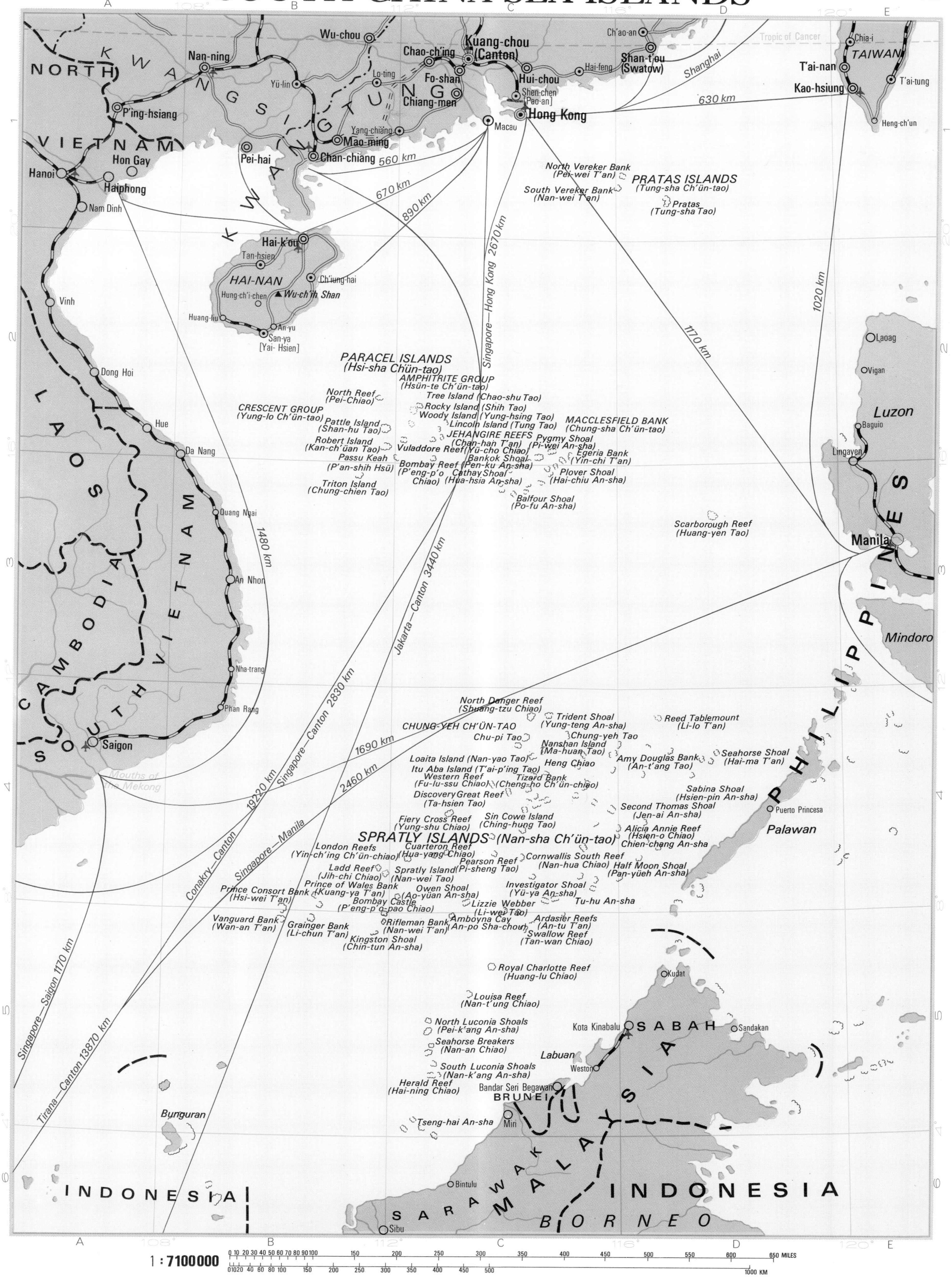

NORTH VIETNAM
KWANGSI
KWANGTUNG
Wu-chou
Nan-ning
Kuang-chou (Canton)
Chao-ch'ing
Fo-shan
Lo-ting
Yü-lin
Chiang-men
Hui-chou
Hai-feng
Ch'ao-an
Shan-t'ou (Swatow)
Shen-chen [Pao-an]
Hong Kong
Macau
Shanghai
Tropic of Cancer
630 km
Chia-i
TAIWAN
T'ai-nan
Kao-hsiung
T'ai-tung
Heng-ch'un
P'ing-hsiang
VIETNAM
Hon Gay
Hanoi
Haiphong
Nam Dinh
Pei-hai
Chan-chiang
Mao-ming
Yang-chiang
560 km
670 km
890 km
Hai-k'ou
Tan-hsien
HAI-NAN
Ch'iung-hai
Hung-ch'i-chen
Wu-ch'ih Shan
Huang-liu
An-yu
San-ya [Yai-Hsien]
Vinh
North Vereker Bank (Pei-wei T'an)
South Vereker Bank (Nan-wei T'an)
PRATAS ISLANDS (Tung-sha Ch'ün-tao)
Pratas (Tung-sha Tao)
Singapore—Hong Kong 2670 km
1170 km
1020 km
Laoag
Vigan
Luzon
Baguio
Lingayen
Manila
PHILIPPINES
Mindoro
PARACEL ISLANDS (Hsi-sha Chün-tao)
AMPHITRITE GROUP (Hsün-te Ch'ün-tao)
North Reef (Pei-Chiao)
Tree Island (Chao-shu Tao)
Rocky Island (Shih Tao)
Woody Island (Yung-hsing Tao)
Lincoln Island (Tung Tao)
CRESCENT GROUP (Yung-lo Ch'ün-tao)
Pattle Island (Shan-hu Tao)
Robert Island (Kan-ch'üan Tao)
Passu Keah (P'an-shih Hsü)
Triton Island (Chung-chien Tao)
Vuladdore Reef (Yü-cho Chiao)
JEHANGIRE REEFS (Chan-han T'an)
Bankok Shoal (Pen-ku An-sha)
Bombay Reef (P'eng-p'o Chiao)
Cathay Shoal (Hua-hsia An-sha)
MACCLESFIELD BANK (Chung-sha Ch'ün-tao)
Pygmy Shoal (Pi-wei An-sha)
Egeria Bank (Yin-chi T'an)
Plover Shoal (Hai-chiu An-sha)
Balfour Shoal (Po-fu An-sha)
Scarborough Reef (Huang-yen Tao)
Dong Hoi
LAOS
Hue
Da Nang
Quang Ngai
1480 km
SOUTH VIETNAM
An Nhon
CAMBODIA
Nha-trang
Phan Rang
Saigon
Mouths of the Mekong
Jakarta—Canton 3440 km
Singapore—Canton 2830 km
1690 km
2460 km
Conakry—Canton 19220 km
Singapore—Manila
Singapore—Saigon 1170 km
Tirana—Canton 13870 km
North Danger Reef (Shuang-tzu Chiao)
Trident Shoal (Yung-teng An-sha)
Reed Tablemount (Li-lo T'an)
CHUNG-YEH CH'ÜN-TAO
Chung-yeh Tao
Chu-pi Tao
Nanshan Island (Ma-huan Tao)
Loaita Island (Nan-yao Tao)
Itu Aba Island (T'ai-p'ing Tao)
Heng Chiao
Amy Douglas Bank (An-t'ang Tao)
Seahorse Shoal (Hai-ma T'an)
Western Reef (Fu-lu-ssu Chiao)
Tizard Bank (Cheng-ho Ch'ün-chiao)
Discovery Great Reef (Ta-hsien Tao)
Sabina Shoal (Hsien-pin An-sha)
Second Thomas Shoal (Jen-ai An-sha)
Puerto Princesa
Palawan
Fiery Cross Reef (Yung-shu Chiao)
Sin Cowe Island (Ching-hung Tao)
Alicia Annie Reef (Hsien-o Chiao)
SPRATLY ISLANDS (Nan-sha Ch'ün-tao)
Chien-chang An-sha
London Reefs (Yin-ch'ing Ch'ün-chiao)
Cuarteron Reef (Hua-yang Chiao)
Cornwallis South Reef (Nan-hua Chiao)
Pearson Reef (Pi-sheng Tao)
Half Moon Shoal (Pan-yüeh An-sha)
Ladd Reef (Jih-chi Chiao)
Spratly Island (Nan-wei Tao)
Prince of Wales Bank (Kuang-ya T'an)
Owen Shoal (Ao-yüan An-sha)
Investigator Shoal (Yü-ya An-sha)
Prince Consort Bank (Hsi-wei T'an)
Bombay Castle (P'eng-p'o-pao Chiao)
Lizzie Webber (Li-wei Tao)
Tu-hu An-sha
Vanguard Bank (Wan-an T'an)
Grainger Bank (Li-chun T'an)
Rifleman Bank (Nan-wei T'an)
Amboyna Cay (An-po Sha-chou)
Ardasier Reefs (An-tu T'an)
Swallow Reef (Tan-wan Chiao)
Kingston Shoal (Chin-tun An-sha)
Royal Charlotte Reef (Huang-lu Chiao)
Kudat
Louisa Reef (Nan-t'ung Chiao)
North Luconia Shoals (Pei-k'ang An-sha)
Kota Kinabalu
SABAH
Sandakan
Seahorse Breakers (Nan-an Chiao)
Labuan
Weston
South Luconia Shoals (Nan-k'ang An-sha)
Herald Reef (Hai-ning Chiao)
Bandar Seri Begawan
BRUNEI
Bunguran
Tseng-hai An-sha
Miri
MALAYSIA
SARAWAK
Bintulu
Sibu
INDONESIA
BORNEO
1 : 7100000
MILES
KM

THE SOUTH CHINA SEA ISLANDS

CHINA claims possession of some 160 islands, mostly very small, in the South China Sea. These have been placed under the provincial administration of Kwangtung Province. There are four main groups.

The Tung-sha Chün-tao comprises Tung-sha Tao, which has deposits of guano, and two coral reefs lying south-east of Hong Kong. Chinese possession of these islands is uncontested.

The Hsi-sha Chün-tao (The Paracel Islands) lie to the south-east of Hainan Island. The Chinese claim sovereignty over these islands since Ming times, although they are also claimed by South Vietnam, to which they were ceded by France. The main islands are Yung-hsing Tao, Shih Tao, Chao-shu Tao and Tung Tao. The group is a source of phosphates, guano and fish, and there are suspected deposits of oil.

The Chung-sha Chün-tao, lying to the east of the Paracels, is a group of sandbanks and shoals of little importance.

The Nan-sha Chün-tao (Spratly Islands), lying north of Borneo and west of Palawan, is the most extensive of the groups. It comprises, besides a large number of coral reefs and sandbanks, nine main islands, the largest of which are Ching-hung Tao, T'ai-p'ing Tao, Li-wei Tao and Chung-ye Tao, known collectively as the Nan-hai Chiu-tao.

Sovereignty of the islands is disputed. Vietnam claims that the islands appeared as Vietnamese on their maps as long ago as 1834. Phosphate mining under Japanese management began in 1917 and ceased in 1929. Operations were resumed in 1937 and Japan annexed the islands in 1939, but renounced her claim at the San Francisco Peace Conference in 1951. France occupied certain of the main islands in 1930 and erected a number of lighthouses. In 1933 the French claimed sovereignty over T'ai-p'ing Tao, Shuang-tzu Chiao, Nan-yao Tao and Chu-pi Tao. A Chinese garrison was stationed on T'ai-p'ing Tao from 1946 to 1949. The Philippines lodged a claim in 1955. The British, too, have a historical connection with the islands but no claim has been lodged in public for several decades.

TAIWAN

THE Chinese first discovered Taiwan at the beginning of the 7th century, when it was given the name Liu-ch'iu. But no permanent relations were established. Chinese fishermen and a few settlers from the coast of Fukien landed and settled on the west coast in the late Ming period (1368–1644), but this colonisation was ended by the arrival first of the Portuguese, and then of the Dutch, who conquered the island in 1642, and set up a colonial government in the south of the island. They in turn were ousted by a loyalist leader of the defeated Ming, Cheng Cheng-kung (Koxinga), who defeated the Dutch in 1661. This conquest was followed by a wave of immigration from the mainland, which continued after the Manchu forces invaded the island in 1683 and incorporated it into Fukien province. The Chinese settlers soon occupied the fertile western plains, and drove the aboriginal peoples into the mountains. Taiwan became an independent province in 1887, and under a forceful governor made some rapid steps towards modernisation. However, in 1895 Taiwan was transferred to Japan, as part of the settlement following the disastrous Sino–Japanese War of 1894–5.

Under the Japanese the island underwent rapid economic expansion, producing tropical goods and natural resources to supply the Japanese market. Good road and rail systems were established, large-scale irrigation and water-conservancy schemes built in the western plains, and a major hydro-electric scheme built at the Jih-yüeh-t'an lake in the central mountains. A certain amount of industry was also begun, including a large aluminium smelter at Kao-hsiung. Chinese settlement also began in the small plains and valleys of the west coast.

In 1945, the province was returned to China. There was considerable resistance to the Nationalist government, leading to a rising of the Taiwanese in 1947, which was harshly suppressed. In 1949 the island came firmly under the Nationalist regime, when the Chinese government, driven from the mainland, established itself in T'ai-pei, bringing with it an influx of some 2,000,000 persons from the mainland.

Sustained in its early years by lavish US aid, and protected by US military power, the Nationalist government has nevertheless contributed to a great advance in the province's economy. An effective land reform was carried through after 1949, but attempts to encourage co-operatives came to nothing. The result is a highly fragmented agriculture. Attempts to extend irrigation in the north-west were made after 1954, and output of grain rose markedly in the late 1950s and early 1960s. There was also a very rapid increase in industry, particularly in textile and light industries producing consumer goods. In recent years Japanese capital has again begun to be invested in Taiwan, and the rate of growth remains very high.

The island has a tropical climate similar to that of Kwangtung province, with January temperatures ranging from 14°C (57°F) in the north to 20°C (68°F) in the extreme south, and July temperatures around 26°C (79°F) to 28°C (82°F). Rainfall is very heavy. Except for the western coastal strip, all Taiwan has more than 1,500 mm, and the central mountainous districts have 3,000 mm and more. In the south there is a marked difference between a very dry winter and very wet summer, but in the north there is also much winter rain, and Chi-lung actually has a winter maximum. The island was naturally covered with rich tropical forest, but the western plain has been almost entirely cleared for cultivation.

The western plain The western coastal plain, which is very densely populated, was the site of early Dutch and Chinese colonisation, and was mostly settled by Chinese farmers before 1895. It is highly fertile, but because of the uneven distribution of rainfall, irrigation is desirable. A major irrigation system, the Chia-nan canal scheme, was built by the Japanese between 1920–30 in the southern area around T'ai-nan, and this continues to service a large and intensively cultivated area. The plain also has an excellent network of rail-lines and roads. The whole coastal area from Chi-lung to Kao-hsiung is a region of intensive paddy rice cultivation. Two rice crops per year, followed by a catch crop in winter, is normal. Sweet potatoes are also widely grown, and in the southern part of the plain wheat is common.

Sugar-cane was introduced under the Dutch, and became a major economic crop under the Japanese, especially in the southern half of the plain, where the irrigation system is best developed.

In the hilly area of the north-western coast, and in the central western mountain areas, where there is more rain in winter, tea is grown extensively. Throughout the western foothills of the central mountains, fruit production is important, especially in the area around T'ai-chung and to the south. Pineapples, bananas, mango, citrus fruits, persimmons and peaches are widely grown, and large quantities of those fruits are canned and exported. The plain around T'ai-chung produces sisal and jute.

T'ai-pei is the administrative capital of Taiwan, and the chief cultural centre. A city of some 600,000 people, it is a centre of the textile and light industries making consumer goods. It produces chemical fertilisers, paper and cement, and has a small engineering industry. Much of the raw materials for these industries is imported through Chi-lung.

T'ai-nan, with a population of 250,000, is the main market and commercial centre of the southern plain. It is a major centre of sugar refining and has a small textile industry.

Kao-hsiung was developed into a major port under the Japanese, replacing T'ai-nan which had silted up and could no longer be used. In 1935 they also set up an aluminium smelter here, which remains important. Since 1949, Kao-hsiung has become the main heavy industrial centre in Taiwan, with iron and steel works, engineering, shipbuilding, oil refining, chemical and fertiliser plants and cement works. It also has a textile industry.

Chi-lung is Taiwan's other major port. It has a very flourishing trade, and a small shipbuilding and chemical industry. The island's only substantial coal mines, producing about 2,700,000 tons annually, are nearby.

Hsin-chu at the northern end of the coastal plain has also developed diversified industries: textiles, paper-making, glass making, cement, chemical fertilisers and oil refining.

The central mountains The eastern half of Taiwan is very mountainous, with high ranges of mountains with peaks of up to 3,950 m, and very rugged terrain. The westernmost range is called the A-li Shan, which is much faulted, with a number of depressions, one of which contains the Jih-yüeh-t'an lake. The eastern ranges are even higher, and mostly composed of ancient metamorphic rocks.

This area is heavily forested, much of it with hardwoods. The Japanese built a lumber railway into the A-li Shan to exploit the timber, particularly camphor wood. But extensive exploitation of the forests is difficult because of inadequate transportation. In these upland areas live most of the island's aboriginal population. There are only a few scattered areas of Chinese settlement.

The T'ai-tung area On the east, this mountain zone is abruptly broken by a major rift valley, separating the main mountains from the T'ai-tung range, which drops precipitously to the east coast. This valley, which extends from T'ai-tung in the south to Hua-lien, was first settled during the Japanese occupation, and is an area of intensive rice and sugar cultivation..

The I-lan basin is a small coastal basin in the north-east, again settled from the 19th century onwards, and intensively cultivated with double-cropped rice.

The P'ing-tung plain Situated on the west coast at the southern end of the island, this basin is the valley of the Hsia-t'an Shui river, which has built up an extensive alluvial plain. This area is a region of intensive cultivation of rice and sugar, and also an important producer of fruit, especially bananas.

TAIWAN		臺灣
TAI-WAN		
5 shih	*municipalities*	
16 hsien	*counties*	
capital **T'ai-pei Shih**	C1	臺北市
Chi-lung Shih	C1	基隆市
Kao-hsiung Shih	B4	高雄市
T'ai-chung Shih	B2	臺中市
T'ai-nan Shih	B4	臺南市
Chang-hua Hsien	B2	彰化縣
Chia-i Hsien	B3	嘉義縣
Hsin-chu Hsien	B2	新竹縣
Hua-lien Hsien	C3	花蓮縣
I-lan Hsien	C2	宜蘭縣
Kao-hsiung Hsien	B4	高雄縣
Miao-li Hsien	B2	苗栗縣
Nan-t'ou Hsien	B3	南投縣
P'eng-hu Hsien		澎湖縣
centre: Ma-kung	A3	馬公
P'ing-tung Hsien	B4	屛東縣
T'ai-chung Hsien	B2	臺中縣
T'ai-nan Hsien	B4	臺南縣
T'ai-pei Hsien	C1	臺北縣
T'ai-tung Hsien	C4	臺東縣
T'ao-yüan Hsien	C2	桃園縣
Yün-lin Hsien		雲林縣
centre: Tou-liu	B3	斗六

AREA
36,000 square kilometres

POPULATION
15,000,000

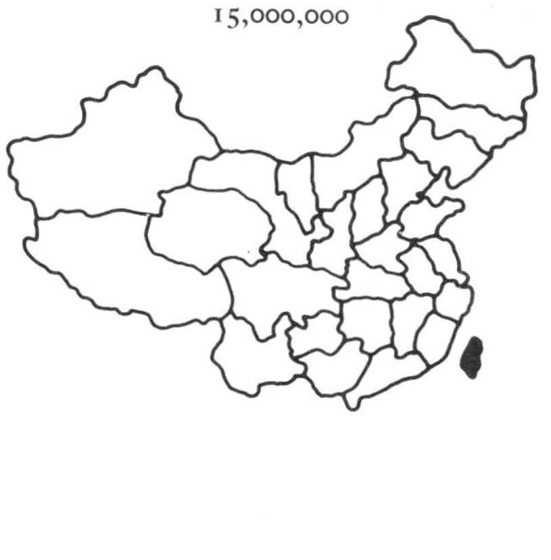

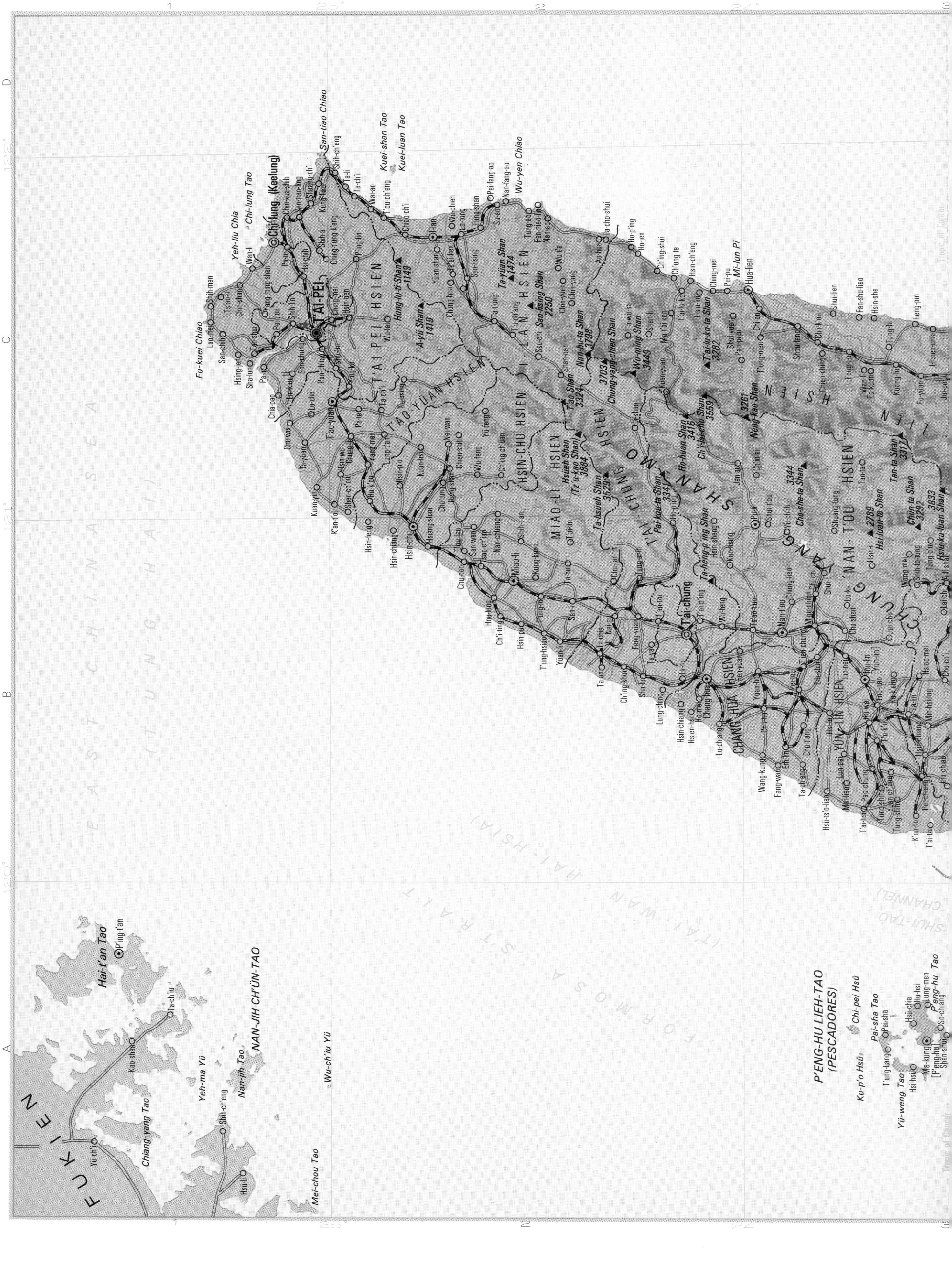
EAST CHINA SEA
(TUNG HAI)
FORMOSA STRAIT
(T'AI-WAN HAI-HSIA)
SHUI-TAO
CHANNEL)
T'AI-PEI
Chi-lung (Keelung)
T'AI-PEI HSIEN
T'AO-YÜAN HSIEN
HSIN-CHU HSIEN
MIAO-LI HSIEN
T'AI-CHUNG HSIEN
CHANG-HUA HSIEN
YÜN-LIN HSIEN
NAN-T'OU HSIEN
I-LAN HSIEN
HSIEN
LIEN
SHAN-MO
CHUNG-YANG
Hsin-chu
T'ai-chung
Chang-hua
Miao-li
T'ao-yüan
I-lan
Hua-lien
Nan-t'ou
Tou-liu
San-tiao Chiao
Fu-kuei Chiao
Yeh-liu Chia
Chi-lung Tao
Kuei-shan Tao
Kuei-luan Tao
Wu-yen Chiao
Mi-lun Pi
Ta-yüan Shan 1474
Hung-lu-ti Shan 1149
A-yü Shan 1419
San-hsing Shan 2250
Nan-hu-ta Shan 3798
Tao Shan 3324
Wu-ming Shan 3449
Chung-yang-chien Shan 3703
T'ai-lu-ko-ta Shan 3282
Ch'i-lai-chu Shan 3559
Ho-huan Shan 3416
Neng-kao Shan 3261
Hsüeh Shan (Tz'u-kao Shan) 3884
Ta-hsüeh Shan 3529
Pai-kou-ta Shan 3341
Ta-heng-p'ing Shan
Cho-she-ta Shan 3344
Tan-ta Shan 3317
Ch'ün-ta Shan 3292
Hsi-luan-ta Shan 2789
Hsiu-ku-luan Shan 3833
P'ENG-HU LIEH-TAO
(PESCADORES)
Ma-kung
[P'eng-hu]
P'eng-hu Tao
Chi-pei Hsü
Pai-sha Tao
Ku-p'o Hsü
Yü-weng Tao
FUKIEN
Hai-t'an Tao
P'ing-t'an
NAN-JIH CH'ÜN-TAO
Nan-jih Tao
Yeh-ma Yü
Wu-ch'iu Yü
Chiang-yang Tao
Mei-chou Tao
Yü-ch'i
Kao-shan
Shih-ch'eng
Hsü-li
Ta-ch'iu
Tropic of Cancer
25°
24°
122°
121°
120°
1
2
A
B
C
D

TAIWAN

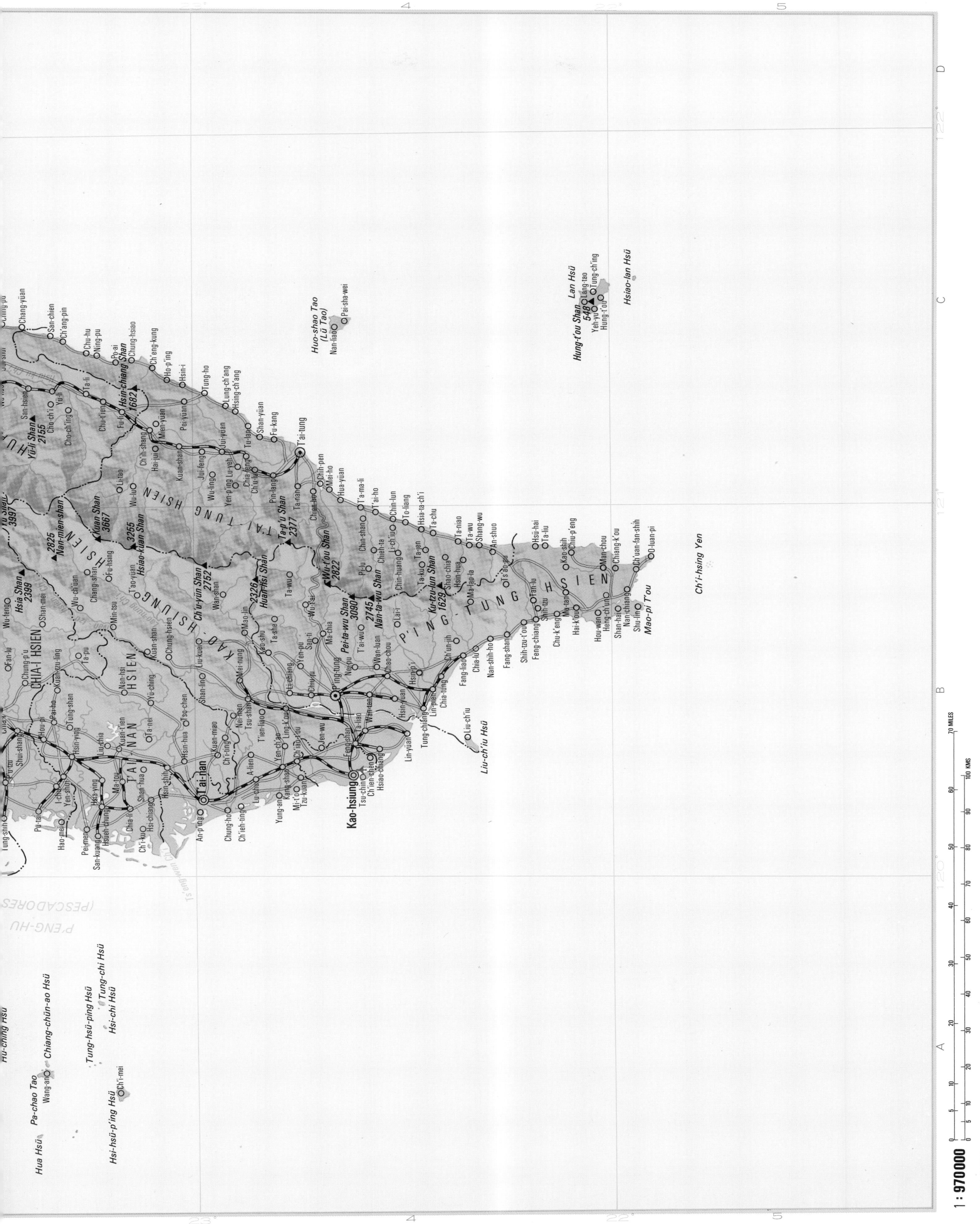

Lan Hsü
Hsiao-lan Hsü
Hung-t'ou Shan 548
Huo-shao Tao (Lü Tao)
Ch'i-hsing Yen
Mao-pi T'ou
Liu-ch'iu Hsü
T'ai-tung
Kao-hsiung
T'ai-nan
P'ing-tung
P'ING TUNG HSIEN
KAO HSIUNG HSIEN
T'AI TUNG HSIEN
CHIA-I HSIEN
T'AI NAN HSIEN
Pei-ta-wu Shan 3090
Wu-t'ou Shan 2822
Kuan Shan 3667
Hsiao-kuan Shan 3255
Ch'u-yün Shan 2752
Hsin-chiang Shan 1682
Yü-li Shan 2155
Hsia Shan 2399
Nan-ta-wu Shan 2745
Ku-tzu-lun Shan 1629
Ta-p'u Shan 2377
Huan-hsi Shan 2326
Nan-mien-shan 2825
P'ENG-HU (PESCADORES)
Hua Hsü
Pa-chao Tao
Chiang-chün-ao Hsü
Tung-hsü-p'ing Hsü
Tung-chi Hsü
Hsi-chi Hsü
Hsi-hsü-p'ing Hsü
70 MILES
100 KMS
1 : 970000

CITIES OF CHINA

PEKING
(PEI-CHING)
Population 2,768,000 (1953); 7,570,000 (1973 estimate)*

Peking, now a municipality under direct central administration, has always occupied a strategic position in the North China Plain, near the gateways to Mongolia and Manchuria. The city was established in very early times and became the capital of the Liao dynasty in the 10th century, under the name of Yen-ching. During the China dynasty in the 12th century, it was known as Ch'ung-tu, and then, under the Mongols, as Khanbalyk (or Ta-tu, its Chinese name) during the golden age of the city when Kublai Khan made it his capital. After 1368, during the early years of the Ming dynasty, Nan-ching was the capital, but Peking resumed its position in 1421 under its present name, and has retained this status, except between 1928 and 1949 when, under the Nationalists, Nan-ching once again replaced it.

The plan of the present city dates from the 13th century. It consists of two walled cities: the Inner City, now the seat of government, which contains the palace of the Mings and the Manchus, known as the Forbidden City; and the Outer City, the main commercial quarters, which adjoins it on the south.

Peking is the cultural and educational capital of the country. Its universities and institutes are situated for the most part in the western suburbs, though housing and educational establishments have also been built to the west and north-west of the city proper.

Industry has been concentrated in the east. The industrial development of Peking before 1949 was based largely on anthracite mines at Men-t'ou-kou, the Shih-ching-shan iron and steel plant west of the city and the engineering industry to the south-west. During the 1950s there was rapid industrial growth east of Peking on the road to T'ung-chou. The Great Leap Forward accelerated expansion and many new industries were established. The steel industry was fully integrated in 1969 and supports a major machine-building and engineering industry which produces heavy constructional steel, locomotives, machine tools, motor vehicles and ball bearings. There is a large chemical industry, electronics and textiles.

Increasing industrialisation and Peking's revived political role as the capital of China led to extension of its municipal area. Soon after 1949, the area almost doubled in size, from 270 to 500 square miles, and by 1958 the total area of the municipality area of Peking was 6,600 square miles.

In the past Peking was linked, through its canal port, T'ung-chou, with the southern parts of the country. The city's importance as a focus for transport and a centre for distribution has been maintained by extensive railway construction and lines radiate from Peking to Wu-han, Canton, Chang-chia-k'ou, Pao-t'ou, Tientsin, Shen-yang, T'ung-chou and Ch'eng-te.

SHANGHAI
(SHANG-HAI)
Population 6,204,000 (1953); 12,000,000 (1973 estimate)

Shanghai is China's largest city and the largest city on the continent of Asia. The municipality covers approximately 2,250 square miles, since its extension in 1958, but its population is concentrated in the central urban area. The city was a relatively insignificant port until 1842 when it was opened to foreign trade. Thanks to its position near the estuary of the Yangtze, the most important waterway of China, it rapidly became China's chief port for foreign trade and the main centre of Western commercial and cultural influence. From the late 19th century it also became China's principal industrial city. Before 1937 it contained more than half of China's textile industry and a wide range of other industries, many of which were foreign-owned.

Before 1949 nearly half of China's imports and exports passed through Shanghai. The principal exports were raw silk, tea, tung-oil, eggs, hog bristles and ores; and food, manufactured goods, including cotton and woollen goods, petrol, steel and chemicals were imported. After 1949 this trade and the industry which it had generated sharply declined. The government deliberately developed other areas of the interior in an attempt to re-locate industry, both for strategic reasons and to encourage rational economic planning. In the 1950s, however, it became clear that Shanghai was unique as an industrial centre and that its growth should continue. Shanghai's industrial base changed: the city's textile industry, though still very important, was eclipsed by the development of heavy industry. Iron and steel production began in the 1950s and during the Great Leap Forward this already flourishing industry was expanded until Shanghai became the second largest steel producer of China. The city is also a major producer of copper, lead and zinc. There are large chemical, electrical and engineering industries, oil refineries, glass, cement and fertiliser plants and a variety of light industries.

Shanghai is an important cultural centre and supports a thriving publishing industry. The city has many universities, research institutes, libraries, museums and theatres.

TIENTSIN
(T'IEN-CHIN)
Population 2,694,000 (1953); 4,280,000 (1970 estimate)

Tientsin is the third largest city in China and an independent municipality under central government. The city was of little importance until the mid-19th century, when it was opened to foreign trade and concessions were granted to several European powers. The city was destroyed during the Boxer Rebellion in 1900 and has been entirely reconstructed. It is situated on the Hai Ho, 25 miles from the sea, and with the aid of continuous dredging and the construction of an artificial harbour on the north bank of the estuary, it has been developed as an outlet for the products of North China and Inner Mongolia.

Tientsin's land communications complement its function as one of China's major ports. It is on the Peking–Shen-yang railway, through which it has access to Manchuria and Inner Mongolia, and is the northern terminus of the Tientsin–P'u-k'ou railway. Small junks, which still carry a considerable proportion of freight, use the network of waterways converging at Tientsin, particularly the Grand Canal–Wei Ho route leading to Hsin-hsiang in Honan.

The city was already a major centre of modern industry before 1937, when large cotton and woollen textile plants, and a variety of other industries were established. Since 1949 Tientsin has been rapidly developed as a centre of heavy industry, with an emphasis on iron and steel production, machinery and engineering. There is also a chemical industry, producing pharmaceuticals and industrial chemicals; and oil refining and petrochemicals using oil from the Ta-kang field on the northern outskirts of the city. Light industry, particularly textiles, food processing, rubber, paper making and electronics, remains important.

Tientsin is not a historic city, but it is a cultural centre with three universities and several specialised institutions of higher learning. It has libraries, museums and an observatory.

NAN-CHING
(NANKING)
Population 1,092,000 (1953); 1,700,000 (1970 estimate)

Nan-ching, the provincial capital of Kiangsu since 1952, has been an important administrative centre from the 2nd century BC. In 221 AD it became capital of the southern kingdom of Wu and remained the main cultural and political city of southern China until 589. It again became capital of an independent state between 937–75 and grew rapidly as the Yangtze valley developed into the economic hub of the empire under the Sung (10th–13th centuries). Between 1368 and 1403 the city was the capital of the Empire under the Ming and it remained a secondary capital until 1644. During this period it became a national centre of culture and learning and grew into a very prosperous commercial city. Nan-ching was taken by the T'ai-p'ing rebels in 1853 and stayed in their hands until 1864, during which period the city suffered a great deal of damage. From 1927–37, and again in 1945–49, it was the capital of the Nationalist government of China. Between 1937 and 1945 it had been occupied by the Japanese and large parts of the city had been destroyed.

Until 1949 it was predominantly an administrative and commercial city, with little modern industry, although it was famous for its traditional textiles and handicrafts. Since 1950 it has been developed into a major industrial city. The textile industry has been expanded, and iron and steel, engineering, machinery, electronics, chemical, synthetic fibre and plastics, fertiliser and cement industries have been established. A bridge across the Yangtze was opened in 1969.

Nan-ching has many notable historical sites, museums and institutes of higher education.

HANG-CHOU
(HANGCHOW)
Population 697,000 (1953); 800,000 (1970 estimate)

The provincial capital of Chekiang, Hang-chou, is situated on the estuary of the Ch'ien-t'ang river, at the southern terminus of the Grand Canal which was completed in 609 AD. Already a great and prosperous city in the 7th century, Hang-chou was capital of China under the Southern Sung (1127–1280) and grew immensely wealthy, with a population of well over a million. It was never again as significant as a political centre, but it remained a very important regional city, renowned for its beauty, its scenery and for the culture and elegance of its people.

Commercially it went into a decline after the 14th century, as its trade moved to Ning-po and later to Shanghai. The city's transport system was improved by the construction of railways to Shanghai (1909), to Kiangsi and Hunan (1936–8) and to Ning-po (1937). It is the focus of all rail traffic from the south-east to Shanghai.

Since 1949 while Hang-chou has been carefully preserved as a beauty spot and tourist attraction, it has also been developed as an industrial city. It is a major producer of cotton and silk textiles, has a large chemical industry and works producing machinery and machine tools, and some food processing industry. The city has a large university and several other institutions of higher education.

CANTON
(KUANG-CHOU)
Population 1,599,000 (1953); 3,000,000 (1970 estimate)

Canton (the name is a corruption of Kwangtung, the province of which the city is capital) is an ancient city and the main centre of the province since its final conquest by the Chinese in the 2nd century BC. From the 5th century AD it became the major port for sea trade with Indonesia, South-east Asia, India and the Near East, with a very large foreign community. Although its role in overseas trade was reduced by the growth of the rival ports of Chang-chou and Hsia-men (Amoy) between the 11th–14th centuries, it remained a major port and the centre of an increasingly prosperous and populous province. In the 17th and 18th centuries all foreign sea-borne trade was concentrated here, under strict government control. The city became the scene of the confrontation with the western powers which ended in the Opium War of 1839–42.

Canton flourished for a while after it had been opened to foreign trade in the mid-19th century, but the rapid growth of Shanghai and the development and prosperity of nearby Hong Kong, which had been ceded to the British after 1842, soon reduced its share of foreign trade. It remained a focus of western influence, both cultural and commercial, and in the late 19th century became a forum for various revolutionary movements. The city was an important centre for national politics until the foundation of the Nationalist regime in 1928.

After the completion of the railway to Han-k'ou in 1936, Canton's trade was predominantly with the interior of the country. The city is the centre of the river trade in the Canton Delta and junks, the chief means of transport, carry goods up the Hsi Chiang, the Pei Chiang and the Tung Chiang into the interior of Kwangtung and Kwangsi. Its principal industries are sugar refining, newsprint manufacture, cement, chemicals, engineering and ship building, and the city also has a range of light industry. Canton is the site of an important annual trade fair, the main showcase for China's produce for buyers from the rest of the world.

Canton is a very important cultural centre. It has several museums, a number of major libraries, several universities and institutes for research.

CH'ANG-CH'UN
(CHANGCHUN)
Population 855,000 (1953); 975,000 (1958 estimate)

When southern Kirin was opened to Chinese colonisation in the 18th century, Ch'ang-ch'un was established to administer the peasant settlers from Shantung and Hopei who had moved there. The completion of the Chinese Eastern Railway in 1901 and later Japanese dominance in the area promoted a new period of growth, until in 1932 Ch'ang-ch'un became the capital of Manchukuo under the name of Hsin-ching. A pleasant modern city was constructed as an administrative centre, with a university and only a limited development of light industry.

Under the Communist regime the character of Ch'ang-ch'un underwent a radical change. Although it remained an important administrative centre, and the provincial capital of Kirin province, Ch'ang-ch'un now became the rapidly expanding centre of a large engineering industry, manufacturing, in particular, trucks, tractors, buses, railway stock and cars. It is now the chief centre of the Chinese automotive industry. In recent years a large chemical and pharmaceutical industry has also grown up. The city has two universities, colleges and research institutes.

HA-ERH-PIN
(HARBIN)
Population 1,163,000 (1953); 2,000,000 (1970 estimate)

Ha-erh-pin, the capital of the province of Heilungkiang, was an insignificant fishing village before the construction of the Chinese Eastern Railway, when it developed into the centre of rail communications in northern Manchuria. The city has long established flour mills, tobacco and soy bean processing plants and dairy and sugar-refining industries. Heavy industry was developed under Japanese rule, and the city now produces a large number of turbines, electric motors and machine tools.

LAN-CHOU
(LANCHOW)
Population 397,000 (1953); 699,000 (1958 estimate)

When Kansu was made an independent province in 1666, Lan-chou, a major strategic and commercial centre since early times, became its capital. Since the war, the Communist administration has developed Lan-chou from the administrative centre of a poverty-stricken and backward province into a major industrial city. Its rail communications have been greatly improved, and the highways constructed in the 1930s, when Lan-chou was a focus of Soviet influence, are still the arterial routes of the north-west. Major power resources have been established – a thermal generating plant, a hydro-electric station and a large multi-purpose dam at the Liu-chia gorge. Lan-chou has also become a centre of the petro-chemical industry, with a large refinery serving the fields at Yü-men, and the site for China's nuclear industry. Oil industry equipment, railway stock and machine tools are manufactured, and there are large industrial chemical and rubber industries. Lan-chou remains the market for produce from the surrounding well-irrigated region and has a large woollen industry. It is the cultural centre of Kansu, with a university and a complex of technical schools and institutes.

* The only reliable population figures available are those given in the 1953 census. All other figures are estimates only.

CHENG-CHOU

(CHENGCHOW)

Population 595,000 (1953); 1,100,000 (1970 estimate)

The city has been provincial capital of Honan since 1954, situated to the south of the Huang Ho river and at the eastern extremity of the Hsiung-erh Shan mountain range. It is generally identified with the Shang capital city of Ao. It achieved its greatest importance under the Sui, T'ang and early Sung when, as the terminus of the Pien-ho canal, it was near a vast granary complex from which provisions were shipped westwards to the capitals at Lo-yang and Ch'ang-an, or northwards to the armies on the frontier around Peking. In 1903 the Peking–Han-k'ou railway arrived at Cheng-chou, and thereafter it became a major rail junction for handling agricultural produce. After 1949, because Cheng-chou was in the centre of a densely peopled cotton-growing district with excellent communications, it was deliberately developed into a modern industrial city. Its industries remain largely based on local agriculture and textiles. This rapid industrial growth has involved a phenomenal increase in the city's population, and there has been an enormous building programme, involving the reconstruction of much of the old city.

CHI-NAN

(TSINAN, JINAN)

Population 680,000 (1953); 862,000 (1958 estimate)

When Shantung province was created under the Ming (1368–1644), Chi-nan, a city which had enjoyed considerable importance as an administrative and religious centre for many centuries, was a natural choice as capital. The modern phase of Chi-nan's growth began in 1852, when the Huang Ho shifted its course to flow in the old bed of the Chi river just north of the city and provided a link for small craft with the Grand Canal and the waterways of Shantung and Hopeh. The construction of excellent rail communications in the early years of this century meant that Chi-nan rapidly became a commercial centre for the agricultural region to the north and developed much light industry.

Since 1949 it has been swiftly and deliberately developed both as an administrative centre and also as a major centre of modern industry. The pre-war textile and flour-milling industries have been expanded and iron and steel, automotive and machine-building industries established. Chi-nan has also become the chief cultural centre of Shantung, with agricultural, medical and engineering colleges and a large university.

T'AI-YÜAN

(TAIYUAN)

Population 721,000 (1953); 1,020,000 (1958 estimate)

Situated on both banks of the Fen Ho river, commanding the north–south route through Shansi and natural lines of communication through the mountains to Hopeh and northern Shansi, T'ai-yüan has been an important city throughout Chinese history. The modern city dates from the Sung period, when it was built to replace the old, heavily-fortified city a few miles further east, which had been destroyed to prevent rebellion. Under the Ming and the Ch'ing, Tai-yüan became the capital of Shansi province and grew in size and importance.

Shansi was fortunate that in the decades of political chaos after 1911 the province remained under a powerful war-lord, Yen Hsi-shan, who maintained political stability. Real growth began with Yen's adoption, in 1933, of a 10-year Industrial Development Plan, based on the Soviet model. Under this plan T'ai-yüan was to become the heavy industrial base for his regime and development was partly completed when the Japanese invaded in 1937. They developed the city's industry still further. Since 1949, in accord with the government's strategy of moving industry away from the coastal zone, T'ai-yüan has become a very large industrial centre, notable for the sheer size of its capacity and for its diversity. Local coal production is considerable; there is a large thermal generating plant; the iron and steel, engineering and chemical industries are extremely important. Industry is supported by many centres of education and research, particularly for technology and applied science.

CH'ANG-SHA

(CHANGSHA)

Population 651,000 (1953); 800,000 (1970 estimate)

The city has been the provincial capital of Hunan since 1664. Its position on the Hsiang Chiang river, some 50 km south of the Tung-t'ing Lake, with excellent water communications to southern and south-western Hunan, has made it a natural commercial centre for centuries. Under the Ming (1368–1644) and the Ch'ing (1644–1911) it became very wealthy as one of China's chief rice markets. Ch'ang-sha was opened to foreign trade in 1904, following the Treaty of Shanghai between China and Japan. Further development followed the opening of the railway to Han-k'ou in 1918.

Ch'ang-sha was in the front line of the Sino-Japanese War from 1938 onwards. It was the site of three major battles in 1939 and 1941 and was virtually destroyed by fire in 1938–9. Since 1949 the city has been rebuilt and has regained its former importance. It is now both a major port, handling enormous tonnages of rice, cotton, timber and livestock, and the most important collection and distribution point on the railway from Han-k'ou to Canton. It is also a major centre of industry and has plants for the manufacture of machine and precision tools, cement, ceramics and paper-making; plants for rice milling, and processing of agricultural products, such as oil-extraction, tea and tobacco curing and textiles; a large chemical and fertiliser industry, and a thermal generating station. Ch'ang-sha has a long tradition of learning and now has a variety of colleges and institutes of higher education.

SHEN-YANG

(MUKDEN)

Population 2,299,000 (1953); 3,000,000 (1970 estimate)

Shen-yang, which was known as Mukden under the Manchus, who made this city their capital before their conquest of China, is now the capital city of Liaoning province. Its position to the south of the Manchurian plain, at the junction of important north–south and east–west rail routes, has made the city the natural economic and political centre of Manchuria. Shen-yang developed particularly during the period of Japanese rule, when a new city was constructed in the former Japanese railway concession zone, to the west of the old Chinese city. The proximity of the city to the iron and steel plants of An-shan and Pen-ch'i has led to further development of heavy industry since the early 1950s, and Shen-yang is now one of the principal metal and machinery producers of China. It also produces electrical equipment, aircraft and vehicles, including tractors.

YIN-CH'UAN

(YINCHWAN)

Population 84,000 (1953)

Yin-ch'uan has been the capital of Ningsia Autonomous Region since its foundation in 1958. It is located on the upper Huang Ho river in the middle of the Ningsia plain. It has a river port at Heng-ch'eng, about 15 km to the east, and is a rail and road centre. The immediate plain area is intensely irrigated and extremely productive. Yin-ch'uan, traditionally an administrative and commercial centre, has grown considerably since 1949, although it is still largely non-industrial. It is primarily a grain market, with flour mills and rice hulling plants, and it serves as a market for the hides, wool and other animal products of the nomadic herdsmen from the surrounding grasslands. The wool produced in the steppe has been the foundation for a modern woollen textile mill which came into operation in 1954.

Yin-ch'uan is an important centre for the Moslem (Hui) minority peoples who constitute one third of the population, and who have established their own schools, cultural centres and hospitals.

HO-FEI

(HOFEI)

Population 184,000 (1953); 500,000 (1970 estimate)

Ho-fei, the provincial capital of Anhwei province, is an important natural communication centre, situated to the north of Ch'ao Hu lake, on a low saddle in the north-eastern extension of the Ta-pieh mountain range. Major east–west and north–south routes run through the city. In the pre-war period Ho-fei remained essentially a traditional city, an administrative centre and the regional market for the fertile plain to the south. The construction in 1912 of the Tientsin–P'u-k'ou railway for a while made Ho-fei a provincial backwater, but between 1932–6 a railway built primarily to exploit the rich coal field in northern Anhwei did much to revive the economy of the Ho-fei area.

Under the Communist regime, it has developed rapidly into a major industrial city. A very large thermal generating plant was established in the early 1950s and a cotton mill and iron and steel complex opened later in the decade. There is a chemical and an aluminium industry, engineering works and a variety of light industries.

FU-CHOU

(FOOCHOW)

Population 553,000 (1953); 700,000 (1970 estimate)

Fu-chou, the provincial capital of Fukien, is situated on the north bank of the estuary of Fukien's largest river, the Min Chiang. During Sung times (960–1278) the province became extremely prosperous, largely through overseas trade, and established itself as a centre of culture and education. Between the 16th and the 19th centuries the port of Fu-chou flourished, its prosperity reaching its highest point after it was opened as a Treaty Port in 1842 and became the chief port for the tea trade. The decline of the tea trade in the late 19th century reduced its importance, although Fu-chou remained a commercial centre and a port until the Second World War.

Since the start of the Communist regime, Fu-chou has developed considerably. Its communications with the interior have been greatly improved by the clearing of the Min Chiang for navigation by medium-sized craft and by the construction of the railway in 1956, which links the city with the main Chinese railway system. Fu-chou is no longer accessible to sea-going ships, but Ma-wei and an outer harbour at Kuan-t'ou handle the export of timber, fruits, paper and foodstuffs. Important chemical, engineering and textile industries have been established in the city.

KUEI-YANG

(KWEIYANG)

Population 271,000 (1953); 504,000 (1958 estimate)

Kuei-yang, provincial capital of Kweichow province, is a natural route centre, with comparatively easy access northwards to Szechwan and north-east to Hunan. Originally the area was peopled with non-Chinese tribes, and it was not until the Yüan invasion of the south-west in 1253 that it was made the seat of an army and a 'pacification office'. Chinese settlement in the area also began at this time. Although Kuei-yang was an important administrative and commercial centre, however, it remained merely the capital of one of China's backward provinces until progress was stimulated by the Second World War, and road and rail communications were greatly improved.

Since 1949 the development of the city has been accelerated and Kuei-yang has become a major industrial base. Coal is mined in the locality of Kuei-yang and An-shun and large deposits of bauxite have been discovered in the north. Aluminium is also produced. In the late 1950s an iron and steel plant was built and the city has become an important manufacturer of industrial, railway and mining plant. There are also large chemical, rubber and textile industries.

NAN-NING

(NANNING, YUNG-NING)

Population 195,000 (1953); 400,000 (1970 estimate)

Nan-ning became the provincial capital of Kwangsi province in 1949, and in 1958, the capital of the Kwangsi Chuang Autonomous Region which replaced it. Until this time Nan-ning, like the other major cities in Kwangsi, Liu-chou and Wu-chou, had been essentially a commercial centre dependent on Canton and on the Hsi Chiang river system. It had been laid out as a spacious modern city under the warlord Li Tsung-jen in the 1930s, but had been much affected by the war and had been occupied twice by the Japanese, in 1940 and 1944. Since 1949 the city's industry has grown considerably and its rail communications have been improved. It is in the middle of a fertile agricultural region and leather manufacture, flour milling, sugar refining, meat packing and the production of fertiliser are important industries. It is a centre of printing and paper manufacture and is also a major producer of aluminium and iron and steel.

After the establishment of the Chuang Autonomous Region in 1958, Nan-ning became the chief cultural centre for the training of cadres from the minority groups, as well as supporting Kwangsi University, a large medical school and a school of Agriculture.

WU-HAN

(WUHAN)

Population 1,427,000 (1953); 2,700,000 (1973 estimate)

Wu-han, situated at the confluence of the Han Shui and the Yangtze is the most extensive conurbation of central China, comprising three cities: Wu-ch'ang, Han-k'ou and Han-yang. The cities were formed into a single municipality in 1950. Wu-ch'ang has been the administrative capital of Hupeh since the 13th century. It is on the right bank of the Yangtze, opposite Han-k'ou and Han-yang, to which it was linked by a great bridge in 1957. It contains the administrative centre of the province, its universities and other public buildings. Outside the old city walls a very large industrial complex has grown up, based on an integrated iron and steel mill constructed in 1956–9 and later expanded. This mill produces steel rails and heavy constructional steel, and supplies a machine-building industry. There are also aluminium, glass and cement works.

Han-k'ou, the largest of the three cities, developed from the late 19th century into the chief centre of foreign trade in the central Yangtze area. It is linked by a second bridge, built in 1954, to Han-yang, which was the site of China's earliest iron and steel works, constructed at the beginning of this century. This was dismantled in 1937 and removed to Ch'ung-ch'ing. Han-yang and Han-k'ou are both centres of very large cotton textile mills and of paper making.

HSI-AN

(SIAN)

Population 787,000 (1953); 1,310,000 (1958 estimate)

The valley of the Wei Ho river, where Hsi-an, the capital of Shensi province, is situated has been one of the cradles of Chinese civilisation since Neolithic times. It was chosen as the seat of the Chou and Ch'in states. Their successors, the Han, built their capital at Ch'ang-an in 200 BC which became the hub of their vast empire's new administration and an important commercial centre. The city fell into decline at the end of the Former Han period and only revived at the re-unification of the empire by the Sui, who built a new city, Ta-hsing-ch'eng, just to the south-east of the Han city. It remained the capital of the T'ang empire under the old name of Ch'ang-an, and became the richest, most populous city in the world of its time. The decline of T'ang power after about AD 880, however, marked the end of the city's prosperity. In the suceeding periods the much reduced city, sacked in 882 and dismantled in 904, became the provincial capital of Shensi, a province which sank steadily in importance until in the

19th century it was one of the most backward in China. The name Hsi-an was given to the city under the Ming (1368–1644).

Its modern growth is very recent and has been remarkably rapid. After the Communist victory in 1949, it became a major centre in the north-west, not only of administration and politics, but also of industry. It has a very large electric generating station and is a centre for the production of electrical equipment and electronic instruments. The city also has one of China's largest modern cotton mills, and engineering and chemical industries.

Although little remains of the old capital, Hsi-an has many ancient monuments, a museum and a famous collection of stone inscriptions. It is a cultural centre with two universities and a number of technical institutes.

NAN-CH'ANG

(NANCHANG)

Population 398,000 (1953); 508,000 (1958 estimate)

Since the foundation and walling of the city in 201 BC, Nan-ch'ang, the provincial capital of Kiangsi on the Kan Chiang river, has been an important administrative and commercial centre. In the 1850s, however, it suffered considerably as a result of the T'ai-p'ing rebellion, and although it was afterwards ruled by a series of progressive governors, its pre-eminence as a commercial centre declined as overland trade routes were replaced by coastal steamship services, and Kiu-kiang, with direct access for the large ships of the Yangtze, became a rival.

Under the Communist regime, Nan-ch'ang has been extensively industrialised. It is a large-scale producer of cotton yarn and textiles and has large paper-making, food-processing and rice-milling industries. Heavy industry was developed in the mid-1950s, with the installation of a large thermal power plant, an iron-smelting plant, and a machinery industry concentrating on agricultural equipment and diesel engines. Later Nan-ch'ang became a centre of the automotive industry, producing trucks and tractors, and has developed a large chemical industry.

CH'UNG-CH'ING

(CHUNGKING)

Population 1,773,000 (1953); 4,400,000 (1970 estimate)

Situated to the south-east of the Szechwan basin, at the confluence of the Yangtze and the Chia-ling rivers, Ch'ung-ch'ing, the war-time capital of Nationalist China, is a centre of communications. Railways lead west to Ch'eng-tu and from there to north-west China, and south to Kuei-yang in Kweichow province, Kwangsi and Yunnan. Freight is trans-shipped between the railways and the Yangtze, which provides a route westward into central China.

Ch'ung-ch'ing is the largest and most rapidly growing industrial city in south-west China. This industrial growth is very recent. The iron and steel industry of Ch'ung-ch'ing was established after 1938 when plants were moved here from Han-yang and Huang-shih, out of the path of the Japanese advance, and the city now produces about one million tons of steel a year. Its other industries include engineering, shipyards, chemicals, fertilisers, plastics, textiles and a wide range of light industry.

Ch'ung-ch'ing has an important university, a number of specialised institutes, museums and libraries.

CH'ENG-TU

(CHENGTU)

Population 857,000 (1953); 1,700,000 (1970 estimate)

The provincial capital of Szechwan province, Ch'eng-tu, has always been a great city and administrative centre, with river communications throughout the Szechwan Basin and beyond, and overland communications north to Lan-chou, north-east to Hsi-an and the traditional centres of political authority, and south-west and west into Yunnan and Tibet. Ch'eng-tu grew rapidly during the Second World War, when many refugees from the east settled there, and its trade and commerce expanded. Since 1949 the growth of Ch'eng-tu has continued. Its road and rail communications have been modernised and improved and it now has air services to all parts of the south-west. It has become a major industrial centre. A very large thermal generating station and two important radio and electronic plants (installed by Soviet engineers) were built in the 1950s, and engineering, chemical and aluminium industries have been established. The city's oldest industry, textiles, is still flourishing and now produces not only the traditional silks but also some cotton and woollen textiles.

Ch'eng-tu is a city with strong local character, whose inhabitants are proud of their sophistication. Its three universities, many institutes and technical schools and historical monuments make it an important cultural centre.

K'UN-MING

(KUNMING)

Population 699,000 (1953); 880,000 (1958 estimate)

K'un-ming, the provincial capital of Yunnan province, has always played a very important part in the communications of the Chinese south-west as it was the junction of two major trading routes, one westwards into Upper Burma, the other southwards to northern Indo-China. Trade trails over the mountains ran east to Hunan and north-east to I-pin in Szechwan.

The opening of the K'un-ming area began with the completion in 1906–10 of the railway to Haiphong, and when K'un-ming became a Treaty Port in 1908 it rapidly became a major commercial centre. But K'un-ming's transformation into a great modern city resulted from the outbreak of the Japanese War in 1937 when great numbers of Chinese flooded into the south-west, bringing with them many dismantled industrial plants which were erected beyond the range of the Japanese bombers. In addition, many universities and institutes of higher education were evacuated here. After the beginning of the Communist period, the expansion of industry which had started during the Second World War continued. The chief industries remain the production of copper, lead and zinc; iron and steel; engineering and chemical works and textiles. K'un-ming is a major cultural centre–there are universities, technical colleges and a number of research institutes.

HSI-NING

(SINING)

Population 94,000 (1953); 300,000 (1970 estimate)

Hsi-ning, the provincial capital of Tsinghai province since 1928, has always been an important strategic point on the Chinese western frontier. It is situated in a fertile mountain basin in the valley of the Huang Shui river, on what were traditionally the main trade routes from northern China into Tibet and the Tsaidam basin, now replaced by modern highways. With the rise of Lamaistic Buddhism, it became an important religious centre, with Tsinghai's biggest Lamasery at Kun-bum to the south-east.

Since the late 1950s, when the Liu-chia Gorge dam and hydro-electric scheme came into operation, Hsi-ning has been linked by high-tension grid to Liu-chia and Lan-chou. It has also developed local coal supplies from mines at Ta-t'ung and has a medium-sized iron and steel works. The city has developed a woollen industry, using wool produced by the nomads of the surrounding pastoral areas, and has a thriving leather industry. It is also an important market for salt from the Tsaidam region.

WU-LU-MU-CH'I

(URUMCHI)

Population 141,000 (1953); 400,000 (1970 estimate)

The city, formerly known as Ti-hua, has been the provincial capital of Sinkiang since it became a province in 1882. It grew rapidly into the greatest city and centre of trade in Central Asia, with a population estimated at about 40,000 at the beginning of the Republic in 1912. Its commercial importance was coupled, in the last days of the empire, with its growing strategic significance as the British and Russians attempted to establish influence in Sinkiang.

Under the Communists, Wu-lu-mu-ch'i has been developed not only as the regional capital and cultural centre of Sinkiang, but also, with the aid of improved road and rail communications, as a major industrial base. Wu-lu-mu-ch'i's new prosperity derives from the oilfield discovered at Karamai in 1955, which has become one of China's major sources of oil, and from extensive coal deposits around the city. In the late 1950s large iron and steel and engineering industries were developed and cement works, chemical and fertiliser plants and cotton textile mills have also been founded.

Wu-lu-mu-ch'i remains an Uighur city with a predominantly Moslem population. There are many schools and institutes of higher education which include colleges for minorities, and for the study of the Russian language, medicine and agriculture.

HU-HO-HAO-T'E

(HUHEHOT)

Population 148,000 (1953); 320,000 (1958 estimate)

Since 1952 Hu-ho-hao-t'e has been the provincial capital of the Inner Mongolian Autonomous Region and Command Headquarters of the Inner Mongolian Military Region. The area was traditionally at the very edge of Chinese settlement and the city grew up as a frontier trading centre, but in the late 18th century Chinese settlers began to farm the fertile plain and a new Chinese city was founded to the north of the Mongol city. The cities later combined under the name of Kuei-sui and became a considerable market with a large Moslem community. Its importance grew rapidly after the completion in 1922 of the railway linking the city to Peking and Tientsin in the east, and Pao-t'ou to the west. Since 1949 Hu-ho-hao-t'e has developed into a fairly important centre of industry, with grain mills, tanneries, plants for oil extraction and a large woollen textile industry. The city also has iron and steel and chemical plants. Cultivation has recently expanded north of Hu-ho-hao-t'e and to support this a major tractor plant and diesel engine factory have been developed. In 1957 the city became the seat of the first university in Inner Mongolia, with an important Medical and Veterinary College. Schools, hospitals, a palace of culture and theatres have made it an important regional cultural centre.

LA-SA

(LHASA)

Population 85,000 (1973 estimate)

La-sa, capital city of the Tibetan Autonomous Region, was founded, according to tradition, in 600 AD by Srong-btsan sgampo, architect of the first Tibetan state. Either La-sa itself or near-by Samye continued as the Tibetan capital until the dissolution of the kingdom in 842. After this La-sa remained an important religious centre. In 1642 the fifth Dalai Lama established La-sa as the capital of Tibet. Following the Manchu conquest in the 18th century, La-sa became the residence of the Manchu governor (*Amban*) and it has been the administrative centre of Tibet ever since. The Manchus were expelled in 1912.

Until the 1950s the country remained, in spite of Chinese government representatives, firmly in the hands of the Tibetan religious hierarchy. A third of its population were monks, and La-sa has many great religious buildings and monasteries, the most famous of which is the Potala, once the residence of the Dalai Lama. After the re-occupation of Tibet by the Chinese in 1951 there were some years of tension between the Communist administration and the Tibetan hierarchy, which led to the rebellion of 1959. Subsequently the Buddhist church was suppressed, many of the monks returned to lay life and the political control of the church destroyed completely.

La-sa has been greatly increased in size and the municipal area now covers some 30,000 square miles of central Tibet. Once almost exclusively Tibetan in population, the city now has large numbers of Chinese inhabitants and a military garrison. There has been some development of minor industry and pharmaceuticals, fertilisers and agricultural machinery are manufactured.

T'AI-PEI

(TAIPEI)

Population 1,117,000 (1964 estimate)

T'ai-pei is the chief city and provincial capital of Taiwan province and, since 1949, the seat of the Chinese Nationalist government in exile. A minor city, founded in 1708, it remained comparatively unimportant until 1887, when Taiwan became an independent province, and T'ai-pei replaced T'ai-nan as provincial capital in 1892. It remained the capital during the Japanese occupation of the island from 1895 to 1945. The city has a very large population of Chinese from the mainland.

Originally the centre of a fertile agricultural area and the hub of Taiwan's excellent rail and road systems, T'ai-pei has developed a considerable range of industries, particularly cotton and synthetic textiles, fertilisers, chemicals, cement and paper manufacture and a variety of consumer goods.

T'ai-pei has also become the cultural centre for the Nationalist regime. It has two major universities and several other institutes of higher education, theatres and museums.

MACAU

(MACAO)

Population 300,000

The oldest European foothold in the Orient, Macau is a Portuguese colony. It was ceded to the Portuguese as a trading outpost in 1557 as a reward for clearing the South China Sea of pirates. Rent was paid to Kwangtung province for the territory until Macau declared itself independent in 1849. China recognised this claim in 1887 when the Portuguese undertook not to alienate Macau without the agreement of China, but it was not officially declared an overseas province by Portugal until 1951.

Macau, a peninsula and two small islands, covers an area of six and a half square miles and lies 40 miles south-west of Hong Kong across the Pearl River estuary. An important bishopric and centre for missionary activity, it grew rich in the 17th century but declined when Japan closed its doors to foreign trade and later under competition from the English and Dutch traders. It is now principally a commercial and tourist dependency of Hong Kong but it has an important gold trade and some light industry based for the most part on textiles.

HONG KONG

Population 4,500,000

Hong Kong, one of the finest natural harbours of the Chinese coast, was founded as an entrepôt for the opium trade. The Chinese empire insisted that all foreign trade should be conducted at Canton and foreign traders settled in nearby Macau. The sale of tea and silk brought into China a great deal of silver. This adverse balance of bullion strained the resources of the Western traders and they began to sell Indian opium illegally to the Chinese in exchange for silver. Eventually the Chinese insisted that the trade should cease and this confrontation led to the Opium War of 1839–42. After their defeat the Chinese ceded Hong Kong Island to the British, and Kowloon peninsula was added in 1870. In 1898 Britain secured a 99-year lease on a further 366 square miles, which included the New Territories on the mainland and some islands.

Hong Kong thrived on trade between China and the West. When this was reduced by American policy in the 1950s and 1960s Hong Kong developed a successful light industrial sector. Today Hong Kong earnings are provided principally by textiles, electronics, banking and financial services, plastics and tourism. The population was 600,000 in 1945 but has swollen to its present level after several waves of immigration from the Chinese mainland. There is a railway from Kowloon to Canton through the New Territories. Frequent ferry services link Hong Kong Island to Kowloon and a road tunnel has been recently completed.

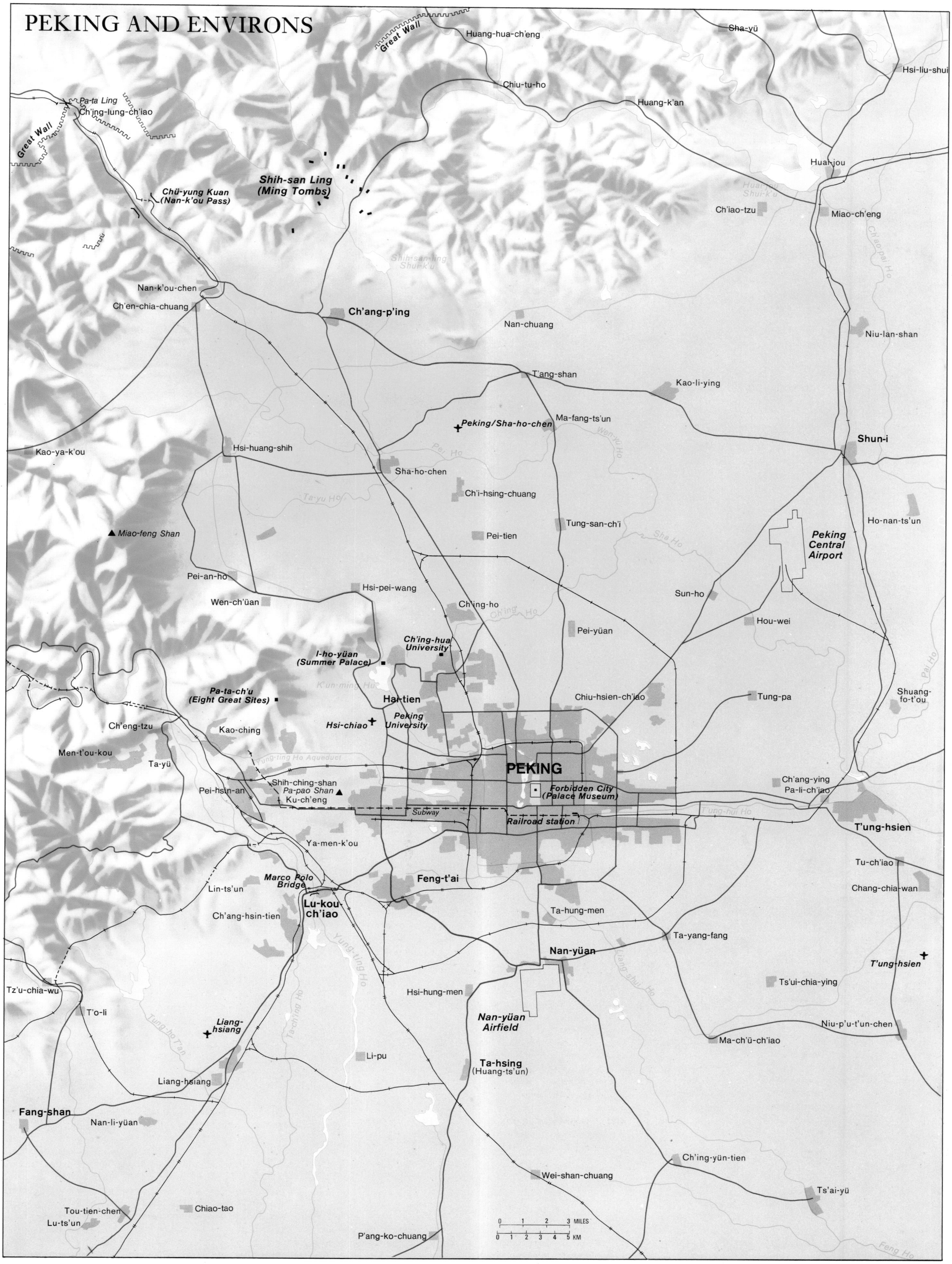

PEKING AND ENVIRONS
Great Wall
Huang-hua-ch'eng
Sha-yü
Hsi-liu-shui
Chiu-tu-ho
Huang-k'an
Pa-ta Ling
Ch'ing-lung-ch'iao
Great Wall
Huai-jou
Shih-san Ling (Ming Tombs)
Chü-yung Kuan (Nan-k'ou Pass)
Ch'iao-tzu
Miao-ch'eng
Nan-k'ou-chen
Ch'en-chia-chuang
Ch'ang-p'ing
Nan-chuang
Niu-lan-shan
T'ang-shan
Kao-li-ying
Ma-fang-ts'un
Peking/Sha-ho-chen
Kao-ya-k'ou
Hsi-huang-shih
Shun-i
Sha-ho-chen
Ch'i-hsing-chuang
Ho-nan-ts'un
Tung-san-ch'i
Miao-feng Shan
Pei-tien
Peking Central Airport
Pei-an-ho
Hsi-pei-wang
Sun-ho
Wen-ch'üan
Ch'ing-ho
Hou-wei
Pei-yüan
Ch'ing-hua University
I-ho-yüan (Summer Palace)
Pa-ta-ch'u (Eight Great Sites)
Hai-tien
Chiu-hsien-ch'iao
Tung-pa
Shuang-fo-t'ou
Ch'eng-tzu
Hsi-chiao
Peking University
Kao-ching
Men-t'ou-kou
Ta-yü
PEKING
Ch'ang-ying
Pa-li-ch'iao
Shih-ching-shan
Pa-pao Shan
Pei-hsin-an
Ku-ch'eng
Forbidden City (Palace Museum)
Subway
Railroad station
T'ung-hsien
Ya-men-k'ou
Tu-ch'iao
Marco Polo Bridge
Feng-t'ai
Lin-ts'un
Chang-chia-wan
Lu-kou-ch'iao
Ch'ang-hsin-tien
Ta-hung-men
Ta-yang-fang
Nan-yüan
T'ung-hsien
Tz'u-chia-wu
Ts'ui-chia-ying
Hsi-hung-men
T'o-li
Nan-yüan Airfield
Liang-hsiang
Niu-p'u-t'un-chen
Ma-ch'ü-ch'iao
Li-pu
Ta-hsing (Huang-ts'un)
Liang-hsiang
Fang-shan
Nan-li-yüan
Ch'ing-yün-tien
Wei-shan-chuang
Ts'ai-yü
Tou-tien-chen
Chiao-tao
Lu-ts'un
P'ang-ko-chuang
0 1 2 3 MILES
0 1 2 3 4 5 KM

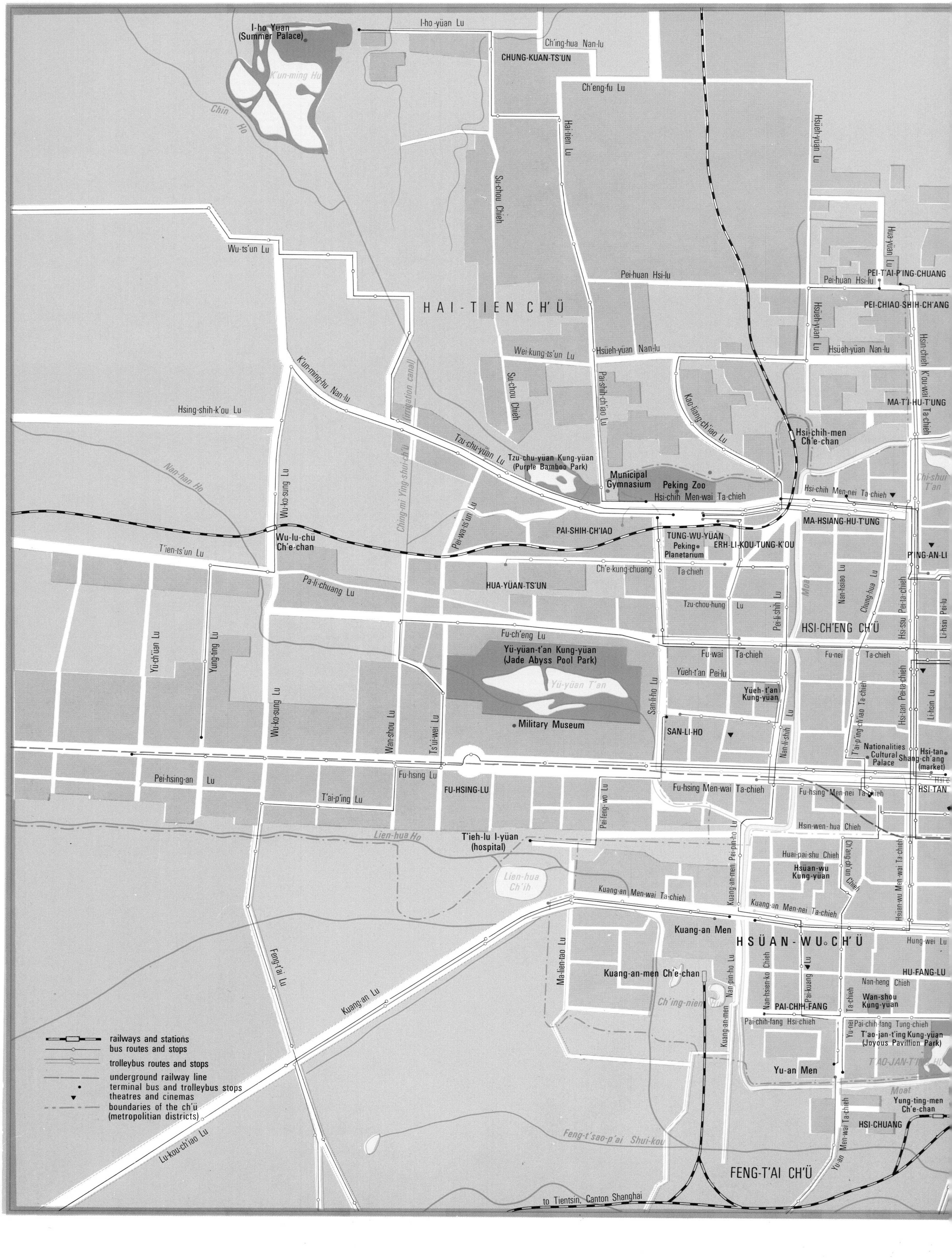
I-ho Yüan
(Summer Palace)
K'un-ming Hu
Chin Ho
I-ho-yüan Lu
Ch'ing-hua Nan-lu
CHUNG-KUAN-TS'UN
Ch'eng-fu Lu
Hai-tien Lu
Hsüeh-yüan Lu
Su-chou Chieh
Wu-ts'un Lu
Pei-huan Hsi-lu
Hua-yüan Lu
PEI-T'AI-P'ING-CHUANG
Pei-huan Hsi-lu
PEI-CHIAO-SHIH-CH'ANG
HAI-TIEN CH'Ü
Hsüeh-yüan Lu
Wei-kung-ts'un Lu
Hsüeh-yüan Nan-lu
Hsüeh-yüan Nan-lu
Hsin-chieh K'ou-wai Ta-chieh
K'un-ming-hu Nan-lu
Su-chou Chieh
Pai-shih-ch'iao Lu
Kao-liang-ch'iao Lu
MA-T'I-HU-T'UNG
Hsing-shih-k'ou Lu
(irrigation canal)
Hsi-chih-men
Ch'e-chan
Tzu-chu-yüan Lu
Tzu-chu-yüan Kung-yüan
(Purple Bamboo Park)
Nan-han Ho
Municipal
Gymnasium
Peking Zoo
Hsi-chih Men-wai Ta-chieh
Hsi-chih Men-nei Ta-chieh
Chi-shui T'an
Wu-ko-sung Lu
Ch'ing-mi Ying-shui-ch'ü
Pei-wa-ts'un Lu
PAI-SHIH-CH'IAO
TUNG-WU-YÜAN
ERH-LI-KOU-TUNG-K'OU
MA-HSIANG-HU-T'UNG
Wu-lu-chü
Ch'e-chan
Peking
Planetarium
P'ING-AN-LI
T'ien-ts'un Lu
Ch'e-kung-chuang
Ta-chieh
Pa-li-chuang Lu
HUA-YÜAN-TS'UN
Nan-hsiao Lu
Chung-hua Lu
Hsi-ssu Pei-ta-chieh
Li-hsin Pei-lu
Tzu-chou-hung Lu
Pei-li-shih Lu
Moat
Yü-ch'üan Lu
Yung-ting Lu
Fu-ch'eng Lu
HSI-CH'ENG CH'Ü
Yü-yüan-t'an Kung-yüan
(Jade Abyss Pool Park)
Fu-wai Ta-chieh
Fu-nei Ta-chieh
Yüeh-t'an Pei-lu
Yü-yüan T'an
Yüeh-t'an
Kung-yüan
Hsi-ssu Pei-ta-chieh
Li-hsin Lu
San-li-ho Lu
Wu-ko-sung Lu
Wan-shou Lu
Ts'ui-wei Lu
Military Museum
SAN-LI-HO
Nan-li-shih Lu
T'ai-p'ing-ch'iao Ta-chieh
Hsi-tan Pei-ta-chieh
Nationalities
Cultural
Palace
Hsi-tan
Shang-ch'ang
(market)
Pei-hsing-an Lu
Fu-hsing Lu
T'ai-p'ing Lu
FU-HSING-LU
Pei-feng-wo Lu
Fu-hsing Men-wai Ta-chieh
Fu-hsing Men-nei Ta-chieh
HSI-TAN
Hsin-wen-hua Chieh
Lien-hua Ho
T'ieh-lu I-yüan
(hospital)
Pei-pin-ho Lu
Huai-pai-shu Chieh
Hsüan-wu
Kung-yüan
Ch'ang-ch'un Chieh
Hsüan-wu Men-wai Ta-chieh
Lien-hua Ch'ih
Kuang-an Men-wai Ta-chieh
Kuang-an-men Pei-pin-ho Lu
Kuang-an Men-nei Ta-chieh
Kuang-an Men
HSÜAN-WU CH'Ü
Hung-wei Lu
Feng-t'ai Lu
Ma-lien-tao Lu
Nan-pin-ho Lu
Nan-hsien-ko Chieh
Pai-kuang Lu
HU-FANG-LU
Kuang-an-men Ch'e-chan
Nan-heng Chieh
Wan-shou
Kung-yüan
Kuang-an Lu
Ch'ing-nien Hu
PAI-CHIH-FANG
Ta-chieh
Kuang-an-men Nan-pin-ho Lu
Pai-chih-fang Hsi-chieh
Pai-chih-fang Tung-chieh
Yu-nei
T'ao-jan-t'ing Kung-yüan
(Joyous Pavillion Park)
T'AO-JAN-T'ING HU
Yu-an Men
Moat
Yung-ting-men
Ch'e-chan
Yu-an Men-wai Ta-chieh
HSI-CHUANG
Feng-t'sao-p'ai Shui-kou
Lu-kou-ch'iao Lu
FENG-T'AI CH'Ü
to Tientsin, Canton Shanghai
railways and stations
bus routes and stops
trolleybus routes and stops
underground railway line
terminal bus and trolleybus stops
theatres and cinemas
boundaries of the ch'ü
(metropolitian districts)

PEKING
HSIAO-KUAN
CHAO-YANG CH'Ü
TUNG-CH'ENG CH'Ü
CH'UNG-WEN CH'Ü
HO-P'ING-CHIEH PEI-K'OU
AN-TE-LI PEI-CHIEH
Ti-t'an Kung-yüan
An-ting Men
Te-sheng Men
Jen-ting-hu Kung-yüan
Ch'ing-nien-hu Kung-yuan
Municipal Library
Overseas Chinese Tourist Office
Tung-chih Men
HSING-FU SAN-TS'UN
Japanese Embassy
Agricultural Exhibition Hall
Ti-an Men
Pei-hai Kung-yüan
Tung-hsi Lü-kuan (hotel)
Workers' Gymnasium
Workers' Stadium
People's Market
National Art Gallery
Ching-shan Kung-yüan
Peking Library
Chao-yang Men
CHIN-T'AI-LU
Chao-yang Kung-yüan
SHA-T'AN
Overseas Chinese Building
Palace Museum
Jih-t'an Kung-yüan
Peace Hotel
Department Store
Peking Hotel
Chung-shan Kung-yüan
Worker's Palace of Culture
KUANG-HUI LU PEI-K'OU
SHIH-LI-PAO
T'ien-an Men
Monument to the People's Heroes
Great Hall of the People
Museum of the Chinese Revolution
Museum of Chinese History
Tung-tan Kung-yüan
Underground railway station
Pei-ching Ch'e-chan
Tung-chiao Ch'e-chan
Ch'ien Men
Ch'ung-wen Men
Kuang-ch'ü Men
Chienmen Hotel
HUA-KUNG-LU HSI-K'OU
TA-CHIAO-T'ING
Nature Museum
KUANG-MING-LOU
SHA-PAN-CHUANG
KUNG-YEH TA-HSÜEH
T'IEN-CH'IAO
T'ien-ch'iao Shang-ch'ang (market)
Pei-ching T'i-yü-kuan (gymnasium)
Ch'ien-nung-t'an T'i-yü-ch'ang (stadium)
T'ien-t'an Kung-yüan (Temple of Heaven)
Yung-ting Men
P'U-HUANG-YÜ
T'IEH-CHIANG-YING
Tso-chia-chuang Shang-ch'ang (market)
Chin-hsien-ch'iao Shang-ch'ang (market)
Pei-huan Tung-lu
Pei-yüan Lu
Ch'ang-p'ing Lu
Tung-chih Lu
Chin-hsin-ch'iao Lu
Tung-chih Men-wai Ta-chieh
Tung-huan Pei-lu
Chao-yang Lu
Ch'ang-cheng Lu
Chien-kuo Men-wai Ta-chieh
Chien-kuo Men-nei Ta-chieh
Ching-ch'eng Hsien (Peking-Ch'eng-te Line)
Pai-tzu-wan Lu
Kuang-ch'ü Lu
Kuang-ch'ü Men-wai Ta-chieh
Tung-huan Nan-lu
Tso-an Lu
Nan-huan Tung-lu
Fang-chuang Lu
Yung-ting Men-wai Ta-chieh
Ma-chia-pao Lu
Hung-kuang Lu
Shu-kuang Lu
Lung-t'an Lu
Fan-ti Lu
Fan-ti Hsi-lu
Hua-shih Ta-chieh
Hsing-lung Chieh
Kuang-ch'ü Men-nei Ta-chieh
Chao-nei Ta-chieh
Chao-wai Ta-chieh
Kuang-hua Lu
Kung-jen T'i-yü-ch'ang Pei-lu
Tung-ssu Shih-t'iao
Tung-chih Men-nei Ta-chieh
Ku-lou Tung-ta-chieh
An-te Lu
Ho-p'ing-li Pei-chieh
Ho-p'ing-li Chung-chieh
Huang-ssu Ta-chieh
Wen-chin Chieh
Wang-fu-ching
Moat
0 1 MILE
0 1 KM

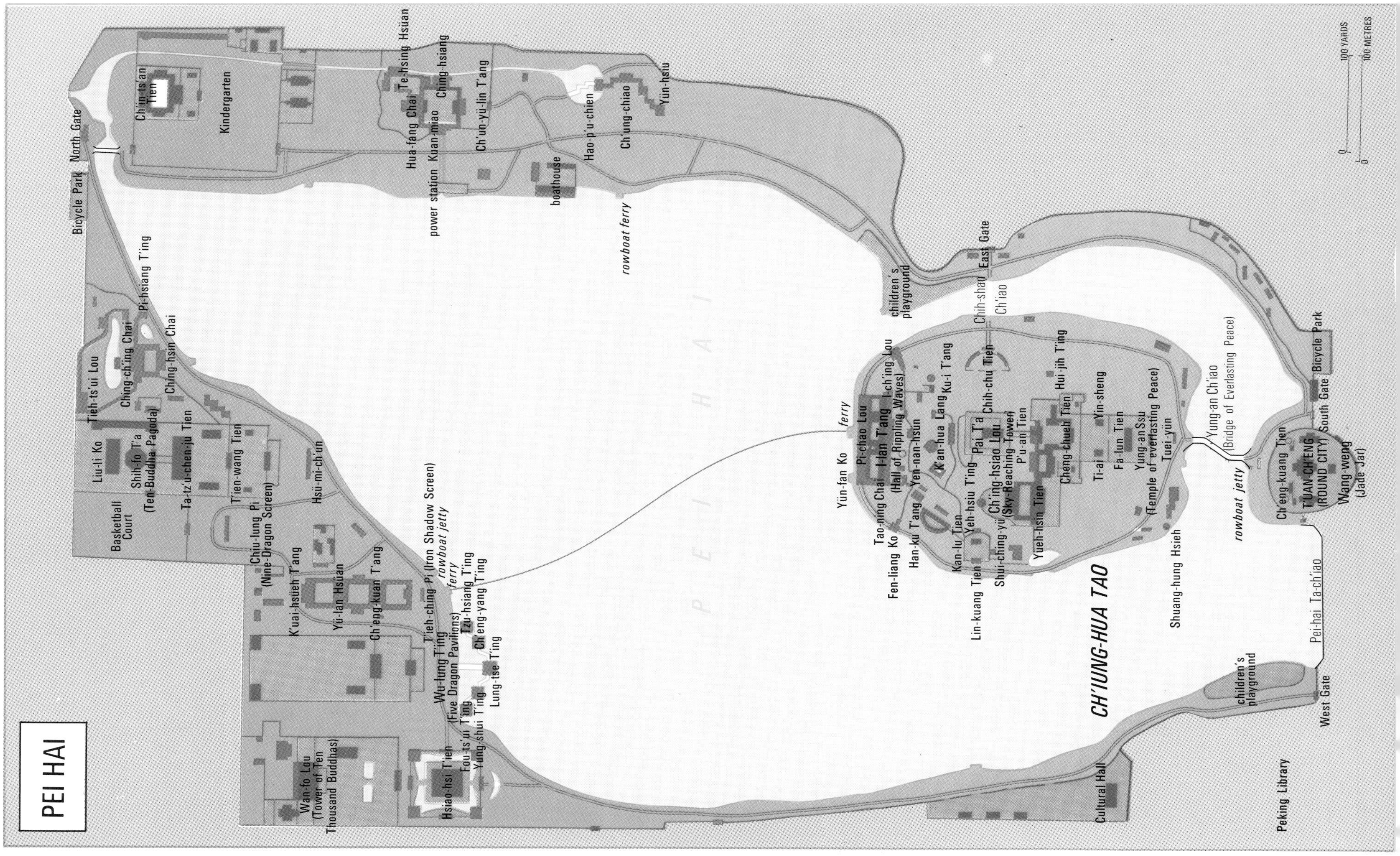
PEI HAI
PEI HAI
CH'IUNG-HUA TAO
North Gate
East Gate
South Gate
West Gate
Bicycle Park
Kindergarten
Chih-tsai Men
Hua-fang Chai
boathouse
rowboat ferry
children's playground
Pai T'a
Yung-an Ssu (Temple of Everlasting Peace)
Yung-an Ch'iao (Bridge of Everlasting Peace)
T'UAN CH'ENG (ROUND CITY)
Wang-weng (Jade Jar)
Ch'eng-kuang Tien
Pei-hai Ta-ch'iao
Peking Library
Cultural Hall
Shuang-hung Hsieh
Yün-fan Ko
Wu-lung T'ing (Five Dragon Pavilions)
T'ieh-ying Pi (Iron Shadow Screen)
Chiu-lung Pi (Nine-Dragon Screen)
Shih-fo T'a (Ten Buddha Pagoda)
Wan-fo Lou (Tower of Ten Thousand Buddhas)
Hsiao-hsi Tien
Basketball Court
Liu-li Ko
T'ien-wang Tien
Hsü-mi-ch'un
Lung-tse T'ing
100 YARDS
100 METRES

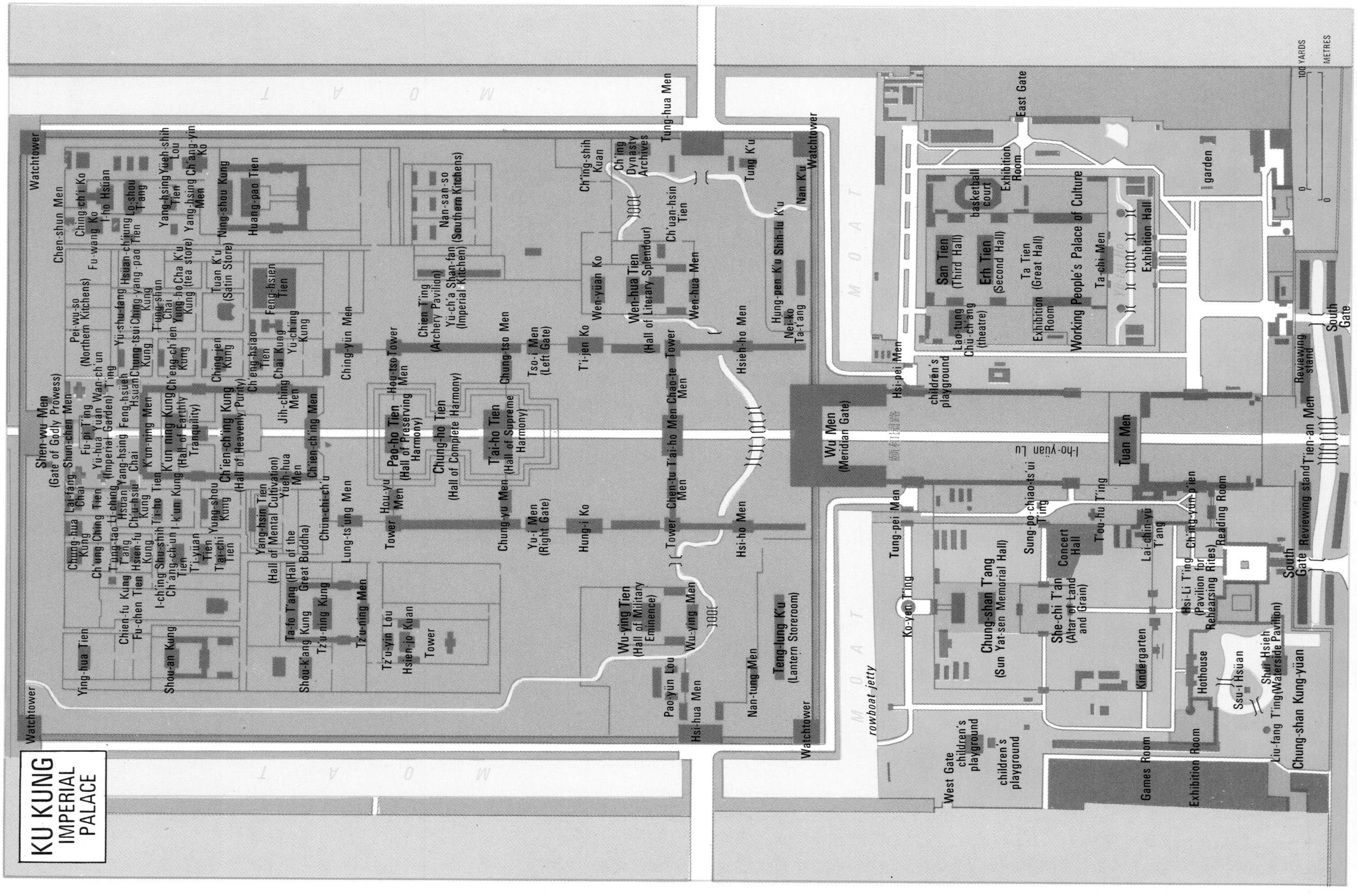
KU KUNG IMPERIAL PALACE
MOAT
Watchtower
Shen-wu Men (Gate of Godly Prowess)
Tung-hua Men
Hsi-hua Men
Wu Men (Meridian Gate)
T'ai-ho Tien (Hall of Supreme Harmony)
Chung-ho Tien (Hall of Complete Harmony)
Pao-ho Tien (Hall of Preserving Harmony)
T'ai-ho Men
Ch'ien-ch'ing Kung (Hall of Heavenly Purity)
K'un-ning Kung (Hall of Earthly Tranquility)
Wen-hua Tien (Hall of Literary Splendour)
Wu-ying Tien (Hall of Military Eminence)
Yang-hsin Tien (Hall of Mental Cultivation)
Huang-chi Tien
Ning-shou Kung
Nan-san-so (Southern Kitchens)
Tuan Men
T'ien-an Men
I-ho-yuan Lu
Working People's Palace of Culture
Chung-shan Kung-yuan
Chung-shan T'ang (Sun Yat-sen Memorial Hall)
She-chi T'an (Altar of Land and Grain)
Concert Hall
Exhibition Hall
Exhibition Room
Reading Room
Reviewing stand
Games Room
Hothouse
Kindergarten
children's playground
East Gate
West Gate
South Gate
rowboat jetty
100 YARDS
METRES

PEKING

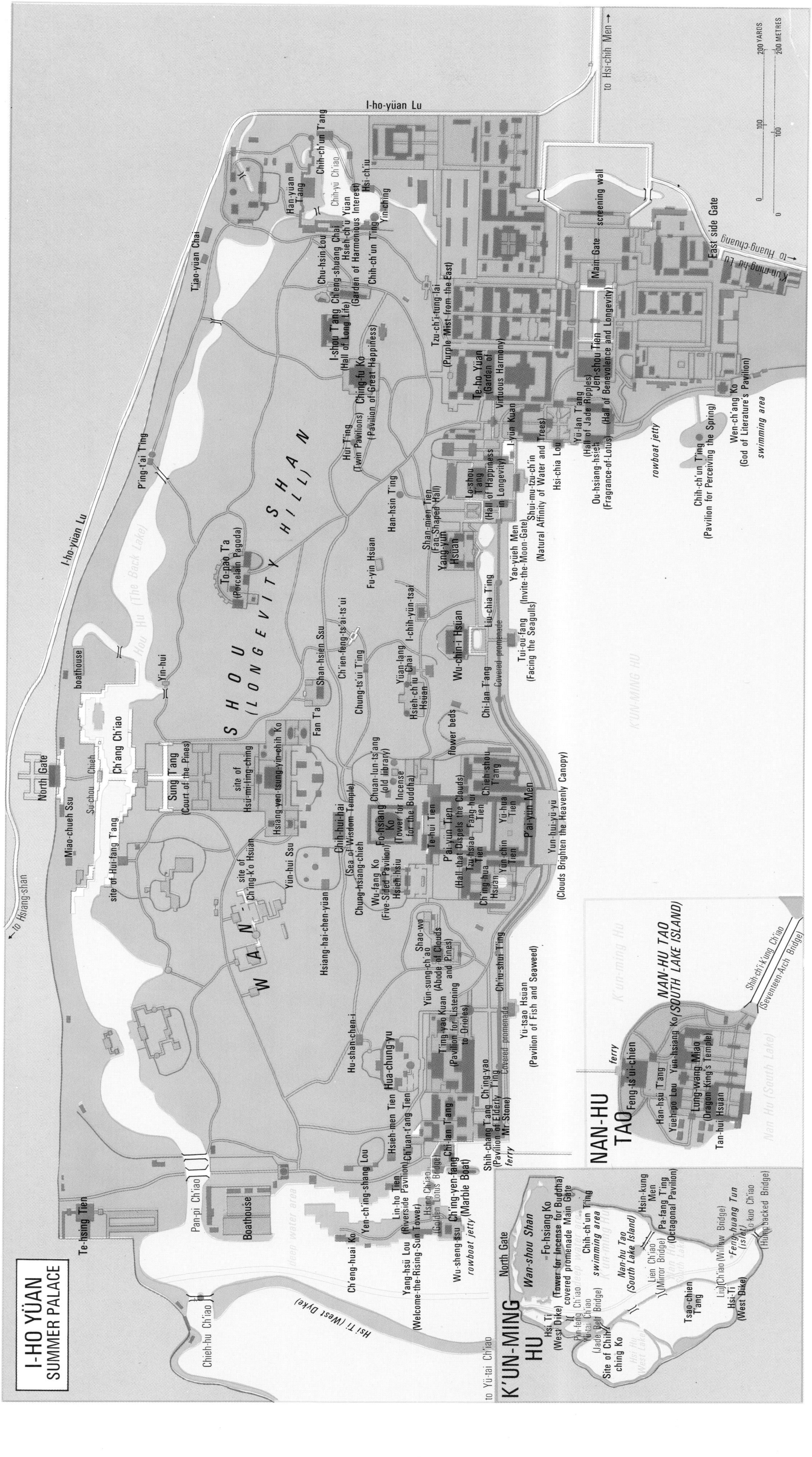
I-HO YÜAN
SUMMER PALACE
WAN SHOU SHAN (LONGEVITY HILL)
K'UN-MING HU
NAN-HU TAO
NAN-HU TAO (SOUTH LAKE ISLAND)
I-ho-yüan Lu
to Hsi-chih Men
to Huang-chuang
to Hsiang-shan
to Yü-tai Ch'iao
North Gate
East side Gate
Main Gate
screening wall
Hou Hu (The Back Lake)
Hsi Ti (West Dyke)
Su-chou Chieh
Ch'ang Ch'iao
boathouse
Boathouse
Chieh-hu Ch'iao
Pan-pi Ch'iao
Te-hsing Tien
Miao-chueh Ssu
site of Hui-fang T'ang
Sung T'ang (Court of the Pines)
site of Hsü-mi-ling-ching
Hsiang-yen-tsung-yin-chih Ko
To-pao T'a (Porcelain Pagoda)
Yin-hui
Fan T'a
Shan-hsien Ssu
Yün-hui Ssu
site of Ch'ing-ko Hsüan
Hsiang-hai-chen-yüan
Hu-shan-chen-i
Hua-chung-yü
Chih-hui-hai (Sea of Wisdom Temple)
Chung-hsiang-chieh
Wu-fang Ko (Five-Sided Pavilion)
Chuan-lun-tsang (old library)
Fo-hsiang Ko (Tower for Incense for the Buddha)
P'ai-yün Tien (Hall that Dispels the Clouds)
Te-hui Tien
Yü-hua Tien
Chieh-shou T'ang
P'ai-yün Men
Yün-hui-yü-yü (Clouds Brighten the Heavenly Canopy)
Chi-lan T'ang
Liu-chia T'ing
Tui-ou-fang (Facing the Seagulls)
Yao-yüeh Men (Invite-the-Moon-Gate)
Shui-mu-tzu-ch'in (Natural Affinity of Water and Trees)
Lo-shou T'ang (Hall of Happiness in Longevity)
Yü-lan T'ang (Hall of Jade Ripples)
Jen-shou Tien (Hall of Benevolence and Longevity)
Te-ho Yüan (Garden of Virtuous Harmony)
Wen-ch'ang Ko (God of Literature's Pavilion)
Chih-ch'un T'ing (Pavilion for Perceiving the Spring)
Ou-hsiang-hsieh (Fragrance-of-Lotus)
Hsi-chia Lou
I-shou T'ang (Hall of Long Life)
Ching-fu Ko (Pavilion of Great Happiness)
Hsieh-ch'ü Yüan (Garden of Harmonious Interest)
Chih-ch'un T'ing
T'iao-yüan Chai
P'ing-t'ai T'ing
Ch'ing-yen-fang (Marble Boat)
Yü-tsao Hsüan (Pavilion of Fish and Seaweed)
Shih-chang T'ang
rowboat jetty
swimming area
ferry
Shih-ch'i-k'ung Ch'iao (Seventeen-Arch Bridge)
Lung-wang Miao (Dragon King's Temple)
Feng-ts'ui-chien
Han-hsü T'ang
Hsi Ti (West Dike)
Yü-tai Ch'iao (Jade Belt Bridge)
Ching-ming Ko
Hsieh-ch'iu T'ing
Lien Ch'iao (Mirror Bridge)
Liu Ch'iao (Willow Bridge)
Feng-huang Tun (islet)
Lo-kuo Ch'iao (Humpbacked Bridge)
Pa-fang T'ing (Octagonal Pavilion)
Nan-hu Tao (South Lake Island)
0 100 200 YARDS
0 100 200 METRES

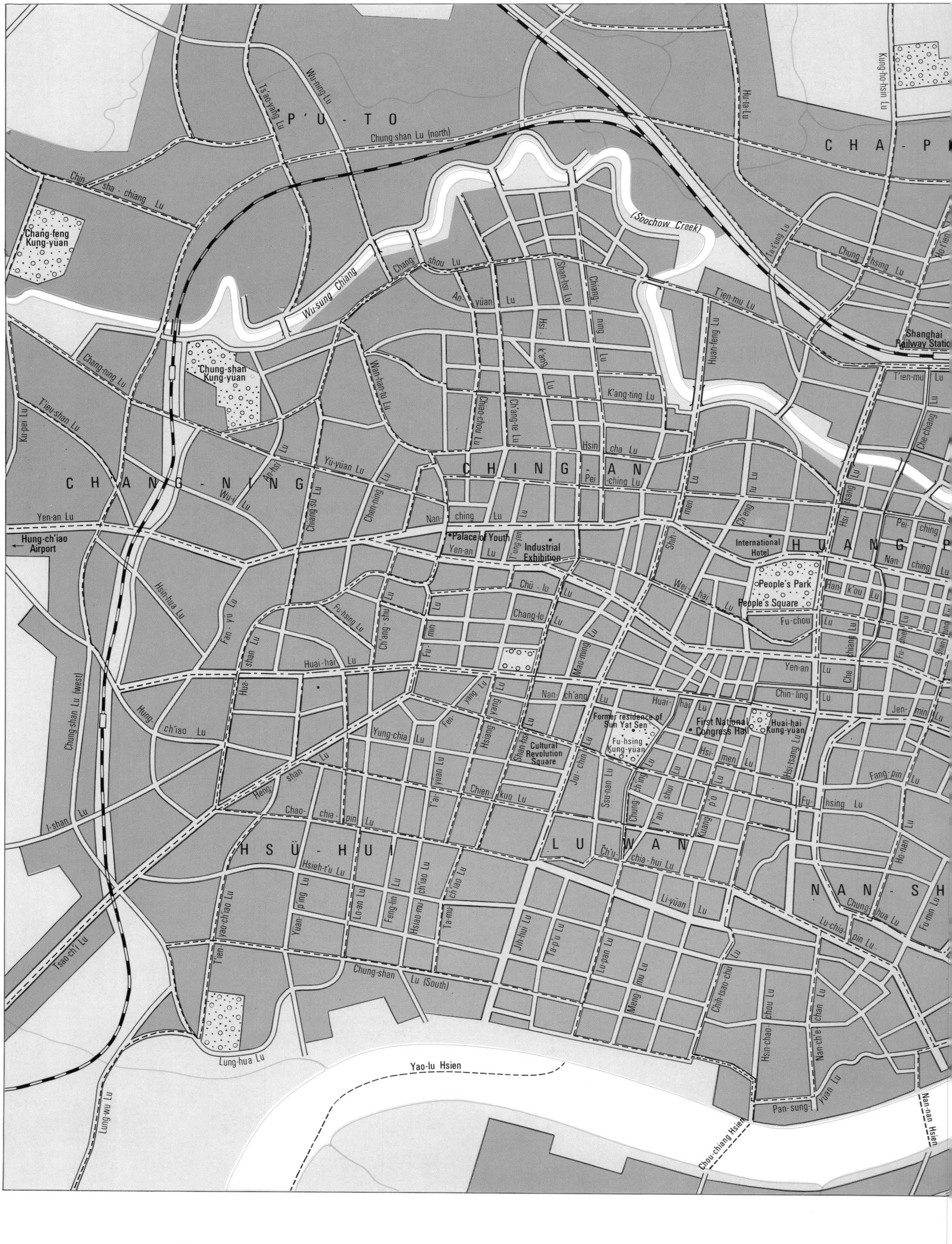
P'U-TO
CH'ANG-NING
CHING-AN
HUANG-P
HSÜ-HUI
LU-WAN
NAN-SH
CHA-P
Chung-shan Lu (north)
Chin-sha-chiang Lu
Chang-feng Kung-yüan
Chung-shan Kung-yüan
Wu-sung Chiang
(Soochow Creek)
Shanghai Railway Station
Hung-ch'iao Airport
Yen-an Lu
Palace of Youth
Industrial Exhibition
International Hotel
People's Park
People's Square
Former residence of Sun Yat Sen
First National Congress Hall
Huai-hai Kung-yüan
Fu-hsing Kung-yüan
Cultural Revolution Square
Chung-shan Lu (South)
Lung-hua Lu
Yao-lu Hsien
Chou-chiang Hsien
Nan-nan Hsien

SHANGHAI

Gymnasium
Han-tan Lu
Hsiang-yin Lu
Kuo-ch'üan Lu
Ning-kuo Lu
Kuang-chung Lu
Hsi-pao-hsing Lu
Chung-shan Lu (north)
Shui-tien Lu
T'i-yü-hui Lu
Tung-fang-hung T'i-yü-ch'ang (sports ground)
Tomb of Lu Hsün
Hung-k'ou Kung-yüan
Ta-lien Lu
Ou-yang Lu
Ssu-p'ing Lu
Pao-shan Lu
Ssu-ch'uan Lu
Ho-p'ing Kung-yüan
H U N G K'O U
Yen-chi Lu
K'ung-chiang Lu
Hai-ning Lu
Ho-nan Lu
Ch'ang-p'u Kung-yüan
Chou-chia-tsui Lu
Hsü-ch'ang Lu
Chiang-p'u Lu
Y A N G - P'U
Wu-sung Lu
T'ang-shan Lu
Kao-yang Lu
Kung-p'ing Lu
Ta-lien Lu
Chang-yang Lu
Ning-kuo Lu
Nei-ch'iang Lu
Shanghai University
Su-chou Lu
Chang-chih Lu
Ta-ming Lu
Ho-chien Lu
Seamen's club
Huang-p'u Kung-yüan
P'ing-liang Lu
Chiang-hsi Lu
H U A N G - P'U
T'ai-kung Hsien
C H I A N G
Ch'ang-shu-p'u Lu
Chün-kung Lu
Kung-ch'ing Lu
Ch'ang-shu-p'u Lu
Ch'i-t'ai Hsien
Lu-yen Hsien
Lu-chia-tsui Lu
(W H A N G P O O
R I V E R)
Shang-ting Hsien
Min-tan Hsien
Hsi-ning Hsien
Ssu-ch'uan Lu
Chung-shan Lu (East)
P'u-tung Lu
H U A N G - P'U
Tung-tung Hsien
Tung-ch'ang Lu
P'u-tung Lu
Ch'ang-fu Hsien
Chung-shan Lu (South)
T'ang-tung Hsien
P'u-tung Lu
tram routes
trolleybus routes
bus routes
0
1 MILE
0
1 KM

TIENTSIN

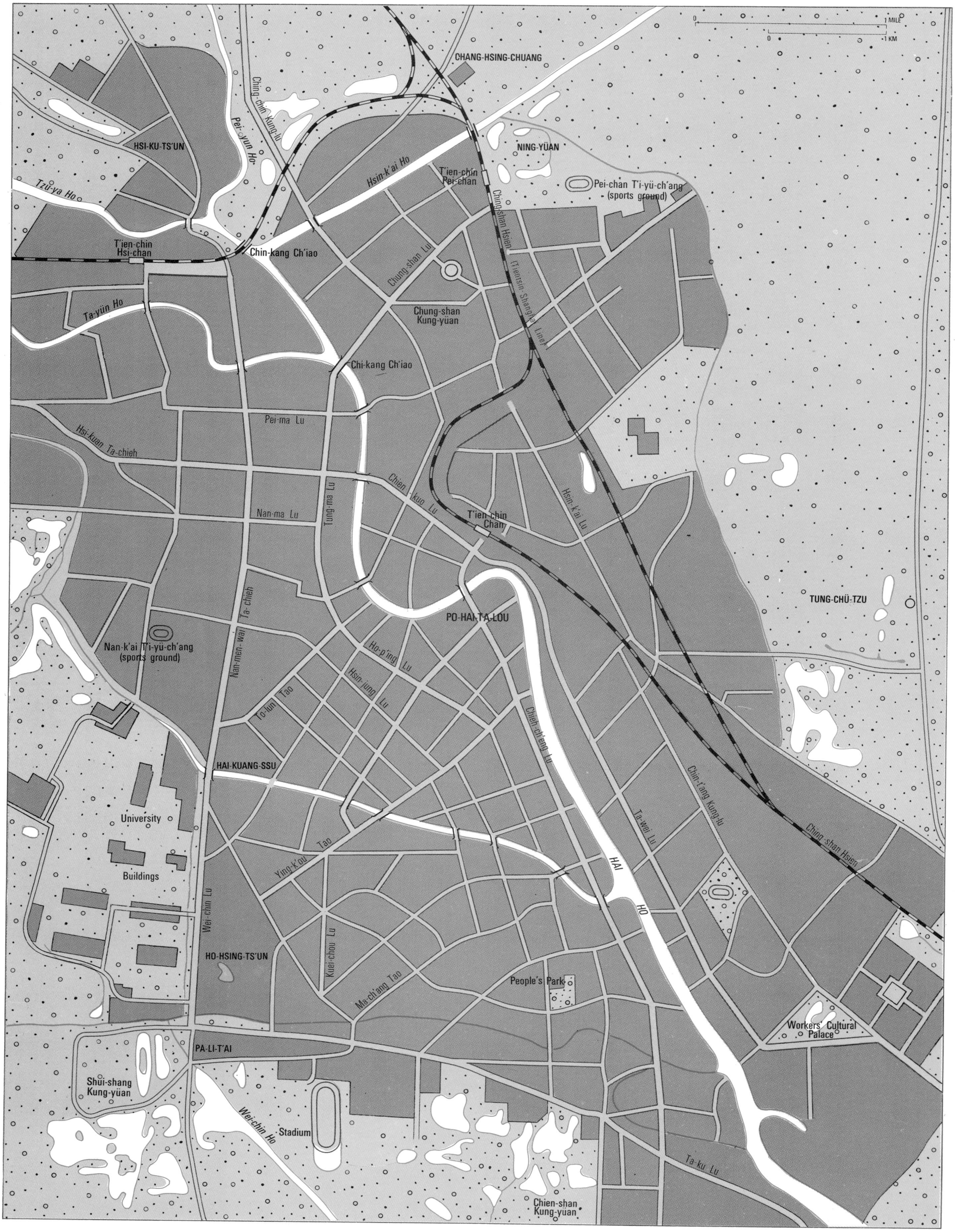
0 1 MILE
0 1 KM
CHANG-HSING-CHUANG
HSI-KU-TS'UN
NING-YÜAN
Ching-chin Kung-lu
Pei-yün Ho
Tzŭ-ya Ho
Hsin-k'ai Ho
T'ien-chin Pei-chan
Pei-chan T'i-yü-ch'ang (sports ground)
T'ien-chin Hsi-chan
Chin-kang Ch'iao
Ching-shan Hsien (Tientsin-Shanghai Line)
Chung-shan Lu
Chung-shan Kung-yüan
Ta-yün Ho
Chi-kang Ch'iao
Pei-ma Lu
Hsi-kuan Ta-chieh
Chien-kuo Lu
Nan-ma Lu
Tung-ma Lu
T'ien-chin Chan
Hsin-k'ai Lu
TUNG-CHÜ-TZU
Nan-men-wai Ta-chieh
PO-HAI-TA-LOU
Nan-k'ai T'i-yü-ch'ang (sports ground)
Ho-p'ing Lu
Hsin-jung Lu
To-lun Tao
Chieh-ch'eng Lu
HAI-KUANG-SSU
Chin-t'ang Kung-lu
Ching-shan Hsien
University
Ta-wei Lu
Ying-k'ou Tao
HAI HO
Buildings
Wei-chin Lu
HO-HSING-TS'UN
Kuei-chou Lu
Ma-ch'ang Tao
People's Park
Workers' Cultural Palace
PA-LI-T'AI
Shui-shang Kung-yüan
Wei-chin Ho
Stadium
Ta-ku Lu
Chien-shan Kung-yüan

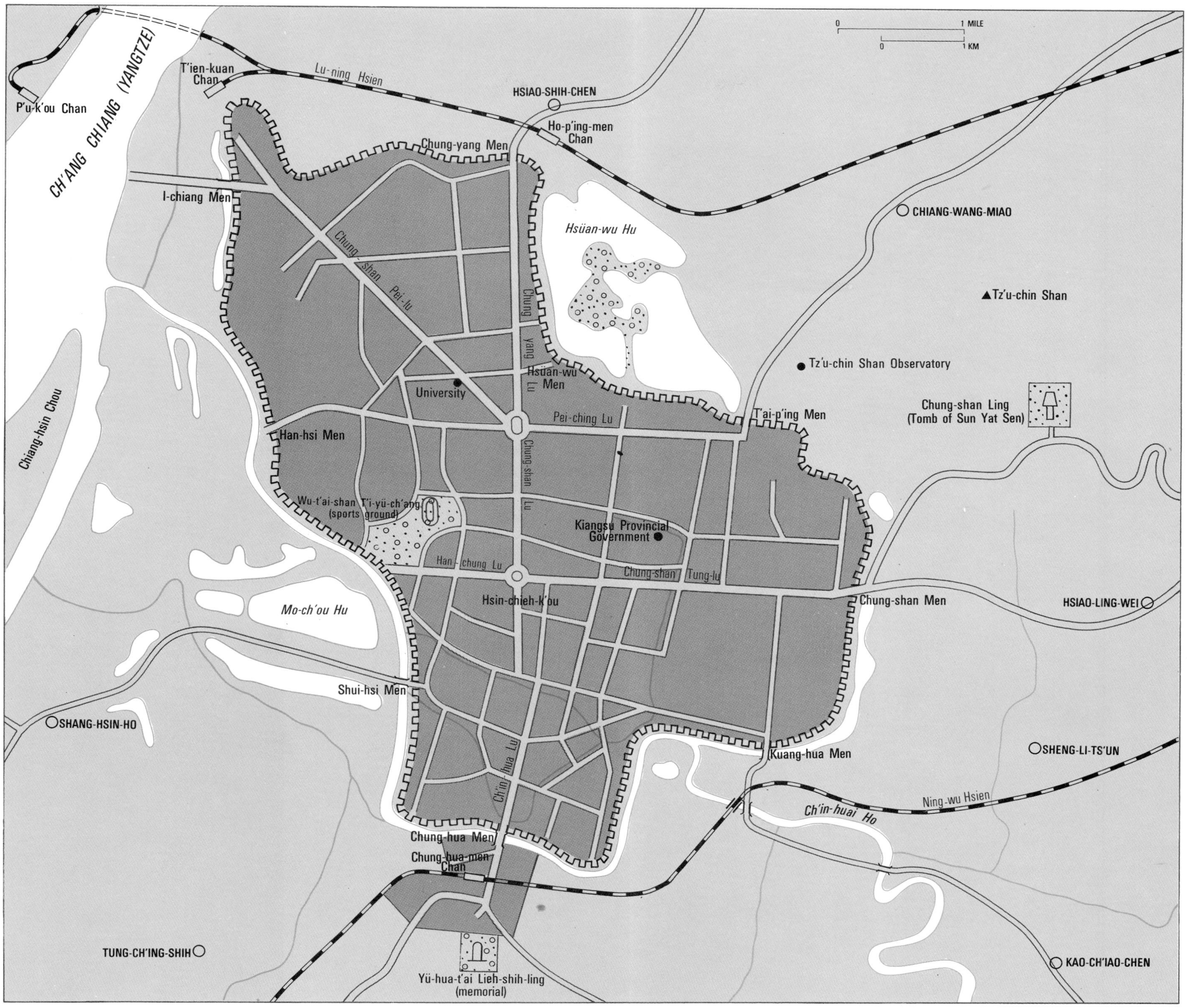
0
1 MILE
0
1 KM
P'u-k'ou Chan
T'ien-kuan Chan
Lu-ning Hsien
HSIAO-SHIH-CHEN
Ho-p'ing-men Chan
CH'ANG CHIANG (YANGTZE)
Chung-yang Men
I-chiang Men
CHIANG-WANG-MIAO
Hsüan-wu Hu
Chung-shan Pei-lu
Chung yang Lu
Tz'u-chin Shan
Tz'u-chin Shan Observatory
Hsüan-wu Men
University
Chung-shan Ling
(Tomb of Sun Yat Sen)
T'ai-p'ing Men
Pei-ching Lu
Chiang-hsin Chou
Han-hsi Men
Chung-shan Lu
Wu-t'ai-shan T'i-yü-ch'ang
(sports ground)
Kiangsu Provincial Government
Han-chung Lu
Chung-shan Tung-lu
Hsin-chieh-k'ou
Chung-shan Men
HSIAO-LING-WEI
Mo-ch'ou Hu
Shui-hsi Men
SHANG-HSIN-HO
SHENG-LI-TS'UN
Kuang-hua Men
Ch'in-hua Lu
Ning-wu Hsien
Ch'in-huai Ho
Chung-hua Men
Chung-hua-men Chan
TUNG-CH'ING-SHIH
Yü-hua-t'ai Lieh-shih-ling
(memorial)
KAO-CH'IAO-CHEN

NAN-CHING
NANKING

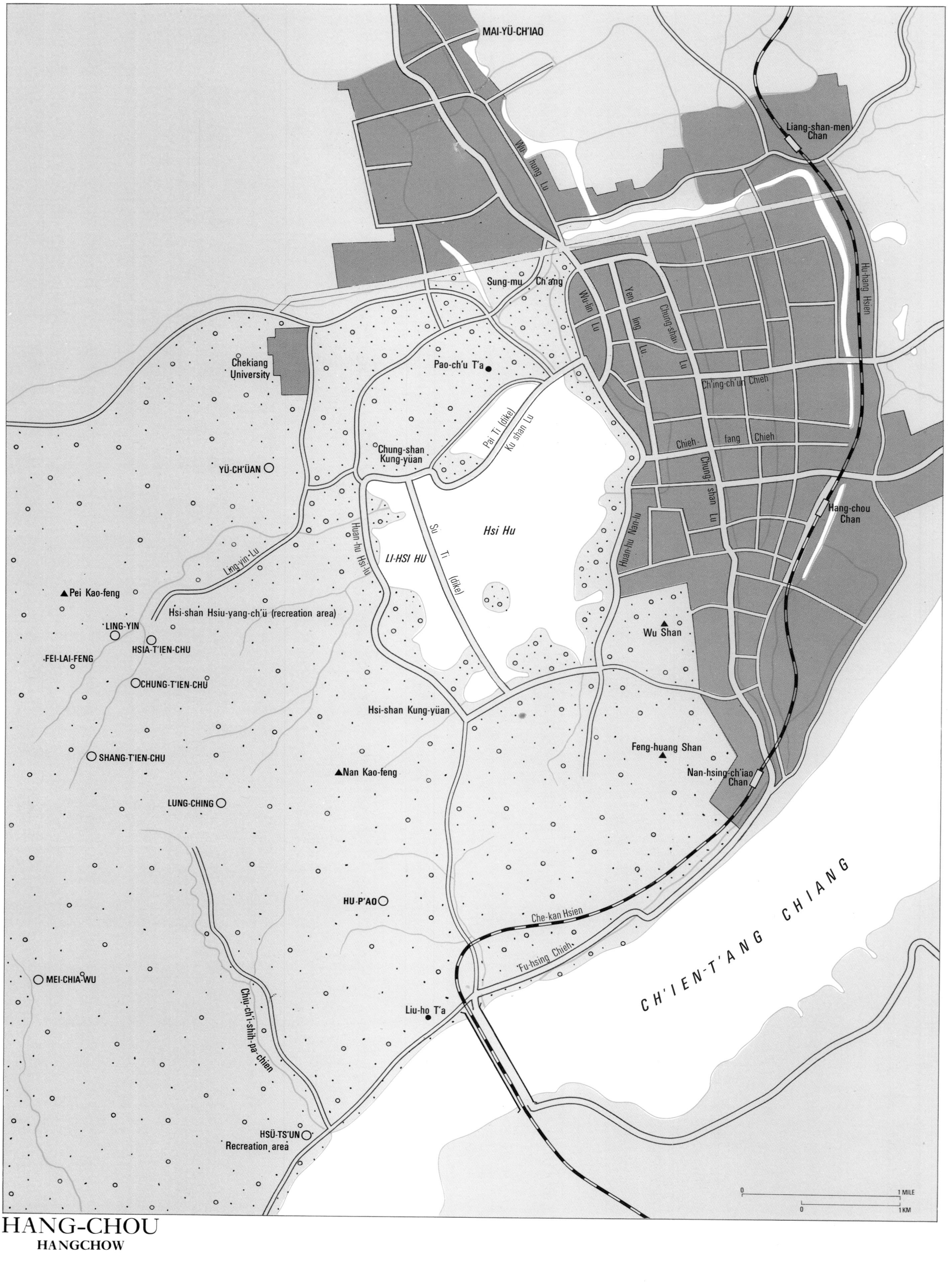
MAI-YÜ-CH'IAO
Wu-lin Lu
Liang-shan-men Chan
Hu-hang Hsien
Sung-mu Ch'ang
Wu-lin Lu
Yen ling Lu
Chung-shan Lu
Chekiang University
Pao-ch'u T'a
Ch'ing-ch'un Chieh
Chieh- fang Chieh
Pai Ti (dike)
Ku shan Lu
Chung-shan Kung-yüan
YÜ-CH'ÜAN
Chung- shan Lu
Hang-chou Chan
Hsi Hu
Su Ti (dike)
LI-HSI HU
Huan-hu Hsi-lu
Huan-hu Nan-lu
Ling-yin Lu
Pei Kao-feng
Hsi-shan Hsiu-yang-ch'ü (recreation area)
LING-YIN
HSIA-T'IEN-CHU
FEI-LAI-FENG
Wu Shan
CHUNG-T'IEN-CHU
Hsi-shan Kung-yüan
SHANG-T'IEN-CHU
Feng-huang Shan
Nan Kao-feng
Nan-hsing-ch'iao Chan
LUNG-CHING
HU-P'AO
Che-kan Hsien
CH'IEN-T'ANG CHIANG
Fu-hsing Chieh
MEI-CHIA-WU
Liu-ho T'a
Chiu-ch'i-shih-pa-chien
HSÜ-TS'UN
Recreation area
0 1 MILE
0 1 KM

HANG-CHOU
HANGCHOW

CANTON

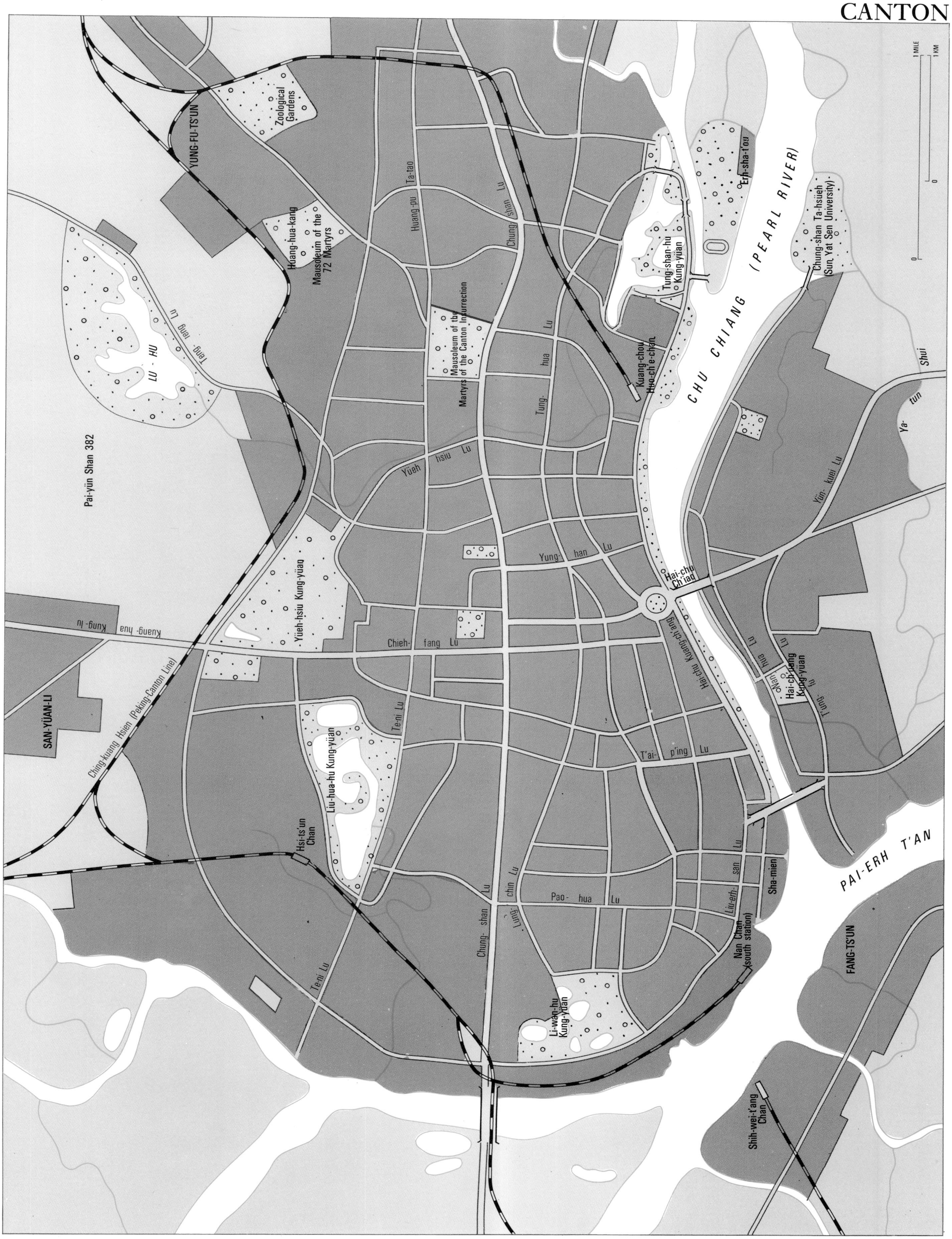
1 MILE
1 KM
0
0
Zoological Gardens
YUNG-FU-TS'UN
Erh-sha-t'ou
CHU CHIANG (PEARL RIVER)
Chung-shan Ta-hsüeh (Sun Yat Sen University)
Ta-tao
Huang-pu
Chung-shan Lu
Huang-hua-kang
Mausoleum of the 72 Martyrs
Tung-shan-hu Kung-yüan
Teng-feng Lu
LU HU
Mausoleum of the Martyrs of the Canton Insurrection
Tung-hua Lu
Kuang-chou Huo-ch'e-chan
Shui
Ya-tun
Pai-yün Shan 382
Yüeh-hsiu Lu
Yün-kuei Lu
Yung-han Lu
Hai-chu Ch'iao
Yüeh-hsiu Kung-yüan
Kuang-hua Kung-lu
Chieh-fang Lu
Hai-chu Kuang-ch'ang
Tung-hua Lu
Hai-ch'uang Kung-yüan
SAN-YÜAN-LI
Ching-kuang Hsien (Peking-Canton Line)
Te-ni Lu
T'ai-p'ing Lu
Liu-hua-hu Kung-yüan
Hsi-ts'un Chan
PAI-ERH T'AN
Liu-erh-san Lu
Sha-mien
Pao-hua Lu
Lung-chin Lu
Chung-shan Lu
Nan Chan (south station)
FANG-TS'UN
Te-ni Lu
Li-wan-hu Kung-yüan
Shih-wei-t'ang Chan

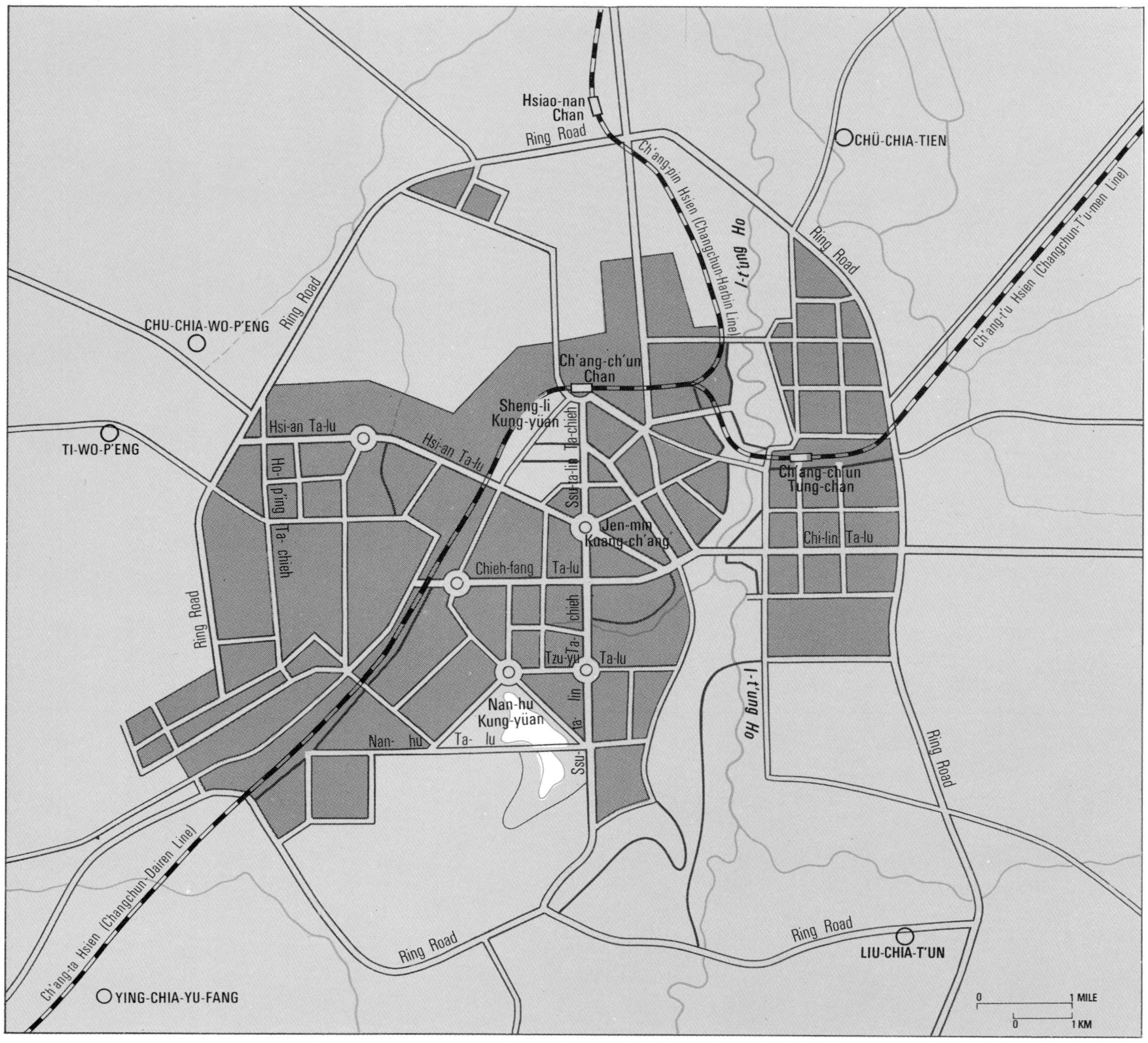

CH'ANG-CH'UN
CHANGCHUN

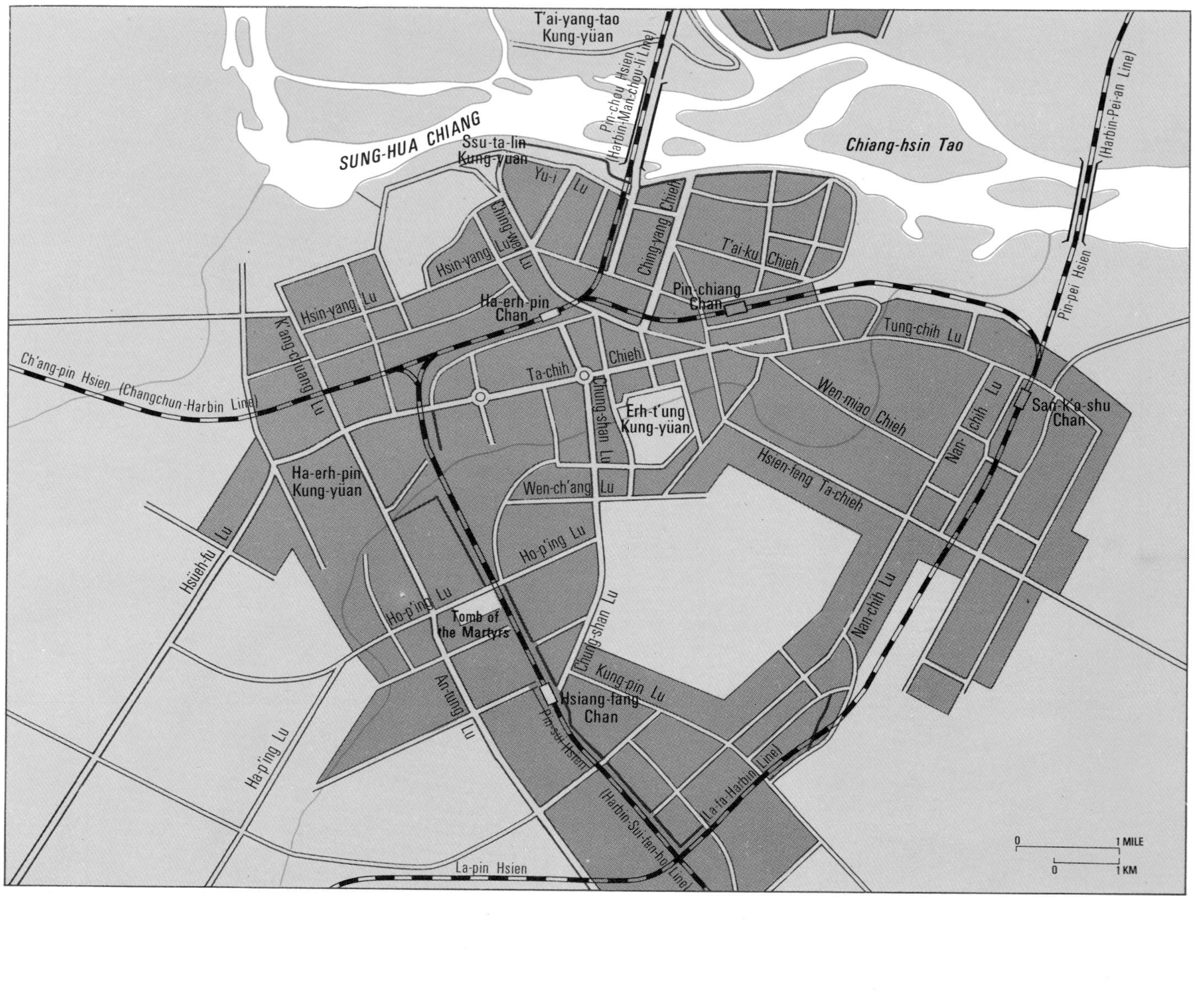

HA-ERH-PIN
HARBIN

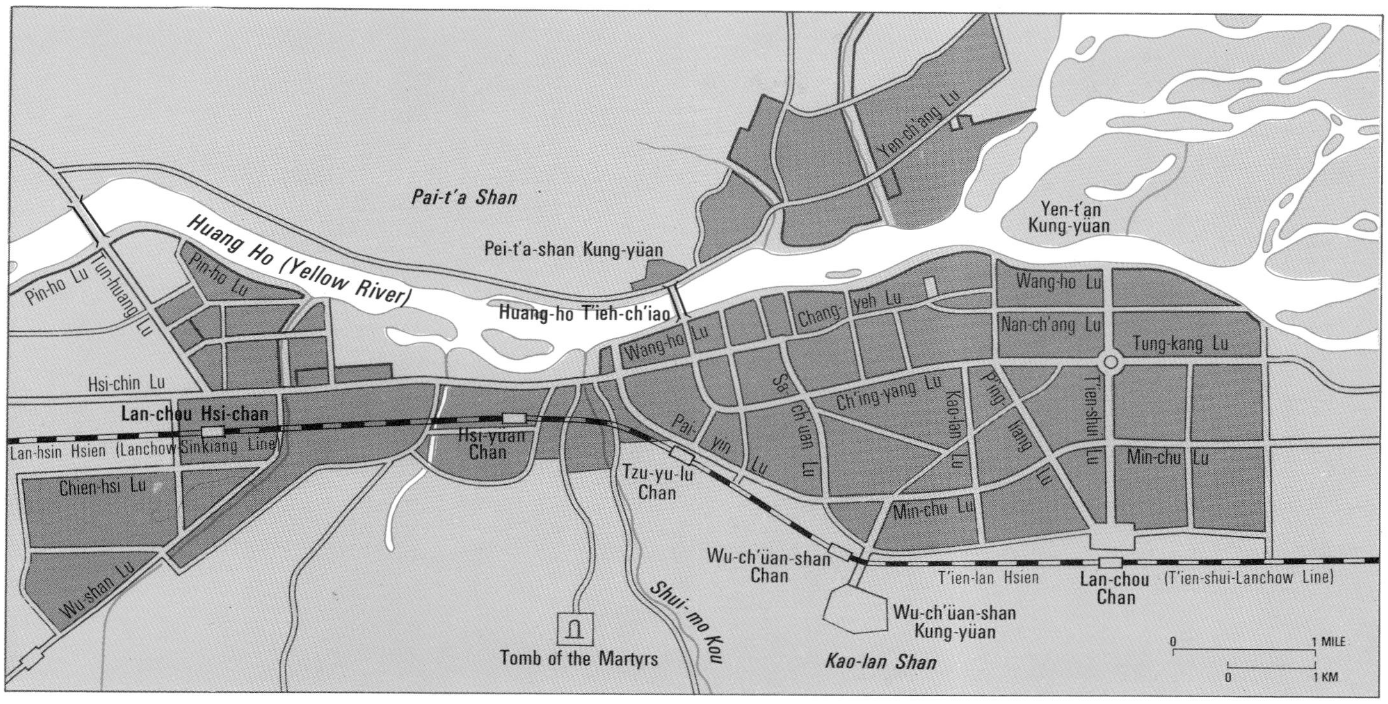

LAN-CHOU
LANCHOW

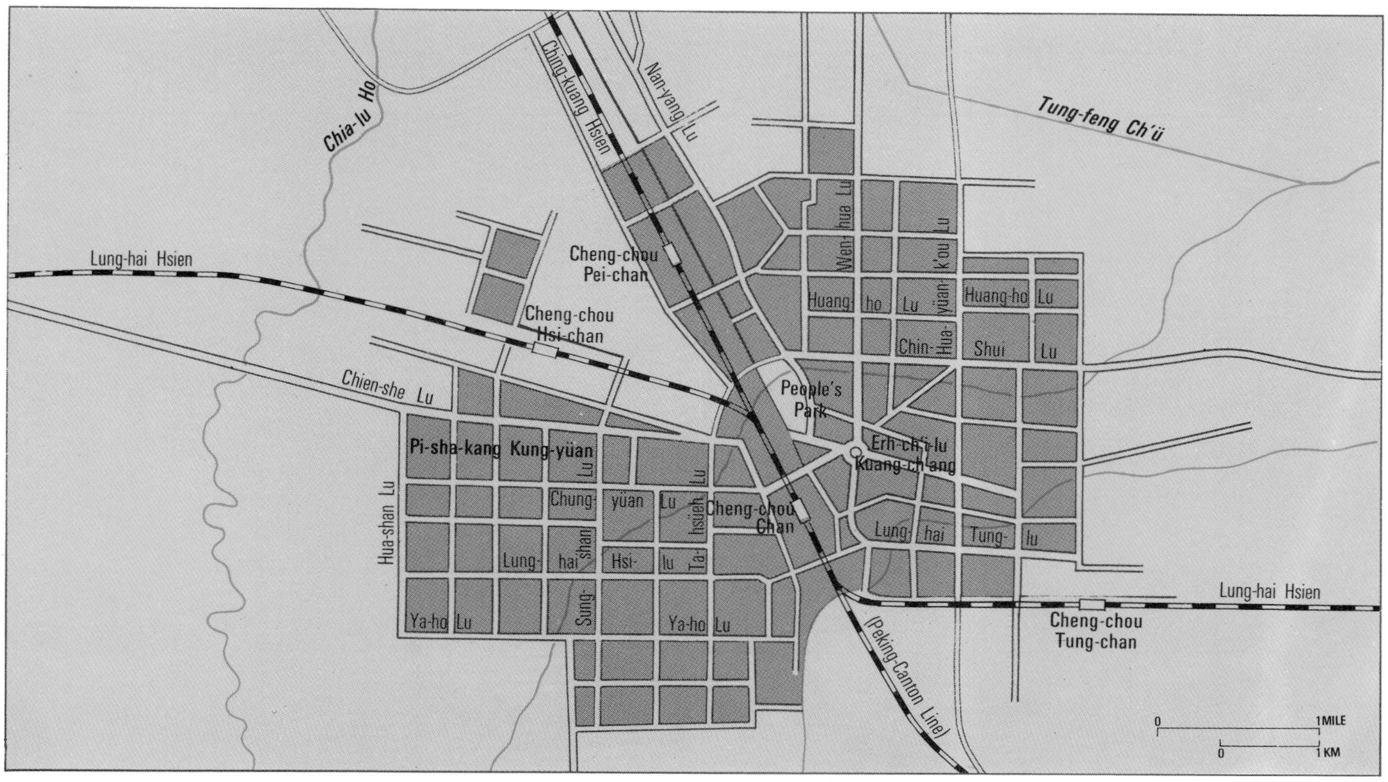

CHENG-CHOU
CHENGCHOW

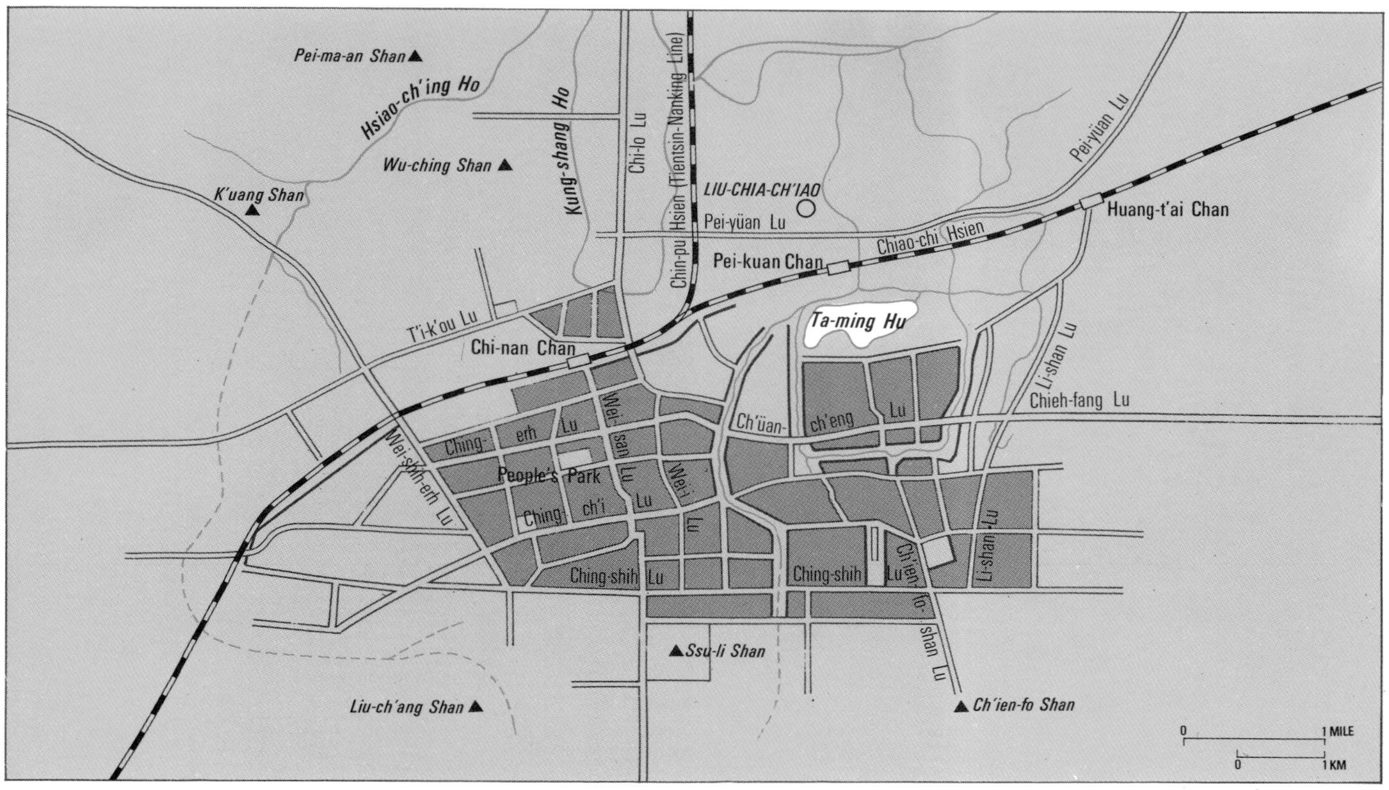

CHI-NAN
TSINAN

T'AI-YÜAN
TAIYUAN

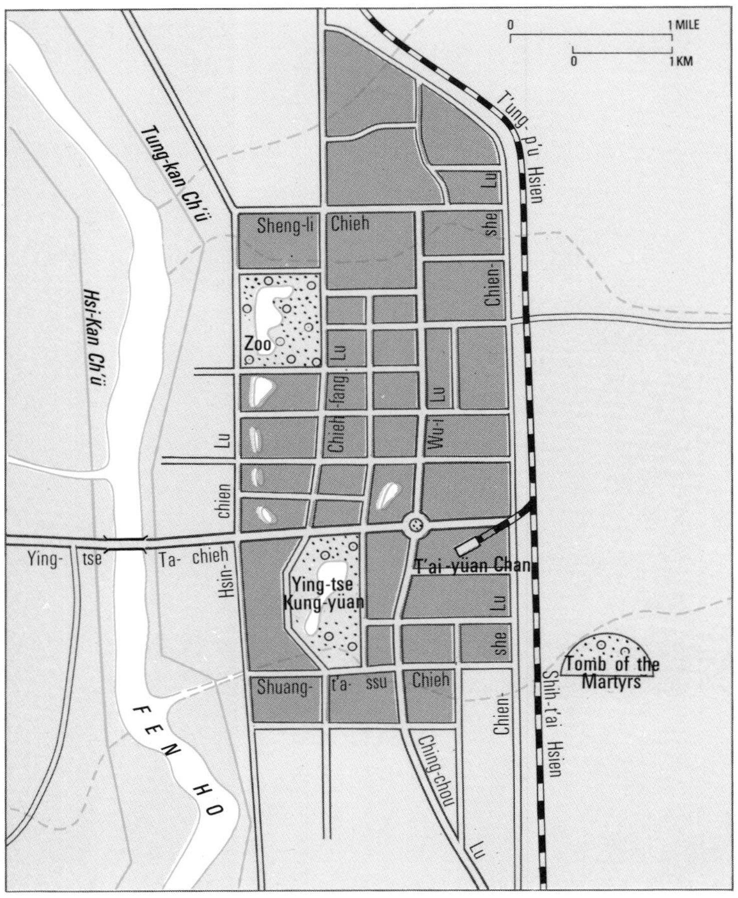

CH'ANG-SHA
CHANGSHA

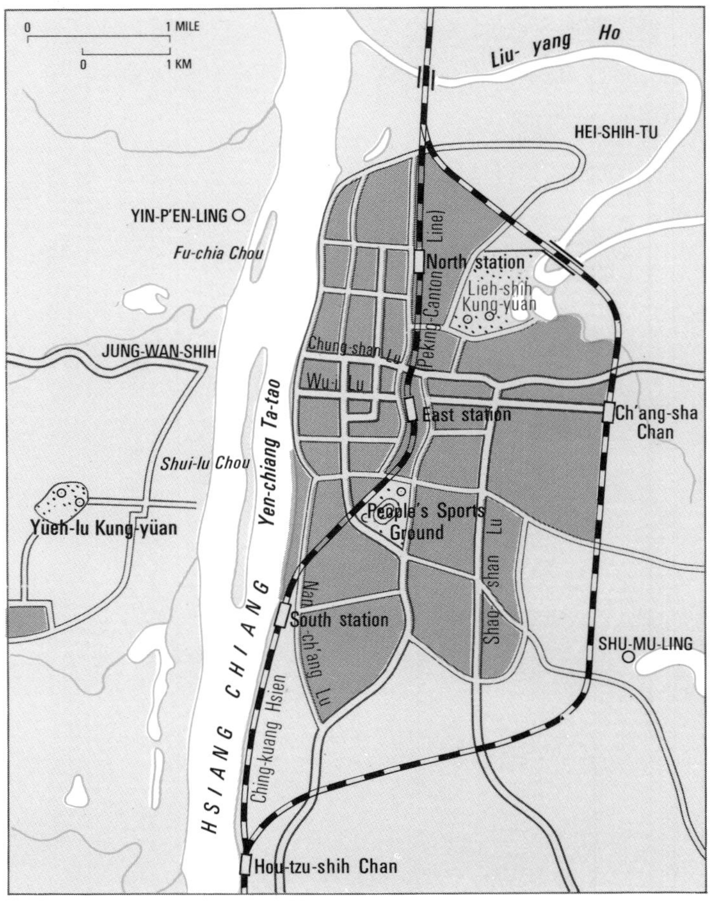

SHEN-YANG
MUKDEN

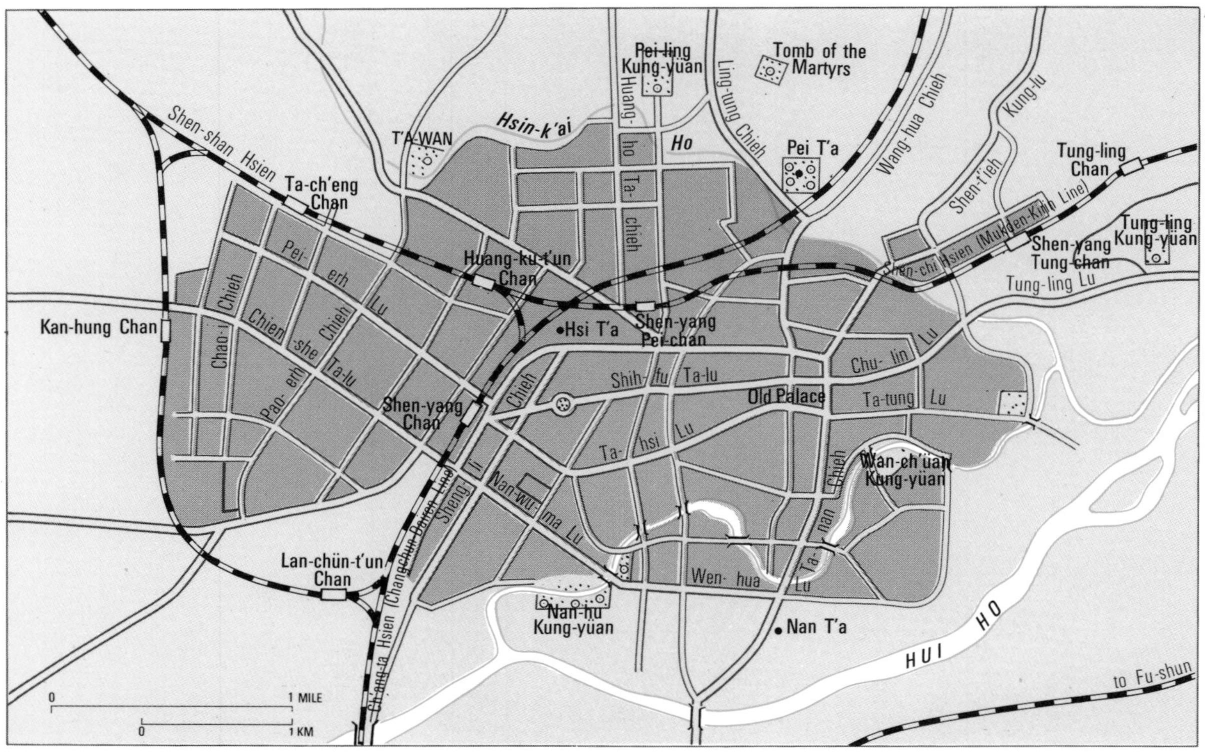

YIN-CH'UAN
YINCHWAN

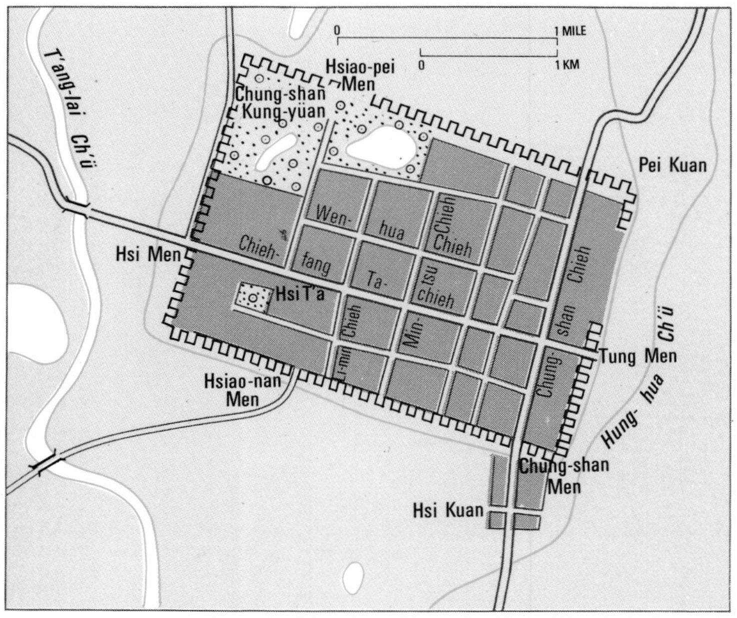

HO-FEI
HOFEI

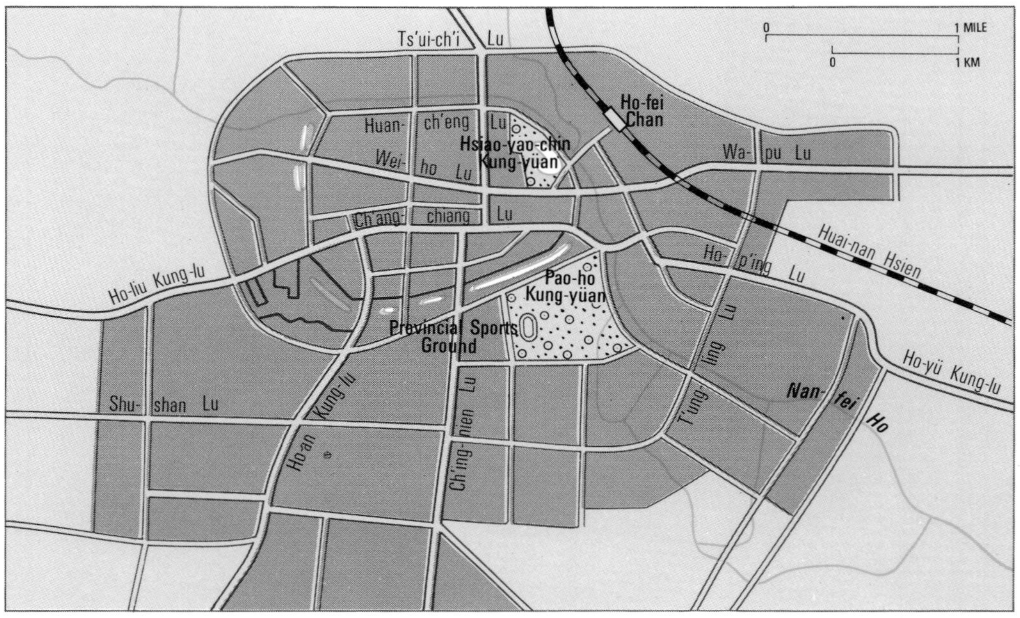

FU-CHOU
FOOCHOW

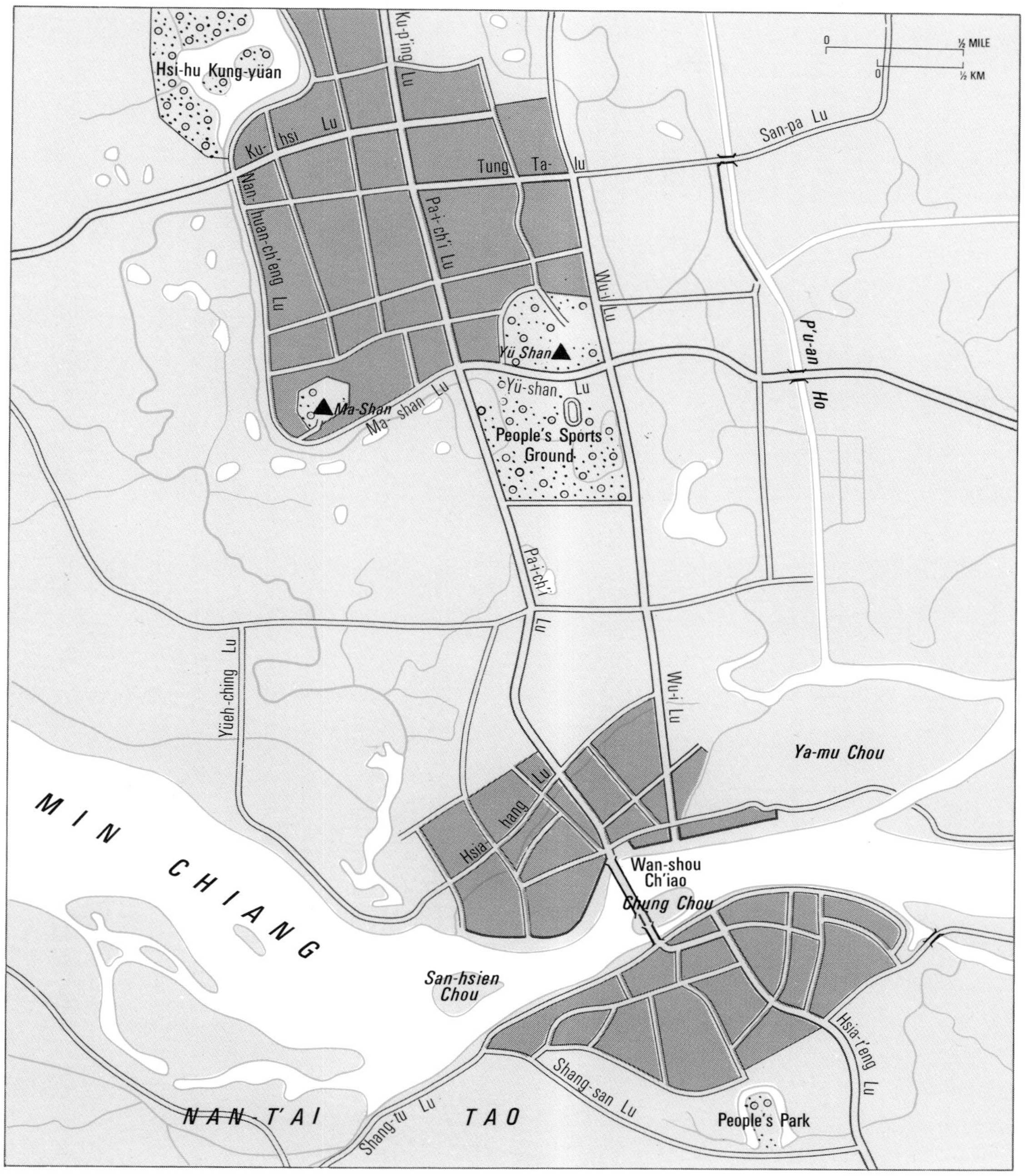

KUEI-YANG
KWEIYANG

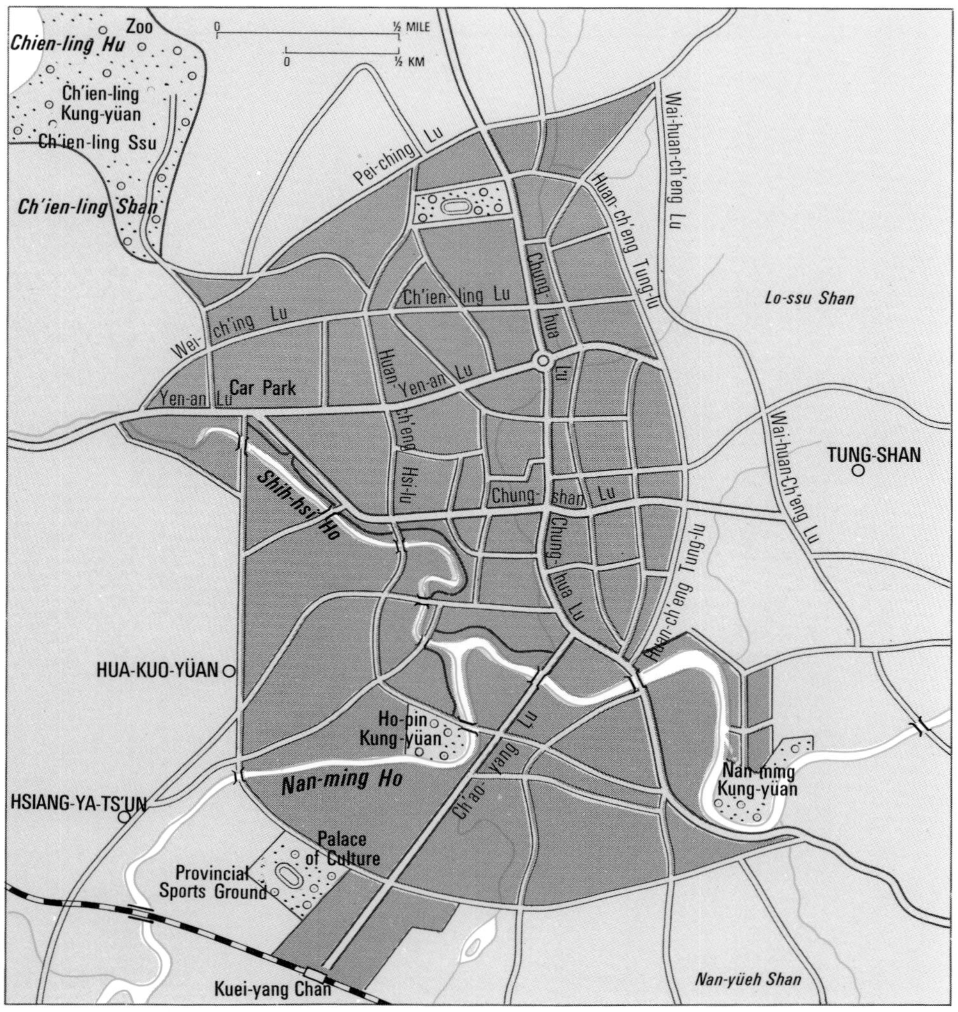

NAN-NING
NANNING

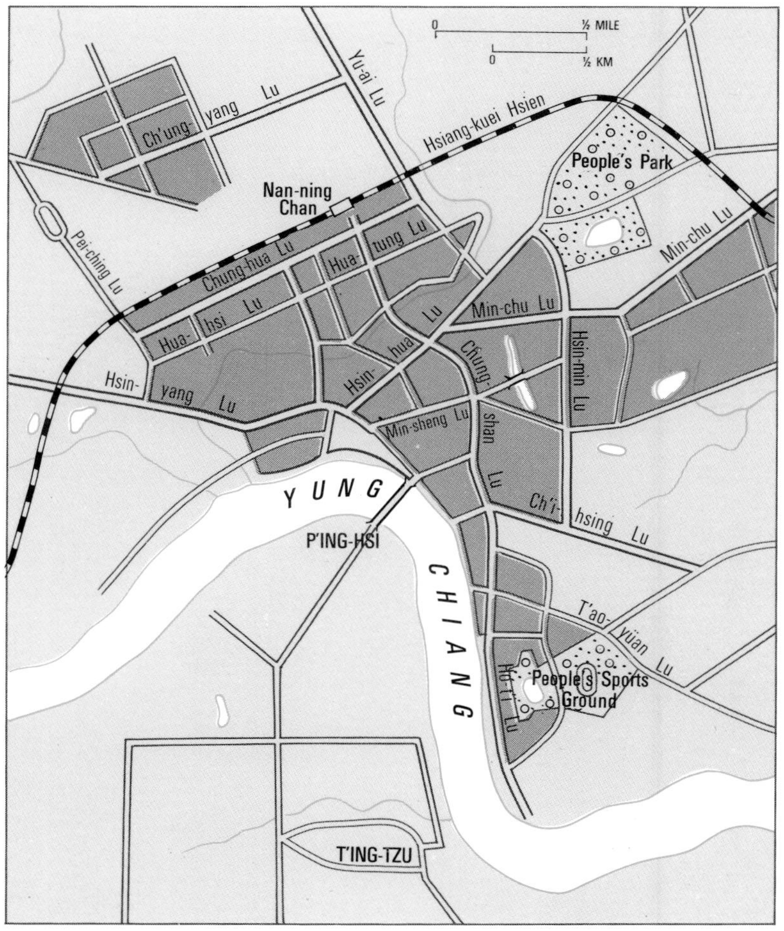

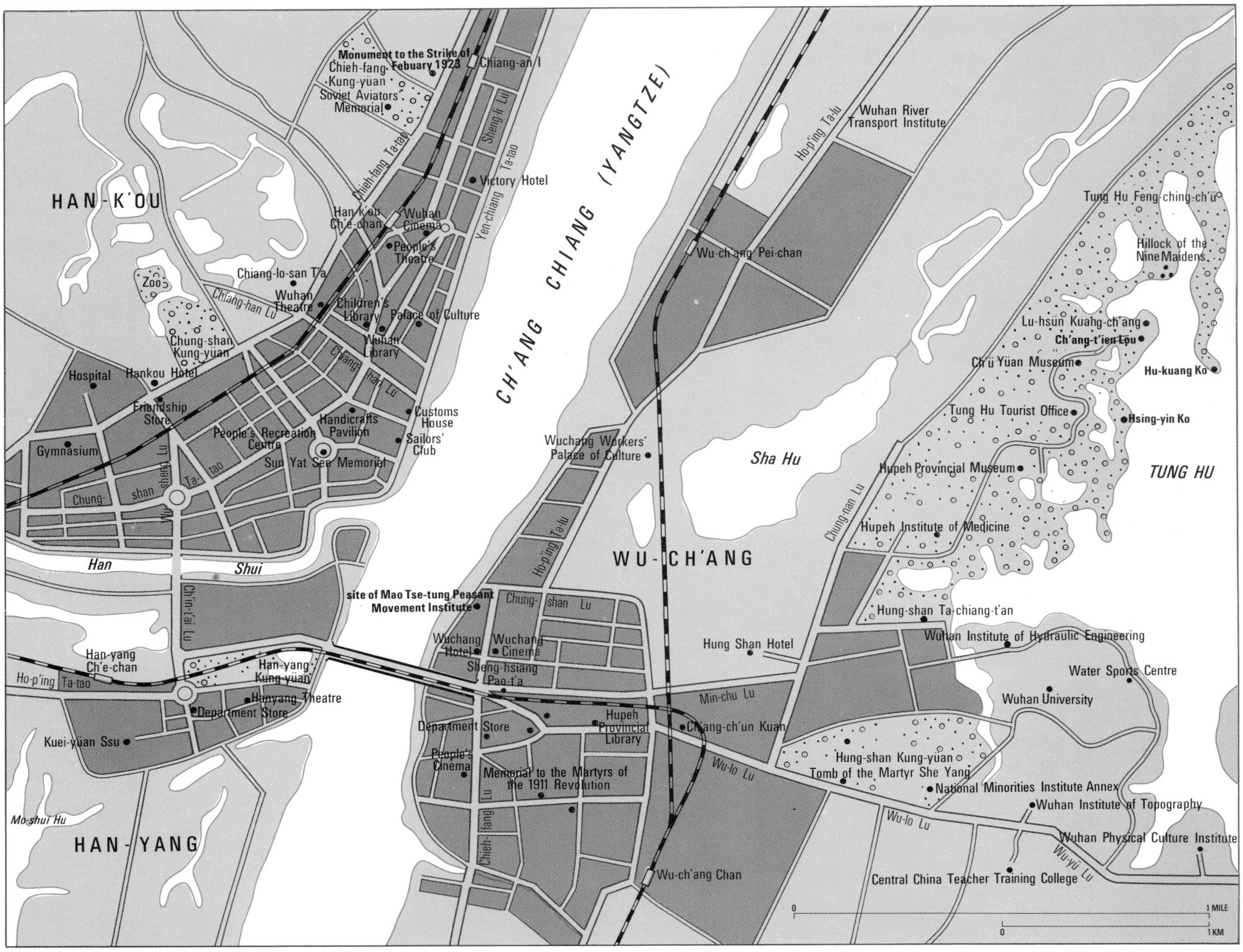
HAN-K'OU
WU-CH'ANG
HAN-YANG
CH'ANG CHIANG (YANGTZE)
Han Shui
Sha Hu
TUNG HU
Monument to the Strike of Febuary 1923
Chieh-fang Kung-yuan
Soviet Aviators' Memorial
Chiang-an
Victory Hotel
Han-k'ou Ch'e-chan
Wuhan Cinema
People's Theatre
Chiang-lo-san T'a
Wuhan Theatre
Children's Library
Palace of Culture
Wuhan Library
Zoo
Chung-shan Kung-yuan
Hospital
Hankou Hotel
Friendship Store
Gymnasium
People's Recreation Centre
Handicrafts Pavilion
Customs House
Sailors' Club
Sun Yat Sen Memorial
Han-yang Ch'e-chan
Han-yang Kung-yuan
Hanyang Theatre
Department Store
Kuei-yuan Ssu
Mo-shui Hu
site of Mao Tse-tung Peasant Movement Institute
Wuchang Hotel
Wuchang Cinema
Sheng-hsiang Pao-t'a
Department Store
Hupeh Provincial Library
People's Cinema
Memorial to the Martyrs of the 1911 Revolution
Wuchang Workers' Palace of Culture
Wu-ch'ang Pei-chan
Wuhan River Transport Institute
Hung Shan Hotel
Ch'ang-ch'un Kuan
Wu-ch'ang Chan
Tung Hu Feng-ching-ch'ü
Hillock of the Nine Maidens
Lu-hsün Kuang-ch'ang
Ch'ang-t'ien Lou
Ch'ü Yüan Museum
Hu-kuang Ko
Tung Hu Tourist Office
Hsing-yin Ko
Hupeh Provincial Museum
Hupeh Institute of Medicine
Hung-shan Ta-chiang-t'an
Wuhan Institute of Hydraulic Engineering
Water Sports Centre
Wuhan University
Hung-shan Kung-yuan
Tomb of the Martyr She Yang
National Minorities Institute Annex
Wuhan Institute of Topography
Wuhan Physical Culture Institute
Central China Teacher Training College
Chieh-fang Ta-tao
Sheng-li Lu
Yen-chiang Ta-tao
Chiang-han Lu
Chung-shan Ta-tao
Wu-sheng Lu
Ch'in-t'ai Lu
Ho-p'ing Ta-tao
Ho-p'ing Ta-lu
Chung-shan Lu
Chieh-fang Lu
Min-chu Lu
Wu-lo Lu
Wu-yü Lu
Chung-nan Lu
0 1 MILE
0 1 KM

WU-HAN
WUHAN

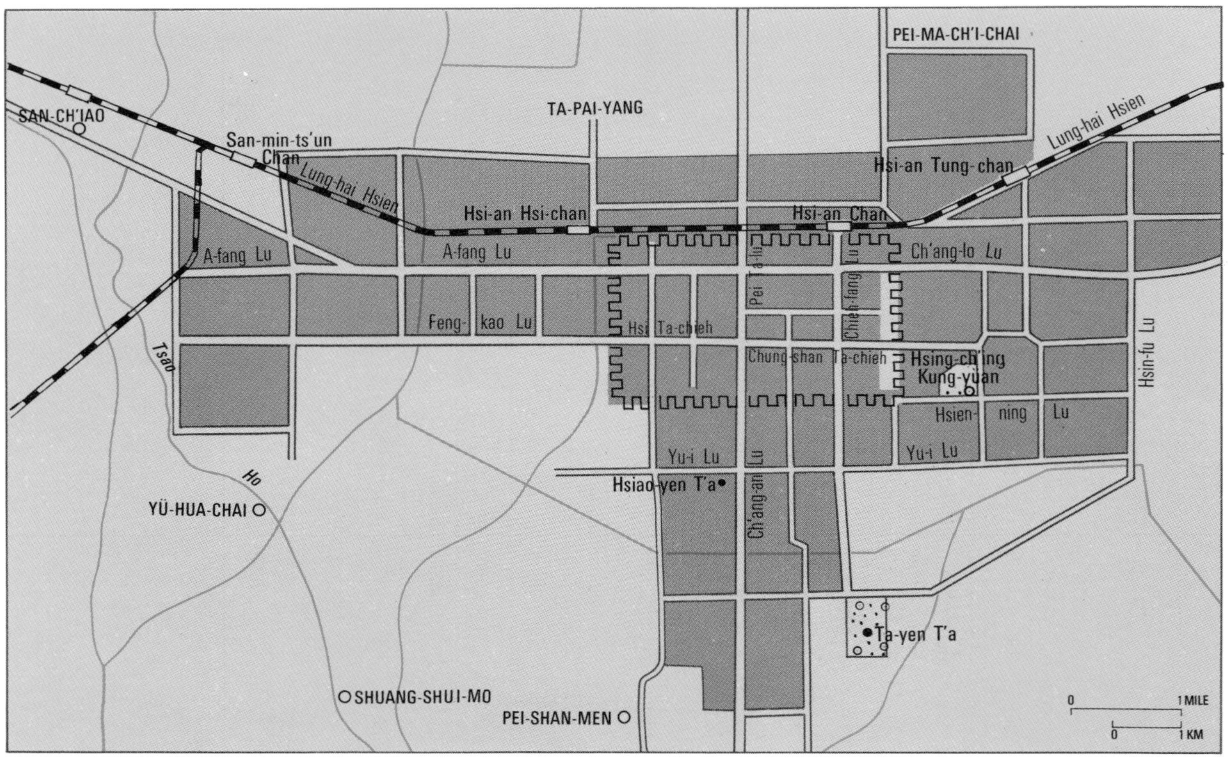
PEI-MA-CH'I-CHAI
TA-PAI-YANG
SAN-CH'IAO
San-min-ts'un Chan
Lung-hai Hsien
Hsi-an Hsi-chan
Hsi-an Chan
Hsi-an Tung-chan
A-fang Lu
Ch'ang-lo Lu
Feng-kao Lu
Hsi Ta-chieh
Pei Ta-lu
Chieh-fang Lu
Chung-shan Ta-chieh
Hsing-ch'ing Kung-yuan
Hsien-ning Lu
Hsin-fu Lu
Yu-i Lu
Hsiao-yen T'a
Ch'ang-an Lu
Tsao Ho
YÜ-HUA-CHAI
Ta-yen T'a
SHUANG-SHUI-MO
PEI-SHAN-MEN
0 1 MILE
0 1 KM

HSI-AN
SIAN

NAN-CH'ANG
NANCHANG

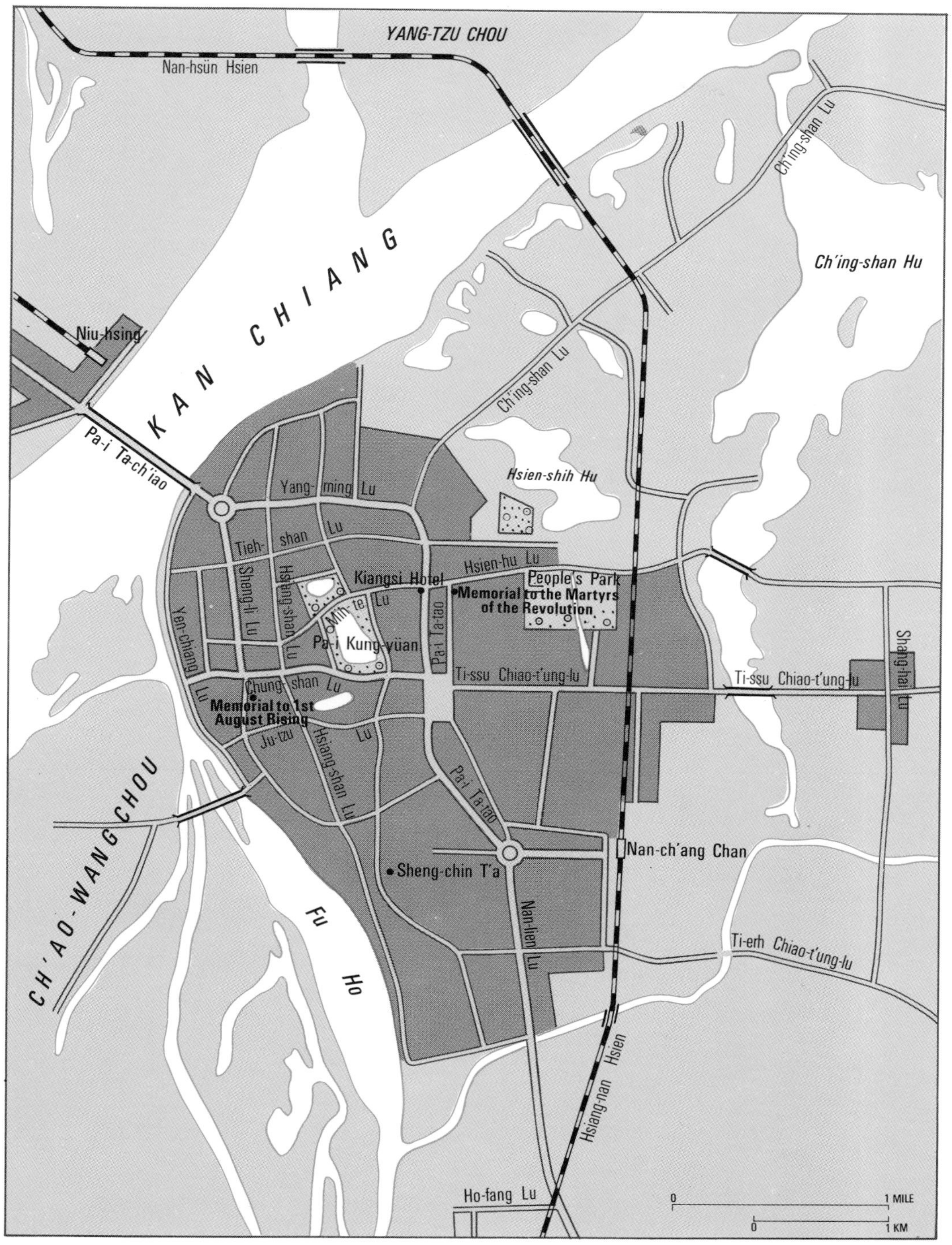
YANG-TZU CHOU
Nan-hsün Hsien
Ch'ing-shan Lu
Ch'ing-shan Hu
KAN CHIANG
Niu-hsing
Ch'ing-shan Lu
Pa-i Ta-ch'iao
Hsien-shih Hu
Yang-ming Lu
Tieh-shan Lu
Hsien-hu Lu
Kiangsi Hotel
People's Park
Memorial to the Martyrs of the Revolution
Shang-li Lu
Hsiang-shan Lu
Min-te Lu
Pa-i Ta-tao
Yen-chiang Lu
Pa-i Kung-yüan
Ti-ssu Chiao-t'ung-lu
Ti-ssu Chiao-t'ung-lu
Shang-hai Lu
Chung-shan Lu
Memorial to 1st August Rising
Ju-tzu Lu
Hsiang-shan Lu
Pa-i Ta-tao
CH'AO-WANG CHOU
Nan-ch'ang Chan
Sheng-chin T'a
FU HO
Nan-lien Lu
Ti-erh Chiao-t'ung-lu
Hsiang-nan Hsien
Ho-fang Lu
0 1 MILE
0 1 KM

CH'UNG-CH'ING
CHUNGKING

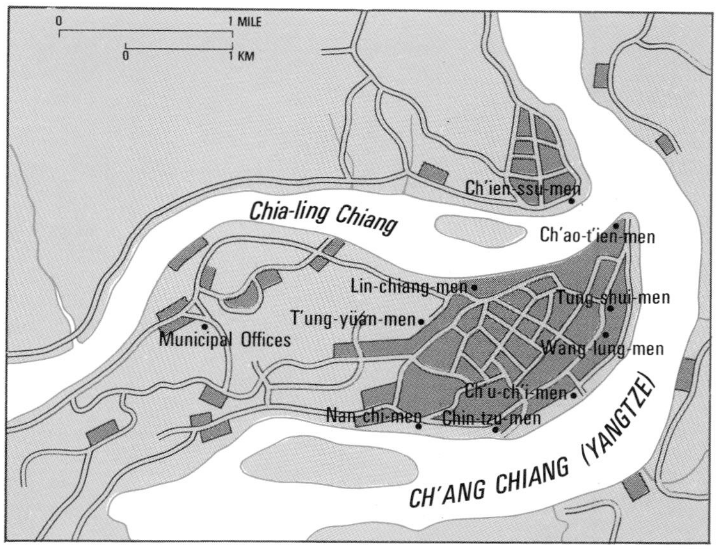
0 1 MILE
0 1 KM
Ch'ien-ssu-men
Chia-ling Chiang
Ch'ao-t'ien-men
Lin-chiang-men
T'ung-yüan-men
Tung-shui-men
Municipal Offices
Wang-lung-men
Ch'u-ch'i-men
Nan-chi-men
Chin-tzu-men
CH'ANG CHIANG (YANGTZE)

CH'ENG-TU
CHENGTU

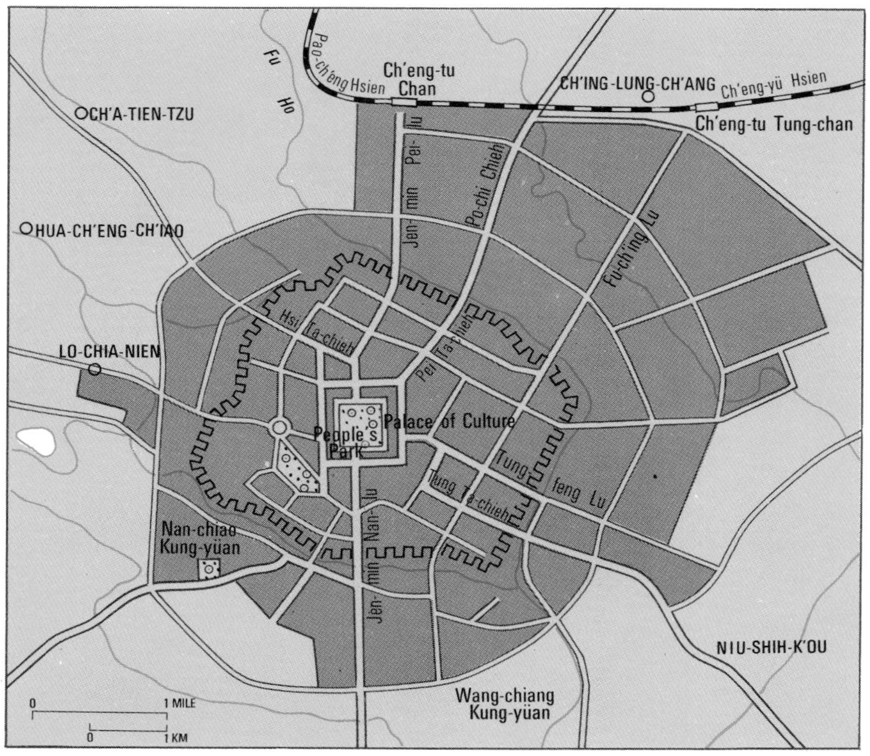
Pao-ch'eng Hsien
Fu Ho
Ch'eng-tu Chan
CH'ING-LUNG-CH'ANG
Ch'eng-yü Hsien
CH'A-TIEN-TZU
Ch'eng-tu Tung-chan
Jen-min Pei-lu
Po-chi Chieh
HUA-CH'ENG-CH'IAO
Fu-ch'ing Lu
LO-CHIA-NIEN
Hsi Ta-chieh
Pei Ta-chieh
Palace of Culture
People's Park
Tung Ta-chieh
Tung-feng Lu
Nan-chiao Kung-yüan
Jen-min Nan-lu
NIU-SHIH-K'OU
Wang-chiang Kung-yüan
0 1 MILE
0 1 KM

K'UN-MING
KUNMING

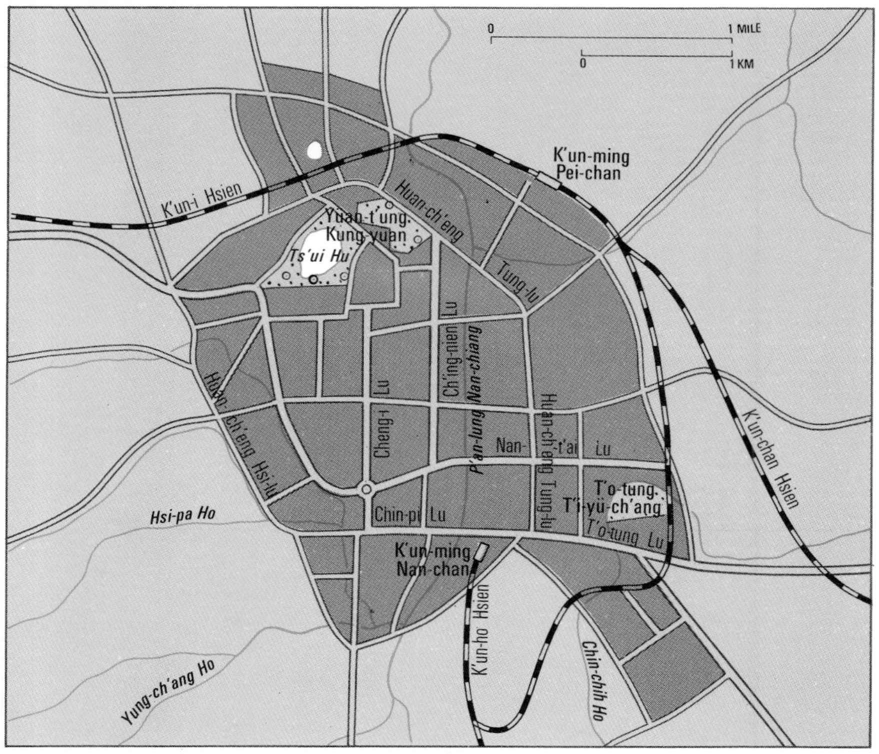
0 1 MILE
0 1 KM
K'un-ming Pei-chan
K'un-i Hsien
Yüan-t'ung Kung-yüan
Huan-ch'eng
Ts'ui Hu
Tung-lu
Ch'ing-nien Lu
Huan-ch'eng Hsi-lu
Cheng-i Lu
P'an-lung Nan-chiang
Huan-ch'eng Tung-lu
Nan-t'ai Lu
K'un-chan Hsien
T'o-tung T'i-yü-ch'ang
T'o-tung Lu
Hsi-pa Ho
Chin-pi Lu
K'un-ming Nan-chan
K'un-ho Hsien
Yung-ch'ang Ho
Chin-chih Ho

HSI-NING
SINING

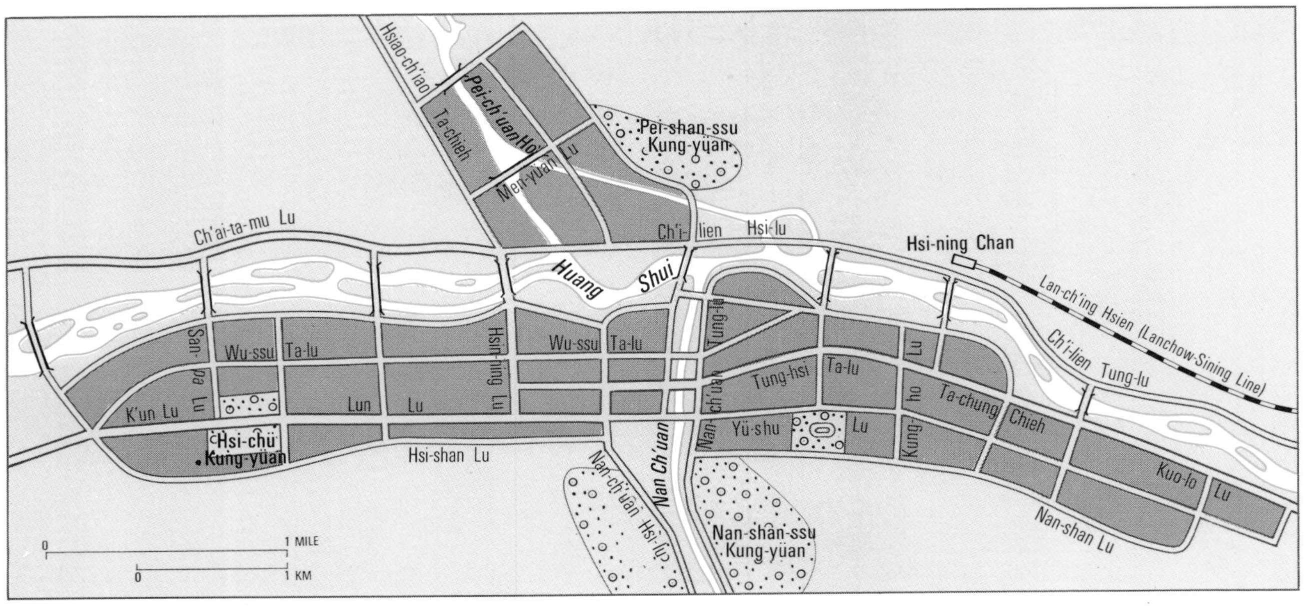

HU-HO-HAO-T'E
HUHEHOT

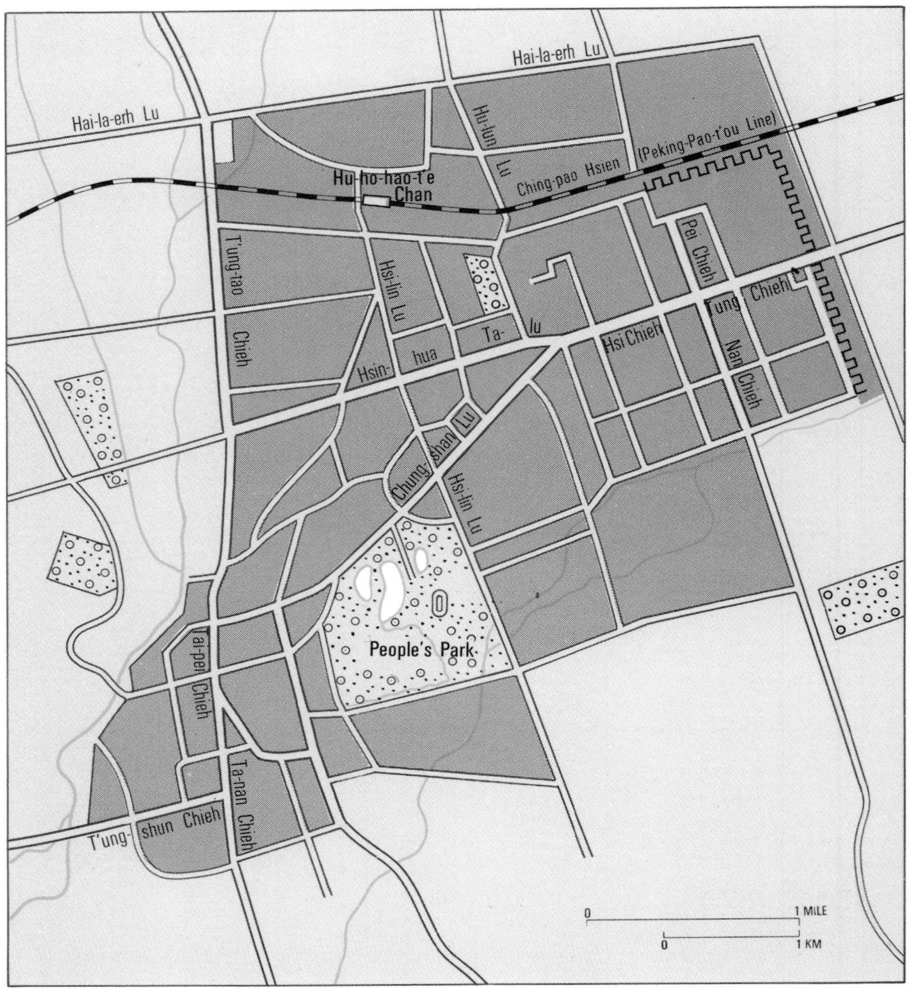

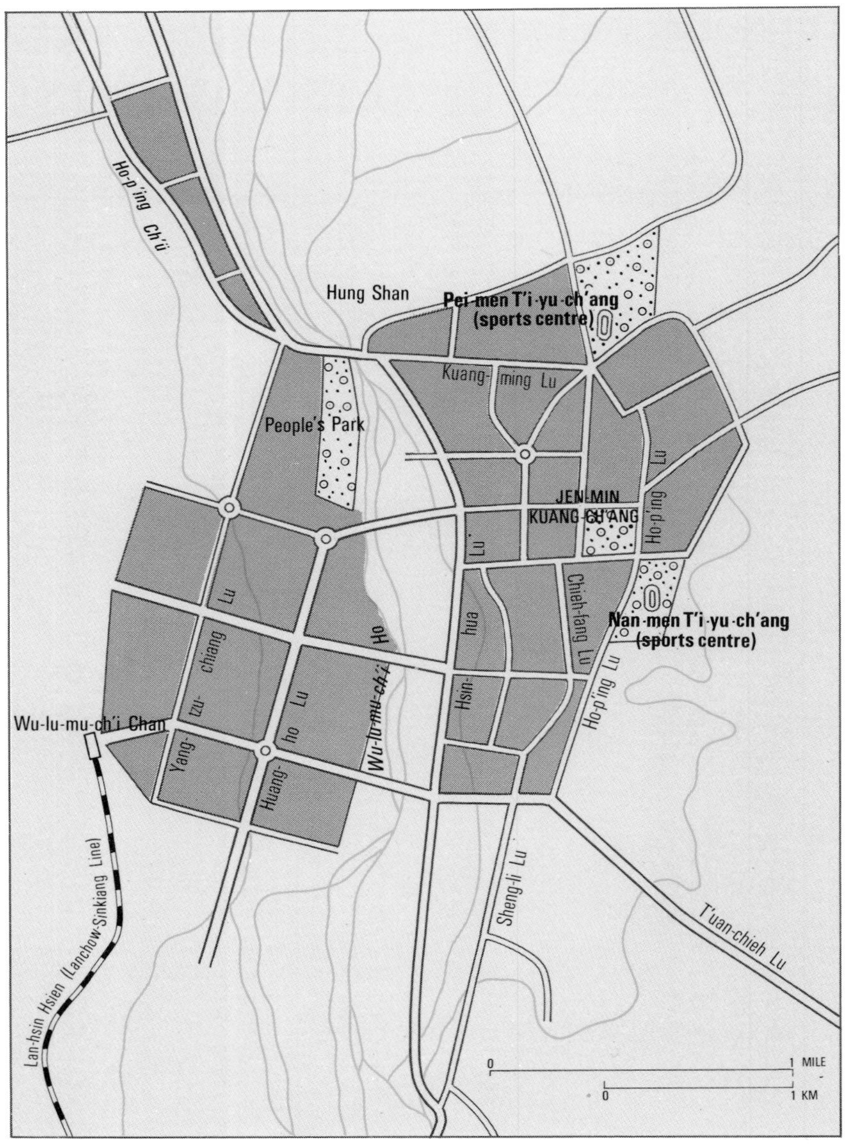

WU-LU-MU-CH'I
URUMCHI

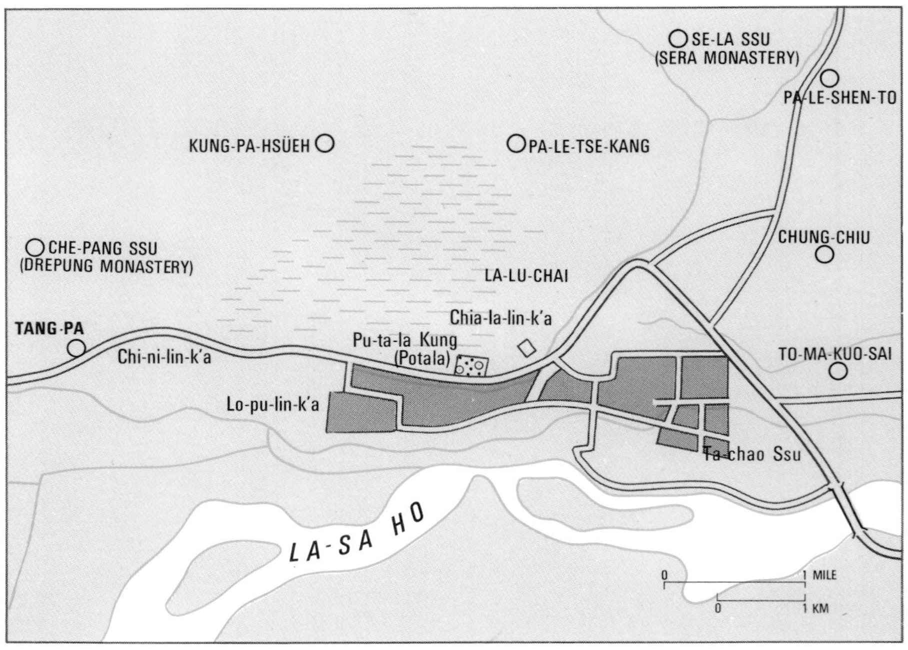

LA-SA
LHASA

T'AI-PEI
TAIPEI

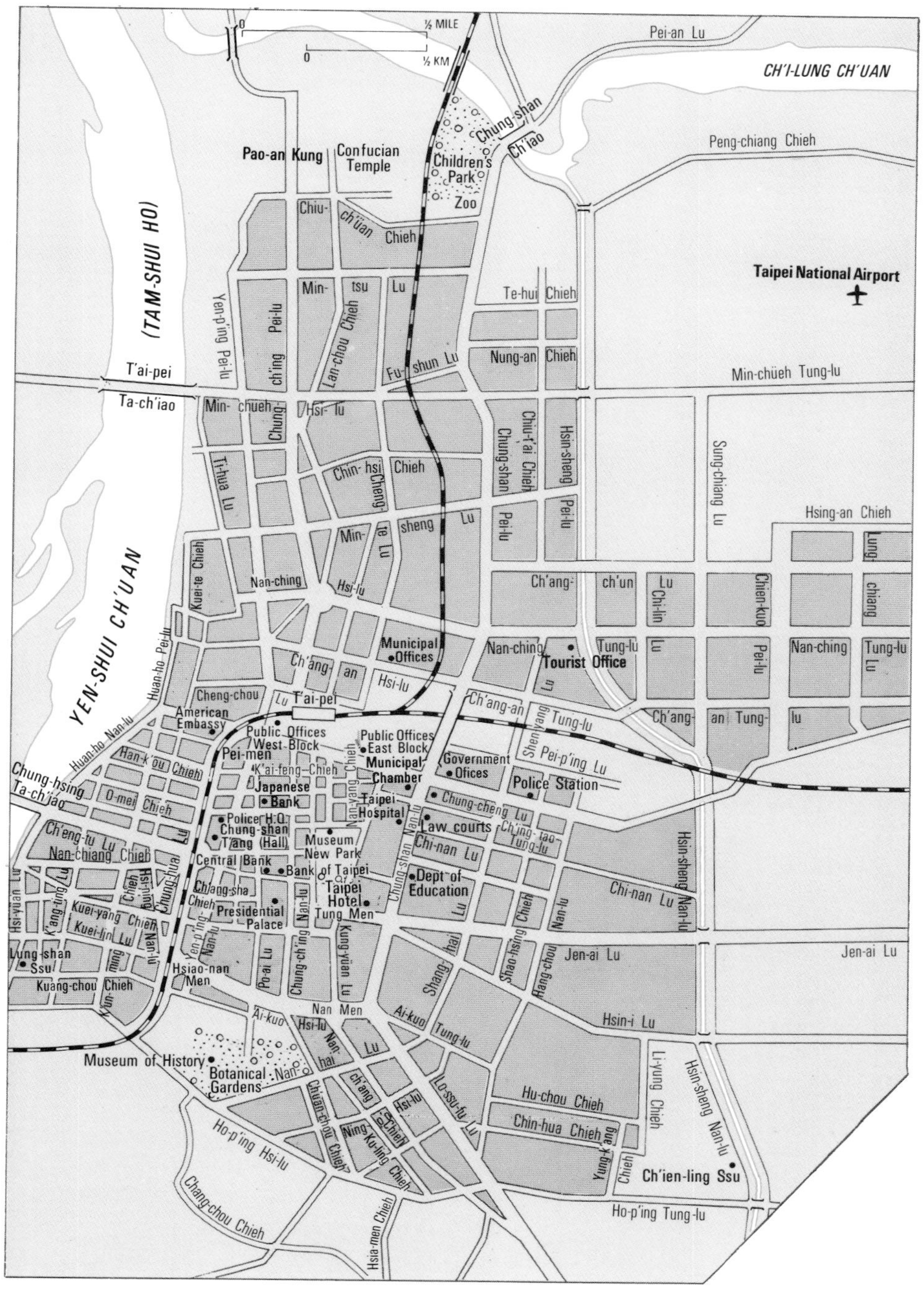

½ MILE
½ KM
Pei-an Lu
CH'I-LUNG CH'UAN
Chung-shan Ch'iao
Pao-an Kung
Confucian Temple
Children's Park
Zoo
Peng-chiang Chieh
(TAM-SHUI HO)
Taipei National Airport
Te-hui Chieh
Nung-an Chieh
Min-chüeh Tung-lu
T'ai-pei
Ta-ch'iao
YEN-SHUI CH'UAN
Sung-chiang Lu
Hsing-an Chieh
Nan-ching
Municipal Offices
Tourist Office
Cheng-chou
American Embassy
T'ai-pei
Public Offices West Block
Public Offices East Block
Pei-men
Municipal Chamber
Government Offices
Police Station
Pei-p'ing Lu
Japanese Bank
Taipei Hospital
Chung-hsing Ta-ch'iao
Police H.Q.
Chung-shan T'ang (Hall)
Museum New Park
Law courts
Central Bank
Bank of Taipei
Dept of Education
Presidential Palace
Taipei Hotel
Tung Men
Lung-shan Ssu
Hsiao-nan Men
Nan Men
Jen-ai Lu
Hsin-i Lu
Museum of History
Botanical Gardens
Hu-chou Chieh
Chin-hua Chieh
Ch'ien-ling Ssu
Ho-p'ing Hsi-lu
Ho-p'ing Tung-lu
Chang-chou Chieh
Hsia-men Chieh

MACAU

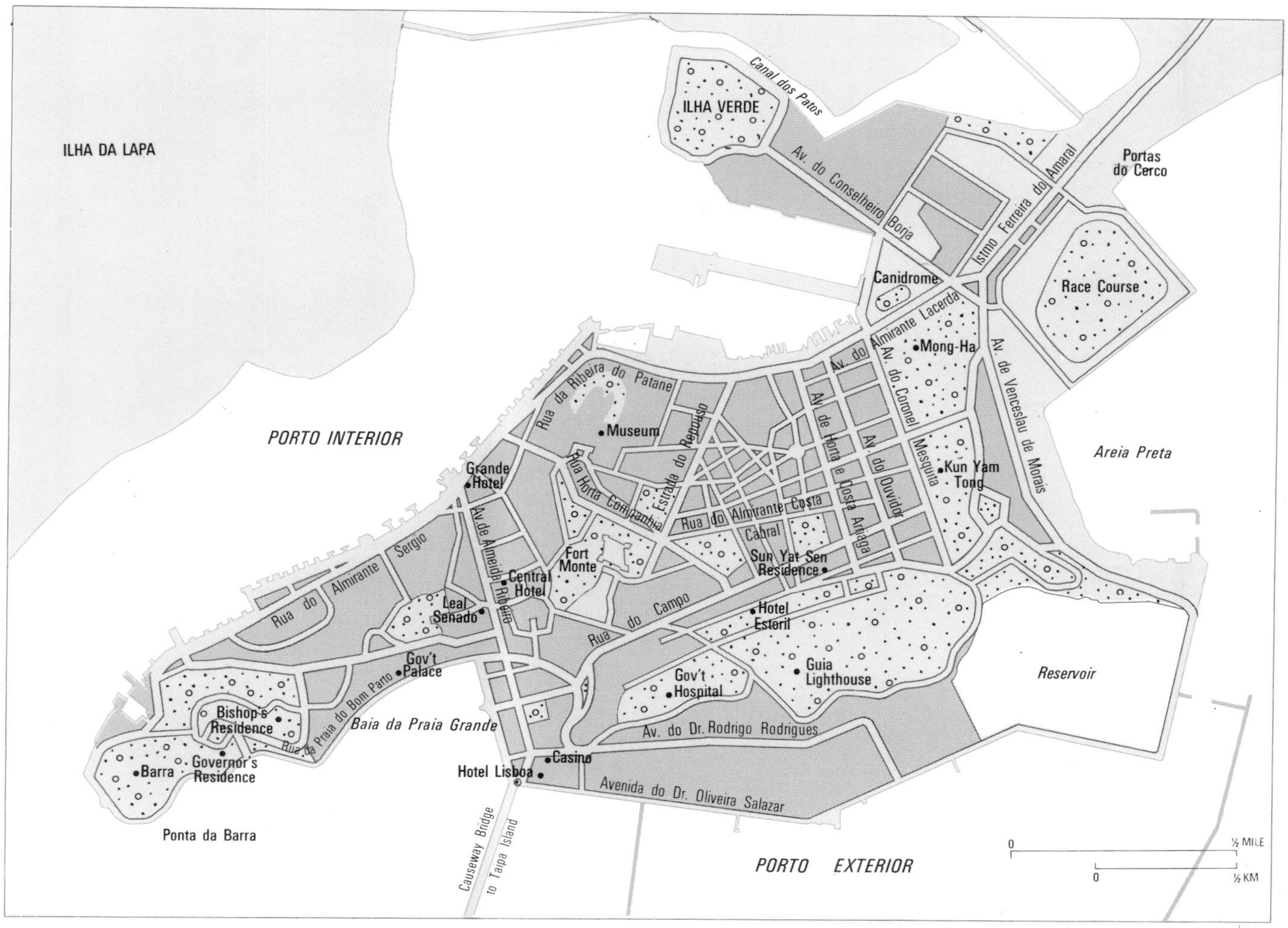

ILHA DA LAPA
Canal dos Patos
ILHA VERDE
Av. do Conselheiro Borja
Portas do Cerco
Istmo Ferreira do Amaral
Canidrome
Race Course
Av. do Almirante Lacerda
Mong-Ha
Av. de Venceslau de Morais
Rua da Ribeira do Patane
Museum
PORTO INTERIOR
Areia Preta
Grande Hotel
Kun Yam Tong
Rua do Almirante Costa Cabral
Fort Monte
Sun Yat Sen Residence
Central Hotel
Rua do Almirante Sergio
Leal Senado
Hotel Estoril
Rua do Campo
Gov't Palace
Gov't Hospital
Guia Lighthouse
Reservoir
Bishop's Residence
Baia da Praia Grande
Rua da Praia do Bom Parto
Av. do Dr. Rodrigo Rodrigues
Barra
Governor's Residence
Hotel Lisboa
Casino
Avenida do Dr. Oliveira Salazar
Ponta da Barra
Causeway Bridge to Taipa Island
PORTO EXTERIOR
½ MILE
½ KM

NOTES ON TRANSCRIPTION

MUCH use is being made today by western commercial cartographers of the Pinyin system for transcribing Chinese names. It is therefore necessary for the editors of the present atlas to explain why they believe the use of Pinyin for this purpose to be ill-advised and why they have adhered unhesitatingly to the Wade–Giles system.

There are a number of different transcription systems for Chinese (Legeza's 'Guide' lists 21), as there are transliteration systems for other scripts, and there is as strong an inclination towards international standardisation in this field as there is in weights and measures. Since Pinyin was developed by the Chinese themselves within the People's Republic it is widely but illogically seen on these grounds alone as being preferable to Wade–Giles or other 'national' systems. It is also claimed, and with some justification, that it is a better system than Wade–Giles.

But the question is not whether Pinyin or Wade–Giles is the better system from a linguistic point of view, but rather, which system is more useful in the context of geographical names? A new context may indeed require a fresh system, and Pinyin appears to be serving adequately the pedagogic and allied purposes for which it was devised. The problem of dealing with Chinese geographical names, however, is not a new one. It is an old and difficult one, but one which has been largely solved by the use of the Wade–Giles system since 1942 for the transcription of names on all official British and American maps of China, hydrographic charts and sailing directions, air charts and gazetteers. There is almost complete coverage of China at 1 : 1,000,000 scale and significant coverage at larger scales, much of which is on sale or available in reference libraries throughout the English-speaking world. The United States Board on Geographic Names published in 1968 a Gazetteer of China listing over 100,000 names in Wade–Giles spellings. It is estimated that something in the order of a quarter of a million Chinese geographical names have been romanised in the Wade–Giles system over the last thirty years.

This represents a formidable mass of interlocking reference material. A small-scale map or atlas which adopts Pinyin spellings of Chinese names succeeds only in cutting the user off totally from any possibility of relating it to this larger-scale reservoir of information, defeating the very purpose of an atlas, which is to serve as a work of reference.

Pinyin can thus cause a great deal of unnecessary confusion among unsuspecting atlas users. There will be those, however, who need to relate spellings in the two systems and for this purpose are appended complete Wade–Giles/Pinyin and Pinyin/Wade–Giles conversion tables. Further, every Wade–Giles names in the index is followed by its Pinyin equivalent. This has involved the minor but none the less practical problem that while rules for the application of Wade–Giles to geographical names were long ago formulated and have been consistently applied by the United States Board on Geographic Names and the Permanent Committee on Geographical Names for over a quarter of a century, no such rules for the application of Pinyin exist. Thus the same name may be found written in different atlases and guide books as Măfánggōu, Mafanggou, Ma Fang Gou or Ma fang gou. The second example seems to come closest to what is known of current Chinese practice and the Pinyin equivalents given in the index are in this form.

Before the introduction of Wade–Giles Chinese names were most commonly romanised in what is known as the Post Office system. Post Office spellings may still be encountered from time to time. The following table may be helpful:

Post Office	Wade–Giles	Post Office	Wade–Giles
ah	a	low	lou
chow	chou	ow	ou
chwan	ch'uan	peh	pei
chwang	chuang	seh	se
fow	fou	show	shou
hing	hsing	shwang	shuang
hwa	hua	si	hsi
hwai	huai	sia	hsia
hwan	huan	siang	hsiang
hwfing	huang	siao	hsiao
hwei	hui	sien	hsien
ki	chi, ch'i	sih	hsi
		sin	hsin
kia	chia	siu	hsiu
kiang	chiang	süeh	hsüeh
kiao	chiao, ch'iao	sze	ssu
		teh	te
kieh	chieh	tow	tou, t'ou
kien	chien, ch'ien	tseh	tse
kin	chin	tsi	chi, ch'i
king	ching, ch'ing	tsiao	chiao
kio, kioh	chiao, ch'üeh	tsin	chin, ch'in
kiu	chiu	tsing	ching, ch'ing
kiung	chiung, ch'iung	tze	tzu, tz'u
kow	kou, k'ou	yi	i
kwei	kuei, k'uei	yo	yüeh
kwo	kuo, k'uo		

WADE–GILES/PINYIN

Wade–Giles	Pinyin
a	a
ai	ai
an	an
ang	ang
ao	ao
cha	zha
ch'a	cha
chai	zhai
ch'ai	chai
chan	zhan
ch'an	chan
chang	zhang
ch'ang	chang
chao	zhao
ch'ao	chao
che	zhe
ch'e	che
chei	zhei
chen	zhen
ch'en	chen
cheng	zheng
ch'eng	cheng
chi	ji
ch'i	qi
chia	jia
ch'ia	qia
chiang	jiang
ch'iang	qiang
chiao	jiao
ch'iao	qiao
chieh	jie
ch'ieh	qie
chien	jian
ch'ien	qian
chih	zhi
ch'ih	chi
chin	jin
ch'in	qin
ching	jing
ch'ing	qing
chiu	jiu
ch'iu	qiu
chiung	jiong
ch'iung	qiong
cho	zhuo
ch'o	chuo
chou	zhou
ch'ou	chou
chu	zhu
ch'u	chu
chua	zhua
ch'ua	chua
chuai	zhuai
ch'uai	chuai
chuan	zhuan
ch'uan	chuan
chuang	zhuang
ch'uang	chuang
chui	zhui
ch'ui	chui
chun	zhun
ch'un	chun
chung	zhong
ch'ung	chong
chü	ju
ch'ü	qu
chüan	juan
ch'üan	quan
chüeh	jue
ch'üeh	que
chün	jun
ch'ün	qun
en	en
eng	eng
erh	er
fa	fa
fan	fan
fang	fang
fei	fei
fen	fen
feng	feng
fo	fo
fou	fou
fu	fu
ha	ha
hai	hai
han	han
hang	hang
hao	hao
hei	hei
hen	hen
heng	heng
ho	he
hou	hou
hsi	xi
hsia	xia
hsiang	xiang
hsiao	xiao
hsieh	xie
hsien	xian
hsin	xin
hsing	xing
hsiu	xiu
hsiung	xiong
hsü	xu
hsüan	xuan
hsüeh	xue
hsün	xun
hu	hu
hua	hua
huai	huai
huan	huan
huang	huang
hui	hui
hun	hun
hung	hong
huo	huo
i	yi
jan	ran
jang	rang
jao	rao
je	re
jen	ren
jeng	reng
jih	ri
jo	ruo
jou	rou
ju	ru
juan	ruan
jui	rui
jun	run
jung	rong
ka	ga
k'a	ka
kai	gai
k'ai	kai
kan	gan
k'an	kan
kang	gang
k'ang	kang
kao	gao
k'ao	kao
kei	gei
ken	gen
k'en	ken
keng	geng
k'eng	keng
ko	ge
k'o	ke
kou	gou
k'ou	kou
ku	gu
k'u	ku
kua	gua
k'ua	kua
kuai	guai
k'uai	kuai
kuan	guan
k'uan	kuan
kuang	guang
k'uang	kuang
kuei	gui
k'uei	kui
kun	gun
k'un	kun
kung	gong
k'ung	kong
kuo	guo
k'uo	kuo
la	la
lai	lai
lan	lan
lang	lang
lao	lao
le	le
lei	lei
leng	leng
li	li
lia	lia
liang	liang
liao	liao
lieh	lie
lien	lian
lin	lin
ling	ling
liu	liu
lo	luo
lou	lou
lu	lu
luan	luan
lun	lun
lung	long
lü	lü
lüan	lüan
lüeh	lüe
ma	ma
mai	mai
man	man
mang	mang
mao	mao
mei	mei
men	men
meng	meng
mi	mi
miao	miao
mieh	mie
mien	mian
min	min
ming	ming
miu	miu
mo	mo
mou	mou
mu	mu
na	na
nai	nai
nan	nan
nang	nang
nao	nao
ne	ne
nei	nei
nen	nen
neng	neng
ni	ni
niang	niang
niao	niao
nieh	nie
nien	nian
nin	nin
ning	ning
niu	niu
no	nuo
nou	nou
nu	nu
nuan	nuan
nun	nun
nung	nong
nü	nü
nüe	nüe
o	e
ou	ou
pa	ba
p'a	pa
pai	bai
p'ai	pai
pan	ban
p'an	pan
pang	bang
p'ang	pang
pao	bao
p'ao	pao
pei	bei
p'ei	pei
pen	ben
p'en	pen
peng	beng
p'eng	peng
pi	bi
p'i	pi
piao	biao
p'iao	piao
pieh	bie
p'ieh	pie
pien	bian
p'ien	pian
pin	bin
p'in	pin
ping	bing
p'ing	ping
po	bo
p'o	po
p'ou	pou
pu	bu
p'u	pu
sa	sa
sai	sai
san	san
sang	sang
sao	sao
se	se
sen	sen
seng	seng
sha	sha
shai	shai
shan	shan
shang	shang
shao	shao
she	she
shei	shei
shen	shen
sheng	sheng
shih	shi
shou	shou
shu	shu
shua	shua
shuai	shuai
shuan	shuan
shuang	shuang
shui	shui
shun	shun
shuo	shuo
so	suo
sou	sou
ssu	si
su	su
suan	suan
sui	sui
sun	sun
sung	song
ta	da
t'a	ta
tai	dai
t'ai	tai
tan	dan
t'an	tan
tang	dang
t'ang	tang
tao	dao
t'ao	tao
te	de
t'e	te
tei	dei
teng	deng
t'eng	teng
ti	di
t'i	ti
tiao	diao
t'iao	tiao
tieh	die
t'ieh	tie
tien	dian
t'ien	tian
ting	ding
t'ing	ting
tiu	diu
to	duo
t'o	tuo
tou	dou
t'ou	tou
tsa	za
ts'a	ca
tsai	zai
ts'ai	cai
tsan	zan
ts'an	can
tsang	zang
ts'ang	cang
tsao	zao
ts'ao	cao
tse	ze
ts'e	ce
tsei	zei
tsen	zen
ts'en	cen
tseng	zeng
ts'eng	ceng
tso	zuo
ts'o	cuo
tsou	zou
ts'ou	cou
tsu	zu
ts'u	cu
tsuan	zuan
ts'uan	cuan
tsui	zui
ts'ui	cui
tsun	zun
ts'un	cun
tsung	zong
ts'ung	cong
tu	du
t'u	tu
tuan	duan
t'uan	tuan
tui	dui
t'ui	tui
tun	dun
t'un	tun
tung	dong
t'ung	tong
tzu	zi
tz'u	ci
wa	wa
wai	wai
wan	wan
wang	wang
wei	wei
wen	wen
weng	weng
wo	wo
wu	wu
ya	ya
yai	yai
yang	yang
yao	yao
yeh	ye
yen	yan
yin	yin
ying	ying
yu	you
yung	yong
yü	yu
yüan	yuan
yüeh	yue
yün	yun

PINYIN/WADE–GILES

Pinyin	Wade–Giles
a	a
ai	ai
an	an
ang	ang
ao	ao
ba	pa
bai	pai
ban	pan
bang	pang
bao	pao
bei	pei
ben	pen
beng	peng
bi	pi
bian	pien
biao	piao
bie	pieh
bin	pin
bing	ping
bo	po
bu	pu
ca	ts'a
cai	ts'ai
can	ts'an
cang	ts'ang
cao	ts'ao
ce	ts'e
cen	ts'en
ceng	ts'eng
cha	ch'a
chai	ch'ai
chan	ch'an
chang	ch'ang
chao	ch'ao
che	ch'e
chen	ch'en
cheng	ch'eng
chi	ch'ih
chong	ch'ung
chou	ch'ou
chu	ch'u
chua	ch'ua
chuai	ch'uai
chuan	ch'uan
chuang	ch'uang
chui	ch'ui
chun	ch'un
chuo	ch'o
ci	tz'u
cong	ts'ong
cou	ts'ou
cu	ts'u
cuan	ts'uan
cui	ts'ui
cun	ts'un
cuo	ts'o
da	ta
dai	tai
dan	tan
dang	tang
dao	tao
de	te
dei	tei
deng	teng
di	ti
dian	tien
diao	tiao
die	tieh
ding	ting
diu	tiu
dong	tung
dou	tou
du	tu
duan	tuan
dui	tui
dun	tun
duo	to
e	o
en	en
eng	eng
er	erh
fa	fa
fan	fan
fang	fang
fei	fei
fen	fen
feng	feng
fo	fo
fou	fou
fu	fu
ga	ka
gai	kai
gan	kan
gang	kang
gao	kao
ge	ko
gei	kei
gen	ken
geng	keng
gong	kung
gou	kou
gu	ku
gua	kua
guai	kuai
guan	kuan
guang	kuang
gui	kuei
gun	kun
guo	kuo
ha	ha
hai	hai
han	han
hang	hang
hao	hao
he	ho
hei	hei
hen	hen
heng	heng
hong	hung
hou	hou
hu	hu
hua	hua
huai	huai
huan	huan
huang	huang
hui	hui
hun	hun
huo	huo
ji	chi
jia	chia
jian	chien
jiang	chiang
jiao	chiao
jie	chieh
jin	chin
jing	ching
jiong	chiung
jiu	chiu
ju	chü
juan	chüan
jue	chüeh
jun	chün
ka	k'a
kai	k'ai
kan	k'an
kang	k'ang
kao	k'ao
ke	k'o
ken	k'en
keng	k'eng
kong	k'ung
kou	k'ou
ku	k'u
kua	k'ua
kuai	k'uai
kuan	k'uan
kuang	k'uang
kui	k'uei
kun	k'un
kuo	k'uo
la	la
lai	lai
lan	lan
lang	lang
lao	lao
le	le
lei	lei
leng	leng
li	li
lia	lia
lian	lien
liang	liang
liao	liao
lie	lieh
lin	lin
ling	ling
liu	liu
long	lung
lou	lou
lu	lu
luan	luan
lun	lun
luo	lo
lü	lü
lüan	lüan
lüe	lüeh
ma	ma
mai	mai
man	man
mang	mang
mao	mao
mei	mei
men	men
meng	meng
mi	mi
mian	mien
miao	miao
mie	mieh
min	min
ming	ming
miu	miu
mo	mo
mou	mou
mu	mu
na	na
nai	nai
nan	nan
nang	nang
nao	nao
ne	ne
nei	nei
nen	nen
neng	neng
ni	ni
nian	nien
niang	niang
niao	niao
nie	nieh
nin	nin
ning	ning
niu	niu
nong	nung
nou	nou
nu	nu
nuan	nuan
nun	nun
nuo	no
nü	nü
nüe	nüeh
ou	ou
pa	p'a
pai	p'ai
pan	p'an
pang	p'ang
pao	p'ao
pei	p'ei
pen	p'en
peng	p'eng
pi	p'i
pian	p'ien
piao	p'iao
pie	p'ieh
pin	p'in
ping	p'ing
po	p'o
pou	p'ou
pu	p'u
qi	ch'i
qia	ch'ia
qian	ch'ien
qiang	ch'iang
qiao	ch'iao
qie	ch'ien
qin	ch'in
qing	ch'ing
qiong	ch'iung
qiu	ch'iu
qu	chü
quan	ch'üan
que	ch'üeh
qun	ch'ün
ran	jan
rang	jang
rao	jao
re	je
ren	jen
reng	jeng
ri	jih
rong	jung
rou	jou
ru	ju
ruan	juan
rui	jui
run	jun
ruo	jo
sa	sa
sai	sai
san	san
sang	sang
sao	sao
se	se
sen	sen
seng	seng
sha	sha
shai	shai
shan	shan
shang	shang
shao	shao
she	she
shei	shei
shen	shen
sheng	sheng
shi	shih
shou	shou
shu	shu
shua	shua
shuai	shuai
shuan	shuan
shuang	shuang
shui	shui
shun	shun
shuo	shuo
si	ssu
song	sung
sou	sou
su	su
suan	suan
sui	sui
sun	sun
suo	so
ta	t'a
tai	t'ai
tan	t'an
tang	t'ang
tao	t'ao
te	t'e
teng	t'eng
ti	t'i
tian	t'ien
tiao	t'iao
tie	t'ieh
ting	t'ing
tong	t'ung
tou	t'ou
tu	t'u
tuan	t'uan
tui	t'ui
tun	t'un
tuo	t'o
wa	wa
wai	wai
wan	wan
wang	wang
wei	wei
wen	wen
weng	weng
wo	wo
wu	wu
xi	hsi
xia	hsia
xian	hsion
xiang	hsiang
xiao	hsiao
xie	hsieh
xin	hsin
xing	hsing
xiong	hsiung
xiu	hsiu
xu	hsü
xuan	hsüan
xue	hsüeh
xun	hsün
ya	ya
yai	yai
yan	yan
yang	yang
yao	yao
ye	yeh
yi	i
yin	yin
ying	ying
yong	yung
you	yu
yu	yü
yuan	yüan
yue	yüeh
yun	yün
za	tsa
zai	tsai
zan	tsan
zang	tsang
zao	tsao
ze	tse
zei	tsei
zen	tsen
zeng	tseng
zha	cha
zhai	chai
zhan	chan
zhang	chang
zha	chao
zhe	che
zhei	chei
zhen	chen
zheng	cheng
zhi	chih
zhong	chung
zhou	chou
zhu	chu
zhua	chua
zhuai	chuai
zhuan	chuan
zhuang	chuang
zhui	chui
zhun	chun
zhuo	cho
zi	tzu
zong	tsung
zou	tsou
zu	tsu
zuan	tsuan
zui	tsui
zun	tsun
zuo	tso

GLOSSARY

隘	**Ai**	defile, pass
暗沙	**An-sha**	shoal
澳	**Ao**	islet
岙	**Ao**	bay, inlet
站	**Chan**	railway station
嶂	**Chang**	mountain
车站	**Ch'e-chan**	railway station
镇	**Chen**	town (administrative division)
城	**Ch'eng**	town, especially a walled town
旗	**Ch'i**	banner (administrative division in Mongol areas)
溪	**Ch'i**	river, stream
岬	**Chia**	point
江	**Chiang**	river
江口	**Chiang-k'ou**	estuary
礁	**Chiao**	reef, bank
角	**Chiao**	point, headland, cape
桥	**Ch'iao**	bridge
街	**Chieh**	street
尖	**Chien**	mountain; island
池	**Ch'ih**	lake
井	**Ching**	well
旧	**Chiu-**	old
洲	**Chou**	island
渠	**Ch'ü**	canal
曲	**Ch'ü**	river (transcription of Tibetan *chhu*)
区	**Ch'ü**	municipal ward (administrative division)
川	**Ch'uan**	river
泉	**Ch'üan**	spring, well
群礁	**Ch'ün-chiao**	bank
群岛	**Ch'ün-tao**	group of islands
峰	**Feng**	mountain, peak
分洪区	**Fen-hung-ch'ü**	flood dispersal area
海	**Hai**	sea; lake
海峡	**Hai-hsia**	strait
海子	**Hai-tsu**	lake
河	**Ho**	river
河口	**Ho-k'ou**	river-mouth
西	**Hsi-**	West(ern)
峡	**Hsia**	gorge
小	**Hsiao-**	little
县	**Hsien**	county (tertiary administrative division)
线	**Hsien**	line, route (railway, ferry, etc.)
新	**Hsin-**	new
行政区	**Hsing-cheng-ch'ü**	district (administrative division)
新港	**Hsin-kang**	new harbour
西	**Hsi-yüan**	western branch (of a stream)
屿	**Hsü**	islet, rock
蓄洪区	**Hsü-hung-ch'ü**	water catchment area
湖	**Hu**	lake, reservoir
港	**Kang**	harbour; inlet; stream
岗	**Kang**	mountain
高原	**Kao-yüan**	plateau
沟	**Kou**	stream
口	**K'ou**	pass; river-mouth
关	**Kuan**	pass
库勒	**K'u-le**	lake (transcription of Turkic *köl*)
库里	**K'u-li**	
崆	**K'ung**	mountain
公路	**Kung-lu**	main road
公园	**Kung-yüan**	park
果勒	**Kuo-le**	river (transcription of Mongol *gol*)
拉	**La**	pass (transcription of Tibetan)
列岛	**Lieh-tao**	group of islands
联合旗	**Lien-ho-ch'i**	united banner (administrative division in Mongol area)
岭	**Ling**	mountain(s)
泷	**Lung**	fast-flowing stream
门	**Men**	pass; strait, marine channel; city gate
盟	**Meng**	league (administrative division in Mongol areas)
庙	**Miao**	temple, shrine
牧场	**Mu-ch'ang**	ranch
南	**Nan-**	South(ern)
南山	**Nan-shan**	southern mountains
淖	**Nao**	lake
內澳	**Nei-ao**	harbour, bay
诺尔	**No-erh**	lake (transcription of Mongol *nuur*)
农场	**Nung-ch'ang**	farm

半岛	**Pan-tao**	peninsula
泡	**P'ao**	lake
泡子	**P'ao-tzu**	lake
北	**Pei-**	North(ern)
北源	**Pei-yüan**	northern branch (of a stream)
盆地	**P'en-ti**	basin
鼻	**Pi**	point
泊	**P'o**	lake
布拉克	**Pu-la-k'o**	spring (transcription of Turkic *bulak*)
沙	**Sha**	tidal flat, shoal
沙洲	**Sha-chou**	cay, sandy islet
沙漠	**Sha-mo**	desert
山	**Shan**	mountain(s), island
山口	**Shan-k'ou**	pass
山脉	**Shan-mo**	mountain range
省	**Sheng**	province (primary administrative division)
市	**Shih**	municipality (administrative division)
石窟	**Shih-k'u**	caves
水	**Shui**	river
水泉	**Shui-ch'üan**	spring
水库	**Shui-k'u**	reservoir
水道	**Shui-tao**	strait
寺	**Ssu**	monastery
大	**Ta-**	great
塔	**T'a**	pagoda
大街	**Ta-chieh**	street
塔格	**T'a-ko**	mountain (transcription of Turkic *tagh*)
大路	**Ta-lu**	street
滩	**T'an**	bank, shoal
潭	**T'an**	rapids
岛	**Tao**	island
道	**Tao**	road
达坂	**Ta-pan**	pass; mountains (transcription of Turkic *dawan* or Mongol *dabaan*)
大山	**Ta-shan**	mountains
大道	**Ta-tao**	road
地区	**Ti-ch'ü**	region (secondary administrative division)
淀	**Tien**	lake
顶	**Ting**	mountain
头	**T'ou**	point
藏布	**Tsang-pu**	river (transcription of Tibetan *tsangpo*)
错	**Ts'o**	lake (transcription of Tibetan *tsho*)
咀	**Tsui**	point
东	**Tung-**	East(ern)
东源	**Tung-yüan**	eastern branch (of a stream)
自治旗	**Tzu-chih-ch'i**	autonomous banner (administrative division in Mongol areas)
自治州	**Tzu-chih-chou**	autonomous district (secondary administrative division)
自治区	**Tzu-chih-ch'ü**	autonomous region (primary administrative division)
自治县	**Tzu-chih-hsien**	autonomous county (tertiary administrative division)
湾	**Wan**	bay, inlet
洋	**Yang**	bay, sound, sea
岩	**Yen**	rocky islet
盐池	**Yen-ch'ih**	salt lake
屿	**Yü**	islet

INDEX

INDEX

THE index is a complete record of all places on the provincial maps. Streets and other locations on the town maps and places on the thematic maps in the preliminary section are not listed, nor are the names on the historical maps. All names are listed alphabetically according to the Wade–Giles transcription used on the maps, and names in the old Post Office spellings are cross-referred to their Wade–Giles equivalent, as are variant spellings of names from Tibetan and other minority languages. The first element of each entry is the page and grid number. The second element is the place-name transcribed in Wade–Giles, and the third the name in Pinyin. This is followed by a description, where relevant, such as *mt*, *est* (mountain, estuary). The last name which appears is that of the province. Certain abbreviations have been used throughout the index.

Province abbreviations

Chekiang	Chek.
Heilungkiang	Heilung.
Inner Mongolia	In. Mong.
Kwangsi-Chuang	Kwangsi
Kwangtung	Kwangt.
Kweichow	Kwei.
Liaoning	Liao.
Shantung	Shant.
Sinkiang	Sink.
S China Sea Islands	China Sea
Szechwan	Szech.
Tsinghai	Tsing.
Yunnan	Yun.

Other abbreviations

est	estuary
mt	mountain
mts	mountains
pen	peninsula
pt	point
res	reservoir

26 B4 Cha-kan-te-jih-ssu *Zhaganderisi* In. Mong.
26 E3 Cha-kan-t'e-ko *Zhagantege* In. Mong.
114 C1 Ch'a-kan-te-le-ssu *Chagandelesi* Ningsia
27 F3 Ch'a-kan-wu-su *Chaganwusu* In. Mong.
Chakar *see* Ch'ia-ha
107 F2 Ch'a-k'a Yen-ch'ih *Chaka Yanchi* (salt lake) Tsing.
106 C3 Cha-ko Ch'ü *Zhage Qu* (river) Tsing.
19 F4 Ch'a-kou *Chagou* Liao.
38 C4 Ch'a-k'ou *Chakou* Shansi
38 E3 Ch'a-k'ou *Chakou* Shansi
83 F6 Cha-k'ou *Zhakou* Kwangsi
102 C3 Cha-la-fu-tun *Zhalafudun* Sink.
22 B3 Cha-lai-no-erh *Zhalainuoer* Heilung.
11 B4 Cha-lai-t'e Ch'i *Zhalaite Qi* Heilung.
114 B3 Ch'a-la-ko-erh *Chalageer* Ningsia
107 E3 Ch'a-la-kou *Chalagou* Tsing.
10 B3 Cha-lan-t'un *Zhalantun* Heilung.
22 E3 Cha-lan-t'un *Zhalantun* Heilung.
27 E2 Cha-lan-wu-la *Zhalanwula* In. Mong.
107 E3 Ch'a-la-p'ing *Chalaping* Tsing.
114 B2 Ch'a-la-t'ung-hu *Chalatonghu* Ningsia
106 C1 Ch'a-leng-k'ou *Chalengkou* Tsing.
Chalhan Lake *see* Ch'a-erh-han Yen-ch'ih
94 B1 Ch'a-li *Chali* Yun.
75 F5 Ch'a-ling *Chaling* Hunan
107 E3 Cha-ling *Zhaling* Tsing.
107 E3 Cha-ling Hu *Zhaling Hu* (lake) Tsing.
Cha-lin Hu *see* Chia-jen Ts'o
86 D1 Ch'a-li-ssu *Chalisi* Szech.
110 B2 Ch'a-lo-erh Ts'o *Chaluoer Cuo* (lake) Tibet
22 D3 Cha-lo-mu-te *Zhaluomude* Heilung.
14 F4 Ch'a-lu-ho *Chaluhe* Kirin
46 C4 Ch'a-lu-k'ou *Chalukou* Anhwei
14 G3 Ch'a-lu-k'ou *Chalukou* Kirin
14 A3 Cha-lu-t'e Ch'i *Zhalute Qi* Kirin
107 G2 Ch'a-ma-lung *Chamalong* Tsing.
Chamchu *see* Ch'a-ch'u
Chamdo Region *see* Ch'ang-tu Ti-ch'ü
78 A4 Ch'a-miao *Chamiao* Kwangt.
111 E3 Cha-mu *Zhamu* Tibet
106 C3 Cha-na-ma *Zhanama* Tsing.
Cha-nang *see* Cha-t'ang
111 D3 Cha-nang Hsien *Zhanang Xian* Tibet
106 D1 Ch'a-na-t'o-k'o *Chanatuoke* Tsing.
34 C2 Chan-ch'eng *Zhancheng* Shant.
55 G3 Chan-chi *Zhanji* Honan
70 C3 Chan-ch'i *Zhanqi* Kiangsi
78 B3 Chan-chiang *Zhanjiang* Kwangt.
99 H5 Chan-erh-hsiang *Zhanerxiang* Kansu
Ch'ang-an *see* Hsi-an
15 H3 Ch'ang-an *Changan* Kirin
83 F2 Ch'ang-an *Changan* Kwangsi
83 F3 Ch'ang-an *Changan* Kwangsi
63 D6 Ch'ang-an *Changan* Shensi
51 D2 Ch'ang-an-chen *Changanzhen* Chek.
78 B4 Ch'ang-ch'ang *Changchang* Kwangt.
38 C2 Ch'ang-chen *Changzhen* Shansi
51 D3 Chang-chen *Zhangzhen* Chek.
78 A4 Ch'ang-ch'eng *Changcheng* Kwangt.
39 E4 Ch'ang-ch'eng *Changcheng* Shansi
34 D5 Ch'ang-ch'eng *Changcheng* Shant.
102 H1 Ch'ang-chi *Changji* Sink.
103 D1 Ch'ang-chi *Changji* Sink.
46 B3 Chang-chi *Zhangji* Anhwei
47 D4 Chang-chi *Zhangji* Anhwei
47 D6 Chang-ch'i *Zhangqi* Anhwei
42 C1 Chang-chi *Zhangji* Kiangsu
59 E3 Chang-chia-chi *Zhangjiaji* Hupeh
98 B1 Chang-chia-ch'üan *Zhangjiaquan* Kansu
99 H4 Chang-chia-ch'uan *Zhangjiachuan* Kansu
34 C2 Ch'ang-chia-chuang *Changjiazhuang* Shant.
30 G4 Chang-chia-chuang *Zhangjiazhuang* Hopeh
38 C2 Chang-chia-chuang *Zhangjiazhuang* Shansi
39 C5 Chang-chia-chuang *Zhangjiazhuang* Shansi
102 H1 Chang-chia-chuang *Zhangjiazhuang* Sink.
99 H4 Chang-chia-ch'uan Hui Antonomous Hsien Kansu
Chang-chia-ch'uan Hui-tsu Tzu-chih-hsien *see* Chang-chia-ch'uan Hui Autonomous Hsien
74 G3 Chang-chia-fang *Zhangjiafang* Hunan
30 B3 Chang-chia-k'ou *Zhangjiakou* Hopeh
70 D2 Chang-chia-ling *Zhangjialing* Kiangsi
35 E4 Chang-chia-lou *Zhangjialou* Shant.
43 F4 Ch'ang Chiang *Chang Jiang* Kiangsu
82 D3 Ch'ang-chiang *Changjiang* Kwangsi
79 C1 Ch'ang-chiang *Changjiang* Kwangt.
47 E5 Ch'ang Chiang *Chang Jiang* (river) Anhwei
59 H5 Ch'ang Chiang *Chang Jiang* (river) Hupeh
70 C2 Ch'ang Chiang *Chang Jiang* (river) Kiangsi
70 E2 Ch'ang Chiang *Chang Jiang* (river) Kiangsi
78 A4 Ch'ang Chiang *Chang Jiang* (river) Kwangt.
87 F3 Ch'ang Chiang *Chang Jiang* (river) Szech.
19 F2 Chang-ch'iang-chen *Zhangqiangzhen* Liao.
78 A4 Ch'ang-chiang Hsien *Changjiang Xian* Kwangt.
43 F4 Ch'ang Chiang-k'ou *Chang Jiangkou* Kiangsu
59 F4 Ch'ang-chiang-pu *Changjiangbu* Hupeh
66 D4 Ch'ang-ch'iao *Changqiao* Fukien
67 C6 Ch'ang-ch'iao *Changqiao* Fukien
71 D5 Ch'ang-ch'iao *Changqiao* Kiangsi
46 D4 Chang-ch'iao *Zhangqiao* Anhwei
55 F4 Chang-ch'iao *Zhangqiao* Honan
62 D3 Chang-chia-p'an *Zhangjiapan* Shensi
59 H4 Chang-chia-p'ang *Zhangjiapang* Hupeh
74 C3 Chang-chia-p'ing *Zhangjiaping* Hunan
63 E6 Chang-chia-p'ing *Zhangjiaping* Shensi
35 H2 Chang-chia-pu *Zhangjiabu* Shant.
70 C3 Chang-chia-shan *Zhangjiashan* Kiangsi
62 F4 Chang-chia-t'an *Zhangjiatan* Shensi
47 C5 Chang-chia-tien *Zhangjiadian* Anhwei
15 J4 Chang-chia-tien *Zhangjiadian* Kirin
51 D4 Chang-chia-tu *Zhangjiadu* Chek.
10 E3 Ch'ang-chia-t'un *Changjiatun* Heilung.
30 D4 Chang-chia-wan *Zhangjiawan* Hopeh
11 C4 Ch'ang-chia-wei-tzu *Changjiaweizi* Heilung.
14 C2 Chang-chia-wo-pao *Zhangjiawobao* Kirin
23 E5 Chang-chia-wo-pao *Zhangjiawobao* Kirin
14 D4 Chang-chia-yao *Zhangjiayao* Kirin
18 C3 Chang-chia-ying-tzu *Zhangjiayingzi* Liao.
51 E3 Ch'ang-chieh *Changjie* Chek.
38 E3 Ch'ang-ch'ih *Changchi* Shansi
39 E5 Ch'ang-chih *Changzhi* Shansi
87 F1 Ch'ang-ch'ih *Changchi* Szech.
103 E1 Ch'ang-chi Hui Autonomous District Sink.
Ch'ang-chi Hui-tsu Tzu-chih-chou *see* Ch'ang-chi Hui Autonomous District
34 B3 Ch'ang-ch'ing *Changqing* Shant.
43 E4 Chang-ching-ch'iao *Zhangjingqiao* Kiangsu
18 C3 Chang-ching-ying-tzu *Zhangjingyingzi* Liao.
59 E4 Chang-chin-ho *Zhangjinhe* Hupeh
30 B2 Chang-chi-ts'un *Zhangjicun* Hopeh
34 B3 Chang-ch'iu *Zhangqiu* Shant.
34 C3 Chang-ch'iu Hsien *Zhangqiu Xian* Shant.
43 D4 Ch'ang-chou *Changzhou* Kiangsu
67 C6 Chang-chou *Zhangzhou* Fukien
Changchow *see* Ch'ang-chou
Changchow *see* Chang-chou
79 D2 Ch'ang-chu *Changzhu* Kwangt.
43 D4 Chang-chu *Zhangzhu* Kiangsu
34 B4 Ch'ang-chuang *Changzhuang* Shant.
34 C3 Ch'ang-chuang *Changzhuang* Shant.
55 G5 Chang-chuang *Zhangzhuang* Honan
71 B4 Chang-chuang *Zhangzhuang* Kiangsi
34 B2 Chang-chuang *Zhangzhuang* Shant.
34 C4 Chang-chuang *Zhangzhuang* Shant.
34 D3 Chang-chuang *Zhangzhuang* Shant.
35 D3 Chang-chuang *Zhangzhuang* Shant.
66 F4 Ch'ang-ch'un *Changchun* Fukien
10 C4 Ch'ang-ch'un *Changchun* Heilung.
14 F4 Ch'ang-ch'un *Changchun* Kirin
23 F6 Ch'ang-ch'un *Changchun* Kirin
Ch'ang-ch'un - city plan *see* Page 134
14 F2 Ch'ang-ch'un-ling *Changchunling* Kirin
55 G3 Chang-chün-mu *Zhangjunmu* Honan
14 F4 Ch'ang-ch'un-pao *Changchunbao* Kirin
90 C3 Ch'ang-ch'un-pao *Changchunbao* Kwei.
14 F3 Ch'ang-ch'un Shih *Changchun Shi* Kirin
55 G6 Ch'ang-chu-yüan *Changzhuyuan* Honan
83 H4 Ch'ang-fa *Changfa* Kwangsi
30 C4 Chang-fang *Zhangfang* Hopeh
11 F4 Ch'ang-fa-t'un *Changfatun* Heilung.
94 A3 Chang-feng *Zhangfeng* Yun.
34 B4 Chang-feng-chi *Zhangfengji* Shant.
46 D4 Ch'ang-feng Hsien *Changfeng Xian* Anhwei
62 D2 Chang-feng-p'an *Zhangfengpan* Shensi
Changgin Hudag *see* Ch'uan-ching
19 F5 Ch'ang-hai Hsien *Changhai Xian* Liao.
51 D2 Ch'ang-ho *Changhe* Chek.
47 C6 Ch'ang Ho *Chang He* (river) Anhwei
31 D5 Chang-ho *Zhanghe* Hopeh
31 B7 Chang Ho *Zhang He* (river) Hopeh
63 D8 Chang-ho-p'ing *Zhangheping* Shensi
51 E2 Ch'ang-ho-shih *Changheshi* Chek.
31 B7 Chang-ho-tien *Zhanghedian* Hopeh
83 G2 Chang-hsia *Zhangxia* Kwangsi
34 B3 Chang-hsia *Zhangxia* Shant.
99 G4 Chang-hsien *Zhangxian* Kansu
30 D3 Chang-hsin *Zhangxin* Hopeh
19 F3 Ch'ang-hsin-chen *Changxinzhen* Liao.
51 C1 Ch'ang-hsing *Changxing* Chek.
63 C6 Ch'ang-hsing *Changxing* Shensi
35 F2 Chang-hsing *Zhangxing* Shant.
43 F4 Ch'ang-hsing Tao *Changxing Dao* (island) Kiangsu
18 E5 Ch'ang-hsing Tao *Changxing Dao* (island) Liao.
18 E3 Ch'ang-hsing-tien *Changxingdian* Liao.
30 D4 Ch'ang-hsin-tien *Changxindian* Hopeh
59 G3 Ch'ang-hsüan-ling *Changxuanling* Hupeh
59 E4 Ch'ang Hu *Chang Hu* (lake) Hupeh
50 C2 Ch'ang-hua *Changhua* Chek.
54 D3 Ch'ang-hua *Changhua* Honan
118 B2 Chang-hua *Zhanghua* Taiwan
118 B2 Chang-hua Hsien *Zhanghua Xian* Taiwan
83 F5 Chang-huang *Zhanghuang* Kwangsi
66 D4 Chang-hu-fan *Zhanghufan* Fukien
35 E3 Ch'ang-i *Changyi* Shant.
114 C4 Chang-i *Zhangyi* Ningsia
70 D3 Ch'ang-k'ai *Changkai* Kiangsi
71 C5 Ch'ang-kang *Changgang* Kiangsi
91 D3 Ch'ang-kang *Changgang* Kwei.
67 E5 Chang-kang *Zhanggang* Fukien
59 E4 Chang-kang *Zhanggang* Hupeh
18 E3 Ch'ang-kao *Changgao* Liao.
67 C5 Ch'ang-k'eng *Changkeng* Fukien
Changki *see* Ch'ang-chi
Changkiakow *see* Chang-chia-k'ou
Changkiu *see* Chang-ch'iu
35 F3 Chang-ko-chuang *Zhanggezhuang* Shant.
55 E3 Ch'ang-ko Hsien *Changge Xian* Honan
46 D3 Ch'ang-kou *Changgou* Anhwei
51 C3 Ch'ang-k'ou *Changkou* Chek.
30 C4 Ch'ang-kou *Changgou* Hopeh
46 B4 Ch'ang-kuan *Changguan* Anhwei
34 B2 Ch'ang-kuan *Changguan* Shant.
46 D4 Chang-kuang *Zhangguang* Anhwei
11 E5 Chang-kuang-ts'ai Ling *Zhangguangcai Ling* (mts) Heilung.
15 I3 Chang-kuang-ts'ai Ling *Zhangguangcai Ling* (mts) Kirin
55 G3 Chang-kung *Zhanggong* Honan
70 C2 Chang-kung-tu *Zhanggongdu* Kiangsi
19 F2 Chang-ku-t'ai *Zhanggutai* Liao.
87 D1 Chang-la *Zhangla* Szech.
39 D4 Chang-lan *Zhanglan* Shansi
47 D5 Ch'ang-lan-tien *Changlandian* Anhwei
82 D3 Ch'ang-lao *Changlao* Kwangsi
30 G4 Ch'ang-li *Changli* Hopeh
35 E3 Ch'ang-li *Changli* Shant.
39 C6 Chang-li *Zhangli* Shansi
38 D3 Ch'ang-liang-kou *Changlianggou* Shansi
54 E4 Chang-liang-tien *Zhangliangdian* Honan
58 B4 Ch'ang-liang-tzu *Changliangzi* Hupeh
47 C6 Ch'ang-ling *Changling* Anhwei
14 D3 Ch'ang-ling *Changling* Kirin
14 F4 Ch'ang-ling *Changling* Kirin
23 E5 Ch'ang-ling *Changling* Kirin
63 C8 Ch'ang-ling *Changling* Shensi
10 B1 Chang-ling *Zhangling* Heilung.
35 E3 Chang-ling *Zhangling* Shant.
47 C5 Ch'ang-ling-an *Changlingan* Anhwei
55 G5 Ch'ang-ling-chi *Changlingji* Honan
95 E4 Ch'ang-ling-chieh *Changlingjie* Yun.
59 F3 Ch'ang-ling-kang *Changlinggang* Hupeh
18 E5 Ch'ang-ling-tzu *Changlingzi* Liao.
18 E6 Ch'ang-ling-tzu *Changlingzi* Liao.
19 F5 Chang-ling-tzu *Zhanglingzi* Liao.
47 D5 Ch'ang-lin-ho *Changlinhe* Anhwei
114 C2 Ch'ang-liu-shui *Changliushui* Ningsia
47 D5 Ch'ang-lo *Changluo* Anhwei
51 D3 Ch'ang-lo *Changluo* Chek.
67 E5 Ch'ang-lo *Changluo* Fukien
74 F3 Ch'ang-lo *Changluo* Hunan
82 D3 Ch'ang-lo *Changluo* Kwangsi
83 F6 Ch'ang-lo *Changluo* Kwangsi
35 D3 Ch'ang-lo *Changluo* Shant.
87 F2 Ch'ang-lo *Changluo* Szech.
114 C3 Ch'ang-lo-pao *Changluobao* Ningsia
58 C4 Ch'ang-lo-p'ing *Changluoping* Hupeh
42 B1 Chang-lou *Zhanglou* Kiangsu
34 C4 Ch'ang-lu *Changlu* Shant.
34 A3 Chang-lu *Zhanglu* Shant.
39 D5 Ch'ang-lung *Changlong* Shansi
98 C2 Ch'ang-ma *Changma* Kansu
107 F3 Ch'ang-ma-ho *Changmahe* Tsing.
31 D5 Chang-man-chuang *Zhangmanzhuang* Hopeh
54 C3 Chang-mao *Zhangmao* Honan
98 C1 Ch'ang-ma-ta-pa *Changmadaba* Kansu
91 E4 Ch'ang-ming *Changming* Kwei.
83 F4 Chang-mu *Zhangmu* Kwangsi
83 F5 Chang-mu *Zhangmu* Kwangsi
83 H3 Chang-mu *Zhangmu* Kwangsi
47 C5 Chang-mu-ch'iao *Zhangmuqiao* Anhwei
111 E3 Ch'ang-mu-kung *Changmugong* Tibet
75 E4 Chang-mu-shih *Zhangmushi* Hunan
79 D2 Chang-mu-t'ou *Zhangmutou* Kwangt.
30 F4 Ch'ang-ning *Changning* Hopeh
75 E5 Ch'ang-ning *Changning* Hunan
38 D4 Ch'ang-ning *Changning* Shansi
63 D6 Ch'ang-ning *Changning* Shensi
87 E3 Ch'ang-ning *Changning* Szech.
94 B3 Ch'ang-ning *Changning* Yun.
99 F2 Ch'ang-ning-pao *Changningbao* Kansu
15 I6 Ch'ang-pai *Changbai* Kirin
Ch'ang-pai Ch'ao-hsien-tsu Tzu-chih-hsien *see* Ch'ang-pai Korean Autonomous Hsien
15 I6 Ch'ang-pai Korean Autonomous Hsien Kirin
15 H6 Ch'ang-pai Shan *Changbai Shan* (mts) Kirin
30 E3 Chang-pai-wan *Zhangbaiwan* Hopeh
46 E4 Chang-pa-ling *Zhangbaling* Anhwei
34 B3 Chang-pao-t'un *Zhangbaotun* Shant.
30 B2 Chang-pei *Zhangbei* Hopeh
66 F4 Ch'ang-piao Tao *Changbiao Dao* (island) Fukien
119 C3 Ch'ang-pin *Changbin* Taiwan
30 D3 Ch'ang-p'ing *Changping* Hopeh
75 B5 Ch'ang-p'ing *Changping* Hunan
58 D3 Ch'ang-p'ing *Changping* Hupeh
79 D2 Ch'ang-p'ing *Changping* Kwangt.
67 C5 Chang-p'ing *Zhangping* Fukien
75 C5 Ch'ang-p'u *Changpu* Hunan
79 D2 Ch'ang-p'u *Changpu* Kwangt.
67 C6 Chang-p'u *Zhangpu* Fukien
43 E4 Chang-pu *Zhangbu* Kiangsu
78 B4 Ch'ang-sa *Changsa* Kwangt.
55 F2 Chang-san-chai *Zhangsanzhai* Honan
30 E2 Chang-san-ying *Zhangsanying* Hopeh
74 E3 Ch'ang-sha *Changsha* Hunan
79 E1 Ch'ang-sha *Changsha* Kwangt.
43 F2 Ch'ang Sha *Chang Sha* (shoal) Kiangsu
Ch'ang-sha - city plan *see* Page 136
50 B4 Ch'ang-shan *Changshan* Chek.
67 C7 Ch'ang-shan *Changshan* Fukien
15 G4 Ch'ang-shan *Changshan* Kirin
34 C3 Ch'ang-shan *Changshan* Shant.
119 B3 Chang-shan *Zhangshan* Taiwan
46 E4 Chang-shan-chi *Zhangshanji* Anhwei
19 F6 Ch'ang-shan Ch'ün-tao *Changshan Qundao* (islands) Liao.
50 B4 Ch'ang-shan Kang *Changshan Gang* (river) Chek.
114 C3 Ch'ang-shan-t'ou *Changshantou* Ningsia
102 H1 Ch'ang-shan-tzu *Changshanzi* Sink.
30 E3 Ch'ang-shan-yü *Changshanyu* Hopeh
30 D3 Ch'ang-shao-ying *Changshaoying* Hopeh
35 G2 Ch'ang-sha-p'u *Changshapu* Shant.
35 E3 Chang-she *Zhangshe* Shant.
71 C5 Ch'ang-sheng *Changsheng* Kiangsi
14 F5 Ch'ang-sheng *Changsheng* Kirin
14 C5 Ch'ang-sheng-ts'un *Changshengcun* Kirin
23 E6 Ch'ang-sheng-ts'un *Changshengcun* Kirin
90 C3 Ch'ang-shih *Changshi* Kwei.
55 F3 Chang-shih *Zhangshi* Honan
87 F3 Ch'ang-shou *Changshou* Szech.
74 F3 Ch'ang-shou-chieh *Changshoujie* Hunan
59 E3 Ch'ang-shou-tien *Changshoudian* Hupeh
Changshow *see* Ch'ang-shou
43 E4 Ch'ang-shu *Changshu* Kiangsu
70 C3 Chang-shu-chen *Zhangshuzhen* Kiangsi
75 E6 Chang-shu-hsia *Zhangshuxia* Hunan
54 C3 Ch'ang-shui *Changshui* Honan
58 D3 Chang Shui *Zhang Shui* (river) Hupeh
71 B6 Chang Shui *Zhang Shui* (river) Kiangsi
74 E3 Chang-shu-kang *Zhangshugang* Hunan
91 D4 Ch'ang-shun *Changshun* Kwei.
58 D3 Chang-shu-p'ing *Zhangshuping* Hupeh
50 B4 Chang-shu-t'an *Zhangshutan* Chek.
70 E3 Chang-shu-tun *Zhangshudun* Kiangsi
50 B4 Ch'ang-t'ai *Changtai* Chek.
67 C6 Ch'ang-t'ai *Changtai* Fukien
55 F5 Ch'ang-t'ai-kuan *Changtaiguan* Honan
19 G3 Chang-t'ai-tzu *Zhangtaizi* Liao.
51 E4 Ch'ang-t'an *Changtan* Chek.
59 E4 Ch'ang-t'an *Changtan* Hupeh
83 G3 Ch'ang-t'an *Changtan* Kwangsi
83 E5 Ch'ang-t'ang *Changtang* Kwangsi
19 H3 Chang-tang *Zhangdang* Liao.
43 D4 Ch'ang-tang Hu *Changdang Hu* (lake) Kiangsu
55 F5 Chang-t'ao *Zhangtao* Honan
35 F2 Ch'ang-tao Hsien *Changdao Xian* Shant.
74 D2 Ch'ang-te *Changde* Hunan
Changteh *see* Ch'ang-te
31 C5 Chang-teng *Zhangdeng* Hopeh
22 D1 Ch'ang-tien *Changdian* Heilung.
19 H4 Ch'ang-tien *Changdian* Liao.
43 E3 Chang-t'ien *Zhangtian* Kiangsu
39 C7 Chang-tien *Zhangdian* Shansi
39 D5 Chang-tien *Zhangdian* Shansi
39 D6 Chang-tien *Zhangdian* Shansi
34 D3 Chang-tien *Zhangdian* Shant.
67 B5 Ch'ang-t'ing *Changting* Fukien
11 E5 Ch'ang-t'ing *Changting* Heilung.
51 E2 Chang-t'ing *Zhangting* Chek.
10 D2 Chang-ti-ying-tzu *Zhangdiyingzi* Heilung.
98 B2 Ch'ang-ts'ao-kou *Changcaogou* Kansu
Changtsing *see* Ch'ang-ch'ing
54 E4 Ch'ang-ts'un *Changcun* Honan
39 D5 Ch'ang-ts'un *Changcun* Shansi
46 B3 Chang-ts'un *Zhangcun* Anhwei
50 C2 Chang-ts'un *Zhangcun* Chek.
51 D3 Chang-ts'un *Zhangcun* Chek.
54 C5 Chang-ts'un *Zhangcun* Honan
70 E3 Chang-ts'un *Zhangcun* Kiangsi
71 D4 Chang-ts'un *Zhangcun* Kiangsi
62 E5 Chang-ts'un-i *Zhangcunyi* Shensi
19 H2 Ch'ang-t'u *Changtu* Liao.
111 F3 Ch'ang-tu *Changdu* Tibet
47 E6 Chang-tu *Zhangdu* Anhwei
59 G4 Chang-tu Hu *Zhangdu Hu* (lake) Hupeh
27 F3 Ch'ang-t'u-su-mu *Changtusumu* In. Mong.
111 F3 Ch'ang-tu Ti-ch'ü *Changdu Diqu* Tibet
27 F3 Ch'ang-tu-yin Kuo-le *Changduyin Guole* (river) In. Mong.
39 D5 Chang-tzu *Zhangzi* Shansi
19 F6 Chang-tzu Tao *Zhangzi Dao* (island) Liao.
66 E4 Chang-wan *Zhangwan* Fukien
58 E2 Chang-wan *Zhangwan* Hupeh
35 E3 Ch'ang-wei *Changwei* Shant.
106 C1 Ch'ang-wei-liang *Changweiliang* Tsing.
35 E3 Ch'ang-wei Ti-ch'ü *Changwei Diqu* Shant.
11 D4 Chang-wei-t'un *Zhangweitun* Heilung.
11 C4 Ch'ang-wu *Changwu* Heilung.
63 C5 Ch'ang-wu *Changwu* Shensi
50 C2 Chang-wu *Zhangwu* Chek.
19 F2 Chang-wu *Zhangwu* Liao.
58 D4 Ch'ang-yang *Changyang* Hupeh
98 E2 Chang-yeh *Zhangye* Kansu
59 G3 Ch'ang-yen *Changyan* Hupeh
43 F5 Chang-yen *Zhangyan* Kiangsu
55 F3 Ch'ang-ying *Changying* Honan
55 F2 Ch'ang-yüan *Changyuan* Honan
39 D5 Chang-yüan *Zhangyuan* Shansi
119 B3 Chang-yüan *Zhangyuan* Taiwan
39 D4 Ch'ang-yüan Ho *Changyuan He* (river) Shansi
10 D3 Chan Ho *Zhan He* (river) Heilung.
94 C2 Chan-ho *Zhanhe* Yun.
91 F3 Ch'an-hsi *Chanxi* Kwei.
34 D2 Chan-hua Hsien *Zhanhua Xian* Shant.
95 D3 Chan-i *Zhanyi* Yun.
Chankiang *see* Chan-chiang
99 G4 Ch'an-k'ou *Chankou* Kansu
46 C4 Chan-kou-chi *Zhangouji* Anhwei
38 E4 Chan-shang *Zhanshang* Shansi
71 B4 Chan Shui *Zhan Shui* (river) Kiangsi
55 E2 Chan-tien *Zhandian* Honan
59 G3 Chan-tien *Zhandian* Hupeh
14 C3 Chan-yü *Zhanyu* Kirin
23 E5 Chan-yü *Zhanyu* Kirin
79 E2 Ch'ao-an *Chaoan* Kwangt.
67 C7 Chao-an *Zhaoan* Fukien
67 C7 Chao-an Wan *Zhaoan Wan* (bay) Fukien
87 E2 Chao-chen *Zhaozhen* Szech.
39 C5 Chao-ch'eng *Zhaocheng* Shansi
34 A3 Chao-ch'eng *Zhaocheng* Shant.
46 C3 Chao-chi *Zhaoji* Anhwei
55 G5 Chao-chi *Zhaoji* Honan
42 C1 Chao-chi *Zhaoji* Kiangsu
87 F2 Chao-chia-ch'ang *Zhaojiachang* Szech.
34 D2 Chao-chia-chü *Zhaojiaju* Shant.
31 C6 Chao-ch'iao *Zhaoqiao* Hopeh
86 D3 Chao-chiao *Zhaojiao* Szech.
31 E5 Chao-chia-pao *Zhaojiabao* Hopeh
58 D3 Chao-chia-tien *Zhaojiadian* Hupeh
19 E3 Chao-chia-t'un *Zhaojiatun* Liao.
19 E3 Chao-chia-t'un *Zhaojiatun* Liao.
54 B4 Chao-chia-wan *Zhaojiawan* Honan
63 D5 Chao-chin *Zhaojin* Shensi
79 C2 Chao-ch'ing *Zhaoqing* Kwangt.
11 C5 Chao-chou *Zhaozhou* Heilung.
119 B4 Chao-chou *Zhaozhou* Taiwan
Chaochow *see* Ch'ao-an
39 C6 Chao-ch'ü *Zhaoqu* Shansi
63 F7 Chao-ch'uan *Zhaochuan* Shensi
55 F3 Ch'ao-chuang *Chaozhuang* Honan
46 C2 Chao-chuang *Zhaozhuang* Anhwei
42 A1 Chao-chuang *Zhaozhuang* Kiangsu
30 C3 Chao-ch'uan-pao *Zhaochuanbao* Hopeh
Chao-chüeh *see* Chao-chiao
22 D2 Ch'ao-chung *Chaozhong* Heilung.
22 D3 Ch'ao-erh *Chaoer* Heilung.
23 D4 Ch'ao-erh Ho *Chaoer He* (river) Heilung.
10 B3 Ch'ao-han Shan *Chaohan Shan* (mt) Heilung.
22 E3 Ch'ao-han Shan *Chaohan Shan* (mt) Heilung.
30 E3 Ch'ao Ho *Chao He* (river) Hopeh
35 E4 Ch'ao-ho *Chaohe* Shant.
54 D4 Chao-ho *Zhaohe* Honan
54 D5 Chao Ho *Zhao He* (river) Honan
71 C4 Chao-hsi *Zhaoxi* Kiangsi
47 D5 Ch'ao-hsien *Chaoxian* Anhwei
50 B4 Chao-hsien *Zhaoxian* Chek.
31 B6 Chao-hsien *Zhaoxian* Hopeh
38 B4 Chao-hsien *Zhaoxian* Shansi
35 D4 Chao-hsien *Zhaoxian* Shant.
63 C6 Chao-hsien *Zhaoxian* Shensi
11 F4 Chao-hsing *Zhaoxing* Heilung.
47 D5 Ch'ao-hu *Chaohu* Anhwei
47 D5 Ch'ao Hu *Chao Hu* (lake) Anhwei
54 E3 Ch'ao-hua *Chaohua* Honan
87 E1 Chao-hua *Zhaohua* Szech.
87 E3 Chao-hua *Zhaohua* Szech.
26 C6 Chao-huang-miao *Zhaohuangmiao* In. Mong.
47 D5 Ch'ao-hu Ti-ch'ü *Chaohu Diqu* Anhwei
63 F6 Ch'ao-i *Chaoyi* Shensi
39 C6 Chao-k'ang *Zhaokang* Shansi
Chaoking *see* Chao-ch'ing
Chaokioh *see* Chao-chiao
55 F2 Ch'ao-ko *Chaoge* Honan
26 B4 Ch'ao-ko Ch'i *Chaoge Qi* In. Mong.
30 F4 Chao-ko-chuang *Zhaogezhuang* Hopeh
35 E3 Chao-ko-chuang *Zhaogezhuang* Shant.
35 F2 Chao-ko-chuang *Zhaogezhuang* Shant.
95 D3 Chao-k'ua *Zhaokua* Yun.
47 E5 Chao-kuan *Zhaoguan* Anhwei
34 B3 Chao-kuan-chen *Zhaoguanzhen* Shant.
10 D3 Chao-kuang *Zhaoguang* Heilung.
18 A2 Chao-ku-tu-le *Zhaogudule* Liao.
90 B4 Chao-la *Zhaola* Kwei.
59 F5 Chao-li-ch'iao *Zhaoliqiao* Hupeh
35 F4 Chao-lien Tao *Zhaolian Dao* (island) Shant.
74 F4 Chao-ling *Zhaoling* Hunan
46 B3 Chao-miao *Zhaomiao* Anhwei
34 B3 Chao-niu Ho *Zhaoniu He* (river) Shant.
30 E4 Ch'ao-pai-hsin Ho *Chaobaixin He* (river) Hopeh
54 E3 Chao-pao *Zhaobao* Honan
38 F2 Chao-pei *Zhaobei* Shansi
31 D5 Chao-pei-k'ou *Zhaobeikou* Hopeh
39 E4 Chao-pi *Zhaobi* Shansi
83 G3 Chao-p'ing *Zhaoping* Kwangsi
54 D4 Ch'ao-p'o *Chaopo* Honan
74 B2 Chao-shih *Zhaoshi* Hunan
62 E3 Chao-shih-p'an *Zhaoshipan* Shensi
35 F2 Ch'ao-shui *Chaoshui* Shant.
31 B7 Chao-ssu-shui *Zhaosishui* Hopeh
102 C2 Chao-su *Zhaosu* Sink.
19 G1 Chao-su-t'ai Ho *Zhaosutai He* (river) Liao.
47 C7 Chao-t'an *Zhaotan* Anhwei
91 F2 Ch'ao-ti *Chaodi* Kwei.
54 C4 Chao-tien *Zhaodian* Honan
87 E1 Chao-t'ien-i *Zhaotianyi* Szech.
54 D4 Chao-ts'un *Zhaocun* Honan
42 B1 Chao-tun *Zhaodun* Kiangsu
83 H2 Ch'ao-tung *Chaodong* Kwangsi
11 C4 Chao-tung *Zhaodong* Heilung.
95 D2 Chao-t'ung *Zhaotong* Yun.
63 E8 Chao-wan *Zhaowan* Shensi
34 A4 Chao-wang Ho *Zhaowang He* (river) Shant.
18 B2 Chao-wu-ta Meng *Zhaowuda Meng* Liao.
10 F3 Ch'ao-yang *Chaoyang* Heilung.
14 F3 Ch'ao-yang *Chaoyang* Kirin
14 G3 Ch'ao-yang *Chaoyang* Kirin
14 G5 Ch'ao-yang *Chaoyang* Kirin
15 G3 Ch'ao-yang *Chaoyang* Kirin
79 E2 Ch'ao-yang *Chaoyang* Kwangt.
91 E5 Ch'ao-yang *Chaoyang* Kwei.
18 D3 Ch'ao-yang *Chaoyang* Liao.
46 D3 Ch'ao-yang-chi *Chaoyangji* Anhwei
15 J5 Ch'ao-yang-ch'uan *Chaoyangchuan* Kirin
34 B5 Chao-yang Hu *Zhaoyang Hu* (lake) Shant.
10 C2 Ch'ao-yang-kou *Chaoyanggou* Heilung.
14 E4 Ch'ao-yang-p'o *Chaoyangpo* Kirin
14 F4 Ch'ao-yang-shan *Chaoyangshan* Kirin
22 F2 Ch'ao-yang-ts'un *Chaoyangcun* Heilung.
30 E1 Ch'ao-yang-wan-tzu *Chaoyangwanzi* *Hopeh*
11 C5 Chao-yüan *Zhaoyuan* Heilung.
35 F2 Chao-yüan *Zhaoyuan* Shant.
62 E2 Chao-yüan-wan *Zhaoyuanwan* Shensi
107 G2 Cha-pa *Zhaba* Tsing.
78 B3 Cha-p'o *Zhapo* Kwangt.
66 C3 Ch'a-pu *Chabu* Fukien
51 E2 Cha-p'u *Zhapu* Chek.
110 B2 Cha-pu *Zhabu* Tibet
102 C2 Ch'a-pu-ch'a-erh *Chabuchaer* Sink.
Ch'a-pu-ch'a-erh Hsi-po Tzu-chih-hsien *see* Chapchal Sibo Autonomous Hsien
107 E2 Cha-pu-sa-ka-hsiu *Zhabusagaxiu* Tsing.
Charatai Dabasu *see* Chi-lan-t'ai Yen-ch'ih
Charkhlik *see* Jo-ch'iang
Charol Tsho *see* Ch'a-lo-erh Ts'o
Charulung Gongma *see* Ch'a-k'a
75 E5 Ch'a-shan-ao *Chashanao* Hunan
86 C4 Cha-shih *Zhashi* Szech.
63 E7 Cha-shui *Zhashui* Shensi
58 C4 Cha-shu-p'ing *Zhashuping* Hupeh
26 D4 Ch'a-su-ch'i *Chasuqi* In. Mong.
Cha-ta *see* T'o-lin
110 A3 Cha-ta Hsien *Zhada Xian* Tibet
14 D2 Ch'a-t'ai *Chatai* Kirin
111 D3 Cha-t'ang *Zhatang* Tibet
106 C4 Ch'a-tang-sung-to *Chadangsongduo* Tsing.
30 C3 Ch'a-tao *Chadao* Hopeh
31 E4 Ch'a-tien *Chadian* Hopeh
91 G3 Ch'a-tien *Chadian* Kwei.
58 C4 Ch'a-tien-tzu *Chadianzi* Hupeh
71 D4 Ch'a-t'ing *Chating* Kiangsi
43 D4 Ch'a-t'ing *Chating* Kiangsu
Cha-to-mu *see* Cha-tung
91 D4 Cha-tso *Zhazuo* Kwei.
74 B3 Ch'a-tung *Chadong* Hunan
78 B2 Ch'a-tung *Chadong* Kwangt.
110 C3 Cha-tung *Zhadong* Tibet
35 F3 Cha-tzu *Zhazi* Shant.
102 B3 Cha-wa *Zhawa* Sink.
47 E5 Ch'a-wan *Chawan* Anhwei
74 E4 Ch'a-wan *Chawan* Hunan
Ch'a-ya *see* Yen-to
111 F3 Ch'a-ya Hsien *Chaya Xian* Tibet
79 E1 Ch'a-yang *Chayang* Kwangt.
55 E4 Ch'a-ya-shan *Chayashan* Honan
Ch'a-yü *see* Chi-kung
111 F3 Ch'a-yü *Chayu* Tibet
51 E3 Ch'a-yüan *Chayuan* Chek.
58 D4 Ch'a-yüan-ssu *Chayuansi* Hupeh
27 E2 Cha-yüeh-a-so-mu *Zhayueasuomu* In. Mong.
111 F3 Ch'a-yü Hsien *Chayu Xian* Tibet
34 C2 Ch'e-chen *Chezhen* Shant.
55 G3 Che-ch'eng *Zhecheng* Honan
74 D3 Che-ch'i *Zheqi* Hunan
75 E5 Ch'e-chiang *Chejiang* Hunan
75 E5 Che-ch'iao *Zheqiao* Hunan
62 F3 Che-chia-p'ing *Zhejiaping* Shensi
14 B2 Ch'e-chia-ying-tzu *Chejiayingzi* Kirin
23 D5 Ch'e-chia-ying-tzu *Chejiayingzi* Kirin
95 D2 Che-chi-chieh *Zhejijie* Yun.
103 D3 Ch'e-erh-ch'en Ho *Cheerchen He* (river) Sink.
95 D2 Ch'e-fan *Chefan* Yun.
Chefoo *see* Yen-t'ai
95 D2 Che-hai *Zhehai* Yun.
82 D3 Ch'e-ho *Chehe* Kwangsi
30 F3 Ch'e-ho-ch'iao *Cheheqiao* Hopeh
90 C5 Che-hsiang *Zhexiang* Kwei.
91 D6 Che-hsiang *Zhexiang* Kwei.
66 E3 Che-jung *Zherong* Fukien
47 D5 Che-kao *Zhegao* Anhwei
Chekiang Province *see* Pages 49-52
102 I1 Che-k'o-sen-ching *Zhekesenjing* Sink.
51 E4 Ch'e-k'ou *Chekou* Chek.
34 C4 Che-kou *Zhegou* Shant.
111 D3 Che-ku Ts'o *Zhegu Cuo* (lake) Tibet
79 D2 Che-lang *Zhelang* Kwangt.
27 F3 Ch'e-le-t'u-miao *Cheletumiao* In. Mong.
14 B3 Che-li-mu Meng *Zhelimu Meng* Kirin
70 C2 Che-lin *Zhelin* Kiangsi
43 F5 Che-lin *Zhelin* Kiangsu
79 E2 Che-lin *Zhelin* Kwangt.
90 C6 Che-lou *Zhelou* Kwei.
102 H1 Ch'e-ma-tien *Chemadian* Sink.
91 E5 Che-mi *Zhemi* Kwei.
14 F5 Chen-an *Zhenan* Kirin
63 E7 Chen-an *Zhenan* Shensi
94 B3 Chen-an *Zhenan* Yun.
46 C2 Ch'en-chai *Chenzhai* Anhwei
14 F3 Chen-ch'ai-kang *Zhenchaigang* Kirin
30 C4 Chen-ch'ang *Zhenchang* Hopeh
67 C7 Ch'en-ch'eng *Chencheng* Fukien
38 D4 Chen-ch'eng-ti *Zhenchengdi* Shansi
55 G5 Ch'en-chi *Chenji* Honan
74 C3 Ch'en-ch'i *Chenqi* Hunan
42 C2 Ch'en-chi *Chenji* Kiangsu
43 D1 Ch'en-chi *Chenji* Kiangsu
43 D2 Ch'en-chi *Chenji* Kiangsu
43 D3 Ch'en-chi *Chenji* Kiangsu
43 F4 Ch'en-chia-chen *Chenjiazhen* Kiangsu
59 G4 Ch'en-chia-chi *Chenjiaji* Hupeh
38 E3 Ch'en-chia-chuang *Chenjiazhuang* Shansi
34 D2 Ch'en-chia-chuang *Chenjiazhuang* Shant.
114 C3 Ch'en-chia-ho Shui-k'u *Chenjiahe Shuiku* (res) Ningsia
47 E5 Ch'en-chia-hsiang *Chenjiaxiang* Anhwei
43 D1 Ch'en-chia-kang *Chenjiagang* Kiangsu
43 D3 Chen-chiang *Zhenjiang* Kiangsu
87 D1 Chen-chiang-kuan *Zhenjiangguan* Szech.
74 C2 Chen-chia-p'ing *Zhenjiaping* Hunan
18 D3 Ch'en-chia-t'ai *Chenjiatai* Liao.
35 G2 Ch'en-chia-t'uan *Chenjiatuan* Shant.
39 C4 Ch'en-chia-wan *Chenjiawan* Shansi
Chen-chieh *see* Chin-chieh
66 E3 Chen-ch'ien *Zhenqian* Fukien
51 F2 Ch'en-ch'ien Shan *Chenqian Shan* (island) Chek.
10 D3 Ch'en-ch'ing-ch'iao *Chenqingqiao* Heilung.
55 G4 Ch'en-ch'iu-ch'eng *Chenqiucheng* Honan
55 G4 Ch'en-ch'iu Hsien *Chenqiu Xian* Honan
75 F6 Ch'en-chou *Chenzhou* Hunan
75 F6 Ch'en-chou Ti-ch'ü *Chenzhou Diqu* Hunan
Chenchow *see* Ch'en-hsien
31 B5 Ch'en-chuang *Chenzhuang* Hopeh
38 E2 Chen-chuang *Zhenzhuang* Shansi
38 E1 Chen-ch'uan-pao *Zhenchuanbao* Shansi
62 F3 Chen-ch'uan-pao *Zhenchuanbao* Shensi
70 E2 Chen-chu-shan *Zhenzhushan* Kiangsi
74 D2 Ch'en-erh-p'u *Chenerpu* Hunan
Chen-fan *see* Min-ch'in
70 E3 Ch'en-fang *Chenfang* Kiangsi
90 C5 Chen-feng *Zhenfeng* Kwei.
Chen-feng Pu-i-tsu Miao-tsu Tzu-chih-hsien *see* Chen-feng Puyi-Miao Autonomous Hsien
90 C5 Chen-feng Puyi-Miao Autonomous Hsien Kwei.
47 D6 Ch'eng-an *Chengan* Anhwei
31 B7 Ch'eng-an *Chengan* Hopeh
55 E3 Cheng-an *Zhengan* Honan
91 E2 Cheng-an Hsien *Zhengan Xian* Kwei.
19 E3 Cheng-an-pao *Zhenganbao* Liao.
63 E5 Ch'eng-ch'eng *Chengcheng* Shensi
34 C4 Cheng-ch'eng *Zhengcheng* Shant.
67 C6 Ch'eng-ch'i *Chengqi* Fukien
43 D2 Ch'eng-chi *Chengji* Kiangsu
42 B1 Cheng-chi *Zhengji* Kiangsu
94 B2 Ch'eng-chia *Chengjia* Yun.
34 C2 Cheng-chia *Zhengjia* Shant.
34 B2 Cheng-chia-chai *Zhengjiazhai* Shant.
42 C3 Ch'eng-chia-ch'iao *Chengjiaqiao* Kiangsu
34 B4 Ch'eng-chia-chuang *Chengjiazhuang* *Shant.*
74 D3 Cheng-chia-i *Zhengjiayi* Hunan
31 C6 Cheng-chia-k'ou *Zhengjiakou* Hopeh
71 C6 Ch'eng-chiang *Chengjiang* Kiangsi
95 D3 Ch'eng-chiang *Chengjiang* Yun.
58 C3 Cheng-chia-p'ing *Zhengjiaping* Hupeh
47 E5 Ch'eng-chia-shih *Chengjiashi* Anhwei
14 D4 Cheng-chia-t'un *Zhengjiatun* Kirin
51 D3 Cheng-chia-wu *Zhengjiawu* Chek.
27 F3 Cheng-chia-ying-tzu *Zhengjiayingzi* In. Mong.
34 C4 Ch'eng-ch'ien *Chengqian* Shant.
10 B4 Ch'eng-chi-ssu-han *Chengjisihan* Heilung.
22 E4 Ch'eng-chi-ssu-han *Chengjisihan* Heilung.
55 E3 Cheng-chou *Zhengzhou* Honan
Cheng-chou - city plan *see* Page 135
Chengchow *see* Cheng-chou
26 C6 Ch'eng-ch'uan *Chengchuan* In. Mong.
38 C3 Ch'eng-chuang *Chengzhuang* Shansi
50 B4 Cheng-chuang *Zhengzhuang* Chek.
39 D6 Cheng-chuang *Zhengzhuang* Shansi
55 G3 Ch'eng-chuang-chai *Chengzhuangzhai* Honan
75 D6 Cheng-ch'ung *Zhengchong* Hunan
70 E3 Cheng-fang *Zhengfang* Kiangsi
79 E2 Ch'eng-hai *Chenghai* Kwangt.
94 C2 Ch'eng Hai *Cheng Hai* (lake) Yun.
70 D3 Ch'eng-hsiang-chen *Chengxiangzhen* *Kiangsi*
27 F3 Cheng-hsiang-pai Ch'i *Zhengxiangbai Qi* In. Mong.
99 G5 Ch'eng-hsien *Chengxian* Kansu
46 C4 Ch'eng-hsi Hu *Chengxi Hu* (lake) Anhwei
83 F5 Ch'eng-huang *Chenghuang* Kwangsi
43 E4 Cheng-i *Zhengyi* Kiangsu
71 C5 Ch'eng-kang *Chenggang* Kiangsi
Chengkiatun *see* Shuang-liao
35 E3 Ch'eng-ko *Chengge* Shant.
67 C5 Ch'eng-k'ou *Chengkou* Fukien
79 C1 Ch'eng-k'ou *Chengkou* Kwangt.
34 C1 Ch'eng-k'ou *Chengkou* Shant.
87 G2 Ch'eng-k'ou Hsien *Chengkou Xian* Szech.
63 C7 Ch'eng-ku *Chenggu* Shensi
119 C3 Ch'eng-kung *Chenggong* Taiwan
95 D3 Ch'eng-kung *Chenggong* Yun.
79 C2 Cheng-kuo *Zhengguo* Kwangt.
23 E5 Cheng-lan *Zhenglan* Kirin
27 G3 Cheng-lan Ch'i *Zhenglan Qi* In. Mong.
74 F2 Ch'eng-ling-chi *Chenglingji* Hunan
54 D2 Ch'eng-liu *Chengliu* Honan
71 B7 Ch'eng-lung *Chenglong* Kiangsi
99 F3 Cheng-lu-pao *Zhenglubao* Kansu
78 A4 Ch'eng-mai *Chengmai* Kwangt.
Cheng-ning *see* Shan-ho
99 I4 Cheng-ning Hsien *Zhengning Xian* Kansu
34 A2 Cheng-pao-t'un *Zhengbaotun* Shant.
75 F5 Ch'eng-p'ing *Chengping* Hunan
71 B6 Cheng-p'ing *Zhengping* Kiangsi
78 A4 Ch'eng-p'o *Chengpo* Kwangt.
75 C5 Ch'eng-pu Miao Autonomous Hsien Hunan
Ch'eng-pu Miao-tsu Tzu-chih-hsien *see* Ch'eng-pu Miao Autonomous Hsien
35 H2 Ch'eng-shan Chiao *Chengshan Jiao* (point) Shant.
75 E4 Cheng Shui *Zheng Shui* (river) Hunan
51 D3 Ch'eng-t'an *Chengtan* Chek.
86 C1 Cheng-ta-sang *Zhengdasang* Szech.

30 E3 Ch'eng-te Chengde Hopeh
Chengteh see Ch'eng-te
30 F3 Ch'eng-te Hsien Chengde Xian Hopeh
30 F3 Ch'eng-te Hsien Chengde Xian Hopeh
34 C2 Cheng-tien Zhengdian Shant.
31 B5 Cheng-ting Zhengding Hopeh
Ch'eng-to see Chou-chün
107 G4 Ch'eng-to Hsien Chengduo Xian Tsing.
42 C1 Ch'eng-t'ou Chengtou Kiangsu
70 B3 Cheng-ts'un Zhengcun Kiangsi
87 E2 Ch'eng-tu Chengdu Szech.
Ch'eng-tu - city plan see Page 139
66 D3 Cheng-tun Zhengdun Fukien
90 C5 Cheng-t'un Zhengtun Kwei.
94 C4 Cheng-tung Zhengdong Yun.
46 C4 Ch'eng-tung Hu Chengdong Hu Anhwei
30 E2 Ch'eng-tzu Chengzi Hopeh
14 F3 Ch'eng-tzu-chieh Chengzijie Kirin
11 F5 Ch'eng-tzu-ho Chengzihe Heilung.
42 C2 Ch'eng-tzu Hu Chengzi Hu (inlet) Kiangsu
19 F5 Ch'eng-tzu-t'an Chengzitan Liao.
34 A5 Ch'eng-wu Chengwu Shant.
46 B4 Cheng-wu-chi Zhengwuji Anhwei
50 C3 Ch'eng-yang Chengyang Chek.
35 F3 Ch'eng-yang Chengyang Shant.
11 F5 Cheng-yang Zhengyang Heilung.
55 F5 Cheng-yang Zhengyang Honan
46 C4 Cheng-yang-kuan Zhengyangguan Anhwei
66 E3 Ch'eng-yüan Chengyuan Fukien
51 E3 Chen-hai Zhenhai Chek.
67 D6 Chen-hai Zhenhai Fukien
79 C3 Chen-hai Zhenhai Kwangt.
47 B6 Ch'en-han-kou Chenhangou Anhwei
Chenhsi see Pa-li-k'un
14 C2 Chen-hsi Zhenxi Kirin
23 E5 Chen-hsi Zhenxi Kirin
11 C4 Chen-hsiang Zhenxiang Heilung.
19 G3 Ch'en-hsiang-t'un Chenxiangtun Liao.
75 F6 Ch'en-hsien Chenxian Hunan
19 H2 Chen-hsing Zhenxing Liao.
19 G2 Chen-hsi-pao Zhenxibao Liao.
95 E2 Chen-hsiung Zhenxiong Yun.
59 F4 Ch'en Hu Chen Hu (lake) Hupeh
35 E5 Ch'e-niu Shan Cheniu Shan (island) Shant.
51 E2 Ch'en-kang Chengang Chek.
71 C6 Chen-kang Zhengang Kiangsi
94 B4 Chen-k'ang Hsien Zhenkang Xian Yun.
Chenkieh see Chin-chieh
31 D5 Ch'en-kuan-t'un Chenguantun Hopeh
14 D2 Chen-lai Zhenlai Kirin
23 E5 Chen-lai Zhenlai Kirin
46 E4 Ch'en-ling Chenling Anhwei
55 F3 Ch'en-liu Chenliu Honan
19 F2 Ch'en-liu-ho Chenliuhe Liao.
63 E5 Ch'en-lu Chenlu Shensi
43 D3 Ch'en-lun Chenlun Kiangsu
83 E5 Chen-lung Zhenlong Kwangsi
83 F4 Chen-lung Zhenlong Kwangsi
78 B2 Chen-lung Zhenlong Kwangt.
11 E4 Ch'en-ming Chenming Heilung.
43 E4 Ch'en-mu Chenmu Kiangsu
14 D2 Chen-nan Zhennan Kirin
91 E2 Chen-nan Zhennan Kwei.
Chen-nan-kuan see Yu-i-kuan
90 C4 Chen-ning Zhenning Kwei.
Chen-ning Pu-i-tsu Miao-tsu Tzu-chih-hsien see Chen-ning Puyi-Miao Autonomous Hsien
90 C4 Chen-ning Puyi-Miao Autonomous Hsien Kwei.
63 C8 Chen-pa Zhenba Shensi
Ch'en-pa-erh-hu Ch'i see Old Barga Banner
83 G1 Chen-pao Ting Zhenbao Ding (mt) Kwangsi
38 E1 Chen-pian-pao Zhenbianbao Shansi
54 D4 Chen-p'ing Zhenping Honan
63 E9 Chen-p'ing Hsien Zhenping Xian Shensi
34 A4 Ch'en-p'o Chenpo Shant.
74 D3 Chen-shang Zhenshang Hunan
31 C5 Ch'en-shih Chenshi Hopeh
43 D2 Ch'en-shih-an Chenshian Kiangsu
74 B4 Ch'en Shui Chen Shui (river) Hunan
74 D2 Ch'en Shui Chen Shui (river) Hunan
79 D1 Chen Shui Zhen Shui (river) Kwangt.
67 C7 Ch'en-tai Chendai Fukien
83 G4 Ch'en-t'ang Chentang Kwangsi
39 C5 Chen-t'ou Zhentou Shansi
74 F3 Chen-tou-shih Zhendoushi Hunan
51 D3 Ch'en-ts'ai Chencai Chek.
43 E3 Ch'en-tsao Chenzao Kiangsu
43 E5 Chen-tse Zhenze Kiangsu
63 C6 Ch'en-ts'un Chencun Shensi
35 E4 Ch'en-t'uan Chentuan Shant.
14 B2 Ch'en-t'un Chentun Kirin
23 D5 Ch'en-t'un Chentun Kirin
Chen-tung see Chen-lai
67 B6 Ch'en-tung Chendong Fukien
30 F4 Chen-tzu-chen Zhenzizhen Hopeh
58 C3 Chen-tzu-ling Zhenziling Hupeh
38 C4 Chen-wu Shan Zhenwu Shan (mt) Shansi
62 E4 Chen-wu-tung Zhenwudong Shensi
43 E2 Ch'en-yang Chenyang Kiangsu
47 D6 Ch'en-yao Hu Chenyao Hu (lake) Anhwei
70 E3 Ch'en-ying Chenying Kiangsi
99 H4 Chen-yüan Zhenyuan Kansu
91 F3 Chen-yüan Hsien Zhenyuan Xian Kwei.
94 C4 Chen-yüan Hsien Zhenyuan Xian Yun.
Cheongkong see Ch'ang-chiang
102 H1 Ch'e-p'ai-tzu Chepaizi Sink.
102 H1 Ch'e-p'ai-tzu-ssu-ch'ang Chepaizisichang Sink.
70 E4 Ch'e-p'an Chepan Kiangsi
82 B3 Che-pao Zhebao Kwangsi
59 F5 Ch'e-pi Chebi Hupeh
Cherchen see Ch'ieh-mo
Cherchen Darya see Ch'e-erh-ch'en Ho
95 E4 Che-sang Zhesang Yun.
82 B3 Che-ta Zheda Kwangsi
95 E3 Che-t'ai Zhetai Yun.
Ch'e-ta-mu see Chi-t'ang
42 C4 Che-t'ang Zhetang Kiangsu
35 G2 Ch'e-tao Chedao Shant.
83 G1 Ch'e-t'ien Chetian Kwangsi
79 C2 Ch'e-t'ien Chetian Kwangt.
86 C2 Che-to Shan Zheduo Shan (mts) Szech.
86 C3 Che-to Shan-k'ou Zheduo Shankou (pass) Szech.
71 C6 Ch'e-t'ou Chetou Kiangsi
54 C4 Ch'e-ts'un Checun Honan
43 D1 Che-wang Zhewang Kiangsu
67 C6 Ch'e-yü Cheyu Fukien
Chhushu see Ch'ü-shui
91 F3 Chia-ao Jiaao Kwei.
Chia-ch'a see Chung-pa
111 E3 Chia-ch'a Jiacha Tibet
111 E3 Chia-ch'a Hsien Jiacha Xian Tibet
55 G3 Chia-chai Jiazhai Honan
34 A3 Chia-chen Jiazhen Shant.
110 C3 Chia-chia Jiajia Tibet
87 D3 Chia-chiang Jiajiang Szech.
91 E5 Chia-ch'iao Jiaqiao Kwei.
38 F1 Chia-chia-t'un Jiajiatun Shansi
106 D4 Chia-chi-po-lo-ko Jiajiboluoge Tsing.
82 D3 Chia-chuan Jiazhuan Kwangsi
87 F1 Chia-ch'uan-chen Jiachuanzhen Szech.
86 C1 Chia-ch'ung-ma Jiachongma Szech.
83 E4 Chia-fang Jiafang Kwangsi
119 C4 Chia-feng Jiafeng Taiwan
83 E4 Chia-fu Jiafu Kwangsi
102 C3 Ch'ia-ha Qiaha Sink.
75 E6 Chia-ho Jiahe Hunan
58 C2 Chia-ho Jiahe Hupeh
58 B1 Chia Ho Jia He (river) Hupeh
42 B1 Chia-ho-chai Jiahezhai Kiangsu
54 E4 Chia-hsien Jiaxian Honan
38 B3 Chia-hsien Jiaxian Shansi
62 F2 Chia-hsien Jiaxian Shensi
86 C3 Ch'ia-hsin Qiaxin Szech.
51 D2 Chia-hsing Jiaxing Chek.
51 D2 Chia-hsing Jiaxing Chek.
51 D2 Chia-hsing Ti-ch'ü Jiaxing Diqu Chek.
11 E5 Chia-hsin-tzu Jiaxinzi Heilung.
87 E2 Chia-hua-yüan Jiahuayuan Szech.
83 G3 Chia-hui Jiahui Kwangsi
74 F3 Chia-i Jiayi Hunan
119 B3 Chia-i Jiayi Taiwan
118 B3 Chia-i Hsien Jiayi Xian Taiwan
102 B3 Ch'ia-je-k'o Qiareke Sink.
110 D3 Chia-jen Ts'o Jiaven Cuo (lake) Tibet
91 D5 Chia-jung Jiarong Kwei.
99 F4 Chia-ka-t'an Jiagatan Kansu
10 C2 Chia-ko-ta-ch'i Jiagedaqi Heilung.
22 F2 Chia-ko-ta-ch'i Jiagedaqi Heilung.
103 F1 Ch'ia-k'o-t'a-k'u-tu-k'o Qiaketakuduke Sink.
46 D3 Chia-kou Jiagou Anhwei
50 C2 Chia-k'ou Jiakou Chek.
42 B1 Chia-k'ou Jiakou Kiangsu
83 E3 Chia-kuei Jiagui Kwangsi
110 D3 Ch'ia-la Qiala Tibet
14 F3 Ch'ia-la-mu Qialamu Kirin
110 C3 Chia-la Shan-k'ou Jiala Shankou Tibet
119 B3 Chia-li Jiali Taiwan
111 E3 Chia-li Jiali Tibet
91 E5 Chia-liang Jialiang Kwei.
19 F3 Ch'ia-li-ma Qialima Liao.
39 D4 Chia-l'ing Jialing Shansi
63 B7 Chia-ling Chiang Jialing Jiang (river) Shensi
87 F2 Chia-ling Chiang Jialing Jiang (river) Szech.
119 B4 Chia-lu Jialu Taiwan
47 E6 Chia-lu-chen Jialuzhen Anhwei
55 F3 Chia-lu Ho Jialu He (river) Honan
58 A5 Chia-ma-ch'ih Jiamachi Hupeh
110 D2 Chia-man-t'e-k'a-mu Hu Jiamantekamu Hu (lake) Tibet
102 C1 Chia-ma-t'e Jiamate Sink.
14 C3 Chia-ma-t'u Jiamatu Kirin
23 E5 Chia-ma-t'u Jiamatu Kirin
34 A2 Chia-ma-ying Jiamaying Shant.
11 F4 Chia-mu-ssu Jiamusi Heilung.
71 B4 Chi-an Jian Kiangsi
14 G6 Chi-an Jian Kirin
118 C3 Chi-an Jian Taiwan
43 F3 Ch'i-an-chen Qianzhen Kiangsu
87 E3 Chiang-an Jiangan Szech.
63 C6 Chiang-chang Jiangzhang Shensi
31 C5 Chiang-ch'eng Jiangcheng Hopeh
94 C4 Chiang-ch'eng Jiangcheng Yun.
Chiang-ch'eng Ha-ni-tsu I-tsu Tzu-chih-hsien see Chiang-ch'eng Hani-Yi Autonomous Hsien
94 C4 Chiang-ch'eng Hani-Yi Autonomous Hsien Yun.
46 C3 Chiang-chi Jiangji Anhwei
55 G5 Chiang-chi Jiangji Honan
11 B4 Chiang-ch'iao Jiangqiao Heilung.
23 E4 Chiang-ch'iao Jiangqiao Heilung.
35 F3 Chiang-chia-p'o Jiangjiapo Shant.
70 D3 Chiang-chia-pu Jiangjiabu Kiangsi
14 G5 Chiang-chia-tien Jiangjiadian Kirin
19 F5 Chiang-chia-t'un Jiangjiatun Liao.
14 C4 Chiang-chia-wo-pao Jiangjiawobao Kirin
23 E6 Chiang-chia-wo-pao Jiangjiawoba Kirin
91 E3 Chiang-chieh-ho Jiangjiehe Kwei.
66 D3 Chiang-ch'i-k'ou Jiangqikou Fukien
87 E3 Chiang-chin Jiangjin Szech.
87 F3 Chiang-chin Jiangjin Szech.
110 D3 Ch'iang-ch'in-hsüeh Qiangqinxue Tibet
87 E3 Chiang-chin Ti-ch'ü Jiangjin Diqu Szech.
91 E4 Chiang-chou Jiangzhou Kwei.
86 D4 Chiang-chou Jiangzhou Szech.
86 D2 Chiang-chü Jiangju Szech.
95 D3 Chiang-ch'uan Jiangchuan Yun.
35 E3 Chiang-chuang Jiangzhuang Shant.
119 A3 Chiang-chün-ao Hsü Jiangjunao Xu (island) Taiwan
111 E3 Chiang-chung Jiangzhong Tibet
58 C2 Chiang-chün-ho Jiangjunhe Hupeh
47 D6 Chiang-chün-miao Jiangjunmiao Anhwei
102 I1 Chiang-chün-miao Jiangjunmiao Sink.
103 E1 Chiang-chün-miao Jiangjunmiao Sink.
31 B6 Chiang-chün-mu Jiangjunmu Hopeh
18 E5 Chiang-chün-shih Jiangjunshi Liao.
98 C1 Chiang-chün-t'ai Jiangjuntai Kansu
51 E4 Chiang-erh Ao Jianger Ao (islet) Chek.
94 C4 Chiang-hsi Jiangxi Yun.
46 D4 Chiang-hsiang Jiangxiang Anhwei
70 D3 Chiang-hsiang Jiangxiang Kiangsi
47 C5 Chiang-hsia-tien Jiangxiadian Anhwei
39 C6 Chiang-hsien Jiangxian Shansi
107 G2 Chiang-hsi-kou Jiangxigou Tsing.
75 D7 Chiang-hua Yao Autonomous Hsien Hunan
Chiang-hua Yao-tsu Tzu-chih-hsien see Chiang-hua Yao Autonomous Hsien
78 A3 Chiang-hung Jianghong Kwangt.
94 C2 Chiang-i Jiangyi Yun.
110 C3 Chiang-ka Jiangga Tibet
43 E3 Ch'iang-kang Qianggang Kiangsu
30 G4 Chiang-ko-chuang Jianggezhuang Hopeh
51 E3 Chiang-k'ou Jiangkou Chek.
66 D3 Chiang-k'ou Jiangkou Fukien
67 E5 Chiang-k'ou Jiangkou Fukien
74 B4 Chiang-k'ou Jiangkou Hunan
74 C4 Chiang-k'ou Jiangkou Hunan
75 C4 Chiang-k'ou Jiangkou Hunan
58 C5 Chiang-k'ou Jiangkou Hupeh
58 D4 Chiang-k'ou Jiangkou Hupeh
70 B4 Chiang-k'ou Jiangkou Kiangsi
71 B6 Chiang-k'ou Jiangkou Kiangsi
71 C4 Chiang-k'ou Jiangkou Kiangsi
71 C6 Chiang-k'ou Jiangkou Kiangsi
83 F3 Chiang-K'ou Jiangkou Kwangsi
83 G3 Chiang-k'ou Jiangkou Kwangsi
83 G4 Chiang-k'ou Jiangkou Kwangsi
78 B2 Chiang-k'ou Jiangkou Kwangt.
91 F3 Chiang-k'ou Jiangkou Kwei.
63 C7 Chiang-k'ou Jiangkou Shensi
119 B5 Chiang-k'ou Jiangkou Taiwan
87 F3 Chiang-k'ou-chen Jiangkouzhen Szech.
87 G2 Chiang-k'ou-chen Jiangkouzhen Szech.
46 C4 Chiang-k'ou-chi Jiangkouji Anhwei
34 B3 Chiang-kuan-t'un Jiangguantun Shant.
86 D2 Ch'iang-lai Shan Qionglai Shan (mts) Szech.
58 E4 Chiang-ling Hsien Jiangling Xian Hupeh
66 C4 Chiang-lo Jiangluo Fukien
99 G5 Chiang-lo-chen Jiangluozhen Kansu
107 F3 Chiang-lu Jianglu Tsing.
91 C5 Chiang-lung Jianglong Kwei.
106 E4 Chiang-lung-ssu Jianglongsi Tsing.
79 C2 Chiang-men Jiangmen Kwangt.
87 E3 Chiang-men-ch'ang Jiangmenchang Szech.
43 D3 Chiang-miao Jiangmiao Kiangsu
15 G4 Chiang-mi-feng Jiangmifeng Kirin
67 E5 Chiang-ming Tao Jiangming Dao (island) Fukien
74 D3 Chiang-nan Jiangnan Hunan
106 E4 Chiang-nan Jiangnan Tsing.
83 F5 Chiang-ning Jiangning Kwangsi
42 C4 Chiang-ning-chen Jiangningzhen Kiangsu
42 C4 Chiang-ning Hsien Jiangning Xian Kiangsu
42 C2 Chiang-pa Jiangba Kiangsu
63 E6 Ch'iang-pai Qiangbai Shensi
74 F3 Chiang-pei Jiangbei Hunan
71 C5 Chiang-pei Jiangbei Kiangsi
15 G4 Chiang-pei Jiangbei Kirin
87 F3 Chiang-pei Hsien Jiangbei Xian Szech.
70 C2 Chiang-p'en Jiangpen Kiangsi
82 E6 Chiang-p'ing Jiangping Kwangsi
42 C3 Chiang-p'u Hsien Jiangpu Xian Kiangsu
106 D4 Chiang-sai Jiangsai Tsing.
50 B4 Chiang-shan Jiangshan Chek.
51 E3 Chiang-shan Jiangshan Chek.
35 F3 Chiang-shan-chen Jiangshanzhen Shant.
51 E4 Chiang-shan Tao Jiangshan Dao (island) Chek.
74 E4 Chiang-shih-chieh Jiangshijie Hunan
31 A6 Chiang-shui Jiangshui Hopeh
111 F3 Chiang-ta Jiangda Tibet
14 F5 Chiang-ta-fang Jiangdafang Kirin
114 C4 Chiang-t'ai Jiangtai Ningsia
39 E5 Chiang-t'ang Jiangtang Shansi
95 D2 Chiang-ti Jiangdi Yun.
47 C5 Chiang-tien Jiangdian Anhwei
67 E5 Chiang-t'ien Jiangtian Fukien
46 C3 Chiang-t'ing-chi Jiangtingji Anhwei
43 E3 Chiang-to Jiangduo Kiangsu
59 G4 Chiang-tsu Jiangzu Hupeh
75 D6 Chiang-ts'un Jiangcun Hunan
70 E2 Chiang-ts'un Jiangcun Kiangsi
70 E3 Chiang-ts'un Jiangcun Kiangsi
79 C2 Chiang-ts'un Jiangcun Kwangt.
38 E3 Chiang-ts'un Jiangcun Shansi
Chiang-tu see Yang-chou
43 D3 Chiang-tu Hsien Jiangdu Xian Kiangsu
74 C4 Chiang-tung Jiangdong Hunan
110 D3 Chiang-tzu Jiangzi Tibet
30 E3 Ch'iang-tzu-lu Qiangzilu Hopeh
70 F2 Chiang-wan Jiangwan Kiangsi
79 C1 Chiang-wan Jiangwan Kwangt.
42 C1 Ch'iang-wei Ho Qiangwei He (river) Kiangsu
74 C2 Chiang-ya Jiangya Hunan
43 E3 Chiang-yen Jiangyan Kiangsu
43 E4 Chiang-yin Jiangyin Kiangsu
74 E4 Chiang-yü Jiangyu Hunan
34 D3 Chiang-yü Jiangyu Shant.
87 E2 Chiang-yu Hsien Jiangyou Xian Szech.
75 D6 Chiang-yung Jiangyong Hunan
58 C3 Chiao-ch'ang-pa Jiaochangba Hupeh
87 D1 Chiao-ch'ang-pa Jiaochangba Szech.
62 D4 Ch'iao-chen Qiaozhen Shensi
39 D4 Chiao-ch'eng Jiaocheng Shansi
95 D2 Chiao-ch'e-tu Jiaochedu Yun.
66 C3 Chiao-ch'i Jiaoqi Fukien
43 E4 Chiao-ch'i Jiaoqi Kiangsu
66 E3 Chiao Ch'i Jiao Qi (river) Fukien
43 E4 Ch'iao-ch'i Qiaoqi Kiangsu
86 D2 Ch'iao-ch'i Qiaoqi Szech.
118 C2 Chiao-ch'i Qiaoqi Taiwan
95 D2 Ch'iao-chia Qiaojia Yun.
74 C4 Ch'iao-chiang Qiaojiang Hunan
91 F2 Ch'iao-chia-p'u Qiaojiapu Kwei.
39 C5 Ch'iao-chia-wan Qiaojiawan Shansi
82 D4 Ch'iao-chien Qiaojian Kwangsi
35 F3 Chiao-chou Wan Jiaozhou Wan (bay) Shant.
55 F4 Chiao-chuang Jiaozhuang Honan
31 D5 Chiao-ho Jiaohe Hopeh
15 H4 Chiao-ho Jiaohe Kirin
15 H4 Chiao Ho Jiaohe (river) Kirin
35 E3 Chiao Ho Jiao He (river) Shant.
106 E4 Chiao-ho-k'a Jiaoheka Tsing.
62 E5 Chiao-ho-kou Jiaohegou Shensi
94 B2 Ch'iao-hou Qiaohou Yun.
91 F3 Chiao-hsi Jiaoxi Kwei.
51 D4 Ch'iao-hsia-chieh Qiaoxiajie Chek.
43 E3 Chiao-hsieh Jiaoxie Kiangsu
63 E6 Chiao-hsieh Jiaoxie Shensi
35 F3 Chiao-hsien Jiaoxian Shant.
55 F2 Chiao-hu-chi Jiaohuji Honan
83 F5 Chiao-i Jiaoyi Kwangsi
102 B4 Ch'iao-ko-li Feng Qiaogeli Feng (mt) Sink.
39 C5 Chiao-k'ou Jiaokou Shansi
39 D5 Chiao-k'ou Jiaokou Shansi
62 F4 Chiao-k'ou Jiaokou Shensi
55 G5 Ch'iao-kou Qiaogou Honan
75 F6 Ch'iao-k'ou Qiaokou Hunan
35 D3 Ch'iao-kuan Qiaoguan Shant.
14 B4 Chiao-lai Ho Jiaolai He (river) Kirin
23 E6 Chiao-lai Ho Jiaolai He (river) Kirin
35 E3 Chiao-lai Ho Jiaolai He (river) Shant.
82 E4 Ch'iao-li Qiaoli Kwangsi
110 B2 Ch'iao-li-ma Qiaolima Tibet
42 C4 Ch'iao-lin Qiaolin Kiangsu
79 E1 Chiao-ling Jiaoling Kwangt.
14 B2 Chiao-liu Ho Jiaoliu He (river) Kirin
23 D4 Chiao-liu Ho Jiaoliu He (river) Kirin
110 D3 Chiao-lo Jiaoluo Tibet
95 D2 Ch'iao-mai-ti Qiaomaidi Yun.
34 B3 Chiao-miao Jiaomiao Shant.
35 E4 Chiao-nan Hsien Jiaonan Xian Shant.
63 D5 Chiao-p'ing Jiaoping Shensi
83 E3 Ch'iao-shan Qiaoshan Kwangsi
39 E6 Ch'iao-shang Qiaoshang Shansi
70 C3 Ch'iao-she Qiaoshe Kiangsi
14 G3 Ch'iao-shui Qiaoshui Kirin
51 D2 Ch'iao-ssu Qiaosi Chek.
70 E2 Chiao-t'an Jiaotan Kiangsi
70 C2 Chiao-t'ang Jiaotang Kiangsi
62 E5 Chiao-tao Jiaodao Shensi
54 C3 Chiao-ti Jiaodi Honan
39 C6 Chiao-ti Jiaodi Shansi
55 F5 Chiao-t'ing-hu Shui-k'u Jiaotinghu Shuiku (res) Honan
51 F3 Chiao-t'ou Jiaotou Chek.
54 D4 Ch'iao-t'ou Qiaotou Honan
75 D6 Ch'iao-tou Qiaodou Hunan
75 G5 Ch'iao-tou Qiaodou Hunan
99 F4 Ch'iao-t'ou Qiaotou Kansu
71 B5 Ch'iao-t'ou Qiaotou Kiangsi
91 E5 Ch'iao-t'ou Qiaotou Kwei.
18 B2 Ch'iao-t'ou Qiaotou Liao.
19 G3 Ch'iao-t'ou Qiaotou Liao.
38 C3 Ch'iao-t'ou Qiaotou Shansi
35 H2 Ch'iao-t'ou Qiaotou Shant.
119 B4 Ch'iao-t'ou Qiaotou Taiwan
107 G2 Ch'iao-t'ou Qiaotou Tsing.
94 C2 Ch'iao-t'ou Qiaotou Yun.
47 D5 Ch'iao-t'ou-chi Qiaotouji Anhwei
74 D4 Ch'iao-tou-ho Qiaodouhe Hunan
51 E3 Ch'iao-t'ou-hu Qiaotouhu Chek.
47 E6 Ch'iao-t'ou-p'u Qiaotoupu Anhwei
75 D6 Ch'iao-tou-p'u Qiaodoupu Hunan
54 E2 Chiao-tso Jiaozuo Honan
47 E6 Chiao-ts'un Jiaocun Anhwei
54 B3 Chiao-ts'un Jiaocun Honan
54 D4 Ch'iao-tuan Qiaoduan Honan
51 D5 Ch'iao-tun Qiaodun Chek.
35 F3 Chiao-tung Jiaodong Shant.
70 C3 Ch'iao-tung Qiaodong Kiangsi
74 C2 Chiao-tzu-ya Jiaoziya Hunan
98 C1 Ch'iao-wan Qiaowan Kansu
67 C6 Chiao-wei Jiaowei Fukien
67 D5 Chiao-wei Jiaowei Fukien
86 B1 Chiao-wu-ssu Jiaowusi Szech.
67 B5 Chiao-yang Jiaoyang Fukien
82 D3 Ch'iao-yin Qiaoyin Kwangsi
83 F5 Ch'iao-yü Qiaoyu Kwangsi
58 B4 Chiao-yüan Jiaoyuan Hupeh
34 A4 Chiao-yüan Jiaoyuan Shant.
118 C1 Chia-pao Jiabao Taiwan
111 E3 Chia-pa-se-la Jiabasela Tibet
79 D3 Chia-p'eng Lieh-tao Jiapeng Liedao (islands) Kwangt.
15 H5 Chia-p'i-kou Jiapigou Kirin
19 H4 Chia-p'i-kou Jiapigou Liao.
91 E5 Ch'ia-p'u Qiapu Kwei.
107 G2 Ch'ia-pu-ch'ia Qiabuqia Tsing.
111 E3 Ch'ia-pu-na Qiabuna Tibet
94 C3 Chia-sa Jiasa Yun.
51 D2 Chia-shan Jiashan Chek.
46 D4 Chia-shan Hsien Jiashan Xian Anhwei
31 B6 Chia-shih-chuang Jiashizhuang Hopeh
54 D5 Chia-sung Jiasong Honan
55 G4 Chia-t'an Jiatan Honan
114 C3 Chia-t'ang Jiatang Ningsia
43 F4 Chia-ting Jiading Kiangsu
110 C3 Chia-to Jiaduo Tibet
38 F2 Chia-tou Jiadou Shansi
71 D4 Ch'ia-ts'un Qiacun Kiangsi
119 B4 Chia-tung Jiadong Taiwan
38 D4 Chia-tung-ch'üan Jiadongquan Shansi
79 E2 Chia-tzu Jiazi Kwangt.
63 E8 Ch'ia-tzu-chieh Qiazijie Shensi
79 E2 Chia-tzu Kang Jiazi Gang Kwangt.
86 C3 Chia-wa Jiawa Szech.
71 D4 Ch'ia-wan Qiawan Kiangsi
42 B1 Chia-wang Jiawang Kiangsu
91 F5 Chia-ya Jiaya Kwei.
34 B4 Chia-yang Jiayang Shant.
Chia-yin see Ch'ao-yang
10 F3 Chia-yin Hsien Jiayin Xian Heilung.
59 F5 Chia-yü Jiayu Hupeh
82 C3 Chia-yu Jiayou Kwangsi
111 E3 Chia-yü Jiayu Tibet
111 F3 Chia-yü-ch'iao Jiayuqiao Tibet
98 D2 Chia-yü-kuan Jiayuguan Kansu
Chibchang Tso see Ch'ih-pu-chang Hu
10 C2 Ch'i-chan Qizhan Heilung.
14 F4 Chi-ch'ang Jichang Kirin
90 C3 Chi-ch'ang Jichang Kwei.
91 D4 Chi-ch'ang Jichang Kwei.
91 E5 Chi-ch'ang Jichang Kwei.
31 C6 Chi-ch'ang-chuang Jichangzhuang Hopeh
90 B5 Chi-ch'ang-p'ing Jichangping Kwei.
15 G5 Chi-ch'ang-tzu Jichangzi Kirin
62 F3 Chi-chen Jizhen Shensi
66 E3 Ch'i-chen Qizhen Fukien
47 E6 Chi-ch'i Jiqi Anhwei
118 B3 Chi-chi Jiji Taiwan
50 B3 Ch'i-ch'i Qiqi Chek.
31 C6 Ch'i-chi Qiji Hopeh
78 A3 Chi-chia Jijia Kwangt.
30 F2 Ch'i-chia Qijia Hopeh
14 F4 Ch'i-chia Qijia Kirin
30 B3 Chi-chia-chuang Jijiazhuang Hopeh
74 D2 Ch'i-chia-ho Qijiahe Hunan
39 C7 Ch'i-chia-ho Qijiahe Shansi
87 F3 Ch'i-chiang Qijiang Szech.
42 C4 Ch'i-ch'iao Qiqiao Kiangsu
103 E2 Ch'i-chiao-ching Qijiaojing Sink.
19 G4 Ch'i-chia-pao Qijiabao Liao.
74 C3 Ch'i-chia-p'ing Qijiaping Hunan
43 E3 Chi-chia-shih Jijiashi Kiangsu
35 D4 Chi-chia-tien-tzu Jijiadianzi Shant.
14 E2 Ch'i-chia-tzu Qijiazi Kirin
59 G4 Ch'i-chia-wan Qijiawan Hupeh
31 E5 Ch'i-chia-wu Qijiawu Hopeh
22 D1 Ch'i-ch'ien Qiqian Heilung.
11 B4 Ch'i-ch'i-ha-erh Qiqihaer Heilung.
23 E4 Ch'i-ch'i-ha-erh Qiqihaer Heilung.
102 I1 Chi-chi-hu Jijihu Sink.
110 C2 Chi-chin Jijin Tibet
70 C4 Ch'i-ch'in Qiqin Kiangsi
74 D4 Chi-ch'ing Jiqing Hunan
78 B3 Ch'i-ching Qijing Kwangt.
22 D4 Chi-ch'in-ho Jiqinhe Heilung.
23 E4 Chi-ch'in Ho Jiqin He (river) Heilung.
22 E3 Ch'i-ch'i Shan Qiqi Shan (mt) Heilung.
103 E2 Chi-chi-t'ai Jijitai Sink.
102 H2 Chi-chi-tsao-tzu Jijizaozi Sink.
59 H4 Ch'i-chou Qizhou Hupeh
78 B4 Ch'i-chou Lieh-Tao Qizhou Liedao (islands) Kwangt.
106 D4 Chi Ch'ü Ji Qu (river) Tsing.
86 C3 Chi-chü Jiju Szech.
102 I2 Ch'i-ch'uan-hu Qichuanhu Sink.
103 E2 Ch'i-ch'üan-hu Qiquanhu Sink.
74 D2 Ch'i-chung-yen Qizhongyan Hunan
59 H4 Ch'i-ch'un Hsien Qichun Xian Hupeh
106 D4 Chieh-cha Jiezha Tsing.
106 E5 Chieh-cha Jiezha Tsing.
91 D2 Chieh-ch'en-hsi Jiechenxi Kwei.
11 B4 Chieh-chi Jieji Heilung.
23 E4 Chieh-chi Jieji Heilung.
42 C2 Chieh-chi Jieji Kiangsu
107 F2 Ch'ieh-chi Qieji Tsing.
39 C6 Chieh Ch'ih Jie Chi (lakes) Shansi
10 G4 Chieh-chin-k'ou Jiejinkou Heilung.
Chieh-chou see Wu-tu
39 B7 Chieh-ch'ou Jeizhou Shansi
54 D5 Chieh-chung-tien Jiezhongdian Honan
70 E3 Chieh-chu-tu Jiezhudu Kiangsi
34 C4 Chieh-ho Jiehe Shant.
38 C3 Chieh-ho-k'ou Jiehekou Shansi
58 D4 Chieh-ho-shih Jieheshi Hupeh
31 B7 Chieh-ho-tien Jiehedian Hopeh
79 D2 Chieh-hsi Hsien Jiexi Xian Kwangt.
39 C4 Chieh-hsiu Jiexiu Shansi
34 D4 Chieh-hu Jiehu Shant.
71 A4 Chieh-hua-lung Jiehualong Kiangsi
86 C2 Ch'ieh-i Qieyi Szech.
47 E7 Chieh-k'ou Jiekou Anhwei
107 G4 Chieh-ku Jiegu Tsing.
75 D5 Chieh-li-ch'iao Jieliqiao Hunan
67 D5 Chieh-mien Jiemian Fukien
102 D3 Ch'ieh-mo Qiemo Sink.
47 F6 Chieh-p'ai Jiepai Anhwei
59 F3 Chieh-p'ai Jiepai Hupeh
34 D4 Chieh-p'ai Jiepai Shant.
46 D4 Chieh-p'ai-chi Jiepaiji Anhwei
70 C3 Chieh-pu Jiebu Kiangsi
59 F5 Chieh-shang Jieshang Hupeh
79 D2 Chieh-shih Jieshi Kwangt.
102 B3 Ch'ieh-shih Qieshi Sink.
99 G4 Chieh-shih-p'u Jieshipu Kansu
30 G4 Chieh-shih Shan Jieshi Shan (mt) Hopeh
79 D2 Chieh-shih Wan Jieshi Wan (bay) Kwangt.
46 B3 Chieh-shou Jieshou Anhwei
66 C3 Chieh-shou Jieshou Fukien
75 F5 Chieh-shou Jieshou Hunan
70 B4 Chieh-shou Jieshou Kiangsi
43 D2 Chieh-shou Jieshou Kiangsu
83 G2 Chieh-shou Jieshou Kwangsi
46 E4 Chieh-shou-chen Jieshouzhen Anhwei
119 B4 Chieh-ta Jieda Taiwan
31 E5 Chieh-ti-chien Ho Jiedijian He (river) Hopeh
39 B6 Chieh-tien Jiedian Shansi
119 B4 Ch'ieh-ting Qieding Taiwan
51 D3 Chieh-t'ou Jietou Chek.
38 E4 Chieh-tu Jiedu Shansi
47 D5 Chieh-tun-chi Jiedunji Anhwei
79 E2 Chieh-yang Jieyang Kwangt.
14 F4 Chien-an Jianan Kirin
30 F3 Ch'ien-an Qianan Hopeh
14 E2 Ch'ien-an Qianan Kirin
23 F5 Ch'ien-an Qianan Kirin
Chien-cha see Ma-k'o-t'ang
91 E2 Chien-ch'a-hsi Jiachaxi Kwei.
107 G3 Chien-cha Hsien Jianzha Xian Tsing.
38 D2 Ch'ien-chai Qianzhai Shansi
18 C4 Chien-ch'ang Jianchang Liao.
19 H3 Chien-ch'ang Jianchang Liao.
115 D4 Chien-chang An-sha Jianzhang Ansha (shoal) China Sea
30 F3 Chien-ch'ang-ying Jianchangying Hopeh
119 B4 Ch'ien-chen Qianzhen Taiwan
78 B2 Chien-ch'eng Jiancheng Kwangt.
75 B4 Ch'ien-ch'eng Qiancheng Hunan
46 E4 Chien-ch'i Jianqi Anhwei
66 D3 Chien Ch'i Jian Qi (river) Fukien
66 F3 Ch'ien-ch'i Qianqi Fukien
42 C2 Ch'ien-chi Qianji Kiangsu
78 A4 Ch'ien-chia Qianjia Kwangt.
74 D3 Chien-chia-ch'i Jianjiaqi Hunan
63 E8 Ch'ien-chia-ling Qianjialing Shensi
66 E4 Chien-chiang Jianjiang Fukien
59 E4 Ch'ien-chiang Qianjiang Hupeh
83 E4 Ch'ien-chiang Qianjiang Kwangsi
83 F4 Ch'ien Chiang Qian Jiang (river) Kwangsi
87 G3 Ch'ien-chiang Qianjiang Szech.
51 D2 Chien-ch'iao Jianqiao Chek.
31 D6 Chien-ch'iao Jianqiao Hopeh
14 C4 Ch'ien-chia-tien Qianjiadian Kirin
23 E6 Ch'ien-chia-tien Qianjiadian Kirin
75 D5 Chien-chia-ts'un Jianjiacun Hunan
35 E4 Ch'ien-chieh-t'ou Qianjietou Shant.
14 D3 Ch'ien-ch'i-hao Qianqihao Kirin
23 E5 Ch'ien-ch'i-hao Qianqihao Kirin
63 E8 Chien-ch'ih-p'u Jianchipu Shensi
15 I3 Ch'ien-chin Qianjin Kirin
107 F3 Ch'ien-chin Quanjin Tsing.
118 C3 Chien-ching Jianjing Taiwan
51 D2 Ch'ien-ch'ing Qianqing Chek.
27 F4 Ch'ien-chin-kou Qianjingou In. Mong.
67 D5 Ch'ien-chin-miao Qianjinmiao Fukien
54 C3 Ch'ien-ch'iu Qianqiu Honan
43 E2 Ch'ien-ch'iu Qianqiu Kiangsu
47 F6 Ch'ien-ch'iu Kuan Qianqiu Guan (pass) Anhwei
50 C2 Ch'ien-ch'iu Kuan Qianqiu Guan (pass) Chek.
74 B3 Chien-chou-chen Jianzhouzhen Hunan
94 B2 Chien-ch'uan Jianchuan Yun.
98 C1 Chien-ch'üan-tzu Jianquanzi Kansu
63 D6 Chien-chün Jianjun Shensi
31 C7 Chien-chung Jianzhong Hopeh
62 E1 Ch'ien-erh-lin-t'u Qianerlintu Shensi
67 C5 Ch'ien-fan Qianfan Fukien
70 D3 Ch'ien-fang Qianfang Kiangsi
26 D5 Ch'ien-fang-tzu Qianfangzi In. Mong.
78 A4 Chien-feng-ling Jiandengling Kwangt.
26 C4 Chien-feng Ning-ch'ang Jianfeng Ningchang In. Mong.
87 F2 Ch'ien-fo Qianfo Szech.
98 B1 Ch'ien-fo-tung Qianfodong Kansu
102 C2 Ch'ien-fo-tung Qianfodong Sink.
63 B6 Chien-ho Jianhe Shensi
119 C4 Chien-ho Jianhe Taiwan
50 B4 Ch'ien-ho Qianhe Chek.
46 C3 Ch'ien Ho Qian He (river) Anhwei
63 C6 Ch'ien Ho Qian He (river) Shensi
91 F4 Chien-ho Hsien Jianhe Xian Kwei.
99 F2 Chien-ho-pa Jianheba Kansu
66 C4 Chien-hsi Jianxi Fukien
91 D3 Ch'ien-hsi Qianxi Kwei.
106 C2 Ch'ien-hsiao-man Qianxiaoman Tsing.
63 D6 Ch'ien-hsien Qianxian Shensi
30 F3 Ch'ien-hsi Hsien Qianxi Xian Hopeh
87 E2 Chien-hsing Jianxing Szech.
Chienhua see Hu-t'u-pi
23 D6 Chien-hua-ts'un Jianhuacun Kirin
43 D2 Chien-hu Hsien Jianhu Xian Kiangsu
63 B6 Ch'ien-hui Ch'ü Qianhui Qu (canal) Shensi
87 E1 Chien-ko Jiange Szech.
67 D6 Ch'ien-ko Qiange Fukien
47 E7 Ch'ien-k'ou Qiankou Anhwei
55 G1 Ch'ien-k'ou Qiankou Honan
27 E3 Chien-kuang Jianguang In. Mong.
14 E2 Ch'ien-kuo-chen Qianguozhen Kirin
23 F5 Ch'ien-kuo-chen Qianguozhen Kirin
Ch'ien-kuo-erh-lo-ssu Meng-ku-tsu Tzu-chih-hsien see South Gorlos Mongol Autonomous Hsien
74 C4 Ch'ien-ku-yao Qianguyao Hunan
59 E5 Chien-li Jianli Hupeh
54 E5 Chien-ling Jianling Honan
94 C4 Ch'ien-liu Qianliu Yun.
87 E1 Chien-men-kuan Jianmenguan Szech.
31 C6 Ch'ien-mo-t'ou Qianmotou Hopeh
58 A4 Chien-nan Jiannan Hupeh
Ch'ien-nan Pu-i-tsu Miao-tsu Tzu-chih-chou see South Kweichow Puyi-Miao Autonomous District
66 B4 Chien-ning Jianning Fukien
86 C2 Ch'ien-ning Qianning Szech.
66 D3 Chien-ou Jianou Fukien
43 D4 Ch'ien-pai-shu Qianbaishu Kiangsu
14 F3 Chien-pao Jianbao Kirin
43 D3 Chien-pi Jianbi Kiangsu
31 A5 Chien-p'ing Jianping Hopeh
18 C3 Chien-p'ing Jianping Liao.
67 C5 Ch'ien-p'ing Qianping Fukien
18 C3 Chien-p'ing Hsien Jianping Xian Liao.
51 D3 Chien-shan Jianshan Chek.
58 A5 Chien-shan Jianshan Hupeh
87 G2 Chien-shan Jianshan Szech.
47 C6 Ch'ien-shan Qianshan Anhwei
19 G3 Ch'ien Shan Qianshan (mt) Liao.
19 G4 Ch'ien Shan Qian Shan (mts) Liao.
70 E3 Ch'ien-shan Hsien Qianshan Xian Kiangsi
102 D1 Ch'ien-shan-lao-pa Qianshanlaoba Sink.
102 H1 Ch'ien-shan-lao-pa Qianshanlaoba Sink.
11 G4 Chien-shan-tzu Jianshanzi Heilung.
67 C5 Chien-she Jianshe Fukien
58 B4 Chien-shih Jianshi Hupeh
118 C2 Chien-shih Jianshi Taiwan
98 D2 Chien-shui Jianshui Kansu
95 D4 Chien-shui Jianshui Yun.
47 C6 Ch'ien Shui Qian Shui (river) Anhwei
51 E4 Ch'ien-so Qiansuo Chek.
18 C4 Ch'ien-so Qiansuo Liao.
94 C3 Ch'ien-so Qiansuo Yun.
10 C3 Ch'ien-ta-la-pin Qiandalabin Heilung.
51 D2 Ch'ien-t'ang Chiang Qiantang Jiang (est) Chek.
50 C3 Chien-te Hsien Jiande Xian Chek.
51 E3 Chien-t'iao Jiantiao Chek.
70 D2 Chien-t'ien Jiantian Kiangsi
67 C5 Chien-tou Jiandou Fukien
34 C5 Chien-t'ou-chi Jiantouji Shant.
51 D5 Ch'ien-ts'ang Qiancang Chek.
51 D4 Ch'ien-ts'un Qiancun Chek.
55 G2 Ch'ien-tu-ku Qiandugu Honan
Ch'ien-tung-nan Miao-tsu T'ung-tsu Tzu-chih-chou see South-east Kweichow Miao-Tung Autonomous District
18 D4 Ch'ien-wei Jianwei Liao.
87 D3 Chien-wei Jianwei Szech.
66 D3 Chien-yang Jianyang Fukien
43 D2 Chien-yang Jianyang Kiangsu
87 E2 Chien-yang Jianyang Szech.
50 C2 Ch'ien-yang Qianyang Chek.
66 E3 Ch'ien-yang Qianyang Fukien
63 C6 Ch'ien-yang Qianyang Shensi
75 C4 Ch'ien-yang Hsien Qianyang Xian Hunan
58 E4 Chien-yang-i Jianyangyi Hupeh
42 C2 Ch'ien-yao Qianyao Kiangsu
63 E7 Ch'ien-yu Ho Qianyou He (river) Shensi
14 C4 Chi-erh-ka-lang Jiergalang Kirin
23 E6 Chi-erh-ka-lang Jiergalang Kirin
59 E2 Ch'i-fang-kang Qifanggang Hupeh
10 B2 Chi-feng Jifeng Heilung.
58 B5 Ch'i-feng Kuan Qifengguan (pass) Hupeh
Chigetai Tsho see I-chi-t'ai Ts'o
27 E3 Ch'i-ha-jih-ko-t'u Qiharigetu In. Mong.
107 G4 Ch'i-ha-ma Qihama Tsing.
51 D3 Ch'ih-an Chian Chek.
27 F3 Ch'i-hao-ts'un Qihaocun In. Mong.
47 E5 Ch'ih-chen Chizhen Anhwei
30 C3 Ch'ih-ch'eng Chicheng Hopeh
58 D4 Chih-ch'eng Zhicheng Hupeh
87 E2 Chih-ch'eng Zhicheng Szech.
70 D3 Ch'ih-ch'i Chiqi Kiangsi
79 C3 Ch'ih-ch'i Chiqi Kwangt.
67 B5 Chih-ch'i Zhiqi Fukien
71 B6 Ch'ih-chiang Chijiang Kiangsi
74 B4 Chih-chiang Zhijiang Hunan
58 D4 Chih-chiang Hsien Zhijiang Xian Hupeh
43 D4 Chih-ch'i-ch'iao Zhiqiqiao Kiangsu
90 C4 Chih-chin Zhijin Kwei.
107 F4 Chih-ch'ing-sung-to Zhiqingsongduo Tsing.
98 C1 Ch'ih-chin-pao Chijinbao Kansu
51 D4 Chih-ch'i-t'ou Zhiqitou Chek.
47 D6 Ch'ih-chou Chizhou Anhwei
Chihchow see Ch'ih-chou
63 F5 Chih-ch'uan-chen Zhichuanzhen Shensi
54 D3 Chih-fang Zhifang Honan
59 G4 Chih-fang Zhifang Hupeh
18 B2 Ch'ih-feng Chifeng Liao.
35 G2 Chih-fu Tao Zhifu Dao (pen.) Shant.
46 D4 Ch'ih-ho Chihe Anhwei
46 D4 Ch'ih Ho Chi He (river) Anhwei
67 D5 Ch'ih-hsi Chixi Fukien

Dre Chu *see* Mu-lu-wu-su Ho
Dre Chu *see* T'ung-t'ien Ho
Dulaan Hiid *see* Tu-lan-ssu
Dulankit Gompa *see* Tu-lan-ssu
23 F4 Durbet Mongol Autonomous Hsien Heilung.
Durbuldzhin *see* O-min
Dzaba *see* Ch'a-k'a
Dza Chu *see* Cha Ch'ü
Dza Chu *see* Ya-lung Chiang
Dzamdo *see* Tsang-to
Dzang Chu *see* Cha Ch'ü
Dze Chu *see* Tzu Ch'ü
Dzun *see* Tsung-chia-fang-tzu
Dzungar Banner *see* Chun-ko-erh Ch'i
Dzungarian Basin *see* Chun-ka-erh P'en-ti
Dzungarian Gate *see* A-la Shan-k'ou
Dzun Makhai Nor *see* Te-tsung-ma-hai Hu

51 F4 East China Sea Chek.
67 F5 East China Sea Fukien
118 C1 East China Sea Taiwan
27 G2 East Ujumuchin Banner In. Mong.
Ebi Nor *see* Ai-pi Hu
Ed Dzong *see* Te-tsung
98 E1 Edsin Banner Kansu
Edsin Gol *see* Jo Shui
115 C2 Egeria Bank China Sea
Em Chu *see* Chi Ch'ü
34 B2 En-ch'eng *Encheng* Shant.
Engteng *see* Yung-ting
22 D1 En-ho-ha-ta *Enhehada* Heilung.
22 C2 En-ho-ts'un *Enhecun* Heilung.
114 B1 En-ko-jih-wu-su *Engeriwusu* Ningsia
94 C3 En-lo *Enluo* Yun.
79 C2 En-p'ing *Enping* Kwangt.
58 B4 En-shih *Enshi* Hupeh
111 F3 En-ta *Enda* Tibet
87 F2 En-yang *Enyang* Szech.
43 E3 Erh-an *Eran* Kiangsu
10 D3 Erh-chan *Erzhan* Heilung.
11 C5 Erh-chan *Erzhan* Heilung.
19 I3 Erh-cha-tien-tzu *Erzhadianzi* Liao.
43 F3 Erh-chia-chen *Erjiazhen* Kiangsu
26 B4 Erh-chi-t'u-miao *Erjitumiao* In. Mong.
26 D4 Erh-fen-tzu *Erfenzi* In. Mong.
94 C3 Erh Hai *Er Hai* (lake) Yun.
19 I3 Erh-hu-lai *Erhulai* Liao.
102 H1 Erh-i-ch'ang *Eryichang* Sink.
86 C2 Erh-ka-li *Ergali* Szech.
70 E4 Erh-k'ou *Erkou* Kiangsi
11 E4 Erh-ku *Ergu* Heilung.
102 H4 Erh-kung *Ergong* Sink.
47 C6 Erh-lang-ho *Erlanghe* Anhwei
47 E5 Erh-lang-k'ou *Erlangkou* Anhwei
54 D4 Erh-lang-miao *Erlangmiao* Honan
54 C4 Erh-lang-p'ing *Erlangping* Honan
59 G3 Erh-lang-t'ien *Erlangtian* Hupeh
26 D3 Erh-lien-hao-t'e *Erlianhaote* In. Mong.
118 B3 Erh-lin *Erlin* Taiwan
43 D4 Erh-ling *Erling* Kiangsu
14 D2 Erh-lung *Erlong* Kirin
10 D3 Erh-lung-shan *Erlongshan* Heilung.
11 G4 Erh-lung-shan *Erlongshan* Heilung.
14 E4 Erh-lung-shan *Erlongshan* Kirin
15 I4 Erh-lung Shan *Erlong Shan* (mt) Kirin
14 F6 Erh-mi-ho *Ermihe* Kirin
47 E5 Erh-pa *Erba* Anhwei
103 F2 Erh-pao *Erbao* Sink.
102 C2 Erh-pa-t'ai *Erbatai* Sink.
23 C5 Erh-pa-ti *Erbadi* Liao.
91 D4 Erh-p'u *Erpu* Kwei.
86 B2 Erh Shan *Er Shan* (mts) Szech.
10 C1 Erh-shih-chan *Ershizhan* Heilung.
18 D3 Erh-shih-chia-tzu *Ershijiazi* Liao.
19 G2 Erh-shih-chia-tzu *Ershijiazi* Liao.
14 D3 Erh-shih-ch'i-hao *Ershiqihao* Kirin
10 C1 Erh-shih-i-chan *Ershiyizhan* Heilung.
47 D5 Erh-shih-li-p'u *Ershilipu* Anhwei
35 F3 Erh-shih-li-p'u *Ershilipu* Shensi
18 E5 Erh-shih-li-t'ai *Ershilitai* Liao.
102 H1 Erh-shih-li-tien-tzu *Ershilidianzi* Sink.
50 B4 Erh-shih-pa-tu *Ershibadu* Chek.
10 C1 Erh-shih-san-chan *Ershisanzhan* Heilung.
10 B1 Erh-shih-wu-chan *Ershiwuzhan* Heilung.
22 E1 Erh-shih-wu-chan *Ershiwuzhan* Heilung.
118 B3 Erh-shui *Ershui* Taiwan
30 B2 Erh-t'ai *Ertai* Hopeh
103 E1 Erh-t'ai *Ertai* Sink.
107 G2 Erh-ta-la *Erdala* Tsing.
75 E5 Erh-t'ang *Ertang* Hunan
83 F4 Erh-t'ang *Ertang* Kwangsi
83 G3 Erh-t'ang *Ertang* Kwangsi
90 B4 Erh-t'ang *Ertang* Kwei.
14 G6 Erh-tao-chiang *Erdaojiang* Kirin
15 H5 Erh-tao Chiang *Erdao Jiang* (river) Kirin
27 E3 Erh-tao-ching *Erdaojing* In. Mong.
23 D4 Erh-tao-ho *Erdaohe* Kirin
11 E5 Erh-tao-ho-tzu *Erdaohezi* Heilung.
22 D3 Erh-tao-ho-tzu *Erdaohezi* Heilung.
114 B2 Erh-tao-hu *Erdaohu* Ningsia
15 H5 Erh-tao-hua-yüan *Erdaohuayuan* Kirin
15 I6 Erh-tao-kang *Erdaogang* Kirin
Erhtaokiang *see* Erh-tao-chiang
106 C3 Erh-tao-kou *Erdaogou* Tsing.
15 I5 Erh-tao-pai-ho *Erdaobaihe* Kirin
15 I5 Erh-tao-pai Ho *Erdaobai He* (river) Kirin
10 D2 Erh-tao-p'an-ch'a *Erdaopancha* Heilung.
15 H4 Erh-tao-tien-tzu *Erdaodianzi* Kirin
10 C4 Erh-tao-wan *Erdaowan* Heilung.
71 D4 Erh-tu *Erdu* Kiangsi
14 C2 Erh-tuan *Erduan* Kirin
23 E5 Erh-tuan *Erduan* Kirin
26 D5 Erh-tzu-hao *Erzihao* In. Mong.
94 B2 Erh-yüan *Eryuan* Yun.
22 C3 Evenki Autonomous Banner Heilung.

35 F2 Fa-ch'eng *Facheng* Shant.
15 G3 Fa-ch'ih *Fachi* Kirin
90 B3 Fa-ch'ung *Fachong* Kwei.
39 D5 Fa-chung *Fazhong* Shansi
Fahsien *see* Hua-chou
19 G2 Fa-k'u *Faku* Liao.
47 E5 Fan-ch'ang *Fanchang* Anhwei
34 C3 Fan-chen *Fanzhen* Shant.
55 E4 Fan-ch'eng *Fancheng* Honan
58 E2 Fan-ch'eng *Fancheng* Hupeh
74 D2 Fan-ch'i *Fanqi* Hunan
50 B4 Fan-chia *Fanjia* Chek.
46 D4 Fan-chia-lan *Fanjialan* Anhwei
74 E4 Fan-chiang *Fanjiang* Hunan
51 E4 Fan-ch'iao *Fanqiao* Chek.
70 C2 Fan-chia-p'u *Fanjiapu* Kiangsi
75 D4 Fan-chia-shan *Fanjiashan* Hunan
14 F4 Fan-chia-t'un *Fanjiatun* Kirin
23 F6 Fan-chia-t'un *Fanjiatun* Kirin
58 C3 Fan-chia-ya *Fanjiaya* Hupeh
38 E2 Fan-chih *Fanzhi* Shansi
95 E4 Fan-chih-hua *Fanzhihua* Yun.
91 F3 Fan-ching Shan *Fanjing Shan* (mt) Kwei.
43 D3 Fan-ch'uan *Fanchuan* Kiangsu
63 F5 Fang-chen *Fangzhen* Shensi
11 E6 Fang-cheng *Fangzheng* Heilung.
54 D4 Fang-ch'eng *Fangcheng* Honan
83 E6 Fang-ch'eng *Fangcheng* Kwangsi
46 B4 Fang-chi *Fangji* Anhwei
70 B3 Fang-ch'i *Fangqi* Kiangsi
59 E3 Fang-chia-chi *Fangjiaji* Hupeh
19 G2 Fang-chia-t'un *Fangjiatun* Liao.
35 D4 Fang-ch'ien *Fangqian* Shant.
34 C3 Fang-hsia *Fangxia* Shant.
58 C2 Fang-hsien *Fangxian* Hupeh
38 E3 Fang-lan *Fanglan* Shansi
55 F2 Fang-li *Fangli* Honan
119 B4 Fang-liao *Fangliao* Taiwan
71 A4 Fang-lou *Fanglou* Kiangsi
19 H2 Fang-mu-t'un *Fangmutun* Liao.
30 C4 Fang-shan *Fangshan* Hopeh
42 C1 Fang-shan *Fangshan* Kiangsu
38 C4 Fang-shan *Fangshan* Shansi
119 B4 Fang-shan *Fangshan* Taiwan
19 F3 Fang-shan-chen *Fangshanzhen* Liao.
31 C5 Fang-shun-ch'iao *Fangshunqiao* Hopeh
34 B3 Fang-ssu *Fangsi* Shant.
66 D3 Fang-tao *Fangdao* Fukien
70 E3 Fang-t'ou *Fangtou* Kiangsi
102 H1 Fang-ts'ao-hu *Fangcaohu* Sink.
50 B3 Fang-ts'un *Fangcun* Chek.
50 B3 Fang-ts'un *Fangcun* Chek.
66 D4 Fang-ts'un *Fangcun* Fukien
42 B1 Fang-ts'un *Fangcun* Kiangsu
35 E3 Fang-tzu *Fangzi* Shant.
118 B3 Fang-wan *Fanwan* Taiwan
67 C6 Fang-yang *Fangyang* Fukien
75 E6 Fang-yüan-yü *Fangyuanyu* Hunan
55 F2 Fan-hsiang *Fanxiang* Honan
55 G2 Fan Hsien *Fan Xian* Honan
34 A4 Fan-hsien *Fanxian* Shant.
Fankiatun *see* Fan-chia-t'un
59 G4 Fan-k'ou *Fankou* Hupeh
79 C1 Fan-k'ou *Fankou* Kwangt.
87 G2 Fan-k'uai-tien *Fankuaidian* Szech.
54 C3 Fan-li *Fanli* Honan
119 B3 Fan-lu *Fanlu* Taiwan
67 D4 Fan-mien *Fanmian* Fukien
47 D5 Fan-shan *Fanshan* Anhwei
51 D5 Fan-shan *Fanshan* Chek.
30 C3 Fan-shan *Fanshan* Hopeh
51 E2 Fan-shih *Fanshi* Chek.
43 D2 Fan-shui *Fanshui* Kiangsu
118 C3 Fan-shu-liao *Fanshuliao* Taiwan
55 G6 Fan-tien *Fandian* Honan
39 D4 Fan-ts'un *Fancun* Shansi
67 D4 Fan-tung *Fandong* Fukien
10 D2 Fa-pieh-la *Fabiela* Heilung.
Fatshan *see* Fo-shan
34 B3 Fei-ch'eng *Feicheng* Shant.
55 H4 Fei-ch'iao *Feiqiao* Honan
46 B3 Fei-ho-chi *Feiheji* Anhwei
31 B7 Fei-hsiang *Feixiang* Hopeh
34 C4 Fei-hsien *Feixian* Shant.
75 E6 Fei-hsien-ch'iao *Feixianqiao* Hunan
47 D5 Fei-hsi Hsien *Feixi Xian* Anhwei
42 C2 Fei-huang Ho *Feihuang He* (river) Kiangsu
79 C2 Fei-lai Hsia *Feilai Xia* (gorge) Kwangt.
66 E4 Fei-luan *Feiluan* Fukien
83 E5 Fei-lung *Feilong* Kwangsi
74 D4 Fei-shui-yen *Feishuiyan* Hunan
75 E5 Fei-t'ien *Feitian* Hunan
47 D5 Fei-tung Hsien *Feidong Xian* Anhwei
87 E6 Fei-yün Chiang *Feiyun Jiang* (river) Chek.
39 C6 Fen-ch'eng *Fencheng* Shensi
26 E4 Feng-chen *Fengzhen* In. Mong.
98 E2 Feng-ch'eng *Fengcheng* Kansu
70 C3 Feng-ch'eng *Fengcheng* Kiangsi
43 F6 Feng-ch'eng *Fengcheng* Kiangsu
19 H4 Feng-ch'eng *Fengcheng* Liao.
34 D3 Feng-ch'eng *Fengcheng* Shant.
35 G3 Feng-ch'eng *Fengcheng* Shant.
66 B4 Feng-ch'i *Fengqi* Fukien
79 E2 Feng-ch'i *Fengqi* Kwangt.
19 F2 Feng-chia *Fengjia* Liao.
35 G2 Feng-chia *Fengjia* Shant.
31 D5 Feng-chia-k'ou *Fengjiakou* Hopeh
79 E2 Feng-chiang *Fengjiang* Kiangsi
119 B4 Feng-chiang *Fengjiang* Taiwan
51 D3 Feng-ch'iao *Fengqiao* Chek.
87 F1 Feng-chia-pa *Fengjiaba* Szech.
31 E5 Feng-chia-pao *Fengjiabao* Hopeh
87 G2 Feng-chieh *Fengjie* Szech.
94 B3 Feng-ch'ing *Fengqing* Yun.
55 F3 Feng-ch'iu *Fengqiu* Honan
67 D6 Feng-chou *Fengzhou* Fukien
71 A6 Feng-chou *Fengzhou* Kiangsi
63 B7 Feng-chou *Fengzhou* Shensi
79 C2 Feng-ch'uan *Fengchuan* Kwangt.
31 B7 Feng-feng *Fengfeng* Hopeh
54 E4 Feng Ho *Feng He* (river) Honan
11 F4 Feng-hsiang *Fengxiang* Heilung.
63 C6 Feng-hsiang *Fengxiang* Shensi
91 D3 Feng-hsiang-pa *Fengxiangba* Kwei.
42 A1 Feng-hsien *Fengxian* Kiangsu
63 B7 Feng Hsien *Feng Xian* Shensi
43 F5 Feng-hsien Hsien *Fengxian Xian* Kiangsu
70 C3 Feng-hsin *Fengxin* Kiangsi
51 E3 Feng-hua *Fenghua* Chek.
74 B4 Feng-huang *Fenghuang* Hunan
82 D3 Feng-huang *Fenghuang* Kwangsi
79 E2 Feng-huang *Fenghuang* Kwangt.
Feng-huang-ch'eng *see* Feng-ch'eng
11 G5 Feng-huang-t'e *Fenghuangte* Heilung.
63 E7 Feng-huang-tsui *Fenghuangzui* Shensi
51 D3 Feng-hui *Fenghui* Chek.
Fenghwa *see* Feng-hua
Fenghwang *see* Feng-huang
91 E2 Feng-i *Fengyi* Kwei.
39 D5 Feng-i *Fengyi* Shansi
94 C3 Feng-i *Fengyi* Yun.
87 D2 Feng-i-chen *Fengyizhen* Szech.
67 B6 Feng-jen *Fengren* Fukien
30 F4 Feng-jun *Fengrun* Hopeh
38 C3 Feng-jun *Fengrun* Shansi
78 B2 Feng-k'ai Hsien *Fengkai Xian* Kwangt.
70 E2 Feng-kang *Fenggang* Kiangsi
71 D4 Feng-kang *Fenggang* Kiangsi
91 E3 Feng-kang Hsien *Fenggang Xian* Kwei.
Fengkieh *see* Feng-chieh
35 F3 Feng-ko-chuang *Fenggezhuang* Shant.
63 B6 Feng-ko-ling *Fenggeling* Shensi
14 D3 Feng-k'u *Fengku* Kirin
15 G3 Feng-kuang *Fengguang* Kirin
87 E2 Feng-ku-chen *Fengguzhen* Szech.
11 C5 Feng-le *Fengle* Heilung.
43 E3 Feng-li *Fengli* Kiangsu
79 E2 Feng-liang *Fengliang* Kwangt.
51 D4 Feng-lin *Fenglin* Chek.
10 E3 Feng-lin *Fenglin* Heilung.
118 C3 Feng-lin *Fenglin* Taiwan
50 B4 Feng-ling Kuan *Fengling Guan* (pass) Chek.
66 D2 Feng-ling Kuan *Fengling Guan* (pass) Fukien
70 C3 Feng-ling-t'ou *Fenglingtou* Kiangsi
54 B3 Feng-ling-tu *Fenglingdu* Honan
39 B7 Feng-ling-tu *Fenglingdu* Shansi
66 D3 Feng-lo *Fengluo* Fukien
59 E3 Feng-lo *Fengluo* Hupeh
91 E2 Feng-lo *Fengluo* Kwei.
47 D5 Feng-lo-ho *Fengluohe* Anhwei
15 G4 Feng-man *Fengman* Kirin
46 D3 Feng-miao *Fengmiao* Anhwei
18 E5 Feng-ming Tao *Fengming Dao* (island) Liao.
30 F4 Feng-nan Hsien *Fengnan Xian* Hopeh
30 F4 Feng-nan Hsien *Fengnan Xian* Hopeh
30 D2 Feng-ning Hsien *Fengning Xian* Hopeh
30 D2 Feng-ning Hsien *Fengning Xian* Hopeh
118 C3 Feng-pin *Fengbin* Taiwan
51 C3 Feng-p'u *Fengpu* Chek.
11 E4 Feng-shan *Fengshan* Heilung.
30 E2 Feng-shan *Fengshan* Hopeh
71 D5 Feng-shan *Fengshan* Kiangsi
82 D3 Feng-shan *Fengshan* Kwangsi
83 F3 Feng-shan *Fengshan* Kwangsi
83 F5 Feng-shan *Fengshan* Kwangsi
119 B4 Feng-shan *Fengshan* Taiwan
67 B6 Feng-shih *Fengshi* Fukien
75 E5 Feng-shih-yen *Fengshiyan* Hunan
34 D3 Feng-shui *Fengshui* Shant.
66 C3 Feng-shui Kuan *Fengshui Guan* (pass) Fukien
10 B1 Feng-shui Shan *Fengshui Shan* (mt) Heilung.
22 E1 Feng-shui Shan *Fengshui Shan* (mt) Heilung.
79 E2 Feng-shun *Fengshun* Kwangt.
Fengsiang *see* Feng-hsiang
Fengsin *see* Feng-hsin
46 C4 Feng-t'ai *Fengtai* Anhwei
30 D4 Feng-t'ai *Fengtai* Hopeh
70 B3 Feng-t'ien *Fengtian* Kiangsi
71 B4 Feng-t'ien *Fengtian* Kiangsi
71 C6 Feng-t'ien *Fengtian* Kiangsi
Fengtienfu *see* Shen-yang
70 B3 Feng-ting Shan *Fengding Shan* (mt) Kiangsi
66 D4 Feng-tu *Fengdu* Fukien
87 F3 Feng-tu *Fengdu* Szech.
91 E5 Feng-tung *Fengdong* Kwei.
94 B4 Feng-wei-pa *Fengweiba* Yun.
82 D4 Feng-wu *Fengwu* Kwangsi
46 D4 Feng-yang *Fengyang* Anhwei
91 E3 Feng-yen *Fengyan* Kwei.
63 E5 Feng-yüan *Fengyuan* Shensi
118 B2 Feng-yüan *Fengyuan* Taiwan
59 H4 Feng-yüan-k'ou *Fengyuankou* Hupeh
55 F4 Fen Ho *Fen He* (river) Honan
38 D3 Fen Ho *Fen He* (river) Shansi
39 D4 Fen Ho *Fen He* (river) Shansi
39 C5 Fen-hsi *Fenxi* Shansi
58 D4 Fen-hsiang-ch'ang *Fenxiangchang* Hupeh
70 B4 Fen-i *Fenyi* Kiangsi
50 B3 Fen-k'ou *Fenkou* Chek.
118 C2 Fen-niao-lin *Fenniaolin* Taiwan
75 E6 Fen-shih *Fenshi* Hunan
19 F4 Fen-shui *Fenshui* Liao.
35 E4 Fen-shui *Fenshui* Shant.
87 G2 Fen-shui-chen *Fenshuizhen* Szech.
50 C3 Fen-shui Chiang *Fenshui Jiang* (river) Chek.
51 D5 Fen-shui-kuan *Fenshuiguan* Chek.
67 C7 Fen-shui Kuan *Fenshui Guan* (pass) Fukien
70 E4 Fen-shui Kuan *Fenshui Guan* (pass) Kiangsi
87 E2 Fen-shui-ling *Fenshuiling* Szech.
59 F4 Fen-shui-tsui *Fenshuizui* Hupeh
46 B3 Fen-t'ai *Fentai* Anhwei
39 C4 Fen-yang *Fenyang* Shansi
118 B2 Fen-yüan *Fenyuan* Taiwan
115 C4 Fiery Cross Reef China Sea
Fo-hai *see* Meng-hai
79 C2 Fo-kang Hsien *Fogeng Xian* Kwangt.
Fongshing *see* Fang-ch'eng
Foochow *see* Fu-chou
63 D7 Fo-p'ing Hsien *Foping Xian* Shensi
67 E6 Formosa Strait Fukien
118 B2 Formosa Strait Taiwan
Fort Bayard *see* Chan-chiang
79 C2 Fo-shan *Foshan* Kwangt.
67 C6 Fo-t'an *Fotan* Fukien
51 D3 Fo-t'ang *Fotang* Chek.
Fotzeling Reservoir *see* Fo-tzu-ling Shui-k'u
67 D5 Fo-tzu-ko *Fozige* Fukien
47 C5 Fo-tzu-ling *Foziling* Anhwei
47 C5 Fo-tzu-ling Shui-k'u *Foziling Shuiku* (res) Anhwei
Fou-hsin *see* Fu-hsin
70 E2 Fou-liang *Fouliang* Kiangsi
Fou-ling *see* Fu-ling
74 D3 Fou-wan *Fouwan* Hunan
Fou-yang *see* Fu-yang
79 E2 Fou-yang *Fouyang* Kwangt.
Fow Kiang *see* Fu Chiang
Fowling *see* Fu-ling
Fowyang *see* Fu-yang
18 C4 Fo-yeh-tung *Foyedong* Liao.
66 E3 Fu-an *Fuan* Fukien
66 E4 Fu-an *Fuan* Fukien
43 E3 Fu-an *Fuan* Kiangsu
66 E3 Fu-an Ti-ch'ü *Fuan Diqu* Fukien
59 F4 Fu-ch'ang *Fuchang* Hupeh
31 D6 Fu-ch'eng *Fucheng* Hopeh
82 E4 Fu-ch'eng *Fucheng* Kwangsi
39 D5 Fu-ch'eng *Fucheng* Shansi
39 E6 Fu-ch'eng *Fucheng* Shansi
66 E3 Fu-ch'i *Fuqi* Fukien
87 E3 Fu-chi *Fuji* Szech.
75 D5 Fu-chia-ch'iao *Fujiaqiao* Hunan
11 C4 Fu-ch'iang *Fuqiang* Heilung.
87 E2 Fu Chiang *Fu Jiang* (river) Szech.
34 C2 Fu-chia-t'ai-tzu *Fujiataizi* Shant.
39 C5 Fu-chia-t'an *Fujiatan* Shansi
114 C1 Fu-chia-wan *Fujiawan* Ningsia
59 H5 Fu-ch'ih-k'ou *Fuchikou* Hupeh
11 G4 Fu-chin *Fujin* Heilung.
67 E5 Fu-ch'ing *Fuqing* Fukien
67 E4 Fu-chou *Fuzhou* Fukien
70 D3 Fu-chou *Fuzhou* Kiangsi
18 E5 Fu-chou-ch'eng *Fuzhoucheng* Liao.
Fu-chou - city plan *see* Page 137
19 E5 Fu-chou Ho *Fuzhou He* (river) Liao.
18 E5 Fu-chou Wan *Fuzhou Wan* (bay) Liao.
18 E5 Fu-chou-wan *Fuzhouwan* Liao.
Fu-chow *see* Fu-hsien
Fuchow *see* Fu-chou
83 H3 Fu-ch'uan *Fuchuan* Kwangsi
91 E4 Fu-ch'üan *Fuquan* Kwei.
34 D5 Fu-chuang *Fuzhuang* Shant.
31 D5 Fu-chuang-i *Fuzhuangyi* Hopeh
70 E2 Fu-ch'un *Fuchun* Kiangsi
50 C3 Fu-ch'un-chiang *Fuchunjiang* Chek.
50 C3 Fu-ch'un Chiang *Fuchun Jiang* (river) Chek.
51 C3 Fu-ch'un Chiang *Fuchun Jiang* (river) Chek.
19 I3 Fu-erh Chiang *Fuer Jiang* (river) Liao.
15 H5 Fu-erh Ho *Fuer He* (river) Kirin
71 D5 Fu-fang *Fufang* Kiangsi
63 C6 Fu-feng *Fufeng* Shensi
10 C4 Fu-hai *Fuhai* Heilung.
22 F4 Fu-hai *Fuhai* Heilung.
103 D1 Fu-hai *Fuhai* Sink.
67 E5 Fu-hsi *Fuxi* Fukien
14 D4 Fu-hsien *Fuxian* Kirin
19 E5 Fu Hsien *Fu Xian* Liao.
62 E5 Fu-hsien *Fuxian* Shensi
95 D3 Fu-hsien Hu *Fuxian Hu* (lake) Yun.
18 E2 Fu-hsin *Fuxin* Liao.
18 E2 Fu-hsin-chen *Fuxinzhen* Liao.
26 B4 Fu-hsing *Fuxing* In. Mong.
15 K4 Fu-hsing *Fuxing* Kirin
90 C2 Fu-hsing *Fuxing* Kwei.
91 D5 Fu-hsing *Fuxing* Kwei.
87 F2 Fu-hsing *Fuxing* Szech.
87 F2 Fu-hsing *Fuxing* Szech.
118 C2 Fu-hsing *Fuxing* Taiwan
119 B3 Fu-hsing *Fuxing* Taiwan
74 B3 Fu-hsing-ch'ang *Fuxingchang* Hunan
Fu-hsing-chen *see* Ssu-mao
47 C7 Fu-hsing-chen *Fuxingzhen* Anhwei
87 G2 Fu-hsing-chen *Fuxingzhen* Szech.
46 D4 Fu-hsing-chi *Fuxingji* Anhwei
18 E2 Fu-hsing-ti *Fuxingdi* Liao.
14 A1 Fu-hsing-t'un *Fuxingtun* Kirin
23 D4 Fu-hsing-t'un *Fuxingtun* Kirin
Fu-hsin Meng-ku-tsu Tzu-chih-hsien *see* Fu-hsin Mongol Autonomous Hsien
18 E2 Fu-hsin Mongol Autonomous Hsien Liao.
19 E2 Fu-hsin Shih *Fuxin Shi* Liao.
51 C4 Fu-i *Fuyi* Chek.
87 E2 Fu-i *Fuyi* Szech.
75 C5 Fu-i Shui *Fuyi Shui* (river) Hunan
51 E4 Fu-jung *Furong* Chek.
91 E2 Fu-jung Chiang *Furong Jiang* (river) Kwei.
71 C4 Fu-jung Shan *Furong Shan* (mt) Kiangsi
102 H1 Fu-k'ang *Fukang* Sink.
103 D1 Fu-k'ang *Fukang* Sink.
119 C4 Fu-kang *Fugang* Taiwan
Fukiatan *see* Fu-chia-t'an
Fukien Province *see* Pages 65-68
66 C4 Fu-k'ou *Fukou* Fukien
55 F3 Fu-kou *Fugou* Honan
74 D4 Fu-k'ou *Fukou* Hunan
38 C2 Fu-ku *Fugu* Shansi
62 G1 Fu-ku *Fugu* Shensi
118 C1 Fu-kuei Chiao *Fugui Jiao* (point) Taiwan
67 C6 Fu-kung *Fugong* Fukien
94 B2 Fu-kung *Fugong* Yun.
34 D2 Fu-kuo *Fuguo* Shant.
11 B4 Fu-la-erh-chi *Fulaerji* Heilung.
23 E4 Fu-la-erh-chi *Fulaerji* Heilung.
Fularki *see* Fu-la-erh-chi
10 C1 Fu-le *Fule* Heilung.
11 F4 Fu-li *Fuli* Heilung.
83 G3 Fu-li *Fuli* Kwangsi
83 H3 Fu-li *Fuli* Kwangsi
119 C3 Fu-li *Fuli* Taiwan
95 D3 Fu-liang-p'eng *Fuliangpeng* Yun.
46 C3 Fu-li-chi *Fuliji* Anhwei
86 D3 Fu-lin *Fulin* Szech.
47 E6 Fu-ling *Fuling* Anhwei
66 D3 Fu-ling *Fuling* Fukien
87 F3 Fu-ling *Fuling* Szech.
74 F3 Fu-lin-p'u *Fulinpu* Hunan
Fulitsi *see* Fu-li-chi
75 B4 Fu-lo *Fuluo* Hunan
83 H3 Fu-lo *Fuluo* Kwangsi
95 E3 Fu-lo *Fuluo* Yun.
11 C4 Fu-lu *Fulu* Heilung.
43 F4 Fu-lu *Fulu* Kiangsu
82 C4 Fu-lu *Fulu* Kwangsi
83 F2 Fu-lu *Fulu* Kwangsi
14 E3 Fu-lung-ch'üan *Fulongquan* Kirin
23 F5 Fu-lung-ch'üan *Fulongquan* Kirin
83 G5 Fu-mien *Fumian* Kwangsi
95 D3 Fu-min *Fumin* Yun.
14 G5 Fu-min-t'un *Fumintun* Kirin
46 B4 Fu-nan *Funan* Anhwei
19 G3 Fu-nan *Funan* Liao.
30 G4 Fu-ning *Funing* Hopeh
43 D2 Fu-ning *Funing* Kiangsu
95 E4 Fu-ning *Funing* Yun.
66 F4 Fu-ning Wan *Funing Wan* (bay) Fukien
54 D4 Fu-niu Shan *Funiu Shan* (mts) Honan
31 B5 Fu-p'ing *Fuping* Hopeh
63 E6 Fu-p'ing *Fuping* Shensi
46 E3 Fu-shan *Fushan* Anhwei
70 C3 Fu-shan *Fushan* Kiangsi
43 E4 Fu-shan *Fushan* Kiangsu
78 A4 Fu-shan *Fushan* Kwangt.
79 E2 Fu-shan *Fushan* Kwangt.
39 C6 Fu-shan *Fushan* Shansi
35 G2 Fu-shan *Fushan* Shant.
26 E4 Fu-sheng-chuang *Fushengzhuang* In. Mong.
Fu-shih *see* Yen-an
67 B6 Fu-shih *Fushi* Fukien
83 F2 Fu-shih *Fushi* Kwangsi
70 E4 Fu-shu *Fushu* Kiangsi
82 D5 Fu-shu *Fushu* Kwangsi
59 G5 Fu Shui *Fu Shui* (river) Hupeh
71 C5 Fu Shui *Fu Shui* (river) Kiangsi
63 F7 Fu-shui *Fushui* Shensi
59 F3 Fu-shui-kang *Fushuigang* Hupeh
19 G3 Fu-shun *Fushun* Liao.
87 E3 Fu-shun *Fushun* Szech.
19 G3 Fu-shun-ch'eng *Fushuncheng* Liao.
19 G3 Fu-shun Hsien *Fushun Xian* Liao.
Fusin *see* Fu-hsin
82 D5 Fu-sui *Fusui* Kwangsi
15 H5 Fu-sung *Fusong* Kirin
82 B3 Fu-ta *Fuda* Kwangsi
14 G5 Fu-t'ai *Futai* Kirin
54 D3 Fu-tien *Fudian* Honan
71 B4 Fu-t'ien *Futian* Kiangsi
71 C5 Fu-t'ien *Futian* Kiangsi
59 H3 Fu-t'ien-ho *Futianhe* Hupeh
66 F3 Fu-ting *Fuding* Fukien
67 C7 Fu-t'ou Wan *Futou Wan* Fukien
95 E3 Fu-ts'un *Fucun* Yun.
62 D4 Fu-ts'un-chen *Fucunzhen* Shensi
66 C3 Fu-t'un Ch'i *Futun Qi* (river) Fukien
15 J5 Fu-tung *Fudong* Kirin
14 A4 Fu-t'ung-chen *Futongzhen* Kirin
23 D6 Fu-t'ung-chen *Futongzhen* Kirin
83 F5 Fu-wang *Fuwang* Kwangsi
Fu-wen *see* Fu-yün
50 C3 Fu-wen *Fuwen* Chek.
66 C4 Fu-wen *Fuwen* Fukien
46 B4 Fu-yang *Fuyang* Anhwei
51 C2 Fu-yang *Fuyang* Chek.
91 E2 Fu-yang *Fuyang* Kwei.
87 F1 Fu-yang *Fuyang* Szech.
31 C6 Fu-yang Ho *Fuyang He* (river) Hopeh
66 F4 Fu-ying Tao *Fuying Dao* (island) Fukien
10 C4 Fu-yü *Fuyu* Heilung.
22 F4 Fu-yü *Fuyu* Heilung.
14 E2 Fu-yü *Fuyu* Kirin
23 F5 Fu-yü *Fuyu* Kirin
Fu-yüan *see* Chi-mu-sa-erh
10 H3 Fu-yüan *Fuyuan* Heilung.
118 C3 Fu-yüan *Fuyuan* Taiwan
95 E3 Fu-yüan *Fuyuan* Yun.
103 E1 Fu-yün *Fuyun* Sink.
94 B4 Fu-yung *Fuyong* Yun.

Gaden Gompa *see* Ka-tan-ssu
Gan *see* Ken Ho
Gangto *see* Kang-t'o
Gansi *see* Kan-sen
Gar Dzong *see* K'un-sa
Gargunsa *see* K'un-sa
Garhun Tso *see* Ka-yün Ts'o
Gartang Tsangpo *see* Ka-erh Ch'ü
Gartok *see* Ka-erh-ya-sha
Gashun Nur *see* Ka-shun No-erh
Gass Kul *see* Ko-tzu K'u-li
Gata *see* Ch'ien-ning
Gawlam *see* Ku-lang
Ghaz K *see* Ko-tzu K'u-li
Godwin Austin (Mt.) *see* Ch'iao-ko-li Feng
Golmo *see* Ko-erh-mu
Gomo *see* Ko-mu
Gonjo *see* Kung-chiao
Goring Tso *see* Ch'i-lin Ts'o
115 B5 Grainger Bank China Sea
Grand Canal *see* Yün Ho
Grand Canal *see* Yün Ho
Grand Canal *see* Ta-yün Ho
Greater Khingan Range *see* Ta-hsing-an Ling
83 E6 Gulf of Tongking Kwangsi
Gulo Gompa *see* Ku-lo-kung-pa
Guma *see* P'i-shan
Gurab Angir *see* Ku-erh-pan-an-ko-erh
Gyangtse *see* Chiang-tzu
Gyatsa Dzong *see* Chia-ch'a

105 E3 Ha-ch'iang *Haqiang* Tsing.
102 B2 Ha-erh-chün *Haerjun* Sink.
22 C3 Ha-erh-hung-te *Heerhongde* Heilung.
107 G2 Ha-erh-kai *Haergai* Tsing.
14 B5 Ha-erh-kao *Haergao* Kirin
23 D6 Ha-erh-kao *Haergao* Kirin
15 I4 Ha-erh-pa-ling *Haerbaling* Kirin
11 D5 Ha-erh-pin *Haerbin* Heilung.
Ha-erh-pin - city plan *see* Page 134
19 F2 Ha-erh-t'ao *Haertao* Liao.
Ha-erh-t'eng-kuo-le Ho *see* Ha-na-t'eng Ho
27 E2 Ha-erh-tsan *Haerzan* In. Mong.
14 E4 Ha-fu *Hafu* Kirin
43 E3 Hai-an *Haian* Kiangsu
78 B3 Hai-an *Haian* Kwangt.
Haicheng *see* Hai-yüan
67 C6 Hai-ch'eng *Haicheng* Fukien
82 D4 Hai-ch'eng *Haicheng* Kwangsi
19 F4 Hai-ch'eng *Haicheng* Liao.
10 C3 Hai-chiang *Haijiang* Heilung.
10 H4 Hai-ch'ing *Haiqing* Heilung.
43 D1 Hai-chou *Haizhou* Kiangsu
43 D1 Hai-chou Wan *Haizhou Wan* (bay) Kiangsu
79 D2 Hai-feng *Haifeng* Kwangt.
43 F4 Hai-fu-chen *Haifuzhen* Kiangsu
Hai-hsi-meng-ku-tsu-tsang-tsu-ka-sa-k'o-tsu Tzu-chih-chou *see* Hai-hsi Mongol-Tibetan-kazakh Autonomous District
107 F2 Hai-hsi Mongol-Tibetan-Kazakh Autonomous District Tsing.
11 D4 Hai-hsing *Haixing* Heilung.
31 E5 Hai-hsing Hsien *Haixing Xian* Hopeh
107 G2 Hai-hsin Shan *Haixin Shan* (mt) Tsing.
70 D2 Hai-hui *Haihui* Kiangsi
119 C3 Hai-jui *Hairui* Taiwan
78 B3 Hai-k'ang Hsien *Haikang Xian* Kwangt.
51 D4 Hai-k'ou *Haikou* Chek.
67 E5 Hai-k'ou *Haikou* Fukien
70 E2 Hai-k'ou *Haikou* Kiangsi
78 B3 Hai-k'ou *Haikou* Kwangt.
119 B4 Hai-k'ou *Haikou* Taiwan
95 D3 Hai-k'ou *Haikou* Yun.
22 C3 Hai-la-erh *Hailaer* Heilung.
22 D3 Hai-la-erh Ho *Hailaer He* (river) Heilung.
10 B2 Hai-la-i *Hailayi* Heilung.
Hailar *see* Hai-la-erh
11 E5 Hai-lin *Hailin* Heilung.
78 B3 Hai-ling Tao *Hailing Dao* (island) Kwangt.
14 A3 Hai-lin-miao *Hailinmiao* Kirin
23 D5 Hai-lin-miao *Hailinmiao* Kirin
26 B4 Hai-li-su *Hailisu* In. Mong.
26 C4 Hai-liu-t'u *Hailiutu* In. Mong.
11 D4 Hai-lun *Hailun* Heilung.
14 F5 Hai-lung-chen *Hailongzhen* Kirin
14 F5 Hai-lung Hsien *Hailong Xian* Kirin
91 E2 Hai-lung-pa *Hailongba* Kwei.
79 E2 Hai-men *Haimen* Kwangt.
51 E4 Hai-men *Maimen* Chek.
43 F4 Hai-men Hsien *Haimen Xian* Kiangsu
22 D4 Hai-min-ts'ai-mu *Haimincaimu* Heilung.
78 A4 Hai-nan Hsing-cheng-ch'ü *Hainan Xingzhengqu* Kwangt.
78 A4 Hainan Li-Miao Autonomous District Kwangt.
Hai-nan Li-tsu Miao-tsu Tzu-chih-chou *see* Hainan Li-Miao Autonomous District
78 A4 Hai-nan Tao *Hainan Dao* (island) Kwangt.
107 G3 Hai-nan Tibetan Autonomous District Tsing.
Hai-nan Tsang-tsu Tzu-chih-chou *see* Hai-nan Tibetan Autonomous District
51 D2 Hai-ning Hsien *Haining Xian* Chek.
11 D4 Hai-pei *Haibei* Heilung.
107 F1 Hai-pei Tibetan Autonomous District Tsing.
Hai-pei Tsang-tsu Tzu-chih-chou *see* Hai-pei Tibetan Autonomous District
26 B5 Hai-po-wan *Haibowan* In. Mong.
102 B3 Hai-san-le-pa-ko *Haisanlebage* Sink.
14 C4 Hai-ssu-kai *Haisigai* Kirin
23 E6 Hai-ssu-kai *Haisigai* Kirin
67 E5 Hai-t'an Tao *Haitan Dao* (island) Fukien
14 D2 Hai-t'o *Haituo* Kirin
30 C3 Hai-t'o Shan *Haituo Shan* (mt) Hopeh
43 D1 Hai-t'ou *Haitou* Kiangsu
78 A4 Hai-t'ou *Haitou* Kwangt.
67 C6 Hai-ts'ang *Haicang* Fukien
98 C2 Hai-t'un *Haitun* Kansu
90 C3 Hai-tzu-chieh *Haizijie* Kwei.
90 C3 Hai-tzu-chieh *Haizijie* Kwei.
114 C3 Hai-tzu-ching *Haizijing* Ningsia
90 B5 Hai-tzu-pao *Haizibao* Kwei.
94 C3 Hai-tzu-ti *Haizidi* Yun.
30 G4 Hai-yang *Haiyang* Hopeh
83 G2 Hai-yang *Haiyang* Kwangsi
35 G3 Hai-yang Hsien *Haiyang Xian* Shant.
83 G2 Hai-yang Shan *Haiyang Shan* (mts) Kwangsi
35 G3 Hai-yang-so *Haiyangsuo* Shant.
19 G5 Hai-yang Tao *Haiyang Dao* (island) Liao.
94 C2 Hai-yao-p'u *Haiyaopu* Yun.
22 E2 Hai-ya-ssu-te *Hayaside* Heilung.
Hai-yen *see* San-chiao-ch'eng
79 C3 Hai-yen *Haiyan* Kwangt.
51 D2 Hai-yen Hsien *Haiyan Xian* Chek.
107 G2 Hai-yen Hsien *Haiyan Xian* Tsing.
51 E3 Hai-yu *Haiyou* Chek.
82 D5 Hai-yüan *Haiyuan* Kwangsi
114 C3 Hai-yüan *Haiyuan* Ningsia
22 D3 Ha-k'o *Hake* Heilung.
102 B2 Ha-la-ch'i *Halaqi* Sink.
14 F3 Ha-la-ha *Halaha* Kirin
14 F3 Ha-la-hai *Halahai* Kirin
23 F5 Ha-la-hai *Halahai* Kirin
26 B5 Ha-la-ha-t'eng *Halahateng* In. Mong.
14 B1 Ha-la-hei *Halahei* Kirin
23 D4 Ha-la-hei *Halahei* Kirin
26 D4 Ha-la-ho-sha *Halahesha* In. Mong.
107 E1 Ha-la Hu *Hala Hu* (lake) Tsing.
27 E3 Ha-la-kan *Halagan* In. Mong.
31 D4 Ha-la-kang *Halagang* Hopeh
22 D3 Ha-la-kou *Halagou* Heilung.
86 D1 Ha-la-ma *Halama* Szech.
114 B1 Ha-la-mu-lin-pai *Halamulinbai* Ningsia
103 D3 Ha-la-mu-lun Shan-k'ou *Halamulun Shankou* (pass) Sink.
102 C3 Ha-lang-kou *Halanggou* Sink.
22 B3 Ha-la-ni-tun *Halanidun* Heilung.
102 C1 Ha-la-pu-la *Halabula* Sink.
22 E3 Ha-la-su *Halasu* Heilung.
102 C2 Ha-la-t'a *Halata* Sink.
18 C2 Ha-la-tao-k'ou *Haladaokou* Liao.
103 E1 Ha-la-t'ung-ku *Halatonggu* Sink.
26 B4 Ha-la-tzu-lao-miao *Halazilaomiao* In. Mong.
Haldan Gol *see* Ha-na-t'eng Ho
26 D4 Ha-le *Hale* In. Mong.
115 D4 Half Moon Shoal China Sea
Haltin Gol *see* Ha-na-t'eng Ho
103 F2 Ha-mi *Hami* Sink.
23 C5 Ha-na-nu-erh *Hananuer* Kirin
106 E1 Ha-na-t'eng Ho *Hanateng He* (river) Tsing.
62 E3 Han-ch'a *Hancha* Shensi
54 C3 Han-ch'eng *Hancheng* Honan
30 F4 Han-ch'eng *Hancheng* Hopeh
63 F5 Han-ch'eng *Hancheng* Shensi
34 A5 Han-chi *Hanji* Shant.
99 F4 Han-chia-chi *Hanjiaji* Kansu
91 E2 Han-chia-kou *Hanjiagou* Kwei.
38 C2 Han-chia-lou *Hanjialou* Shansi
67 E5 Han-chiang *Hanjiang* Fukien
79 E1 Han Chiang *Han Jiang* (river) Kwangt.
43 D3 Han-chiang Hsien *Hanjiang Xian* Kiangsu
114 C3 Han-chiao-shui *Hanjiaoshui* Ningsia
30 E2 Han-chia-tien *Hanjiadian* Hopeh
18 E3 Han-chia-tien *Hanjiadian* Liao.
31 B5 Han-chia-wa *Hanjiawa* Hopeh
10 C1 Han-chia-wei-tzu *Hanjiaweizi* Heilung.
30 B2 Han-chia-ying *Hanjiaying* Hopeh
63 E5 Han-ching *Hanjing* Shensi
59 F4 Han-ch'uan *Hanchuan* Hupeh
34 C5 Han-chuang *Hanzhuang* Shant.
63 C7 Han-chung *Hanzhong* Shensi
71 C6 Han-fang *Hanfang* Kiangsi
Hang-chin Ch'i *see* Hanggin Banner

70 C3 Hsiao-kang-k'ou *Xiaogangkou* Kiangsi
47 D5 Hsiao-ko *Xiage* Anhwei
31 E5 Hsiao-ku *Xiaogu* Hopeh
102 D1 Hsiao-kuai *Xiaoguai* Sink.
102 H1 Hsiao-kuai *Xiaoguai* Sink.
58 B5 Hsiao-kuan *Xiaoguan* Hupeh
119 B3 Hsiao-kuan Shan *Xiaoguan Shan* (mt) Taiwan
15 H4 Hsiao-ku-chia *Xiaogujia* Kirin
14 E4 Hsiao-ku-shan *Xiaogushan* Kirin
19 G5 Hsiao-ku-shan *Xiaogushan* Liao.
79 C2 Hsiao-lan *Xiaolan* Kwangt.
119 C5 Hsiao-lan Hsü *Xiaolan Xu* (island) Taiwan
14 C2 Hsiao-lao-yeh-miao *Xiaolaoyemiao* Kirin
23 E5 Hsiao-lao-yeh-miao *Xiaolaoyemiao* Kirin
19 F2 Hsiao-liang-shan *Xiaoliangshan* Liao.
55 E3 Hsiao-li-chuang *Xiaolizhuang* Honan
51 E2 Hsiao-lin *Xiaolin* Chek.
11 D5 Hsiao-ling *Xiaoling* Heilung.
18 D3 Hsiao-ling Ho *Xiaoling He* (river) Liao.
59 F2 Hsiao-lin-tien *Xiaolindian* Hupeh
34 B3 Hsiao-li-p'u *Xiaolipu* Shant.
34 A4 Hsiao-liu-chi *Xiuliuji* Shant.
46 E3 Hsiao-liu-hsiang *Xiaoliuxiang* Anhwei
30 E2 Hsiao-luan Ho *Xiaoluan He* (river) Hopeh
83 E3 Hsiao-lung *Xiaolong* Kwangsi
95 D4 Hsiao-lung-t'an *Xiaolongtan* Yun.
18 D6 Hsiao-lun-shan Tao *Xiaolongshan* (island) Liao.
91 C4 Hsiao-mao-ch'ang *Xiaomaochang* Kwei.
30 D2 Hsiao-mao-shan *Xiaomaoshan* Hopeh
91 E2 Hsiao-ma-ts'un *Xiaomacun* Kwei.
50 B5 Hsiao-mei *Xiaomei* Chek.
118 B3 Hsiao-mei *Xiaomei* Taiwan
71 B6 Hsiao-mei Kuan *Xiaomei Guan* (pass) Kiangsi
79 D1 Hsiao-mei Kuan *Xiaomei Guan* (pass) Kwangt.
94 B3 Hsiao-meng-t'ung *Xiaomengtong* Yun.
87 F2 Hsiao-mien-chen *Xiaomianzhen* Szech.
11 G4 Hsiao-mu-ho *Xiaomuhe* Heilung.
106 D3 Hsiao-nan-ch'uan *Xiaonanchuan* Tsing.
30 D2 Hsiao-nan-kuan *Xiaonanguan* Hopeh
30 B2 Hsiao-nan-ying *Xiaonanying* Hopeh
63 B8 Hsiao-pa *Xiaoba* Shensi
11 E4 Hsiao-pai *Xiaobai* Heilung.
30 E3 Hsiao-pai-ch'i *Xiaobaiqi* Hopeh
23 D6 Hsiao-p'ao-tzu *Xiaopaozi* Liao.
95 D2 Hsiao-pao-tzu *Xiaobaozi* Yun.
22 D3 Hsiao-pei *Xiaobei* Heilung.
19 F3 Hsiao-pei-ho *Xiaobeihe* Liao.
91 D4 Hsiao-pi *Xiaobi* Kwei.
34 A4 Hsiao-p'i-k'ou *Xiaopikou* Shant.
74 C3 Hsiao-p'ing *Xiaoping* Hunan
83 G5 Hsiao-p'ing-shan *Xiaopingshan* Kwangsi
83 F4 Hsiao-p'ing-yang *Xiaopingyang* Kwangsi
10 C2 Hsiao-p'o-le Shan *Xiaopole Shan* (mt) Heilung.
71 C5 Hsiao-p'u *Xiaopu* Kiangsi
47 C6 Hsiao-sha *Xiaosha* Anhwei
59 F5 Hsiao-sha-k'ou *Xiaoshakou* Hupeh
51 D2 Hsiao-shan *Xiaoshan* Chek.
31 E5 Hsiao-shan *Xiaoshan* Hopeh
54 C3 Hsiao Shan *Xiao Shan* (mts) Honan
55 E4 Hsiao-shang-ch'iao *Xiaoshangqiao* Honan
19 H3 Hsiao-shih *Xiaoshi* Liao.
87 E3 Hsiao-shih *Xiaoshi* Szech.
54 E4 Hsiao-shih-tien *Xiaoshidian* Honan
51 C2 Hsiao-shu *Xiaoshu* Chek.
75 D6 Hsiao Shui *Xiao Shui* (river) Hunan
71 B4 Hsiao Shui *Xiao Shui* (river) Kiangsi
75 E5 Hsiao-shui-p'u *Xiaoshuipu* Hunan
51 C3 Hsiao-shun *Xiaoshun* Chek.
30 F3 Hsiao-ssu-kou *Xiaosigou* Hopeh
14 F5 Hsiao-ssu-p'ing *Xiaosiping* Kirin
39 B4 Hsiao-suan *Xiaosuan* Shansi
30 B3 Hsiao-suan-kou *Xiaosuangou* Hopeh
107 D4 Hsiao-su-mang *Xiaosumang* Tsing.
66 D3 Hsiao-sung *Xiaosong* Fukien
71 D5 Hsiao-sung *Xiaosong* Kiangsi
47 E5 Hsiao-tan-yang *Xiaodanyang* Anhwei
67 C5 Hsiao-t'ao *Xiaotao* Fukien
19 G2 Hsiao-t'a-tzu *Xiaotazi* Liao.
31 C5 Hsiao-t'i *Xiaoti* Hopeh
47 C5 Hsiao-t'ien *Xiaotian* Anhwei
54 D3 Hsiao-tien *Xiaodian* Honan
42 C1 Hsiao-tien *Xiaodian* Kiangsu
46 B4 Hsiao-t'ien-chi *Xiaotianji* Anhwei
58 D2 Hsiao-tien-tzu *Xiaodianzi* Hupeh
66 E4 Hsiao-ts'ang *Xiaocang* Fukien
102 I2 Hsiao-ts'ao-hu *Xiaocaohu* Sink.
103 E2 Hsiao-ts'ao-hu *Xiaocaohu* Sink.
95 E2 Hsiao-ts'ao-pa *Xiaocaoba* Yun.
67 D6 Hsiao-tso *Xiaozuo* Fukien
19 G3 Hsiao-t'un *Xiaotun* Liao.
83 E5 Hsiao-tung *Xiaodong* Kwangsi
107 F3 Hsiao-tung-liang *Xiaodongliang* Tsing.
75 F6 Hsiao-wan *Xiaowan* Hunan
19 G5 Hsiao-wang-chia Tao *Xiaowangjia Dao* (island) Liao.
46 E4 Hsiao-wang-ling *Xiaowangling* Anhwei
51 E3 Hsiao-wang-miao *Xiaowangmiao* Chek.
11 F5 Hsiao-wu-chan *Xiaowuzhan* Heilung.
22 D3 Hsiao-wu-erh-ch'i-han *Xiaowuerqihan* Heilung.
30 B4 Hsiao-wu-t'ai Shan *Xiaowutai Shan* (mt) Hopeh
10 C2 Hsiao-yang-ch'i *Xiaoyangqi* Heilung.
95 D3 Hsiao-yang-chieh *Xiaoyangjie* Yun.
51 F2 Hsiao-yang Shan *Xiaoyang Shan* (island) Chek.
55 F4 Hsiao-yao-chen *Xiaoyaozhen* Honan
58 D3 Hsiao-yen *Xiaoyan* Hupeh
34 D2 Hsiao-ying *Xiaoying* Shant.
46 D3 Hsiao-yü *Xiaoyu* Anhwei
58 C2 Hsia-pa *Xiaba* Hupeh
59 H4 Hsia-pa-ho *Xiabahe* Hupeh
102 H1 Hsia-pa-hu *Xiabahu* Sink.
30 F3 Hsia-pan-ch'eng *Xiabancheng* Hopeh
38 E4 Hsia-p'an-shih *Xiapanshi* Shansi
58 D3 Hsia-pao-p'ing *Xiabaoping* Hupeh
91 G5 Hsia-p'i-lin *Xiapilin* Kwei.
58 C4 Hsia-p'ing *Xiaping* Hupeh
31 B5 Hsia-p'ing-yang *Xiapingyang* Hopeh
51 E2 Hsia-p'u *Xiapu* Chek.
66 E4 Hsia-p'u *Xiapu* Fukien
70 B4 Hsia-p'u *Xiapu* Kiangsi
70 D3 Hsia-pu-chi *Xiabuji* Kiangsi
102 H1 Hsia-san-chiang *Xiasanjiang* Sink.
90 C5 Hsia-shan *Xiashan* Kwei.
119 B3 Hsia Shan *Xia Shan* (mt) Taiwan
70 A4 Hsia-shan-k'ou *Xiashankou* Kiangsi
23 C5 Hsia-shan-wan *Xiashanwan* Liao.
38 E2 Hsia-she *Xiashe* Shansi
74 E4 Hsia-she-ssu *Xiashesi* Hunan
51 D2 Hsia-shih *Xiashi* Chek.
82 C5 Hsia-shih *Xiashi* Kwangsi
38 C3 Hsia-shih-chia-chuang *Xiashijiazhuang* Shansi
43 D3 Hsia-shu *Xiashu* Kiangsu
38 D2 Hsia-shui-t'ou *Xiashuitou* Shansi
75 D6 Hsia-shu-p'u *Xiashupu* Hunan
91 E4 Hsia-ssu *Xiasi* Kwei.
91 E4 Hsia-ssu *Xiasi* Kwei.
99 F2 Hsia-ssu-fen *Xiasifen* Kansu
119 B4 Hsia-ta-ch'i *Xiadaqi* Taiwan
54 D4 Hsia-t'ang *Xiatang* Honan
75 F5 Hsia-t'ang *Xiatang* Hunan
46 D4 Hsia-t'ang-chi *Xiatangji* Anhwei
66 D4 Hsia-tao *Xiadao* Fukein
30 D4 Hsia-tien *Xiadian* Hopeh
39 D5 Hsia-tien *Xiadian* Shansi
35 E3 Hsia-tien *Xiadian* Shant.
35 F2 Hsia-tien *Xiadian* Shant.
15 J5 Hsia-t'ien-p'ing *Xiatianping* Kirin
42 C2 Hsia-ts'ao-wan *Xiacaowan* Kiangsu
50 C2 Hsia-ts'un *Xiacun* Chek.
70 B4 Hsia-ts'un *Xiacun* Kiangsi
35 G3 Hsia-ts'un *Xiacun* Shant.
98 B1 Hsia-tung *Xiadong* Kansu
82 C5 Hsia-tung *Xiadong* Kwangsi
91 E3 Hsia-tzu-ch'ang *Xiazichang* Kwei.
103 D1 Hsia-tzu-chieh *Xiazijie* Sink.
18 D2 Hsia-wa *Xiawa* Liao.
83 G4 Hsia-wan *Xiawan* Kwangsi
34 D4 Hsia-wei *Xiawei* Shant.
71 C6 Hsia-wen-t'an *Xiawentan* Kiangsi
66 D4 Hsia-yang *Xiayang* Fukien
67 B6 Hsia-yang *Xiayang* Fukien
67 C5 Hsia-yang *Xiayang* Fukien
22 D2 Hsia-yang-ko-ch'i *Xiayanggeqi* Heilung.
82 D3 Hsia-yao *Xiayao* Kwangsi
83 H4 Hsia-ying *Xiaying* Kwangsi
35 E2 Hsia-ying *Xiaying* Shant.
63 E6 Hsia-ying *Xiaying* Shensi
119 B3 Hsia-ying *Xiaying* Taiwan
90 C4 Hsia-ying-p'an *Xiayingpan* Kwei.
50 C2 Hsia-yü-ch'iao *Xiayuqiao* Chek.
66 E4 Hsia-yüeh-shih *Xiayueshi* Fukien
74 E2 Hsia-yü-k'ou *Xiayukou* Hunan
79 D2 Hsia-yung *Xiayong* Kwangt.
63 C7 Hsi-ch'a-ho *Xichahe* Shensi
58 D5 Hsi-chai *Xizhai* Hupeh
39 E4 Hsi-chai *Xizhai* Shansi
83 E6 Hsi-ch'ang *Xichang* Kwangsi
86 D4 Hsi-ch'ang *Xichang* Szech.
59 G3 Hsi-chang-tien *Xizhangdian* Hupeh
31 B5 Hsi-ch'a-t'ou *Xichatou* Hopeh
74 B2 Hsi-ch'e *Xiche* Hunan
10 C3 Hsi-ch'eng *Xicheng* Heilung.
22 F3 Hsi-ch'eng *Xicheng* Heilung.
55 G2 Hsi-ch'eng *Xicheng* Honan
30 B3 Hsi-ch'eng *Xicheng* Hopeh
82 D5 Hsi-ch'eng *Xicheng* Kwangsi
39 D6 Hsi-ch'eng Shan *Xicheng Shan* (mt) Shansi
66 D4 Hsi-ch'i *Xiqi* Fukien
11 D4 Hsi-chi *Xiji* Heilung.
74 C3 Hsi-ch'i *Xiqi* Hunan
74 C4 Hsi-ch'i *Xiqi* Hunan
114 C4 Hsi-chi *Xiji* Ningsia
67 C5 Hsi Ch'i *Xi Qi* (river) Fukien
67 C6 Hsi Ch'i *Xi Qi* (river) Fukien
34 C5 Hsi-chi *Xiji* Shant.
71 C6 Hsi-chiang *Xijiang* Kiangsi
78 B2 Hsi Chiang *Xi Jiang* (river) Kwangt.
119 B3 Hsi-chiang *Xijiang* Taiwan
43 D2 Hsi-ch'iao *Xiqiao* Kiangsu
106 B3 Hsi-chieh *Xijie* Tsing.
118 C1 Hsi-chih *Xizhi* Taiwan
119 A3 Hsi-chi Hsü *Xiji Xu* (island) Taiwan
66 D3 Hsi-chin *Xijin* Fukien
66 D4 Hsi-ch'in *Xiqin* Fukien
83 F5 Hsi-chin *Xijin* Kwangsi
39 E5 Hsi-ching *Xijing* Shansi
107 G3 Hsi-ch'ing Shan *Xiqing Shan* (mts) Tsing.
86 C2 Hsi-ch'ing-ssu *Xiqingsi* Szech.
106 B3 Hsi-chin-wu-lan Hu *Xijinwulan Hu* (lake) Tsing.
99 F3 Hsi-chi-shui *Xijishui* Kansu
51 E3 Hsi-chou *Xizhou* Chek.
94 C3 Hsi-chou *Xizhou* Yun.
95 E4 Hsi-ch'ou *Xichou* Yun.
95 E4 Hsi-ch'ou-hsin-chieh *Xichouxinjie* Yun.
38 D3 Hsi-chou Shan *Xizhou Shan* (mts) Shansi
18 C1 Hsi-ch'ü *Xiqu* Kansu
39 C4 Hsi-ch'üan *Xiquan* Shansi
46 D4 Hsi-ch'üan-chieh *Xiquanjie* Anhwei
63 F5 Hsi-chuang-chen *Xizhuangzhen* Shensi
54 C4 Hsi-ch'uan Hsien *Xichuan Xian* Honan
67 E5 Hsi-ch'üan Tao *Xiquan Dao* (island) Fukien
87 E2 Hsi-ch'ung *Xichong* Szech.
18 E5 Hsi-chung Tao *Xizhong Dao* (island) Liao.
47 E5 Hsieh-chen *Xiezhen* Anhwei
55 G3 Hsieh-chi *Xieji* Honan
14 F5 Hsieh-chia *Xiejia* Kirin
18 E3 Hsieh-chia *Xiejia* Liao.
47 B5 Hsieh-chia-chi *Xiejiaji* Anhwei
43 D3 Hsieh-chia-chi *Xiejiaji* Kiangsu
34 C2 Hsieh-chia-chi *Xiejiaji* Shant.
46 C4 Hsieh-ch'iao *Xieqiao* Anhwei
51 D2 Hsieh-ch'iao *Xieqiao* Chek.
58 D5 Hsieh-ch'iao *Xieqiao* Hopeh
43 E3 Hsieh-ch'iao *Xieqiao* Kiangsu
70 D2 Hsieh-chia-t'an *Xiejiatan* Kiangsi
55 E3 Hsieh-chuang *Xiezhuang* Honan
34 D4 Hsieh-chuang *Xiezhuang* Shant.
71 C6 Hsieh-fang *Xiefang* Kiangsi
91 D3 Hsieh-ho *Xiehe* Kwei.
Hsieh-ka *see* **Hsieh-ko-erh**
110 C3 Hsieh-ko-erh *Xiegeer* Tibet
23 C5 Hsieh-li-fu *Xielifu* Liao.
102 C4 Hsieh-li-k'o-k'o-shih *Xielikekeshi* Sink.
58 D3 Hsieh-ma-ho *Xiemahe* Hupeh
34 C4 Hsieh-ming-t'ing *Xiemating* Shant.
70 D2 Hsieh Shan *Xie Shan* (mt) Kiangsi
66 E3 Hsieh-t'an *Xietan* Fukien
70 C2 Hsieh-t'an *Xietan* Kiangsi
51 C3 Hsieh-t'ang *Xietang* Chek.
18 E3 Hsieh-t'un *Xietun* Liao.
18 E5 Hsieh-t'un *Xietun* Liao.
110 D3 Hsieh-t'ung-men *Xietongmen* Tibet
34 D4 Hsieh-wu *Xiewu* Shant.
107 F4 Hsieh-wu-ssu *Xiewusi* Tsing.
70 E2 Hsien-ch'a *Xiancha* Kiangsi
99 H3 Hsien-ch'eng-pao *Xianchengbao* Kansu
74 D3 Hsien-ch'i *Xianqi* Hunan
35 F3 Hsien-chia-chai *Xianjiazhai* Shant.
55 D5 Hsien-chiang *Xianjiang* Chek.
75 B5 Hsien-ch'i-chen *Xianqizhen* Hunan
51 D4 Hsien-chü *Xianju* Chek.
58 E3 Hsien-chü *Xianju* Hupeh
39 B5 Hsien-ch'uan-k'ou *Xianchuankou* Shansi
62 F4 Hsien-ch'uan-k'ou *Xianchuankou* Shensi
74 F3 Hsien-chung *Xianzhong* Hunan
58 B5 Hsien-feng *Xianfeng* Hupeh
94 C4 Hsien-ho-chieh *Xianhejie* Yun.
58 B2 Hsien-ho-p'u *Xianhepu* Hupeh
118 B2 Hsien-hsi *Xianxi* Taiwan
47 F6 Hsien-hsia *Xianxia* Anhwei
71 C5 Hsien-hsia *Xianxia* Kiangsi
50 B4 Hsien-hsia Ling *Xianxia Ling* (mt) Chek.
50 C4 Hsien-hsia Ling *Xianxia Ling* (mts) Chek.
66 D2 Hsien-hsia Ling *Xianxia Ling* (mts) Fukien
31 D5 Hsien-hsien *Xianxian* Hopeh
38 E3 Hsien-jen *Xianren* Shansi
58 D2 Hsien-jen-tu *Xianrendu* Hupeh
63 C6 Hsien-kung-chen *Xiangongzhen* Shensi
107 G2 Hsien-mi *Xianmi* Tsing.
59 G5 Hsien-ning *Xianning* Hupeh
59 G5 Hsien-ning *Xianning* Hupeh
59 G5 Hsien-ning Ti-ch'ü *Xianning Diqu* Hupeh
43 D3 Hsien-nü-miao *Xiannümiao* Kiangsu
71 B6 Hsien-nü-pu *Xiannübu* Kiangsi
83 G2 Hsien-shui *Xianshui* Kwangsi
86 C2 Hsien-shui Ho *Xianshui He* (river) Szech.
31 E5 Hsien-shui-ku *Xianshuigu* Hopeh
106 D1 Hsien-shuilch'üan *Xianshuiquan* Tsing.
87 F3 Hsien-t'an *Xiantan* Szech.
91 D5 Hsien-t'ang *Xiantang* Kwei.
59 F4 Hsien-t'ao-chen *Xiantaozhen* Hupeh
83 G5 Hsien-ti *Xiandi* Kwangsi
66 E4 Hsien-ts'un *Xiancun* Fukien
47 D5 Hsien-tsung *Xianzong* Anhwei
67 C5 Hsien-tu *Xiandu* Fukien
75 D6 Hsien-tzu-chiao *Xianzijiao* Hunan
66 D2 Hsien-yang *Xianyang* Fukien
67 C5 Hsien-yang *Xianyang* Fukien
63 D6 Hsien-yang *Xianyang* Shensi
63 D6 Hsien-yang *Xianyang* Shensi
51 D3 Hsien-yen *Xianyan* Chek.
67 D5 Hsien-yu *Xianyou* Fukien
70 B3 Hsien-yüan *Xianyuan* Kiangsi
91 D2 Hsien-yüan *Xianyuan* Kwei.
95 D3 Hsi-erh *Xier* Yun.
14 B5 Hsi-erh-tao-hu *Xierdaohu* Kirin
23 D6 Hsi-erh-tao-hu *Xierdaohu* Kirin
38 E2 Hsi-fang-ch'eng *Xifangcheng* Shansi
46 C4 Hsi-fei Ho *Xifei He* (river) Anhwei
11 G4 Hsi-feng *Xifeng* Heilung.
91 D3 Hsi-feng *Xifeng* Kwei.
19 H2 Hsi-feng *Xifeng* Liao.
99 H4 Hsi-feng-chen *Xifengzhen* Kansu
30 F3 Hsi-feng-k'ou *Xifengkou* Hopeh
55 F3 Hsi-feng-ling *Xifengling* Honan
75 F6 Hsi-feng-tu *Xifengdu* Hunan
19 F3 Hsi-fo *Xifo* Liao.
35 F3 Hsi-fu *Xifu* Shant.
23 E6 Hsi-ha-la-ka *Xihalaga* Kirin
18 B1 Hsi-ha-la-mao-tao *Xihalamaodao* Liao.
99 G5 Hsi-han Shui *Xihan Shui* (river) Kansu
58 C3 Hsi-hao-p'ing *Xihaoping* Hupeh
23 C6 Hsi-ha-ta-ying-ko *Xihadayingge* Liao.
47 E6 Hsi-ho *Xihe* Anhwei
59 F3 Hsi-ho *Xihe* Hupeh
26 D4 Hsi-ho *Xihe* In. Mong.
99 G4 Hsi-ho *Xihe* Kansu
47 D5 Hsi Ho *Xi He* (river) Anhwei
58 D3 Hsi Ho *Xi He* (river) Hupeh
98 E1 Hsi Ho *Xi He* (river) Kansu
18 E3 Hsi Ho *Xi He* (river) Liao.
87 F2 Hsi Ho *Xi He* (river) Szech.
34 C3 Hsi-ho *Xihe* Shant.
35 F3 Hsi-ho *Xihe* Shant.
63 D8 Hsi-ho *Xihe* Shensi
63 C8 Hsi-ho *Xihe* Szech.
63 C8 Hsi-ho-k'ou *Xihekou* Shensi
39 E6 Hsi-ho-ti *Xihedi* Shansi
30 B4 Hsi-ho-ying *Xiheying* Hopeh
54 C4 Hsi-hsia *Xixia* Honan
35 F2 Hsi-hsia *Xixia* Shant.
54 D2 Hsi-hsiang *Xixiang* Honan
70 B3 Hsi-hsiang *Xixiang* Kiangsi
63 B8 Hsi-hsiang *Xixiang* Shensi
110 C3 Hsi-hsia-pang-ma Feng *Xixiabangma Feng* (mt) Tibet
43 D4 Hsi-hsia-shu *Xixiashu* Kiangsu
55 F5 Hsi-hsien *Xixian* Honan
39 B5 Hsi-hsien *Xixian* Shansi
51 D2 Hsi-hsing *Xixing* Chek.
118 A3 Hsi-hsü *Xixu* Taiwan
119 A3 Hsi-hsü-p'ing Hsü *Xixuping Xu* (island) Taiwan
70 E2 Hsi-hu *Xihu* Kiangsi
55 F4 Hsi-hua *Xihua* Honan
99 I4 Hsi-hua-ch'ih *Xihuachi* Kansu
31 B6 Hsi-huang-ts'un *Xihuangcun* Hopeh
114 C2 Hsi-kang *Xigang* Ningsia
34 C5 Hsi-kang *Xigang* Shant.
10 D3 Hsi-kang-tzu *Xigangzi* Heilung.
59 G5 Hsi-k'eng *Xikeng* Hupeh
79 D2 Hsi-k'eng *Xikeng* Kwangt.
102 H1 Hsi-ko-pi *Xigebi* Sink.
98 C2 Hsi-kou *Xigou* Kansu
23 D4 Hsi-k'ou *Xikou* Kirin
39 E4 Hsi-kou *Xigou* Shansi
39 E5 Hsi-kou-ts'un *Xigoucun* Shansi
22 D1 Hsi-k'ou-tzu *Xikouzi* Heilung.
74 D4 Hsi-k'uang-shan *Xikuangshan* Hunan
22 D3 Hsi-kuei-t'u Ch'i *Xiguitu Qi* Heilung.
14 A2 Hsi-k'un-tu-le *Xikundule* Kirin
23 D5 Hsi-k'un-tu-le *Xikundule* Kirin
26 E3 Hsi-la-ha-t'a *Xilahata* In. Mong.
Hsi-la-mu-lun Ho *see* **T'a-pu Ho**
18 C1 Hsi-la-mu-lun Ho *Xilamulun He* (river) Liao.
26 E3 Hsi-li *Xili* In. Mong.
106 D2 Hsi-li *Xili* Tsing.
106 C1 Hsi-liang-tzu *Xiliangzi* Tsing.
14 C4 Hsi-liao Ho *Xiliao He* (river) Kirin
23 E5 Hsi-liao Ho *Xiliao He* (river) Kirin
78 A3 Hsi-lien *Xilian* Kwangt.
107 F2 Hsi-li-kou *Xiligou* Tsing.
11 E4 Hsi-lin *Xilin* Heilung.
83 G3 Hsi-ling *Xiling* Kwangsi
79 C2 Hsi-ling *Xiling* Kwangt.
58 C4 Hsi-ling Hsia *Xiling Xia* (gorge) Hupeh
55 F3 Hsi-ling-ssu *Xilingsi* Honan
27 G3 Hsi-lin-hao-t'e *Xilinhaote* In. Mong.
11 F5 Hsi-lin-ho *Xilinhe* Heilung.
82 B3 Hsi-lin Hsien *Xilin Xian* Kwangsi
27 G3 Hsi-lin Kuo-le *Xilin Guole* (river) In. Mong.
27 G3 Hsi-lin Kuo-le *Xilin Guok* (river) In. Mong.
27 G2 Hsi-lin-kuo-le Meng *Xilinguole Meng* In. Mong.
38 D3 Hsi-ling-ching *Xilingjing* Shansi
110 D3 Hsi-lin-t'o *Xilintuo* Tibet
31 C6 Hsi-liu *Xiliu* Hopeh
59 F4 Hsi-liu-ho *Xiliuhe* Hupeh
63 F5 Hsi-li-yü *Xiliyu* Shensi
118 B3 Hsi-lo *Xiluo* Taiwan
118 B3 Hsi-lo-mu Ho *Xiluomu He* (river) Tibet
111 E3 Hsi-luan-ta Shan *Xiluanda Shan* (mt) Taiwan
59 H4 Hsi-ma-fan *Ximafan* Hupeh
59 G3 Hsi-ma-ho *Ximahe* Kwei.
18 E5 Hsi-ma-i Tao *Ximayi Dao* (island) Liao.
59 F4 Hsi-ma-k'ou *Ximakou* Hupeh
23 D4 Hsi-ma-la-t'u *Ximalatu* Kirin
Hsi-ma-la-ya Shan *see* **Himalayas**
30 B3 Hsi-ma-lin *Ximalin* Hopeh
94 B4 Hsi-meng *Ximeng* Yun.
94 B4 Hsi-meng Wa Autonomous Hsien Yun.
Hsi-meng Wa-tsu Tzu-chih-hsien *see* **Hsi-meng Wa Autonomous Hsien**
98 E1 Hsi-miao *Ximiao* Kansu
38 D4 Hsi-ming *Ximing* Shansi
39 B7 Hsi-mo *Ximo* Shensi
19 F4 Hsi-mu-ch'eng *Ximucheng* Liao.
26 C4 Hsi-na-ko-erh-miao *Xinageermiao* In. Mong.
10 C3 Hsin-an *Xinan* Heilung.
11 E5 Hsin-an *Xinan* Heilung.
55 E3 Hsin-an *Xinan* Honan
31 D4 Hsin-an *Xinan* Hopeh
74 D2 Hsin-an *Xinan* Hunan
71 D5 Hsin-an *Xinan* Kiangsi
42 C1 Hsin-an *Xinan* Kiangsu
43 E4 Hsin-an *Xinan* Kiangsu
14 F4 Hsin-an *Xinan* Kirin
15 H3 Hsin-an *Xinan* Kirin
79 C2 Hsin-an *Xinan* Kwangt.
79 D2 Hsin-an *Xinan* Kwangt.
35 F3 Hsin-an *Xinan* Shant.
30 E4 Hsin-an-chen *Xinanzhen* Hopeh
26 C4 Hsin-an-chen *Xinanzhen* In. Mong.
43 D1 Hsin-an-chen *Xinanzhen* Kiangsu
14 D3 Hsin-an-chen *Xinanzhen* Kirin
23 E5 Hsin-an-chen *Xinanzhen* Kirin
55 G4 Hsin-an-chi *Xinanji* Honan
50 C3 Hsin-an-chiang *Xinanjiang* Chek.
50 B3 Hsin-an Chiang *Xinan Jiang* (river) Chek.
50 C3 Hsin-an-chiang Shui-k'u *Xinanjiang Shuiku* (res) Chek.
35 E2 Hsin-an-chuang *Xinanzhuang* Shant.
62 D3 Hsin-an-pien *Xinanbian* Shensi
95 D4 Hsin-an-so *Xinansuo* Yun.
55 F5 Hsin-an-tien *Xinandian* Honan
31 B5 Hsin-an-ts'un *Xinancun* Hopeh
47 C6 Hsin-an-tu *Xinandu* Anhwei
30 F4 Hsin-chai *Xinzhai* Hopeh
34 C3 Hsin-chai *Xinzhai* Shant.
34 D3 Hsin-chai *Xinzhai* Shant.
11 C5 Hsin-chan *Xinzhan* Heilung.
55 F4 Hsin-chan *Xinzhan* Honan
14 F3 Hsin-chan *Xinzhan* Kirin
15 H4 Hsin-chan *Xinzhan* Kirin
91 D2 Hsin-chan *Xinzhan* Kwei.
51 D3 Hsin-ch'ang *Xinchang* Chek.
75 B5 Hsin-ch'ang *Xinchang* Hunan
63 D3 Hsin-ch'ang *Xinchang* Hupeh
59 E5 Hsin-ch'ang *Xinchang* Hupeh
70 E2 Hsin-ch'ang *Xinchang* Kiangsi
43 F4 Hsin-ch'ang *Xinchang* Kiangsu
79 C2 Hsin-ch'ang *Xinchang* Kwangt.
87 E2 Hsin-ch'ang *Xinchang* Szech.
22 D2 Hsin-chang-fang *Xinzhangfang* Heilung.
30 E3 Hsin-chang-tzu *Xinzhangzi* Hopeh
26 B5 Hsin-chao-miao *Xinzhaomiao* In. Mong.
70 C2 Hsin-che-lin *Xinzhelin* Kiangsi
55 F2 Hsin-chen *Xinzhen* Honan
31 D4 Hsin-chen *Xinzhen* Hopeh
34 D2 Hsin-chen *Xinzhen* Shant.
87 F2 Hsin-chen *Xinzhen* Szech.
51 D2 Hsin-ch'eng *Xincheng* Chek.
51 D5 Hsin-cheng *Xinzheng* Chek.
11 F4 Hsin-ch'eng *Xincheng* Heilung.
11 F5 Hsin-ch'eng *Xincheng* Heilung.
55 E3 Hsin-cheng *Xinzheng* Honan
31 C6 Hsin-ch'eng *Xincheng* Hopeh
59 F2 Hsin-ch'eng *Xincheng* Hupeh
59 G3 Hsin-ch'eng *Xincheng* Hupeh
98 E2 Hsin-ch'eng *Xincheng* Kansu
99 F4 Hsin-ch'eng *Xincheng* Kansu
71 B5 Hsin-ch'eng *Xincheng* Kiangsi
71 B6 Hsin-ch'eng *Xincheng* Kiangsi
43 D3 Hsin-ch'eng *Xincheng* Kiangsu
83 E3 Hsin-ch'eng *Xincheng* Kwangsi
78 A4 Hsin-cheng *Xinzheng* Kwangt.
114 C2 Hsin-ch'eng *Xincheng* Ningsia
38 D4 Hsin-ch'eng *Xincheng* Shansi
118 C2 Hsin-ch'eng *Xincheng* Taiwan
30 C4 Hsin-ch'eng Hsien *Xincheng Xian* Hopeh
30 C4 Hsin-ch'eng Hsien *Xincheng Xian* Hopeh
62 D3 Hsin-ch'eng-pao *Xinchengbao* Shensi
31 B5 Hsin-ch'eng-p'u *Xinchengpu* Hopeh
19 G2 Hsin-ch'eng-tzu *Xinchengzi* Liao.
102 D1 Hsin-ch'e-p'ai-tzu *Xinchepaizi* Sink.
102 H1 Hsin-ch'e-p'ai-tzu *Xinchepaizi* Sink.
46 D3 Hsin-chi *Xinji* Anhwei
30 F3 Hsin-chi *Xinji* Hopeh
31 C6 Hsin-chi *Xinji* Hopeh
59 E3 Hsin-chi *Xinji* Hupeh
34 A4 Hsin-chi *Xinji* Shant.
63 B7 Hsin-chi *Xinji* Shensi
74 F2 Hsin-chiang *Xinjiang* Hunan
70 D3 Hsin Chiang *Xin Jiang* (river) Kiangsi
39 C6 Hsin-chiang *Xinjiang* Shansi
118 B2 Hsin-chiang *Xinjiang* Taiwan
118 B3 Hsin-chiang *Xinjiang* Taiwan
22 C3 Hsin-chiang-chün-miao *Xinjiangjunmiao* Heilung.
58 D4 Hsin-chiang-k'ou *Xinjiangkou* Hupeh
119 C3 Hsin-chiang Shan *Xinjiang Shan* (mt) Taiwan
66 C3 Hsin-ch'iao *Xinqiao* Fukien
67 B5 Hsin-ch'iao *Xinqiao* Fukien
67 C4 Hsin-ch'iao *Xinqiao* Fukien
67 C5 Hsin-ch'iao *Xinqiao* Fukien
55 F4 Hsin-ch'iao *Xinqiao* Honan
74 C4 Hsin-ch'iao *Xinqiao* Hunan
83 G5 Hsin-ch'iao *Xinqiao* Kwangsi
90 C5 Hsin-ch'iao *Xinqiao* Kwei.
67 C5 Hsin-ch'iao Ho *Xinqiao He* (river) Fukien
70 C3 Hsin-ch'i-chou *Xinqizhou* Kiangsi
46 E4 Hsin-chieh *Xinjie* Anhwei
26 C5 Hsin-chieh *Xinjie* In. Mong.
83 H2 Hsin-chieh *Xinjie* Kwangsi
78 A4 Hsin-chieh *Xinjie* Kwangt.
86 D4 Hsin-chieh *Xinjie* Szech.
107 G3 Hsin-chieh *Xinjie* Tsing.
94 B3 Hsin-chieh *Xinjie* Yun.
95 D4 Hsin-chieh *Xinjie* Yun.
63 B6 Hsin-chieh-chen *Xinjiezhen* Shensi
10 D1 Hsin-chieh-chi *Xinjieji* Heilung.
51 D4 Hsin-chien *Xinjian* Chek.
74 C4 Hsin-chien *Xinjian* Hunan
70 C3 Hsin-chien *Xinjian* Kiangsi
70 E2 Hsin-chien *Xinjian* Kiangsi
34 D2 Hsin-ch'ien-hu *Xinqianhu* Shant.
70 B4 Hsin-chih *Xinzhi* Kiangsi
39 C5 Hsin-chih *Xinzhi* Shansi
87 D2 Hsin-chin *Xinjin* Szech.
Hsin-ching *see* **Ch'ang-ch'un**
10 E3 Hsin-ch'ing *Xinqing* Heilung.
98 E2 Hsin-ching *Xinjing* Kansu
19 E5 Hsin-chin Hsien *Xinjin Xian* Liao.
18 E2 Hsin-ch'iu *Xinqiu* Liao.
74 D2 Hsin-chou *Xinzhou* Hunan
59 G4 Hsin-chou *Xinzhou* Hupeh
78 A4 Hsi'n-chou *Xinzhou* Kwangt.
79 C3 Hsin-chou *Xinzhou* Kwangt.
91 E2 Hsin-chou *Xinzhou* Kwei.
91 E3 Hsin-chou *Xinzhou* Kwei.
Hsinchow *see* **Hsin-hsien**
118 B2 Hsin-chu *Xinzhu* Taiwan
67 B5 Hsin-ch'üan *Xinquan* Fukien
43 E4 Hsin-chuang *Xinzhuang* Kiangsu
43 F4 Hsin-chuang *Xinzhuang* Kiangsu
34 C3 Hsin-chuang *Xinzhuang* Shant.
34 C4 Hsin-chuang *Xinzhuang* Shant.
35 F2 Hsin-chuang *Xinzhuang* Shant.
30 C3 Hsin-chuang-tzu *Xinzhuangzi* Hopeh
18 E3 Hsin-chuang-tzu *Xinzhuangzi* Liao.
63 E6 Hsin-chu-chen *Xinzhuzhen* Shensi
118 C2 Hsin-chu Hsien *Xinzhu Xian* Taiwan
30 E4 Hsin-chün-t'un *Xinjuntun* Hopeh
87 E2 Hsin-fan *Xinfan* Szech.
51 D2 Hsin-feng *Xinfeng* Chek.
71 B6 Hsin-feng *Xinfeng* Kiangsi
71 D4 Hsin-feng *Xinfeng* Kiangsi
71 D4 Hsin-feng *Xinfeng* Kiangsi
43 D3 Hsin-feng *Xinfeng* Kiangsu
83 G5 Hsin-feng *Xinfeng* Kwangsi
79 D1 Hsin-feng *Xinfeng* Kwangt.
79 E1 Hsin-feng *Xinfeng* Kwangt.
118 B2 Hsin-feng *Xinfeng* Taiwan
43 E2 Hsin-feng-chen *Xinfengzhen* Kiangsu
63 E6 Hsin-feng-chen *Xinfengzhen* Shensi
10 B2 Hsing-a *Xinga* Heilung.
22 D3 Hsing-an *Xingan* Heilung.
31 B5 Hsing-an *Xingan* Hopeh
83 G2 Hsing-an *Xingan* Kwangsi
14 B1 Hsing-an-chen *Xinganzhen* Kirin
23 D4 Hsing-an-chen *Xinganzhen* Kirin
22 E3 Hsing-an-li *Xinganli* Heilung.
119 C4 Hsing-ch'ang *Xingchang* Taiwan
30 F3 Hsing-ch'eng *Xingcheng* Hopeh
18 D4 Hsing-ch'eng *Xingcheng* Liao.
38 D4 Hsing-ch'eng *Xingcheng* Shansi
55 E5 Hsing-chi *Xingji* Honan
31 B6 Hsing-chi *Xingji* Hopeh
31 B6 Hsing-chia-wan *Xingjiawan* Hopeh
30 E2 Hsing-chou Ho *Xingzhou He* (river) Hopeh
91 C2 Hsing-chüeh-hsi *Xingjuexi* Kwei.
34 D2 Hsing-fu *Xingfu* Shant.
Hsing-hai *see* **Tzu-k'o-t'an**
107 F3 Hsing-hai Hsien *Xinghai Xian* Tsing.
27 E4 Hsing-ho *Xinghe* In. Mong.
38 C3 Hsing-hsien *Xingxian* Shansi
103 F2 Hsing-hsing-hsia *Xingxingxia* Sink.
10 D1 Hsing-hua *Xinghua* Heilung.
11 D4 Hsing-hua *Xinghua* Heilung.
54 C3 Hsing-hua *Xinghua* Honan
43 D3 Hsing-hua *Xinghua Xian* Kiangsu
39 C4 Hsing-hua-ts'un *Xinghuacun* Shansi
67 E5 Hsing-hua Wan *Xinghua Wan* (bay) Fukien
55 F3 Hsing-hua-ying *Xinghuaying* Honan
31 C5 Hsing-i *Xingyi* Hopeh
90 B5 Hsing-i *Xingyi* Kwei.
11 D4 Hsing-jen *Xingren* Heilung.
90 C5 Hsing-jen *Xingren* Kwei.
91 E4 Hsing-jen *Xingren* Kwei.
118 C1 Hsing-jen *Xingren* Taiwan
114 C3 Hsing-jen-pao *Xingrenbao* Ningsia
11 G5 Hsing-k'ai *Xingkai* Heilung.
11 G5 Hsing-k'ai Hu *Xingkai Hu* (lake) Heilung.
71 C5 Hsing-kuo *Xingguo* Kiangsi
91 E5 Hsing-lang *Xinglang* Kwei.
67 D6 Hsing-lin *Xinglin* Fukien
46 B3 Hsing-liu *Xingliu* Anhwei
10 C2 Hsing-lung *Xinglong* Heilung.
11 F4 Hsing-lung *Xinglong* Heilung.
55 F3 Hsing-lung *Xinglong* Honan
30 E3 Hsing-lung *Xinglong* Hopeh
59 E2 Hsing-lung *Xinglong* Hupeh
99 G4 Hsing-lung *Xinglong* Kansu
14 D4 Hsing-lung *Xinglong* Kirin
78 B4 Hsing-lung *Xinglong* Kwangt.
91 E3 Hsing-lung *Xinglong* Kwei.
114 C4 Hsing-lung *Xinglong* Ningsia
34 B2 Hsing-lung *Xinglong* Shant.
87 F2 Hsing-lung *Xinglong* Szech.
87 F3 Hsing-lung *Xinglong* Szech.
10 C1 Hsing-lung-chan *Xinglongzhan* Heilung.
63 D8 Hsing-lung-ch'ang *Xinglongchang* Shensi
74 B3 Hsing-lung-ch'ang Ta-lan *Xinglongchang Dalan* Hunan
11 D4 Hsing-lung-chen *Xinglongzhen* Heilung.
46 E4 Hsing-lung-chi *Xinglongji* Anhwei
74 D3 Hsing-lung-chieh *Xinglongjie* Hunan
10 B3 Hsing-lung-ch'üan *Xinglongquan* Heilung.
10 C3 Hsing-lung-pao *Xinglongbao* Heilung.
19 F2 Hsing-lung-pao *Xinglongbao* Liao.
14 F4 Hsing-lung-shan *Xinglongshan* Kirin
23 E5 Hsing-lung-shan *Xinglongshan* Kirin
19 G3 Hsing-lung-tien *Xinglongdian* Liao.
14 C1 Hsing-mu-t'un *Xingmutun* Kirin
23 E4 Hsing-mu-t'un *Xingmutun* Kirin
10 B3 Hsing-nan-chen *Xingnanzhen* Heilung.
82 D4 Hsing-ning *Xingning* Kwangsi
79 D1 Hsing-ning *Xingning* Kwangt.
83 G3 Hsing-p'ing *Xingping* Kwangsi
63 D6 Hsing-p'ing *Xingping* Shensi
11 B4 Hsing-shan *Xingshan* Heilung.
11 C5 Hsing-shan *Xingshan* Heilung.
23 E4 Hsing-shan *Xingshan* Heilung.
55 E3 Hsing-shan *Xingshan* Honan
58 C3 Hsing-shan *Xingshan* Hupeh
63 E6 Hsing-shih-chen *Xingshizhen* Shensi
11 F5 Hsing-shu *Xingshu* Heilung.
19 F5 Hsing-shu-ho *Xingshuhe* Liao.
26 D4 Hsing-shun-hsi *Xingshunxi* In. Mong.
31 B6 Hsing-t'ai *Xingtai* Hopeh
31 B5 Hsing-t'ang *Xingtang* Hopeh
46 B3 Hsing-t'ang-chi *Xingtangji* Anhwei
103 D2 Hsing-ti *Xingdi* Sing.
66 D3 Hsing-t'ien *Xingtian* Fukien
42 C3 Hsing-tien *Xingdian* Kiangsu
66 C3 Hsing-ts'un *Xingcun* Fukien
34 C4 Hsing-ts'un *Xingcun* Shant.
35 F3 Hsing-ts'un *Xingcun* Shant.
10 F4 Hsing-tung-chen *Xingdongzhen* Heilung.
70 D2 Hsing-tzu *Xingzi* Kiangsi
79 C1 Hsing-tzu *Xingzi* Kwangt.
87 E3 Hsing-wen *Xingwen* Szech.
54 E3 Hsing-yang *Xingyang* Honan
Hsin-hai-lien *see* **Lien-yün-kang**
27 F2 Hsin-hao-t'e *Xinhaote* In. Mong.
51 E4 Hsin-ho *Xinhe* Chek.
31 C6 Hsin-ho *Xinhe* Hopeh
31 E4 Hsin-ho *Xinhe* Hopeh
82 D5 Hsin-ho *Xinhe* Kwangsi
35 E3 Hsin-ho *Xinhe* Shant.
102 C2 Hsin-ho *Xinhe* Sink.
47 E5 Hsin-ho-chuang *Xinhezhuang* Anhwei
55 E2 Hsin-hsiang *Xinxiang* Honan
67 E5 Hsin-hsien *Xinxian* Fukien
55 F6 Hsin-hsien *Xinxian* Honan
31 E6 Hsin-hsien *Xinxian* Hopeh
38 D3 Hsin-hsien *Xinxian* Shansi
34 A3 Hsin-hsien *Xinxian* Shant.
43 D3 Hsin-hsing *Xinxing* Kiangsu
43 E2 Hsin-hsing *Xinxing* Kiangsu
14 C3 Hsin-hsing *Xinxing* Kirin
15 I5 Hsin-hsing *Xinxing* Kirin
15 J4 Hsin-hsing *Xinxing* Kirin
23 E5 Hsin-hsing *Xinxing* Kirin
78 A4 Hsin-hsing *Xinxing* Kwangt.
78 B4 Hsin-hsing *Xinxing* Kwangt.
79 C2 Hsin-hsing *Xinxing* Kwangt.
35 E3 Hsin-hsing *Xinxing* Shant.
46 C3 Hsin-hsing-chi *Xinxingji* Anhwei
102 H1 Hsin-hu *Xinhu* Sink.
74 D4 Hsin-hua *Xinhua* Hunan
26 B4 Hsin-hua *Xinhua* In. Mong.
98 E2 Hsin-hua *Xinhua* Kansu
82 C3 Hsin-hua *Xinhua* Kwangsi
119 B3 Hsin-hua *Xinhua* Taiwan
119 B4 Hsin-hua *Xinhua* Taiwan
43 D1 Hsin-huai Ho *Xinhuai He* (river) Kiangsu
75 B4 Hsin-huang *Xinhuang* Hunan
75 B4 **Hsin-huang Tung Autonomous Hsien** Hunan
Hsin-huang T'ung-tsu Tzu-chih-hsien *see* **Hsin-huang Tung Autonomous Hsien**
79 C2 Hsin-hui *Xinhui* Kwangt.
18 C2 Hsin-hui *Xinhui* Liao.
78 B2 Hsin-i *Xinyi* Kwangt.
39 C4 Hsin-i *Xinyi* Shansi
118 B3 Hsin-i *Xinyi* Taiwan
119 C3 Hsin-i *Xinyi* Taiwan
26 C5 Hsi-ni-chen *Xinizhen* In. Mong.
22 D2 Hsi-ni-ch'i *Xiniqi* Heilung.
43 D1 Hsin-i Ho *Xinyi He* (river) Kiangsu
22 D3 Hsi-ni-ho-hsi *Xinihexi* Heilung.
22 D3 Hsi-ni-ho-tung *Xinihetong* Heilung.
42 C1 Hsin-i Hsien *Xinyi Xian* Kiangsu
86 D3 Hsi-ning *Xining* Szech.
107 G2 Hsi-ning *Xining* Tsing.
Hsi-ning - city plan *see* **Page 140**
114 C3 Hsi-ning-pao *Xiningbao* Ningsia
71 B6 Hsi-niu *Xiniu* Kiangsi
114 C1 Hsi-ni-wu-su *Xiniwusu* Ningsia
114 C2 Hsi-ni-wu-su *Xiniwusu* Ningsia
43 F4 Hsin-k'ai-ho *Xinkaihe* Kiangsu
19 F3 Hsin-k'ai-ho *Xinkaihe* Liao.
14 D4 Hsin-k'ai Ho *Xinkai He* (river) Kirin
23 E5 Hsin-k'ai Ho *Xinkai He* (river) Kirin
74 F2 Hsin-k'ai-t'ang *Xinkaitang* Hunan
70 C4 Hsin-kan *Xingan* Kiangsi
47 E5 Hsin-kang *Xingang* Anhwei
38 D2 Hsin-kao *Xingao* Shansi
Hsin-kao Shan *see* **Yü Shan**
22 D3 Hsin-k'en-t'i *Xinkendi* Heilung.
Hsinking *see* **Ch'ang-ch'un**
103 E2 Hsin-ko-erh *Xingeer* Sink.
67 C4 Hsin-k'ou *Xinkou* Fukien
59 F4 Hsin-kou *Xingou* Hupeh
59 F5 Hsin-kou *Xingou* Hupeh
38 D3 Hsin-k'ou *Xinkou* Shansi
102 H1 Hsin-kuang *Xinguang* Sink.
38 D2 Hsin-kuang-wu *Xinguangwu* Shansi
31 C6 Hsin-lei-t'ou *Xinleitou* Hopeh
14 C2 Hsin-li *Xinli* Kirin
15 G3 Hsin-li *Xinli* Kirin
23 E5 Hsin-li *Xinli* Kirin
78 B3 Hsin-liao Tao *Xinliao Dao* (island) Kwangt.
10 C2 Hsin-lin *Xinlin* Heilung.
23 C6 Hsin-lin *Xinlin* Liao.
10 D2 Hsin-li-t'un *Xinlitun* Heilung.
14 A5 Hsin-li-t'un *Xinlitun* Kirin
23 D6 Hsin-li-t'un *Xinlitun* Kirin
19 F2 Hsin-li-t'un *Xinlitun* Liao.
91 F4 Hsin-liu *Xinliu* Kwei.
14 D3 Hsin-li-yao *Xinliyao* Kirin
30 F4 Hsin-lo *Xinluo* Hopeh
31 B5 Hsin-lo *Xinluo* Hopeh
31 B5 Hsin-lo Hsien *Xinluo Xian* Hopeh
31 B5 Hsin-lo Hsien *Xinluo Xian* Hopeh
86 B2 Hsin-lu-hai *Xinluhai* Szech.
67 E5 Hsin-lung *Xinlong* Fukien
86 C2 Hsin-lung *Xinlong* Szech.
14 C3 Hsin-lung-shan *Xinlongshan* Kirin
50 C4 Hsin-lu-wan *Xinluwan* Chek.
46 D3 Hsin-ma-ch'iao *Xinmaqiao* Anhwei
27 H2 Hsin-miao *Xinmiao* In. Mong.
14 E2 Hsin-miao *Xinmiao* Kirin
10 D3 Hsin-min *Xinmin* Heilung.
19 F3 Hsin-min *Xinmin* Liao.
86 D3 Hsin-min *Xinmin* Szech.
62 F1 Hsin-min-chen *Xinminzhen* Shensi
62 F5 Hsin-min-chieh *Xinminjie* Shensi
Hsin-ming *see* **Hua-te**
98 C2 Hsin-min-pao *Xinminbao* Kansu
18 D2 Hsin-min-ts'un *Xinmincun* Liao.
19 G3 Hsin-min-t'un *Xinmintun* Liao.
75 C5 Hsin-ning *Xinning* Hunan
37 D3 Hsin-o-ts'un *Xinecun* Heilung.
43 D1 Hsin-pa *Xinba* Kiangsu

111 E3 Hsin-pa *Xinba* Tibet
Hsin-pa-erh-hu Tso-ch'i *see* New Barga East Banner
Hsin-pa-erh-hu Yu-ch'i *see* New Barga West Banner
30 B3 Hsin-pao *Xinbao* Hopeh
30 C3 Hsin-pao-an *Xinbaoan* Hopeh
27 E3 Hsin-pao-li-ko *Xinbaolige* In. Mong.
22 C3 Hsin-pao-li-ko-tung *Xinbaoligedong* Heilung.
119 B4 Hsin-p'i *Xinpi* Taiwan
19 I3 Hsin-pin *Xinbin* Liao.
94 C3 Hsin-p'ing *Xinping* Yun.
38 F1 Hsin-p'ing-pao *Xinpingbao* Shansi
30 E1 Hsin-po *Xinbo* Hopeh
63 B7 Hsin-p'u *Xinpu* Shensi
63 C7 Hsin-p'u *Xinpu* Shensi
118 B2 Hsin-pu *Xinbu* Taiwan
118 C2 Hsin-p'u *Xinpu* Taiwan
51 E2 Hsin-p'u-yen *Xinpuyan* Chek.
75 D4 Hsin-shao Hsien *Xinshao Xian* Hunan
118 C3 Hsin-she *Xinshe* Taiwan
15 G5 Hsin-sheng *Xinsheng* Kirin
118 B2 Hsin-sheng *Xinsheng* Taiwan
34 B2 Hsin-sheng-tien *Xinshengdian* Shant.
10 D2 Hsin-sheng-ts'un *Xinshengcun* Heilung.
51 D2 Hsin-shih *Xinshi* Chek.
74 F3 Hsin-shih *Xinshi* Hunan
75 E5 Hsin-shih *Xinshi* Hunan
75 F4 Hsin-shih *Xinshi* Hunan
43 E3 Hsin-shih *Xinshi* Kiangsu
119 B3 Hsin-shih *Xinshi* Taiwan
87 D3 Hsin-shih-chen *Xinshizhen* Szech.
86 D3 Hsin-shih-pa *Xinshiba* Szech.
43 E1 Hsin-shih-ts'un *Xinshicun* Kiangsu
42 C1 Hsin-shu Ho *Xinshu He* (river) Kiangsu
39 B5 Hsin-shui Ho *Xinshui He* (river) Shansi
99 G4 Hsin-ssu *Xinsi* Kansu
51 E2 Hsin-tai *Xindai* Chek.
34 C4 Hsin-t'ai *Xintai* Shant.
19 G2 Hsin-t'ai-tzu *Xintaizi* Liao.
58 B4 Hsin-t'ang *Xintang* Hupeh
79 C2 Hsin-t'ang *Xintang* Kwangt.
70 C2 Hsin-t'ang-p'u *Xintangpu* Kiangsi
59 F4 Hsin-t'an-k'ou *Xintankou* Hupeh
59 G5 Hsin-t'an-p'u *Xintanpu* Hupeh
19 H5 Hsin Tao *Xin Dao* (island) Liao.
Hsin-teng *see* Ch'eng-yang
59 F5 Hsin-t'i *Xinti* Hupeh
83 H4 Hsin-ti *Xindi* Kwangsi
18 C2 Hsin-ti *Xindi* Liao.
67 D6 Hsin-tien *Xindian* Fukien
10 C2 Hsin-t'ien *Xintian* Heilung.
11 D5 Hsin-tien *Xindian* Heilung.
23 F4 Hsin-tien *Xindian* Heilung.
54 D4 Hsin-tien *Xindian* Honan
54 D5 Hsin-tien *Xindian* Honan
31 B6 Hsin-tien *Xindian* Hopeh
75 E6 Hsin-t'ien *Xintian* Hunan
59 F5 Hsin-tien *Xindian* Hupeh
99 F4 Hsin-tien *Xindian* Kansu
70 B4 Hsin-t'ien *Xintian* Kiangsi
70 B4 Hsin-tien *Xindian* Kiangsi
71 C6 Hsin-t'ien *Xintian* Kiangsi
42 C1 Hsin-tien *Xindian* Kiangsu
91 D4 Hsin-tien *Xiandian* Kwei.
39 D5 Hsin-tien *Xindian* Shansi
34 B2 Hsin-tien *Xindian* Shant.
34 C2 Hsin-tien *Xindian* Shant.
34 D2 Hsin-tien *Xindian* Shant.
34 D3 Hsin-tien *Xindian* Shant.
118 C2 Hsin-tien *Xindian* Taiwan
95 D3 Hsin-tien *Xindian* Yun.
74 B4 Hsin-tien-p'ing *Xindianping* Hunan
46 C4 Hsin-tien-pu *Xindianbu* Anhwei
75 D4 Hsin-t'ien-p'u *Xintianpu* Hunan
30 F3 Hsin-tien-tzu *Xindianzi* Hopeh
87 G2 Hsin-tien-tzu *Xindianzi* Szech.
55 F5 Hsin-ts'ai *Xincai* Honan
51 D2 Hsin-ts'ang *Xincang* Chek.
79 D2 Hsin-tso-t'ang *Xinzuotang* Kwangt.
Hsin-ts'un *see* T'ung-ch'uan
83 F3 Hsin-ts'un *Xincun* Kwangsi
78 A4 Hsin-ts'un *Xincun* Kwangt.
38 C3 Hsin-ts'un *Xincun* Shansi
46 B4 Hsin-ts'un-chi *Xincunji* Anhwei
83 H3 Hsin-tu *Xindu* Kwangsi
87 E2 Hsin-tu *Xindu* Szech.
86 C2 Hsin-tu-ch'iao *Xinduqiao* Szech.
99 F3 Hsin-t'un-ch'uan *Xintunchuan* Kansu
67 E5 Hsin-tung-chang *Xindongzhang* Fukien
43 D3 Hsin-t'ung-yang-yün Ho *Xintongyangyun He* (river) Kiangsu
34 C4 Hsin-wen Hsien *Xinwen Xian* Shant.
51 D4 Hsin-wo *Xinwo* Chek.
118 C2 Hsin-wu *Xinwu* Taiwan
55 F5 Hsin-yang *Xinyang* Honan
99 G4 Hsin-yang-chen *Xinyangzhen* Kansu
55 F4 Hsin-yang Hsien *Xinyang Xian* Honan
43 E2 Hsin-yang Kang *Xinyang Gang* (river) Kiangsu
54 D5 Hsin-yeh *Xinye* Honan
70 E3 Hsin-ying *Xinying* Kiangsi
78 A4 Hsin-ying *Xinying* Kwangt.
114 C3 Hsin-ying *Xinying* Ningsia
119 B3 Hsin-ying *Xinying* Taiwan
67 C6 Hsin-yü *Xinyu* Fukien
70 B4 Hsin-yü *Xinyu* Kiangsi
82 C4 Hsin-yü *Xinyu* Kwangsi
83 F3 Hsin-yü *Xinyu* Kwangsi
83 G3 Hsin-yü *Xinyu* Kwangsi
83 G5 Hsin-yü *Xinyu* Kwangsi
83 H2 Hsin-yü *Xinyu* Kwangsi
83 H5 Hsin-yü *Xinyu* Kwangsi
102 C2 Hsin-yüan *Xinyuan* Sink.
119 B4 Hsin-yüan *Xinyuan* Taiwan
107 F2 Hsin-yüan *Xinyuan* Tsing.
38 E3 Hsi-p'an *Xipan* Shansi
31 B5 Hsi-pao-shui *Xibaoshui* Hopeh
19 G2 Hsi-p'ao-tzu *Xipaozi* (lake) Liao.
38 C3 Hsi-pao-yü *Xibaoyu* Shansi
15 H4 Hsi-pei-ch'a *Xibeicha* Kirin
14 B3 Hsi-pei-hua *Xibeihua* Kirin
23 D5 Hsi-pei-hua *Xibeihua* Kirin
58 D3 Hsi-pei-k'ou *Xibeikou* Hupeh
50 C4 Hsi-p'ing *Xiping* Chek.
67 C5 Hsi-p'ing *Xiping* Fukien
54 C4 Hsi-p'ing *Xiping* Honan
55 E4 Hsi-p'ing *Xiping* Honan
82 B3 Hsi-p'ing *Xiping* Kwangsi
39 D6 Hsi-p'ing *Xiping* Shansi
22 C3 Hsi-po-erh-t'u *Xiboertu* Heilung.
31 A5 Hsi-po-p'o *Xibopo* Hopeh
47 E5 Hsi-pu *Xibu* Anhwei
67 C7 Hsi-pu *Xibu* Fukien
30 F3 Hsi-p'u-ts'un *Xipucun* Hopeh
94 C4 Hsi-sa *Xisa* Yun.
27 H1 Hsi-sang-ao-huo-no-mu *Xisangaohuonuomu* In. Mong.
46 D4 Hsi-san-shih-li-tien *Xisanshilidian* Anhwei
18 E5 Hsi-san-t'ai *Xisantai* Liao.
70 C3 Hsi-shan *Xishan* Kiangsi
31 C4 Hsi-shan-chuang *Xishanzhuang* Hopeh
Hsi-shan-tsui *see* Wu-la-t'e-ch'ien-ch'i
63 B8 Hsi-shen-pa *Xishenba* Shensi
43 E4 Hsi-shih-ch'iao *Xishiqiao* Kiangsu
31 A7 Hsi-shu *Xishu* Hopeh
31 B6 Hsi-shu *Xishu* Hopeh
34 D2 Hsi-shuang-ho *Xishuanghe* Shant.
Hsi-shuang-pan-na T'ai-tsu Tzu-chih-chou *see* Hsi-shuang-pan-na Thai Autonomous District
94 C4 Hsi-shuang-pan-na Thai Autonomous District Yun.
59 H4 Hsi-shui *Xishui* Hupeh
54 C4 Hsi Shui *Xi Shui* (river) Honan
59 H4 Hsi Shui *Xi Shui* (river) Hupeh
91 D2 Hsi-shui Hsien *Xishui Xian* Kwei.
46 D3 Hsi-ssu-p'o *Xisipo* Anhwei
46 C3 Hsi-ssu-p'u *Xisipu* Anhwei
31 A7 Hsi-ta *Xida* Hopeh
31 A7 Hsi-ta *Xida* Hopeh
110 C3 Hsi-t'ai *Xitai* Tibet
106 C2 Hsi-t'ai-chi-nai-erh Hu *Xitaijinaier Hu* (lake) Tsing.
102 H1 Hsi-ta-kou *Xidagou* Sink.
67 C7 Hsi-t'an *Xitan* Fukien
51 D2 Hsi-t'ang *Xitang* Chek.
47 C5 Hsi-t'ang-ch'ih *Xitangchi* Anhwei
114 C2 Hsi-ta-t'an *Xidatan* Ningsia
18 D3 Hsi-ta-ying-tzu *Xidayingzi* Liao.
86 D3 Hsi-te Hsien *Xide Xian* Szech.
102 I1 Hsi-ti *Xidi* Sink.
110 B2 Hsi-ti *Xidi* Tibet
50 C2 Hsi-t'iao Ch'i *Xitiao Qi* (river) Chek.
106 D2 Hsi-t'ieh-shan *Xitieshan* Tsing.
51 E3 Hsi-tien *Xidian* Chek.
50 C2 Hsi-t'ien-mu Shan *Xitianmu Shan* (mt) Chek.
102 B3 Hsi-ti-la *Xidila* Sink.
43 F3 Hsi-t'ing *Xiting* Kiangsu
31 E4 Hsi-ti-t'ou *Xiditou* Hopeh
87 G2 Hsi-t'o-chen *Xituozhen* Szech.
67 C5 Hsi-t'ou *Xitou* Fukien
70 C3 Hsi-t'ou *Xitou* Kiangsi
26 C4 Hsi-tou-p'u *Xidoupu* In. Mong.
110 C2 Hsi-tsang Kao-yüan *Xizang Gaoyuan* (plat) Tibet
54 C3 Hsi-ts'un *Xicun* Honan
75 E5 Hsi-tu *Xidu* Hunan
14 B2 Hsi-tu-erh-chi *Xiduerji* Kirin
23 D5 Hsi-tu-erh-chi *Xiduerji* Kirin
43 E4 Hsi-tung-t'ing Shan *Xidongting Shan* (mt) Kiangsu
18 C3 Hsi-tzu *Xizi* Liao.
74 C4 Hsiu-ch'i-k'ou *Xiuqikou* Hunan
10 C1 Hsiu-feng *Xiufeng* Heilung.
83 G3 Hsiu-jen *Xiuren* Kwangsi
106 D3 Hsiu-kou *Xiugou* Tsing.
106 D3 Hsiu-kou-kuo-le Ho *Xiugouguole He* (river) Tsing.
106 D3 Hsiu-kou-tu-k'ou *Xiugoudukou* Tsing.
119 C3 Hsiu-ku Ch'i *Xiugu Qi* (river) Taiwan
118 C3 Hsiu-ku-luan Shan *Xiuguluan Shan* (mt) Taiwan
118 C2 Hsiu-lin *Xiulin* Taiwan
107 E4 Hsiu-ma-ssu *Xiumasi* Tsing.
107 E4 Hsiu-ma-t'an *Xiumatan* Tsing.
55 F5 Hsiung-chai *Xiongzhai* Honan
86 C2 Hsiung-chi-ling *Xiongjiling* Szech.
54 C3 Hsiung-erh Shan *Xionger Shan* (mts) Honan
30 B3 Hsiung-erh Shan *Xionger Shan* (mts) Hopeh
31 D4 Hsiung-hsien *Xiongxian* Hopeh
59 E4 Hsiung-k'ou *Xiongkou* Hupeh
47 E6 Hsiung-lu *Xionglu* Anhwei
67 C7 Hsiung-ti Yü *Xiongdi Yu* (islet) Fukien
71 E4 Hsiung-ts'un *Xiongcun* Kiangsi
19 F4 Hsiung-yüeh-ch'eng *Xiongyuecheng* Liao.
47 E7 Hsiu-ning *Xiuning* Anhwei
83 E3 Hsiuo-huan Chiang *Xiaohuan Jiang* (river) Kwangsi
87 G3 Hsiu-shan *Xiushan* Szech.
70 B2 Hsiu-shui *Xiushui* Kiangsi
70 C2 Hsiu Shui *Xiu Shui* (river) Kiangsi
90 A4 Hsiu-shui-hai-tzu *Xiushuihaizi* Kwei.
19 G2 Hsiu-shui Ho *Xiushui He* (river) Liao.
19 G2 Hsiu-shui-ho-tzu *Xiushuihezi* Liao.
102 D3 Hsiu-tang *Xiudang* Sink.
70 C4 Hsiu-ts'ai-pu *Xiucaibu* Kiangsi
91 D4 Hsiu-wen *Xiuwen* Kwei.
54 E2 Hsiu-wu *Xiuwu* Honan
19 G4 Hsiu-yen *Xiuyan* Liao.
78 B3 Hsiu-ying *Xiuying* Kwangt.
46 D4 Hsi-wang-chi *Xiwangji* Anhwei
30 B3 Hsi-wan-pao *Xiwanbao* Hopeh
30 C3 Hsi-wan-tzu *Xiwanzi* Hopeh
18 C2 Hsi-wo-p'u *Xiwopu* Liao.
51 E3 Hsi-wu *Xiwu* Chek.
22 C3 Hsi-wu-chu-erh *Xiwuzhuer* Heilung.
Hsi-wu-chu-mu-ch'in Ch'i *see* West Ujumuchin Banner
22 D2 Hsi-wu-li-t'un *Xiwulitun* Heilung.
27 F2 Hsi-ya-la-huo-tuo-chia *Xiyalahuoduojia* In. Mong.
66 D4 Hsi-yang *Xiyang* Fukien
14 G4 Hsi-yang *Xiyang* Kirin
38 E4 Hsi-yang *Xiyang* Shansi
46 C3 Hsi-yang-chi *Xiyangji* Anhwei
82 B3 Hsi-yang Chiang *Xiyang Jiang* (river) Kwangsi
95 E4 Hsi-yang-chieh *Xiyangjie* Yun.
66 F4 Hsi-yang Tao *Xiyang Dao* (island) Fukien
83 E4 Hsi-yen *Xiyan* Kwangsi
38 E3 Hsi-yen *Xiyan* Shansi
103 E2 Hsi-yen-ch'ih *Xiyanchi* Sink.
75 C5 Hsi-yen-shih *Xiyanshi* Hunan
39 E5 Hsi-ying *Xiying* Shansi
34 C3 Hsi-ying *Xiying* Shant.
66 F4 Hsi-yin Tao *Xiyin Dao* (island) Fukien
31 B6 Hsi-yin-ts'un *Xiyincun* Hopeh
35 E2 Hsi-yu *Xiyou* Shant.
47 E6 Hsüan-ch'eng *Xuancheng* Anhwei
43 D3 Hsüan-chia-p'u *Xuanjiapu* Kiangsu
75 E4 Hsüan-chou *Xuanzhou* Hunan
58 B4 Hsüan-en *Xuanen* Hupeh
70 B4 Hsüan-feng *Xuanfeng* Kiangsi
87 F2 Hsüan-han *Xuanhan* Szech.
114 C3 Hsüan-ho-pao *Xuanhebao* Ningsia
30 C3 Hsüan-hua *Xuanhua* Hopeh
59 G3 Hsüan-hua-tien *Xuanhuadian* Hupeh
38 D3 Hsüan-kang *Xuangang* Shansi
91 F4 Hsüan-tung *Xuandong* Kwei.
91 E4 Hsüan-wei *Xuanwei* Kwei.
95 E2 Hsüan-wei *Xuanwei* Yun.
55 G4 Hsüan-wu *Xuanwu* Honan
55 E3 Hsü-ch'ang *Xuchang* Honan
55 G2 Hsü-chen *Xuzhen* Honan
34 B4 Hsü-ch'eng *Xucheng* Shant.
47 C5 Hsü-chi *Xuji* Anhwei
47 C6 Hsü-chia *Xujia* Anhwei
118 A3 Hsü-chia *Xujia* Taiwan
47 C6 Hsü-chia-ch'iao *Xujiaqiao* Anhwei
63 C7 Hsü-chia-miao *Xujiamiao* Shensi
91 F3 Hsü-chia-pa *Xujiaba* Kwei.
70 D2 Hsü-chia-pu *Xujiabu* Kiangsi
63 B7 Hsü-chia-p'ung *Xujiaping* Shensi
35 E4 Hsü-chia-ta-ts'un *Xujiadacun* Shant.
35 F2 Hsü-chia-tien *Xujiadian* Shant.
70 B3 Hsü-chia-tu *Xujiadu* Kiangsi
95 D3 Hsü-chia-tu *Xujiadu* Yun.
19 F4 Hsü-chia-t'un *Xujiatun* Liao.
75 F6 Hsü-chia-tung *Xujiadong* Hunan
11 C5 Hsü-chia-wei-tzu *Xujiaweizi* Heilung.
42 B1 Hsü-chou *Xuzhou* Kiangsu
34 C4 Hsü-chuang *Xuzhuang* Shant.
34 C5 Hsüeh-ch'eng *Xuecheng* Shant.
86 D2 Hsüeh-ch'eng *Xuecheng* Szech.
58 C3 Hsüeh-chia-p'ing *Xuejiaping* Hupeh
35 F4 Hsüeh-chia-tao *Xuejiadao* Shant.
54 B3 Hsüeh-chia-ying *Xuejiaying* Honan
119 B3 Hsüeh-chung *Xuezhong* Taiwan
35 F3 Hsüeh-fang *Xuefang* Shant.
42 C2 Hsüeh-feng *Xuefeng* Kiangsu
74 D3 Hsüeh-feng Shan *Xuefeng Shan* (mts) Hunan
111 D4 Hsüeh-hsia *Xuexia* Tibet
55 H3 Hsüeh-hu *Xuehu* Honan
111 E3 Hsüeh-k'a *Xueka* Tibet
47 E7 Hsüeh-k'eng-k'ou *Xuekengkou* Anhwei
51 D5 Hsüeh-k'ou *Xuekou* Chek.
39 C5 Hsüeh-kuan *Xueguan* Shansi
38 D2 Hsüeh-k'uo-lun *Xuekuolun* Shansi
58 D3 Hsüeh-p'ing *Xueping* Hupeh
43 D4 Hsüeh-pu *Xuebu* Kiangsu
118 C2 Hsüeh Shan *Xue Shan* (mt) Taiwan
10 E3 Hsüeh-shui-wen *Xueshuiwen* Heilung.
54 E3 Hsüeh-tien *Xuedian* Honan
55 E3 Hsüeh-tien *Xuedian* Honan
51 E3 Hsüeh-tou Shan *Xuedou Shan* (mt) Chek.
34 C3 Hsüeh-yeh-chuang *Xueyezhuang* Shant.
43 E4 Hsüeh-yen-ch'iao *Xueyanqiao* Kiangsu
119 B4 Hsü-hai *Xuhai* Taiwan
110 B2 Hsü-hei-no *Xuheinuo* Tibet
47 C6 Hsü-ho *Xuhe* Anhwei
14 E5 Hsü-ho *Xuhe* Kirin
42 C2 Hsü-i *Xuyi* Kiangsu
30 F4 Hsü-ko-chuang *Xugezhuang* Hopeh
43 D1 Hsü-kou *Xugou* Kiangsu
39 D4 Hsü-kou *Xugou* Shansi
59 G4 Hsü-ku *Xugu* Hupeh
22 E2 Hsü-kuang *Xuguang* Heilung.
42 C2 Hsü-liu *Xuliu* Kiangsu
35 E4 Hsü-meng *Xumeng* Shant.
38 C2 Hsün-chen *Xunzhen* Shansi
83 G2 Hsün Chiang *Xun Jiang* (river) Kwangsi
83 G4 Hsün Chiang *Xun Jiang* (river) Kwangsi
58 D3 Hsün-chia-ya *Xunjiaya* Hupeh
58 D3 Hsün-chien-ssu *Xunjiansi* Hupeh
59 F3 Hsün-chien-ssu *Xunjiansi* Hupeh
62 E3 Hsün-chien-ssu *Xunjiansi* Shensi
63 F6 Hsün-chien-ssu *Xunjiansi* Shensi
95 D4 Hsün-chien-szu *Xunjiansi* Yun.
10 E3 Hsün-ho *Xunhe* Heilung.
63 D7 Hsün Ho *Xun He* (river) Shensi
63 E7 Hsün Ho *Xun He* (river) Shensi
55 F2 Hsün-hsien *Xunxian* Honan
Hsün-hua Sa-la-tsu Tzu-chih-hsien *see* Hsün-hua Salar Autonomous Hsien
63 D5 Hsün-i *Xunyi* Shensi
107 F3 Hsün-jih-ssu *Xunrisi* Tsing.
Hsün-k'o *see* Ch'i-k'o
10 E3 Hsün-k'o Hsien *Xunke Xian* Heilung.
55 F3 Hsün-mu-k'ou *Xunmukou* Honan
35 H2 Hsün-shan-so *Xunshansuo* Shant.
95 D3 Hsün-tien *Xundian* Yun.
71 C7 Hsün-wu *Xunwu* Kiangsi
63 E8 Hsün-yang *Xunyang* Shensi
63 D7 Hsün-yang-pa *Xunyangba* Shensi
38 E1 Hsü-pao *Xubao* Shansi
74 C4 Hsü-p'u *Xupu* Hunan
74 C4 Hsü-p'u *Xupu* Hunan
43 E4 Hsü-p'u *Xupu* Kiangsu
98 D2 Hsü-san-wan *Xusanwan* Kansu
43 D4 Hsü-she *Xushe* Kiangsu
66 D3 Hsü-shih *Xushi* Fukien
43 E4 Hsü-shih *Xushi* Kiangsu
55 E3 Hsü-shui *Xushui* Honan
31 C4 Hsü-shui *Xushui* Hopeh
74 C4 Hsü Shui *Xu Shui* (river) Hunan
42 C1 Hsü-t'ang *Xutang* Kiangsu
118 B3 Hsü-ts'o-liao *Xucuoliao* Taiwan
47 E6 Hsü-ts'un *Xucun* Anhwei
51 D2 Hsü-ts'un *Xucun* Chek.
70 E2 Hsü-ts'un *Xucun* Kiangsi
78 B3 Hsü-wen *Xuwen* Kwangt.
43 D1 Hsü-yü *Xuyu* Kiangsu
87 E3 Hsü-yung *Xuyong* Szech.
67 C5 Hua-an *Huaan* Fukien
98 E2 Hua-chai-tzu *Huazhaizi* Kansu
79 C2 Hua-ch'eng *Huacheng* Kwangt.
79 D1 Hua-ch'eng *Huacheng* Kwangt.
46 B4 Hua-chi *Huaji* Anhwei
51 D3 Hua-ch'i *Huaqi* Chek.
71 B4 Hua-ch'i *Huaqi* Kiangsi
91 D4 Hua-ch'i *Huaqi* Kwei.
91 D4 Hua-ch'i *Huaqi* Kwei.
14 F3 Hua-chia *Huajia* Kirin
99 G4 Hua-chia-ling *Huajialing* Kansu
75 D6 Hua-chiang *Huajiang* Hunan
83 G2 Hua-chiang *Huajiang* Kwangsi
90 C5 Hua-chiang *Huajiang* Kwei.
50 B5 Hua-ch'iao *Huaqiao* Chek.
51 E4 Hua-ch'iao *Huaqiao* Chek.
66 C3 Hua-ch'iao *Huaqiao* Fukien
66 D3 Hua-ch'iao *Huaqiao* Fukien
74 C4 Hua-ch'iao *Huaqiao* Hunan
74 D4 Hua-ch'iao *Huaqiao* Hunan
75 D5 Hua-ch'iao *Huaqiao* Hunan
75 F5 Hua-ch'iao *Huaqiao* Hunan
70 E3 Hua-ch'iao *Huaqiao* Kiangsi
70 E4 Hua-ch'iao *Huaqiao* Kiangsi
91 F3 Hua-ch'iao *Huaqiao* Kwei.
91 G4 Hua-ch'iao *Huaqiao* Kwei.
87 F2 Hua-ch'iao *Huaqiao* Szech.
75 E6 Hua-ch'iao-shih *Huaqiaoshi* Hunan
14 B3 Hua-chieh *Huajie* Kirin
23 D5 Hua-chieh *Huajie* Kirin
19 I3 Hua-chien-tzu *Huajianzi* Liao.
Hua-ch'ih *see* Jou-yüan-ch'eng-tzu
99 H3 Hua-ch'ih Hsien *Huachi Xian* Kansu
91 D2 Hua-ch'iu *Huaqiu* Kwei.
78 B3 Hua-chou *Huazhou* Kwangt.
90 C4 Hua-ch'u *Huachu* Kwei.
Hua-ch'uan *see* Yüeh-lai
55 G5 Hua-chuang *Huazhuang* Honan
11 F4 Hua-ch'uan Hsien *Huachuan Xian* Heilung.
42 C1 Hua-chung *Huazhong* Kiangsu
39 C6 Hua-feng *Huafeng* Shansi
34 C4 Hua-feng *Huafeng* Shant.
98 C1 Hua-hai *Huahai* Kansu
55 F2 Hua Hsien *Hua Xian* Honan
79 C2 Hua-hsien *Huaxian* Kwangt.
63 E6 Hua-hsien *Huaxian* Shensi
119 A3 Hua Hsü *Hua Xu* (island) Taiwan
27 G2 Hua-hu-shu *Huahushu* In. Mong.
43 D2 Huai-an *Huaian* Kiangsu
30 B3 Huai-an-chen *Huaianzhen* Hopeh
30 B3 Huai-an Hsien *Huaian Xian* Hopeh
30 B3 Huai-an Hsien *Huaian Xian* Hopeh
87 E2 Huai-chen *Huaizhen* Szech.
79 C2 Huai-chi *Huaiji* Kwangt.
83 E3 Huai-ch'ün *Huaiqun* Kwangsi
71 B4 Huai-chung *Huaizhong* Kiangsi
55 G5 Huai-feng-chi *Huaifengji* Honan
46 D4 Huai Ho *Huai He* (river) Anhwei
55 F5 Huai Ho *Huai He* (river) Honan
31 B6 Huai Ho *Huai He* (river) Hopeh
74 B4 Huai-hua Hsien *Huaihua Xian* Hunan
38 E2 Huai-jen *Huaiyan* Shansi
34 C2 Huai-jen *Huairen* Shant.
30 D3 Huai-jou *Huairou* Hopeh
10 D1 Huai-jou-chan *Huairouzhan* Heilung.
30 C3 Huai-lai Hsien *Huailai Xian* Hopeh
30 C3 Huai-lai Hsien *Huailai Xian* Hopeh
47 D5 Huai-lin *Huailin* Anhwei
46 D4 Huai-nan *Huainan* Anhwei
67 C5 Huai-nan *Huainan* Fukien
47 C6 Huai-ning Hsien *Huaining Xian* Anhwei
62 E5 Huai-pai *Huaibai* Shensi
46 C3 Huai-pei *Huaibei* Anhwei
55 G5 Huai-pin Hsien *Huaibin Xian* Honan
62 D5 Huai-shu-chuang *Huaishuzhuang* Shensi
42 C2 Huai-shu Ho *Huaishu He* (river) Kiangsu
23 F6 Huai-te *Huaide* Kirin
14 E4 Huai-te-chen *Huaidezhen* Kirin
23 F6 Huai-te-chen *Huaidezhen* Kirin
14 E4 Huai-te Hsien *Huaide Xian* Kirin
55 G4 Huai-tien *Huaidian* Honan
106 E2 Huai-t'ou-t'a-la *Huaitoutala* Tsing.
70 E3 Huai-wang Shan *Huaiwang Shan* (mts) Kiangsi
63 C6 Huai-ya *Huaiya* Shensi
55 F4 Huai-yang *Huaiyang* Honan
Huai-yin *see* Ch'ing-chiang
43 D3 Huai-yin *Huaiyin* Kiangsu
43 D2 Huai-yin Hsien *Huaiyin Xian* Kiangsu
43 D2 Huai-yin Ti-ch'ü *Huaiyin Diqu* Kiangsu
46 D4 Huai-yüan *Huaiyuan* Anhwei
83 E3 Huai-yüan *Huaiyuan* Kwangsi
86 D2 Huai-yüan *Huaiyuan* Szech.
70 E3 Huai-yü-shan *Huaiyushan* Kiangsi
74 E2 Hua-jung *Huarong* Hunan
47 D5 Hua-lan *Hualan* Anhwei
34 B3 Hua-lan-tien *Hualandian* Shant.
91 E3 Hua-li *Huali* Kwei.
63 E8 Hua-li *Huali* Shensi
118 C3 Hua-lien *Hualian* Taiwan
118 C3 Hua-lien Hsien *Hualian Xian* Taiwan
70 C3 Hua-lin *Hualin* Kiangsi
Hua-lung *see* Pa-yen
Hua-lung Hui-tsu Tzu-chih-hsien *see* Hua-lung Hui Autonomous Hsien
11 F4 Hua-ma *Huama* Heilung.
75 E4 Hua-men-lou *Huamenlou* Hunan
11 F4 Hua-nan *Huanan* Heilung.
75 F5 Huan-ch'i *Huanqi* Hunan
82 E3 Huan-chiang *Huanjiang* Kwangsi
99 H3 Huan Chiang *Huan Jiang* (river) Kansu
34 A4 Huang-an *Huangan* Shant.
71 B5 Huang-ao *Huangao* Kiangsi
51 C3 Huang-chai *Huangzhai* Chek.
38 D3 Huang-chai *Huangzhai* Shansi
59 G3 Huang-chan *Huangzhan* Hupeh
35 F2 Huang-ch'eng-chi *Huangchengji* Shant.
66 E4 Huang-ch'i *Huangqi* Fukien
58 E2 Huang-chi *Huangji* Hupeh
70 C3 Huang-ch'i *Huangqi* Kiangsi
42 B1 Huang-chi *Huangji* Kiangsu
42 C2 Huang-chi *Huangji* Kiangsu
34 C2 Huang-chia *Huangjia* Shant.
43 E2 Huang-chia-chien *Huangjiajian* Kiangsu
43 E3 Huang-ch'iao *Huangqiao* Kiangsu
91 E3 Huang-chia-pa *Huangjiaba* Kwei.
75 E5 Huang-chia-tu *Huangjiadu* Hunan
27 E4 Huang-ch'i Hai *Huangqi Hai* (lake) In. Mong.
66 C3 Huang-ch'i-k'ou *Huangqikou* Fukien
83 E3 Huang-chin *Huangjin* Kwangsi
74 C4 Huang-chin-ching *Huangjinjing* Hunan
43 F4 Huang-ching *Huangjing* Kiangsu
87 E3 Huang-ching-kou *Huangjinggou* Szech.
66 E3 Huang-chin-k'eng Kang *Huangjinkeng Gang* (mt) Fukien
70 D3 Huang-chin-pu *Huangjinbu* Kiangsi
74 B4 Huang-chin-yao *Huangjinyao* Hunan
27 G3 Huang-ch'i-ta-ying-tzu *Huangqidayingzi* In. Mong.
59 G4 Huang-chou *Huangzhou* Hupeh
78 B4 Huang-chu *Huangzhu* Kwangt.
47 E7 Huang-ch'uan *Huangchuan* Anhwei
55 G5 Huang-ch'uan *Huangchuan* Honan
30 E4 Huang-chuang *Huangzhuang* Hopeh
34 C3 Huang-chuang *Huangzhuang* Shant.
114 C2 Huang-ch'ü-ch'iao *Huangquqiao* Ningsia
43 D3 Huang-chüeh-ch'iao *Huangjueqiao* Kiangsu
58 E2 Huang-ch'ü-ho *Huangquhe* Hupeh
Huang-chung *see* Lu-sha-erh
107 G2 Huang-chung Hsien *Huangzhong Xian* Tsing.
75 F4 Huang-feng-ch'iao *Huangfengqiao* Hunan
106 C2 Huang-feng-shan *Huangfengshan* Tsing.
Huang Hai *see* Yellow Sea
55 F3 Huang Ho *Huang He* Honan
99 G3 Huang Ho *Huang He* Kansu
114 C2 Huang Ho *Huang He* Ningsia
26 B5 Huang Ho *Huang He* (river) In. Mong.
39 B5 Huang Ho *Huang He* (river) Shansi
107 G3 Huang Ho *Huang He* (river) Tsing.
38 C2 Huang Ho *Huang He* Shansi
34 A4 Huang Ho *Huang He* Shant.
34 B4 Huang-ho *Huanghe* Shant.
34 D2 Huang Ho *Huang He* Shant.
35 D2 Huang Ho-k'ou *Huang Hekou* (est.) Shant.
34 B2 Huang-ho-ya *Huangheya* Shant.
107 F3 Huang-ho-yen *Huangheyan* Tsing.
35 F2 Huang-hsien *Huangxian* Shant.
51 C2 Huang-hu *Huanghu* Chek.
31 E5 Huang-hua *Huanghua* Hopeh
58 D3 Huang-hua *Huanghua* Hupeh
30 D3 Huang-hua-ch'eng *Huanghuacheng* Hopeh
74 F3 Huang-hua-shih *Huanghuashi* Hunan
19 G4 Huang-hua-tien *Huanghuadian* Liao.
35 E4 Huang-hua-tien *Huanghuadian* Shant.
47 D6 Huang-i Hu *Huangyi Hu* (lake) Anhwei
70 B3 Huang-kang *Huanggang* Kiangsi
70 C4 Huang-kang *Huanggang* Kiangsi
79 C2 Huang-kang *Huanggang* Kwangt.
79 E2 Huang-kang *Huanggang* Kwangt.
34 B5 Huang-kang-chi *Huanggangji* Shant.
59 G4 Huang-kang Hsien *Huanggang Xian* Hupeh
59 H4 Huang-kang-miao *Huanggangmiao* Hupeh
66 C3 Huang-kang Shan *Huanggang Shan* (mt) Fukien
70 A4 Huang-kang Shan *Huanggang Shan* (mt) Kiangsi
66 C3 Huang-k'eng *Huangkeng* Fukien
46 C2 Huang-k'ou *Huangkou* Anhwei
74 F2 Huang-k'ou *Huangkou* Hunan
106 B1 Huang-kua-liang *Huanggualiang* Tsing.
83 H2 Huang-kuan *Huangguan* Kwangsi
63 B8 Huang-kuan-ling *Huangguanling* Shensi
47 D5 Huang-ku-cha *Huangguzha* Anhwei
102 H1 Huang-kung *Huanggong* Sink.
90 C5 Huang-kuo-shu *Huangguoshu* Kwei.
30 E2 Huang-ku-t'un *Huanggutun* Hopeh
46 B4 Huang-lan *Huanglan* Anhwei
87 D3 Huang-lang *Huanglang* Szech.
70 C2 Huang-lao-men *Huanglaomen* Kiangsi
43 D4 Huang-li *Huangli* Kiangsu
58 C3 Huang-liang-p'ing *Huangliangping* Hupeh
63 C6 Huang-li-chen *Huanglizhen* Shensi
94 B3 Huang-lien-p'u *Huanglianpu* Yun.
46 B3 Huang-ling *Huangling* Anhwei
63 E5 Huang-ling *Huangling* Shensi
59 G4 Huang-ling-chi *Huanglingji* Hupeh
58 D4 Huang-ling-miao *Huanglingmiao* Hupeh
78 A4 Huang-liu *Huangliu* Kwangt.
59 E3 Huang-lung *Huanglong* Hupeh
71 C6 Huang-lung *Huanglong* Kiangsi
63 E5 Huang-lung Hsien *Huanglong Xian* Shensi
55 F3 Huang-lung-ssu *Huanglongsi* Honan
58 C2 Huang-lung-t'an *Huanglongtan* Hupeh
54 D4 Huang-lu-tien *Huangludian* Honan
70 B3 Huang-mao *Huangmao* Kiangsi
83 F4 Huang-mao *Huangmao* Kwangsi
74 C4 Huang-mao-wan *Huangmaowan* Hunan
59 H4 Huang-mei *Huangmei* Hupeh
47 E5 Huang-mu-tu *Huangmudu* Anhwei
107 G3 Huang-nan Tibetan Autonomous District Tsing.
Huang-nan Tsang-tsu Tzu-chih-chou *see* Huang-nan Tibetan Autonomous District
39 E5 Huang-nien *Huangnian* Shansi
95 E3 Huang-ni-ho *Haungnihe* Yun.
47 D5 Huang-ni-ho *Huangnihe* Anhwei
14 F5 Huang-ni-ho *Huangnihe* Kirin
15 H4 Huang-ni-ho *Huangnihe* Kirin
47 C6 Huang-ni-kang *Huangnigang* Anhwei
75 E5 Huang-ni-t'ang *Huangnitang* Hunan
63 B6 Huang-niu-p'u *Huangniupu* Shensi
63 B8 Huang-pa-i *Huangbayi* Shensi
91 G2 Huang-pan *Huangban* Kwei.
63 E5 Huang-pao *Huangbao* Shensi
54 D2 Huang-pei-chiao *Huangbeijiao* Honan
59 G4 Huang-p'i *Huangpi* Hupeh
91 E4 Huang-p'ing Hsien *Huangping Xian* Kwei.
70 E3 Huang-po *Huangbo* Kiangsi
71 C5 Huang-p'o *Huangpo* Kiangsi
71 D4 Huang-p'o *Huangpo* Kiangsi
14 G6 Huang-po *Huangbo* Kirin
78 B3 Huang-p'o *Huangpo* Kwangt.
19 H3 Huang-po-yü *Huangboyu* Liao.
79 C2 Huang-p'u *Huangpu* Kwangt.
43 F4 Huang-p'u Chiang *Huangpu Jiang* (river) Kiangsu
43 F4 Huang Sha *Huang Sha* (island) Kiangsu
70 C3 Huang-sha *Huangsha* Kiangsi
70 B3 Huang-sha-ch'iao *Huangshaqiao* Kiangsi
74 F3 Huang-sha-chieh *Huangshajie* Hunan
83 H1 Huang-sha-ho *Huangshahe* Kwangsi
70 B3 Huang-sha-kang *Huangshagang* Kiangsi
51 D3 Huang-shan *Huangshan* Chek.
47 E6 Huang Shan *Huang Shan* (mt) Anhwei
35 H3 Huang-shan *Huangshan* Shant.
102 I1 Huang-shan-chieh *Huangshanjie* Sink.
35 F2 Huang-shan-kuan *Huangshanguan* Shant.
55 F5 Huang-shan-p'o *Huangshanpo* Honan
58 E5 Huang-shan-t'ou *Huangshantou* Hupeh
75 E6 Huang-sha-pao *Huangshabao* Hunan
19 F3 Huang-sha-t'o *Huangshatuo* Liao.
87 D1 Huang-sheng-kuan *Huangshengguan* Szech.
59 H4 Huang-shih *Huangshi* Hupeh
31 B4 Huang-shih-k'ou *Huangshikou* Hopeh
71 C5 Huang-shih-kuan *Huangshiguan* Kiangsi
59 G4 Huang-shih Shih *Huangshi Shi* Hupeh
70 D4 Huang-shih-tu *Huangshidu* Kiangsi
71 D4 Huang Shui *Huang Shui* (river) Kiangsi
38 D2 Huang-shui Ho *Huangshui He* (river) Shansi
31 B6 Huang-ssu *Huangsi* Hopeh
34 B5 Huang-ssu *Huangsi* Shant.
15 H4 Huang-sung-tien *Huangsongdian* Kirin
43 E4 Huang-tai-chen *Huangdaizhen* Kiangsu
51 E3 Huang-t'an *Huangtan* Chek.
66 C4 Huang-t'an *Huangtan* Fukien
70 E2 Huang-t'an *Huangtan* Kiangsi
58 D3 Huang-t'an-chou *Huangtanzhou* Hupeh
43 D4 Huang-t'ang *Huangtang* Kiangsu
79 D2 Huang-t'ang *Huangtang* Kwangt.
59 G4 Huang-t'ang Hu *Huangtang Hu* (lake) Hupeh
67 B5 Huang-t'an Ho *Huangtan He* (river) Fukien
50 B4 Huang-t'an-k'ou *Huangtankou* Chek.
26 C5 Huang-t'ao-lao-kai *Huangtaolaogai* In. Mong.
51 F2 Huang-ta Yang *Huangda Yang* (sea) Chek.
30 F2 Huang-ti *Huangdi* Hopeh
18 D4 Huang-ti *Huangdi* Liao.
51 D4 Huang-t'ien *Huangtian* Chek.
75 D5 Huang-t'ien-p'u *Huangtianpu* Hunan
75 D4 Huang-t'ing-shih *Huangtingshi* Hunan
74 E3 Huang-ts'ai *Huangcai* Hunan
102 I1 Huang-ts'ao-hu *Huangcaohu* Sink.
102 H2 Huang-ts'ao-liang *Huangcaoliang* Sink.
94 C4 Huang-ts'ao-pa *Huangcaoba* Yun.
51 D3 Huang-tse *Huangze* Chek.
51 F2 Huang-tse Yang *Huangze Yang* (sea) Chek.
51 D4 Huang-ts'un *Huangcun* Chek.
30 D4 Huang-ts'un *Huangcun* Hopeh
83 G3 Huang-ts'un *Huangcun* Kwangsi
79 D2 Huang-ts'un *Huangcun* Kwangt.
83 H1 Huang-t'u-ching *Huangtujing* Kwangsi
19 G5 Huang-t'u-k'an *Huangtukan* Liao.
55 G6 Huang-tu-kang *Huangdugang* Honan
59 H3 Huang-t'u-kang *Huangtugang* Hupeh
75 C5 Huang-tu-k'eng *Huangdukeng* Hunan
30 F2 Huang-t'u-liang-tzu *Huangtuliangzi* Hopeh
74 F4 Huang-t'u-ling *Huangtuling* Hunan
19 F4 Huang-t'u-ling *Huangtuling* Liao.
35 E4 Huang-tun *Huangdun* Shant.
70 D4 Huang-t'ung *Huangtong* Kiangsi
46 D3 Huang-tun-miao *Huangdunmiao* Anhwei
90 B4 Huang-t'u-p'o *Huangtupo* Kwei.
75 D5 Huang-tu-p'u *Huangdupu* Hunan
74 D3 Huang-t'u-tien *Huangtudian* Hunan
43 F2 Huang-tzu Sha *Huangzi Sha* (shoal) Kiangsu
51 D2 Huang-wan *Huangwan* Chek.
83 F3 Huang-wan *Huangwan* Kwangsi
47 C5 Huang-wei-ho *Huangweihe* Anhwei
83 E6 Huang-wu *Huangwu* Kwangsi
51 C5 Huang-yang *Huangyang* Chek.
99 F3 Huang-yang-chen *Huangyangzhen* Kansu
75 D5 Huang-yang-ssu *Huangyangsi* Hunan
114 C2 Huang-yang-tan *Huangyangdan* Ningsia
83 H3 Huang-yao *Huangyao* Kwangsi
51 E4 Huang-yen *Huangyan* Chek.
43 D2 Huang-ying *Huangying* Kiangsu
107 G2 Huang-yüan *Huangyuan* Tsing.
58 C1 Huang-yün-p'u *Huangyunpu* Hupeh
99 H3 Huan-hsien *Huanxian* Kansu
119 B4 Huan-hsi Shan *Huanxi Shan* (mt) Taiwan
51 F2 Hua-niao Shan *Huaniao Shan* (island) *Chek.*
95 D3 Hua-nien *Huanian* Yun.
95 D3 Hua-ning *Huaning* Yun.
98 B1 Hua-niu-shan *Huaniushan* Kansu
19 I3 Huan-jen *Huanren* Liao.
42 A1 Huan-k'ou *Huankou* Kiangsu
51 E4 Huan-shan *Huanshan* Chek.
59 G3 Huan Shui *Huan Shui* (river) Hupeh
34 C3 Huan-t'ai-ch'eng *Huantaicheng* Shant.
34 D3 Huan-t'ai Hsien *Huantai Xian* Shant.
59 F3 Huan-t'an *Huantan* Hupeh
42 C1 Huan-tun-pu *Huandunbu* Kiangsu
38 D3 Hua-pei-t'un *Huabeitun* Shansi
30 D3 Hua-p'en *Huapen* Hopeh
14 G4 Hua-p'i-ch'ang *Huapichang* Kirin
10 D2 Hua-p'i-mi *Huapimi* Heilung.
58 B4 Hua-p'ing *Huaping* Hupeh
79 C1 Hua-p'ing *Huaping* Kwangt.
91 E2 Hua-p'ing *Huaping* Kwei.
94 C2 Hua-p'ing *Huaping* Yun.
50 B3 Hua-pu *Huabu* Chek.
Hua Shan *see* Ch'in-ling Shan-mo
42 A1 Hua-shan *Huashan* Kiangsu
15 G6 Hua-shan *Huashan* Kirin
63 F6 Hua Shan *Hua Shan* (mt) Shensi
30 B3 Hua-shao-ying *Huashaoying* Hopeh
74 E4 Hua-shih *Huashi* Hunan
43 E4 Hua-shih *Huashi* Kiangsu
82 E6 Hua-shih *Huashi* Kwangsi
107 F3 Hua-shih-hsia *Huashixia* Tsing.
15 H6 Hua-shu *Huashu* Kirin
102 I2 Hua-shu-lin *Huashulin* Sink.
15 H4 Hua-shu-lin-tzu *Huashulinzi* Kirin
39 C5 Hua-sung *Huasong* Shansi
86 D3 Hua-t'an *Huatan* Szech.
75 E6 Hua-t'ang-p'u *Huatangpu* Hunan
27 E4 Hua-te *Huade* In. Mong.
15 G5 Hua-tien *Huadian* Kirin
14 F6 Hua-tien-tzu *Huadianzi* Kirin
67 D5 Hua-t'ing *Huating* Fukien
99 H4 Hua-t'ing *Huating* Kansu
51 E3 Hua-ting Shan *Huading Shan* (mt) Chek.
106 B1 Hua-t'u-kou *Huatugou* Tsing.
14 C4 Hua-t'u-ku-la *Huatugula* Kirin
23 E6 Hua-t'u-ku-la *Huatugula* Kirin
19 E4 Hua-t'ung *Huatong* Liao.
19 G3 Hua-tzu *Huazi* Liao.
62 E3 Hua-tzu-p'ing *Huaziping* Shensi
75 C5 Hua-wan *Huawan* Hunan
94 B1 Hua-weng-p'ing *Huawengping* Yun.
47 C6 Hua-yang *Huayang* Anhwei
51 D3 Hua-yang *Huayang* Chek.
63 C7 Hua-yang-chen *Huayangzhen* Shensi
63 F6 Hua-yin *Huayin* Shensi
87 F2 Hua-ying Shan *Huaying Shan* (mt) Szech.
30 C3 Hua-yüan *Huayuan* Hopeh
74 B3 Hua-yüan *Huayuan* Hunan
59 F3 Hua-yüan *Huayuan* Hupeh
119 C4 Hua-yüan *Huayuan* Taiwan
42 C3 Hua-yüan-chü *Huayuanju* Kiangsu
19 F5 Hua-yüan-k'ou *Huayuankou* Liao.
39 C6 Hu-chang *Huzhang* Shansi
91 D4 Hu-ch'ao *Huchao* Kwei.
50 C3 Hu-chen *Huzhen* Chek.
51 D4 Hu-chen *Huzhen* Chek.
67 D5 Hu-ch'eng *Hucheng* Fukien
46 B3 Hu-chi *Huji* Anhwei
51 D3 Hu-ch'i *Huqi* Chek.
59 E3 Hu-chi *Huji* Hupeh
71 B5 Hu-ch'i *Huqi* Kiangsi
42 C2 Hu-chi *Huji* Kiangsu
43 E3 Hu-chi *Huji* Kiangsu
19 E3 Hu-chia *Hujia* Liao.

42 B1 Kuan-hu *Guanhu* Kiangsu
47 C7 Kuan-kang *Guangang* Anhwei
67 C6 Kuan-k'ou *Guankou* Fukien
59 H4 Kuan-k'ou *Guankou* Hupeh
63 D7 Kuan-k'ou *Guankou* Shensi
46 D4 Kuan-kou-chi *Guangouji* Anhwei
91 E2 K'uan-k'uo-pa *Kuankuoba* Kwei.
35 F2 Kuan-li *Guanli* Shant.
43 D4 Kuan-lin *Guanlin* Kiangsu
75 E5 Kuan-ling *Guanling* Hunan
90 C5 Kuan-ling Hsien *Guanling Xian* Kwei.
51 D4 Kuan-lu *Guanlu* Chek.
119 B4 Kuan-miao *Guanmiao* Taiwan
43 D1 Kuan-nan Hsien *Guannan Xian* Kiangsu
67 C6 Kuan-p'o *Guanpo* Fukien
54 B4 Kuan-p'o *Guanpo* Honan
71 A4 Kuan-p'o *Guanpo* Kiangsi
59 G5 Kuan-pu-ch'iao *Guanbuqiao* Hupeh
71 C4 Kuan-shan *Guanshan* Kiangsi
119 B3 Kuan Shan *Guan Shan* (mt) Taiwan
119 B3 Kuan-shan *Guanshan* Taiwan
119 C3 Kuan-shan *Guanshan* Taiwan
39 C4 Kuan-shang *Guanshang* Shansi
51 D5 Kuan-shan Tao *Guanshan Dao* (island) Chek.
19 H4 Kuan-shui *Guanshui* Liao.
90 C5 Kuan-so *Guansuo* Kwei.
31 B7 Kuan-t'ai *Guantai* Hopeh
26 D5 K'uan-t'an *Kuantan* In. Mong.
74 E2 Kuan-tang *Guandang* Hunan
59 G5 Kuan-t'ang-i *Guantangyi* Hupeh
31 C7 Kuan-t'ao Hsien *Guantao Xian* Hopeh
31 C7 Kuan-t'ao Hsien *Guantao Xian* Hopeh
54 C3 Kuan-tao-k'ou *Guandaokou* Honan
30 D2 Kuan-ti *Guandi* Hopeh
15 I4 Kuan-ti *Guandi* Kirin
18 B2 Kuan-ti *Guandi* Liao.
46 E4 Kuan-tien *Guandian* Anhwei
71 B4 Kuan-t'ien *Guantian* Kiangsi
91 D2 Kuan-tien *Guantian* Kwei.
119 B3 Kuan-t'ien *Guantian* Taiwan
71 C5 K'uan-t'ien *Kuantian* Kiangsi
19 H4 K'uan-tien *Kuandian* Liao.
42 C1 Kuan-tien-chieh *Guandianjie* Kiangsu
58 C4 Kuan-tien-k'ou *Guandiankou* Hupeh
75 E5 Kuan-ti-miao *Guandimiao* Hunan
47 C5 Kuan-t'ing *Guanting* Anhwei
55 E3 Kuan-t'ing *Guanting* Honan
30 C3 Kuan-t'ing *Guanting* Hopeh
99 G5 Kuan-t'ing *Guanting* Kansu
107 H3 Kuan-t'ing *Guanting* Tsing.
95 D4 Kuan-t'ing *Guanting* Yun.
30 C3 Kuan-t'ing Shui-k'u *Guanting Shuiku* (res.) Hopeh
74 C2 Kuan-ti-p'ing *Guandiping* Hunan
38 C4 Kuan-ti Shan *Guandi Shan* (mt) Shansi
67 E4 Kuan-t'ou *Guantou* Fukien
39 B5 Kuan-t'ou *Guantou* Shansi
38 D3 Kuan-ts'en Shan *Guancen Shan* (mt) Shansi
38 D2 Kuan-ts'en Shan *Guancen Shan* (mts) Shansi
74 F3 Kuan-tu *Guandu* Hunan
58 C3 Kuan-tu *Guandu* Hupeh
79 C1 Kuan-tu *Guandu* Kwangt.
91 D2 Kuan-tu *Guandu* Kwei.
87 G2 Kuan-tu *Guandu* Szech.
58 C3 Kuan-tu-k'ou *Guandukou* Hupeh
91 G5 Kuan-tung *Guandong* Kwei.
18 B2 Kuan-tung-p'u-tzu *Guandongpuzi* Liao.
27 E4 Kuan-t'un-ying *Guantunying* In. Mong.
119 B3 Kuan-tzu-ling *Guanziling* Taiwan
90 B5 Kuan-tzu-yao *Guanziyao* Kwei.
39 C6 Kuan-wang-miao *Guanwangmiao* Shansi
66 F3 Kuan-yang *Guanyang* Fukien
83 H2 Kuan-yang *Guanyang* Kwangsi
58 B2 Kuan-ya-tzu *Guanyazi* Hupeh
63 E8 Kuan-ya-tzu *Guanyazi* Shensi
83 G2 Kuan-yin *Guanyin* Kwangsi
118 C1 Kuan-yin *Guanyin* Taiwan
87 E3 Kuan-yin-chen *Guanyinzhen* Szech.
74 C4 Kuan-yin-chiao *Guanyinjiao* Hunan
75 E5 Kuan-yin-ch'iao *Guanyinqiao* Hunan
63 B6 Kuan-yin-shan *Guanyinshan* Shensi
58 D3 Kuan-yin-ssu *Guanyinsi* Hupeh
63 B7 Kuan-yin-ssu *Guanyinsi* Shensi
75 D5 Kuan-yin-t'an *Guanyintan* Hunan
54 C3 Kuan-yin-t'ang *Guanyintang* Honan
55 E3 Kuan-yin-t'ang *Guanyintang* Honan
63 D8 Kuan-yin-t'ang *Guanyintang* Shensi
78 B2 Kuan-yü *Guanyu* Kwangt.
118 C2 Kuan-yüan *Guanyuan* Taiwan
47 B5 Kuan-yüeh-miao *Guanyuemiao* Anhwei
43 D1 Kuan-yün Hsien *Guanyun Xian* Kiangsu
42 C3 Kua-pu *Guabu* Kiangsu
51 D4 Kua-ts'ang Shan *Guacang Shan* (mt) Chek.
51 D4 Kua-ts'ang Shan *Guacang Shan* (mts) Chek.
Kucha *see* K'u-ch'e
83 F3 Ku-chai *Guzhai* Kwangsi
74 B3 Ku-chang *Guzhang* Hunan
102 C2 K'u-ch'e *Kuche* Sink.
46 D3 Ku-chen *Guzhen* Anhwei
39 D6 Ku-chen *Guzhen* Shansi
46 B3 Ku-ch'eng *Gucheng* Anhwei
46 D4 Ku-ch'eng *Gucheng* Anhwei
67 B5 Ku-ch'eng *Gucheng* Fukien
10 C4 Ku-ch'eng *Gucheng* Heilung.
55 F4 Ku-ch'eng *Gucheng* Honan
31 C4 Ku-ch'eng *Gucheng* Hopeh
31 D6 Ku-ch'eng *Gucheng* Hopeh
58 D2 Ku-ch'eng *Gucheng* Hupeh
26 D4 Ku-ch'eng *Gucheng* In. Mong.
99 F3 Ku-ch'eng *Gucheng* Kansu
70 F3 Ku-ch'eng *Gucheng* Kiangsi
71 B5 Ku-ch'eng *Gucheng* Kiangsi
42 C3 Ku-ch'eng *Gucheng* Kiangsu
83 H3 Ku-ch'eng *Gucheng* Kwangsi
38 E1 Ku-ch'eng *Gucheng* Shansi
39 B6 Ku-ch'eng *Gucheng* Shansi
39 C6 Ku-ch'eng *Gucheng* Shansi
39 D5 Ku-ch'eng *Gucheng* Shansi
34 A4 Ku-ch'eng *Gucheng* Shant.
87 E1 Ku-ch'eng *Gucheng* Szech.
31 C6 Ku-ch'eng Hsien *Gucheng Xian* Hopeh
31 C6 Ku-ch'eng Hsien *Gucheng Xian* Hopeh
42 C4 Ku-ch'eng Hu *Gucheng Hu* (lake) Kiangsu
71 D4 Ku-ch'eng-kang *Guchenggang* Kiangsi
Kuchengtze *see* Ch'i-t'ai
55 F4 Ku-ch'iang *Guqiang* Honan
71 B4 Ku-chiang *Gujiang* Kiangsi
82 A3 Ku-chiang *Gujiang* Kwangsi
46 C4 Ku-ch'iao *Guqiao* Anhwei
91 D4 Ku-chiao *Gujiao* Kwei.
38 D4 Ku-chiao *Gujiao* Shansi
39 E6 Ku-chiao *Gujiao* Shansi
70 E3 K'u-ch'iao *Kuqiao* Kiangsi
14 E4 Ku-chia-tzu *Gujiazi* Kirin
23 F6 Ku-chia-tzu *Gujiazi* Kirin
23 C5 Ku-chih-lin *Guzhilin* Liao.
10 C1 Ku-ch'i-ku *Guqigu* Heilung.
91 F5 Ku-chou *Guzhou* Kwei.
71 D5 Ku-chu *Guzhu* Kiangsi
79 D2 Ku-chu *Guzhu* Kwangt.
63 B6 Ku-ch'uan *Guchuan* Shensi
87 G2 Ku-chün-pa *Gujunba* Szech.
46 C4 Kuei-chi *Guiji* Anhwei
70 E3 Kuei-ch'i *Guiqi* Kiangsi
83 H4 Kuei Chiang *Gui Jiang* (river) Kwangsi
47 D6 Kuei-ch'ih Hsien *Guichi Xian* Anhwei
95 D1 Kuei-hsi *Guixi* Yun.
95 E2 K'uei-hsiang *Kuixiang* Yun.
83 F4 Kuei-hsien *Guixian* Kwangsi
66 C4 Kuei-hua *Guihua* Fukien
10 C3 K'uei-le Ho *Kuile He* (river) Heilung.
22 F3 K'uei-le Ho *Kuile He* (river) Heilung.
83 G2 Kuei-lin *Guilin* Kwangsi
83 H3 Kuei-ling *Guiling* Kwangsi
23 D4 Kuei-liu-ho *Guiliuhe* Kirin
23 F5 Kuei-liu Ho *Guiliu He* (river) Kirin
118 C2 Kuei-luan Tao *Guiluan Dao* (island) Taiwan
51 D3 Kuei-men *Guimen* Chek.
34 C4 Kuei-meng Ting *Guimeng Ding* (mt) Shant.
Kuei-nan *see* Mang-la
107 G3 Kuei-nan Hsien *Guinan Xian* Tsing.
83 G4 Kuei-p'ing *Guiping* Kwangsi
95 D3 Kuei-shan *Guishan* Yun.
11 F5 K'uei-shan *Kuishan* Heilung.
118 C2 Kuei-shan Tao *Guishan Dao* (island) Taiwan
75 E6 Kuei Shui *Gui Shui* (river) Hunan
103 F2 K'uei-su *Kuisu* Sink.
Kuei-sui *see* Hu-ho-hao-t'e
82 E5 Kuei-t'ai *Guitai* Kwangsi
79 D2 K'uei-t'an *Kuitan* Kwangt.
Kuei-te *see* Ho-yin
34 B3 Kuei-te *Guide* Shant.
107 G2 Kuei-te Hsien *Guide Xian* Tsing.
62 E2 Kuei-te-pao *Guidebao* Shensi
18 C3 K'uei-te-su *Kuidesu* Liao.
91 E4 Kuei-ting *Guiding* Kwei.
79 C1 Kuei-t'ou *Guitou* Kwangt.
102 D1 K'uei-t'un *Kuitun* Sink.
102 H1 K'uei-t'un *Kuitun* Sink.
75 F6 Kuei-tung *Guidong* Hunan
102 H1 K'uei-t'un Ho *Kuitun He* (river) Sink.
78 B2 Kuei-tzu *Guizi* Kwangt.
82 E6 Kuei-wei *Guiwei* Kwangsi
75 E6 Kuei-yang *Guiyang* Hunan
91 D4 Kuei-yang *Guiyang* Kwei.
Kuei-yang - city plan *see* Page 137
82 C4 K'uei-yü *Kuiyu* Kwangsi
79 D2 K'uei-yung *Kuiyong* Kwangt.
27 F3 K'u-erh-ch'a-kan No-erh *Kuerchagan Nuoer* (lake) In. Mong.
102 D2 K'u-erh-ch'u *Kuerchu* Sink.
103 D2 K'u-erh-le *Kuerle* Sink.
107 E2 Ku-erh-pan-an-ko-erh *Guerbanangeer* Tsing.
27 G2 Ku-erh-pan-t'ao-pu-ko *Guerbantaobuge* In. Mong.
Ku-erh-pan-t'ung-ku-t'e Sha-mo *Guerbantonggute Shamo* (desert) Sink.
103 D1 Ku-erh-pan-t'ung-ku-t'e Sha-mo *Guerbantonggute Shamo* (desert) Sink.
26 B3 Ku-erh-pan-wu-lan Ching *Guerbanwulan Jing* (spring) In. Mong.
10 E3 K'u-erh-pin Ho *Kuerbin He* (river) Heilung.
10 B2 K'u-erh-pin-ying-lin-ts'un *Kuerbinyinglincun* Heilung.
102 C1 Ku-erh-t'u *Guertu* Sink.
Kueshan Islands *see* Chiu-shan Lieh-tao
66 D4 Ku-fen *Gufen* Fukien
47 D5 Ku-ho *Guhe* Anhwei
71 D5 Ku-hou *Guhou* Kiangsi
79 E2 Ku-hsiang *Guxiang* Kwangt.
54 C3 Ku-hsien *Guxian* Honan
55 E5 Ku-hsien *Guxian* Honan
70 C3 Ku-hsien *Guxian* Kiangsi
71 C4 Ku-hsien *Guxian* Kiangsi
39 C5 Ku-hsien *Guxian* Shansi
39 D5 Ku-hsien *Guxian* Shansi
39 D6 Ku-hsien *Guxian* Shansi
35 F3 Ku-hsien *Guxian* Shant.
35 G2 Ku-hsien *Guxian* Shant.
47 C4 Ku-hsien-ssu *Guxiansi* Anhwei
70 D2 Ku-hsien-tu *Guxiandu* Kiangsi
31 A7 Ku-hsin *Guxin* Hopeh
31 A7 Ku-hsin *Guxin* Hopeh
86 B3 Ku-hsüeh *Guxue* Szech.
67 E5 Ku-huai *Guhuai* Fukien
67 D5 Ku-i *Guyi* Fukien
83 F2 Ku-i *Guyi* Kwangsi
42 C2 Kui-jen *Guiren* Kiangsu
46 C3 Ku-jao-chi *Guraoji* Anhwei
90 C3 Ku-k'ai *Gukai* Kwei.
102 D3 K'u-kan *Kugan* Sink.
74 F3 Ku-kang *Gugang* Hunan
118 B3 Ku-k'eng *Gukeng* Taiwan
Kükong *see* Shao-kuan
66 D4 Ku-k'ou *Gukou* Fukien
102 B3 K'u-k'o-ya *Kukeya* Sink.
63 B6 Ku-kuan-chen *Guguanzhen* Shensi
34 B3 Ku-kuan-t'un *Guguantun* Shant.
Kuku Nor *see* Ch'ing-hai Hu
106 B3 K'u-k'u-shih-li-lai-k'en *Kukushililaiken* Tsing.
Kukushili *see* K'o-k'o-hsi-li Shan
51 D3 Ku-lai *Gulai* Chek.
102 D3 K'u-la-mu-le-k'o *Kulamuleke* Sink.
99 F3 Ku-lang *Gulang* Kansu
94 B2 Ku-lang *Gulang* Yun.
67 D6 Ku-lang-yü *Gulangyu* Fukien
114 B1 K'u-lan-t'u-miao *Kulantumiao* Ningsia
58 D4 Ku-lao-pei *Gulaobei* Hupeh
Kuldja *see* I-ning
67 C7 Ku-lei-t'ou *Guleitou* Fukien
91 D4 Ku-li *Guli* Kwei.
34 C4 Ku-li *Guli* Shant.
10 B1 Ku-lien *Gulian* Heilung.
22 E1 Ku-lien *Gulian* Heilung.
87 E3 Ku-lin *Gulin* Szech.
83 E4 Ku-ling *Guling* Kwangsi
87 G2 Ku-ling-chen *Gulingzhen* Szech.
34 A3 Ku-liu-shu *Guliushu* Shant.
86 B2 Ku-lo *Guluo* Szech.
110 C2 Ku-lo-kung-pa *Guluogongba* Tibet
54 E5 Ku-lou *Gulou* Honan
74 D3 Ku-lou *Gulou* Hunan
46 D4 Ku-lou-lan *Guloulan* Anhwei
103 F2 K'u-lu-k'o Kuo-le *Kuluke Guole* Sink.
103 E2 K'u-lu-k'o Shan *Kuluke Shan* (mts) Sink.
10 B2 Ku-lu-nai *Gulunai* Heilung.
14 B5 K'u-lun-chen *Kulunzhen* Kirin
23 D6 K'u-lun-chen *Kulunzhen* Kirin
14 B5 K'u-lun Ch'i *Kulun Qi* Kirin
11 C5 Ku-lung *Gulong* Heilung.
83 G4 Ku-lung *Gulong* Kwangsi
71 C5 Ku-lung-kang *Gulonggang* Kiangsi
26 D4 K'u-lun-t'u *Kuluntu* In. Mong.
106 C4 K'u-mao-lung-a-jih-la-tu-k'ou *Kumaolongariladukou* Tsing.
82 C4 Ku-mei *Gumei* Kwangsi
54 E5 Ku-miao *Gumiao* Honan
103 E2 K'u-mi-shih *Kumishi* Sink.
10 C3 K'u-mo-t'un *Kumotun* Heilung.
95 E4 Ku-mu *Gumu* Yun.
103 E2 K'u-mu-k'u-tu-k'o *Kumukuduke* Sink.
Kumul *see* Ha-mi
Kumush *see* K'u-mi-shih
102 H1 Ku-mu-ti *Gumudi* Sink.
103 D2 Ku-mu-ti *Gumudi* Sink.
82 D6 Kung-an *Gongan* Kwangsi
83 H3 Kung-an *Gongan* Kwangsi
58 E4 Kung-an Hsien *Gongan Xian* Hupeh
Kung-ch'ang *see* Lung-hsi
19 G3 Kung-ch'ang-ling *Gongchangling* Liao.
83 E6 Kung-ch'e *Gongche* Kwangsi
43 D4 K'ung-chen *Kongzhen* Kiangsu
34 C2 K'ung-chen *Kongzhen* Shant.
82 E5 Kung-cheng *Gongzheng* Kwangsi
83 G3 Kung-ch'eng *Gongcheng* Kwangsi
47 D5 K'ung-ch'eng *Kongcheng* Anhwei
70 C4 Kung-ch'i *Gongqi* Kiangsi
30 B3 K'ung-chia-chuang *Kungjiazhuang* Hopeh
19 G2 Kung-chia-fang *Gongjiafang* Liao.
26 B5 Kung-ch'ia-han *Gongqiahan* In. Mong.
86 C3 Kung-chia-ling *Gongjialing* Szech.
Kung-chiao *see* Mo-lo
111 F3 Kung-chiao *Gongjiao* Tibet
103 E2 K'ung-ch'iao Ho *Kongqiao He* (river) Sink.
111 F3 Kung-chiao Hsien *Gongjiao Xian* Tibet
55 F6 Kung-chia-p'eng *Gongjiapeng* Honan
31 C6 Kung-chia-t'ai *Gongjiatai* Hopeh
58 E3 K'ung-chia-wan *Kongjiawan* Hupeh
54 C3 Kung-ch'ien *Gongqian* Honan
23 B6 Kung-chih-keng *Gongzhigeng* Liao.
87 E3 Kung-ching *Gongjing* Szech.
102 H1 Kung-ch'ing-t'uan Nung-ch'ang *Gongqingtuan Nongchang* Sink.
103 D1 Kung-ch'ing-t'uan Nung-ch'ang *Gongqingtuan Nongchang* Sink.
26 E4 Kung-chi-t'ang *Gongjitang* In. Mong.
91 G4 Kung-chou *Gongzhou* Kwei.
67 C4 Kung-ch'uan *Gongchuan* Fukien
82 D4 Kung-ch'uan *Gongchuan* Kwangsi
14 E4 Kung-chu-ling *Gongzhuling* Kirin
110 B3 Kung-chu Ts'o *Gongzhu Cuo* (lake) Tibet
19 F2 Kung-chu-t'un *Gongzhutun* Liao.
71 C4 Kung-fang *Gongfang* Kiangsi
70 D4 K'ung-fang *Kongfang* Kiangsi
Kung-ha *see* Ni-le-k'o
Kung-ho *see* Ch'ia-pu-ch'ia
107 G2 Kung-ho Hsien *Gonghe Xian* Tsing.
14 D5 Kung-ho-lai *Gonghelai* Kirin
110 C3 Kung-hsieh-ya *Gongxieya* Tibet
54 D3 Kung Hsien *Gong Xian* Honan
87 E3 Kung-hsien *Gongxian* Szech.
14 B4 Kung-hsing-tang *Gongxingdang* Kirin
23 D6 Kung-hsing-tang *Gongxingdang* Kirin
30 B2 Kung-hui *Gonghui* Hopeh
83 H3 Kung-hui *Gonghui* Kwangsi
14 G6 Kung-i *Gongyi* Kirin
79 C2 Kung-i *Gongyi* Kwangt.
Kung-ka *see* Chi-hsiung
111 E3 Kung-k'a *Gongka* Tibet
111 D3 Kung-ka Hsien *Gongga Xian* Tibet
86 C3 Kung-ka Shan 7590 *Gongga Shan* (mt) Szech.
102 A3 Kung-ko-erh Shan *Gonggeer Shan* (mt) Sink.
83 F6 Kung-kuan *Gongguan* Kwangsi
78 B3 Kung-kuan *Gongguan* Kwangt.
118 B2 Kung-kuan *Gongguan* Taiwan
22 D2 Kung-k'u-li *Gongkuli* Heilung.
94 B3 Kung-kuo-ch'iao *Gongguoqiao* Yun.
26 D4 Kung-la-ma *Gonglama* In. Mong.
94 C3 Kung-lang *Gonglang* Yun.
34 C4 Kung-li *Gongli* Shant.
118 C1 Kung-liao *Gongliao* Taiwan
102 C2 Kung-liu *Gongliu* Sink.
59 H5 K'ung-lung *Konglong* Hupeh
107 G3 Kung-ma-ts'ang *Gongmacang* Tsing.
26 C4 Kung-miao-tzu *Gongmiaozi* In. Mong.
102 C2 Kung-nai-ssu-ch'ang *Gongnaisichang* Sink.
102 C2 Kung-nai-ssu Ho *Gongnaisi He* (river) Sink.
102 H2 Kung-nai-ssu Ho *Gongnaisi He* (river) Sink.
102 D2 Kung-nai-ssu-lin-ch'ang *Gongnaisilinchang* Sink.
102 H2 Kung-nai-ssu-lin-ch'ang *Gongnaisilinchang* Sink.
14 F2 Kung-p'eng-tzu *Gongpengzi* Kirin
14 G3 Kung-p'eng-tzu *Gongpengzi* Kirin
83 G2 Kung-p'ing *Gongping* Kwangsi
79 D2 Kung-p'ing *Gongping* Kwangt.
75 E5 Kung-p'ing-hsü *Gongpingxu* Hunan
98 C1 Kung-p'o-ch'üan *Gongpoquan* Kansu
Kung-pu-chiang-ta *see* Hsia-lung-hsiang
111 E3 Kung-pu-chiang-ta Hsien *Gongbujiangda Xian* Tibet
94 B2 Kung-shan *Gongshan* Yun.
95 D3 Kung-shan *Gongshan* Yun.
94 B2 Kung-shan Tulung-Nu Autonomous Hsien Yun.
Kung-shan Tu-lung-tsu Nu-tsu Tzu-chih-hsien *see* Kung-shan Tulung-Nu Autonomous Hsien
71 C6 Kung Shui *Gong Shui* (river) Kiangsi
87 G3 Kung-t'an *Gongtan* Szech.
87 E3 K'ung-t'an *Kongtan* Szech.
74 F2 Kung-t'ien *Gongtian* Hunan
46 D4 K'ung-tien *Kongdian* Anhwei
71 C7 K'ung-t'ien *Kongtian* Kiangsi
30 D4 Kung-ts'un *Gongcun* Hopeh
99 H4 K'ung-t'ung Shan *Kongtong Shan* (mt) Kansu
35 G2 K'ung-t'ung Tao *Kongtong Dao* (island) Shant.
63 E6 Kung-wang-ling *Gongwangling* Shensi
86 B2 Kung-ya *Gongya* Szech.
Kung-ya-ssu *see* Chieh-cha
18 C3 Kung-ying-tzu *Gongyingzi* Liao.
59 E2 Kun Ho *Gun He* (river) Hupeh
11 E4 K'un-lun-ch'i *Kunlunqi* Heilung.
83 E4 K'un-lun Kuan *Kunlun Guan* (pass) Kwangsi
102 B3 K'un-lun Shan *Kunlun Shan* (mts) Sink.
106 C3 K'un-lun Shan *Kunlun Shan* (mts) Tsing.
106 D3 K'un-lun Shan-k'ou *Kunlun Shankou* (pass) Tsing.
95 D3 K'un-ming *Kunming* Yun.
K'un-ming - city plan *see* Page 139
110 B3 K'un-mi-teng-li *Kunmidengli* Tibet
83 E2 Kun-pei *Gunbei* Kwangsi
110 A2 K'un-sa *Kunsa* Tibet
43 E4 K'un-shan *Kunshan* Kiangsu
22 D3 K'un-t'o-la *Kuntuola* Heilung.
23 C5 K'un-tu *Kundu* Liao.
27 F3 K'un-tui-ao-ssu *Kunduiaosi* In. Mong.
26 C4 K'un-tu-lun-chao *Kundulunzhao* In. Mong.
35 G2 K'un-yu Shan *Kunyou Shan* (mt) Shant.
111 F3 Kuo-cha *Guozha* Tibet
74 F2 Kuo-chen *Guozhen* Hunan
63 C6 Kuo-chen *Guozhen* Shensi
99 G3 Kuo-ch'eng-i *Guochengyi* Kansu
54 E5 Kuo-chi *Guoji* Honan
43 D1 Kuo-chi *Guoji* Kiangsu
14 F3 Kuo-chia *Guojia* Kirin
35 F3 Kuo-chia-chai *Guojiazhai* Shant.
99 G4 Kuo-chia-chen *Guojiazhen* Kansu
35 F3 Kuo-chia-chuang *Guojiazhuang* Shant.
70 D2 Kuo-ch'iao *Guoqiao* Kiangsi
38 E1 Kuo-chia-pao *Guojiabao* Shansi
14 E4 Kuo-chia-tien *Guojiadian* Kirin
23 F6 Kuo-chia-tien *Guojiadian* Kirin
35 F2 Kuo-chia-tien *Guojiadian* Shant.
30 E2 Kuo-chia-t'un *Guojiatun* Hopeh
43 E3 Kuo-chia-yüan *Guojiayuan* Kiangsu
51 F3 Kuo-chü *Guoju* Chek.
31 B5 Kuo-chuang *Guozhuang* Hopeh
43 D4 Kuo-chuang-miao *Guozhuangmiao* Kiangsu
27 E3 Kuo-erh-pen-ao-pao *Guoerbenaobao* In. Mong.
11 D4 Kuo-fu *Guofu* Heilung.
55 F3 Kuo Ho *Guo He* (river) Honan
118 B2 Kuo-hsing *Guoxing* Taiwan
82 D4 Kuo-hua *Guohua* Kwangsi
67 C6 Kuo-k'eng *Guokeng* Fukien
103 E2 K'uo-k'o-su *Kuokesu* Sink.
30 B3 Kuo-lei-chuang *Guoleizhuang* Hopeh
34 B4 Kuo-li-chi *Guoliji* Shant.
Kuo-lo Tsang-tsu Tzu-chih-chou *see* Ngolog Tibetan Autonomous District
54 B3 Kuo-lüeh-chen *Guoluezhen* Honan
55 G5 Kuo-lu-t'an *Guolutan* Honan
107 G3 Kuo-ma-ying *Guomaying* Tsing.
39 D4 Kuo-pao *Guobao* Shansi
102 C3 K'uo-shih-la-shih *Kuoshilashi* Sink.
14 G6 Kuo-sung *Guosong* Kirin
54 D5 Kuo-t'an *Guotan* Honan
39 D5 Kuo-tao *Guodao* Shansi
Kuo-te *see* P'ing-kuo
55 E3 Kuo-tien *Guodian* Honan
34 C3 Kuo-tien *Guodian* Shant.
34 A3 Kuo-tien-t'un *Guodiantun* Shant.
30 C3 Kuo-ts'un *Goucun* Hopeh
47 D6 Kuo-ts'un *Guocun* Anhwei
39 D5 Kuo-ts'un *Guocun* Shansi
34 C4 Kuo-tu *Guodu* Shant.
114 B2 K'uo-t'u-hu *Kuotuhu* Ningsia
46 C3 Kuo-yang *Guoyang* Anhwei
38 D3 Kuo-yang-chen *Guoyangzhen* Shansi
27 G3 Kuo-ying Mu-ch'ang *Guoying Muchang* In. Mong.
46 D4 Ku-p'ei *Gupei* Anhwei
47 B5 Ku-pei *Gubei* Anhwei
30 E3 Ku-pei-k'ou *Gubeikou* Hopeh
83 E4 Ku-p'eng *Gupeng* Kwangsi
42 B1 Ku-p'i *Gupi* Kiangsu
71 C6 Ku-p'o *Gupo* Kiangsi
82 D5 Ku-p'o *Gupo* Kwangsi
87 E3 Ku-po *Gubo* Szech.
118 A3 Ku-p'o Hsü *Gupo Xu* (island) Taiwan
75 D7 Ku-p'o Shan *Gupo Shan* (mt) Hunan
83 H3 Ku-p'o Shan *Gupo Shan* (mt) Kwangsi
26 C4 K'u-pu-ch'i Sha-mo *Kubuqi Shamo* (desert) In. Mong.
106 C3 K'u-sai Hu *Kusai Hu* (lake) Tsing.
51 D4 Ku-shan *Gushan* Chek.
70 B3 Ku-shan *Gushan* Kiangsi
18 C2 Ku-shan *Gushan* Liao.
19 F4 Ku-shan *Gushan* Liao.
19 G5 Ku-shan *Gushan* Liao.
38 E1 Ku-shan *Gushan* Shansi
34 B3 Ku-shan *Gushan* Shant.
62 F1 Ku-shan *Gushan* Shensi
107 H2 Ku-shan *Gushan* Tsing.
14 G5 Ku-shan-tzu *Gushanzi* Kirin
50 C4 Ku-shih *Gushi* Chek.
55 G5 Ku-shih *Gushi* Honan
70 B2 Ku-shih *Gushi* Kiangsi
63 E6 Ku-shih *Gushi* Shensi
55 G3 Ku-shu-chi *Gushuji* Honan
54 D3 Ku-shui *Gushui* Honan
79 C2 Ku-shui *Gushui* Kwangt.
103 F2 K'u-shui *Kushui* Sink.
98 B1 K'u-shui-ching *Kushuijing* Kansu
102 B3 K'u-ssu-la-fu *Kusilafu* Sink.
102 C1 K'u-ssu-t'ai *Kusitai* Sink.
10 E3 K'u-ssu-t'e *Kusite* Heilung.
87 E3 Ku-sung *Gusong* Szech.
67 C6 Ku-t'ang *Gutang* Fukien
38 F1 Ku-ta-t'un *Gudatun* Shansi
35 E3 Ku-t'i *Guti* Shant.
66 D4 Ku-t'ien *Gutian* Fukien
67 B5 Ku-t'ien *Gutian* Fukien
67 B5 Ku-t'ien *Gutian* Fukien
14 E3 Ku-tien *Gudian* Kirin
38 E1 Ku-tien *Gudian* Shansi
66 D4 Ku-t'ien Ch'i *Gutian Qi* (river) Fukien
71 B6 Ku-t'ing *Guting* Kiangsi
34 B5 Ku-t'ing *Guting* Shant.
38 E2 Ku-ting-ch'iao *Gudingqiao* Shansi
79 C2 Ku-tou Shan *Gudou Shan* (mt) Kwangt.
Kütsing *see* Ch'ü-ching
71 C4 Ku-ts'un *Gucun* Kiangsi
71 D5 Ku-ts'un *Gucun* Kiangsi
39 B6 Ku-ts'un *Gucun* Shansi
22 D3 K'u-tu-erh *Kuduer* Heilung.
39 C6 Ku-tui *Gudui* Shansi
91 E4 Ku-tung *Gudong* Kwei.
94 B3 Ku-tung *Gudong* Yun.
15 I5 Ku-tung Ho *Gudong He* (river) Kirin
119 B4 Ku-tzu-lun Shan *Guzilun Shan* (mt) Taiwan
50 C3 Ku-wan *Guwan* Chek.
Küwo *see* Ch'ü-wo
102 C3 K'u-ya-k'o *Kuyake* Sink.
55 F3 Ku-yang *Guyang* Honan
26 D4 Ku-yang *Guyang* In. Mong.
39 D5 Ku-yang *Guyang* Shansi
30 F4 Ku-yeh *Guye* Hopeh
26 D5 K'u-yeh Ho *Kuye He* (river) In. Mong.
62 F2 K'u-yeh Ho *Kuye He* (river) Shensi
Kuyi *see* Ku-i
10 C2 Ku-yüan *Guyuan* Heilung.
114 C3 Ku-yüan *Guyuan* Ningsia
30 C2 Ku-yüan Hsien *Guyuan Xian* Hopeh
35 E3 Ku-yüeh *Guyue* Shant.
98 B1 Ku-yü-men-kuan *Guyumenguan* (site) Kansu
94 B3 Ku-yung *Guyong* Yun.
19 G1 Ku-yü-shu *Guyushu* Liao.
Kwanghwa *see* Lao-ho-k'ou
Kwang-nan-fu *see* Ch'ü-ching
Kwangsi Chuang Autonomous Region *see* Pages 81-84
Kwangsin *see* Shang-jao
Kwangtseh *see* Kuang-tse
Kwangtung Province *see* Pages 77-80
Kwangyüan *see* Kuang-yüan
Kweichow Province *see* Pages 89-92
Kweihsien *see* Kuei-hsien
Kweihwa *see* Hu-ho-hao-t'e
Kweiki *see* Kuei-ch'i
Kwei Kiang *see* Kuei Chiang
Kweilin *see* Kuei-lin
Kweiping *see* Kuei-p'ing
Kweisui *see* Hu-ho-hao-t'e
Kweitch *see* Ho-yin
Kweiyang *see* Kuei-yang
Kwo Ho *see* Kuo Ho
Kwoteh *see* P'ing-kuo
Kwotsang Mountains *see* K'uo-ts'ang Shan
Kyerong *see* Chi-lung
Kyimdong *see* Chin-tung

Labrang *see* La-pu-leng
111 E3 La-chia-li *Lajiali* Tibet
107 G3 La-chia-ssu *Lajiasi* Tsing.
110 B2 La-chu-lung *Lazhulong* Tibet
110 C2 La-chung *Lazhong* Tibet
106 C4 La-chung-ko-yüeh *Lazhonggeyue* Tsing.
115 B4 Ladd Reef China Sea
15 H4 La-fa *Lafa* Kirin
10 C3 La-ha *Laha* Heilung.
22 F3 La-ha *Laha* Heilung.
95 D4 La-ha-ti *Lahadi* Yun.
111 E2 La-hsi-t'ang *Laxitang* Tibet
110 C2 La-hsiung Ts'o *Laxiung Cuo* (lake) Tibet
106 E4 La-hsiu-ssu *Laxiusi* Tsing.
46 E4 Lai-an *Laian* Anhwei
118 B3 Lai-chi *Laiji* Taiwan
66 D4 Lai-chou *Laizhou* Fukien
35 E2 Lai-chou Wan *Laizhou Wan* (bay) Shant.
58 B5 Lai-feng *Laifeng* Hupeh
35 F3 Lai-hsi-chan *Laixizhan* Shant.
35 F3 Lai-hsi Hsien *Laixi Xian* Shant.
119 B4 Lai-i *Laiyi* Taiwan
47 C6 Lai-pang *Laibang* Anhwei
83 F4 Lai-pin *Laibin* Kwangsi
35 G2 Lai-shan *Laishan* Shant.
30 C4 Lai-shui *Laishui* Hopeh
102 C2 La-i-su *Layisu* Sink.
71 C5 Lai-ts'un *Laicun* Kiangsi
82 D5 Lai-t'uan *Laituan* Kwangsi
34 C3 Lai-wu *Laiwu* Shant.
35 F3 Lai-yang *Laiyang* Shant.
35 F3 Lai-yang-chan *Laiyangzhan* Shant.
67 C5 Lai-yüan *Laiyuan* Fukien
55 F2 Lai-yüan *Laiyuan* Honan
30 B4 Lai-yüan *Laiyuan* Hopeh
39 D4 Lai-yüan *Lai Yuan* Shansi
82 E3 La-jen *Laren* Kwangsi
111 E3 La-ju *Laru* Tibet
110 C3 La-ka *Laga* Tibet
La-ka Ch'ih *see* Lan-chia Ts'o
110 C2 La-ka-la-pu Shan-k'ou *Lagalabu Shankou* (pass) Tibet
107 G3 La-kan *Lagan* Tsing.
111 F3 La-k'ang-ssu *Lakangsi* Tibet
110 C3 La-k'a Tsang-pu *Laka Zangbu* (river) Tibet
110 C2 La-k'o Hu *Lake Hu* (lake) Tibet
110 C3 La-kuo *Laguo* Tibet
19 H4 La-ku-shao *Lagushao* Liao.
82 E3 La-lang *Lalang* Kwangsi
14 F4 La-la-t'un *Lalatun* Kirin
82 E3 La-lieh *Lalie* Kwangsi
11 D5 La-lin *Lalin* Heilung.
11 D5 La-lin Ho *Lalin He* (river) Heilung.
11 D5 La-lin Ho *Lalin He* (river) Heilung.
14 E3 La-ma-huang *Lamahuang* Kirin
94 B2 La-ma-ti *Lamadi* Yun.
14 E4 La-ma-tien *Lamadian* Kirin
11 C4 La-ma-tien-tzu *Lamadianzi* Heilung.
18 C4 La-ma-tung *Lamadong* Liao.
26 D4 La-ma-wan *Lamawan* In. Mong.
14 B3 La-ma-ying-tzu *Lamayingzi* Kirin
23 D5 La-ma-ying-tzu *Lamayingzi* Kirin
38 C3 Lan-ch'eng *Lancheng* Shansi
34 C5 Lan-ch'eng *Lancheng* Shant.
47 D5 Lan-chi *Lanji* Anhwei
50 C3 Lan-ch'i *Lanqi* Chek.
59 H4 Lan-ch'i *Lanqi* Hupeh
50 C3 Lan Chiang *Lan Jiang* (river) Chek.
63 E6 Lan-ch'iao *Lanqiao* Shensi
110 B3 Lan-chia Ts'o *Lanjia Cuo* (lake) Tibet
67 B6 Lan-chia-tu *Lanjiadu* Fukien
99 F4 Lan-chou *Lanzhou* Kansu
Lan-chou - city plan *see* Page 135
47 F5 Lang-ch'i *Langqi* Anhwei
67 E4 Lang-ch'i *Langqi* Fukien
111 E3 Lang-chia *Langjia* Tibet
47 E6 Lang-ch'iao *Langqiao* Anhwei
43 F3 Lang-chia Sha *Langjia Sha* (shoal) Kiangsu
70 D2 Lang-ch'i-kang *Langqigang* Kiangsi
51 E4 Lang-chi Shan *Langji Shan* (island) Chek.
70 D4 Lang-chü *Langju* Kiangsi
Lang-ch'u Ho *see* Sutlej
87 E2 Lang-chung *Langzhong* Szech.
110 B2 Lang-chü-ts'a-ch'ü *Langjucaqu* Tibet
30 D4 Lang-fang *Langfang* Hopeh
22 D3 Lang-feng *Langfeng* Heilung.
58 D2 Lang-ho-tien *Langhedian* Hupeh
11 E4 Lang-hsiang *Langxiang* Heilung.
Lang-hsien *see* La-to
111 E3 Lang Hsien *Lang Xian* Tibet
102 B3 Lang-ju *Langru* Sink.
111 D3 Lang-ka *Langga* Tibet
51 F2 Lang-kang-shan Lieh-tao *Langgangshan Liedao* (islands) Chek.
111 D3 Lang-k'a-tzu *Langkazi* Tibet
74 F3 Lang-li-shih *Langlishi* Hunan
111 D3 Lang-lung Shan-k'ou *Langlong Shankou* (pass) Tibet
110 D3 Lang-ma *Langma* Tibet
86 D1 Lang-mu-ssu *Langmusi* Szech.
58 C4 Lang-p'ing *Langping* Hupeh
82 C3 Lang-p'ing *Langping* Kwangsi
30 C3 Lang-shan *Langshan* Hopeh
75 C5 Lang-shan *Langshan* Hunan
26 B4 Lang-shan *Langshan* In. Mong.
43 E4 Lang Shan *Lang Shan* (mt) Kiangsu
26 B4 Lang Shan *Lang Shan* (mts) In. Mong.
90 C4 Lang-tai *Langdai* Kwei.
74 D3 Lang-t'ang *Langtang* Hunan
Lang Tao *see* Hsi-yin Tao
119 C4 Lang-tao *Langdao* Taiwan
75 F6 Lang-t'ien *Langtian* Hunan
19 H4 Lang-t'ou *Langtou* Liao.
23 D4 Lang-t'ou-t'un *Langtoutun* Heilung.
91 F4 Lang-tung *Langdong* Kwei.
30 B2 Lang-wo-kou *Langwogou* Hopeh
31 C4 Lang-ya Shan *Langya Shan* (mt) Hopeh
50 C3 Lang-yeh *Langye* Chek.
35 E4 Lang-yeh Shan *Langye Shan* Shant.
63 D8 Lan Ho *Lan He* (river) Shensi
58 B2 Lan-ho-p'u *Lanhepu* Hupeh
11 D4 Lan-hsi *Lanxi* Heilung.
38 C3 Lan Hsien *Lan Xian* Shansi
119 C4 Lan Hsü *Lan Xu* (island) Taiwan
38 C3 Lan-i Ho *Lanyi He* (river) Shansi
106 D3 La-ni-kung-tu *Lanigongdu* Tsing.
46 D3 Lan-kan-chi *Langanji* Anhwei
11 E5 Lan-kang *Langang* Heilung.
55 F3 Lan-k'ao *Lankao* Honan
63 D8 Lan-kao *Langao* Shensi
79 D2 Lan-k'ou *Lankou* Kwangt.
66 D3 Lan-ku *Langu* Fukien
74 B4 Lan-li *Lanli* Hunan
11 D5 Lan-ling *Lanling* Heilung.
34 C5 Lan-ling *Lanling* Shant.
90 C4 Lan-pa *Lanba* Kwei.
86 D4 Lan-pa *Lanba* Szech.
94 B2 Lan-p'ing *Lanping* Yun.
75 E6 Lan-shan *Lanshan* Hunan
75 F5 Lan-shih *Lanshi* Hunan
79 D2 Lan-t'ang *Lantang* Kwangt.
35 E3 Lan-ti *Landi* Shant.
74 D4 Lan-t'ien *Lantian* Hunan
79 D2 Lan-t'ien *Lantian* Kwangt.
91 G3 Lan-t'ien *Lantian* Kwei.
63 E6 Lan-t'ien *Lantian* Shensi
11 D5 Lan-ts'ai-ch'iao *Lancaiqiao* Heilung.
Lan-ts'ang Chiang *see* Mekong
Lan-t'sang Chiang *see* Mekong
94 C4 Lan-ts'ang Chiang (River) Yun.
111 F3 Lan-t'sang Chiang *Lancang Jiang* (river) Tibet
94 B4 Lan-ts'ang Lahu Autonomous Hsien Yun.
Lan-ts'ang La-hu-tsu Tzu-chih-hsien *see* Lan-ts'ang Lahu Autonomous Hsien
87 F2 Lan-ts'ao-tu *Lancaodu* Szech.
35 F3 Lan-ts'un *Lancun* Shant.
46 D4 Lan-tzu-chi *Lanziji* Anhwei
14 D3 Lan-tzu-ching *Lanzijing* Kirin
82 D5 Lan-yü *Lanyu* Kwangsi
90 B5 Lao-ch'ang *Laochang* Kwei.
95 E3 Lao-ch'ang *Laochang* Yun.
58 D4 Lao-ch'eng *Laocheng* Hupeh
19 G2 Lao-ch'eng *Laocheng* Liao.
63 B7 Lao-ch'eng *Laocheng* Shensi
19 H2 Lao-ch'eng-chen *Laochengzhen* Liao.
46 B4 Lao-chi *Laoji* Anhwei
11 D5 Lao-chieh-chi *Laojieji* Heilung.
10 B1 Lao-chin-kou *Laojingou* Heilung.
102 I2 Lao-ch'i-t'ai *Laoqitai* Sink.
47 C7 Lao-chou-t'ou *Laozhoutou* Anhwei
50 C4 Lao-chu *Laozhu* Chek.
55 F4 Lao-chung *Laozhong* Honan
55 F5 Lao-chün-miao *Laojunmiao* Honan
62 E3 Lao-chün-tien *Laojundian* Shensi
102 C1 Lao-feng-k'ou *Laofengkou* Sink.
18 B2 Lao-fu *Laofu* Liao.
18 C3 Lao-ha Ho *Laohe He* (river) Liao.
23 D5 Lao-han-ying-tzu *Laohanyingzi* Liao.
10 D3 Lao-hei-shan *Laoheishan* Heilung.
11 F6 Lao-hei-shan *Laoheishan* Heilung.
54 D5 Lao-ho *Laohe* Honan
70 C3 Lao Ho *Lao He* (river) Kiangsi
58 D2 Lao-ho-k'ou *Laohekou* Hupeh
63 E8 Lao-hsien *Laoxian* Shensi
102 H1 Lao-hsi-hu *Laoxihu* Sink.
59 E4 Lao-hsin-k'ou *Laoxinkou* Hupeh
95 D3 Lao-hu *Laohu* Yun.
18 E5 Lao-hu-t'un *Laohutun* Liao.
46 D4 Lao-jen-ts'ang *Laorencang* Anhwei
14 E2 Lao-k'an *Laokan* Kirin
82 E5 Lao-k'ou *Laokou* Kwangsi
70 A4 Lao-kuan *Laoguan* Kiangsi
59 G4 Lao-kuan-tsui *Laoguanzui* Hupeh
30 F3 Lao-kuo *Laoguo* Hopeh
10 C3 Lao-lai *Laolai* Heilung.
22 F3 Lao-lai *Laolai* Heilung.
14 G6 Lao-ling *Laoling* Kirin
14 G6 Lao Ling *Lao Ling* (mts) Kirin
79 D1 Lao-lung *Laolong* Kwangt.
118 C1 Lao-mei *Laomei* Taiwan
15 H5 Lao-niu-kou *Laoniugou* Kirin
38 C2 Lao-niu-wan *Laoniuwan* Shansi
119 B3 Lao-nung Ch'i *Laonong Qi* (river) Taiwan
83 F2 Lao-pao *Laobao* Kwangsi
19 F4 Lao-pien *Laobian* Liao.
35 D4 Lao-p'o *Laopo* Shant.
91 E3 Lao-p'u-ch'ang *Laopuchang* Kwei.

51 E3 Li-yang *Liyang* Chek.
43 D4 Li-yang *Liyang* Kiangsu
39 E4 Li-yang *Liyang* Shansi
74 B3 Li-yeh *Liye* Hunan
70 D3 Li-yü *Liyu* Kiangsi
39 C6 Li-yüan *Liyuan* Shansi
75 F6 Li-yü-chiang *Liyujiang* Hunan
83 F3 Li-yung *Liyong* Kwangsi
75 F5 Li-yü-t'ang *Liyutang* Hunan
115 C4 Lizzie Webber (island) China Sea
115 C4 Loaita Island China Sea
71 C4 Lo-an *Luoan* Kiangsi
70 D3 Lo-an Chiang *Luoan Jiang* (river) Kiangsi
71 C6 Lo-ao *Luoao* Kiangsi
Lo-cha *see* Ka-po
111 D3 Lo-cha Hsien *Luozha Xian* Tibet
79 C1 Lo-ch'ang *Luochang* Kwangt.
47 D5 Lo-ch'ang-ho *Luochanghe* Anhwei
34 D2 Lo-chen *Luozhen* Shant.
98 D2 Lo-ch'eng *Luocheng* Kansu
83 E3 Lo-ch'eng *Luocheng* Kwangsi
46 D4 Lo-chi *Luoji* Anhwei
70 B2 Lo-ch'i *Luoqi* Kiangsi
87 F3 Lo-ch'i *Luoqi* Szech.
34 D3 Lo-chia-chuang *Luojiazhuang* Shant.
47 D6 Lo-chia-ling *Luojialing* Anhwei
87 E2 Lo-chiang *Luojiang* Szech.
66 E4 Lo-ch'iao *Luoqiao* Fukien
70 E3 Lo-ch'iao *Luoqiao* Kiangsi
90 C4 Lo-chih *Luozhi* Kwei.
87 E2 Lo-chih *Luozhi* Szech.
51 D4 Lo-ch'ing *Luoqing* Chek.
78 B2 Lo-ching *Luojing* Kwangt.
98 D1 Lo Ching *Luo Jing* (well) Kansu
83 F3 Lo-ch'ing Chiang *Luoqing Jiang* (river) Kwangsi
51 E4 Lo-ch'ing Wan *Luoqing Wan* (bay) Chek.
74 B4 Lo-chiu *Luojiu* Hunan
67 E5 Lo-chou *Luozhou* Fukien
62 E5 Lo-ch'üan *Luochuan* Shensi
34 D5 Lo-chuang *Luozhuang* Shant.
67 B5 Lo-fang *Luofang* Fukien
70 C3 Lo-fang *Luofang* Kiangsi
70 C4 Lo-fang *Luofang* Kiangsi
82 D3 Lo-fu *Luofu* Kwangsi
79 D1 Lo-fu *Luofu* Kwangt.
79 D2 Lo-fu Shan *Luofu Shan* (mt) Kwangt.
67 E5 Lo-han Shan *Luohan Shan* (mt) Fukien
55 F4 Lo-ho *Luohe* Honan
51 D3 Lo Ho *Luo He* (river) Honan
62 D4 Lo Ho *Luo He* (river) Shensi
63 E5 Lo Ho *Luo He* (river) Shensi
63 E8 Lo-ho *Luohe* Shensi
35 D4 Lo-ho-ai *Luoheai* Shant.
83 E3 Lo-hsi *Luoxi* Kwangsi
75 F5 Lo-hsiao Shan *Luoxiao Shan* (mts) Hunan
27 H1 Lo-hsien-su-mu *Luoxiansumu* In. Mong.
83 F3 Lo-hsiu *Luoxiu* Kwangsi
83 G4 Lo-hsiu *Luoxiu* Kwangsi
86 C1 Lo-hsüeh *Luoxue* Szech.
95 D2 Lo-hsüeh *Luoxue* Yun.
63 E6 Lo-hui Ch'ü *Luohui Qu* (canal) Shensi
74 D4 Lo-hung *Luohong* Hunan
74 B3 Lo-i-ch'i *Luoyiqi* Hunan
86 C1 Lo-jo-ssu *Luoruosi* Szech.
95 E2 Lo-k'an *Luokan* Yun.
Loka Region *see* Shan-nan Ti-ch'ü
Lokchong *see* Lo-ch'ang
79 C1 Lo-k'eng *Luokeng* Kwangt.
111 E3 Lo-ko *Luoge* Tibet
70 E3 Lo-k'ou *Luokou* Kiangsi
71 C6 Lo-k'ou *Luokou* Kiangsi
71 D5 Lo-k'ou *Luokou* Kiangsi
34 B3 Lo-k'ou *Luokou* Shant.
Loktung *see* Lo-tung
22 D1 Lo-ku-ho *Luoguhe* Heilung.
91 D5 Lo-k'un *Luokun* Kwei.
86 C2 Lo-ku-ssu *Luogusi* Szech.
82 C3 Lo-li *Luoli* Kwangsi
91 F4 Lo-li *Luoli* Kwei.
82 C3 Lo-li Ho *Luoli He* (river) Kwangsi
34 C2 Lo-ling *Luoling* Shant.
82 C3 Lo-lou *Luolou* Kwangsi
34 A4 Lo-lou *Luolou* Shant.
91 D5 Lo-lu *Luolu* Kwei.
Lo-lung *see* Tzu-t'o
91 E1 Lo-lung *Luolong* Kwei.
111 F3 Lo-lung *Luolong* Tibet
111 E3 Lo-lung Hsien *Luolong Xian* Tibet
83 F3 Lo-man *Luoman* Kwangsi
99 G4 Lo-men *Luomen* Kansu
78 A4 Lo-nan *Luonan* Kwangt.
63 F6 Lo-nan *Luonan* Shensi
115 C4 London Reefs China Sea
54 C3 Lo-ning *Luoning* Honan
82 D5 Lo-pai *Luobai* Kwangsi
Lop Bazar *see* Lo-p'u
11 F4 Lo-pei Hsien *Luobei Xian* Heilung.
90 C4 Lo-pieh *Luobie* Kwei.
70 E3 Lo-p'ing *Luoping* Kiangsi
95 E3 Lo-p'ing *Luoping* Yun.
Lop Nor *see* Lo-pu Po
66 C4 Lo-p'o Ting *Luopo Ding* (mt) Fukien
70 B3 Lo-p'o-t'ou *Luopotou* Kiangsi
83 F3 Lo-pu *Luobu* Kwangsi
102 C3 Lo-p'u *Luopu* Sink.
26 B4 Lo-pu-chao *Luobuzhao* In. Mong.
103 E3 Lo-pu-chuang *Luobuzhuang* Sink.
103 E2 Lo-pu Po *Luobu Bo* (lake) Sink.
55 F5 Lo-shan *Luoshan* Honan
59 F5 Lo-shan *Luoshan* Hupeh
87 D3 Lo-shan *Luoshan* Szech.
43 E4 Lo-she *Luoshe* Kiangsu
38 F2 Lo-shui-ho *Luoshuihe* Shansi
58 A4 Lo-shui-k'an *Luoshuikan* Hupeh
99 F5 Lo-ta *Luoda* Kansu
71 B5 Lo-t'ang *Luotang* Kiangsi
62 F3 Lo-t'ang-pao *Luotangbao* Shensi
59 F3 Lo-tien *Luodian* Hupeh
59 H4 Lo-t'ien *Luotian* Hupeh
43 F4 Lo-tien *Luodian* Kiangsu
58 D4 Lo-t'ien-ch'i *Luotianqi* Hupeh
91 D5 Lo-tien Hsien *Luodian Xian* Kwei.
30 F4 Lo-t'ing *Luoting* Hopeh
78 B2 Lo-ting *Luoding* Kwangt.
98 C1 Lo-t'o-ching *Luotuojing* Kansu
103 F2 Lo-t'o-ch'üan-tzu *Luotuoquanzi* Sink.
15 J4 Lo-t'o-shan *Luotuoshan* Kirin
55 E5 Lo-t'o-t'ien *Luotuotian* Honan
18 D3 Lo-t'o-ying *Luotuoying* Liao.
39 B5 Lo-ts'un *Luocun* Shansi
Lo-tu *see* Nien-po
34 B4 Lo-t'un *Luotun* Shant.
83 E3 Lo-tung *Luodong* Kwangsi
78 A4 Lo-tung *Luodong* Kwangt.
118 C2 Lo-tung *Luodong* Taiwan
46 C3 Lo-t'u-p'u *Luotupu* Anhwei
95 D3 Lo-tz'u *Luoci* Yun.
15 K4 Lo-tzu-kou *Luozigou* Kirin
46 D3 Lou-chuang *Louzhuang* Anhwei
38 C3 Lou-fan *Loufan* Shansi
115 C5 Louisa Reef China Sea
38 C2 Lou-kou *Lougou* Shansi
103 E2 Lou-lan *Loulan* (site) Sink.
38 D3 Lou-pan-chai *Loubanzhai* Shansi
11 E5 Lou-shan *Loushan* Heilung.
91 E2 Lou-shan-kuan *Loushanguan* Kwei.
74 C2 Lou Shui *Lou Shui* (river) Hunan
43 F4 Lou-t'ang *Loutang* Kiangsu
34 C4 Lou-te *Loude* Shant.
31 B6 Lou-ti *Loudi* Hopeh
74 D4 Lou-ti *Loudi* Hunan
67 B5 Lou-tzu-pa *Louziba* Fukien
18 C2 Lou-tzu-tien *Louzidian* Liao.
43 D2 Lo-wang *Luowang* Kiangsu
55 F3 Lo-wang *Luowang* Honan
91 D5 Lo-wang *Luowang* Kwei.
87 F2 Lo-wen-pa *Luowenba* Szech.
38 E1 Lo-wen-tsao *Luowenzao* Shansi
Lowti *see* Lou-ti
83 F3 Lo-yai *Luoyai* Kwangsi
67 C5 Lo-yang *Luoyang* Fukien
67 D6 Lo-yang *Luoyang* Fukien
54 D3 Lo-yang *Luoyang* Honan
82 E3 Lo-yang *Luoyang* Kwangsi
59 F3 Lo-yang-tien *Luoyangdian* Hupeh
82 C3 Lo-yeh *Luoye* Kwangsi
82 E4 Lo-yü *Luoyu* Kwangsi
66 E4 Lo-yüan *Luoyuan* Fukien
91 C5 Lo-yüan *Luoyuan* Kwei.
66 E4 Lo-yüan Wan *Luoyuan Wan* (bay) Fukien
38 B3 Lo-yü-k'ou *Luoyukou* Shansi
83 G4 Lo-yün *Luoyun* Kwangsi
31 B6 Luan-ch'eng *Luancheng* Hopeh
83 E5 Luan-ch'eng *Luancheng* Kwangsi
114 C3 Luan-ching *Luanjing* Ningsia
54 C4 Luan-ch'uan *Luanchuan* Honan
63 F7 Luan-chuang *Luanzhuang* Shensi
104 C3 Luan-hai-tzu *Luanhaizi* Tsing.
30 C3 Luan-ho *Luanhe* Hopeh
30 E2 Luan Ho *Luan He* (river) Hopeh
30 F3 Luan Ho *Luan He* (river) Hopeh
30 F4 Luan-hsien *Luanxian* Hopeh
30 F4 Luan-nan Hsien *Luannan Xian* Hopeh
30 E3 Luan-p'ing Hsien *Luanping Xian* Hopeh
83 F3 Lu-chai *Luzhai* Kwangsi
86 D4 Lu-ch'ang *Luchang* Szech.
94 B3 Lu-chang-chieh *Luzhangjie* Yun.
74 F2 Lu-ch'eng *Lucheng* Hunan
43 D4 Lü-ch'eng *Lücheng* Kiangsu
82 C3 Lu-ch'eng *Lucheng* Kwangsi
39 E5 Lu-ch'eng *Lucheng* Shansi
39 E6 Lu-ch'eng *Lucheng* Shansi
47 C5 Lu-chen-kuan *Luzhenguan* Anhwei
67 C6 Lu-ch'i *Luqi* Fukien
70 B4 Lu-ch'i *Luqi* Kiangsi
87 E2 Lu-ch'i *Luqi* Szech.
43 F4 Lu-chia *Lujia* Kiangsu
14 G3 Lu-chia *Lujia* Kirin
34 C3 Lü-chia-chai *Lüjiazhai* Shant.
31 E5 Lü-chia-ch'iao *Lüjiaqiao* Hopeh
38 E4 Lu-chia-chuang *Lujiazhuang* Shansi
47 D5 Lu-chiang *Lujiang* Anhwei
118 B2 Lu-chiang *Lujiang* Taiwan
46 D4 Lu-ch'iao *Luqiao* Anhwei
51 E4 Lu-ch'iao *Luqiao* Chek.
34 B4 Lu-ch'iao *Luqiao* Shant.
51 E3 Lu-chia-pu *Lujiabu* Chek.
59 F3 Lu-chia-shan *Lujiashan* Hupeh
19 F4 Lu-chia-t'un *Lujiatun* Liao.
43 E4 Lu-chih-chen *Luzhizhen* Kiangsu
74 C3 Lu-ch'i Hsien *Luqi Xian* Hunan
43 D3 Lu-chin *Lujin* Kiangsu
99 G4 Lü-ching *Lüjing* Kansu
83 G5 Lu-ching *Lujing* Kwangsi
63 F5 Lu-ching *Lujing* Shensi
87 E3 Lu-chou *Luzhou* Szech.
Luchow *see* Lu-chou
Luchow *see* Ho-fei
Lu-ch'ü *see* Ch'iao-t'ou
118 C1 Lu-chu *Luzhu* Taiwan
119 B4 Lu-chu *Luzhu* Taiwan
83 G5 Lu-ch'uan *Luchuan* Kwangsi
95 D3 Lu-ch'üan *Luquan* Yun.
99 F4 Lu-ch'ü Hsien *Luqu Xian* Kansu
95 D4 Lü-ch'un *Lüchun* Yun.
63 B7 Lüeh-yang *Lueyang* Shensi
67 B6 Lu-feng *Lufeng* Fukien
79 D2 Lu-feng *Lufeng* Kwangt.
95 D3 Lu-feng *Lufeng* Yun.
11 D4 Lu-ho *Luhe* Heilung.
10 B4 Lu Ho *Luhe* (river) Heilung.
62 E3 Lu Ho *Lu He* (river) Shensi
94 C3 Lü-ho *Lühe* Yun.
55 F5 Lü-ho-tien *Lühedian* Honan
95 D3 Lu-hsi *Luxi* Yun.
66 F4 Lü-hsia *Lüxia* Fukien
87 E3 Lu Hsien *Lu Xian* Szech.
94 B3 Lu-hsi Hsien *Luxi Xian* Yun.
59 F5 Lu-hsi-k'ou *Luxikou* Hupeh
43 E4 Lu-hsü *Luxu* Kiangsu
114 C2 Lu-hua-t'ai *Luhuatai* Ningsia
31 D5 Lü-hung-pao *Lügongbao* Hopeh
75 D5 Lu-hung-shih *Luhongshi* Hunan
86 C2 Lu-huo *Luhuo* Szech.
55 G4 Lu-i *Luyi* Honan
Luichow *see* Lei-chou
Luichow Peninsula *see* Lei-chou Pan-tao
54 D4 Lu-i-miao *Luyimiao* Honan
74 F4 Lui-ta-shih *Luidashi* Hunan
Luitung *see* Tung-shan
47 E5 Lu-kang *Lugang* Anhwei
43 F5 Lü-kang *Lügang* Kiangsu
102 I2 Lu-k'o-ch'in *Lukeqin* Sink.
103 E2 Lu-k'o-ch'in *Lukeqin* Sink.
74 F4 Lu-k'ou *Lukou* Hunan
70 C2 Lu-k'ou *Lukou* Kiangsi
71 B4 Lu-k'ou *Lukou* Kiangsi
30 D4 Lu-kou-ch'iao *Lugouqiao* Hopeh
74 F2 Lu-k'ou-p'u *Lukoupu* Hunan
46 C4 Lu-k'ou-tzu *Lukouzi* Anhwei
74 F3 Lu-k'ou-yü *Lukouyu* Hunan
86 D3 Lu-ku *Lugu* Szech.
118 B3 Lu-ku *Lugu* Taiwan
47 C6 Lu-kuan *Luguan* Anhwei
74 D4 Lu-kuan *Luguan* Hunan
83 E4 Lu-kuan *Luguan* Kwangsi
111 E3 Lu-kung Shan-k'ou *Lugong Shankou* (pass) Tibet
95 D3 Lu-liang *Luliang* Yun.
43 D2 Lü-liang-ch'iao *Lüliangqiao* Kiangsu
38 C4 Lü-liang Shan *Lüliang Shan* (mts) Shansi
54 B3 Lu-ling Kuan *Lulingguan* (pass) Honan
31 A6 Lu-lo *Luluo* Hopeh
110 B2 Lu-lo *Luluo* Tibet
42 A1 Lu-lou *Lulou* Kiangsu
30 F4 Lu-lung *Lulong* Hopeh
110 C3 Lu-ma-hsia *Lumaxia* Tibet
42 C1 Lu-ma Hu *Luma Hu* (lake) Kiangsu
107 F2 Lü-mang-k'ou *Lümangkou* Tsing.
43 E4 Lu-mu *Lumu* Kiangsu
95 D3 Lu-nan *Lunan* Yun.
Lu-nan I-tsu Tzu-chih-hsien *see* Lu-nan Yi Autonomous Hsien
95 D3 Lu-nan Yi Autonomous Hsien Yun.
34 B3 Lun-chen *Lunzhen* Shant.
71 D4 Lung-an *Longan* Kiangsi
82 D4 Lung-an *Longan* Kwangsi
83 E2 Lung-an *Longan* Kwangsi
62 E4 Lung-an *Longan* Shensi
11 C4 Lung-an-ch'iao *Longanqiao* Heilung.
83 F6 Lung-chang *Longzhang* Kwangsi
90 B4 Lung-ch'ang *Longchang* Kwei.
90 C5 Lung-ch'ang *Longchang* Kwei.
91 E4 Lung-ch'ang *Longchang* Kwei.
19 G4 Lung-ch'ang *Longchang* Liao.
87 E3 Lung-ch'ang *Longchang* Szech.
119 C4 Lung-ch'ang *Longchang* Taiwan
11 F5 Lung-chao *Longzhao* Heilung.
14 D2 Lung-chao *Longzhao* Kirin
19 H4 Lung-chao-kou *Longzhaogou* Liao.
10 D3 Lung-chen *Longzhen* Heilung.
39 E5 Lung-chen *Longzhen* Shansi
75 B5 Lung-ch'eng *Longcheng* Hunan
67 C6 Lung-ch'i *Longqi* Fukien
42 C1 Lung-chi *Longji* Kiangsu
42 C2 Lung-chi *Longji* Kiangsu
74 B2 Lung-chia-chai *Longjiazhai* Hunan
66 C4 Lung-chiang *Longjiang* Fukien
11 B4 Lung-chiang *Longjiang* Heilung.
23 E4 Lung-chiang *Longjiang* Heilung.
79 E2 Lung-chiang *Longjiang* Kwangt.
59 G5 Lung-chiao-shan *Longjiaoshan* Hupeh
14 F3 Lung-chia-pao *Longjiabao* Kirin
79 D1 Lung-chieh *Longjie* Kwangt.
94 B3 Lung-chieh *Longjie* Yun.
94 C3 Lung-chieh *Longjie* Yun.
95 E2 Lung-chieh *Longjie* Yun.
90 B3 Lung-chieh-tzu *Longjiezi* Kwei.
86 D3 Lung-ch'ih *Longchi* Szech.
87 F2 Lung-ch'i Ho *Longqi He* (river) Szech.
15 J5 Lung-ching *Longjing* Kirin
118 B2 Lung-ching *Longjing* Taiwan
67 C6 Lung-ch'i Ti-ch'ü *Longqi Diqu* Fukien
82 C5 Lung-chou *Longzhou* Kwangsi
Lungchow *see* Lung-chou
43 D1 Lung-chü *Longju* Kiangsu
50 C4 Lung-ch'üan *Longquan* Chek.
67 C6 Lung-ch'üan *Longquan* Fukien
11 D4 Lung-ch'üan *Longquan* Heilung.
14 C2 Lung-ch'üan *Longquan* Kirin
15 G5 Lung-ch'üan *Longquan* Kirin
23 E5 Lung-ch'üan *Longquan* Kirin
82 C3 Lung-ch'uan *Longchuan* Kwangsi
91 E3 Lung-ch'üan *Longquan* Kwei.
91 E4 Lung-ch'üan *Longquan* Kwei.
94 A3 Lung-ch'uan *Longchuan* Yun.
50 C4 Lung-ch'üan Ch'i *Longquan Qi* (river) Chek.
79 D1 Lung-ch'uan Hsien *Longchuan Xian* Kwangt.
31 A5 Lung-ch'üan-kuan *Longquanguan* Hopeh
63 F7 Lung-chü-chai *Longjuzhai* Shensi
58 E3 Lung-chung *Longzhong* Hupeh
87 G2 Lung-chü-pa *Longjuba* Szech.
Lungdo *see* Lun-to
11 C4 Lung-feng *Longfeng* Heilung.
58 B4 Lung-feng-pa *Longfengba* Hupeh
67 C6 Lung-hai Hsien *Longhai Xian* Fukien
95 D3 Lung-hai-t'ang *Longhaitang* Yun.
10 B1 Lung-ho *Longhe* Heilung.
10 C3 Lung-ho *Longhe* Heilung.
82 C4 Lung-ho *Longhe* Kwangsi
91 E4 Lung Ho *Long He* (river) Kwei.
99 G4 Lung-hsi *Longxi* Kansu
91 E3 Lung-hsi *Longxi* Kwei.
79 D1 Lung-hsien *Longxian* Kwangt.
63 B6 Lung-hsien *Longxian* Shensi
91 E2 Lung-hsing *Longxian* Kwei.
38 E2 Lung-hsing *Longxing* Shansi
14 C4 Lung-hsing-tang *Longxingdang* Kirin
23 E6 Lung-hsing-tang *Longxingdang* Kirin
66 C4 Lung-hsi Shan *Longxi Shan* (mt) Fukien
83 H4 Lung-hsü *Longxu* Kwangsi
47 C6 Lung Hu *Longhu* Anhwei
71 D4 Lung-hu *Longhu* Kiangsi
83 G3 Lung-hu *Longhu* Kwangsi
67 D5 Lung-hua *Longhua* Fukien
31 D6 Lung-hua *Longhua* Hopeh
79 D2 Lung-hua *Longhua* Kwangt.
39 C6 Lung-hua *Longhua* Shansi
30 E2 Lung-hua Hsien *Longhua Xian* Hopeh
71 B6 Lung-hui *Longhui* Kiangsi
75 D4 Lung-hui Hsien *Longhui Xian* Hunan
75 C6 Lung-hu Kuan *Longhu Guan* (pass) Hunan
83 G2 Lung-hu Kuan *Longhu Guan* (pass) Kwangsi
82 B3 Lung-huo *Longhuo* Kwangsi
70 D3 Lung-hu Shan *Longhu Shan* (mt) Kiangsi
86 D1 Lung-jih-pa *Longriba* Szech.
59 G5 Lung-kang *Longgang* Hupeh
71 C5 Lung-kang *Longgang* Kiangsi
71 D5 Lung-kang *Longgang* Kiangsi
43 E2 Lung-kang *Longgang* Kiangsu
79 D2 Lung-kang *Longgang* Kwangt.
91 E4 Lung-kang *Longgang* Kwei.
34 D3 Lung-kang *Longgang* Shant.
46 C3 Lung-k'ang-chi *Longkangji* Anhwei
14 G5 Lung-kang Shan *Longgang Shan* (mts) Kirin
71 C5 Lung-kang-t'ou *Longgangtou* Kiangsi
Lungkar *see* Lung-ka-erh
Lungki *see* Chang-chou
Lungki River *see* Lung-ch'i Ho
55 F5 Lung-k'ou *Longkou* Honan
59 F5 Lung-k'ou *Longkou* Hupeh
71 C5 Lung-k'ou *Longkou* Kiangsi
34 C3 Lung-k'ou *Longkou* Shant.
35 F2 Lung-k'ou *Longkou* Shant.
102 H1 Lung-k'ou *Longkou* Sink.
35 F2 Lung-k'ou Wan *Longkou Wan* (bay) Shant.
42 A1 Lung-ku *Longgu* Kiangsu
30 C3 Lung-kuan *Longguan* Hopeh
82 C4 Lung-Kuang *Longguang* Kwangsi
90 C5 Lung-kuang *Longguang* Kwei.
34 A4 Lung-ku-chi *Longguji* Shant.
78 B4 Lung-kun *Longgun* Kwangt.
50 B5 Lung-kung *Longgong* Chek.
70 D4 Lung-ku-tu *Longgudu* Kiangsi
91 D4 Lung-li *Longli* Kwei.
82 B3 Lung-lin *Longlin* Kwangsi
82 C4 Lung-lin *Longlin* Kwangsi
83 F4 Lung-ling *Longling* Kwangsi
94 B3 Lung-ling *Longling* Yun.
Lung-lin Ko-tsu Tzu-chih-hsien *see* Lung-lin Multi-national Autonomous Hsien
82 B3 Lung-lin Multi-national Autonomous Hsien Kwangsi
47 E6 Lung-men *Longmen* Anhwei
67 B5 Lung-men *Longmen* Fukien
67 D6 Lung-men *Longmen* Fukien
10 D3 Lung-men *Longmen* Heilung.
54 D3 Lung-men *Longmen* Honan
82 D5 Lung-men *Longmen* Kwangsi
83 E6 Lung-men *Longmen* Kwangsi
83 F5 Lung-men *Longmen* Kwangsi
78 B3 Lung-men *Longmen* Kwangt.
78 B4 Lung-men *Longmen* Kwangt.
79 D2 Lung-men *Longmen* Kwangt.
39 B6 Lung Men *Long Men* Shansi
118 A3 Lung-men *Longmen* Taiwan
74 G3 Lung-men-ch'ang *Longmenchang* Hunan
39 B6 Lung-men Shan *Longmen Shan* (mt) Shansi
87 E1 Lung-men Shan *Longmen Shan* (mts) Szech.
30 C3 Lung-men-suo *Longmensuo* Hopeh
82 D5 Lung-ming *Longming* Kwangsi
Lungmoon *see* Lung-men
71 B7 Lung-nan *Longnan* Kiangsi
106 E4 Lung-pao *Longbao* Tsing.
95 D4 Lung-p'eng *Longpeng* Yun.
58 C4 Lung-p'ing *Longping* Hupeh
59 H5 Lung-p'ing *Longping* Hupeh
91 D5 Lung-p'ing *Longping* Kwei.
91 E3 Lung-p'ing *Longping* Kwei.
71 C6 Lung-pu *Longbu* Kiangsi
46 C3 Lung-shan *Longshan* Anhwei
67 C6 Lung-shan *Longshan* Fukien
74 B2 Lung-shan *Longshan* Hunan
83 F4 Lung-shan *Longshan* Kwangsi
63 B6 Lung Shan *Long Shan* (mts) Shensi
83 G2 Lung-sheng *Longsheng* Kwangsi
83 G5 Lung-sheng *Longsheng* Kwangsi
79 C2 Lung-sheng *Longsheng* Kwangt.
27 E4 Lung-sheng-chuang *Longshengzhuang* In. Mong.
Lung-sheng Ko-tsu Tzu-chih-hsien *see* Lung-sheng Multi-national Autonomous Hsien
83 G2 Lung-sheng Multi-national Autonomous Hsien Kwangsi
71 A5 Lung-shih *Longshi* Kiangsi
98 E2 Lung-shou Shan *Longshou Shan* (mts) Kansu
83 H1 Lung-shui *Longshui* Kwangsi
87 E3 Lung-shui *Longshui* Szech.
74 C4 Lung-t'an *Longtan* Hunan
43 D3 Lung-t'an *Longtan* Kiangsu
87 F3 Lung-t'an *Longtan* Szech.
87 G3 Lung-t'an *Longtan* Szech.
118 C2 Lung-t'an *Longtan* Taiwan
55 G3 Lung-t'ang *Longtang* Honan
74 D3 Lung-t'ang *Longtang* Hunan
71 C7 Lung-t'ang *Longtang* Kiangsi
78 B3 Lung-t'ang *Longtang* Kwangt.
78 B4 Lung-t'ang *Longtang* Kwangt.
90 C4 Lung-t'ang *Longtang* Kwei.
91 F3 Lung-t'ang *Longtang* Kwei.
62 E5 Lung-tang *Longfang* Shensi
74 D2 Lung-t'an-ho *Longtanhe* Hunan
46 B4 Lung-t'an-ssu *Longtansi* Anhwei
75 E6 Lung-t'an-yü *Longtanyu* Hunan
98 E2 Lung-tao-pao *Longdaobao* Kansu
114 C4 Lung-te *Longde* Ningsia
67 E5 Lung-t'ien *Longtian* Fukien
74 D3 Lung-t'ien *Longtian* Hunan
91 F3 Lung-t'ien *Longtian* Kwei.
63 F5 Lung-t'ing *Longting* Shensi
63 C7 Lung-t'ing-p'u *Longtingpu* Shensi
82 D5 Lung-t'ou *Longtou* Kwangsi
82 E3 Lung-t'ou *Longtou* Kwangsi
83 F3 Lung-t'ou *Longtou* Kwangsi
18 E6 Lung-t'ou *Longtou* Liao.
74 C4 Lung-tou-an *Longdouan* Hunan
Lungtsing *see* Lung-ching
79 D2 Lung-ts'un *Longcun* Kwangt.
42 C4 Lung-tu *Longdu* Kinagsu
74 C2 Lung-tung-p'ing *Longdongping* Hunan
Lung-tzu *see* Hsin-pa
111 E3 Lung-tzu Hsien *Longzi Xian* Tibet
47 C6 Lung-wan *Longwan* Anhwei
51 E4 Lung-wan *Longwan* Chek.
14 E3 Lung-wang *Longwang* Kirin
58 D2 Lung-wang-chi *Longwangji* Hupeh
47 D6 Lung-wang-chü *Longwangju* Anhwei
46 D3 Lung-wang-miao *Longwangmiao* Anhwei
11 G5 Lung-wang-miao *Longwangmiao* Heilung.
30 G3 Lung-wang-miao *Longwangmiao* Hopeh
31 C7 Lung-wang-miao *Longwangmiao* Hopeh
19 G4 Lung-wang-miao *Longwangmiao* Liao.
34 B5 Lung-wang-miao *Longwangmiao* Shant.
46 B4 Lung-wang-t'ang *Longwangtang* Anhwei
39 B5 Lung-wang-yen *Longwangyan* Shansi
79 D2 Lung-wo *Longwo* Kwangt.
107 H3 Lung-wu *Longwu* Tsing.
95 D3 Lung-wu *Longwu* Yun.
107 G3 Lung-yang Hsia *Longyang Xia* (gorge) Tsing.
31 B6 Lung-yao *Longyao* Hopeh
67 C5 Lung-yen *Longyan* Fukien
83 F4 Lung-yen *Longyan* Kwangsi
34 C4 Lung-yen *Longyan* Shant.
75 F5 Lung-ying-shih *Longyingshi* Hunan
Lung-yü *see* Lung-hsü
50 C3 Lung-yu *Longyou* Chek.
71 B7 Lung-yüan-pa *Longyuanba* Kiangsi
11 D4 Lun-ho *Lunhe* Heilung.
86 C3 Lu-ning *Luning* Szech.
Lunkar Gompa *see* Lung-ka-erh
118 B3 Lun-pei *Lunbei* Taiwan
102 D2 Lun-t'ai *Luntai* Sink.
110 B2 Lun-to *Lunduo* Tibet
91 D3 Lu-pan *Luban* Kwei.
79 C2 Lu-pao *Lubao* Kwangt.
14 A3 Lu-pei *Lubei* Kirin
23 D5 Lu-pei *Lubei* Kirin
95 D3 Lu-piao *Lubiao* Yun.
91 E4 Lu-p'ing *Luping* Kwei.
79 C2 Lu-pu *Lubu* Kwangt.
107 G2 Lu-sha-erh *Lushaer* Tsing.
54 D4 Lu-shan *Lushan* Honan
70 C2 Lu-shan *Lushan* Kiangsi
70 C2 Lu Shan *Lu Shan* (mt) Kiangsi
34 D3 Lu Shan *Lu Shan* (mt) Shant.
34 D3 Lu Shan *Lu Shan* (mts) Shant.
86 D2 Lu-shan *Lushan* Szech.
54 C3 Lu-shih *Lushi* Honan
59 F4 Lu-shih *Lushi* Hupeh
102 C3 Lü-shih *Lüshi* Sink.
94 C3 Lu-shih *Lushi* Yun.
51 D3 Lu-shih-k'ou *Lushikou* Chek.
74 F4 Lu Shui *Lu Shui* (river) Hunan
15 H5 Lu-shui-ho *Lushuihe* Kirin
94 B3 Lu-shui Hsien *Lushui Xian* Yun.
18 E6 Lü-shun *Lüshun* Liao.
Lusi *see* Lu-hsi
43 F3 Lü-ssu *Lüsi* Kiangsu
55 G4 Lu-t'ai *Lutai* Honan
30 E4 Lu-t'ai *Lutai* Hopeh
55 F3 Lü-t'an *Lütan* Honan
75 E6 Lu-t'ang *Lutang* Hunan
Lü Tao *see* Huo-shao Tao
11 E6 Lu-tao-kou *Ludaogou* Heilung.
19 F5 Lü-ta Shih *Lüda Shi* Liao.
54 E3 Lu-tien *Ludian* Honan
70 D3 Lu-t'ien *Lutian* Kiangsi
79 C2 Lü-t'ien *Lütian* Kwangt.
95 D2 Lu-tien Hsien *Ludian Xian* Yun.
47 D5 Lü-t'ing *Lüting* Anhwei
86 D3 Lu-ting *Luding* Szech.
43 D2 Lu-to *Luduo* Kiangsu
59 E2 Lu-t'ou *Lutou* Hupeh
106 D2 Lü-ts'ao-shan *Lücaoshan* Tsing.
47 F6 Lu-ts'un *Lucun* Anhwei
83 E5 Lu-ts'un *Lucun* Kwangsi
34 D3 Lu-ts'un *Lucun* Shant.
58 C4 Lü-ts'ung-p'o *Lücongpo* Hupeh
74 C4 Lu-tu-chai *Luduzhai* Hunan
70 D3 Lu-tz'u-k'ou *Lucikou* Kiangsi
67 E5 Lu-tz'u Yü *Luci Yu* (islet) Fukien
83 E5 Lu-wu *Luwu* Kwangsi
74 C4 Lu-yang *Luyang* Hunan
18 E3 Lü-yang *Lüyang* Liao.
38 C3 Lu-ya Shan *Luya Shan* (mt) Shansi
38 C3 Lu-ya Shan *Luya Shan* (mts) Shansi
38 C3 Lu-ya Shan *Luyashan* (mts) Shansi
119 C4 Lu-yeh *Luye* Taiwan
58 E2 Lü-yen-i *Lüyanyi* Hupeh
83 F4 Lu-yü *Luyu* Kwangsi
43 E4 Lu-yüan *Luyan* Kiangsu
Lwan Ho *see* Luan Ho
Lwanhsien *see* Luan-hsien

51 D2 Ma-an *Maan* Chek.
58 C2 Ma-an *Maan* Hupeh
Ma-an Lieh-tao *see* Sheng-ssu Lieh-tao
15 H3 Ma-an-ling *Maanling* Kirin
47 E5 Ma-an-shan *Maanshan* Anhwei
70 B2 Ma-ao *Maao* Kiangsi
Macau - city plan *see* Page 141
115 C2 Macclesfield Bank (Reefs, shoals) China Sea
102 B3 Ma-cha *Mazha* Sink.
102 C3 Ma-cha *Mazha* Sink.
51 D5 Ma-chan *Mazhan* Chek.
34 D3 Ma-chan *Mazhan* Shant.
46 D3 Ma-ch'ang *Machang* Anhwei
31 D5 Ma-ch'ang *Machang* Hopeh
42 C1 Ma-ch'ang *Machang* Kiangsu
91 D3 Ma-ch'ang *Machang* Kwei.
91 D4 Ma-ch'ang *Machang* Kwei.
18 C2 Ma-ch'ang *Machang* Liao.
39 E5 Ma-ch'ang *Machang* Shansi
18 D4 Ma-chang-fang *Mazhangfang* Liao.
91 E4 Ma-ch'ang-p'ing *Machangping* Kwei.
63 D6 Ma-chao-chen *Mazhaozhen* Shensi
102 C3 Ma-cha-t'a-ko *Mazhatage* Sink.
38 B3 Ma-chen *Mazhen* Shansi
62 F2 Ma-chen *Mazhen* Shensi
59 H3 Ma-ch'eng *Macheng* Hupeh
50 C2 Ma-che-pu *Mazhebu* Chek.
42 C3 Ma-chi *Maji* Kiangsu
34 A4 Ma-chi *Maji* Shant.
67 D5 Ma-chia *Majia* Fukien
119 B4 Ma-chia *Majia* Taiwan
71 B5 Ma-chia-chou *Majiazhou* Kiangsi
34 C2 Ma-chia Ho *Majia He* (river) Shant.
114 C3 Ma-chia-ho-wan *Majiahewan* Ningsia
11 G5 Ma-chia-kang *Majiagang* Heilung.
75 F5 Ma-chiang *Majiang* Hunan
83 H4 Ma-chiang *Majiang* Kwangsi
91 E4 Ma-chiang *Majiang* Kwei.
111 D3 Ma-chiang *Majiang* Tibet
59 G5 Ma-ch'iao *Maqiao* Hupeh
102 H1 Ma-ch'iao *Maqiao* Sink.
103 D1 Ma-ch'iao *Maqiao* Sink.
55 H4 Ma-ch'iao-chi *Maqiaoji* Honan
11 F5 Ma-ch'iao-ho *Maqiaohe* Heilung.
87 E1 Ma-chiao-pa *Majiaoba* Szech.
58 D4 Ma-chia-tien *Majiadian* Hupeh
38 F1 Ma-chia-tsao *Majiazao* Shansi
10 C2 Ma-chia-tzu *Majiazi* Heilung.
22 F2 Ma-chia-tzu *Majiazi* Heilung.
14 B5 Ma-chia-tzu *Majiazi* Kirin
23 D6 Ma-chia-tzu *Majiazi* Kirin
18 C2 Ma-chia-tzu *Majiazi* Liao.
14 B5 Ma-chia-wa-tzu *Majiawazi* Kirin
23 D6 Ma-chia-wa-tzu *Majiawazi* Kirin
99 F4 Ma-chia-yao *Majiayao* Kansu
63 E7 Ma-chieh *Majie* Shensi
95 D3 Ma-chieh *Majie* Yun.
95 E4 Ma-chieh *Majie* Yun.
50 C3 Ma-chien *Majian* Chek.
51 C3 Ma-chien *Majian* Chek.
Ma-ch'in *see* Ta-wu
50 B3 Ma-chin *Majin* Chek.
50 B3 Ma-chin Ch'i *Majin Qi* (river) Chek.
74 B3 Ma-ching-yao *Majingyao* Hunan
107 G3 Ma-ch'in Hsien *Maqin Xian* Tsing.
74 C3 Ma-ch'i-p'u *Maqipu* Hunan
74 D3 Ma-chi-t'ang *Majitang* Hunan
71 C6 Ma-chou *Mazhou* Kiangsi
Ma-ch'ü *see* Cho-ko-ni-ma
51 E2 Ma-chu *Mazhu* Chek.
55 F5 Ma-chuang *Mazhuang* Honan
82 C3 Ma-chuang *Mazhuang* Kwangsi
34 D4 Ma-chuang *Mazhuang* Shant.
110 B3 Ma-ch'üan Ho *Maquan He* (river) Tibet
82 E2 Ma-Ch'uan-lo *Machuanluo* Kwangsi
99 F4 Ma-ch'ü Hsien *Maqu Xian* Kansu
19 H2 Ma-chung-ho *Mazhonghe* Liao.
86 D2 Ma-erh-k'ang *Maerkang* Szech.
86 C1 Ma-erh-k'o Ho *Maerke He* (river) Szech.
110 B3 Ma-fa-mu-ts'o Hu *Mafamucuo Hu* (lake) Tibet
55 F6 Ma-fan *Mafan* Honan
38 C3 Ma-fang *Mafang* Shansi
39 E4 Ma-fang *Mafang* Shansi
86 D3 Ma-fang-kou *Mafanggou* Szech.
82 A3 Ma-feng *Mafeng* Kwangsi
63 C6 Ma-fu-chen *Mafuzhen* Shensi
106 D1 Ma-hai *Mahai* Tsing.
15 I4 Ma-hao *Mahao* Kirin
26 C5 Ma-ha-t'u-miao *Mahatumiao* In. Mong.
99 G4 Ma-ho-chen *Mahezhen* Kansu
91 F3 Ma-hsi *Maxi* Kwei.
86 C2 Ma-hsi *Maxi* Szech.
99 H4 Ma-hsia *Maxia* Kansu
55 F5 Ma-hsiang *Maxiang* Honan
78 B3 Ma-hsieh *Maxie* Kwangt.
106 D2 Ma-huang-kou *Mahuanggou* Tsing.
114 D3 Ma-huang-shan *Mahuangshan* Ningsia
70 C2 Ma-hui-ling *Mahuiling* Kiangsi
99 H4 Mai-chi Shan *Maiji Shan* (mt) Kansu
78 A3 Mai-ch'u *Maichu* Kwangt.
86 D1 Mai-erh-ma *Maerma* Szech.
67 D5 Mai-hsieh *Maixie* Fukien
70 C4 Mai-hsieh *Maixie* Kiangsi
102 B3 Mai-kai-t'i *Maigaiti* Sink.
118 B3 Mai-liao *Mailiao* Taiwan
83 H2 Mai-ling *Mailing* Kwangsi
59 F5 Mai-shih *Maishi* Hupeh
86 C3 Mai-ti-lung *Maidilong* Szech.
94 C3 Ma-i-tui *Mayidui* Yun.
59 F4 Mai-wang *Maiwang* Hupeh
67 C5 Mai-yüan *Maiyuan* Fukien
86 B2 Ma-jung *Marong* Szech.
104 E3 Ma-ka-hsiao-ko *Magaxiaoge* Tsing.
110 B2 Ma-k'a-mu Ts'o *Makamu Cuo* (lake) Tibet
31 C6 Ma-kan *Magan* Hopeh
67 D6 Ma-kang *Magang* Fukien
35 E3 Ma-ko-chuang *Magezhuang* Shant.
35 F3 Ma-ko-chuang *Magezhuang* Shant.
Ma-k'o-ha Ts'o *see* Ma-k'a-mu Ts'o
107 G3 Ma-k'o-t'ang *Maketang* Tsing.
70 C3 Ma-k'ou *Makou* Kiangsi
95 D2 Ma-k'ou *Makou* Yun.
90 B4 Ma-ku *Magu* Kwei.
107 G4 Ma-k'u *Maku* Tsing.
95 E4 Ma-kuan *Maguan* Yun.
78 B2 Ma-kuei *Magui* Kwangt.
79 D2 Ma-kung *Magong* Kwangt.
118 A3 Ma-kung *Magong* Taiwan
71 D4 Ma-ku-shan *Magushan* Kiangsi
54 E5 Ma-ku-t'ien *Magutian* Honan
107 F3 Ma-la-i-wan *Malayiwan* Tsing.
35 F3 Ma-lan *Malan* Shant.
63 D5 Ma-lan-chen *Malanzhen* Shensi
59 E4 Ma-lang *Malang* Hupeh
58 D3 Ma-lang-p'ing *Malangping* Hupeh
30 E3 Ma-lan-yü *Malanyu* Hopeh
119 B4 Ma-lao-la *Malaola* Taiwan
Mal Hab *see* Ma-chiang
86 D4 Ma-li *Mali* Szech.
46 C2 Ma-liang-chi *Maliangji* Anhwei
83 G4 Ma-lien *Malian* Kwangsi
98 B1 Ma-lien-ching *Malianjing* Kansu
98 E2 Ma-lien-ching *Malianjing* Kansu
35 F2 Ma-lien-chuang *Malianzhuang* Shant.
99 I4 Ma-lien Ho *Malian He* (river) Kansu
75 C5 Ma-lin *Malin* Hunan
83 G3 Ma-ling *Maling* Kwangsi
90 B5 Ma-ling *Maling* Kwei.
31 B6 Ma-ling Kuan *Maling Guan* (pass) Hopeh
95 E4 Ma-li-p'o *Malipo* Yun.
99 F4 Ma-lu *Malu* Kansu
99 H4 Ma-lu *Malu* Kansu
83 G2 Ma-lu-ch'iuo *Maluqiao* Kwangsi
10 C1 Ma-lun *Malun* Heilung.
94 C3 Ma-lung Ho *Malong He* (river) Yun.
95 D3 Ma-lung Hsien *Malong Xian* Yun.
95 D2 Ma-lu-t'ang *Malutang* Yun.
34 B4 Ma-miao *Mamiao* Shant.
95 D3 Ma-ming *Maming* Yun.
Mamoi *see* Ma-wei
55 G3 Ma-mu-chi *Mamuji* Honan
102 I1 Ma-na-nu-i-k'u-tu-k'o *Mananuyikuduke* Sink.
Manas *see* Ma-na-ssu
Ma-na-sa-lo-wu Ch'ih *see* Ma-fa-mu-ts'o Hu
102 H1 Ma-na-ssu *Manasi* Sink.
103 D1 Ma-na-ssu *Manasi* Sink.
102 H1 Ma-na-ssu Ho *Manasi He* (river) Sink.
102 H1 Ma-na-ssu Hu *Manasi Hu* (lake) Sink.
103 D1 Ma-na-ssu Hu *Manasi Hu* (lake) Sink.
31 C5 Man-ch'eng *Mancheng* Hopeh
15 H6 Man-chiang *Manjiang* Kirin
15 H6 Man Chiang *Man Jiang* (river) Kirin
119 B4 Man-chou *Manzhou* Taiwan
22 B3 Man-chou-li *Manzhouli* Heilung.
34 C3 Man-chuang *Manzhuang* Shant.
63 F7 Man-ch'uan-kuan *Manchuanguan* Shensi
82 D2 Mang-ch'ang *Mangchang* Kwangsi
55 F5 Mang-chang-tien *Mangzhangdian* Honan
Mang-k'ang *see* Chu-k'a
111 F3 Mang-k'ang Hsien *Mangkang Xian* Tibet
107 G3 Mang-la *Mangla* Tsing.
Mango *see* Man-ko
95 E2 Mang-pu *Mangbu* Yun.
94 B3 Mang-shih *Mangshi* Yun.
55 H3 Mang-tang Shan *Mangdang Shan* (mt) Honan
106 B2 Mang-yai *Mangya* Tsing.
106 B1 Mang-yai-chen *Mangyaizhen* Tsing.
114 A1 Man-han-ch'a-ko *Manhanchage* Ningsia
95 D4 Man-hao *Manhao* Yun.
58 E3 Man Ho *Man He* (river) Hupeh
110 C2 Ma-ni *Mani* Tibet
86 B2 Ma-ni-kan-ko *Manigange* Szech.
Manikengo *see* Ma-ni-kan-ko
110 C3 Man-k'a-pa *Mankaba* Tibet
110 B2 Man-ko *Mange* Tibet

34 B5 Man-k'ou *Mankou* Shant.
14 C5 Man-k'o-ying-tzu *Mankeyingzi* Kirin
23 E6 Man-k'o-ying-tzu *Mankeyingzi* Kirin
10 B1 Man-kuei *Mangui* Heilung.
22 E1 Man-kuei *Mangui* Heilung.
26 C5 Man-lai *Manlai* In. Mong.
58 B5 Man-shui *Manshui* Hupeh
47 C5 Man-shui-ho *Manshuihe* Anhwei
27 E2 Man-ta-la-t'u-miao *Mandalatumiao* In. Mong.
27 E2 Man-ta-la-t'u-miao *Mandalatumiao* In. Mong.
103 E3 Man-t'e-li-k'o *Mantelike* Sink.
38 D2 Man-t'ou Shan *Mantou Shan* (mt) Shansi
19 F3 Man-tu-hu *Manduhu* Liao.
Man-tung-kung-pa *see* **Men-tung**
94 A3 Man-yün-chieh *Manyunjie* Yun.
91 D4 Mao-ch'ang *Maochang* Kwei.
14 E4 Mao-ch'eng-tzu *Maochengzi* Kirin
46 C4 Mao-chi *Maoji* Anhwei
55 E5 Mao-chi *Maoji* Honan
43 F4 Mao-chia-chen *Maojiazhen* Kiangsu
70 E3 Mao-chia-ling *Maojialing* Kiangsi
74 E2 Mao-chia-t'an *Maojiatan* Hunan
38 E2 Mao-chia-tsao *Maojiazao* Shansi
99 H3 Mao-ching *Maojing* Kansu
54 C3 Mao-chin-tu *Maojindu* Honan
39 C7 Mao-chin-tu *Maojindu* Shansi
31 D5 Mao-chou *Maozhou* Hopeh
75 E6 Mao-chün-yü *Maojunyu* Hunan
86 D1 Mao-erh-kai *Maoergai* Szech.
11 D5 Mao-erh-shan *Maoershan* Heilung.
Mao-hsien *see* **Feng-i-chen**
11 C5 Mao-hsing *Maoxing* Heilung.
74 C2 Mao-kang *Maogang* Hunan
19 G4 Mao-k'uei Shan *Maokui Shan* (mt) Liao.
91 F4 Mao-kung *Maogong* Kwei.
94 C3 Mao-lan *Maolan* Yun.
47 E6 Mao-lin *Maolin* Anhwei
14 D4 Mao-lin *Maolin* Kirin
23 E6 Mao-lin *Maolin* Kirin
119 B4 Mao-lin *Maolin* Taiwan
83 E6 Mao-ling *Maoling* Kwangsi
99 F3 Mao-mao Shan *Maomao Shan* (peak) Kansu
91 D4 Mao-mao-tung *Maomaodong* Kwei.
78 B3 Mao-ming *Maoming* Kwangt.
Mao-mu *see* **Ting-hsin**
86 C2 Mao-niu *Maoniu* Szech.
87 E1 Mao-niu Shan *Maoniu Shan* (mt) Szech.
107 E2 Mao-niu-shan *Maoniushan* Tsing.
58 B4 Mao-pa *Maoba* Hupeh
58 B5 Mao-pa *Maoba* Hupeh
91 D3 Mao-pa *Maoba* Kwei.
63 D8 Mao-pa-kuan *Maobaguan* Shensi
74 B2 Mao-p'ing *Maoping* Hunan
58 C4 Mao-p'ing *Maoping* Hupeh
71 B4 Mao-p'ing *Maoping* Kiangsi
71 B5 Mao-p'ing *Maoping* Kiangsi
91 E3 Mao-p'ing *Maoping* Kwei.
119 B5 Mao-pi T'ou *Maobi Tou* (pt) Taiwan
107 G2 Mao-po-sheng *Maobosheng* Tsing.
30 E3 Mao-shan *Maoshan* Hopeh
71 B7 Mao-shan *Maoshan* Kiangsi
43 D4 Mao Shan *Mao Shan* (mts) Kiangsu
59 F5 Mao-shih *Maoshi* Hupeh
74 E2 Mao-ssu-p'u *Maosipu* Hunan
14 B4 Mao-ta-lai *Maodalai* Kirin
23 D6 Mao-ta-lai *Maodalai* Kirin
47 C5 Mao-t'an-ch'ang *Maotanchang* Anhwei
27 G2 Mao-teng *Maodeng* In. Mong.
91 D4 Mao-t'iao Ho *Maotiao* (river) Kwei.
58 B4 Mao-t'ien *Maotian* Hupeh
71 C6 Mao-tien *Maodian* Kiangsi
19 H4 Mao-tien-tzu *Maodianzi* Liao.
74 E2 Mao-ts'ao-chieh *Maocaojie* Hunan
91 D3 Mao-ts'ao-p'u *Maocaopu* Kwei.
95 D2 Mao-tsu *Maozu* Yun.
59 F4 Mao-tsui *Maozui* Hupeh
42 B1 Mao-ts'un *Maocun* Kiangsu
27 E4 Mao-tu *Maodu* In. Mong.
75 E7 Mao-tung-ch'iao *Maodongqiao* Hunan
59 E3 Mao-tz'u-fan *Maocifan* Hupeh
106 E4 Ma-ou-la *Maoula* Tsing.
87 D2 Mao-wen Chiang Autonomous Hsien *Maowen Jiang* Szech.
Mao-wen Ch'iang-tsu Tzu-chih-hsien *see* **Mao-wen Chiang Autonomous Hsien**
26 C5 Mao-wu-su Sha-mo *Maowusu Shamo* (desert) In. Mong.
51 C5 Mao-yang *Maoyang* Chek.
91 D5 Mao-ying *Maoying* Kwei.
42 C3 Ma-pa *Maba* Kiangsu
79 C1 Ma-pa *Maba* Kwangt.
94 B1 Ma-pa-t'ing *Mabating* Yun.
66 E4 Ma-pi *Mabi* Fukien
39 D6 Ma-pi *Mabi* Shansi
90 C5 Ma-pieh Ho *Mabie He* (river) Kwei.
87 D3 Ma-pien *Mabian* Szech.
59 F3 Ma-p'ing *Maping* Hupeh
83 F6 Ma-p'ing *Maping* Kwangsi
42 B1 Ma-p'o *Mapo* Kiangsu
83 G5 Ma-p'o *Mapo* Kwangsi
34 B4 Ma-p'o *Mapo* Shant.
51 D5 Ma-pu *Mabu* Chek.
67 C6 Ma-p'u *Mapu* Fukien
70 C4 Ma-pu *Mabu* Kiangsi
91 C4 Ma-p'u *Mapu* Kwei.
Markang *see* **Ma-erh-k'ang**
Markham Lake *see* **Ma-k'a-mu Ts'o**
19 G3 Ma-san-chia *Masanjia* Liao.
110 A3 Ma-sao *Masao* Tibet
66 C5 Ma-sha *Masha* Fukien
58 C4 Ma-sha *Masha* Hupeh
11 F5 Ma-shan *Mashan* Heilung.
82 E4 Ma-shan *Mashan* Kwangsi
34 C3 Ma-shang *Mashang* Shant.
54 D4 Ma-shan-k'ou *Mashankou* Honan
30 E3 Ma-shen-ch'iao *Mashenqiao* Hopeh
79 D1 Ma-shih *Mashi* Kwangt.
30 B3 Ma-shih-k'ou *Mashikou* Hopeh
54 D4 Ma-shih-p'ing *Mashiping* Honan
35 G2 Ma-shih-tien *Mashidian* Shant.
95 D2 Ma-shu-t'ang *Mashutang* Yun.
83 E3 Ma-ssu *Masi* Kwangsi
35 D3 Ma-sung *Masong* Shant.
87 D3 Ma-t'a-ching *Matajing* Szech.
118 C2 Ma-t'ai-kan *Mataigan* Taiwan
114 C2 Ma-t'ai-kou *Mataigou* Ningsia
102 B2 Ma-t'an *Matan* Sink.
74 F2 Ma-t'ang *Matang* Hunan
70 D2 Ma-tang *Madang* Kiangsi
43 F3 Ma-t'ang *Matang* Kiangsu
14 F6 Ma-tang *Madang* Kirin
95 E4 Ma-t'ang *Matang* Yun.
38 E4 Ma-tao *Madao* Shansi
63 B7 Ma-tao *Madao* Shensi
75 E8 Ma-tao-t'ou *Madaotou* Shansi
86 A1 Ma-ta-ssu *Madasi* Szech.
54 C5 Ma-teng *Madeng* Honan
94 B2 Ma-teng *Madeng* Yun.
83 G2 Ma-t'i *Mati* Kwangsi
46 C3 Ma-tien *Madian* Anhwei
46 C4 Ma-tien *Madian* Anhwei
31 C5 Ma-tien *Madian* Hopeh
43 D3 Ma-tien *Madian* Kiangsu
39 E5 Ma-t'ien *Matian* Shansi
35 F3 Ma-tien *Madian* Shant.
35 F3 Ma-tien *Madian* Shant.
75 E5 Ma-t'ien-hsü *Matianxu* Hunan
74 C3 Ma-ti-i *Madiyi* Hunan
62 G1 Ma-ti-kou *Madigou* Shensi
15 K5 Ma-ti-ta *Madida* Kirin
86 D1 Ma-t'i-tzu *Matizi* Szech.
Ma-to *see* **Huang-ho-yen**
107 F3 Ma-to Hsien *Maduo Xian* Tsing.
67 D5 Ma-t'ou *Matou* Fukien
30 D4 Ma-t'ou *Matou* Hopeh
30 D4 Ma-t'ou *Matou* Hopeh
31 B7 Ma-t'ou *Matou* Hopeh
31 C7 Ma-t'ou *Matou* Hopeh
31 D6 Ma-t'ou *Matou* Hopeh
70 C2 Ma-t'ou *Matou* Kiangsi
118 B3 Ma-tou *Madou* Taiwan
47 E6 Ma-t'ou-chen *Matouzhen* Anhwei
34 D5 Ma-t'ou-chen *Matouzhen* Shant.
47 C4 Ma-t'ou-chi *Matouji* Anhwei
34 A4 Ma-t'ou-chi *Matouji* Shant.
31 C6 Ma-t'ou-li *Matouli* Hopeh
91 E2 Ma-t'ou-shan *Matoushan* Kwei.
83 D3 Ma-t'ou-ya *Matouya* Hopeh
30 F4 Ma-t'ou-ying *Matouying* Hopeh
Matow *see* **Ma-t'ou**
Matsang Tsangpo *see* **Ma-ch'üan Ho**
67 F4 Ma-tsu Lieh-tao *Mazu Liedao* (islands) Fukien
Ma-ts'un *Macun* Shansi
39 D6 Ma-ts'un *Macun* Shansi
98 C1 Ma-tsung Shan *Mazong Shan* (mt) Kansu
67 E4 Ma-tsu Tao *Mazu Dao* (island) Fukien
83 G5 Ma-t'ung *Matong* Kwangsi
62 E4 Ma-tung-ch'uan *Madongchuan* Shensi
98 C2 Ma-tzu-hsüan-ch'üan *Mazixuanquan* Kansu
Ma-tzu-t'a-ma-ssu Feng *Mazitamasi Feng* (peak) Sink.
87 G3 Ma-wang *Mawang* Szech.
67 E5 Ma-wei *Mawei* Fukien
91 E5 Ma-wei *Mawei* Kwei.
99 G4 Ma-wu *Mawu* Kansu
87 G3 Ma-wu-pa *Mawuba* Szech.
99 F5 Ma-ya *Maya* Kansu
59 F4 Ma-yang *Mayang* Hupeh
74 B4 Ma-yang Hsien *Mayang Xian* Hunan
11 D5 Ma-yen *Mayan* Heilung.
99 G4 Ma-yen *Mayan* Kansu
99 G4 Ma-ying *Maying* Kansu
107 H2 Ma-ying *Maying* Tsing.
47 D6 Ma-yü *Mayu* Anhwei
51 D5 Ma-yü *Mayu* Chek.
Mayum La *see* **Ma-yu-mu Shan-k'ou**
110 B3 Ma-yu-mu Shan-k'ou *Mayoumu Shankou* (pass) Tibet
50 C3 Mei-ch'eng *Meicheng* Chek.
74 D3 Mei-ch'eng-chen *Meichengzhen* Hunan
47 C2 Mei-ch'i *Meiqi* Anhwei
50 C2 Mei-ch'i *Meiqi* Chek.
83 G1 Mei-ch'i *Meiqi* Kwangsi
71 C5 Mei Chiang *Mei Jiang* (river) Kiangsi
79 E1 Mei Chiang *Mei Jiang* (river) Kwangt.
46 D3 Mei-ch'iao *Meiqiao* Anhwei
47 D6 Mei-chieh *Meijie* Anhwei
51 D3 Mei-ch'ih *Meichi* Chek.
67 C7 Mei-chou *Meizhou* Fukien
67 E5 Mei-chou Tao *Meizhou Dao* (island) Fukien
67 E5 Mei-chou Wan *Meizhou Wan* (bay) Fukien
47 F5 Mei-chu *Meizhu* Anhwei
59 H4 Mei-ch'uan *Meichuan* Hupeh
99 G4 Mei-ch'uan *Meichuan* Kansu
99 G4 Mei-chuang *Meizhuang* Kiangsi
119 C4 Mei-ho *Meihe* Taiwan
14 F5 Mei-ho-k'ou *Meihekou* Kirin
11 E4 Mei-hsi *Meixi* Heilung.
66 D4 Mei-hsien *Meixian* Fukien
74 F3 Mei-hsien *Meixian* Hunan
79 E1 Mei-hsien *Meixian* Kwangt.
63 C6 Mei-hsien *Meixian* Shensi
67 E4 Mei-hua *Meihua* Fukien
75 D6 Mei-hua-yü *Meihuayu* Hunan
110 C3 Mei-k'ang-sha *Meikangsha* Tibet
47 D6 Mei-keng *Meigeng* Anhwei
79 D1 Mei-k'eng *Meikeng* Kwangt.
66 C4 Mei-k'ou *Meikou* Fukien
86 D3 Mei-ku *Meigu* Szech.
78 B4 Mei-lan *Meilan* Kwangt.
43 E4 Mei-li *Meili* Kiangsu
47 F6 Mei-lin *Meilin* Anhwei
51 E3 Mei-lin *Meilin* Chek.
67 C6 Mei-lin *Meilin* Fukien
71 C6 Mei-lin *Meilin* Kiangsi
70 C3 Mei Ling *Mei Ling* (mt) Kiangsi
11 B4 Mei-li-ssu *Meilisi* Heilung.
23 E4 Mei-li-ssu *Meilisi* Heilung.
67 D5 Mei-lou *Meilou* Fukien
91 E5 Mei-lu *Meilu* Kwangt.
79 D2 Mei-lung *Meilong* Kwangt.
Mei-mao *see* **Mei-lu**
110 B2 Mei-ma Ts'o *Meima Cuo* (lake) Tibet
119 B4 Mei-nung *Meinong* Taiwan
47 B5 Mei-shan *Meishan* Anhwei
50 C1 Mei-shan *Meishan* Chek.
67 C5 Mei-shan *Meishan* Fukien
75 D5 Mei-shan *Meishan* Hunan
87 D2 Mei-shan *Meishan* Szech.
47 B5 Mei-shan Shui-k'u *Meishan Shuiku* (res) Anhwei
67 C5 Mei-shui-k'eng *Meishuikeng* Fukien
26 D4 Mei-tai-chao *Meidaizhao* In. Mong.
91 E3 Mei-t'an Hsien *Meitan Xian* Kwei.
74 E3 Mei-t'an-pa *Meitanba* Hunan
22 D3 Mei-t'ien *Meitian* Heilung.
75 E6 Mei-t'ien *Meitian* Hunan
14 B2 Mei-yao *Meiyao* Kirin
23 D5 Mei-yao *Meiyao* Kirin
102 I1 Mei-yao *Meiyao* Sink.
103 E1 Mei-yao *Meiyao* Sink.
86 C4 Mei-yü *Meiyu* Szech.
50 C4 Mei-yüan *Meiyuan* Chek.
38 E1 Mei-yü-k'ou *Meiyukou* Shansi
Mekong *see* **Lan-ts'ang Chiang**
Mekong *see* **Lan-ts'ang Chiang**
Memar Tshakha *see* **Mei-ma Ts'o**
Mendong *see* **Men-tung**
94 C5 Meng-che *Mengzhe* Yun.
46 C3 Meng-ch'eng *Mengcheng* Anhwei
39 C6 Meng-ch'eng *Mengcheng* Shansi
46 C4 Meng-chi *Mengji* Anhwei
11 F4 Meng-chia-kang *Mengjiagang* Heilung.
54 C5 Meng-chia-lou *Mengjialou* Honan
83 G4 Meng-chiang *Mengjiang* Kwangsi
83 G4 Meng Chiang *Meng Jiang* (river) Kwangsi
62 E2 Meng-chia-wan *Mengjiawan* Shensi
54 D3 Meng-chin Hsien *Mengjin Xian* Honan
75 D7 Meng-chu Ling *Mengzhu Ling* (mts) Hunan
39 D4 Meng-feng *Mengfeng* Shansi
94 C5 Meng-hai *Menghai* Yun.
43 D3 Meng-ho *Menghe* Kiangsu
54 D3 Meng-hsien *Mengxian* Honan
94 C5 Meng-hsing *Mengxing* Yun.
Meng-hua *see* **Wei-shan**
94 C5 Meng-hun *Menghun* Yun.
Menghwa *see* **Weishan**
27 F2 Meng-ken-wu-su *Menggenwusu* In. Mong.
55 G2 Meng-k'o-chi *Mengkeji* Honan
18 D2 Meng-k'o Ho *Mengke He* (river) Liao.
94 B4 Meng-ku *Mengku* Yun.
74 D4 Meng-kung-shih *Menggongshi* Hunan
10 C1 Meng-ku-shan *Mengguashan* Heilung.
30 B2 Meng-ku-ying *Mengguying* Hopeh
94 C5 Meng-la *Mengla* Yun.
94 B4 Meng-lang-pa *Menglangba* Yun.
34 D4 Meng-liang-ku *Mengliangu* Shant.
94 B4 Meng-lien *Menglian* Yun.
94 B4 Meng-lien Shan-Lahu-Wa Autonomous Hsien Yun.
Meng-lien T'ai-tsu La-hu-tsu Wa-tsu Tzu-chih-hsien *see* **Meng-lien Shan-Lahu-Wa Autonomous Hsien**
94 C5 Meng-lun *Menglun* Yun.
86 B1 Meng-lung-ssu *Menglongsi* Szech.
94 C4 Meng-man *Mengman* Yun.
55 F4 Meng-miao *Mengmiao* Honan
19 H1 Meng-niu-hsiao *Mengniuxiao* Liao.
99 H4 Meng-pa *Mengba* Kansu
94 C4 Meng-pan *Mengban* Yun.
94 C5 Meng-p'eng *Mengpeng* Yun.
94 B3 Meng-pin *Mengbin* Yun.
83 G3 Meng-shan *Mengshan* Kwangsi
34 D4 Meng Shan *Meng Shan* (mts) Shant.
94 B4 Meng-sheng *Mengsheng* Yun.
34 C2 Meng-ssu *Mengsi* Shant.
94 B4 Meng-ting-chieh *Mengdingjie* Yun.
83 F4 Meng-ts'un *Mengcun* Kwangsi
31 E5 Meng-ts'un Hui Autonomous Hsien *Mengcun Hui* Hopeh
Meng-ts'un Hui-tsu Tzu-chih-hsien *see* **Meng-ts'un Hui Autonomous Hsien**
35 E3 Meng-t'uan *Mengtuan* Shant.
95 D4 Meng-tzu *Mengzi* Yun.
94 C4 Meng-wang *Mengwang* Yun.
34 C4 Meng-yin *Mengyin* Shant.
94 B3 Meng-yu *Mengyou* Yun.
63 F6 Meng-yüan *Mengyuan* Shensi
94 B4 Meng-yung *Mengyong* Yun.
Menkhap *see* **Man-k'a-pa**
Menkong *see* **Men-kung**
58 C2 Men-ku *Mengu* Hupeh
111 F3 Men-kung *Mengong* Tibet
10 C3 Men-lu Ho *Menlu He* (river) Heilung.
110 B3 Men-shih *Menshi* Tibet
14 D4 Men-ta *Menda* Kirin
14 D4 Men-t'ai-tzu *Mentaizi* Anhwei
30 D4 Men-t'ou-kou *Mentougou* Hopeh
Mentowkow *see* **Men-t'ou-kou**
35 E3 Men-ts'un *Mencun* Shant.
110 C3 Men-tung *Mendong* Tibet
Men-yüan *see* **Hao-men**
Men-yüan Hui-tsu Tzu-chih-hsien *see* **Men-yüan Hui Autonomous Hsien**
Menze *see* **Men-shih**
Mergen *see* **Nen-chiang**
Merket *see* **Mai-kai-t'i**
62 C3 Miao-chai-tzu *Miaozhaizi* Shensi
43 F4 Miao-chen *Miaozhen* Kiangsu
14 C2 Miao-chia *Miaojia* Kirin
23 E5 Miao-chia *Miaojia* Kirin
47 D6 Miao-ch'ien *Miaoqian* Anhwei
70 C2 Miao-ch'ien *Miaoqian* Kiangsi
19 G3 Miao-erh-kou *Miaoergou* Liao.
102 C1 Miao-erh-kou *Miaoergou* Sink.
102 H2 Miao-erh-kou *Miaoergou* Sink.
83 G2 Miao-erh Shan *Miaoer Shan* (mt) Kwangsi
30 D3 Miao-feng Shan *Miaofeng Shan* (mt) Hopeh
54 D3 Miao-hsia *Miaoxia* Honan
71 B6 Miao-hsia *Miaoxia* Kiangsi
55 F2 Miao-k'ou *Miaokou* Honan
62 F1 Miao-kou-men *Miaogoumen* Shensi
118 B2 Miao-li *Miaoli* Taiwan
118 B2 Miao-li Hsien *Miaoli Xian* Taiwan
15 J4 Miao-ling *Miaoling* Kirin
87 F2 Miao-pa *Miaoba* Szech.
83 G2 Miao-p'ing *Miaoping* Kwangsi
34 C3 Miao-shan *Miaoshan* Shant.
74 B3 Miao-shih *Miaoshi* Hunan
47 E6 Miao-shou *Miaoshou* Anhwei
63 B7 Miao-t'ai-tzu *Miaotaizi* Shensi
58 D2 Miao-t'an *Miaotan* Hupeh
91 E2 Miao-t'ang *Miaotang* Kwei.
35 F2 Miao Tao *Miao Dao* (island) Shant.
35 F1 Miao-tao Ch'ün-tao *Miaodao Qundao* (islands) Shant.
51 C1 Miao-t'ou *Miaotou* Kiangsu
83 H1 Miao-tou *Miaodou* Kwangsi
54 C4 Miao-tzu *Miaozi* Honan
55 F4 Miao-wan *Miaowan* Honan
19 H4 Miao-yang *Miaoyang* Liao.
83 G5 Mi-ch'ang *Michang* Kwangsi
34 B2 Mi-chen *Mizhen* Shant.
62 F3 Mi-chih *Mizhi* Shensi
102 D2 Mi-ch'üan Hsien *Miquan Xian* Sink.
Mi-ch'ün *see* **Ku-mu-ti**
Middle Seshan *see* **T'an-hu Shan**
59 F4 Mien-ch'eng *Miancheng* Hupeh
54 C3 Mien-ch'ih *Mianchi* Honan
71 B5 Mien-chin *Mianjin* Kiangsi
87 E2 Mien-chu *Mianzhu* Szech.
87 E2 Mien-hsien *Mianxian* Shensi
79 E2 Mien-hu *Mianhu* Kwangt.
86 D2 Mien-hu-chen *Mianhuzhen* Szech.
86 D3 Mien-ning *Mianning* Szech.
86 D3 Mien-shan *Mianshan* Szech.
7,1 C6 Mien Shui *Mian Shui* (river) Kiangsi
95 D4 Mien-tien *Miandian* Yun.
107 F3 Mien-ts'ao-wan *Miancaowan* Tsing.
22 D3 Mien-tu-ho *Mianduhe* Heilung.
87 E2 Mien-yang *Mianyang* Szech.
59 F4 Mien-yang Hsien *Mianyang Xian* Hupeh
82 E4 Mien-yü *Mianyu* Kwangsi
119 C3 Mien-yüan *Mianyuan* Taiwan
55 G4 Mi Ho *Mi He* (river) Shant.
54 E3 Mi-hsien *Mixian* Honan
38 F1 Mi-hsin-kuan *Mixinguan* Shansi
86 D4 Mi-i *Miyi* Szech.
111 F3 Mi-ku *Migu* Tibet
103 E3 Mi-lan *Milan* Sink.
103 E3 Mi-lan Ho *Milan He* (river) Sink.
95 D3 Mi-le *Mile* Yun.
70 C2 Mi-liang-p'u *Milianqpu* Kiangsi
Mi-lin *see* **Tung-to**
Miling *see* **Mi-lin**
111 E3 Mi-lin Hsien *Milin Xian* Tibet
Milo *see* **Mi-le**
74 F3 Mi-lo *Miluo* Hunan
74 F3 Mi-lo Chiang *Miluo Jiang* (river) Hunan
118 C2 Mi-lun Pi *Milun Bi* (point) Taiwan
66 D4 Min Chiang *Min Jiang* (river) Fukien
87 D1 Min Chiang *Min Jiang* (river) Szech.
67 E4 Min Chiang-kou *Min Jianggou* (est) Fukien
43 D3 Min-ch'iao *Minqiao* Kiangsu
14 G3 Min-chia-t'un *Minjiatun* Kirin
99 F2 Min-ch'in *Minqin* Kansu
67 D4 Min-ch'ing *Minqing* Fukien
11 E4 Min-chu *Minzhu* Heilung.
90 B5 Min-chu *Minzhu* Kwei.
55 G3 Min-ch'üan *Minquan* Honan
37 B2 Min-feng *Minfeng* Shant.
103 B2 Min-feng *Minfeng* Sink.
14 F4 Ming-ch'eng *Mingcheng* Kirin
79 C2 Ming-ch'eng *Mingcheng* Kwangt.
82 D5 Ming-chiang *Mingjiang* Kwangsi
82 D5 Ming Chiang *Ming Jiang* (river) Kwangsi
118 B3 Ming-chien *Mingjian* Taiwan
66 C4 Ming-ch'i Hsien *Mingqi Xian* Fukien
66 D4 Ming-ch'ing *Mingqing* Fukien
31 C6 Ming-hua *Minghua* Hopeh
55 F5 Ming-kang *Minggang* Honan
54 D3 Ming-kao *Minggao* Honan
Mingkiang *see* **Ming-chiang**
46 D4 Ming-kuang *Mingguang* Anhwei
94 B4 Ming-lang *Minglang* Yun.
38 D4 Ming-li *Mingli* Shansi
18 D3 Ming-iun *Minglun* Kwangsi
114 C3 Ming-sha-chou *Mingshazhou* Ningsia
11 F4 Ming-shan *Mingshan* Heilung.
86 D2 Ming-shan *Mingshan* Szech.
11 C4 Ming-shui *Mingshui* Heilung.
98 C1 Ming-shui *Mingshui* Kansu
14 E3 Ming-shui *Mingshui* Kirin
23 D4 Ming-shui *Mingshui* Kirin
34 D4 Ming-shui *Mingshui* Shant.
102 A3 Ming-t'ieh-kai *Mingtiegai* Sink.
102 A3 Ming-t'ieh-kai Ta-pan *Mingtiegai Daban* (pass) Sink.
94 C2 Ming-yin *Mingyin* Yun.
87 F3 Ming-yü *Mingyu* Szech.
15 I4 Ming-yüeh-kou *Mingyuegou* Kirin
107 H2 Min-ho *Minhe* Tsing.
67 D5 Min-hou *Minhou* Fukien
67 E4 Min-hou Hsien *Minhou Xian* Fukien
67 D5 Min-hou Ti-ch'ü *Minhou Diqu* Fukien
91 F3 Min-hsiao *Minxiao* Kwei.
99 F4 Min-hsien *Minxian* Kansu
43 F4 Min-hsing *Minxing* Kiangsu
118 B3 Min-hsiung *Minxiong* Taiwan
98 E2 Min-le *Minle* Kansu
Min-lo *see* **Min-le**
Min-lo Hsien *see* **Min-le Hsien**
86 D1 Min Shan *Min Shan* (mts) Szech.
Mintaka Pass *see* **Ming-t'ieh-kai Ta-pan**
119 B3 Min-tsu *Minzu* Taiwan
Minya Konka *see* **Kung-ka Shan**
Miran *see* **Mi-lan**
102 C3 Mi-sha-lieh-i *Mishalieyi* Sink.
11 F5 Mi-shan *Mishan* Heilung.
14 F3 Mi-sha-tzu *Mishazi* Kirin
75 F5 Mi Shui *Mishui* (river) Hunan
Missar *see* **Men-shih**
119 B4 Mi-t'o *Mituo* Taiwan
110 B2 Mi-to *Miduo* Tibet
58 E4 Mi-t'o-ssu *Mituosi* Hupeh
63 C8 Mi-ts'ang Shan *Micang Shan* (mts) Shensi
94 C3 Mi-tu *Midu* Yun.
14 C3 Mi-tzu-huang *Mizihuang* Kirin
23 E5 Mi-tzu-huang *Mizihuang* Kirin
86 D2 Mi-ya-lo *Miyaluo* Szech.
38 C4 Mi-yü-chen *Miyuzhen* Shansi
30 D3 Mi-yün *Miyun* Hopeh
30 D3 Mi-yung Shui-k'u *Miyong Shuiku* (res.) Hopeh
Mobaishun *see* **Mao-po-sheng**
18 D2 Mo-ch'eng-tzu *Mochengzi* Liao.
94 C4 Mo-chiang *Mojiang* Yun.
70 C2 Mo-ch'i-t'ou *Moqitou* Kiangsi
86 D1 Mo Ch'ü *Mo Qu* (river) Szech.
83 G2 Mo-ch'uan *Mochuan* Kwangsi
Mo-chu-kung-k'a *see* **Kung-k'a**
111 E3 Mo-chu-kung-k'a Hsien *Mozhugongka Xian* Tibet
91 E4 Mo-ch'ung *Mochong* Kwei.
22 C3 Mo-erh-jen-ssu *Moerrensi* Heilung.
22 D3 Mo-erh-ko-le Ho *Moergele He* (river) Heilung.
110 C3 Mo-erh-k'o-sung *Moerkesong* Tibet
22 D2 Mo-erh-tao-ka *Moerdaoga* Heilung.
22 D2 Mo-erh-tao-ka Ho *Moerdaoga He* (river) Heilung.
94 C4 Mo-hei *Mohei* Yun.
10 B1 Mo-ho *Mohe* Heilung.
22 E1 Mo-ho *Mohe* Heilung.
107 F2 Mo-ho *Mohe* Tsing.
22 D3 Mo-ho-erh-t'u *Moheertu* Heilung.
35 H3 Mo-hsieh Tao *Moxie Dao* (island) Shant.
51 C2 Mo-kan Shan *Mogan Shan* (mt) Chek.
54 B4 Mo-kou-k'ou *Mogoukou* Honan
23 E4 Mo-ku-ch'i *Moguqi* Heilung.
102 H1 Mo-ku-hu Shui-k'u *Moguhu Shuiku* (res.) Sink.
Mo-ku-t'ai *see* **T'ai-k'ang**
107 G2 Mo-le *Mole* Tsing.
22 E2 Mo-leng-ko *Molengge* Heilung.
14 B4 Mo-li-miao *Molimiao* Kirin
23 D6 Mo-li-miao *Molimiao* Kirin
14 C4 Mo-li-miao Shui-k'u *Molimiao Shuiku* (res) Kirin
23 D6 Mo-li-miao Shui-k'u *Molimiao Shuiku* (res) Kirin
42 C4 Mo-ling-kuan *Molingguan* Kiangsu
Mo-li-ta-wa Ta-wo-erh-tsu Tzu-chih-ch'i *see* **Moroi-Daba Daghor Autonomous Banner**
111 F3 Mo-lo *Moluo* Tibet
Momein *see* **Tung-ch'eng**
14 D2 Mo-mo-ke *Momoge* Kirin
39 B7 Mo-nan *Monan* Shansi
Mg Lem *see* **Meng-lien**
34 B2 Mo-ni *Moni* Szech.
103 E3 Mo-no-ma-ha Shan *Monuomaha Shan* (mt) Sink.
106 B2 Mo-no-ma-ha Shan *Monuomaha Shan* (mt) Tsing.
107 G4 Mo-pa *Moba* Tsing.
46 D3 Mo-p'an-chi *Mopanji* Anhwei
58 D4 Mo-p'an-chou *Mopanzhou* Hupeh
15 J5 Mo-p'an-shan *Mopanshan* Kirin
58 B4 Mo-pin *Mobin* Hunan
54 E4 Mo-p'o *Mopo* Honan
10 C3 Moroi-Daba Daghor Autonomous Banner Heilung.
M Us *see* **Mu-lu-wu-su Ho**
34 D5 Mo-shan *Moshan* Shant.
74 C2 Mo-shih *Moshi* Hunan
102 H1 Mo-so-wan *Mosuowan* Sink.
103 D1 Mo-so-wan *Mosuowan* Sink.
102 H1 Mo-so-wan-erh-ch'ang *Mosuowanerchang* Sink.
Mosün *see* **Wu-hsüan**
11 E5 Mo-tao-shih *Modaoshi* Heilung.
54 D4 Mo-t'ien-ling *Motianling* Honan
87 E3 Mo-t'o *Motuo* Szech.
111 E3 Mo-t'o *Motuo* Tibet
102 H2 Mo-t'o-sha-la *Motuoshala* Sink.
43 E3 Mo-t'ou *Motou* Kiangsu
79 C2 Mo-ts'un *Mocun* Kwangt.
Motzetan Reservoir *see* **Mo-tzu-t'an Shui-k'u**
47 C5 Mo-tzu-t'an *Mozitan* Anhwei
47 C5 Mo-tzu-t'an Shui-k'u *Mozitan Shuiku* (res) Anhwei
Moukden *see* **Shen-yang**
35 G2 Mou-p'ing *Mouping* Shant.
58 A4 Mou-tao *Moudao* Hupeh
95 C3 Mou-ting *Mouding* Yun.
86 D1 Mo-wa *Mowa* Szech.
Mowming *see* **Mao-ming**
66 C4 Mo-wu *Mowu* Fukien
Mowwen Chiang Autonomous County *see* **Mao-wen Chiang Autonomous Hsien**
78 B2 Mo-yang Chiang *Moyang Jiang* (river) Kwangt.
102 B3 Mo-yü *Moyu* Sink.
104 C4 Mo-yün *Moyun* Tsing.
87 E3 Mu-ai *Muai* Szech.
47 C5 Mu-ch'ang-p'u *Muchangpu* Anhwei
102 C2 Mu-cha-t'i Ho *Muzhati He* (river) Sink.
47 D6 Mu-chen *Muzhen* Anhwei
19 H3 Mu-ch'i *Muqi* Liao.
102 B3 Mu-chi *Muji* Sink.
110 C2 Mu-chia-li-p'u *Mujialipu* Tibet
47 E5 Mu-ch'iao *Muqiao* Anhwei
63 C8 Mu-chia-pa *Mujiaba* Shensi
14 C2 Mu-chia-tien *Mujiadian* Kirin
23 E5 Mu-chia-tien *Mujiadian* Kirin
18 B2 Mu-chia-ying-tzu *Mujiayingzi* Liao.
10 C2 Mu-chi-kung *Mujigong* Heilung.
87 D3 Mu-ch'uan *Muchuan* Szech.
34 B3 Mu-chuang *Muzhuang* Shant.
35 G2 Mu-chu Ho *Muzhu He* (river) Shant.
Mufow Mountains *see* **Mu-fu Shan**
58 B4 Mu-fu *Mufu* Hupeh
74 F2 Mu-Fu Shan *Mufu Shan* (mt) Hunan
70 B2 Mu-fu Shan *Mufu Shan* (mts) Kiangsi
42 C1 Mu Ho *Mu He* (river) Kiangsu
59 H3 Mu-hsi-ho *Muxihe* Hupeh
91 F2 Mu-huang *Muhuang* Kwei.
95 E4 Mu-kan-chieh *Muganjie* Yun.
59 H5 Mu-kang *Mugang* Hupeh
Mukden *see* **Shen-yang**
83 F5 Mu-ko *Muge* Kwangsi
106 C4 Mu-ko Ch'ü *Muge Qu* (river) Tsing.
10 D3 Mu-kou-ho *Mugouhe* Heilung.
83 G4 Mu-kuei *Mugui* Kwangsi
86 C3 Mu-la *Mula* Szech.
11 E5 Mu-lan *Mulan* Heilung.
78 B3 Mu-lan T'ou *Mulan Tou* (cape) Kwangt.
102 I1 Mu-lei *Mulei* Sink.
103 E2 Mu-lei *Mulei* Sink.
Mu-lei Ha-sa-k'o Tzu-chih-hsien *see* **Mu-lei Kazakh Autonomous Hsien**
Mu-leng *see* **Mu-ling**
Mu-leng *see* **Pa-mien-t'ung**
11 G5 Mu-leng Ho *Muleng He* (river) Heilung.
107 F1 Mu-li *Muli* Tsing.
Mu-ling *see* **Pa-mien-t'ung**
11 F5 Mu-ling *Muling* Heilung.
11 F5 Mu-ling Hsien *Muling Xian* Heilung.
34 D3 Mu-ling Kuan *Muling Guan* (pass) Shant.
Mu-lin Ho *see* **Hsi Ho**
86 C4 Mu-li Tibetan Autonomous Hsien *Muli* Szech.
Mu-li Tsang-tsu Tzu-chih-hsien *see* **Mu-li Tibetan Autonomous Hsien**
83 G4 Mu-lo *Muluo* Kwangsi
106 C3 Mu-lu-wu-su Ho *Muluwusu He* (river) Tsing.
38 D3 Mu-ma Ho *Muma He* (river) Shansi
106 D4 Mu-mai-t'ang *Mumaitang* Tsing.
54 C4 Mu-miao Ling *Mumiao Ling* (mt) Honan
94 B4 Mu-nai *Munai* Yun.
Mu-nan-kuan *see* **Yu-i-kuan**
Murui Ussu *see* **Mu-lu-wu-su Ho**
14 G3 Mu-shih-ho *Mushihe* Kirin
14 G3 Mu-shih Ho *Mushi He* (river) Kirin
102 C3 Mu-shih Shan *Mushi Shan* (mt) Sink.
119 B4 Mu-tan *Mudan* Taiwan
11 E5 Mu-tan-chiang *Mudanjiang* Heilung.
11 E5 Mu-tan Chiang *Mudan Jiang* (river) Heilung.
15 H4 Mu-tan Chiang *Mudan Jiang* (river) Kirin
Mutankiang *see* **Mu-tan-chiang**
18 B2 Mu-t'ou-kou *Mutougou* Liao.
30 G3 Mu-t'ou-teng *Mutoudeng* Hopeh
83 F5 Mu-tzu *Muzi* Kwangsi
110 C1 Mu-tzu T'a-ko *Muzi Tage* (mt) Tibet
103 D3 Mu-tzu T'a-ko *Muzi Tage* (peak) Sink.
102 H2 Mu-tzu Ta-pan *Muzi Daban* (pass) Sink.
59 H3 Mu-tzu-tien *Muzidian* Hupeh
Muu Bayshin *see* **Mao-po-sheng**
66 E3 Mu-yang *Muyang* Fukien
66 E3 Mu-yang Ch'i *Muyang Qi* (river) Fukien
22 D3 Mu-yüan *Muyuan* Heilung.
35 F2 Mu-yü-tien *Muyudian* Shant.
Muzart *see* **Mu-cha-t'i Ho**
Muz Tagh *see* **Mu-shih Shan**
82 E5 Na-ch'en *Nachen* Kwangsi
22 D3 Na-chi *Naji* Heilung.
87 E3 Na-ch'i *Naqi* Szech.
106 D3 Na-ch'ih-t'ai *Nachitai* Tsing.
14 C2 Na-chin *Najin* Kirin
23 E5 Na-chin *Najin* Kirin
82 E5 Na-ch'in *Naqin* Kwangsi
10 D2 Na-chin-k'ou-tzu *Najinkouzi* Heilung.
10 B3 Na-chi-t'un *Najitun* Heilung.
22 E3 Na-chi-t'un *Najitun* Heilung.
Na-ch'ü *see* **Hei-ho**
111 E3 Na Ch'ü *Naqu* (river) Tibet
111 E3 Na-ch'ü Hsien *Naqu Xian* Tibet
111 E3 Na-ch'ü Ti-ch'ü *Naqu Diqu* Tibet
15 H5 Na-erh-hung *Naerhong* Kirin
79 C2 Na-fu *Nafu* Kwangt.
Nag Chhu *see* **Na Ch'ü**
Nagchhu Region *see* **Na-ch'ü**
78 B3 Na-huo *Nahuo* Kwangt.
Naichi Gol *see* **Nai-ch'i-kuo-le Ho**
106 C3 Nai-ch'i-kuo-le Ho *Naiqiguole He* (river) Tsing.
Naijin Gol *see* **Nai-ch'i-kuo-le Ho**
18 C3 Nai-lin *Nailin* Liao.
14 A5 Nai-man Ch'i *Naiman Qi* Kirin
103 E1 Nai-ming Shui-ch'üan *Naiming Shuiquan* (spring) Sink.
15 I5 Nai-t'ou-shan *Naitoushan* Kirin
111 D3 Nai-tung *Naidong* Tibet
15 H4 Nai-tzu-shan *Naizishan* Kirin
98 C1 Na-jan-pa-pu-ssu-t'ai-yin Pu-la-ko *Naranbabusitaiyin Bulage* (spring) Kansu
106 C2 Na-jen-kuo-le Ho *Narenguole He* (river) Tsing.
27 F2 Na-jen-pao-li-ko *Narenbaolige* In. Mong.
27 F3 Na-jih-t'u *Naritu* In. Mong.
82 C5 Na-k'an *Nakan* Kwangsi
82 D5 Na-k'an *Nakan* Kwangsi
Nak Chu *see* **Na Ch'ü**
66 C3 Na-k'ou *Nakou* Fukien
Naksh *see* **Pi-ju**
94 B1 Na-ku *Nagu* Yun.
106 E3 Na-ku-tsung-lieh Ch'ü *Naguzonglie Qu* (river) Tsing.
82 B3 Na-lao *Nalao* Kwangsi
102 D2 Na-la-t'i *Nalati* Sink.
Na-leng-kuo-le Ho *see* **Na-jen-kuo-le Ho**
83 E6 Na-li *Nali* Kwangsi
27 E3 Na-lin *Nalin* In. Mong.
82 D5 Na-ling *Naling* Kwangsi
Na-lin Ho *see* **Tung Ho**
26 C5 Na-lin-nao *Nalinnao* In. Mong.
26 C5 Na-lin-shih-li *Nalinshili* In. Mong.
114 C2 Na-lin-su-hai-t'u *Nalinsuhaitu* Ningsia
26 D5 Na-lin-t'a *Nalinta* In. Mong.
83 E5 Na-lou *Nalou* Kwangsi
82 D5 Na-lung *Nalong* Kwangsi
82 E5 Na-lung *Nalong* Kwangsi
111 D3 Na-lung-chia-mu *Nalongjiamu* Tibet
Na-ma *see* **Chou-lu**
82 C4 Na-man *Naman* Kwangsi
Namling Dzong *see* **Nan-mu-lin**
Namoa *see* **Nan-ao**
Nam Tso *see* **Na-mu Hu**
110 B3 Na-mu-cha Shan-k'ou *Namuzha Shankou* (pass) Tibet
27 E3 Na-mu-han-jan-chin-so-mu *Namuhanranjinsuomu* In. Mong.
111 D3 Na-mu Hu *Namu Hu* (lake) Tibet
Namyung *see* **Nan-hsiung**
67 D6 Nan-an *Nanan* Fukien
82 D6 Nan-an *Nanan* Kwangsi
79 D2 Nan-ao *Nanao* Kwangt.
79 E2 Nan-ao *Nanao* Kwangt.
118 C2 Nan-ao *Nanao* Taiwan
79 E2 Nan-ao Tao *Nanao Dao* (island) Kwangt.
11 E4 Nan-ch'a *Nancha* Heilung.
55 E2 Nan-chai *Nanzhai* Honan
58 D3 Nan-chang *Nanzhang* Hupeh
70 C3 Nan-ch'ang *Nanchang* Kiangsi
39 D5 Nan-chang *Nanzhang* Shansi
31 B6 Nan-chang-ch'eng *Nanzhangcheng* Hopeh
Nan-ch'ang - city plan *see* **Page 139**
70 C3 Nan-ch'ang Hsien *Nanchang Xian* Kiangsi
35 F2 Nan-ch'ang-shan Tao *Nanchangshan Dao* (island) Shant.
54 D4 Nan-chao *Nanzhao* Honan
35 E4 Nan-ch'ao *Nanchao* Shant.
46 B4 Nan-chao-chi *Nanzhaoji* Anhwei
66 F3 Nan-chen *Nanzhen* Fukien
78 A4 Nan-ch'en *Nanchen* Kwangt.
67 D5 Nan-ch'eng *Nancheng* Fukien
70 D4 Nan-ch'eng *Nancheng* Kiangsi
40 D4 Nan-ch'eng *Nancheng* Kiangsi
63 B7 Nan-cheng Hsien *Nanzheng Xian* Shensi
47 B5 Nan-ch'i *Nanqi* Anhwei
51 D4 Nan-ch'i *Nan Qi* (river) Chek.
39 D4 Nan-ch'i *Nanqi* Shansi
87 E3 Nan-ch'i *Nanqi* Szech.
91 F4 Nan-chia *Nanjia* Kwei.
87 F1 Nan-chiang *Nanjiang* Szech.
119 B5 Nan-chiang *Nanjiang* Taiwan
74 F3 Nan-chiang-ch'iao *Nanjiangqiao* Hunan
78 B2• Nan-chiang-k'ou *Nanjiangkou* Kwangt.
58 E3 Nan-ch'iao *Nanqiao* Hupeh
43 F5 Nan-ch'iao *Nanqiao* Kiangsu
78 B4 Nan-ch'iao *Nanqiao* Kwangt.
79 C2 Nan-chieh *Nanjie* Kwangt.
86 C2 Nan-chieh *Nanjie* Szech.
94 C3 Nan-chien *Nanjian* Yun.
Nan-chien I-tsu Tzu-chih-hsien *see* **Nan-chien Yi Autonomous Hsien**
94 C3 Nan-chien Yi Autonomous Hsien Yun.

31 C6 Nan-chih-ch'iu *Nanzhiqiu* Hopeh
71 B7 Nan-ching *Nanjing* Kiangsi
42 C3 Nan-ching *Nanjing* Kiangsu
Nan-ching - city plan *see* Page 131
67 C6 Nan-ching Hsien *Nanjing Xian* Fukien
58 D4 Nan-chin-kuan *Nanjinguan* Hupeh
51 E5 Nan-chi Shan *Nanji Shan* (island) Chek.
38 E2 Nan-ch'üan *Nanquan* Shansi
35 F3 Nan-ch'üan *Nanquan* Shant.
87 F3 Nan-ch'uan *Nanchuan* Szech.
54 D3 Nan-chuang *Nanzhuang* Honan
39 D4 Nan-chuang *Nanzhuang* Shansi
102 H2 Nan-chuang *Nanzhuang* Sink.
118 C2 Nan-chuang *Nanzhuang* Taiwan
47 E5 Nan-chu Hu *Nanzhu Hu* (lake) Anhwei
87 F2 Nan-ch'ung *Nanchong* Szech.
87 F2 Nan-ch'ung *Nanchong* Szech.
Nanchwan *see* Nan-ch'uan
118 C2 Nan-fang-ao *Nanfangao* Taiwan
43 E4 Nan-fang-ch'üan *Nanfangquan* Kiangsu
19 G3 Nan-fen *Nanfen* Liao.
70 D2 Nan-feng *Nanfeng* Kiangsi
71 D4 Nan-feng *Nanfeng* Kiangsi
78 B2 Nan-feng *Nanfeng* Kwangt.
Nang-ch'ien *see* Hsiang-ta
106 E4 Nang-ch'ien Hsien *Nangqian Xian* Tsing.
Nan Hai *see* South China Sea
Nan Hai *see* South China Sea
79 C2 Nan-hai Hsien *Nanhai Xian* Kwangt.
30 A2 Nan-hao-ch'ien *Nanhaoqian* Hopeh
31 B6 Nan-ho *Nanhe* Hopeh
58 D2 Nan Ho *Nan He* (river) Hupeh
35 D2 Nan-ho *Nanhe* Shant.
54 D4 Nan-ho-tien *Nanhedian* Honan
55 F3 Nan-hsi *Nanxi* Honan
119 B3 Nan-hsi *Nanxi* Taiwan
31 D6 Nan-hsia-k'ou *Nanxiakou* Hopeh
43 F4 Nan-hsiang *Nanxiang* Kiangsu
83 F5 Nan-hsiang *Nanxiang* Kwangsi
83 H3 Nan-hsiang *Nanxiang* Kwangsi
83 E5 Nan-hsiao *Nanxiao* Kwangsi
74 E2 Nan-hsien *Nanxian* Hunan
42 C2 Nan-hsien-chi *Nanxianji* Kiangsu
34 C4 Nan-hsin *Nanxin* Shant.
63 B7 Nan-hsing *Nanxing* Shensi
79 D1 Nan-hsiung *Nanxiong* Kwangt.
51 D2 Nan-hsün *Nanxun* Chek.
98 B2 Nan-hu *Nanhu* Kansu
99 G4 Nan-hu *Nanhu* Kansu
94 C3 Nan-hua *Nanhua* Yun.
23 D5 Nan-hua-hu-shao *Nanhuahushao* Kirin
35 G3 Nan-huang *Nanhuang* Shant.
35 F1 Nan-huang-ch'eng Tao *Nanhuangcheng Dao* (island) Shant.
15 I4 Nan-huang-ni-ho *Nanhuangnihe* Kirin
58 C1 Nan-hua-t'ang *Nanhuatang* Hupeh
43 F4 Nan-hui *Nanhui* Kiangsu
106 D2 Nan-huo-lu-hsün Hu *Nanhuoluxun Hu* (lake) Tsing.
118 C2 Nan-hu-ta Shan *Nanhuda Shan* (mt) Taiwan
11 E6 Nan-hu-t'ou *Nanhutou* Heilung.
34 C4 Nan-i *Nanyi* Shant.
67 E5 Nan-jih Ch'ün-tao *Nanri Qundao* (islands) Fukien
67 E5 Nan-jih Tao *Nanri Dao* (island) Fukien
90 B4 Nan-k'ai *Nankai* Kwei.
47 C5 Nan-kang *Nangang* Anhwei
71 B6 Nan-k'ang *Nankang* Kiangsi
83 F6 Nan-k'ang *Nankang* Kwangsi
15 J5 Nan-kang Shan *Nangang Shan* (mts) Kirin
42 C1 Nan-kang-shang *Nangangshang* Kiangsu
70 A4 Nan-k'eng *Nankeng* Kiangsi
Nankien *see* Nan-chien
Nanking *see* Nan-ching
66 C4 Nan-k'ou *Nankou* Fukien
15 I4 Nan-kou *Nangou* Kirin
39 C7 Nan-kou *Nangou* Shansi
30 D3 Nan-k'ou-chen *Nankouzhen* Hopeh
19 H3 Nan-k'ou-ch'ien *Nankouqian* Liao.
39 D4 Nan-kuan *Nanguan* Shansi
18 E5 Nan-kuan-ling *Nanguanling* Liao.
31 C7 Nan-kuan-t'ao *Nanguantao* Hopeh
39 C5 Nan-kuan-ts'un *Nanguancun* Shansi
98 E2 Nan-ku-ch'eng *Nangucheng* Kansu
34 D5 Nan-ku-chuang *Nanguzhuang* Shant.
31 C6 Nan-kung *Nangong* Hopeh
18 C4 Nan-kung-ying-tzu *Nangongyingzi* Liao.
11 C4 Nan-lai *Nanlai* Heilung.
79 C2 Nan-lang *Nanlang* Kwangt.
39 D5 Nan-li *Nanli* Shansi
30 B2 Nan-liang *Nanliang* Hopeh
39 C6 Nan-liang *Nanliang* Shansi
119 C4 Nan-liao *Nanliao* Taiwan
59 G5 Nan-lin-ch'iao *Nanlinqiao* Hupeh
47 E6 Nan-ling *Nanling* Anhwei
79 D2 Nan-ling *Nanling* Kwangt.
18 D3 Nan-ling *Nanling* Liao.
75 E6 Nan Ling *Nan Ling* (mts) Hunan
106 D2 Nan-ling-ch'iu *Nanlingqiu* Tsing.
39 C6 Nan-liu *Nanliu* Shansi
35 E3 Nan-liu *Nanliu* Shant.
83 F6 Nan-liu Chiang *Nanliu Jiang* (river) Kwangsi
55 G1 Nan-lo *Nanluo* Honan
15 G4 Nan-lou Shan *Nanlou Shan* (mt) Kirin
34 A4 Nan-lu-chi *Nanluji* Shant.
51 D3 Nan-ma *Nanma* Chek.
34 D3 Nan-ma *Nanma* Shant.
70 B4 Nan-miao *Nanmiao* Kiangsi
119 B3 Nan-mien-shan *Nanmianshan* (mt) Taiwan
22 E3 Nan-mu *Nanmu* Heilung.
87 F2 Nan-mu *Nanmu* Szech.
110 D3 Nan-mu-lin *Nanmulin* Tibet
75 B4 Nan-mu-p'ing *Nanmuping* Hunan
86 C1 Nan-mu-ta *Nanmuda* Szech.
58 C4 Nan-mu-yüan *Nanmuyuan* Hupeh
Nan-ning - city plan *see* Page 137
82 E5 Nan-ning (Nanning) *Nanning* Kwangsi
62 E4 Nan-ni-wan *Nanniwan* Shensi
87 E1 Nan-pa *Nanba* Szech.
87 G2 Nan-pa-chen *Nanbazhen* Szech.
106 D2 Nan-pa-hsien *Nanbaxian* Tsing.
91 D3 Nan-pai-chen *Nanbaizhen* Kwei.
82 B3 Nan-p'an Chiang *Nanpan Jiang* (river) Kwangsi
95 E3 Nan-p'an Chiang *Nanpan Jiang* (river) Yun.
30 F4 Nan-pao *Nanbao* Hopeh
31 F4 Nan-pao *Nanbao* Hopeh
79 C3 Nan-p'eng Tao *Nanpeng Dao* Kwangt.
31 D5 Nan-p'i *Nanpi* Hopeh
18 D3 Nan-p'iao *Nanpiao* Liao.
66 D3 Nan-p'ing *Nanping* Fukien
66 D4 Nan-p'ing *Nanping* Fukien
74 C1 Nan-p'ing *Nanping* Hunan
75 F5 Nan-p'ing *Nanping* Hunan
58 E5 Nan-p'ing *Nanping* Hupeh
15 J5 Nan-p'ing *Nanping* Kirin
87 E1 Nan-p'ing *Nanping* Szech.
46 C3 Nan-p'ing-chi *Nanpingji* Anhwei
66 D3 Nan-p'ing Ti-ch'ü *Nanping Diqu* Fukien
82 C4 Nan-p'o *Nanpo* Kwangsi
87 F2 Nan-pu *Nanbu* Szech.
66 D3 Nan-p'u Ch'i *Nanpu Qi* (river) Fukien
94 C4 Nan-sang-tu *Nansangdu* Yun.
47 D5 Nan-san-shih-lan *Nansanshilan* Anhwei
34 C4 Nan-sha-ho *Nanshahe* Shant.
19 I2 Nan-shan-ch'eng *Nanshancheng* Liao.
34 C3 Nan-shang-chuang *Nanshangzhuang* Shant.
30 B4 Nan-shang-t'un *Nanshangtun* Hopeh
115 D4 Nanshan Island China Sea
103 F2 Nan-shan-k'ou *Nanshankou* Sink.
67 C6 Nan-sheng *Nansheng* Fukien
119 B4 Nan-shih-ho *Nanshihe* Taiwan
31 B6 Nan-shih-men *Nanshimen* Hopeh
18 D3 Nan-shuang-miao *Nanshuangmiao* Liao.
66 F4 Nan-shuang Tao *Nanshuang Dao* (island) Fukien
Nansiung *see* Nan-hsiung
19 F4 Nan-t'ai *Nantai* Liao.
31 C5 Nan-ta-jan *Nandaran* Hopeh
82 D3 Nan-tan *Nandan* Kwangsi
71 C5 Nan-t'ang *Nantang* Kiangsi
74 E2 Nan-ta-shan *Nandashan* Hunan
119 B4 Nan-ta-wu Shan *Nandawu Shan* (mt) Taiwan
51 C5 Nan-t'ien *Nantian* Chek.
51 E3 Nan-t'ien *Nantian* Chek.
19 H3 Nan-tien-tzu *Nandianzi* Liao.
34 D3 Nan-ting *Nanding* Shant.
94 B4 Nan-ting Ho *Nanding He* (river) Yun.
67 D6 Nan-ting Tao *Nanding Dao* (island) Fukien
79 C2 Nan-t'ou *Nantou* Kwangt.
118 B3 Nan-t'ou *Nantou* Taiwan
118 B3 Nan-t'ou Hsien *Nantou Xian* Taiwan
19 H3 Nan-tsa-mu *Nanzamu* Liao.
55 E2 Nan-ts'un *Nancun* Honan
71 C4 Nan-ts'un *Nancun* Kiangsi
38 F2 Nan-ts'un *Nancun* Shansi
35 F3 Nan-ts'un *Nancun* Shant.
43 D4 Nan-tu *Nandu* Kiangsu
83 G5 Nan-tu *Nandu* Kwangsi
46 C3 Nan-tu-chi *Nanduji* Anhwei
78 B4 Nan-tu Chiang *Nandu Jiang* (river) Kwangt.
22 C3 Nan-t'un *Nantun* Heilung.
43 E3 Nan-t'ung *Nantong* Kiangsu
43 F3 Nan-t'ung Hsien *Nantong Xian* Kiangsu
43 E3 Nan-t'ung-kang *Nantonggang* Kiangsu
119 B3 Nan-tzu-hsien Ch'i *Nanzixian Qi* (river) Taiwan
94 C5 Na-nung *Nanong* Yun.
55 E5 Nan-wan *Nanwan* Honan
34 B4 Nan-wang *Nanwang* Shant.
55 E5 Nan-wan Shui-k'u *Nanwan Shuiku* (res) Honan
39 E5 Nan-wei-ch'üan *Nanweiquan* Shansi
27 F3 Nan-wei-tzu *Nanweizi* In. Mong.
63 D7 Nan-wu-t'ai *Nanwutai* (mt) Shensi
66 D4 Nan-ya *Nanya* Fukien
66 E3 Nan-yang *Nanyang* Fukien
54 D4 Nan-yang *Nanyang* Honan
43 E2 Nan-yang *Nanyang* Kiangsu
83 E5 Nan-yang *Nanyang* Kwangsi
34 B4 Nan-yang *Nanyang* Shant.
38 F1 Nan-yang Ho *Nanyang He* (river) Shansi
34 B4 Nan-yang Hu *Nanyang Hu* (section of lake) Shant.
67 E5 Nan-yen *Nanyan* Fukien
51 D5 Nan-yen-t'ang Shan *Nanyantang Shan* (mt) Chek.
66 F4 Nan Yü *Nan Yu* (islet) Fukien
82 D4 Nan-yü *Nanyu* Kwangsi
107 F2 Nan-yü *Nanyu* Tsing.
47 D6 Nan-yüan *Nanyuan* Anhwei
50 C5 Nan-yüan *Nanyuan* Chek.
30 D4 Nan-yüan *Nanyuan* Hopeh
75 E4 Nan-yüeh *Nanyue* Hunan
38 E2 Nan-yü-k'ou *Nanyukou* Shansi
102 B3 Nao-erh Hu *Naoer Hu* (lake) Sink.
114 C2 Nao-kan-t'ao-le *Naogantaole* Ningsia
107 E1 Nao-ko-cha *Naogezha* Tsing.
55 F2 Nao-li *Naoli* Honan
11 G4 Nao-li Ho *Naoli He* (river) Heilung.
103 F2 Nao-mao-hu *Naomaohu* Sink.
10 C1 Nao-ta-han *Naodahan* Heilung.
14 C5 Nao-te-hai *Naodehai* Kirin
23 E6 Nao-te-hai *Naodehai* Kirin
82 E5 Na-pai *Nabai* Kwangsi
83 E6 Na-p'eng *Napeng* Kwangsi
82 B4 Na-p'o *Napo* Kwangsi
82 C4 Na-p'o *Napo* Kwangsi
110 B2 Na-p'o *Napo* Tibet
83 F6 Na-pu *Nabu* Kwangsi
95 E4 Na-sa *Nasa* Yun.
71 B5 Na-shan *Nashan* Kiangsi
58 A4 Na-shui-ch'i *Nashuiqi* Hupeh
78 A4 Na-ta *Nanda* Kwangt.
82 D6 Na-tang *Nadang* Kwangsi
14 F4 Na-tan-po *Nadanbo* Kirin
82 B3 Na-tso *Nazuo* Kwangsi
10 C2 Na-tu-li Ho *Naduli He* (river) Heilung.
22 F2 Na-tu-li Ho *Naduli He* (river) Heilung.
82 D4 Na-t'ung *Natong* Kwangsi
Nausa Bay *see* Liu-sha Wan
22 F2 Na-wen Ho *Nawen He* (river) Heilung.
110 B3 Na-wu Tsang-pu *Nawu Zangbu* (river) Tibet
83 F5 Na-yang *Nayang* Kwangsi
90 C4 Na-yung *Nayong* Kwei.
Near Lake *see* Yang Ts'o
87 E3 Nei-chiang *Neijiang* Szech.
31 B6 Nei-ch'iu *Neiqiu* Hopeh
54 C4 Nei-hsiang *Neixiang* Honan
55 F2 Nei-huang *Neihuang* Honan
55 F3 Nei-huang-chi *Neihuangji* Honan
Neikiang *see* Nei-chiang
99 G4 Nei-kuan-ying *Neiguanying* Kansu
71 B6 Nei-liang *Neiliang* Kiangsi
119 B4 Nei-men *Neimen* Taiwan
54 D3 Nei-pu *Neibu* Honan
118 B2 Nei-pu *Neibu* Taiwan
119 B4 Nei-pu *Neibu* Taiwan
118 C2 Nei-wan *Neiwan* Taiwan
10 C3 Ne-nan *Nenan* Heilung.
10 C3 Nen-chiang *Nenjiang* Heilung.
10 C3 Nen Chiang *Nen Jiang* (river) Heilung.
22 F3 Nen Chiang *Nen Jiang* (river) Heilung.
23 F5 Nen Chiang *Nen Jiang* (river) Kirin
10 C4 Nen-chiang Ti-ch'ü *Nenjiang Diqu* Heilung.
18 D3 Neng-chia *Nengjia* Liao.
118 C3 Neng-kao Shan *Nenggao Shan* (mt) Taiwan
22 C3 New Barga East Banner Heilung.
22 B3 New Barga West Banner Heilung.
New Shu Ho *see* Hsin-shu Ho
New Yi Ho *see* Hsin-i Ho
Neymo *see* Ni-ma
Nganglaring Tsho *see* Ang-la-jen Ts'o
Ngemda *see* En-ta
107 F3 Ngolog Tibetan Autonomous District Tsing.
Ngoring Nor *see* O-ling Hu
75 D4 Niang-ch'i *Niangqi* Hunan
63 B6 Niang-niang-miao *Niangniangmiao* Shensi
99 G4 Niang-niang-pa *Niangniangba* Kansu
Niangtzekwan *see* Niang-tzu Kuan
38 E4 Niang-tzu-kuan *Niangziguan* Shansi
59 G4 Niao-lung-ch'üan *Niaolongquan* Hupeh
83 G5 Niao-shih *Niaoshi* Kwangsi
74 C3 Niao-su *Niaosu* Hunan
Niari Lake *see* Ang-tse Ts'o
51 C4 Ni-chai *Nizhai* Chek.
43 F5 Ni-ch'eng *Nicheng* Kiangsu
95 D3 Ni-chiao *Nijiao* Yun.
47 C7 Ni-ch'i-ch'ung *Niqichong* Anhwei
46 B3 Ni-ch'iu *Niqiu* Anhwei
86 B1 Ni Ch'ü *Ni Qu* (river) Szech.
58 D4 Nieh-chia-ho *Niejiahe* Hupeh
70 C2 Nieh-ch'iao *Nieqiao* Kiangsi
Nieh-jung *see* Se-kung
111 E2 Nieh-jung Hsien *Nierong Xian* Tibet
Nieh-la-mu *see* Ch'ung-tui
110 C3 Nieh-la-mu Hsien *Nielamu Xian* Tibet
71 B6 Nieh-tu *Niedu* Kiangsi
46 D4 Nien-chia-lan *Nianjialan* Anhwei
111 D3 Nien-ch'ing-t'ang-ku-la Shan *Nianqingtanggula Shan* (peak) Tibet
111 E3 Nien-ch'ing-t'ang-ku-la Shan-mo *Nianqingtanggula Shanmo* (mts) Tibet
42 B1 Nien-chuang *Nianzhuang* Kiangsu
107 H2 Nien-po *Nianbo* Tsing.
70 F3 Nien-ssu-tu *Niansidu* Kiangsi
42 C1 Nien-t'ou-chi *Niantouji* Kiangsu
59 G3 Nien-tzu-kang *Nianzigang* Hupeh
11 B4 Nien-tzu-shan *Nianzishan* Heilung.
23 E4 Nien-tzu-shan *Nianzishan* Heilung.
74 E2 Nien-yü-hsü *Nianyuxu* Hunan
70 E2 Nien-yü-shan *Nianyushan* Kiangsi
10 C3 Ni-erh-chi *Nierji* Heilung.
22 F3 Ni-erh-chi *Nierji* Heilung.
18 E3 Ni-ho-tzu *Nihezi* Liao.
94 B2 Ni-hsi *Nixi* Yun.
102 C2 Ni-le-k'o *Nileke* Sink.
Nilki *see* Ni-le-k'o
110 C3 Ni-ma *Nima* Tibet
14 A3 Ni-ma-la-ku *Nimalagu* Kirin
23 D5 Ni-ma-la-ku *Nimalagu* Kirin
Ni-mu *see* T'a-jung
111 D3 Ni-mu Hsien *Nimu Xian* Tibet
11 E5 Ning-an *Ningan* Heilung.
Ning-an-pao *see* Chung-ning
18 C3 Ning-ch'eng Hsien *Ningcheng Xian* Liao.
51 D4 Ning-ch'i *Ningqi* Chek.
63 B8 Ning-ch'iang *Ningqiang* Shensi
31 B6 Ning-chin *Ningjin* Hopeh
34 B2 Ning-chin *Ningjin* Shant.
111 F3 Ning-ching Shan *Ningjing Shan* (mts) Tibet
35 H3 Ning-chin-so *Ningjinsuo* Shant.
Ning-erh *see* P'u-erh
Ning-hai *see* Mou-p'ing
51 E3 Ning-hai *Ninghai* Chek.
30 E4 Ning-ho Hsien *Ninghe Xian* Hopeh
30 E4 Ning-ho Hsien *Ninghe Xian* Hopeh
74 E3 Ning-hsiang *Ningxiang* Hunan
99 H4 Ning-hsien *Ningxian* Kansu
66 B4 Ning-hua *Ninghua* Fukien
38 D3 Ning-hua *Ninghua* Shansi
71 A5 Ning-kang Hsien *Ninggang Xian* Kiangsi
Ningkiang *see* Ning-chiang
39 D4 Ning-ku *Ninggu* Shansi
47 E6 Ning-kuo *Ningguo* Anhwei
47 E6 Ning-kuo Hsien *Ningguo Xian* Anhwei
94 C2 Ning-lang *Ninglang* Yun.
Ning-lang I-tsu Tzu-chih-hsien *see* Ning-lang Yi Autonomous Hsien
94 C2 Ning-lang Yi Autonomous Hsien Yun.
55 G3 Ning-ling *Ningling* Honan
82 D5 Ning-ming *Ningming* Kwangsi
86 D4 Ning-nan *Ningnan* Szech.
Ning-nien *see* Fu-yü
51 E3 Ning-po *Ningbo* Chek.
119 C3 Ning-pu *Ningbu* Taiwan
63 D7 Ning-shan Hsien *Ningshan Xian* Shensi
Ningsia *see* Yin-ch'uan
Ningsiafu *see* Yin-ch'uan
Ningsia Hui Autonomous Region *see* Pages 113-114
66 E4 Ning-te *Ningde* Fukien
71 C5 Ning-tu *Ningdu* Kiangsi
47 F6 Ning-tun *Ningdun* Anhwei
Ninguta *see* Ning-an
38 D2 Ning-wu *Ningwu* Shansi
34 B4 Ning-yang *Ningyang* Shant.
62 D3 Ning-yen-ch'eng *Ningyancheng* Shensi
Ning-yüan *see* Hsi-ch'ang
75 D6 Ning-yüan *Ningyuan* Hunan
110 C2 Ni-shan *Nishan* Tibet
74 C2 Ni-shih *Nishi* Hunan
58 E2 Ni-tsui *Nizui* Hupeh
82 A3 Ni-tung *Nidong* Kwangsi
90 C5 Niu-ch'ang *Niuchang* Kwei.
91 E4 Niu-ch'ang *Niuchang* Kwei.
91 D3 Niu-ch'ang-p'o *Niuchangpo* Kwei.
74 C2 Niu-ch'e-ho *Niuchehe* Hunan
11 D5 Niu-chia *Niujia* Heilung.
31 B6 Niu-chia-ch'iao *Niujiaqiao* Hopeh
34 B3 Niu-chiao-tien *Niujiaodian* Shant.
18 B2 Niu-chia-ying-tzu *Niujiayingzi* Liao.
35 F3 Niu-ch'i-pu *Niuqibu* Shant.
19 F4 Niu-chuang *Niuzhuang* Liao.
34 D2 Niu-chuang *Niuzhuang* Shant.
22 D2 Niu-erh-ho *Niuerhe* Heilung.
22 D2 Niu-erh-ho *Niuerhou* Heilung.
23 D4 Niu-fen-t'ai *Niufentai* Kirin
71 B5 Niu-hou Ho *Niuhou He* (river) Kiangsi
14 F5 Niu-hsing-ting-tzu *Niuxindingzi* Kirin
19 G3 Niu-hsin-t'ai *Niuxintai* Liao.
30 G4 Niu-kuan-ying *Niuguanying* Hopeh
86 B3 Niu-ku-tu *Niugudu* Szech.
95 D2 Niu-lan Chiang *Niulan Jiang* (river) Yun.
91 G3 Niu-lang *Niulang* Kwei.
30 D3 Niu-lan-shan *Niulanshan* Hopeh
19 I4 Niu-mao-wu *Niumaowu* Liao.
83 H3 Niu-miao *Niumiao* Kwangsi
90 A3 Niu-p'eng-tzu *Niupengzi* Kwei.
106 C1 Niu-pi-tzu-liang *Niubiziliang* Tsing.
47 D5 Niu-pu *Niubu* Anhwei
42 C1 Niu-shan *Niushan* Kiangsu
39 B6 Niu-she *Niushe* Shansi
55 F2 Niu-shih-t'un *Niushitun* Honan
58 D2 Niu-shou *Niushou* Hupeh
71 C4 Niu-t'ien *Niutian* Kiangsi
30 D4 Niu-t'o *Niutuo* Hopeh
71 C7 Niu-tou-kuang *Niudouguang* Kiangsi
47 D6 Niu-t'ou-shan *Niutoushan* Anhwei
51 E3 Niu-t'ou Shan *Niutou Shan* (island) Chek.
50 C4 Niu-t'ou Shan *Niutou Shan* (mt) Chek.
63 E8 Niu-t'ou-tien *Niutoudian* Shensi
38 E3 Niu-ts'un *Niucun* Shansi
62 E4 Niu-wu *Niuwu* Shensi
111 E3 Ni-wu-mu *Niwumu* Tibet
Niya *see* Min-feng
102 C3 Ni-ya Ho *Niya He* (river) Sink.
107 E3 Ni-ya-mu-ts'o *Niyamucuo* Tsing.
Noh *see* Shan-ho
10 C3 No-ho *Nuohe* Heilung.
22 F3 No-ho *Nuohe* Heilung.
Nomhon *see* No-mu-hung
10 B3 No-min Ho *Nuomin He* (river) Heilung.
22 E3 No-min Ho *Nuomin He* (river) Heilung.
10 B2 No-min Ta-shan *Nuomin Dashan* (mt) Heilung.
22 E2 No-min-ta Shan *Nuominda Shan* (mt) Heilung.
Nomohon Hoto *see* No-mu-hung
106 E2 No-mu-hung *Nuomuhong* Tsing.
22 F3 No-nan *Nuonan* Heilung.
115 C4 North Danger Reef China Sea
98 B2 North Kansu Mongol Autonomous Hsien Kansu
North Kiangsu Canal *see* *Su-pei Kuan-kai-tsung-ch'ü*
115 C5 North Luconia Shoals China Sea
115 B2 North Reef China Sea
115 D1 North Vereker Bank China Sea
83 H4 No-tung *Nuodong* Kwangsi
30 B4 Nuan-ch'üan *Nuanquan* Hopeh
114 C2 Nuan-ch'üan *Nuanquan* Ningsia
39 B4 Nuan-ch'üan *Nuanquan* Shansi
70 E3 Nuan-shui *Nuanshui* Kiangsi
Nu Chiang *see* Salween
111 F3 Nu Chiang *Nu Jiang* (river) Tibet
94 B3 Nu Chiang *Nu Jiang* (river) Yun.
111 F3 Nu-chiang *Nujiang* Tibet
94 B2 Nu-chiang Lisu Autonomous District Yun.
Nu-chiang Li-su-tsu Tzu-chih-chou *see* Nu-chiang Lisu Autonomous District
18 E3 Nü-erh-ho *Nüerhe* Liao.
18 D4 Nü-erh Ho *Nüer He* (river) Liao.
102 C3 Nu-jih *Nuri* Sink.
Nukiang Lisu Autonomous District *see* Nu-chiang Lisu Autonomous District
18 C3 Nu-lu-erh-hu Shan *Nuluerhu Shan* (mts) Liao.
14 F3 Nung-an *Nongan* Kirin
23 F5 Nung-an *Nongan* Kirin
74 B2 Nung-ch'e *Nongche* Hunan
10 G4 Nung Chiang *Nong Jiang* (river) Heilung.
11 E4 Nung-ho *Nonghe* Heilung.
27 H2 Nung-nao-miao *Nongnaomiao* In. Mong.
Nunkiang *see* Nen-chiang
Nura *see* Nu-jih
Nurture *see* Nu-t'u-le
94 B3 Nu Shan *Nu Shan* (mts) Yun.
46 E4 Nü-shan Hu *Nüshan Hu* (lake) Anhwei
106 C2 Nu-t'u-le *Nutule* Tsing.
Nya Chu *see* Ya-lung Chiang
59 G4 O-ch'eng *Echeng* Hupeh
94 C3 O-chia *Ejia* Yun.
47 E5 O-ch'iao *Eqiao* Anhwei
86 B1 O-chih *Ezhi* Szech.
O-chi-na-ch'i *see* Ta-lan-l'u-pu
O-chi-na Ch'i *see* Edsin Banner
27 G2 O-chi-na-erh-su-mo *Ejinaersumo* In. Mong.
O-chi-na Ho *see* Jo Shui
34 D4 O-chuang *Ezhuang* Shant.
10 C3 O-erh-ho *Eerhe* Heilung.
22 F3 O-erh-ho *Eerhe* Heilung.
22 D2 O-erh-ku-ha Ho *Eerguha He* (river) Heilung.
O-erh-ku-na Tso-ch'i *see* Argun East Banner
O-erh-ku-na Yu-ch'i *see* Argun West Banner
70 E2 O-hu *Ehu* Kiangsi
Oitoghrak *see* Ao-i-t'e-ko-la-k'o
27 G2 O-jen-ko-pi Mu-ch'ang *Erengebi Muchang* In. Mong.
86 C2 O-jih *Eri* Szech.
Oka Dzong *see* Wo-ka
98 E2 O-k'en-hu-tu-ko *Ekenhuduge* Kansu
106 D1 O-k'o-t'u-le *Eketule* Tsing.
38 E2 O-k'ou *Ekou* Shansi
22 C3 Old Barga Banner Heilung.
107 E3 O-ling *Eling* Tsing.
107 E3 O-ling Hu *Eling Hu* (lake) Tsing.
86 C2 O-lo *Eluo* Szech.
22 B3 O-lo-fu-nei *Eluofunei* Heilung.
119 B5 O-luan-pi *Eluanbi* Taiwan
O-lun-ch'un-tsu Tzu-chih-ch'i *see* Oronchon Autonomous Banner
27 F3 O-lung-so-mu *Elongsuomu* In. Mong.
102 H1 O-lun-pu-la-k'o *Elunbulake* Sink.
Ombo *see* Wen-po
19 G3 O-mei *Emei* Liao.
86 D3 O-mei *Emei* Szech.
86 D3 O-mei Shan *Emei Shan* (mt) Szech.
102 C1 O-min *Emin* Sink.
102 C1 O-min Ho *Emin He* (river) Sink.
15 I4 O-mu *Emu* Kirin
O-mu Ch'ü *see* Chi Ch'ü
10 C1 O-mu-erh *Emuer* Heilung.
10 B1 O-mu-erh Ho *Emuer He* (river) Heilung.
22 E1 O-mu-erh Ho *Emuer He* (river) Heilung.
Ongniut Banner *see* Weng-niu-t'e Ch'i
86 D3 O-pien *Ebian* Szech.
106 C4 O-po *Ebo* Tsing.
107 G2 O-po *Ebo* Tsing.
106 C1 O-po-liang *Eboliang* Tsing.
Oring Nor *see* O-ling Hu
10 B2 Oronchon Autonomous Banner Heilung.
95 D3 O-shan *Eshan* Yun.
O-shan I-tsu Tzu-chih-hsien *see* O-shan Yi Autonomous Hsien
95 D3 O-shan Yi Autonomous Hsien Yun.
75 F5 O-shih *Eshi* Hunan
Otok Banner *see* O-t'o-k'o Ch'i
26 B5 O-t'o-k'o Ch'i *Etuoke Qi* In. Mong.
10 G3 O-t'u *Etu* Heilung.
51 D4 Ou Chiang *Ou Jiang* (river) Chek.
74 E3 Ou-chiang-ch'a *Oujiangcha* Hunan
38 D1 Ou-chia-ts'un *Oujiacun* Shansi
59 E5 Ou-ch'ih-k'ou *Ouchikou* Hupeh
98 E4 Ou-la *Oula* Kansu
14 D4 Ou-li *Ouli* Kirin
67 C6 Ou-liao *Ouliao* Fukien
58 E3 Ou-miao *Oumiao* Hupeh
10 D1 Ou-p'u *Oupu* Heilung.
75 F6 Ou Shui *Ou Shui* (river) Hunan
46 D4 Ou-t'ang *Outang* Anhwei
83 E3 Ou-t'ung *Outong* Kwangsi
22 D3 O-wen-k'o *Ewenke* Heilung.
O-wen-k'o Tzu-chih-ch'i *see* Evenki Autonomous Banner
115 C4 Owen Shoal China Sea
66 D4 O-yang *E-yang* Fukien
Ozero Khanka *see* Hsing-k'ai Hu
Paan *see* Pa-t'ang
10 G3 Pa-ch'a *Bacha* Heilung.
10 C2 Pa-chan *Bazhan* Heilung.
91 F4 Pa-ch'ang *Bachang* Kwei.
119 A3 Pa-chao Tao *Bazhao Dao* (island) Taiwan
43 E4 Pa-ch'eng *Bacheng* Kiangsu
78 B3 Pa-chia *Bajia* Kwangt.
Pa-chia-ch'ai-ta-mu Hu *see* Hsiao-ch'ai-ta-mu Hu
104 D1 Pa-chia-na-lin *Bajianalin* Tsing.
79 C2 P'a-chiang-k'ou *Pajiangkou* Kwangt.
58 B4 Pa-chiao *Bajiao* Hupeh
38 C2 Pa-chiao *Bajiao* Shansi
63 E6 Pa-ch'iao *Baqiao* Shensi
43 D3 Pa-ch'iao-chen *Baqiaozhen* Kiangsu
43 D3 Pa-ch'iao-chen *Baqiaozhen* Kiangsu
18 E3 Pa-chiao-t'ai *Bajiaotai* Liao.
15 J5 Pa-chia-tzu *Bajiazi* Kirin
18 D4 Pa-chia-tzu *Bajiazi* Liao.
18 E2 Pa-chia-tzu *Bajiazi* Liao.
19 H2 Pa-chia-tzu *Bajiazi* Liao.
90 B6 Pa-chieh *Bajie* Kwei.
79 D1 Pa-ch'ih *Bachi* Kwangt.
14 E3 Pa-chi-lei *Bajilei* Kirin
Pa-ch'ing *see* La-hsi-t'ang
70 C3 Pa-ching *Bajing* Kiangsi
111 E2 Pa-ch'ing Hsien *Baqing Xian* Tibet
66 D4 Pa-ch'ü *Baqu* Fukien
102 B3 Pa-ch'u *Bachu* Sink.
87 F2 Pa-chung *Bazhong* Szech.
Pading *see* P'a-ting
111 E2 P'a-erh *Baer* Tibet
22 C4 Pa-erh-t'u *Baertu* Heilung.
26 C5 Pa-han Nao *Bahan Nao* (lake) In. Mong.
14 G2 Pa-hao *Bahao* Kirin
82 C4 Pa-ho *Bahe* Kwangsi
63 E8 Pa Ho *Ba He* (river) Shensi
31 D4 Pa-hsien *Baxian* Hopeh
63 E8 Pa-hsien *Baxian* Shensi
87 F3 Pa Hsien *Baxian* Szech.
14 B4 Pa-hsien-t'ung *Baxiantong* Kirin
23 D6 Pa-hsien-t'ung *Baxiantong* Kirin
27 E2 Pa-hsi-ha-lu-erh *Baxihaluer* In. Mong.
95 D4 Pa-hsin *Baxin* Yun.
86 B2 Pa-hsi-to-ch'ia *Baxiduoqia* Szech.
91 G3 Pa-huang-ch'ang *Bahuangchang* Kwei.
14 C4 Pa-hu-t'a *Bahuta* Kirin
23 E6 Pa-hu-t'a *Bahuta* Kirin
10 D3 Pai-an *Beian* Heilung.
86 D2 Pai-chang *Baizhang* Szech.
51 C5 Pai-chang-k'ou *Baizhangkou* Chek.
14 C2 Pai-ch'eng *Baicheng* Kirin
23 E5 Pai-ch'eng *Baicheng* Kirin
102 C2 Pai-ch'eng *Baicheng* Sink.
47 D7 Pai-ch'i *Baiqi* Anhwei
51 E4 Pai-ch'i *Baiqi* Chek.
42 B1 Pa-i-chi *Bayiji* Kiangsu
83 E5 Pai-chi *Baiji* Kwangsi
87 E3 Pai-ch'i *Baiqi* Szech.
71 B5 Pai-chia *Baijia* Kiangsi
62 F3 Pai-chia-ch'uan *Baijiachuan* Shensi
38 D4 Pai-chia-chuang *Baijiazhuang* Shansi
102 H1 Pai-chia Hai *Baijia Hai* (lake) Sink.
50 C3 P'ai-chiang *Baijiang* Chek.
75 D6 Pai-chia-p'ing *Baijiaping* Hunan
99 F2 Pai-chia-tsui *Baijiazui* Kansu
30 C4 Pai-chien *Baijian* Hopeh
102 D1 Pai-chien-t'an *Baijiantan* Sink.
102 H1 Pai-chien-t'an *Baijiantan* Sink.
55 F4 Pai-ch'ih *Baichi* Honan
39 E6 Pai-ch'ih *Baichi* Shansi
35 E3 Pai-ch'ih-ho *Baichihe* Shant.
15 J5 Pai-chin *Baijin* Kirin
91 D4 Pai-chin *Baijin* Kwei.
38 E4 Pai-ching *Baijing* Shansi
54 D5 Pai-ch'iu *Baiqiu* Honan
59 F4 P'ai-chou *Paizhou* Hupeh
43 E2 Pai-chü *Baiju* Kiangsu
51 F2 Pai-ch'üan *Baiquan* Chek.
11 D4 Pai-ch'üan *Baiquan* Heilung.
55 E2 Pai-ch'üan *Baiquan* Honan
14 E5 Pai-ch'üan *Baiquan* Kirin
63 B7 Pai-ch'üeh-ssu *Baiquesi* Shensi
55 G6 Pai-ch'üeh-yüan *Baiqueyuan* Honan
106 C4 Pai-ch'ü-k'a *Baiquka* Tsing.
75 E5 Pai-fang *Baifang* Hunan
58 B5 Pai-fu-ssu *Baifusi* Hupeh
106 D4 Pai-ha *Baiha* Tsing.
94 C2 Pai-han-ch'ang *Baihanchang* Yun.
54 D3 Pai-ho *Baihe* Honan
31 B5 Pai-ho *Baihe* Hopeh
83 F5 Pai-ho *Baihe* Kwangsi
54 D5 Pai Ho *Bai He* (river) Honan
30 C3 Pai Ho *Bai He* (river) Hopeh
30 G4 Pai Ho *Bai He* (river) Hopeh
63 F8 Pai-ho *Baihe* Shensi
119 B3 Pai-ho *Baihe* Taiwan
51 D3 Pai-hou *Baihou* Chek.
79 E1 Pai-hou *Baihou* Kwangt.
54 D2 Pai-hsiang *Baixiang* Honan
31 B6 Pai-hsiang *Baixiang* Hopeh
14 B2 Pai-hsing *Baixing* Kirin
23 D5 Pai-hsing *Baixing* Kirin
90 C4 Pai-hsing *Baixing* Kwei.
47 D5 Pai Hu *Bai Hu* (lake) Anhwei
59 F4 P'ai Hu *Pai Hu* (lake) Hupeh
10 C2 Pai-hua-p'ai *Baihuapai* Heilung.
30 C4 Pai-hua Shan *Baihua Shan* (mt) Hopeh
30 E2 Pai-hu-kou *Baihugou* Hopeh
39 D5 Pai-hu-yao *Baihuyao* Shansi
74 E3 Pai-jo-p'u *Bairuopu* Hunan
31 D4 Pai-kou *Baigou* Hopeh
102 H1 Pai-k'ou-ch'üan *Baikouquan* Sink.
118 C2 Pai-kou-ta Shan *Baigouda Shan* (mt) Taiwan
51 D2 Pai-kuan *Baiguan* Chek.
59 G3 Pai-kuo *Baiguo* Hupeh
58 B5 Pai-kuo-pa *Baiguoba* Hupeh
75 E5 Pai-kuo-shih *Baiguoshi* Hunan
91 D3 Pai-la-k'an *Bailakan* Kwei.
Pai-lang *see* Chiao-lo
23 D4 Pai-lang *Bailang* Kirin
35 E3 Pai-lang Ho *Bailang He* (river) Shant.
110 D3 Pai-lang Hsien *Bailang Xian* Tibet
26 D3 Pai-lan-t'e *Bailante* In. Mong.
15 I5 Pai-li *Baili* Kirin
86 B2 Pai-li *Baili* Szech.
63 F5 Pai-liang-chen *Bailiangzhen* Shensi
66 C4 Pai-lien *Bailian* Fukien
78 B4 Pai-lien *Bailian* Kwangt.
66 F3 Pai-lin *Bailin* Fukien
75 F5 Pai-lin *Bailin* Hunan
50 C3 P'ai-ling *Pailing* Chek.
26 D4 Pai-ling-miao *Bailingmiao* In. Mong.
26 D4 Pai-ling-nao *Bailingnao* In. Mong.
83 G2 Pai-li-ts'un *Bailicun* Kwangsi
82 C3 Pai-lo *Bailuo* Kwangsi
59 F5 Pai-lo-chi *Bailuozhi* Hupeh
47 D6 P'ai-lou *Pailou* Anhwei
75 B4 P'ai-lou-yao *Pailouyao* Hunan
99 G4 Pai-lung *Bailong* Kansu
63 C7 Pai-lung *Bailong* Shensi
99 G5 Pai-lung Chiang *Bailong Jiang* (river) Kansu
51 D2 Pai-lu-t'ang *Bailutang* Chek.
83 G5 Pai-ma *Baima* Kwangsi
111 F3 Pai-ma *Baima* Tibet
78 A4 Pai-ma-ching *Baimajing* Kwangt.
55 G4 Pai-ma-i *Baimayi* Honan
99 F2 Pai-ma-kang *Baimagang* Kansu
91 E4 Pai-mang *Baimang* Kwei.
38 E2 Pai-mang-shen *Baimangshen* Shansi
75 D7 Pai-mang-ying *Baimangying* Hunan
43 E4 Pai-mao *Baimao* Kiangsu
75 C5 Pai-mao-p'ing *Baimaoping* Hunan
50 B3 Pai-ma-shih *Baimashi* Chek.
54 D3 Pai-ma-ssu *Baimasi* Honan
74 E3 Pai-ma-ssu *Baimasi* Hunan
63 F5 Pai-ma-t'an *Baimatan* Shensi
43 D4 Pai-mian *Baimian* Kiangsu
55 G3 Pai-miao *Baimiao* Honan
18 D4 Pai-miao-tzu *Baimiaozi* Liao.
63 C7 Pai-mien-hsia *Baimianxia* Shensi
43 E3 Pai-mu *Baimu* Kiangsu
90 C3 Pai-na *Baina* Kwei.
26 E3 Pai-nai-miao *Bainaimiao* In. Mong.
91 E3 Pai-ni *Baini* Kwei.
59 G5 Pai-ni-ch'iao *Bainiqiao* Hupeh
26 D4 Pai-ni-ching *Bainijing* In. Mong.
54 D5 Pai-niu *Bainiu* Honan
102 H1 Pa-i Nung-ch'ang *Bayi Nongchang* Sink.
82 D5 Pai-pao *Baibao* Kwangsi
58 D4 Pai-pao-chai *Baibaozhai* Hupeh
83 F3 Pai-p'eng *Baipeng* Kwangsi
55 F1 Pai-pi *Baibi* Honan
39 D4 Pai-pi *Baibi* Shansi
74 B3 P'ai-pi *Paibi* Hunan
70 C4 Pai-p'o *Baipo* Kiangsi
43 E3 Pai-p'u *Baipu* Kiangsu
79 D2 Pai-pu *Baibu* Kwangt.
35 E3 Pai-pu *Baibu* Shant.
70 B3 P'ai-pu *Paibu* Kiangsi
58 C2 Pai-sang *Baisang* Hupeh
Pai-se *see* Po-se
50 C3 Pai-sha *Baisha* Chek.
67 B5 Pai-sha *Baisha* Fukien
67 C5 Pai-sha *Baisha* Fukien
67 D5 Pai-sha *Baisha* Fukien
54 D3 Pai-sha *Baisha* Honan
54 E3 Pai-sha *Baisha* Honan
55 E3 Pai-sha *Baisha* Honan
74 G3 Pai-sha *Baisha* Hunan
75 E5 Pai-sha *Baisha* Hunan
71 C5 Pai-sha *Baisha* Kiangsi
83 F4 Pai-sha *Baisha* Kwangsi
83 F6 Pai-sha *Baisha* Kwangsi
83 G3 Pai-sha *Baisha* Kwangsi
79 C1 Pai-sha *Baisha* Kwangt.
79 C2 Pai-sha *Baisha* Kwangt.
91 F3 Pai-sha *Baisha* Kwei.
87 F3 Pai-sha *Baisha* Szech.
118 A3 Pai-sha *Baisha* Taiwan
67 E4 Pai-sha-chen *Baishazhen* Fukien
78 A4 Pai-sha Hsien *Baisha Xian* Kwangt.
70 F2 Pai-sha-kuan *Baishaguan* Kiangsi
70 B2 Pai-sha-ling *Baishaling* Kiangsi
15 H5 Pai-shan *Baishan* Kirin
15 I5 Pai-shan *Baishan* Kirin
83 F3 Pai-shan *Baishan* Kwangsi
98 A1 Pai Shan *Bai Shan* (mt) Kansu
46 C3 Pai-shan-chi *Baishanji* Anhwei
35 G3 Pai-shan-t'an *Baishantan* Shant.
50 C5 Pai-shan-tsu *Baishanzu* (mt) Chek.
59 H5 Pai-sha-p'u *Baishapu* Hupeh
54 E3 Pai-sha Shui-k'u *Baisha Shuiku* (res) Honan
118 A3 Pai-sha Tao *Baisha Dao* (island) Taiwan
119 C4 Pai-sha-wei *Baishawei* Taiwan
71 D4 Pai-she *Baishe* Kiangsi
51 D4 Pai-shih *Baishi* Chek.
59 H5 P'ai-shih *Paishi* Hupeh
66 B4 Pai-shih Feng *Baishi Feng* (mountain) Fukien
87 F3 Pai-shih-i *Baishiyi* Szech.

111 F3 Sa-yen *Sayan* Tibet
95 D2 Sa-ying-p'an *Sayingpan* Yun.
115 D3 **Scarborough Reef** China Sea
115 C5 **Seahorse Breakers** China Sea
115 D4 **Seahorse Shoal** China Sea
111 E3 Se-cha *Sezha* Tibet
115 C4 **Second Thomas Shoal** China Sea
63 E7 Se-ho-p'u *Sehepu* Shensi
86 A1 Se-hsü-ssu *Sexusi* Szech.
111 E3 Se-ju-sung-to *Serusongduo* Tibet
55 F6 Se-kang *Segang* Honan
111 E2 Se-kung *Segong* Tibet
Seling Tsho *see* Ch'i-lin Ts'o
102 B3 Se-li-pu-ya *Selibuya* Sink.
22 E2 Sen-ching *Senjing* Heilung.
30 D2 Sen-chi-t'u *Senjitu* Hopeh
39 C5 Seng-nien *Sengnian* Shansi
106 D2 Se-nieh Hu *Senie Hu* (lake) Tsing.
110 B2 Sen-ko Tsang-pu *Senge Zangbu* (river) Tibet
15 K4 Sen-lin Shan *Senlin Shan* (mt) Kirin
103 E1 Sen-t'a-ssu *Sentasi* Sink.
86 B3 Se-pa *Seba* Szech.
30 C4 Se-shu-fen *Seshufen* Hopeh
86 C1 Se-ta *Seda* Szech.
106 D3 Se-wu Ch'ü *Sewu Qu* (river) Tsing.
106 D3 Se-wu-kou *Sewugou* Tsing.
91 C3 Sha-ch'ang *Shachang* Kwei.
34 A3 Sha-chen *Shazhen* Shant.
58 C4 Sha-chen-ch'i *Shazhenqi* Hupeh
66 F3 Sha-ch'eng *Shacheng* Fukien
30 C3 Sha-ch'eng *Shacheng* Hopeh
50 C5 Sha-ch'i *Shaqi* Chek.
51 E3 Sha-ch'i *Shaqi* Chek.
75 B5 Sha-ch'i *Shaqi* Hunan
70 F3 Sha-ch'i *Shaqi* Kiangsi
71 B6 Sha-ch'i *Shaqi* Kiangsi
71 C5 Sha-ch'i *Shaqi* Kiangsi
43 F4 Sha-ch'i *Shaqi* Kiangsu
66 C4 Sha Ch'i *Sha Qi* (river) Fukien
67 C4 Sha Ch'i *Sha Qi* (river) Fukien
62 D4 Sha-chi *Shaji* Shensi
66 E4 Sha-chiang *Shajiang* Fukien
74 D4 Sha-chiang *Shajiang* Hunan
94 C3 Sha-ch'iao *Shaqiao* Yun.
67 C6 Sha-chien *Shajian* Fukien
19 I3 Sha-chien-tzu *Shajianzi* Liao.
110 B2 Sha-chih-ya *Shazhiya* Tibet
99 F2 Sha-ching *Shajing* Kansu
102 B2 Sha-ching-tzu *Shajingzi* Sink.
15 I5 Sha-chin-kou *Shajingou* Kirin
102 I1 Sha-ch'iu-ho *Shaqiuhe* Sink.
62 F3 Sha-chiu-tien *Shajiudian* Shensi
43 E4 Sha-chou Hsien *Shazhou Xian* Kiangsu
71 C6 Sha-chou-pa *Shazhouba* Kiangsi
75 E4 Sha-ch'üan *Shaquan* Hunan
38 C2 Sha-ch'üan *Shaquan* Shansi
26 D3 Sha-erh-mo-jen-so-mu *Shaermorensuomu* In. Mong.
114 B1 Sha-erh-pu-jih-tu *Shaerburidu* Ningsia
103 D1 Sha-erh-t'a-le *Shaertale* Sink.
Shag Paserab *see* Chia-pa-se-la
18 C3 Sha-hai *Shahai* Liao.
30 D3 Sha-ho *Shahe* Hopeh
31 B7 Sha-ho *Shahe* Hopeh
42 C1 Sha-ho *Shahe* Kiangsu
83 F5 Sha-ho *Shuhe* Kwangsi
54 D4 Sha Ho *Sha He* (river) Honan
59 E2 Sha Ho *Sha He* (river) Hupeh
34 C2 Sha Ho *Sha He* (river) Shant.
38 E2 Sha-ho *Shahe* Shansi
35 E2 Sha-ho *Shahe* Shant.
34 B4 Sha-ho-chan *Shahezhan* Shant.
70 C2 Sha-ho-chen *Shahezhen* Kiangsi
14 F5 Sha-ho-chen *Shahezhen* Kirin
46 E4 Sha-ho-chi *Shaheji* Anhwei
31 D5 Sha-ho-ch'iao *Shaheqiao* Hopeh
31 B7 Sha-ho Hsien *Shahe Xian* Hopeh
31 B7 Sha-ho Hsien *Shahe Xian* Hopeh
30 F4 Sha-ho-i *Shaheyi* Hopeh
63 C8 Sha-ho-k'an *Shahekan* Shensi
98 E2 Sha-ho-pao *Shahebao* Kansu
55 E5 Sha-ho-tien *Shahedian* Honan
11 D5 Sha-ho-tzu *Shahezi* Heilung.
87 G2 Sha-ho-tzu *Shahezi* Szech.
18 D4 Sha-hou-so *Shahousuo* Liao.
15 I4 Sha-ho-yen *Shaheyan* Kirin
66 C4 Sha-hsien *Shaxian* Fukien
59 F4 Sha-hu *Shahu* Hupeh
38 D1 Sha-hu-k'ou *Shahukou* Shansi
75 F4 Shai-pu-chiang *Shaibujiang* Hunan
59 E4 Sha-kang *Shagang* Hupeh
19 F4 Sha-kang *Shagang* Liao.
74 E2 Sha-kang-shih *Shagangshi* Hunan
110 B2 Sha-k'o-ti *Shakedi* Tibet
26 D5 Sha-ko-tu *Shagedu* In. Mong.
43 D2 Sha-kou *Shagou* Kiangsu
79 C1 Sha-k'ou *Shakou* Kwangt.
34 C5 Sha-kou *Shagou* Shant.
63 D7 Sha-kou-chieh *Shagoujie* Shensi
18 D3 Sha-kuo-t'un *Shaguotun* Liao.
19 E2 Sha-la *Shala* Liao.
Sha-la-mu-lun-miao *see* Sha-erh-mo-jen-so-mu
11 E5 Sha-lan *Shalan* Heilung.
78 B3 Sha-lang *Shalang* Kwangt.
82 B3 Sha-li *Shali* Kwangsi
110 C2 Sha-li *Shali* Tibet
104 C2 Sha-liang-tzu *Shaliangzi* Tsing.
14 A5 Sha-li-hao-lai *Shalihaolai* Kirin
23 D6 Sha-li-hao-lai *Shalihaolai* Kirin
19 F3 Sha-ling *Shaling* Liao.
19 G3 Sha-ling *Shaling* Liao.
30 B3 Sha-ling-tzu *Shalingzi* Hopeh
51 E3 Sha-liu *Shaliu* Chek.
30 E4 Sha-liu-ho *Shaliuhe* Hopeh
107 G2 Sha-liu-ho *Shaliuhe* Tsing.
118 B2 Sha-lu *Shalu* Taiwan
86 B2 Sha-lu-li Shan *Shaluli Shan* (mts) Szech.
118 C1 Sha-lun *Shalun* Taiwan
Shamal *see* Hsia-ma-le
62 F2 Sha-mao-t'ou *Shamaotou* Shensi
102 H1 Sha-men-tzu *Shamenzi* Sink.
102 H2 Sha-men-tzu *Shamenzi* Sink.
106 E5 Sha-mu-ta *Shamuda* Tsing.
67 C6 Shan-ch'eng-chen *Shanchengzhen* Fukien
14 F5 Shan-ch'eng-chen *Shanchengzhen* Kirin
51 D5 Shan-ch'i *Shanqi* Chek.
82 D3 Shan-chiao *Sanjiao* Kwangsi
94 B3 Shan-chieh *Shanjie* Yun.
66 C3 Shan-ch'ien *Shanqian* Fukien
35 F2 Shan-ch'ien-tien *Shanqiandian* Shant.
70 B4 Shan-chuang *Shanzhuang* Kiangsi
39 B5 Shan-chung *Shanzhong* Shansi
18 C4 Shan-chü-tzu *Shanjuzi* Liao.
86 C1 Shang-a-pa *Shangaba* Szech.
91 E2 Shang-ba *Shangba* Kwei.
38 F2 Shang-chai *Shangzhai* Shansi
86 C1 Shang-chai *Shangzhai* Szech.
95 D2 Shang-cha-ko *Shangzhage* Yun.
82 E2 Shang-ch'ao *Shangchao* Kwangsi
107 G3 Shang-cha-ssu *Shangzhasi* Tsing.
55 G6 Shang-ch'eng *Shangcheng* Honan
62 D5 Shang-chen-tzu *Shangzhenzi* Shensi
59 F5 Shang-ch'e-wan *Shangchewan* Hupeh
51 C3 Shang-ch'i *Shangqi* Chek.
11 D4 Shang-chi *Shangji* Heilung.
54 C4 Shang-chi *Shangji* Honan
11 C4 Shang-chia *Shangjia* Heilung.
19 H3 Shang-chia-ho *Shangjiahe* Liao.
51 C4 Shang-chiao-tao *Shangjiaodao* Chek.
11 D5 Shang-chih *Shangzhi* Heilung.
34 C4 Shang-chih *Shangzhi* Shant.
58 C1 Shang-chin *Shangjin* Hupeh
82 D5 Shang-chin *Shangjin* Kwangsi
67 C5 Shang-ching *Shangjing* Fukien
70 E3 Shang-ch'ing *Shangqing* Kiangsi
55 G3 Shang-ch'iu *Shangqiu* Honan
55 G3 Shang-ch'iu *Shangqiu* Honan
55 G3 Shang-ch'iu Ti-ch'ü *Shangqiu Diqu* Honan
54 D4 Shang-chiu-wu *Shangjiuwu* Honan
54 D2 Shang-chuang *Shangzhuang* Honan
30 B4 Shang-chuang *Shangzhuang* Hopeh
35 E4 Shang-chuang *Shangzhuang* Shant.
35 G2 Shang-chuang *Shangzhuang* Shant.
79 C3 Shang-ch'uan Tao *Shangchuan Dao* (island) Kwangt.
91 F4 Shang-chung *Shangzhong* Kwei.
50 B3 Shang-fang *Shangfang* Chek.
31 B5 Shang-fang *Shangfang* Hopeh
70 B3 Shang-fu *Shangfu* Kiangsi
43 F4 Shang-hai *Shanghai* Kiangsu
Shang-hai - city plan *see* Pages 128-129
43 F4 Shang-hai Hsien *Shanghai Xian* Kiangsu
43 F4 Shang-hai Shih *Shanghai Shi* Kiangsu
67 B5 Shang-hang *Shanghang* Fukien
34 C2 Shang-ho *Shanghe* Shant.
14 G3 Shang-ho-wan *Shanghewan* Kirin
38 D2 Shang-hsi-chuang *Shangxizhuang* Shansi
63 E7 Shang-hsien *Shangxian* Shensi
43 D4 Shang-hsing-chen *Shangxingzhen* Kiangsu
42 C3 Shang-hsin-ho *Shangxinhe* Kiangsu
51 D3 Shang-hu *Shanghu* Chek.
51 E3 Shang-hu *Shanghu* Chek.
38 E4 Shang-hu *Shanghu* Shansi
43 D4 Shang-huang *Shanghuang* Kiangsu
30 D2 Shang-huang-ch'i *Shanghuangqi* Hopeh
107 F2 Shang-huan-ts'ang *Shanghuancang* Tsing.
22 D2 Shang-hu-lin *Shanghulin* Heilung.
30 A2 Shang-i Hsien *Shangyi Xian* Hopeh
30 A2 Shang-i Hsien *Shangyi Xian* Hopeh
70 E3 Shang-jao *Shangrao* Kiangsi
75 D6 Shang-jen-li *Shangrenli* Hunan
67 E5 Shang-kan *Shanggan* Fukien
58 C3 Shang-k'an *Shangkan* Hupeh
43 E2 Shang-kang *Shanggang* Kiangsu
10 E4 Shang-kan-ling *Shangganling* Heilung.
70 B3 Shang-kao *Shanggao* Kiangsi
Shangkin *see* Shang-chin
Shangkiu *see* Shang-ch'iu
35 D3 Shang-k'ou *Shangkou* Shant.
30 F3 Shang-ku *Shanggu* Hopeh
55 F2 Shang-kuan-ts'un *Shangguancun* Honan
22 D2 Shang-k'u-li *Shangkuli* Heilung.
114 C3 Shang-kun-ch'üan *Shanggunquan* Ningsia
107 G4 Shang-kung-ma *Shanggongma* Tsing.
23 C6 Shang-kung-ti *Shanggongdi* Liao.
39 B6 Shang-kuo *Shangguo* Shansi
67 B5 Shang-kuo-ch'e *Shangguoche* Fukien
50 C2 Shang-lang *Shanglang* Chek.
86 C1 Shang-lang-t'ang *Shanglangtang* Szech.
38 D3 Shang-lan-ts'un *Shanglancun* Shansi
83 F3 Shang-lei *Shanglei* Kwangsi
87 F1 Shang-liang *Shangliang* Szech.
31 D5 Shang-lin *Shanglin* Hopeh
83 E4 Shang-lin *Shanglin* Kwangsi
79 C2 Shang-lin *Shanglin* Kwangt.
79 D1 Shang-ling *Shangling* Kwangt.
70 A4 Shang-li-shih *Shanglishi* Kiangsi
63 F7 Shang-lo *Shangluo* Shensi
63 F7 Shang-lo-chen *Shangluozhen* Shensi
63 F7 Shang-lo Ti-ch'ü *Shangluo Diqu* Shensi
66 D3 Shang-mei *Shangmei* Fukien
63 F7 Shang-nan *Shangnan* Shensi
59 H4 Shang-pa-ho *Shangbahe* Hupeh
47 D5 Shang-p'ai-ho *Shangpaihe* Anhwei
66 E3 Shang-pai-shih *Shangbaishi* Fukien
55 E2 Shang-pa-li *Shangbali* Honan
51 E4 Shang-p'an *Shangpan* Chek.
30 F3 Shang-pan-ch'eng *Shangbancheng* Hopeh
67 C5 Shang-p'ing *Shangping* Fukien
71 C6 Shang-p'ing *Shangping* Kiangsi
79 D1 Shang-p'ing *Shangping* Kwangt.
51 D3 Shang-p'u *Shangpu* Chek.
70 B4 Shang-pu *Shangbu* Kiangsi
71 C5 Shang-she *Shangshe* Kiangsi
38 D3 Shang-she *Shangshe* Shansi
38 E3 Shang-she *Shangshe* Shansi
55 G5 Shang-shih-ch'iao *Shangshiqiao* Honan
59 F3 Shang-shih-tien *Shangshidian* Hupeh
55 F4 Shang-shui Hsien *Shangshui Xian* Honan
82 D5 Shang-ssu *Shangsi* Kwangsi
91 E5 Shang-ssu *Shangsi* Kwei.
114 B1 Shang-tan *Shangdan* Ningsia
70 C3 Shang-t'ang *Shangtang* Kiangsi
71 D4 Shang-t'ang *Shangtang* Kiangsi
42 C2 Shang-t'ang *Shangtang* Kiangsu
18 D2 Shang-t'ang-kou *Shangtanggou* Liao.
10 E3 Shang-tao-kan *Shangdaogan* Heilung.
54 D3 Shang-tien *Shangdian* Honan
54 E4 Shang-tien *Shangdian* Honan
34 C2 Shang-tien *Shangdian* Shant.
58 B1 Shang-tien-tzu *Shangdianzi* Hupeh
55 F4 Shang-ts'ai *Shangcai* Honan
30 E4 Shang-ts'ang *Shangcang* Hopeh
75 F6 Shang-tu *Shangdu* Hunan
27 E4 Shang-tu *Shangdu* In. Mong.
54 D5 Shang-t'un *Shangtun* Honan
70 D4 Shang-tun-tu *Shangdundu* Kiangsi
119 B4 Shang-wu *Shangwu* Taiwan
22 D2 Shang-wu-erh-ken *Shangwuergen* Heilung.
38 D3 Shang-yang-wu *Shangyangwu* Shansi
51 D3 Shang-yen-t'an *Shangyantan* Chek.
15 H3 Shang-ying *Shangying* Kirin
82 C4 Shang-ying *Shangying* Kwangsi
71 B6 Shang-yu *Shangyou* Kiangsi
18 D3 Shang-yüan *Shangyuan* Liao.
71 B6 Shang-yu Chiang *Shangyou Jiang* (river) Kiangsi
51 D2 Shang-yü Hsien *Shangyu Xian* Chek.
102 C2 Shang-yu-i-ch'ang *Shangyouyichang* Sink.
22 D2 Shang-yu-ling *Shangyouling* Heilung.
94 B4 Shang-yün *Shangyun* Yun.
67 D5 Shang-yung *Shangyong* Fukien
102 C2 Shang-yu Shui-k'u *Shangyou Shuiku* (res.) Sink.
119 B5 Shan-hai *Shanhai* Taiwan
30 G3 Shan-hai-kuan *Shanhaiguan* Hopeh
99 I4 Shan-ho *Shanhe* Kansu
110 A2 Shan-ho *Shanhe* Tibet
11 D5 Shan-ho-t'un *Shanhetun* Heilung.
75 D6 Shan-hsiang *Shanxiang* Hunan
54 C3 Shan Hsien *Shan Xian* Honan
34 B5 Shan-hsien *Shanxian* Shant.
83 F5 Shan-hsin *Shanxin* Kwangsi
119 B3 Shan-hua *Shanhua* Taiwan
Shanjakur *see* Shang-chia-ssu
107 G2 Shan-ken *Shangen* Tsing.
114 C2 Shan-ken-ta-lai *Shangendalai* Ningsia
67 C6 Shan-ko *Shange* Fukien
51 D4 Shan-k'ou *Shankou* Chek.
74 D3 Shan-k'ou *Shankou* Hunan
70 B3 Shan-k'ou *Shankou* Kiangsi
83 F6 Shan-k'ou *Shankou* Kwangsi
63 E7 Shan-k'ou *Shankou* Shensi
103 F2 Shan-k'ou *Shankou* Sink.
66 C3 Shan Kuan *Shan Guan* (pass) Fukien
71 E4 Shan Kuan *Shan Guan* (pass) Kiangsi
86 D3 Shan-leng-kang *Shanlenggang* Szech.
47 D7 Shan-li *Shanli* Anhwei
118 C2 Shan-li *Shanli* Taiwan
51 D2 Shan-lien *Shanlian* Chek.
119 B4 Shan-lin *Shanlin* Taiwan
119 B3 Shan-mei *Shanmei* Taiwan
75 C4 Shan-men *Shanmen* Hunan
99 H4 Shan-men *Shanmen* Kansu
90 A4 Shan-mu-ch'ing *Shanmuqing* Kwei.
118 C2 Shan-nan *Shannan* Taiwan
47 C5 Shan-nan-kuan *Shannanguan* Anhwei
111 D3 Shan-nan Ti-ch'ü *Shannan Diqu* Tibet
26 B4 Shan-pa *Shanba* In. Mong.
47 F5 Shan-pei *Shanbei* Anhwei
91 D3 Shan-p'en *Shanpen* Kwei.
55 E2 Shan-piao *Shanbiao* Honan
59 G4 Shan-p'o *Shanpo* Hupeh
102 I2 Shan-shan *Shanshan* Sink.
103 E2 Shan-shan *Shanshan* Sink.
11 E5 Shan-shih *Shanshi* Heilung.
118 A3 Shan-shui *Shanshui* Taiwan
114 C3 Shan-shui Ho *Shanshui He* (river) Ningsia
74 E3 Shan-shu-ts'ang *Shanshucang* Hunan
Shansi Province *see* Pages 37-40
14 G5 Shan-sung-kang *Shansonggang* Kirin
98 E2 Shan-tan *Shandan* Kansu
74 C4 Shan-t'ang-i *Shantangyi* Hunan
27 F3 Shan-tan-so *Shandansuo* In. Mong.
27 G3 Shan-tien Ho *Shandian He* (river) In. Mong.
34 C4 Shan-t'ing *Shanting* Shant.
26 D3 Shan-ting-hu-la-erh *Shandinghulaer* In. Mong.
71 C4 Shan-t'ou *Shantou* Kiangsi
79 E2 Shan-t'ou *Shantou* Kwangt.
46 E3 Shan-t'ou-chi *Shantouji* Anhwei
74 E4 Shan-tsao *Shanzao* Hunan
35 G2 Shan-tung Pan-tao *Shandong Bandao* (pen) Shant.
Shantung Province *see* Pages 33-36
47 C5 Shan-wang-ho *Shanwanghe* Anhwei
30 E1 Shan-wan-tzu *Shanwanzi* Hopeh
79 D2 Shan-wei *Shanwei* Kwangt.
66 E4 Shan-yang *Shanyang* Fukien
63 E7 Shan-yang *Shanyang* Shensi
67 D5 Shan-yao *Shanyao* Fukien
38 D2 Shan-yin-ch'eng *Shanyincheng* Shansi
38 D2 Shan-yin Hsien *Shanyin Xian* Shansi
82 D5 Shan-yü *Shanyu* Kwangsi
119 C4 Shan-yüan *Shanyuan* Taiwan
119 B4 Shao-chia *Shaojia* Taiwan
Shaohing *see* Shao-hsing
19 G4 Shao Ho *Shao He* (river) Liao.
51 D2 Shao-hsing *Shaoxing* Chek.
55 F3 Shao-kang-chi *Shaogangji* Honan
23 D6 Shao-ken *Shaogen* Liao.
79 C1 Shao-kuan *Shaoguan* Kwangt.
14 F4 Shao-kuo *Shaoguo* Kirin
14 D2 Shao-kuo-chen *Shaoguozhen* Kirin
43 D3 Shao-po *Shaobo* Kiangsu
74 E4 Shao-shan *Shaoshan* Hunan
83 G2 Shao-shui *Shaoshui* Kwangsi
55 F4 Shao-tien *Shaodian* Honan
42 C1 Shao-tien *Shaodian* Kiangsu
75 D4 Shao-tung Hsien *Shaodong Xian* Hunan
19 G4 Shao-tzu-ho *Shaozihe* Liao.
11 C4 Shao-wen *Shaowen* Heilung.
66 C3 Shao-wu *Shaowu* Fukien
75 D4 Shao-yang *Shaoyang* Hunan
75 D5 Shao-yang Hsien *Shaoyang Xian* Hunan
54 D2 Shao-yüan *Shaoyuan* Honan
78 B3 Sha-pa *Shaba* Kwangt.
91 E4 Sha-pao-pao *Shabaobao* Kwei.
19 F5 Sha-pao-tzu *Shabaozi* Liao.
79 C2 Sha-p'ing *Shaping* Kwangt.
114 B3 Sha-p'o-t'ou *Shapotou* Ningsia
59 G5 Sha-p'u *Shapu* Hupeh
83 F3 Sha-pu *Shabu* Kwangsi
Shara Bürdü *see* Sha-erh-pu-jih-tu
Shara M Süme *see* Sha-erh-mo-jen-so-mu
Shara Muren (river) *see* Hsi-la-mu-lun Ho
Sharasume *see* A-le-t'ai
Sharha *see* Hsia-jih-ha
Sharu Lake *see* Hsia-ju Ts'o
11 E4 Sha-shan *Shashan* Heilung.
102 C1 Sha-shan-tzu *Shashanzi* Sink.
58 E4 Sha-shih *Shashi* Hupeh
74 F3 Sha-shih-chieh *Shashijie* Hunan
Shasi *see* Sha-shih
114 C4 Sha-t'ang-pu *Shatangpu* Ningsia
58 B5 Sha-tao-kou *Shadaogou* Hupeh
58 D4 Sha-tao-kuan *Shadaoguan* Hupeh
86 C3 Sha-te *Shade* Szech.
71 B5 Sha-ti *Shadi* Kiangsi
79 C3 Sha-ti *Shadi* Kwangt.
75 F6 Sha-t'ien *Shatian* Hunan
59 G3 Sha-tien *Shadian* Hupeh
71 B5 Sha-t'ien *Shatian* Kiangsi
83 G5 Sha-t'ien *Shatian* Kwangsi
83 H3 Sha-t'ien *Shatian* Kwangsi
55 F2 Sha-tien-chi *Shadianji* Honan
111 E3 Sha-ting *Shading* Tibet
74 E3 Sha-tou *Shadou* Hunan
83 H4 Sha-t'ou *Shatou* Kwangsi
98 B2 Sha-tsao-yüan *Shazaoyuan* Kansu
71 C5 Sha-ts'un *Shacun* Kiangsi
91 D3 Sha-t'u *Shatu* Kwei.
34 A4 Sha-t'u-chi *Shatuji* Shant.
59 F5 Sha-tui *Shadui* Hupeh
106 D3 Sha-tung-t'a *Shadongta* Tsing.
83 G3 Sha-tzu *Shazi* Kwangsi
91 C5 Sha-tzu-kou *Shazigou* Kwei.
90 C5 Sha-tzu-ling *Shaziling* Kwei.
91 F2 Sha-tzu-p'o *Shazipo* Kwei.
58 B4 Sha-tzu-ti *Shazidi* Hupeh
Sha-wan *see* San-tao-ho-tzu
75 C4 Sha-wan *Shawan* Hunan
91 D3 Sha-wan *Shawan* Kwei.
87 D3 Sha-wan *Shawan* Szech.
86 D3 Sha-wan-chen *Shawanzhen* Szech.
102 D1 Sha-wan Hsien *Shawan Xian* Sink.
55 G6 Sha-wo *Shawo* Honan
91 C4 Sha-wo *Shawo* Kwei.
67 B4 Sha-wu-t'ang *Shawutang* Fukien
102 C2 Sha-ya *Shaya* Sink.
59 E4 Sha-yang *Shayang* Hupeh
Shayizamka *see* Chia-yü-ch'iao
54 D3 Sha-yü-kou *Shayugou* Honan
Shazga *see* Hsia-tzu-chieh
39 D4 She-ch'eng *Shecheng* Shansi
54 D4 She-ch'i *Sheqi* Honan
71 B6 She-ch'i *Sheqi* Kiangsi
55 F4 She-ch'iao *Sheqiao* Honan
74 D3 She-chia-p'ing *Shejiaping* Hunan
She Chu *see* Hsien-shui Ho
43 D4 She-chu *Shezhu* Kiangsu
63 E7 She-ch'uan Ho *Shechuan He* (river) Shensi
71 C5 She-fu *Shefu* Kiangsi
47 E7 She Hsien *She Xian* Anhwei
31 A7 She-hsien *Shexian* Hopeh
87 E2 She-hung Hsien *Shehong Xian* Szech.
74 F3 She-kang-shih *Shegangshi* Hunan
Shekar *see* Hsieh-ko-erh
70 D3 She-keng *Shigeng* Kiangsi
Shekki *see* Shih-ch'i
59 G4 She-k'ou *Shekou* Hupeh
14 D2 She-li *Sheli* Kirin
14 F2 She-li *Sheli* Kirin
23 E5 She-li *Sheli* Kirin
26 C5 She-li-miao *Shelimiao* In. Mong.
14 F4 She-ling *Sheling* Kirin
Shemen Lake *see* Ch'a-lo-erh Ts'o
110 D3 Shen-cha *Shenzha* Tibet
79 D2 Shen-chen *Shenzhen* Kwangt.
34 A4 Shen-chi *Shenji* Shant.
11 D4 Shen-chia *Shenjia* Heilung.
102 I2 Shen-chia *Shenjia* Sink.
59 E4 Shen-chia-chi *Shenjiaji* Hupeh
38 D2 Shen-ch'ih *Shenchi* Shansi
79 C3 Shen-ching *Shenjing* Kwangt.
114 B3 Shen-ching *Shenjing* Ningsia
30 B3 Shen-ching-ts'un *Shenjingcun* Hopeh
14 E3 Shen-ching-tzu *Shenjingzi* Kirin
19 G3 Shen-ching-tzu *Shenjingzi* Liao.
Shen-ch'iu *see* Ch'en-ch'iu
118 C2 Shen-ch'ou *Shenchou* Taiwan
51 E3 Shen-ch'üan *Shenquan* Chek.
79 E2 Shen-ch'üan *Shenquan* Kwangt.
79 E2 Shen-ch'üan Kang *Shenquan Gang* Kwangt.
47 D5 Sheng-chia-ch'iao *Shengjiaqiao* Anhwei
47 E6 Sheng-chia-ch'iao *Shengjiaqiao* Anhwei
90 B5 Sheng-ching Kuan *Shengjing Guan* (pass) Kwei.
102 I2 Sheng-chin-t'ai *Shengjintai* Sink.
103 E2 Sheng-chin-t'ai *Shengjintai* Sink.
51 D3 Sheng-hsien *Shengxian* Chek.
59 G4 Sheng-hung-ch'ing *Shenghongqing* Hupeh
11 E4 Sheng-lang *Shenglang* Heilung.
11 D5 Sheng-li *Shengli* Heilung.
59 H3 Sheng-li *Shengli* Hupeh
23 E5 Sheng-li *Shengli* Kirin
106 D2 Sheng-li-k'ou *Shenglikou* Tsing.
102 C2 Sheng-li-shih-chiu-ch'ang *Shenglishijiuchang* Sink.
102 H2 Sheng-li Ta-pan *Shendi Daban* (pass) Sink.
103 D2 Sheng-li Ta-pan *Shengli Daban* (pass) Sink.
70 C3 Sheng-mi-chieh *Shengmijie* Kiangsi
11 C4 Sheng-p'ing *Shengping* Heilung.
14 F5 Sheng-shui-ho-tzu *Shengshuihezi* Kirin
51 F2 Sheng-ssu Hsien *Shengsi Xian* Chek.
51 F2 Sheng-ssu Lieh-tao *Shengsi Liedao* (islands) Chek.
58 D2 Sheng-tai *Shengdai* Hupeh
79 C2 Sheng-t'ang *Shengtang* Kwangt.
43 E5 Sheng-tse *Shengze* Kiangsu
43 E3 Sheng-tz'u-chen *Shengcizhen* Kiangsu
63 E8 Shen-ho-k'ou *Shenhekou* Shensi
31 C5 Shen-hsien *Shenxian* Hopeh
67 D6 Shen-hu *Shenhu* Fukien
94 A3 Shen-hu-kuan *Shenhuguan* Yun.
39 C7 Shen-jen-chien *Shenrenjian* Shansi
71 D4 Shen-kang *Shengang* Kiangsi
43 E4 Shen-kang *Shengang* Kiangsu
54 E3 Shen-kou *Shengou* Honan
34 B4 Shen-li-p'u *Shenlipu* Shant.
54 E4 Shen-lou *Shenlou* Honan
62 F2 Shen-mu *Shenmu* Shensi
31 B5 Shen-nan *Shennan* Hopeh
58 C3 Shen-nung-chia *Shennongjia* Hupeh
31 D4 Shenq-fang *Shengfang* Hopeh
51 E2 Shen-shih-ch'iao *Shenshiqiao* Chek.
11 E4 Shen-shu *Shenshu* Heilung.
Shensi Province *see* Pages 61-64
51 D2 Shen-tang *Shendang* Chek.
38 D2 Shen-t'ou *Shentou* Shansi
34 B2 Shen-t'ou *Shentou* Shant.
31 C5 Shen-tse *Shenze* Hopeh
47 E7 Shen-tu *Shendu* Anhwei
67 C6 Shen-t'u *Shentu* Fukien
14 E4 Shen-yang *Shenyang* Kirin
19 G3 Shen-yang *Shenyang* Liao.
Shen-yang - city plan *see* Page 136
19 G2 Shen-yang Ti-ch'ü *Shenyang Diqu* Liao.
She-p'an Yang *see* San-men Wan
14 B3 She-po-t'u *Shebotu* Kirin
23 E5 She-po-t'u *Shebotu* Kirin
74 E4 She-pu *Shebu* Hunan
83 G4 She-pu *Shebu* Kwangsi
Shershik Gompa *see* Sa-hsi-k'o-kung-pa
75 C5 She Shui *She Shui* (river) Hunan
59 G3 She Shui *She Shui* (river) Hupeh
75 D4 She-t'ien-ch'iao *Shetianqiao* Hunan
Shetsuishan *see* Shih-tsui-shan
54 C4 She-wei *Shewei* Honan
43 D2 She-yang *Sheyang* Kiangsu
43 D2 She-yang Ho *Sheyang He* (river) Kiangsu
43 E2 She-yang Hsien *Sheyang Xian* Kiangsu
Shigatse *see* Jih-k'a-tse
Shigatse Region *see* Jih-k'a-tse Ti-ch'ü
Shigatze *see* Jih-k'a-tse
63 E9 Shih-chai-ho *Shizhaihe* Shensi
10 C2 Shih-chan *Shizhan* Heilung.
91 C3 Shih-ch'ang *Shichang* Kwei.
91 F3 Shih-ch'ang *Shichang* Kwei.
35 E4 Shih-ch'ang *Shichang* Shant.
18 C4 Shih-chang-tzu *Shizhangzi* Liao.
39 D5 Shih-che *Shizhe* Shansi
70 D3 Shih-chen-chieh *Shizhenjie* Kiangsi
67 E5 Shih-ch'eng *Shicheng* Fukien
71 D5 Shih-ch'eng *Shicheng* Kiangsi
79 D1 Shih-cheng *Shizheng* Kwangt.
19 H4 Shih-ch'eng *Shicheng* Liao.
39 E5 Shih-ch'eng *Shicheng* Shansi
118 C2 Shih-ch'eng *Shicheng* Taiwan
19 F5 Shih-ch'eng Tao *Shicheng Dao* (island) Liao.
66 C4 Shih-ch'i *Shiqi* Fukien
70 E3 Shih-ch'i *Shiqi* Kiangsi
14 F4 Shih-ch'i *Shiqi* Kirin
79 C2 Shih-ch'i *Shiqi* Kwangt.
83 F5 Shih-ch'ia *Shiqia* Kwangsi
47 C5 Shih-chia-ch'iao *Shijiaqiao* Anhwei
51 D2 Shih-chia-ch'iao *Shijiaqiao* Chek.
43 D3 Shih-chia-ch'iao *Shijiaqiao* Kiangsu
31 B5 Shih-chia-chuang *Shijiazhuang* Hopeh
47 F6 Shih-ch'iao *Shiqiao* Anhwei
54 D4 Shih-ch'iao *Shiqiao* Honan
55 E4 Shih-ch'iao *Shiqiao* Honan
58 E3 Shih-ch'iao *Shiqiao* Hupeh
70 D4 Shih-ch'iao *Shiqiao* Kiangsi
71 B5 Shih-ch'iao *Shiqiao* Kiangsi
83 H4 Shih-ch'iao *Shiqiao* Kwangsi
79 C2 Shih-chiao *Shijiao* Kwangt.
79 C2 Shih-ch'iao *Shiqiao* Kwangt.
79 C2 Shih-ch'iao *Shiqiao* Kwangt.
34 D3 Shih-ch'iao *Shiqiao* Shant.
34 D4 Shih-ch'iao *Shiqiao* Shant.
87 F2 Shih-ch'iao *Shiqiao* Szech.
87 E2 Shih-ch'iao-chen *Shiqiaozhen* Szech.
19 G3 Shih-ch'iao-tzu *Shiqiaozi* Liao.
87 E2 Shih-chia-pa *Shijiaba* Szech.
14 E4 Shih-chia-pao *Shijiabao* Kirin
18 E3 Shih-chia-pao *Shijiabao* Liao.
110 D2 Shih-chia-sha-lung *Shijiashalong* Tibet
39 B6 Shih-chia-t'an *Shijiatan* Shansi
30 C4 Shih-chia-ying *Shijiaying* Hopeh
15 I5 Shih-ch'i-chieh *Shiqijie* Kirin
47 F6 Shih-chieh-tu *Shijiedu* Anhwei
79 C2 Shih-chien *Shijian* Kwangt.
91 F3 Shih-ch'ien *Shiqian* Kwei.
47 D5 Shih-chien-pu *Shijianbu* Anhwei
67 D6 Shih-ching *Shijing* Fukien
54 D3 Shih-ching *Shijing* Honan
35 D4 Shih-ching *Shijing* Shant.
30 D4 Shih-ching-shan *Shijingshan* Hopeh
10 C1 Shih-chiu-chan *Shijiuzhan* Heilung.
47 E5 Shih-chiu Hu *Shijiu Hu* (lake) Anhwei
42 C4 Shih-chiu Hu *Shijiu Hu* (lake) Kiangsu
35 E4 Shih-chiu-so *Sijiusuo* Shant.
51 D4 Shih-chu *Shizhu* Chek.
14 G4 Shih-chü *Shiju* Kirin
83 G4 Shih-chü *Shiju* Kwangsi
38 E3 Shih-chü *Shiju* Shansi
86 B1 Shih-ch'ü *Shiqu* Szech.
87 G3 Shih-chu *Shizhu* Szech.
63 D7 Shih-ch'üan *Shiquan* Shensi
43 E3 Shih-chuang *Shizhuang* Kiangsu
39 D6 Shih-chuang *Shizhuang* Shansi
63 D6 Shih-ch'uan Ho *Shichuan He* (river) Shensi
110 A2 Shih-ch'üan-ho *Shiquanhe* Tibet
103 F2 Shih-ch'üan-tzu *Shiquanzi* Sink.
62 F3 Shih-chü-i *Shijuyi* Shensi
67 C6 Shih-chung *Shizhong* Fukien
10 C2 Shih-erh-chan *Shierzhan* Heilung.
50 B3 Shih-erh Shan *Shier Shan* (mt) Chek.
70 F2 Shih-erh Shan *Shier Shan* (mt) Kiangsi
15 H6 Shih-erh-tao-kou *Shierdaogou* Kirin
67 B5 Shih-fang *Shifang* Fukien
87 E2 Shih-fang *Shifang* Szech.
51 D3 Shih-feng Ch'i *Shifeng Qi* (river) Chek.
54 D4 Shih-fo-ssu *Shifosi* Honan
118 B3 Shih-fo-tung *Shifodong* Taiwan
34 B3 Shih-heng *Shiheng* Shant.
Shihhing *see* Shih-hsing
46 B3 Shih-ho *Shihe* Anhwei
18 E5 Shih-ho *Shihe* Liao.
102 D1 Shih-ho-tzu *Shihezi* Sink.
102 H1 Shih-ho-tzu *Shihezi* Sink.
99 G5 Shih-hsia *Shixia* Kansu
39 E4 Shih-hsia *Shixia* Shansi
75 C4 Shih-hsia-chiang *Shixiajiang* Hunan
79 D1 Shih-hsing *Shixing* Kwangt.
42 C1 Shih-hu *Shihu* Kiangsu
58 D2 Shih-hua-chieh *Shihuajie* Hupeh
87 G3 Shih-hui *Shihui* Szech.
59 E4 Shih-hui-ch'iao *Shihuiqiao* Hupeh
30 F3 Shih-hui-yao *Shihuiyao* Hopeh
19 G4 Shih-hui-yao *Shihuiyao* Liao.
102 H1 Shih-hui-yao-tzu *Shihuiyaozi* Sink.
78 A4 Shih-i *Shiyi* Kwangt.
10 C2 Shih-i-chan *Shiyizhan* Heilung.
70 F3 Shih-i-tu *Shiyidu* Kiangsi
43 E4 Shih-i-yü *Shiyiyu* Kiangsu
79 D1 Shih-jen-chang *Shirenzhang* Kwangt.
11 D4 Shih-jen-ch'eng *Shirencheng* Heilung.
30 E2 Shih-jen-kou *Shirengou* Hopeh
54 C5 Shih-kang *Shigang* Honan
43 E3 Shih-kang *Shigang* Kiangsu
83 F6 Shih-k'ang *Shikang* Kwangsi
94 C4 Shih-kao-ching *Shigaojing* Yun.
79 C1 Shih-k'eng k'ung *Shikeng Kong* (mt) Kwangt.
Shihkiachwang *see* Shih-chia-chuang
66 E3 Shih-k'ou *Shikou* Fukien
70 C4 Shih-k'ou *Shikou* Kiangsi
70 D3 Shih-k'ou *Shikou* Kiangsi
79 C2 Shih-kou *Shigou* Kwangt.
39 C5 Shih-k'ou *Shikou* Shansi
34 D2 Shih-k'ou *Shikou* Shant.
114 C3 Shih-kou-i *Shigouyi* Ningsia
78 B3 Shih-ku *Shigu* Kwangt.
94 B2 Shih-ku *Shigu* Yun.
39 E4 Shih-kuai *Shiguai* Shansi
26 D4 Shih-kuai-kou *Shiguaigou* In. Mong.
15 J4 Shih-kuan *Shiguan* Kirin
46 E4 Shih-kuan-chi *Shiguanji* Anhwei
47 E5 Shih-kuei *Shigui* Anhwei
58 D2 Shih-ku-kuan *Shiguguan* Hupeh
98 B1 Shih-kung *Shigong* Kansu
114 C3 Shih-k'ung *Shikong* Ningsia
46 C3 Shih-kung-shan *Shigongshan* Anhwei
55 E5 Shih-kun-ho *Shigunhe* Honan
31 B7 Shih-ku Shan *Shigu Shan* (mt) Hopeh
34 C4 Shih-lai *Shilai* Shant.
39 D6 Shih-li *Shili* Shansi
50 B3 Shih-liang *Shiliang* Chek.
55 G4 Shih-liang *Shiliang* Honan
39 E5 Shih-liang *Shiliang* Shansi
35 F2 Shih-liang *Shiliang* Shant.
19 G3 Shih-li-ho *Shilihe* Liao.
39 C5 Shih-lin *Shilin* Shansi
118 C1 Shih-lin *Shilin* Taiwan
14 E4 Shih-ling *Shiling* Kirin
106 C3 Shih-li-no-erh *Shilinuoer* Tsing.
46 C3 Shih-li-pao *Shilibao* Anhwei
15 K4 Shih-li-p'ing *Shiliping* Kirin
58 E4 Shih-li-p'u *Shilipu* Hupeh
10 C1 Shih-liu-chan *Shiliuzhan* Heilung.
67 C6 Shih-liu-fan *Shiliufan* Fukien
42 C1 Shih-liu-shu *Shiliushu* Kiangsu
39 B4 Shih-lou *Shilou* Shansi
78 A4 Shih-lu *Shilu* Kwangt.
82 C5 Shih-lung *Shilong* Kwangsi
83 F4 Shih-lung *Shilong* Kwangsi
79 C2 Shih-lung *Shilong* Kwangt.
67 C6 Shih-ma *Shima* Fukien
71 C5 Shih-ma *Shima* Kiangsi
79 D1 Shih-ma *Shima* Kwangt.
55 E4 Shih-man-t'an Shui-k'u *Shimantan Shuiku* (res) Honan
51 D2 Shih-men *Shimen* Chek.
54 D4 Shih-men *Shimen* Honan
30 C3 Shih-men *Shimen* Hopeh
30 E3 Shih-men *Shimen* Hopeh
30 F4 Shih-men *Shimen* Hopeh
74 D2 Shih-men *Shimen* Hunan
58 D3 Shih-men *Shimen* Hupeh
99 F4 Shih-men *Shimen* Kansu
70 D4 Shih-men *Shimen* Kiangsi
34 D5 Shih-men *Shimen* Shant.
35 E4 Shih-men *Shimen* Shant.
118 C1 Shih-men *Shimen* Taiwan
30 G3 Shih-men-chai *Shimenzhai* Hopeh
94 B3 Shih-men-chen *Shimenzhen* Yun.
31 D5 Shih-men-ch'iao *Shimenqiao* Hopeh
74 D3 Shih-men-ch'iao *Shimenqiao* Hunan
70 D2 Shih-men-chieh *Shimenjie* Kiangsi
58 A5 Shih-men-k'an *Shimenkan* Hupeh
70 B3 Shih-men-lou *Shimenlou* Kiangsi
46 D4 Shih-men-shan *Shimenshan* Anhwei
75 C5 Shih-men-shan *Shimenshan* Hunan
22 D3 Shih-men-tzu *Shimenzi* Heilung.
34 C2 Shih-miao *Shimiao* Shant.
86 D3 Shih-mien *Shimian* Szech.
83 F5 Shih-nan *Shinan* Kwangsi
67 D5 Shih-n'u Shan *Shiniu Shan* (mt) Fukien
46 E4 Shih-pa *Shiba* Anhwei
10 C1 Shih-pa-chan *Shibazhan* Heilung.
22 F1 Shih-pa-chan *Shibazhan* Heilung.
27 E4 Shih-pa-ch'ing *Shibaqing* In. Mong.
47 C6 Shih-p'ai *Shipai* Anhwei
59 E4 Shih-p'ai *Shipai* Hupeh
46 B3 Shih-pa-li-p'u *Shibalipu* Anhwei
99 F3 Shih-pa-li-p'u *Shibalipu* Kansu
63 C7 Shih-pa-li-p'u *Shibalipu* Shensi
39 D4 Shih-p'an *Shipan* Shansi
98 D1 Shih-pan Ching *Shiban Jing* (well) Kansu
59 F3 Shih-pan-ho *Shibanhe* Hupeh
74 D2 Shih-pan-t'an *Shibantan* Hunan
55 E1 Shih-pan-yen *Shibanyan* Honan
63 E5 Shih-pao *Shibao* Shensi
98 C2 Shih-pao-ch'eng *Shibaocheng* Kansu
91 D2 Shih-pao-szu *Shibaosi* Kwei.
67 C5 Shih-pei *Shibei* Fukien
70 C3 Shih-pi *Shibi* Kiangsi
83 E3 Shih-pieh *Shibie* Kwangsi
27 G3 Shih-pieh-su-mu *Shibiesumu* In. Mong.
Shih-p'ing *see* Ch'ih-p'ing
91 F3 Shih-ping *Shibing* Kwei.
95 D4 Shih-p'ing *Shiping* Yun.
70 D2 Shih-pi-shan *Shibishan* Kiangsi
66 D3 Shih-p'o *Shipo* Fukien
63 F6 Shih-p'o *Shipo* Shensi
47 C5 Shih-p'o-tien *Shipodian* Anhwei
51 E3 Shih-p'u *Shipu* Chek.
35 E3 Shih-pu *Shibu* Shant.
10 C2 Shih-san-chan *Shisanzhan* Heilung.
22 F2 Shih-san-chan *Shisanzhan* Heilung.
103 E2 Shih-san-chien-fang *Shisanjianfang* Sink.
10 D4 Shih-san-ching-tzu *Shisanjingzi* Heilung.
67 D5 Shih-shan *Shishan* Fukien
18 E3 Shih-shan *Shishan* Liao.
71 D5 Shih-shang *Shishang* Kiangsi
67 D6 Shih-shih *Shishi* Fukien
71 B5 Shih-shih-k'ou *Shishikou* Kiangsi
59 E5 Shih-shou *Shishou* Hupeh
63 B6 Shih-shu-lin *Shishulin* Shensi
10 C2 Shih-ssu-chan *Shisizhan* Heilung.
15 H6 Shih-ssu-tao-kou *Shisidaogou* Kirin
47 D6 Shih-t'ai Hsien *Shitai Xian* Anhwei
74 E4 Shih-t'an *Shitan* Hunan
70 C3 Shih-t'an *Shitan* Kiangsi
79 C1 Shih-t'an *Shitan* Kwangt.
79 C2 Shih-t'an *Shitan* Kwangt.
118 B2 Shih-t'an *Shitan* Taiwan
114 C2 Shih-t'an-ching *Shitanjing* Ningsia
50 C4 Shih-t'ang *Shitang* Chek.
51 E4 Shih-t'ang *Shitang* Chek.
70 E3 Shih-t'ang *Shitang* Kiangsi
71 C4 Shih-t'ang *Shitang* Kiangsi
83 F5 Shih-t'ang *Shitang* Kwangsi
83 H2 Shih-t'ang *Shitang* Kwangsi
34 C3 Shih-t'an-wu *Shitanwu* Shant.
35 H3 Shih-tao *Shidao* Shant.
35 H3 Shih-tao Wan *Shidao Wan* (bay) Shant.
118 C1 Shih-ti *Shidi* Taiwan
74 C2 Shih-t'i-ch'i *Shitiqi* Hunan

106 C2 Su-ts'ai-k'o-su-a-chia-tzu *Sucaikesuajiazi* Tsing.
31 B7 Su-ts'ao *Sucao* Hopeh
31 C6 Su-ts'un *Sucun* Hopeh
34 D4 Su-ts'un *Sucun* Shant.
19 H3 Su-tzu Ho *Suzi He* (river) Liao.
19 G4 Su-tzu-kou *Suzigou* Liao.
42 B1 Su-yang-shan *Suyangshan* Kiangsu
82 E5 Su-yü *Suyu* Kwangsi
Swabue *see* Shan-wei
115 C5 Swallow Reef China Sea
Swatow *see* Shan-t'ou
Szechwan Basin *see* Ssu-ch'ua P'en-ti
Szechwan Province *see* Pages 85-88
Szefang *see* Ssu-fang
Szemao *see* Ssu-mao
Sze-nan-fu *see* Ssu-nan
Szeping *see* Ssu-p'ing
Szepingkai *see* Ssu-p'ing
Szeshui *see* Ssu-shui
Szewui *see* Ssu-hui
Szu- *see* Ssu-
91 F2 Szu-ch'ü *Siqu* Kwei.
11 G4 Szu-p'ai *Sipai* Heilung.

51 C5 Ta-an *Daan* Chek.
66 C3 Ta-an *Daan* Fukien
83 E3 Ta-an *Daan* Kwangsi
83 G4 Ta-an *Daan* Kwangsi
79 D2 Ta-an *Daan* Kwangt.
63 B7 Ta-an *Daan* Shensi
118 B2 Ta-an *Daan* Taiwan
14 E2 Ta-an Hsien *Daan Xian* Kirin
74 B2 Ta-an-p'ing *Daanping* Hunan
39 E4 Ta-chai *Dazhai* Shansi
99 F3 Ta-ch'ai-kou *Dachaigou* Kansu
106 C1 Ta-ch'ai-kou *Dachaigou* Tsing.
106 D2 Ta-ch'ai-ta-mu Hu *Dachaidamu* (lake) Tsing.
106 D2 Ta-ch'ai-tan *Dachaidan* Tsing.
102 D1 T'a-ch'a-k'ou *Tachakou* Sink.
102 H1 T'a-ch'a-k'ou *Tachakou* Sink.
51 F2 Ta-chan *Dazhan* Chek.
54 C3 Ta-chang *Dazhang* Honan
30 D4 Ta-ch'ang *Dachang* Hopeh
43 F4 Ta-ch'ang *Dachang* Kiangsu
82 D3 Ta-ch'ang *Dachang* Kwangsi
83 F4 Ta-chang *Dazhang* Kwangsi
106 E3 Ta-ch'ang *Dachang* Tsing.
42 C3 Ta-ch'ang-chen *Dachangzhen* Kiangsu
87 G2 Ta-ch'ang-chen *Dachangzhen* Szech.
67 E5 Ta-chang Ch'i *Dazhang Qi* (river) Fukien
30 D4 Ta-ch'ang Hui Autonomous Hsien Hopeh
30 D4 Ta-ch'ang Hui Autonomous Hsien *Dachang Hui* Hopeh
Ta-ch'ang Hui-tsu Tzu-chih-hsien *see* Ta-ch'ang Hui Autonomous Hsien
19 F5 Ta-ch'ang-shan Tao *Dachangshan Dao* (island) Liao.
51 F2 Ta-ch'ang-t'u Shan *Dachangtu Shan* (island) Chek.
30 F3 Ta-chang-tzu *Dazhangzi* Hopeh
55 E2 Ta-chao-ying *Dazhaoying* Honan
50 C4 Ta-che *Dazhe* Chek.
98 E2 Ta-ch'e-ch'ang *Dachechang* Kansu
51 D3 Ta-ch'en *Dachen* Chek.
62 E4 Ta-chen *Daozhen* Shensi
31 B6 Ta-ch'en-chuang *Dachenzhuang* Hopeh
31 D5 Ta-ch'eng *Dacheng* Hopeh
70 C3 Ta-ch'eng *Dacheng* Kiangsi
118 B3 Ta-ch'eng *Dacheng* Taiwan
102 C1 T'a-ch'eng *Tacheng* Sink.
94 B2 T'a-ch'eng *Tacheng* Yun.
43 D3 Ta-ch'eng-ch'iao *Dachengqiao* Kiangsu
19 F5 Ta-cheng-chia-t'un *Dazhengjiatun* Liao.
102 C1 T'a-ch'eng Ti-ch'ü *Tacheng Diqu* Sink.
18 C3 Ta-ch'eng-tzu *Dachengzi* Liao.
31 C5 Ta-ch'eng-wei *Dachengwei* Hopeh
50 C5 Ta-chi *Daji* Chek.
51 E4 Ta-ch'i *Daqi* Chek.
118 C2 Ta-ch'i *Daqi* Taiwan
118 B2 Ta-chia *Dajia* Taiwan
118 B2 Ta-chia Ch'i *Dajia Qi* (river) Taiwan
11 G4 Ta-chia-ho *Dajiahe* Heilung.
95 D4 Ta-chia-i *Dajiayi* Yun.
14 F3 Ta-chia-kou *Dajiagou* Kirin
83 F2 Ta-chiang *Dajiang* Kwangsi
83 G3 Ta-chiang *Dajiang* Kwangsi
47 E5 Ta-ch'iao *Daqiao* Anhwei
50 B4 Ta-ch'iao *Daqiao* Chek.
66 D4 Ta-ch'iao *Daqiao* Fukien
58 B4 Ta-ch'iao *Daqiao* Hupeh
70 B3 Ta-ch'iao *Daqiao* Kiangsi
70 C2 Ta-ch'iao *Daqiao* Kiangsi
70 E3 Ta-ch'iao *Daqiao* Kiangsi
43 D3 Ta-ch'iao *Daqiao* Kiangsu
43 E3 Ta-ch'iao *Daqiao* Kiangsu
15 I4 Ta-ch'iao *Daqiao* Kirin
83 G5 Ta-ch'iao *Daqiao* Kwangsi
79 C1 Ta-ch'iao *Daqiao* Kwangt.
39 C6 Ta-chiao *Dajiao* Shansi
86 D3 Ta-ch'iao *Daqiao* Szech.
86 D4 Ta-ch'iao *Daqiao* Szech.
95 D2 Ta-ch'iao *Daqiao* Yun.
55 F4 T'a-ch'iao *Taqiao* Honan
58 D4 Ta-ch'iao-pien *Daqiaobian* Hupeh
74 F4 Ta-ch'iao-wan *Daqiaowan* Hunan
19 F2 Ta-chia-tzu *Dajiazi* Liao.
35 D2 Ta-chia-wa *Dajiawa* Shant.
58 B5 Ta-chi-ch'ang *Dajichang* Hupeh
35 G2 Ta-chieh-shih *Dajieshi* Shant.
70 E2 T'a-ch'ien *Taqian* Kiangsi
83 E6 Ta-chih *Dazhi* Kwangsi
78 B4 Ta-chih-p'o *Dazhipo* Kwangt.
67 B5 Ta-ch'ih-yu *Dachiyu* Fukien
22 E3 Ta-chi-lu-ch'i-na Shan *Dajiluqina Shan* (mt) Heilung.
71 C4 Ta-chin-chu *Dajinzhu* Kiangsi
51 E4 Ta-ching *Dajing* Chek.
99 F3 Ta-ching *Dajing* Kansu
71 B5 Ta-ching *Dajing* Kiangsi
78 B2 Ta-ching *Dajing* Kwangt.
114 B3 Ta-ching *Dajing* Ningsia
34 B4 Ta-ching *Dajing* Shant.
63 E6 Ta-ching *Dajing* Shensi
102 I1 Ta-ching *Dajing* Sink.
95 D2 Ta-ching *Dajing* Yun.
14 F3 Ta-ch'ing-chü *Daqingju* Kirin
31 F4 Ta-ch'ing-ho *Daqinghe* Hopeh
31 D4 Ta-ch'ing Ho *Daqing He* (river) Hopeh
30 B2 Ta-ch'ing-kou *Daqinggou* Hopeh
26 D4 Ta-ch'ing Shan *Daqing Shan* (mts) In. Mong.
19 G2 Ta-ch'ing-tui-tzu *Daqingduizi* Liao.
59 H4 Ta-chin-p'u *Dajinpu* Hupeh
91 C2 Ta-chin-sha *Dajinsha* Kwei.
14 A5 Ta-ch'in-t'a-la *Daqintala* Kirin
23 D6 Ta-ch'in-t'a-la *Daqintala* Kirin
35 F1 Ta-ch'in Tao *Daqin Dao* (island) Shant.
54 D3 Ta-chin-tien *Dajindian* Honan
70 D3 Ta-ch'i-tu *Daqidu* Kiangsi
67 E5 Ta-ch'iu *Daqiu* Fukien
103 E3 Ta-chiu-pa *Dajiuba* Sink.
118 C2 Ta-cho-shui *Dazhuoshui* Taiwan
50 C4 Ta-chou *Dazhou* Chek.
43 D2 Ta-chou *Dazhou* Kiangsu
86 B1 Ta Ch'ü *Da Qu* (river) Szech.
87 F2 Ta-chu *Dazhu* Szech.
119 B4 Ta-chu *Dazhu* Taiwan
98 B1 Ta-ch'üan *Daquan* Kansu
98 C2 Ta-ch'üan *Daquan* Kansu
15 H4 Ta-ch'uan *Dachuan* Kirin
102 I1 Ta-ch'üan *Daquan* Sink.
46 D3 Ta-chuang *Dazhuang* Anhwei
67 D4 T'a-chuang *Tazhuang* Fukien
55 F3 Ta-chuang-t'ou *Dazhuangtou* Honan
38 E1 Ta-ch'üan-shan *Daquanshan* Shansi
103 F2 Ta-ch'üan-wan *Daquanwan* Sink.
14 F6 Ta-ch'üan-yüan *Daquanyuan* Kirin
110 D3 Ta-chu-ch'ia *Dazhuqia* Tibet
43 E2 Ta-chung-chi *Dazhongji* Kiangsu
75 D5 Ta-chung-ch'iao *Dazhongqiao* Hunan
51 F2 Ta-ch'ü Shan *Daqu Shan* (island) Chek.
110 D2 Ta-erh-cho *Daerzhuo* Tibet
Ta-erh-han-mao Ming-an Lien-ho-ch'i *see* Darhan-Mow Mingan United Banner
30 D2 Ta-erh-hao *Daerhao* Hopeh
26 B4 T'a-erh-hu *Taerhu* In. Mong.
102 I2 T'a-erh-lan *Taerlan* Sink.
106 C2 T'a-erh-ting *Taerding* Tsing.
59 F3 T'a-erh-wan *Taerwan* Hupeh
59 G5 Ta-fan *Dafan* Hupeh
90 C3 Ta-fang *Dafang* Kwei.
14 F3 Ta-fang-shen *Dafangshen* Kirin
18 E5 Ta-fang-shen *Dafangshen* Liao.
19 G2 Ta-fan-ho *Dafanhe* Liao.
71 B5 Ta-fen *Dafen* Kiangsi
11 E4 Ta-feng *Dafeng* Heilung.
43 E2 Ta-feng Hsien *Dafeng Xian* Kiangsu
15 G4 Ta-feng-man *Dafengman* Kirin
106 C1 Ta-feng-shan *Dafengshan* Tsing.
51 E3 Ta-fo Shan *Dafo Shan* (island) Chek.
47 E7 Ta-fu *Dafu* Anhwei
59 F3 Ta-fu Shui *Dafu Shui* (river) Hupeh
11 C4 T'a-ha *Taha* Heilung.
23 F4 T'a-ha *Taha* Heilung.
10 C2 T'a-ha Ho *Taha He* (river) Heilung.
22 F2 T'a-ha Ho *Taha He* (river) Heilung.
30 E4 Ta-hai-pei *Dahaibei* Hopeh
14 C4 Ta-han *Dahan* Kirin
23 E6 Ta-han *Dahan* Kirin
Tahcheng *see* T'a-ch'eng
26 D4 Ta-hei Ho *Dahei He* (river) In. Mong.
107 F3 Ta-hei Ho *Dahei He* (river) Tsing.
14 E4 Ta-hei Shan *Dahei Shan* (mts) Kirin
67 C5 Ta-heng *Daheng* Fukien
118 B2 Ta-heng-p'ing Shan *Dahengping Shan* (mt) Taiwan
67 B5 Ta-ho *Dahe* Fukien
78 B4 Ta-ho *Dahe* Kwangt.
79 C2 Ta-ho *Dahe* Kwangt.
10 C1 T'a-ho *Tahe* Heilung.
22 F1 T'a-ho *Tahe* Heilung.
11 G4 Ta-ho-chen *Dahezhen* Heilung.
27 G3 Ta-ho-k'ou *Dahekou* In. Mong.
27 G3 Ta-ho-k'ou *Dahekou* In. Mong.
63 D8 Ta-ho-k'ou *Dahekou* Shensi
30 C4 Ta-ho-nan *Dahenan* Hopeh
58 B5 Ta-ho-pa *Daheba* Hupeh
54 E5 Ta-ho-t'un *Dahetun* Honan
102 I2 Ta-ho-yen *Daheyan* Sink.
14 E3 Ta-hsi *Daxi* Kirin
90 C3 Ta-hsi *Daxi* Kwei.
102 D2 Ta-hsi *Daxi* Sink.
10 D3 T'a-hsi *Taxi* Heilung.
107 H2 Ta-hsia *Daxia* Tsing.
58 C3 Ta-hsia-k'ou *Daxiakou* Hupeh
86 D3 Ta-hsiang Ling *Daxiang Ling* (mts) Szech.
51 E3 Ta-hsieh-t'ou *Daxietou* Chek.
87 F2 Ta-hsien *Daxian* Szech.
103 D2 Ta-hsi-hai-tzu Shui-k'u *Daxihaizi Shuiku* (res.) Sink.
82 D5 Ta-hsin *Daxin* Kwangsi
83 G4 Ta-hsin *Daxin* Kwangsi
42 C2 Ta-hsing *Daxing* Kiangsu
14 D3 Ta-hsing *Daxing* Kirin
82 D3 Ta-hsing *Daxing* Kwangsi
91 G3 Ta-hsing *Daxing* Kwei.
95 D2 Ta-hsing *Daxing* Yun.
10 B2 Ta-hsing-an Ling *Daxingan Ling* (mts) Heilung.
10 C2 Ta-hsing-an-ling Ti-ch'ü *Daxinganling Diqu* Heilung.
14 F5 Ta-hsing-chen *Daxingzhen* Kirin
34 D5 Ta-hsing-chen *Daxingzhen* Shant.
30 D4 Ta-hsing Hsien *Daxing Xian* Hopeh
30 D4 Ta-hsing Hsien *Daxing Xian* Hopeh
15 J4 Ta-hsing-kou *Daxinggou* Kirin
55 E4 Ta-hsin-tien *Daxindian* Honan
35 F2 Ta-hsin-tien *Daxindian* Shant.
51 E3 Ta-hsü *Daxu* Chek.
83 G4 Ta-hsüan *Daxuan* Kwangsi
42 B1 Ta-hsü-chia *Daxujia* Kiangsu
51 D5 Ta-hsüeh *Daxue* Chek.
118 C2 Ta-hsüeh Shan *Daxue Shan* (mt) Taiwan
86 C2 Ta-hsüeh Shan *Daxue Shan* (mts) Szech.
70 D4 Ta-hsü Shan *Daxu Shan* (mt) Kiangsi
70 F3 Ta-hsü-ts'un *Daxucun* Kiangsi
67 C4 Ta-hu *Dahu* Fukien
74 F3 Ta-hu *Dahu* Hunan
118 B2 Ta-hu *Dahu* Taiwan
82 D4 Ta-hua *Dahua* Kwangsi
79 C2 Ta-huai *Dahuai* Kwangt.
82 E2 Ta-huan Chiang *Dahuan Jiang* (river) Kwangsi
14 G5 Ta-huang-kou *Dahuanggou* Kirin
15 K4 Ta-huang-kou *Dahuanggou* Kirin
51 F2 Ta-huang-lung Shan *Dahuanglong Shan* (island) Chek.
71 B5 Ta-hu-chiang *Dahujiang* Kiangsi
30 C2 Ta-hu-lun *Dahulun* Hopeh
26 D4 Ta-hung-ch'eng *Dahongcheng* In. Mong.
19 F3 Ta-hung-ch'i *Dahongqi* Liao.
54 E2 Ta-hung-ch'iao *Dahongqiao* Honan
102 B4 Ta-hung-liu-t'an *Dahongliutan* Sink.
59 E3 Ta-hung Shan *Dahong Shan* (mt) Hupeh
106 D2 Ta-hung-shan *Dahongshan* Tsing.
14 C3 Ta-huo-fang *Dahuofang* Kirin
23 E5 Ta-huo-fang *Dahuofang* Kirin
19 F3 Ta-hu-shan *Dahushan* Liao.
91 D5 Ta-i *Dayi* Kwei.
34 B4 Ta-i *Dayi* Shant.
86 D2 Ta-i *Dayi* Szech.
19 F3 T'ai-an *Taian* Liao.
34 C3 T'ai-an *Taian* Shant.
118 B2 T'ai-an *Taian* Taiwan
43 F4 T'ai-an-kang *Taiangang* Kiangsu
111 E3 T'ai-chao *Taizhao* Tibet
51 D2 Tai-ch'i *Daiqi* Chek.
66 E4 Tai-ch'i *Daiqi* Fukien
43 D3 Ta-i-chi *Dayiji* Kiangsu
34 A5 Ta-i-chi *Dayiji* Shant.
34 B4 Ta-i-chi *Dayiji* Shant.
67 D4 T'ai-ch'i *Taiqi* Fukien
66 E4 Tai Chiang *Dai Jiang* (river) Fukien
91 E4 T'ai-chiang Hsien *Taijiang Xian* Kwei.
43 E3 Tai-chia-yao *Daijiayao* Kiangsu
14 A2 T'ai-chia-ying-tzu *Taijiayingzi* Kirin
23 D5 T'ai-chia-ying-tzu *Taijiayingzi* Kirin
74 D4 T'ai-chih-miao *Taizhimiao* Hunan
14 B2 Tai-ch'in-t'a-la *Daiqintala* Kirin
23 D5 Tai-ch'in-t'a-la *Daiqintala* Kirin
51 E4 T'ai-chou *Taizhou* Chek.
43 D3 T'ai-chou *Taizhou* Kiangsu
51 E4 T'ai-chou Lieh-tao *Taizhou Liedao* (islands) Chek.
51 E4 T'ai-chou Wan *Taizhou Wan* (bay) Chek.
Taichow *see* Tai-hsien
Taichow *see* T'ai-chou
118 B2 T'ai-chung *Taizhong* Taiwan
118 B2 T'ai-chung Hsien *Taizhong Xian* Taiwan
34 C5 T'ai-erh-chuang *Taierzhuang* Shant.
71 C4 Tai-fang *Daifang* Kiangsi
26 E4 Tai Hai *Dai Hai* (lake) In. Mong.
31 B4 T'ai-hang Shan *Taihang Shan* (mts) Hopeh
Taihing *see* T'ai-hsing
46 B3 T'ai-ho *Taihe* Anhwei
71 B5 T'ai-ho *Taihe* Kiangsi
71 D4 T'ai-ho *Taihe* Kiangsi
34 D3 T'ai-ho *Taihe* Shant.
119 B4 T'ai-ho *Taihe* Taiwan
87 E2 T'ai-ho-chen *Taihezhen* Szech.
Taihoku *see* T'ai-pei
75 E6 T'ai-ho-yü *Taiheyu* Hunan
118 B3 T'ai-hsi *Taixi* Taiwan
38 D2 Tai-hsien *Daixian* Shansi
43 E3 T'ai Hsien *Tai Xian* Kiangsu
43 D3 T'ai-hsing *Taixing* Kiangsu
47 C6 T'ai-hu *Taihu* Anhwei
43 E4 T'ai Hu *Taihu* (lake) Kiangsu
91 D5 Tai-hua *Daihua* Kwei.
11 C4 T'ai-k'ang *Taikang* Heilung.
23 F4 T'ai-k'ang *Taikang* Heilung.
55 F3 T'ai-k'ang *Taikang* Honan
Taikiang *see* T'ai-kung
39 D4 T'ai-ku *Taigu* Shansi
91 F4 T'ai-kung *Taigong* Kwei.
11 B4 T'ai-lai *Tailai* Heilung.
22 E4 T'ai-lai *Tailai* Heilung.
27 F2 Tai-la-min-su-mo *Dailaminsumo* In. Mong.
26 C4 T'ai-liang *Tailiang* In. Mong.
91 F4 T'ai-lieh *Tailie* Kwei.
39 C5 T'ai-lin *Tailin* Shansi
11 E4 Tai-ling *Dailing* Heilung.
118 C2 T'ai-lu-ko *Tailuge* Taiwan
118 C2 T'ai-lu-ko Hsia *Tailuge Xia* (gorge) Taiwan
118 C2 T'ai-lu-ko-ta Shan *Tailugeda Shan* (mt) Taiwan
79 D2 T'ai-mei *Taimei* Kwangt.
106 E4 T'ai-nai Ch'ü *Tainai Qu* (river) Tsing.
43 E3 Tai-nan *Dainan* Kiangsu
119 B4 T'ai-nan *Tainan* Taiwan
119 B3 T'ai-nan Hsien *Tainan Xian* Taiwan
66 C4 T'ai-ning *Taining* Fukien
67 B6 T'ai-pa *Taiba* Fukien
99 I3 T'ai-pai *Taibai* Kansu
70 E2 T'ai-pai *Taibai* Kiangsi
91 E2 T'ai-pai *Taibai* Kwei.
63 C6 T'ai-pai Hsien *Taibai Xian* Shensi
38 F2 T'ai-pai Shan *Taibai Shan* (mt) Shansi
63 C7 T'ai-pai Shan *Taibai Shan* (mt) Shensi
43 D1 T'ai-pei *Taibei* Kiangsu
118 C1 T'ai-pei *Taibei* Taiwan
T'ai-pei - city plan *see* Page 141
118 C2 T'ai-pei Hsien *Taibei Xian* Taiwan
27 H2 T'ai-pen-miao *Taibenmiao* In. Mong.
T'ai-p'ing *see* Wen-ling
66 D4 T'ai-p'ing *Taiping* Fukien
11 F4 T'ai-p'ing *Taiping* Heilung.
74 D2 T'ai-p'ing *Taiping* Hunan
75 E6 T'ai-p'ing *Taiping* Hunan
59 E2 T'ai-p'ing *Taiping* Hupeh
82 D4 T'ai-p'ing *Taiping* Kwangsi
82 D5 T'ai-p'ing *Taiping* Kwangsi
83 E3 T'ai-p'ing *Taiping* Kwangsi
83 E5 T'ai-p'ing *Taiping* Kwangsi
83 F3 T'ai-p'ing *Taiping* Kwangsi
79 C1 T'ai-p'ing *Taiping* Kwangt.
79 C2 T'ai-p'ing *Taiping* Kwangt.
118 B2 T'ai-p'ing *Taiping* Taiwan
30 F3 T'ai-p'ing-chai *Taipingzhai* Hopeh
79 C2 T'ai-p'ing-ch'ang *Taipingchang* Kwangt.
54 C4 T'ai-p'ing-chen *Taipingzhen* Honan
58 B5 T'ai-p'ing-chen *Taipingzhen* Hupeh
34 D2 T'ai-ping-chen *Taibingzhen* Shant.
34 B4 T'ai-p'ing-ch'iao *Taipingqiao* Shant.
22 D2 T'ai-p'ing-ch'uan *Taipingchuan* Heilung.
14 D3 T'ai-p'ing-ch'uan *Taipingchuan* Kirin
15 H5 T'ai-p'ing-ch'uan *Taipingchuan* Kirin
23 E5 T'ai-p'ing-ch'uan *Taipingchuan* Kirin
30 E2 T'ai-ping-chuang *Taibingzhuang* Hopeh
47 E6 T'ai-p'ing Hsien *Taiping Xian* Anhwei
10 F3 T'ai-p'ing-kou *Taipinggou* Heilung.
58 E4 T'ai-p'ing-k'ou *Taibingkou* Hupeh
15 K4 T'ai-p'ing-kou *Taipinggou* Kirin
18 C3 T'ai-p'ing-kou *Taipinggou* Liao.
70 D2 T'ai-p'ing-kuan *Taipingguan* Kiangsi
75 F6 T'ai-p'ing-li *Taipingli* Hunan
74 D4 T'ai-p'ing-p'u *Taipingpu* Hunan
11 D4 T'ai-p'ing-shan *Taipingshan* Heilung.
14 E3 T'ai-p'ing-shan *Taipingshan* Kirin
23 F5 T'ai-p'ing-shan *Taipingshan* Kirin
19 F4 T'ai-p'ing-shan *Taipingshan* Liao.
19 I4 T'ai-p'ing-shao *Taipingshao* Liao.
74 E4 T'ai-p'ing-ssu *Taipingsi* Hunan
58 D2 T'ai-p'ing-tien *Taipingdian* Hupeh
31 E5 T'ai-p'ing-ts'un *Taipingcun* Hopeh
87 F3 T'ai-p'ing-tu *Taipingdu* Szech.
75 E6 T'ai-p'ing-yü *Taipingyu* Hunan
46 D4 Tai-pu *Daibu* Anhwei
43 D4 Tai-pu *Daibu* Kiangsu
51 F2 Tai Shan *Dai Shan* (island) Chek.
43 D1 Ta-i-shan *Dayishan* Kiangsu
79 C2 T'ai-shan *Taishan* Kwangt.
34 C3 T'ai Shan *Tai Shan* (mt) Shant.
34 C3 T'ai Shan *Tai Shan* (mts) Shant.
38 E2 T'ai-shan *Taishan* Shansi
14 F6 T'ai-shang *Taishang* Kirin
51 F2 Tai-shan Hsien *Daishan Xian* Chek.
66 F4 T'ai-shan Lieh-tao *Taishan Liedao* (island group) Fukien
87 F2 Tai-shih *Daishi* Szech.
50 C5 T'ai-shun *Taishun* Chek.
103 E3 T'ai-t'e-ma Hu *Taitema Hu* (lake) Sink.
67 E5 Tai-t'ou *Daitou* Fukien
30 G3 T'ai-t'ou-ying *Taitouying* Hopeh
43 F4 T'ai-ts'ang *Taicang* Kiangsu
83 G2 T'ai-ts'un *Taicun* Kwangsi
10 C4 T'ai-tung *Taidong* Heilung.
119 C4 T'ai-tung *Taidong* Taiwan
119 B3 T'ai-tung Hsien *Taidong Xian* Taiwan
118 B3 T'ai-tzu *Taizi* Taiwan
19 G3 T'ai-tzu Ho *Taizi He* (river) Liao.
74 D3 T'ai-tzu-miao *Taizimiao* Hunan
99 F4 T'ai-tzu-ssu *Taizisi* Kansu
Taiwan *see* Pages 117-119
54 E2 Tai-wang *Daiwang* Honan
30 B4 Tai-wang-ch'eng *Daiwangcheng* Hopeh
82 C3 T'ai-wang Lao-shan *Taiwang Laoshan* (mt) Kwangsi
T'ai-wan Hai-hsia *see* Formosa Strait
T'ai-wan Hai-hsia *see* Formosa Strait
T'ai-wan Shan *see* Chung-yang Shan-mo
119 B4 T'ai-wu *Taiwu* Taiwan
58 B4 T'ai-yang-ho *Taiyanghe* Hupeh
10 C2 T'ai-yang-kou *Taiyanggou* Heilung.
63 B7 T'ai-yang Shan *Taiyang Shan* (mt) Shensi
39 B6 T'ai-yang-ts'un *Taiyangcun* Shansi
63 D6 T'ai-yü *Taiyu* Shensi
38 D4 T'ai-yüan *Taiyuan* Shansi
T'ai-yüan - city plan *see* Page 136
75 E4 Tai-yüan-ssu *Daiyuansi* Hunan
38 D2 Tai-yüeh *Daiyue* Shansi
39 D5 T'ai-yüeh Shan *Taiyue Shan* (mts) Shansi
Taiyuenfu *see* T'ai-yüan
67 D5 Tai-yün Shan *Daiyun Shan* (mt) Fukien
119 B4 Ta-jen *Daren* Taiwan
T'a-je Ts'o *see* T'e-li-na-mu Ts'o
Ta-jih *see* Chi-mai
107 F4 Ta-jih *Dari* Tsing.
107 F4 Ta-jih-chin-tu *Darijindu* Tsing.
111 D3 T'a-jung *Tavong* Tibet
83 G2 Ta-jung-chiang *Tarongjiang* Kwangsi
83 G4 Ta-jung Shan *Darong Shan* (mts) Kwangsi
66 C4 Ta-kan *Dagan* Fukien
70 D3 Ta-kang *Dagang* Kiangsi
43 D3 Ta-kang *Dagang* Kiangsu
43 E2 Ta-kang *Dagang* Kiangsu
55 F2 T'a-kang *Tagang* Honan
50 C4 Ta-kang-t'ou *Dagangtou* Chek.
75 F6 Ta-ken-ch'iao *Dagenqiao* Hunan
71 C5 Ta-k'eng *Dakeng* Kiangsi
79 C1 Ta-k'eng-k'ou *Dakengkou* Kwangt.
106 D1 Ta-k'en-ta-pan Shan *Dakendaban Shan* (mts) Tsing.
Takhing *see* Te-ch'ing
Taklakhar *see* P'u-lan
Taklakot *see* P'u-lan
Takla Makan *see* T'a-k'o-la-ma-kan Sha-mo
30 D2 Ta-ko-chen *Dagezhen* Hopeh
102 C3 T'a-k'o-la-ma-kan Sha-mo *Takelamagan Shamo* (desert) Sink.
102 B4 T'a-ko-ma-po *Tagemabo* Sink.
107 F1 Ta-ko-ta *Dageda* Tsing.
14 B2 T'a-k'o-t'u *Taketu* Kirin
23 D5 T'a-k'o-t'u *Taketu* Kirin
54 D2 Ta-k'ou *Dakou* Honan
39 D6 Ta-k'ou *Dakou* Shansi
30 E4 Ta-k'ou-t'un *Dakoutun* Hopeh
31 E5 Ta-ku *Dagu* Hopeh
119 B4 Ta-ku *Dagu* Taiwan
102 H1 Ta-kuai *Daguai* Sink.
91 D4 Ta-kuan *Daguan* Kwei.
87 E3 Ta-kuan *Daguan* Szech.
118 C3 Ta-kuan *Daguan* Taiwan
95 D2 Ta-kuan *Daguan* Yun.
35 F3 Ta-k'uang *Dakuang* Shant.
47 C6 Ta-kuan Hu *Daguan Hu* Anhwei
11 C4 Ta-kuan-t'un *Daguantun* Heilung.
19 H2 Ta-ku-chia *Dagujia* Liao.
19 G2 Ta-ku-chia-tzu *Dagujiazi* Liao.
11 D4 Ta-kuei *Dagui* Heilung.
35 F3 Ta-ku Ho *Dagu He* (river) Shant.
35 G2 Ta-ku Ho *Dagu He* (river) Shant.
110 C2 T'a-ku-k'o *Taguke* Tibet
51 E3 Ta-kung *Dagong* Chek.
98 C2 Ta-kung-ch'a *Dagongcha* Kansu
86 C2 T'a-kung-ssu *Tagongsi* Szech.
35 F4 Ta-kung Tao *Dagong Dao* (island) Shant.
34 C3 Ta-k'un-lun *Dakunlun* Shant.
74 D3 Ta-kuo-kang *Daguogang* Hunan
14 F4 Ta-ku-shan *Dagushan* Kirin
19 G3 Ta-ku-shan *Dagushan* Liao.
47 C5 Ta-ku-tien *Dagudian* Anhwei
15 I4 T'a-la-chan *Talazhan* Kirin
99 G3 Ta-la-ch'ih *Dalachi* Kansu
23 F4 T'a-la-ha *Talaha* Heilung.
11 C4 T'a-la-ho *Talahe* Heilung.
22 B3 Ta-lai *Dalai* Heilung.
14 E2 Ta-lai *Dalai* Kirin
23 F5 Ta-lai *Dalai* Kirin
22 D2 Ta-lai-kou *Dalaigou* Heilung.
102 D2 Ta-la-k'o *Dalake* Sink.
26 C4 T'a-la-kou *Talagou* In. Mong.
26 E4 Ta-la-ma-miao *Dalamamiao* In. Mong.
79 D2 Ta-lan *Dalan* Kwangt.
102 I2 Ta-lang-k'an *Dalangkan* Sink.
79 C3 Ta-lang-wan *Dalangwan* Kwangt.
98 E1 Ta-lan-k'u-pu *Dalankubu* Kansu
102 C2 Ta-lao-pa *Dalaoba* Sink.
62 E4 Ta-lao-shan *Dalaoshan* Shensi
35 D3 Ta-lao-tzu *Dalaozi* Shant.
14 E3 Ta-lao-yeh-fu *Dalaoyefu* Kirin
106 D4 Ta-la-ssu *Dalasi* Tsing.
26 D4 Ta-la-t'e Ch'i *Dalate Qi* In. Mong.
114 B2 T'a-la-t'u *Talatu* Ningsia
10 E3 Ta-la-tzu *Dalazi* Heilung.
15 J5 Ta-la-tzu *Dalazi* Kirin
82 C4 Ta-leng *Daleng* Kwangsi
83 G4 Ta-li *Dali* Kwangsi
63 E6 Ta-li *Dali* Shensi
118 C2 Ta-li *Dali* Taiwan
119 C3 Ta-li *Dali* Taiwan
94 C3 Ta-li *Dali* Yun.
30 E4 Ta-liang *Daliang* Hopeh
83 F3 Ta-liang *Daliang* Kwangsi
79 C2 Ta-liang *Daliang* Kwangt.
107 G2 Ta-liang *Daliang* Tsing.
119 B4 Ta-liao *Daliao* Taiwan
46 D4 Ta-li-chi *Daliji* Anhwei
42 B2 Ta-li-chi *Daliji* Kiangsu
34 B2 Ta-li-chia *Dalijia* Shant.
31 B7 Ta-lien *Dalian* Hopeh
91 E2 Ta-lien *Dalian* Kwei.
18 E6 Ta-lien *Dalian* Liao.
11 E4 Ta-lien-ho *Dalianhe* Heilung.
67 E5 Ta-lien Tao *Dalian Dao* (island) Fukien
19 F5 Ta-lien Tao *Dalian Dao* (island) Liao.
62 E3 Ta-li Ho *Dali He* (river) Shensi
66 C4 Ta-li-k'ou *Dalikou* Fukien
102 C2 Ta-li-mu *Dalimu* Sink.
102 D2 T'a-li-mu Ho *Talimu He* (river) Sink.
102 C3 T'a-li-mu P'en-ti *Talimu Pendi* Sink.
14 C4 Ta-lin *Dalin* Kirin
23 E6 Ta-lin *Dalin* Kirin
118 B3 Ta-lin *Dalin* Taiwan
34 C3 Ta-lin-ch'ih *Dalinchi* Shant.
14 E4 Ta-ling *Daling* Kirin
15 G2 Ta-ling *Daling* Kirin
82 D5 Ta-ling *Daling* Kwangsi
46 C3 Ta-ling-chi *Dalingji* Anhwei
18 D3 Ta-ling Chiang *Daling Jiang* (river) Liao.
18 E3 Ta-ling-ho *Dalinghe* Liao.
46 D3 Ta-ling-tzu *Dalingzi* Anhwei
38 E2 Ta-lin-ho *Dalinhe* Shansi
23 B6 Ta-li No-erh *Dali Nuoer* (lake) Liao.
14 B2 Ta-lin-t'un *Dalintun* Kirin
23 D5 Ta-lin-t'un *Dalintun* Kirin
14 F2 Ta-lin-tzu *Dalinzi* Kirin
14 E2 Ta-li-pa *Daliba* Kirin
94 B2 Ta-li Pai Autonomous District Yun.
Ta-li Pai-tsu Tzu-chih-chou *see* Ta-li Pai Autonomous District
22 C3 Ta-li-su-lin *Dalisulin* Heilung.
14 C4 Ta-li-t'u *Dalitu* Kirin
23 E6 Ta-li-t'u *Dalitu* Kirin
Talitze *see* Ta-li-tzu
15 G6 Ta-li-tzu *Dalizi* Kirin
119 B4 Ta-liu *Daliu* Taiwan
103 D2 T'a-liu-ch'ang *Taliuchang* Sink.
55 F4 Ta-liu-chuang *Daliuzhuang* Honan
62 F1 Ta-liu-t'a *Daliuta* Shensi
55 E4 Ta-liu-tien *Daliudian* Honan
19 F2 Ta-liu-t'un *Daliutun* Liao.
46 D3 Ta-li-yüan *Daliyuan* Anhwei
94 C5 Ta-lo *Daluo* Yun.
11 D4 Ta-lo-chen *Daluozhen* Heilung.
103 D2 Ta-lo-li-k'o *Daluolike* Sink.
11 E5 Ta-lo-mi *Daluomi* Heilung.
79 C2 Ta-lo Shan *Daluo Shan* (mt) Kwangt.
91 E2 Ta-lou Shan *Dalou Shan* (mts) Kwei.
99 G3 Ta-lu *Dalu* Kansu
14 F6 Ta-lu *Dalu* Kirin
82 E6 Ta-lü *Dalü* Kwangsi
35 F2 Ta-lü-chia *Dalüjia* Shant.
27 E4 Ta-lu-hao *Daluhao* In. Mong.
70 A4 Ta-lu-li *Daluli* Kiangsi
71 B5 Ta-lung *Dalong* Kiangsi
111 D3 Ta-lung *Dalong* Tibet
30 C4 Ta-lung-hua *Dalonghua* Hopeh
79 D1 Ta-lung-t'ien *Dalongtian* Kwangt.
111 D3 Ta-lun Ts'o *Dalun Cuo* (lake) Tibet
19 G5 Ta-lu Tao *Dalu Dao* (island) Liao.
47 E4 Ta-ma-ch'ang *Damachang* Anhwei
30 C2 Ta-ma-chün Shan *Damajun Shan* (mts) Hopeh
39 C4 Ta-mai-chiao *Damaijiao* Shansi
119 B4 T'a-ma-li *Tamali* Taiwan
70 E3 Ta-mao Shan *Damao Shan* (mt) Kiangsi
106 D2 Ta-mei-kou *Dameigou* Tsing.
11 E5 Ta-mei-lin *Dameilin* Heilung.
38 D3 Ta-meng *Dameng* Shansi
94 C5 Ta-meng-lung *Damenglong* Yun.
94 B4 Ta-meng-o *Damenge* Yun.
51 E5 Ta-men Tao *Damen Dao* (island) Chek.
30 E2 Ta-miao *Damiao* Hopeh
26 B5 Ta-miao *Damiao* In. Mong.
26 D4 Ta-miao *Damiao* In. Mong.
70 B3 Ta-miao *Damiao* Kiangsi
42 B1 Ta-miao *Damiao* Kiangsu
18 B2 Ta-miao *Damiao* Liao.
87 G2 Ta-miao *Damiao* Szech.
75 D5 Ta-miao-k'ou *Damiaokou* Hunan
Ta-miao-shan *see* Jung-shui
67 A5 Ta-ming *Daming* Fukien
31 C7 Ta-ming *Daming* Hopeh
19 G2 Ta-ming-pei *Damingbei* Liao.
83 E4 Ta-ming Shan *Daming Shan* (mt) Kwangsi
19 F3 Ta-min-t'un *Damintun* Liao.
58 C2 Ta-mu-ch'ang *Damuchang* Hupeh
67 D4 Ta-mu-chih Shan *Damuzhi Shan* (mt) Fukien
114 B1 T'a-mu-su-pu-lu-k'o *Tamusubuluge* Ningsia
70 F3 Ta-nan *Danan* Kiangsi
119 C4 Ta-nan *Danan* Taiwan
103 F2 Ta-nan-hu *Dananhu* Sink.
14 F4 Ta-nan-t'un *Danantun* Kirin
38 C2 Tan-chai *Danzhai* Shansi
91 E4 Tan-chai Hsien *Danzhai Xian* Kwei.
102 H2 T'an-ch'ang *Tanchang* Sink.
51 E3 Tan-ch'eng *Dancheng* Chek.
55 G4 Tan-ch'eng *Dancheng* Honan
34 D5 T'an-ch'eng *Tancheng* Shant.
42 B1 Tan-chi *Danji* Kiangsu
74 B3 T'an-ch'i *Tanqi* Hunan
70 C3 T'an-ch'i *Tanqi* Kiangsi
91 F2 T'an-chia-ch'ang *Tanjiachang* Kwei.
47 E6 T'an-chia-ch'iao *Tanjiaqiao* Anhwei
99 F3 T'an-chia-ching *Tanjiajing* Kansu
34 D3 T'an-chia-fang *Tanjiafang* Shant.
75 D6 Tan-chiang *Danjiang* Hunan
58 D2 Tan-chiang *Danjiang* Hupeh
63 F7 Tan Chiang *Dan Jiang* (river) Shensi
79 C2 T'an Chiang *Tan Jiang* (river) Kwangt.
59 E4 T'an-ch'iao *Tanqiao* Hupeh
74 C3 T'an-chia-wan *Tanjiawan* Hunan
70 C4 T'an-ch'iu *Tanqiu* Kiangsi
83 F2 Tan-chou *Danzhou* Kwangsi
83 G4 Tan-chu *Danzhu* Kwangsi
55 F4 T'an-chuang *Tanzhuang* Honan
119 B3 Ta-nei *Danei* Taiwan
70 D4 T'an-fang *Tanfang* Kiangsi
95 D3 Tan-feng *Danfeng* Yun.
63 F7 Tan-feng Hsien *Danfeng Xian* Shensi
Tangar *see* Huang-yüan
43 E3 T'ang-cha *Tangzha* Kiangsu
99 G5 Tang-ch'ang *Dangchang* Kansu
31 B5 Tang-ch'eng *Dangcheng* Hopeh
39 D5 T'ang-ch'eng *Tangcheng* Shansi
98 B2 Tang-ch'eng-wan *Dangchengwan* Kansu
50 C3 T'ang-ch'i *Tangqi* Chek.
43 D2 T'ang-chi *Tangji* Kiangsu
34 B3 Tang-chia-chuang *Dangjiazhuang* Shant.
30 F4 T'ang-chia-chuang *Tangjiazhuang* Hopeh
47 D6 T'ang-chia-kou *Tangjiagou* Anhwei
47 E5 T'ang-chia-kou *Tangjiakou* Anhwei
110 C3 T'ang-chia La *Tangjia La* (pass) Tibet
106 D4 Tang-chiang *Dangjiang* Tsing.
71 B6 T'ang-chiang *Tangjiang* Kiangsi
35 F2 T'ang-chia-p'o *Tangjiapo* Shant.
62 F4 Tang-chia-wan *Dangjiawan* Shensi
50 C2 T'ang-chia-wan *Tangjiawan* Chek.
79 C2 T'ang-chia-wan *Tangjiawan* Kwangt.
107 G4 T'ang-ch'ien-kou *Tangqiangou* Tsing.
11 B4 T'ang-ch'ih *Tangchi* Heilung.
23 E4 T'ang-ch'ih *Tangchi* Heilung.
111 D3 Tang-ch'ing *Dangqing* Tibet
106 D1 Tang-chin Shan-k'ou *Dangjin Shankou* (pass) Tsing.
31 B6 T'ang-ch'iu *Tangqiu* Hopeh
106 C4 Tang Ch'ü *Dang Qu* (river) Tsing.
99 H4 Tang-ch'uan *Dangchuan* Kansu
67 C5 T'ang-ch'üan *Tangquan* Fukien
67 D4 T'ang-ch'uan *Tangchuan* Fukien
34 D5 T'ang-chuang *Tangzhuang* Shant.
31 D4 T'ang-erh-li *Tangerli* Hopeh
71 D5 T'ang-fang *Tangfang* Kiangsi
30 F4 T'ang-feng *Tangfeng* Hopeh
98 B2 Tang Ho *Dang He* (river) Kansu
54 D5 T'ang-ho *Tanghe* Honan
46 D3 T'ang Ho *Tang He* (river) Anhwei
31 C5 T'ang Ho *Tang He* (river) Hopeh
30 D3 T'ang-ho-k'ou *Tanghekou* Hopeh
Tang-ho Nan-shan *see* Wu-lan-ta-pan Shan
18 D3 T'ang-ho-tzu *Tanghezi* Liao.
51 D2 T'ang-hsi *Tangxi* Chek.
51 D5 T'ang-hsia *Tangxia* Chek.
75 F6 T'ang-hsia *Tangxia* Hunan
51 D3 T'ang-hsien *Tangxian* Chek.
31 B5 T'ang-hsien *Tangxian* Hopeh
59 F3 T'ang-hsien-chen *Tangxianzhen* Hupeh
111 D3 Tang-hsiung *Dangxiung* Tibet
111 D3 Tang-hsü *Dangxu* Tibet
71 B5 T'ang-hu *Tanghu* Kiangsi
83 E4 T'ang-hung *Tanghong* Kwangsi
34 A3 T'ang-i *Tangyi* Shant.
Tangin Pass *see* Tang-chin Shan-k'ou
19 F3 T'ang-kang-tzu *Tanggangzi* Liao.
Tangkiachwan *see* T'ang-chia-chuang
86 D1 T'ang-k'o *Tangke* Szech.
107 G2 T'ang-ko-mu *Tanggemu* Tsing.
47 E6 T'ang-k'ou *Tangkou* Anhwei
42 C2 T'ang-kou *Tanggou* Kiangsu
43 E4 T'ang-k'ou *Tangkou* Kiangsu
31 E4 T'ang-ku *Tanggu* Hopeh
31 D5 T'ang-kuan-t'un *Tangguantun* Hopeh
106 C4 T'ang-ku-la-chia-k'a *Tanggulajiaka* Tsing.
111 D2 T'ang-ku-la Shan-k'ou *Tanggula Shankou* (pass) Tibet
106 B4 T'ang-ku-la Shan-k'ou *Tanggula Shankou* Tsing.
111 D3 T'ang-ku-la Shan-mo *Tanggula Shanmo* (mts) Tibet
110 C3 T'ang-ku-la-yu-mu Ts'o *Tanggulayoumu Cuo* (lake) Tibet
111 E3 T'ang-kuo *Tangguo* Tibet
102 C3 T'ang-ku-tzu-pa-ssu-t'e *Tangguzibasite* Sink.
27 E4 Tang-lang-hu-t'ung *Danglanghutong* In. Mong.
Tanglha Range *see* T'ang-ku-la Shan-mo
42 A1 T'ang-lou *Tanglou* Kiangsu
107 F3 Tang-lu *Danglu* TS1Tsinghai
63 E6 Tang-mu *Dangmu* Shensi
105 G3 T'ang-nai-hai *Tangnaihai* Tsing.
46 D3 T'ang-nan-chi *Tangnanji* Anhwei
86 C3 T'ang-o *Tange* Szech.
30 F3 Tang-pa *Dangba* Hopeh
87 E2 T'ang-pa *Tangba* Szech.
78 B3 T'ang-p'eng *Tangpeng* Kwangt.
11 G5 Tang-pi-chen *Dangbizhen* Heilung.
51 D3 T'ang-p'u *Tangpu* Chek.
70 B3 T'ang-p'u *Tangpu* Kiangsi
70 C3 T'ang-pu *Tangbu* Kiangsi
Tangra Tso *see* T'ang-ku-la-yu-mu Ts'o
19 F4 T'ang-sha *Tangsha* Liao.
46 C2 Tang-shan *Dangshan* Anhwei
30 F4 T'ang-shan *Tangshan* Hopeh
43 D3 T'ang-shan *Tangshan* Kiangsu
19 H4 T'ang-shan-ch'eng *Tangshancheng* Liao.
19 H4 T'ang-sha-tzu *Tangshazi* Liao.
43 E4 T'ang-shih *Tangshi* Kiangsu
10 E3 Tang-shih-ho *Dangshihe* Heilung.
95 D2 T'ang-tan *Tangdan* Yun.
95 E2 T'ang-t'ang *Tangtang* Yun.
30 F3 T'ang-tao-ho *Tangdaohe* Hopeh
75 F5 T'ang-t'ien *Tangtian* Hunan
75 D5 T'ang-t'ien-shih *Tangtianshi* Hunan
91 F3 T'ang-t'ou *Tangtou* Kwei.
34 D4 T'ang-t'ou *Tangtou* Shant.
79 D2 T'ang-t'ou-hsia *Tangtouxia* Kwangt.
30 E2 T'ang-t'ou-kou *Tangtougou* Hopeh
50 B3 T'ang-ts'un *Tangcun* Chek.
50 C3 T'ang-ts'un *Tangcun* Chek.
34 C4 T'ang-ts'un *Tangcun* Shant.
75 E6 T'ang-ts'un-yü *Tangcunyu* Hunan
47 E5 Tang-t'u *Dangtu* Anhwei
75 D5 T'ang-tu-k'ou *Tangdukou* Hunan
30 E3 T'ang-tzu-chuang *Tangzizhuang* Hopeh
75 C4 T'ang-wan *Tangwan* Hunan
70 E3 T'ang-wan *Tangwan* Kiangsi
10 E3 T'ang-wang *Tangwang* Heilung.
11 E4 T'ang-wang Ho *Tangwang He* (river) Heilung.
35 D3 T'ang-wu *Tangwu* Shant.
51 C3 T'ang-ya *Tangya* Chek.
58 D4 Tang-yang *Dangyang* Hupeh
43 E3 T'ang-yang *Tangyang* Kiangsu
55 F2 T'ang-yin *Tangyin* Honan
71 D4 T'ang-yin *Tangyin* Kiangsi
63 E7 T'ang-yü *Tangyu* Shensi
11 E4 T'ang-yüan *Tangyuan* Heilung.

39 D6 Tan Ho Dan He (river) Shansi
78 A4 Tan Hsien Dan Xian Kwangt.
75 F5 T'an-hu Tanhu Hunan
51 E2 T'an-hu Shan Tanhu Shan (island) Chek.
34 D4 T'an-i Tanyi Shant.
119 B4 Ta-niao Daniao Taiwan
111 F3 T'a-nien-t'a-weng Shan Taniantaweng Shan (mts) Tibet
83 H3 Ta-ning Daning Kwangsi
39 B5 Ta-ning Daning Shansi
87 G2 Ta-ning-ch'ang Daningchang Szech.
87 G2 Ta-ning Ho Daning He (river) Szech.
38 D3 Ta-niu-tien Daniudian Shansi
70 C3 T'an-kang Tangang Kiangsi
79 D2 Tan-kan Lieh-tao Dangan Liedao (islands) Kwangt.
67 C6 T'an-kou Tangou Fukien
71 B6 T'an-k'ou Tankou Kiangsi
86 D4 Tan-kuei Dangui Szech.
86 D2 Tan-leng Danleng Szech.
82 D5 T'an-lo Tanluo Kwangsi
119 B4 Tan-lu Danlu Taiwan
62 D4 Tan-pa Danba Shensi
86 C2 Tan-pa Danba Szech.
111 E3 Tan-pa Ch'ü Danba Qu (river) Tibet
75 E4 T'an-p'o Tanpo Hunan
47 D6 T'an-pu Tanbu Anhwei
70 B3 T'an-pu Tanbu Kiangsi
34 D4 T'an-pu Tanbu Shant.
70 B3 T'an-shan Tanshan Kiangsi
38 E3 T'an-shang Tanshang Shansi
50 B4 T'an-shih Tanshi Chek.
74 E4 T'an-shih Tanshi Hunan
54 C4 Tan-shui Danshui Honan
78 B3 Tan-shui Danshui Kwangt.
79 D2 Tan-shui Danshui Kwangt.
118 C1 Tan-shui Danshui Taiwan
118 C1 Tan-shui Ho Danshui He (river) Taiwan
79 C2 Tan-shui-k'ou Danshuikou Kwangt.
118 C3 Tan-ta Danda Taiwan
14 D1 Tan-tai Dandai Kirin
83 F4 Tan-t'ang Dantang Kwangsi
58 D3 T'an-tang-ho Tandanghe Hupeh
118 C3 Tan-ta Shan Danda Shan (mt) Taiwan
59 H4 Tan-tien Dandian Hupeh
19 H4 T'an-tien Tandian Liao.
50 C3 T'an-t'ou Tantou Chek.
51 E3 T'an-t'ou Tantou Chek.
67 E4 T'an-t'ou Tantou Fukien
54 C3 T'an-t'ou Tantou Honan
71 C5 T'an-t'ou Tantou Kiangsi
43 D3 Tan-tou-chen Dandouzhen Kiangsu
63 E6 Tan-ts'un Dancun Shensi
14 D1 T'an-t'u Tantu Kirin
23 E4 T'an-t'u Tantu Kirin
43 D3 Tan-t'u Hsien Dantu Xian Kiangsu
19 H4 Tan-tung Dandong Liao.
86 C2 Tan-tung Dandong Szech.
19 G4 Tan-tung Shih Dandong Shi Liao.
46 E4 Tan-tzu Danzi Anhwei
118 B2 T'an-tzu Tanzi Taiwan
75 E5 T'an-tzu-shan Tanzishan Hunan
74 C4 T'an-wan Tanwan Hunan
66 E4 Tan-yang Danyang Fukien
43 D4 Tan-yang Danyang Kiangsu
103 F1 T'an-yao Tanyao Sink.
83 F5 T'an-yü Tanyu Kwangsi
14 C2 T'ao-an Hsien Taoan Xian Kirin
86 C3 Tao-ch'eng Daocheng Szech.
47 F5 T'ao-ch'eng Taocheng Anhwei
55 F4 T'ao-ch'eng Taocheng Honan
91 E2 Tao-chen Hsien Daozhen Xian Kwei.
47 C5 T'ao-ch'i Taoqi Anhwei
50 C4 T'ao-ch'i Taoqi Chek.
67 B5 T'ao-ch'i Taoqi Fukien
59 H4 T'ao-chia-ho Taojiahe Hupeh
83 F3 Tao-chiang Daojiang Kwangsi
74 E3 T'ao-chiang Taojiang Hunan
99 F4 T'ao-chiang Taojiang Kansu
71 C6 T'ao Chiang Tao Jiang (river) Kiangsi
T'ao-chou see Lin-t'an
51 E4 T'ao-chu Taozhu Chek.
75 D6 T'ao-ch'uan Taochuan Hunan
34 D2 Tao-chuang Daozhuang Shant.
34 C5 T'ao-chuang Taozhuang Shant.
47 E5 T'ao-ch'ung Taochong Anhwei
14 C2 T'ao-erh Ho Taoer He (river) Kirin
23 E5 T'ao-erh Ho Taoer He (river) Kirin
18 C4 Tao-erh-teng Daoerdeng Liao.
86 C2 Tao-fu Daofu Szech.
11 F5 Tao-ho Daohe Heilung.
99 F4 T'ao Ho Tao He Kansu
75 D6 Tao-hsien Daoxian Hunan
38 D4 T'ao-hsing Taoxing Shansi
34 D2 Tao-hsü Daoxu Shant.
86 B3 Tao-hsüeh Daoxue Szech.
30 B3 T'ao-hua-pao Taohuabao Hopeh
75 D4 T'ao-hua-p'ing Taohuaping Hunan
51 F3 T'ao-hua Tao Taohua Dao (island) Chek.
59 G3 T'ao-hua-tien Taohuadian Hupeh
18 D3 T'ao-hua-t'u Taohuatu Liao.
54 E3 T'ao-hua-yü Taohuayu Honan
59 F4 Tao-jen-ch'iao Daorenqiao Hupeh
18 D2 Tao-ko-lang-ying-tzu Daogelangyingzi Liao.
23 C5 T'ao-ko-ssu Taogesi Kirin
55 F2 Tao-k'ou Daokou Honan
30 C3 Tao-la-chü Daolaju Hopeh
34 B3 Tao-lang Daolang Shant.
14 C3 Tao-lan-t'ao-pu Daolantaobu Kirin
23 E5 Tao-lan-t'ao-pu Daolantaobu Kirin
55 G5 T'ao-lin Taolin Honan
74 E4 T'ao-lin Taolin Hunan
74 F2 T'ao-lin Taolin Hunan
75 C5 T'ao-lin Taolin Hunan
42 C1 T'ao-lin Taolin Kiangsu
35 E4 T'ao-lin Taolin Shant.
74 F3 T'ao-lin-ssu Taolinsi Hunan
T'ao-lo see Ma-t'ai-kou
35 E4 T'ao-lo Taolvo Shant.
114 C2 T'ao-lo Hsien Taoluo Xian Ningsia
31 B4 Tao-ma-kuan Daomaguan Hopeh
14 C2 T'ao-nan Taonan Kirin
23 E5 T'ao-nan Taonan Kirin
14 D2 T'ao-pao Taobao Kirin
23 E5 T'ao-pao Taobao Kirin
91 D3 Tao-pa-shuDaobashui (Kwei.)
91 E4 Tao-p'ing Daoping Kwei.
43 D3 Tao-p'u Daopu Kiangsu
26 E4 T'ao-pu-ch'i Taobuqi In. Mong.
70 D3 T'ao-sha Taosha Kiangsi
51 D5 T'ao-shan Taoshan Chek.
11 E4 T'ao-shan Taoshan Heilung.
118 C2 T'ao Shan Tao Shan (mt) Taiwan
46 D2 T'ao-shan-chi Taoshanji Anhwei
58 C3 Tao-shih-p'ing Daoshiping Hupeh
50 B2 Tao-shih-wu Daoshiwu Chek.
83 H4 Tao-shui Daoshui Kwangsi
59 G3 Tao Shui Dao Shui (river) Hupeh
26 B4 T'ao-ssu-t'u Taositu In. Mong.
11 E4 Tao-t'ai-ch'iao Daotaiqiao Heilung.
107 G2 Tao-t'ang-ho Daotanghe Tsing.
23 D6 Tao-te-miao Daodemiao Liao.
14 B4 Tao-te-ying Daodeying Kirin
23 D6 Tao-te-ying Daodeying Kirin
30 F4 Tao-ti Daodi Hopeh
35 D3 Tao-t'ien Daotian Shant.
10 F3 Tao-t'ien-ti Daotiandi Heilung.
34 D4 Tao-to Daoduo Shant.
35 F2 Tao-t'ou Daotou Shant.
51 F2 Tao-tou-ao Daodouao Chek.
35 G2 T'ao-ts'un Taocun Shant.
42 C4 T'ao-wu Taowu Kiangsu
51 D2 T'ao-yen Taoyan Chek.
91 F3 T'ao-ying Taoying Kwei.
83 F5 T'ao-yü Taoyu Kwangsi
31 B5 Tao-yüan Daoyuan Hopeh
67 C5 T'ao-yüan Taoyuan Fukien
74 D3 T'ao-yüan Taoyuan Hunan
42 B2 T'ao-yüan Taoyuan Kiangsu
34 A4 T'ao-yüan Taoyuan Shant.
118 C2 T'ao-yüan Taoyuan Taiwan
119 B3 T'ao-yüan Taoyuan Taiwan
118 C2 T'ao-yüan Hsien Taoyuan Xian Taiwan
83 G3 Ta-pa Daba Kwangsi
79 E1 Ta-pa Daba Kwangt.
91 D2 Ta-pa Daba Kwei.
19 F2 Ta-pa Daba Liao.
114 C3 Ta-pa Daba Ningsia
91 F3 Ta-pa-ch'ang Dabachang Kwei.
71 C5 Ta-pai Dabai Kiangsi
50 C4 Ta-pai-an Dabaian Chek.
23 C6 Ta-pa-lin-wang-fu Dabalinwangfu Liao.
59 F4 Ta-pan Daban Hupeh
18 B1 Ta-pan Daban Liao.
102 I2 Ta-pan-ch'eng Dabancheng Sink.
103 E2 Ta-pan-ch'eng Dabancheng Sink.
95 D3 Ta-pan-ch'iao Dabanqiao Yun.
90 C5 Ta-pang Dabang Kwei.
90 C5 Ta-pang Ho Dabang He (river) Kwei.
59 F3 Ta-pang-tien Dabangdian Hupeh
107 H2 Ta-pan Shan Daban Shan (mts) Tsing.
19 H4 Ta-pao Dabao Liao.
86 D3 Ta-pao Dabao Szech.
75 B5 Ta-pao-tzu Dabaozi Hunan
63 E9 Ta-pa Shan Daba Shan (mts) Shensi
87 G2 Ta-pa Shan Daba Shan (mts) Szech.
47 D7 Ta-pei-pu Dabeibu Anhwei
78 A4 Ta-pen Daben Kwangt.
27 H2 T'a-pen-ch'a-kan Tabenchagan In. Mong.
83 G4 Ta-p'eng Dapeng Kwangsi
59 H3 Ta-pieh Shan Dabie Shan (mt) Hupeh
47 B5 Ta-pieh Shan Dabie Shan (mts) Anhwei
91 D6 Ta-pin Dabin Kwei.
74 C2 Ta-p'ing Daping Hunan
83 H3 Ta-p'ing Daping Kwangsi
91 F3 Ta-p'ing Daping Kwei.
63 E7 Ta-p'ing Daping Shensi
63 B7 T'a-p'ing Taping Shensi
18 D3 Ta-p'ing-fang Dapingfang Liao.
15 I4 Ta-p'ing-ling Dapingling Kirin
98 E2 Ta-p'ing-pao Dapingbao Kansu
91 G2 Ta-p'ing-ying Dapingying Kwei.
67 C7 Ta-p'ing-yü Dapingyu Fukien
83 F2 Ta-p'o Dapo Kwangsi
83 H4 Ta-p'o Dapo Kwangsi
78 A4 Ta-p'o Dapo Kwangt.
15 I5 Ta-po-ch'ai-ho Dabochaihe Kirin
15 G5 Ta-po-chi Daboji Kirin
66 D3 Ta-pu Dabu Fukien
71 C6 Ta-pu Dabu Kiangsi
83 F3 Ta-p'u Dapu Kwangsi
34 D5 Ta-p'u Dapu Shant.
119 B3 Ta-pu Dabu Taiwan
26 C5 Ta-pu-ch'an Dabuchan In. Mong.
75 E4 Ta-p'u-chieh Dapujie Hunan
102 H2 Ta-pu-erh-ku-ssu-t'ai Dabuergusitai Sink.
26 D4 T'a-pu Ho Tabu He (river) In. Mong.
79 E1 Ta-pu Hsien Dabu Xian Kwangt.
102 I1 Ta-pu-hsün Dabuxun Sink.
103 E1 Ta-pu-hsün Dabuxun Sink.
Ta-pu-hsün Hu see Ch'a-erh-han Yen-ch'ih
66 C3 Ta-pu-kang Dabugang Fukien
119 B4 Ta-p'u Shan Dapu Shan (mt) Taiwan
14 D3 Ta-pu-su P'ao Dabusu Pao (lake) Kirin
23 E5 Ta-pu-su P'ao Dabusu Pao (lake) Kirin
Tarbagatai see T'a-ch'eng
Tardin see T'a-erh-ting
Tarim see T'a-li-mu Ho
Tarim Basin see T'a-li-mu P'en-ti
Tarnguk see T'a-ku-k'o
Tartin see T'a-erh-ting
63 C6 Ta-san Kuan Dasan Guan (pass) Shensi
19 E6 Ta-san-shan Tao Dasanshan Dao (island) Liao.
30 C2 Ta-san-yen-ching Dasanyanjing Hopeh
79 C2 Ta-sha Dasha Kwangt.
43 F2 Ta Sha Da Sha (shoal) Kiangsu
15 I5 Ta-sha-ho Dashahe Kirin
90 C5 Ta-shan Dashan Kwei.
34 C1 Ta-shan Dashan Shant.
35 F3 Ta-Shan Dashan Shant.
18 D4 T'a-shan Tashan Liao.
19 F4 T'a-shan Tashan Liao.
15 I4 Ta-shan-chü Dashanju Kirin
91 C4 Ta-shan-shao Dashanshao Kwei.
59 F5 Ta-sha-p'ing Dashaping Hupeh
119 B4 Ta-she Dashe Taiwan
67 C5 Ta-shen Dashen Fukien
30 E1 Ta-sheng-t'ang Shan Dashengtang Shan (mt) Hopeh
58 C3 Ta-shen-nung-chia Dashennongjia (mt) Hupeh
26 C4 Ta-she-t'ai Dashetai In. Mong.
38 C3 Ta-she-t'ou Dashetou Shansi
86 B2 Ta-she-tung Dashedong Szech.
Tashi Bhup Tsho see Cha-hsi-pu Ts'o
Tashigong see Cha-hsi-kang
50 B3 Ta-shih Dashi Chek.
18 E3 Ta-shih Dashi Liao.
50 C3 T'a-shih Tashi Chek.
98 B1 T'a-shih Tashi Kansu
23 D4 Ta-shih-chai Dashizhai Kirin
19 F4 Ta-shih-ch'iao Dashiqiao Liao.
51 E3 Ta-shih-chin Dashijin Chek.
31 B6 Ta-shih-chuang Dashizhuang Hopeh
74 E2 T'a-shih-i Tashiyi Hunan
102 A3 T'a-shih-k'u-erh-kan Tashikuergan Sink.
T'a-shih-k'u-erh-kan T'a-chi-k'o Tzu-chih-hsien see Tash Kurghan Tajik Autonomous Hsien
102 C3 Ta-shih-man Dashiman Sink.
18 A2 Ta-shih-men Dashimen Liao.
22 B3 Ta-shih-mi-k'o Dashimike Heilung.
87 E1 Ta-shih-pan Dashiban Szech.
30 E1 Ta-shih-t'ou Dashitou Hopeh
15 I4 Ta-shih-t'ou Dashitou Kirin
103 E2 Ta-shih-t'ou Dashitou Sink.
Tash Kurghan see T'a-shih-k'u-erh-kan
34 C4 Ta-shu Dashu Shant.
87 E3 Ta-shu Dashu Szech.
47 D4 Ta-shu-chieh Dashujie Anhwei
107 F2 Ta-shui-ch'iao Dashuiqiao Tsing.
95 D2 Ta-shui-ching Dashuijing Yun.
114 C3 Ta-shui-k'eng Dashuikeng Ningsia
23 B6 Ta-shui-no-erh Dashuinuoer Liao.
35 H2 Ta-shui-p'o Tashuipo Shant.
23 B5 Ta-shui-po-lo Dashuiboluo Liao.
99 G3 Ta-shui-t'ou Dashuitou Kansu
51 C4 Ta-shun Dashun Chek.
14 A4 Ta-shu-ying-tzu Dashuyingzi Kirin
23 D6 Ta-shu-ying-tzu Dashuyingzi Kirin
111 E2 Ta-so-jih Dasuori Tibet
83 E5 Ta-ssu Dasi Kwangsi
46 B3 Ta-ssu-chi Dasiji Anhwei
31 C4 Ta-ssu-ko-chuang Dasigezhuang Hopeh
26 D4 Ta-su-chi Dasuji In. Mong.
Tasüeh Mountains see Ta-hsüeh Shan
14 G4 Ta-sui-ho Dasuihe Kirin
106 E4 Ta-su-mang Dasumang Tsing.
95 D4 Ta-t'a Data Yun.
30 C4 Ta-t'ai Datai Hopeh
75 F5 Ta-t'ai Datai Hunan
10 D2 Ta-t'ai-shan Dataishan Heilung.
102 D3 T'a-t'a-lang Tatalang Sink.
106 E2 T'a-t'a-leng Ho Tataleng He (river) Tsing.
30 D2 Ta-t'an Datan Hopeh
26 E4 Ta-t'an Datun In. Mong.
71 B6 Ta-t'ang Datang Kiangsi
83 E3 Ta-t'ang Datang Kwangsi
83 E5 Ta-t'ang Datang Kwangsi
91 F4 Ta-t'ang Datang Kwei.
86 B1 Ta-t'ang-pa Datangba Szech.
83 F4 Ta-t'eng Hsia Dateng Xia (gorge) Kwangsi
87 F3 Ta-t'iao-teng Datiaodeng Szech.
46 B4 Ta-t'ien Datian Anhwei
46 D3 Ta-tien Dadian Anhwei
51 E4 Ta-t'ien Datian Chek.
67 C5 Ta-t'ien Datian Fukien
71 C6 Ta-t'ien Datian Kiangsi
79 C2 Ta-t'ien Datian Kwangt.
34 D4 Ta-tien Dadian Shant.
78 B2 Ta-t'ien Ting Datian Ding (mt) Kwangt.
15 I5 Ta-tien-tzu Dadianzi Kirin
19 H2 Ta-tien-tzu Dadianzi Liao.
Tatlin Gol see T'a-t'a-leng Ho
43 E3 Ta-to Daduo Kiangsu
74 E3 Ta-to-p'u Daduopu Hunan
66 D4 T'a-tou Tadou Fukien
86 D1 Ta-ts'ang-ssu Dacangsi Szech.
106 D2 Ta-tsao-huo Dazaohuo Tsing.
10 B1 Ta-ts'ao-tien-tzu Dacaodianzi Heilung.
111 D3 Ta-tse Daze Tibet
110 C3 Ta-tse Ts'o Daze Cuo (lake) Tibet
Tatsienlu see K'ang-ting
67 D6 Ta-tso Dazuo Fukien
87 E3 Ta-tsu Dazu Szech.
59 G4 Ta-tsui Dazui Hupeh
82 E6 Ta-ts'un Dacun Kwangsi
87 F3 Ta-ts'un Dacun Szech.
43 D2 Ta-tsung Hu Dazong Hu (lake) Kiangsu
75 D5 Ta-ts'un-tien Dacundian Hunan
118 B2 Ta-tu Dadu Taiwan
43 F5 Ta-t'uan Datuan Kiangsu
14 B4 Ta-tuan Daduan Kirin
23 D6 Ta-tuan Daduan Kirin
118 B2 Ta-tu Ch'i Dadu Qi (river) Taiwan
86 D2 Ta-tu Ho Dadu He (river) Szech.
94 C4 Ta-tu-kang Dadugang Yun.
47 D6 Ta-tu-k'ou Dadukou Anhwei
102 H1 Ta-t'u-ku-li Datuguli Sink.
14 D2 Ta-t'un Datun Kirin
14 F4 Ta-t'un Datun Kirin
95 D4 Ta-t'un-chieh Datunjie Yun.
Ta-t'ung see Ch'iao-t'ou
46 D4 Ta-t'ung Datong Anhwei
46 E4 Ta-t'ung Datong Anhwei
47 D6 Ta-t'ung Datong Anhwei
50 C3 Ta-t'ung Datong Chek.
11 C4 Ta-t'ung Datong Heilung.
83 E5 Ta-tung Dadong Kwangsi
19 H5 Ta-tung Dadong Liao.
38 E1 Ta-t'ung Datong Shansi
118 C2 Ta-t'ung Datong Taiwan
95 E3 Ta-t'ung Datong Yun.
38 E1 Ta-t'ung Tatung Shansi
43 F3 Ta-t'ung-chen Datongzhen Kiangsu
99 F3 Ta-t'ung Ho Datung He (river) Kansu
107 G2 Ta-t'ung Ho Datung He (river) Tsing.
38 E1 Ta-t'ung Hsien Datong Xian Shansi
107 G2 Ta-t'ung Hsien Datung Xian Tsing.
74 E2 Ta-t'ung Hu Datong Hu (lake) Hunan
102 H1 Ta-tung-kou Dadonggou Sink.
50 C4 Ta-tung-pa Dadongba Chek.
107 F2 Ta-t'ung Shan Datong Shan (mts) Tsing.
14 D4 Ta-t'u-shan Datushan Kirin
Ta-tzu see Te-ch'ing
11 B4 T'a-tzu-ch'eng Tazicheng Heilung.
23 E4 T'a-tzu-ch'eng Tazicheng Heilung.
111 D3 Ta-tzu Hsien Tazi Xian Tibet
86 C2 T'a-tzu-pa Taziba Szech.
31 C5 Ta-tzu-wen Daziwen Hopeh
38 E2 Ta-tz'u-yao Daciyao Shansi
Taushkan see T'o-shih-kan Ho
14 E2 Ta-wa Dawa Kirin
14 E2 Ta-wa Dawa Kirin
19 F4 Ta-wa Dawa Liao.
19 G1 Ta-wa Dawa Liao.
86 C1 T'a-wa Tawa Szech.
98 D1 Ta-wan Dawan Kansu
83 F4 Ta-wan Dawan Kwangsi
78 B2 Ta-wan Dawan Kwangt.
79 C1 Ta-wan Dawan Kwangt.
95 D2 Ta-wan Dawan Yun.
95 E2 Ta-wan Dawan Yun.
102 C2 Ta-wan-ch'i Dawanqi Sink.
Tawang see Ta-wang
83 G4 Ta-wang Dawang Kwangsi
34 D3 Ta-wang Dawang Shant.
111 D4 Ta-wang Dawang Tibet
42 B2 Ta-wang-chi Dawangji Kiangsu
34 A5 Ta-wang-chi Dawangji Shant.
19 F5 Ta-wang-chia Tao Dawangjia Dao (island) Liao.
23 B6 Ta-wang-miao Dawangmiao Liao.
71 D4 Ta-wang-shan Dawangshan Kiangsi
31 C4 Ta-wang-tien Dawangdian Hopeh
86 D2 Ta-wei Dawei Szech.
55 E3 Ta-wei-chen Daweizhen Honan
34 B4 Ta-wen Ho Dawen He (river) Shant.
34 C4 Ta-wen-k'ou Dawenkou Shant.
Tawilgha see Ho-shuo
74 B2 T'a-wo Tawo Hunan
74 C3 Ta-wo-p'ing Dawoping Hunan
38 C4 Ta-wu Dawu Shansi
34 B4 Ta-wu Dawu Shant.
119 B4 Ta-wu Dawu Taiwan
119 B4 Ta-wu Dawu Taiwan
105 G3 Ta-wu Dawu Tsing.
91 E3 Ta-wu-chiang Dawujiang Kwei.
10 D3 Ta-wu-chia-tzu Tawujiazi Heilung.
59 G3 Ta-wu Hsien Dawu Xian Hupeh
30 G3 Ta-wu-kang Dawugang Hopeh
18 E3 Ta-wu-lan Dawulan Liao.
118 C2 T'a-wu-sai Tawusai Taiwan
59 G3 Ta-wu Shan Dawu Shan (mt) Hupeh
106 B2 Ta-wu-ssu Dawusi Tsing.
118 B2 Ta-ya Daya Taiwan
110 B2 Ta-ya-erh Dayaer Tibet
46 B3 Ta-yang Dayang Anhwei
67 D5 Ta-yang Dayang Fukien
83 F4 Ta-yang Dayang Kwangsi
39 C5 Ta-yang Dayang Shansi
34 B3 Ta-yang Dayang Shant.
10 C2 Ta-yang-ch'i Dayangqi Heilung.
19 G4 Ta-yang Ho Dayang He (river) Liao.
51 F2 Ta-yang Shan Dayang Shan (island) Chek.
10 C3 Ta-yang-shu Dayangshu Heilung.
22 F3 Ta-yang-shu Dayangshu Heilung.
75 D6 Ta-yang-tung Dayangdong Hunan
74 F4 Ta-yao Dayao Hunan
94 C3 Ta-yao Dayao Yun.
Ta-yao-shan see Chin-hsiu
83 G3 Ta-yao Shan Dayao Shan (mts) Kwangsi
79 D2 Ta-ya Wan Daya Wan (bay) Kwangt.
59 G4 Ta-yeh Daye Hupeh
51 E3 Ta-yen Dayan Chek.
58 C2 Ta-yen Dayan Hupeh
74 D2 Ta-yen-tang Dayandang Hunan
51 E3 Ta-yin Dayin Chek.
42 B1 Ta-yin-chai Dayinzhai Kiangsu
54 D4 Ta-ying Daying Honan
54 E4 Ta-ying Daying Honan
31 C6 Ta-ying Daying Hopeh
15 H5 Ta-ying Daying Kirin
38 D3 Ta-ying Daying Shansi
38 E2 Ta-ying Daying Shansi
30 B2 Ta-ying-p'an Dayingpan Hopeh
18 B3 Ta-ying-tzu Dayingzi Liao.
23 B6 Ta-ying-tzu Dayingzi Liao.
75 D7 Ta-yü Dayu Hunan
71 B6 Ta-yü Dayu Kiangsi
71 D5 Ta-yu Dayou Kiangsi
43 D1 Ta-yu Dayou Kiangsu
83 F4 Ta-yü Dayu Kwangsi
83 G2 Ta-yü Dayu Kwangsi
102 I2 Ta-yu Dayou Sink.
51 C2 Ta-yüan Dayuan Chek.
51 D4 Ta-yüan Dayuan Chek.
35 E2 Ta-yüan Dayuan Shant.
118 C1 Ta-yüan Dayuan Taiwan
10 C2 T'a-yüan Tayuan Heilung.
22 F2 T'a-yüan Tayuan Heilung.
118 C2 Ta-yüan Shan Dayuan Shan (mt) Taiwan
43 E1 Ta-yu-chien Dayoujian Kiangsu
35 D3 Ta-yü-ho Dayuhe Shant.
74 C2 Ta-yung Dayong Hunan
90 C4 Ta-yung Dayong Kwei.
91 F4 Ta-yung Dayong Kwei.
74 D3 Ta-yung-t'ang Dayongtang Hunan
51 D2 Ta-yün Ho Dayun He (river) Chek.
34 B4 Ta-yün Ho Dayun He (river) Shant.
18 E6 Ta-yün Wan Dayun Wan (bay) Liao.
18 E5 Ta-yün-wan Dayunwan Liao.
78 B2 Ta-yün-wu Shan Dayunwu Shan (mts) Kwangt.
66 F4 Ta-yü Shan Dayu Shan (island) Fukien
11 B4 Ta-yü-shu Dayushu Heilung.
23 E4 Ta-yü-shu Dayushu Heilung.
14 B4 Ta-yü-shu Dayushu Kirin
14 C2 Ta-yü-shu Dayushu Kirin
14 E4 Ta-yü-shu Dayushu Kirin
23 D6 Ta-yü-shu Dayushu Kirin
23 E5 Ta-yü-shu Dayushu Kirin
18 E3 Ta-yü-shu-pao Dayushubao Liao.
70 C2 Te-an Dean Kiangsi
86 D4 Te-ch'ang Dechang Szech.
91 F2 Te-chiang Dejiang Kwei.
94 B1 Te-ch'in Deqin Yun.
51 D2 Te-ch'ing Deqing Chek.
78 B2 Te-ch'ing Deqing Kwangt.
111 D3 Te-ch'ing Deqing Tibet
34 B2 Te-chou Dezhou Shant.
106 C4 Te-erh-ha-ta Deerhada Tsing.
23 D4 T'e-erh-mo Shan Teermo Shan (mt) Kirin
22 D2 Te-erh-pu-erh Deerbuer Heilung.
22 D2 Te-erh-pu-erh Ho Deerbuer He (river) Heilung.
26 C5 T'e-erh-pu-hai Teerbuhai In. Mong.
91 G4 Te-feng Defeng Kwei.
107 F4 T'e-ha-t'u Tehatu Tsing.
Tehchow see Te-chou
Tehjung see Te-jung
95 D4 Te-hou-chieh Dehoujie Yun.
70 E3 Te-hsing Dexing Kiangsi
14 C3 Te-hsing-t'ai Dexingtai Kirin
23 E5 Te-hsing-t'ai Dexingtai Kirin
Tehtsin see Te-ch'in
Tehtsing see Te-ch'ing
67 D5 Te-hua Dehua Fukien
14 F3 Te-hui Dehui Kirin
94 B3 Te-hung Shan-Kachin Autonomous District Yun.
Te-hung T'ai-tsu Ching-p'o-tsu Tzu-chih-chou see Te-hung Shan-Chin Autonomous District
111 E4 Te-jang-tsung Derangzong Tibet
27 E3 Te-jih-ssu-t'u Derisitu In. Mong.
86 B3 Te-jung Derong Szech.
Tekes see T'e-k'o-ssu
86 B2 Te-ko Dege Szech.
102 C2 T'e-k'o-ssu Tekesi Sink.
102 C2 T'e-k'o-ssu Ho Tekesi He (river) Sink.
27 E3 T'e-ko-t'u-so-mu Tegetusuomu In. Mong.
86 B2 Te-lai Delai Szech.
Te-la-to-mu see Cha-tung
22 F1 Te-li Deli Heilung.
106 C4 Te-lieh-ch'u-k'a Deliechuka Tsing.
106 D3 Te-lieh-ch'u-la-po-teng Deliechulabodeng Tsing.
110 C3 T'e-li-na-mu Ts'o Telinamu Cuo (lake) Tibet
105 E2 Te-ling-ha Delingha Tsing.
107 E2 Te-ling-ha Nung-ch'ang Delingha Nongchang Tsing.
19 F5 Te-li-ssu Delisi Liao.
82 B4 Te-lung Delong Kwangsi
Temerlik see T'ieh-mu-li-k'o
Te-mo see Te-mu
111 E3 Te-mu Demu Tibet
19 F3 T'eng-ao-pao Tengaobao Liao.
55 F4 Teng-ch'eng Dengcheng Honan
30 D2 Teng-chia-cha-tzu Dengjiazhazi Hopeh
35 H2 T'eng-chia-chi Tengjiaji Shant.
70 D4 T'eng-ch'iao Tengqiao Kiangsi
78 A4 T'eng-ch'iao Tengqiao Kwangt.
75 C5 Teng-chia-p'u Dengjiapu Hunan
70 D3 Teng-chia-pu Dengjiabu Kiangsi
75 F6 Teng-chia-t'ang Dengjiatang Hunan
Tengchow see P'eng-lai
94 C3 Teng-ch'uan Dengchuan Yun.
34 B2 T'eng-chuang Tengzhuang Shant.
94 B3 T'eng-ch'ung Tengchong Yun.
54 E3 Teng-feng Dengfeng Honan
Tenghai see Ch'eng-hai
54 D5 Teng-hsien Dengxian Honan
83 G4 T'eng-hsien Tengxian Kwangsi
34 C4 T'eng-hsien Tengxian Shant.
86 A1 Teng-k'o Dengke Szech.
26 D3 T'eng-ko-erh No-erh Tenggeer Nuoer (lake) In. Mong.
99 G2 T'eng-ko-li Sha-mo Tenggeli Shamo (desert) Kansu
114 B2 T'eng-ko-li Sha-mo Tenggeli Shamo (desert) Ningsia
26 B4 Teng-k'ou Hsien Dengkou Xian In. Mong.
87 E3 Teng-kuan-chen Dengguanzhen Szech.
110 B3 Teng-lung Denglong Tibet
31 D6 Teng-ming-ssu Dengmingsi Hopeh
Tengri see T'eng-ko-li Sha-mo
Tengri Nuur see T'eng-ko-erh No-erh
19 F5 Teng-sha-ho Dengshahe Liao.
86 D2 Teng-sheng Dengsheng Szech.
106 E3 Teng-ssu-o-po Dengsiebo Tsing.
79 D1 Teng-t'a Dengta Kwangt.
19 G3 Teng-t'a Dengta Liao.
71 C4 T'eng-t'ien Tengtian Kiangsi
30 B2 Teng-yu-fang Dengyoufang Hopeh
Tengyün see T'eng-hsien
22 D3 T'e-ni-ho-ts'un Tenihecun Heilung.
Tenkar see Huang-yüan
82 C4 Te-pao Debao Kwangsi
34 B2 Te-p'ing Deping Shant.
18 D1 Te-po-le-miao Debolemiao Liao.
106 C2 Te-pu-t'e-li Debuteli Tsing.
83 E3 Te-sheng Desheng Kwangsi
71 D4 Te-sheng-kuan Deshengguan Kiangsi
38 E1 Te-sheng-pao Deshangbao Shansi
90 B4 Te-sheng-p'o Deshengpo Kwei.
58 B2 Te-sheng-p'u Deshengpu Hupeh
94 B3 Te-tang-chen Dedangzhen Yun.
107 E4 Te-tang-ssu Dedangsi Tsing.
111 F3 Te-teng-ssu Dedengsi Tibet
111 D2 Te-tsung Dezong Tibet
106 D1 Te-tsung-ma-hai Hu Dezongmahai Hu (lake) Tsing.
Te-tu see Ch'ing-shan
10 D3 Te-tu Hsien Dedu Xian Heilung.
91 F3 Te-wang Dewang Kwei.
90 B4 Te-wu Dewu Kwei.
Te-wu-lu see Ho-tso
87 E2 Te-yang Deyang Szech.
87 E3 Te-yao-kuan Deyaoguan Szech.
Thangkar see Huang-yüan
Thok Jalung see Ts'o-k'o-cha
Thongmon see Hsieh-t'ung-men
59 F4 Tiao-ch'a Hu Diaocha Hu (lake) Hupeh
66 E4 T'iao-ch'eng Tiaocheng Fukien
78 B3 Tiao-feng Diaofeng Kwangt.
27 H1 Tiao-han-t'ai-lo Diaohantailuo In. Mong.
59 E5 T'iao-hsien-k'ou Tiaoxiankou Hupeh
34 D2 Tiao-k'ou-chen Diaokouzhen Shant.
11 F5 Tiao-ling Diaoling Heilung.
30 C3 Tiao-o-ts'un Diaoecun Hopeh
87 F3 T'iao-shih Tiaoshi Szech.
Tibet Autonomous Region see Pages 109-112
99 G3 Ti-chia-t'ai Dijiatai Kansu
94 B2 Ti-ch'ing Tibetan Autonomous District Yun.
Ti-ch'ing Tsang-tsu Tzu-chih-chou see Ti-ch'ing Tibetan Autonomous District
82 C4 Ti-chou Dizhou Kwangsi
74 C3 Ti-chuang Dizhuang Hunan
14 G6 T'ieh-ch'ang Tiechang Kirin
79 D1 T'ieh-ch'ang Tiechang Kwangt.
63 E7 T'ieh-ch'ang Tiechang Shensi
30 D2 T'ieh-chia-ying Tiejiaying Hopeh
63 D7 T'ieh-fo-ssu Tiefosi Shensi
46 C3 T'ieh-fo-szu Tiefosi Anhwei
63 C7 T'ieh-ho Tiehe Shensi
103 D2 T'ieh-kan-li-k'o Tieganlike Sink.
102 C3 T'ieh-k'o-li-k'o Shan Tiekelike Shan (mt) Sink.
35 G2 T'ieh-k'ou Tiekou Shant.
11 E4 T'ieh-li Tieli Heilung.
19 G2 T'ieh-ling Tieling Liao.
55 E3 T'ieh-lu Tielu Honan
102 B4 T'ieh-lung-t'an Tielongtan Sink.
70 C4 T'ieh-lu-t'ou Tielutou Kiangsi
107 G2 T'ieh-mai Tiemai Tsing.
54 D3 T'ieh-men Tiemen Honan
102 D1 T'ieh-mi-t'a-mu Tiemitamu Sink.
106 B1 T'ieh-mu-li-k'o Tiemulike Tsing.
66 C3 T'ieh-niu Kuan Tieniu Guan (pass) Fukien
70 E4 T'ieh-niu Kuan Tieniu Guan (pass) Kiangsi
62 C4 T'ieh-pien-ch'eng Tiebiancheng Shensi
Tieh-pu see Tien-ka-ssu
99 F4 Tieh-pu Hsien Diebu Xian Kansu
26 E4 T'ieh-sha-kai Tieshagai In. Mong.
66 D3 T'ieh-shan Tieshan Fukien
59 G4 T'ieh-shan Tieshan Hupeh
55 E4 T'ieh-shan-miao Tieshanmiao Honan
83 F6 T'ieh-shan Wan Tieshan Wan (bay) Kwangsi
114 B2 T'ieh-shih-kan Tieshigan Ningsia
46 E4 T'ien-ch'ang Tianchang Anhwei
38 F1 T'ien-chen Tianzhen Shansi
34 C2 T'ien-chen Tianzhen Shant.
78 B3 Tien-ch'eng Diancheng Kwangt.
98 D2 T'ien-ch'eng Tiancheng Kansu
35 F3 Tien-chi Dianji Shant.
19 E5 T'ien-chia Tianjia Liao.
T'ien-chia-an see Huai-nan
59 H5 T'ien-chia-chen Tianjiazhen Hupeh
14 F4 T'ien-chia-chieh Tianjiajie Kirin
87 F2 Tien-chiang Dianjiang Szech.
15 J4 T'ien-ch'iao-ling Tianqiaoling Kirin
58 C2 T'ien-chia-pa Tianjiaba Hupeh
51 D4 Tien-ch'ien Dianqian Chek.
47 C6 Tien-ch'ien-ho Dianqianhe Anhwei
95 D3 Tien Ch'ih Dian Chi (lake) Yun.
102 I1 T'ien Ch'ih Tianchi (lake) Sink.
31 E4 T'ien-chin Tianjin Hopeh
39 D6 T'ien-ching-kuan Tianjingguan Shansi
31 E5 T'ien-chin Hsin-kang Tianjin Xingang (harbour) Hopeh
31 E5 T'ien-chin Shih Tianjin Shi Hopeh
30 E4 T'ien-chin Ti-ch'ü Tianjin Diqu Hopeh
T'ien-chu see An'yüan-i
91 G4 T'ien-chu Tianzhu Kwei.
86 D2 T'ien-ch'üan Tianquan Szech.
30 E4 T'ien-chuang Tianzhuang Hopeh
75 F6 T'ien-chuang Tianzhuang Hunan
62 F3 T'ien-chuang Tianzhuang Shensi
19 F4 T'ien-chuang-t'ai Tianzhuangtai Liao.
T'ien-chün see Hsin-yüan
67 D4 T'ien-chung Tianzhong Fukien
118 B3 T'ien-chung Tianzhong Taiwan
107 F2 T'ien-chün Hsien Tianjun Xian Tsing.
47 C5 T'ien-chu Shan Tianzhu Shan (mt) Anhwei
99 F3 T'ien-chu Tibetan Autonomous Hsien Tianzhu Zangzu Zizhixian Kansu
T'ien-chu Tsang-tsu Tzu-chih-hsien see T'ien-chu Tibetan Autonomous Hsien
59 F4 T'ien-erh-ho Tianerhe Hupeh
39 B6 Tien-erh-p'ing Dianerping Shansi
70 D2 T'ien-fan-chieh Tianfanjie Kiangsi
35 F3 T'ien-heng Tao Tianheng Dao (island) Shant.
58 C2 T'ien-ho Tianhe Hupeh
71 B5 T'ien-ho Tianhe Kiangsi
83 E3 T'ien-ho Tianhe Kwangsi
59 F2 T'ien-ho-k'ou Tianhekou Hupeh
23 D6 T'ien-ho-lung Tianhelong Liao.
82 D5 T'ien-hsi Tianxi Kwangsi
70 C4 Tien-hsia Dianxia Kiangsi
74 D4 T'ien-hsin Tianxin Hunan
74 F4 T'ien-hsin Tianxian Hunan
70 B3 T'ien-hsin Tianxin Kiangsi
95 E2 T'ien-hsin Tianxin Yun.
54 D3 T'ien-hu Tianhu Honan
71 C7 T'ien-hua Tianhua Kiangsi
34 C4 T'ien-huang Tianhuang Shant.
67 C5 T'ien-hu-shan Tianhushan Fukien
18 C3 T'ien-i Tianyi Liao.
15 H4 T'ien-kang Tiangang Kirin
99 F4 Tien-ka-ssu Diangasi Kansu
Tienkian see Huai-nan
34 A5 T'ien-kuan-miao Tianguanmiao Shant.
119 B4 T'ien-liao Tianliao Taiwan
82 C3 T'ien-lin Hsien Tianlin Xian Kwangsi
34 D2 T'ien-liu Tianliu Shant.
43 D1 T'ien-lou Tianlou Kiangsu
91 D4 T'ien-lung Tianlong Kwei.
91 F3 T'ien-ma Tianma Kwei.
75 E4 Tien-men Dianmen Hunan
59 F4 T'ien-men Tianmen Hupeh
59 F4 T'ien-men Ho Tianmen He (river) Hupeh
50 C2 T'ien-mu Ch'i Tianmu Qi Chek.
50 C2 T'ien-mu Shan Tianmu Shan (mts) Chek.
51 D2 T'ien-ning Tianning Chek.
82 D2 T'ien-o Hsien Tiane Xian Kwangsi
78 B3 Tien-pai Dianbai Kwangt.
67 C6 T'ien-pao Tianbao Fukien
15 I5 T'ien-pao-shan Tianbaoshan Kirin
74 D4 T'ien-p'ing Tianping Hunan
83 G4 T'ien-p'ing Tianping Kwangsi
91 G3 T'ien-p'ing Tianping Kwei.
47 D5 Tien-pu Dianbu Anhwei
23 D6 T'ien-shan Tianshan Liao.
102 C2 T'ien Shan Tian Shan (mts) Sink.
103 E2 T'ien Shan Tian Shan (mts) Sink.
39 E6 Tien-shang Dianshang Shansi
43 E4 Tien-shan Hu Dianshan Hu (lake) Kiangsu
23 D6 T'ien-shan-k'ou Tianshankou Liao.
11 D4 T'ien-sheng Tiansheng Heilung.
95 D3 T'ien-sheng-ch'iao Tianshengqiao Yun.
43 E3 T'ien-sheng-kang Tianshenggang Kiangsu
19 H3 T'ien-shih-fu Tianshifu Liao.
T'ien-shui see Pei-tao-pu
99 G4 T'ien-shui Tianshui Kansu
99 H3 T'ien-shui Tianshui Kansu
114 C3 T'ien-shui Tianshui Ningsia
98 B1 T'ien-shui-ching Tianshuijing Kansu
103 F3 T'ien-shui-ch'üan Tianshuiquan Sink.
102 B4 T'ien-shui-hai Tianshuihai Sink.
T'ien-shui-hsien see Pei-tao-pu
99 G4 T'ien-shui Hsien Tianshui Xian Kansu
94 C4 Tien-so-t'ang Diansuotang Yun.
51 E3 T'ien-t'ai Tiantai Chek.
51 E3 T'ien-t'ai Shan Tiantai Shan (mts) Chek.
18 A2 T'ien-t'ai-shui Tiantaishui Liao.
78 B2 T'ien-t'ang Tiantang Kwangt.
63 C6 T'ien-t'ang-chen Tiantangzhen Shensi
91 F2 T'ien-t'ang-shao Tiantangshao Kwei.
15 G3 T'ien-te Tiande Kirin
82 D4 T'ien-teng Tiandeng Kwangsi
99 F3 T'ien Tibetan Autonomous Hsien Tianzhu Zangzu Zizhixian Kansu
66 F3 Tien-t'ou Diantou Fukien
79 C1 T'ien-t'ou Tiantou Kwangt.
98 D1 T'ien-ts'ang Tiancang Kansu
94 C3 Tien-ts'ang Shan Diancang Shan (mt) Yun.
Tientsin see T'ien-chin
Tientsin - city plan see Page 130
71 C5 T'ien-ts'un Tiancun Kiangsi
78 A4 T'ien-tu Tiandu Kwangt.
63 C6 T'ien-tu Tiandu Shensi
82 D4 T'ien-tung Hsien Tiandong Xian Kwangsi
18 B3 Tien-tzu Dianzi Liao.
23 F4 T'ien-wa Tianwa Kirin
74 C3 T'ien-wan Tianwan Hunan
63 C6 T'ien-wang Tianwang Shensi
43 D4 T'ien-wang-ssu Tianwangsi Kiangsu
95 D3 Tien-wei Dianwei Yun.
82 C4 T'ien-yang Tianyang Kwangsi

23 F4 T'ien-yen-cha-kan *Tianyanzhagan* Heilung.
Ti-erh-sung-hua Chiang *see* Sung-hua Chiang
34 C4 Ti-fang *Difang* Shant.
95 E3 Ti-hsü *Dixu* Yun.
Ti-huo *see* Wu-lu-mu-ch'i
Tihwa *see* Wu-lu-mu-ch'i
102 I2 Ti-k'an-erh *Dikaner* Sink.
103 E2 Ti-k'an-erh *Dikaner* Sink.
47 E5 Ti-kang *Digang* Anhwei
Tikelik Tagh *see* T'ieh-k'o-li-k'o Shan
Tikenlik *see* T'ieh-kan-li-k'o
55 F3 Ti-ko *Dige* Honan
66 D4 Ti-k'ou *Dikou* Fukien
46 B4 Ti-li-ch'eng *Dilicheng* Anhwei
Timurlik *see* T'ieh-mu-li-k'o
82 B3 Ting-an *Dingan* Kwangsi
78 B4 Ting-an *Dingan* Kwangt.
58 B5 Ting-chai *Dingzhai* Hupeh
46 C4 Ting-chi *Dingji* Anhwei
55 F4 Ting-chi *Dingji* Honan
71 C4 Ting-chiang *Dingjiang* Kiangsi
67 B5 T'ing Chiang *Ting Jiang* (river) Fukien
43 E3 Ting-chia-so *Dingjiasuo* Kiangsu
110 D3 Ting-chieh *Dingjie* Tibet
110 C3 Ting-chieh Hsien *Dingjie Xian* Tibet
59 H4 T'ing-ch'ien *Tingqian* Hupeh
111 E3 Ting-ch'ing *Dingqing* Tibet
86 B3 Ting-ch'ü Ch'ü *Dingqu Qu* (river) Szech.
63 B7 Ting-chün Shan *Dingjun Shan* (mt) Shensi
Tingfan *see* Hui-shui
51 F2 Ting-hai *Dinghai* Chek.
54 C4 Ting-ho *Dinghe* Honan
99 G4 Ting-hsi *Dingxi* Kansu
51 E3 T'ing-hsia *Tingxia* Chek.
38 D3 Ting-hsiang *Dingxiang* Shansi
47 D6 Ting-hsiang-shu *Dingxiangshu* Anhwei
90 C5 Ting-hsiao *Dingxiao* Kwei.
31 B5 Ting-hsien *Dingxian* Hopeh
74 D2 T'ing-hsien-tu *Tingxiandu* Hunan
98 D1 Ting-hsin *Dingxin* Kansu
30 C4 Ting-hsing *Dingxing* Hopeh
79 C2 Ting-hu *Dinghu* Kwangt.
62 E3 Ting-hui Ch'ü *Dinghui Qu* (canal) Shensi
Ting-jih *see* Hsieh-ko-erh
110 C3 Ting-jih *Dingri* Tibet
110 C3 Ting-jih Hsien *Dingri Xian* Tibet
111 F2 Ting-k'o *Dingke* Tibet
Tingkou *see* Chiu-teng-k'ou
43 D3 Ting-kou *Dinggou* Kiangsu
63 C5 T'ing-k'ou-chen *Tingkouzhen* Shensi
82 D5 T'ing-liang *Tingliang* Kwangsi
43 F5 T'ing-lin *Tinglin* Kiangsu
30 F4 T'ing-liu-ho *Tingliuhe* Hopeh
55 F2 Ting-luan *Dingluan* Honan
71 C7 Ting-nan *Dingnan* Kiangsi
51 E3 T'ing-p'ang *Tingpang* Chek.
62 C3 Ting-pien *Dingbian* Shensi
75 C5 T'ing-p'ing *Tingping* Hunan
47 B5 Ting-pu-chieh *Dingbujie* Anhwei
Tingri *see* Ting-jih
103 D1 Ting-shan *Dingshan* Sink.
43 D4 Ting-shu-chen *Dingshuzhen* Kiangsu
59 G5 T'ing-ssu-ch'iao *Tingsiqiao* Hupeh
91 F5 Ting-tan *Dingdan* Kwei.
51 E3 Ting-t'ang *Dingtang* Chek.
82 D4 Ting-tang *Dingdang* Kwangsi
34 A4 Ting-t'ao *Dingtao* Shant.
110 A2 Ting-to *Dingduo* Tibet
51 D5 Ting-ts'ao Yü *Dingcao Yu* (island) Chek.
66 C3 Ting-ts'o *Dingcuo* Fukien
91 F5 T'ing-tung *Tingdong* Kwei.
82 E5 T'ing-tzu *Tingzi* Kwangsi
35 F3 Ting-tzu Kang *Dingzi Gang* (inlet) Shant.
106 C1 Ting-tzu-k'ou *Dingzikou* Tsing.
43 E3 Ting-yen *Dingyan* Kiangsu
55 E4 Ting-ying *Dingying* Honan
46 D4 Ting-yüan *Dingyuan* Anhwei
Ting-yüan-ying *see* Pa-yen-hao-t'e
Tinki *see* Ting-chieh
Tinkye Dzong *see* Ting-chieh
Tinpak *see* Tien-pai
Tinq-chieh *see* Chiang-ka
38 B3 Ti-pa-pao *Dibabao* Shansi
22 D3 Ti-san-chan *Disanzhan* Heilung.
38 D2 Ti-san-tso *Disanzuo* Shansi
102 I1 Ti-shui Ch'üan *Dishui Quan* (spring) Sink.
51 E2 Ti-t'ang *Ditang* Chek.
11 F5 Ti-tao *Didao* Heilung.
39 B6 Ti-tien *Didian* Shansi
43 E3 Ti-to *Diduo* Kiangsu
Titsing Tibetan Autonomous District *see* Ti-ch'ing Tibetan Autonomous District
15 K4 Ti-yin-kou *Diyingou* Kirin
115 C4 Tizard Bank China Sea
110 D3 To-cha-chung *Duozhazhong* Tibet
22 E2 T'o-cha-ming *Tuozhaming* Heilung.
10 B2 T'o-cha-min-nu-t'u-k'o *Tuozhaminnutuke* Heilung.
79 D1 T'o-ch'eng *Tuocheng* Kwangt.
75 D6 T'o-chiang *Tuojiang* Hunan
87 E2 T'o Chiang *Tuo Jiang* (river) Szech.
90 C4 To-chiao *Duojiao* Kwei.
35 F1 T'o-chi Tao *Tuoji Dao* (island) Shant.
79 D2 To-chu *Duozhu* Kwangt.
34 D4 To-chuang *Duozhuang* Shant.
70 C3 T'o-ch'uan-pu *Tuochuanbu* Kiangsi
107 G3 To-fu-tun *Duofudun* Tsing.
Tamiin Süme *see* T'u-ho-mu-miao
46 D3 T'o Ho *Tuo He* Anhwei
46 D3 T'o-ho-chi *Tuoheji* Anhwei
110 B2 T'o-ho-p'ing Ts'o *Tuoheping Cuo* (lake) Tibet
74 B3 To-hsi *Duoxi* Hunan
To Huping Lake *see* T'o-ho-p'ing Ts'o
Toishan *see* T'ai-shan
Tokak *see* To-k'a-k'o
106 C2 To-k'a-k'o *Duokake* Tsing.
106 C2 To-k'a-k'o Ho *Duokake He* (river) Tsing.
102 I2 T'o-k'o-hsün *Tuokexun* Sink.
103 E2 T'o-k'o-hsün *Tuokexun* Sink.
110 C2 T'o-k'o-ting-ling *Tuokedingling* Tibet
26 D4 T'o-k'o-t'o *Tuoketuo* In. Mong.
75 B4 To-k'ou *Duokou* Hunan
Toksun *see* T'o-k'o-hsün
Toktomal Ulan Muran *see* T'o-t'o Ho
106 D2 T'o-la *Tuola* Tsing.
106 C4 To-la-hsing-ko *Duolaxingge* Tsing.
T'o-lai-kung-chuang *see* T'o-le
T'o-lai-mu-ch'ang *see* T'o-le
107 F1 T'o-lai Nan-shan *Tuolai Nanshan* (mts) Tsing.
106 E4 To-la-ma-k'ang *Duolamakang* Tsing.
106 D2 T'o-la-t'o-la-lin *Tuolatuolalin* Tsing.
106 D2 T'o-le *Tuole* Tsing.
107 F1 T'o-le *Tuole* Tsing.
102 C1 T'o-li *Tuoli* Sink.
119 B4 To-liang *Duoliang* Taiwan
110 A3 T'o-lin *Tuolin* Tibet
Ting *see* T'o-lin
106 C2 T'o-lo-i *Tuoluoyi* Tsing.
82 D5 T'o-lu *Tuolu* Kwangsi
27 G3 To-lun *Duolun* In. Mong.
106 C4 T'o-lun-ch'ih-p'ing-erh *Tuolunchipinger* Tsing.
110 A2 T'o-ma-erh *Tuomaer* Tibet
Tomar *see* To-ma-erh
86 D4 T'o-mu-kou *Tuomugou* Szech.
110 B2 To-mu-la *Duomula* Tibet
11 B4 To-nai *Duonai* Heilung.
23 E4 To-nai *Duonai* Heilung.
Tonga *see* T'a-ku-k'o
Tongkow *see* Chiu-teng-k'ou
Tongkyuk *see* Tung-chiu
Tonguz Baste *see* T'ang-ku-tzu-pa-ssu-t'e
82 B3 T'o-niang Chiang *Tuoniang Jiang* (river) Kwangsi
Tonori Tso Nor *see* T'o-so Hu (sic)
107 G2 To-pa *Duoba* Tsing.
59 E4 To-pao-wan *Duobaowan* Hupeh
10 C2 To-pu-k'u-erh *Duobukuer* Heilung.
10 C2 To-pu-k'u-erh Ho *Duobukuer He* (river) Heilung.
22 F2 To-pu-k'u-erh Ho *Duobukuer He* (river) Heilung.
63 B6 T'o-shih *Tuoshi* Shensi
102 B2 T'o-shih-kan Ho *Tuoshigan He* (river) Sink.
107 F3 T'o-so Hu *Tuosuo Hu* (lake) Tsing.
Toson Nuur *see* T'o-su Hu (sic)
Tossun Nor *see* T'o-su Hu
107 E2 T'o-su Hu *Tuosu Hu* (lake) Tsing.
Totalyn Gol *see* T'a-t'a-leng Ho
58 E4 To-tao *Duodao* Hupeh
Totling *see* T'o-lin
102 C1 T'o-t'o *Tuotuo* Sink.
106 B3 T'o-t'o Ho *Tuotuo He* (river) Tsing.
106 C3 T'o-t'o-ho *Tuotuohe* Tsing.
107 E2 T'o-t'u *Tuotu* Tsing.
30 D4 Tou-chang-chuang *Douzhangzhuang* Hopeh
118 C2 T'ou-ch'eng *Toucheng* Taiwan
83 F2 Tou-chiang *Doujiang* Kwangsi
118 B2 T'ou-fen *Toufen* Taiwan
19 H2 Tou-hu-t'un *Douhutun* Liao.
34 A3 Tou-hu-t'un *Douhutun* Shant.
94 C4 Tou-ko *Douge* Yun.
55 F5 Tou-kou *Dougou* Honan
87 E1 Tou-k'ou *Doukou* Szech.
11 E6 Tou-kou-tzu *Dougouzi* Heilung.
55 F1 Tou-kung *Dougong* Honan
98 B1 T'ou-kung *Tougong* Kansu
102 I1 T'ou-kung *Tougong* Sink.
11 G4 T'ou-lin *Toulin* Heilung.
118 B3 Tou-liu *Douliu* Taiwan
38 D3 Tou-lo *Douluo* Shansi
55 F3 Tou-men *Doumen* Honan
79 C2 Tou-men *Doumen* Kwangt.
63 D6 Tou-men-chen *Doumenzhen* Shensi
79 C2 Tou-men Hsien *Doumen Xian* Kwangt.
74 D3 Tou-mu-hu *Doumuhu* Hunan
95 D4 Tou-mu-ko *Doumuge* Yun.
118 B3 Tou-nan *Dounan* Taiwan
83 G3 Tou-p'ai *Doupai* Kwangsi
30 B3 T'ou-pai-hu *Toubaihu* Hopeh
51 D2 T'ou-p'eng *Toupeng* Chek.
71 D5 T'ou-p'o *Toupo* Kiangsi
95 E1 Tou-sha-kuan *Doushaguan* Yun.
58 E4 Tou-shih *Doushi* Hupeh
71 B6 Tou-shui *Doushui* Kiangsi
11 C5 T'ou-t'ai *Toutai* Heilung.
102 H1 T'ou-t'ai *Toutai* Sink.
14 F6 T'ou-tao *Toudao* Kirin
15 H5 T'ou-tao Chiang *Toudao Jiang* (river) Kirin
26 B4 T'ou-tao-ch'iao *Toudaoqiao* In. Mong.
18 E3 T'ou-tao-ho *Toudaohe* Liao.
102 I2 T'ou-tao-ho *Toudaohe* Sink.
62 E2 T'ou-tao-ho-tzu *Toudaohezi* Shensi
114 C2 T'ou-tao-hu *Toudaohu* Ningsia
15 J5 T'ou-tao-kou *Toudaogou* Kirin
38 E3 Tou-ts'un *Doucun* Shansi
102 H2 T'ou-t'un Ho *Toutun He* (river) Sink.
102 H2 T'ou-t'un-ho *Toutunhe* Sink.
114 C3 T'ou-ying *Touying* Ningsia
31 B6 Tou-yü *Douyu* Hopeh
78 A4 To-wen *Duowen* Kwangt.
86 D3 T'o-wu *Tuowu* Szech.
110 B3 T'o-ya *Tuoya* Tibet
106 D2 To-ya-ho *Duoyahe* Tsing.
14 F5 T'o-yao-ling *Tuoyaoling* Kirin
11 F4 T'o-yao-tzu *Tuoyaozi* Heilung.
107 E3 To-yün Ho *Duoyun He* (river) Tsing.
Tradom *see* Cha-tung
115 C2 Tree Island China Sea
115 C4 Trident Shoal China Sea
115 B3 Triton Island China Sea
Tsa-ch'u Ho *see* Ya-lung Chiang
Tsagaan Tologoy Hudag *see* Ch'a-kan-t'ao-le-kai-hu-tu-ko
Tsagaan Us *see* Ch'ai-ta-mu Ho
67 B5 Ts'ai-ch'i *Caiqi* Fukien
75 D5 Ts'ai-chia *Caijia* Hunan
35 E3 Ts'ai-chia-chuang *Caijiazhuang* Shant.
59 H4 Ts'ai-chia-ho *Caijiahe* Hupeh
46 C4 Ts'ai-chia-lan *Caijialan* Anhwei
63 C6 Ts'ai-chia-p'o *Caijiapo* Shensi
30 C2 Ts'ai-chia-ying *Caijiaying* Hopeh
55 F3 Ts'ai-chuang *Caizhuang* Honan
30 F3 Ts'ai-chuang *Caizhuang* Hopeh
Tsaidam Basin *see* Ch'ai-ta-mu P'en-ti
39 B7 Ts'ai-hsia *Caixia* Shansi
58 C4 Ts'ai-hua *Caihua* Hupeh
107 F3 Ts'ai-jih-wa *Cairiwa* Tsing.
55 F4 Ts'ai-kou *Caigou* Honan
118 C2 Ts'ai-lien *Cailian* Taiwan
91 F4 Tsai-ma *Zaima* Kwei.
82 D5 Tsai-miao *Zaimiao* Kwangsi
91 F5 Tsai-pien *Zaibian* Kwei.
90 B3 Ts'ai-shen-t'ang *Caishentang* Kwei.
47 E5 Ts'ai-shih *Caishi* Anhwei
59 G4 Ts'ai-tien *Caidian* Hupeh
30 E4 Ts'ai-t'ing-ch'iao *Caitingqiao* Hopeh
47 E6 Ts'ai-ts'un-pa *Caicunba* Anhwei
47 D6 Ts'ai-tzu Hu *Caizi Hu* (lake) Anhwei
14 D3 Ts'ai-tzu-kung *Caizigong* Kirin
83 G2 Ts'ai-wan *Caiwan* Kwangsi
51 F2 Ts'ai-yüan-chen *Caiyuanzhen* Chek.
86 D2 Tsa-ku-nao *Zagunao* Szech.
Tsamkong *see* Chan-chiang
55 H4 Tsan-ch'eng *Zancheng* Honan
14 E4 Tsan-chia *Zanjia* Kirin
35 F2 Ts'an-chuang *Canzhuang* Shant.
87 E2 Ts'ang-ch'i *Cangqi* Szech.
55 E5 Tsang-chi *Zangji* Honan
31 D5 Tsang-chia-ch'iao *Zangjiaqiao* Hopeh
66 D4 Ts'ang-ch'ien *Cangqian* Fukien
31 D5 Ts'ang-chou *Cangzhou* Hopeh
Tsangchow *see* Ts'ang-chou
39 C4 Ts'ang-erh-hui *Cangerhui* Shansi
31 D5 Ts'ang Hsien *Cang Xian* Hopeh
74 D3 Ts'ang-kang *Canggang* Hunan
90 B6 Ts'ang-keng *Canggeng* Kwei.
35 F2 Ts'ang-ko-chuang *Canggezhuang* Shant.
35 F3 Ts'ang-k'ou *Cangkou* Shant.
102 B3 Tsang-kui *Zanggui* Sink.
Tsangpo *see* Brahmaputra
59 G4 Ts'ang-pu *Cangbu* Hupeh
10 B2 Ts'ang-shan *Cangshan* Heilung.
87 E2 Ts'ang-shan-chen *Cangshanzhen* Szech.
34 D5 Ts'ang-shan Hsien *Cangshan Xian* Shant.
19 H3 Ts'ang-shih *Cangshi* Liao.
74 E3 Ts'ang-shui-p'u *Cangshuipu* Hunan
110 C3 Tsang-to *Zangduo* Tibet
47 D5 Ts'ang-t'ou *Cangtou* Anhwei
38 D1 Ts'ang-t'ou Ho *Cangtou He* (river) Shansi
Ts'ang-wu *see* Lung-hsü
83 H4 Ts'ang-wu Hsien *Cangwu Xian* Kwangsi
94 B4 Ts'ang-yüan *Cangyuan* Yun.
94 B4 Ts'ang-yüan Wa Autonomous Hsien Yun.
Ts'ang-yüan Wa-tsu Tzu-chih-hsien *see* Ts'ang-yüan Wa Autonomous Hsien
31 B6 Tsan-huang *Zanhuang* Hopeh
Tsan-lan *see* Yin-ch'uan
31 D4 Tsan-lan *Zanlan* Hopeh
46 D4 Ts'ao-an *Caoan* Anhwei
70 E3 Ts'ao-ch'i *Caoqi* Kiangsi
50 C2 Tsao-ch'i *Zaoqi* Chek.
46 B4 Ts'ao-chia-chi *Caojiaji* Anhwei
39 C7 Ts'ao-chia-ch'uan *Caojiachuan* Shansi
59 H4 Ts'ao-chia-ho *Caojiahe* Hupeh
31 C6 Tsao-ch'iang *Zaoqiang* Hopeh
43 D4 Ts'ao-ch'iao *Caoqiao* Kiangsu
118 B2 Tsao-ch'iao *Zaoqiao* Taiwan
107 G2 Ts'ao-chia-pao *Caojiabao* Tsing.
63 E7 Ts'ao-chia-p'ing *Caojiaping* Shensi
63 B6 Ts'ao-chia-wan *Caojiawan* Shensi
94 B3 Ts'ao-chien *Caojian* Yun.
39 B5 Ts'ao-ching *Caojing* Shansi
Tsaochow *see* Ho-tse
34 D5 Ts'ao-chuang *Caozhuang* Shant.
34 C5 Tsao-chuang *Zaozhuang* Shant.
Tsaochwang *see* Tsao-chuang
90 B4 Ts'ao Hai *Caohai* (lake) Kwei.
31 C5 Ts'ao-ho *Caohe* Hopeh
19 H4 Ts'ao Ho *Cao He* (river) Liao.
42 C1 Tsao-ho *Zaohe* Kaingsu
19 H3 Ts'ao-ho-chang *Caohezhang* Liao.
19 H4 Ts'ao-ho-ch'eng *Caohecheng* Liao.
19 G4 Ts'ao-ho-k'ou *Caohekou* Liao.
71 B5 Tsao-ho-shih *Zaoheshi* Kiangsi
34 A5 Ts'ao-hsien *Caoxian* Shant.
102 D2 Ts'ao-hu *Caohu* Sink.
34 C2 Tsao-hu-li *Zaohuli* Shant.
106 D2 Tsao-huo Ho *Zaohuo He* (river) Tsing.
46 D3 Ts'ao-kou *Caogou* Anhwei
30 B4 Ts'ao-kou-pao *Caogoubao* Hopeh
46 D3 Ts'ao-lao-chi *Caolaoji* Anhwei
118 C1 Ts'ao-li *Caoli* Taiwan
71 B5 Tsao-lin *Zaolin* Kiangsi
38 E2 Tsao-lin *Zaolin* Shansi
62 F3 Tsao-lin-p'ing *Zaolinping* Shensi
34 B5 Ts'ao-ma-chi *Caomaji* Shant.
114 C3 Ts'ao-miao *Caomiao* Ningsia
Tsaongo River *see* Ts'ao-o Chiang
43 E3 Ts'ao-nien *Caonian* Kiangsu
51 D3 Ts'ao-o *Caoe* Chek.
51 D3 Ts'ao-o Chiang *Caoe Jiang* (river) Chek.
86 D3 Ts'ao-pa *Caoba* Szech.
95 D4 Ts'ao-pa *Caoba* Yun.
59 H4 Ts'ao-p'an-ti *Caopandi* Hupeh
63 C6 Ts'ao-pi-chen *Caobizhen* Shensi
43 E3 Ts'ao-p'ieh *Caopie* Kiangsu
75 F4 Tsao-p'o *Zaopo* Hunan
42 C1 Ts'ao-p'u *Caopu* Kiangsu
119 B4 Ts'ao-pu *Caobu* Taiwan
99 I4 Tsao-sheng *Zaosheng* Kansu
46 C3 Ts'ao-shih *Caoshi* Anhwei
75 F5 Ts'ao-shih *Caoshi* Hunan
19 I2 Ts'ao-shih *Caoshi* Liao.
74 D2 Tsao-shih *Zaoshi* Hunan
75 E5 Tsao-shih *Zaoshi* Hunan
59 F4 Tsao-shih *Zaoshi* Hupeh
51 D3 Ts'ao-t'a *Caota* Chek.
78 A3 Ts'ao-t'an *Caotan* Kwangt.
91 E3 Ts'ao-t'ang *Caotang* Kwei.
87 G2 Ts'ao-t'ang-pa *Caotangba* Szech.
58 D2 Ts'ao-tien *Caodian* Hupeh
43 D2 Ts'ao-tien *Caodian* Kiangsu
46 D2 Ts'ao-ts'un *Caocun* Anhwei
63 E5 Ts'ao-ts'un *Caocun* Shensi
91 E5 Ts'ao-tu Ho *Caodu He* (river) Kwei.
118 B3 Ts'ao-t'un *Caotun* Taiwan
30 G4 Ts'ao-tung-chuang *Caodongzhuang* Hopeh
74 E2 Ts'ao-wei *Caowei* Hunan
59 E2 Tsao-yang *Zaoyang* Hupeh
43 D2 Ts'ao-yen *Caoyan* Kiangsu
67 E5 Ts'ao Yü *Cao Yu* (islet) Fukien
102 H1 Ts'ao-yüan *Caoyuan* Sink.
31 C7 Tsao-yüan *Zaoyuan* Hopeh
34 C3 Tsao-yüan *Zaoyuan* Shant.
62 E4 Tsao-yüan *Zaoyuan* Shensi
Tsaring Nor *see* Cha-ling Hu
Tsa-to *see* Yü-yü-jih-pen
106 D4 Tsa-to Hsien *Zaduo Xian* Tsing.
Tsaydamiin Uula *see* Ch'ai-ta-mu Shan
39 C6 Tse-chang *Zezhang* Shansi
74 B3 Tse-chia-hu *Zejiahu* Hunan
Tsehchowfu *see* Chin-ch'eng
Ts'e-heng Pu-i-tsu Tzu-chih-hsien *see* Ts'e-heng Puyi Autonomous Hsien
90 C6 Ts'e-heng Puyi Autonomous Hsien Kwei.
Tsehleh *see* Ts'e-le
Tsehpu *see* Tse-p'u
98 E1 Ts'e-k'o *Ceke* Kansu
Tse-k'u *see* So-nai-hai
107 G3 Tse-k'u Hsien *Zeku Xian* Tsing.
51 E4 Tse-kuo *Zeguo* Chek.
111 E3 Tse-la *Zela* Tibet
100 C3 Ts'e-le *Cele* Sink.
82 D3 Tse-ling *Zeling* Kwangsi
107 E2 Tse-ling-kou *Zelinggou* Tsing.
83 H5 Ts'en-ch'i *Cenqi* Kwangsi
79 C2 Tseng-ch'eng *Zengcheng* Kwangt.
79 C2 Tseng Chiang *Zeng Jiang* (river) Kwangt.
15 I5 Tseng-feng Shan *Zengfeng Shan* (mt) Kirin
115 C5 Tseng-hai An-sha *Zenghai Ansha* China Sea
34 D5 Ts'eng-shan *Cengshan* Shant.
14 F3 Tseng-sheng *Zengsheng* Kirin
Tsengshing *see* Tseng-ch'eng
79 D1 Ts'eng-t'ien *Cengtian* Kwangt.
71 C4 Tseng-t'ien *Zengtian* Kiangsi
119 B3 Ts'eng-wen Ch'i *Cengwen* (river) Taiwan
59 E4 Ts'en-ho *Cenhe* Hupeh
91 F3 Ts'en-kung Hsien *Cengong Xian* Kwei.
102 B3 Tse-p'u *Zepu* Sink.
38 E4 Ts'e-shih *Ceshi* Shansi
111 D3 Tse-tang *Zedang* Tibet
102 D2 Ts'e-ta-ya *Cedaya* Sink.
Tsethang *see* Tse-tang
35 G2 Tse-t'ou-chi *Zetouji* Shant.
111 F3 Tse-wei *Zewei* Tibet
90 C6 Ts'e-yang *Ceyang* Kwei.
43 E4 Tse-yang-chen *Zeyangzhen* Kiangsu
31 B6 Ts'e-yü *Ceyu* Hopeh
Tsian *see* Chi-an
Tsiaotso *see* Chiao-tso
Tsientang River *see* Ch'ien-t'ang Chiang
Tsiho *see* Ch'i-ho
Tsimo *see* Chi-mo
Tsinan *see* Chi-nan
Tsinchow *see* Ch'in-hsien
Tsingan *see* Ching-an
Tsinghai Province *see* Pages 105-108
Tsingi *see* Ch'ing-i Chiang
Tsing-ki *see* Han-yüan
Tsingkiang *see* Ch'ing-chiang
Tsingpu *see* Ch'ing-p'u
Tsingshan *see* Ch'ing-shan
Tsingshih *see* Chin-shih
Tsingshui *see* Chang-chia-ch'uan
Tsingshui Ho *see* Ch'ing-shui Ho
Tsingsi *see* Ching-hsi
Tsingsing *see* Ching-hsing
Tsingtao *see* Ch'ing-tao
Tsingtien *see* Ch'ing-t'ien
Tsingtungsia *see* Ch'ing-t'ung-hsia
Tsing-yuen *see* Ching-yüan
Tsingyün *see* Ch'ing-yüan
Tsining *see* Chi-ning
Tsining *see* Chi-ning
Tsinkiang *see* Ch'üan-chou
Tsinkong *see* Ch'ien-chiang
Tsinling Mountains *see* Ch'in-ling Shan-mo
Tsinsien *see* Chin-hsien
Tsinyün *see* Chin-yün
Tsishih Shan *see* Chi-shih Shan
Tsitaokow *see* Ch'i-tao-kou
Tsitsihar *see* Ch'i-ch'i-ha-erh
Tsiyang *see* Chi-yang
71 B5 Tso-an *Zuoan* Kiangsi
47 D5 Ts'o-chen *Cuozhen* Anhwei
119 B3 Tso-chen *Zuozhen* Taiwan
55 F2 Tso-ch'eng *Zuocheng* Honan
14 G3 Tso-chia-chen *Zuojiazhen* Kirin
82 D5 Tso Chiang *Zuo Jiang* (river) Kwangsi
Ts'o-ch'in *see* Men-tung
110 C3 Ts'o-chin Hsien *Cuojin Xian* Tibet
82 D5 Tso-chou *Zuozhou* Kwangsi
39 E4 Tso-ch'üan *Zuoquan* Shansi
39 E5 Tso-hui *Zuohui* Shansi
22 C3 Ts'o-kang *Cuogang* Heilung.
110 B2 Ts'o-k'o-cha *Cuokezha* Tibet
Tso-kung *see* Ya-chung
111 F3 Tso-kung Hsien *Zuogong Xian* Tibet
63 D8 Tso-lung-kou *Zuolonggou* Shensi
Ts'o-mei *see* Tang-hsü
111 D3 Ts'o-mei Hsien *Cuomei Xian* Tibet
Ts'o-na *see* Hsüeh-hsia
111 D4 Ts'o-na Hsien *Cuona Xian* Tibet
Tsonji *see* Ch'üan-chi
111 F3 Tso-pa *Zuoba* Tibet
105 E3 Ts'o-pa-jih-ka-tse *Cuobarigaze* Tsing.
Tso-shui *see* Cha-shui
79 D2 Tso-t'an *Zuotan* Kwangt.
82 D4 Tso-teng *Zuodeng* Kwangsi
70 C2 Tsou-ch'iao *Zouqiao* Kiangsi
34 B4 Tsou-hsien *Zouxian* Shant.
107 F1 Tsou-lang Nan-shan *Zoulang Nanshan* (mts) Tsing.
83 G3 Tsou-ma *Zouma* Kwangsi
31 B4 Tsou-ma-i *Zoumayi* Hopeh
58 C5 Tsou-ma-p'ing *Zoumaping* Hupeh
34 C3 Tsou-p'ing *Zouping* Shant.
74 D2 Tsou-shih *Zoushi* Hunan
43 E3 Ts'ou-t'ung *Coutong* Kiangsu
34 C5 Tsou-wu *Zouwu* Shant.
30 B3 Tso-wei *Zuowei* Hopeh
38 D2 Tso-yün *Zuoyun* Shansi
63 D6 Tsu-an-chen *Zuanzhen* Shensi
119 B4 Tsu-chin *Zujin* Taiwan
110 B2 Tsu-hsia-kung-pu *Zuxiagongbu* Tibet
51 E3 Ts'ui-chia-ao *Cuijaao* Chek.
35 E3 Ts'ui-chia-chi *Cuijiaji* Shant.
55 F3 Ts'ui-ch'iao *Cuiqiao* Honan
58 B4 Ts'ui-chia-pa *Cuijiaba* Hupeh
34 D4 Ts'ui-chia-yü *Cuijiayu* Shant.
59 H5 Ts'ui-chou *Cuizhou* Hupeh
30 E4 Ts'ui-huang-k'ou *Cuihuangkou* Hopeh
10 C1 Ts'ui-kang *Cuigang* Heilung.
10 B2 Ts'ui-ling *Cuiling* Heilung.
11 E4 Ts'ui-luan *Cuiluan* Heilung.
Tsuimen *see* Hsü-wen
54 E3 Ts'ui-miao *Cuimiao* Honan
63 C6 Ts'ui-mu *Cuimu* Shensi
63 C6 Tsui-t'ou-chen *Zuitouzhen* Shensi
71 C5 Ts'ui-wei Feng *Cuiwei Feng* (mt) Kiangsi
82 C4 Tsu-jung *Zurong* Kwangsi
34 C3 Ts'u-lai Shan *Cilai Shan* (mt) Shant.
46 C2 Tsu-lou *Zulou* Anhwei
70 C3 Ts'un-ch'ien *Cunqian* Kiangsi
38 E3 Tsung-ai *Zongai* Shansi
98 D2 Tsung-chai *Zongzhai* Kansu
107 E2 Tsung-chia-fang-tzu *Zongjiafangzi* Tsing.
91 F5 Ts'ung-chiang Hsien *Congjiang Xian* Kwei.
83 F6 Tsung-chiang-k'ou *Zongjiangkou* Kwangsi
79 C2 Ts'ung-hua *Conghua* Kwangt.
110 C3 Tsung-ka *Zongga* Tibet
59 E4 Tsung-k'ou *Zongkou* Hupeh
38 B4 Ts'ung-lo-yü *Congluoyu* Shansi
46 D4 Tsung-p'u *Zongpu* Anhwei
Tsungteh *see* Ch'ung-te
39 D5 Ts'ung-tzu-yü *Congziyu* Shansi
107 E2 Tsung-wu-lung *Zongwulong* Tsing.
47 D6 Tsung-yang *Zongyang* Anhwei
30 E3 Tsun-hua *Zunhua* Hopeh
91 D3 Tsun-i *Zunyi* Kwei.
91 D3 Tsun-i Hsien *Zunyi Xian* Kwei.
Tsunyi *see* Tsun-i
35 E3 Tsuo-shan *Zuoshan* Shant.
119 B4 Tsu-shan *Zushan* Taiwan
31 C6 Tsu-yang-chuang *Zuyangzhuang* Hopeh
Tsuyung Yi Autonomous District *see* Ch'u-hsiung Yi Autonomous District
82 C4 Tu-an *Duan* Kwangsi
82 E4 Tu-an *Duan* Kwangsi
55 G6 Tuan-chi *Duanji* Honan
107 E1 T'uan-chieh Feng *Tuanjie Feng* (peak) Tsing.
39 C5 Tuan-ch'un *Duanchun* Shansi
59 G4 T'uan-feng *Tuanfeng* Hupeh
54 C5 Tuan Ho *Duan He* (river) Honan
91 E3 T'uan-hsi *Tuanxi* Kwei.
70 E2 Tuan-hsin *Duanxin* Kiangsi
50 C2 T'uan-k'ou *Tuankou* Chek.
58 E4 T'uan-lin *Tuanlin* Hupeh
14 G5 T'uan-lin *Tuanlin* Kirin
58 B4 T'uan-pao-ssu *Tuanbaosi* Hupeh
39 E4 T'uan-pi *Tuanbi* Shansi
59 H4 T'uan-p'o *Tuanpo* Hupeh
91 D5 Tuan-shan *Duanshan* Kwei.
59 E5 T'uan-shan-ssu *Tuanshansi* Hupeh
39 D6 Tuan-shih *Duanshi* Shansi
38 C4 T'uan-shui-t'ou *Tuanshuitou* Shansi
59 G4 Tuan-tien *Duandian* Hupeh
38 D4 Tuan-t'ing *Duanting* Shansi
39 D4 Tuan-ts'un *Duancun* Shansi
39 D5 Tuan-ts'un *Duancun* Shansi
35 F3 T'uan-wan *Tuanwan* Shant.
35 F3 T'uan-wang *Tuanwang* Shant.
83 G2 Tu-an Yao Autonomous Hsien Kwangsi
Tu-an Yao-tsu Tzu-chih-hsien *see* Tu-an Yao Autonomous Hsien
67 D6 T'u-chai *Tuzhai* Fukien
70 D2 Tu-ch'ang *Duchang* Kiangsi
118 C2 T'u-ch'ang *Tuchang* Taiwan
58 C3 T'u-ch'eng *Tucheng* Hupeh
91 C2 T'u-ch'eng *Tucheng* Kwei.
30 B2 T'u-ch'eng-tzu *Tuchengzi* Hopeh
30 D2 T'u-ch'eng-tzu *Tuchengzi* Hopeh
14 A5 T'u-ch'eng-tzu *Tuchengzi* Kirin
14 G3 T'u-ch'eng-tzu *Tuchengzi* Kirin
23 D6 T'u-ch'eng-tzu *Tuchengzi* Kirin
19 G4 T'u-ch'eng-tzu *Tuchengzi* Liao.
58 C4 Tu-chen-wan *Duzhenwan* Hupeh
55 G3 Tu-chi *Duji* Honan
34 B2 Tu-chi *Duji* Shant.
110 D3 Tu-chia-li *Dujiali* Tibet
91 F5 Tu-chiang *Dujiang* Kwei.
91 F5 Tu Chiang *Du Jiang* (river) Kwei.
75 C5 Tu-ch'iao *Duqiao* Hunan
47 D5 T'u-ch'iao *Tuqiao* Anhwei
43 D4 T'u-ch'iao *Tuqiao* Kiangsu
15 G3 T'u-ch'iao *Tuqiao* Kirin
34 B2 T'u-ch'iao *Tuqiao* Shant.
63 D5 T'u-ch'iao *Tuqiao* Shensi
63 D7 T'u-chia-p'ing *Tujiaping* Shensi
70 C2 T'u-chia-pu *Tujiabu* Kiangsi
59 F4 Tu-chia-t'ai *Dujiatai* Hupeh
82 D4 Tu-chieh *Dujie* Kwangsi
82 E3 Tu-chieh *Dujie* Kwangsi
90 B3 T'u-chieh-tzu *Tujiezi* Kwei.
50 B3 Tu-ching *Dujing* Chek.
31 D4 T'u-ch'ing-t'o *Tuqingtuo* Hopeh
14 B2 T'u-ch'üan *Tuquan* Kirin
23 D5 T'u-ch'üan *Tuquan* Kirin
38 E2 Tu-chuang *Duzhuang* Shansi
39 E4 Tu-chuang *Duzhuang* Shansi
78 A4 T'u-ch'ü Wan *Tuqu Wan* (bay) Kwangt.
Tu-erh-po-t'e *see* T'ai-k'ang
Tu-erh-po-t'e Meng-ku-tsu Tzu-chih-hsien *see* Durbet Mongol Autonomous Hsien
67 B5 T'u-fang *Tufang* Fukien
34 C2 T'u-hai Ho *Tuhai He* (river) Shant.
58 C2 Tu Ho *Du He* (river) Hupeh
26 D3 T'u-ho-mo-miao *Tuhemomiao* In. Mong.
91 E2 T'u-hsi *Tuxi* Kwei.
51 E4 Tu-hsia-ch'iao *Duxiaqiao* Chek.
87 G2 T'u-hsiang *Tuxiang* Szech.
102 C3 Tu-hsien-pai-pa-cha *Duxianbaibazha* Sink.
67 C7 Tu-hsün *Duxun* Fukien
79 C2 Tu-hu *Duhu* Kwangt.
115 C5 Tu-hu An-sha *Duhu Ansha* (shoal) China Sea
94 C2 T'u-huan-ts'un *Tuhuancun* Yun.
91 D5 Tu-i *Duyi* Kwei.
39 C4 Tui-chen *Duizhen* Shansi
71 B5 Tui-ch'ien *Duiqian* Kiangsi
11 D5 Tui-ch'ing-shan *Duiqingshan* Heilung.
26 D4 Tui-la-ma-miao *Duilamamiao* In. Mong.
Tui-lung-te-ch'ing *see* Lang-ka
111 D3 Tui-lung-te-ch'ing Hsien *Duilongdeqing Xian* Tibet
10 E4 Tui-mien Shan *Duimian Shan* (mt) Heilung.
15 H4 T'ui-po *Tuibo* Kirin
62 D3 Tui-tzu-liang *Duiziliang* Shensi
103 E1 Tu-je *Dure* Sink.
114 B2 Tu-jih-le-chi *Durileji* Ningsia
91 F2 Tu-ju *Duru* Kwei.
51 E4 Tu-kang *Dugang* Chek.
23 D5 T'u-ken-t'a-la-miao *Tugentalamiao* Liao.
31 B7 Tu-k'ou *Dukou* Hopeh
70 F3 Tu-k'ou *Dukou* Kiangsi
82 C2 Tu-k'ou *Dukou* Kwangsi
86 C4 Tu-k'ou *Dukou* Szech.
94 C2 Tu-k'ou *Dukou* Yun.
Tuktsitukar Tso *see* Ta-tse Ts'o
118 B3 T'u-k'u *Tuku* Taiwan
54 B3 Tu-kuan *Duguan* Honan
95 D3 T'u-kuan-chuang *Tuguanzhuang* Yun.
95 D3 T'u-kuan-ts'un *Tuguancun* Yun.
94 C4 Tu-kuei *Dugui* Yun.
26 C5 Tu-kuei-chia-han *Duguijiahan* In. Mong.
26 C4 Tu-kuei-t'e-la *Duguitela* In. Mong.
27 E4 T'u-kuei-wu-la *Tuguiwula* In. Mong.
114 C1 T'u-k'u-mu *Tukumu* Ningsia
103 D3 T'u-la *Tula* Sink.
Tu-lan *see* Ch'a-han-wu-su
119 C4 Tu-lan *Dulan* Taiwan
107 F2 Tu-lan Hsien *Dulan Xian* Tsing.
107 F2 Tu-lan-ssu *Dulansi* Tsing.
114 B2 T'u-lan-t'ai *Tulantai* Ningsia
91 D4 Tu-la-ying *Dulaying* Kwei.
102 C3 T'u-le-k'o-ch'i-k'u-le *Tulekeqikule* Sink.
14 A2 T'u-lieh-mao-tu *Tuliemaodu* Kirin
23 D5 T'u-lieh-mao-tu *Tuliemaodu* Kirin
22 D2 T'u-li-ho *Tulihe* Heilung.
30 D1 T'u-li-ken Ho *Tuligen He* (river) Hopeh
31 D5 Tu-lin *Dulin* Hopeh
54 C4 Tu-li-p'ing *Duliping* Honan
31 D4 Tu-liu *Duliu* Hopeh
46 C2 Tu-lou *Dulou* Anhwei
102 I2 T'u-lu-fan *Tulufan* Sink.
102 I2 T'u-lu-fan *Tulufan* Sink.
103 E2 T'u-lu-fan *Tulufan* Sink.
103 E2 T'u-lu-fan Chan *Tulufan Zhan* Sink.
11 F4 Tu-lu-ho *Duluhe* Heilung.
102 A2 T'u-lu-ka-erh-t'e Shan-k'ou *Tulugaerte Shankou* (pass) Sink.
95 E4 Tu-lung-hsin-chieh *Dulongxinjie* Yun.
103 E1 Tu-lung-ko-k'u-tu-k'o *Dulonggekuduke* Sink.
11 F4 T'u-lung-shan *Tulongshan* Heilung.
67 C6 Tu-mei *Dumei* Fukien
58 C1 T'u-men *Tumen* Hupeh
15 J5 T'u-men *Tumen* Kirin
63 F7 T'u-men *Tumen* Shensi
15 J5 T'u-men Chiang *Tumen Jiang* (river) Kirin
15 K5 T'u-men Chiang *Tumen Jiang* (river) Kirin
14 G3 T'u-men-ling *Tumenling* Kirin
30 G3 T'u-men-tzu *Tumenzi* Hopeh
99 F3 T'u-men-tzu *Tumenzi* Kansu
58 D4 T'u-men-ya *Tumenya* Hupeh
26 D4 Tumet East Banner In. Mong.
26 D4 Tumet West Banner In. Mong.
83 G3 Tu-mo *Dumo* Kwangsi
T'u-mo-t'e Tso-ch'i *see* Tumet East Banner
T'u-mo-t'e Yu-ch'i *see* Tumet West Banner
74 E4 Tu-mu-ch'iao *Dumuqiao* Hunan
27 E4 T'u-mu-erh-t'ai *Tumuertai* In. Mong.
11 G4 Tu-mu-ho *Dumuhe* Heilung.
102 B2 T'u-mu-hsiu-k'o *Tumuxiuke* Sink.
30 B2 T'u-mu-lu *Tumulu* Hopeh
78 B4 T'un-ch'ang *Tunchang* Kwangt.
47 E7 T'un-ch'i *Tunqi* Anhwei
90 C5 T'un-chiao *Tunjiao* Kwei.
83 F3 T'un-ch'iu *Tunqiu* Kwangsi
34 B3 Tung-a-chen *Dongazhen* Shant.
34 B3 Tung-a Hsien *Donga Xian* Shant.
47 E6 Tung-an *Dongan* Anhwei
11 H4 Tung-an *Dongan* Heilung.
67 D6 T'ung-an *Tongan* Fukien
70 B3 T'ung-an *Tongan* Kiangsi
83 G3 T'ung-an *Tongan* Kwangsi
86 D4 T'ung-an *Tongan* Szech.
43 F4 Tung-an-chen *Donganzhen* Kiangsu
75 D5 Tung-an Hsien *Dongan Xian* Hunan
75 D5 Tung-an Hsien *Dongan Xian* Hunan
99 G4 T'ung-an-i *Tonganyi* Kansu
118 C2 Tung-ao *Dongao* Taiwan
38 D3 Tung-chai *Dongzhai* Shansi
54 D5 T'ung-chai-p'u *Tongzhaipu* Honan
43 D3 Tung-ch'ang-chieh *Dongchangjie* Kiangsu
98 C1 T'ung-ch'ang-k'ou *Tongchangkou* Kansu
31 B5 Tung-ch'ang-shou *Dongchangshou* Hopeh
54 D3 Tung-chao-pao *Dongzhaobao* Honan
31 B6 Tung-chen *Dongzhen* Hopeh
99 F2 Tung-chen *Dongzhen* Kansu
43 E3 Tung-ch'en *Dongchen* Kiangsu
39 C6 Tung-chen *Dongzhen* Shansi
63 D7 Tung-chen-chieh *Dongzhenjie* Shensi
51 E4 Tung-cheng *Dongzheng* Chek.
30 B3 Tung-ch'eng *Dongcheng* Hopeh
102 I2 Tung-ch'eng *Dongcheng* Sink.
46 A3 T'ung-ch'eng *Tongcheng* Anhwei
46 E4 T'ung-ch'eng *Tongcheng* Anhwei
47 C5 T'ung-ch'eng *Tongcheng* Anhwei
59 F5 T'ung-ch'eng *Tongcheng* Hupeh
34 B3 T'ung-ch'eng *Tongcheng* Shant.
47 E5 T'ung-ch'eng-cha *Tongchengzha* Anhwei
58 D3 T'ung-ch'eng-ho *Tongchenghe* Hupeh
43 D1 Tung-chi *Dongji* Kiangsu
67 C7 Tung Ch'i *Dong Qi* (river) Fukien
67 D5 Tung Ch'i *Dong Qi* (river) Fukien
87 F3 Tung-ch'i *Dongqi* Szech.
70 C3 Tung-chia *Dongjia* Kiangsi
35 E3 Tung-chia *Dongjia* Shant.
70 E3 T'ung-chia *Tongjia* Kiangsi
30 C3 Tung-chia-fang *Dongjiafang* Hopeh
19 E5 Tung-chia-kou *Dongjiagou* Liao.
75 F6 Tung-chiang *Dongjiang* Hunan
82 E3 Tung-chiang *Dongjiang* Kwangsi
83 F2 Tung-chiang *Dongjiang* Kwangsi
79 D2 Tung Chiang *Dong Jiang* (river) Kwangt.
119 B4 Tung-chiang *Dongjiang* Taiwan
11 D4 T'ung-chiang *Tongjiang* Heilung.
11 G4 T'ung-chiang *Tongjiang* Heilung.
50 C3 T'ung-Chiang *Tong Jiang* (river) Chek.
87 F2 T'ung-chiang *Tongjiang* Szech.
63 D7 Tung-chiang-k'ou *Dongjiangkou* Shensi
19 G2 T'ung-chiang-k'ou *Tongjiangkou* Liao.
70 C2 T'ung-chiang-ling *Tongjiangling* Kiangsi
59 E3 Tung-ch'iao *Dongqiao* Hupeh
71 A4 Tung-ch'iao *Dongqiao* Kiangsi
43 D2 Tung-ch'iao *Dongqiao* Kiangsu
111 D3 Tung-ch'iao *Dongqiao* Tibet
14 D3 T'ung-chia-tien *Tongjiadian* Kirin
47 E6 Tung-chia-wan *Dongjiawan* Anhwei
87 F1 Tung-ch'i-chen *Dongqizhen* Szech.
54 D4 Tung-chieh *Dongjie* Honan
51 E3 Tung-ch'ien Hu *Dongqian Hu* (lake) Chek.
99 H4 Tung-chih *Dongzhi* Kansu
47 D6 Tung-chih Hsien *Dongzhi Xian* Anhwei
119 A3 Tung-chi Hsü *Dongji Xu* (island) Taiwan
38 E4 Tung-chih-t'ou *Dongzhitou* Shansi
11 D4 Tung-chin *Dongjin* Heilung.
83 F4 Tung-chin *Dongjin* Kwangsi
62 F2 T'ung-ch'in-chai *Tongqinzhai* Shensi
11 C4 Tung-ch'ing *Dongqing* Heilung.
119 C4 Tung-ch'ing *Dongqing* Taiwan
42 C4 T'ung-ching *Tongjing* Kiangsu
34 D4 T'ung-ching *Tongjing* Shant.
11 E5 Tung-ching-ch'eng *Dongjingcheng* Heilung.
30 B3 Tung-ching-chi *Dongjingji* Hopeh
114 B2 Tung-ch'ing-hu *Dongqinghu* Ningsia
19 G3 Tung-ching-ling *Dongjingling* Liao.
Tung-ching Wan *see* Gulf of Tongking

70 B3 Tung-chin Shui *Dongjin Shui* (river) Kiangsi
58 E2 Tung-chin-wan *Dongjinwan* Hupeh
111 E3 Tung-chiu *Dongjiu* Tibet
31 C6 Tung-chiu-kung *Dongjiugong* Hopeh
50 B4 Tung-chou *Dongzhou* Chek.
91 E5 T'ung-chou *Tongzhou* Kwei.
31 C6 Tung-chu *Dongzhu* Hopeh
83 F3 Tung-ch'üan *Dongquan* Kwangsi
62 C3 Tung Ch'uan *Dong Chuan* (river) Shensi
39 D4 Tung-ch'üan *Dongquan* Shansi
103 F1 Tung-chüan *Dongquan* Sink.
95 D2 Tung-ch'uan *Dongchuan* Yun.
63 E5 T'ung-ch'uan *Tongchuan* Shensi
95 D3 T'ung-ch'üan-chen *Tongquanzhen* Yun.
63 D7 Tung-ch'üan-chieh *Dongchuanjie* Shensi
55 F2 Tung-chuang *Dongzhuang* Honan
67 E5 Tung-ch'üan Tao *Dongquan Dao* (island) Fukien
111 D3 Tung-ch'ü-k'a *Dongquka* Tibet
66 E4 Tung-ch'ung *Dongchong* Fukien
55 F5 T'ung-chung *Tongzhong* Honan
Tungchwan *see* T'ung-ch'uan
19 G3 T'ung-erh-pao *Tongerbao* Liao.
43 E4 Tung-fang *Dongfang* Kiangsu
78 A4 Tung-fang Hsien *Dongfang Xian* Kwangt.
11 G4 Tung-fang-hung *Dongfanghong* Heilung
66 D3 Tung-feng *Dongfeng* Fukien
14 F5 Tung-feng *Dongfeng* Kirin
39 D6 Tung-feng *Dongfeng* Shansi
102 D3 Tung-feng *Dongfeng* Sink.
30 E4 Tung-feng-t'ai *Dongfengtai* Hopeh
15 J5 T'ung-fo-ssu *Tongfosi* Kirin
118 C3 Tung-fu *Dongfu* Taiwan
26 D4 Tung-ha-hao *Donghahao* In. Mong.
Tung Hai *see* East China Sea
Tung Hai *see* East China Sea
95 D3 T'ung-hai *Tonghai* Yun.
46 E3 T'ung-hai-chi *Tonghaiji* Anhwei
42 C1 Tung-hai Hsien *Donghai Xian* Kiangsu
59 F4 T'ung-hai-k'ou *Tonghaikou* Hupeh
114 C3 Tung-hai-pa *Donghaiba* Ningsia*
78 B3 Tung-hai Tao *Donghai Dao* (island) Kwangt.
Tunghing *see* Tung-hsing
98 E1 Tung Ho *Dong He* (river) Kansu
63 D8 Tung-ho *Donghe* Shensi
119 C4 Tung-ho *Donghe* Taiwan
11 E4 T'ung-ho *Tonghe* Heilung.
54 D5 T'ung-ho *Tonghe* Honan
83 G4 T'ung-ho *Tonghe* Kwangsi
14 F5 T'ung Ho *Tong He* (river) Kirin
43 E4 Tung-ho-chen *Donghezhen* Kiangsu
38 F2 Tung-ho-nan *Donghenan* Shansi
26 C4 T'ung-ho-t'ai Mu-ch'ang *Tonghetai Muchang* In. Mong.
47 F5 Tung-hsia *Dongxia* Anhwei
Tung-hsiang *see* So-nan-pa
70 D3 Tung-hsiang *Dongxiang* Kiangsi
83 F4 Tung-hsiang *Dongxiang* Kwangsi
51 D2 T'ung-hsiang *Tongxiang* Chek.
99 F4 Tunghsiang Autonomous Hsien Kansu
67 E5 Tung-hsiang Tao *Dongxiang Dao* (island) Fukien
Tung-hsiang Tzu-chih-hsien *see* Tunghsiang Autonomous Hsien
118 B2 T'ung-hsiao *Tongxiao* Taiwan
15 H6 Tung-hsiao-shan *Dongxiaoshan* Kirin
55 F4 Tung-hsia-t'ing *Dongxiating* Honan
30 D4 T'ung-hsien *Tongxian* Hopeh
15 J4 Tung-hsin *Dongxin* Kirin
114 C3 T'ung-hsin *Tongxin* Ningsia
18 D4 Tung-hsin-chuang *Dongxinzhuang* Liao.
11 D4 Tung-hsing *Dongxing* Heilung.
82 E6 Tung-hsing *Dongxing* Kwangsi
83 E2 Tung-hsing *Dongxing* Kwangsi
43 E2 T'ung-hsing *Tongxing* Kiangsu
23 B6 T'ung-hsing *Tongxing* Liao.
43 D1 T'ung-hsing-chieh *Tongxingjie* Kiangsu
Tung-hsing Ko-tsu Tzu-chih-hsien *see* Tung-hsing Multi-national Autonomous Hsien
82 E6 Tung-hsing Multi-national Autonomous Hsien Kwangsi
38 C3 Tung-hsiu-chuang *Dongxiuzhuang* Shansi
43 D1 Tung-hsi-yün Tao *Dongxiyun Dao* (island) Kiangsu
39 C5 Tung-hsü *Dongxu* Shansi
55 F3 T'ung-hsü *Tongxu* Honan
119 A3 Tung-hsü-p'ing Hsü *Dongxuping Xu* (island) Taiwan
75 F5 Tung-hu *Donghu* Hunan
102 I1 Tung-hu *Donghu* Sink.
70 C3 Tung-hua *Donghua* Kiangsi
14 F6 T'ung-hua *Tonghua* Kirin
39 B6 T'ung-hua *Tonghua* Shansi
86 D2 T'ung-hua *Tonghua* Szech.
99 I3 Tung-hua-ch'ih *Donghuachi* Kansu
14 F6 T'ung-hua Hsien *Tonghua Xian* Kirin
91 D2 Tung-huang-ch'ang *Donghuangchang* Kwei.
38 D3 Tung-huang-shui *Donghuangshui* Shansi
59 G3 Tung-huang-tien *Donghuangdian* Hupeh
31 B5 Tung-hui-she *Donghuishe* Hopeh
55 F4 Tung-hung *Donghong* Honan
Tunghwa *see* T'ung-hua
86 C3 Tung-i *Dongyi* Szech.
46 D3 Tung-i-chi *Dongyiji* Anhwei
T'ung-jen *see* Lung-wu
91 G3 T'ung-jen *Tongren* Kwei.
107 H3 T'ung-jen Hsien *Tongren Xian* Tsing.
43 D1 Tung-k'an *Dongkan* Kiangsu
95 E4 Tung-kan *Donggan* Yun.
10 C1 Tung-kang *Donggang* Heilung.
70 E2 Tung-kang *Donggang* Kiangsi
15 H5 Tung-kang *Donggang* Kirin
54 D5 Tung-kao-ying *Donggaoying* Honan
50 C5 Tung-k'eng *Dongkeng* Chek.
70 B4 Tung-k'eng *Dongkeng* Kiangsi
71 B7 Tung-k'eng *Dongkeng* Kiangsi
50 B3 Tung-k'eng-k'ou *Dongkengkou* Chek.
11 D4 T'ung-k'en Ho *Tongken He* (river) Heilung.
Tungki *see* Tung-ch'i
Tungkiangkow *see* Tung-chiang-k'ou
75 C4 Tung-k'ou *Dongkou* Hunan
42 C3 Tung-kou *Donggou* Kiangsu
43 D2 Tung-kou *Donggou* Kiangsu
39 D6 Tung-kou *Donggou* Shansi
34 A4 Tung-k'ou *Dongkou* Shant.
102 H2 Tung-kou *Donggou* Sink.
102 I2 Tung-kou *Donggou* Sink.
31 C5 T'ung-k'ou *Tongkou* Hopeh
14 F6 T'ung-kou *Tonggou* Kirin
19 H5 Tung-kou Hsien *Donggou Xian* Liao.
71 C5 Tung-ku *Donggu* Kiangsi
70 B3 T'ung-ku *Tonggu* Kiangsi
T'ung-kuan *see* T'ung-ch'uan
47 D5 Tung-kuan *Dongguan* Anhwei
31 E5 Tung-kuan *Dongguan* Hopeh
70 D4 Tung-kuan *Dongguan* Kiangsi
79 C2 Tung-kuan *Dongguan* Kwangt.
39 D4 Tung-kuan *Dongguan* Shansi
74 E3 T'ung-kuan *Tongguan* Hunan
63 F6 T'ung-kuan *Tongguan* Shensi
94 C4 T'ung-kuan *Tongguan* Yun.
51 D2 Tung-kuan-chen *Dongguanzhen* Chek.
31 D6 Tung-kuang *Dongguang* Hopeh
87 F3 T'ung-kuan-i *Tongguanyi* Szech.
T'ung-kuan-shan *see* T'ung-ling
18 D3 Tung-kuan-ying-tzu *Dongguanyingzi* Liao.
79 E1 T'ung-ku Chang *Tonggu Zhang* (mt) Kwangt.
114 C2 T'ung-ku-le-nao-erh *Tonggulenaoer* Ningsia
22 C3 Tung-kung *Donggong* Heilung.
58 D3 Tung-kung *Donggong* Hupeh
50 C5 Tung-kung Shan *Donggong Shan* (mts) Chek.
34 C4 Tung-kuo *Dongguo* Shant.
Tungkwan *see* T'ung-ch'uan
Tungkwanshan *see* T'ung-ling
14 B4 Tung-lai *Donglai* Kirin
23 D6 Tung-lai *Donglai* Kirin
82 D3 Tung-lan *Donglan* Kwangsi
58 C2 Tung-lang *Donglang* Hupeh
98 E2 Tung-le *Dongle* Kansu
11 D4 T'ung-le *Tongle* Heilung.
43 E4 T'ung-li *Tongli* Kiangsu
15 J5 Tung-liang *Dongliang* Kirin
18 E3 Tung-liang *Dongliang* Liao.
38 E3 Tung-liang *Dongliang* Shansi
87 F3 T'ung-liang *Tongliang* Szech.
118 A3 T'ung-liang *Tongliang* Taiwan
34 C4 Tung-liang-chuang *Dongliangzhuang* Shant.
14 C4 T'ung-liao *Tongliao* Kirin
23 E6 T'ung-liao *Tongliao* Kirin
14 E4 Tung-liao Ho *Dongliaohe* (river) Kirin
23 E6 Tung-liao Ho *Dongliao He* (river) Kirin
14 C4 Tung-liao Hsien *Dongliao Xian* Kirin
91 F4 T'ung-lin *Tonglin* Kwei.
82 C4 Tung-ling *Dongling* Kwangsi
19 G3 Tung-ling *Dongling* Liao.
38 D3 Tung-ling *Dongling* Shansi
47 D6 T'ung-ling *Tongling* Anhwei
47 D6 T'ung-ling *Tongling* Anhwei
83 F4 T'ung-ling *Tongling* Kwangsi
30 C3 Tung-ling Shan *Dongling Shan* (mt) Hopeh
34 D3 Tung-li-tien *Donglidian* Shant.
47 C6 Tung-liu *Dongliu* Anhwei
70 E2 Tung-liu *Dongliu* Kiangsi
43 D3 Tung-lo *Dongluo* Kiangsu
82 D5 Tung-lo *Dongluo* Kwangsi
118 B2 T'ung-lo *Tongluo* Taiwan
66 E4 Tung-lo Tao *Dongluo Dao* (island) Fukien
38 D3 Tung-lou *Donglou* Shansi
10 E3 Tung-lu *Donglu* Heilung.
50 C3 T'ung-lu *Tonglu* Chek.
79 E2 Tung-lung *Donglong* Kwangt.
30 D4 Tung-ma-ch'üan *Dongmaquan* Hopeh
111 E3 T'ung-mai *Tongmai* Tibet
30 D3 Tung-mao *Dongmao* Hopeh
74 G3 Tung-men *Dongmen* Hunan
82 D5 Tung-men *Dongmen* Kwangsi
118 C3 T'ung-men *Tongmen* Taiwan
14 C3 Tung-min-chu-t'un *Dongminzhutun* Kirin
23 E5 Tung-min-chu-t'un *Dongminzhutun* Kirin
14 B4 Tung-ming *Dongming* Kirin
23 D6 Tung-ming *Dongming* Kirin
34 A4 Tung-ming *Dongming* Shant.
34 A4 Tung-ming-chi *Dongmingji* Shant.
70 A4 T'ung-mu *Tongmu* Kiangsi
83 G3 T'ung-mu *Tongmu* Kwangsi
74 C4 T'ung-mu-ch'i *Tongmuqi* Hunan
10 C3 T'ung-nan *Tongnan* Heilung.
87 E2 T'ung-nan *Tongnan* Szech.
11 F5 Tung-ning *Dongning* Heilung.
30 D4 Tung-pa *Dongba* Hopeh
98 D1 Tung-pa *Dongba* Kansu
43 D4 Tung-pa *Dongba* Kiangsu
106 C4 Tung-pa *Dongba* Tsing.
106 D4 Tung-pa *Dongba* Tsing.
107 G2 Tung-pa *Dongba* Tsing.
54 E5 T'ung-pai *Tongbai* Honan
70 F3 T'ung-pan *Tongban* Kiangsi
38 D2 Tung-pan-ch'uan *Dongbanchuan* Shansi
98 B1 Tung-pa-t'u *Dongbatu* Kansu
10 D4 T'ung-pei *Tongbei* Heilung.
34 C3 Tung-pei-chi-p'o *Dongbeijipo* Shant.
11 D4 Tung-pien-chin *Dongbianjin* Heilung.
66 D3 Tung-p'ing *Dongping* Fukien
74 D3 Tung-p'ing *Dongping* Hunan
14 D1 Tung-p'ing *Dongping* Kirin
79 C3 Tung-p'ing *Dongping* Kwangt.
34 B4 Tung-p'ing *Dongping* Shant.
34 B3 Tung-p'ing Hu *Dongping Hu* (lake) Shant.
71 D4 Tung-p'o *Dongpo* Kiangsi
78 B3 Tung-p'o *Dongpo* Kwangt.
79 C1 Tung-p'o *Dongpo* Kwangt.
95 D3 Tung-p'o *Dongpo* Yun.
67 B5 T'ung-po *Tongbo* Fukien
51 D2 Tung-p'u *Dongpu* Chek.
118 B3 Tung-p'u *Dongpu* Taiwan
70 E2 T'ung-pu *Tongbu* Kiangsi
106 C3 Tung-pu-li-ling *Dongbuliling* Tsing.
23 C6 Tung-pu-ling *Dongbuling* Liao.
14 E3 Tung-san-chia-tzu *Dongsanjiazi* Kirin
46 D3 Tung-san-p'u *Dongsanpu* Anhwei
51 F2 Tung-sha-chiao *Dongshajiao* Chek.
19 F3 Tung-sha Ho *Dongsha He* (river) Liao.
Tung-shan *see* Hsü-chou
46 C4 Tung-shan *Dongshan* Anhwei
75 B5 Tung-shan *Dongshan* Hunan
42 C4 Tung-shan *Dongshan* Kiangsu
43 E4 Tung-shan *Dongshan* Kiangsu
83 H2 Tung-shan *Dongshan* Kwangsi
78 B3 Tung-shan *Dongshan* Kwangt.
118 C2 Tung-shan *Dongshan* Taiwan
119 B3 Tung-shan *Dongshan* Taiwan
47 D6 T'ung-shan *Tongshan* Anhwei
59 G5 T'ung-shan *Tongshan* Hupeh
42 C4 T'ung-shan *Tongshan* Kiangsu
15 H6 T'ung-shan *Tongshan* Kirin
39 C6 T'ung-shan *Tongshan* Shansi
67 C7 Tung-shan Hsien *Dongshan Xian* Fukien
42 B1 T'ung-shan Hsien *Tongshan Xian* Kiangsu
67 C7 Tung-shan Nei-ao *Dongshan Neiao* Fukien
67 C7 Tung-shan Tao *Dongshan Dao* (island) Fukien
Tungshap *see* T'ung-shih
67 F4 Tung-sha Tao *Dongsha Dao* (island) Fukien
38 D3 Tung-she *Dongshe* Shansi
38 D4 Tung-she *Dongshe* Shansi
39 C4 Tung-she *Dongshe* Shansi
26 C5 Tung-sheng *Dongsheng* In. Mong.
14 B2 Tung-sheng *Dongsheng* Kirin
23 D5 Tung-sheng *Dongsheng* Kirin
87 F3 Tung-sheng *Dongsheng* Szech.
15 J5 Tung-sheng-yung *Dongshengyong* Kirin
T'ung-shih *see* Hung-ch'i-chen
67 D6 Tung-shih *Dongshi* Fukien
74 D3 Tung-shih *Dongshi* Hunan
58 D4 Tung-shih *Dongshi* Hupeh
118 B2 Tung-shih *Dongshi* Taiwan
118 B3 Tung-shih *Dongshi* Taiwan
118 B3 Tung-shih *Dongshi* Taiwan
119 B3 Tung-shih *Dongshi* Taiwan
34 C4 T'ung-shih *Tongshi* Shant.
55 F5 Tung-shuang-ho *Dongshuanghe* Honan
79 D1 Tung-shui *Dongshui* Kwangt.
71 B4 T'ung-shu-p'ing *Tongshuping* Kiangsi
Tungsiang *see* Tung-hsiang
63 B7 Tung-su-ho *Dongsuhe* Shensi
14 C3 Tung-su-lin-yang *Dongsulinyang* Kirin
23 E5 Tung-su-lin-yang *Dongsulinyang* Kirin
11 C4 T'ung-ta *Tongda* Heilung.
66 E4 Tung-tai *Dongdai* Fukien
43 E3 Tung-t'ai *Dongtai* Kiangsu
106 C2 Tung-t'ai-chi-nai-erh Ho *Dongtaijinaier He* (river) Tsing.
106 C2 Tung-t'ai-chi-nai-erh Hu *Dongtaijinaier Hu* (lake) Tsing.
43 E3 Tung-t'ai Ho *Dongtai He* (river) Kiangsu
54 D4 Tung-t'ai-t'ou *Dongtaitou* Honan
39 E5 Tung-t'an *Dongtan* Shansi
10 E3 Tung-t'ang *Dongtang* Heilung.
10 E3 Tung-t'ang *Dongtang* Heilung.
82 C3 T'ung-t'ang *Tongtang* Kwangsi
47 D5 Tung-t'ang-ch'ih *Dongtangchi* Anhwei
75 B5 T'ung-tao Tung Autonomous Hsien Hunan
T'ung-tao T'ung-tsu Tzu-chih-hsien *see* T'ung-tao Tung Autonomous Hsien
30 E2 Tung-ta-pa *Dongdaba* Hopeh
18 D3 Tung-ta-tao *Dongdadao* Liao.
39 D6 Tung-ta-yang *Dongdayang* Shansi
T'ung-te *see* Ka-pa-sung-tou
107 G3 T'ung-te Hsien *Tongde Xian* Tsing.
51 D2 Tung-t'iao Ch'i *Dongtiao Qi* (river) Chek.
106 D3 T'ung-t'ien Ho *Tongtian He* (river) Tsing.
106 C4 T'ung-t'ien-ho-yen *Tongtianheyan* Tsing.
50 C2 Tung-t'ien Shan *Dongtianmu Shan* (mt) Chek.
31 C5 Tung-t'ing *Dongting* Hopeh
74 C3 Tung-t'ing-ch'i *Dongtingqi* Hunan
74 E3 Tung-t'ing Hu *Dongting Hu* (lake) Hunan
67 D6 Tung-ting Tao *Dongding Dao* (island) Fukien
111 E3 Tung-to *Dongduo* Tibet
51 E5 Tung-t'ou *Dongtou* Chek.
83 E2 Tung-t'ou *Dongtou* Kwangsi
51 E5 Tung-t'ou Shan *Dongtou Shan* (island) Chek.
38 C3 Tung-ts'un *Dongcun* Shansi
39 B7 Tung-ts'un *Dongcun* Shansi
35 G3 Tung-ts'un *Dongcun* Shant.
31 C7 T'ung-ts'un *Tongcun* Hopeh
107 E4 Tung-tsung-ssu *Dongzongsi* Tsing.
34 C4 Tung-tu *Dongdu* Shant.
14 B2 Tung-tu-erh-chi *Dongduerji* Kirin
23 D5 Tung-tu-erh-chi *Dongduerji* Kirin
11 C4 Tung-t'u-mo *Dongtumo* Heilung.
43 E4 Tung-tung-t'ing Shan *Dongdongting Shan* (mt) Kiangsu
Tungtze *see* T'ung-tzu
91 D2 T'ung-tzu *Tongzi* Kwei.
87 F3 T'ung-tzu *Tongzi* Szech.
74 D3 T'ung-tzu-ts'un *Tongzicun* Hunan
31 D5 Tung-tzu-ya *Dongziya* Hopeh
35 E3 Tung-wa-kou *Dongwagou* Shant.
102 H1 Tung-wan *Dongwan* Sink.
83 F4 T'ung-wan *Tongwan* Kwangsi
31 B5 Tung-wang-chuang *Dongwangzhuang* Hopeh
30 D2 Tung-wan-k'ou *Dongwankou* Hopeh
99 G4 T'ung-wei *Tongwei* Kansu
34 D4 Tung-wen Ho *Dongwen He* (river) Shant.
22 C3 Tung-wu-chu-erh *Dongwuzhuer* Heilung.
Tung-wu-chu-mu-ch'in Ch'i *see* East Ujumuchin Banner
51 D3 Tung-yang *Dongyang* Chek.
10 C3 Tung-yang *Dongyang* Heilung.
22 F3 Tung-yang *Dongyang* Heilung.
39 D4 Tung-yang *Dongyang* Shansi
34 C4 Tung-yang *Dongyang* Shant.
30 B3 Tung-yang Ho *Dongyang He* (river) Hopeh
43 E2 T'ung-yang-kang *Tongyanggang* Kiangsu
39 E5 Tung-yang-kuan *Dongyangguan* Shansi
75 E5 Tung-yang-tu *Dongyangdu* Hunan
55 E2 Tung-yao *Dongyao* Honan
39 C6 Tung-yao *Dongyao* Shansi
38 E3 Tung-yeh *Dongye* Shansi
39 D6 Tung-yeh *Dongye* Shansi
66 F4 Tung-yin Tao *Dongyin Dao* (island) Fukien
66 D3 Tung-yu *Dongyou* Fukien
39 D5 Tung-yü *Dongyu* Shansi
67 D6 Tung-yüan *Dongyuan* Fukien
79 E2 Tung-yüan *Dongyuan* Kwangt.
51 D2 T'ung-yüan *Tongyuan* Chek.
70 D3 T'ung-yüan *Tongyuan* Kiangsi
19 G4 T'ung-yüan-pao *Tongyuanbao* Liao.
74 D2 Tung-yüeh-kuan *Dongyueguan* Hunan
58 D5 Tung-yüeh-miao *Dongyuemiao* Hupeh
14 D3 T'ung-yü Hsien *Tongyu Xian* Kirin
38 D2 Tung-yü-lin *Dongyulin* Shansi
38 D2 Tung-yü-lin *Dongyulin* Shansi
71 B4 Tun-hou *Dunhou* Kiangsi
15 I4 Tun-hua *Dunhua* Kirin
98 B1 Tun-huang *Dunhuang* Kansu
Tunhwa *see* Tun-hua
Tunki *see* T'un-ch'i
59 G4 Tun-k'ou *Dunkou* Hupeh
30 B2 T'un-k'un *Tunkun* Hopeh
83 E5 T'un-li *Tunli* Kwangsi
39 B5 T'un-li *Tunli* Shansi
103 E3 Tun-li-k'o *Dunlike* Sink.
39 D5 T'un-liu *Tunliu* Shansi
58 B4 T'un-pao *Tunbao* Hupeh
43 D1 Tun-shang *Dunshang* Kiangsu
34 B3 T'un-t'ou *Tuntou* Shant.
46 E4 T'un-ts'ang *Tuncang* Anhwei
55 F2 T'un-tzu *Tunzi* Honan
39 E6 Tuo-huo *Duohuo* Shansi
38 B3 T'u-pan *Tuban* Shansi
75 D6 Tu-p'ang Ling *Dupang Ling* (mts) Hunan
91 E2 T'u-p'ing *Tuping* Kwei.
83 F3 T'u-po *Tubo* Kwangsi
59 G4 Tu-p'u-k'ou *Dupukou* Hupeh
Turbator Mongol Autonomous Hsien *see* Durbet Mongol Autonomous Hsien
Turfan *see* T'u-lu-fan
47 C5 Tu-shan *Dushan* Anhwei
91 E5 Tu-shan *Dushan* Kwei.
30 F3 Tu Shan *Du Shan* (mt) Hopeh
42 B1 T'u-shan *Tushan* Kiangsu
34 B4 Tu-shan-chi *Dushanji* Shant.
34 B4 Tu-shan Hu *Dushan Hu* (lake) Shant.
98 B2 Tu-shan-tzu *Dushanzi* Kansu
102 D1 Tu-shan-tzu *Dushanzi* Sink.
102 H1 Tu-shan-tzu *Dushanzi* Sink.
31 D5 Tu-sheng *Dusheng* Hopeh
30 C2 Tu-shih-k'ou *Dushikou* Hopeh
54 E4 Tu-shu *Dushu* Honan
34 D4 Tu-shu-t'ou *Dushutou* Shant.
26 B5 Tu-ssu-t'u Ho *Dusitu He* (river) In. Mong.
31 B7 Tu-tang *Dudang* Hopeh
70 D2 T'u-t'ang *Tutang* Kiangsi
91 F2 T'u-ti-ao *Tudiao* Kwei.
14 F4 T'u-ting-tzu *Tudingzi* Kirin
59 G4 T'u-ti-t'ang *Tuditang* Hupeh
75 F6 Tu-tou *Dudou* Hunan
50 B3 Tu-tse *Duze* Chek.
35 E3 Tu-ts'un *Ducun* Shant.
67 D5 Tu-wei *Duwei* Fukien
62 F2 T'u-wei Ho *Tuwei He* Shensi
67 E4 Tu-wu *Duwu* Fukien
103 E2 T'u-wu *Tuwu* Sink.
82 D4 Tu-yang *Duyang* Kwangsi
91 E4 Tu-yün *Duyun* Kwei.
Tyngeri Desert *see* T'eng-ko-li Sha-mo
Tzechung *see* Tzu-chung
Tzehing *see* Tzu-hsing
Tzehu *see* Pa-yen-hao-t'e
Tzekam *see* Tzu-chin
Tzeki *see* Tzu-ch'i
Tzeki *see* Tz'u-ch'i
Tzekung *see* Tzu-kung
Tzepo *see* Tzu-po
Tzeshan *see* Tz'u-shan
Tze Shui *see* Tzu Shui
Tzeyang *see* Tzu-yang
Tzeya River *see* Tzu-ya Ho
Tzeyün *see* Tzu-yün
62 E3 Tzu-ch'ang Hsien *Zichang Xian* Shensi
51 E3 Tz'u-ch'eng *Cicheng* Chek.
75 D5 Tzu-ch'i *Ziqi* Hunan
70 E3 Tzu-ch'i *Ziqi* Kiangsi
70 E4 Tzu-ch'i *Ziqi* Kiangsi
Tzu-chiang *see* Pa-yen-hao-t'e
34 C2 Tzu-chiao *Zijiao* Shant.
30 C4 Tz'u-chia-wu *Cijiawu* Hopeh
54 D3 Tz'u-chien *Cijian* Honan
51 E3 Tz'u-ch'i Hsien *Ciqi Xian* Chek.
58 D2 Tzu-chin *Zijin* Hupeh
79 D2 Tzu-chin *Zijin* Kwangt.
30 C4 Tzu-ching-kuan *Zijingguan* Hopeh
91 F3 Tzu-ching-kuan *Zijingguan* Kwei.
39 C5 Tzu-ching Shan *Zijing Shan* (mt) Shansi
42 C3 Tzu-chin Shan *Zijin Shan* (mt) Kiangsu
34 B4 Tz'u-ch'iu *Ciqiu* Shant.
58 C4 Tzu-ch'iu *Ziqiu* Hupeh
62 F3 Tzu-chou Hsien *Zizhou Xian* Shensi
106 E4 Tzu-ch'ü *Zi Qu* (river) Tsing.
34 C3 Tzu-chuan *Zizhuan* Shant.
87 E3 Tzu-chung *Zizhong* Szech.
104 D4 Tzu-ch'ü-tu-k'ou *Zigudukou* Tsing.
58 D2 Tz'u-ho *Cihe* Hupeh
34 D3 Tzu Ho *Zi He* (river) Shant.
86 C3 Tzu-ho *Zihe* Szech.
34 D3 Tzu-ho-tien *Zihedian* Shant.
31 B7 Tz'u-hsien *Cixian* Hopeh
75 F6 Tzu-hsing *Zixing* Hunan
Tzu-hu *see* Pa-yen-hao-t'e
70 F3 Tzu-hu *Zihu* Kiangsi
58 D4 Tz'u-hua *Cihua* Hupeh
70 B3 Tz'u-hua *Cihua* Kiangsi
39 D4 Tzu-hung *Zihong* Shansi
38 D2 Tzu-jun *Zirun* Shansi
Tz'u-kao Shan *see* Hsüeh Shan
107 F3 Tzu-k'o-t'an *Ziketan* Tsing.
55 E4 Tz'u-kou *Cigou* Honan
59 G5 Tz'u-k'ou *Cikou* Hupeh
22 E3 Tzu-kou *Zigou* Heilung.
66 C4 Tzu-k'ou-fang *Zikoufang* Fukien
119 B4 Tzu-kuan *Ziguan* Taiwan
58 C3 Tzu-kuei *Zigui* Hupeh
87 E3 Tzu-kung *Zigong* Szech.
46 E4 Tzu-lai-ch'iao *Zilaiqiao* Anhwei
74 D2 Tz'u-li *Cili* Hunan
74 D1 Tzu-liang-p'ing *Ziliangping* Hunan
74 E4 Tzu-men-ch'iao *Zimenqiao* Hunan
102 I1 Tzu-ni-ch'üan *Ziniquan* Sink.
114 C2 Tzu-ni-hu *Zinihu* Ningsia
71 B5 Tz'u-p'ing *Ciping* Kiangsi
31 B7 Tz'u-shan *Cishan* Hopeh
59 E3 Tzu-shan *Zishan* Hupeh
71 C6 Tzu-shan *Zishan* Kiangsi
86 D2 Tzu-shih *Zishi* Szech.
74 D3 Tzu Shui *Zi Shui* (river) Hunan
111 E3 Tzu-t'o *Zituo* Tibet
67 D6 Tz'u-tsao *Cizao* Fukien
87 E2 Tzu-t'ung *Zitong* Szech.
83 G4 Tzu-wang *Ziwang* Kwangsi
63 D6 Tzu-wu-chen *Ziwuzhen* Shensi
63 D7 Tzu-wu Ho *Ziwu He* (river) Shensi
31 D5 Tzu-ya Ho *Ziya He* (river) Hopeh
46 E3 Tzu-yang *Ziyang* Anhwei
63 D8 Tzu-yang *Ziyang* Shensi
87 E2 Tzu-yang *Ziyang* Szech.
34 C4 Tz'u-yao *Ciyao* Shant.
31 B5 Tz'u-yü *Ciyu* Hopeh
83 G1 Tzu-yüan *Ziyuan* Kwangsi
91 D5 Tzu-yün *Ziyun* Kwei.
91 D5 Tzu-yün Miao-Puyi Autonomous Hsien Kwei.
Tzu-yün Miao-tsu Pu-i-tsu Tzu-chih-hsien *see* Tzu-yün Miao-Puyi Autonomous Hsien
67 C5 Tzu-yün-tung Shan *Ziyundong Shan* (mt) Fukien
19 F3 Tz'u-yü-t'o *Ciyutuo* Liao.

Ubusue Dzag *see* Wu-pu-su-i-cha-ha
Ugampu *see* Wei yüan
Ulanchab League *see* Wu-lan-sh'a-pu Meng
Ulanhot *see* Wu-lan-hao-t'e
26 C4 Urat Centre and North United Banner In. Mong.
26 C4 Urat South Banner In. Mong.
Urumchi *see* Wu-lu-mu-ch'i
Urungu *see* Wu-lun-ku Ho
Ushak Tal *see* Ho-shuo
Ushin Banner *see* Wu-shen Ch'i
Ussuri *see* Wu-su-li Chiang
Uta M *see* Wu-t'u-mei-jen Ho
Ut Muren *see* Wu-t'u-mei-jen Ho
Uyug *see* Wu-yü

115 B5 Vanguard Bank China Sea
115 C2 Vuladdore Reef China Sea

86 C3 Wa-ch'ang *Wachang* Szech.
86 D1 Wa-ch'ieh *Waqie* Szech.
86 C3 Wa-erh-chai *Waerzhai* Szech.
14 B4 Wa-fang *Wafeng* Kirin
14 C2 Wa-fang *Wafang* Kirin
14 C5 Wa-fang *Wafang* Kirin
23 D6 Wa-fang *Wafang* Kirin
23 E5 Wa-fang *Wafang* Kirin
23 E6 Wa-fang *Wafang* Kirin
19 E5 Wa-fang-tien *Wafangdian* Liao.
63 D8 Wa-fang-tien *Wafangdian* Shensi
11 D4 Wa-hsing-chen *Waxingzhen* Heilung.
118 C2 Wai-ao *Waiao* Taiwan
51 D3 Wai-ch'en *Waichen* Chek.
Waichow *see* Hui-chou
22 C3 Wai-erh-t'a-pu-erh-t'a *Waiertabuerta* Heilung.
67 E5 Wai-k'eng *Waikeng* Fukien
30 D2 Wai-kou-men *Waigoumen* Hopeh
78 B3 Wai-lo *Wailuo* Kwangt.
99 G5 Wai-na-p'u *Wainapu* Kansu
50 C4 Wai-she *Waishe* Chek.
107 G3 Wai-ssu *Waisi* Tsing.
19 G3 Wai-t'ou-shan *Waitoushan* Liao.
Waitsap *see* Huai-chi
54 D5 Wai-tzu *Waizi* Honan
54 C4 Wai-wan Shan *Waiwan Shan* (mts) Honan
66 D4 Wai-yang *Waiyang* Fukien
86 D4 Wa-kang *Wagang* Szech.
111 F3 Wa-kung *Wagong* Tibet
30 F4 Wa-li *Wali* Hopeh
86 C3 Wa-li *Wali* Szech.
Walong *see* Wa-nung
59 F4 Wa-miao *Wamiao* Hupeh
66 C4 Wan-an *Wanan* Fukien
71 B5 Wan-an *Wanan* Kiangsi
39 C5 Wan-an *Wanan* Shansi
67 C5 Wan-an Ch'i *Wanan Qi* (river) Fukien
38 C2 Wan-chia-chai *Wanjiazhai* Shansi
19 F5 Wan-chia-ling *Wanjialing* Liao.
70 C3 Wan-chia-pu *Wanjiabu* Kiangsi
18 C4 Wan-chia-t'un *Wanjiatun* Liao.
47 E5 Wan-chih *Wanzhi* Anhwei
14 F3 Wan-chin-t'a *Wanjinta* Kirin
30 B3 Wan-ch'üan *Wanquan* Hopeh
30 D4 Wan-chuang *Wanzhuang* Hopeh
78 B4 Wan-ch'üan Ho *Wanquan He* (river) Kwangt.
14 F2 Wan-fa *Wanfa* Kirin
Wanfow *see* Yün-fu
71 B4 Wan-fu *Wanfu* Kiangsi
19 F4 Wan-fu *Wanfu* Liao.
34 B4 Wan-fu Ho *Wanfu He* (river) Shant.
119 A3 Wang-an *Wangan* Taiwan
30 B4 Wang-an-chen *Wanganzhen* Hopeh
46 C2 Wang-chai *Wangzhai* Anhwei
50 C4 Wang-chai *Wangzhai* Chek.
70 C3 Wang-ch'eng-kang *Wangchenggang* Kiangsi
58 E3 Wang-chi *Wangji* Hupeh
42 C2 Wang-chi *Wangji* Kiangsu
15 G4 Wang-ch'i *Wangqi* Kirin
74 D2 Wang-chia-ch'ang *Wangjiachang* Hunan
39 C4 Wang-chia-ch'ih *Wangjiachi* Shansi
31 C6 Wang-chia-ching *Wangjiajing* Hopeh
70 D3 Wang-chia-chou *Wangjiazhou* Kiangsi
95 D3 Wang-chia-chuang *Wangjiazhuang* Yun.
47 C6 Wang-chiang *Wangjiang* Anhwei
55 G3 Wang-ch'iao *Wangqiao* Honan
59 E5 Wang-ch'iao *Wangqiao* Hupeh
19 G4 Wang-chia-pao *Wangjiabao* Liao.
75 B5 Wang-chia-p'ing *Wangjiaping* Hunan
62 E4 Wang-chia-p'ing *Wangjiaping* Shensi
70 C2 Wang-chia-p'u *Wangjiapu* Kiangsi
58 C3 Wang-chia-t'an *Wangjiatan* Hupeh
10 F4 Wang-chia-tien *Wangjiadian* Heilung.
10 G3 Wang-chia-tien *Wangjiadian* Heilung.
59 F3 Wang-chia-tien *Wangjiadian* Hupeh
58 A4 Wang-chia-ying *Wangjiaying* Hupeh
70 C3 Wang-chia-yü *Wangjiayu* Kiangsi
94 C4 Wang-chieh *Wangjie* Yun.
15 J4 Wang-ch'ing *Wangqing* Kirin
19 I3 Wang-ch'ing-men *Wangqingmen* Liao.
67 D5 Wang-ch'uan *Wangchuan* Fukien
39 C5 Wang-chuang *Wangzhuang* Shansi
63 E5 Wang-chuang *Wangzhuang* Shensi
42 C1 Wang-chuang-chi *Wangzhuangji* Kiangsu
38 E2 Wang-chuang-pao *Wangzhuangbao* Shansi
Wangdan *see* Wang-tan
70 E3 Wang-erh *Wanger* Kiangsi
54 C3 Wang-fan *Wangfan* Honan
34 A3 Wang-feng *Wangfeng* Shant.
62 F5 Wang-feng-ch'iao *Wangfengqiao* Shensi
14 F3 Wang-fu *Wangfu* Kirin
18 E2 Wang-fu *Wangfu* Liao.
23 C6 Wang-fu *Wangfu* Liao.
18 E3 Wang-hai Shan *Wanghai Shan* (mt) Liao.
39 D5 Wang-ho *Wanghe* Shansi
74 F4 Wang-hsien *Wangxian* Hunan
71 C4 Wang-hsien *Wangxian* Kiangsi
39 B6 Wang-hsien *Wangxian* Shansi
31 E5 Wang-hsü-chuang *Wangxuzhuang* Hopeh
70 B4 Wang-hua *Wanghua* Kiangsi
31 B7 Wang-hua-pao *Wanghuabao* Hopeh
82 C3 Wang-hung *Wanghong* Kwangsi
34 A4 Wang-huo-t'un *Wanghuotun* Shant.
107 F2 Wang-ka-hsiu *Wanggaxiu* Tsing.
83 H3 Wang-kao *Wanggao* Kwangsi
35 E4 Wang-ko-chuang *Wanggezhuang* Shant.
35 F3 Wang-ko Chuang *Wangge Zhuang* Shant.
31 D5 Wang-k'ou *Wangkou* Hopeh
34 D4 Wang-kou *Wanggou* Shant.
38 E2 Wang-ku *Wanggu* Shansi
38 E1 Wang-kuan-jen-t'un *Wangguanrentun* Shansi
Wang-k'uei *see* Shuang-lung
11 D4 Wang-k'uei Hsien *Wangkui Xian* Heilung.
118 B3 Wang-kung *Wanggong* Taiwan
46 B3 Wang-lao-jen-chi *Wanglaorenji* Anhwei
75 F4 Wang-ling *Wangling* Hunan
55 G5 Wang-liu *Wangliu* Honan
91 C2 Wang-lung *Wanglong* Kwei.
118 B3 Wang-mei *Wangmei* Taiwan
Wang-mo Pu-i-tsu Miao-tsu Tzu-chih-hsien *see* Wang-mo Puyi-Miao Autonomous Hsien
91 D5 Wang-mo Puyi-Miao Autonomous Hsien Kwei.
83 F5 Wang-mou *Wangmou* Kwangsi
71 B6 Wang-mu-tu *Wangmudu* Kiangsi
34 C2 Wang-p'an-chen *Wangpanzhen* Shant.
51 E2 Wang-p'an Shan *Wangpan Shan* (island) Chek.
51 E2 Wang-p'an Yang *Wangpan Yang* (bay) Chek.
14 D4 Wang-pen *Wangben* Kirin
39 D6 Wang-pi *Wangbi* Shansi
58 B4 Wang-p'ing *Wangping* Hupeh
46 C3 Wang-shih *Wangshi* Anhwei
63 E5 Wang-shih-ao *Wangshiao* Shensi
74 E4 Wang-shih-wan *Wangshiwan* Hunan
31 D6 Wang-ssu *Wangsi* Hopeh
91 E4 Wang-ssu *Wangsi* Kwei.
66 C4 Wang-t'ai *Wangtai* Fukien
35 F3 Wang-t'ai *Wangtai* Shant.
110 D3 Wang-tan *Wangdan* Tibet
51 D3 Wang-t'ang *Wangtang* Chek.
39 D5 Wang-t'ao *Wangtao* Shansi
51 D2 Wang-tien *Wangdian* Chek.
10 B3 Wang-tien *Wangdian* Heilung.
82 C3 Wang-tien *Wangdian* Kwangsi
63 D6 Wang-tien *Wangdian* Shensi
43 E4 Wang-t'ing *Wangting* Kiangsu
87 F1 Wang-ts'ang Hsien *Wangcang Xian* Szech.
91 E2 Wang-ts'ao-pa *Wangcaoba* Kwei.
47 D7 Wang-ts'un *Wangcun* Anhwei
47 E7 Wang-ts'un *Wangcun* Anhwei
31 E6 Wang-ts'un *Wangcun* Hopeh
74 B3 Wang-ts'un *Wangcun* Hunan
38 D2 Wang-ts'un *Wangcun* Shansi
34 C3 Wang-ts'un *Wangcun* Shant.
35 F3 Wang-ts'un *Wangcun* Shant.
63 F5 Wang-ts'un *Wangcun* Shensi
50 B4 Wang-ts'un-k'ou *Wangcunkou* Chek.
34 B2 Wang-ts'un-tien *Wangcundian* Shant.
31 C5 Wang-tu *Wangdu* Hopeh
31 D6 Wang-t'uan *Wangtuan* Hopeh
35 G2 Wang-t'uan *Wangtuan* Shant.
46 C3 Wang-t'uan-chi *Wangtuanji* Anhwei
114 C3 Wang-t'uan-chuang *Wangtuanzhuang* Ningsia
Wang-tzu-chuang *see* Chin-t'a
34 B3 Wang-tzu-chuang *Wangzizhuang* Shant.
99 G5 Wang-tzu-kuan *Wangziguan* Kansu
114 C3 Wang-wa *Wangwa* Ningsia
54 D2 Wang-wu *Wangwu* Honan
55 F5 Wang-wu-ch'iao *Wangwuqiao* Honan
Wang Ye Fu *see* Pa-yen-hao-t'e
Wang-yeh-miao *see* Wu-lan-hao-t'e
18 B3 Wang-yeh-tien *Wangyedian* Liao.
34 B4 Wang-yin *Wangyin* Shant.
43 D2 Wang-ying *Wangying* Kiangsu
39 C6 Wang-yü-k'ou *Wangyukou* Shansi
59 F2 Wan-ho-tien *Wanhedian* Hupeh
31 C5 Wan-hsien *Wanxian* Hopeh
87 G2 Wan Hsien *Wan Xian* Szech.
87 G2 Wan-hsien *Wanxian* Szech.
39 B6 Wan-jung Hsien *Wanrong Xian* Shansi
99 F4 Wan-ka-t'an *Wangatan* Kansu
15 G5 Wan-kou *Wangou* Kirin
Wankow *see* Wan-k'ou
22 C3 Wan-kung *Wangong* Heilung.
47 E5 Wan-li *Wanli* Anhwei
118 C1 Wan-li *Wanli* Taiwan
118 C3 Wan-li *Wanli* Taiwan
15 H5 Wan-liang *Wanliang* Kirin
119 B4 Wan-luan *Wanluan* Taiwan
11 C5 Wan-lung *Wanlong* Heilung.
70 E3 Wan-nien Hsien *Wannian Xian* Kiangsi
78 B4 Wan-ning *Wanning* Kwangt.
83 G2 Wan-pan-ch'iao *Wanban Qiao* Kwangsi
14 F3 Wan-pao *Wanbao* Kirin
91 G3 Wan-shan *Wanshan* Kwei.
119 B4 Wan-shan *Wanshan* Taiwan
79 C3 Wan-shan Ch'üan-tao *Wanshan Qundao* (islands) Kwangt.
87 F3 Wan-sheng-ch'ang *Wanshengchang* Szech.
47 C6 Wan Shui *Wan Shui* (river) Anhwei
14 E3 Wan-shun *Wanshun* Kirin
55 E3 Wan-t'an *Wantan* Honan
58 C4 Wan-t'an *Wantan* Hupeh
119 B4 Wan-tan *Wandan* Taiwan
95 D4 Wan-t'ang *Wantang* Yun.
34 B3 Wan-te *Wande* Shant.
35 F3 Wan-ti *Wandi* Shant.
19 I3 Wan-tien-tzu *Wandianzi* Liao.
94 B3 Wan-ting *Wanding* Yun.
94 B3 Wan-ting Chen *Wanding Zhen* Yun.
75 C5 Wan-tou-ch'iao *Wandouqiao* Hunan
70 B3 Wan-tsai *Wanzai* Kiangsi
111 F3 Wa-nung *Wanong* Tibet
75 F5 Wan-yang Shan *Wanyang Shan* (mts) Hunan
87 G1 Wan-yüan *Wanyuan* Szech.
46 C4 Wa-pu *Wabu* Anhwei

46 C4 Wa-pu Hu *Wabu Hu* (lake) Anhwei
103 D3 Wa-shih-hsia *Washixia* Sink.
83 F5 Wa-t'ang *Watang* Kwangsi
38 B3 Wa-t'ang *Watang* Shansi
Watiam *see* Yü-lin
54 D5 Wa-tien *Wadian* Honan
Watnam *see* Yü-nan
62 F5 Wa-tzu-chieh *Wazijie* Shensi
30 F2 Wa-tzu-tien *Wazidian* Hopeh
75 E6 Wa-wan *Wawan* Hunan
86 C2 Wa-wu-kou *Wawugou* Szech.
54 D4 Wa-wu-miao *Wawumiao* Honan
75 C5 Wa-wu-t'ang *Wawutang* Hunan
42 C1 Wa-yao *Wayao* Kiangsu
94 B3 Wa-yao *Wayao* Yun.
62 E3 Wa-yao-pao *Wayaobao* Shensi
107 F2 Wa-yü-hsiang-k'a *Wayuxiangka* Tsing.
30 E2 Wei-ch'ang Hsien *Weichang Xian* Hopeh
30 E2 Wei-ch'ang Hsien *Weichang Xian* Hopeh
91 D4 Wei-ch'eng *Weicheng* Kwei.
86 C4 Wei-ch'eng *Weicheng* Szech.
87 E2 Wei-ch'eng *Weicheng* Szech.
54 D5 Wei-chia-chi *Weijiaji* Honan
34 C2 Wei-chia-ch'iao *Weijiaqiao* Shant.
42 C2 Wei-ch'iao *Weiqiao* Kiangsu
38 C3 Wei-chia-t'an *Weijiatan* Shansi
59 F3 Wei-chia-tien *Weijiadian* Hupeh
14 F5 Wei-chin *Weijin* Kirin
43 E4 Wei-ching-t'ang *Weijingtang* Kiangsu
55 F2 Wei-ch'iu-chi *Weiqiuji* Honan
31 B5 Wei-chou *Weizhou* Hopeh
114 C3 Wei-chou *Weizhou* Ningsia
114 C3 Wei-chou *Weizhou* Ningsia
86 D2 Wei-chou *Weizhou* Szech.
83 F6 Wei-chou Tao *Weizhou Dao* (island) Kwangsi
55 E3 Wei-ch'uan *Weichuan* Honan
39 B6 Wei-chuang *Weizhuang* Shansi
35 E3 Wei-fang *Weifang* Shant.
38 C3 Wei-fen Ho *Weifen He* (river) Shansi
35 H2 Wei-hai *Weihai* Shant.
Weihaiwei *see* Wei-hai
11 E5 Wei-ho *Weihe* Heilung.
55 F2 Wei Ho *Wei He* (river) Honan
99 H4 Wei Ho *Wei He* (river) Kansu
35 E3 Wei Ho *Wei He* (river) Shant.
63 E6 Wei Ho *Wei He* (river) Shensi
94 B2 Wei-hsi *Weixi* Yun.
55 F2 Wei-hsien *Weixian* Honan
31 B7 Wei-hsien *Weixian* Hopeh
31 C7 Wei-hsien *Weixian* Hopeh
35 E3 Wei Hsien *Wei Xian* Shant.
90 C3 Wei-hsin *Weixin* Kwei.
74 D2 Wei-hsin-ch'ang *Weixinchang* Hunan
95 E2 Wei-hsin Hsien *Weixin Xian* Yun.
63 D6 Wei-hui Ch'ü *Weihui Qu* (canal) Shensi
15 H4 Wei-hu Ling *Weihu Ling* (mts) Kirin
99 G4 Wei-jung *Weirong* Kansu
58 B4 Wei-kan-pao *Weiganbao* Hupeh
10 E3 Wei-kuo *Weiguo* Heilung.
Wei-li *see* Yü-li
Wei-li Hsien *see* Yü-li Hsien
63 F6 Wei-lin-chen *Weilinzhen* Shensi
11 E4 Wei-ling *Weiling* Heilung.
82 B3 Wei-lo *Weiluo* Kwangsi
82 E5 Wei-lo *Weiluo* Kwangsi
38 D1 Wei-lu-pao *Weilubao* Shansi
39 E4 Wei-ma *Weima* Shansi
66 C3 Wei-ming *Weiming* Fukien
63 E6 Wei-nan *Weinan* Shensi
90 B4 Wei-ning *Weining* Kwei.
19 G3 Wei-ning *Weining* Liao.
Wei-ning I-tsu Hui-tsu Miao-tsu Tzu-chih-hsien *see* Wei-ning Yi-Hui-Miao Autonomous Hsien
90 B4 Wei-ning Yi-Hui-Miao Autonomous Hsien Kwei.
31 C5 Wei-po *Weibo* Hopeh
51 D3 Wei-shan *Weishan* Chek.
74 D3 Wei-shan *Weishan* Hunan
94 C3 Wei-shan *Weishan* Yun.
30 D4 Wei-shan-chuang *Weishanzhuang* Hopeh
34 C5 Wei-shan Hsien *Weishan Xian* Shant.
34 C5 Wei-shan Hu *Weishan Hu* (lake) Shant.
Wei-shan I-tsu Hui-tsu Tzu-chih-hsien *see* Wei-shan Yi-Hui Autonomous Hsien
94 C3 Wei-shan Yi-Hui Autonomous Hsien Yun.
55 F3 Wei-shih *Weishi* Honan
31 B5 Wei-shui *Weishui* Hopeh
74 E3 Wei Shui *Wei Shui* (river) Hunan
Weisi *see* Wei-hsi
66 D3 Wei-t'ien *Weitian* Fukien
67 D6 Wei-t'ou *Weitou* Fukien
67 D6 Wei-t'ou Wan *Weitou Wan* (bay) Fukien
43 D4 Wei-ts'un *Weicun* Kiangsu
83 F4 Wei-tu *Weidu* Kwangsi
10 C1 Wei-tung *Weidong* Heilung.
19 G4 Wei-tzu *Weizi* Liao.
39 E5 Wei-tzu-chen *Weizizhen* Shansi
19 H3 Wei-tzu-yü *Weiziyu* Liao.
34 A3 Wei-wan *Weiwan* Shant.
34 A5 Wei-wan *Weiwan* Shant.
103 F2 Wei-ya *Weiya* Sink.
42 C2 Wei-ying *Weiying* Kiangsu
99 G4 Wei-yüan *Weiyuan* Kansu
87 E3 Wei-yüan *Weiyuan* Szech.
107 G2 Wei-yüan *Weiyuan* Tsing.
94 C4 Wei-yüan Chiang *Weiyuan Jiang* (river) Yun.
19 H2 Wei-yüan-pao *Weiyuanbao* Liao.
38 D2 Wei-yüan-pao *Weiyuanbao* Shansi
31 D5 Wen-an *Wenan* Hopeh
58 D4 Wen-an *Wenan* Hupeh
50 C3 Wen-ch'ang *Wenchang* Chek.
78 B4 Wen-ch'ang *Wenchang* Kwangt.
39 B5 Wen-ch'eng *Wencheng* Shansi
51 D5 Wen-ch'eng Hsien *Wencheng Xian* Chek.
51 D4 Wen-ch'i *Wenqi* Chek.
70 D3 Wen-chia-ch'ou *Wenjiachou* Kiangsi
87 D2 Wen-chiang *Wenjiang* Szech.
70 D2 Wen-ch'iao *Wenqiao* Kiangsi
88 B4 Wen-chiao *Wenjiao* Kwangt.
74 F3 Wen-chia-shih *Wenjiashi* Hunan
91 E3 Wen-chia-tien *Wenjiadian* Kwei.
34 C2 Wen-chia-tien *Wenjiadian* Shant.
94 C3 Wen-ching *Wenjing* Yun.
Wen-chou *see* Wen-ch'uan
51 D4 Wen-chou *Wenzhou* Chek.
51 D5 Wen-chou *Wenzhou* Chek.
51 D5 Wen-chou Wan *Wenzhou Wan* (bay) Chek.
Wenchow *see* Wen-chou
54 C5 Wen-ch'ü *Wenqu* Honan
71 A5 Wen-chu *Wenzhu* Kiangsi
23 D4 Wen-ch'üan *Wenquan* Kirin
91 D3 Wen-ch'üan *Wenquan* Kwei.
91 E2 Wen-ch'üan *Wenquan* Kwei.
18 D4 Wen-ch'üan *Wenquan* Liao.
102 C1 Wen-ch'üan *Wenquan* Sink.
87 G2 Wen-ch'üan *Wenquan* Szech.
106 B4 Wen-ch'üan *Wenquan* Tsing.
107 F3 Wen-ch'üan *Wenquan* Tsing.
59 G5 Wen-ch'üan-chen *Wenquanzhen* Hupeh
86 D2 Wen-ch'üan Hsien *Wenchuan Xian* Szech.
110 C2 Wen-ch'üan Hu *Wenquan Hu* (lake) Tibet
19 H3 Wen-ch'üan-ssu *Wenquansi* Liao.
35 H2 Wen-ch'üan-t'ang *Wenquantang* Shant.
106 D2 Wen-ch'u-k'o-pu-la-k'o *Wenchukebulake* Tsing.
11 E5 Wen-ch'un *Wenchun* Heilung.
70 E3 Wen-fang *Wenfang* Kiangsi
99 G4 Wen-feng-chen *Wenfengzhen* Kansu
91 E3 Weng-an Hsien *Wengan Xian* Kwei.
79 C1 Weng-ch'eng *Wengcheng* Kwangt.
74 F3 Weng-chiang *Wengjiang* Hunan
79 C1 Weng Chiang *Weng Jiang* (river) Kwangt.
18 B2 Weng-niu-t'e Ch'i *Wengniute Qi* Liao.
94 B1 Weng-shui *Wengshui* Yun.
86 C2 Weng-ta *Wengda* Szech.
91 G3 Weng-tung *Wengdong* Kwei.
51 D4 Weng-yang *Wengyang* Chek.
79 D1 Weng-yüan Hsien *Wengyuan Xian* Kwangt.
67 B5 Wen-heng *Wenheng* Fukien
35 E3 Wen Ho *Wen He* (river) Shant.
39 C6 Wen-hsi *Wenxi* Shansi
54 E3 Wen-hsien *Wenxian* Honan
99 G5 Wen-hsien *Wenxian* Kansu
31 C5 Wen-jen *Wenren* Hopeh
22 E3 Wen-k'u-t'u *Wenkutu* Heilung.
83 G5 Wen-li *Wenli* Kwangsi
51 E4 Wen-ling *Wenling* Chek.
71 B7 Wen-lung *Wenlong* Kiangsi
75 F6 Wen-meng *Wenmeng* Hunan
75 D5 Wen-ming-p'u *Wenmingpu* Hunan
91 F2 Wen-p'ing *Wenping* Kwei.
95 D2 Wen-p'ing-chen *Wenpingzhen* Yun.
110 C3 Wen-po *Wenbo* Tibet
86 B1 Wen-po-ssu *Wenbosi* Szech.
95 E4 Wen-shan *Wenshan* Yun.
95 E4 Wen-shan Chuang-Miao Autonomous District Yun.
Wen-shan Chuang-tsu Miao-tsu Tzu-chih-chou *see* Wen-shan Chuang-miao Autonomous District
34 B4 Wen-shang *Wenshang* Shant.
83 H2 Wen-shih *Wenshi* Kwangsi
105 G3 Wen-shih-chia *Wenshijia* Tsing.
91 D2 Wen-shui *Wenshui* Kwei.
39 D4 Wen-shui *Wenshui* Shansi
102 C2 Wen-su *Wensu* Sink.
Wensuh *see* Wen-su
70 B2 Wen-t'ang *Wentang* Kiangsi
70 B4 Wen-t'ang *Wentang* Kiangsi
34 C3 Wen-teng *Wendeng* Shant.
83 G6 Wen-ti *Wendi* Kwangsi
103 E1 Wen-ti-erh-k'a-la *Wendierkala* Sink.
58 A5 Wen-tou *Wendou* Hupeh
34 C3 Wen-tsu *Wenzu* Shant.
114 B1 Wen-tu-erh-mao-tao *Wenduermaodao* Ningsia
27 E3 Wen-tu-erh-miao *Wenduermiao* In. Mong.
14 A3 Wen-tu-ha-ta *Wenduhada* Kirin
23 D5 Wen-tu-ha-ta *Wenduhada* Kirin
71 B6 Wen-ying *Wenying* Kiangsi
54 C3 Wen-yü *Wenyu* Honan
38 C4 Wen-yü Ho *Wenyu He* (river) Shansi
115 C4 Western Reef China Sea
74 B3 West Hunan Tuchia-Miao Autonomous District Hunan
27 G2 West Ujumuchin Banner In. Mong.
Whampoa *see* Huang-p'u
Whangpoo River *see* Huang-p'u Chiang
14 A4 Wo-feng-tien-tzu *Wofengdianzi* Kirin
23 D6 Wo-feng-tien-tzu *Wofengdianzi* Kirin
43 D4 Wo Ho *Wo Hu* (lake) Kiangsu
14 D4 Wo-hu-t'un *Wohutun* Kirin
23 E6 Wo-hu-t'un *Wohutun* Kirin
111 E3 Wo-ka *Woga* Tibet
11 F5 Wo-k'en *Woken* Heilung.
71 C7 Wo-kung *Wogong* Kiangsi
15 I5 Wo-lung *Wolong* Kirin
86 C2 Wo-lung-shih *Wolongshi* Szech.
Wompo *see* Wen-po
22 E3 Wo-niu-ho *Woniuhe* Heilung.
11 B4 Wo-niu-t'u *Woniutu* Heilung.
23 E4 Wo-niu-t'u *Woniutu* Heilung.
115 C2 Woody Island China Sea
58 E4 Wo-shih *Woshi* Hupeh
82 D3 Wu-ai *Wuai* Kwangsi
31 B7 Wu-an *Wuan* Hopeh
34 A4 Wu-an-chi *Wuanji* Shant.
50 C3 Wu-chai *Wuzhai* Chek.
38 C3 Wu-chai *Wuzhai* Shansi
23 D4 Wu-ch'a-kou *Wuchagou* Kirin
10 C2 Wu-chan *Wuzhan* Heilung.
11 D5 Wu-chan *Wuzhan* Heilung.
11 D5 Wu-ch'ang *Wuchang* Heilung.
59 G4 Wu-ch'ang *Wuchang* Hupeh
59 G4 Wu-ch'ang Hsien *Wuchang Xian* Hupeh
59 G4 Wu-ch'ang Hu *Wuchang Hu* (lake) Anhwei
51 D2 Wu-chen *Wuzhen* Chek.
58 D3 Wu-chen *Wuzhen* Hupeh
62 E3 Wu-chen *Wuzhen* Shensi
47 E7 Wu-ch'eng *Wucheng* Anhwei
55 E4 Wu-ch'eng *Wucheng* Honan
55 E5 Wu-ch'eng *Wucheng* Honan
31 C6 Wu-ch'eng *Wucheng* Hopeh
70 C2 Wu-ch'eng *Wucheng* Kiangsi
38 E2 Wu-ch'eng *Wucheng* Shansi
39 B5 Wu-ch'eng *Wucheng* Shansi
39 C4 Wu-ch'eng *Wucheng* Shansi
34 C2 Wu-cheng *Wucheng* Shant.
31 B5 Wu-chi *Wuji* Hopeh
31 C7 Wu-chi *Wuji* Hopeh
74 C3 Wu-ch'i *Wuqi* Hunan
74 C3 Wu-ch'i *Wuqi* Hunan
75 E4 Wu-chi *Wuji* Hunan
43 D3 Wu-chi *Wuji* Kiangsu
50 B4 Wu Ch'i *Wu Qi* (river) Chek.
35 E4 Wu-chi *Wuji* Shant.
35 G2 Wu-chi *Wuji* Shant.
62 D4 Wu-ch'i *Wuqi* Shensi
87 G2 Wu-ch'i *Wuqi* Szech.
11 D5 Wu-chia *Wujia* Heilung.
83 F6 Wu-chia *Wujia* Kwangsi
102 A3 Wu-ch'ia *Wuqia* Sink.
14 F3 Wu-chia-chan *Wujiazhan* Kirin
102 H1 Wu-chia-ch'ü *Wujiaqu* Sink.
26 C4 Wu-chia-ho *Wujiahe* In. Mong.
26 B4 Wu-chia Ho *Wujia He* (river) In. Mong.
47 E4 Wu-chia-lan *Wujialan* Anhwei
47 E5 Wu-chiang *Wujiang* Anhwei
22 D3 Wu-chiang *Wujiang* Heilung.
55 G3 Wu-ch'iang *Wuqiang* Honan
71 C4 Wu-chiang *Wujiang* Kiangsi
43 E4 Wu-chiang *Wujiang* Kiangsu
83 G3 Wu-chiang *Wujiang* Kwangsi
71 C4 Wu Chiang *Wu Jiang* (river) Kiangsi
91 E3 Wu Chiang *Wu Jiang* (river) Kwei.
31 C5 Wu-ch'iang Hsien *Wuqiang Xian* Hopeh
31 C5 Wu-ch'iang Hsien *Wuqiang Xian* Hopeh
98 E2 Wu-chiang-pao *Wujiangbao* Kansu
91 D3 Wu-chiang-tu *Wujiangdu* Kwei.
31 D6 Wu-ch'iao Hsien *Wuqiao Xian* Hopeh
31 D6 Wu-ch'iao Hsien *Wuqiao Xian* Hopeh
66 C3 Wu-chia-t'ang *Wujiatang* Fukien
55 E5 Wu-chia-tien *Wujiadian* Honan
47 D6 Wu-ch'i-ch'iao *Wuqiqiao* Anhwei
118 C2 Wu-chieh *Wujie* Taiwan
43 D4 Wu-chien Hsien *Wujin Xian* Kiangsu
54 E2 Wu-chih *Wuzhi* Honan
31 C6 Wu-chih *Wuzhi* Hopeh
30 F3 Wu-chih Shan *Wuzhi Shan* (mt) Hopeh
78 A4 Wu-chih Shan *Wuzhi Shan* (mt) Kwangt.
11 D5 Wu-chi-mi *Wujimi* Heilung.
Wu-chin *see* Ch'ang-chou
79 D1 Wu-ching *Wujing* Kwangt.
34 D3 Wu-ching *Wujing* Shant.
79 E2 Wu-ching-fu *Wujingfu* Kwangt.
30 E4 Wu-ch'ing Hsien *Wuqing Xian* Hopeh
30 E4 Wu-ch'ing Hsien *Wuqing Xian* Hopeh
14 D3 Wu-ching-tzu *Wujingzi* Kirin
67 E6 Wu-ch'iu Yü *Wuqiu Yu* (islet) Fukien
83 H4 Wu-chou *Wuzhou* Kwangsi
Wuchow *see* Wu-chou
63 E7 Wu-chu *Wuzhu* Shensi
26 D4 Wu-ch'uan *Wuchuan* In. Mong.
119 B3 Wu-ch'uan *Wuquan* Taiwan
78 B3 Wu-ch'uan Hsien *Wuchuan Xian* Kwangt.
91 F2 Wu-ch'uan Hsien *Wuchuan Xian* Kwei.
114 C2 Wu-chung *Wuzhong* Ningsia
22 D3 Wu-erh-ch'i-han *Wuerqihan* Heilung.
102 D1 Wu-erh-ho *Wuerhe* Sink.
22 B3 Wu-erh-hsün Ho *Wuerxun He* (river) Heilung.
102 H2 Wu-erh-kou *Wuergou* Sink.
103 D2 Wu-erh-kou *Wuergou* Sink.
106 B2 Wu-erh-t'eng *Wuerteng* Tsing.
43 E2 Wu-fan *Wufan* Kiangsu
58 C4 Wu-feng *Wufeng* Hupeh
19 F2 Wu-feng *Wufeng* Liao.
118 B2 Wu-feng *Wufeng* Taiwan
118 C2 Wu-feng *Wufeng* Taiwan
119 B3 Wu-feng *Wufeng* Taiwan
75 D5 Wu-feng-p'u *Wufengpu* Hunan
18 B1 Wu-fen-ti *Wufendi* Liao.
99 G3 Wu-fo-ssu *Wufosi* Kansu
66 D3 Wu-fu *Wufu* Fukien
71 B5 Wu-fu-t'ing *Wufuting* Kiangsi
59 G4 Wu-han *Wuhan* Hupeh
Wu-han - city plan *see* Page 138
119 C3 Wu-hao *Wuhao* Taiwan
Wuhing *see* Wu-hsing
46 D3 Wu-ho *Wuhe* Anhwei
47 C6 Wu-ho *Wuhe* Anhwei
11 D5 Wu-ho *Wuhe* Heilung.
43 E4 Wu-hsi *Wuxi* Kiangsu
58 C3 Wu Hsia *Wu Xia* (gorge) Hupeh
87 H2 Wu Hsia *Wu Xia* (gorge) Szech.
51 E3 Wu-hsiang-ch'i *Wuxiangqi* Chek.
39 D5 Wu-hsiang Hsien *Wuxiang Xian* Shansi
43 E4 Wu Hsien *Wu Xian* Kiangsu
14 D3 Wu-hsing *Wuxing* Kirin
51 D2 Wu-hsing Hsien *Wuxing Xian* Chek.
83 F4 Wu-hsüan *Wuxuan* Kwangsi
59 H5 Wu-hsüeh *Wuxue* Hupeh
47 E5 Wu-hu *Wuhu* Anhwei
79 D2 Wu-hua *Wuhua* Kwangt.
19 E2 Wu-huan-ch'ih *Wuhuanchi* Liao.
43 D4 Wu-huang *Wuhuang* Kiangsu
47 E5 Wu-hu Hsien *Wuhu Xian* Anhwei
46 E4 Wu-i *Wuyi* Anhwei
51 C4 Wu-i *Wuyi* Chek.
31 C6 Wu-i *Wuyi* Hopeh
51 C4 Wu-i Chiang *Wuyi Jiang* (river) Chek.
102 H2 Wu-i-kung-she *Wuyigongshe* Sink.
10 E3 Wu-i-ling *Wuyiling* Heilung.
66 C3 Wu-i Shan-mo *Wuyi Shanmo* (mts) Fukien
67 B4 Wu-i Shan-mo *Wuyi Shanmo* (mts) Fukien
70 E4 Wu-i Shan-mo *Wuyi Shanmo* (mts) Kiangsi
31 C5 Wu-jen-ch'iao *Wurenqiao* Hopeh
27 E3 Wu-jih-te-no-erh *Wuridenuoer* In. Mong.
51 C2 Wu-k'ang *Wukang* Chek.
75 C5 Wu-kang *Wugang* Hunan
43 D2 Wu-kang *Wugang* Kiangsu
Wukiang *see* Wu-chiang
67 B5 Wu-ko *Wuge* Fukien
26 D4 Wu-k'o-hu-tung *Wukehudong* In. Mong.
14 D1 Wu-k'o-shu *Wukeshu* Kirin
14 G3 Wu-k'o-shu *Wukeshu* Kirin
23 E4 Wu-k'o-shu *Wukeshu* Kirin
102 I1 Wu-k'o-shu *Wukeshu* Sink.
74 F3 Wu-k'ou *Wukou* Hunan
55 F4 Wu-kou-ying *Wugouying* Honan
102 C3 Wu-k'u *Wuku* Sink.
63 F7 Wu-kuan *Wuguan* Shensi
31 C6 Wu-kuan-chai *Wuguanzhai* Hopeh
63 B7 Wu-kuan-ho *Wuguanhe* Shensi
55 E4 Wu-kung *Wugong* Honan
31 C5 Wu-kung *Wugong* Hopeh
63 D6 Wu-kung Hsien *Wugong Xian* Shensi
75 F5 Wu-kung Shan *Wugong Shan* (mts) Hunan
70 B4 Wu-kung Shan *Wugong Shan* (mts) Kiangsi
18 C2 Wu-kuo-t'ao-hai *Wuguotaohai* Liao.
14 G3 Wu-la-chieh *Wulajie* Kirin
118 C2 Wu-lai *Wulai* Taiwan
10 C1 Wu-la-kan *Wulagan* Heilung.
27 H1 Wu-la-ken Kuo-le *Wulagen Guole* (river) In. Mong.
102 H2 Wu-la-leng-ko *Wulalengge* Sink.
103 D2 Wu-la-leng-ko *Wulalengge* Sink.
Wu-lan *see* Hsi-li-kou
106 D1 Wu-lan *Wulan* Tsing.
107 E2 Wu-lan *Wulan* Tsing.
26 C4 Wu-lan-ai-li-kai-miao *Wulanailigaimiao* In. Mong.
14 C4 Wu-lan-ao-tao *Wulanaodao* Kirin
23 E6 Wu-lan-ao-tao *Wulanaodao* Kirin
27 D3 Wu-lan-ch'a-pu Meng *Wulanchabu Meng* In. Mong.
98 E1 Wu-lan-ch'üan-chi *Wulanquanji* Kansu
111 E3 Wu-lang *Wulang* Tibet
26 B5 Wu-lan-ha-la-ka-su *Wulanhalagasu* In. Mong.
26 C4 Wu-lan-hao-lai *Wulanhaolai* In. Mong.
14 C1 Wu-lan-hao-t'e *Wulanhaote* Kirin
23 E4 Wu-lan-hao-t'e *Wulanhaote* Kirin
27 E4 Wu-lan-ha-ta *Wulanhada* In. Mong.
14 A2 Wu-lan-ha-ta *Wulanhada* Kirin
14 C1 Wu-lan-ha-ta *Wulanhada* Kirin
23 D5 Wu-lan-ha-ta *Wulanhata* Kirin
23 E4 Wu-lan-ha-ta *Wulanhada* Kirin
27 F2 Wu-lan-hou-pu-erh *Wulanhoubuer* In. Mong.
107 F2 Wu-lan Hsien *Wulan Xian* Tsing.
26 D4 Wu-lan-hua *Wulanhua* In. Mong.
14 D4 Wu-lan-hua *Wulanhua* Kirin
23 E5 Wu-lan-hua *Wulanhua* Kirin
114 B1 Wu-lan-hu-hai *Wulanhuhai* Ningsia
106 D1 Wu-lan-ku-cha-erh *Wulanguzhaer* Tsing.
114 B2 Wu-lan-mao-tao *Wulanmaodao* Ningsia
23 D4 Wu-lan-mao-tu *Wulanmaodu* Kirin
26 B4 Wu-lan-pu-ho Sha-mo *Wulanbuhe Shamo* (desert) In. Mong.
114 C2 Wu-lan-pu-ho Sha-mo *Wulanbuhe Shamo* Ningsia
26 D4 Wu-lan-pu-lang *Wulanbulang* In. Mong.
14 C3 Wu-lan-shan *Wulanshan* Kirin
26 B4 Wu-lan-so-hai *Wulansuohai* In. Mong.
23 C6 Wu-lan-t'ao-hai *Wulantaohai* Liao.
107 E1 Wu-lan-ta-pan *Wulandaban Shan* (mts) Tsing.
106 B3 Wu-lan-wu-la Hu *Wulanwula Hu* (lake) Tsing.
39 B7 Wu-lao Feng *Wulao Feng* (mt) Shansi
102 H2 Wu-la-ssu-t'ai *Wulasitai* Sink.
Wu-la-su Hai *see* Wu-liang-su Hai
Wu-la-t'e Ch'ien-ch'i *see* Urat South Banner
Wu-la-t'e Chung-hou-lien-ho-ch'i *see* Urat Centre and North United Banner
35 G3 Wu-lei-tao Wan *Wuleidao Wan* (bay) Shant.
83 F5 Wu-li *Wuli* Kwangsi
106 C3 Wu-li *Wuli* Tsing.
94 C3 Wu-liang Shan *Wuliang Shan* (mt) Yun.
94 C3 Wu-liang Shan *Wuliang Shan* (mts) Yun.
26 C4 Wu-liang-su Hai *Wuliangsu Hai* (lake) In. Mong.
23 C6 Wu-li-chi-mu-jen Ho *Wulijimuren He* (river) Liao.
54 C4 Wu-li-ch'uan *Wulichuan* Honan
30 F2 Wu-lieh Ho *Wulie He* (river) Hopeh
87 E2 Wu-lien *Wulian* Szech.
35 E4 Wu-lien Hsien *Wulian Xian* Shant.
11 E5 Wu-lin *Wulin* Heilung.
83 G4 Wu-lin *Wulin* Kwangsi
54 D4 Wu-ling *Wuling* Honan
83 E4 Wu-ling *Wuling* Kwangsi
119 C4 Wu-ling *Wuling* Taiwan
87 G2 Wu-ling-chen *Wulingzhen* Szech.
30 E3 Wu-ling Shan *Wuling Shan* (mt) Hopeh
74 C3 Wu-ling Shan *Wuling Shan* (mts) Hunan
63 C8 Wu-li-pa *Wuliba* Shensi
63 D8 Wu-li-pa *Wuliba* Shensi
58 C5 Wu-li-p'ing *Wuliping* Hupeh
58 E4 Wu-li-p'u *Wulipu* Hupeh
55 F5 Wu-li-tien *Wulidian* Honan
71 B7 Wu-li-t'ing *Wuliting* Kiangsi
27 G2 Wu-li-ya-ssu-t'ai *Wuliyasitai* In. Mong.
91 F2 Wu-lo *Wuluo* Kwei.
91 F4 Wu-lo *Wuluo* Kwei.
119 C3 Wu-lu *Wulu* Taiwan
14 A3 Wu-lu-ken-ha-ta *Wulugenhada* Kirin
23 D5 Wu-lu-ken-ha-ta *Wulugenhada* Kirin
22 F2 Wu-lu-k'o *Wuluke* Heilung.
102 A3 Wu-lu-k'o-ch'ia-t'i *Wulukeqiati* Sink.
102 H2 Wu-lu-mu-ch'i *Wulumuqi* Sink.
103 D2 Wu-lu-mu-ch'i *Wulumuqi* Sink.
Wu-lu-mu-ch'i - city plan *see* Page 140
102 H2 Wu-lu-mu-ch'i Ho *Wulumuqi He* (river) Sink.
87 F3 Wu-lung *Wulong* Szech.
55 G5 Wu-lung-chi *Wulongji* Honan
35 F3 Wu-lung Ho *Wulong He* (river) Shant.
19 H4 Wu-lung-pei *Wulongbei* Liao.
62 F3 Wu-lung-p'u *Wulongpu* Shensi
103 E1 Wu-lun-ku Ho *Wulungu He* (river) Sink.
10 C3 Wu-lun-pu-t'ieh *Wulunbutie* Heilung.
22 D1 Wu-ma *Wuma* Heilung.
11 E4 Wu-ma-ho *Wumahe* Heilung.
70 B3 Wu-mei Shan *Wumei Shan* (mt) Kiangsi
90 B4 Wu-meng Shan *Wumeng Shan* (mts) Kwei.
95 E2 Wu-meng Shan *Wumeng Shan* (mts) Yun.
82 E4 Wu-ming *Wuming* Kwangsi
82 E4 Wu-ming Ho *Wuming He* (river) Kwangsi
118 C2 Wu-ming Shan *Wuming Shan* (mt) Taiwan
11 E4 Wu-min-ho *Wuminhe* Heilung.
71 B5 Wu-mu *Wumu* Kiangsi
102 H1 Wu-mu-k'o *Wumuke* Sink.
43 F3 Wu-nan Sha *Wunan Sha* (shoal) Kiangsu
70 C2 Wu-ning *Wuning* Kiangsi
70 B3 Wu-ning Shui *Wuning Shui* (river) Kiangsi
22 D3 Wu-nu-erh *Wunuer* Heilung.
55 E3 Wu-nü-tien *Wunüdian* Honan
26 B4 Wu-pai-erh-ha *Wubaierha* In. Mong.
39 B4 Wu-pao *Wubao* Shansi
62 F3 Wu-pao Hsien *Wubao Xian* Shensi
14 F3 Wu-p'i *Wupi* Kirin
67 B5 Wu-p'ing *Wuping* Fukien
86 D3 Wu-p'o *Wupo* Szech.
22 C3 Wu-pu-erh-pao-li-ko *Wubuerbaolige* Heilung.
23 D4 Wu-pu-lin-chia-la-ka *Wubulinjialaga* Kirin
106 D2 Wu-pu-su-i-cha-ha *Wubusuyizhaha* Tsing.
47 D6 Wu-sha *Wusha* Anhwei
90 B5 Wu-sha *Wusha* Kwei.
47 D4 Wu-shan *Wushan* Anhwei
59 F2 Wu-shan *Wushan* Hupeh
99 G4 Wu-shan *Wushan* Kansu
87 H2 Wu Shan *Wu Shan* (mts) Szech.
87 G2 Wu-shan *Wushan* Szech.
Wushek *see* Wu-shih
26 C5 Wu-shen-chao *Wushenzhao* In. Mong.
26 C5 Wu-shen Ch'i *Wushen Qi* In. Mong.
50 C3 Wu-sheng *Wusheng* Chek.
87 F2 Wu-sheng *Wusheng* Szech.
99 F3 Wu-sheng-i *Wushengyi* Kansu
55 F6 Wu-sheng Kuan *Wusheng Guan* (pass) Honan
59 F3 Wu-sheng Kuan *Wusheng Guan* (pass) Hupeh
70 D4 Wu-shih *Wushi* Kiangsi
78 A3 Wu-shih *Wushi* Kwangt.
78 A4 Wu-shih *Wushi* Kwangt.
79 C1 Wu-shih *Wushi* Kwangt.
102 B2 Wu-shih *Wushi* Sink.
103 D2 Wu-shih-ta-la *Wushidala* Sink.
74 B3 Wu Shui *Wu Shui* (river) Hunan
75 D5 Wu Shui *Wu Shui* (river) Hunan
79 C1 Wu Shui *Wu Shui* (river) Kwangt.
91 F3 Wu Shui *Wu Shui* (river) Kwei.
99 G4 Wu-shu Shan *Wushu Shan* (mt) Kansu
Wusih *see* Wu-hsi
102 D3 Wu-ssu-teng-t'a-ko Shan *Wusidengtage Shan* (mts) Sink.
67 B5 Wu-su *Wusuo* Fukien
102 D1 Wu-su *Wusu* Sink.
102 H1 Wu-su *Wusu* Sink.
Wusüeh *see* Wu-hsüeh
10 B1 Wu-su-li *Wusuli* Heilung.
22 E1 Wu-su-li *Wusuli* Heilung.
10 H4 Wu-su-li Chiang (River) Heilung.
43 F4 Wu-sung *Wusong* Kiangsu
43 F4 Wu-sung Chiang *Wusong Jiang* (river) Kiangsu
26 B5 Wu-ta *Wuda* In. Mong.
118 C2 Wu-t'a *Wuta* Taiwan
55 G4 Wu-t'ai *Wutai* Honan
38 E3 Wu-t'ai *Wutai* Shansi
34 C4 Wu-t'ai *Wutai* Shant.
102 C1 Wu-t'ai *Wutai* Sink.
119 B4 Wu-t'ai *Wutai* Taiwan
38 E2 Wu-t'ai Shan *Wutai Shan* (mt) Shansi
38 E3 Wu-t'ai Shan *Wutai Shan* (mts) Shansi
10 D3 Wu-ta-lien-ch'ih *Wudalianchi* Heilung.
74 D3 Wu-t'an *Wutan* Hunan
18 B2 Wu-tan *Wudan* Liao.
67 E5 Wu-t'ang *Wutang* Fukien
83 E5 Wu-t'ang *Wutang* Kwangsi
91 D4 Wu-tang *Wudang* Kwei.
58 D2 Wu-tang Shan *Wudang Shan* (mt) Hupeh
58 D2 Wu-tang Shan *Wudang Shan* (mts) Hupeh
18 E5 Wu-tao *Wudao* Liao.
14 G6 Wu-tao-chiang *Wudaojiang* Kirin
10 D2 Wu-tao-kou *Wudaogou* Heilung.
11 E4 Wu-tao-kou *Wudaogou* Heilung.
14 F5 Wu-tao-kou *Wudaogou* Kirin
15 K4 Wu-tao-kou *Wudaogou* Kirin
106 C3 Wu-tao-liang *Wudaoliang* Tsing.
74 B2 Wu-tao-shui *Wudaoshui* Hunan
23 E5 Wu-tao-ying-tzu *Wudaoyingzi* Kirin
50 C5 Wu-ta-pao *Wudabao* Chek.
82 C5 Wu-te *Wude* Kwangsi
34 C2 Wu-ti *Wudi* Shant.
46 D4 Wu-tien *Wudian* Anhwei
47 B5 Wu-tien *Wudian* Anhwei
67 C7 Wu-t'ien *Wutian* Fukien
59 E3 Wu-tien *Wudian* Hupeh
95 D3 Wu-ting *Wuding* Yun.
62 F3 Wu-ting Ho *Wuding He* (river) Shensi
119 B4 Wu-t'ou Shan *Wutou Shan* (mt) Taiwan
62 D3 Wu-ts'ang-pao *Wucangbao* Shensi
Wutsin *see* Ch'ang-chou
54 E2 Wu-ts'un *Wucun* Honan
82 C4 Wu-ts'un *Wucun* Kwangsi
79 E2 Wu-ts'un *Wucun* Kwangt.
34 C4 Wu-ts'un *Wucun* Shant.
102 D1 Wu-tsun-pu-la-k'o *Wuzunbulake* Sink.
103 E2 Wu-tsun Pu-la-k'o *Wuzun Bulake* (spring) Sink.
50 B5 Wu-tu *Wudu* Chek.
99 G5 Wu-tu *Wudu* Kansu
70 F3 Wu-tu *Wudu* Kiangsi
87 E2 Wu-tu *Wudu* Szech.
58 D3 Wu-tu-ho *Wuduhe* Hupeh
106 C2 Wu-t'u-mei-jen *Wutumeiren* Tsing.
106 C2 Wu-t'u-mei-jen Ho *Wutumeiren He* (river) Tsing.
63 C7 Wu-tu-men *Wudumen* Shensi
67 D5 Wu-t'ung *Wutong* Fukien
83 G2 Wu-t'ung *Wutong* Kwangsi
39 C4 Wu-t'ung *Wutong* Shansi
87 D3 Wu-t'ung-ch'iao *Wutongqiao* Szech.
18 D2 Wu-t'ung-hao-lai *Wutonghaolai* Liao.
11 F4 Wu-t'ung-ho *Wutonghe* Heilung.
103 E2 Wu-t'ung-kou *Wutonggou* Sink.
103 F2 Wu-t'ung-wo-tzu Ch'üan *Wutongwozi Quan* (spring) Sink.
103 D1 Wu-t'u-pu-la-k'o *Wutubulake* Sink.
102 A3 Wu-tzu-pieh-li Shan-k'ou *Wuzibieli Shankou* (pass) Sink.
102 H2 Wu-wa-men *Wuwamen* Sink.
31 B4 Wu-wang-k'ou *Wuwangkou* Hopeh
47 D5 Wu-wei *Wuwei* Anhwei
99 F3 Wu-wei *Wuwei* Kansu
55 E4 Wu-yang *Wuyang* Honan
75 C5 Wu-yang *Wuyang* Hunan
71 C6 Wu-yang *Wuyang* Kiangsi
91 F3 Wu-yang *Wuyang* Kwei.
39 E5 Wu-yang *Wuyang* Shansi
11 E5 Wu-ya-p'ao *Wuyapao* Heilung.
51 D5 Wu-yen *Wuyan* Chek.
118 C2 Wu-yen Chiao *Wuyan Jiao* (point) Taiwan
Wuyi *see* Wu-i
Wuyi Mountains *see* Wu-i Shan
Wuyi Mountains *see* Wu-i Shan-mo
10 E3 Wu-ying *Wuying* Heilung.
43 E2 Wu-yu *Wuyou* Kiangsu
82 E5 Wu-yü *Wuyu* Kwangsi
110 D3 Wu-yü *Wuyu* Tibet
26 C4 Wu-yüan *Wuyuan* In. Mong.
70 E2 Wu-yüan *Wuyuan* Kiangsi
51 D2 Wu-yüan-chen *Wuyuanzhen* Chek.
54 C3 Wu-yüan-ts'un *Wuyuancun* Honan
10 E3 Wu-yün *Wuyun* Heilung.
71 B5 Wu-yün-ch'iao *Wuyunqiao* Kiangsi
86 D3 Ya-an *Yaan* Szech.
111 E3 Ya-an-to *Yaanduo* Tibet
111 E3 Ya-an-to *Yaanduo* Tibet
78 A4 Ya-ch'a *Yacha* Kwangt.
82 C3 Ya-ch'ang *Yachang* Kwangsi
66 F4 Ya-ch'eng *Yacheng* Fukien
78 A4 Ya-ch'eng *Yacheng* Kwangt.
107 H2 Ya-ch'eng *Yacheng* Tsing.
43 D4 Ya-ch'i *Yaqi* Kiangsu
86 C2 Ya-chiang *Yajiang* Szech.
75 F4 Ya-chiang-ch'iao *Yajiangqiao* Hunan
47 C6 Ya-ch'ien *Yaqian* Anhwei
70 D3 Ya-ch'ien *Yaqian* Kiangsi
71 B5 Ya-ch'ien *Yaqian* Kiangsi
91 D3 Ya-ch'ih Ho *Yachi He* (river) Kwei.
43 E3 Ya-chou *Yazhou* Kiangsu
91 E5 Ya-chou *Yazhou* Kwei.
Yachow *see* Ya-an
91 E3 Ya-ch'uan *Yachuan* Kwei.
34 D3 Ya-chuang *Yazhuang* Shant.
58 D4 Ya-ch'üeh-ling *Yaqueling* Hupeh
58 B4 Ya-ch'üeh-shui *Yaqueshui* Hupeh
111 F3 Ya-chung *Yazhong* Tibet
50 C3 Ya-fan *Yafan* Chek.
Yagmo *see* Ya-ko-mu
11 F5 Ya-ho *Yahe* Heilung.
106 D3 Ya-ho-la-ta-ho-tse Shan *Yaheladaheze Shan* (mt) Tsing.
91 D3 Ya-hsi *Yaxi* Kwei.
110 B2 Ya-hsieh Ts'o *Yaxie Cuo* (lake) Tibet
78 A4 Ya-hsing *Yaxing* Kwangt.
30 E4 Ya-hung-ch'iao *Yahongqiao* Hopeh
78 A4 Yai Hsien *Yai Xian* Kwangt.
Yak Lake *see* Ya-k'o Ts'o
106 C4 Ya-ko-chang-k'a *Yagezhangka* Tsing.
106 D4 Ya-ko Ch'ü *Yage Qu* (river) Tsing.
110 D2 Ya-ko-mu *Yagemu* Tibet
22 D3 Ya-k'o-shih *Yakeshi* Heilung.
110 C2 Ya-k'o Ts'o *Yake Cuo* (lake) Tibet
31 B6 Ya-ko-ying *Yageying* Hopeh
111 E3 Ya-la *Yala* Tibet
31 B7 Ya-li Chi *Yali Ji* Hopeh
22 E3 Ya-lu *Yalu* Heilung.
19 H4 Ya-lü Chiang (River) Liao.
22 E3 Ya-lu Ho *Yalu He* (river) Heilung.
86 C2 Ya-lung Chiang *Yalong Jiang* (river) Szech.
Ya-lung-tsang-pu Chiang *see* Brahmaputra
Yalu River *see* Ya-lü Chiang
111 D3 Ya-lu-tsang-pu Chiang *Yaluzangbu Jiang* (river) Tibet
Ya-lu-tsung-pu Chiang *see* Brahmaputra
103 F2 Ya-man-su *Yamansu* Sink.
102 C2 Ya-ma-tu *Yamadu* Sink.
Yamchow Bay *see* Ch'in-chou Wan
Yamdrok Tso *see* Yang-cho-yung Hu
107 G2 Ya-men-chuang *Yamenzhuang* Tsing.
23 C6 Ya-men-miao *Yamenmiao* Liao.
14 B5 Ya-men-ying-tzu *Yamenyingzi* Kirin
14 C4 Ya-men-ying-tzu *Yamenyingzi* Kirin
23 D6 Ya-men-ying-tzu *Yamenyingzi* Kirin
23 E6 Ya-men-ying-tzu *Yamenyingzi* Kirin
Yanchow *see* Ch'in-chou
Yangamdo *see* Ya-an-to
83 G3 Yang-an *Yangan* Kwangsi
34 C2 Yang-an *Yangan* Shant.
43 D2 Yang-chai *Yangzhai* Kiangsu
90 C4 Yang-ch'ang *Yangchang* Kwei.
91 D4 Yang-ch'ang *Yangchang* Kwei.
91 D5 Yang-ch'ang *Yangchang* Kwei.
91 E4 Yang-ch'ang *Yangchang* Kwei.
91 F3 Yang-ch'ang *Yangchang* Kwei.
95 E2 Yang-ch'ang *Yangchang* Yun.
90 C3 Yang-ch'ang-pa *Yangchangba* Kwei.
39 D6 Yang-ch'eng *Yangcheng* Shansi
47 E6 Yang-ch'i *Yangqi* Anhwei
50 C3 Yang-ch'i *Yangqi* Chek.
66 C4 Yang-ch'i *Yangqi* Fukien
55 G2 Yang-chi *Yangji* Honan
55 H3 Yang-chi *Yangji* Honan
74 D4 Yang-ch'i *Yangqi* Hunan
70 D3 Yang-ch'i *Yangqi* Kiangsi
71 B4 Yang-ch'i *Yangqi* Kiangsi
43 D1 Yang-chi *Yangji* Kiangsu
34 D5 Yang-chi *Yangji* Shant.
59 G3 Yang-chia-chai *Yangjiazhai* Hupeh
34 D4 Yang-chia-chai *Yangjiazhai* Shant.
18 D4 Yang-chia-chang-tzu *Yangjiazhangzi* Liao.
59 E4 Yang-chia-chiang *Yangjiajiang* Hupeh
39 C4 Yang-chia-chuang *Yangjiazhuang* Shansi
63 C8 Yang-chia-ho *Yangjiahe* Shensi
63 E7 Yang-chia-hsieh *Yangjiaxie* Shensi
62 E4 Yang-chia-ling *Yangjialing* Shensi
70 B4 Yang-chiang *Yangjiang* Kiangsi
78 B3 Yang-chiang *Yangjiang* Kwangt.
31 C7 Yang-ch'iao *Yangqiao* Hopeh
70 B4 Yang-ch'iao *Yangqiao* Hunan
74 B4 Yang-ch'iao *Yangqiao* Kiangsi
87 F3 Yang-chiao-chen *Yangjiaozhen* Szech.
35 D2 Yang-chiao-kou *Yangjiaogou* Shant.
62 E3 Yang-chiao-p'an *Yangjiaopan* Shensi
75 E5 Yang-chiao-t'ang *Yangjiaotang* Hunan
74 D4 Yang-chia-t'an *Yangjiatan* Hunan
18 E5 Yang-chia-tien *Yangjiadian* Liao.
63 D5 Yang-chia-tien *Yangjiadian* Shensi
90 B3 Yang-chia-wan *Yangjiawan* Kwei.
38 C2 Yang-chia-ying *Yangjiaying* Shansi
62 E3 Yang-chia-yüan-tzu *Yangjiayuanzi* Shensi
95 D3 Yang-chieh *Yangjie* Yun.
90 B3 Yang-chieh-tzu *Yangjiezi* Kwei.
67 D6 Yang-chih *Yangzhi* Fukien
62 C3 Yang-ching *Yangjing* Shensi
39 E5 Yang-ching-ti *Yangjingdi* Shansi
43 D3 Yang-chou *Yangzhou* Kiangsu
Yangchow *see* Yang-chou
111 D3 Yang-cho-yung Hu *Yangzhuoyong Hu* (lake) Tibet
35 F2 Yang-ch'u *Yangchu* Shant.
75 E5 Yang-chüan *Yangjuan* Hunan
91 E3 Yang-ch'uan *Yangchuan* Kwei.
38 E4 Yang-ch'üan *Yangquan* Shansi
62 E5 Yang-ch'üan *Yangquan* Shensi
39 C4 Yang-ch'üan-ch'ü *Yangquanqu* Shansi
38 E2 Yang-chuang *Yangzhuang* Shansi
34 C5 Yang-chuang *Yangzhuang* Shant.
34 B4 Yang-chuang-chi *Yangzhuangji* Shant.
102 H2 Yang-chuan-kou *Yangzhuangou* Sink.
34 C3 Yang-ch'ün-tzu *Yangqunzi* Liao.
38 D4 Yang-chü-chen *Yangjuzhen* Shansi
38 D3 Yang-ch'ü Hsien *Yangqu Xian* Shansi
78 B2 Yang-ch'un *Yangchun* Kwangt.
66 D4 Yang-chung *Yangzhong* Fukien
43 D3 Yang-chung *Yangzhong* Kiangsu
86 B1 Yang-chung *Yangzhong* Szech.
31 E5 Yang-erh-chuang *Yangerzhuang* Hopeh
38 D2 Yang-fang-k'ou *Yangfangkou* Shansi

59 G5 **Yang-fang-lin** *Yangfanglin* Hupeh
42 C2 **Yang-ho** *Yanghe* Kiangsu
19 G4 **Yang-ho** *Yanghe* Liao.
114 C2 **Yang-ho** *Yanghe* Ningsia
30 C3 **Yang Ho** *Yang He* (river) Hopeh
58 D4 **Yang-hsi** *Yangxi* Hupeh
102 D2 **Yang-hsia** *Yangxia* Sink.
43 D4 **Yang-hsiang** *Yangxiang* Kiangsu
63 C7 **Yang-hsien** *Yangxian* Shensi
59 G5 **Yang-hsin** *Yangxin* Hupeh
59 H5 **Yang-hsin** *Yangxin* Hupeh
34 C2 **Yang-hsin** *Yangxin* Shant.
38 D3 **Yang-hsing** *Yangxing* Shansi
42 C2 **Yang-hua** *Yanghua* Kiangsu
90 B4 **Yang-huai-shu** *Yanghuaishu* Kwei.
46 C4 **Yang-hu-chen** *Yanghuzhen* Anhwei
31 A7 **Yang-i** *Yangyi* Hopeh
39 D4 **Yang-i** *Yangyi* Shansi
11 G5 **Yang-kang** *Yanggang* Heilung.
38 E1 **Yang-kao** *Yanggao* Shansi
Yangkiachangtze *see* **Yang-chia-chang-tzu**
Yangkiokow *see* **Yang-chiao-kou**
30 D3 **Yang-ko-chuang** *Yanggezhuang* Hopeh
66 C4 **Yang-k'ou** *Yangkou* Fukien
70 F3 **Yang-k'ou** *Yangkou* Kiangsi
50 B4 **Yang-k'ou-shih** *Yangkoushi* Chek.
55 F3 **Yang-ku** *Yanggu* Honan
34 A3 **Yang-ku** *Yanggu* Shant.
47 C5 **Yang-kung-miao** *Yanggongmiao* Anhwei
70 C3 **Yang-kung-yü** *Yanggongyu* Kiangsi
63 E6 **Yang-kuo** *Yangguo* Shensi
59 E5 **Yang-lin** *Yanglin* Hupeh
95 D3 **Yang-lin** *Yanglin* Yun.
74 E3 **Yang-lin-chai** *Yanglinzhai* Hunan
75 F4 **Yang-lin-ch'iao** *Yanglinqiao* Hunan
63 D6 **Yang-ling** *Yangling* Shensi
59 F4 **Yang-lin-wei** *Yanglinwei* Hupeh
91 E4 **Yang-liu-chieh** *Yangliujie* Kwei.
58 C4 **Yang-liu-ch'ih** *Yangliuchi* Hupeh
31 E4 **Yang-liu-ch'ing** *Yangliuqing* Hopeh
47 E6 **Yang-liu-p'u** *Yangliupu* Anhwei
34 B4 **Yang-liu-tien** *Yangliudian* Shant.
34 C3 **Yang-liu-tien** *Yangliudian* Shant.
59 G4 **Yang-lo** *Yangluo* Hupeh
46 C2 **Yang-lou** *Yanglou* Anhwei
34 B5 **Yang-lou** *Yanglou* Shant.
74 F2 **Yang-lou-ssu** *Yanglousi* Hunan
59 F5 **Yang-lou-tung** *Yangloudong* Hupeh
91 D3 **Yang-lung-chan** *Yanglongzhan* Kwei.
35 G2 **Yang-ma Tao** *Yangma Dao* (island) Shant.
83 G5 **Yang-mei** *Yangmei* Kwangsi
118 C2 **Yang-mei** *Yangmei* Taiwan
71 B6 **Yang-mei-ssu** *Yangmeisi* Kiangsi
55 F3 **Yang-miao** *Yangmiao* Honan
18 B3 **Yang-mi Ho** *Yangmi He* (river) Liao.
79 D1 **Yang-ming** *Yangming* Kwangt.
38 D2 **Yang-ming-pao** *Yangmingbao* Shansi
75 D5 **Yang-ming Shan** *Yangming Shan* (mt) Hunan
118 C1 **Yang-ming-shan** *Yangmingshan* Taiwan
11 G5 **Yang-mu-kang** *Yangmugang* Heilung.
14 F5 **Yang-mu-lin** *Yangmulin* Kirin
91 C6 **Yang-pa** *Yangba* Kwei.
111 D3 **Yang-pa-ching** *Yangbajing* Tibet
94 B3 **Yang-pi** *Yangbi* Yun.
54 B3 **Yang-p'ing** *Yangping* Honan
58 D3 **Yang-p'ing** *Yangping* Hupeh
91 F3 **Yang-p'ing** *Yangping* Kwei.
38 C3 **Yang-p'ing** *Yangping* Shansi
63 B8 **Yang-p'ing-kuan** *Yangpingguan* Shensi
38 D3 **Yang-p'o** *Yangpo* Shansi
51 C1 **Yang-p'u** *Yangpu* Chek.
55 F5 **Yang-pu** *Yangbu* Honan
78 A4 **Yang-p'u Wan** *Yangpu Wan* (bay) Kwangt.
67 D5 **Yang-shan** *Yangshan* Fukien
79 C1 **Yang-shan** *Yangshan* Kwangt.
18 D3 **Yang-shan** *Yangshan* Liao.
34 B4 **Yang-shan** *Yangshan* Shant.
26 D4 **Yang-shan Shan-mo** *Yangshan Shanmo* (mts) In. Mong.
54 C3 **Yang-shao** *Yangshao* (site) Honan
43 E4 **Yang-she** *Yangshe* Kiangsu
30 F2 **Yang-shu-ling** *Yangshuling* Hopeh
83 G3 **Yang-shuo** *Yangshuo* Kwangsi
Yangsin *see* **Yang-hsin**
Yangsiu *see* **Yung-hsiu**
14 E4 **Yang-ta-ch'eng-tzu** *Yangdachengzi* Kirin
23 F6 **Yang-ta-ch'eng-tzu** *Yangdachengzi* Kirin
102 C2 **Yang-t'a-k'o-k'u-tu-k'o** *Yangtakekuduke* Sink.
47 F6 **Yang-t'an** *Yangtan* Anhwei
39 C6 **Yang-t'an** *Yangtan* Shansi
59 E2 **Yang-tang** *Yangdang* Hupeh
27 F3 **Yang-tao-su-mu** *Yangdaosumu* In. Mong.
103 E3 **Yang-ta-shih-k'o** *Yangdashike* Sink.
91 D2 **Yang-teng** *Yangdeng* Kwei.
54 B3 **Yang-tien** *Yangdian* Honan
59 G3 **Yang-tien** *Yangdian* Hupeh
43 D4 **Yang-tien** *Yangdian* Kiangsu
30 F3 **Yang-tien-tzu** *Yangdianzi* Hopeh
46 D3 **Yang-t'ing** *Yangting* Anhwei
35 H2 **Yang-t'ing** *Yangting* Shant.
94 C3 **Yang-t'ou-yen** *Yangtouyan* Yun.
54 E5 **Yang-ts'e** *Yangce* Honan
110 B2 **Yang Ts'o** *Yangcuo* (lake) Tibet
30 E4 **Yang-ts'un** *Yangcun* Hopeh
31 C4 **Yang-ts'un** *Yangcun* Hopeh
70 E3 **Yang-ts'un** *Yangcun* Kiangsi
71 B7 **Yang-ts'un** *Yangcun* Kiangsi
79 D2 **Yang-ts'un** *Yangcun* Kwangt.
46 E4 **Yang-ts'un-chen** *Yangcunzhen* Anhwei
50 C3 **Yang-ts'un-ch'iao** *Yangcunqiao* Chek.
Yangtze *see* **T'ung-t'ien Ho**
Yangtze *see* **Chin-sha Chiang**
Yangtze *see* **Ch'ang Chiang**
Yangtze *see* **Ch'ang Chiang**
Yangtze *see* **Ch'ang Chiang**
Yangtze *see* **Chin-sha Chiang**
Yangtze *see* **Ch'ang Chiang**
Yangtze *see* **Ch'ang Chiang**
59 E3 **Yang-tzu** *Yangzi* Hupeh
70 D2 **Yang-tzu-ch'iao** *Yangziqiao* Kiangsi
14 D2 **Yang-tzu-ching** *Yangzijing* Kirin
14 G5 **Yang-tzu-shao** *Yangzishao* Kirin
58 C2 **Yang-wei** *Yangwei* Hupeh
95 D4 **Yang-wu** *Yangwu* Yun.
82 C4 **Yang-yü** *Yangyu* Kwangsi
82 E4 **Yang-yü** *Yangyu* Kwangsi
30 B3 **Yang-yüan Hsien** *Yangyuan Xian* Hopeh
30 B3 **Yang-yüan Hsien** *Yangyuan Xian* Hopeh
Yanping *see* **En-p'ing**
34 A3 **Yan-tien** *Yandian* Shant.
94 C3 **Yao-an** *Yaoan* Yun.
82 D3 **Yao-chai** *Yaozhai* Kwangsi
10 C2 **Yao-chan** *Yaozhan* Heilung.
62 F2 **Yao-chen** *Yaozhen* Shensi
31 B6 **Yao-ch'eng** *Yaocheng* Hopeh
59 G3 **Yao-chia-chi** *Yaojiaji* Hupeh
74 F4 **Yao-chia-pa** *Yaojiaba* Hunan
91 D4 **Yao-chia-shao** *Yaojiashao* Kwei.
34 D4 **Yao-chia-tien-tzu** *Yaojiadianzi* Shant.
99 F3 **Yao-chieh** *Yaojie* Kansu
14 D3 **Yao-ching** *Yaojing* Kirin
98 C2 **Yao-ch'üan-tzu** *Yaoquanzi* Kansu
47 C5 **Yao-hsiao-chuang** *Yaoxiaozhuang* Anhwei
10 D3 **Yao-hsiao-ling** *Yaoxiaoling* Heilung.
63 D6 **Yao-hsien** *Yaoxian* Shensi
75 F6 **Yao-kang-hsien** *Yaogangxian* Hunan
35 E3 **Yao-ko-chuang** *Yaogezhuang* Shant.
47 D5 **Yao-kou** *Yaogou* Anhwei
34 D3 **Yao-kou** *Yaogou* Shant.
46 C4 **Yao-k'ou-chi** *Yaokouji* Anhwei
79 C2 **Yao-ku** *Yaogu* Kwangt.
94 B3 **Yao-kuan** *Yaoguan* Yun.
31 D5 **Yao-kuan-t'un** *Yaoguantun* Hopeh
70 E2 **Yao-li** *Yaoli* Kiangsi
14 C3 **Yao-li-mao-tu** *Yaolimaodu* Kirin
23 E5 **Yao-li-mao-tu** *Yaolimaodu* Kirin
47 C5 **Yao-li-miao** *Yaolimiao* Anhwei
15 G6 **Yao-lin** *Yaolin* Kirin
79 C1 **Yao-ling** *Yaoling* Kwangt.
47 B5 **Yao-ling-t'ou** *Yaolingtou* Anhwei
47 C5 **Yao-lo-p'ing** *Yaoluoping* Anhwei
18 C4 **Yao-lu-kou** *Yaolugou* Liao.
23 E5 **Yao-min-wang-t'un** *Yaominwangtun* Kirin
114 C2 **Yao-pa** *Yaoba* Ningsia
19 F2 **Yao-pao** *Yaobao* Liao.
75 F5 **Yao-p'o** *Yaopo* Hunan
46 E4 **Yao-p'u** *Yaopu* Anhwei
43 E2 **Yao Sha** *Yao Sha* (shoal) Kiangsu
67 B5 **Yao-shan** *Yaoshan* Fukien
79 C1 **Yao-Shan** *Yaoshan* (mts) Kwangt.
114 C3 **Yao-shan** *Yaoshan* Ningsia
30 E3 **Yao-shang** *Yaoshang* Hopeh
75 B5 **Yao-shang** *Yaoshang* Hunan
75 F6 **Yao-shang** *Yaoshang* Hunan
74 B4 **Yao-shih** *Yaoshi* Hunan
99 H4 **Yao-tien** *Yaodian* Kansu
62 E4 **Yao-tien-tzu** *Yaodianzi* Shensi
102 I2 **Yao-tien-tzu** *Yaodianzi* Sink.
71 B5 **Yao-t'ou** *Yaotou* Kiangsi
38 C3 **Yao-t'ou** *Yaotou* Shansi
39 B5 **Yao-t'ou** *Yaotou* Shansi
47 F6 **Yao-ts'un** *Yaocun* Anhwei
55 E1 **Yao-ts'un** *Yaocun* Honan
31 C4 **Yao-ts'un** *Yaocun* Hopeh
34 B4 **Yao-ts'un** *Yaocun* Shant.
47 D6 **Yao-tu** *Yaodu* Anhwei
10 D3 **Yao-t'un** *Yaotun* Heilung.
62 D4 **Yao-tzu-ch'uan** *Yaozichuan* Shensi
38 D2 **Yao-tzu-t'ou** *Yaozitou* Shansi
26 C4 **Yao-tzu-wan** *Yaoziwan* In. Mong.
42 C1 **Yao-wan** *Yaowan* Kiangsu
14 C2 **Yao-yen** *Yaoyan* Kirin
23 E5 **Yao-yen** *Yaoyan* Kirin
70 C4 **Yao-yü** *Yaoyu* Kiangsi
99 F2 **Ya-pu-lai** *Yabulai* Kansu
99 F2 **Ya-pu-lai Shan** *Yabulai Shan* (mts) Kansu
99 F2 **Ya-pu-lai-yen-ch'ih** *Yabulaiyanchi* Kansu
11 E5 **Ya-pu-li** *Yabuli* Heilung.
Yarkand *see* **So-ch'e**
Yarkand Darya *see* **Yeh-erh-ch'iang Ho**
47 E6 **Ya-shan** *Yashan* Anhwei
106 D2 **Ya-sha-t'u** *Yashatu* Tsing.
Yashil Tso *see* **Ya-hsieh Ts'o**
47 C6 **Ya-t'an** *Yatan* Anhwei
35 H2 **Ya-t'ou** *Yatou* Shant.
10 B3 **Ya-tung** *Yadong* Heilung.
22 E3 **Ya-tung** *Yadong* Heilung.
110 D4 **Ya-tung** *Yadong* Tibet
102 C3 **Ya-t'ung-ku-tzu-lan-kan** *Yatongguzilangan* Sink.
75 B5 **Ya-t'un-pao** *Yatunbao* Hunan
35 G2 **Ya-tzu** *Yazi* Shant.
74 E3 **Ya-tzu-kang** *Yazigang* Hunan
86 B2 **Ya-wa** *Yawa* Szech.
34 C3 **Ya-wang-k'ou** *Yawangkou* Shant.
106 C4 **Ya-yün Ch'ü** *Yayun Qu* (river) Tsing.
102 B3 **Yeh-ch'eng** *Yecheng* Sink.
30 F4 **Yeh-chi-t'o** *Yejituo* Hopeh
102 B3 **Yeh-erh-ch'iang Ho** *Yeerqiang He* (river) Sink.
54 E4 **Yeh-hsien** *Yexian* Honan
35 E2 **Yeh-hsien** *Yexian* Shant.
102 C3 **Yeh-i-k'o** *Yeyike* Sink.
111 E3 **Yeh-kung** *Yegong* Tibet
111 E3 **Yeh-kung Ch'ü** *Yegongqu* (river) Tibet
14 A5 **Yeh-la-ma-t'u** *Yelamatu* Kirin
23 D6 **Yeh-la-ma-t'u** *Yelamatu* Kirin
99 F4 **Yeh-li-kuan** *Yeliguan* Kansu
118 C1 **Yeh-liu Chia** *Yeliu Jia* (point) Taiwan
106 C3 **Yeh-lu-su Hu** *Yelusu Hu* (lake) Tsing.
90 B3 **Yeh-ma-ch'uan** *Yemachuan* Kwei.
98 C2 **Yeh-ma Ho** *Yema He* (river) Kansu
98 B2 **Yeh-ma Nan-shan** *Yema Nanshan* (mts) Kansu
19 F2 **Yeh-mao-t'ai** *Yemaotai* Liao.
105 E3 **Yeh-ma-t'an** *Yematan* Tsing.
107 F2 **Yeh-ma-t'an** *Yematan* Tsing.
14 B2 **Yeh-ma-t'u** *Yematu* Kirin
23 D5 **Yeh-ma-t'u** *Yematu* Kirin
106 B2 **Yeh-men-k'o** *Yemenke* Tsing.
107 E3 **Yeh-niu-kou** *Yeniugou* Tsing.
107 F1 **Yeh-niu-kou** *Yeniugou* Tsing.
18 C3 **Yeh-pai-shou** *Yebaishou* Liao.
71 D6 **Yeh-p'ing** *Yeping* Kiangsi
Yehposhow *see* **Yeh-pai-shou**
58 C4 **Yeh-san-kuan** *Yesanguan* Hupeh
106 D4 **Yeh-ta Ch'ü** *Yeda Qu* (river) Tsing.
31 B6 **Yeh-ts'ao-wan** *Yecaowan* Hopeh
63 F7 **Yeh-ts'un** *Yecun* Shensi
119 C4 **Yeh-yu** *Yeyou* Taiwan
102 D2 **Yeh-yün-kou** *Yeyungou* Sink.
Yellow River *see* **Huang Ho**
Yellow River *see* **Huang Ho**
35 G4 **Yellow Sea** Shant.
62 E4 **Yen-an** *Yanan* Shensi
62 E4 **Yen-an Hsien** *Yanan Xian* Shensi
39 D5 **Yen-chai** *Yanzhai* Shansi
39 C6 **Yen-chang** *Yanzhang* Shansi
62 F4 **Yen-ch'ang** *Yanchang* Shensi
62 C3 **Yen-ch'ang-pao** *Yanchangbao* Shensi
31 B5 **Yen-chao** *Yanzhao* Hopeh
119 B4 **Yen-ch'ao** *Yanchao* Taiwan
55 E4 **Yen-ch'eng** *Yancheng* Honan
43 E2 **Yen-ch'eng** *Yancheng* Kiangsu
34 B3 **Yen-ch'eng** *Yancheng* Shant.
67 C6 **Yen-ch'i** *Yanqi* Fukien
30 C3 **Yen-ch'i** *Yanqi* Hopeh
74 C3 **Yen-ch'i** *Yanqi* Hunan
70 C4 **Yen-ch'i** *Yanqi* Kiangsi
42 C1 **Yen-chi** *Yanji* Kiangsu
15 J5 **Yen-chi** *Yanji* Kirin
103 D2 **Yen-ch'i** *Yanqi* Sink.
18 E3 **Yen-chia** *Yanjia* Liao.
11 F4 **Yen-chia** *Yenjia* Heilung.
55 F6 **Yen-chia-ho** *Yanjiahe* Honan
63 B6 **Yen-chia-ho** *Yanjiahe* Shensi
82 D4 **Yen-chiang** *Yanjiang* Kwangsi
74 B4 **Yen-ch'iao** *Yanqiao* Hunan
90 C4 **Yen-chiao** *Yanjiao* Kwei.
66 C4 **Yen-ch'ien** *Yanqian* Fukien
67 B6 **Yen-ch'ien** *Yenqian* Fukien
114 D3 **Yen-ch'ih** *Yanchi* Ningsia
103 F2 **Yen-ch'ih** *Yanchi* Sink.
98 E2 **Yen-chih Shan** *Yanzhi Shan* (mt) Kansu
15 J5 **Yen-chi Hsien** *Yanji Xian* Kirin
Yen-ch'i Hui-tsu Tzu-chih-hsien *see* **Yen-ch'i Hui Autonomous Hsien**
98 B2 **Yen-ch'ih-wan** *Yanchiwan* Kansu
27 H2 **Yen-chi-ko-miao** *Yanjigemiao* In. Mong.
55 F2 **Yen-chin** *Yanjin* Honan
95 E1 **Yen-chin** *Yanjin* Yun.
30 C3 **Yen-ch'ing** *Yanqing* Hopeh
39 B6 **Yen-ching** *Yanjing* Shansi
87 F3 **Yen-ching** *Yanjing* Szech.
111 F3 **Yen-ching** *Yanjing* Tibet
71 B5 **Yen-ch'i-tu** *Yanqidu* Kiangsi
54 D3 **Yen-ch'iu** *Yanqiu* Honan
55 F2 **Yen-chou** *Yanzhou* Honan
34 B4 **Yen-chou** *Yanzhou* Shant.
Yenchow *see* **Chien-te**
62 F4 **Yen-ch'uan** *Yanchuan* Shensi
38 D3 **Yen-chuang** *Yanzhuang* Shansi
34 C3 **Yen-chuang** *Yanzhuang* Shant.
Yenchwan *see* **Yen-ch'uan**
38 E2 **Yen-erh-yai** *Yanerya* Shansi
95 E3 **Yen-fang** *Yanfang* Yun.
94 C3 **Yen-feng** *Yanfeng* Yun.
59 H3 **Yen-ho** *Yanhe* Hupeh
91 F2 **Yen-ho** *Yanhe* Kwei.
43 D2 **Yen Ho** *Yan He* (river) Kiangsu
62 F4 **Yen Ho** *Yan He* (river) Shensi
30 C3 **Yen-ho-ch'eng** *Yanhecheng* Hopeh
62 E4 **Yen-ho-wan** *Yanhewan* Shensi
30 G3 **Yen-ho-ying** *Yanheying* Hopeh
10 F4 **Yen-hsing** *Yanxing* Heilung.
102 I2 **Yen-hu** *Yanhu* Sink.
103 E2 **Yen-hu** *Yanhu* Sink.
106 D2 **Yen-hu** *Yanhu* Tsing.
38 E4 **Yen-hui** *Yanhui* Shansi
Yenki *see* **Yen-chi**
30 F4 **Yen-ko-chuang** *Yangezhuang* Hopeh
46 C4 **Yen-k'ou** *Yankou* Anhwei
43 D4 **Yen-k'ou** *Yankou* Kiangsu
51 D2 **Yen-kuan** *Yanguan* Chek.
99 G4 **Yen-kuan** *Yanguan* Kansu
83 G2 **Yen-kuan-hsiang** *Yanguanxiang* Kwangsi
47 E6 **Yen-kung-t'ang** *Yangongtang* Anhwei
82 D4 **Yen-li** *Yanli* Kwangsi
39 D6 **Yen-li** *Yanli* Shansi
63 E6 **Yen-liang** *Yanliang* Shensi
55 F3 **Yen-ling** *Yanling* Honan
43 D4 **Yen-ling** *Yanling* Kiangsu
47 C4 **Yen-liu-miao** *Yenliumiao* Anhwei
30 B4 **Yen-mei-tung** *Yenmeidong* Hopeh
74 B4 **Yen-men** *Yanmen* Hunan
87 E1 **Yen-men-pa** *Yanmenba* Szech.
38 E2 **Yen-pei** *Yanbei* Shansi
38 E1 **Yen-pei Ti-ch'ü** *Yanbei Diqu* Shansi
86 C4 **Yen-pien** *Yanbian* Szech.
Yen-pien Ch'ao-hsien-tsu Tzu-chih-chou *see* **Yen-pien Korean Autonomous District**
15 J4 **Yen-pien Korean Autonomous District** Kirin
119 C4 **Yen-p'ing** *Yanping* Taiwan
75 E4 **Yen-p'o-ch'iao** *Yanpoqiao* Hunan
74 C2 **Yen-p'o-tu** *Yanpodu* Hunan
119 B4 **Yen-pu** *Yanbu* Taiwan
59 H5 **Yen-pu-t'ou** *Yanbutou* Hupeh
59 G5 **Yen-sha** *Yansha* Hupeh
66 C3 **Yen-shan** *Yanshan* Fukien
22 D3 **Yen-shan** *Yanshan* Heilung.
31 E5 **Yen-shan** *Yanshan* Hopeh
83 G2 **Yen-shan** *Yanshan* Kwangsi
91 E4 **Yen-shan** *Yanshan* Kwei.
95 E4 **Yen-shan** *Yanshan* Yun.
54 D3 **Yen-shih** *Yanshi* Honan
106 C4 **Yen-shih-p'ing** *Yanshiping* Tsing.
11 E5 **Yen-shou** *Yanshou* Heilung.
75 F6 **Yen-shou** *Yanshou* Hunan
119 B3 **Yen-shui** *Yanshui* Taiwan
39 B5 **Yen-shui-kuan** *Yanshuiguan* Shansi
62 F4 **Yen-shui-kuan** *Yanshuiguan* Shensi
47 E7 **Yen-ssu** *Yensi* Anhwei
35 G2 **Yen-t'ai*** *Yantai* Shant.
51 D4 **Yen-t'an** *Yantan* Chek.
74 D4 **Yen-t'ang** *Yantang* Hunan
75 F5 **Yen-t'ang** *Yantang* Hunan
51 D4 **Yen-tang Shan** *Yandang Shan* (mts) Chek.
14 C3 **Yen-teng-t'u** *Yandengtu* Kirin
23 E5 **Yen-teng-t'u** *Yandengtu* Kirin
66 E4 **Yen-t'ien** *Yantian* Fukien
26 D5 **Yen-tien** *Yandian* In. Mong.
71 B4 **Yen-t'ien** *Yantian* Kiangsi
87 E2 **Yen-t'ing** *Yanting* Szech.
111 F3 **Yen-to** *Yanduo* Tibet
51 D4 **Yen-t'ou** *Yantou* Chek.
38 E2 **Yen-t'ou** *Yantou* Shansi
58 C3 **Yen-tu-ho** *Yenduhe* Hupeh
11 C4 **Yen-t'un** *Yantun* Heilung.
78 B4 **Yen-tun** *Yandun* Kwangt.
103 F2 **Yen-tun** *Yandun* Sink.
59 E4 **Yen-tun-chi** *Yandunji* Hupeh
82 C4 **Yen-t'ung** *Yantong* Kwangsi
82 D3 **Yen-tung** *Yandong* Kwangsi
14 G4 **Yen-t'ung-shan** *Yantongshan* Kirin
30 C3 **Yen-t'ung Shan** *Yantong Shan* (mts) Hopeh
11 C4 **Yen-t'ung-t'un** *Yantongtun* Heilung.
47 E6 **Yen-tun-p'u** *Yandunpu* Anhwei
42 C3 **Yen-tzu-fan** *Yanzifan* Kiangsu
90 C3 **Yen-tzu-k'ou** *Yanzikou* Kwei.
63 B8 **Yen-tzu-pien** *Yanzibian* Shensi
59 G4 **Yen-tzu-wo** *Yanziwo* Hupeh
94 B2 **Yen-wa** *Yanwa* Yun.
43 D1 **Yen-wei-kang** *Yanweigang* Kiangsu
39 C4 **Yen-wu** *Yanwu* Shansi
91 G3 **Yen-wu-p'ing** *Yanwuping* Kwei.
62 D5 **Yen-yao-pien** *Yanyaobian* Shensi
86 C4 **Yen-yüan** *Yanyuan* Szech.
Yen-yüan I-tsu Tzu-chih-hsien *see* **Yen-yüan Yi Autonomous Hsien**
86 C4 **Yen-yüan Yi Autonomous Hsien** *Yanyuan Yi* Szech.
Yeungchun *see* **Yang-ch'un**
Yeungkong *see* **Yang-chiang**
Yigrong Chu *see* **Yek-kung Ch'ü**
22 E2 **Yin-a** *Yina* Heilung.
82 D4 **Yin-ch'a** *Yincha* Kwangsi
79 C2 **Yin-chan-yao** *Yinzhanyao* Kwangt.
39 E6 **Yin-ch'eng** *Yincheng* Shansi
46 D3 **Yin-chi** *Yinji* Anhwei
34 B3 **Yin-chi** *Yinji* Shant.
47 D6 **Yin-chia-hui** *Yinjiahui* Anhwei
91 F2 **Yin-chiang** *Yinjiang* Kwei.
67 E5 **Yin-ch'ien** *Yinqian* Fukien
114 C2 **Yin-ch'uan** *Yinchuan* Ningsia
Yin-ch'uan - city plan *see* **Page 136**
Yinchwan *see* **Yin-ch'uan**
10 C3 **Ying-ch'en** *Yingchen* Heilung.
59 F4 **Ying-ch'eng** *Yingcheng* Hupeh
14 F3 **Ying-ch'eng** *Yingcheng* Kirin
14 F4 **Ying-ch'eng-tzu** *Yingchengzi* Kirin
18 E6 **Ying-ch'eng-tzu** *Yingchengzi* Liao.
19 H2 **Ying-ch'eng-tzu** *Yingchengzi* Liao.
83 H3 **Ying-chia** *Yingjia* Kwangsi
70 F3 **Ying-chia-k'ou** *Yingjiakou* Kiangsi
94 A3 **Ying-chiang** *Yingjiang* Yun.
55 E4 **Ying-ch'iao** *Yingqiao* Honan
71 B6 **Ying-ch'ien** *Yingqian* Kiangsi
86 D3 **Ying-ching** *Yingjing* Szech.
18 C2 **Ying-chin Ho** *Yingjin He* (river) Liao.
102 B3 **Ying-chi-sha** *Yingjisha* Sink.
Yingchow *see* **Fu-yang**
55 F2 **Ying-chü** *Yingju* Honan
50 C5 **Ying-ch'uan** *Yingchuan* Chek.
11 G4 **Ying-ch'un** *Yingchun* Heilung.
35 F3 **Ying-fang** *Yingfang* Shant.
74 E3 **Ying-feng-ch'iao** *Yingfengqiao* Hunan
54 C3 **Ying-hao** *Yinghao* Honan
46 C4 **Ying-ho** *Yinghe* Anhwei
46 B3 **Ying Ho** *Ying He* (river) Anhwei
38 E2 **Ying-hsien** *Yingxian* Shansi
14 D2 **Ying-hua** *Yinghua* Kirin
Yingkisha *see* **Ying-chi-sha**
118 C2 **Ying-ko** *Yingge* Taiwan
19 F4 **Ying-k'ou** *Yingkou* Liao.
19 F4 **Ying-k'ou Hsien** *Yingkou Xian* Liao.
Yingkow *see* **Ying-k'ou**
31 A5 **Ying-li** *Yingli* Hopeh
19 G5 **Ying-na Ho** *Yingna He* (river) Liao.
19 I2 **Ying-o-men** *Yingemen* Liao.
14 F6 **Ying-o-pu** *Yingebu* Kirin
83 F6 **Ying-p'an** *Yingpan* Kwangsi
19 H3 **Ying-p'an** *Yingpan* Liao.
94 B3 **Ying-p'an** *Yingpan* Yun.
63 E7 **Ying-p'an-chieh** *Yingpanjie* Shensi
94 B3 **Ying-p'an-chieh** *Yingpanjie* Yun.
114 B3 **Ying-p'an-shui** *Yingpanshui* Ningsia
59 F3 **Ying-shan** *Yingshan* Hupeh
59 H4 **Ying-shan** *Yingshan* Hupeh
87 F2 **Ying-shan** *Yingshan* Szech.
46 C4 **Ying-shang** *Yingshang* Anhwei
66 B4 **Ying-shang** *Yingshang* Fukien
35 F3 **Ying-shang** *Yingshang* Shant.
67 C5 **Ying-shih** *Yingshi* Fukien
67 C5 **Ying-shih Ch'i** *Yingshi Qi* (river) Fukien
30 E3 **Ying-shou-ying-tzu** *Yingshouyingzi* Hopeh
103 D2 **Ying-su** *Yingsu* Sink.
70 E3 **Ying-t'an** *Yingtan* Kiangsi
55 G2 **Ying-t'ao-yüan** *Yingtaoyuan* Honan
79 C1 **Ying-te** *Yingde* Kwangt.
74 E3 **Ying-t'ien** *Yingtian* Hunan
102 D2 **Ying-t'ou-lai** *Yingtoulai* Sink.
67 D6 **Ying-tu** *Yingdu* Fukien
62 E4 **Ying-wang** *Yingwang* Shensi
91 F2 **Ying-wu-hsi** *Yingwuxi* Kwei.
54 D3 **Ying-yang** *Yingyang* Honan
83 H3 **Ying-yang Kuan** *Yingyang Guan* (pass) Kwangsi
26 D4 **Yin-hao** *Yinhao* In. Mong.
10 B3 **Yin Ho** *Yin He* (river) Heilung.
63 E6 **Yin-ho-hui** *Yinhehui* Shensi
34 C2 **Yin-hsiang** *Yinxiang* Shant.
Yin-hsien *see* **Ning-po**
51 E3 **Yin Hsien** *Yin Xian* Chek.
46 C4 **Yin-hsien-chi** *Yinxianji* Anhwei
55 F1 **Yin-hsü** *Yinxu* (site) Honan
114 B1 **Yin-ken** *Yingen* Ningsia
71 C5 **Yin-k'eng** *Yinkeng* Kiangsi
34 A4 **Yin-ma** *Yinma* Shant.
98 C1 **Yin-ma-ch'ang** *Yinmachang* Kansu
14 F4 **Yin-ma Ho** *Yinma He* (river) Kirin
95 D2 **Yin-min** *Yinmin* Yun.
83 H4 **Yin-nan** *Yinnan* Kwangsi
42 C1 **Yin-p'ing** *Yinping* Kiangsu
87 E3 **Yin-shan-chen** *Yinshanzhen* Szech.
11 B4 **Yin-te-erh** *Yindeer* Heilung.
23 E4 **Yin-te-erh** *Yindeer* Heilung.
90 C3 **Yin-ti** *Yindi* Kwei.
75 E5 **Yin-t'ien** *Yintian* Hunan
59 F2 **Yin-tien** *Yindian* Hupeh
74 E4 **Yin-t'ien-ssu** *Yintiansi* Hunan
102 B4 **Yin-ti-la-k'o-li Shan-k'ou** *Yindilakeli Shankou* Sink.
59 G5 **Yin-tsu** *Yinzu* Hupeh
31 B6 **Yin-ts'un** *Yincun* Hopeh
35 H2 **Yin-tzu-k'uang** *Yinzikuang* Shant.
43 F4 **Yin-yang** *Yinyang* Kiangsu
38 E4 **Yin-ying** *Yinying* Shansi
Yisa *see* **Hung-ho**
Yitang *see* **I-t'ang**
Yitu *see* **I-tu**
Yiyang *see* **I-yang**
Yotsing *see* **Lo-ch'ing**
Yoyang *see* **Yüeh-yang**
58 D3 **Yüan-an** *Yuanan* Hupeh
118 B3 **Yüan-ch'ang** *Yuanchang* Taiwan
63 D7 **Yüan-chia-chuang** *Yuanjiazhuang* Shensi
46 B3 **Yüan-ch'iang** *Yuanqiang* Anhwei
74 E3 **Yüan-chiang** *Yuanjiang* Hunan
74 C3 **Yüan Chiang** *Yuan Jiang* (river) Hunan
94 D4 **Yüan Chiang** *Yuan Jiang* (river) Yun.
94 C4 **Yüan-chiang** *Yuanjiang* Yun.
51 E4 **Yüan-ch'iao** *Yuanqiao* Chek.
38 C3 **Yüan-chia-ts'un** *Yuanjiacun* Shansi
70 B3 **Yüan-ch'ien** *Yuanqian* Kiangsi
34 D3 **Yüan-ch'üan** *Yuanquan* Shant.
39 C6 **Yüan-ch'ü Hsien** *Yuanqu Xian* Shansi
55 F3 **Yüan-fang** *Yuanfang* Honan
91 C2 **Yüan-hou** *Yuanhou* Kwei.
55 G3 **Yüan-hsiang** *Yuanxiang* Honan
38 D4 **Yüan-hsiang** *Yuanxiang* Shansi
59 I5 **Yüan Hu** *Yuan Hu* (lake) Hupeh
87 F2 **Yüan-i** *Yuanyi* Szech.
66 C4 **Yüan-k'eng** *Yuankeng* Fukien
35 G2 **Yüan-ko-chuang** *Yuangezhuang* Shant.
91 G4 **Yüan-k'ou** *Yuankou* Kwei.
63 D8 **Yüan-k'ou** *Yuankou* Shensi
118 B2 **Yüan-li** *Yuanli* Taiwan
19 F3 **Yüan-liang-tien** *Yuanliangdian* Liao.
22 D3 **Yüan-lin** *Yuanlin* Heilung.
118 B3 **Yüan-lin** *Yuanlin* Taiwan
74 C3 **Yüan-ling** *Yuanling* Hunan
94 C3 **Yüan-mou** *Yuanmou* Yun.
63 B8 **Yüan-pa** *Yuanba* Shensi
11 E5 **Yüan-pao** *Yuanbao* Heilung.
18 C2 **Yüan-pao-shan** *Yuanbaoshan* Liao.
83 F2 **Yüan-pao Shan** *Yuanbao Shan* (mt) Kwangsi
26 C4 **Yüan-pao-wan** *Yuanbaowan* In. Mong.
38 D3 **Yüan-p'ing** *Yuanping* Shansi
87 E2 **Yüan-shan** *Yuanshan* Szech.
118 C2 **Yüan-shan** *Yuanshan* Taiwan
98 D2 **Yüan-shan-tzu** *Yuanshanzi* Kansu
31 B6 **Yüan-shih** *Yuanshi* Hopeh
70 B4 **Yüan Shui** *Yuan Shui* (river) Kiangsi
47 C6 **Yüan-t'an** *Yuantan* Anhwei
54 D5 **Yüan-t'an** *Yuantan* Honan
74 F2 **Yüan-t'an** *Yuantan* Hunan
79 C2 **Yüan-t'an** *Yuantan* Kwangt.
91 D2 **Yüan-t'ien** *Yuantian* Kwei.
31 B6 **Yüan-t'ou** *Yuantou* Hopeh
83 G3 **Yüan-tou** *Yuandou* Kwangsi
55 G1 **Yüan-ts'un** *Yuancun* Honan
99 F3 **Yüan-tun** *Yuandun* Kansu
38 D2 **Yüan-tzu Ho** *Yuanzi He* (river) Shansi
55 E2 **Yüan-wu** *Yuanwu* Honan
54 D3 **Yüan-ya** *Yuanya* Honan
55 E2 **Yüan-yang** *Yuanyang* Honan
95 D4 **Yüan-yang** *Yuanyang* Yun.
99 G4 **Yüan-yang-chen** *Yuanyangzhen* Kansu
94 C3 **Yüan-yung-ching** *Yuanyongjing* Yun.
Yüanyungtsing *see* **Yüan-yung-ching**
50 C5 **Yü-chang** *Yuzhang* Chek.
90 C5 **Yü-chang** *Yuzhang* Kwei.
55 F3 **Yü-chen** *Yuzhen* Honan
70 D2 **Yu-ch'eng** *Youcheng* Kiangsi
43 D1 **Yü-ch'eng** *Yucheng* Kiangsu
34 B3 **Yü-ch'eng** *Yucheng* Shant.
34 B5 **Yü-ch'eng** *Yucheng* Shant.
55 G3 **Yü-ch'eng Hsien** *Yucheng Xian* Honan
46 D3 **Yu-chi** *Youji* Anhwei
51 E4 **Yu-ch'i** *Youqi* Chek.
67 D4 **Yu-ch'i** *Youqi* Fukien
74 D4 **Yu-ch'i** *Youqi* Hunan
67 D4 **Yu Ch'i** *You Qi* (river) Fukien
87 F3 **Yu-ch'i** *Youqi* Szech.
67 E5 **Yü-ch'i** *Yuqi* Fukien
31 D6 **Yü-chi** *Yuji* Hopeh
58 D4 **Yü-ch'i** *Yuqi* Hupeh
43 E4 **Yü-ch'i** *Yuqi* Kiangsu
91 E2 **Yü-ch'i** *Yuqi* Kwei.
34 B3 **Yü-chi** *Yuji* Shant.
95 D3 **Yü-ch'i** *Yuqi* Yun.
70 D4 **Yu-chia** *Youjia* Kiangsi
70 D3 **Yü-chia** *Yujia* Kiangsi
74 C2 **Yü-chia-ch'i** *Yujiaqi* Hunan
47 C6 **Yü-chia-ching** *Yujiajing* Anhwei
70 D2 **Yü-chia-i** *Yujiayi* Kiangsi
82 D4 **Yu Chiang** *You Jiang* (river) Kwangsi
83 F5 **Yü Chiang** *Yu Jiang* (river) Kwangsi
70 D3 **Yü-chiang Hsien** *Yujiang Xian* Kiangsi
70 D4 **Yu-chia-pien** *Youjiabian* Kiangsi
59 E4 **Yü-chia-pu** *Yujiabu* Hupeh
15 G3 **Yu-chia-t'un** *Youjiatun* Kirin
74 D4 **Yu-chia-wan** *Youjiawan* Hunan
87 F2 **Yu-ch'i-chen** *Youqizhen* Szech.
118 B3 **Yü-ch'ih** *Yuchi* Taiwan
66 D4 **Yu-ch'i-k'ou** *Youqikou* Fukien
47 E5 **Yü-ch'i-k'ou** *Yuqikou* Anhwei
63 E6 **Yü-chin-chen** *Yujinzhen* Shensi
38 D2 **Yü-ching** *Yujing* Shansi
119 B3 **Yü-ching** *Yujing* Taiwan
91 E3 **Yü-ch'ing Hsien** *Yuqing Xian* Kwei.
70 B3 **Yu-chü** *Youju* Kiangsi
11 D5 **Yü-ch'üan** *Yuquan* Heilung.
38 D3 **Yü-chuang** *Yuzhuang* Shansi
91 E3 **Yu-ch'üan-pa** *Youquanba* Kwei.
58 D4 **Yü-ch'üan-ssu** *Yuquansi* Hupeh
106 B1 **Yu-ch'üan-tzu** *Youquanzi* Tsing.
99 G4 **Yü-chung** *Yuzhong* Kansu
86 C2 **Yüeh-cha** *Yuezha* Szech.
46 C4 **Yüeh-chang-chi** *Yuezhangji* Anhwei
55 F5 **Yüeh-ch'eng** *Yuecheng* Honan
31 B7 **Yüeh-ch'eng** *Yuecheng* Hopeh
79 C2 **Yüeh-ch'eng** *Yuecheng* Kwangt.
83 G1 **Yüeh-ch'eng Ling** *Yuecheng Ling* (mts) Kwangsi
30 F4 **Yüeh-chih** *Yuezhi* Hopeh
87 F2 **Yüeh-ch'ih** *Yuechi* Szech.
102 H1 **Yüeh-chih-hsin-ts'un** *Yuezhixincun* Sink.
102 H1 **Yueh-chin Shui-k'u** *Yuejin Shuiku* (res.) Sink.
Yüeh-chi-t'ai Ts'o *see* **I-chi-t'ai Ts'o**
110 D3 **Yüeh-chu** *Yuezhu* Tibet
34 D3 **Yüeh-chuang** *Yuezhuang* Shant.
103 F2 **Yüeh-fei-ch'üan** *Yuefeiquan* Sink.
55 E5 **Yüeh-ho-tien** *Yuehedian* Honan
86 D3 **Yüeh-hsi** *Yuexi* Szech.
47 C6 **Yüeh-hsi Hsien** *Yuexi Xian* Anhwei
Yüeh Kiang *see* **Chu Chiang**
59 F4 **Yüeh-k'ou** *Yuekou* Hupeh
70 D4 **Yüeh-k'ou** *Yuekou* Kiangsi
11 F4 **Yüeh-lai** *Yuelai* Heilung.
87 G2 **Yüeh-lai** *Yuelai* Szech.
87 F3 **Yüeh-lai-ch'ang** *Yuelaichang* Szech.
99 H3 **Yüeh-le** *Yuehle* Kansu
82 D2 **Yüeh-li** *Yueli* Kwangsi
14 D2 **Yüeh-liang P'ao** *Yueliangpao* (lake) Kirin
23 E5 **Yüeh-liang P'ao** *Yueliang Pao* (lake) Kirin
74 F3 **Yüeh-lung-shih** *Yuelongshi* Hunan
74 E3 **Yüeh-lu Shan** *Yuelu Shan* (mt) Hunan
106 B2 **Yüeh-po-k'a-li-k'o** *Yuebokalike* Tsing.
102 B3 **Yüeh-p'u-hu** *Yuepuhu* Sink.
47 C6 **Yüeh-shan** *Yueshan* Anhwei
74 E4 **Yüeh-shan** *Yueshan* Hunan
74 F2 **Yüeh-t'ien** *Yuetian* Hunan
71 C7 **Yüeh-tzu** *Yuezi* Kiangsi
114 C2 **Yüeh-ya-hu** *Yueyahu* Ningsia
74 F2 **Yüeh-yang** *Yueyang* Hunan
39 C5 **Yüeh-yang** *Yueyang* Shansi
Yüen King *see* **Red River**
30 F3 **Yü-erh-yai** *Yueryai* Hopeh
30 D4 **Yü-fa** *Yufa* Hopeh
31 C6 **Yu-fang** *Youfang* Hopeh
43 D3 **Yu-fang** *Youfang* Kiangsu
38 D2 **Yu-fang** *Youfang* Shansi
63 B6 **Yu-fang-kou** *Youfanggou* Shensi
63 E5 **Yu-fang-t'ai** *Youfangtai* Shensi
66 C4 **Yü-fang-wei** *Yufangwei* Fukien
82 D4 **Yü-feng** *Yufeng* Kwangsi
118 C2 **Yü-feng** *Yufeng* Taiwan
51 D2 **Yü-hang Hsien** *Yuhang Xian* Chek.
10 E4 **Yu-hao** *Youhao* Heilung.
87 F2 **Yu-ho** *Youhe* Szech.
55 E2 **Yü-ho** *Yuhe* Honan
38 E1 **Yü Ho** *Yu He* (river) Shansi
62 E3 **Yü-ho-pao** *Yuehebao* Shensi
Yü-hsi *see* **Yü-ch'i**
43 F3 **Yü-hsi** *Yuxi* Kiangsu
63 D6 **Yü-hsia** *Yuxia* Shensi
95 E3 **Yü-hsia** *Yuxia* Yun.
58 C4 **Yü-hsia-k'ou** *Yuxiakou* Hupeh
39 B7 **Yü-hsiang** *Yuxiang* Shansi
34 C2 **Yü-hsiang** *Yuxiang* Shant.
75 F4 **Yu-hsien** *Youxian* Hunan
54 E3 **Yü-hsien** *Yuxian* Honan
30 B4 **Yü-hsien** *Yuxian* Hopeh
38 E3 **Yü-hsien** *Yuxian* Shansi
59 F4 **Yü-hsin** *Yuxin* Hupeh
51 D5 **Yü-hu** *Yuhu* Chek.
43 E2 **Yü-hua** *Yuhua* Kiangsu
51 E4 **Yü-huan Hsien** *Yuhuan Xian* Chek.
51 E4 **Yü-huan Tao** *Yuhuan Dao* (island) Chek.
11 F4 **Yu-i** *Youyi* Heilung.
70 D3 **Yü-i** *Yuyi* Kiangsi
82 C6 **Yu-i-kuan** *Youyiguan* Kwangsi
106 D1 **Yü-k'a** *Yuka* Tsing.
106 D1 **Yü-k'a Ho** *Yuka He* (river) Tsing.
70 D3 **Yü-kan** *Yugan* Kiangsi
14 D2 **Yu-kan-nao** *Yougannao* Kirin
107 G3 **Yu-kan-t'an** *Yongantan* Tsing.
79 D1 **Yü-k'eng** *Yukeng* Kwangt.
Yüki *see* **Yü-ch'i**
Yü Kiang *see* **Yü Chiang**
Yükikow *see* **Yü-ch'i-k'ou**
31 C6 **Yü-k'o** *Yuke* Hopeh
86 C2 **Yü-k'o** *Yuke* Szech.
46 D3 **Yü-kou** *Yugou* Anhwei
30 E3 **Yü-k'ou** *Yukou* Hopeh
42 C2 **Yü-kou** *Yugou* Kiangsu
38 C4 **Yü-k'ou** *Yukou* Shansi
30 G4 **Yü-kuan** *Yuguan* Hopeh
11 F4 **Yü-kung** *Yugong* Heilung.
19 G3 **Yü-kuo** *Yuguo* Liao.
70 D3 **Yu-lan** *Youlan* Kiangsi
83 F3 **Yu-lan** *Youlan* Kwangsi
110 C2 **Yu-lang-lo-p'u-chiang-ssu** *Youlangluopujiangsi* Tibet
78 B2 **Yü-lao** *Yulao* Kwangt.
35 G2 **Yü-li** *Yuli* Shant.
103 D2 **Yü-li** *Yuli* Sink.
119 C3 **Yü-li** *Yuli* Taiwan
14 B4 **Yü-liang-pao** *Yuliangbao* Kirin
23 D6 **Yü-liang-pao** *Yuliangbao* Kirin
23 D6 **Yü-liang-p'u** *Yuliangpu* Kirin
35 D2 **Yu-lin** *Youlin* Shant.
22 D3 **Yü-lin** *Yulin* Heilung.
83 G5 **Yü-lin** *Yulin* Kwangsi
78 A4 **Yü-lin** *Yulin* Kwangt.
62 E2 **Yü-lin** *Yulin* Shensi
11 D4 **Yü-lin-chen** *Yulinzhen* Heilung.
62 E2 **Yü-lin Ho** *Yulin He* (river) Shensi
30 B3 **Yü-lin-pao** *Yulinbao* Hopeh
119 C3 **Yü-li Shan** *Yuli Shan* (mt) Taiwan
Yülung *see* **Ya-lung Chiang**
86 B2 **Yü-lung** *Yulong* Szech.
87 E2 **Yü-lung** *Yulong* Szech.
102 B3 **Yü-lung-k'a-shih Ho** *Yulongkashi He* (river) Sink.
94 C2 **Yü-lung Shan** *Yulong Shan* (mt) Yun.
83 G4 **Yu-ma** *Youma* Kwangsi
83 G3 **Yu-ma-k'ou** *Youmakou* Kwangsi
98 C2 **Yü-men** *Yumen* Kansu
98 C1 **Yü-men-chen** *Yumenzhen* Kansu
39 B6 **Yü-men-k'ou** *Yumenkou* Shansi
98 A1 **Yü-men-kuan** *Yumenguan* Kansu
98 C2 **Yü-men Tung-chan** *Yumen Dongzhan* Kansu
Yü-min *see* **Ha-la-pu-la**
102 C1 **Yü-min Hsien** *Yumin Xian* Sink.
Yumrang Lopchang *see* **Yu-lang-lo-p'u-ch'iang-ssu**
15 G4 **Yü-mu-ch'iao-tzu** *Yumuqiaozi* Kirin
78 B2 **Yü-nan** *Yunan* Kwangt.
87 G2 **Yün-an-chen** *Yunanzhen* Szech.
31 B5 **Yün-ch'eng** *Yuncheng* Hopeh
39 B6 **Yün-ch'eng** *Yuncheng* Shansi
34 A4 **Yün-ch'eng** *Yuncheng* Shant.
74 F2 **Yün-ch'i** *Yunqi* Hunan
83 F3 **Yün-chiang** *Yunjiang* Kwangsi
94 C5 **Yün-ching-hung** *Yunjinghong* Yun.
30 C2 **Yün-chou** *Yunzhou* Hopeh
39 D4 **Yün-chou-hsi-ts'un** *Yunzhouxicun* Shansi
38 D3 **Yün-chung Shan** *Yunzhong Shan* (mt) Shansi
38 D3 **Yün-chung Shan** *Yunzhong Shan* (mts) Shansi
Yün-fou *see* **Yün-fu**
79 C2 **Yün-fu** *Yunfu* Kwangt.
46 D3 **Yung-an** *Yongan* Anhwei
67 C5 **Yung-an** *Yongan* Fukien
11 D4 **Yung-an** *Yongan* Heilung.
11 F5 **Yung-an** *Yongan* Heilung.
75 E6 **Yung-an** *Yongan* Hunan
82 E2 **Yung-an** *Yongan* Kwangsi
91 E2 **Yung-an** *Yongan* Kwei.
34 D2 **Yung-an** *Yongan* Shant.
119 B4 **Yung-an** *Yongan* Taiwan
51 D4 **Yung-an Ch'i** *Yongan Qi* (river) Chek.
75 D6 **Yung-an Kuan** *Yongan Guan* (pass) Hunan
83 H2 **Yung-an Kuan** *Yongan Guan* (pass) Kwangsi
74 F3 **Yung-an-shih** *Yonganshi* Hunan
50 C3 **Yung-ch'ang** *Yongchang* Chek.
71 B5 **Yung-ch'ang** *Yongchang* Kiangsi
55 H4 **Yung-ch'eng** *Yongcheng* Honan
39 B7 **Yung-chi** *Yongji* Shansi
Yung-chia *see* **Wen-chou**
51 D4 **Yung-chia** *Yongjia* Chek.
51 E2 **Yung Chiang** *Yong Jiang* Chek.
38 F1 **Yung-chia-pao** *Yongjiabao* Shansi
74 F2 **Yung-chia-wan** *Yongjiawan* Hunan

Sources

Historical maps: In the absence of any adequate modern historical atlas of China, extensive use has been made in the compilation of the historical maps of *An Historical Atlas of China* by Albert Herrmann, Edinburgh University Press, Edinburgh, 1966; and *Ajia rekishi chizu* edited by Matsuda and Mori, Heibonsha, Tokyo, 1966.

Province maps and city plans: The base for all province maps and most of the town plans in this atlas is *Chung-kuo Ti-t'u-ts'e* (Collection of Maps of China), Peking, 1966. The following later sources: *Chung-hua Jen-min Kung-ho-kuo Ti-t'u-chi* (Atlas of the People's Republic of China), Peking, 1972, and *Chung-hua Jen-min Kung-ho-kuo Ti-t'u* (Map of the People's Republic of China), Peking, (a) 1:4,000,000, Dec. 1971 (b) 1:6,000,000, Jan. 1973, have been used extensively to update the province maps in respect of communications and administrative information, including internal boundary changes, and to provide a considerable number of new and additional names. The following sources for city plans have also been used: the *Hong Kong Official Guide Map* (2nd edition), 1:100,000, Crown Lands and Survey office, Hong Kong, 1973; and Portuguese Chart No. 520: *Provincia de Macau. Plano hidrográfico de Macau, Taipa e Coloane* (2a Edição), 1:20,000 Lisbon, 1972.

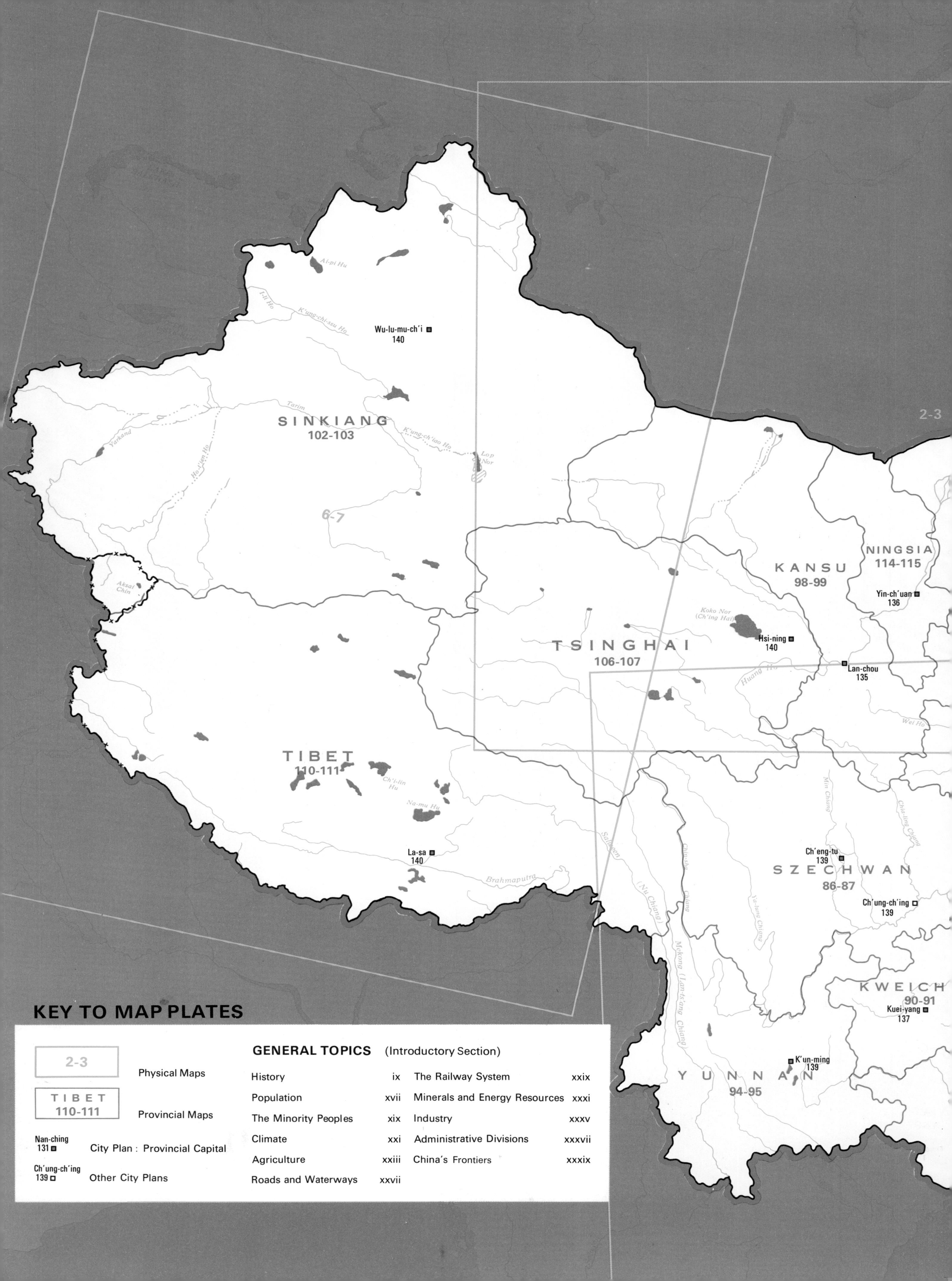

KEY TO MAP PLATES

2-3	Physical Maps
TIBET 110-111	Provincial Maps
Nan-ching 131 ■	City Plan : Provincial Capital
Ch'ung-ch'ing 139 □	Other City Plans

GENERAL TOPICS (Introductory Section)